Understanding Post-traumatic Stress

Understanding Post-traumatic Stress
A Psychosocial Perspective on PTSD and Treatment

Stephen Joseph
University of Essex, UK

Ruth Williams
Institute of Psychiatry, London, UK

William Yule
Institute of Psychiatry, London, UK

JOHN WILEY & SONS
Chichester · Weinheim · New York · Brisbane · Singapore · Toronto

National   01243 779777
International (+44) 1243 779777
e-mail (for orders and customer service enquires): cs-books@wiley.co.uk
Visit our Home Page on http://www.wiley.co.uk
or http://www.wiley.com

Other Wiley Editorial Offices

John Wiley & Sons, Inc., 605 Third Avenue,
New York, NY 10158-0012, USA

VCH Verlagsgesellschaft mbH,
Pappelallee 3, 0-69469 Weinheim, Germany

Jacaranda Wiley Ltd, 33 Park Road, Milton,
Queensland 4064, Australia

John Wiley & Sons (Asia) Pte Ltd, 2 Clementi Loop #02-01,
Jin Xing Distripark, Singapore 129809

John Wiley & Sons (Canada) Ltd, 22 Worcester Road,
Rexdale, Ontario M9W 1L1, Canada

Library of Congress Cataloging-in-Publication Data

Joseph, Stephen.
    Understanding post-traumatic stress: a psychosocial perspective
  on PTSD and treatment / Stephen Joseph, Ruth Williams, William Yule.
        p.   cm.
    Includes bibliographical references and index.
    ISBN 0-471-96800-5 (cloth).—ISBN 0-471-96801-3 (pbk.)
    1. Post-traumatic stress disorder.   2. Psychic trauma.
  3. Adjustment (Psychology)   I. Williams, Ruth, MA (Oxon), Dip.
  Psych.   II. Yule, William.   III. Title.
  RC552.P67J67   1997
  616.85'21—dc20
                                                    96-41655
                                                         CIP

British Library Cataloguing in Publication Data

A catalogue record for this book is available from the British Library

ISBN 0-471-96800-5 (cased)
ISBN 0-471-96801-3 (paper)

Typeset 10/12 pt Plantin from the authors' disks by Vision Typesetting, Manchester
Printed and bound in Great Britain by Bookcraft Ltd, Midsomer Norton, Somerset
This book is printed on acid-free paper responsibly manufactured from sustainable forestation,
for which at least two trees are planted for each one used for paper production.

TABLE OF CONTENTS

ABOUT THE AUTHORS

Stephen Joseph is a lecturer in psychology at the University of Essex. Trained in social psychology at the London School of Economics he went on to work with survivors of disaster at the Institute of Psychiatry where he addressed the issues of why some people cope very well with traumatic events while others struggle to come to terms with their experiences. Following this he returned to Ireland to take up a lectureship at the University of Ulster. There he turned his interest to political violence and its consequences before moving back to England in 1994 to take up work at the University of Essex where he has continued to conduct research into post-traumatic stress disorder. He has published articles in *British Journal of Clinical Psychology*, *British Journal of Medical Psychology*, *British Journal of Psychiatry*, *Journal of Child Psychology and Psychiatry*, and *Behaviour Research and Therapy*.

Ruth Williams is a Senior Lecturer in the Psychology Department of the Institute of Psychiatry where she has worked for some 20 years. Her main interests are in Cognitive Therapy and in the application of cognitive-behavioural approaches to general adult problems. She is a founder of the Institute of Psychiatry's well-known post-qualification course in Cognitive-Behavioural Therapy.

William Yule trained as a clinical psychologist at the Institute of Psychiatry and Maudsley Hospital in London where he was for many years head of the clinical psychology services and Professor of Applied Child Psychology. He has published over 300 articles and nine books on a wide range of topics in child psychology. For the past eight years, he has been heavily involved in the study and treatment of PTSD in both adults and children. He has shown that PTSD is both a commoner and more chronic reaction in children and adolescents than had hitherto been suspected. Since the summer of 1993, he has been an adviser to UNICEF on its psychosocial programme for war-effected children in former Yugoslavia and is Technical Director of a major programme to develop services for war-affected children in Mostar, Bosnia. He is a member of the Board of the International Society for Traumatic Stress Studies, and is on the boards of both the Journal of Traumatic Stress and the new electronic journal, *Traumatology*. He was elected Chair of ACCP in June 1996.

I have returned
from a world beyond knowledge
and now must unlearn
for otherwise I clearly see
I can no longer live.

(Charlotte Delbo (1995), *Auschwitz and After*)

PREFACE

The field of traumatic stress research has grown enormously in recent years. So much more is now known about the psychological consequences of traumatic events and their treatment than when we first became involved in this field in the late 1980s. We became involved in the study of traumatic stress following the capsize of the *Herald of Free Enterprise* in 1987 when survivors were referred to the Institute of Psychiatry in London for assessment and treatment. Then, traumatic stress research was still very much in its infancy in Britain. However, the pace of development since then has been remarkable and shows no sign of slowing down. Not everyone who is exposed to trauma goes on to develop severe and chronic psychological problems and it is this observation that has driven our work. Why do some people cope very well with trauma while others struggle a great deal? It is this interest in the individual and in how he or she interrogates and reconstructs his or her memories and past experiences which sums up the character of this book.

The book has been written for undergraduates doing an advanced clinical option, postgraduate clinical psychologists, and practising clinicians who want to understand more about post-traumatic stress and its treatment. Over the years many people have collaborated with us in our work on traumatic stress and many of the ideas in the book have their origins in discussions with them. In particular, we would like to thank Bernice Andrews, Chris Brewin, Sandra Ten Bruggencate, Ed Cairns, Tim Dalgleish, Peter Hodgkinson, Willem Kuyken, Gerry Mulhern, Sian Thrasher, Troy Tranah, Andrew Walker, and Ronnie Wilson. Grateful thanks also to Michael Coombs, Wendy Hudlass, and Mike Shardlow at Wiley. But most of all, our thanks must go to the survivors themselves who have worked with us and have kindly agreed to take part in our research. This book is dedicated to them.

Stephen Joseph
Ruth Williams
William Yule

ACKNOWLEDGEMENTS

The authors are grateful to Yale University Press for permission to reproduce the quotation on p. ix and to Plenum Publishing Corp. for permission to reproduce the quotations from Manton and Talbot (1991) on pages 116 and 117.

Permission has been sought for all the other copyright material that is quoted in the book and acknowledgements are made at appropriate points in the text.

Chapter 1

GENERAL INTRODUCTION

On 21 December 1988, a bomb exploded on board a Pan Am jet flying above Scotland at 31,000 feet on route to JFK at New York from London. Two hundred and fifty-nine passengers and crew were killed as well as eleven people on the ground. The bodies and wreckage were strewn over almost 900 square miles around the town of Lockerbie.

Tragic events such as at Lockerbie can strike at any time and at any place. There is approximately a 1 in 5 million probability of being killed in an air crash. These are good odds. After all, there is a 1 in 10,000 probability of being struck by lightning (Krantz, 1992). Although it is unlikely that you will die in an air crash or be struck by lightning, between 1967 and 1991 there were 7766 disasters world wide involving the death of more than 7 million people and affecting nearly 3 trillion individual lives (International Federation of Red Cross and Red Crescent Societies World Disaster Report, 1993). One survivor of the capsize of the *Herald of Free Enterprise* ferry in 1987, when later asked about her views on life, replied that she now felt that something bad was just waiting around the corner to happen. A fear of future catastrophe is common among survivors of disaster. Fears of future catastrophe constituted an important part of Pauline's problems shown in Case History 1.

Such fears are often based on an overestimation of the probability of such events. However, there is evidence that most people see bad events as more unlikely to happen than they actually are. Most of us live in a bubble of perceived invulnerability to the numerous everyday personal tragedies of car accidents, house fires, muggings, sexual assaults, and illnesses. Increasingly in recent years, psychologists and psychiatrists have come to recognise that such events can have a profound and long-lasting effect on the people involved. Such an example is provided by Henry (see Case History 2).

Although the topic of post-traumatic stress disorders has become popular over the last few years, one of the first people to develop a post-traumatic paradigm was Freud whose original view of neurosis, the 'seduction theory', emphasised the role of actual sexual abuse in the development of later emotional disorders. Freud soon revised this theory because, it has been suggested, the emphasis on sexual abuse was not well received in Vienna and because he found it difficult to accept how widespread sexual abuse might be if his theory were correct. He revised his theory to suggest that the memories of patients

CASE HISTORY 1

Pauline—an unmarried woman aged 22 years, working in marketing for a drug company—was first seen seven months after suffering from an accidental gas poisoning at her home in which two other young people, close friends, were killed. She reported intrusive and distressing recollections of experiences during her period of partial suffocation in the house when she felt trapped and wanted to break a window and also of her time in hospital when she witnessed her friend dying and thought she would die next. Pauline was convinced that something awful was going to happen to herself or to one of her friends in the near future. She reported extreme anxiety in situations involving confinement (queues, trains and the tube) or when driving or being driven (sweating, raised heart rate, hyperventilation). She felt apathetic, feeling there was no point in doing things; she had a sense that she would not live much longer. She also reported signs of general hyperarousal: she had difficult staying asleep, concentration at work was poor, she was always 'on edge' and startled easily. Although she continued working and showed little behavioural avoidance, she reported trying to avoid thoughts and feelings about the tragedy. She distracted herself and feared losing control of her thoughts. She had given up smoking but was abusing alcohol at weekends (up to 15 pints of beer).

Pauline's boyfriend, also a survivor, had also been referred for help but failed to attend. Pauline was very angry about his failure to support her. He refused to talk about the tragedy and seemed dazed. Pauline said that she didn't think he wanted to get better. He had lost two jobs and she had now asked him to leave their house.

CASE HISTORY 2

Henry is a 52-year-old single man who is a political refugee from Pakistan, having suffered imprisonment and torture for political opposition. He had been diagnosed by the psychiatric service as suffering from a chronic depressive illness with marked suicidal ideation, having made at least one suicidal attempt. The diagnosis of a dependent personality disorder had also been made. He had been treated for at least 10 years with antidepressant medication and several hospital admissions without clear benefit, though compliance was thought poor. He had been referred for psychotherapy on two occasions but had not attended beyond a few sessions. He was working as a cleaner for the local council although he has a degree in political sciences, law and industrial relations. He had been accustomed to a life of comfort and status in his own country. He escaped and came to the UK 14 years ago and sought asylum because of death threats. He had left his wife and two children at home and they were now dead. He felt extreme guilt at having escaped and survived them. His previous experience of torture had caused severe damage to his body which had since been reconstructed surgically. Henry was very-selfconscious and aware of the unusual appearance of his face. He was extremely anxious in public places, afraid of being looked at and laughed at and tried to prevent people from seeing his face. He referred to his profound distrust of strangers, as if 'every human being is wicked and cruel'. He reported wandering around in London, 'searching for a moment of calm'. Reported symptoms included tension and difficulty in breathing. As well as extreme sadness at his multiple losses, he reported reliving his torture experiences, nightmares 3–4 times per week and marked sleep disturbance. He was having difficulty concentrating at work and was profoundly alienated from the people he worked with. Henry referred to himself as a 'spoilt child', not able to compromise and accept the reality of his new situation with his social status as the 'lowest member of society'.

seeking treatment may have been fantasies of such events (see Herman, 1992b for an excellent discussion of this 'forgotten history').

THE APPROACH OF THIS BOOK

The approach which we have taken in this book is that post-traumatic stress reactions have multiple causes. By definition, the experience of a traumatic event is the necessary cause. But not all survivors of traumatic events go on to develop severe or chronic distress. So, although the experience of a traumatic event may be a necessary cause, it is not a sufficient cause and various psychosocial factors must either mediate or moderate the effects of traumatic events.

The psychosocial perspective which we have adopted on post-traumatic stress reactions brings together the current thinking in social and cognitive psychology relevant to understanding adaptation to a wide range of life-stressors. It is not just what happens to people that is important, but also what it means to those people in relation to their sense of who they are, the world they live in and what their expectations are for the future. Exposure to traumatic events can challenge the whole meaning of a person's life and his or her sense of purpose. One person might construe an event as a lucky escape from which some benefit has in some way been derived, whereas another person might construe the same event as a catastrophic misfortune which proves that life is meaningless. The effects of the traumatic event on the emotional and behavioural reactions of these two people will invariably be influenced by these different appraisals.

The importance of understanding the role of psychosocial factors in the development of post-traumatic stress reactions is that, unlike the traumatic event itself, they are potentially modifiable and are therefore possible targets for therapeutic intervention. For example, techniques can be aimed at examining the way in which a person makes sense of the experience and how he or she copes with what has happened.

In Chapter 2 we will provide a more detailed description of the psychological reactions experienced by survivors and outline some of the difficulties involved in the psychiatric classification and assessment of trauma-related reactions. Chapter 2 will also provide coverage of the historical development of the diagnostic category of post-traumatic stress disorder (PTSD. APA, 1994). A major issue is whether or not the symptoms outlined as diagnostic of PTSD should be regarded as indicative of abnormal or normal processes. Although PTSD provides a useful framework for conceptualising psychological reactions, our approach has a broader focus that encompasses normal functioning and views the symptoms of PTSD as indicative of unresolved processing of the traumatic event. Measurement is the cornerstone of psychological science and, in Chapter 3, we discuss some of the commonly used instruments as well as some theoretical and practical issues in assessment. In Chapter 4 we will consider the psychological effects of different traumatic events and raise the question of whether all events are interchangeable with regard to their effects or whether different kinds of event lead to variations in symptoms and functional impairment. In Chapter 5 we will outline the main theoretical approaches to understanding post-traumatic stress reactions and present our psychosocial model of adjustment to traumatic stressors. In Chapter 6 we will review the evidence for the role of psychosocial factors and in Chapter 7 we will review what is known about the efficacy of various treatments within a framework derived from our model of psychosocial adjustment. Finally, in Chapter 8, we will summarise the key issues that have emerged and discuss their implications.

Chapter 2

NORMAL AND ABNORMAL REACTIONS TO TRAUMA

INTRODUCTION

An avalanche in the Italian Alps in 1775 trapped three women in their house for 37 days without open air or daylight and with only minimal nourishment. Looking back at the medical account provided at the time, the authors of a recent report concluded that one of the women developed what might be described today as moderately severe post-traumatic stress disorder (PTSD) with a chronic course of two years (Parry-Jones & Parry-Jones, 1994). Going back another hundred years to 1666, Samuel Pepys's description of his psychological symptoms following the Great Fire of London also corresponds to the description of PTSD (Daly, 1983).

But although psychological suffering in response to traumatic events has always been with us, it wasn't until 1980 that the term PTSD was officially introduced into the psychiatric literature. The term PTSD provided a common language which has succeeded in bringing together research in a wide range of fields under one, unifying, theoretical umbrella. Prior to 1980, the effects of traumatic events on psychological health had been discussed using a variety of different terms. For example, Rape Trauma Syndrome and Combat Stress Reaction (Herman, 1992b). Undoubtedly, the introduction of PTSD has led to more efficient research programmes and consequently better treatment. This chapter will provide an overview of the history of PTSD and some of the issues surrounding this concept.

Key Topics

Historical perspectives
Horowitz's two-factor model
Post-traumatic stress disorder
Course of disorder
Associated symptoms
Children and adolescents
Conclusion

HISTORICAL PERSPECTIVES

The nineteenth century saw the advent of the railway and with it descriptions of post-traumatic stress reactions in relation to railway collisions, e.g., spinal concussion and railway spine (Erichsen, 1866). Since then, the effects of traumatic events on psychological health have been recognised under various names (see Gersons & Carlier, 1992; Trimble, 1981 for reviews); most of these labels have been chosen in relation to combat, e.g., nervous shock (Page, 1885), traumatic neurosis (Oppenheim, 1892), anxiety neurosis (Freud, 1894, 1919), fright neuroses (Kraepelin, 1886), and shell shock (Mott, 1919; Southward, 1919).

Shell shock is perhaps the most well known of these terms and retains some common currency today when people talk about the effects of traumatic events. Originally it referred to the belief that combat-related disorder was caused by minute brain haemorrhages which resulted from the lodging of shrapnel in the brain during explosions. But the observation that soldiers could develop shell shock even in the absence of explosions led to the belief that shell shock implied weakness of character with the consequence that many soldiers of the First World War, who today would be diagnosed as suffering from PTSD, were executed for cowardice. Fortunately, our understanding of post-traumatic stress reactions has moved beyond this view to recognise that anyone may develop severe and chronic disturbance as a result of traumatic experience—although some people may be more vulnerable or more resistant to the development of disorder.

By the Second World War, further descriptions of post-traumatic stress reactions were provided by psychiatrists. For example, post-trauma-syndrome (Kardiner, 1941), traumatophobia (Rado, 1942), and war neurosis (Grinker & Spiegel, 1943). The clinical descriptions of these terms were remarkably similar to each other as well as to the earlier descriptions provided during the First World War. For example, the post-trauma-syndrome described by Kardiner (1941) included increased feelings of irritability and outbursts of aggression, exaggerated startle response and fixation on the trauma, disrupted personality functioning, and disturbed dreams.

Similar reactions were also being described in adult civilian survivors of traumatic events around this time. For example, Adler (1943), in her most influential study of survivors of Boston's Coconut Grove nightclub fire, made reference to trauma related intrusive thinking, nightmares and insomnia, as well as avoidance behaviours. Other work in the second half of the twentieth century documented increased psychological symptoms in civilian survivors of Hiroshima (Lifton, 1967), natural disasters such as floods (e.g., Abrahams, Price, Whitlock, & Williams, 1976; Bennet, 1970; Logue, Hansen & Struening, 1979; Powell & Penick, 1983; Gleser, Green, & Winget, 1981) and cyclones (e.g., Patrick & Patrick, 1981; Parker, 1977); as well as accidents (e.g., Wilkinsòn, 1983); combat (e.g., Keane, Zimering, & Caddell, 1985b); rape (e.g.,

Burgess & Holmstrom, 1974a, 1974b, 1978; Steketee & Foa, 1987); child sexual abuse (e.g., Frank & Stewart, 1984), political violence in Northern Ireland (e.g., Lyons, 1974), and other events such as the Three Mile Island incident (e.g., Bromet, Parkinson, Schulberg, Dunn, & Gondek, 1982a).

Many research studies have now also accumulated which show that children and adolescents may also develop post-traumatic stress reactions following various stressors such as witnessing mother's sexual assault (e.g., Pynoos & Nader, 1988); a fatal school shooting (e.g., Schwarz & Kowalski, 1991); a sniper attack (e.g., Pynoos et al., 1987); a concentration camp (e.g., Kinzie, Sack, Angell, et al., 1986); warfare (e.g., Arroyo & Eth, 1985; Saigh, 1989); sexual abuse (e.g., Burgess, Hartman, McCausland, & Powers, 1984; Frederick, 1985b; Kiser et al, 1988; McLeer, Deblinger, Atkins, Foa, & Ralphe, 1988; Wolfe, Gentile, & Wolfe, 1989; Wolfe, Sas & Wekerle, 1994); and boating accidents (e.g., Martini, Ryan, Nakayama, et al., 1990).

However, the literature on the subject of trauma-related reactions lay scattered and lacked a common language until the Vietnam War provided the impetus for the current interest in post-traumatic phenomena (see Figley, 1978) and the introduction of the term post-traumatic stress disorder (PTSD: APA, 1980).

HOROWITZ'S TWO-FACTOR MODEL

The diagnostic specification of PTSD was influenced by Horowitz's (1975, 1976, 1979) work on the phenomenology of trauma-related reactions. Horowitz described reactions to trauma within an information-processing model in which, post-trauma, the person is initially assailed by intrusive and emotionally disturbing memories of the trauma and tends to use avoidant strategies to ward off these distressing thoughts, images, and feelings. Phases of intrusion and avoidance occur as the person attempts to process or 'work through' the experience. We shall consider Horowitz's work in more detail in Chapter 5, but for the moment it is important to note that Horowitz considered reactions to consist of alternating phases of intrusions and avoidance or 'denial' and that these symptom categories constituted the architecture of post-traumatic stress reactions (see Table 2.1). This two-factor model, as it became known, was adopted to a large extent by those preparing the American Psychiatric Association's third edition of the *Diagnostic and Statistical Manual of Mental Disorders* (DSM-III) (APA, 1980) as the framework for the new concept of PTSD.

Table 2.1   Operational definitions of signs and symptoms of intrusion and denial

---

Signs and symptoms of intrusion:
   pangs of emotion;
   rumination or preoccupation;
   fear of losing bodily control or hyperactivity in any bodily system;
   intrusive ideas in word form;
   difficulty in dispelling ideas;
   hypervigilance;
   re-enactments;
   bad dreams;
   intrusive thoughts or images while trying to sleep; intrusive images;
   startle reactions;
   illusions; and hallucinations.

Signs and symptoms of denial:
   avoidance of associational connections;
   numbness;
   reduced level of feeling responses to other stimuli;
   rigid role adherence;
   loss of reality appropriacy of thought by switching attitudes;
   unrealistic narrowing of attention;
   vagueness;
   inattention;
   inflexibility or constriction of thought;
   loss of train of thought;
   loss of reality appropriacy of thought by sliding meanings;
   memory failure;
   loss of reality appropriacy of thought by use of disavowal;
   warding of reality-orientated thought by use of phantasy.

Adapted from Horowitz (1979).

POST-TRAUMATIC STRESS DISORDER

Diagnostic and Statistical Manual of the American Psychiatric Association

Within the DSM-III criteria for PTSD (see Table 2.2), symptoms were grouped into three sections: (1) re-experiencing of the traumatic event; (2) numbing of responsiveness to or reduced involvement in the external world; and (3) a miscellaneous section which included memory impairment, difficulty concentrating, hyperalertness or an exaggerated startle response. Patients with PTSD were described as psychophysiologically hyperaroused and they showed an intensification of symptoms following exposure to events associated with the trauma.

In addition, DSM-III described three forms of PTSD: acute (the onset of symptoms within six months from the event and a duration of less than six months); chronic (a duration of symptoms for six months or more); and delayed (the onset of symptoms at least six months after the trauma) (APA,

Table 2.2   DSM-III criteria for PTSD

1.   The existence of a recognizable stressor that would evoke significant symptoms of distress in almost anyone.

2.   Re-experiencing of the trauma as evidenced by at least one of the following:
     (a)   Recurrent and intrusive recollections of the event.
     (b)   Recurrent dreams of the event.
     (c)   Sudden acting or feeling as if the traumatic event were re-occurring, because of an association with an environmental or ideational stimulus.

3.   Numbing of responsiveness to or reduced involvement with the external world, beginning some time after the trauma, as shown by at least one of the following:
     (a)   Markedly diminished interest in one or more significant activities.
     (b)   Feeling of detachment or estrangment from others.
     (c)   Constricted affect.

4.   At least two of the following symptoms that were not present before the trauma:
     (a)   Hyperalertness or exaggerated startle response.
     (b)   Sleep disturbance.
     (c)   Guilt about surviving when others have not, or about behavior required for survival.
     (d)   Memory impairment or trouble concentrating.
     (e)   Avoidance of activities that arouse recollection of the traumatic event.
     (f)   Intensification of symptoms by exposure to events that symbolize or resemble the traumatic event.

Reprinted with permission from the *Diagnostic and Statistical Manual of Mental Disorders,* Third Edition. Copyright 1980 American Psychiatric Association.

1980). These forms of PTSD reflected the clinical experience that there seemed to be no time constraints on the development of PTSD, often taking the form of an immediate reaction, or appearing after weeks, months, or after a period of prolonged incubation, perhaps lasting several years.

What was unique about this disorder was that, with the exception of organic brain syndromes, substance abuse disorders, and puerperal psychosis, the symptoms were thought to arise as the direct result of a psychologically traumatic event (although DSM-III did note that pre-existing psychopathology may increase the likelihood of an individual developing PTSD). The introduction of the diagnostic classification of PTSD was important to the scientific community as it provided the essential constituent for scientific generalisation, a common language with which to describe phenomena, leading to a sharp increase in published work on the topic of post-traumatic stress reactions (Blake, Albano, & Keane, 1992).

However, diagnostic classification is constantly evolving to take account of new knowledge and in 1987 a revised version of the third edition of the *Diagnostic and Statistical Manual* was introduced (DSM-III-R) (APA, 1987) with slight changes to the criteria for the diagnosis of PTSD (see Table 2.3). DSM-III-R asserted that to meet diagnostic criteria, symptoms must usually begin in the immediate aftermath of a traumatic event and last for no less than one month. However, it was also noted that the re-experiencing may not occur for a number of years and that a number of avoidance symptoms may occur

Table 2.3 DSM-III-R criteria for PTSD

A. The person has experienced an event that is outside the range of usual human experience and that would be markedly distressing to almost anyone, e.g., serious threat to one's life or physical integrity; serious threat or harm to one's children, spouse, or other close relatives and friends; sudden destruction of one's home or community; or seeing another person who has recently been, or is being, seriously injured or killed as the result of an accident or physical violence.

B. The traumatic event is persistently reexperienced in at least one of the following ways:
   (1)   recurrent and intrusive distressing recollections of the event(in young children, repetitive play in which themes or aspects of the trauma are expressed)
   (2)   recurrent distressing dreams of the event
   (3)   sudden acting or feeling as if the traumatic event were recurring (includes a sense of reliving the experience, illusions, hallucinations, and dissociative [flashback] episodes, even those that occur upon awakening or when intoxicated)
   (4)   intense psychological distress or exposure to events that symbolize or resemble an aspect of the traumatic event, including anniversaries of the trauma

C. Persistent avoidance of stimuli associated with the trauma or numbing of responsiveness (not present before the trauma), as indicated by at least three of the following:
   (1)   efforts to avoid thoughts or feelings associated with the trauma
   (2)   efforts to avoid activities or situations that arouse recollections of the trauma
   (3)   inability to recall an important aspect of the trauma (psychogenic amnesia)
   (4)   markedly diminished interest in significant activities (in young children, loss of recently acquired developmental skills such as toilet training or language skills)
   (5)   feeling of detachment or estrangement from others
   (6)   restricted range of affect, e.g., unable to have loving feelings
   (7)   sense of a foreshortened future, e.g., child does not expect to have a career, marriage, or children, or a long life

D. Persistent symptoms of increased arousal (not present before the trauma), as indicated by at least two of the following:
   (1)   difficulty falling or staying asleep
   (2)   irritability or outbursts of anger
   (3)   difficulty concentrating
   (4)   hypervigilance
   (5)   exaggerated startle response
   (6)   physiologic reactivity at exposure to events that symbolize or resemble an aspect of the traumatic event (e.g., a woman who was raped in an elevator breaks out in a sweat when entering any elevator)

E. Duration of the disturbance (symptoms in B, C, and D) of at least one month.

Specify delayed onset if the onset of symptoms was at least six months after the trauma.

throughout this period of delayed onset. As with DSM-III, in the DSM-III-R system there were also three sections of symptoms: re-experiencing, avoidance, and hyperarousal. However, the re-experiencing section now included distress caused by re-exposure to trauma-relevant stimuli which had been included in DSM-III's miscellaneous section. This was an important shift in thinking which recognised that re-experiencing was often accompanied by strong emotional responses. Similarly, the numbing section now included efforts to avoid thoughts, feelings, and activities associated with the trauma from DSM-III's miscellaneous section. This, too, was important in recognising that avoidance reactions can take many forms. These changes illustrate how diagnostic criteria are constantly evolving as more becomes known about the phenomenology of a disorder. In this case, the changes in criteria reflected the view that symptoms could be grouped into two main clusters, intrusions and denials, as proposed by Horowitz; although some symptoms of PTSD, i.e., difficulty falling or staying asleep and difficulty concentrating, remained outside of the two-factor model despite these symptoms being viewed by Horowitz as indicators of intrusion and denials respectively. Another change in the diagnostic criteria between DSM-III and DSM-III-R was the omission of survivor guilt. Although guilt is commonly observed in survivors of traumatic events (Raphael, 1986), its specificity is likely to be low in the presence of bereavement or major depression where guilt is also common (March, 1990).

The role of prior psychopathology

Both DSM-III and DSM-III-R represented an important shift in understanding from previous editions of the DSM which had emphasised the role of prior psychopathology in understanding emotional reactions to trauma. The DSM-I (APA, 1952) contained the diagnosis 'gross stress reaction' which, although characterised by an individual's exposure to extreme emotional and physical stress, was thought to diminish rather rapidly unless maintained by premorbid personality traits. Similarly, in the DSM-II (APA, 1968) the category of 'gross stress reaction' was deleted and trauma-related stress was considered only in the context of adult adjustment reactions where a diagnosis of 'transient situational disturbance' could be given. As the name of this reaction implies, stress responses were thought of as time-limited phenomena with prolonged responses to stress having their roots in early individual history and personality. A role for early individual history and personality has, however, been reintroduced in DSM-IV (APA, 1994). An example which illustrates the role of early experiences is given by Mary in Case History 3.

Here it could be possible that Mary's early established belief in physical injury as a consequence of sexual abuse had led her to catastrophise physical symptoms as indicative of extreme pathology. Also her distrust of others had led to multiple investigations despite nothing being found. Her experience of an extremely unpleasant muscular reaction, together with her mother's attribu-

CASE HISTORY 3

Mary is a 28-year-old single Afro-Caribbean woman, born in Jamaica. She lives with her mother and is unemployed. She was seen only after the encouragement of her boyfriend, four years after having experienced an adverse reaction to medication while a patient in hospital. She reported that nightmares began three days after the experience. She reported that in her dream her body is arching up and she cannot breathe. She calls a nurse's name and asks for water and says that she does not want to die. She believes she cannot move and that she is about to die. In consequence she is afraid to sleep at night and tries to stay awake. She also experiences intrusive thoughts about the experience while awake. She sees images of the nurse, of a doctor and hears her mother's voice saying that she will die or be paralysed. These memories are also triggered by coming to the clinic, reading in the newspaper about medical mistakes and watching TV programmes about hospitals. She attempts to avoid such thoughts and feelings. She does not talk about her experiences because she does not want to burden others. In particular she avoids the hospital where she was taken and the area immediately around it. She has lost interest in former interests. She has given up her psychology course, she rarely goes out socially and does not want to be with people.

Mary has a lengthy medical history dating from the age of 15 years when she was referred for psychiatric assessment and found to be depressed with behavioural disturbances. She subsequently underwent numerous physical investigations for abdominal pain, 'fits', respiratory symptoms and menstrual irregularities and migraine. She has had three laparoscopies with no major abnormalities found. A previous muscular dystonic reaction to Maxilon, an anti-emetic had been observed. Four years ago a psychologist obtained a history of repeated sexual abuse at the age of 11 years committed by her step-father. Mary is reported to have believed that she suffered internal physical damage during this forced intercourse. Currently, Mary was being treated for migraine and arthritic knees.

tions, was sufficient to make Mary reach the traumatic conclusion that she was dying—a conclusion which she was unable to check out with others. Hence previous psychological problems may interact with severity of an event in accounting for individual variation—a point we shall return to later.

As well as containing the diagnostic criteria for PTSD (see Table 2.4), DSM-IV reintroduced the category of acute stress disorder (see Table 2.5). Acute stress disorder is specified as lasting for a minimum of two days and a maximum of four weeks in contrast to PTSD which has a specified duration criteria of at least one month. Survivors must have had the symptoms for at least this amount of time to meet the criteria for diagnosis. The main change in DSM-IV, however, was the shift in thinking regarding Criterion A (the criterion for assessing whether or not the person has been exposed to a traumatic event).

What is a traumatic event?

The example of Mary may lead us to question the definition of 'trauma'. Despite the attempt in previous editions of DSM to define traumatic events

Table 2.4 DSM-IV Criteria for PTSD

A. The person has been exposed to a traumatic event in which both the following were present:
  (1) The person experienced, witnessed, or was confronted with an event or events that involved actual or threatened death or serious injury, or a threat to the physical integrity of self or others.
  (2) The person's response involved fear, helplessness, or horror. *Note:* In children, this may be expressed instead by disorganised or agitated behaviour.

B. The traumatic event is persistently re-experienced in one (or more) of the following ways:
  (1) Recurrent and intrusive distressing recollections of the event, including images, thoughts, or perceptions. *Note:* In young children, repetitive play may occur in which themes or aspects of the trauma are expressed.
  (2) Recurrent distressing dreams of the event. *Note:* In children, there may be frightening dreams without recognisable content.
  (3) Acting or feeling as if the traumatic event were recurring (includes a sense of reliving the experience, illusions, hallucinations, and dissociative flashback episodes, including those that occur on awakening or when intoxicated). *Note:* In young children, trauma-specific re-enactment may occur.
  (4) Intense psychological distress at exposure to internal or external cues that symbolise or resemble an aspect of the traumatic event.
  (5) Physiological reactivity on exposure to internal or external cues that symbolise or resemble an aspect of the traumatic event.

C. Persistent avoidance of stimuli associated with the trauma and numbing of general responsiveness (not present before the trauma), as indicated by three (or more) of the following:
  (1) Efforts to avoid thoughts, feelings, or conversations associated with the trauma.
  (2) Efforts to avoid activities, places, or people that arouse recollections of the trauma.
  (3) Inability to recall an important aspect of the trauma.
  (4) Markedly diminished interest or participation in significant activities.
  (5) Feeling of detachment or estrangement from others.
  (6) Restricted range of affect (e.g., unable to have loving feelings).
  (7) Sense of foreshortened future (e.g., does not expect to have a career, marriage, children, or a normal life span).

D. Persistent symptoms of increased arousal (not present before the trauma) as indicated by two (or more) of the following:
  (1) Difficulty falling or staying asleep.
  (2) Irritability or outbursts of anger.
  (3) Difficulty concentrating.
  (4) Hypervigilance.
  (5) Exaggerated startle response.

E. Duration of the disturbance (symptoms in criteria B, C, and D) is more than one month.

F. The disturbance causes clinically significant distress or impairment in social, occupational, or other important areas of functioning.

Specify if:
  Acute: if duration of symptoms is less that three months.
  Chronic: if duration of symptoms is three months or more.

Specify if:
  With delayed onset: if onset of symptoms is at least six months after the stressor.

Reprinted with permission from the *Diagnostic and Statistical Manual of Mental Disorders*, Fourth Edition. Copyright 1994 American Psychiatric Association.

Table 2.5 DSM-IV criteria for Acute Stress Disorder

A. The person has been exposed to a traumatic event in which both of the following were present:
    (1) The person experienced, witnessed, or was confronted with an event or events that involved actual or threatened death or serious injury, or a threat to the physical integrity of self or others.
    (2) The person's response involved fear, helplessness, or horror.

B. Either while experiencing or after experiencing the distressing event, the individual has three (or more) of the following dissociative symptoms:

    (1) A subjective sense of numbing, detachment, or absence of emotional responsiveness.
    (2) A reduction in awareness of his or her surroundings (e.g., 'being in a daze').
    (3) Derealisation.
    (4) Depersonalisation.
    (5) Dissociative amnesia (i.e., inability to recall an important aspect of the trauma).

C. The traumatic event is persistently re-experienced in at least one of the following ways: recurrent images, thoughts, dreams, illusions, flashback episodes, or a sense of reliving the experience; or distress on exposure to reminders of the traumatic event.

D. Marked avoidance of stimuli that arouse recollections of the trauma (e.g., thoughts, feelings, conversations, activities, places, people).

E. Marked symptoms of anxiety or increased arousal (e.g., difficulty sleeping, irritability, poor concentration, hypervigilance, exaggerated startle response, motor restlessness).

F. The disturbance causes clinically significant distress or impairment in social, occupational, or other important areas of functioning or impairs the individual's ability to pursue some necessary task, such as obtaining necessary assistance or mobilising personal resources by telling family members about the traumatic experience.

G. The disturbance lasts for a minimum of two days and a maximum of four weeks and occurs within four weeks of the traumatic event.

H. The disturbance is not due to the direct physiological effects of a substance (e.g., a drug of abuse, a medication) or a general medical condition, is not better accounted for by Brief Psychotic Disorder, and is not merely an exacerbation of a preexisting Axis I or Axis II disorder.

Reprinted with permission from the *Diagnostic and Statistical Manual of Mental Disorders*, Fourth Edition. Copyright 1994 American Psychiatric Association.

objectively as events outside the range of usual human experience (see Tables 2.2 and 2.3), the question of what actually constitutes a traumatic event has proved to be a definitional quagmire. But it is a question of considerable importance because, by definition, criterion A has traditionally served as the gatekeeper to the diagnosis of PTSD.

> . . . If a person does not meet the required definition of a stressful event, it matters little whether all the other criteria are met because the person cannot be diagnosed

with PTSD. If Criterion A is loosely defined and over inclusive, then the prevalence of PTSD is likely to increase, whereas a restrictive definition will reduce its
prevalence. (Davidson & Foa, 1991, p. 346).

Some events, such as an aeroplane disaster or ferry sinking, were clearly
understood to fulfil criterion A as specified in DSM-III and DSM-III-R.
However, there remained much debate on whether other events, such as the
death of a spouse through cancer, met the criterion (Baum, 1987; March,
1993). If a person can develop all the emotional and behavioural symptoms of
PTSD without having experienced an event outside the range of usual human
experience, then it could be argued that the definition of what constitutes a
traumatic event must change. It was argued that what was important was how
the person perceived the event and thus that criterion A should include reference to subjective factors. Clearly, what is traumatic to one person may not be
so to another. But others argued that by broadening the definition to include
subjective factors, criterion A would become all but abolished so that trauma
was defined in terms of its effects. In response, it was argued that previous
definitions, despite attempting to define the event objectively, implied subjective perception as well as objective environmental factors, anyway. For
example, judgements of unusualness of the event, the chief criterion in DSM-
III and DSM-III-R, were necessarily based on the clinicians assessment of what
the average person in similar circumstances and with similar sociocultural
values would experience (see March, 1993).

In response to these arguments, the authors of the DSM-IV reformulated
criterion A (of both Acute Stress Disorder and PTSD) to include: (1) exposure
to a traumatic event coupled with (2) the person's reaction to it (see Tables 2.4
and 2.5). The inclusion of subjective factors into criterion A of DSM-IV was an
important theoretical shift, one which is central to the model of psychosocial
adaptation which we shall describe in Chapter 5.

International Classification of Diseases

As already noted, the APA's classification system provided researchers with the
common language with which to facilitate research throughout the world on
PTSD. Following this lead, the World Health Organisation (WHO) also
included the category of PTSD within the most recent edition of the International Classification of Diseases, ICD-10 (WHO, 1993).

Prior to this, ICD-9 (WHO, 1978) acknowledged two diagnoses to cover the
emotional problems which follow trauma. The first was 'Acute Reaction to
Stress'. This was defined as a very transient disorder of any severity and nature,
which occurred in individuals without any apparent mental disorder in response to exceptional physical or mental stress, such as disaster or combat, and
which was thought to subside usually within hours or days. In addition to this
diagnosis, there was 'Adjustment Reaction' which was defined as a mild or
transient disorder lasting longer than an acute stress reaction and which occur-

Table 2.6   ICD-10 criteria for acute stress reaction

There must be an immediate and clear temporal connection between the impact of an exceptional stressor and the onset of symptoms; onset is usually within a few minutes, if not immediate. In addition, the symptoms:

(a)   show a mixed and usually changing picture; in addition to the initial state of 'daze', depression, anxiety, anger, despair, overactivity, and withdrawal may all be seen, but no one type of symptoms predominates for long;

(b)   resolve rapidly (within a few hours at the most) in those cases where removal from the stressful environment is possible; in cases where the stress continues or cannot by its nature be reversed, the symptoms usually begin to diminish after 24–48 hours and are usually minimal after about three days.

This diagnosis should not be used to cover sudden exacerbations of symptoms in individuals already showing symptoms that fulfil the criteria of any other psychiatric disorder, except for those in F60 (personality disorders). However, a history of previous psychiatric disorder does not invalidate the use of this diagnosis.

Includes: acute crisis reaction
                combat fatigue
                crisis state
                psychic shock

Reprinted with permission from the *International Classification of Diseases*, Tenth Edition. Copyright 1993 World Health Organization.

red in individuals of any age without any apparent pre-existing psychopathology. Such disorder was thought to be often relatively circumscribed or situation specific and usually closely related in time and content to stressors such as bereavement, or separation.

ICD-10 introduced the new category of 'reaction to severe stress and adjustment disorders'. As with the APA system, the experience of a traumatic event is thought to be a necessary aetiological factor in the disorders contained within this category. Within this category, ICD-10 considers three diagnoses: (1) acute stress reaction, (2) post-traumatic stress disorder, and (3) adjustment disorder.

Acute stress reaction (see Table 2.6) describes a transient disorder which develops in an individual without any other apparent mental disorder in response to exceptional physical and/or mental stress. Symptoms are thought to appear usually within minutes of the impact of the stressful stimulus and, often, to disappear within hours. Notably, symptoms, expected to last no longer than 2–3 days at the most, include an initial state of 'daze' with some constriction of the field of consciousness and narrowing of attention, inability to comprehend stimuli, and disorientation. Autonomic signs of panic anxiety (tachycardia, sweating, flushing) are commonly present. With regard to the stressor itself, ICD-10 notes that the stressor may be an overwhelming traumatic experience involving serious threat to the security or physical integrity of the individual or of a loved one (e.g., natural catastrophe, accident, battle, criminal assault, rape), or an unusually sudden and threatening change in the social position and/or network of the individual, such as multiple bereavement or domestic fire. The risk of this disorder developing is increased if physical exhaustion or

Table 2.7   ICD-10 criteria for Post-traumatic Stress Disorder

This disorder should not generally be diagnosed unless there is evidence that it arose within six months of a traumatic event of exceptional severity. A 'probable' diagnosis might still be possible if the delay between the event and the onset was longer than six months, provided that the clinical manifestations are typical and no alternative identification of the disorder (e.g., as an anxiety or obsessive–compulsive disorder or depressive episode) is plausible. In addition to evidence of trauma, there must be a repetitive, intrusive recollection or re-enactment of the event in memories, daytime imagery, or dreams. Conspicuous emotional detachment, numbing of feeling, and avoidance of stimuli that might arouse recollection of the trauma are often present but are not essential for the diagnosis. The autonomic disturbances, mood disorder, and behavioural abnormalities all contribute to the diagnosis but are not of prime importance.

The late chronic sequelae of devastating stress, i.e., those manifest decades after the stressful experience, should be classified under F62.0.

Includes:traumatic neurosis.

Reprinted with permission from the *International Classification of Diseases*, Tenth Edition. Copyright 1993 World Health Organization.

organic factors (e g., in the elderly) are also present. Individual vulnerability and coping capacity play a role in the occurrence and severity of acute stress reactions, as evidenced by the fact that not all people exposed to exceptional stress develop the disorder.

The diagnostic criteria of post-traumatic stress disorder outlined by the WHO (see Table 2.7) are similar to those of the APA and involve the identification of a threatening event which is thought to be necessary in the onset of disorder, although the approach to making the diagnosis is very different. As with the APA system, it is recognised that other factors, such as pre-existing disorder, may play a role in the aetiology of PTSD, but they are not thought to be either necessary or sufficient. Symptoms are thought to arise as a delayed and/or protracted response to a stressful event or situation (either short- or long-lasting) that is exceptionally threatening or catastrophic and which is likely to cause pervasive distress in almost anyone (e.g., natural or man-made disaster, combat, serious accident, witnessing the violent death of others, or being the victim of torture, terrorism, rape, or other crime). Predisposing factors such as personality traits (e.g., compulsive, asthenic) or previous history of neurotic illness may lower the threshold for the development of the syndrome or aggravate its course, but they are neither necessary nor sufficient to explain its occurrence. Typical symptoms include episodes of repeated reliving of the trauma in intrusive memories or 'flashbacks' or dreams, which occur against the persisting background of a sense of 'numbness' and emotional blunting, detachment from other people, unresponsiveness to surroundings, anhedonia, and avoidance of activities and situations reminiscent of the trauma. Commonly, there is fear and avoidance of cues that remind the sufferer of the original trauma. Rarely, there may be dramatic, acute bursts of fear, panic or aggression, triggered by stimuli arousing a sudden recollection and/or re-enactment of the trauma or of the original reaction to it. There is usually a

Table 2.8 ICD-10 criteria for adjustment disorders

Diagnosis depends on a careful evaluation of the relationship between:

(a)   form, content, and severity of symptoms;
(b)   previous history and personality; and
(c)   stressful event, situation, or life crisis.

The presence of this third factor should be clearly established and there should be strong, though perhaps presumptive, evidence that the disorder would not have arisen without it. If the stressor is relatively minor, or if a temporal connection (less than three months) cannot be demonstrated, the disorder should be classified elsewhere, according to its presenting features.

Includes: culture shock
            grief reaction
            hospitalism in children.

Excludes: separation anxiety disorder of childhood (F93.0).

If the criteria for adjustment disorder are satisfied, the clinical form or predominant features can be specified by a fifth character:

F43.20   *Brief depressive reaction*
A transient, mild depressive state of duration not exceeding 1 month.

F43.21   *Prolonged depressive reaction*
A mild depressive state occurring in response to a prolonged exposure to a stressful situation but of duration not exceeding 2 years.

F43.22   *Mixed anxiety and depressive reaction*
Both anxiety and depressive symptoms are prominent, but at levels no greater than specified in mixed anxiety and depressive disorder (F41.2) or other mixed anxiety disorder (F41.3).

F43.23   *With predominant disturbance of other emotions*
The symptoms are usually of several types of emotion, such as anxiety, depression, worry, tensions, and anger. Symptoms of anxiety and depression may fulfil the criteria for mixed anxiety and depressive disorder (F41.2) or other mixed anxiety disorder (F41.3), but they are not so predominant that other more specific depressive or anxiety disorders can be diagnosed. This category should also be used for reactions in children in which regressive behaviour such as bed-wetting or thumb-sucking are also present.

F43.24   *With predominant disturbance of conduct*
The main disturbance is one involving conduct, e.g., an adolescent grief reaction resulting in aggressive or dissocial behaviour.

F43.25   *With mixed disturbance of emotions and conduct*
Both emotional symptoms and disturbance of conduct are prominent features.

F43.28   *With other specified predominant symptoms*

state of autonomic hyperarousal with hypervigilance, an enhanced startle reaction, and insomnia. Anxiety and depression are commonly associated with the above symptoms and signs, and suicidal ideation may be present. Excessive use of alcohol or drugs may also be a complicating factor. The onset follows the trauma with a latency period which may range from a few weeks to months (but rarely exceeds six months). The course is thought to be fluctuating but recovery can be expected in the majority of cases. In a small proportion of patients, the ICD-10 notes, the condition may show a chronic course over many years and a transition into an enduring personality change.

The category of 'Adjustment disorders' (see Table 2.8) refers to states of subjective and emotional disturbance which arise in the period of adaptation to a significant life change or to the consequences of a stressful event. ICD-10 also notes that the stressor involved may have affected the person's social network through, for example, bereavement. Although it is assumed that the condition would not have arisen without the stressor, what differentiates this category from that of post-traumatic stress disorder is the acknowledgement of the role of individual difference variables. Symptoms are thought to include depressed mood, anxiety, worry, a feeling of inability to cope, plan ahead, or continue in the present situation, and some degree of disability in the performance of daily routine. With adolescents, conduct disorders are thought to be an associated feature and in children, regressive behaviour such as thumb sucking may be part of the symptom pattern. The onset is usually within one month of the occurrence of the stressful event and the duration of symptoms does not usually exceed six months, except in the case of prolonged depressive reaction where the duration is not thought to exceed two years.

The importance of the ICD-10, in contrast to that of the DSM-III-R, was that it drew attention to the varieties of stress response and the relative roles of the traumatic event and psychosocial factors. With regard to PTSD, however, the major difference between the WHO and APA systems is that ICD-10 states that symptoms of emotional numbing are not necessary for the diagnosis of PTSD—although emotional numbing is viewed as a frequent accompaniment to the disorder.

It is the re-experiencing symptoms which are the hallmark signs of PTSD. (Symptoms in common to each of our three case examples so far.) In particular, sleep disturbances have been characterised as a hallmark of PTSD (Ross, Ball, Sullivan, & Caroff, 1989) and, along with nightmares, are referred to frequently in the PTSD literature (e.g., Glaubman, Mikulincer, Porat, Wasserman, & Birger, 1990; Hefez, Metz, & Lavie, 1987; Inman, Silver, & Doghramji, 1990; Lavie, Hefez, Halperin, & Enoch, 1979; Marshall, 1975; Mellman, Kulick-Bell, Ashlock, & Nolan, 1995; Rosen, Reynolds, Yeager, Houck, & Hurwitz, 1991; van der Kolk, Blitz, Burr, Sherry, & Hartmann, 1984a).

COURSE OF DISORDER

Understandably, the very long-term effects of traumatic events are not as well documented as the shorter term effects. However, the evidence beginning to accumulate does suggest that, for survivors of some events, the effects can be very long-lasting. Holen (1991), for example, found that some survivors of an oil rig collapse in the North Sea continued to show psychological problems eight years after the event. PTSD has been reported 14 years on in 17% of survivors of the Buffalo Creek disaster (Green et al., 1990a). Some events appear to be particularly likely to lead to long-term distress. Kilpatrick, Saunders, Veronen, Best, & Von (1987) reported that almost 17% of their sample of women met full PTSD criteria 17 years after a sexual assault. Longer-term studies have shown PTSD up to 40 years later in Second World War combat veterans and POWs (Davidson, Kudler, Saunders, & Smith, 1990; Hierholzer, Munson, Peabody, & Rosenberg, 1992; Kluznik, Speed, Van Valkenburg, & Magraw, 1986; Rosen, Fields, Hand, Falsettie, & Van Kammen, 1989; Speed, Engdahl, Schwartz, & Eberly, 1989; Spiro, Schnurr, & Aldwin, 1994; Zeiss & Dickman, 1989) and Jewish survivors of the Holocaust (Krystal, 1970; Kuch & Cox, 1992).

Although these data suggest that PTSD can continue many years after an event, survivors often report only being intermittently troubled by their symptoms (Zeiss & Dickman, 1989) and PTSD can have a varied course (Blank, 1993). Evidence for this comes chiefly from McFarlane (1988b) who assessed over 300 firefighters for psychiatric 'caseness' using the General Health Questionnaire at 4, 11, and 29 months after the event (see Box 2.1). McFarlane identified eight patterns of response: (1) 50% fell into the no-disorder group (i.e., not reaching caseness at any of the three time points); (2) 9% fell into the acute group (i.e., reaching caseness at 4 months but not at 11 or 29 months); (3) 10% were identified as persistent and chronic (i.e., reaching caseness at all three time points); (4) 6% fell into the resolved chronic group (i.e., reaching caseness at 4 and 11 months but not at 29 months); (5) 5% fell into the recurrent group (i.e., reaching caseness at 4 and 29 months but not at 11 months); (6) 3% fell into the persistent delayed onset group (i.e., not reaching caseness at 4 months but reaching caseness at 11 and 29 months); (7) 5% fell into the 11 month delayed onset group (i.e., not reaching caseness at 4 or 29 months but reaching caseness at 11 months); and (8) 11% fell into the 29 month delayed onset group (i.e., not reaching caseness at 4 or 11 months but only at 29 months).

ASSOCIATED SYMPTOMS

The diagnosis of PTSD represents only a circumscribed set of symptoms experienced by survivors of traumatic events. As well as enduring personality changes, which Horowitz (1986a, 1986b) refers to as post-traumatic character disorder, many studies of survivors report high levels of both anxiety and depressive symptoms in association with PTSD. Such an example is provided by Sarah (see Case History 4)

Sarah suffered multiple losses as a consequence of the accident, her injuries

---

Box 2.1   Assessment of psychological health using the GHQ

The General Health Questionnaire was originally designed as a screening instrument with the general population. However, it has been used satisfactorily with disaster victims in a number of studies (e.g., Joseph et al., 1993g; Parker, 1977; McFarlane, 1988a, 1988b, 1989, 1992a), railway accidents (Karlehagen et al., 1993; Malt et al., 1993) and has been extensively employed in the population surveys conducted in Northern Ireland to assess the effects of political violence (Cairns & Wilson, 1989). There are several versions of this instrument available ranging from the short 12 item version to the 60-item version (Goldberg, 1972, 1978; Goldberg & Hillier, 1979; Goldberg & Williams, 1988). However, it is the 28-item version (Goldberg & Hillier, 1979) which has generally been adopted as the GHQ-28 consists of four subscales: somatic symptoms, anxiety and insomnia, social dysfunction, and severe depression. However, several studies have used the 12-item General Health Questionnaire (Goldberg, 1972) which, despite its brevity, has been found to be a valid measure of psychiatric impairment (Henderson, Byrne, & Duncan-Jones, 1981; Tennant, 1977) with a 90% specificity and a 78% sensitivity of PTSD using a structured interview (McFarlane, 1986b). Using this questionnaire patients can be grouped into those scoring above or below a certain cutoff point; depending on the version used, those scoring above the cutoff point are classified as cases. Other general self-report measures which have been used include the 90-item Symptom Checklist (SCL-90: Derogatis, 1977, 1983). The SCL-90 has been used extensively in the work by Baum and his colleagues on residents living near Three Mile Island (e.g., Baum, Gatchel, & Schaeffer, 1983b; Davidson, Weiss, O'Keefe, & Baum, 1991).

---

and her prolonged period of immobility: her job, her financial security, her plans for the future, her relationship, her independence and her very personality. Sarah blamed herself for the feelings of grief and rage she felt, was unable to express these feeings and remained psychologically stuck in a chronic depression.

McFarlane and Papay (1992) investigated multiple diagnoses in the victims of a natural disaster. Over 450 firefighters who had been exposed to the bush fire that devastated large areas of southeastern Australia in 1983 were screened using the General Health Questionnaire at 4, 11, and 29 months subsequent to the event (see Box 2.1).

On the basis of these data, a high-risk group of 147 firefighters were interviewed using a standard interview schedule—the Diagnostic Interview Schedule (DIS: Robins & Helzer, 1985) at 42 months to examine the prevalence of PTSD as well as affective and anxiety disorders. PTSD was the most common disorder (18%) followed by major depression (10%). Only 23% of the 70 subjects who had developed PTSD did not attract a further diagnosis, usually of major depression. McFarlane and Papay's data are particularly important because theirs was a community sample and thus the coexistence of disorders was not simply a consequence of treatment-seeking or some other factor. Of course it may be that exposure to bushfire is particularly depressogenic. The generalisability of these data needs to be established. However, other research

CASE HISTORY 4

Sarah, a 34-year-old woman, of Afro-Caribbean background, was seen three years after a major car accident in which she was the passenger and suffered multiple and serious fractures requiring long periods of hospitalisation. Indeed, Sarah still suffered considerable pain, was badly scarred and walked with difficulty and with a stick. She was still awaiting further surgery on her wrist and leg and was involved in a claim for financial compensation. She was unable to work, was relying upon benefits and was forced to live at home with her parents. She expressed extreme frustration at her necessary dependency and loss of control over her life.

Sarah spoke about her memories of the accident in a flat, unemotional voice and generally presented herself as cheerful and outgoing. But she reported recurrent intrusive memories of the accident and of her experiences in hospital. She felt she was much more anxious than before the accident, especially when being reminded of the accident (e.g., a film depicting a car crash on TV) or in situations such as walking down the street alone. She was phobic of travelling by bus, train, and tube and extremely reluctant to go outside alone. She was particularly concerned with the probability of further accidents, with meeting people and having to talk about her difficulties and being vulnerable in a public place. She reported making efforts to shut off distressing memories using music as a distractor.

Notably, Sarah spoke of herself as a changed person: formerly carefree and independent, she reported feeling insignificant, without purpose, and uncertain of her changed identity. Before the accident she had been a professional athlete and involved in fashion design, intending to set up her own business. It was clear that her whole world had changed dramatically. She was now largely confined to her parents' home, inactive, unable to see friends and overcome with sadness and irritation. She felt guilty about her feelings.

---

suggests that depression is also common among survivors of other events. For example, North, Smith, and Spitznagel (1994) also report that the most frequent additional post-disaster diagnosis in survivors of a mass shooting was major depression, which was present in 35% of women and 25% of men. Furthermore, Loughrey, Bell, Kee, Roddy, and Curran (1988) investigated the incidence of PTSD among 499 people exposed to various types of civilian trauma in Northern Ireland, finding that out of those who developed PTSD, 35% showed a diagnosis of depression compared to 12% of those not suffering from PTSD. In addition, co-morbidity appeared to be an important predictor of chronic PTSD.

Substance abuse

There have been many reports of increased substance use in survivors of traumatic events, particularly in combat veterans (Jelinek & Williams, 1984; Lacoursiere, Godfrey, & Ruby, 1980; Penk et al., 1981; Solomon, Mikulincer, & Kotler, 1987b) where substance abuse is a common co-diagnosis along with depression and anxiety (Davidson & Foa, 1991). In one study of 40 Vietnam veterans with PTSD, it was found that 63% reported heavy and often abusive alcohol consumption (Keane, Caddell, Martin, Zimering, & Fairbank, 1983).

In a larger study of 268 Vietnam veterans, Roth (1986) found that almost half of the combat veterans with stress disorders were heavy drinkers and that over half used drugs other than alcohol. Friedman and colleagues surveyed a large sample of veterans who had applied for outpatient services. Of those diagnosed as suffering from PTSD, 19% were also diagnosed with current alcohol abuse or dependence (Friedman et al., 1987). In another study, it was found that of 440 veterans suffering from PTSD, 22% had a current diagnosis of alcohol abuse or dependence and 6% as suffering from drug abuse or dependence (Kulka et al., 1990). What is particularly interesting, however, is that when past history was investigated, Kulka et al. (1990) found that 75% of these same veterans could have been diagnosed as alcohol abusing or dependent and 23% drug abusing or dependent prior to the war.

But although substance abuse seems to be particularly prevalent among combat veterans, it is not confined to this population, and it has also been reported in survivors of sexual assault and child sexual abuse (Yeary, 1982) as well as survivors of disaster (Abrahams et al., 1976; Logue et al., 1979; Gleser et al., 1981; Goenjian, 1993).

In our 30-month follow up of the survivors of the *Herald of Free Enterprise* (Joseph, Yule, Williams, & Hodgkinson, 1993f) several questions were asked about changes in substance use. Respondents were asked to rate whether they had used alcohol, cigarettes, sleeping tablets, antidepressants, and tranquillisers more than they usually did. We found that retrospective ratings for the six months immediately following the disaster showed that 73% reported that their alcohol consumption had increased; 44% that their cigarette consumption had increased; 40% that their use of sleeping tablets had increased; 28% that their use of antidepressants had increased; and 21% that their use of tranquillisers had increased. What was interesting was that although all ratings of use had significantly decreased at 30 months after the event, compared to the retrospective ratings for the first six months, many were still using alcohol and cigarettes at an increased level suggesting that, for some survivors at least, the increased use of cigarettes and alcohol may become stable and long-term habits. An interesting example of alcohol abuse in an adult survivor of childhood abuse is provided by Rose (see Case History 5).

As well as presenting serious health risks, alcohol problems may have serious effects on other areas of a person's life. For example, with Vietnam veterans there is evidence that alcohol abuse, along with other factors such as low levels of social support, may lead to later homelessness (Rosenheck & Fontana, 1994).

Cognitive impairment

There is evidence suggesting that impairment of memory and cognition are major characteristics of PTSD. Wilkinson (1983), in his report on survivors of the Hyatt Regency Hotel skywalk collapse, found that 44% of his 102 subjects

CASE HISTORY 5

Rose, a 70-year-old retired teacher, was referred because of fears of driving and of travelling by train. These problems dated from having suffered a fracture of the right humerus six months before. Rose was also reported to be drinking heavily and she had been previously suspended from work suspected of being intoxicated while on duty although, on inquiry, she had been cleared of this misdemeanour. A year ago she had been referred to two services for alcohol abuse but had not been engaged. Rose described the fracture as having been subjectively 'traumatic'. She had broken her arm in a fall at home alone. She had not sought help. She couldn't see how she could manage travelling and she didn't want to go to hospital fearing she 'wouldn't come home again.' (She had always had a horror of anaesthesia.) She couldn't undress herself and sat on the floor all night, fearful of looking at her arm and hoping that the swelling would go down. Eventually she called the doctor. In retrospect she thought she could have killed herself. Rose thought she had been drinking too much since the death of her mother, five years previously, also after a fall. Rose continued to think of her a great deal, to blame herself for not doing more for her mother. She also recounted an upsetting experience at the funeral when she was informed that her mother's body had not been in the chapel of rest as she had expected. All of these events had culminated in Rose being on leave from work for a prolonged period, being confined to the home, being dependent upon others and having difficulty coping with everyday tasks. On her expected return to work she felt vulnerable to another adverse experience and feared an assault on the train. This fear resulted in avoidance and finally in her taking retirement. Without the structure and meaning her work gave her, Rose felt more depressed and pitied herself, leading her to feel she deserved a drink. She had no plans for the future, she tended to procrastinate in day-to-day tasks and had little contact with others. After some sessions in therapy, Rose began to telephone in distress, often in an intoxicated state and disclosed that she had been assaulted by a man in childhood who tried to strangle her and subsequently killed himself. This experience had never been discussed and had given her a sense of guilt and responsibility.

had difficulty concentrating and 27% had memory difficulties. A more recent study that has evaluated the cognitive deficits in PTSD patients by means of objective tests, such as the Wechsler Adult Intelligence Scale, reports evidence that patients with PTSD have substantial impairment of cognitive functioning (Gil, Calev, Greenberg, Kugelmass, & Lerer, 1990). Gil et al. (1990) argue that their results are consistent with the view that PTSD patients have a generalised cognitive deficit similar to that encountered in other psychiatric disorders such as depression and schizophrenia. However, they do suggest that the deficits observed are likely to be a secondary consequence of general psychiatric symptomatology rather than a primary feature of the disorder. Other more recent work has documented autobiographical memory disturbance in PTSD patients (McNally, Lasko, Macklin, & Pitman, 1995). A complex example of severe PTSD where cognitive impairment was important is provided by Mark (see Case History 6).

CASE HISTORY 6

Mark is a 60-year-old single man of Jamaican origin who was first seen for assessment in connection with his compensation claim seven months after experiencing an objectively minor road traffic accident in which he was the driver. Mark had suffered injury to his neck in the accident, was phobic of driving and was unable to work as a lorry driver. He worried about his financial security and had exhausted his savings. Mark experienced intrusive imagery of the accident, in which he had thought he might be killed, and also disturbing related images of his own death and of his own grave and tombstone. He was seriously depressed, believing himself to be useless and his life over. He had withdrawn from social activities and his cohabitee of some years had left unable to tolerate his disturbed sleeping pattern, lack of affection, and irritability. Mark complained particularly of difficulties in concentration and claimed only to be able to maintain concentration for about five minutes. He reported going into another room in his house and being unable to remember the reason. He attempted to read and do puzzles but lost concentration easily. In therapy, he benefited from behavioural work to lift his mood but he was unable to remember and utilise the simple principles and was extremely vulnerable to relapse. Four years prior to the accident Mark had suffered a left cerebral infarction.

Physical health

As well as psychological problems, there is evidence that there may also be physical health consequences of exposure to traumatic events. Although operational definitions of physical health vary from study to study, research has shown that trauma is associated with declines in subjective health ratings (Logue et al., 1979; Melick, 1978; Price, 1978), an increased use of medical services (Abrahams et al., 1976; Bennet, 1970; Price, 1978), and the development of a wide variety of physical health conditions, including tiredness, headaches, chest pains, gastrointestinal disorders, cardiovascular disorders, renal disorders, respiratory diseases, and infectious diseases as well as impairments in the immune system (Abrahams et al., 1976; Clayer, Bookless-Pratz, & Harris, 1985; Logue et al., 1979; McFarlane, Atchison, Rafalowicz, & Papay, 1994; Price, 1978; Raphael, 1986; Solomon et al., 1987b).

Social relationships

Exposure to traumatic events may also have a number of effects on social relationships. Evidence for this is provided by McFarlane (1987) who reported longitudinal data on the impact of the 1983 Australian bushfire on the patterns of social interaction in the families involved. A group of 183 disaster-affected families were compared with 497 families who had not been exposed to the disaster. At both 8 and 26 months after the event, the interaction in the disaster-affected families was characterised by increased levels of irritability, fighting, withdrawal, and decreased enjoyment from shared activities. Furthermore, a substantial proportion of the variance of irritable distress could be

CASE HISTORY 7

Frank is a 55-year-old married man who was self-employed before his involvement in a major shipping disaster. Frank had a particularly miraculous escape, having been in the lower side of the ship at the moment of capsize. His wife, Maureen, was also a vicarious victim because she had been intended to make the crossing herself and had been prevented by a bout of 'flu. Before the disaster, Maureen had also run a small business of her own. Frank had travelled a good deal, so to some extent their lives had been independent. Frank had physical injuries as well as severe PTSD following the disaster. Being self-employed, his business fell apart, Frank was virtually housebound and Maureen was unable to continue with her business. The couple began to suffer financially and Frank's rage at the injustice of these events was a prominent component of his post-trauma reaction. His rage was compounded by the discovery of a pronounced visual field defect on one examination which placed his driving licence in jeopardy. The couple began to drink heavily and Frank admitted to hitting his wife. Part of their frequent rows stemmed from Frank's inability to understand Maureen's problems when, from his point of view, she had nothing to do with the tragedy. He had no interest in sexual relations and Maureen felt bitter and depressed about her perceived rejection by him. The couple were referred for conjoint therapy but Frank refused and filed for divorce.

accounted for by disaster-related variables which suggested that the event played an important aetiological role in the increase of irritable distress. These data provide evidence in a civilian population that there is a relationship between exposure to traumatic events and poorer subsequent interpersonal functioning. Other evidence is provided by Goenjian (1993) who has also noted the increased prevalence of marital discord, intrafamilial and interpersonal violence in civilian survivors of the Armenia earthquake. Data with male Vietnam veterans also shows that PTSD is associated with increased social maladjustment (Kulka et al., 1990). An example of interpersonal problems is provided by Frank (see Case History 7).

CHILDREN AND ADOLESCENTS

Although less is known of the manifestations of post-traumatic stress reactions in children and adolescents compared to adults, their reactions are now explicitly considered in the diagnostic criteria for PTSD (APA, 1994). DSM-IV emphasises repetitive play and trauma-specific re-enactment as well as distressing dreams in children (see Table 2.4). However, up until relatively recently there were few studies on the effects of traumatic events on children (see Yule, 1990, 1991). In part, this was because of the difficulty in conducting adequate studies of the immediate aftermath of traumatic events, but also because adults are often very protective towards children and are often unwilling to acknowledge what children may have suffered. Consequently, adults may deny that

children have major psychological sequelae that warrant investigation (Yule & Williams, 1990). Thus, there were fewer systematic studies of the effects of major trauma on children and many of the earlier published ones suffered from major methodological weaknesses (Garmezy, 1986). For example, Garmezy and Rutter (1985) summed up the findings from published studies concluding that

> ... behavioural disturbances appear to be less intense than might have been anticipated; a majority of children show a moderate amount of fear and anxiety but this subsides; regressive behaviour marked by clinging to parents and heightened dependency on adults appears and then moderately mild sleep disturbance persists for several months; a later less severe stressor such as a storm may lead to a temporary increase in emotional distress, although this is variable; enuresis occurs in some cases, while hypersensitivity to loud noises may be evident in others. (Garmezy & Rutter, 1985, p. 162)

In their view, severe acute stressors, such as major disasters, resulted in socially handicapping emotional disorders in some children, but in the majority of those cases, the disturbances were short lived. Because children tend not to show amnesia for the event, nor to show 'psychic numbing' or intrusive flashbacks, they argued that there was no need for a specific diagnostic category for children parallel to PTSD in adults.

However, more recent research has questioned this view (e.g., McNally, 1993; Yule, 1990, 1991). Yule (1991) has noted that the evidence reviewed by Garmezy and Rutter (1985) rarely dealt with the aftermath of major civilian disasters in which the children have been exposed to life-threatening events. Other evidence suggests that children, like adults, may experience severe and chronic post-traumatic reactions. Yule (1991) concludes that up to 30–50% of children may experience significant impairment following major disaster. As with adults, Yule (1991) also notes that bereavement reactions will complicate the presenting picture of symptoms. What is interesting, however, is that children's symptoms are almost identical with those recognised by the American Psychiatric Association as comprising PTSD (see Case History 8).

This case illustrates the low priority too often given to dealing with the emotional sequelae of road traffic accidents. It is probable that Hazel's reactions were potentiated by the facts that one brother had been killed in a previous road accident and a sister had been badly injured in another. None of these pertinent details had been picked up at the time. Then, the school, while sympathetic, did nothing to arrange help. It was only after medico-legal assessment that help was eventually arranged. Some three to four years of unnecessary suffering was the result.

Another example is given by Alison (Case History 9). This case illustrates the acute reaction to a traumatic event in a child and how prompt intervention may have prevented a full-blown PTSD developing. A single case like this can never prove that the natural course of recovery would not have been as dramatic, but

CASE HISTORY 8

Hazel (15) was crossing the road at a pedestrian-controlled crossing with members of her family. A bus was stopped as she walked past it, the next she recalls was being on the ground with her mother screaming and other people rushing around her. She was taken to the Casualty Department of the local hospital where she was found to have various sprains, bruises, and cuts, but was discharged home. She was not offered any counselling for herself. Treatment was suggested when she was assessed a year later for medico-legal purposes, but it was a further year before she was referred for treatment.

In the five years since the accident, Hazel had changed. She avoided all reminders of the accident and especially avoided crossing the road at that crossing, despite its being the most convenient for many journeys. She could not watch the television news for fear she would see an accident. She could not talk about it to friends or family, and would start crying when it was mentioned. She had always regarded herself as a strong, self-reliant person, but said of the accident, 'That's one of the things that makes me angry. Every other bit of my life, I'm in control. But that bit, *it* is in control.' In fact, she had developed a very strong sense of anger towards the van driver as he had overtaken the bus at the crossing and hit her.

She still thought about the accident all the time and that still upset her. When these thoughts came into her mind, she would try to make herself not think about them, but this rarely worked. She had had bad dreams about it initially, but these had stopped over the years. She worried that a similar accident might happen to other members of her family, as it had in the past.

When the accident first happened, she had just been settling in to her secondary school. She had been a bright pupil, interested in everything. She became lethargic with no interest in anything, staying indoors a lot and rarely going out. Her sleep suffered badly and even at the time of treatment, it would often be 2 a.m. before she got off to sleep. She still has problems concentrating and also complains of having a poor memory.

On the Impact of Event Scale, she scored 55. She scored 14 on the Birleson Depression Scale, but only 4 on the Children's Manifest Anxiety Scale. She was taken on for treatment and while this was complicated by illness and death in the immediate family, she made slow but steady progress and was able to return to leading a full and active life.

This case illustrates the low priority too often given to dealing with the emotional sequelae of road traffic accidents. It is probable that Hazel's reactions reflected the fact that one brother had been killed in a previous RTA and a sister had been badly injured in yet another one. None of this had been picked up by those dealing with her. Then, the school, while sympathetic, did nothing to arrange help and it was only after a medico-legal assessment that help was eventually arranged. Some three to four years of unnecessary suffering was the result.

---

given the very high scores on the Impact of Event Scale, it is unlikely that the stress reaction would have resolved spontaneously as quickly.

It is on the basis of many cases like these that we would argue that children and adolescents are at risk of PTSD following exposure to a traumatic event. Generally, the reactions of children share the same thematic content as for adults (Weiss, 1993b) (see Table 2.9).

CASE HISTORY 9

Alison (12) was on her way home from school. She was late for her train and as she ran down the stairs to the platform, she saw it pulling away. Then she saw an old man fall under the wheels of the train and she recoiled in horror as she saw his decapitated head roll along the track. She fled home in terror and was crying inconsolably.

She was seen in a specialist clinic a few days later, having been referred by the railways counselling service. She had not attended school for a few days and then only went if taken by car, a considerable imposition for her parents. She had become very clingy, from being a very confident, outgoing girl. She had to sleep in her mother's bed at night for comfort and security. She had recurring, intrusive images and thoughts about the decapitated head, and thought that it moved and talked to her. She tried unsuccessfully to push these thoughts and images from consciousness. She was avoiding travelling by train. She had great difficulty sleeping, difficulty in concentrating at school and was much more alert to dangers around her as well as being much more jumpy when there were unexpected noises.

It turned out that she thought that the man may have committed suicide and she was angry at him for doing so when she saw it. On investigation, it transpired that the elderly man's clothing had got trapped in the train door and he was dragged under the wheels. It was an accident. The dilemma was whether to tell Alison that it was an accident and thereby confirm any fears that travelling by train was dangerous, or let her continue to believe he had killed himself. It was decided to tell her the truth.

At the initial interview, it was explained to her that she was experiencing a normal, if distressing, reaction to an abnormal event. She was not going mad. Advice was given about managing the distress and a month later things had got much better. Alison was again able to travel to school by train and the intrusive images had all but stopped. Her scores on various questionnaires confirmed this improvement:

	Referral	*One month later*
Impact of Events	49	26
Depression	12	3
Anxiety	17	2

This case illustrates the acute reaction to a traumatic event and how prompt intervention may have prevented a full-blown PTSD developing. A single case like this can never prove that the natural course of recovery would not have been as dramatic, but given the very high scores on the Impact of Event Scale, it is unlikely that the stress reaction would have resolved spontaneously as quickly.

The case also illustrates a fine diagnostic point. As Alison was first assessed within a week of the trauma, then she is not eligible to receive a diagnosis of PTSD since symptoms must have been present for at least four weeks. Thus, one cannot claimed to have 'cured' a disorder that technically was not present. At least she satisfied the criteria for a diagnosis of 'Acute Stress Reaction'.

A Broader Syndrome Continuous with Normal Behaviour

Traumatic events act as a powerful trigger to the onset of depressive and anxiety disorders as well as PTSD. As our examples have shown, a survivor of a traumatic event with only the symptoms of PTSD would be an exception. McFarlane and Papay (1992) note that in the published studies examining co-morbidity, more than 80% of subjects with PTSD appear to have another disorder, although what this is seems to depend on the population studied.

Table 2.9 Common reactions of children after exposure to trauma

- Not wanting to sleep alone, wanting to sleep with parents.
- Being afraid of things that are reminders of the trauma, as in an earthquake, loud noises or feeling buildings shake with passing traffic.
- Crying and fearful clinging—being worried about where parents are.
- Unusual aches and pains; headaches, tummyaches.
- Regressive behaviours—that is, going back to habits that had been overcome like thumb-sucking, bed-wetting, 'babytalk'.
- Play that is aggressive or re-creates the disaster.
- Being confused about what the trauma is and what it means.
- Being worried and/or confused about death.
- Trouble concentrating and doing work in school.
- Worries about their own parents' or siblings' and friends' safety.
- Shame or guilt about things they did or didn't do.
- Worry about the future—'if I grow up'.
- Worry about how parents have reacted to the trauma.

Reproduced, with permission, from Weiss (1993b, p. 19).

Most survivors diagnosed with PTSD will have a range of depressive and anxious reactions whether or not they meet the full criteria to receive a secondary diagnosis. The menu for the diagnostic category of PTSD may simply describe a circumscribed set of symptoms that form part of a broader syndrome that sits astride other major diagnostic groupings. The general exclusion of anxious and depressive symptoms from the criteria for PTSD, McFarlane and Papay (1992) argue, has been significantly determined by the preponderant view that PTSD symptoms are organised around the two-factor model of intrusive and avoidant phenomena.

Negative emotional states (e.g., rage, anger, guilt, shame) are common. Feelings of guilt and shame have been documented in many populations which have been studied. For example, in our 30-month follow up of survivors of the *Herald of Free Enterprise* disaster we were interested in the levels and patterns of guilt and shame. It was found that over half of our sample of 73 survivors felt guilt for being alive when so many died; approximately one-third said that they felt guilty about things they did; and two-thirds said that they felt guilty about things they failed to do. In addition, almost one-third said that they felt they had let themselves down during the disaster; and almost half said that they felt they had let others down (Joseph, Hodgkinson, Yule, & Williams, 1993b).

As well as guilt and shame, there may be intense feelings of rage and anger. Such negative emotional states are distressing and can lead to destructive behaviours, such as substance abuse, in an attempt to dull or block them.

Although it is helpful for communication purposes (arguably one of the principle scientific functions of diagnosis) to classify people into those with and without PTSD, in reality, survivors suffer from a wide range of emotional and behavioural reactions which might be envisaged as continuous with normal emotional and behavioural reactions. We consider that the diagnostic classification of PTSD has been important in providing a common language for the scientific community but, in reality, people's reactions to severe life-stressors can be viewed as ranging along a continuum of adaptation. Work akin to that of Kendall (1976), who investigated the distribution of 'neurotic' and 'endogenous' symptoms finding no 'point of rarity' that would distinguish two syndromes, needs to be done to further establish our view.

Another role of diagnostic classification, reinforced by the needs of courts of law, is to draw a line across this continuum to separate those survivors who are distressed and dysfunctional and 'psychiatrically damaged' from those who are not. Post-traumatic stress reactions follow particular events, although not all people who are exposed to an event will go on to develop severe and chronic problems. The reactions have a recognisable form and early course. However, as we have seen it is a changeable function of classificatory practice whether these reactions are called a 'psychiatric disorder' or not, and these practices may be influenced by factors other than scientific understanding of 'illnesses'. For example, Norris (1992), in an epidemiological study, noted that the rates of PTSD would double if the avoidance criterion were to use a cut-off of two symptoms rather than three. Such a change could have significant implications for compensation judgements and for the planning of services.

Although statistical evidence supports the existence of a constellation of cognitive, emotional, and behavioural phenomena similar to those contained within the diagnostic category of PTSD (e.g., Keane, Wolfe, & Taylor, 1987), there remains debate over whether or not PTSD merits its status as a discrete disorder rather than being considered an amalgam of other disorders. PTSD is at present classified as an anxiety disorder. Certainly it has much in common with panic disorder, phobic anxiety, generalised anxiety disorder (GAD), and obsessive-compulsive disorder (OCD) (Davidson & Foa, 1991). But PTSD also has much in common with mood disorders, and depression would seem to be a common feature. Many of the characteristics of PTSD also invite its consideration as a dissociative disorder (Spiegel, 1988). Complete amnesia, but, more often, partial amnesia of the event (particularly of the reactive feelings) has been noted in combat veterans (Silver, 1984). Psychogenic amnesia and flashbacks may also be considered as dissociative symptoms.

It can be concluded that the range of reactions following exposure to a traumatic event is wide. Exposure to trauma may have a variety of cognitive, emotional, behavioural, and social consequences as well as impaired physical health. Of course, epidemiological findings about reactions to traumatic events are dependent on the criteria used in the assessment of those reactions. PTSD is a syndrome that sits astride other major diagnostic groupings such as anxiety and depression and there remains much debate over the phenomenology of the reactions experienced by survivors of traumatic events.

We would encourage a wider psychosocial perspective to be taken which emphasises the survivor's overall subjective well-being. The literature has focused on pathological adjustment and testifies to the severity and chronicity of distress often experienced by survivors of traumatic events. But there are often positive psychological reactions following trauma such as an increased ability to appreciate life and to show more compassion towards others (Collins, Taylor, & Skokan, 1990; Lehman et al., 1993; Taylor, Lichtman, & Wood, 1984; Zeidner & Ben-Zur, 1994).

With a sample of 35 adult survivors of the *Jupiter* cruise ship, we found that most agreed that they no longer took life for granted (94%), valued their relationships more (91%), valued other people more (88%), felt more experienced about life (83%), and no longer took people or things for granted (91%). A large number also agreed that they tried to live life to the full now (71%), were more understanding and tolerant (71%), and looked upon each day as a bonus (77%). Just over half said that they had a greater faith in human nature (54%) and were more determined to succeed in life (50%). Just under half agreed that they no longer worry about death (44%).

However, greater endorsement of these items were not associated with lower symptom scores as was predicted, instead we found a trend contrary to what we had predicted for those endorsing these beliefs to have higher intrusive and avoidant symptoms (Joseph, Williams, & Yule, 1993c). This might reflect the need for meaning that survivors have, the most distressed having the greatest need to find meaning. It might also be that positive responses such as these are symptomatic of distress at the time of assessment but would predict lower distress later on.

CONCLUSION

Although clinicians working with survivors will conduct standardised interviews based on either the APA or WHO systems, these systems have provided only a temporary gold standard because of the changing criteria within and across each system. For example, it is possible that someone suffering from excessive guilt and who would have fulfilled the DSM-III criteria in 1980 would not have fulfilled the DSM-III-R criteria in 1987. Alternatively, someone suffering from distressing intrusive recollections might fulfil the ICD-10 (WHO, 1993) criteria but not the DSM-IV criteria if they did not also present with symptoms of emotional numbing and avoidance. Nevertheless, such problems are not unusual within the psychiatric literature. For example, even the validity of the concept of schizophrenia remains in question (Boyle, 1990) and it is likely that the concept of PTSD will continue to evolve as more about the phenomenology of reactions to extreme stress becomes understood. Furthermore, the fact of frequent psychiatric co-morbidity raises the question of what exactly researchers and clinicians should be trying to assess. The overlap with other and more generally recognised depressive and anxiety disorders highlights the need for specificity in the classification of PTSD. But although a circumscribed menu of symptoms is a requirement of psychiatric classification, in reality, the range of post-traumatic stress reactions is wide. Thus, on the one hand, psychiatric classification requires that the menu of symptoms be fairly circumscribed to avoid overlap with other disorders, but on the other, there is a need for an extended menu of symptoms that recognises the wide range of trauma-related reactions.

SUMMARY POINTS

1. The problems in psychological functioning that people often experience following exposure to traumatic events have a recognisable form and early course. The hallmark symptoms are intrusive thoughts, feelings, and images. The term PTSD was first introduced into the clinical literature by the American Psychiatric Association in 1980 (APA, 1980) in an attempt to describe the clinical characteristics exhibited by survivors of traumatic events.

2. Although there have been several revisions to the criteria necessary for the diagnosis of PTSD since 1980, much debate remains over the architecture of PTSD symptomatology and in particular the definition of trauma. Recent theoretical work emphasises the role of subjective perception in the development of trauma-related disorder.

3. The diagnosis of PTSD is often accompanied by other related disorders as well as a wide range of cognitive, emotional and behavioural problems. Research suggests that depression is the major co-diagnosis. A broader perspective on symptoms which recognises the multifaceted nature of post-traumatic stress reactions is encouraged.

4. The reactions of children and adolescents to trauma are similar to those of adults. Post-traumatic stress disorder has been reported in children and adolescents following a wide range of different events.

5. Finally, a perspective which views symptoms of PTSD as continuous with symptoms of normal adaptation is advocated.

Chapter 3

ASSESSMENT AND MEASUREMENT

Reliable and valid measurement is the cornerstone of psychological science. Since the original formulation of PTSD in DSM-III (APA, 1980) there has been much interest in standardised measurement of PTSD (e.g., Allen, 1994; Ollendick & Hoffman, 1982; Litz, Penk, Gerardi, & Keane, 1992). The range of psychological reactions that people experience after trauma is wide and, as we have seen, includes not only the symptoms necessary for the diagnosis of PTSD but also those of depression, anxiety, as well as problems in cognitive and social functioning. The clinician working with survivors of traumatic events is faced with the task of collecting relevant information about the patient in an attempt to understand what the problem areas are and of formulating the case with a view to deciding upon a treatment plan. The clinician will probably also assess the client at several stages during the course of treatment to see how he or she is responding to the treatment and again at the end of treatment to determine whether it has been effective. Research scientists may want to pool the information collected by many clinicians to find out in a more systematic and controlled way the most effective methods of treatment. Alternatively, they may want to conduct surveys of groups of survivors to find out about the effects of a particular event or to run experiments to find out how survivors react to certain stimuli. In all of these cases, the reliability and validity of the assessments will determine the value of the research. Most of the assessment techniques used with survivors of traumatic events are either based on data obtained from interviews or from self-report questionnaires.

Key Topics

Interviews
Self-report
Associated symptoms
Children and adolescents
Issues and recommendations
Conclusion

INTERVIEWS

Several standard structured psychiatric interview schedules now include questions to assess PTSD symptoms (see Watson, 1990 for a review), e.g., the Diagnostic Interview Schedule (DIS: Robins & Helzer, 1985) and the Structured Clinical Interview (SCID: Spitzer, Williams, & Gibbon, 1987). These interview schedules are fairly lengthy and are used by clinicians to assess for various psychiatric disorders. Other interview schedules have been developed solely for the assessment of PTSD. To illustrate the format of interview schedules, as well as some theoretical issues concerning the nature of disorder and its assessment, we will consider two of the most recently developed tools, the PTSD Interview (PTSD-I: Watson, Juba, Manifold, Kucala, & Anderson, 1991a) and the Clinician-Administered Post-Traumatic Stress Disorder Scale (CAPS: Blake, Weathers, Nagy, et al., 1990).

The PTSD Interview (PTSD-I: Watson et al., 1991a) asks whether the interviewee has experienced an unusual, extremely distressful event (the DSM-III/III-R definition of trauma). This question is then followed by a request for details and reflects section A of the DSM manual criteria. Seventeen items follow which closely reflect the symptoms of PTSD as described by DSM-III-R, each of which is answered on a 7-point Likert scale that ranges from 'no; never' to 'extremely; always'. Respondents provide a verbal response which is recorded by the examiner. This provides information on the frequency of symptoms. A score of 4 ('somewhat; commonly') is considered sufficient to meet the relevant DSM criteria. This provides information on whether or not the person qualifies for a diagnosis of PTSD. Two additional questions are asked to determine whether the section E requirement of a duration of at least one month has been met. The authors report very high test–retest reliability and internal reliability for the PTSD-I.

PTSD, as defined by DSM, is a disorder which a person either has or does not have. Although this is how psychiatric classification works, there is much debate in the field of abnormal psychology over whether disorder should be viewed in this way or whether abnormal behaviour should be viewed as continuous with normal behaviour. The reader will note that the PTSD-I can be used to make a diagnosis of disorder (i.e., answers of somewhat/commonly or above to all of the questions) or to provide a continuous score of symptom frequency.

The Clinician-Administered Post-Traumatic Stress Disorder Scale (CAPS: Blake, Weathers, Nagy, et al., 1990a) also consists of 17 questions based on DSM-III-R which are administered by the clinician. The CAPS assesses both lifetime and present presence of PTSD as well as both the frequency and intensity of PTSD symptoms. Using clinicians' diagnosis, it has been found to have good agreement with clinical diagnosis and convergent validity with self-report scales of PTSD symptomatology (e.g., Hovens et al., 1994b). Hovens et al. (1994b) conclude that the CAPS appears to be an adequate instrument for the assessment of PTSD and there is now a version developed for use with children.

Both instruments are based on diagnostic criteria that have now been revised (APA, 1994). It is inevitable, given the time it takes to conduct and publish research, that assessment procedures will tend to be one step behind the latest thinking in classification. Like the PTSD-I, the CAPS yields both dichotomous diagnostic information about PTSD and continuous symptom scores. However, with regard to continuous scores, the CAPS distinguishes between the frequency and the intensity of symptoms. For example, one person may have slightly upsetting nightmares several times a month whereas another person may have extremely upsetting nightmares several times a month, but if only the frequency of nightmares is assessed, both individuals would receive the same score. It may be useful to take into account both the frequency and intensity of symptoms separately.

If one accepts a continuity between normal and pathological states, interviews that simply dichotomise survivors into those who qualify for a diagnosis and those who do not provide less information than those that provide an indication of the intensity of the person's emotional experiences and the relative position of this person's symptoms compared to other people's. Many people will not meet the full criteria for PTSD but they may be just as impaired in functioning and require the same level of care as those who do. These people might be said to have partial PTSD or subthreshold PTSD (Blank, 1993; Carlier & Gersons, 1995).

SELF-REPORT

Due to practical constraints in research, self-report scales are widely used. The PTSD Inventory (Solomon, Weisenberg, Schwarzwald, & Mikulincer, 1987c) is a self-report scale originally based on DSM-III criteria, but it has since been revised following publication of DSM-III-R (Solomon et al., 1993a). The questionnaire consists of 17 statements corresponding to the 17 PTSD symptoms listed in DSM-III-R and has been shown to have a satisfactory internal reliability (Cronbach's alpha = 0.86) and convergent validity with the SCID.

The Mississippi Scale for combat related PTSD (M-PTSD) is a 35-item self-report Likert scale developed by Keane, Caddell, and Taylor (1988) and is one of the most widely used measures for veterans seeking treatment. Items were derived from the original DSM-III criteria to provide a measure of combat-related PTSD. Ratings are made for each item on a 5-point Likert scale and are summated to provide a continuous measure of PTSD symptom severity ranging from 35 to 175. The M-PTSD assesses the standard PTSD symptoms as well as the associated features of depression, substance abuse, and suicidal tendencies. With a sample of 362 male Vietnam veterans who had sought professional help, Keane et al. (1988) found the scale to have satisfactory internal reliability (Cronbach's alpha = 0.94) and test–retest reliability over a one-week period ($r = 0.97$). Other data have confirmed the reliability and validity of the M-PTSD (Hyer, Davis, Boudewyns, & Woods, 1991; McFall, Smith, MacKay, & Tarver, 1990a; McFall, Smith, Roszell, Tarver, & Malas, 1990b) and the M-PTSD has been used in numerous studies (e.g., King, King, Gudanowski, & Vreven, 1995; Marmar et al., 1994; McNally, Lasko, Macklin, & Pitman, 1995) and translated into several languages (e.g., Hovens & van der Ploeg, 1993). Using a cutoff score of 107 (Keane, Caddell, & Taylor, 1988), the M-PTSD had a sensitivity (i.e, true positives/true positives + false negatives) of 93% in identifying PTSD patients and a specificity (i.e., true negatives/true negatives + false positives) of 88% in discriminating them from substance-abusing controls patients. Keane et al. (1988) note, however, that the cutoff score may vary with the populations studied.

The Penn Inventory is a 26-item self-report inventory which provides a continuous measure of the degree, frequency, and intensity of PTSD symptomatology (Hammarberg, 1992). Developed on the basis of DSM-III-R criteria, the Penn Inventory was validated on both survivors of civilian trauma and Vietnam veterans and it showed satisfactory internal reliability (Cronbach's alpha = 0.94) and test–retest reliability ($r = 0.96$) as well as convergent validity with other scales.

There are two major approaches to the development of self-report measures. First, the development of new tests for assessing PTSD symptoms, and second, the study of existing tests and their usefulness in diagnosing PTSD. The Mississippi Scale, the Penn Inventory, and the PTSD Inventory are examples of the first approach and are based on the DSM criteria. However, much work has also been concerned with the latter approach using the Minnesota Multiphasic Personality Inventory.

Minnesota Multiphasic Personality Inventory

The Minnesota Multiphasic Personality Inventory (MMPI) has been widely used in the assessment of PTSD. This is an interesting approach as it is informative about the wider phenomenology of post-traumatic stress reactions. The MMPI is the most widely used personality self-report inventory in the USA (Colligan & Offord, 1992) and consists of 550 self-statements which are rated as true or false. The items in the MMPI make up 10 clinical scales: hypochondriasis, depression, conversion hysteria, psychopathic deviate, masculinity–feminity, paranoia, psychasthenia, schizophrenia, hypomania, and social introversion. Studies have shown that PTSD patients show general elevation on many or all subscales (Fairbank, Keane, & Malloy, 1983b; Foy, Sipprelle, Rueger, & Carroll, 1984; Silver & Salamone-Genovese, 1991) but also that some survivor groups may have particular profiles. To illustrate, it has been found that substance-abuse veterans with PTSD showed MMPI elevations on the psychopathic, paranoia, and social introversion scales (Roberts,

Penk, Robinowitz, & Patterson, 1982) whereas sexual-abuse survivors have MMPI elevations on the psychopathic deviate and schizophrenia scales (Belkin, Greene, Rodrigue, & Boggs, 1994).

Although such data are informative, the MMPI was developed long before the recognition of PTSD and other research has attempted to develop a PTSD scale on the basis of the MMPI items. Keane, Malloy, and Fairbank (1984) compared PTSD patients with non-PTSD patients on each of the 550 MMPI items. On the basis of these data, Keane et al. (1984) developed a 49-item MMPI-PTSD subscale (PK-MMPI) which differentiated the two groups. Although the PK-MMPI has been used in numerous studies (e.g., Marmar et al., 1994) and there is some evidence for its reliability and validity (Burke & Mayer, 1985; Gerardi, Keane, & Penk, 1989; Watson, 1990), overall the evidence is mixed (Denny, Robinowitz, & Penk, 1987) and it has been suggested that some caution might be employed in its use due to low diagnostic accuracy (Silver & Salamone-Genovese, 1991) and a tendency to identify false positives. False positives refer to those people diagnosed as suffering from the disorder when they are not. This is a problem to a greater or lesser extent with all assessment techniques which aim to classify people into groups which correspond to other external criteria, in this case, the DSM criteria for PTSD. Furthermore, these data have been collected with Vietnam veterans and there is a need to validate the PK-MMPI with survivors of civilian trauma (McCaffrey, Hickling, & Marrazo, 1989).

Although the PK-MMPI has been widely used and is popular among clinicians in the USA because of their familiarity with the MMPI, the main limitation of the PK-MMPI is that the MMPI was designed before PTSD was first defined by the APA (1980) and therefore does not include items that might be thought of as directly testing for all of the core PTSD criteria. Moody and Kish (1989) have suggested that the PK-MMPI measures general psychological maladjustment and dysphoric feelings rather than any specific syndrome.

However, a new version of the MMPI has recently been introduced, the MMPI-2 (Butcher, 1990). Several changes have been made to the PK-MMPI resulting in the PK-MMPI-2 (Lyons & Keane, 1992). The MMPI-2 also includes a new PTSD scale, the PS-MMPI-2 (Schlenger & Kulka, 1989). This is a 60-item scale with 46 items taken from the PK-MMPI with 14 new items which have been shown to discriminate for PTSD. However, the properties of these newer scales await further research.

Multifactorial Assessment

Although PTSD as a disorder consists of groupings of symptoms characterised as re-experiencing, denial, and hyperarousal, most of the instruments we have reviewed are not usually used to yield separate scores for these groupings but instead either a dichotomous assessment of whether or not the person fulfils the diagnostic criteria for PTSD or a continuous score of PTSD intensity.

A further consideration in assessment is whether to treat PTSD symptoms as a homogeneous or a heterogeneous grouping of symptoms. For example, it might be that a person scoring high on re-experiencing symptoms and low on avoidance symptoms may yield the same score as someone scoring moderately high on both re-experiencing and avoidance. Both individuals would, however, receive the same score if the symptoms are simply summated to give a total score which would hide the psychologically significant differences in the presenting symptoms of these two people. Adopting Horowitz's perspective on post-traumatic stress reactions as alternating between intrusions and denials the description of survivors in terms of these two dimensions would seem to be a minimum requirement.

Impact of Event Scale

One of the most widely used instruments worldwide for the assessment of post-traumatic phenomena has been the Impact of Event Scale (IES: Horowitz, Wilner, & Alvarez, 1979). The IES is a self-report measure which was developed on the basis of Horowitz's two-factor theory that can be anchored to any specific life event and taps: (1) intrusively experienced ideas, images, feelings and dreams, and (2) the avoidance of ideas, feelings, or situations. The items on the IES were developed from statements most frequently used to describe episodes of distress by people who had experienced recent life-events and was initially tested on 66 individuals admitted to an outpatient clinic for the treatment of stress-response syndromes, about half of whom had experienced bereavement. The remainder had personal injuries resulting from road accidents, violence, illness, or surgery. Horowitz et al. (1979) report satisfactory internal reliability (Cronbach's alpha = 0.78 for intrusion and 0.82 for avoidance) and test–retest reliability ($r = 0.89$ for intrusion and 0.79 for avoidance). In addition, other research has largely confirmed these findings and the separate factors of intrusion and avoidance (Joseph, Williams, Yule, & Walker, 1992b; Joseph, Yule, Williams, & Hodgkinson, 1993g; Schwarzwald, Solomon, Weisenberg, & Mikulincer, 1987; Zilberg, Weiss, & Horowitz, 1982). The IES correlates well with other PTSD measures (Kulka et al., 1990; Schlenger et al., 1992; Weisenberg, Solomon, Schwarzwald, & Mikulincer, 1987) and has been used in numerous studies with victims of sexual abuse (e.g., Rowan, Foy, Rodriguez, & Ryan, 1993), battered women (e.g., Houskamp & Foy, 1991), train drivers following railway accidents (Malt et al., 1993; Karlehagen et al., 1993) and translated into many languages including Hebrew (Schwarzwald et al., 1987), and Dutch (Brom, Kleber, & Defares, 1986). The IES is most useful because it can be anchored to any life-event making data comparable across studies. In addition, the IES provides a continuous score for both the intrusion and avoidance subscales making it useful for correlational studies. However, the IES was developed to test Horowitz's two-factor structure of post-traumatic stress reactions and does not assess the full range of symptoms associated with PTSD.

Analysis of PTSD symptoms, however, does not usually show a clear structure corresponding to the DSM groupings of intrusions, denials, and hyperarousal raising the question of whether these groupings provide the best description of the architecture of post-traumatic stress reactions. Principal component analysis of the M-PTSD identified six factors (Keane, Caddell & Taylor, 1988) labelled as: 'intrusive memories and depression', 'interpersonal adjustment problems', 'liability of affect and memory', 'rumination features', 'other interpersonal difficulties', and 'sleep problems'. The last four factors were, however, defined by fewer than four items which, Keane et al. (1988) note, raises questions about the reliability of their measurement. Other research has, however, suggested a three-factor structure to the M-PTSD: intrusive re-experiencing; numbing-avoidance and anger; lability and social alienation (McFall et al., 1990a). The architecture of PTSD symptoms is an issue that we will return to in Chapter 8.

Assessment can often be very time consuming and researchers and clinicians have also been interested in devising short scales that can assess for PTSD. For example, Hyer et al. (1991) identify a subset of 10 items that can be used in short screening batteries (Miss-10). Two groups of Vietnam veterans were used and all had been treated on a specialised PTSD unit subsequent to a series of screenings that confirmed PTSD. The first group of 52 veterans were administered the Mississippi Scale twice, on entry and at six weeks. The test–retest reliability was found to be 0.64, and the internal reliability was high at both times (Cronbach's alpha = 0.91 and 0.94 respectively). The second group consisted of 95 veterans who were administered the measure on entry only. Again, internal reliability was high (Cronbach's alpha = 0.92). Hyer et al. (1991) also inspected individual item correlations with the overall scale to identify 10 items with a good test–retest reliability (0.66), and high internal reliability (Cronbach's alpha = 0.94 and 0.96 respectively). For the 95 veterans, internal reliability was high for the Miss-10 (Cronbach's alpha = 0.85) and correlated highly with the total Mississippi Scale (r = 0.95). Other variations of the M-PTSD have included a version designed to assess symptoms in female veterans of operation 'Desert Storm' (Wolfe, Brown, & Buscela, 1992) as well as a civilian version (Kulka et al., 1990).

Dissociative Experiences Scale

Investigators are becoming increasingly interested in the dissociation component of PTSD. The Dissociative Experiences Scale (Bernstein & Putnam, 1986) is a 28-item self-report measure of trait dissociation. The scale assesses absorption, depersonalization and derealization, and amnesic experiences. A shorter measure which can be easily included as part of a battery of different measures is the Peritraumatic Dissociative Experiences Questionnaire

(Marmar et al., 1994). This is an 8-item interview based questionnaire for assessing retrospective reports of depersonalization, derealization, amnesia, out of body experience, and altered time perception. Internal reliability was found to be satisfactory (Cronbach's alpha = 0.80) and convergent validity found with other measures of post-traumatic functioning. Dissociation appears to be a particular feature of sexual abuse and forms one component of the Trauma Symptom Checklist (TSC: Briere & Runtz, 1989). Briere and Runtz (1989) report that the TSC has satisfactory internal reliability and that it was able to classify 79% of women as to whether or not they had a history of CSA. Other research points to the validity of the TSC as a measure of the consequences of sexual trauma (Gold, Milan, Mayall, & Johnson, 1994).

Several other self-rating scales have been developed recently to assess PTSD. For example, the Self-Rating Inventory for Posttraumatic Stress (SIP: Hovens et al., 1994a) is a 47-item questionnaire reflecting DSM-III-R criteria and associated features. Although the SIP appears to have excellent reliability and validity it remains to be investigated with an English-speaking population.

Other researchers have developed scales for use following specific events. For example, Zeidner and Ben-Zur (1994) constructed a 6-item scale to assess post-traumatic symptoms following the Gulf War and the SCUD missile attacks on Israel. Subjects rated the frequency (1 = not at all to 5 = almost all the time) of each item: (1) nightmares about missile attacks, (2) attempts to escape or avoid things or people which bring back memories of the crisis period, (3) heightened sensitivity to rooms/places which served as sealed shelters during the war, (4) recurring intrusive thoughts about the crisis, (5) heightened sensitivity to events which occurred during the war, and (6) active attempts at avoiding information relating to events during the war.

ASSOCIATED SYMPTOMS

The General Health Questionnaire has been widely used in traumatic stress research (see Box 2.1) as a measure of global dysfunction. The Beck Depression Inventory (BDI: Beck, 1967), and the State-Trait Anxiety Inventory (STAI: Spielberger, Gorsuch, & Lushene, 1970) are also widely used and well-validated measures which have received some attention in the growing PTSD literature. For example, Fairbank et al. (1983a) reported that PTSD Vietnam veteran's BDI scores were higher than both psychiatric and healthy combat control subjects, and that their STAI scores were significantly higher than those of healthy combat control subjects. In addition, Orr et al. (1990) found Vietnam veterans diagnosed as suffering from PTSD scored higher on the BDI and STAI than healthy combat control subjects. These findings provide psychometric support for PTSD's reported co-morbidity with major depression and anxiety disorders. The BDI and the STAI have been used in numerous other studies (e.g., Basoglu & Paker, 1995; Joseph, Yule, & Williams, 1994; McNally, Lasko, Macklin, & Pitman, 1995).

However, although self-report measures of anxiety and depression, such as the BDI and the STAI, are thought to tap distinct constructs, scores on the BDI and the STAI have been found to be strongly correlated (e.g., Joseph, Yule, & Williams, 1995a) questioning this distinction. This is echoed within the psychometric literature where it has actually proved difficult to distinguish the constructs of anxiety and depression (Feldman, 1993). There is growing evidence for a tripartite model of depression and anxiety that divides symptoms into three groups: manifestations of anhedonia specific to depression, somatic arousal unique to anxiety, and symptoms of general distress that are largely non-specific (Clark & Watson, 1991; Watson & Clark, 1984; Watson et al., 1995b; Watson et al., 1995a).

Depending on the nature of the event, many survivors may also be bereaved and investigators will often want to measure grief reactions. One commonly used scale is the Texas Inventory of Grief (TIG: Faschingbauer, Devaul, & Zisook, 1977) although several versions of this scale now exist (see Hodgkinson, Joseph, Yule, & Williams, 1995).

CHILDREN AND ADOLESCENTS

As with adults, assessment of children and adolescents can be through interview or self-report measures. However, assessment with these age groups has received less attention than adults (McNally, 1991). The Post-Traumatic Stress Disorder Reaction Index is a 20-item structured interview based on DSM-III criteria for assessing childhood PTSD (Frederick, 1985a). It has also been validated with adults (Frederick, 1987) and a translated version has been used by Goenjian and colleagues in their study of the effects of the Armenia earthquake (Goenjian, 1993; Goenjian et al., 1994; Pynoos et al., 1993) and found to be a valid index in evaluating PTSD (Goenjian et al., 1994). It is therefore a useful instrument for studies which wish to compare the responses of children and adults and is suitable for use cross-culturally.

Often parents or teachers are called upon to make ratings of children's behaviour. Several scales designed for this purpose are available. For example, the Behaviour Problem Checklist (Quay & Peterson, 1979), the Child Behaviour Checklist (Achenbach & Edelbrock, 1983), and the Rutter parent and teacher rating scales (Goodman, 1994; Rutter, 1967). However, these parent or teacher scales may underestimate the level of distress experienced by the child (Terr, 1985; Yule & Williams, 1990), possibly because of the tendency for adults to underestimate children's emotional distress but also because the scales do not contain items sensitive to traumatic stress reactions. In addition, children are often afraid of admitting how they feel to anyone. Each child may feel that he or she is either unusual or will be teased by others. For these reasons, both adult report data as well as self-report measures are recommended (Saigh, 1989). Various self-report measures have been employed to assess post-traumatic stress reactions, depression, anxiety, fears, and the consequences of sexual abuse. Often self-reports may reveal differences between PTSD positive and PTSD negative groups where parent reports do not (Wolfe, Sas, & Wekerle, 1994) although Wolfe, Gentile, & Wolfe (1989) have emphasised that the right questions must be asked of children if they are to report on their subjective state.

Impact of Event Scale

Although originally developed for use with adults, the Impact of Event Scale (IES: Horowitz, Wilner, & Alvarez, 1979) has been used successfully with children (e.g., Joseph, Brewin, Yule, & Williams, 1993a; Marmar et al., 1994; Yule, Udwin, & Murdoch, 1990b) and has been described as probably the best questionnaire available for evaluating childhood PTSD (McNally, 1991). It has been used with children who survived the *Herald of Free Enterprise* disaster (Yule & Williams, 1990) and children who survived the capsize of the *Jupiter* cruise ship (Yule, Ten Brugencate, & Joseph, 1994; Yule & Udwin, 1991; Yule et al., 1990b). Yule and Williams (1990) reported that children as young as 8 years found the scale to be generally meaningful and relevant to their experiences although more recent work has identified some items as too difficult and a shorter version of the scale for children has been developed (Dyregrov & Yule, 1995a, 1995b).

But, as with adults, the range of symptomatology reported by children and adolescents following trauma is wide and other self-report scales that have been employed with child survivors are the Birleson Depression Scale (Birleson, 1981) and the Revised Children's Manifest Anxiety Scale (Reynolds & Richmond, 1978). Yule and Udwin (1991) were able to contact 24 teenage girls 10 days after the sinking of the *Jupiter* cruise ship. During a debriefing session, all 24 completed the Impact of Event Scale, the Birelson Depression Scale, and the Revised Children's Manifest Anxiety Scale. On the basis of their scores on these measures at 10 days after the sinking, 10 girls aged 14 years were judged to be at high risk of developing problems. When help was offered on an individual or group basis (and without disclosing which girls were considered to be at high risk,) 8 of the 10 high-risk group came forward for help on the first day. The other two attended the second meeting. Only five others ever attended any group meeting. This was, Yule and Udwin (1991) note, a highly significant relationship between scores on the screening scales and later help seeking. They concluded that this battery of measures showed considerable promise in identifying those children who are most in need of help after a disaster.

Fear Survey Schedule

In another study, Yule, Udwin and Murdoch (1990b) asked the same 24 girls (and three control groups) to complete the Revised Fear Survey Schedule for Children (Ollendick, 1983). In the affected school, three subgroups of girls were distinguished: those who went on the cruise and were traumatised, those who had wanted to go but could not get a place, and those who showed no interest in going in the first place. However, this latter group could not be considered as an unaffected control group as the whole school was badly affected by the aftermath of the disaster. Accordingly, fourth-year girls in a nearby school also completed the fear schedule. The fear survey items were rated as being related to the events on the cruise or not. There was agreement among the authors that 11 items were related and 33 were unrelated. It was found that there were no differences across the four exposure groups on unrelated fears (e.g., spiders). In contrast, on related fears (e.g., drowning), only the girls who experienced the traumatic events showed a significant increase in reported fears. On this basis, this self-report measure may also have potential as a valuable screening instrument, but only when items specific to the event are used.

Sexual Abuse

Other self-report measures which have been used include the Children's Depression Inventory (Kovacs, 1983) as well as specific measures such as the Sexual Abuse Fear Evaluation (Wolfe & Wolfe, 1986; Wolfe et al., 1989, 1994). This is a 27-item scale that is embedded within the Fear Survey Schedule for Children—Revised (Ollendick, 1983) to assess fears related to events and situations that sexually abused children report as more distressing. Several studies have found that scores on standardised self-report measures of depression or anxiety may not be elevated although scores on measures such as the Sexual Abuse Fear Evaluation are (see Wolfe et al., 1994). For this reason, other measures such as the Child Sexual Behaviour Inventory (CITES: Friedrich et al., 1992) and the Children's Impact of Traumatic Events (Wolfe, Wolfe, Gentile, & LaRose, 1986) may be useful in the assessment of sexual abuse. The CITES, since revised (CITES R: Wolfe, Gentile, Michienzi, et al., 1991), has 78 questions and can be either used as a self-report or administered as an interview. The CITES-R has four subscales: PTSD (intrusive thoughts, avoidance, hyperarousal, sexual anxiety); social reactions (negative reactions from others, social support); abuse attributions (self-blame, guilt, empowerment, vulnerability, dangerous world); and eroticism. McNally (1991), in his review of children's measures, notes that the CITES-R cannot be used to provide a PTSD diagnosis because it fails to assess the full range of symptoms.

However, the use of self-report scales or clinical interviews is not always possible with children and it may be necessary to use some other form of assessment. For example, Gleser, Green, & Winget (1981) report data using the Psychiatric evaluation Form (PEF: Endicott & Spitzer, 1972) completed by the research team on the basis of psychiatric reports from lawsuit proceedings. Fears are thought to be common. Dollinger, O'Donnell and Staley (1984) studied the effects of a lightening strike on 27 soccer players and two spectators all aged 10 to 13 years. All had been knocked flat by the lightening strike in which one boy was killed and six required immediate medical treatment. The survivors later completed the Louisville Fear Survey for Children, 104 items rated on 5-point scales. The investigators found that the children on the soccer field showed more fear of storms than did matched controls, and these fears were more intense. But also, it was found that responses showed a clear generalisation gradient with fears of storms being strongest, followed by fears relating to sleep, noise, disasters, death, and dying while there was no effect on fears of people or embarrassment. Similar findings are reported by Yule et al. (1990b) with children who survived the *Jupiter* sinking. Recent evidence also suggests that infants and young children (i.e., less that 4 years of age) can develop post-traumatic disorders after traumatic events, although it does not seem that they exhibit symptoms in a way that can be diagnosed by DSM-IV criteria but instead require more behaviourally anchored and developmentally sensitive criteria (Scheeringa, Zeanah, Drell, & Larrieu, 1995).

ISSUES AND RECOMMENDATIONS

Although cutoff scores are often proposed for self-report scales so that they can be used diagnostically, the use of cutoff scores reflects a dichotomous categorisation and there will often be very little difference between those respondents scoring just below the cutoff point and those scoring just above the cutoff point. Furthermore, appropriate cutoff points will vary with the population under study (Watson, 1990). Recommended cutoff points for classification should be used with great caution.

A further limitation of the various self-report measures is the possibility that respondents can easily fake psychopathology. This has been demonstrated in studies with the IES (Lees-Haley, 1990) although other work using the MMPI has suggested that when asked to fake symptoms, respondents will tend to overendorse PTSD symptoms (Fairbank, McCaffrey, & Keane, 1985). The possibility of factitious presentations (Lacoursiere, 1993) has prompted researchers to find other objective methods of assessment. In addition to clinical interviews and self-report instruments, there has been some interest in the development of psychophysiological measures of PTSD. This refers to the assessment of autonomic activity when survivors are re-exposed to traumatic stimuli. In an early study, Blanchard, Kolb, Pallmeyer, and Gerardi (1982) found that heart rate, skin conductance, and electromyography responses to combat stimuli discriminated PTSD patients from normal control subjects.

More recently, Blanchard, Kolb, Gerardi, Ryan, and Pallmeyer (1986) proposed that heart rate reactivity to combat stimuli could serve as a marker for PTSD because it accurately classified 88% of PTSD patients. In addition, the use of cognitive and neuropsychological measures also appear to be promising (Wolfe & Charney, 1991).

Changes in Outlook

Generally the literature has focused on pathological adjustment and testifies to the severity and chronicity of distress often experienced by survivors of traumatic events. But there are often positive psychological reactions following trauma such as an increased ability to appreciate life and to show more compassion towards others (Collins, Taylor, & Skokan, 1990; Lehman et al., 1993; Taylor, Lichtman, & Wood, 1984; Zeidner & Ben-Zur, 1994). One self-report instrument that has been designed to assess both negative and positive trauma-related reactions is the Changes in Outlook Questionnaire (Joseph, Williams, & Yule, 1993c). This is a 26-item self-report measure (see Figure 3.1) that contains two scales tapping positive changes (e.g., I value my relationships much more now) as well as negative changes (e.g., I have very little trust in other people now). Many people who are involved in disaster and who are not identified as overtly suffering from severe psychological disturbance can undergo major changes in their approach to life and we would argue that, at present, disaster research is constrained by its focus on psychopathological responses. It is through the assessment of both positive and negative responses that it should become possible to identify more accurately those at risk of long-term disturbance.

Assessment of Psychosocial Factors

Although exposure to a traumatic event is a necessary aetiological factor in the development of PTSD, exposure would not appear to be sufficient and reactions to trauma are thought to be multiply determined. For this reason some researchers have advocated an assessment procedure compatible with research and clinical purposes. For example, Freedy, Kilpatrick, and Resnick (1993) outline an assessment instrument that they have used with survivors of Hurricane Hugo. This includes questions on pre-disaster factors, within-disaster factors, post-disaster factors as well as mental health outcome. Various self-report instruments exist for the measurement of coping resources and behaviour (e.g., Carver, Scheier, & Weintraub, 1989; Folkman, Lazarus, Dunkel-Schetter, DeLongis, & Gruen, 1986a; Hobfoll, Lilly, & Jackson, 1991; Matheny, Curlette, Aycock, Pugh, & Taylor, 1987; Matheny, Aycock, Curlette, & Junker, 1993; Muris, van Zuuren, de Jong, de Beurs, & Hanewald, 1994; Tobin, Holroyd, Reynolds, & Wigal, 1989), social support (Joseph, Andrews, Williams, & Yule, 1992a; Power, 1988; Sarason, Levine, Basham, &

Each of the following statements have been made by survivors of disaster at some time. Please read each one and indicate, by circling one of the numbers next to it, how much you agree or disagree with it at the present time:
1 = Strongly disagree; 2 = Disagree; 3 = Disagree a little; 4 = Agree a little;
5 = Agree; 6 = Strongly agree

1.	I don't take life for granted any more	1	2	3	4	5	6
2.	I value my relationships much more now..............	1	2	3	4	5	6
3.	I feel more experienced about life now..............	1	2	3	4	5	6
4.	I don't worry about death at all any more..............	1	2	3	4	5	6
5.	I live everyday to the full now...........	1	2	3	4	5	6
6.	I look upon each day as a bonus.........	1	2	3	4	5	6
7.	I'm a more understanding and tolerant person now........................	1	2	3	4	5	6
8.	I have greater faith in human nature now..............	1	2	3	4	5	6
9.	I no longer take people or things for granted............................	1	2	3	4	5	6
10.	I value other people more now..........	1	2	3	4	5	6
11.	I am more determined to succeed in life now........................	1	2	3	4	5	6
12.	I don't look forward to the future any more..............	1	2	3	4	5	6
13.	My life has no meaning any more......	1	2	3	4	5	6
14.	I no longer feel able to cope with things................................	1	2	3	4	5	6
15.	I fear death very much now..............	1	2	3	4	5	6
16.	I feel as if something bad is just waiting around the corner to happen.	1	2	3	4	5	6
17.	I desperately wish I could turn the clock back to before it happened.......	1	2	3	4	5	6
18.	I sometimes think it's not worth being a good person............................	1	2	3	4	5	6
19.	I have very little trust in other people now..............	1	2	3	4	5	6
20.	I feel very much as if I'm in limbo.......	1	2	3	4	5	6
21.	I have very little trust in myself now...	1	2	3	4	5	6
22.	I feel harder towards other people.....	1	2	3	4	5	6
23.	I am less tolerant of others now.........	1	2	3	4	5	6
24.	I am much less able to communicate with other people..........................	1	2	3	4	5	6
25.	Nothing makes me happy any more...	1	2	3	4	5	6
26.	I feel as if I'm dead from the neck downwards.....................	1	2	3	4	5	6

N.B. Items 1 to 11 are summated to give a total score for the positive response scale. Items 12 to 26 are summated to give a total score for the negative response scale.

Figure 3.1   Changes in Outlook Questionnaire

Sarason, 1983; Sarason, Shearin, Pierce, & Sarason, 1987), attributional style and locus of control (e.g., Peterson et al., 1982; Rotter, 1966) and life-events (e.g., Brugha, Bebbington, Tennant, & Hurry, 1985; Paykel, 1983; Sarason, Johnson, & Siegal, 1978; Smith, 1992; Zuckerman, Oliver, Hollingsworth, & Austrin, 1986).

CONCLUSION

A large number of operational definitions for the assessment of trauma-related reactions have appeared. These definitions can be grouped into either (1) highly structured interviews, or (2) self-report symptomatology measures. The use of structured interviews and self-report rating scales not only assist in making a diagnosis, but also allow quantification and reduce the subjectivity inherent in clinical judgements of the severity of what are private phenomena. However, regardless of the individual reliability and validity of the various assessment tools, researchers have advocated the use of multiple assessment measures prior to conferring the diagnosis of PTSD (Denny, Robinowitz, & Penk, 1987; Malloy, Fairbank, & Keane, 1983; Keane, Caddell, & Taylor, 1988; Wolfe & Keane, 1993). Included in such an approach is an emphasis on the clinical interview, self-report instruments, and psychophysiological assessment. The range of psychological problems experienced by survivors is wide and includes not only the symptoms of PTSD but also those of depression and anxiety as well as difficulties in social functioning and substance abuse. On this basis, a multimethod approach to assessment is encouraged, one that includes not only pathological outcomes but an evaluation of the person's attitudes towards life.

SUMMARY POINTS

1. Several standardised interview schedules have been developed on the basis of the DSM criteria. However, there remains some debate on how best to conceptualise reactions to extreme stressors and measures will all need to be updated and validated with respect to DSM-IV criteria.
2. Self-report questionnaires have been developed on the basis of psychometric evidence. There have been two approaches to the development of self-report measures: first, the development of new tests for assessing PTSD; second, the study of existing tests and their usefulness in diagnosing PTSD. The MMPI has received much attention.
3. Adults often appear to underestimate children's reactions and therefore self-report measures are especially valuable when working with children. Several measures that have been developed that focus on child sexual abuse, and appear promising.

4.   Other work has shown that survivors often experience both negative and positive reactions and there is a need also to ask about other changes that survivors may experience. There is some evidence that positive existential changes in outlook are common following some events and that survivors may sometimes report that the experience of the traumatic event has been in some way beneficial to them.

Chapter 4

TYPES OF TRAUMA: FROM NATURAL DISASTER TO POLITICAL VIOLENCE

INTRODUCTION

Earlier definitions of what constitutes a traumatic event emphasised unusual experiences (APA, 1980), i.e., mass transportation disasters. But this definition was fraught with problems (see Davidson & Foa, 1991) and it became clear that what was needed was an indication of the tendency of the stressor to produce psychological problems rather than attempt to define a trauma by its frequency. As our cases have shown, the individual experience of an event as traumatic may be highly idiosyncratic. This chapter, however, will review the types of event that have usually been found to produce post-traumatic stress reactions. Over the last 15 years there has been an explosion in research on the psychological effects of various traumatic events. Typical PTSD-inducing events are generally outside of individual control, unpredictable, involve the potential for physical injury or death, and possess the capacity to elicit affect-laden visual imagery (see March, 1993). However, there is tremendous variability in the prevalence of disorder found between studies of different events (Rubonis & Bickman, 1991) raising the question of whether different events lead to different rates of disorder and different symptoms.

Key Topics

Epidemiological findings
Natural disaster
Technological disaster
Combat
Criminal victimisation
Sexual assault
Childhood sexual abuse
Political violence
Refugees
Event factors
Conclusion

EPIDEMIOLOGICAL FINDINGS

Estimates of psychological impairment in the first year following natural disaster reported in the review by Raphael (1986) range from around 20% in survivors of Cyclone Tracy (Parker, 1977) to around 50% in survivors of the Xenia Tornado (Taylor, Ross, & Quarantelli, 1976) demonstrating the variability in prevalence rates between studies. The incidence of psychological impairment in any population exposed to a traumatic event is expected to be a function of the intensity of the event. But if we want to compare the incidence rates between different events it is necessary that each of the studies uses the same methods of assessing psychological impairment. Most of the studies reviewed by Raphael, however, were conducted before the introduction of PTSD and investigated the prevalence of distress using different measures. So, the results are a function of the measurement tools used as well as the actual differences that might exist between populations, making it difficult to reach meaningful conclusions about which events are the most distressing. But with the introduction of the diagnostic category of PTSD investigators have increasingly been working under the same conceptual umbrella using compatible measures of impairment allowing for generalisations to be made about which events are most likely to lead to high levels of impairment.

NATURAL DISASTERS

Epidemiological findings suggest that events involving death and destruction on a massive scale are especially likely to lead to psychological problems. In 1985 a volcanic explosion in Columbia destroyed the small town of Armero killing 80% of its 30,000 inhabitants. Seven months after the incident, a sample of 200 adult survivors were screened for evidence of psychological impairment using a self-report questionnaire. Fifty-five per cent were found, on the basis of their scores on the questionnaire, to be severely distressed (Lima, Pai, Santacruz, & Lozano, 1987). In a two-year follow up study, Lima, Pai, Lozano, and Santacruz (1991) report data on a representative sample of 40 people who were included in their 1987 study. Interestingly, at two years using the same self-report questionnaire, they identified 78% as emotionally distressed. Contrary to what one might have expected, these findings indicate an increase rather than a decrease in distress over time. Lima et al. (1991) suggest that this may, at least in part, be due to the adverse environmental conditions experienced by survivors subsequently, such as poor housing and unemployment. However, the authors also note that a small number of survivors showed no evidence of emotional distress during the first two years, raising the question of what makes some individuals emotionally resilient. In a further study Lima et al. (1993) found that 30% of survivors were emotionally distressed at five years. This study makes some interesting points that illustrate very well the usefulness of the psychosocial approach to understanding post-traumatic stress reactions. In particular, the fact that distress might actually be maintained or exacerbated by other post-trauma psychosocial stressors such as poor housing conditions demonstrates that psychological impairment following exposure to trauma is a function of factors which may or may not be a function of the traumatic event itself. This is another reason why even when apparently similar events are compared the prevalence rates can vary widely. For example, studies of the psychological effects of earthquakes have yielded mixed findings, some studies indicating that the psychological effects are often mild and transient (e.g., Popovic & Petrovic, 1964; Takuma, 1978; Tierney, 1985), whereas others have showed more severe and long-lasting effects (e.g., Carr, 1991; Galante & Foa, 1986; Lima et al., 1989; Maj et al., 1989; Bourque, Aneshensel, & Goltz, 1991). The fact that different assessment measures were used across these studies confounds the picture even further.

However, one finding that is largely consistent, although it might be argued that it does not take a psychologist to tell us, is that those events involving widespread death and destruction are associated with the most severe and long-lasting psychological symptomatology. For example, De La Fuente (1990) reported that over 30% of the survivors of the 1985 earthquakes in Mexico displayed PTSD. Work with almost 600 adult survivors of the 1988 Armenia earthquake found a PTSD prevalence rate of 74% at 3 to 6 months (Goenjian, 1993). In further studies, Goenjian and colleagues present evidence that the frequency and severity of post-traumatic stress reactions remained high at one and a half years in adults (Goenjian et al., 1994) and children (Pynoos et al., 1993).

Other work by Galante and Foa (1986) of children badly traumatised by the massive earthquakes in a remote mountainous region of central Italy in November 1980 also shows that the effects on children can be severe and long-lasting. But other research on natural disasters with lower death rates suggests that although symptoms may persist for as long as three to five years, most abate in about 18 months (Cook & Bickman, 1990; Krause, 1987; Phifer & Norris, 1989; Shore, Tatum, & Vollmer, 1986; Steinglass & Gerrity, 1990). This finding that symptoms abate in around 18 months would also seem to be true of children (Vogel & Vernberg, 1993).

TECHNOLOGICAL DISASTER

Green and her colleagues have conducted a most impressive series of studies on adult and child survivors of the Buffalo Creek dam collapse in which 125 people were killed and the community destroyed. They followed a group of survivors from 2 to 14 years following the event (Gleser, Green, & Winget, 1981; Green et al., 1990a). At 14 years, they found that 28% of the adult sample had PTSD whereas a comparison group had a rate of 8%. Green et al.,

(1994) conducted a 17-year follow-up of 99 of the 207 children who survived the Buffalo Creek disaster in 1972. In contrast to the earlier findings with adults, their results with children showed little evidence of psychiatric impairment. Green et al. (1994) conclude that '. . . some optimism is warranted with regard to long-term recovery in children exposed to severe events' (p. 78). Although these data are encouraging, work with children and adolescents who survived the sinking of the *Herald of Free Enterprise* ferry in 1987 has found severe distress at 12–15 months and six years post-disaster, suggesting that in the short term at least there may be serious problems (Yule & Williams, 1990).

Interestingly, technological accidents, such as Three Mile Island, have been found to be associated with long-term effects up to six years later in adults (Baum, 1990; Baum & Fleming, 1993; Baum, Fleming, & Singer, 1983a; Baum, Gatchel, & Schaeffer, 1983b; Davidson, Fleming, & Baum, 1986) despite the fact that the Three Mile Island nuclear incident involved no apparent physical damage to people or property. Handford et al. (1983) conducted a study at one and a half years on thirty-five 5 to 19 years olds living within 30 miles of the Three Mile plant. Unlike the work with adults they did not find evidence of increased impairment. There were no cases of PTSD, two children received a diagnosis of anxiety disorder, one, dysthymic disorder, and one, conduct disorder. This rate represents an incidence consistent with what might be expected in the general population. But as discussed in Chapter 3 it may be that these data under-represent the level of distress through the use of parents' ratings of their children's symptoms. Alternatively, since there were no signs of the effects of radiation, the children may have been less frightened by this event in the first place.

Natural versus Technological Disaster

Green and Lindy (1994), in a brief review of the literature on the psychological outcomes following disaster, conclude that it is difficult to distinguish natural and technological disasters from each other in terms of their early impact, but that the persistence of responses may differentiate the two and that the effects of natural disasters seem to be no longer detectable after two years. This may be the case for natural disasters with very limited death and destruction, but for those events involving widespread destruction and death the effects would seem to be extremely severe and it might be that these events have very long-term effects although no evidence is yet available to confirm this. However, the long-term effects of technological disasters are documented and it might be suggested that the fact that technology is involved makes these events particularly traumatic as, unlike acts of God, they may have been avoidable accidents caused by human negligence.

As we shall discuss in Chapter 6, the fact of human involvement in traumatic events can have important implications for how the event is understood, leading to very strong emotions, i.e., anger, rage, guilt, shame, which serve to impede emotional processing. It has been argued that human-caused events such as combat, criminal victimisation, and sexual assault where there is a clear intention to harm appear to have the most severe and chronic effects of all.

COMBAT

Compared to all other events, the effects of war have been particularly well documented. Kulka et al. (1990) have presented data from the National Vietnam Veterans Readjustment Study (NVVRS). This is a comprehensive and rigorous study of the prevalence of PTSD and other psychological problems in readjusting to civilian life among Vietnam veterans. The NVVRS was a national epidemiological study involving face-to-face interviews. NVVRS estimated that 15% of all male Vietnam veterans were current cases of PTSD, 15 or more years after service. This represents about 479,000 of the estimated 3.14 million men who served in Vietnam. Among veteran women, current PTSD prevalence is estimated to be 8.5% of the approximately 7,200 women who served. In addition, NVVRS estimate that approximately one-third of male and one-fourth of women veterans have had PTSD at some time in their lives (Kulka et al., 1990; Schlenger et al., 1992). The NVVRS study indicates that nearly half a million Vietnam veterans are current cases of PTSD. In addition to these analyses, Kulka et al. (1990) also estimated the prevalence of partial PTSD, a subdiagnostic constellation of symptoms, finding lifetime and current prevalence to be 22.5% and 11.1% for male theatre veterans and 21.2% and 7.8% for female theatre veterans, respectively. Together, full and partial prevalence estimates for lifetime PTSD suggest that half of all male (53.4%) and almost half of all female (48.1%) Vietnam veterans have experienced clinically significant symptomatology.

Although the data are sparse, high prevalence rates have also been reported for British servicemen who served in the Falklands War (O'Brien & Hughes, 1991; Orner, Lynch, & Seed, 1993). Five years after the war, O'Brien and Hughes (1991) compared a unit of 64 soldiers who had fought in the 1982 Falklands conflict with a matched unit of 64 who had remained on home duties. O'Brien and Hughes (1991) found a higher reported rate of self-reported symptoms in the veteran group and 22% reported symptoms fulfilling the diagnostic criteria of PTSD, suggesting that in the wider population of Falklands veterans many may be seriously affected five years later.

CRIMINAL VICTIMISATION

In an American survey, it was estimated that the prevalence of civilian trauma and crime-related PTSD was around 1% in the general population (Helzer, Robins, & McEvoy, 1987). There is evidence from a variety of studies that the experience of criminal victimisation is associated with poorer mental health (Kilpatrick, Saunders, Veronen, Best, & Von, 1987; Resnick, Kilpatrick, Dansky, Saunders, & Best, 1993; Sorenson & Golding, 1990). The immediate aftermath of crime can be particularly distressing. Davis and Friedman (1985) in a study of victims of burglary, robbery, and assault found that 45% of victims were experiencing distress 1–3 weeks after the incident, and if sleeping disorders were included, this rose to 75%.

Crime involving random violence can be particularly distressing. Several studies have been carried out following multiple shooting events. Following one shooting which took place in a McDonald's restaurant in San Ysidro killing 21 people and injuring 15, it was found that nearly a third of the community surveyed reported that they were seriously affected by the incident. Those who reported having family or friends involved in the incident were the most likely to exhibit PTSD symptoms (Hough et al., 1990). In another study of a multiple shooting in a small Arkansas town, 80% exhibited some symptoms of PTSD (North, Smith, McCool, & Shea, 1989). A later study by North, Smith, and Spitznagel (1994) investigated the emotional reactions of people after a gunman mounted a firearm assault for almost 15 minutes on a crowd of nearly 150 civilians in a cafeteria in Texas. Twenty-four of those present were killed and many others were wounded. Initially, the gunman drove his truck through the window of the restaurant injuring several people. Then he walked around the room systematically shooting his victims, mainly women, at point-blank range. The police arrived within 15 minutes and cornered the gunman who then shot himself dead. Interviews were carried out within 6–8 weeks with those present. Overall, nearly all had some symptoms of PTSD and 20% of men and 36% of women met the full criteria for PTSD. Other research has shown PTSD symptoms in children at one month (Pynoos & Nader, 1988) and at 14 months (Nader, Pynoos, Fairbanks, & Frederick, 1990) following a fatal sniper shooting in a Californian school. Other research has reported a 19% prevalence rate of PTSD in children after a mass shooting incident at a school (Schwarz & Kowalski, 1991).

Solomon and Horn (1986), in their study of police officers following post-shooting incidents, found that 37% of victims experienced a mild reaction, 35% moderate, and 28% severe distress. Similarly, Gersons (1989) investigated the degree and intensity of post-traumatic reactions in 37 police officers of the Amsterdam police force who were involved in serious shooting incidents in the period between 1977 and 1984. In these seven years 62 officers were involved in a shooting incident that involved injury. Gersons (1989) was able to obtain an interview with 37 of these officers. It was not known if this sample was representative of the whole group. Out of the 37, only 3 were found to be symptom free, 17 suffered from some PTSD symptoms, and 17 fulfilled PTSD criteria. Gersons reports that none had looked for help or treatment from doctors, psychologists, or social workers within the police force. It was suggested that this was because of police culture in which officers do not generally complain about psychological issues or discuss emotional reactions. Duckworth (1986) found that 35% of a sample of the police officers involved with the Bradford football club fire were suffering from PTSD, and a further 21% met three of the four DSM-III criteria for PTSD.

SEXUAL ASSAULT

A survey of over 4000 American women found that one-third had experienced a crime such as physical or sexual assault (Resnick et al., 1993). For those exposed to such events, PTSD is a likely outcome. Kilpatrick, Saunders, Veronen, Best, & Von (1987) found a 75% lifetime prevalence rate of exposure to a variety of crimes in a community sample of women. Furthermore, 27.8% of those women exposed to any crime acquired lifetime PTSD. In addition, Kilpatrick et al. (1987) found that there was an overall rate of sexual assault of around 50% and a rate of approximately 20% for completed rape (see also Koss, 1993). The crime of rape was associated with a lifetime PTSD prevalence rate of 57.1%. This and other evidence suggests that rape is one of the most traumatic events and produces rates of PTSD higher than that produced by other events (Breslau, Davis, Andreski, & Peterson, 1991; Kilpatrick et al., 1989; Norris, 1992). Other survey work indicates that over 30% of all rape victims may develop PTSD at some time in their lives (National Victims Center, 1992). Resnick, Veronen, Saunders, Kilpatrick, and Cornelison (1989) found that 76% of rape victims met the diagnostic criteria for PTSD at some point within a year of the assault. Similarly, high rates have been reported by others (Crummier & Green, 1991).

In a prospective study by Rothbaum, Foa, Riggs, Murdock, and Walsh (1992), 64 women who had been subjected to rape or attempted rape were interviewed within a month of the event. Further interviews were conducted weekly over 12 weeks during which time the women completed a variety of self-report measures of psychiatric symptoms. Women who had a prior history of mental disorder were excluded from the study. Most of the remaining women were black, unmarried, and of low income and had been referred by the police. Rothbaum et al. (1992) found that although the incidence of PTSD decreased over the 12 weeks, at the initial interview 94% of the women met the symptomatic criteria for PTSD. By assessment 4, when the DSM-III-R duration criterion of one-month was met, the incidence of PTSD was 65%, and by assessment 12 the incidence of PTSD was 47%.

In addition, there is evidence that women who have experienced sexual assault are likely to suffer from a range of psychological problems including anxiety and fear (Calhoun, Atkeson, & Resick, 1982; Ellis, Atkeson, & Calhoun, 1981; Kilpatrick, Resick, & Veronen, 1981; Kimerling & Calhoun, 1994), depression (Atkeson, Calhoun, Resick, & Ellis, 1982; Frank, Turner, & Duffy, 1979; Kilpatrick, Veronen, & Resick, 1979; Kimerling & Calhoun,

1994), sexual dysfunction (Becker, Skinner, Abel, & Treacy, 1982; Orlando & Koss, 1983), and problems in social adjustment (Kilpatrick et al., 1979; Resick, Calhoun, Atkeson, & Ellis, 1982).

CHILDHOOD SEXUAL ABUSE

Terr (1991) has delineated two classes of trauma that may lead to the development of PTSD. First, Type I trauma involves single traumatic events that are sudden and unexpected. Examples of such an event would be involvement in a road traffic accident or being a victim of criminal or sexual assault.

Type II trauma, on the other hand, involves repeated exposure to a traumatic event that may be predictable and expected. For example, this might include repetitive and prolonged physical or sexual abuse. PTSD, as outlined by the APA and the WHO, is largely concerned with survivors of Type I trauma. Evidence has begun to accumulate, however, for another more complex form of PTSD in survivors of Type II trauma. It has been noted that the problems that occur in child abuse victims reflect a different emphasis from the DSM classification for PTSD (Herman, 1992a; Terr, 1991). A recent review of the evidence for the existence of a complex form of PTSD concludes that there is

> . . . unsystematised but extensive empirical support for the concept of a complex post-traumatic syndrome in survivors of prolonged, repeated victimisation. This previously undefined syndrome may coexist with simple PTSD, but extends beyond it. The syndrome is characterised by enduring personality changes, and high risk for repeated harm, either self-inflicted or at the hands of others. (Herman, 1992a, p. 387)

Herman (1992a) goes on to say that patients suffering from this risk being misdiagnosed as having personality disorders.

A personality disorder refers to pervasive, enduring, inflexible, and distressing patterns of thought and behaviour that deviate from social norms. DSM-IV (APA, 1994) distinguishes between 10 personality disorders grouped into three clusters: (1) paranoid, schizoid, and schizotypal personality disorders characterised by eccentric behaviours; (2) antisocial, borderline, histrionic, and narcissistic personality disorders characterised by dramatic, emotional, or erratic behaviours; and (3) avoidant, dependent, and obsessive-compulsive personality disorders characterised by fearful or anxious behaviours.

Borderline personality disorder, in particular, has been discussed in relation to early trauma and studies show a heightened prevalence of childhood physical and sexual abuse among people with this disorder (Beitchman, Zucker, Hood, DaCosta, & Cassavia, 1992; Browne & Finkelhor, 1986; Finkelhor, 1990; Marcus, 1989). Adults with borderline personality disorder display a pervasive pattern of instability in interpersonal relationships, sexual dysfunction, poor self-image, mood shifts, impulsivity, and destructive behaviour reminiscent of the character Alex Forrest in the film 'Fatal Attraction'.

A wide variety of short- and long-term consequences of child sexual abuse (CSA) have been described (Browne & Finkelhor, 1986; Finkelhor, 1990) and a recent national survey of over 2500 Americans has indicated that 27% of women and 16% of men report CSA experiences (Finkelhor, Hotaling, Lewis, & Smith, 1990). Furthermore, there is evidence that the experience of CSA is associated with the development of PTSD (Burgess et al., 1984; Frederick, 1985b; McLeer et al., 1988; Wolfe, Gentile, & Wolfe, 1989; Wolfe, Sas, & Wekerle, 1994) and related symptoms.

Sexually abused female children may exhibit a wide range of dissociative symptoms and autodestructive behaviours. Increased aggression, feelings of fear, anger, guilt, shame, as well as eating and sleeping disturbances, inappropriate sexual behaviour, truancy from school, are all common in childhood sexual abuse. Women who have been sexually abused as children are more likely to suffer social and interpersonal difficulties in adult life (Browne & Finkelhor, 1986; Mullen, Martin, Anderson, Romans, & Herbison, 1994) as well as inappropriate sexual behaviour and sexual dysfunction and self-harming behaviour. Feelings of isolation, depression, anxiety, low self-esteem, as well as substance abuse have also been shown to be related to early abuse.

Although most of the research into sexual abuse has been with women, recent reports into the sexual abuse of men as children have also suggested that there may be similar problems in long-term functioning (Lisak, 1994; Lisak & Luster, 1994; Schulte, Dinwiddie, Pribor, & Yutzy, 1995). As with women, the evidence suggests that men who have been sexually abused as children may show disturbed attitudes towards sexuality, producing difficulties ranging from fear of sexual contact to a tendency to engage in frequent brief sexual encounters. Mood disorders, anxiety disorder, and substance-use disorders are common and victims often appear to meet criteria for many different psychiatric disorders.

POLITICAL VIOLENCE

For over 25 years Northern Ireland has been exposed to civil disturbance in which over 3000 people have died and over 100,000 people have been injured out of a total population of around only 1.5 million. Since the beginning of the conflict, researchers have been interested in its possible psychological effects (Fraser, 1971). An early study by Lyons (1974) of 100 people who had been directly involved in a bomb explosion found that in the majority of cases there was evidence for affective disturbance, most commonly anxiety with various phobic symptoms. Depression, often with irritability, was also frequently reported. Some PTSD symptoms such as exaggerated startle responses to loud noises were also reported.

In a subsequent study, Hadden, Rutherford and Merret (1978) investigated 1532 patients admitted to the accident and emergency unit of a Belfast hospital because of involvement in a bomb explosion. They found that 50% had sustained 'psychological shock'. Although studies such as that by Fraser (1971), Lyons (1974), and Hadden et al. (1978) were conducted before the introduction of PTSD, more recent data confirms that PTSD may be a consequence of exposure to such violence (Kee, Bell, Loughrey, Roddy, & Curran, 1987). In one study it was found that 50% of a sample assessed following the Enniskillen bombing satisfied the DSM-III criteria for PTSD (Curran, Bell, Loughrey, Roddy, & Rocke, 1988). However, other prevalence estimates have been found to be lower. For example, Loughrey, Bell, Kee, Roddy, & Curran (1988) investigated the incidence of PTSD among 499 people exposed to various types of civilian trauma in Northern Ireland finding that 23% had developed PTSD.

Other work which has been carried out in Northern Ireland have been community-based surveys which have shown that most people in Northern Ireland were not suffering from severe psychological problems (Cairns & Wilson, 1984, 1985, 1989). This might seem surprising given the relentless violence in that society. But it should be noted that for most people in Northern Ireland the political violence was not something that they were directly exposed to. A study of the emotional reactions of civilians resident in Israel during the Persian Gulf War and the SCUD missile attacks was conducted by Zeidner and Ben-Zur (1994) who gathered data on a sample of over 800 adults about three months following the June 1991 cease fire. They found that the effects of the war were weak and in keeping with an 'evaporation model' of stress response (Worthington, 1977). One explanation for this, Zeidner and Ben-Zur suggest, is that the Israeli people have over the years experienced many past traumas including the holocaust and the Israel–Arab conflict. Such an explanation might also apply to the findings of Cairns and Wilson that the people of Northern Ireland appeared to suffer little residual effects of the violence.

REFUGEES

Psychiatric problems have long been documented in refugees (Eitinger, 1959) and evidence suggests that disturbance is not only influenced by migration and subsequent adjustment but also by pre-migration factors such as torture and imprisonment (Westermeyer, Vang, & Neider, 1983). Arroyo and Eth (1985) interviewed 30 central American refugees under the age of 17 years who had been exposed to war before arrival in the United States finding that 10 met diagnostic criteria for PTSD while 9 met criteria for adjustment disorder. Kinzie et al. (1986) interviewed 40 children four years after they had been imprisoned in Cambodian concentration camps where they had undergone starvation, beatings and witnessed the death of others. Twenty met APA criteria for PTSD, 17 of whom had concurrent depressive disorder. Students who had fled Cambodia before Pol Pot came to power received no diagnoses, leading the authors to conclude that their findings did not appear to be a result of migration but of pre-migration factors.

EVENT FACTORS

Although there is evidence throughout the epidemiological literature that bereavement is associated with more severe and chronic disturbance (e.g., Gleser et al., 1981; Goenjian et al., 1994; Singh & Raphael, 1981; Solkoff, Gray, & Keill, 1986; Green, Grace, Lindy, Titchener, & Lindy, 1983; Murphy, 1986; Shore et al., 1986), and generally the higher the rate of death, the higher the later psychological disturbance, these factors alone do not account for the individual differences in reactions among any group of survivors or between groups of survivors.

Various researchers have tried to identify what it is about traumatic events that is most distressing and much research has accumulated showing that the extent of personal injury as well as the degree of life-threat also influence the course of symptomatology in combat veterans (e.g., Breslau & Davis, 1987; Card, 1987; Fontana, Rosenheck, & Brett, 1992; Foy, Resnick, Sipprelle, & Carroll, 1987; Frye & Stockton, 1982; Helzer et al., 1987; Orner, Lynch & Seed, 1993; Solkoff et al., 1986; Yehuda, Southwick, & Giller, 1992) as well as in civilian survivors of a variety of events (e.g., Cluss, Boughton, Frank, Stewart, & West, 1983; Ellis et al., 1981; Green et al., 1983; Gleser et al., 1981; Helzer et al., 1987; Kilpatrick et al., 1989; Maida, Gordon, Steinberg, & Gordon, 1989; Parker, 1977; Resnick, Kilpatrick, Best, & Crummier, 1992; Shore et al., 1986; Smith et al., 1986; Weisaeth, 1983; Western & Milne, 1979).

It would seem that some events can be so traumatic, i.e., involve a high degree of life-threat and personal injury, that almost everyone who is exposed will develop PTSD. For example, Kilpatrick et al. (1989) found that for those women who had experienced rape, life-threat, and physical injury, 80% went on to develop PTSD. The prevalence of disorder thus depends on the nature and intensity of the experience. For example, Helzer et al. (1987) reported a prevalence rate of about 3.5% in Vietnam veterans who were not wounded in battle compared to about 20% in veterans who were. Card (1987) found that 19% of all veterans, and 27% of veterans exposed to heavy combat suffered from PTSD. Even higher estimates have been made for those who were exposed to particularly heavy combat. Foy et al. (1987) observed that 25–30% of low-combat-exposed subjects in their clinical samples met full DSM-III criteria for PTSD, and 70% of their high-combat-exposed subjects were diagnosed as having PTSD. Foy et al. (1987) observe that being wounded, involvement in the deaths of non-combatants, and exposure to atrocities are critical elements in the development of PTSD in combat veterans. With over 5000 veterans from the Second World War, Korea, and Vietnam, it has been shown that symptoms are more severe the more intense the traumatic exposure is, and that responsibility for killing another human being or having been a target of killing are associated with emotional distress (Fontana & Rosenheck, 1994a). The role of combat exposure has received much attention and other research has shown that Second World War veterans exposed to moderate or heavy combat had 13.3 times greater risk of PTSD symptoms measured 45 years later compared with non-combat veterans (Spiro, Schnurr, & Aldwin, 1994).

Intensity of exposure has been defined in a variety of different ways in the above studies. One other factor, however, which appears to be a common defining criterion is that of witnessing death and exposure to the grotesque. Solkoff et al. (1986) found that the stressor variable accounting for most of the variance in PTSD symptoms in survivors of Vietnam was exposure to death and injury. They found support for the hypothesis that PTSD patients would have experienced more intense combat and would have been involved with more death and killing than controls. PTSD subjects were found to perceive themselves as having been closer to personal death and the death of others. They reported more personal involvement in killing, more friends killed, and that they were more likely to have observed their death. PTSD subjects were also in combat for a longer time and more frequently sustained injuries. Witnessing death has also been found to affect children adversely, even as young as 5 years (Malmquist, 1986).

Furthermore, Lund, Foy, Sipprelle, and Strachan (1984) suggested that stress may build cumulatively through exposure to a traumatic event. Lund et al. (1984) employed a Guttman scaling technique to construct a measure of trauma in the Vietnam War. Developed from dichotomous questions about traumatic events, the scale was associated with PTSD symptoms confirming their prediction that stress may build cumulatively. Events involving repeated and prolonged exposure may be most harmful. For example, the duration and frequency of child sexual abuse have been shown to be associated with PTSD diagnostic status (Rowan, Foy, Rodriguez, & Ryan, 1993). In a survey of over 3000 Los Angeles community residents it was found that criminal victimisation was associated with increased thoughts of suicide and depression. Furthermore, those people reporting two or more victimising experiences were more likely to suffer depression than those people reporting only one such event (Sorenson & Golding, 1990).

However, although much of this work has attempted to demonstrate the dose–response relationship, it is difficult to find indices of objective exposure and invariably much of the work has had to rely on the subjective assessment of exposure variables, such as retrospectively assessed perceived life-threat. From this evidence, it is impossible to untangle the effects of objective and subjective factors. However, there is other work which has demonstrated an objective exposure–response relationship. In his study of the aftermath of a paint factory fire, Weisaeth (1983) showed that those workers nearest the centre of the explosion suffered most post-traumatic distress; those furthest from it suffered the least. Similarly, poorer psychological health was demonstrated in Three Mile Island residents living within 5 miles of the plant compared to those living further away within three months of the leak (Bromet, Parkinson, Schulberg, Dunn, & Gondek, 1982a). Furthermore, Baum, Gatchel, and Schaeffer (1983b) evaluated the psychophysiological impact on residents one year after the Three Mile Island accident compared to people living near an undamaged power plant, people living near a traditional coal-fired power plant, and people living in an area more than 20 miles from any power plant. Results indicated that residents of the Three Mile Island area exhibited more self-reported symptoms of stress as measured by the Beck Depression Inventory and the 90-item Symptom Checklist.

In a similar study by Davidson, Weiss, O'Keffe, and Baum (1991) 70 residents of the Three Mile Island accident area were compared to a control group of 29 subjects who lived some 80 miles southwest of Three Mile Island. All subjects were randomly selected and completed the 90-item Symptom Checklist (Derogatis, 1977). The results of this study suggested that accident area residents continued to exhibit more symptoms of chronic anxiety and somatic complaints than controls even after six years. In addition, measures of heart rate and blood pressure were obtained and it was found that for Three Mile Island residents, both measures were elevated relative to controls.

Similarly, Realmuto, Wagner, and Bartholow (1991) investigated the impact of a gasline explosion in a small midwestern suburban city in 1986 which caused the death of a mother and her daughter and severely injured one other person as well as causing much damage to private property. Thirteen months after the explosion, 3 of the 24 people living at the disaster site satisfied diagnostic criteria for PTSD whereas no subject within the control site was similarly affected. The two groups differed significantly on the mean number of PTSD symptoms reported, those from the disaster site exhibiting the most symptoms. These differences were particularly pronounced on avoidance symptoms, amnesia, disinterest, and detachment. These symptoms were not seen in the control group. The symptom of difficulty sleeping was the most accurate of the PTSD symptom list in identifying a disaster victim.

A higher PTSD prevalence rate was reported for adult and children survivors who lived in cities closer to the epicentre of the Armenian earthquake (Goenjian, 1993; Goenjian et al., 1994; Pynoos et al., 1993). Interviews with survivors of the Armenia earthquake revealed that the worst experiences were seeing mutilated corpses, hearing the screams of people in agony trapped in the rubble, and seeing the expressions on people's faces as they searched for loved ones (Goenjian et al., 1994).

Pynoos and Nader (1988) demonstrated that following a fatal sniper shooting of children in a Californian school, children trapped in the playground had the strongest post-traumatic reactions, with those not attending school that day showing the least. Of those attending, nearly 40% of the 9-year-old children were found to have moderate to severe PTSD approximately one month after the event. Fourteen months later, Nader et al. (1990) report that 74% of the most severely exposed children in the playground still reported moderate to severe levels of PTSD.

In addition to the objective severity of the event, current thinking on the coping process emphasises the role of stimulus appraisal (e.g., Folkman, 1984; Folkman & Lazarus, 1980, 1985, 1988; Folkman, Lazarus, Dunkel-Schetter, DeLongis, & Gruen, 1986a; Folkman, Lazarus, Gruen, & DeLongis, 1986b; Lazarus, 1966; Lazarus & Folkman, 1984). Lazarus and his colleagues distinguish between primary appraisal, the assessment of the stressor, from secondary appraisal, the estimation of personal resources to deal with the stressor. The choice of coping strategy, they argue, results from these appraisals. The idiosyncratic way in which events can be appraised is illustrated by Pynoos and Nader (1988) who reported that although the psychological effects appeared to be a function of objective exposure to the sniper shooting, there were individual differences. They provide an example of one boy who had left school early that day leaving his sister in the playground and who went on to develop a severe reaction to the event. Although some experiences are particularly likely to give rise to PTSD, this study illustrates the necessity to take into account individual differences in the appraisal of the stressor and what it represents to the person. Speculatively, the reactions of this boy, for example, might have resulted from a self-appraisal that he had let his sister down.

Other appraisals might be less concerned with personal culpability. Yule, Udwin, and Murdoch (1990b) found that within one school that had sent a party of children on the *Jupiter* cruise, children who had wanted to go on the cruise but failed to get a place showed scores on depression and anxiety that were intermediate between controls and the victims. A similar finding was reported by Fraser (1971) who examined psychiatric admission rates and outpatient referrals in Belfast during 1969 when street riots where at their peak. He divided the city into three areas: (1) where the worst violence had occurred; (2) where signs of tension were present, but violence was not widespread; and (3) the remainder of the city. He found no evidence for increased admissions or referrals in the area of worst violence compared to the rest of the city. However, in the intermediate area, an increase was noted in referrals of male psychotics and male neurotics leading him to conclude that stress reactions were highest in areas which were under threat of attack.

In another study, Cairns and Wilson (1984) investigated reactions of Northern Irish residents in two towns. Both towns were similar in most respects except that one had suffered considerably more violence than the other. It was found that those who lived in the more violent town had higher symptom scores. Also, regardless of which town they lived in, those who perceived their town to have experienced a good deal of violence scored higher than those who perceived their town to have experienced little or no violence. This study demonstrates the main effects of both objective and subjective factors. But those who both lived in the violent town and perceived most violence had considerably higher symptom scores than the other groups.

However, the exposure variables which may predict the onset of disorder are not necessarily those which predict the severity or chronicity of symptoms. For example, Green, Grace, Lindy, and Gleser (1990b) examined the impact of a variety of specific war stressor experiences on the development and chronicity of the PTSD syndrome in a large sample of Vietnam veterans. They addressed a broader range of stressors than are typically explored. In terms of predicting type and persistence of symptoms, there was some differentiation among the stressors studied. Extent of injury, loss, life threat, and injuring or killing Vietnamese predicted developing PTSD symptoms at some point in time, but not maintaining symptoms over many years which was predicted by exposure to grotesque death and special assignment. Fontana and Rosenheck (1994a) report that for war veterans, responsibility for killing another human being is the single most pervasive, traumatic experience of war. Having been a target of killing and having participated in abusive violence were also found to be associated with greater emotional distress.

Although some studies have not found exposure to predict outcome and have emphasised prior vulnerability factors, the bulk of the evidence suggests that the intensity of exposure (both objectively and subjectively assessed) is associated with poorer outcome, at least for the relatively short periods after the event that have usually been studied. Goenjian et al. (1994), in their study of the Armenia earthquake, suggest that at very high levels of exposure most individuals will develop post-traumatic reactions regardless of premorbid vulnerabilities. What this literature seems to suggest is that as the objective (insofar as they can be measured) intensity (whatever that means precisely) of an event increases, so does the likelihood of psychological problems, which should then be viewed as *normal functions of adaptation*. Events involving massive death and destruction, human intention, life-threat and personal injury, are likely to give rise to post-traumatic stress reactions. But despite the fact that some events may be so overwhelming that nearly all will develop post-traumatic stress reactions, most events that are commonly associated with PTSD do not affect the total population in this way. Indeed, post-traumatic stress reactions have been documented following a variety of other stressors which are not generally associated with PTSD, for example, difficult child birth (Ballard, Stanley, & Brockington, 1995). Ballard et al present four case studies of women with a symptom profile suggestive of PTSD. To illustrate, one women, with no history of psychiatric illness, underwent emergency caesarean section. The epidural was not fully effective and she experienced excruciating pain during the operation which took 10 minutes. Afterwards, she experienced nightmares and would re-experience the operation along with intense physiological reactions.

Also, although the evidence is less clear cut, it has been suggested that some events lead to a different pattern of disorder. Severe depressive reactions such as suicidal thoughts and violence towards the self are particularly common in war veterans (e.g., Fontana & Rosenheck, 1994a), rape victims and child sexual abuse victims (e.g., Steketee and Foa, 1987) suggesting that the experience of traumatic events involving human intention may be particularly depressogenic.

Providing an estimate of impairment within any population of survivors is complicated by the fact that the rate of disorder may not be uniformly spread across the population. For example, in a study of over 500 community survivors of the Mt St Helen's volcano, Shore et al. (1986) found that 11% of men compared to 21% of women exposed to high levels of trauma developed either depression, anxiety, or PTSD within the first two years. Natural disasters such as the Mt St Helen's volcano affect whole communities and it is possible to investigate the differential incidence rate among men and women. Some events, however, are more likely to happen to women than men, i.e., sexual assault, whereas other events are more likely to happen to men than women, i.e., combat, making it difficult to compare between events. A different incidence of impairment between sexual assault and combat may reflect the differences in these events or it may be that one group is more vulnerable than the other. Other group differences such as socio-economic status may also be important. Ideally epidemiological studies into the effects of traumatic events should use compatible measures and report the prevalence rate of impairment for various social groupings separately.

CONCLUSION

In this chapter we have reviewed the typical events which have been found to lead to post-traumatic stress reactions. There is evidence that different events may lead to different levels of disorder and different patterns of disorder. But despite the vast amount of research, the evidence does remain relatively sparse due to the methodological difficulties inherent in trauma-related research. For example, difference in the populations studied, the measures used, and the time frames of investigation make it difficult to compare and contrast data across studies. Estimates of PTSD prevalence vary from study to study. Few epidemiological studies have been able to survey total populations and what knowledge we have is based on partial samples which may overestimate or underestimate the level of distress. Although epidemiological work should aim to survey all the survivors of a traumatic event, this is an ideal difficult to achieve as survivors may be geographically scattered, hard to contact, or reluctant to take part in research. Where PTSD is concerned, severe dysfunction is characterised by avoidant behaviour. It is possible, therefore, that much of the research evidence underestimates the levels of distress in disaster populations as the most severely affected may also be the people most likely not to seek professional help or take part in surveys. This is particularly a problem for research that relies on self-identification such as in the case of sexual assault. The issue of representativeness is particularly at question in studies where survivors have been obtained through referral via solicitors dealing with litigation. McFarlane (1986a,b) has argued for the importance of studying individuals who present unsolicited for treatment. He argues that the study of compensation litigants complicates the naturalistic assessment of psychological problems since individual attitudes towards the reporting of symptoms may be affected. Nevertheless, the effects of compensation seeking is an interesting area of investigation in its own right and should be studied.

In conclusion, it would seem that post-traumatic reactions characterise an expected response and normal response to certain traumatic events. Some events, such as rape, will frequently result in predictable distressing responses that meet the diagnostic criteria for PTSD. However, it is also possible that PTSD may appear to be a less normal or expected reaction following other types of events which, on the face of it, do not seem traumatic but can be revealed as being subjectively so when individual experiences and perceptions are taken into account. Clearly, the event is the necessary aetiological factor for the onset of PTSD. However, it would not appear to be sufficient and so there is a need to identify the other factors that may contribute to the development of symptoms.

SUMMARY POINTS

1. Typical PTSD-inducing events are generally perceived as being outside individual control and usually involve the potential for physical injury or death as well as possessing the capacity to elicit affect-laden visual imagery.
2. For most events symptoms of PTSD appear to diminish by around 18 months although for other events there may be very long-lasting effects. Events involving massive death and destruction as well as human agency seem particularly likely to have chronic effects. The long-term effects of the Vietnam War have been well documented.
3. Prolonged repeated trauma can result in deep-seated personality changes and the term post-traumatic character disorder has been suggested. Events such as repeated child sexual abuse seem to be most likely to effect personality development in adverse ways.
4. Although some events such as rape seem particularly likely to lead to post-traumatic stress reactions, other events such as difficult childbirth which are unlikely to lead to post-traumatic stress reactions will nevertheless have severe and long-lasting effects for some individuals.

Chapter 5

THEORETICAL PARADIGMS AND PERSPECTIVES

INTRODUCTION

If we are to be able to help survivors of traumatic events who are suffering from some form of post-traumatic stress reaction, a theoretical model explaining onset and maintenance will be called for. In this chapter we will discuss the main theoretical perspectives which have been applied to understanding post-traumatic stress reactions. As we have seen in Chapter 4, survivors of different events may have different symptoms; some survivors will be more affected than others, and some will remain affected for considerably longer than others. Various theoretical paradigms have been applied to understanding post-traumatic stress reactions but each model is only partially successful so that it has become increasingly clear to us that an integrative approach is necessary to account for the full range of reactions experienced by survivors.

Key Topics

Emotional processing
Conditioning theory
Learned helplessness
Information processing
Social-cognitive perspectives
Towards an integrative psychosocial model
Conclusion

EMOTIONAL PROCESSING

Rachman's (1980) concept of 'emotional processing' provides a useful theoretical framework for conceptualising the psychological reactions of survivors. In a discussion which aimed to link a variety of phenomena such as reactions to disturbing events, nightmares, obsessions and abnormal grief, Rachman suggested that emotional processing results in emotional reactions being 'absorbed' so that exposure to the problematic cue no longer elicits a strong

Table 5.1   Indices of unsatisfactory emotional processing

Direct signs
   Test probes elicit disturbances
   Obsessions
   Disturbing dreams
   Unpleasant intrusive thoughts
   Inappropriate expressions of emotion
   Behavioural disruptions
   Pressure of talk
   Hallucinations
   Return of fear

Indirect signs
   Subjective distress
   Fatigue
   Insomnia
   Anorexia
   Inability to direct constructive thoughts
   Preoccupations
   Restlessness
   Irritability
   Resistance to distraction

Reproduced, with some adaptation, from Rachman (1980) with kind permission from Elsevier Science Ltd, The Boulevard, Langford Lane, Kidlington OX5 1GB, UK.

emotional reaction. He outlines several direct and indirect signs of unsatisfactory emotional processing, many of which are diagnostic criteria for PTSD (see Table 5.1).

> Broadly, successful processing can be gauged from the person's ability to talk about, see, listen to or be reminded of the emotional events without experiencing distress or disruptions. (Rachman, 1980, p. 52).

Rachman points to various factors which give rise to difficulties in emotional processing: these are stimulus factors, personality factors, state factors, and associated activity factors. For example, if the stimulus is predictable, controllable, the person is high in self-efficacy, in a relaxed state at the time, and increases his or her sense of control through associated activity, the person might avoid difficulties in emotional processing. In contrast, if the stimulus is sudden, intense, dangerous, uncontrollable, unpredictable, the person is high on neuroticism, in a state of fatigue, and there are concurrent stressors and the person has a need to suppress appropriate emotional expression, emotional processing will be impeded. Factors thought to promote satisfactory emotional processing are, engaged exposure, sense of control, and relevant conversation. Those likely to impede processing are an avoidance of the disturbing situation, refusal or inability to talk about them, and absence of perceived control.

We have found Rachman's concept of emotional processing to be extremely useful in our thinking. Although his thinking gives emphasis to stimulus characteristics rather than appraisal, Rachman's theory provides a useful conceptual umbrella which links neurotic phenomena previously unrelated which might usefully be thought of as direct and indirect signs of incomplete emotional processing. Post-traumatic stress reactions are therefore seen as indicative of a process which is incomplete.

Goal of Theory

The goal of any theory is to explain: (1) the constellation of reactions that arise following traumatic events; (2) the individual differences in reactions; and (3) the course of those reactions over time. Rachman's theory allows us to understand the constellation of reactions as signs of incomplete emotional processing, as opposed to an abnormal process, and helps to account for individual differences in severity and chronicity of these reactions by reference to the various factors found to promote or impede emotional processing. Although Rachman's work provides the framework for the development of a theory of adaptation to post-traumatic stress, his theory is largely descriptive and a theoretical perspective needs also to explain the mechanisms that are involved.

CONDITIONING THEORY

One of the earliest paradigms to be applied to understanding reactions to traumatic events was that of learning theory. Post-traumatic reactions were viewed as a result of classical conditioning at the time of the trauma. The conditioned links between fear and traumatic stimuli, including those that resemble the trauma, are maintained through the individual's avoidance of memories and situations that elicit them. This theoretical explanation is similar to that given for the development of phobias although higher order conditioning is also invoked to explain the generalised overarousal seen in PTSD.

While helpful in giving an account of mechanisms related to fear maintenance, the theory gives no explanation of the differences between phobias and PTSD nor does it give any explanation of the wide range of other emotional states and problems often found in PTSD.

LEARNED HELPLESSNESS

Signalling the entry of cognitive-behavioural models of emotional disorder into clinical psychology and building upon the principles of operant conditioning, the theory of 'learned helplessness' was developed by Seligman and his colleagues to explain the reactions of animals that had been exposed to extreme stressors such as electric shocks (Overmier & Seligman, 1967; Seligman, 1975; Seligman & Maier, 1967). For example, it was shown that when dogs were immobilised and given inescapable electric shocks, they exhibited a later marked impairment in learning a response which would terminate the shock. Demonstrations of learned helplessness have often used a paradigm in which one animal was yoked to another. Both animals received exactly the same aversive stimulus, but the second animal was able to terminate the stimulus by making an operant response, at which time the first animal's aversive stimulus was also terminated, irrespective of its own response. In this relationship, the first animal has no control, and learns that there is a lack of contingency between what it does and the termination of the aversive stimulus. This intervening belief that action is futile thus accounts for impairments character-ised by, first, a failure to initiate escape responses (motivational deficit); sec-ond, an inability to profit from an occasionally successful escape response (cognitive deficit); and, third, a passive acceptance of the shock (emotional deficit). Together these deficits constitute the learned helplessness syndrome. Learned helplessness was originally offered as a model for depression (Selig-man, 1975) but more recently has been suggested as analogous to PTSD (e.g., Kolb, 1987; van der Kolk, 1983, 1987; van der Kolk et al., 1984b). This dual explanation is interesting in view of the observed overlap in symptoms already discussed. It has been proposed that the similarity between the reactions of animals exposed to uncontrollable and unpredictable events and human sur-vivors of traumatic events may reflect a common biochemical aetiology.

An animal model of PTSD holds considerable theoretical intrigue and van der Kolk and his colleagues (van der Kolk, Boyd, Krystal, & Greenberg, 1984b) have formulated a biochemical model to explain development of PTSD symptoms in humans. This model is based upon the neurochemical alterations that are known to occur in animals exposed to inescapable shock. They argue that traumatic events and associated stimuli may cause profound cat-echolamine depletion similar to the norepinephrine depletion found in animals suffering from learned helplessness and that this might account for such symptoms as loss of motivation. Their model also provides some evidence for a human equivalent of the stress-induced analgesia seen in animals. It is known that some traumatised individuals voluntarily re-expose themselves to trauma-associated stimuli, and then subjectively report a rather paradoxical sense of calm. Van der Kolk and his colleagues suggest that this is due to endorphin release. Cessation of exposure will be followed by physiological hyperactivity and symptoms of opiate withdrawal, but this in turn is modified by re-exposure to the trauma. Furthermore, van der Kolk and his colleagues have pointed out the striking similarities between the symptoms of hyperalertness, anxiety, in-somnia, emotional lability, uncontrollable anger, and the almost identical symptoms of opiate withdrawal syndrome. But although the learned helpless-ness paradigm provides a useful framework for understanding a wider range of reactions and complements the classical conditioning perspective, together these learning theories cannot provide an adequate account of the hallmark re-experiencing symptoms.

INFORMATION PROCESSING

More recently, Foa, Zinbarg, & Rothbaum (1992) have also proposed that the symptoms observed in animals subjected to unpredictable and uncontrollable aversive events resemble PTSD. They also argue that the similarity in symptoms between animals and trauma victims may reflect common aetiological factors and that it is the lack of predictability and controllability that leads to the syndrome of learned helplessness.

However, their synthesis of the animal and PTSD literatures also suggests that information-processing constructs are important. The suggestion that information-processing constructs are involved in the aetiology of post-traumatic stress reactions is not a new one. For example, Freud (1919) discussed the nightmares experienced by veterans of the First World War. He argued that emotionally intense events penetrate the ego's defence, flooding it with uncontrollable anxiety. The patient was thought by Freud to remain fixated on the trauma and that this was expressed through dreams of the event.

Furthermore, Janet (1889) suggested that intense emotional reactions cause memories of particular events to be dissociated from consciousness and to be stored as visceral sensations (panic and anxiety) or visual images (nightmares and flashbacks). These intense emotions interfere with the integration of the experience into existing memory schemas. These ideas are remarkably similar to those of today.

Horowitz's Theory

Horowitz's (1975, 1976, 1979, 1982, 1986a, 1986b) information-processing approach is based on the idea that individuals have mental models, or schemata, of the world and of themselves which they use to interpret incoming information. He also proposes that there is an inherent drive to make our mental models coherent with current information (the 'completion principle'). A traumatic event presents information which is incompatible with existing schemas. This incongruity gives rise to a stress response requiring reappraisal and revision of the schema. As traumatic events generally require massive schematic changes, complete integration and cognitive processing take some time to occur. During this time, active memory tends to repeat its representations of the traumatic event causing emotional distress. However, to prevent emotional exhaustion, there are processes of inhibition and facilitation which act as a feedback system modulating the flow of information. The symptoms observed during stress responses, which Horowitz categorises as involving denials and intrusion, occur as a result of opposite actions of a control system

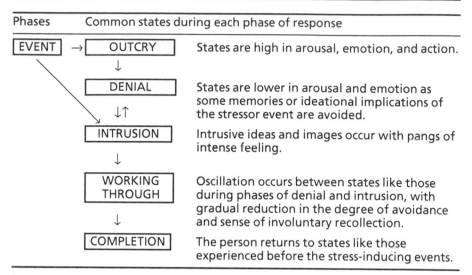

Phases	Common states during each phase of response
EVENT → OUTCRY ↓	States are high in arousal, emotion, and action.
DENIAL ↓↑	States are lower in arousal and emotion as some memories or ideational implications of the stressor event are avoided.
INTRUSION ↓	Intrusive ideas and images occur with pangs of intense feeling.
WORKING THROUGH ↓	Oscillation occurs between states like those during phases of denial and intrusion, with gradual reduction in the degree of avoidance and sense of involuntary recollection.
COMPLETION	The person returns to states like those experienced before the stress-inducing events.

Figure 5.1   Phases of response following trauma (Horowitz, 1979)

that regulates the incoming information to tolerable doses. If inhibitory control is not strong enough, intrusive symptoms such as nightmares and flashbacks emerge. When inhibitory efforts are too strong in relation to active memory, symptoms indicative of the avoidance phase occur. Typically, avoidance and intrusion symptoms fluctuate in a way particular to the individual without causing flooding or exhaustion that would prevent adaptation. The person oscillates between the states of avoidance and intrusion until a relative equilibrium is reached when the person is said to have worked through the experience (see Figure 5.1). The emotional numbing symptoms are thus viewed as a defence mechanism against intrusion.

The information-processing approach of Horowitz draws our attention to the central role that memory plays in the development of post-traumatic stress reactions. Such an approach is compatible with Rachman's concept of emotional processing; both emphasise that post-traumatic stress reactions are signs of incomplete processing, but whereas Horowitz emphasises the need to assimilate and integrate information regarding the event, Rachman emphasises the importance of emotional arousal.

Fear Structures

Applying Lang's (1977, 1985) concept of 'fear structures', Foa and her colleagues (Foa & Kozak, 1986; Foa, Steketee & Rothbaum, 1989; Foa et al., 1992; Foa & Riggs, 1993) have put forward a theory of PTSD which centres around the conditioned formation of a 'fear network' in memory, as a result of traumatisation. This network encompasses: (1) stimulus information about the traumatic event; (2) information about cognitive, behavioural, and physiological reactions to the event; and (3) interoceptive information which links these stimulus and response elements.

This theory leads to the prediction that people characterised by an extensive fear network will show a number of information-processing biases such as an attentional hypervigilance towards trauma-related stimuli (e.g., Foa, Feske, Murdock, Kozac, & McCarthy, 1991; McNally, English, & Lipke, 1993) and consequently an increased probability estimation that traumatic events are likely to happen—it is known that the probability of occurrence accorded a given event is a function of the availability in memory of instances similar to that event (Tversky & Kahneman, 1974).

Activation of the fear network by triggering stimuli (i.e., reminders of the event) causes information to enter consciousness (re-experiencing symptoms). Attempts to suppress such activation leads to the cluster of avoidance symptoms. Successful resolution of the trauma can only occur by integrating the information in the fear network with existing memory structures. Such integration requires, first, the activation of the fear network so that it becomes accessible for modification and, second, availability of information that is incompatible with the fear network so that overall memory structure can be modified.

A number of factors make such integration problematic. Foa and her colleagues argue that the unpredictability and uncontrollability of the event make it difficult to assimilate into existing models in which the world is controllable and predictable. In addition, factors such as the severity of the event disrupt the cognitive processes of attention and memory at the time of the trauma. Foa and her colleagues argue that this disruption leads to the formation of a disjointed and fragmented fear network which is consequently difficult to integrate with existing organised models.

Foa et al.'s theory, whilst useful in explaining fear maintenance and associated cognitive factors, also suffers from the exclusive concentration upon fear. The theory also relies upon a model of stimulus representation which has been found to be inadequate (Teasdale & Barnard, 1993).

Cognitive Action Theory

The cognitive action theory of Chemtob, Roitblat, Hamada, Carlson, and Twentyman (1988) presents a similar perspective to that of Foa and her colleagues but with more detailed analysis of the structure of the fear network which is formulated as a parallel-distributed hierarchical system. Chemtob et al. (1988) argue that, in individuals with PTSD, the fear network is permanently activated causing them to function in 'survival mode' that has proved adaptive during the traumatic event. This permanent activation leads to the symptoms of hyperarousal and re-experiencing.

A possible synthesis?

The cognitive-processing model of PTSD put forward by Creamer, Burgess, and Pattison (1992) is presented as a 'synthesis and reconceptualisation of existing formulations' (p. 453). It combines the central ideas of Horowitz with the network architecture of Foa et al. (1989) and Chemtob et al. (1988).

Creamer et al. (1992) propose that the fear network must be activated for recovery to take place—a mechanism referred to as 'network resolution processing'. This is a concept similar to Horowitz's completion tendency. Creamer et al. (1992) argue for an initial period of intrusion (due to activation of the fear network) which the individual copes with by using a range of defensive and avoidant strategies. Creamer et al. (1992) argue that the extent of initial intrusive symptomatology is an index of the degree of network resolution processing that is occurring. Thus, high levels of initial intrusion are a predictor of successful recovery whereas low levels of intrusion are a predictor of poor outcome and chronic symptoms. Creamer et al. (1992) also argue that intrusion precedes avoidance which is conceptualised as a coping strategy in response to the discomfort that arises from intrusive memories. Although avoidance may reduce immediate distress, excessive reliance on this strategy may be maladaptive because it prevents fear network activation and thus network resolution processing (see Figure 5.2).

Creamer et al's. (1992) model is significant in that it is based on longitudinal data and makes clear predictions about outcome. In a test of the model with 158 office workers following shootings, it was found that intrusive activity at 4 months, as measured using the IES, was predictive of lower distress scores at 8 months, and intrusion at 8 months was predictive of lower distress at 14 months. Avoidance was not found to predict distress.

However, the opposite pattern of results were found by McFarlane (1992a). McFarlane also noted that, although intrusive thinking is diagnostic of disorder, it also represents part of the normal process of trauma appraisal. But, in contrast to Creamer et al., he suggested that greater frequency of intrusive thinking should be predictive of poorer subsequent outcome.

In a test of this prediction, McFarlane (1992a) examined data from 290 firefighters who had completed questionnaires at 4, 11, and 29 months after exposure to bush fires in Australia. A higher frequency of intrusive thinking at 4 months, as assessed using the IES, was predictive of greater distress at 11 months and a higher frequency of intrusive thinking at 11 months was predictive of greater distress at 29 months.

Findings similar to those of McFarlane have been reported in longitudinal studies of survivors of the *Herald of Free Enterprise* disaster (Joseph, Yule, & Williams, 1994) and for survivors of the *Jupiter* cruise ship disaster (Joseph, Yule, & Williams, 1995a).

The reason for these discrepant results is not clear and, to further complicate the picture, other research has failed to show a relationship between early

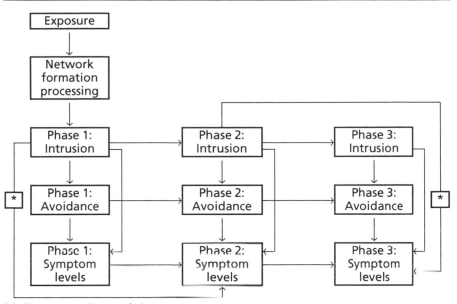

* Indicates a negative association.

Figure 5.2 The longitudinal model of cognitive processing proposed by Creamer et al. (1992). (Copyright © 1992 by the American Psychological Association. Reprinted with permission)

intrusion and avoidance and later symptoms in survivors of a terrorist attack (Shalev, 1992). This might be, as McFarlane (1992b) suggests, because Shalev's data were collected only days following the attack:

> In the initial days after a traumatic event, intrusive memories are a universal phenomena indicative of a normal process of reappraisal of the experience. Various representations of the trauma are developed and an attempt is made to integrate them with existing psychological schemata. It is unclear at which state traumatic memories develop the relatively inflexible quality that represents the failure to resolve the issue of meaning. (McFarlane, 1992b, p. 599)

The importance of the timing of intrusions has also been noted by Brewin and colleagues (Brewin, Dalgleish, & Joseph, 1996) who, in an attempt to provide a conceptual framework for these data suggest that two factors need to be considered: first, the intensity of the event and, second, the timing of the assessment of intrusive and avoidant activity. Like McFarlane, Brewin et al. suggest that the presence of intrusive memories immediately after substantial trauma is a normal reaction that, as Shalev (1992) found, will not predict subsequent adjustment. After some weeks or months, however, continuing intrusive activity, as argued by Rachman (1980), signals a failure to emotionally process the experience and the longer the time elapsed since the trauma, the more likely that intrusive thoughts will predict poor outcome.

One study which would seem to support this possibility was carried out with hospitalised burn patients in which it was found that the severity of intrusive and avoidant thoughts during the first week of hospitalisation did not predict the development of PTSD. This is consistent with the findings of Shalev (1992). But the severity of intrusive thoughts at two months predicted PTSD at six months and the severity of avoidant thoughts at six months predicted PTSD at 12 months (Perry, Difede, Musngi, Frances, & Jacobsberg, 1992). The authors of this study conclude, like McFarlane (1992a), that intrusive and avoidant mental processes immediately after a severe trauma may be normal and should only be defined as pathological if they persist.

With survivors of the *Herald of Free Enterprise* disaster, we found that greater frequency of intrusive thinking and avoidance behaviour at three years, as assessed using the IES, following the event was predictive of greater distress at five years (Joseph, Dalgleish, Thrasher, Yule, Williams, & Hodgkinson, 1996).

But what of the prediction by Creamer et al. that intrusions represent network resolution processing and so should predict less PTSD? It may be that there is a period of time after which intrusions become indicative of a failure to process the experience but before which they are normal reactions, in which emotional processing is ongoing. For some people, this initial period will lead to unsatisfactory emotional processing and chronic distress, but for others this stage will lead to satisfactory emotional processing and recovery. It is the content of the intrusive thinking that will determine whether emotional processing is satisfactory or unsatisfactory.

Similarly, an ambiguity in the role of avoidance has been discussed (Williams, Joseph, & Yule, 1994) and it might be suggested that, early on, avoidance is a normal response and that as the weeks and months pass it becomes increasingly pathological. But before it becomes indicative of unsatisfactory emotional processing some forms of avoidance may be helpful whereas other forms may be harmful. This would require analysis of the specific avoidant cognitions and behaviours used in any given situation.

SOCIAL-COGNITIVE PERSPECTIVES

The work of Janoff-Bulman (1985, 1989, 1992) is of interest in that it focuses on the cognitive schemata that individuals hold, and thus complements the work of Horowitz. Janoff-Bulman suggests that there are common psychological experiences shared by victims who have experienced a wide range of traumatic situations. She proposed that post-traumatic stress following victimisation is largely due to the shattering of basic assumptions that victims hold about themselves and the world.

The number and extent of assumptions that are shattered are dependent upon the individual, but central to Janoff-Bulman's thesis is a common and core belief in personal invulnerability. She argues that although we may recognise that crimes, accidents, and illness occur to a large proportion of the population, it is also possible to believe simultaneously that these misfortunes will not happen to us. There is evidence that people will rate themselves as less likely than others to be victims of diseases, crimes, and accidents (Perloff, 1983), and to underestimate their likelihood of experiencing negative events (Weinstein & Lachendro, 1982). Victimisation shatters this assumption of invulnerability, Janoff-Bulman argues, leaving the person feeling vulnerable to future victimisation.

The sense of vulnerability appears to be tied, Janoff-Bulman believes, to the disruption of three core beliefs: (1) the world as benevolent; (2) the world as meaningful; and (3) the self as worthy (Janoff-Bulman, 1985, 1989, 1992). However, one of the most important underlying assumptions, Janoff-Bulman believes, is that of justice and fairness.

According to the just world hypothesis formulated by Lerner (1975, 1980; Lerner & Miller, 1978), individuals have a need to believe that they live in a world where people get what they deserve and deserve what they get. The belief in a just world enables the individual to confront the physical and social environment as if it were stable and orderly. It is a belief that individuals are reluctant to give up, and evidence that the world is not really just can be extremely distressing.

Janoff-Bulman (1985, 1989, 1992) also writes that people generally operate under the assumption that they are worthy decent people. Victimisation may lead to a questioning of these self-perceptions. This rests, in part, on the notion of the just world. If one deserves what one gets, the experience of victimisation would suggest that one is not a worthy decent person after all. Coping with victimisation involves the person coming to terms with these shattered assumptions and re-establishing a conceptual system that will allow him or her to function effectively.

While bringing out the cognitive contents of the survivor's shattered experience and having considerable face validity, little work has been done as yet to test out these ideas. Janoff-Bulman (1989) has devised a 32-item 'World Assumptions Scale' self-report questionnaire which has been found to have adequate reliability and to distinguish between traumatised and non-traumatised university students. One might question the appropriateness of a questionnaire, however, to assess tacit meaning, which, by definition may not be accessible to consciousness. This level of assessment represents a challenge to cognitive scientists.

TOWARDS AN INTEGRATIVE PSYCHOSOCIAL MODEL

A common theme in the above theories is the integration within memory of trauma-related information with pre-existing schemas. Horowitz suggests that there are phases of intrusion and avoidance as the people gradually dose themselves with information. Although Horowitz's model remains the single most influential perspective in understanding post-traumatic stress reactions there are a number of important criticisms.

Jones and Barlow (1990) note that although Horowitz's model accommodates the signs and symptoms characteristic of PTSD, it is limited in that it fails explicitly to incorporate psychosocial factors that may influence the differential development in the severity and chronicity of symptoms. Indeed, it has been suggested that the most important function of any aetiological model is to explain the absence of symptoms in some individuals (Jones & Barlow, 1990). We will outline those psychosocial factors, based on the work of Rachman (1980) which might operate to impede or promote emotional processing.

Furthermore, little attention is given to the process of appraisal and how the individual's interpretations may mediate between the traumatic event and adjustment. Our approach emphasises the role of appraisal processes as emphasised in the social-cognitive theory of Janoff-Bulman.

Finally, Chemtob et al. (1988) note that Horowitz places an emphasis on a 'drive for completion' for which there is little evidence. An integrative model must therefore outline those psychosocial factors which might operate to impede or promote emotional processing as well as explicate the process of how the individual's interpretations may mediate between the traumatic event and adjustment. Although we will also argue that there is a drive for completion it will be recognised that the emotional processing of traumatic experiences can become blocked so that intrusive and avoidant phenomena are indicative of psychopathology.

However, it is argued that different types of intrusion and avoidance are distinguishable: whereas phenomena indicative of processing or working through seem to be under conscious control, i.e., ruminative thoughts and behavioural avoidance, states viewed as pathological are less under conscious control, i.e., nightmares, and dissociation. Differentiating between types of intrusion and types of avoidance might help to clarify the conflicting data discussed above concerning the predictive role of these phenomena.

Janet (1909) considered dissociation in the context of trauma to result from a state of physiological hyperarousal which results in memory disturbance. The information conveyed by the traumatic event is not available to ordinary conscious representation and so cannot be processed. Instead it persists as a fixed idea that is split off from consciousness and experienced in nightmares. Available empirical data substantiate the view that dissociation at the time of trauma is associated with later post-traumatic symptomatology (Bremner et al., 1992; Holen, 1993; Marmar et al., 1994).

Each of the theories reviewed can tell us about some of the clinical characteristics. We would argue that there are two main assumptions that need to be made before understanding the psychological processes underlying PTSD (see Weiss, 1993b). First, that the symptoms of PTSD have an evolutionary origin, and, second, that both conscious and nonconscious processes are involved.

An Evolutionary Perspective

It has been argued that the cognitive features of chronic PTSD found in combat veterans, such as hyperalertness, excessive startle responses, focused concentration, appear to be derivative of a special 'survival mode' of functioning (Chemtob et al., 1988). Such reactions are likely to be adaptive in a combat situation as they enable the soldier to react quickly to threat, thus increasing the chance of survival. From an evolutionary perspective, post-traumatic reactions might be considered to be a normal and adaptive reaction. A similar evolutionary significance might be attached to the protective function of dissociation when stress exceeds the capacity of coping resources.

A similar argument is presented by Marks and Nesse (1994) who review the evolutionary origins and functions of the capacity for anxiety. However, the persistence of these reactions into civilian life interferes with everyday social functioning and can be highly distressing. Thus, theoretical approaches need, first, to explain the development of post-traumatic reactions as a normal psychological reaction to an extreme stressor; and second, to account for the persistence of these post-traumatic reactions once the stressor is no longer present.

One mechanism which might help to explain the persistence of reactions in the time subsequent to the traumatic event has been described by Brown and Kulik (1977) as flashbulb memory. Brown and Kulik argued that there is a special mechanism which exists for encoding emotion-laden memories. Such a mechanism would have evolutionary survival value. Flashbulb memories might enable the organism to learn quickly about threat in the environment without having to undergo repeated exposure to the stimulus, e.g., if a lion jumps out suddenly and our ancestor was able to escape from the lion, having learnt from that one experience to stay away from lions in future will have survival value. Such a mechanism of encoding emotional-laden information might help to account for the re-experiencing phenomena. Wright and Gaskell (1992) have presented a view of flashbulb memories which is compatible with current thinking on the nature of trauma-related imagery. Flashbulb memories, they argue, develop initially as a result of the person having difficulty storing the event within an existing memory structure.

Conscious and Nonconscious Processes

The acceptance that nonconscious as well as conscious mental processes are involved is important. Research suggests that sensory input is subject to conscious and nonconscious processing (see Brewin, 1988, 1989; Epstein, 1994, for reviews). It has been proposed that dual representations in memory of traumatic experience are the minimum cognitive architecture necessary to understand PTSD (Brewin, Dalgleish, & Joseph, 1996). The first set of representations are the person's conscious experience of trauma, which Brewin (1989) refers to as 'verbally accessible knowledge' because it can in principle be deliberately retrieved from the store of autobiographical experiences. The second set of representations is not verbally accessible but refers to the output of extensive nonconscious processing which may be accessed automatically when the person is in a context whose physical features or meaning are similar to those of the traumatic situation. Later we will argue that this information can be accessed through imagery. Brewin (1989) refers to this second set of representations as 'situationally accessible knowledge'. Briefly, Brewin et al. (1996), in applying this theoretical structure to PTSD, propose that the sensory (i.e., visual, auditory, olfactory, etc.), physiological and motor aspects of traumatic experience are represented in situationally accessible knowledge in the form of analogical codes that enable the original experience to be recreated. The person may only become aware that these representations have been accessed when emotional arousal, motor impulses, flashbacks, or dissociative states are experienced. Verbally accessible knowledge, on the other hand, is viewed as consisting of a series of autobiographical memories that can be deliberately and progressively edited in an attempt to assign meaning to the trauma in terms of verbally accessible constructs (Brewin et al., 1996). A dual representation theory, Brewin et al. believe, provides the minimum cognitive architecture needed to synthesise the various theories reviewed earlier. Teasdale and Barnard (1993) suggest a more complex theory of cognitive representation, the 'interacting cognitive subsystems approach' in which nine different kinds of information and their interrelationships are explicitly recognised. Teasdale and Barnard's emphasis has as yet been upon the explication of depression. The implications for PTSD remain to be explored.

A further set of representations are the person's pre-existing schematic representations about the self and the world which reflect prior experience. These representations would be similar to those discussed by Janoff-Bulman and include beliefs about the self and the world—beliefs that are themselves not easily accessible to verbalisation. Prior life-experiences, particularly those in early childhood between the infant and caregiver, can have an important bearing on later schematic representations which influence how the traumatic event is processed.

Psychosocial Factors in the Post-trauma Environment

There has been much interest in the possible psychosocial factors that contribute to adjustment following exposure to a traumatic event. Green, Wilson, and Lindy (1985c) presented a psychosocial framework for understanding positive and negative outcomes following a traumatic event. Their model starts with exposure to specific aspects of the event, such as violent loss, threat to life, and exposure to grotesque injury. Exposure leads to psychological processing such as that proposed by Horowitz which takes place in the context of two sets of factors: (1) those which the person brings to the situation (e.g., past psychological problems); and (2) those in the recovery environment (e.g., social support). Although not addressing the issue of PTSD specifically, Hobfoll (1989) proposed the Conservation of Resources model. This model focuses on the extent to which individuals are able to maintain social and personal resources. Hobfoll's model proposes that the loss of these resources leads to diminished coping capacity and psychological distress and that it is through replenishing resources that the individuals are able to enhance their coping and reduce their distress.

We suggest that a traumatic event presents an individual with stimulus information which, as perceived *at the time*, gives rise to extreme emotional arousal but interferes with immediate processing. Representations of these *event stimuli* are held in memory, due to their personal salience and to the difficulty they present for easy assimilation with other stored representations. These *event cognitions* take two forms corresponding to the dual representation theory of Brewin et al. (1996): information that is not available to conscious inspection and information which is deliberately retrievable and can be easily edited. Event cognitions provide the basis for the re-experiencing phenomena or intrusive recollections of the trauma which are sometimes full and realistic enough to be experienced as if the event were really happening again (flashbacks). These traumatic cognitions will idiosyncratically reflect the individual's prior experience, personality, basic assumptions, and the specific components of an event that presented the individual with the greatest subjective threat. Intrusive ideation is therefore influenced by *personality* and/or representations of earlier experience (i.e., 'top-down processing').

These images can then form the subject of further cognitive activity called *appraisals* and *reappraisals*. Any stimulus is capable of being perceived in a variety of ways: what is dangerous to an inhabitant of Manhattan may not seem so to someone who has lived on the Ganges and vice versa. Although it is the appraisal that is important in determining subsequent reactions, some stimulus characteristics may render a stimulus to be perceived in the same way by all observers. To this extent we can say that some stimuli are universally judged to be objectively dangerous, unpredictable and uncontrollable: factors which are thought to be important in the aetiology of PTSD (Foa & Kozak, 1986; Foa et al., 1989, 1992).

Appraisal cognitions are distinguished from traumatic cognitions in being thoughts about the information depicted and its further meanings, drawing more extensively and consciously upon past representations of experience and/ or aspects of personality. (This analysis is similar to Salkovskis (1985) cognitive model for Obsessional-Compulsive Disorder which also features ego-dystonic intrusive cognitions.) These appraisal cognitions might therefore take two forms: (1) automatic thoughts (Beck, 1976; Hollon & Kendall, 1980) associated with automatic schematic activation and with strong emotional states and reappraisals; and (2) conscious thinking through of alternative meanings, influenced by disclosure to others in the social network. These appraisal cognitions might be considered as ruminative behaviour and constitute a further form of intrusive activity. Depending on the content of this intrusive activity, emotional processing might be impeded or promoted. For example, self-blaming ruminative activity which encourages a sense of control and appropriate activity might be expected to promote emotional processing. In contrast, self-blaming ruminative activity which encourages a sense of shame and withdrawal from social support sources might be expected to impede emotional processing.

Current views of how personality and environmental influences are represented in memory encompass various concepts such as associative networks, cognitive styles, schema and other theoretical models (e.g., Teasdale & Barnard, 1993). This part of the model awaits further work. Examples of these representational concepts are noted in Figure 5.3 with a two-way interaction with appraisals (and reappraisals), the specific contents of conscious cognition. In other words, appraisals are influenced by representations and representations are modified by new appraisals (assimilation).

The occurrence of event cognitions and automatic thoughts will be associated with strong *emotional states* (e.g., fear, panic, grief, guilt, and shame) which will themselves become the subjects of cognitive appraisal, influenced by personality. Hence, we suggest that there is a two-way interaction between emotional states and appraisals, each being influenced by the other. As a result of the appraisal process, emotional states are capable of generating further emotional states, e.g., shame about fear, depression about anger, etc.

The occurrence of these event cognitions, appraisals, and emotional states will all engender distress and attempts at *coping* including, most notably, avoidance thoughts and behaviours: avoidance of stimuli (triggers for re-experiencing), thoughts and images (intrusive and automatic), emotions and activities. Some avoidance may take the form of thinking: voluntary, ruminative, worry thoughts directed at problem-solving and the avoidance of strongly emotive imagery and associated with generalised anxiety (Wells & Matthews, 1994). It is suggested that some successful avoidance may be an important aspect of coping but that too much emotional suppression (avoidance) will result in the emotional state of numbness and the dissociation of cognitive and emotional activity. Cognitive suppression will result in the recurrence of intrusive trauma cognitions (Wegner, Shortt, Blake & Page, 1990; Clark, Ball & Pape, 1991). An important component of coping will be the seeking of *social support* from the environment. Input from others can interact via appraisal processes to influence the individual's meaning attributions, emotional states, memory structures and coping in a helpful manner or to induce more distress.

In the 'normal' case, then, following Horowitz, the individual goes through a repetitive cycle of intrusions and appraisals and associated emotional reappraisals and coping resulting in more intrusive cognitions and more appraisals, with feedback into memorial representations until such time that mental models are adjusted to produce new models that are coherent but allow for the new information. On examination the factors distinguished in this analysis bear

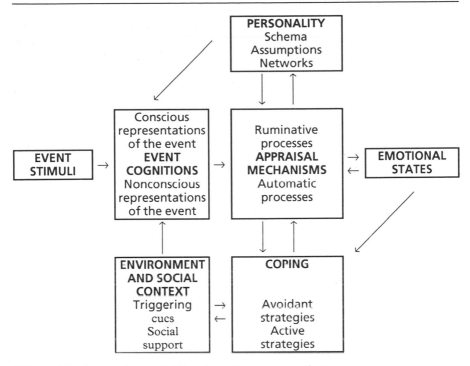

Figure 5.3 Integrative model for adaptation to traumatic stress

close resemblance to Rachman's factors that may impede 'emotional processing', although we are suggesting that the factors that impair emotional processing *at the time* of an event continue into the post-event period, event cognitions acting for event stimuli.

The process of adaptation is extended over time and involves a number of states of mind rather than one static mental state. Some have suggested stages of adaptation characterised by a sequence of emotions (e.g., Kubler-Ross, 1969) whereas others have questioned the necessity of a standard sequence to these states and have emphasised the multifaceted nature of the processes of adaptation. For example, there are likely to be differing needs for support over time (Jacobson, 1986). In this model, adaptation to trauma is seen as a function of both conscious and nonconscious processes.

In this model, which is schematically represented in Figure 5.3, individual variation is attributable to a complex interaction between components that constitute variables which may contribute to outcomes at different points in time. The model offers a way of integrating research findings and points the way to multivariate research which may investigate the patterns of interrelationships.

From a therapeutic perspective, the model delineates phenomenological components of individual experience which may be valuable to analyse and offers points at which therapeutic intervention can be addressed. For example, while emotional states are intense and intolerable, an individual may need help with coping techniques which provide relief, involving avoidance and distraction. When coping is established, individuals who fear 'going crazy' as a result of their intense emotions may need help in reappraising their emotional state before they will risk eliciting the emotion in talking about the incident in detail. Other individuals who have no such emotion cognitions may be able to enter straight into reappraising the event stimuli in a supportive environment where appraisals of culpability and weakness can be examined and reality tested. Seen within this framework, the criteria for PTSD above are observable or introspectable products of emotional processing (an in principle unobservable process) viz.: thoughts of and about the trauma, corresponding highly emotional states, and coping responses including avoidance.

CONCLUSION

In this chapter we have reviewed the main theories that have been put forward to explain post-traumatic reactions. We have outlined an integrative psychosocial model of adaptation which emphasises the role of appraisal factors, personality factors, emotional state factors, and activity factors. In Chapter 6 we shall discuss the evidence for each of the components of this model.

SUMMARY POINTS

1. A number of theoretical paradigms have been applied to the understanding of PTSD. These include 'emotional processing', conditioning theory, learned helplessness, and information processing models.
2. All models have their advantages and limitations to the extent that they explain the phenomena of post-trauma responses.
3. Some attempts to integrate and reconceptualise earlier theories are described, including a new psychosocial model which brings into the picture the importance of the social environment in influencing an individual's adaptation after trauma.
4. Our psychosocial model points to the interactions between a number of key elements, environmental, personal and social in determining an individual's symptomatic 'outcome' and emphasises the importance of appraisal in mediating response to the environment.
5. Important distinctions are drawn between re-experiencing cognitive representations of aspects of the traumatic event itself and ruminations about both the event and emotional reactions. All might be influenced by the individual's personality, coping techniques and social environment.
6. Implications for therapeutic intervention are suggested.

Chapter 6

EVIDENCE FOR AN INTEGRATIVE MODEL OF ADJUSTMENT

INTRODUCTION

Although exposure to a traumatic event is a necessary causal factor in the development of post-traumatic reactions, it is not thought to be sufficient and there has been much interest in the possible factors that may mediate the effects of traumatic events and moderate their impact on mental health. In Chapter 5 we introduced our integrative model of adjustment following traumatic stressors. The main components of this model are stimulus factors, appraisal factors, personality factors, activity factors, and emotional state factors. Stimulus factors were reviewed in Chapter 4. In this chapter we will discuss the experimental literature about the impact of each of these factors.

Key Topics

Appraisal factors
Personality factors
Emotional state factors
Activity factors
Sociocultural factors
Conclusion

APPRAISAL FACTORS

Although appraisal is very much an idiosyncratic process that does not lend itself easily to empirical studies having group designs, it is central to our model of adaptation presented in the previous chapter. We have argued that appraisal processes mediate between the traumatic event and subsequent adjustment. Appraisal processes can constitute one type of intrusive experience; one that is potentially under conscious control although the roots of such activity may be in the form of less consciously accessible 'automatic thoughts' (Beck, 1976). For example, an automatic thought such as 'I should have acted differently' can pop into mind spontaneously, but having done so, that thought is then accessible to conscious inspection and controllable rumination, perhaps in an attempt to resolve questions such as, 'But could I really have done things differently?', 'What would other people have done in that situation?', and so on.

Rumination, in itself, will not necessarily lead to better or worse outcome although, as discussed in the previous chapter, it is likely to become pathological after a certain amount of time if it becomes repetitive and stereotyped, indicating that emotional processing has been unsatisfactory and issues of meaning have not yet been resolved. However, early on, depending on the content of the ruminative activity, it might promote or impede processing.

Attributional Perspectives

One aspect of appraisal that helps us to understand some of the processes involved in adaptation is causal attribution. As we have seen, several theorists have noted the importance of the constructs of controllability and predictability in post-traumatic stress reactions. The reason why the constructs of uncontrollability and unpredictability might be important rests on the general theoretical viewpoint that people have a need to predict the future and control events (e.g., Harvey & Weary, 1985; Heider, 1958; Rotter, 1966). The consequence of this is that people who are exposed to unpredictable and uncontrollable events are strongly motivated to explain why the event occurred (Weiner, 1985, 1986; Wong & Weiner, 1981). This has been demonstrated following physical illness (Watts, 1982), cancer (Taylor, 1983), and accidents (Dollinger, 1986) and evidence shows that perceptions of being out of control are predictive of poorer adjustment (e.g., Craig, Hancock, & Dickson, 1994).

As well as the need for perceived predictability and controllability, people also have a need for self-esteem (e.g., Steele, 1988; Tesser & Cambell, 1980). Self-esteem, like perceptions of predictability and controllability, is thought to serve a stress-buffering function (Greenberg et al., 1992, 1993). Causal attribution is the central cognitive mechanism involved in the attempt to establish and maintain self-esteem as well as perceptions of the world as predictable and controllable.

One study which illustrates the need to explain misfortune was carried out by Taylor (1983) who reported that 95% of her sample of women diagnosed as having cancer made some explanation for its occurrence. Women attributed their cancer to stress, the taking of birth-control pills, living near a chemical dump, hereditary factors, or diet. The question is: Do different explanations lead to different ways of coping with the event and different emotional states? Attribution theorists believe that they do (e.g., Antaki & Brewin, 1982; Brewin, 1985, 1988; Janoff-Bulman, 1979; Joseph, Yule, & Williams, 1993d; Shaver & Drown, 1986; Tennen & Affleck, 1990; Turnquist, Harvey & Anderson, 1988; Weiner, 1986) and several theoretical perspectives exist which can help us to make predictions regarding particular types of explanation.

Hopelessness theory

One model that has received much attention is the reformulated model of learned helplessness (Abramson, Seligman, & Teasdale, 1978), since revised as the hopelessness theory of depression (Abramson, Metalsky, & Alloy, 1988, 1989; Alloy, Abramson, Metalsky, & Hartledge, 1988). This theory predicts that, following a negative event, individuals who make causal attributions for the event's occurrence to stable factors (i.e., the cause is perceived as something that persists across time) and global factors (i.e., the cause is perceived as something that affects a wide range of outcomes in one's life) will experience an expectation of hopelessness which may lead to a subtype of depression characterised by hopelessness. Feelings of hopelessness have been observed to underlie a variety of mental health problems (e.g., MacLeod & Tarbuck, 1994) and the hopelessness theory has been applied to understanding a wide variety of illnesses and injuries (e.g., DeVellis, & Blalock, 1992). Although the hopelessness theory does not make explicit predictions regarding PTSD, hopelessness is a common theme expressed by survivors of traumatic events (e.g., Harvey et al., 1995) and the expectation of hopelessness is echoed throughout Janoff-Bulman's (1985, 1992) theory of shattered assumptions. Many of the new beliefs about the world that survivors develop can be considered under the conceptual umbrella of hopelessness expectation. For example, Janoff-Bulman suggests that the cognitive schemata of traumatised populations emphasises the randomness and malevolence of the world, beliefs that reflect stable and global perceptions that bad things will continue to happen. Symptoms are further compounded by lowered self-esteem if the stable and global attributions are also internal (i.e., the cause is perceived as residing within the person). Other variables, such as the lack of social support, are thought to contribute to this expectation of hopelessness.

Although there is evidence for the role of causal attributions with a variety of outcomes (Brewin, 1985; 1988; Sweeney, Anderson, & Bailey, 1986), the hopelessness model remains to be tested in its application to PTSD. However, there is reason to suggest that the hopelessness theory might be an appropriate model for predicting at least some of the clinical characteristics of PTSD. As we have seen in Chapter 2, many of the symptoms of hopelessness depression are diagnostic criteria for PTSD.

It is suggested that a syndrome of post-traumatic hopelessness provides a core construct that can help to resolve some of the discrepancies over the classification of symptoms associated with PTSD by providing a bridge between anxious and depressive phenomena. Although anxiety and depression are considered to be phenomenologically distinct, it has proven difficult to distinguish these constructs empirically (Feldman, 1993).

Although the hopelessness theory may be an appropriate model for predicting at least some aspects of PTSD it does not adequately account for the full range of symptoms associated with the diagnosis of PTSD. To extend attribution theory to account for other PTSD symptomatology, the work of Weiner (1986) is useful. Weiner suggests that there are links between causal attributions and specific emotional states. Weiner draws attention to the way in which specific emotional states appear to depend on causal attributions for events. For example, feelings of rage and anger are generally experienced in the context of negative and externally controllable outcomes.

So, although self-blame has been associated with negative outcomes among victims of threatening events in a variety of studies, there is other evidence that blaming others may also be associated with poorer adjustment in a variety of circumstances (Tennen & Affleck, 1990). One reason for this may be that blaming others leads to the emotional states of rage and anger, states which are frequently reported by survivors of assault and which may lead to the development and maintenance of PTSD (Riggs, Dancu, Gershuny, Greenberg, & Foa, 1992). Other work has shown that anger and hostility in Vietnam veterans was associated with detachment (Silver & Iacono, 1984) and it may be that such emotional states which result out of other-blame may be seen as a form of defence or denial (Tennen & Affleck, 1990).

However, it may be important to differentiate between causal attributions for the events occurrence and causal attributions for what takes place during the event. Guilt and shame are common reactions. In survivors of the *Herald of Free Enterprise* disaster it was found that between one-third and two-thirds said that they felt guilty about things they did or failed to do during the capsize (Joseph, Hodgkinson, Yule, & Williams, 1993b). Feelings of guilt are generally experienced in the context of negative and internally controllable outcomes. Shame, on the other hand, tends to be experienced when an attribution is made to an internal stable cause (Weiner, 1986).

Two studies based on Weiner's (1986) work have investigated the causal attributions made by survivors about events that occurred during a disaster and their relationship to symptomatology. In the first, Joseph, Brewin, Yule, and Williams (1991) investigated the relationship between causal attributions and psychiatric symptoms in civilian survivors of a shipping disaster in which 193 people died: the *Herald of Free Enterprise* disaster. For purposes of legal assessment, 20 survivors provided a detailed account of their experiences during the disaster. From these, causal attributions were extracted and rated along external—internal and uncontrollable—controllable dimensions. Although ratings were generally uncontrollable there was much variation on the externality—internality dimension. For example, some of the survivors provided accounts of their attempts to climb up a rope to safety: 'I had several attempts to climb the rope but was unable to do so. There were no knots in it and it was very slippy.' This was rated as external and uncontrollable, whereas the statement 'I was unable to climb the rope because my legs had gone numb' was rated as internal and uncontrollable. Ratings were based on the attributional coding system developed by Stratton and his colleagues (Stratton et al., 1986). In this study it was found that more internal and controllable attributions were related to intrusive thoughts, depression, and anxiety at 8 and 19 months following the disaster. These findings are consistent with Weiner's (1986) cognitive theory of emotions which suggests that internal and controllable causal attributions for negative outcomes are related to feelings of guilt which in turn, it was suggested, may exacerbate symptoms. This finding is also consistent with the prediction of Foa, Steketee, and Rothbaum (1989) that symptoms of PTSD would be exacerbated by the perception of unexercised control.

A second study by Joseph, Brewin, Yule, and Williams (1993a) replicated the above study with 16 adolescents who survived the *Jupiter* cruise ship disaster. In this study, however, attributions were overwhelmingly uncontrollable so only the externality—internality dimension was rated. For example, the statement 'It was not easy swimming because I had my jeans and sweater on' was rated as external whereas the statement 'I found it very hard to swim out of the suction as I am not a strong swimmer' was rated as internal. The results confirmed that for adolescents causal attribution is an important aspect of disaster response. More internal attributions for disaster-related events were associated with greater depression and intrusive thoughts one year later. However, whereas it was hypothesised that the results with the *Herald* survivors reflected the operation of guilt, the virtually complete absence of personally controllable attributions in the *Jupiter* survivors suggested that it might be shame in this case that provides the link with symptoms.

Although both of these studies suggest an intriguing link between causal attributions and post traumatic stress, the samples were small and highly selected. Also, no evidence was found to support a causal relationship between attributions and symptoms, although it should be noted that symptoms were probably too stable to permit the demonstration of causal effects. However, even if causal attributions are not responsible for the onset of symptoms they may be responsible for their maintenance. Attributions may be important in the way survivors cope subsequent to disaster, which in turn may exacerbate symptoms.

In addition, survivors may make causal attributions for their emotional state (Solomon, Benbenishty, & Mikulincer, 1988a; Mikulincer, Solomon, & Benbenishty, 1988). Mikulincer et al. investigated how battle events contribute to the formation of PTSD. It was shown that the experience of particular battle events, notably officers' errors during battle, and problems in unit functioning, were associated with fewer long-term disturbances. One possible explanation for this, they suggested, is that soldiers who experience such events can attribute their combat stress reaction (CSR) to external factors beyond their control. In contrast, those who do not experience such events cannot fall back on situational attributions and, therefore, tend to attribute their CSR to personal weakness. The attribution of CSR to personality deficits would have negative consequences for self-image and long-term mental health. A similar explanation was offered by Solomon et al. (1988a) for their finding that soldiers who experienced physical deprivations such as hunger, or who suffered the consequences of error, such as coming under fire by their own forces, exhibited less severe psychological symptoms than those who did not have such experiences. Both physical deprivations and errors, Solomon et al. (1988a) argue, are external causes that may serve to prevent soldiers attributing their own inappropriate behaviour to internal and controllable factors. Events can therefore be appraised in a variety of ways and these studies indicate how idiosyncratic people's reactions can be. Other data also suggest that self-blame is associated with higher levels of depressive symptomatology in survivors of rape (Frazier, 1990; Frazier & Schauben, 1994; Hill & Zautra, 1989; Meyer & Taylor, 1986).

Causal attributions, therefore, constitute one aspect of stimulus appraisal that may help to account for some variations in PTSD symptoms as well as specific emotional states such as rage, anger, guilt, and shame. However, it would seem to be necessary to differentiate between causal attributions for the occurrence of an event, behaviours during the event, and subsequent emotional reactions. This distinction might help to resolve some of the conflicting findings in the literature regarding the role of perceptions of control. Furthermore, we would suggest that the resolution of causal attribution may be one aspect of internal experience that actually constitutes a form of intrusive thinking. This would correspond to the ruminative activity discussed previously, some forms of ruminative activity might lead to better outcome whereas other forms might lead to worse outcome. This might explain why, as we have seen in the previous chapter, findings regarding the role of intrusive thinking in determining later outcome are mixed. But ruminative behaviour must be distinguished from those intrusions which are symptomatic of disorder, the most symptomatic intrusions would correspond to what Lifton (1967) described as the death imprint. This consisted of intrusive images of the impact, the sight of bodies dismembered or crushed, the sounds of screaming, and the smell of burning flesh occurring in the waking state or in nightmare.

PERSONALITY FACTORS

A recent survey with a national probability sample in America has suggested that the prevalence of psychiatric problems is greater than previously thought. Fifty per cent of respondents reported at least one lifetime disorder and approximately 30% reported at least one disorder in the previous 12 months. Furthermore, this morbidity is highly concentrated in roughly one-sixth of the population who have a history of three or more co-morbid disorders (Kessler et al., 1994). The question that many researchers have asked is whether people with previous psychological problems are more at risk of developing post-traumatic stress reactions than those who do not have previous psychological problems.

The evidence which has accumulated is generally consistent in showing that prior behavioural and psychological problems are associated with greater distress. This conclusion has been drawn from studies of the effects of personal injury and physical attack (Breslau, Davis, Andreski, & Peterson, 1991; Helzer, Robins, & McEvoy, 1987; Hough et al., 1990), rape (Atkeson, Calhoun, Resick, & Ellis, 1982; Burgess & Holmstrom, 1978; Frank & Anderson, 1987; Frank, Turner, Stewart, Jacob, & West, 1981; Ruch, Chandler, & Harter, 1980), mass shooting (North, Smith, & Spitznagel, 1994) disaster (Lopez-Ibor, Soria, Canas, & Rodrigues-Gamazo, 1985; Markowitz & Gutterman, 1986; McFarlane, 1988a, 1988b, 1989; Bromet, Schulberg, & Dunn, 1982b) and previous psychiatric history is recognised as a vulnerability factor for PTSD (APA, 1994).

But interestingly, it has been suggested that the effects of prior psychological problems interact with the intensity of event exposure. For example, Foy, Resnick, Sipprelle, and Carroll (1987) reported that a family history of psychiatric disorders was associated with the development of PTSD in Vietnam veterans but that the effect was greatest for those with the least exposure to combat. This is an interesting suggestion which might help to explain why some other research has not found prior history factors to be associated with distress (Solkoff, Gray, & Keill, 1986; Speed, Engdahl, Schwartz, & Eberly, 1989; Kilpatrick, Veronen, & Best, 1985; Madakasira & O'Brien, 1987). It may be that survivors of these event experienced a traumatic event so intense that the effect of prior psychological problems was minimum. In addition, there are other factors which may need to be taken into account when trying to understand the role of prior psychological problems. For example, in the study by North et al. (1994) of survivors of a mass shooting, it was found that a past history of psychiatric disorder predicted the development of PTSD for women but not for men. Clearly, the role of prior-psychological problems in the development of post-traumatic stress reactions is not straightforward.

Personality is shaped by our life-experiences and some researchers have suggested that particular experiences in the past may lead to a person being vulnerable to the development of psychiatric problems. In particular, childhood experiences are thought to be crucial to later personality development and work has shown that people who are depressed are more likely to have had childhoods characterised by adverse experiences (Brewin, Andrews, & Gotlib, 1993). It might be expected that people with adverse events in their childhood are also prone to the development of post-traumatic stress reactions.

Childhood experiences are thought to be important in the development of our beliefs about ourselves and the world around us and from a cognitive perspective it might be that these belief systems in turn cause the person to be vulnerable to disorder. One set of beliefs that seem relevent to understanding post-traumatic stress are those to do with control.

Attributional style

As we have seen, causal attributions are thought to be important in how a person reacts to an event. Causal attributions themselves reflect not only the situational information available regarding the event but also the person's attributional style (Abramson et al., 1988; Alloy & Tabachnik, 1984; Alloy et al., 1988), a relatively stable personality characteristic (Burns & Seligman, 1989) which refers to people's characteristic way of explaining events.

The hopelessness theory predicts that individuals who characteristically explain negative events in terms of internal, stable, and global causes and explain positive events in terms of external, unstable, and specific causes are vulnerable to the development of depression characterised by feelings of hopelessness accompanied by low self-esteem (Abramson et al., 1988; Alloy et al., 1988). Research which has tested this prediction with a retrospective behavioural high-risk paradigm has presented evidence consistent with the hopelessness theory (Alloy, Lipman, & Abramson, 1992) and there is some correlational evidence that this vulnerable attributional style is also associated with PTSD in Vietnam veterans (McCormick, Taber, & Kruedelbach, 1989) and in women with histories of child sexual abuse and who are suffering from low self-esteem and poorer adjustment (Gold, 1986; Wolfe, Gentile, & Wolfe, 1989).

Another study by Mikulincer and Solomon (1988) investigated whether attributional style was associated with emotional distress in Israeli combat veterans at two and three years following the Lebanon War. They found that intensity of PTSD symptomatology, general psychiatric symptomatology, and problems in social functioning were associated with the attribution of good events to more external and uncontrollable causes and the attribution of bad events to more external, stable, and uncontrollable causes. But in contrast to other research which suggests that internality for negative events is associated with poorer outcome, Mikulincer and Solomon (1988) suggest that their finding that externality for negative outcomes is associated with poorer outcome is explained by the denial of personal responsibility by PTSD veterans. It might be that avoidance manifests itself in this particular attributional pattern. Alternatively, it may be that these data reflect the attribution of blame and feelings of anger towards other people.

Locus of Control

A related concept to attributional style is that of locus of control. It has generally been believed that perceptions of control are adaptive in stressful situations (Benassi, Sweeney, & Dufour, 1988). For example, Taylor (1983) reported that in cancer patients the belief that one could control one's own cancer was associated with positive adjustment and there is growing evidence that perceptions of control are also associated with lower distress in combat veterans (Frye & Stockton, 1982; Orr et al., 1990; Solomon, Mikulincer, & Benbenishty, 1989b). However, although it is likely that attributional style and locus of control are vulnerability factors for disorder following traumatic events, there is as yet no evidence to confirm this suggestion. Obtaining pre-morbid personality measures is a particular problem with trauma research. However, the availability of attributional coding techniques which can be used with written material such as letters (Stratton et al., 1986; Schulman, Castellan, & Seligman, 1989) makes this an intriguing possibility for future research.

If attributional style and locus of control do constitute vulnerability factors, it is likely that the intensity of exposure will moderate the association between locus of control and distress. Solomon et al. (1989b) found an association between locus of control and distress in soldiers who had been exposed to low battle intensity but not in soldiers who had been exposed to high battle intensity. The explanation for this, they suggest, was due to the greater informational value of greater battle intensity in helping the soldier to explain his behaviour to himself. High-intensity battle, they argue, leads the soldier to explain his combat stress reaction entirely by the stressful events whereas low-intensity battle leads to explanations affected by locus of control.

Locus of control refers to the person's perceptions of control and it might be predicted that perceptions of control are most adaptive in situations where control can actually be exercised. Locus of control should, however, be distinguished from self-efficacy, the person's conviction of whether or not he or she is able to exercise control (see Litt, 1988).

Attitudes and Beliefs

Beck and Emery (1985), although they do not discuss PTSD as such, suggest that there may be another mechanism whereby an individual's personality may result in extreme and negative conclusions following traumatisation. They suggest that vulnerable individuals have dysfunctional assumptions which predispose them to the development of depression and anxiety. These asumptions are rules for living acquired during childhood but which can be too rigid, extreme, and absolute in form. For example, the need for control is sometimes represented in absolute black and white terms so that any deviation from absolute control tends to be conceived in terms of absolute lack of control. This could be a mechanism by which a primitive belief could come to be shattered by the operation of automatic, schematic processing rather than discrepant information impacting on a basic belief.

Drawing upon Beck's concept of dysfunctional assumptions, as well as the work of Rachman (1980), Williams (1989) has hypothesised that negative attitudes towards emotional expression (e.g., 'I think you should always keep your feelings under control', 'I think you should not burden other people with your problems', 'I think getting emotional is a sign of weakness', 'I think other people don't understand your feelings') would act to block the processing of emotionally charged information and constitute one vulnerability factor for the development or maintenance of post-traumatic stress reactions.

Tests of this prediction have been carried out with survivors of the *Herald of Free Enterprise* disaster showing that those who held the most negative attitudes towards emotional expression had the highest distress scores (Williams, Hodgkinson, Joseph, & Yule, 1995) and that more negative attitudes towards emotional expression at three years were associated with greater distress at five years (Joseph, Dalgleish, Williams, et al., 1997).

EMOTIONAL STATE FACTORS

The role of emotional state at the time of the event has received some attention and DSM-IV (APA, 1994) has, as we have seen in Chapter 2, introduced the category of Acute Stress Disorder. To qualify for a diagnosis, the person must exhibit dissociative symptoms, persistent re-experiencing, marked avoidance of reminders, anxiety and increased arousal. Acute Stress Disorder is most likely to develop under conditions of extreme stress and it is thought that individuals with this disorder are at increased risk for the development of PTSD although at present the relationship between Acute Stress Disorder and PTSD is not understood and we have to rely on data which have been collected on other acute syndromes such as Combat Stress Reaction (CSR) (see Oei, Lim, & Hennessy, 1990). CSRs may be brief, lasting only a few hours to a few weeks. Israeli soldiers who suffered from CSR in the 1982 Lebanon War were more likely to go on to develop PTSD than those soldiers who had not suffered from CSR but had experienced an equal level of combat exposure. In the first year after the war, the PTSD prevalence rate was 62% for the CSR group compared to 14% in the non-CSR group. At three years, the prevalence rates were 43% and 10% respectively (Solomon, 1993). Although these data provide some evidence in support of the causal link between acute reactions and PTSD, the specific features of acute reactions that are most likely to predict PTSD remain unclear. A prominent feature of Acute Stress Disorder is dissociation and it has been suggested that this may provide the link between acute and chronic reactions. There is some evidence for the role of dissociation with survivors of a North Sea oil rig disaster (Holen, 1993) and Vietnam veterans (Marmar et al., 1994).

In addition, personality variables and pre-existing mental disorders may influence the development of Acute Stress Disorder. However, not all those who develop Acute Stress Disorder go on to develop PTSD and so the relationship between these two states must be moderated by other factors.

Theorists who propose a stage model of processing have drawn attention to the multiple emotional states experienced following trauma. Although some theories have emphasised fear (e.g., Foa et al., 1989) with thoughts of recurrence of the trauma and helplessness in the face of it, PTSD is not synonymous with fear and anxiety. It would appear that the full range of negative emotions are felt, not only fear and anxiety but grief, guilt, and shame as well as rage and anger. Indeed, processing gives rise to not only one state but a series of states as the event comes to be examined from different perspectives.

As already noted, Weiner (1986) points out how specific emotional states appear to depend upon causal attributions for events. It has been suggested that the relationship between internal and controllable attributions and symptoms in a sample of survivors of a ferry disaster was mediated by the emotional state of guilt (Joseph et al., 1991); whereas it was suggested that the internal and uncontrollable attributions of a group of adolescent survivors could reflect the emotional state of shame (Joseph et al., 1993a). However, further research is clearly needed to substantiate these data. In particular, it is not known whether particular emotional states are exclusively related to attributions for specific types of events, for example, events which involve another person. In addition, although causal attributions and attributional style have been found to be associated with post-traumatic symptoms, there is at present no evidence supporting a causal path between these variables. In addition to longitudinal research, it is also suggested that future research should attempt to address the association between causal attributions for real events and attributional style for hypothetical events in order to explore a vulnerability model for the development of post-traumatic stress reactions.

As already discussed, emotional states themselves may be subject to appraisal. Emotional states that are perceived of as inappropriate may be associated with behavioural inhibition, concealment and denial (or avoidance). The emotional states can be appraised as frightening, depressing, etc. and lead to secondary emotional reactions. Foa et al. (1989) emphasise the importance of these secondary reactions because of their association with avoidant coping strategies. As Horowitz (1976) pointed out, an individual may feel threatened by the emotional state itself and use avoidance as self-protection. Such reactions to powerful emotional states may then both block processing and render the individual beyond the scope of social support.

Foa, Zinbarg, and Rothbaum (1992) present evidence that rape victims diagnosed with PTSD two months post-rape were unlikely to recover spontaneously. This and other evidence with survivors of a variety of events suggests that after 3–4 months, PTSD, if present and without treatment, is likely to remain stable over time and that symptoms early on are able to predict later chronicity of symptomatology (McFarlane, 1988a, 1988b; Perry, Difede, Musngi, Frances, & Jacobsberg, 1992; Solomon, Weisenberg, et al., 1987c).

ACTIVITY FACTORS

The role of causal attributions may be to influence the coping strategies employed following adversity which, in turn, may exacerbate PTSD symptoms. There is good evidence for this relationship in normal populations. Brewin, MacCarthy, and Furnham (1989), for example, investigated whether causal attributions concerning negative outcomes were related to seeking social support. It was found that individuals who blamed their own inadequacies for a specific negative event were more likely to have withdrawn socially and were less likely to have used coping strategies involving family and friends. Previously we discussed the role of appraisal in determining specific emotional states such as guilt or shame. Recent work on the role of guilt and shame and psychopathology suggests that they may have a differential relationship to post-traumatic response. Tangney, Wagner, and Gramzow (1992) note that, although both shame and guilt involve negative affect, each has a distinct focus which is related to unique symptom clusters.

> In guilt, the object of concern is some specific action (or failure to act). There is remorse or regret over the 'bad thing that was done' and a sense of tension that often serves as a motivation for reparative action. The tension, remorse, and regret engendered by guilt can be quite uncomfortable, particularly when reparation is blocked for one reason or another... In shame, the object of concern is the entire self. The 'bad thing' is experienced as a reflection of a 'bad self', and the entire self is painfully scrutinized and negatively evaluated. With this painful scrutiny of the self is a corresponding sense of shrinking, of being small, and of being worthless and powerless. Shame also involves a sense of exposure. (Tangney, Wagner, & Gramzow, 1992, p. 469)

One important phenomenological difference between guilt and shame, then, is that shame motivates us to hide whereas guilt motivates us to take reparative action. This has implications for the choice of coping behaviour. It might be expected that shame leads to the use of avoidant coping whereas guilt leads us to use approach coping. However, where reparative action cannot be taken, the person may be obliged to relive the events over in his or her mind. Strong feelings of guilt may then be associated with intrusive thinking whereas shame may be associated with avoidant behaviour. Interestingly, there are similarities here to the distinction drawn by Lifton (1967) between 'animating guilt' and 'static guilt'. Animating guilt is a spur to self-examination whereas static guilt keeps the victim bound to the experience and unable to move on. A variety of strategies may be used to cope with traumatic events. For example, Green, Grace, and Gleser (1985a), in their study of survivors of the Beverly Hills Supper Club fire, assessed coping using an open-ended question to which responses were grouped into one of three categories. These were denial (e.g., using drugs or turning to work to avoid thinking about the situation), philosophical/intellectual (e.g., turning to religion), and interpersonal (e.g., talking to others). North et al. (1994), in their study of survivors of a mass shooting, found that the most widespread method of coping was seeking support from family and friends (88%).

Coping refers to the person's cognitive and behavioural efforts to manage (reduce, tolerate, master) the demands (both internal and external) of a stressful transaction (Lazarus & Folkman, 1984). Much evidence has accumulated showing that coping mediates between stressful events and psychological distress (Billings & Moos, 1981, 1984; Carver et al., 1989; Endler & Parker, 1990; Folkman & Lazarus, 1985, 1988; Folkman, Lazarus, Dunkel-Schetter, De-Longis, & Gruen, 1986a; Pearlin & Schooler, 1978). A basic distinction often employed is between problem-focused and emotion-focused coping (Folkman & Lazarus, 1985). The former refers to acts taken to remove or mitigate the source of stress, the latter to attempts to reduce the psychological distress. Findings regarding the use of emotion-focused and problem-focused strategies seem, at first, somewhat inconsistent and confusing. Greater emotion-focused coping has been found to be associated with less distress following the Three Mile Island leak (Baum, Fleming, & Singer, 1983a), and more distress in Israeli combat veterans (Solomon, Mikulincer, & Flum 1988c), American combat veterans (Nezu & Carnevale, 1987), civilians following the SCUD missile attacks on Israel during the Gulf War (Zeidner & Ben-Zur, 1994), and women with HIV infection (Commerford, Gular, Orr, Reznikoff, & O'Dowd, 1994).

In addition, the role of coping may be modest following events associated with great loss (Freedy, Darlene, Jarrell, & Masters, 1992). There are as yet no clear answers to the question of which strategies, or combination of strategies, are most beneficial. The Conservation of Resources stress model (Hobfoll, 1989) suggests that whichever particular strategy, or combination of strategies, leads to the most efficient acquisition of resource losses will be the most adaptive for psychological health. If event-related resource loss allows for the person to take control, then problem-focused coping should be adaptive. However, if the event-related loss does not allow the person to take control, then emotion-focused strategies should be adaptive (Carver et al., 1989; Folkman & Lazarus, 1988; Hobfoll, 1989). Thus, it would seem that the effects of coping can only be understood in relation to the nature of the event and its appraisal.

Avoidance

Various forms of avoidant coping have been found to be associated with less distress in uncontrollable situations such as the political violence in Northern Ireland (Cairns & Wilson, 1984, 1989), the length of survival following the diagnosis of cancer (Greer, Morris, & Pettingale, 1979). In addition, Whittington and Wykes (1991) found that psychiatric nurses who reported using denial also reported fewer problems in the year following a violent assault. There are some suggestions from empirical studies, then, that using coping strategies that involve avoidance strategies may be helpful. In contrast, McFarlane (1988a/b) found that in a sample of volunteer firefighters exposed to Australian bush fires, a reported tendency to avoid thinking about negative experiences was associated with more symptoms. Also, Green, Grace, and Gleser (1985a), in their study of the Beverly Hills Supper Club fire, found that those using avoidant strategies exhibited higher levels of pathology and it is generally believed that coping which involves exposure (without escape) to feared stimuli can help to ameliorate anxiety (Beck & Emery, 1985; Clark, 1986; Marks, 1981). As a type of coping with perceived threats, avoidance is believed to play a role in the spiralling cycle that characterises anxiety disorders (Beck & Emery, 1985) and to be associated with a range of health problems (Suls & Fletcher, 1985). As we have seen, however, Horowitz (1976, 1979) sheds a different light upon the role of avoidance. According to Horowitz's theory, as a part of normal adaptation, an individual will go through phases of re-experiencing and avoiding thinking about the trauma. Thus the role of avoidance in coping with stress seems ambiguous: first, avoidance impedes emotional processing and maintains anxiety; but second, avoidance may be necessary to protect a traumatised individual from being overwhelmed by emotion and plays a part in normal processing of the event.

Avoidance is not a simple concept and can implicate different coping responses: behavioural avoidance (i.e., staying away from reminders); cognitive avoidance (i.e., not thinking about the event); and affective avoidance (i.e., blocking an affective response). It is possible that different types of avoidance are associated with different outcomes. Specifically, if emotion is required in processing, it might be that affective avoidance would have the most generalised inhibitory effect and would be associated with the greatest signs of blocked emotional processing and functional impairment. The studies which have shown avoidant strategies to be adaptive have generally used measures of either cognitive or behavioural avoidance rather than affective avoidance. It is suggested that affective avoidance may be predictive of emotional disorder.

Inhibition

The inhibition-disease framework developed by Pennebaker and his colleagues (Pennebaker, 1985; Pennebaker & Beall, 1986; Pennebaker & Chew, 1985; Pennebaker & O'Heeron, 1984; Pennebaker, Hughes, & O'Heeron, 1987; Pennebaker, Kiecolt-Glaser, & Glaser, 1988) suggests that the act of restraining ongoing thoughts or behaviour requires physiological work resulting in increased psychosomatic symptoms. One explanation for this effect is that, by disclosure, individuals change the way in which trauma-relevant material is represented in memory. Pennebaker and his colleagues (Pennebaker, 1993; Hughes, Uhlmann, & Pennebaker, 1994) present evidence that what is important is the construction of a coherent story together with the expression of negative emotions.

Similarly, Foa et al. (1989) argue that recovery from victimisation requires that, first, the fear memory be activated, and, second, that new information incompatible with what is already in the fear structure be introduced.

Evidence suggests that a tendency towards thought suppression is associated with obsessive thinking and emotional reactivity. It has been suggested that intention to suppress a thought produces two mental processes: a conscious effortful operating process that searches for distractors, and an unconscious, relatively effortless monitoring process that searches for the unwanted thought (Wegner & Zanakos, 1994). It may be then that avoidant strategies can actually increase the cognitive accessibility of information.

SOCIOCULTURAL FACTORS

Social Support

A considerable body of evidence has been accumulated documenting the stress-buffering effects of social support (Brown & Harris, 1978; Cohen & Wills, 1985; Dalgard, Bjork, & Tambs, 1995; Roy & Steptoe, 1994) and much research has now been carried out showing greater social support to be associated with better outcome following toxic exposure (Bromet, Parkinson, Schulberg, Dunn, & Gondek, 1982a), rape (Burgess & Holmstrom, 1974a, 1974b, 1978; Kilpatrick et al., 1985), combat (Fontana & Rosenheck, 1994c; Foy, Sipprelle, rueger, & Carroll, 1984; Foy et al., 1987; Frye & Stockton, 1982; Keane, Scott, Chavoya, Lamparski, & Fairbank, 1985a; Roberts, Penk, Robinowitz, & Patterson, 1982; Solkoff et al., 1986; Solomon, Mikulincer, & Avitzur, 1988b; Stretch, Vail, & Maloney, 1985) as well as a range of civilian disasters (Cook & Bickman, 1990). However, social support has been variously defined in these studies.

Definitions of social support emphasise behaviour relevant to coping needs. Schaefer, Coyne, and Lazarus (1981) distinguished between the emotional, tangible and informational support functions of support. Emotional support includes intimacy and attachment, reassurance and being able to confide in and rely on another: factors which contribute to the feeling that one is loved, or cared about, and that one belongs. Tangible support involves direct aid, and includes loans, gifts of money, and the provision of services. Informational support includes giving advice and providing feedback.

The demands evoked by any event may unfold over time and Jacobson (1986) has emphasised the need to consider social support in its temporal dimension. To the extent that stressful situations are sequential, different kinds of support will be called for at different times. Weiss (1976) outlined a model in which the types of support are related to the sequencing of stressful events. First, there is 'crisis', which is defined as a situation of sudden onset and limited duration, severely threatening to one's well-being, and marked by emotional arousal. In a crisis the most useful form of help is emotional support which provides a person with reassurance that others are able and willing to help in the struggle to regain equilibrium. Second, there is 'transition', which is defined as a period of personal and relational change involving a shift in the person's 'assumptive world'. In transitions, the primary type of help is cognitive support that helps the individual to come to terms with the meaning of the changes experienced. Third, there are 'deficit states', which are situations in which the individual's life is characterised by excessive demands. Here material aid and direct action are needed to remedy an imbalance between needs and tangible resources.

A study by Cook and Bickman (1990) investigated the relationship of perceived availability of social support to self-reported psychological symptomatology at various points in time over a period of six months following a flood. Their results indicated that respondents experienced severe distress immediately following the disaster, that this distress decreased sharply at six weeks after the flood, and decreased more gradually in the following months. Perceived availability of social support was not related to distress immediately following the disaster nor five months later. Social support and symptomatology were, however, significantly correlated during the intermediate time. Cook and Bickman (1990) suggest that their data have important methodological considerations for the conduct of research following traumatic events:

> Not only did the effects of the distress decay but also the relationship between an important social variable such as social support and symptomatology changes over time. These results can possibly explain some of the inconsistent findings in this field. Differing results may be obtained depending on the time since the occurrence of the stressor. (Cook & Bickman, 1990, p. 555)

Buffering hypothesis

A major debate in the conceptualization of social support has been whether to consider it as acting as an antecedent to stressful life-events that serves to protect individuals from negative health outcomes, versus viewing it as playing a buffering role in situations of high stress (Cohen & Wills, 1985; Gore, 1981; House & Kahn, 1985; Thoits, 1982). Cohen and Wills (1985) reviewed the existing literature in detail in an attempt to consider the process by which support has a beneficial effect on well-being. Their review concludes that there is evidence consistent with both models. Evidence for a main effect model was found when the support measure assessed the person's degree of integration in a social network. Evidence for a buffering model is found when the support measure assesses interpersonal resources that are responsive to the needs elicited by a stressful situation.

Raphael (1986) notes that survivors often have a compelling need to talk about their experiences, and thus empathic listening is a principal component of the necessary emotional support following crisis. One study which has examined the buffering role of support offers impressive evidence that it is related to a reduced risk of depression following a crisis. In a longitudinal study of working-class women, it was found that retrospective reports of crisis support received from a husband, lover, or very close friend following a severe event or major difficulty were strongly associated with a reduced risk of depression. Crisis support was said to have been received if, following a provoking agent, there had been a high level of confiding with a high level of active emotional support, as long as it was not accompanied at some point by a negative response from the person confided in (Andrews & Brown, 1988; Brown, Andrews, Harris, Adler, & Bridge, 1986).

Studies which have investigated the role of crisis support with survivors of the *Jupiter* cruise ship disaster (Joseph, Andrews, Williams, & Yule, 1992a; Joseph, Yule, Williams, & Andrews, 1993e) and the *Herald of Free Enterprise* sinking (Dalgleish, Joseph, Thrasher, Tranah, & Yule, 1996) have also found that higher self-reported ratings of crisis support received from family and friends are predictive of lower levels of distress.

With civilian burns patients, Perry, Difede, Musngi, Frances, and Jacobsberg (1992) found less emotional support to be predictive of PTSD up to 12 months later. Thus, there is growing evidence for the role of social support as a protective factor against emotional distress following exposure to a traumatic event. It has been suggested that one way in which social support works is by enhancing perceptions of control over the environment. For example, social support acts as a vehicle for the transmission of information for problem solving.

Solomon et al. (1988b) examined the relationship between coping, locus of control, social support, and combat-related PTSD. Their sample consisted of 262 Israeli soldiers who suffered a combat stress reaction episode during the 1982 Lebanon War. In contrast to much previous work that has set out to examine the impact of personal and social resources on the development of PTSD among CSR casualties, Solomon et al. (1988b) employed a longitudinal design, focusing on two points in time: two years and three years following combat. They examined, first, the relation between personal resources and social resources and PTSD at each point in time; and, second, the relation between changes in the course of PTSD and changes in both personal and social resources. The intensity of PTSD declined between the two points of time, reflecting a process of recovery. In addition, locus of control became more internal, there was less emotion-focused coping, and more perceived social support. As hypothesised, associations were found at each point in time between PTSD intensity and personal and social resources. Both in the second and third years after the war, more intense PTSD was associated with external locus of control, emotion-focused coping style, and insufficient social support. With regard to locus of control, although correlated at both times with PTSD, the removal of the contributions of coping strategies and social support to PTSD variance cancelled out the significance of locus of control. It is suggested that this is consistent with the idea that internal locus of control is associated with the use of more task-relevant problem-focused coping strategies, and less task-irrelevant emotionally-focused strategies (Anderson, 1977). The findings are thus thought to point to coping strategies as mediating between locus of control and PTSD. However, this study is limited by several methodological problems in common with much of the disaster literature. First, the subjects have PTSD prior to the start of the study, the findings cannot provide definitive evidence as to the direction of causality between resources and PTSD, and once established one would expect a mutually reinforcing relation between resources and PTSD. Second, the conceptualisation of emotion-focused coping as including avoidant strategies can actually be viewed as an expression of PTSD symptomatology rather than as a contributing factor. Third, assessments of personal and social resources are retrospective, and thus may be influenced by the current psychological state. Although people with an internal locus of control may be more able to get support in a time of crisis, other research has suggested that the buffering effect of social support might only apply to those people with an external locus of control (Dalgard et al., 1995).

However, over-reliance on the social network can create dependency and there is some research which suggests that marriage may actually exacerbate the negative psychological consequences of disaster for women (Gleser et al., 1981; Solomon, Smith, Robins, & Fischbach, 1987a). It may be that married women are relied on for support by others, creating additional stress. Other life-events will often occur in the period after disaster, some perhaps triggered by it (Janney, Masuda, & Holmes, 1977) and which might serve to exacerbate symptoms. It is known from numerous studies that stressful life-events are implicated in the onset and maintenance of psychiatric problems (Brown & Harris, 1978; Lloyd, 1980; Breslau & Davis, 1986). McFarlane (1988a, 1988b), in his study of survivors of the Australian bush fire, found that individuals with PTSD had more adverse life-events before and after the trauma. Karlehagen et al. (1993) report that railway drivers who suffered from negative psychological outcomes following railway accidents were more likely to have had previous similar accidents. In their work on Dutch hijackings, van der Ploeg and Kleijn (1988) note that hostages who had to cope with other major life-events besides having been held hostage reported a greater number of negative after-affects. Following extreme catastrophe, post-disaster life-events are inextricably bound up with the traumatic event itself. Goenjian et al. (1994), in their study of the survivors of the Armenia earthquake, note that the persistence of symptoms one and a half years later may also have been related to the unremitting multiple post-disaster adversities such as the relocation of families, loss of possessions, lack of housing and crowded living conditions, unemployment, and so on. Also, they note that the undisposed of debris and destroyed buildings served as constant reminders of the event.

Social Context

Responses to trauma are also linked to sociocultural events. Summerfield (1993), for example, draws attention to the Vietnam War following which the

US veterans were disowned by their society and contrasts this to the Falklands War in which British veterans returned to popular acclaim. The social context helps to determine the meaning of particular experiences and subsequent emotional reactions. The relationship between emotional reactions and social context is illustrated in an interesting study carried out by Bartone and Wright (1990) who investigated group recovery following a military air disaster which showed a response pattern of adaptation that included both intrusion and avoidance. A chartered US Army jetliner crashed in 1985 killing all who were on board. This was the second of three flights carrying soldiers home from the Sinai for Christmas. Bartone and Wright collected monthly data using unstructured interviews over a period of six months following the crash on 140 individuals from the battalion. Their data indicated four relatively distinct phases, each lasting 4–6 weeks: (1) Numb Dedication; (2) Anger–Betrayal; (3) Stoic Resolve; and (4) Integration. This first phase in weeks 1 to 6 was characterised by denial, generalised affective detachment, and numbness.

> The work atmosphere was sombre but business-like. Soldiers working at the battalion staff offices at this time described a 'feeling of unreality, like this isn't really happening,' 'like I'm on automatic pilot,' and feeling as if 'I'm here, but I'm not really here.' Many described feeling numb or 'cold,' with 'no real feelings at all.' (Bartone & Wright, 1990, p. 528).

Bartone and Wright (1990) note that although this phase was dominant, various intrusive reminders sometimes triggered periods of uncontrollable crying and dreams were common. Other symptoms observed included those of startle response and survivor guilt. Near the six-week point, Bartone and Wright describe how this first phase of Numb Dedication shifted to one dominated by Anger–Betrayal. What is interesting about Bartone and Wright's work is that they attempt to integrate these stages with a sociopsychological context. They note that the transition into this phase was marked by the publication of a report indicating poor airline safety practices as contributing to the cause of the crash and also the explosion of the space shuttle *Challenger* in 1986.

> Unit survivors resented what they perceived as greater public concern for seven astronaut lives than for 248 soldier lives. This was attributed to a presumed public attitude that 'a soldier's blood is cheap,' that soldiers represent the lower strata of society and are therefore more expendable than others ... anger was frequently expressed toward the charter airline for alleged safety violations ... and toward the upper-echelons of Army command for not assuring the safety of military charter flights. This was coupled with a sharp sense of betrayal; many felt the trust they placed in the army to care for their safety and welfare had been profoundly violated. (Bartone & Wright, 1990, p. 531)

However, Bartone and Wright also note that during this phase there was a high degree of support within the group and that many members tried to direct their anger into constructive channels, for example, using it to care for the bereaved families. Also, there was no notable decline in symptoms like insomnia, dreams, guilt, or startle reactions and many reported an increased use of alcohol or tranquillisers to relieve tension. At around the tenth week, following the burial of the last dead soldier, there was another marked turning point characterised by a sense of relief.

> Expressions of sadness and anger were replaced by an attitude of 'stoic resolve' to continue on with work and life. Many individuals reported having made a conscious decision to focus attention on the present and future, with the aim of bringing the battalion back to a strong and healthy state. The crash itself became a taboo topic. All emphasis was on training and readiness. When some reference to the crash became necessary, as was the case at memorial services, indirect or euphemistic terms were used (e.g., 'the plane that was lost'; 'our Sinai heroes'; 'our soldiers who didn't make it home'). (Bartone & Wright, 1990, p. 532)

This phase, although still marked by reported symptoms of sleep disturbance and increased alcohol use, was characterised as one of avoidance. Also, during this period a major training exercise was conducted which gave the replacement troops the opportunity to integrate within the unit. The end of the training exercise in week 20 marked the final recovery phase which was characterised by Bartone and Wright as one of integration. As already noted, new replacement troops had by now become incorporated within the unit, and most of the veteran unit members were now looking forward to the future, having accepted the loss. Integration, Bartone and Wright note, was evident in the memorial displays and plaques which have been erected around the post and which they suggest

> ...may serve the paradoxical function of permitting survivors to turn their conscious attention away from the disturbing event, without contributing to a sense of guilt. Survivors consistently walked past such displays without observing them directly, and yet they also reported strong beliefs that it was right and honorable to preserve the memory of the Gander victims through such memorials. (Bartone & Wright, 1990, p. 534)

Bartone and Wright help to put the phenomenology of PTSD within a social context. They suggest that intrusion and avoidance may manifest in different forms at particular times with different functions, depending on the changing social context. Bartone and Wright's work suggests an initial avoidance phase characterised as numb dedication. This was dominated by a detached almost unconscious avoidance, punctuated by a high frequency of intrusive reminders at both the individual and group level. This was followed by an intrusion phase characterised as anger-betrayal followed by an avoidance phase characterised as stoic resolve and finally integration. Interestingly, Bartone and Wright note that those who maintained avoidance throughout fared less well than those who followed this pattern. These 'total-deniers', as they are referred to, never discussed their feelings and avoided memorial services and other reminders. Their model of group recovery shares important features with Horowitz's description of individual responses to trauma and demonstrates the role social events might play in helping survivors to process events.

CONCLUSION

This chapter has provided an overview of empirical work in the area of psychosocial approaches to post-traumatic reactions. It would seem that personality factors (including previous mental history) are associated with an increased likelihood of developing PTSD, although it does not seem that these factors are necessary for the development of the disorder. What does seem likely, however, is that personality factors help to shape the specific cognitions of and about the traumatic event. Cognitions in turn help to determine the nature and intensity of emotional states, such as guilt, shame, fear, or rage. Emotional states in turn influence the choice of coping strategy and the level of social support received. It would seem to us to be useful in helping to explain the individual differences in the severity and chronicity of reactions of survivors to take into account the role of stimulus, appraisal, personality, state, and activity factors. Although we have tried to integrate the results of previous research and, where possible, specify the interactions of the various components of our model, there are inconsistencies in the literature and there remains a lack of data in several areas. The model may offer a useful heuristic for guiding future research and clinical practice.

SUMMARY POINTS

1. Evidence has been reviewed implicating a role for causal attributions in mediating emotional distress. More internal and controllable attributions for events during a shipping disaster were related to measures of intrusive thoughts, depression and anxiety. External attributions for emotional responses during battle may, in reverse, be associated with less emotional distress.
2. Evidence also has been reviewed for a relationship between history of psychological problems and distress after trauma. It seems that such an effect is strongest when the intensity of the trauma is lower. Such an effect may be related to attributional style although there are some inconsistencies in the literature that remain to be explained.
3. Some little evidence has also been described relating dysfunctional beliefs about emotional expression to emotional distress.
4. There are some suggestions that severe emotional distress at the time of

the trauma may be predictive of later PTSD. Different emotional states such as shame and rage may be related to causal attributions.

5. Some inconsistencies exist in the empirical literature relating to coping and distress. It is suggested that choice of coping can only be evaluated in relation to aspects of the traumatic event such that in some instances emotion-focused coping may be more helpful and in others where action is possible, coping related to problem resolution may relieve distress.

7. Some studies show a protective function for coping by avoidance. Others show a positive relation between avoidance and distress. It is suggested that 'avoidance' is a complex construct which needs further examination. Some types of avoidance may be more blocking of processing than others.

8. Some evidence has been reviewed which indicates a protective function of crisis support following trauma. The effects of social support may be mediated by enhancement of self-esteem and appraisals of control. Needs for social support may vary as a function of time.

Chapter 7

INTERVENTION AND TREATMENT

INTRODUCTION

While any particular mental health service may go for years without having to respond to the psychosocial sequelae of a major event, when they do occur, services are all too often ill-prepared and overwhelmed. Given the well-documented increase in morbidity following traumatic events, mental health services need to plan their crisis intervention and longer-term treatment to meet the needs of survivors well in advance. In the absence of such planning, problems arising from failures in communication and coordination and from competition between rival services have been seen. In Chapter 6 we discussed the role of psychosocial factors in the aetiology and maintenance of post-traumatic stress reactions. Although the processes through which these factors may be related to adjustment are not entirely clear at present, the available evidence does suggest that one aim of intervention should be to provide social support where it is lacking. It is often the role of the social services and volunteers to provide emotional or practical support in the form of outreach programmes, whereas mental health professionals may be employed for crisis intervention and longer-term therapy. These services require coordination. In the present chapter we will outline the various outreach programmes that have been employed as well as the various forms of therapeutic intervention that are commonly used.

Key Topics

Outreach to survivors
Key areas in psychosocial care
Crisis intervention
Treatment strategies
Direct exposure therapies
Cognitive-behavioural therapies
Encouraging activity and social support
Planning for the future
Conclusion

OUTREACH TO SURVIVORS

The death and destruction following major natural disasters calls for massive relief. For example, during the 1988 Armenian earthquake on 7 December 1988, four major cities and 350 villages were destroyed. Estimates indicate that up to 100,000 people were killed and 530,000 people left homeless. Many of these people were refugees who had fled the pogroms perpetrated against Armenians in Azerbaijan and had settled in the earthquake zone (Goenjian et al., 1994). The task of the Armenian Relief Society of the Western United States was to organise and implement a mental health relief programme following the earthquake to treat survivors and to provide training to local mental health workers and teachers (Goenjian et al. 1994). In extreme circumstances, organisations such as the Red Cross move in to give help, offering food, clothing, and shelter. Surrounding communities will be called upon to complement this assistance. Outreach may be required on a massive scale bringing together local agencies as well as international bodies and relief from other countries. Such relief must initially be directed towards life-saving and providing basic human needs for food, water, and shelter.

Much of current thinking about planning for the provision of psychological relief has been shaped from the work carried out in the Netherlands in the 1970s. In the 1970s there were a large number of political hijackings in the Netherlands. Civilians were taken hostage and used in negotiation with the authorities. Several people were killed. In response to the suffering of many of the victims, a strategy for outreach treatment was introduced as early as 1975. Van der Ploeg and Kleijn (1988) outline the outreach programme for hijackings. A group of health care providers, consisting of workers at a local level and at a regional and national level, are brought together immediately subsequent to the hijack. Each victim and their family are visited at home within one week of the hostage's release. They are invited to talk about the events and their immediate reactions in a friendly, permissive atmosphere. They are informed about coping strategies, about 'normal' reactions, and about individuals, organisations, and addresses capable of offering help and after care. After a few weeks, a second call is made in most cases. In addition, the family's general practitioner is asked to offer help and to visit the victim. It is essential, however, that outreach is not forced upon the victims. The Netherlands provided the basic model of intervention. However, much experience has since accumulated (see Adshead, Canterbury, & Rose, 1994).

The *Herald* Assistance Unit

In the UK, the *Herald of Free Enterprise* disaster provided much instructive experience. Following the disaster, the Herald Assistance Unit was set up by Kent Social Services. This service provided, over a 15-month period, a 24-hour telephone help line, a newsletter, proactive outreach visits to the passenger survivors and bereaved, and longer term counselling and group work for the crew survivors and bereaved in Dover. Further therapeutic services were also provided by the local mental health services in Dover. The Departments of Psychology and Psychiatry at the Institute of Psychiatry in London were extensively involved in the assessment of survivors and bereaved for the purposes of compensation and became involved in the treatment of some survivors (Yule & Williams, 1990).

Those affected themselves set up the Herald Families Association as both a pressure group and a support network, and across the UK many volunteers and helping professionals became involved with individual families. Some 30 children under the age of 16 years were on board the *Herald of Free Enterprise*. A few months later, most of the children and their families were also referred to the Psychology Department at the Institute of Psychiatry for assessment for legal purposes and for whatever help could be offered.

It is obviously important that survivors and bereaved are put in touch with outreach programmes and self-help groups. It is inevitable, however, that not all survivors will turn to professional services for help. Blake et al. (1990b) found that one-third of the combat veterans in their study reporting PTSD symptoms did not seek psychiatric help. Some populations, then, may be characterised by hiding the levels of distress although other factors may operate such as the availability of community or religious services and the perceived helpfulness of mental health professionals. In particular, work with women following sexual assault has demonstrated that the majority of survivors do not seek services from mental health professionals, rape crisis centres, or victim assistance programmes (Burnam et al., 1988; Kilpatrick, Saunders, Veronen, Best, & Von, 1987; Kimerling & Calhoun, 1994). Other populations, however, may be more willing to seek help. For example, North, Smith, and Spitznagel (1994) reported that 71% of survivors diagnosed with PTSD following a mass shooting had sought help from a doctor or counsellor, although this still leaves a substantial minority who had not sought help. Although services will not be needed by all survivors, it is important that a support team should make an initial proactive contact in which they assess risk factors and potential needs, and refer on to other services for more specialised therapies where appropriate.

Proactive Contact

Since one of the main features of PTSD is avoidance of trauma-related information, many of the severely affected may not present themselves to the services for help. In most cases, survivors will be people unaccustomed to seeking help for psychological problems, and may believe that they should be able to cope without outside help. For this reason it is recommended that an initial contact is made to all those who have been affected in order to offer the opportunity to talk through their experiences with a member of the support team. This initial contact provides an occasion for a debriefing in which the counsellor provides normalising information about how people react to disaster and gives a further point of contact if later help is required.

Following the Australian bush fires, mental health workers developed a leaflet describing common reactions to major personal crises and indicating when and where to seek further help. The leaflet was adapted and distributed after the Bradford fire, the capsize of the *Herald of Free Enterprise*, the Kings Cross fire, and other recent major disasters (Hodgkinson & Stewart, 1991). This leaflet, now entitled 'Coping with a Personal Crisis', is distributed by the British Red Cross. In the 30-month follow-up of survivors of the *Herald of Free Enterprise* disaster (Yule, Hodgkinson, Joseph, Parkes, & Williams, 1990a) we found that, to the majority, the response team's visit and leaflet were helpful. However, we also found that a small minority recalled that they had been upset by these contacts and judged them to be harmful rather than helpful. What sort of help should be provided?

KEY AREAS IN PSYCHOSOCIAL CARE

Much has been written on psychosocial care. The following discussion will highlight what have been recognised as key areas: the prevention of long-term disorder; the identification of vulnerable individuals; and the provision of specialised services for individuals with more severe and chronic problems (Williams, Joseph, & Yule, 1993). It must be stressed, however, that although there is a considerable amount of expertise developing and many theoretical notions about how to achieve these aims, the concrete evidence about the effectiveness of services, particularly for civilian disasters, is still very sparse. In our model of psychosocial adaptation we have emphasised the temporal sequence of reactions and the recognition that the phenomenology of post-traumatic stress reactions alters over time. This has guided our thinking about what psychological provision should be provided.

Immediate Impact Phase

The immediate necessity for the rescue of survivors may obscure the practical needs of individuals who may have lost all their possessions and lost contact with companions and be ignorant of the exact nature of what happened, including loss of lives. Thus, in this phase, assigned volunteer helpers could be useful in providing information, solving practical problems, and in making contact between those separated in the disaster. Brom and Kleber (1989), in describing a programme of preventative work, point out that the importance of practical help in the early stages is often underestimated. Individuals who are in shock may need quiet to rest and protection from the most intrusive agents of the media. When ready, survivors may benefit from talking through their experiences either individually or in groups and giving expression to the strong feelings that these generate. There is some evidence that talking through at a relatively early stage can protect individuals from a more severe reaction later, although such an intervention needs to be held off until the immediate phase of shock has passed (Hodgkinson & Stewart, 1991).

To minimise the agonising uncertainty that relatives and friends may experience as to the fate of their loved ones who are caught up in the disaster, adequate telephone lines for information and support need to be established and be well publicised. The needs of relatives and friends at this time emphasise the central importance of accurate, up-to-date information being available as the details of what happened and to whom become clearer over time. Staff answering information and help lines should be trained to expect to deal with high levels of anxiety and anger in stressed callers.

Space should be assigned, with relevant services, for relatives who wish to visit the site of the disaster. Helpers assigned to individual families can give support, information, and help to solve the practical problems the family may have. In the case of death, a family member will be required by the police to provide identification. Distressed and worried relatives may be further distressed when asked to give the name of the missing person's dentist so that dental records may be compared. Assigned workers should be available to explain procedures such as this, conveying information about the condition of bodies or the likelihood and time of recovery.

Viewing Human Remains

Bereaved individuals may wish to view the body. It has been suggested that this can be helpful in the process of accepting the reality of a sudden, unexpected death, and in finding out how the person died, even if the body is disfigured or if deterioration has occurred (Cathcart, 1988; Hodgkinson & Stewart, 1991). Singh and Raphael (1981) report that following the Granville train disaster, 36 of 44 bereaved had not seen the body, and of these 22 regretted not viewing. Those who had viewed had lower scores on the GHQ at 15-18 months. However, it may be that in some cases where the body is not recovered for some time and begins to decompose, viewing is harmful rather than helpful.

In a study of those bereaved following the *Herald of Free Enterprise* (Hodgkinson, Joseph, Yule, & Williams, 1993), 22 reported that the body was recovered on the night of the disaster, 13 reported that the body was recovered in the following weeks, and 43 reported that the body was recovered when the ship was righted one month later. Each individual was asked if he or she had viewed the body. Of the 22 respondents answering questions concerning bodies recovered on the first night, 10 viewed and 12 did not: only 1 person who viewed said that they regretted it whereas 5 people who did not view regretted this choice. Of the 13 respondents answering questions concerning bodies recovered in the weeks following the disaster, 5 viewed and 8 did not: 3 people

Table 7.1   Viewing human remains following disaster

	Viewed		Did not view	
	Mean	SD	Mean	SD
Body recovered				
on the night:				
IES intrusion	19.90	8.35	28.67	6.85*
IES avoidance	16.50	10.35	26.59	9.10*
GHQ-28	10.10	7.31	12.83	8.65
Body recovered in				
the weeks following disaster:				
IES intrusion	28.00	4.69	21.50	10.21
IES avoidance	15.40	14.26	17.50	11.55
GHQ-28	19.80	5.63	8.38	7.44*
Body recovered when				
the ship was righted:				
IES intrusion	15.00	11.31	23.81	8.27*
IES avoidance	12.00	11.36	20.62	10.40*
GHQ-28	8.60	5.13	12.14	8.71

* Indicates a significant difference between mean scores. Adapted from Hodgkinson, Joseph, Yule, & Williams (1993).

who viewed regretted doing so whereas only 1 person who did not view regretted this choice. Of the 43 respondents answering questions concerning bodies recovered when the ship was righted, 5 viewed and 37 did not: none of those who viewed regretted doing so whereas 19 people who did not view regretted this choice.

These data were part of the survey carried out 30 months after the disaster at which time survivors also completed the GHQ-28 and the IES (see Chapter 3). Those who viewed relatives' bodies where recovery was made on the first night or on the righting of the ship, reported lower scores on intrusive and avoidant symptoms than those who did not view (see Table 7.1). No differences were found between these groups on the GHQ-28. Although these results would seem to support the benefits of viewing, it may be that those who requested to view had less severe symptoms in the first place or differed in some other uncontrolled way.

In contrast, where body recovery was many weeks following disaster, there were no significant differences on the IES between those who viewed their relatives' bodies and those who chose not to, but those who had viewed had significantly higher GHQ-28 scores. Although these results may be due to the small numbers in this sample and factors specific to these families, it may be that the results are due to the state of the bodies themselves having been washed up on the shore.

Hodgkinson et al. (1993) conclude that although no one should be encouraged to view, what must be ensured is that those who wish to do so are not prevented. Even if the person does not wish to view, it will often be the case that recovered bodies are photographed as part of the procedure for the coroner's report and assigned helpers should explain to relatives that they have the right of access to all documents and should, therefore, have access to photographs at a later stage if they so wish.

On this point, relatives are often unclear of the purposes of an inquest and will probably be unfamiliar with the procedures of a coroner's court. The hearing may actually take place several months after the disaster, and this is often the first time the relatives have an opportunity of finding out exactly how their loved one died. At present it is probably true to say that following most of the recent mass civilian disasters in the UK, the needs of relatives have not been well considered, often provoking further distress in the families.

We have so far placed much emphasis on effective communication systems being set up to benefit survivors and their families. This requires further discussion. By their nature, disasters are often unexpected and the immediate impact phase is one of chaos. The specific details necessary in setting up an effective information network cannot always be planned in advance; however, much can be planned and should be. To avoid endlessly overlapping questioning by staff from different agencies and the loss of vital information, standard forms should be drawn up beforehand which can then be adapted, if necessary, to collect information. Accordingly, thought needs to be given to the storage of the information in an accessible and central system. Arguments on the access to this database and considerations on how best to protect survivors' confidentiality should also be discussed and sorted out at the planning stage. Likewise, thought should be given to the ways of accessing the database for later research and evaluation.

CRISIS INTERVENTION

Crisis intervention has received much attention by clinicians in recent years. It is thought that early intervention facilitates emotional processing, although data are sparse on this. It has been noted that post-traumatic stress responses, once they have become chronic, can be extremely difficult to treat (Watson, 1987). Several writers have commented on this and recommended early crisis intervention. Stein (1977), for example, outlines a model of crisis intervention counselling which includes on-the-scene support with follow-up within two days. Similarly, Mitchell (1983) states that interventions within the first 72 hours are effective in reducing the long-term effects of events in emergency workers and Solomon (1986) recommends confidential debriefing within three days and preferably within 24 hours. The function of early crisis intervention is to support and facilitate emotional release in a safe supportive environment (Raphael, 1986) and has been used extensively with victims of rape (Burgess & Holmstrom, 1974a) and armed robbery (Manton & Talbot, 1991).

Manton and Talbot (1991) outline a system they developed to assist victims of armed hold-ups. First, they describe the process of making initial observations. Following the hold-up, the counsellor aims to arrive at the scene within an hour, during which a sense of the atmosphere is obtained.

> There may be people who appear to be working normally, small groups chatting or comforting each other, individuals who are isolated and in shock, and there may be one or more who is visibly and audibly overwrought. Sometimes there is a complete eerie silence and stillness and at other times there is high-pitched out-of-control laughter or someone crying quietly. You can smell the fear. (Manton & Talbot, 1991, p. 511)

Those identified as being highly overwrought are attended to first and contact established with those locked into their own internal processes. The aim is to see all staff members before they leave for home and provide an initial debriefing.

Debriefing

Manton and Talbot (1991) see the purpose of debriefing as one of providing comfort, defusing the frightening situation, allowing expression of anxieties, and normalising reactions. They describe their approach as 'empathic listening, with awareness that people may experience many different emotions, all of which are valid . . .'. The debriefing session, they believe, '. . . is almost certainly the most important preventative measure and an opportunity for rapport building which will be essential later on' (Manton & Talbot, 1991, p. 512).

> With each individual we start by observing their behaviour—observing whether they want to talk to us or not and keeping that in mind while talking to them. Then asking 'How are you?' and if that brings no response we might say 'Would you be willing to tell me what happened?' which can lead to fairly basic level empathy and deepening if necessary or as appropriate. If they are not willing to talk we can then start to give them information. For example, 'I have been to a lot of hold-ups and talked to a lot of people. It seems that reactions vary, sometimes people feel this and sometimes people feel that and some people find it very hard to talk. Later though you may want to.' Sometimes victims do not fully realise what has hit them until they get home and then there may be no one to talk to. The focus of the discussion is to make it clear to them that we are there to listen. We want to hear how it feels for them. Part of the debriefing session is reassurance, caring for the person, making the event smaller and cutting it down to size without minimising their reaction: accepting, supporting and understanding, and permission giving. (Manton & Talbot, 1991, p. 512).

At this stage, Manton and Talbot (1991) note there may be feelings of guilt over letting others down which can become projected as anger directed at the organisation. However, they argue that although at this stage it is useful to empathise with these feelings it may not be appropriate to help the victim to change the projection. 'Victims need to be able to express and vent their feelings. It is a normal response, albeit inappropriately placed' (Manton & Talbot, 1991; p. 512).

Manton and Talbot (1991) note that following armed hold-ups there are issues about returning to work and taking medication that victims need to be aware of. Issues of information giving will be central to the debriefing of survivors of all traumatic events. However, they raise the issue of how this information is presented and argue that it should be done permissively and not as advice. The intervention continues the next day and is seen as a continuation of the previous day. Everyone is seen individually if required or perhaps in small groups, depending on various factors such as the size and cohesiveness of the existing group. Here, Manton and Talbot (1991) note that there are a variety of reactions which may be observed, some of which are coloured by the individuals' previous history or their current life situation. They argue that follow-up is essential in order to identify those at risk of further problems.

Hayman and Scaturo (1993) outline a protocol for debriefing military personnel, although there are clear applications of their protocol to other populations as well. The first general guideline from their procedure is that debriefing should begin as soon as possible so as to help defuse the intensity of reactions and prevent negative coping behaviours from becoming habitual. This last point is particularly important as it is crucial for survivors to be able to make effective use of their social support networks. Second, it is recommended that standardised screening instruments are employed so as to facilitate referral for treatment. Third, they maintain that, throughout the debriefing process, it is essential to reinforce the expectation of returning to pre-combat levels of psychosocial functioning. Fourth, they recommend the use of group sessions for married couples, which might include exploration of the impact of separation and relationship skills enhancement. They also emphasise that the debriefing should proceed at a speed comfortable for the participants. The protocol involves 12 sessions, beginning with a clarification of the purposes of debriefing and the nature of emotional reactions through to the exploration of the personal impact of combat and homecoming, through to learning about managing moods and resolving current life stressors, and finally, facilitating the impact of the group termination (Hayman and Scaturo, 1993).

However, despite the widespread use of debriefing there remains relatively little evidence for its efficacy. One study examined 137 consecutive admissions to a burns unit. Patients completed a battery of standardised self-report measures on admission and were randomly allocated to either a psychological debriefing group or a control group which received no intervention. Three months later most of the 137 were interviewed in their homes where they again completed several self-report measures. It was found that debriefing did not prevent psychological sequelae but it was perceived to be useful by most of those who received it. Furthermore, those who received debriefing were more likely to continue with the research, a finding which the authors suggest points to the important role of debriefing in helping to engage patients in a more comprehensive treatment package (Bisson, Jenkins, & Bannister, in press).

Debriefing involves some kind of exposure to the trauma-related stimuli. According to Fairbank and Nicholson (1987) and van der Kolk, Boyd, Krystal, and Greenberg (1984b), exposure to stimuli related to the trauma is an essential part of treatment. But unlike other treatment intervention strategies which may form part of longer-term support services, i.e., systematic desensitisation and implosive therapy, and which are also based on the principle of exposure, debriefing is concerned with prevention rather than the amelioration of symptoms.

Long-term Support Services

Building on the experiences of services after the Bradford football stadium fire, Kent Social Services quickly set up a longer term response and support team for survivors and relatives from the *Herald of Free Enterprise* disaster. It has now been recommended (Department of Health, 1990) that such a support service should be set up and financed for at least two years following a disaster. As discussed earlier, there is evidence that many survivors remain highly symptomatic even after this time. Indeed, distressed people may still present to services for the first time years after the disaster. Although services will not be needed by all survivors, it is important that a support team should make an initial proactive contact in which they assess risk factors and potential needs, and refer on to other services for more specialised therapies where appropriate.

TREATMENT STRATEGIES

For the mental health professional involved in diagnosis, it becomes necessary to enquire about a range of the clients' emotions and behaviours in order to make a complete assessment. Often the length of time required to capture the full picture is not available, or the client may be reluctant to undergo such a lengthy procedure involving many personal questions. It is necessary, therefore, for mental health professionals to be aware of the range of possible difficulties and the various measurement instruments available. Once the clinician has clearly identified what the focus of treatment is to be, he or she will be in a better position to select the most efficacious method of treatment.

Since the inclusion of PTSD in the diagnostic literature, there have been numerous descriptive summaries of various treatment approaches to PTSD. However, there remains relatively little empirical information concerning the effectiveness of psychological interventions. In addition, much of the work has been with Vietnam veterans and findings may not always generalise to survivors of civilian trauma. However, the work reviewed in Chapter 6 offers evidence that although exposure to a traumatic event is the necessary aetiological factor in the development of PTSD, other psychosocial variables are involved in the development of post-traumatic stress reactions.

Emotional processing in survivors of traumatic events is thought to be a normal adaptation process although processing can be excessively prolonged or even blocked. This process is determined by identifiable factors. Although, it is acknowledged that the role of other variables may be small, particularly following extremely traumatic events, what is important is the fact that they are modifiable. Thus, there is scope for the treatment of distressed individuals. Our model suggests a conceptual framework for planning therapeutic interventions with survivors with post-traumatic stress reactions.

The model contains different components of the adaptation process where it may be possible to intervene:

- promoting re-exposure to the event and to stimuli associated with the event for reappraisal;
- promoting reappraisal of the traumatic experience and its meanings and in promoting reappraisal of the emotional states to which appraisals give rise;
- promoting the direct reduction of emotional arousal;
- promoting helpful coping strategies to deal with emotional arousal; and
- promoting the reviewing of previously held cognitive styles and rules for living, some of which may be maintaining symptoms through blocking re-exposure, others of which may determine primary traumatic appraisal.

The choice of strategy can be determined by the therapist's formulation of the role played by each factor in an individual case. In some cases, stimulus factors may predominate and the individual's needs may best be met by the use of direct exposure techniques (DETs) (Richards & Rose, 1991) which help the survivor to confront the traumatic event. However, given our formulation of stress reactions in terms of blocked processing, the task for the clinician may be the identification of the block to permit natural processes (completion tendency) to continue rather than the indiscriminate treatment of each and every client within an exposure framework.

The importance of such flexibility within an overall conceptualisation echoes the conclusions of McFarlane (1994) who points to the impact of allegiance to therapeutic models in the evaluation of their efficacy and the degree of partiality which is prominent in psychotherapy. Space precludes an exhaustive discussion of treatment options. Our choice is determined by methods that have most empirical support.

DIRECT EXPOSURE THERAPIES

DET techniques have received the most attention by researchers and can be grouped according to the medium of exposure (imaginal vs in vivo), the length of exposure (short vs long), and the amount of arousal induced by the exposure (low vs high) (Rothbaum & Foa, 1992).

Systematic Desensitisation

When the length of exposure is short and the amount of arousal is low it is termed systematic desensitisation. Both forms of systematic desensitisation were based on the conditioning of incompatible relaxation responses with traumatic stimuli (although this explanation of treatment effects has since been challenged). The client is taught a formal relaxation technique and later employs this technique while a graduated series of increasingly anxiety-provoking imaginal or in vivo cues are presented. By remaining relaxed as successive cues are presented, the client learns to associate the cues with feelings of relaxation rather than anxiety (Lyons & Keane, 1989). Systematic desensitisation has been used with combat veterans with some success (e.g., Bowen & Lambert, 1986). Lyons and Keane (1989), however, note that in certain cases desensitisation may not be feasible:

> Memories of combat may be so potent that they override both the therapist's attempts to present very gradual exposure and the patient's capacity to remain relaxed. For such cases, implosive therapy may be the treatment of choice. (Lyons & Keane, 1989, p. 138).

Implosive Therapy

In contrast to systematic desensitisation, which is based on classical conditioning theory, implosive therapy is based on an operant extinction model (Stampfl & Levis, 1967). Implosive therapy involves prolonged exposure to a stimulus during which time high levels of arousal are induced. In practice, clinicians often employ a graded prolonged exposure procedure in which cues are presented in increasing order of threat. The client is exposed to trauma-related cues until there is a reduction in anxiety associated with the cues (Lyons & Keane, 1989). Implosive therapy has been used with some success with adults (e.g., Black & Keane, 1982; Fairbank, Gross, & Keane, 1983a; Fairbank & Keane, 1982; Keane & Kaloupek, 1982), and with children (Saigh, 1987). For example, in the Keane and Kaloupek (1982) study, a 36-year-old Vietnam veteran was treated for the anxiety-related symptoms of PTSD. Therapy consisted of 19 sessions over a 22-day inpatient hospitalisation. The purpose of their study was to test the efficacy of treating a combat-related disorder by imaginally presenting the aversive events surrounding the patient's trauma.

The patient frequently experienced nightmares and flashbacks of three events from Vietnam. For example, one recurrent scene was the death of a buddy in an ambush attack. Measures included daily anxiety ratings, hours of sleep, frequency of nightmares and flashbacks. Following a three-day baseline period, treatment consisted of the presentation of a scene preceded by 10 minutes of relaxation. There was a reduction in anxiety as well as an overall improvement which was maintained over a 12-month period. Keane and Kaloupek (1982) concluded that, for some patients at least, imaginal flooding was an effective treatment.

Gersons (1989) gives case illustrations of treatment with two police officers who had been involved in a shooting incident. Treatment consisted of, first, recalling to mind every detail of the traumatic event. Gersons notes that the use of newspaper articles and photographs are helpful at this stage. Relaxation and closing one's eyes is beneficial in inducing a trance-like state in which experiences can be vividly recalled. The stimulation of re-experiencing the event helps release hidden emotions which, Gersons notes, is often a totally new experience for 'very walled-off' officers. Five to ten sessions, Gersons reports, can be enough to work through all the affects associated with the event, and the PTSD symptoms steadily disappear, although follow-up therapy may be necessary in certain cases. Other uncontrolled single case studies for a variety of types of traumatic event are reported by Richards and Rose (1991) who emphasise the importance of self-exposure in homework assignments, incorporating the use of tape-recorded imaginal exposure sessions and in-vivo exposure exercises to promote extinction. Richards, Lovell, and Marks (1994) have also studied the relative merits of imaginal and in-vivo exposure, finding that in-vivo exposure to trauma-related stimuli was of advantage only for the amelioration of phobic anxiety, in some cases. The authors report improvement in focal PTSD symptoms, measures of general psychiatric well-being and in work and social adjustment. However, self-reported depression before treatment was low in this group. Treatment gains reported were highly significant (65–80% reduction) and were maintained over one year's follow-up.

Implosive therapy has also been used in the treatment of an adult victim of sexual abuse (Rychtarik, Silverman, & Van Landingham, 1984).

A cautionary note is sounded by Pitman et al. (1991). These authors report six illustrative case vignettes where unforeseen complications have arisen during prolonged exposure. They suggest that concurrent problems such as depression and alcohol abuse may lead to emotional problems such as panic and guilt which do not extinguish with exposure, pointing to the importance of other therapeutic methods being needed. It is sometimes unclear to what extent therapists are using a more complex therapeutic regime from their descriptions. Thompson, Charlton, Kerry, Lee, and Turner (1995), for example, describe their open trial under the rubric of 'deconditioning' although explicitly employing cognitive as well as behavioural exposure methods.

The use of these exposure techniques is illustrated in the case of David,

CASE HISTORY 10

(An adult case involving exposure therapy)

David is a 29-year-old lecturer in design and technology who also runs a successful computer graphics consultancy. He had a good relationship with his long-standing partner and they enjoyed a very comfortable lifestyle until this was shattered in a boating accident. They were celebrating with friends on a river boat when, late at night, the boat was sunk in collision with a barge. David and his partner were among those who survived.

At first, he felt lucky to be alive, but then he was haunted with guilt that he had not done enough to help his partner, nor managed to save any of his friends who had drowned. He found it very difficult to sleep and was constantly fending off intrusive images of what had happened to him when he was under the water. On one occasion, he was travelling home on a night bus. As the bus crossed a bridge over a river, he saw lights reflecting off the surface of the water and immediately he had a terrifying flashback in which he believed that he was back on the boat as it went under. It took him many hours to calm down and get back in touch with reality.

He found great difficulty concentrating at work and his consultancy business foundered. He began smoking and drinking a great deal, to the point that he was making himself ill. He went to a counsellor for a couple of sessions but did not engage. He was referred for treatment over a year after the accident.

After taking a full and careful history, including a detailed account of his experiences during the accident, David was offered exposure therapy along the lines described by Richards and Rose (1991). It was explained to him that by avoiding dealing with his emotional reactions, the memories remained and interfered with his recovery. While confronting the memories in detail would probably be painful, he should experience a lowering of tension and anxiety and a greater ability to control his reactions. It was emphasised that the treatment would not rid him of the memories as they were now an important part of him. Rather, he would be able to control his reactions to them.

In the first session, he was seated comfortably and the tape recorder was switched on. He was then asked to describe in detail, in the first person present tense, as if it was happening currently, precisely what happened in the accident. He was asked to say what he was seeing, hearing, feeling, tasting, smelling, and so on, as well as what he was thinking and the emotional reactions he was having. What then happened was remarkable. David began in a steady voice describing how they had gone on board the boat and settled to have a drink in the bar as the boat pulled out into the river. They were laughing, joking, and relaxing when suddenly they felt a great bump and heard the noise of the two vessels tearing against each other. Immediately, everything went dark as the lights went out and all he could see was the reflections of lights from the shore on the water pouring in through the smashed windows. As he described all this, so his demeanour changed. His descriptions were graphic, but so was his body language. As he recalled pulling himself through a smashed window, he writhed in his chair; as he recalled hitting the bottom of the river and then surfacing to see people carried away on the current, he began to shiver with cold and almost shake off the water. He rated his anxiety as near maximum while recounting this.

At the end of more than an hour, he was given the recording of the session to take home and asked to listen to it daily. He managed to do so about four times in the week before the second session. Then, he was able to expose himself in imagination to the whole episode, but reporting a much lower level of anxiety. The therapist watched his reactions intently and any time that it appeared that David was blocking on a part of the experience or was otherwise skipping over it, he would ask David to go back to that section and conjure up the image in greater detail. In this way, all the worst memories were confronted and after eight sessions David's levels of distress were lowered to within normal, acceptable levels.

someone who survived a very unpleasant boating disaster. It illustrates how lengthy exposure sessions can initially induce strong, unpleasant emotions which then habituate with repeated exposure (Case History 10).

Children

Although the adult literature is increasingly full of examples of the successful application of behaviour therapy to reduce intrusive thoughts, startle reaction, and phobic and avoidance behaviour, there is little information available on children. One study is, however, reported by Saigh (1986) of the in-vitro flooding treatment of PTSD exhibited by a $6\frac{1}{2}$-year-old Lebanese boy who had been traumatised by a bomb blast. Two years after the event, he suffered nightmares, intrusive thoughts and avoided areas associated with the bombing. Four scenes were successfully worked on in therapy and rapid improvement was obtained in 10 sessions, and improvement was maintained over six months. Saigh (1986) notes that earlier attempts to treat other children with systematic desensitisation failed, and in this case, each session began with 15 minutes of relaxation followed by 24 minutes of flooding. This extended exposure to the fear-inducing stimuli fits in well with Rachman's (1980) views on factors that accelerate successful emotional processing.

It is trickier using exposure therapy with children and adolescents because of the need to ensure that one has informed consent for any treatment and especially for ones which are, in part, unpleasant initially. The rationale is described more fully elsewhere (Saigh, Yule, & Inamdar, 1996). As with interventions with adults, there are a number of successful case studies with children being published but, as yet, no systematic, randomised controlled trials. Work with groups of children has been described and there is some evidence that group approaches to debriefing children after accidents and disasters can be successful.

COGNITIVE-BEHAVIOURAL THERAPIES

The difficulties some clients have in dealing with exposure has led to the suggestion that anxiety management techniques (AMT) (Fairbank & Nicholson, 1987) might be used to help the survivors improve their management of high anxiety and other symptoms. Lyons and Keane (1989) conclude that implosive therapy must be embedded in a strong and supportive therapeutic relationship, and that it appears to be most effective when used in conjunction with skill-building techniques aimed at developing coping skills. Kilpatrick and Veronen (1983) have described a 4–6-hour treatment package for survivors of rape. The package includes behavioural procedures with elements of rape crisis counselling which attempt to promote realistic beliefs and adaptive coping skills.

Meichenbaum (1993) presents detailed instructions for carrying out Stress Innoculation Training (SIT), a therapy consisting of 8–14 sessions in individual and group formats. The therapy protocol has three phases: (1) an educational stage in which the client is introduced to the nature of dysfunctional emotions and their origins; (2) a skills acquisition stage in which coping strategies are introduced in relation to the tripartite model of emotions (physiological, behavioural, and cognitive-emotional); (3) a stage in which the client is helped to apply the training via imagery rehearsal, role-playing, and graded in-vivo exposure.

Cognitive Therapy

Cognitive-behavioural theorists propose that emotional disorders, including anxiety and depression, stem from dysfunctional interpretations of environmental events. Therapy aimed at challenging these interpretations should therefore lead to a change in emotional state. There is a considerable body of outcome research which suggests that cognitive therapy (CT) is effective in comparisons with control therapies for depression (see Hollon, Shelton, & Davis, 1993, for a review) and anxiety disorders (see Chambless & Gillis, 1993, for a review). The high level of success recently reported for the treatment of panic disorder by Clark (1986, 1991) should have clear implications for the treatment of PTSD in view of the overlap in symptomatology. Although there has been little application of CT to PTSD to date, the theoretical approach of CT with its emphasis upon psychoeducation and the acquisition of skills lends itself well to a condition which, as we have seen, may have manifold components with global impact upon the individual's functioning. CT's emphasis is upon the challenging of appraisals and the identification of dysfunctional attitudes that may block processing. (See Treatment 1.)

The identification of psychological vulnerability factors has much implication for therapeutic intervention. For example, causal attributions for trauma-related experience may be connected to emotional states and, as we have outlined earlier in Chapter 6, may be one of the possible mechanisms that may operate to impede or promote emotional processing. If this is true, then there are implications for therapeutic intervention based on attributional style therapy (Layden, 1982). The direction of attributional change will, however, depend on individual circumstances insofar as realistic causal attributions may involve a shift in the direction of greater or less personal controllability (Fösterling, 1985). (See Treatment 2.)

An important methodological issue in the cognitive-behavioural therapies (CBTs) is the degree to which it is necessary to intervene in modifying cognitions to achieve therapeutic ends. Exposure practitioners would assert that cognitions change spontaneously as Horowitz's theory of a 'completion tendency' would perhaps also propose. An interesting variant of CBT called 'Imagery Rescripting' has been described by Smucker, Dancu, Foa, and

TREATMENT 1

(See Case History 1, p. 2)

Pauline had spent some sessions with a CPN prior to referral in which she had talked about the trauma and reported feeling less distressed now when talking about it. This was evidenced by the first interview and Pauline's relatively low avoidance score on the IES, although the score for intrusive experiences was still high. It was therefore decided to start treatment within a cognitive model and to direct intervention at cognitions and symptoms that seemed to reflect event appraisals. Pauline was introduced to the cognitive model on the first sessions and the link was made between her expectation of future catastrophe and her situational anxiety, her depression and pessimism about the future. Pauline began making written records of her 'automatic thoughts' associated with negative emotions, day to day. We became aware of worries that she would have a panic attack in social situations and, when travelling, with thoughts such as 'what will people think?' and 'I'm out of control'. These self-observations led to cognitive intervention addressing panic. At one stage Pauline and her therapist ran together up three flights of stairs to create autonomic arousal. They then sat quietly together and noticed Pauline's relative difficulty in dealing with this physical activation leading to her relative slowness at calming down. An exposure hierarchy was drawn up, including physical activity such as running, medical situations and social situations especially giving a presentation at work, the latter being a problem prior to the trauma. Pauline was also trained in slowed breathing to cope with panic and to use this skill in anxiety-provoking situations. An exploration of Pauline's anger with other people and her alienation from them led to a full examination of her veiws about friendship and the discovery of black and white thinking in this area (viz., if you do not support me all the time you have let me down). A lengthy and important examination of 'What's going to happen next?' led to a changed view of the predominance of adverse events, taking her life as a whole although the fear remained at a lower level of intensity. Discussion of ending sessions after about six months led to a recurrence of worries about future adversity and inability to cope alone. At termination, Pauline was revealing frequent and horrifying images of hospitalisation, being helpless, unable to communicate, staff ignoring her, and of her being unable to cope, screaming and resisting. Some attempts to use both exposure and restructuring of imagery were made but these were relatively unsuccessful. Pauline was not prepared to overcome avoidance of medical situations at present and therapy was terminated. Pauline was considerably less depressed and anxious at termination. There remained some problems, especially with fears of hospitalisation, which maintained her fear of repetition but it was hoped that Pauline had the tools to deal with these if and when she wanted to.

Niederee (1995) which aims to achieve change in deep schemas for PTSD adult survivors of sexual abuse. The procedure combines some initial prolonged exposure with the addition of a modification procedure in which the abusive imagery is altered to introduce mastery and complete the memory with a more positive ending. Throughout the imagery rescripting, dysfunctional schemas underlying abuse cognitions are identified and challenged, the therapist going in and out of the image to work on cognitions or go back to the image. Smucker is clear to point out, however, that modifications to the script follow the client's own wishes and are not directed by the therapist who plays a facilitative role, asking questions to prompt the new imagery. The 10 sessions,

TREATMENT 2

Roy is a 35-year-old single man, currently unemployed and cohabiting with a partner. Roy had suffered a depressive reaction when a successful career in business had ended in bankruptcy in the economic recession. Both Roy and his twin sister had suffered severe psychological difficulties at this time and, associated with severe symptoms, he began to remember incidences of repeated sexual, physical, and emotional abuse in childhood. These memories which were intrusive and highly disturbing were corroborated by two out of his three siblings.

Roy came into therapy wanting to address these traumatic experiences in the past which he felt were holding him back from full recovery and affecting his confidence and his relationships. After some initial sessions in which he was introduced to the cognitive model and the role of avoidance in maintaining beliefs and symptoms and problems, one perceived major block was discovered, namely his attitude to expressed emotion. Roy thought emotions were bad and tended to present himself to others, including his therapist, in a cheerful, confident manner while feeling depressed and anxious inside. He failed to confide in others who had commented that they did not really know him. This 'avoidance' had the result of maintaining his fear that he was unlovable and that others would reject him if they got to know him intimately. In order to deal with these fears, therefore, therapy proceeded to embark on an exploration of his childhood experiences as perceived and remembered as a way of unlocking the emotions and allowing processing to occur. Roy was able progressively to give way to feelings in sessions and to explore the associated cognitions. Prominantly emerged a need for explanation: Why did the abuse happen? The answers that he gave to this question were that his father did not love him and that he was unlovable and that his father was a monster. Since he also loved his father he was unable to hold on to the external attribution. He was enraged by his father's continuing denial of his behaviour which he linked in his mind to being loved and being unlovable: if his father loved him he would admit to his offences. An important discussion of the functions of denial led to a lessening of his hopeless need for validation and to a more complex understanding of human motivation and therefore to the implications he can read into the behaviour about himself.

---

each lasting 90 minutes, also involve the practice of self-comforting or 'nurturing' imagery. Initial outcome results in comparison with SIT are yielding comparable effects (Smucker et al., 1995).

Comparative Outcome Studies

Studies comparing the effects of different therapies are few in the literature. Brom, Kleber, and Defares (1989) compared the effects of brief psychodynamic therapy, hypnotherapy and desensitisation and a waiting-for-therapy-control condition in a group of 112 adults, mainly female and suffering from traumatic bereavements. All treatments were effective in comparison with waiting. At three months' follow-up, psychotherapy had more impact upon avoidant symptoms, desensitisation upon intrusion.

Boudewyns and Hyer (1990) compared implosive therapy and counselling for Vietnam veterans. Both treatments were equally effective at the end of treatment but implosive therapy produced a stronger effect upon overall adjustment at three months' follow-up. Foa, Rothbaum, Riggs, and Murdock (1991) compared implosive therapy, SIT, counselling and waiting-for-therapy in rape survivors. They found that at the end of therapy, SIT was superior in reducing symptoms but at three months' follow-up, the implosion group was superior to both SIT and counselling on all measures. Much more work needs to be done on establishing the relative merits of different interventions for different types of trauma, different combinations of problem, and for different durations after the event.

Eye-movement Desensitisation and Reprocessing Therapy

Shapiro (1995) describes the serendipitous discovery and development of eye-movement desensitisation and reprocessing therapy (EMDR), which is widely practised as a rapid treatment for the symptoms of PTSD (see Box 7.1). Shapiro herself had been troubled by intrusive thoughts until one day, out jogging, she noticed they began to diminish. She linked this to rapid movements of her eyes. She then tried to conjure up the disturbing thoughts and found that they were not so disturbing. She asked colleagues to try pairing eye movements with thinking disturbing thoughts and they too found that the strength of the images waned. She then tried out this technique carefully with clients who had PTSD. The early case studies she reported showed people with distressing intrusive thoughts and images getting symptomatic relief in as little as a single one-hour session. Later, she found that other, non-specific, factors in therapy had to be given greater emphasis and so EMDR was born.

In the session, clients are asked to conjure up their distressing scene and then to follow the therapist's finger with their eyes. The therapist moves the finger across the field of vision at a rapid rate and after 20 or more passes, asks the clients to rest. The clients ask for feedback about what has happened to the image and at various points the clients are asked to rate subjective distress on a 10-point scale. Clients often report that the image changes, more detail may be recalled and then the image fades while, simultaneously, the distress goes down. The therapist, unlike in more orthodox cognitive and exposure therapies, does not interrogate the clients for details or try to make new connections between the changing images and other aspects of the traumatic event.

There have been many case examples and clinical studies published that claim extraordinarily good results, but there is a lack of larger scale studies involving double blind randomised controls and long-term follow-up (see Smith and Yule, in press, for a review). But this is a familiar story in psychotherapy research. More worrying is that there is no clear model of why this inherently implausible therapy should work at all. Is it that the eye-movement procedure permits the subjects to expose themselves in imagination and that it is exposure and habituation that are the processes whereby the treatment is effective? Or is it that the eye movements do somehow have a facilitating or inhibiting effect within the central nervous system? At present, the jury is out.

Box 7.1   Eye Movement Desensitisation and Reprocessing Therapy (EMDR)

Recently, Eye Movement Desensitisation and Reprocessing Therapy (EMDR) has been introduced as a treatment for intrusive traumatic memories (Shapiro, 1989a, 1989b) and some support for its clinical effectiveness has begun to accumulate (Marquis, 1991; Puk, 1991; Wolpe & Abrams, 1991; Vaughan, Wiese, Gold, & Tarrier, 1994) although other studies have not found it to be effective (Jensen, 1994) and the mechanisms underlying this treatment remain unclear (Dyck, 1993).

The EMDR procedure involves the client creating in his or her mind a visual image of the traumatic event and then isolating a word or phrase which represents a belief about the visual image. For example, 'I am helpless', or 'I have no control' (Shapiro, 1989b, p.204). The client then repeats these phrases while bilateral saccadic eye movements are induced by following the clinician's fingers which are moved rapidly across the visual field. Subsequently, negative belief statements are replaced by alternative positive belief statements such as 'I have control', 'I am worthy' (Shapiro, 1989b, p. 204) while the clinician again induces bilateral saccadic eye movements.

What is emerging is that the eye movements themselves may not be a necessary component of the procedure. Renfrey and Spates (1994) found that eye movement versus fixating a blinking light were equally effective in reducing PTSD.

Clearly, any procedure that seems to reduce suffering quickly and inexpensively even in a minority of cases is worthy of further investigation. If one could identify suitable candidates for EMDR then this would potentially save a great deal of suffering and also save on the scarce resource of experienced therapists.

There are other rapid treatment techniques which make extravagant claims for their efficacy in treating PTSD. Sometimes, they are merely variants on exposure therapy that emphasise one particular facet of the treatment. Other rapid treatments have little or no theoretical rationale and cannot be recommended until proper outcome studies have been undertaken. People with PTSD are often vulnerable to promises of rapid cures and the therapeutic community owes them a duty of care that incorporates a healthy scepticism towards brief, miraculous interventions. (See Treatment 3.)

Group Therapy

Many workers in the field of disaster research are agreed that group debriefing sessions are desirable, and that they reduce later morbidity (Stallard & Law, 1993; Yule & Udwin, 1991). If this is true, the explanation may be that de-briefing sessions expose individuals to information of how others react to the same stimuli. Yule and Williams (1990) note that the child survivors of the *Herald of Free Enterprise* disaster who attended group meetings were clear that merely being together was helpful. However, Yule and Williams (1990) also note that

TREATMENT 3

(Geoff: treated by EMDR)

Geoff, aged 10, was referred for treatment three years after he had been badly frightened in an accident in which the car he was seated in was hit from the side by another car, causing quite a bit of damage but no injury to the occupants. Geoff though he was going to be badly hurt, if not killed. Shortly afterwards, Geoff started to have nightmares and kept waking in the night. There were times when he was scared to sleep. He kept seeing pictures of the other car that hit them. He also developed a very strong fear of death.

When seen, he still had worries about travelling by car. He still saw recurring pictures of what happened and these were upsetting. His nightmares occurred at least once per week. He has occasionally had flashbacks when it felt as if it was all happening all over again. He did not like watching programmes on television that involve car crashes. He felt shaky and scared. He often had to sleep in his parents' bed. He had become much more aware of dangers when he was in a car or walking on a pavement. He tried to stay in the middle of the seat when in the car.

He said that he did not feel miserable or depressed, but was anxious. He worried about death. He got upset by sudden loud noises. Geoff completed some questionnaires and scored as follows:

Scale	July	September
Impact of Events	32	2
Birleson Depression	14	6
Child Anxiety	21	1

There were no concerns about his development prior to the accident. It was followed immediately by the appearance of many symptoms of stress reactions and anxiety. As a direct consequence of the accident, Geoff developed a positive psychiatric disorder, namely a Post-Traumatic Stress Disorder of moderate severity but which ran a chronic course and he still met criteria for the diagnosis three-and-a-half years later.

Geoff agreed to try EMDR. In the first session, after the first set of eye movements while he was visualising the accident, he was experiencing a high level of distress but he also began to recall considerable detail of what had happened three years previously. He could describe the type of clothing worn by workmen who were working at the other side of the place they were parked. He could describe details of what his mother and brother did and said at the time of the accident—details that appeared to have been inaccessible to him when he first described the accident to the therapist. With successive exposures and eye movements, he recalled more detail and his subjective distress subsided. Gains made in the clinic generalised to the home.

Following only two sessions of 'Eye-Movement Desensitisation and Reprocessing', there was a remarkable drop in the level of reported symptoms, as can be seen in the table of scores. His mother confirmed that he was greatly improved and he no longer met criteria for a diagnosis of PTSD.

... In the children's group, they were allowed to express their sadness and fears and so learn that others shared similar reactions. They were encouraged to think of strategies for coping and out of the discussions emerged some practical ways of dealing with their problems. In the adults group, parents were also relieved to learn that some of the uncharacteristic behaviours shown by their own children were also exhibited by others. They were able to discuss how to react to problems presented by their children and, lastly but not least, they were able to face their own reactions to the disaster and share these. (Yule & Williams, 1990, p. 292)

Thus, a situation that provides consensual information seems to be welcomed by survivors. From a more cognitive point of view it may be that group experiences enable people to undergo a shift in their attributional patterns. However, it is also possible that debriefing may, depending on individual circumstances, foster an attributional pattern that would serve to increase a person's emotional distress. The concern must be to help the survivor resolve issues of meaning in a way that is not only satisfactory but is also realistic as to the situation.

Resick and Schnicke (1992) report a controlled evaluation of a variant of CT called Cognitive Processing Therapy carried out in a group format with survivors of rape. The therapy consisted of 12 sessions, each lasting 90 minutes. Following some educational and 'exposure' sessions in which clients wrote and experienced the emotions of the trauma, subsequent sessions dealt with cognitive aspects: self-blame and then issues of safety, trust, power, esteem, and intimacy. Written materials addressing these themes were used. In a comparison with a waiting list group, individuals who experienced the group therapy showed significantly reduced PTSD and other symptoms, and improved social adjustment post-therapy.

Children

Therapeutic intervention for child victims of disaster has often been aimed at alleviating the immediate distress of traumatic experiences with counselling techniques. Some workers have found that adjustment may be facilitated through a more guided cognitive and emotional re-experiencing, restructuring and re-enacting of the disaster under controlled circumstances (Galante & Foa, 1986; Pynoos & Eth, 1986). Going over what happened in this way is likely to result in the child changing his or her causal attributions for particular events. Therefore, attribution style therapy may also be beneficial for children suffering from post-traumatic reactions. A similar argument is presented by Stallard and Law (1993) who carried out a group debriefing with school pupils who had been involved in a minibus accident. They found debriefing was effective in reducing intrusive thoughts.

Changing beliefs

The evidence would suggest that some beliefs are more adaptive than others; for example, those that help to maintain a sense of control and protect self-esteem. However, the clinician is faced with the question of whether it is appropriate to encourage such beliefs when they are unrealistic (Calhoun &

Tedeschi, 1991). While discussing the role of attribution therapy, it is important to note the role of the therapist. Milgram (1986) makes the interesting point that the framework within which therapy takes place is in itself important. He suggests that efficacious treatment of PTSD requires the patient to take responsibility for the progress of his or her own therapy.

It is probably true to say that most therapists actively discourage self-blame. However, in her discussion of reactions to rape, Janoff-Bulman (1979) distinguishes between characterological self-blame (attributions to aspects of the self that cannot be changed), versus behavioural self-blame (attributions to aspects of the self that can be changed). She suggests that behavioural self-blame is related to better recovery because it is associated with a sense of future control and, therefore, therapeutic intervention that discourages all self-blame could actually be harmful. However, evidence would suggest that people do not always seem to make the distinction between characterological and behavioural self-blame (Frazier & Schauben, 1994).

ENCOURAGING ACTIVITY AND SOCIAL SUPPORT

Survivors who are overwhelmed with traumatic recollections may benefit from planning activities and structuring their day. Activity planning can serve various functions: to learn control and mastery of distress which may have useful impact upon self-esteem and depression and provide an alternative to drug-use; to address practical problems that may have been overlooked because of the emotional experience (also impacting upon depression and self-esteem and preventing further cascade of disaster); to establish a 'normal' pattern of exposure and avoidance which is managable; to aid integration with family or other social network; to engender hope that life can go on.

Traumatic events often interfere with the normal functioning of social support networks through the death of others, or through disruptions caused by responses to the event (Solomon, 1986). For example, McFarlane (1987) showed that families who had been exposed to the Australian bush fires were characterised by increased levels of irritability and fighting.

Others have, however, commented that communality can increase in the aftermath of disaster (Wright, Ursano, Bartone, & Ingraham, 1990). There is evidence that social support is related to later post-traumatic symptoms. In cases where a low level of social support is identified, intervention aimed at increasing support may be possible. As has been argued earlier, attribution therapy may be feasible in helping survivors deal with specific emotional states such as guilt or shame that may block processing. Such emotional states, it is believed, may also lead to social withdrawal and hence making little use of coping strategies that rely on family and friends. Thus, the alleviation of these feelings may lead to increased support seeking. There is good evidence that higher levels of support received are predictive of later adjustment.

TREATMENT 4

(See Case History 4, p. 22)

Sarah's problems in relating with others was a problem that frequently recurred in therapy. Either she reported feeling very irritable and angry and then guilty about feeling that way or else she was afraid of meeting people and dealing with other people's questions about her problems which added to her general avoidance. Initially we tried getting Sarah to accept her feelings, as components of her reaction to the trauma that anyone would experience, to reduce the guilt. How bad was it to be irritable and snappy, given the full range of bad behaviours a person might engage in? Was her boyfriend unable to deal with it and understand how she felt, given her totally unwanted and unbidden state of dependence? We tackled what might happen if she met someone in the street, role-played how she could deflect intrusive enquiries if she wanted to and looked at her feelings of shame that she still had emotional problems, three years after the accident. Examining her angry feelings further we found that Sarah was angry with her sister for not helping her more and angry that she had to help others with *their* feelings of distress about her problems. They did not understand: they infantilised her and gave her advice or they failed to appreciate the emotional impact of her disabilities and did not see how vulnerable and helpless she felt and how hard she was trying to combat her problems. This exploration led us into thinking more about how she presented herself to others, as the chirpy survivor and did not give them a chance to understand the darker side of her feelings. This led us back into issues of control and lost independence which she characterised in a black and white way, thereby obscuring her awareness of her gradual regrowth of independence.

The support received from others is also a function of the support providers' perception of the victims' need for help. It has been suggested that the self-presentational coping stance taken by victims can play an important role in the support providers' reaction (Silver, Wortman, & Crofton, 1990). Silver et al. (1990) argue that victims who are able to portray 'balanced coping'—conveying that although they are distressed, they are attempting to cope through their own efforts—are most likely to receive support from others. Problems in perceiving and receiving support are demonstrated by our client, Sarah, who was badly physically damaged in a car accident and who was forced to depend upon others over a long period. (See Treatment 4.)

On this basis, it may be feasible for therapists to focus on the self-presentational stance employed by survivors. Part of the self-presentational stance taken by survivors is their expression of causal attributions for the event's occurrence. For example, women who blame themselves for rape have been shown to be perceived as less well-adjusted and as more responsible for the rape (Thornton et al., 1988). Because of their interpersonal nature, group therapies can provide opportunities for social support, social reintegration, and learning more adaptive social behaviours and can be particularly useful for treating patients with PTSD (Allen & Bloom, 1994). Family members who were not involved are often also highly distressed by the event (van der Ploeg & Kleijn, 1988) and may be in need of some form of professional intervention. With regard to research into the efficacy of treatment programmes, Perconte (1988) notes that the wide range of problems associated with PTSD (for example, alcohol and drug abuse, marital and family conflicts) may interfere with any treatment programme that focuses exclusively upon alleviating symptoms and problems associated with re-experiencing the trauma. Perconte notes that:

> Successful treatment of PTSD must follow a number of stages corresponding to the variety of problems experienced, and also directed toward overcoming secondary problems which may interfere with long-term rehabilitation. (Perconte, 1988, p. 133)

Perconte (1988) lists some of the problems found in the course of treatment with veterans. This includes incomplete treatment for addiction. Substance abuse can also be a problem with civilian survivors and deserves special attention. Many survivors will use drugs as a way of coping and the therapist may find it valuable to discuss drug-related beliefs (e.g., 'I can't handle stress without a drink') with a view to introducing cognitive therapy for substance abuse as part of the treatment package (Liese, 1994).

Other problems noted by Perconte (1988) include subsequent life-events resulting in an increase of symptomatology; failure to address phobic behaviour; failure to maintain communication with family and friends; and failure to establish new activities to replace intrusive thoughts and behaviour patterns.

In addition to social support, communities can offer important group experiences that can help survivors to process their memories. Johnson, Feldman, Lubin, and Southwick (1995) report on the therapeutic use of ritual and ceremony in the treatment of Vietnam veterans. The authors have developed four ceremonies that form part of an intensive group inpatient programme which focus on the relations within the veteran's family. They comment that these ceremonies are effective in accessing and containing intense emotions and are rated as extremely helpful by a very high proportion of veterans, family, and staff members.

What is clear, then, from this selective review is that successful treatment must depend on attention to a wide range of factors as well as the core PTSD symptomatology. Furthermore, although data from controlled trials of pharmacotherapy are limited, the available evidence suggests that antidepressants can be helpful for core PTSD symptoms (see Sutherland & Davidson, 1994, for a review of psychopharmacological treatment in PTSD).

PLANNING FOR THE FUTURE

To facilitate an effective and efficient response to an unpredicted traumatic event, working relationships should be established well before any incident between the relevant organisations, which include the emergency services and police, social services, health authorities, education authorities, voluntary agencies, and religious bodies. In the UK, the Report of the Disasters Working Party (Department of Health, 1990) recommended that Local Authority Departments of Social Services should take the lead role in coordinating a response. As far as responding to disasters that affect children, the school system is the obvious means through which to reach and help large numbers. Schools have been urged to develop contingency plans to prepare for both large and small disasters (Yule & Gold, 1993). Some agencies have argued for a central disaster fund to which local authorities could make an application, perhaps along the lines of the US Federal arrangements after a major disaster area is declared centrally.

In addition to the existing plans for rescue, under the responsibility of the police, protocols need to be established with the police for the provision of psychosocial care in the immediate aftermath. Training in the planning phase should include use of communication systems by administrators and for all individuals, across disciplines, in the psychological effects of trauma. It is important to also recognise that all workers involved in the aftercare of survivors should be prepared for the effects of massive stress on themselves. Some have argued for a national disaster squad of expert professionals who could be held in readiness to respond immediately and to consult and supervise a response to a disaster in any particular locality.

The role of such a national squad needs very careful consideration. It would be impossible as well as undesirable for a small specialised team to take responsibility for treating all those affected by a disaster. Far better, local services should be facilitated in responding to local disasters. They would need advice on particular aspects, but they will already have many relevant skills in dealing with anxiety, depression, and bereavement. The function of a specialist unit should not be inadvertently to deskill local staff. Rather, they should have an important role in disseminating information in training, and in mounting high-quality research. In Norway, armed forces mental health professionals are used to attend disasters in times of peace, thereby using resources efficiently in tasks that may be relevant in times of conflict. It may well be worth other countries considering the virtues of this model of service delivery.

The development of effective services for survivors, as we have seen, involves a diversity of professionals. It is crucial, therefore, for researchers to communicate their knowledge of the effects of trauma, and the factors involved in more severe and chronic disturbance, to these interested agencies. Gersons (1989), in his study of police officers involved in a shooting incident, reported that none of the general practitioners visited by the officers recognised or reported a post-traumatic stress reaction. Furthermore, Westermeyer (1989) discusses some of the problems faced by professionals working with patients from other cultures. He notes that often there is a failure to recognise organic factors, such as head injuries, among torture victims, concentration camp internees, and refugees. Westermyer argues that there is a need for professionals with expertise in neuropsychology and neuropsychiatry to be on hand when dealing with such groups.

Support Staff and Vicarious Traumatisation

In the planning stages attention should be drawn to the importance of selecting staff who are able and willing to cope with the nature of the work. There will be volunteer staff involved who should be given clear information about the work being highly stressful. This is true also for volunteers who are trained professionals. Specialised training should be given where possible, for example, in dealing with distressed relatives, being exposed to bodies, or being trained to break difficult and distressing news.

Although mental health professionals have generally spent a considerable amount of time in training it must be remembered that they are not immune to the powerful emotions aroused through exposure to their clients' traumatic memories. Workers may develop many of the symptoms of the survivors themselves and resort to strategies like increasing cigarette and alcohol consumption to cope. McCann and Pearlman (1990) refer to the psychological impact of working with trauma victims as vicarious traumatisation. This may involve symptoms analogous to that of the survivors, a disruption of the therapists' own basic assumptions of trust, safety, invulnerability, independence, self-worth, and so on. McCann and Pearlman (1990) note that helpful coping strategies for the therapists include: striving for balance between their personal and professional lives; and balancing traumatised with non-traumatised treatment work. It is important that helpers are themselves embedded within their own wider support network.

Certain professional groups may develop a 'macho' image and deny any emotional impact of confronting death and disfigurement. It has been recommended that staff involved in disaster work attend a stress debriefing group (Hartsough & Myers, 1985) either immediately following the work or within 24–48 hours. Mitchell (1983) described a structured group usually run by a mental health professional experienced in emergency work, in which, as well as sharing factual experiences, workers are encouraged to express the feelings that they experienced during and after the rescue work with a view to normalising their appraisal of their reactions and preparing them for further symptoms and the availability of further help should the need arise. As has been recommended for the survivors themselves, it is suggested that re-experiencing events in this way can help in emotionally processing the event. However, the effects of such critical incident stress debriefing remains to be fully evaluated.

Also, as McFarlane's (1987) study demonstrated, the experience of disaster and PTSD symptoms are associated with impaired family functioning. There is the recommendation, therefore, that attention be paid to the possible impact on the functioning of the helper's family.

CONCLUSION

This chapter has described strategies for intervention and treatment, focusing upon those methods that have received the most empirical evaluation in the literature. Intervention for trauma is a broad area encompassing planning for emergency services, the provision of information in the immediate aftermath, crisis and outreach approaches, individual and group therapies for the most severely affected.

We are aware of a great increase in professional knowledge and in public awareness over the 10 years since we became involved in this field. Much as this is to be welcomed, there is still a great deal that needs to be researched, particularly in the area of treatment intervention, as we as yet know little about the effectiveness or relative effectiveness of different treatment approaches, nor yet about the indications for treating any individual by any particular method. Although we would like to see people being offered help when suffering post-trauma disorders, we strongly hope that treatments will continue to be researched and funding found for this work, so that these important questions can be addressed and our ability to help others in the future can be improved.

SUMMARY POINTS

1. Recent experiences in dealing with the aftermath of disasters has led to the recommendation that outreach services be set up to locate survivors who may not come forward for help.
2. In the immediate impact phase, the following issues have been discussed as critical: the setting up of good information systems for the relaying of up-to-date news on what has happened to survivors and affected relatives; practical help for survivors and relatives; deciding upon the viewing of human remains.
3. Immediate intervention in the form of crisis counselling and debriefing is popular and carries our wish to prevent the development of later severe and prolonged problems but at present is not well supported by empirical evidence.
4. Various longer term treatment methods are in use and we can relate these to our psychosocial model, indicating at which points they are operating.
5. Direct exposure therapies seem to operate through representing event stimuli for reappraisal and habituation of high arousal that may impede reappraisal.
6. Cognitive-behavioural therapies aim to promote reappraisal more directly and also to teach coping techniques to manage high arousal.
7. Cognitive therapy specifically embraces the reviewing of pre-existing

beliefs and coping strategies which may be dysfunctional in relation to coping with trauma.

8. Eye-movement desensitisation and reprocessing therapy is one of several new approaches that lack any clear rationale but which seem to promise rapid and relatively painless effects for some patients. Controlled trials are called for in the further evaluation of this method.

9. Group therapies seem especially effective in normalising post-trauma reactions and providing a supportive environment for reprocessing trauma experiences.

10. Community support action can provide vital practical and emotional support for survivors. Communities can also supply important communal experiences which some find useful in processing trauma, such as memorial services and official inquiries.

11. Throughout we have emphasised the importance of prior planning to facilitate the coordination of different services. Planning includes the selection and training of personnel and the provision of services for these key people who may also suffer trauma in the context of their work or vicarious traumatisation as a result of working with survivors.

CHAPTER 8

CONCLUSIONS

In the past two decades there has been an explosion of research into the psychological effects of traumatic events. But on reading the preceding chapters it is clear that much remains to be investigated. The present chapter will discuss some of the issues that strike us as promising foci for future work. In particular, although the diagnostic category of PTSD provided the impetus for research, the architecture of post-traumatic stress reactions remains unclear.

Key Topics

Architecture of symptomatology
Implications and directions
Conclusion

ARCHITECTURE OF SYMPTOMATOLOGY

As already noted in Chapter 2, the criteria for PTSD have largely reflected Horowitz's (1975, 1976, 1979) formulation of stress responses as consisting of alternating phases of intrusions and attempts to ward off intrusive thinking. These are the hallmark characteristics of PTSD. But despite the influence of the two-factor model (Gersons, 1989), the grouping of symptoms within the diagnostic criteria remains controversial and only partially reflects Horowitz's operational criteria.

To illustrate, sleep disturbances, hypervigilance, exaggerated startle response (which Horowitz considered as intrusions), memory loss, and difficulties in concentration (which Horowitz considered as denials) have been placed in section D of the DSM criteria for PTSD (APA, 1980, 1987, 1994). Section D has been described as a miscellaneous section and it has been argued that the section D symptoms should be divided between the two dimensions of repetition phenomena and defensive phenomena and that these two symptom groupings should consist of two patterns: (a) a re-experiencing symptom pattern, divided into (1) intrusion symptoms and (2) hyperarousal symptoms; and (b) a denial symptom pattern, divided into (1) numbing and (2) cognitive difficulties (Laufer, Brett, & Gallops, 1985).

Factor Analytic Studies

Although the symptom groupings proposed by Laufer et al. (1985) provide an appealing structure, the question of whether there is an underlying and identifiable symptom structure to post-traumatic reactions or whether they are simply arbitrary groupings of symptoms can only be resolved by psychometric studies. Surprisingly few studies have, however, investigated the grouping of symptoms within a broader perspective on the phenomenology of post-traumatic stress reactions.

Silver and Iacono (1984) carried out a factor analysis of 33 symptoms associated with PTSD which were self-rated by over 400 Vietnam veterans selected from Outreach Centers in the USA. A four-factor solution was obtained which identified a first factor characterised as depression and dysthymic disorder; a second factor characterised as survival guilt; a third factor characterised as re-experiencing the trauma; and a fourth factor identified as numbed responsiveness and detachment including feelings of anger and hostility (see Table 8.1). Although these data provide support for the separate groupings of intrusive and avoidant symptoms, they do not provide evidence that a two-factor structure provides the most parsimonious architecture for conceptualising reactions. Furthermore, their data show that depressive symptoms account for most of the variance in reactions. Silver and Iacono (1984) suggest that their data may more accurately represent the PTSD symptom structure for war veterans than they do for PTSD as defined by the APA, which may be more accurately described as a generic classification.

This is an important point. Although the classification of PTSD has provided a common language for researchers and fuelled interest into the study of the psychological effects of traumatic events, there remains debate over whether or not there is a generic PTSD. It may be that the structure of post-traumatic stress reactions is dependent on the type of event. It has been suggested that the term PTSD should be qualified as in rape-related PTSD, combat-related PTSD, and so on.

Furthermore, the evidence does not strongly support the grouping of symptoms as listed in DSM, i.e., intrusion, avoidance, and hyperarousal. Factor analytic data using the DSM-III criteria with 131 Vietnam veterans have been reported (Watson, Kucala, Juba, Manifold, & Anderson, 1991b). All respondents were male patients at a veteran medical center who had been administered a DSM-III interview schedule (PTSD-I: Watson, Juba, Manifold, Kucala, & Anderson, 1991a) and had qualified for a DSM-III based diagnosis of PTSD. Five factors were generated (see Table 8.2). Factor 1 was labelled as 'intrusive thoughts and their effects'. Factor 2 was labelled as 'increased arousal'. Factor 3 was labelled as 'impoverished relationships'. Factor 4 consisted of 'guilt' items and 'nightmares'. Factor 5 was labelled as 'memory and concentration' problems. Although these data provide some support for the DSM groupings (e.g., factor 2 resembles the DSM-IV arousal section and

Table 8.1 Symptoms loading on each factor

Factor 1: Depression
Trouble concentrating
Low interest in job or other activities
Feeling worthless or unsure about the self
Difficulty keeping a job
Depression
Suicidal feelings or attempts
Problems with memory

Factor 2: Survival guilt and grief
Guilt about what I did in Vietnam
Guilt for surviving Vietnam
Grief or sorrow

Factor 3: Reexperiencing the trauma
Nightmares
Violent dreams or fantasies
Flashbacks to Vietnam
Reacting when surprised, using military training

Factor 4: Detachment and anger
Feeling angry or irritable
Losing temper easily
Difficulty in relations with others
Mistrust of others or government
Jumpiness or hyperalertness
Feeling emotionally distant from family and others
Anxiety
Difficulty feeling emotions
Painful moods and emotions
Feeling separated from others, from country or society
Fear of loss of control
Depression
Having arguments with others

Adapted from Silver and Iacono (1984).

factor 3 resembles the DSM-IV avoidance/numbing section) the evidence does not support the three-factor structure inherent in DSM. Such studies only tell us about the structure of the DSM symptom menu. This point is illustrated by the inclusion of guilt in those studies conducted using DSM-III criteria. Not surprisingly, studies using DSM-III-R criteria in which guilt was omitted do not yield a guilt factor.

Factor analytic data of DSM-III-R criteria have shown four factors: numbing of general responsiveness; intrusion; avoidance; and sleeping problems (Hovens et al., 1994a). A similar four-factor structure has been reported in a variety of other studies of survivors of shipping disasters using the IES (Joseph, Williams, Yule, & Walker, 1992b: Joseph, Yule, Williams, & Hodgkinson, 1993g; Yule, Ten Bruggencate, & Joseph, 1994) and victims of armed robbery (Hodgkinson & Joseph, 1995). However, these data, although informative, do

Table 8.2   Five factors of Watson et al. (1991b)

Factor 1: Intrusive thoughts and their effects
Intrusive memories
Trauma-like stimuli worsen symptoms
Diminished interests
Nightmares
Avoiding trauma-like stimuli
Flashbacks
Detachment

Factor 2: Increased arousal
Hyperalertness
Exaggerated startle response
Sleep difficulties
Nightmares

Factor 3: Impoverished relationships
Numbed to intimacy
Constricted affect
Detachment
Decreased sexual pleasure
Avoiding trauma-like stimuli

Factor 4: Guilt and nightmares
Guilt over behaviours
Guilt over survival
Nightmares

Factor 5: Memory and concentration
Memory problems
Concentration difficulties

Adapted from Watson et al. (1991b).

not tell us about the structure of post-traumatic reactions very broadly defined. In order to obtain a clear idea of the symptom structure of post-traumatic reactions, it would be necessary to have a comprehensive menu of all symptoms associated with trauma, and not just those provided in the diagnostic classification systems.

It might therefore be argued that rather than qualify the term PTSD, the term PTSD should be dropped altogether and retained only as an umbrella term for an area of study in which investigators discuss the specific types of symptoms that are present.

The evidence would suggest that even the groupings of intrusive and avoidant symptoms need to be clarified further as there appear to be two distinct forms of intrusive thinking (the first characterised as deliberate ruminative activity and the second characterised best by 'flashbulb' nightmares and flashbacks) and two distinct forms of avoidance (the first characterised as conscious coping efforts and the second characterised as emotional numbing and detachment).

The empirical distinction between these forms of intrusion and avoidance is important theoretically as it has been suggested that different cognitive mechanisms underlie each of these phenomena. Deliberate ruminative activity and conscious coping efforts are best understood within those theoretical frameworks such as the social-cognition perspective of Janoff-Bulman which reflect the operation of conscious processes, whereas nonconscious processes may underlie the occurrence of nightmares, flashbacks, and symptoms of emotional numbing. In our theoretical model we distinguish between trauma cognitions, which refer to intrusive imagery which has its roots in nonconscious processes and ruminative behaviour which can best be understood in terms of appraisal processes which are largely conscious—although influenced by cognitive schemata which, in themselves, may reflect underlying beliefs about the self and the world which are largely nonconscious.

Anyone may develop post-traumatic stress reactions insofar as such reactions reflect normal cognitive processes with their roots in evolutionary history and which reflect the processes of working through. Post-traumatic stress reactions are not here conceptualised as disorder, although it is recognised that the process of working through can become blocked. Recent thinking on the nature of mental disorder conceptualises one defining quality of 'disorder' as 'dysfunction' where dysfunction is a scientific term referring to the failure of a mental mechanism to perform a natural function for which it was 'designed' by evolution (Wakefield, 1992). Applying this definition to PTSD, we would suggest that PTSD does not represent the dysfunction of a mental mechanism but rather the function of normal cognitive processes of adaptation, most often the case where the completion tendency remains persistently in conflict with defensive mechanisms that impede processing. However, when the process of working through becomes blocked it is not completely clear whether this might in some cases represent a failure of a mental mechanism, e.g., where cognitive deficits result in an impairment in the process of assimilation. We would not want to rule this out.

IMPLICATIONS AND DIRECTIONS

The goal of research is to provide better methods for treatment and much research has compared survivors with and without PTSD on various psychosocial factors in an attempt to identify potentially modifiable targets for intervention. However, because different cognitive mechanisms may be involved in different reactions, we would suggest that specific symptom clusters and their relationship to psychosocial factors be investigated. Certainly, there is growing evidence for a differential relationship between the intrusive and avoidant symptom categories and other variables. For example, evidence suggests that antidepressant medication may be effective in reducing symptoms of intrusion but not symptoms of avoidance (Sutherland & Davidson, 1994). It is of importance that therapeutic goals are stated precisely.

A problem arises when global rather than specific measures of dysfunction are used. It may be that psychosocial variables do not mediate between the traumatic event and either intrusion or avoidance, but rather exert their effect on overlapping depressive or anxious symptomatology. In order to clarify these issues, research needs to examine specific relationships between personal and social factors and post-traumatic symptoms.

As well as emphasising a symptom-based approach to research, we would also emphasise the temporal variation in the nature of post-traumatic reactions and how this might affect research findings. Horowitz (1975, 1976, 1979) suggests that intrusion and avoidance are phasic states which oscillate in ways particular to each person eventually reaching a period of stability when a period of completion is said to have been reached. This has implications for research seeking to demonstrate links between post-traumatic stress and other personal or social factors. Specific personal or social factors may be predictive of particular outcomes only at certain times in the period of adjustment.

Timing is, of course, the main problem confronting trauma researchers. There is the difficulty in obtaining pre-event measures. Also, if respondents have PTSD prior to the start of any study the findings cannot provide definitive evidence as to the direction of causality between PTSD and other variables. Clearly, future studies should attempt to obtain measures before the development of severe and chronic PTSD. In particular, there is also a need to understand the relationship between Acute Stress Reaction and PTSD.

It is often said that further research is needed. But this is especially true in trauma studies as they so often have to rely on naturalistic methods of investigation and where relatively little is known about the generalisabilty of results from one situation to another. For example, the *Herald of Free Enterprise* disaster involved a substantial loss of life and in this respect is a very different event from the *Jupiter* cruise ship capsize in which relatively few lives were lost. But both these events share a number of other common characteristics. Both were uncontrollable and unpredictable sudden disasters at sea which invoked in many the fear of drowning. In turn, both of these events are very different from a flood which results in substantial property loss. Even within a single event, the intensity of exposure, both objectively and subjectively defined, may range from minimal to extreme depending on individual differences in experience and perception. We have attempted to draw together the various approaches to understanding individual differences in adjustment into a coherent and testable framework.

There is accumulating evidence that the suspicion about biased reporting in litigants is exaggerated (Green, Grace, Lindy, Titchener, & Lindy, 1983; Cohen, 1987). But although the issue of compensation litigation may introduce a biasing complication in rare cases, it is nevertheless a social reality that some survivors of disaster have a case for compensation when negligence can be proved and hence the ordeal to 'prove' that they have been adversely affected is a part of the consequences of being a survivor. Furthermore, it may be that disasters resulting from human negligence represent a special case and may result in problems of a particular kind. For these reasons, we would argue that litigants from such disasters are important to study further. It may be that involvement in litigation has a biasing effect on self-reports. It has been suggested that psychological reactions might be produced or maintained by a compensation claim, often referred to as 'compensation neurosis' (Weighill, 1983). However, it is a difficult question to investigate whether this is true as often the only survivors available for study are involved in litigation.

Although there are many unavoidable difficulties in the study of people's reactions following exposure to traumatic events, it should also be emphasised that the study of trauma-affected populations provides a unique opportunity to assess the relationship between adversity and illness that is not possible with traditional life-event methodology. As McFarlane (1985) noted: the occurrence of a natural disaster and its impact are obviously not caused by any illness and are therefore independent events; problems of recall are minimised; documenting the effects of a single event is much simpler than trying to unravel the combined effects of a number of highly personal experiences; all subjects experience the same event on the same day at the same time. However, as we have seen, the definition of trauma is problematic and the boundaries of PTSD indistinct. It may be that findings from trauma research will have implications for understanding reactions to stress over a wider range of severity.

CONCLUSION

It would seem that although post-traumatic stress reactions arise as a direct result of exposure to the experience of a traumatic event, the chronicity and severity of reactions are also a function of other psychosocial factors. In particular, the person's appraisal of his or her experiences, the support received from others, and the life-events experienced subsequent to disaster may all exacerbate symptoms. For this reason, we have adopted an integrative model of adaptation to traumatic stressors which emphasises that post-traumatic stress reactions are indicative that the experience has in some way not yet been assimilated. It is important that mental health professionals should have a thorough knowledge of the main research findings and are familiar with those signs of incomplete emotional processing which may indicate risk of later disorder. It should then be possible for victims at high risk to be identified in the early stages and given help to work through and assimilate their experiences.

REFERENCES

Abrahams, M. J., Price, J., Whitlock, F. A., & Williams, G. (1976). The Brisbane floods, January 1974: Their impact on health. *Medical Journal of Australia*, 2, 936–939.

Abramson, L. Y., Metalsky, G. I., & Alloy, L. B. (1988). The hopelessness theory of depression: Does the research test the theory? In L. Y. Abramson (Ed.), *Social cognition and clinical psychology: A synthesis*. New York: Guilford.

Abramson, L. Y., Metalsky, G. I., & Alloy, L. B. (1989). Hopelessness depression: A theory based subtype of depression. *Psychological Review*, 96, 358–372.

Abramson, L. Y., Seligman, M. E., & Teasdale, J. D. (1978). Learned helplessness in humans; critique and reformulation. *Journal of Abnormal Psychology*, 87, 49–74.

Achenbach, T. M., & Edelbrock, C. (1983). *Manual for the child behaviour checklist and revised child behaviour profile*. Burlington, VT: University of Vermont.

Adler, A. (1943). Neuropsychiatric complications in victims of Boston's Coconut Grove disaster. *Journal of the American Medical Association*, 123, 1098–1101.

Adshead, G., Canterbury, R., & Rose, S. (1994). Current provision and recommendations for the management of psychosocial morbidity following disaster in England. *Criminal Behaviour and Mental Health*, 4, 181–208.

Affleck, G., Tennen, H., Croog, S., & Levine, S. (1987). Causal attribution, perceived benefits, and morbidity after a heart attack: An 8-year study. *Journal of Consulting and Clinical Psychology*, 55, 29–35.

Allen, S. N. (1994). Psychological assessment of post-traumatic stress disorder. *Psychiatric Clinics of North America*, 17, 327–349.

Allen, S. N., & Bloom, S. L. (1994). Group and family treatment of post-traumatic stress disorder. *Psychiatric Clinics of North America*, 17, 425–437.

Alloy, L. B., Abramson, L. Y., Metalsky, G. I., & Hartledge, S. (1988). The hopelessness theory of depression: attributional aspects. *British Journal of Clinical Psychology*, 27, 5–21.

Alloy, L. B., Kelly, K. A., Mineka, S., & Clements, C. M. (1990). Comorbidity in anxiety and depressive disorders: A helplessness–hopelessness perspective. In J. D. Maser & C. R. Cloninger (Eds), *Comorbidity in anxiety and mood disorders* (pp. 499–543). Washington, DC: American Psychiatric Press.

Alloy, L. B., Lipman, A. J., & Abramson, L. Y. (1992). Attributional style as a vulnerability factor for depression: Validation by past history of mood disorders. *Cognitive Therapy and Research*, 16, 391–407.

Alloy, L. B., & Tabachnik, N. (1984). The assessment of covariation by humans and animals: the joint influence of prior expectations and current situational information. *Psychological Review*, 91, 112–149.

Anderson, C. R. (1977). Locus of control, coping behaviours, and performance in a stress setting: A longitudinal study. *Journal of Applied Psychology*, 62, 446–451.

Antaki, C., & Brewin, C. R. (Eds). (1982). *Attributions and psychological change: Applications of attributional theories to clinical and educational practice*. London: Academic Press.

Andrews, B., & Brown, G. W. (1988). Social support, onset of depression and personality. *Social Psychiatry and Psychiatric Epidemiology*, 23, 99–108.

APA (1952). *Diagnostic and statistical manual of mental disorders* (1st edition). Washington, DC: American Psychiatric Association.

APA (1968). *Diagnostic and statistical manual of mental disorders* (2nd edition). Washington, DC: American Psychiatric Association.

APA (1980). *Diagnostic and statistical manual of mental disorders* (3rd edition). Washington, DC: American Psychiatric Association.

APA (1987). *Diagnostic and statistical manual of mental disorders* (3rd edition, revised). Washington, DC: American Psychiatric Association.

APA (1994). *Diagnostic and statistical manual of mental disorders* (4th edition). Washington, DC: American Psychiatric Association.

Arroyo, W., & Eth, S. (1985). Children traumatized by Central American warfare. In S. Eth & R. S. Pynoos (Eds), *Post-traumatic stress disorder in children*. Washington, DC: American Psychiatric Press.

Astor-Dubin, L., & Hammen, C. (1984). Cognitive versus behavioural coping responses of men and women: A brief report. *Cognitive Therapy and Research*, **8**, 85–90.

Atkeson, B. M., Calhoun, K. S., Resick, P. A., & Ellis, E. M. (1982). Victims of rape: Repeated assessment of depressive symptoms. *Journal of Consulting and Clinical Psychology*, **50**, 96–102.

Baider, L., Peretz, T., & Kaplan De-Nour, A. (1992). Effect of the Holocaust on coping with cancer. *Social Science and Medicine*, **34**, 11–15.

Ballard, C. G., Stanley, A. K., & Brockington, I. F. (1995). Post-traumatic stress disorder (PTSD) after childbirth. *British Journal of Psychiatry*, **166**, 525–528.

Bard, M., & Sangrey, D. (1980). Things fall apart. Victims in Crisis. Evaluation Change (Special issue), 28–35.

Bartone, P. T., & Wright, K. M. (1990). Grief and group recovery following a military air disaster. *Journal of Traumatic Stress*, **3**, 523–540.

Basoglu, M., & Paker, M. (1995). Severity of trauma as predictor of long-term psychological status in survivors of torture. *Journal of Anxiety Disorders*, **9**, 339–350.

Baum, A. (1987). Toxins, technology, and natural disasters. In G. R. VandenBos and B. K. Bryant (Eds), *Cataclysms, crises, and catastrophes: Psychology in action*. American Psychological Association.

Baum, A. (1990). Stress, intrusive imagery, and chronic distress. *Health Psychology*, **9**, 653–675.

Baum, A., & Fleming, I. (1993). Implications of psychological research on stress and technological accidents. *American Psychologist*, **48**, 665–672.

Baum, A., Fleming, R., & Singer, J. E. (1983a). Coping with victimization by technological disaster. *Journal of Social Issues*, **39**, 117–138.

Baum, A., Gatchel, R. J., & Schaeffer, M. A. (1983b). Emotional, behavioral, and physiological effects of chronic stress at Three Mile Island. *Journal of Consulting and Clinical Psychology*, **51**, 565–572.

Baum, A., O'Keefe, M. K., & Davidson, L. M. (1990). Acute stressors and chronic response: The case of traumatic stress. *Journal of Applied Social Psychology*, **20**, 1643–1654.

Beck, A. T. (1967). *Depression: Clinical, experimental, and theoretical aspects*. New York: Hoeber.

Beck, A. T. (1976). *Cognitive therapy and the emotional disorder*. New York: International University Press.

Beck, A. T., & Emery, G. (1985). *Anxiety disorders and phobias. A cognitive perspective*. New York: Basic Books.

Beck, A. T., Rush, A. J., Shaw, B. F., & Emery, G. (1979). *Cognitive therapy of depression*. New York: Guilford.

Becker, J. V., Skinner, L. J., Abel, G. G., Howell, J., & Bruce, K. (1982). The effects of sexual assault on rape and attempted rape victims. *Victimology*, **7**, 106–113.

Becker, J. V., Skinner, L. J., Abel, G. G., & Treacy, E. C. (1982). Incidence and types of sexual dysfunctions in rape and incest victims. *Journal of Sex and Marital Therapy*, 8, 65–74.

Bernstein, E. M., & Putnam, F. W. (1986). Development, reliability, and validity of a dissociation scale. *Journal of Nervous and Mental Disease*, 174, 727–735.

Berren, M. R., Beigel, A., & Barker, G. (1982). A typology for the classification of disasters: Implications for intervention. *Community Mental Health Journal*, 18, 120–134.

Beitchman, J. H., Zucker, K. J., Hood, J. E., DaCosta, G. A., & Cassavia, E. (1992). A review of the long-term effects of childhood sexual abuse. *Child Abuse and Neglect*, 16, 101–118.

Belkin, D. S., Greene, A. F., Rodrigue, J. R., & Boggs, S. R. (1994). Psychopathology and history of sexual abuse. *Journal of Interpersonal Violence*, 9, 535–547.

Bell, B. D. (1978). Disaster impact and response: overcoming the thousand natural shocks. *The Gerontologist*, 18, 531–540.

Benassi, V. A., Sweeney, P. D., & Dufour, C. L. (1988). Is there a relation between locus of control orientation and depression? *Journal of Abnormal Psychology*, 97, 357–367.

Bennet, G. (1970). Bristol floods 1968: Controlled survey of effects on health of local community disaster. *British Medical Journal*, 3, 454–458.

Bentall, R. P. (1992). Reconstructing psychopathology. *The Psychologist*, 15, 61–65.

Billings, A. G., & Moos, R. H. (1981). The role of coping responses and social resources in attenuating the stress of life events. *Journal of Behavioural Medicine*, 4, 139–157.

Birleson, P. (1981). The validity of depressive disorder in childhood and the development of a self rating scale: A research report. *Journal of Child Psychology and Psychiatry*, 22, 73–88.

Bisson, J. I., Jenkins, P. L., & Bannister, C. (in press). A randomised controlled trial of psychological debriefing for victims of acute burn trauma.

Black, J. L., & Keane, T. M. (1982). Implosive therapy in the treatment of combat related fears in a world war II veteran. *Behaviour Therapy and Experimental Psychiatry*, 13, 163–165.

Blake, D. D., Albano, A. M., & Keane, T. M. (1992). Twenty years of trauma: Psychological Abstracts 1970 through 1989. *Journal of Traumatic Stress*, 5, 477–484.

Blake, D. D., Keane, T. M., Wine, P. R., Mora, C., Taylor, K. L., & Lyons, J. A. (1990b). Prevalence of PTSD symptoms in combat veterans seeking medical treatment. *Journal of Traumatic Stress*, 3, 15–29.

Blake, D. D., Weathers, F. W., Nagy, L. M., et al. (1990a). A clinician rating scale for assessing current and lifetime PTSD: The CAPS-I. *Behaviour Therapy*, 13, 187–188.

Blanchard, E. B., Hickling, E. J., Taylor, A. E., Loos, W. R., & Geradi, R. J. (1994). Psychological morbidity associated with motor vehicle accidents. *Behaviour Research and Therapy*, 32, 283–290.

Blanchard, E. B., Kolb, L. B., Gerardi, R. J., Ryan, P., & Pallmeyer, T. P. (1986). Cardiac response to relevant stimuli as an adjunctive tool for diagnosing posttraumatic stress disorder in Vietnam veterans. *Behaviour Therapy*, 17, 592–606.

Blanchard, E. B., Kolb, L. B., Pallmeyer, T. P., & Gerardi, R. J. (1982). A psychophysiological study of post-traumatic stress disorder in Vietnam veterans. *Psychiatric Quarterly*, 54, 220–229.

Blank, A. S. (1993). The longitudinal course of posttraumatic stress disorder. In J. R. T. Davidson & E. B. Foa (Eds), *Posttraumatic stress disorder: DSM-IV and beyond*. Washington, DC: American Psychiatric Press.

Bourque, L. B., Aneshensel, C. S., & Goltz, J. D. (1991). Injury and psychological distress following the Whittier Narrows and Loma Prieta earthquakes (abstract). In proceedings of the UCLA International Conference on the Impact of Natural Disasters, Agenda for Future Action. Los Angeles: University of California.

Bowen, G. R., & Lambert, J. A. (1986). Systematic desensitization therapy with post-traumatic stress disorder cases. In C. R. Figley (Ed.), *Trauma and its wake*, Vol. II (pp. 264–279), New York: Brunner/Mazel.

Boudewyns, P. A., & Hyer, L. (1990). Physiological response to combat memories and preliminary treatment outcome in Vietnam veteran PTSD patients treated with direct therapeutic exposure. *Behavior Therapy*, 21, 63–87.

Boyle, M. (1990). *Schizophrenia: A scientific delusion?* London: Routledge.

Bradley, G. W. (1978). Self-serving biases in the attribution process: A re-examination of the fact or fiction question. *Journal of Personality and Social Psychology*, 36, 56–71.

Bravo, M., Rubio-Stipec, M., Canino, G. J., Woodbury, M. A., & Ribera, J. C. (1990). The psychological sequelae of disaster stress prospectively and retrospectively evaluated. *American Journal of Community Psychology*, 18, 661–680.

Bremner, J. D., Southwick, S., Brett, E., Fontana, A., Rosenheck, R., & Charney, D. S. (1992). Dissociation and postraumatic stress disorder in Vietnam combat veterans. *American Journal of Psychiatry*, 149, 328–332.

Breslau, N., & Davis, G. C. (1986). Chronic stress and major depression. *Archives of General Psychiatry*, 43, 309–314.

Breslau, N., & Davis, G. C. (1987). Post-traumatic stress disorder: the etiological specificity of wartime stressors. *American Journal of Psychiatry*, 144, 578–583.

Breslau, N., Davis, G. C., Andreski, P., & Peterson, E. (1991). Traumatic events and posttraumatic stress disorder in an urban population of young adults. *Archives of General Psychiatry*, 48, 216–222.

Brewin, C. R. (1985). Depression and causal attributions: What is their relation? *Psychological Bulletin*, 98, 297–309.

Brewin, C. R. (1988). *Cognitive foundations of clinical psychology*. Hove and London: Lawrence Erlbaum.

Brewin, C. R. (1989). Cognitive change processes in psychotherapy. *Psychological Review*, 96, 379–394.

Brewin, C. R., Andrews, B., & Gotlib, I. H. (1993). Psychopathology and early experience: a reappraisal of retrospective reports. *Psychological Bulletin*, 113, 82–98.

Brewin, C. R., Dalgleish, T., & Joseph, S. (1996). A dual representation theory of posttraumatic stress disorder. *Psychological Review*, 103, 670–686.

Brewin, C. R., MacCarthy, B., & Furnham, A. (1989). Social support in the face of adversity: The role of cognitive appraisal. *Journal of Research in Personality*, 23, 354–372.

Brewin, C. R., & Shapiro, D. A. (1984). Beyond locus of control: Attributions of responsibility for positive and negative outcomes. *British Journal of Psychology*, 75, 43–49.

Briere, J., & Runtz, M. (1989). The Trauma Symptom Checklist (TSC-33): Early data on a new scale. *Journal of Interpersonal Violence*, 4, 151–63.

Brom, D., Kleber, R. J., & Defares, P. B. (1986). *Traumatische ervaringen en psychotherapie* (Traumatic experiences and psychotherapy). Lisse: Swets & Zeitlinger.

Brom, D., & Kleber, R. J. (1989). Prevention of post-traumatic stress disorders. *Journal of Traumatic Stress*, 2, 335–351.

Brom, D., Kleber, R. J., & Defares, P. B. (1989). Brief psychotherapy for posttraumatic stress disorders. *Journal of Consulting and Clinical Psychology*, 57, 607–612.

Brom, D., Kleber, R. J., & Hofman, M. C. (1993). Victims of traffic accidents: Incidence and prevention of post-traumatic stress disorder. *Journal of Clinical Psychology*, 49, 131–140.

Bromet, E. J., Hough, L., & Connell, M. (1984). Mental health of children near the

Three Mile Island reactor. *Journal of Preventive Psychiatry*, 2, 275–301.

Bromet, E. J., Parkinson, D. K., Schulberg, H. C., Dunn, L. O., & Gondek, P. C. (1982a). Mental health of residents near the Three Mile Island reactor: A comparative study of selected groups. *Journal of Preventive Psychiatry*, 1, 225–274.

Bromet, E. J., Schulberg, H. C., & Dunn, L. O. (1982b). Reactions of psychiatric patients to the Three Mile Island nuclear accident. *Archives of General Psychiatry*, 39, 725–730.

Brown, G. W., Andrews, B., Harris, T., Adler, Z., & Bridge, L. (1986). Social support, self-esteem and depression. *Psychological Medicine*, 16, 813–831.

Brown, G. W. & Harris, T. (1978). *Social origins of depression*. London: Tavistock.

Brown, R., & Kulik, J. (1977). Flashbulb memories. *Cognition*, 5, 73–99.

Browne, A., & Finkelhor, D. (1986). The impact of child sexual abuse: A review of the research. *Psychological Bulletin*, 99, 66–77.

Brugha, T., Bebbington, P., Tennant, C., & Hurry, J. (1985). The list of threatening experiences: a subset of 12 life-event categories with considerable long-term contextual threat. *Psychological Medicine*, 15, 189–194.

Bulman, R. J., & Wortman, C. B. (1977). Attributions of blame and coping in the 'real world': Severe accident victims react to their lot. *Journal of Personality and Social Psychology*, 35, 351–363.

Burgess, A. W., Hartman, C. R., McCausland, M. P., & Powers, P. (1984). Response patterns in children and adolescents exploited through sex rings and pornography. *American Journal of Psychiatry*, 141, 656–662.

Burgess, A. W., & Holmstrom, L. L. (1974a). *Rape: Victims of crisis*. Bowie, MD: R. J. Brady Company.

Burgess, A. W., & Holmstrom, L. L. (1974b). Rape trauma syndrome. *American Journal of Psychiatry*, 131, 981–986.

Burgess, A. W., & Holmstrom, L. L. (1978). Recovery from rape and prior life stress. *Research in Nursing and Health*, 1, 165–174.

Burke, H. R., & Mayer, S. M. (1985). The MMPI and the post-traumatic stress syndrome in Vietnam-era veterans. *Journal of Clinical Psychology*, 41, 152–156.

Burnam, M. A., Stein, J. A., Golding, J. M., Siegal, J. M., Sorenson, S. B., Forsythe, A. B., & Telles, C. A. (1988). Sexual assault and mental disorders in a community population. *Journal of Consulting and Clinical Psychology*, 56, 843–850.

Burns, M. O., & Seligman, M. E. P. (1989). Explanatory style across the lifespan: Evidence for stability over 52 years. *Journal of Personality and Social Psychology*, 56, 471–477.

Burnstein, E. M., & Putnam, F. W. (1986). Development, reliability, and validity of a dissociative scale. *Journal of Nervous and Mental Disease*, 174, 727–735.

Butcher, J. N. (1990). *MMPI-2 in psychological treatment*. New York: Oxford UP.

Cairns, E., & Wilson, R. (1984). The impact of political violence on mild psychiatric morbidity in Northern Ireland. *British Journal of Psychiatry*, 145, 631–635.

Cairns, E., & Wilson, R. (1985). Psychiatric aspects of violence in Northern Ireland. *Stress Medicine*, 1, 193–201.

Cairns, E., & Wilson, R. (1989). Mental health aspects of political violence in Northern Ireland. *International Journal of Mental Health*, 18, 38–56.

Calhoun, J. S., Atkeson, B. M., & Resick, P. A. (1982). A longitudinal examination of fear reactions in victims of rape. *Journal of Counselling Psychology*, 29, 655–661.

Calhoun, L. G., & Tedeschi, R. G. (1991). Perceiving benefits in traumatic events: Some issues for practising psychologists. *The Journal of Training and Practice in Professional Psychology*, 5, 45–52.

Card, J. (1987). Epidemiology of PTSD in a national cohort of Vietnam veterans. *Journal of Consulting Psychology*, 43, 6–16.

Carlier, I. V. E., & Gersons, B. P. R. (1995). Partial posttraumatic stress disorder (PTSD): The issue of psychological scars and the occurrence of PTSD symptoms. *The Journal of Nervous and Mental Disease*, **183**, 107–109.

Carr, V. J. (1991). Quake Impact Study: Interim Report. Callaghan, NSW, Australia, University of Newcastle Faculty of Medicine, Discipline of Psychiatry, September.

Carver, C. S., Scheier, M. F., & Weintraub, J.K. (1989). Assessing coping strategies: A theoretically based approach. *Journal of Personality and Social Psychology*, **56**, 267–283.

Cathcart, F. (1988). Seeing the body after death. *British Medical Journal*, **297**, 997–998.

Chambless, D. L., & Gillis, M. M. (1993). Cognitive therapy of anxiety disorders. *Journal of Consulting and Clinical Psychology*, **61**, 248–260.

Chemtob, C., Roitblat, H. L., Hamada, R. S., Carlson, J. G., & Twentyman, C. T. (1988). A cognitive action theory of post-traumatic stress disorder. *Journal of Anxiety Disorders*, **2**, 253–275.

Clark, D. M. (1986). A cognitive approach to panic. *Behaviour Research and Therapy*, **24**, 461–470.

Clark, D. M. (1991). Cognitive therapy for panic disorder. Paper presented at the NIH Consensus Development Conference on the treatment of panic disorder, 23–25 September, Bethesda, MD.

Clark, D. M., Ball, S., & Pape, D. (1991). An experimental investigation of thought suppression. *Behaviour Research and Therapy*, **29**, 253–257.

Clark, L. A., & Watson, D. (1991). Tripartite model of anxiety and depression: Psychometric evidence and taxonomic implications. *Journal of Abnormal Psychology*, **100**, 316–336.

Clayer, J. R., Bookless-Pratz, C., & Harris, R. L. (1985). Some health consequences of a natural disaster. *Medical Journal of Australia*, **143**, 182–184.

Cluss, P. A., Boughton, J., Frank, L. E., Stewart, B. D., & West, D. (1983). The rape victims: psychological correlates of participation in the legal process. *Criminal Justice and Behaviour*, **10**, 342–357.

Cohen, R. I. (1987). Post-traumatic stress disorder: Does it clear up when the litigation is settled? *British Journal of Hospital Medicine*, **27**, 485.

Cohen, S., & McKay, G. (1984). Social support, stress and the buffering hypothesis: A theoretical analysis. In A. Baum, J. E. Singer, & S. E. Taylor (Eds), *Handbook of psychology and health*, Vol. 4 (pp. 253–267). Hillsdale, NJ: Erlbaum.

Cohen, S., & Wills, T. A. (1985). Stress, social support, and the buffering hypothesis. *Psychological Bulletin*, **2**, 310–357.

Colligan, R. C., & Offord, K. P. (1992). The MMPI: A contemporary normative study of adolescents. Norwood, NJ: Ablex Publishing Corporation.

Collins, R. L., Taylor, S. E., & Skokan, L. A. (1990). A better world or a shattered vision? Changes in life perspective following victimization. *Social Cognition*, **8**, 263–285.

Commerford, M. C., Gular, E., Orr, D. A., Reznikoff, M., & O'Dowd, M. A. (1994). Coping and psychological distress in women with HIV/AIDS. *Journal of Community Psychology*, **22**, 224–230.

Cook, J. D., & Bickman, L. (1990). Social support and psychological symptomatology following a natural disaster. *Journal of Traumatic Stress*, **3**, 541–557.

Coyne, J. C. (1978). Depression and responses of others. *Journal of Abnormal Psychology*, **85**, 186–193.

Craig, A. R., Hancock, K. M., & Dickson, H. G. (1994). Spinal cord injury: A search for determinants of depression two years after the event. *British Journal of Clinical Psychology*, **33**, 221–230.

Creamer, M., Burgess, P., & Pattison, P. (1990). Cognitive processing in post-trauma reactions: Some preliminary findings. *Psychological Medicine*, 20, 597–604.

Creamer, M., Burgess, P., & Pattison, P. (1992). Reaction to trauma: A cognitive processing model. *Journal of Abnormal Psychology*, 101, 452–459.

Cronkite, R. C., & Moos, R. H. (1984). The role of predisposing and moderating factors in the stress–illness relationship. *Journal of Health and Social Behaviour*, 25, 372–393.

Crummier, T. L., & Green, B. L. (1991). Posttraumatic stress disorder as an early response to sexual assault. *Journal of Interpersonal Violence*, 6, 160–173.

Curran, P., Bell, P., Loughrey, G., Roddy, R., & Rocke, L. (1988, August). Psychological consequences of the Enniskillen bombing. Paper presented at the First European Conference on Traumatic Stress Studies, Lincoln, UK.

Dakof, G. A., & Taylor, S. E. (1990). Victim's perceptions of social support: What is helpful from whom. *Journal of Personality and Social Psychology*, 58, 80–89.

Dalgard, O. S., Bjork, S., & Tambs, K. (1995). Social support, negative life-events and mental health. *British Journal of Psychiatry*, 166, 29–34.

Dalgleish, T., Joseph, S., Thrasher, S., Tranah, T., & Yule, W. (1996). Crisis support following the *Herald of Free Enterprise* disaster: A longitudinal perspective. *Journal of Traumatic Stress*, 9, 833–846.

Daly, R. J. (1983). Samuel Pepys and post traumatic disorder. *British Journal of Psychiatry*, 143, 64–68.

Davidson, J. R. T., & Foa, E. B. (1991). Diagnostic issues in posttraumatic stress disorder: Considerations for DSM-IV. *Journal of Abnormal Psychology*, 100, 346–355.

Davidson, J. R. T., Kudler, H. S., Saunders, W. B., & Smith, R. D. (1990). Symptoms and comorbidity patterns in World War II and Vietnam veterans with posttraumatic stress disorder. *Comprehensive Psychiatry*, 31, 162–170.

Davidson, L., Fleming, I., & Baum, A. (1986). Post-traumatic stress as a function of chronic stress and toxic exposure. In C. Figley (Ed.), *Trauma and its wake* (pp. 57–77). New York: Brunner/Mazel.

Davidson, L. M., Weiss, L., O'Keffe, M., & Baum, A. (1991). Acute stressors and chronic stress at Three Mile Island. *Journal of Traumatic Stress*, 4, 481–493.

Davis, R. C., & Friedman, L. N. (1985). The emotional aftermath of crime and violence. In C. R. Figley (Ed.), *Trauma and its wake: The study and treatment of Post-Traumatic Stress Disorder*. New York: Brunner/Mazel.

De La Fuente, R. (1990). The mental health consequences of the 1985 earthquakes in Mexico. *International Journal of Mental Health*, 19, 21–29.

Delbo, C. (1995). *Auschwitz and After*. New Haven and London: Yale University Press.

Denny, N., Robinowitz, R., & Penk, W. (1987). Conducting applied research on Vietnam combat-related post-traumatic stress disorder. *Journal of Clinical Psychology*, 43, 56–66.

Department of Health (1990). *Disasters: Planning for a caring response. Draft report of the working party on the psychosocial aspects of disasters.* London: Department of Health.

Derogatis, L. R. (1977). *The SCL-9-R: Administration, scoring, and procedures manual I*. Baltimore: Clinical Psychometrics Research.

Derogatis, L. R. (1983). *SCL-90-R: Administration, scoring and procedures manual—II* (2nd edn.). Baltimore, MD: Clinical Psychometric Research.

DeVellis, B. M., & Blalock, S. J. (1992). Illness attributions and hopelessness depression: The role of hopelessness expectancy. *Journal of Abnormal Psychology*, 101, 257–264.

Di Nardo, P. A., & Barlow, D. H. (1988). *Anxiety Disorders Interview Schedule-Revised (ADIS-R)*. Albany, NY: Phobia and Anxiety Disorders Clinic.

Dollinger, S. J. (1986). The need for meaning following disaster: Attributions and emotional upset. *Personality and Social Psychology Bulletin*, 12, 300–310.

Dollinger, S. J., O'Donnell, J. P., & Staley, A. A. (1984). Lightening-strike disaster: Effects on children's fears and worries. *Journal of Consulting and Clinical Psychology*, 52, 1028–1038.

Duckworth, D.H. (1986). Psychological problems arising from disaster work. *Stress Medicine*, 2, 315–323.

Dyck, M. J. (1993). A proposal for a conditioning model of eye movement desensitization treatment for posttraumatic stress disorder. *Journal of Behaviour Therapy and Experimental Psychiatry*, 24, 201–210.

Dyregrov, A., & Yule, W. (1995a). Screening measures – the development of the UNICEF screening battery. Paper presented at Symposium on 'Children and War' at Fourth European Conference on Traumatic Stress, Paris, 7–11 May 1995.

Dyregrov, A., & Yule, W. (1995b). Screening measures – the development of the UNICEF screening battery. Paper presented at Symposium on 'War Affected Children in Former Yugoslavia' at Eleventh Annual Meeting of the International Society for Traumatic Stress Studies, Boston, 2–6 November 1995.

Earls, F., Smith, E., Reich, W., et al. (1988). Investigating psychopathological consequences of a disaster in children: A pilot study incorporating a structured diagnostic interview. *Journal of the American Academy Child and Adolescent Psychiatry*, 27, 90–95.

Eisler, R. M., Skidmore, J. R., & Ward, C. H. (1988). Masculine gender-role stress: predictor of anger, anxiety, and health-risk behaviours. *Journal of Personality Assessment*, 52, 133–141.

Eitinger, L. (1959). The incidence of mental disease among refugees in Norway. *Journal of Mental Science*, 105, 326–338.

Ellis, E. M., Atkeson, B. M., & Calhoun, K. S. (1981). An assessment of long-term reaction to rape. *Journal of Abnormal Psychology*, 90, 263–266.

Endicott, J., & Spitzer, R. (1972). What! another rating scale? the Psychiatric Evaluation Form. *Journal of Nervous and Mental Disease*, 154, 88–104.

Endler, N. S., & Parker, J. D. A. (1990). Multidimensional assessment of coping: A critical evaluation. *Journal of Personality and Social Psychology*, 58, 844–854.

Epstein, S. (1994). Integration of the cognitive and the psychodynamic unconscious. *American Psychologist*, 49, 709–724.

Erichsen, J. E. (1866). *On railway and other injuries of the nervous system*. London: Walton & Maberly.

Erikson, K. T. (1976). *Everything in its path*. New York: Simon & Schuster.

Eysenck. J., & Eysenck, S. B. G. (1964). *Manual of the Eysenck Personality Inventory*. London: London University Press.

Fairbank, J. A., & Brown, T. A. (1987). Current behavioral approaches to the treatment of posttraumatic stress disorder. *Behaviour Therapist*, 3, 57–64.

Fairbank, J. A., Gross, R. T., & Keane, T. M. (1983a). Treatment of post-traumatic stress disorder: Evaluating outcome with a behavioural code. *Behaviour Modification*, 7, 557–568.

Fairbank, J. A., & Keane, T. M. (1982). Flooding for combat-related stress disorders: Assessment of anxiety reduction across traumatic memories. *Behaviour Therapy*, 13, 499–510.

Fairbank, J. A., Keane, T. M., & Malloy, P. F. (1983b). Some preliminary data on the psychological characteristics of Vietnam veterans with PTSD. *Journal of Consulting and Clinical Psychology*, 51, 912–919.

Fairbank, J. A., McCaffrey, R. J., & Keane, T. M. (1985). Psychometric detection of fabricated symptoms of post-traumatic stress disorder. *American Journal of Psychiatry*, 142, 501–503.

Fairbank, J. A., & Nicholson, R. A. (1987). Theoretical and empirical issues in the treatment of post-traumatic stress disorder in Vietnam veterans. *Journal of Clinical*

Psychology, **43**, 44–55.

Faschingbauer, T. R., Devaul, R., & Zisook, S. (1977). Development of the Texas Inventory of Grief. *American Journal of Psychiatry*, **134**, 696–698.

Feldman, L. A. (1993). Distinguishing depression and anxiety in self-report: Evidence from confirmatory factor analysis on nonclinical and clinical samples, *Journal of Consulting and Clinical Psychology*, **61**, 631–638.

Figley, C. R. (1978). Psychosocial adjustment among Vietnam veterans. In C. R. Figley (Ed.), *Stress disorders among Vietnam veterans*. New York: Brunner/Mazel.

Finkelhor, D. (1990). Early and long-term effects of child sexual abuse: An update. *Professional Psychology: Research and Practice*, **21**, 325–330.

Finkelhor, D., Hotaling, G., Lewis, I. A., & Smith, C. (1990). Sexual abuse in a national survey of adult men and women: Prevalence, characteristics, and risk factors. *Child Abuse and Neglect*, **14**, 19–28.

Flannery, R. B. (1990). Social support and psychological trauma: A methodological review. *Journal of Traumatic Stress*, **3**, 593–612.

Foa, E. B., Feske, U., Murdock, T. B., Kozac, M. J., & McCarthy, P. R. (1991). Processing of threat-related information in rape victims. *Journal of Abnormal Psychology*, **100**, 156–162.

Foa, E. B., & Kozak, M. J. (1986). Emotional processing of fear: Exposure to corrective information. *Psychological Bulletin*, **99**, 20–35.

Foa, E. B., & Riggs, D. S. (1993). Post-traumatic stress disorder in rape victims. In J. Oldham, M. B. Riba, & A. Tasman (Eds), *American Psychiatric Press Review of Psychiatry*, Vol. 12. Washington, DC: American Psychiatric Press.

Foa, E. B., Steketee, G., & Rothbaum, B. O. (1989). Behavioural/cognitive conceptualizations of post-traumatic stress disorder. *Behaviour Therapy*, **20**, 155–176.

Foa, E. B., Rothbaum B. O., Riggs D. S. & Murdock T. B. (1991) Treatment of posttraumatic stress disorder in rape victims: A comparison between cognitive-behavioural procedures and counselling. *Journal of Consulting and Clinical Psychology*, **59**, 715–723.

Foa, E. B., Zinbarg, R., & Rothbaum, B. O. (1992). Uncontrollability and unpredictability in post-traumatic stress disorder: An animal model. *Psychological Bulletin*, **112**, 218–238.

Folkman, S. (1984). Personal control and stress and coping process: A theoretical analysis. *Journal of Personality and Social Psychology*, **46**, 839–852.

Folkman, S., & Lazarus, R. S. (1980). An analysis of coping in a middle-aged community sample. *Journal of Health and Social Behaviour*, **21**, 219–239.

Folkman, S., & Lazarus, R. S. (1985). If it changes it must be a process: Study of emotion and coping during three stages of a college examination. *Journal of Personality and Social Psychology*, **48**, 150–170.

Folkman, S., & Lazarus, R. S. (1988). Coping as a mediator of emotion. *Journal of Personality and Social Psychology*, **54**, 466–475.

Folkman, S., Lazarus, R. S., Dunkel-Schetter, C., DeLongis, A., & Gruen, R. J. (1986a). The dynamics of a stressful encounter: Cognitive appraisal, coping, and encounter outcomes. *Journal of Personality and Social Psychology*, **50**, 992–1003.

Folkman, S., Lazarus, R.S., Gruen, R.L., & DeLongis, A. (1986b). Appraisal, coping, health status, and psychological symptoms. *Journal of Personality and Social Psychology*, **50**, 571–579.

Fontana, A., & Rosenheck, R. (1994a). Traumatic war stressors and psychiatric symptoms among World War II, Korean, and Vietnam war veterans. *Psychology and Aging*, **9**, 27–33.

Fontana, A., & Rosenheck, R. (1994b). Attempted suicide among Vietnam veterans: A model of etiology in a community sample. *American Journal of Psychiatry*, **152**,

102–109.

Fontana, A., & Rosenheck, R. (1994c). Posttraumatic stress disorder among Vietnam theater veterans: A causal model of etiology in a community sample. *Journal of Nervous and Mental Disease*, 182, 677–684.

Fontana, A., Rosenheck, R., & Brett, E. (1992). War zone traumas and posttraumatic stress disorder symptomatology. *Journal of Nervous and Mental Disease*, 180, 748–755.

Fösterling, F. (1985). Attribution retraining: A review. *Psychological Bulletin*, 98, 495–512.

Foy, D. W., Resnick, H. S., Sipprelle, R. C., & Carroll, E. M. (1987). Premilitary, military, and postmilitary factors in the development of combat-related stress disorders. *The Behaviour Therapist*, 10, 3–9.

Foy, D. W., Sipprelle, R., Rueger, D., & Carroll, E. M. (1984). Etiology of posttraumatic stress disorder in Vietnam veterans: Analysis of premilitary, military, and combat exposure influences. *Journal of Consulting and Clinical Psychology*, 52, 79–87.

Frank, E., & Anderson, B. P. (1987). Psychiatric disorders in rape victims: Past history and current symptomatology. *Comprehensive Psychiatry*, 28, 77–82.

Frank, E., & Stewart, B. D. (1984). Depressive symptoms in rape victims. A revisit. *Journal of Affective Disorders*, 7, 77–85.

Frank, E., Turner, S. M., & Duffy, B. (1979). Depressive symptoms in rape victims. *Journal of Affective Disorders*, 1, 269–277.

Frank, E., Turner, S. M., Stewart, B. D., Jacob, M., & West, D. (1981). Past psychiatric symptoms and the response to sexual assault. *Comprehensive Psychiatry*, 22, 479–487.

Frankl, V. E. (1963). *Man's search for meaning*. New York: Washington Square Press.

Fraser, R. M. (1971). The cost of commotion–analysis of psychiatric sequelae of 1969 Belfast riots. *British Journal of Psychiatry*, 118, 257–264.

Frazier, P. (1990). Victim attributions and postrape trauma. *Journal of Personality and Social Psychology*, 59, 298–304.

Frazier, P., & Schauben, L. (1994). Causal attributions and recovery from rape and other stressful life events. *Journal of Social and Clinical Psychology*, 13, 1–14.

Frederick, C. J. (1985a). Selected foci in the spectrum of posttraumatic stress disorders. In J. Laube & S. A. Murphy (Eds), *Perspectives on disaster recovery* (pp. 110–130). East Norwalk, CT: Appleton-Century-Crofts.

Frederick, C. J. (1985b). Children traumatized by catastrophic situations. In S. Eth & R. Pynoos (Eds), *Post-traumatic stress disorder in children*. Washington, DC: American Psychiatric Press.

Frederick, C. J. (1987). Psychic trauma in victims of crime and terrorism. In G. R. Vandenbos & B. K. Bryant (Eds), *Cataclysms, crisis, and catastrophes: Psychology in action*. Washington, DC: American Psychological Association.

Freedy, J. R., Darlene, L. S., Jarrell, M. P., & Masters, C. R. (1992). Towards an understanding of the psychological impact of natural disasters: An application of the Conservation Resources Stress Model. *Journal of Traumatic Stress*, 5, 441–454.

Freedy, J. R., Kilpatrick, D. G., & Resnick, H. S. (1993). Natural disasters and mental health: Theory, assessment, and intervention. In R. Allen (Ed.), *Handbook of post-disaster interventions*. [Special Issue]. *Journal of Social Behaviour and Personality*, 8, 49–103.

Freud, S. (1894). On the grounds for detaching a particular syndrome from neurasthenia under the description 'anxiety neurosis'. *The Standard Edition of the Complete Psychological Works of Sigmund Freud*, Vol. 3. London: Hogarth Press.

Freud, S. (1919). *Introduction to the psychology of the war neurosis (Standard Ed.*, Vol. 18). London: Hogarth Press.

Friedman, M. J., Kolb, L. C., Arnold, A., Baker, R., Falcon, S., Furey, J., Gelsomino, J., Gusman, F., Keane, T., Petty, S., Podkul, T., & Smith, J. R. (1987). *Third Annual*

Report of the Chief Medical Director's Special Committee on Post-Traumatic Stress Disorder. Washington, DC: Veterans Administration.

Friedrich, W. N., Grambsch, P., Damon, C., Hewitt, S., Leonard, T., & Broughton, D. (1992). The Child Sexual Behaviour Inventory: Normative and clinical comparisons. *Psychological Assessment,* 4, 303–311.

Frye, J., & Stockton, R. A. (1982). Discriminant analysis of posttraumatic stress disorder among a group of Vietnam veterans. *American Journal of Psychiatry,* 139, 52–56.

Galante, R., & Foa, D. (1986). An epidemiological study of psychic trauma and treatment effectiveness for children after a natural disaster. *Journal of the American Academy of Child Psychiatry,* 25, 357–363.

Garmezy, N. (1986). Children under severe stress: Critique and comments. *Journal of the American Academy of Child Psychiatry,* 25, 384–392.

Garmezy, N., & Rutter, M. (1985). Acute reactions to stress. In M. Rutter & L. Hersov (Eds) *Child and adolescent psychiatry: Modern approaches* (2nd edition). Oxford: Blackwell.

Genest, M., Bowen, R. C., Dudley, J., & Keegan, D. (1990). Assessment of strategies for coping with anxiety: Preliminary investigations. *Journal of Anxiety Disorders,* 4, 1–14.

Gerardi, R., Keane, T. M., & Penk, W. (1989). Utility: Sensitivity and specificity in developing diagnostic tests of combat-related post-traumatic stress disorder (PTSD). *Journal of Clinical Psychology,* 45, 691–703.

Gersons, B. P. R. (1989). Patterns of PTSD among police officers following shooting incidents: A two-dimensional model and treatment implications. *Journal of Traumatic Stress,* 2, 247–257.

Gersons, P. R., & Carlier, I. V. E. (1992). Post-traumatic stress disorder: The history of a recent concept. *British Journal of Psychiatry,* 161, 742–748.

Gibbs, M. S. (1989). Factors in the victim that mediate between disaster and psychopathology: A review. *Journal of Traumatic Stress,* 2, 489–514.

Gil, T., Calev, A., Greenberg, D., Kugelmass, S., & Lerer, B. (1990). Cognitive functioning in post-traumatic stress disorder. *Journal of Traumatic Stress,* 3, 29–46.

Glaubman, H., Mikulincer, M., Porat, A., Wasserman, O., & Birger, M. (1990). Sleep of chronic posttraumatic patients. *Journal of Traumatic Stress,* 3, 255–263.

Gleser, G. C., Green, B. L., & Winget, C. N. (1981). *Prolonged psychosocial effects of disaster.* New York: Academic Press.

Goenjian, A. (1993). A mental health relief programme in Armenia after the 1988 Earthquake: Implementation and clinical observations. *British Journal of Psychiatry,* 163, 230–239.

Goenjian, A. K., Najarian, L. M., Pynoos, R. S., Steinberg, A. M., Manoukian, G., Tavosian, A., & Fairbanks, L. A. (1994). Posttraumatic stress disorder in elderly and younger adults after the 1988 earthquake in Armenia. *American Journal of Psychiatry,* 151, 895–901.

Goffman, E. (1968). *Stigma: Notes on the management of a spoiled identity.* Harmondsworth, Middlesex: Penguin books.

Gold, E. R. (1986). Long-term effects of sexual victimization in childhood: An attributional approach. *Journal of Consulting and Clinical Psychology,* 54, 471–475.

Gold, S. R., Milan, L. D., Mayall, A., & Johnson, A. E. (1994). A cross-validation study of the Trauma Symptom Checklist: The role of mediating variables. *Journal of Interpersonal Violence,* 9, 12–26.

Goldberg, D. P. (Ed.) (1972). *The detection of psychiatric illness by questionnaire.* London: Oxford University Press.

Goldberg, D. (1978). *Manual of the General Health Questionnaire.* Windsor, England:

NFER Publishing Company.

Golberg, D. P., & Hillier, V. F. (1979). A scaled version of the General Health Questionnaire. *Psychological Medicine*, **9**, 139–145.

Goldberg, D., & Williams, P. (1988). *A user's guide to the General Health Questionnaire.* NFER-NELSON.

Goodman, R. (1994). A modified version of the Rutter Parent Questionnaire including extra items on children's strengths: A research note. *Journal of Child Psychology and Psychiatry*, **35**, 1483–1494.

Gore, S. (1981). Stress buffering functions of social supports: An appraisal and clarification of research models. In B. S. Dohrenwend & B. P. Dohrenwend (Eds), *Stressful life events and their contexts* (pp. 202–222). New York: Prodist.

Green, B. L., Grace, M. C., & Gleser, G. C. (1985a). Identifying survivors at risk: Long-term impairment following the Beverly Hills Supper Club fire. *Journal of Consulting and Clinical Psychology*, **53**, 672–678.

Green, B. L., Grace, M. C., Lindy, J. D., & Gleser, G. C. (1990b). War stressors and symptom persistence in posttraumatic stress disorder. *Journal of Anxiety Disorders*, **4**, 31–39.

Green, B. L., Grace, M. C., Lindy, J. D., Gleser, G. C., Leonard, A. C., & Crummier, T. L. (1990a). Buffalo Creek survivors in the second decade: comparison with unexposed and nonlitigant groups. *Journal of Applied Social Psychology*, **20**, 1033–1050.

Green, B. L., Grace, M. C., Lindy, J. D., Titchener, J. L., & Lindy, J. G. (1983). Levels of functional impairment following a civilian disaster: the Beverly Hills Supper club fire. *Journal of Consulting and Clinical Psychology*, **51**, 573–580.

Green, B. L., Grace, M. C., Vary, M. G., Crummier, T. L., Gleser, G. C., & Leonard, A. C. (1994). Children of disaster in the second decade: A 17-year follow up of Buffalo Creek survivors. *Journal of the American Academy of Child and Adolescent Psychiatry*, **33**, 71–79.

Green, B. L., & Lindy, J. D. (1994). Post-traumatic stress disorder in victims of disaster. *Psychiatric Clinics of North America*, **17**, 301–309.

Green, B.L., Lindy, J.D., & Grace, M.C. (1985b). Posttraumatic stress disorder. Toward DSM-IV. *Journal of Nervous and Mental Disease*, **173**, 406–411.

Green, B. L., Wilson, J., & Lindy. J. (1985c). Conceptualizing post-traumatic stress disorder: A psycho-social framework. In C. Figley (Ed.), *Trauma and its wake* (pp. 53–69). New York: Brunner/Mazel.

Greenberg, J., Pyszczynski, T., Solomon, S., Pinel, E., Simon, L., & Jordan, K. (1993). Effects of self-esteem on vulnerability-denying defensive distortions: Further evidence of an anxiety-buffering function of self-esteem. *Journal of Experimental Social Psychology*, **29**, 229–251.

Greenberg, J., Solomon, S., Pyszczynski, T., Rosenblatt, A., Burling, J., Lyon, D., Simon, L., & Pinel, E. (1992). Why do people need self-esteem? Converging evidence that self-esteem serves an anxiety-buffering function. *Journal of Personality and Social Psychology*, **63**, 913–922.

Greer, S., Morris, T., & Pettingale, K. W. (1979). Psychological response to breast cancer: Effect on outcome. *Lancet*, ii, 785–787.

Grinker, R. R., & Spiegel, J. P. (1943). *War neurosis in North Africa, the Tunisian Campaign, January to May 1943.* New York: Josiah Macy Foundation.

Hadden, W. A., Rutherford, W. H., & Merret, J. D. (1978). The injuries of terrorist bombing: A study of 1,532 consecutive patients. *British Journal of Surgery*, **65**, 525–530.

Hammarberg, M. (1992). Penn Inventory for posttraumatic stress disorder: Psychometric properties. *Psychological Assessment*, **4**, 67–76.

Handford, H. A., Mayes, S. O., Mattison, R. E., Humphrey, F. J., Bagnato, S., Bixler, E. O., & Kales, J. D. (1983). Child and parent reaction to the TMI nuclear accident. *Journal of the American Academy of Child and Adolescent Psychiatry*, 25, 346–355.

Hansson, R., Jones, W., & Carpenter, B. (1984). Relational competence and social support. In P. Shaver (Ed.), *Review of Personality and Social Psychology* (Vol. 5, pp. 265–284). Beverly Hills, CA: Sage.

Harper, H., Oei, T. P. S., Medalgio, S., & Evans, L. (1990). Dimensionality, validity, and utility of the I-E scale with anxiety disorders. *Journal of Anxiety Disorders*, 4, 89–98.

Hartsough, D.M., & Myers, D.G. (1985). *Disaster work and mental health: Prevention and control of stress among workers*. Washington, DC: NIMH.

Harvey, J. H., Stein, S. K., Olsen, N., Roberts, R. J., Lutgendorf, S. K., & Ho, J. A. (1995). Narratives of loss and recovery from a natural disaster. *Journal of Social Behaviour and Personality*, 10, 313–330.

Harvey, J. H., & Weary, G. (1985). *Attribution: Basic issues and applications*. Orlando, FL: Academic.

Hayman, P. M., & Scaturo, D. J. (1993). Psychological debriefing of returning military personnel: a protocol for post-combat intervention. In R. Allen (Ed.), *Handbook of post-disaster interventions* [Special Issue]. *Journal of Social Behaviour and Personality*, 8, 117–130.

Hefez, A., Metz, L., & Lavie, P. (1987). Long-term effects of extreme situational stress on sleep and dreaming. *American Journal of Psychiatry*, 144, 344–347.

Heider, F. (1958). *The psychology of interpersonal relations*. New York: Wiley.

Helzer, J. E., Robins, L. N., & McEvoy, L. (1987). Post-traumatic stress disorder in the general population: Findings of the epidemiological catchment area survey. *New England Journal of Medicine*, 317, 1630–1634.

Henderson, A. S., Byrne, D. G., & Duncan-Jones, P. (1981). *Neurosis and the social environment*. New York and London: Academic Press.

Herman, J. L. (1992a). Complex PTSD: A syndrome in survivors of prolonged and repeated trauma. *Journal of Traumatic Stress*, 5, 377–392.

Herman, J. L. (1992b). *Trauma and recovery: From domestic abuse to political terror*. London: Pandora.

Hickling, E. J., & Blanchard, E. B. (1992). Post-traumatic stress disorder and motor vehicle accidents. *Journal of Anxiety Disorders*, 6, 285–291.

Hierholzer, R., Munson, J., Peabody, C., & Rosenberg, J. (1992). Clinical presentation of PTSD in World War II combat veterans. *Hospital and Community Psychiatry*, 43, 806–820.

Hill, J., & Zautra, A. (1989). Self-blame attributions and unique vulnerability as predictors of postrape demoralization. *Journal of Social and Clinical Psychology*, 8, 368–375.

Hobfoll, S. E. (1989). Conservation of resources: A new attempt at conceptualizing stress. *American Psychologist*, 44, 513–524.

Hobfoll, S. E., Lilly, R. S., & Jackson, A. P. (1991). Conservation of social resources and the self. In H. O. F. Veiel & U. Baumann (Eds), *The meaning and measurement of social support: Taking stock of 20 years of research*. Washington, DC: Hemisphere Publishing.

Hodgkinson, P., & Joseph, S. (1995). Factor analysis of the Impact of Event Scale with female bank staff following a raid. *Personality and Individual Differences*, 5, 773–775.

Hodgkinson, P. E., Joseph, S., Yule, W., & Williams, R. (1993). Viewing human remains following disaster: helpful or harmful? *Medicine, Science, and the Law*, 33, 197–202.

Hodgkinson, P. E., Joseph, S., Yule, W., & Williams, R. (1995). Measuring grief after sudden violent death: Zeebrugge bereaved at 30 months. *Personality and Individual Differences*, **18**, 805–808.

Hodgkinson, P. E., & Stewart, M. (1991). *Coping with catastrophe: A handbook of disaster management*. London: Routledge.

Holen, A. (1991). A longitudinal study of the occurrence and persistence of post-traumatic health problems in disaster survivors. *Stress Medicine*, 7, 11–17.

Holen, A. (1993). The North Sea oil rig disaster. In J. P. Wilson & B. Raphael (Eds), *International Handbook of Traumatic Stress Syndromes*. New York: Plenum.

Hollon, S. D., & Kendall, P. C. (1980). Cognitive self-statements in depression: Development of an automatic thoughts questionnaire. *Cognitive Therapy and Research*, 4, 383–395.

Hollon, S. D., Shelton, R. C., & Davis, D. D. (1993). Cognitive therapy for depression: Conceptual issues and clinical efficacy. *Journal of Consulting and Clinical Psychology*, **61**, 270–275.

Horowitz, M. J. (1975). Intrusive and repetitive thoughts after stress. *Archives of General Psychiatry*, **32**, 1457–1463.

Horowitz, M. J. (1976). *Stress response syndromes*. New York: Jason Aronson.

Horowitz, M. J. (1979). Psychological response to serious life events. In V. Hamilton and D. M. Warburton (Eds), *Human stress and cognition: An information processing approach*. New York: Wiley.

Horowitz, M. J. (1982). Psychological processes induced by illness, injury, and loss. In T. Millon, C. Green, & R. Meagher (Eds), *Handbook of clinical health psychology* (pp. 53–68). New York: Plenum.

Horowitz, M. J. (1986a). *Stress response syndromes*. Northvale, NJ: Jason Aronson.

Horowitz, M. J. (1986b). Stress–response syndromes: A review of posttraumatic and adjustment disorders. *Hospital and Community Psychiatry*, **37**, 241–249.

Horowitz, M. J., Wilner, N., & Alvarez, W. (1979). Impact of Event Scale: A measure of subjective stress. *Psychosomatic Medicine*, **41**, 209–218.

Hough, R. L., Vega, W. A., Valle, R., Kolody, B., Griswald del Castillo, R., & Tarke, H. (1990). Mental health consequences of the San Ysidro McDonald's massacre: A community study. *Journal of Traumatic Stress*, 3, 71–92.

House, J. S., & Kahn, R. L. (1985). Measuring social support. In S. Cohen & S.L. Syme (Eds), *Social support and health* (pp. 83–108). New York: Academic Press.

Houskamp, B. M., & Foy, D. W. (1991). The assessment of posttraumatic stress disorder in battered women. *Journal of Interpersonal Violence*, 6, 365–371.

Hovens, J. E., & van der Ploeg, H. M. (1993). Post Traumatic Stress Disorder in Dutch psychiatric in-patients. *Journal of Traumatic Stress*, 6, 91–101.

Hovens, J. E., van der Ploeg, H. M., Bramsen, I., Klaarenbeek, M. T. A., Schreuder, J. N., & Rivero, V. V. (1994a). The development of the self-rating inventory for posttraumatic stress disorder. *Acta Psychiatric Scandanavia*, **90**, 172–183.

Hovens, J. E., van der Ploeg, H. H., Klaarenbeek, M. T. A., Bramsen, I., Schreuder, J. N., & Rivero, V. V. (1994b). The assessment of posttraumatic stress disorder: with the clinician administered PTSD Scale: Dutch results. *Journal of Clinical Psychology*, **50**, 325–340.

Huerta, F., & Horton, R. (1978). Coping behaviour of elderly flood victims. *The Gerontologist*, **18**, 541–546.

Hughes, C. F., Uhlmann, C., & Pennebaker, J. W. (1994). The body's response to processing emotional trauma: Linking verbal text with autonomic activity. *Journal of Personality*, **62**, 565–585.

Husaini, B. A., & Neff, J. A. (1981). Social class and depressive symptomatology. The role of life change events and locus of control. *Journal of Nervous and Mental Disease*, **169**, 638–647.

Hyer, L., Davis, H., Boudewyns, P., & Woods, M. G. (1991). A short form of the Mississippi Scale for combat related PTSD. *Journal of Clinical Psychology*, **47**, 510–518.

Ingram, R, E., Lumrey, A. E., Cruet, D., & Sieber, W. (1987). Attentional processes in depressive disorders. *Cognitive Therapy and Research*, **11**, 351–360.

Inman, D. J., Silver, S. M., & Doghramji, K. (1990). Sleep disturbance in post-traumatic stress disorder: A comparison with non-PTSD insomnia. *Journal of Traumatic Stress*, **3**, 429–437.

International Federation of Red Cross and Red Crescent Societies World Disaster Report (1993). Dordrecht, The Netherlands: Martinus Nijhoff.

Jacobson, D. E. (1986). Types and timing of social support. *Journal of Health and Social Behaviour*, **27**, 250–264.

Janet, P. (1889). *L'automatisme psychologique*. Paris: Alcan.

Janet, P. (1909). *Les Nervoses*. Paris: Flammarion.

Janney, J. G., Masuda, M., & Holmes, T. H. (1977). Impact of a natural catastrophe on life events. *Journal of Human Stress*, **3**, 22–34.

Janoff-Bulman, R. (1979). Characterological versus behavioral self-blame: Inquiries into depression and rape. *Journal of Personality and Social Psychology*, **37**, 1798–1809.

Janoff-Bulman, R. (1985). The aftermath of victimisation: Rebuilding shattered assumptions. In C. R. Figley (Ed.), *Trauma and its wake*, Vol. 1. New York: Brunner/Mazel.

Janoff-Bulman, R. (1989). Assumptive worlds and the stress of traumatic events: Applications of the schema construct. *Social Cognition*, **7**, 113–136.

Janoff-Bulman, R. (1992). *Shattered assumptions: Towards a new psychology of trauma*. New York: The Free Press.

Jelinek, J.M., & Williams, T. (1984). Post-traumatic stress disorder and substance abuse in Vietnam veterans: Treatment problems, strategies and recommendations. *Journal of Substance Abuse and Treatment*, **1**, 87–97.

Jensen, J. A. (1994). An investigation of eye movement desensitization and reprocessing (EMD/R) as a treatment for posttraumatic stress disorder (PTSD) symptoms of Vietnam combat veterans. *Behavior Therapy*, **25**, 311–325.

Johnson, D. R., Feldman, S. C., Lubin, H., & Southwick, S. M. (1995). The therapeutic use of ritual and ceremony in the treatment of post-traumatic stress disorder. *Journal of Traumatic Stress*, **8**, 283–298.

Jones, D. R. (1985). Secondary disaster victims: The emotional effects of recovering and identifying human remains. *American Journal of Psychiatry*, **142**, 303–307.

Jones, J. C., & Barlow, D. H. (1990). The etiology of posttraumatic stress disorder. *Clinical Psychology Review*, **10**, 299–328.

Joseph, S., Andrews, Williams, R., & Yule, W. (1992a). Crisis support and psychiatric symptomatology in survivors of the Jupiter cruise ship disaster. *British Journal of Clinical Psychology*, **31**, 63–73.

Joseph, S., Brewin, C.R., Yule, W., & Williams, R. (1991). Causal attributions and psychiatric symptoms in survivors of the Herald of Free Enterprise disaster. *British Journal of Psychiatry*, **159**, 542–546.

Joseph, S., Brewin, C.R., Yule, W., & Williams, R. (1993a). Causal attributions and post-traumatic symptoms in adolescent survivors of disaster. *Journal of Child Psychology and Psychiatry*, **34**, 247–253.

Joseph, S., Dalgleish, T., Thrasher, S., Yule, W., Williams, R., & Hodgkinson, P. (1996). Chronic emotional processing in survivors of the Herald of Free Enterprise disaster: The relationship of intrusion and avoidance at 3 years to distress at 5 years. *Behaviour Research and Therapy*, **34**, 357–360.

Joseph, S., Dalgleish, T., Williams, R., Thrasher, S., Yule, W., & Hodgkinson, P.

(1997). Attitudes towards emotional expression and post-traumatic stress in survivors of the Herald of Free Enterprise disaster. *British Journal of Clincial Psychology*, **36**, 133–138.

Joseph, S., Hodgkinson, P., Yule, W., & Williams, R. (1993b). Guilt and distress 30 months after the capsize of the Herald of Free Enterprise. *Personality and Individual Differences*, **14**, 271–273.

Joseph, S., Williams, R., & Yule, W. (1993c). Changes in outlook following disaster: The preliminary development of a measure to assess positive and negative responses. *Journal of Traumatic Stress*, **6**, 271–279.

Joseph, S., Williams, R., Yule, W., & Walker, A. (1992b). Factor analysis of the Impact of Event Scale in survivors of two disasters at sea. *Personality and Individual Differences*, **13**, 693–697.

Joseph, S., Yule, W., & Williams, R. (1993d). Post-traumatic stress: attributional aspects. *Journal of Traumatic Stress*, **6**, 501–513.

Joseph, S., Yule, W., & Williams, R. (1994). The Herald of Free Enterprise disaster: The relationship of intrusion and avoidance to subsequent depression and anxiety. *Behaviour Research and Therapy*, **32**, 115–117.

Joseph, S., Yule, W., & Williams, R. (1995a). Emotional processing in survivors of the Jupiter cruise ship disaster. *Behaviour Research and Therapy*, **33**, 187–192.

Joseph, S., Yule, W., Williams, R., & Andrews, B. (1993e). Crisis support in the aftermath of disaster: A longitudinal perspective. *British Journal of Clinical Psychology*, **32**, 177–185.

Joseph, S., Yule, W., Williams, R., & Hodgkinson, P. (1993f). Increased substance use in survivors of the Herald of Free Enterprise disaster. *British Journal of Medical Psychology*, **66**, 185–191.

Joseph, S., Yule, W., Williams, R., & Hodgkinson, P. (1993g). The Herald of Free Enterprise disaster: Measuring post-traumatic symptoms thirty months on. *British Journal of Clinical Psychology*, **32**, 327–332.

Kardiner, A. (1941). *The traumatic neurosis of war*. Psychosomatic Medicine Monograph II–III. New York: Paul B. Hoeber.

Karlehagen, S., Malt, U. F., Hoff, H., Tibell, E., Herrstromer, U., Hildingson, K., & Leymann, H. (1993). The effect of major railway accidents on the psychological health of train drivers—II. A longitudinal study of the one-year outcome after the accident. *Journal of Psychosomatic Research*, **37**, 807–817.

Keane, T. M. (1993). Symptomatology of Vietnam veterans with posttraumatic stress disorder. In J. R. T. & E. B. Foa (Eds), *Posttraumatic stress disorder: DSM-IV and beyond* (pp. 99–112). Washington, DC: American Psychiatric Press.

Keane, T. M., Caddell, J. M., Martin, B., Zimering, R. T., & Fairbank, J. A. (1983). Substance abuse among Vietnam veterans with posttraumatic stress disorders. *Bulletin of Psychologists and Addictive Behaviour*, **2**, 117–122.

Keane, T. M., Caddell, J. M., & Taylor, K, L. (1988). Mississippi scale for combat-related posttraumatic stress disorder: Three studies in reliability and validity. *Journal of Consulting and Clinical Psychology*, **56**, 85–90.

Keane, T. M., & Kaloupek, D.G. (1982). Imaginal flooding in the treatment of post-traumatic stress disorder. *Journal of Consulting and Clinical Psychology*, **50**, 138–140.

Keane, T. M., Malloy, P. P., & Fairbank, J. A. (1984). Empirical development of an MMPI subscale for the assessment of combat-related PTSD. *Journal of Consulting and Clinical Psychology*, **52**, 888–891.

Keane, T. M., Scott, W. O., Chavoya, G. A., Lamparski, D. M., & Fairbank, J. A. (1985a). Social support in Vietnam veterans: A comparative analysis. *Journal of Consulting and Clinical Psychology*, **53**, 95–102.

Keane, T. M., Wolfe, J. A., & Taylor, K. L. (1987). Post-traumatic stress disorder: Evidence for diagnostic validity and methods of psychological assessment. *Journal of Clinical Psychology*, **43**, 32–43.

Keane, T. M., Zimering, R. T., & Caddell, J. M. (1985b). A behavioural formulation of post-traumatic stress disorder in Vietnam veterans. *The Behaviour Therapist*, **8**, 9–12.

Kee, M., Bell, P., Loughrey, G. C., Roddy, R. J., & Curran, P. S. (1987). Victims of violence: A demographic and clinical study. *Medicine, Science and the Law*, **27**, 241.

Kendall, R. E. (1976). Classification of depressions: A review of contemporary confusion. *British Journal of Psychiatry*, **129**, 15–28.

Kessler, R. C., McGonagle, K. A., Zhao, S., Nelson, C. B., Hughes, M., Eshleman, S., Wittchen, H., & Kendler, K. S. (1994). Lifetime and 12 month prevalence of DSM-III-R psychiatric disorders in the United States: Results from the National Comorbidity Survey. *Archives of General Psychiatry*, **51**, 8–19.

Kilpatrick, D. G., Resick, P. A., & Veronen, L. J. (1981). Effects of a rape experience: A longitudinal study. *Journal of Social Issues*, **37**, 105–122.

Kilpatrick, D. G., Saunders, B. E., Amick-McMullan, A., Best, C. L., Veronen, L. J., & Resnick, H. S. (1989). Victim and crime factors associated with the development of crime-related post-traumatic stress disorder. *Behavior Therapy*, **20**, 199–214.

Kilpatrick, D. G., Saunders, B. E., Veronen, L. J., Best, C. L., & Von, J. M. (1987). Criminal victimization: Lifetime prevalence reporting to police, and psychological impact. *Crime and Delinquency*, **33**, 479–489.

Kilpatrick, D. G., & Veronen, L. J. (1983). Treatment for rape-related problems: crisis intervention is not enough. In L. H. Cohen, W. L. Clauban, & G. A. Specter (Eds), *Crisis Intervention*. New York: Human Sciences Press.

Kilpatrick, D. G., Veronen, L. J., & Best, C. L. (1985). Factors predicting psychological distress among rape victims. In C. R. Figley (Ed.), *Trauma and its wake*. New York: Brunner/Mazel.

Kilpatrick, D. G., Veronen, L. J., & Resick, P. A. (1979). Assessment of the aftermath of rape: Changing patterns of fear. *Journal of Behavioural Assessment*, **1**, 133–148.

Kimerling, R., & Calhoun, K. S. (1994). Somatic symptoms, social support, and treatment seeking among sexual assault victims. *Journal of Consulting and Clinical Psychology*, **62**, 333–340.

King, D. W., King, L. A., Gudanowski, D. M., & Vreven, D. L. (1995). Alternative representations of war zone stressors: Relationships to posttraumatic stress disorder in male and female Vietnam veterans. *Journal of Abnormal Psychology*, **104**, 184–196.

Kinzie, J. D., Sack, W. H., Angell, R. H., et al. (1986). The psychiatric effects of massive trauma on Cambodian children: I. The children. *Journal of the American Academy for Child and Adolescent Psychiatry*, **25**, 370–376.

Kiser, L. J., Ackerman, B. J., Brown, E., Edwards, N. B., McColgan, E., Pugh, R., & Pruitt, D. B. (1988). Posttraumatic stress disorder in young children: A reaction to purported sexual abuse. *Journal of the American Academy for Child and Adolescent Psychiatry*, **27**, 645–649.

Kluznik, J. C., Speed, N., Van Valkenburg, C., & Magraw, R. (1986). Forty year follow up of United States prisoners of war. *American Journal of Psychiatry*, **143**, 1443–1446.

Koss, M. (1993). Detecting the scope of rape: A review of prevalence research methods. *Journal of Interpersonal Violence*, **8**, 198–222.

Kolb, L. C. (1987). A neuropsychological hypothesis explaining post-traumatic stress disorders. *American Journal of Psychiatry*, **144**, 989–995.

Kovacs, M. (1983). A self-rated depression scale for school-aged youngsters. Unpublished manuscript. University of Pittsburgh School of Medicine, Pittsburgh, PA.

Kraepelin, E. (1886). *Psychiatrie*, Vol. 5. Leipzig: Barth.

Krantz, L. (1992). *What the odds are*. New York: Harper Perennial.

Krause, N. (1987). Exploring the impact of a natural disaster on the health and well being of older adults. *Journal of Human Stress*, Summer, 61–69.

Krystal, H. (1970). Trauma and the stimulus barrier. Paper presented at the Annual General Meeting of the Psychoanalytic Association. San Francisco.

Kubler-Ross, E. (1969). *On death and dying*. New York: Macmillan.

Kuch, J., & Cox, B. J. (1992). Symptoms of PTSD in 124 survivors of the Holocaust. *American Journal of Psychiatry*, **149**, 337–340.

Kulka, R. A., Schlenger, W. E., Fairbank, J. A., Hough, R. L., Jordon, B. K., Marmar, C. R., & Weiss, D. S. (1990). *Trauma and the Vietnam war generation: Report of findings from the National Vietnam Veterans Readjustment Study*. New York: Brunner/Mazel.

Kulka, R. A., Schlenger, W. E., Fairbank, J. A., Jordan, B. K., Hough, R. L., Marmar, C. R., & Weiss, D. S. (1991). Assessment of Posttraumatic Stress Disorder in the community: Prospects and pitfalls from recent studies of Vietnam veterans. Psychological Assessment. *Journal of Consulting and Clinical Psychology*, **3**, 547–560.

Lacoursiere, R. B. (1993). Diverse motives for fictitious post-traumatic stress disorder. *Journal of Traumatic Stress*, **6**, 141–149.

Lacoursiere, R. B., Godfrey, K. E., & Ruby, L. M. (1980). Traumatic neurosis in the etiology of alcoholism: Vietnam combat and other trauma. *American Journal of Psychiatry*, **137**, 966–968.

Lang, P. J. (1977). Imagery in therapy: An information processing analysis of fear. *Behavior Therapy*, **8**, 862–886.

Lang, P. J. (1985). The cognitive psychophysiology of emotion: Fear and anxiety. In A. H. Tuma & J. D. Maser (Eds), *Anxiety and the anxiety disorder* (pp. 131–170). Hillsdale, NJ: Erlbaum.

Langer, E. J., & Rodin, J. (1976). The effects of choice and enhanced personal responsibility for the aged: A field experiment in an institutional setting. *Journal of Personality and Social Psychology*, **34**, 191–198.

Laufer, R. S., Brett, E., & Gallops, M. S. (1985). Dimensions of post-traumatic stress disorder among Vietnam veterans. *Journal of Nervous and Mental Disorder*, **173**, 538–545.

Lavie, P., Hefez, A., Halperin, G., & Enoch, D. (1979). Long-term effects of traumatic war-related events on sleep. *American Journal of Psychiatry*, **136**, 175–178.

Layden, M. A. (1982). Attribution style therapy. In C. Antaki & C. Brewin (Eds), *Attributions and psychological change*. London: Academic Press.

Lazarus, R. S. (1966). *Psychological stress and the coping process*. New York: McGraw-Hill.

Lazarus, R. S., & Folkman, S. (1984). *Stress, appraisal, and coping*. (pp. 378–389). New York: Springer.

Lees-Haley, P. R. (1990). Malingering mental disorder on the Impact of Events Scale. *Journal of Traumatic Stress*, **3**, 315–321.

Lehman, D. R., Davis, C. G., DeLongis, A., Wortman, C. B., Bluck, S., Mandel, D. R., & Ellard, J. H. (1993). Positive and negative life changes following bereavement and their relations to adjustment. *Journal of Social and Clinical Psychology*, **12**, 90–112.

Leopold, R. L., & Dillon, H. (1963). Psychanatomy of a disaster: A long-term study of post-traumatic neurosis in survivors of a marine explosion. *American Journal of Psychiatry*, **119**, 913–921.

Lerner, M. J. (1975). The justice motive in social behaviour: Introduction. *Journal of Social Issues*, **31**, 1–19.

Lerner, M. J. (1980). *The belief in a just world*. New York: Plenum Press.

Lerner, M. J., & Miller, D. T. (1978). Just world research and the attribution process: Looking back and ahead. *Psychological Bulletin*, **85**, 1030–1051.

Lewinsohn, P. M., & Talkington, J. (1979). Studies on the measurement of unpleasant events and relations with others. *Applied Psychological Measurement*, **3**, 83–101.

Liese, B. S. (1994). Brief therapy, crisis intervention and the cognitive therapy of substance abuse. *Crisis Intervention*, **1**, 11–29.

Lifton, R. J. (1967). *Death in life: Survivors of Hiroshima*. New York: Random House.

Lifton, R. J., & Olson, E. (1976). The human meaning of total disaster: The Buffalo Creek experience. *Psychiatry*, **39**, 1–18.

Lima, B. R., Chavez, H., Samaniego, N., Pompe, M. S., Pai, S., Santacruz, H., & Lozano, J. (1989). Disaster severity and emotional disturbance: implications for primary mental health care in developing countries. *Acta Psychiatric Scandanavia*, **79**, 74–82.

Lima, B. R., Pai, S., Santacruz, H., & Lozano, J. (1987). Screening for the psychological consequences of a major disaster in a developing country. *Acta Psychiatric Scandanavia*, **76**, 561–567.

Lima, B. R., Pai, S., Toledo, V., Caris, L., Haro, J. M., Lozano, J., & Santacruz, H. (1993). Emotional distress in disaster victims: a follow up study. *Journal of Nervous and Mental Disease*, **181**, 388–393.

Lima, B.R., Pai, S., Lozano, J., & Santacruz, H. (1991). The stability of emotional symptoms among disaster victims in a developing country. *Journal of Traumatic Stress*, **3**, 497–506.

Lisak, D. (1994). The psychological impact of sexual abuse: Content analysis of interviews with male survivors. *Journal of Traumatic Stress*, **7**, 525–548.

Lisak, D., & Luster, L. (1994). Educational, occupational, and relationship histories of men who were sexually and/or physically abused as children. *Journal of Traumatic Stress*, **7**, 507–524.

Litt, M. D. (1988). Cognitive mediators of stressful experience: Self-efficacy and perceived control. *Cognitive Therapy and Research*, **12**, 241–260.

Litz, B. T., & Keane, T. M. (1989). Information processing in anxiety disorders: Application to the understanding of posttraumatic stress disorder. *Clinical Psychology Review*, **9**, 243–257.

Litz, B. T., Penk, W. E., Gerardi, R. J., & Keane, T. M. (1992). In P. A. Saigh (Ed.), *Posttraumatic stress disorder: A behavioral approach to assessment and treatment*. Boston: Allyn & Bacon.

Lloyd, C. (1980). Life events and depressive disorder reviewed. *Archives of General Psychiatry*, **37**, 529 541.

Logue, J.N., Hansen, H., & Struening, E. (1979). Emotional and physical distress following Hurricane Agnes in Wyoming Valley of Pennsylvania. *Public Health Reports*, **4**, 495–502.

Lopez-Ibor, J.J., Soria. J., Canas, F., & Rodrigues-Gamazo, M. (1985). Psychopathological aspects of the toxic oil syndrome catastrophe. *British Journal of Psychiatry*, **147**, 352–365.

Loughrey, G. C., Bell, P., Kee, M., Roddy, R. J., & Curran, P. S. (1988). Posttraumatic stress disorder and civil violence in Northern Ireland. *British Journal of Psychiatry*, **153**, 554–560.

Lund, M., Foy, D., Sipprelle, C., & Strachan, A. (1984). The combat exposure scale: A systematic assessment of trauma in the Vietnam war. *Journal of Clinical Psychology*, **40**, 1323–1328.

Lyons, H. A. (1974). Terrorist bombing and the psychological sequelae. *Journal of the Irish Medical Association*, **67**, 15.

Lyons, J. A. (1991). Strategies for assessing the potential for positive adjustment following trauma. *Journal of Traumatic Stress*, **4**, 93–112.

Lyons, J.A., & Keane, T.M. (1989). Implosive therapy for the treatment of combat related PTSD. *Journal of Traumatic Stress*, **2**, 137–152.

Lyons, J. A., & Keane, T. M. (1992). Keane PTSD scale: MMPI and MMPI-2 update. *Journal of Traumatic Stress*, 5, 111–117.

MacLeod, A. K., & Tarbuck, A. F. (1994). Explaining why negative events will happen to oneself: Parasuicides are pessimistic because they can't see any reason not to be. *British Journal of Clinical Psychology*, 33, 317–326.

Madakasira, S., & O'Brien, K. F. (1987). Acute posttraumatic stress disorder in victims of a natural disaster. *Journal of Nervous and Mental Disease*, 175, 286–290.

Maida, C. A., Gordon, N. S., Steinberg, A., & Gordon, G. (1989). Psychosocial impact of disasters: Victims of the Baldwin fire. *Journal of Traumatic Stress*, 2, 37–48.

Maj, M., Starace, F., Crepet, P., Lobrace, S., Veltro, F., DeMarco, F., & Kemali, D. (1989). Prevalence of psychiatric disorders among subjects exposed to a natural disaster. *Acta Psychiatric Scandanavia*, 79, 544–549.

Malloy, P. F., Fairbank, J. A., & Keane, T. M. (1983). Validation of a multimethod assessment of post-traumatic stress disorders in Vietnam veterans. *Journal of Consulting and Clinical Psychology*, 51, 488–494.

Malmquist, C. P. (1986). Children who witness parental murder: Post-traumatic aspects. *Journal of the American Academy of Child Psychiatry*, 25, 320–325.

Malt, U. F., Karlehagen, S., Hoff, H., Herrstromer, U., Hildingson, K., Tibell, E., & Leymann, H. (1993). The effect of major railway accidents on the psychological health of train drivers—I. Acute psychological responses to accident. *Journal of Psychosomatic Research*, 37, 793–805.

Manton, M., & Talbot, A. (1991). Crisis intervention after an armed hold-up: Guidelines for counsellors. *Journal of Traumatic Stress*, 3, 507–522.

March, J. S. (1990). The nosology of posttraumatic stress disorder. *Journal of Anxiety Disorders*, 4, 61–82.

March, J. S. (1993). What constitutes a stressor? The criterion A issue. In J. R. T. Davidson & E. B. Foa (Eds), *Posttraumatic stress disorder: DSM-IV and beyond.* Washington, DC: The American Psychiatric Press.

Marcus, B. F. (1989). Incest and the borderline syndrome: The mediating role of identity. *Psychoanalytic Psychology*, 6, 199–215.

Markowitz, J. S., & Gutterman, E. (1986). Predictors of psychological distress in the community following two toxic chemical incidents. In A. H. Lebovits., A. Baum., & J. E. Singer (Eds), *Advances in environmental psychology.* Vol. 6: *Exposure to hazardous substances: Psychological parameters* (pp. 89–107). Hillsdale, NJ: Erlbaum.

Marks, I. M. (1969). *Fears and phobias*, London: Heinemann.

Marks, I. M. (1981). *Cure and care of neurosis: Theory and practice of behavioural psychotherapy.* New York: Wiley.

Marks, I. M., & Nesse, R. M. (1994). Fear and fitness: An evolutionary analysis of anxiety disorders. *Ethology and Sociobiology*, 15, 247–261.

Marmar, C. R., Weiss, D. S., Schlenger, W. E., Fairbank, J. A., Jordan, B. K., Kulka, R. A., & Hough, R. L. (1994). Peritraumatic dissociation and posttraumatic stress in male Vietnam theatre veterans. *American Journal of Psychiatry*, 151, 902–907.

Marquis, J. (1991). A report on seventy-eight cases treated by eye movement desensitization. *Journal of Behaviour Therapy and Experimental Psychiatry*, 22, 187–192.

Marshall, J. R. (1975). The treatment of night terrors associated with the posttraumatic syndrome. *American Journal of Psychiatry*, 132, 293–295.

Martini, D. R., Ryan, C., Nakayama, D., et al. (1990). Psychiatric sequelae after traumatic injury: the Pittsburgh Regatta accident. *Journal of the American Academy for Child and Adolescent Psychiatry*, 29, 70–75.

Matheny, K. B., Curlette, W. L., Aycock, D. W., Pugh, J. L., & Taylor, H. F. (1987). *The Coping Resources Inventory for Stress.* Atlanta, GA: Health Prisms.

Matheny, K. B., Aycock, D. W., Curlette, W. L., & Junker, G. N. (1993). The coping resources inventory for stress: A measure of perceived resourcefulness. *Journal of Clinical Psychology*, **49**, 815–830.

Mayou, R. A., Bryant, B. M., & Duthie, R. (1993). Psychiatric consequences of road traffic accidents. *British Medical Journal*, 307, 647–651.

McCaffrey, R. J., Hickling, E. J., & Marrazo, M. J. (1989). Civilian-related post-traumatic stress disorder: Assessment-related issues. *Journal of Clinical Psychology*, **45**, 72–76.

McCann, I. L., & Pearlman, L. A. (1990). *Psychological trauma and the adult survivor: Theory, therapy, and transformation.* New York: Brunner/Mazel.

McCauley, R., & Troy, M. (1983). The impact of urban conflict and violence on children referred to a child guidance clinic. In J. Harbison (Ed.), *Children of the troubles: Children in Northern Ireland.* Belfast: Stranmillis College Learning Resources Unit.

McCormick, R. A., Taber, J. I., & Kruedelbach, N. (1989). The relationship between attributional style and post traumatic stress disorder in addicted patients. *Journal of Traumatic Stress*, **2**, 477–487.

McFall, M. E., Smith, D. E., Mackay, P. W., & Tarver, D. J (1990a). Reliability and validity of Mississipi scale for combat-related posttraumatic stress disorder. *Psychological Assessment*, **2**, 114–121.

McFall, M. E., Smith, D. E, Roszell, D. K., Tarver, D. J., & Malas, K. L. (1990b). Convergent validity of measures of PTSD in Vietnam combat veterans. *American Journal of Psychiatry*, **147**, 645–648.

McFarlane, A.C. (1985). The effects of stressful life events and disasters: Research and theoretical issues. *Australian and New Zealand Journal of Psychiatry*, **19**, 409–421.

McFarlane, A. C. (1986a). Chronic posttraumatic morbidity of a natural disaster: Implications for disaster planners and emergency services. *Medical Journal of Australia*, **145**, 561–563.

McFarlane, A. C. (1986b). Post-traumatic morbidity of a disaster: A study of cases presenting for psychiatric treatment. *Journal of Nervous and Mental Disease*, **174**, 4–14.

McFarlane, A. C. (1987). Family functioning and overprotection following a natural disaster: The longitudinal effects of post-traumatic morbidity. *Australian and New Zealand Journal of Psychiatry*, **21**, 210–218.

McFarlane, A. C. (1988a). The aetiology of post-traumatic stress disorders following a natural disaster. *British Journal of Psychiatry*, **152**, 116–121.

McFarlane, A. C. (1988b). The longitudinal course of posttraumatic morbidity: The range of outcomes and their predictors. *Journal of Nervous and Mental Disease*, **176**, 22–29.

McFarlane, A. (1989). The aetiology of post-traumatic morbidity: Predisposing, pre-cipitating and perpetuating factors. *British Journal of Psychiatry*, **154**, 221–228.

McFarlane, A. C. (1992a). Avoidance and intrusion in posttraumatic stress disorder. *Journal of Nervous and Mental Disease*, **180**, 439–445

McFarlane, A. C. (1992b). Commentary. Posttraumatic stress disorder among injured survivors of a terrorist attack: Predictive value of early intrusion and avoidance symptoms. *Journal of Nervous and Mental Disease*, **180**, 599–600.

McFarlane, A. C. (1994). Individual psychotherapy for post-traumatic stress disorder. *Psychiatric Clinics of North America*, **17**, 393–408.

McFarlane, A. C., & Papay, P. (1992). Multiple diagnoses in posttraumatic stress disorder in the victims of a natural disaster. *Journal of Nervous and Mental Disease*, **180**, 498–504.

McFarlane, A. C., Atchison, M., Rafalowicz, E., & Papay, P. (1994). Physical symp-toms in post-traumatic stress disorder. *Journal of Psychosomatic Research*, **38**, 715–726.

McFarlane, A. C., Policansky, S., & Irwin, C. P. (1987). A longitudinal study of the psychological morbidity in children due to a natural disaster. *Psychological Medicine*, **17**, 727–738.

McNally, R. J. (1991). Assessment of posttraumatic stress disorder in children. *Psychological Assessment*, **3**, 531–537.

McNally, R. J. (1993). Stressors that produce posttraumatic stress disorder in children. In J. R. T. Davidson & E. B. Foa (Eds), *Posttraumatic stress disorder: DSM-IV and beyond*. Washington, DC: American Psychiatric Press.

McNally, R. J., English, G. E., & Lipke, H. J. (1993). Assessment of intrusive cognition in PTSD: Use of the modified Stroop paradigm. *Journal of Traumatic Stress*, **6**, 33–41.

McNally, R. J., Lasko, N. B., Macklin, M. L., & Pitman, R. K. (1995). Autobiographical memory disturbance in combat-related posttraumatic stress disorder. *Behaviour Research and Therapy*, **33**, 619–630.

McLeer, S. V., Deblinger, E., Atkins, M. S., Foa, E. B., & Ralphe, D. L. (1988). Post-traumatic stress disorder in sexually abused children: A prospective study. *Journal of the American Academy of Child and Adolescent Psychiatry*, **27**, 650–654.

Mechanic, D. (1977). Illness behaviour, social adaptation, and the management of illness. *Journal of Nervous and Mental Disease*, **2**, 79–87.

Meichenbaum, D. (1993). Stress inoculation training: A 20-year update. In P. M. Lehrer & R. L. Woolfolk (Eds), *Principles and practice of stress management* (2nd edn.). New York: Guilford.

Melick, M. E. (1978). Life change and illness: Illness behavior of males in the recovery period of a natural disaster. *Journal of Health and Social Behavior*, **19**, 335–342.

Mellman, T. A., Kulick-Bell, R., Ashlock, L. E., & Nolan, B. (1995). Sleep events among veterans with combat-related posttraumatic stress disorder. *American Journal of Psychiatry*, **152**, 110–115.

Meyer, C., & Taylor, S. (1986). Adjustment to rape. *Journal of Personality and Social Psychology*, **50**, 1226–1234.

Mikulincer, M., & Solomon, Z. (1988). Attributional style and combat-related post-traumatic stress disorder. *Journal of Abnormal Psychology*, **97**, 308–313.

Mikulincer, M., Solomon, Z., & Benbenishty, R. (1988). Battle events, acute combat stress reaction and long-term psychological sequelae of war. *Journal of Anxiety Disorders*, **2**, 121–133.

Milgram, N. A. (1986). Attributional analysis of war-related stress: Models of coping and helping. In N. A. Milgram (Ed.), *Generalizations from the Israeli experience*. New York: Brunner/Mazel.

Miranda, J. (1992). Dysfunctional thinking is activated by stressful life events. *Cognitive Therapy and Research*, **16**, 473–483.

Mitchell, J. T. (1983). When disaster strikes. . . . The critical incident stress debriefing process. *Journal of Emergency Medical Services*, **8**, 36–39.

Moody, D. R., & Kish, G. B. (1989). Clinical meaning of the Keane PTSD scale. *Journal of Clinical Psychology*, **45**, 542–546.

Mott, F. W. (1919). *War neuroses and shell shock*. London: Oxford University Press.

Mullen, P. E., Martin, J. L., Anderson, J. C., Romans, S. E., & Herbison, G. P. (1994). The effect of child sexual abuse on social, interpersonal and sexual function in adult life. *British Journal of Psychiatry*, **165**, 35–47.

Muris, P., van Zuuren, F. J., de Jong, P. J., de Beurs, E., & Hanewald, G. (1994). Monitoring and blunting coping styles: The Miller Behavioural Style Scale and its correlates, and the development of an alternative questionnaire. *Personality and Individual Differences*, **17**, 9–19.

Murphy, S. A. (1986). Status of natural disaster victims' health and recovery 1 and 3 years later. *Research in Nursing and Health*, **9**, 331–340.

Murphy, S. A. (1988). Mediating effects of intrapersonal and social support on mental health 1 and 3 years after a natural disaster. *Journal of Traumatic Stress*, 2, 155–172.

Nader, K., Pynoos, R. S., Fairbanks, L., & Frederick, C. (1990). Childhood PTSD reactions one year after a sniper attack at their school. *American Journal of Psychiatry*, 147, 1526–1530.

National Victims Center (1992). *Rape in America: a report to the nation*. National Victims Center.

Nezu, A. M., & Carnevale, G. J. (1987). Interpersonal problem solving and coping reactions of Vietnam veterans with post-traumatic stress disorder. *Journal of Abnormal Psychology*, 96, 155–157.

Norris, F. H. (1992). Epidemiology of trauma: Frequency and impact of different potentially traumatic events on different demographic groups. *Journal of Consulting and Clinical Psychology*, 60, 409–418.

North, C. S., Smith, E. M., McCool, R. E., & Shea, J. M. (1989). Short-term psychopathology in eye witnesses to mass murder. *Hospital and Community Psychiatry*, 40, 1293–1295.

North, C. S., Smith, E. M., & Spitznagel, E. L. (1994). Posttraumatic stress disorder in survivors of a mass shooting. *American Journal of Psychiatry*, 151, 82–88.

O'Brien, L. S., & Hughes, S. J. (1991). Symptoms of post-traumatic stress disorder in Falklands veterans five years after the conflict. *British Journal of Psychiatry*, 159, 135–141.

O'Donahue, W., & Elliot, A. (1992). The current status of post-traumatic stress disorder as a diagnostic category: Problems and proposals. *Journal of Traumatic Stress*, 5, 421–439.

Oei, T. P. S., Lim, B., & Hennessy, B. (1990). Psychological dysfunction in battle: Combat stress reactions and post-traumatic stress disorder. *Clinical Psychology Review*, 10, 355–388.

Ollendick, D., & Hoffman, M. (1982). Assessment of psychological reactions in disaster victims. *Journal of Community Psychology*, 10, 157–167.

Ollendick, T. H. (1983). Reliability and validity of the revised fear survey schedule for children (FSSC-R). *Behaviour Research and Therapy*, 21, 685–692.

Oppenheim, H. (1892). *Die Traumatischen Neurosen*. Berlin: August Hirschwald.

Orlando, J. A., & Koss, M. P. (1983). Effects of sexual victimization on sexual satisfaction: A study of the negative association hypothesis. *Journal of Abnormal Psychology*, 92, 104–106.

Orley, J., & Kuyken, W. (Eds) (1994). *Quality of life assessment: International perspectives*. Berlin: Springer-Verlag.

Orner, R. J., Lynch, T., & Seed, P. (1993). Long-term traumatic stress reactions in British Falklands war veterans. *British Journal of Clinical Psychology*, 32, 457–459.

Orr, S. P., Claiborn, J. M., Altman, B., Forgue, D. F., de Jong, J. B., & Pitman, R. K. (1990). Psychometric profile of posttraumatic stress disorder, anxious, and healthy Vietnam veterans: Correlations with psychophysiological responses. *Journal of Consulting and Clinical Psychology*, 58, 329–335.

Overmier, J. B., & Seligman, M. E. P. (1967). Effects of inescapable shock upon subsequent escape and avoidance learning. *Journal of Comparative Physiological Psychology*, 63, 23–33.

Page, H. (1885). *Injuries of the spine and spinal cord without apparent mechanical lesion*. London: Churchill.

Parker, G. (1977). Cyclone Tracy and Darwin Evacuees: On the restoration of the species. *British Journal of Psychiatry*, 130, 548–555.

Parry-Jones, B., & Parry-Jones, W. L. L. (1994). Post-traumatic stress disorder: Supportive evidence from an eighteenth century natural disaster. *Psychological Medicine*,

24, 15–27.

Patrick, V., & Patrick, W. K. (1981). Cyclone 78 in Sri Lanka: The mental health trail. *British Journal of Psychiatry*, **138**, 210–216.

Paykel, E. S. (1983). Methodological aspects of life events research. *Journal of Psychosomatic Research*, **27**, 341–352.

Pearlin, L. I., & Schooler, C. (1978). The structure of coping. *Journal of Health and Social Behaviour*, **19**, 2–21.

Penk, W. E., Robinowitz, R., Roberts, W. R., Patterson, E. T., Dolan, M. P., & Atkins, H. G. (1981). Adjustment differences among male substance abusers varying in degree of combat experience in Vietnam. *Journal of Consulting and Clinical Psychology*, **49**, 426–437.

Pennebaker, J. W. (1985). Traumatic experience and psychosomatic disease: Exploring the roles of behavioural inhibition, obsession, and confiding. *Canadian Psychology*, **26**, 82–95.

Pennebaker, J. W. (1993). Putting stress into words: Health, linguistic, and therapeutic implications. *Behaviour Research and Therapy*, **31**, 539–548.

Pennebaker, J. W., & Beall, S. (1986). Confronting a traumatic event: Toward an understanding of inhibition and disease. *Journal of Abnormal Psychology*, **95**, 274–281.

Pennebaker, J. W., & Chew, C. H. (1985). Deception, electrodermal activity, and the inhibition of behavior. *Journal of Personality and Social Psychology*, **49**, 1427–1433.

Pennebaker, J. W., Hughes, C. F., & O'Heeron, R. C. (1987). The psychophysiology of confession: Linking inhibitory and psychosomatic processes. *Journal of Personality and Social Psychology*, **52**, 781–793.

Pennebaker, J. W., Kiecolt-Glaser, J., & Glaser, R. (1988). Disclosure of traumas and immune function: Health implications for psychotherapy. *Journal of Consulting and Clinical Psychology*, **56**, 239–245.

Pennebaker, J. W., & O'Heeron, R. C. (1984). Confiding in others and illness rate among spouses of suicide and accidental death victims. *Journal of Abnormal Psychology*, **93**, 473–476.

Perconte, S. T. (1988). Stability of positive outcome and symptom relapse in post-traumatic stress disorder. *Journal of Traumatic Stress*, **2**, 127–135.

Perloff, L. S. (1983). Perceptions of vulnerability to victimization. *Journal of Social Issues*, **39**, 41–61.

Perry, S., Difede, J., Musngi, G., Frances, A. J., & Jacobsberg, L. (1992). Predictors of posttraumatic stress disorder after burn injury. *American Journal of Psychiatry*, **149**, 931–935.

Peterson, C., Semmel, A., von Baeyer, C., Abramson, L. Y., Metalsky, G. I., & Seligman, M. E. P. (1982). The attributional style questionnaire. *Cognitive Therapy and Research*, **6**, 287–300.

Phifer, J., & Norris, F. (1989). Psychological symptoms in older adults following natural disaster: Nature, timing, duration, and course. *Journal of Gerontology: Social Science*, **44**, 207–217.

Pitman, R. K., Altman, B., Greenwald, E., Longpre, R. E., Macklin, M. M., Poire, R. E. & Steketee, G. S. (1991) Psychiatric complications during flooding therapy for posttraumatic stress disorder. *Journal of Clinical Psychiatry*, **52**, 17–20.

Popovic, M., & Petrovic, D. (1964). After the earthquake. *Lancet*, **2**, 1169–1171.

Powell, B. J., & Penick, E. C. (1983). Psychological distress following a natural disaster: A one year follow up of 98 flood victims. *Journal of Community Psychology*, **11**, 269–276.

Power, M. J. (1988). Stress-buffering effects of social support: A longitudinal study. *Motivation and Emotion*, **12**, 197–204.

Price, J. (1978). Some age-related effects of the 1974 Brisbane floods. *Australian and*

New Zealand Journal of Psychiatry, **12**, 55–58.

Puk, G. (1991). Treating traumatic memories: A case report on the eye movement desensitization procedure. *Journal of Behaviour Therapy and Experimental Psychiatry*, **22**, 149–151.

Pynoos, R. S., & Eth, S. (1986). Witness to violence: The child interview. *Journal of the American Academy of Child Psychiatry*, **25**, 3, 306–319.

Pynoos, R. S., Frederick, C., Nader, K., Arroyo, W., Steinberg, A., Eth, S., Nuner, F., & Fairbanks, C. (1987). Life threat and post traumatic stress in school-age children. *Archives of General Psychiatry*, **44**, 1057–1063.

Pynoos, R. S., Goenjian, A., Tashjian, M., Karakashian, M., Manjikian, R., Manoukian, G., Steinberg, A. M., & Fairbanks, L. A. (1993). Post-traumatic stress reactions in children after the 1988 Armenian Earthquake. *British Journal of Psychiatry*, **163**, 239–247.

Pynoos, R. S., & Nader, K. (1988). Psychological first aid and treatment approach for children exposed to community violence: research implications. *Journal of Traumatic Stress*, **1**, 243–267.

Quarantelli, E. L. (1985a). What is disaster? The need for clarification in definition and conceptualization in research. In B. J. Sowder (Ed.,), *Disasters and mental health: Selected contemporary perspectives*. Rockville, MD: US Department of Health and Human Services.

Quarantelli, E. I. (1985b). An assessment of conflicting views on mental health: the consequences of traumatic events. In C. R. Figley (Ed.,), *Trauma and its wake*. New York: Brunner/Mazel.

Quay, H. C., & Peterson, D. R. (1979). Manual of the Behaviour Problem Checklist (Unpublished): cited in Yule, W., & Williams, R. (1990). Post-traumatic stress reactions in children. *Journal of Traumatic Stress*, **3**, 279–296.

Rabkin, J. G., & Struening, E. L. (1976). Life-events, stress, and illness. *Science*, **194**, 1013–1020.

Rachman, S. (1968). *Phobias: Their nature and control*. Springfield, IL: Thomas.

Rachman, S. (1980). Emotional processing. *Behaviour Research and Therapy*, **18**, 51–60.

Rado, S. (1942). Pathodynamics and treatment of traumatic war neurosis (traumatophobin). *Psychosomatic Medicine*, **42**, 363–368.

Raphael, B. (1986). *When disaster strikes*. London: Hutchinson.

Realmuto, G. M., Wagner, N., & Bartholow, J. (1991). The Williams Pipeline disaster: A controlled study of a technological accident. *Journal of Traumatic Stress*, **4**, 469–479.

Renfry, G., & Spates, C. R. (1994). Eye movement desensitisation and reprocessing: A partial dismantling procedure. *Journal of Behaviour Therapy and Experimental Psychiatry*, **25**, 231–239.

Resick, P. A., Calhoun, K. S., Atkeson, B. M., & Ellis, E. M. (1982). Social adjustment in victims of sexual assault. *Journal of Consulting and Clinical Psychology*, **49**, 705–712.

Resick, P. A., & Schnicke, M. K. (1992). Cognitive processing therapy for sexual assault victims. *Journal of Consulting and Clinical Psychology*, **60**, 748–756.

Resnick, H. S., Kilpatrick, D. G., Best, C. L., & Crummier, T. L. (1992). Vulnerability-stress factors in development of post-traumatic stress disorder. *Journal of Nervous and Mental Disease*, **180**, 424–430.

Resnick, H. S., Kilpatrick, D. G., Dansky, B. S., Saunders, B. E., & Best, C. L. (1993). Prevalence of civilian trauma and posttraumatic stress disorder in a representative national sample of women. *Journal of Consulting and Clinical Psychology*, **61**, 984–991.

Resnick, H. S., Veronen, L. J., Saunders, B. E., Kilpatrick, D. G., & Cornelison, V. (1989). Assessment of PTSD in a subset of rape victims at 12 to 36 months post-assault. Unpublished manuscript cited in Rothbaum, B. O., Foa, E. B., Riggs, D. S.,

Murdock, T., & Walsh, W. (1992). A prospective examination of post-traumatic stress disorder in rape victims. *Journal of Traumatic Stress*, 5, 455–475.

Reynolds, C. R., & Richmond, B. O. (1978). What I think and feel: A revised measure of children's manifest anxiety. *Journal of Abnormal Child Psychology*, 6, 271–282.

Richards, D. A., & Rose, J. S. (1991). Exposure therapy for post-traumatic stress disorder. *British Journal of Psychiatry*, 58, 836–840.

Richards, D. A., Lovell K., & Marks I. M. (1994) Post-traumatic stress disorder: Evaluation of a treatment program. *Journal of Traumatic Stress*, 7, 669–680.

Riggs, D. S., Dancu, C. V., Gershuny, B. S., Greenberg, D., & Foa, E. B. (1992). Anger and post-traumatic stress disorder in female crime victims. *Journal of Traumatic Stress*, 5, 613–625.

Roberts, W. R., Penk, W. E., Robinowitz, R., & Patterson, E. (1982). Interpersonal problems of Vietnam veterans with symptoms of PTSD. *Journal of Abnormal Psychology*, 91, 444–450.

Robins, L. N., & Helzer, J. E. (1985). Diagnostic Interview Schedule (DIS) Version III-A. St. Louis, MO: Washington University.

Rosen, J., Fields, R. B., Hand, A. M., Falsettie, G., & Van Kammen, D. P. (1989). Concurrent posttraumatic stress disorder in psychogeriatric patients. *Journal of Geriatric Psychiatry and Neurology*, 2, 65–69.

Rosen, J., Reynolds, C. F., Yeager, A. L., Houck, P. R., & Hurwitz, L. F. (1991). Sleep disturbances in survivors of the Nazi Holocaust. *American Journal of Psychiatry*, 148, 62–66.

Rosenheck, R., & Fontana, A. (1994). A model of homelessness among male veterans of the Vietnam war generation. *American Journal of Psychiatry*, 151, 421–427.

Ross, R. J., Ball, W. A., Sullivan, K. A., & Caroff, S. N. (1989). Sleep disturbance as the hallmark of posttraumatic stress disorder. *American Journal of Psychiatry*, 146, 697–707.

Roth, L. M. (1986). Substance use and mental health among Vietnam veterans. In G. Boulanger & C. Kadushin (Eds), *The Vietnam veteran redefined* (pp. 61–78). Hillsdale, NJ: Erlbaum.

Roth, S., Wayland, K., & Woolsey, M. (1990). Victimization history and victim–assailant relationships as factors in recovery from sexual assault. *Journal of Traumatic Stress*, 3, 169–180.

Rothbaum, B. O., & Foa, E. B. (1992). Cognitive-behavioral treatment of posttraumatic stress disorder. In P. A. Saigh (Ed.), *Posttraumatic stress disorder: A behavioral approach to assessment and treatment*. Boston: Allyn & Bacon.

Rothbaum, B. O., Foa, E. B., Riggs, D. S., Murdock, T., & Walsh, W. (1992). A prospective examination of post-traumatic stress disorder in rape victims. *Journal of Traumatic Stress*, 5, 455–476.

Rotter, J. B. (Ed.) (1966). Generalized expectancies for internal vs. external control of reinforcement. *Psychological Monograph*, 80 (1, Whole No. 609).

Rowan, A. B., Foy, D. W., Rodriguez, N., & Ryan, S. (1993). Posttraumatic stress disorder in a clinical sample of adults sexually abused as children. *Child Abuse and Neglect*, 18, 51–61.

Roy, M. P., & Steptoe, A. (1994). Daily stressors and social support availability as predictors of depressed mood in male firefighters. *Work and Stress*, 8, 210–219.

Rubonis, A. V., & Bickman, L. (1991). Psychological impairment in the wake of disaster: The disaster–psychopathology relationship. *Psychological Bulletin*, 109, 384–399.

Ruch, L. O., Chandler, S. M., & Harter, R. A. (1980). Life change and rape impact. *Journal of Health and Social Behaviour*, 21, 248–260.

Russel, C. K. (1919). War neurosis: Some views on diagnosis and treatment. *Archives of*

Neurological Psychiatry, **25**, 25–38.

Rutter, M. (1967). A children's behaviour questionnaire for completion by teachers: Preliminary findings. *Journal of Child Psychology and Psychiatry*, **8**, 1–11.

Rychtarik, R. G., Silverman, W. K., & Van Landingham, W. P. (1984). Treatment of an incest victims with implosive therapy: A case study. *Behavior Therapy*, **15**, 410–420.

Saigh, P. A. (1987). In vitro flooding of an adolescent post-traumatic stress disorder. *Journal of Clinical Child Psychology*, **16**, 147–150.

Saigh, P. A. (1989). The development and validation of the Children's Posttraumatic Stress Disorder Inventory. *International Journal of Special Education*, **4**, 75–84.

Saigh, P. A., Yule, W., & Inamdar, S. C. (1996). Imaginal flooding of traumatized children and adolescents. *Journal of School Psychology*.

Salkovskis, P. M. (1985). Obsessional-compulsive problems: A cognitive-behavioural analysis. *Behaviour Research and Therapy*, **27**, 677–682.

Sarason, I. G., Johnson, J. H., & Siegal, J. M. (1978). Assessing the impact of life changes: development of the life-experiences survey. *Journal of Consulting and Clinical Psychology*, **46**, 932–946.

Sarason, I. G., Levine., H. M., Basham, R. B., & Sarason, B. R. (1983). Assessing social support: The social support questionnaire. *Journal of Personality and Social Psychology*, **44**, 127–139.

Sarason, B. R., Sarason, I. G., Hacker, T. A., & Basham, R. B. (1985). Concomitants of social support: Social skills, physical attractiveness, and gender. *Journal of Personality and Social Psychology*, **49**, 469–480.

Sarason, B. R., Sarason, I. G., & Pierce, G. R. (1990). Traditional views of social support and their impact on assessment. In B. R. Sarason, I. G. Sarason and G. R. Pierce (Eds), *Social support: An interactional view*. New York: Wiley.

Sarason, I. G., Sarason, B. R., & Shearin, E. N. (1986) Social support as an individual difference variable: Its stability, origins, and relational aspects. *Journal of Personality and Social Psychology*, **4**, 845–855.

Sarason, B. R., Shearin, E. N., Pierce, G. R., & Sarason, I. G. (1987). Interrelations of social support measures: Theoretical and practical implications. *Journal of Personality and Social Psychology*, **52**, 813–832.

Schaefer, C., Coyne, J. C., & Lazarus, R. S. (1981). The health related functions of social support. *Journal of Behavioural Medicine*, **4**, 381–406.

Scheeringa, M. S., Zeanah, C. H., Drell, M. J., & Larrieu, J. A. (1995). Two approaches to the diagnosis of posttraumatic stress disorder in infancy and early childhood. *Journal of the American Academy for Child and Adolescent Psychiatry*, **34**, 191–200.

Schlenger, W. E., & Kulka, R. A. (1989). *PTSD scale development for the MMPI-2*. Research Triangle Park, NC: Research Triangle Institute.

Schlenger, W. E., Kulka, R. A., Fairbank, J. A., Hough, R. L., Jordan, B. K., Marmar, C. R., & Weiss, D. S. (1992). The prevalence of post-traumatic stress disorder in the Vietnam generation: A multimethod, multiscore assessment of psychiatric disorder. *Journal of Traumatic Stress*, **5**, 333–364.

Schulte, J. G., Dinwiddie, S. H., Pribor, E. F., & Yutzy, S. H. (1995). Psychiatric diagnoses of adult male victims of childhood sexual abuse. *Journal of Nervous and Mental Disease*, **183**, 111–113.

Schwarz, E. D., & Kowalski, J. M. (1991). Posttraumatic stress disorder after a school shooting: Effects of symptom threshold selection and diagnosis by DSM-III, DSM-III-R, or proposed DSM-IV. *American Journal of Psychiatry*, **148**, 592–597.

Schwarzwald, J., Solomon, Z., Weisenberg, M., & Mikulincer, M. (1987). Validation of the impact of event scale for psychological sequelae of combat. *Journal of Consulting and Clinical Psychology*, **55**, 251–256.

Schulman, P., Castellan, C., & Seligman, M. E. P. (1989). Assessing explanatory style:

The content analysis of verbatim explanations and the attributional style question-naire. *Behaviour Research and Therapy*, 27, 505–512.

Seligman, M. E. P. (1975). *Helplessness: On depression, development, and death.* San Francisco: Freeman.

Seligman, M. E. P., Abramson, L. Y., Semmel, A., & von Baeyer, C. (1979). Depressive attributional style. *Journal of Abnormal Psychology*, 88, 242–247.

Seligman. M. E. P., & Maier, S. F. (1967). Failure to escape traumatic shock. *Journal of Experimental Psychology*, 74, 1–9.

Shalev, A. Y. (1992). Posttraumatic stress disorder among injured survivors of a terrorist attack. *Journal of Nervous and Mental Disease*, 180, 505–509.

Shapiro, F. (1989a). Efficacy of the eye movement desensitization procedure in the treatment of traumatic memories. *Journal of Traumatic Stress*, 2, 199–223.

Shapiro, F. (1989b). Eye movement desensitization: A new treatment for Post-Traumatic Stress Disorder. *Journal of Behaviour Therapy and Experimental Psychiatry*, 20, 211–217.

Shapiro, F. (1995). *Eye movement desensitization and reprocessing: Basic principles, protocols and procedures.* New York: Guilford Press.

Shaver, K. G., & Drown, D. (1986). On causality, responsibility, and self blame: A theoretical note. *Journal of Personality and Social Psychology*, 50, 697–702.

Shore, J. H., Tatum, E. L., & Vollmer, W. M. (1986). Psychiatric reactions to disaster: The Mount St Helens experience. *American Journal of Psychiatry*, 143, 590–595.

Silver, R. L., Boon, C., & Stones, M. H. (1983). Searching for meaning in misfortune: Making sense of incest. *Journal of Social Issues*, 39, 81–101.

Silver, R., Wortman, C. B., & Crofton, A. (1990). The role of coping in support provision: The self-presentational dilemma of victims of life crisis. In B. R. Sarason, I. G. Sarason, & G. R. Pierce (Eds), *Social support: An interactional view* (pp. 397–426). New York: Wiley.

Silver, S. M. (1984). An inpatient program for post-traumatic stress disorder: Context as treatment. In C. R. Figley (Ed.), *Trauma and its wake*, Vol. II: *Traumatic stress theory, research, and intervention.* New York: Brunner/Mazel.

Silver, S. M., & Iacono, C. U. (1984). Factor-analytic support for DSM-III's post-traumatic stress disorder for Vietnam veterans. *Journal of Clinical Psychology*, 40, 5–14.

Silver, S. M., & Salamone-Genovese, L. (1991). A study of the MMPI Clinical and Research Scales for Post-Traumatic Stress Disorder Diagnostic Utility. *Journal of Traumatic Stress*, 4, 533–548.

Singh, B., & Raphael, B. (1981). Postdisaster morbidity of the bereaved: A possible role for preventative psychiatry? *Journal of Nervous and Mental Disease*, 169, 203–212.

Smith, T. W. (1992). A life-events approach to developing an index of societal well being. *Social Science Research*, 21, 353–379.

Smith, E. M., Robins, L. N., Pryzbeck, T. R., Goldring, E., & Solomon, S. D. (1986). Psychosocial consequences of a disaster. In J. Shore (Ed.), *Disaster stress studies: New methods and findings* (pp. 49–76). Washington, DC: American Psychiatric Press.

Smith, P., & Yule, W. (1997). Eye movement desensitization and reprocessing. Chapter to appear in W. Yule (Ed.), *Post traumatic stress disorder.* Chichester: Wiley.

Smucker, M. R., Dancu, C., Foa, E. B., & Niederee, J. L. (1995) Imagery rescripting: A new treatment for survivors of childhood sexual abuse suffering from posttraumatic stress. *Journal of Cognitive Psychotherapy*, 9, 3–17.

Solkoff, N., Gray, P., & Keill, S. (1986). Which Vietnam veterans develop posttraumatic stress disorders? *Journal of Clinical Psychology*, 42, 687–698.

Solomon, R. M., & Horn, J. M. (1986). Post shooting traumatic reactions: A pilot study. In J. Reese & H. Goldstein (Eds), *Psychological Services for Law Enforcement* (pp. 383–393), Washington, DC: United States Government Printing Office.

Solomon, S. (1986). Mobilizing social support networks in times of disaster. In C. Figley (Ed.), *Trauma and its Wake*. Vol. 2: *Traumatic stress theory, research, and intervention* (pp. 232–263). New York: Brunner/Mazel.

Solomon, S., & Canino, G. (1990). Appropriateness of the DSM-III-R criteria for post-traumatic stress disorder. *Comprehensive Psychiatry*, 31, 227–237.

Solomon, S. D., Smith, E. M., Robins, L. N., & Fischbach, R. L. (1987a). Social involvement as a mediator of disaster induced stress. *Journal of Applied Social Psychology*, 17, 1092–1112.

Solomon, Z. (1993). Immediate and long-term effects of traumatic combat stress among Israeli veterans of the Lebanon war. In J. P. Wilson & B. Raphael (Eds), *International handbook of traumatic stress syndromes* (pp. 321–332). New York: Plenum Press.

Solomon, Z., Avitzur, M., & Mikulincer, M. (1989a). Coping resources and social functioning following combat stress reactions: A longitudinal study. *Journal of Social and Clinical Psychology*, 8, 87–96.

Solomon, Z., Benbenishty, R., & Mikulincer, M. (1988a). A follow-up of Israeli casualties of combat stress reaction ('battle shock') in the 1982 Lebanon war. *British Journal of Clinical Psychology*, 27, 125–135.

Solomon, Z., Benbenishty, R., Neria, Y., Abramowitz, M., Ginzburg, K., & Ohry, A. (1993a). Assessment of PTSD: Validation of the Revised PTSD Inventory. *Israel Journal of Psychiatry and Related Sciences*, 30, 110–115.

Solomon, Z., Laor, N., Weiler, D., Muller, U. F., Hadar, O., Waysman, M., Koslowsky, M., Yakar, M. B., & Bleich, A. (1993b). The psychological impact of the Gulf war: a study of acute stress in Israeli evacuees. *Archives of General Psychiatry*, 50, 320–321.

Solomon, Z., & Mikulincer, M. (1992). Aftermaths of combat stress reactions: A three year study. *British Journal of Clinical Psychology*, 31, 21–32.

Solomon, Z., Mikulincer, M., & Avitzur, E. (1988b). Coping, locus of control, social support, and combat related posttraumatic stress disorder: A prospective study. *Journal of Personality and Social Psychology*, 55, 279–285.

Solomon, Z., Mikulincer, M., & Benbenishty, R. (1989b). Locus of control and combat-related post-traumatic stress disorder: The intervening role of battle intensity, threat appraisal and coping. *British Journal of Clinical Psychology*, 28, 131–144.

Solomon, Z., Mikulincer, M., & Flum, H. (1988c). Negative life events, coping responses, and combat-related psychopathology: A prospective study. *Journal of Abnormal Psychology*, 97, 302–307.

Solomon, Z., Mikulincer, M., & Kotler, M. (1987b). A two year follow-up of somatic complaints among Israeli combat stress reaction casualties. *Journal of Psychosomatic Research*, 31, 463–469.

Solomon, Z., Weisenberg, M., Schwarzwald, J., & Mikulincer, M. (1987c). Posttraumatic stress disorder among frontline soldiers with combat stress reaction: The 1982 Israeli experience. *American Journal of Psychiatry*, 144, 448–454.

Sorenson, S. B., & Golding, J. M. (1990). Depressive sequelae of recent criminal victimization. *Journal of Traumatic Stress*, 3, 337–350.

Southward, E. E. (1919). *Shell shock and neuropsychiatric problems*. Boston: Leonard.

Speed, N., Engdahl, B., Schwartz, J., & Eberly, R. (1989). Post-traumatic stress disorder as a consequence of the POW experience. *Journal of Nervous and Mental Disease*, 177, 147–153.

Spiegel, D. (1988). Dissociation and hypnosis in post-traumatic stress. *Journal of Traumatic Stress*, 1, 17–34.

Spielberger, C. D., Gorsuch, R. L., & Lushene, R. E. (1970). *STAI Manual for the state-trait anxiety inventory*. Palo Alto, CA: Consulting Psychologists Press.

Spiro, A., Schnurr, P. P., & Aldwin, C. M. (1994). Combat-related posttraumatic stress disorder symptoms in older men. *Psychology and Aging*, **9**, 17–26.

Spitzer, R. L., Williams, J. B. W., & Gibbon, M. (1987). *Structured Clinical Interview for DSM-III-R, Version NP-V*. New York: New York State Psychiatric Institute, Biometrics Research Department.

Spitzer, R. L., Williams, J. B. W., Gibbon, M., & First, M. (1992). The Structured Clinical Interview for DSM-III-R (SCID): History, rationale, and description. *Archives of General Psychiatry*, **49**, 624–629.

Stallard, P., & Law, F. (1993). Screening and psychological debriefing of adolescent survivors of life-threatening events. *British Journal of Psychiatry*, **163**, 660–665.

Stampfl, T. G., & Levis, D. J. (1967). Essentials of implosive therapy: A learning theory-based psychodynamic behavioural therapy. *Journal of Abnormal Psychology*, **72**, 157–163.

Steele, C. M. (1988). The psychology of self-affirmation: Sustaining the integrity of the self. In L. Berkowitz (Ed.), *Advances in experimental social psychology* (pp. 261–302), vol. 21. San Diego, CA: Academic Press.

Stein, J. H. (1977). *Better services for crime victims: A perspective package LGAA Grant Report*. Blackstone Institute.

Steinglass, P., & Gerrity, E. (1990). Natural disasters and post-traumatic stress disorder: Short-versus long-term recovery in two disaster-affected communities. *Journal of Applied Social Psychology*, **20**, 1746–1765.

Steketee, G., & Foa, E. B. (1987). Rape victims: Post-traumatic stress responses and their treatment: A review of the literature. *Journal of Anxiety Disorders*, **1**, 69–86.

Stratton, P., Heard, D., Hanks, H. G. I., Munton, A. G., Brewin, C. R., & Davidson, C. (1986). Coding causal beliefs in natural discourse. *British Journal of Social Psychology*, **25**, 299–313.

Stretch, R. (1985). PTSD among US army reserve Vietnam and Vietnam-era veterans. *Journal of Consulting and Clinical Psychology*, **55**, 272–275.

Stretch, R. H., Vail, J. D., & Maloney, J. P. (1985). Posttraumatic stress disorder among army nurse corps Vietnam veterans. *Journal of Consulting and Clinical Psychology*, **53**, 704–708.

Suls, J., & Fletcher, B. (1985). The relative efficacy of avoidant and nonavoidant coping strategies: A meta analysis. *Health Psychology*, **4**, 249–288.

Summerfield, D. (1993). War and posttraumatic stress disorder: The question of social context. *Journal of Nervous and Mental Disease*, **181**, 522.

Sutherland, S. M., & Davidson, J. R. T. (1994). Pharmacotherapy for post-traumatic stress disorder. *Psychiatric Clinics of North America*, **17**, 409–423.

Sweeney, P. D., Anderson, K., & Bailey, S. (1986). Attributional style in depression: A meta-analytic review. *Journal of Personality and Social Psychology*, **50**, 974–991.

Takuma, T. (1978). Human behaviour in the event of earthquakes. In E. L. Quarantelli (Ed.), *Disasters: Theory and Research*. Beverly Hills, CA: Sage.

Tangney, J. P., Wagner, P., & Gramzow, R. (1992). Proneness to shame, proneness to guilt, and psychopathology. *Journal of Abnormal Psychology*, **101**, 469–478.

Tatum, E., Vollmer, W., & Shore. J. H. (1985). High-risk groups of the Mount St. Helen's disaster. Paper presented at 138th Annual General Meeting of the American Psychiatric Association, Dallas, Texas, 18–24 May, 1985.

Taylor, A. J. W., & Frazer, A. G. (1982). The stress of post-disaster body handling and victim identification. *Journal of Human Stress*, **8**, 4–12.

Taylor, P., Abrahams, D., & Hewstone, M. (1988). Cancer, stress and personality: A correlational investigation of life-events, repression-sensitization and locus of control. *British Journal of Medical Psychology*, **61**, 179–183.

Taylor, S. (1981). The interface of cognitive and social psychology. In J. H. Harvey (Ed.), *Cognition, social behaviour, and the environment.* Hillsdale, NJ: Erlbaum.

Taylor, S. (1983). Adjustment to threatening life events: A theory of cognitive adaptation. *American Psychologist,* **38**, 1161–1173.

Taylor, S. E. (1984). Issues in the study of coping: A commentary. *Cancer,* **53**, 2313–2315.

Taylor, S. E., Lichtman, R. R., & Wood, J. V. (1984). Attributions, beliefs about control, and adjustment to breast cancer. *Journal of Personality and Social Psychology,* **46**, 489–502.

Taylor, V. A., Ross, G. A., & Quarantelli, E. L. (1976). *Delivery of mental health services in disasters: The Xenia tornado and some implications.* (Book and Monograph Series II.) Disaster Research Center, The Ohio State University, Colombus.

Teasdale, J. D. (1988). Cognitive vulnerability to persistent depression. *Cognition and Emotion,* **2**, 247–274.

Teasdale, J. D., & Barnard, P. J. (1993). *Affect, cognition and change: Remodelling depressive thought.* Hillsdale, NJ: Laurence Erlbaum.

Tennen, H., & Affleck, G. (1990). Blaming others for threatening events. *Psychological Bulletin,* **108**, 209–232.

Tennant, C. (1977). The General Health Questionnaire: A valid index of psychological impairment in Australian populations. *Medical Journal of Australia,* **2**, 392–394.

Tennant, C., & Andrews, G. (1978). The pathogenic quality of life event stress in neurotic impairment. *Archives of General Psychiatry,* **35**, 859–863.

Terr, L. C. (1985). Children traumatized in small groups. In S. Eth & R. Pynoos (Eds), *Posttraumatic stress disorder in children* (pp. 45–70). Washington, DC: American Psychiatric Association.

Terr, L. C. (1991). Childhood traumas: An outline and overview. *American Journal of Psychiatry,* **148**, 10–20.

Tesser, A., & Campbell, J. (1980). Self-definition and self-evaluation maintenance. In J. Suls & A. G. Greenwald (Eds), *Psychological perspective on the self* (vol. 2). Hillsdale, NJ: Erlbaum.

Thoits, P. A. (1982). Conceptual, methodological and theoretical problems in studying social support as a buffer against life event stress. *Journal of Health and Social Behaviour,* **23**, 145–159.

Thompson, J. A., Charlton, P. F. C., Kerry, R., Lee, D., & Turner, S. W. (1995). An open trial of exposure therapy based on de-conditioning for post-traumatic stress disorder. *British Journal of Clinical Psychology,* **34**, 407–416.

Thornton, B., Ryckman, R., Kirchner, G., Jacobs, J., Kaczor, L., & Kuehnel, R. (1988). Reaction to self-attributed victim responsibility: A comparative analysis of rape crisis counsellors and lay observers. *Journal of Applied Social Psychology,* **18**, 409–422.

Tierney, K. J. (1985). Report on the Coalinga earthquake of May 2, 1983: Report SSC 85–01. Sacramento, State of California Seismic Safety Commission, September 1985.

Tobin, D. L., Holroyd, K. A., Reynolds, R. V., & Wigal, J. K. (1989). The hierarchical factor structure of the coping strategies inventory. *Cognitive Therapy and Research,* **13**, 343–361.

Trimble, M. R. (1981). *Post-traumatic neurosis: From railway spine to the whiplash.* New York: Wiley.

True, W. R., Rice, J., Eisen, S. A., Heath, A. C., Goldberg, J., Lyons, M. J., & Nowak, J. (1993). A twin study of genetic and environmental contributions to liability for posttraumatic stress symptoms. *Archives of General Psychiatry,* **50**, 257–264.

Turner, R. J. (1981). Social support as a contingency in psychological well being. *Journal of Health and Social Behaviour,* **22**, 357–367.

Turnquist, D. C., Harvey, J. H., & Anderson, B. L. (1988). Attributions and adjustment to life-threatening illness. *British Journal of Clinical Psychology*, 27, 55–65.

Tversky, A., & Kahneman, D. (1974). Judgement under uncertainty: Heuristics and biases in judgements reveal some heuristics of thinking under uncertainty. *Science*, 185, 1124–1131.

Vaillant, G. E. (1971). Theoretical hierarchy of adaptive ego mechanisms. *Archives of General Psychiatry*, 24, 107–118.

Vaillant, G. E. (1977). *Adaption to life*. Boston: Little, Brown.

van der Kolk, B. A. (1983). Psychopharmacological issues in post-traumatic stress disorder. *Hospital and Community Psychiatry*, 34, 683–691.

van der Kolk, B. A. (1987). *Psychological trauma*. Washington, DC: American Psychiatric Press.

van der Kolk, B. A., Blitz, R., Burr, W., Sherry, S., & Hartmann, E. (1984a). Nightmares and trauma: A comparison of nightmares after combat with lifelong nightmares in veterans. *American Journal of Psychiatry*, 141, 187–190.

van der Kolk, B.A., Boyd, H., Krystal, J., & Greenberg, M. (1984b). Post-traumatic stress disorder as a biologically based disorder: Implications of the animal model of inescapable shock. In B. A. van der Kolk (Ed.), *Post-traumatic stress disorder: Psychological and biological sequelae* (pp. 124–134). Washington, DC: American Psychiatric Press.

van der Ploeg, H. M., & Kleijn, W. C. (1988). Being held hostage in the Netherlands: A study of long-term aftereffects. *Journal of Traumatic Stress*, 2, 153–169.

Vaughan, K., Wiese, M., Gold, R., & Tarrier, N. (1994). Eye-movement desensitisation: Symptom change in post-traumatic stress disorder. *British Journal of Psychiatry*, 164, 533–541.

Vogel, J. M., & Vernberg, E. M. (1993). Children's psychological responses to disasters. *Journal of Clinical Child Psychology*, 22, 464–484.

Wakefield, J. C. (1992). The concept of mental disorder: On the boundary between biological facts and social values. *American Psychologist*, 47, 373–388.

Warr, P. B., & Jackson, P. R. (1984). Self-esteem and employment among young workers. *Le Travail Humain*, 46, 355–366.

Watson, C. G. (1990). Psychometric posttraumatic stress disorder measurement techniques: A review. *Psychological Assessment*, 2, 460–469.

Watson, C. G., Juba, M. P., Manifold, V., Kucala, T., & Anderson, P. E. D. (1991d). The PTSD interview: Rationale, description, reliability, and concurrent validity of a DSM-III based technique. *Journal of Clinical Psychology*, 47, 179–214.

Watson, C. G., Kucala, T., Juba, M., Manifold, V., & Anderson, P. E. D. (1991b). A factor analysis of the DSM-III post-traumatic stress disorder criteria. *Journal of Clinical Psychology*, 47, 205–214.

Watson, D., & Clark, L. A. (1984). Negative affectivity: The predisposition to experience aversive emotional states. *Psychological Bulletin*, 96, 465–490.

Watson, D., Clark, L. A., Weber, K., Assenheimer, J. S., Strauss, M. E., & McCormick, R. A. (1995a). Testing a tripartite model. II: Exploring the symptom structure of anxiety and depression in student, adult, and patient samples. *Journal of Abnormal Psychology*, 104, 15–25.

Watson, D., Weber, K., Assenheimer, J. S., Clark, L. A., Strauss, M. E., & McCormick, R. A. (1995b). Testing a tripartite model. I: Evaluating the convergent and discriminant validity of anxiety and depression symptom scales. *Journal of Abnormal Psychology*, 104, 3–14.

Watson, P. B. (1987). Post-traumatic stress disorder in Australia and New Zealand: A critical review of the consequences of inescapable horror. *Medical Journal of Australia*, 147, 443–446.

Watts, F. N. (1982). Attributional aspects of medicine. In C. Antaki & C. Brewin (Eds), *Attributions and psychological change* (pp. 135–155). London: Academic Press.

Wayland, K., Roth, S., & Lochman, J. E. (1991). The relation between physical assault and psychological functioning in a sample of university women, and the relative effects of physical and sexual assault. *Journal of Traumatic Stress*, 4, 495–514.

Wegner, D. M., Shortt, J. W., Blake, A. W., & Page, M. S. (1990). The suppression of exciting thoughts. *Journal of Personality and Social Psychology*, 58, 409–418.

Wegner, D. M., & Zanakos, S. (1994). Chronic thought suppression. *Journal of Personality*, 62, 615–640.

Weighill, V. E. (1983). Compensation neurosis: A review of the literature. *Journal of Psychosomatic Research*, 27, 97–104.

Weiner, B. (1972). *Theories of motivation: From mechanism to cognition*. Chicago: Rand McNally.

Weiner, B. (1979). A theory of motivation for some classroom experiences. *Journal of Educational Psychology*, 71, 3–25.

Weiner, B. (1983). Some methodological pitfalls in attributional research. *Journal of Educational Psychology*, 75, 530–543.

Weiner, B. (1985). Spontaneous causal thinking. *Psychological Bulletin*, 97, 74–84.

Weiner, B. (1986). *An attributional theory of motivation and emotion*. New York: Springer Verlag.

Weinstein, N. D., & Lachendro, E. (1982). Egocentrism as a source of unrealistic optimism. *Personality and Social Psychology Bulletin*, 8, 195–200.

Weisaeth, L. (1983). The study of a factory fire. Doctoral dissertation, University of Oslo.

Weisaeth, L. (1989). Research on long term outcome of disasters. Paper presented at the discussion meeting—Post-traumatic stress disorder; prospects for inter-disciplinary investigation. CIBA Foundation, London, UK.

Weisenberg, M., Solomon, Z., Schwarzwald, J., & Mikulincer, M. (1987). Assessing the severity of posttraumatic stress disorder: Relation between dichotomous and continuous measures. *Journal of Consulting and Clinical Psychology*, 55, 432–434.

Weiss, D. S. (1993a). Structured clinical interview techniques. In J. P. Wilson & B. Raphael (Eds), *International handbook of traumatic stress syndromes* (pp. 179–187). New York: Plenum Press.

Weiss, D. S. (1993b). Psychological processes in traumatic stress. In R. Allen (Ed.), *Handbook of post-disaster interventions* [Special Issue]. *Journal of Social Behaviour and Personality*, 8, 3–28.

Weiss, R. (1974). The provisions of social relationships. In Z. Rubin (Ed.), *Doing onto others*. Englewood Cliffs, NJ: Prentice Hall.

Weiss, R. (1976). Transition states and other stressful situations: Their nature and programs for their management. In G. Caplan and M. Killilea (Eds), *Support systems and mutual help: Multidisciplinary explorations*. New York: Grune & Stratton.

Wells, A., & Matthews, G. (1994). *Attention and emotion: A clinical perspective*. Hillsdale, NJ: Laurence Erlbaum.

Westermeyer, J. (1989). Cross-cultural care for PTSD: Research, training, and service needs for the future. *Journal of Traumatic Stress*, 2, 515–536.

Westermeyer, J., Vang, T. F., & Neider, J. (1983). Migration and mental health among refugees: Association of pre- and post-migration factors with self-rating scales. *Journal of Nervous and Mental Disease*, 171, 92–96.

Western, J. S., & Milne, G. (1979). Some social effects of a natural hazard: Darwin residents and cyclone Tracy. In R. L. Heathcote & B. G. Thom (Eds), *Natural hazards in Australia*. Canberra: Australian Academy of Science.

Wethington, E., & Kessler, R. C. (1986). Perceived support, received support, and adjustment to stressful life events. *Journal of Health and Social Behaviour*, 27, 78–89.

Whittington, R., & Wykes, T. (1991). Coping strategies used by staff following assault by a patient: An exploratory study. *Work and Stress*, 5, 37–48.

Wilkinson, C.B. (1983). Aftermath of a disaster: The collapse of the Hyatt Regency Hotel Skywalk. *American Journal of Psychiatry*, 140, 1134–1139.

Williams, J. B. W., Gibbon, M., First, M. B., Spitzer, R. L., Davies, M., Borus, J., Howes, M., Kane, J., Pope, H. G., Rounsaville, B., & Wittchen, H. U. (1992). The Structured Clinical Interview for DSM-III-R (SCID): Multisite test-retest reliability. *Archives of General Psychiatry*, 49, 630–636.

Williams, R. M. (1989). Towards a cognitive model of PTSD. Paper presented at the discussion meeting—Post-traumatic stress disorder; prospects for inter-disciplinary investigation. CIBA Foundation, London, UK.

Williams, R. M., Hodgkinson, P., Joseph, S., & Yule, W. (1995). Attitudes to emotion, crisis support and distress 30 months after the capsize of a passenger ferry. *Crisis Intervention*, 1, 209–214.

Williams, R., Joseph, S., & Yule, W. (1993). Disaster and mental health. In D. Bhugra & J. Leff (Eds), *Principles of social psychiatry*. Oxford: Blackwell Scientific Publications.

Williams, R. M., Joseph, S., & Yule, W. (1994). The role of avoidance in coping with disasters: A study of survivors of the capsize of the *Herald of Free Enterprise*. *Clinical Psychology and Psychotherapy*, 1, 97–94.

Wilson, J. P., & Krause, G. (1985). Predicting PTSD among Vietnam veterans. In W. Kelly (Ed.), *Post-traumatic stress disorder and the war veteran patient* (pp. 102–148). New York: Brunner/Mazel.

Wolfe, D. A., Sas, L., & Wekerle, C. (1994). Factors associated with the development of posttraumatic stress disorder among child victims of sexual abuse. *Child Abuse and Neglect*, 18, 37–50.

Wolfe, J., Brown, P. J., & Buscela, M. L. (1992). Symptom responses of female Vietnam veterans to Operation Desert Storm. *American Journal of Psychiatry*, 149, 676–679.

Wolfe, J., & Charney, D. S. (1991). Use of neuropsychological assessment in posttraumatic stress disorder. *Psychological Assessment*, 3, 573–580.

Wolfe, J., & Keane, T. M. (1993). New perspectives in the assessment and diagnosis of combat-related posttraumatic stress disorder. In J. P. Wilson & B. Raphael (Eds), *International handbook of traumatic stress syndromes* (pp. 165–177). New York: Plenum Press.

Wolfe, V. V., Gentile, C., Michienzi, T. et al. (1991). The Children's Impact of Traumatic Events Scale: A measure of post-sexual abuse PTSD symptoms. *Behaviour Assessment*, 13, 359–383.

Wolfe, V. V., Gentile, C., & Wolfe, D. A. (1989). The impact of sexual abuse on children: A PTSD formulation. *Behavior Therapy*, 20, 215–228.

Wolfe, V. V., & Wolfe, D. A. (1986). The sexual abuse fear evaluation (SAFE): A subscale for the fear survey schedule for children—revised. Unpublished questionnaire. University of Western Ontario, London, Canada.

Wolfe, V. V., Wolfe, D. A., Gentile, C., & LaRose, L. (1986). The children's impact of traumatic events scale (CITES). Available from V. Wolfe, Dept. of Paediatric Psychology, Children's Hospital of Western Ontario, London, Canada.

Wolfenstein, M. (1957). *Disaster: A psychological essay*. Glencoe, IL: Free Press.

Wong, P. T. P., & Weiner, B. (1981). When people ask 'why' questions, and the heuristics of attributional search. *Journal of Personality and Social Psychology*, 40, 650–663.

Wolpe, J., & Abrams, J. (1991). Post-Traumatic Stress Disorder overcome by eye-movement desensitization: A case report. *Journal of Behaviour Therapy and Experimen-*

tal Psychiatry, **22**, 39–43.

World Health Organisation (1978). *Mental disorders: Glossary and guide to their classification in accordance with the ninth revision of the international classification of diseases.* Geneva: WHO.

World Health Organisation (1993). *Mental disorders: Glossary and guide to their classification in accordance with the tenth revision of the international classification of diseases.* Geneva: WHO.

Worthington, E. R. (1977). Pre-service adjustment and Vietnam era veterans. *Military Medicine*, **142**, 865–866.

Wright, D., & Gaskell, G. (1992). The construction and function of vivid memories. In M. A, Conway, D. C. Rubin, H. Spinnler, & W. A. Wagenaar (Eds), *Theoretical perspectives on autobiographical memory* (pp. 275–292). Dordrecht, Netherlands: Kluwer Academic Publishers.

Wright, K. M., Ursano, R. J., Bartone, P. T., & Ingraham, L. H. (1990). The shared experience of catastrophe: An expanded classification of disaster community. *American Journal of Orthopsychiatry*, **60**, 35–42.

Yeary, J. (1982). Incest and chemical dependency. *Journal of Psychoactive Drugs*, **14**, 133–135.

Yehuda, R., Southwick, S. M., & Giller, E. L. (1992). Exposure to atrocities and severity of chronic posttraumatic stress disorder in Vietnam combat veterans. *American Journal of Psychiatry*, **149**, 333–336.

Yule, W. (1990). Post traumatic stress in children who survived the *Jupiter* cruise ship disaster. Paper presented at the 1990 American Psychological Association Conference.

Yule, W. (1991). Children in shipping disasters. *Journal of the Royal Society of Medicine*, **84**, 12–15.

Yule, W., & Gold, A. (1993). *Wise before the event: Coping with crises in school.* London: Calouste Gulbenkian Foundation.

Yule, W., Hodgkinson, P., Joseph, S., Parkes, C. M., & Williams, R. (1990a). The *Herald of Free Enterprise*: 30 months follow-up. Paper presented at the second European Conference on Traumatic Stress, Netherlands, 23–27 September 1990.

Yule, W., & Udwin, O. (1991). Screening child survivors for post-traumatic stress disorders: Experiences from the 'Jupiter sinking'. *British Journal of Clinical Psychology*, **30**, 131–138.

Yule, W., Udwin, O. & Murdoch, K. (1990b). The 'Jupiter' sinking: Effects on children's fears, depression and anxiety. *Journal of Child Psychology and Psychiatry*, **31**, 1051–1061.

Yule, W., & Williams, R. A. (1990). Post-traumatic stress reactions in children. *Journal of Traumatic Stress*, **3**, 279–295.

Yule, W., Ten Bruggencate, S., & Joseph, S. (1994). Principal components analysis of the impact of event scale in adolescents who survived a shipping disaster. *Personality and Individual Differences*, **16**, 685–691.

Zeidner, M., & Ben-Zur, H. (1994). Individual differences in anxiety, coping, and post-traumatic stress in the aftermath of the Persian Gulf war. *Personality and Individual Differences*, **16**, 459–476.

Zeiss, R., & Dickman, H. (1989). PTSD 40 years later: Incidence and person-situation correlates in former POW's. *Journal of Clinical Psychology*, **45**, 80–87.

Zeller, R. A., & Carmines, E. G. (1980). *Measurement in the social sciences. The link between theory and data.* Cambridge: Cambridge University Press.

Zilberg, N. J., Weiss, D. S., & Horowitz, M. J. (1982). Impact of Event Scale: A cross-validation study and some empirical evidence supporting a conceptual model of stress response syndromes. *Journal of Consulting and Clinical Psychology*, **50**, 407–414.

Zuckerman, M. (1979). Attribution of success and failure revisited, or: The motivational bias is alive and well in attribution theory. *Journal of Personality*, 47, 245–287.

Zuckerman, L. A., Oliver, J. M., Hollingsworth, H. H., & Austrin, H. R. (1986). A comparison of life events scoring methods as predictors of psychological symptomatology. *Journal of Human Stress*, 12, 64–70.

SUBJECT INDEX

Related titles of interest from Wiley...

Treating Post-Traumatic Stress Disorder
Donald Meichenbaum

"This book will be new for years to come... it's an extraordinary volume, a crowning contribution to traumascience."

Journal of Trauma Studies

"... more than just a manual - it is a gift of many years of research and dedication to the understanding and impact of PTSD. Adjectives like "definitive" and "indispensable" come to mind."

Journal of Religion and Health

0-471-97241-X 600pp 1997 Paperback

Stress and Policing
Sources and Strategies
Jennifer M. Brown and Elizabeth A. Campbell

Presents an overview of the sources and consequences of stress experienced by police officers and ways to deal with it.

0-471-96176-0 214pp 1995 Paperback

Psychology in Counselling and Therapeutic Practice
Jill D. Wilkinson and Elizabeth A. Campbell

Focusing on the needs of counsellors, this book offers a concise and selective account of psychological concepts and processes, illustrated by examples and cases that relate to problems and processes of counselling.

0-471-95562-0 300pp 1997 Paperback

Research Methods in Stress and Health Psychology
Edited by Stan V. Kasl and Cary L. Cooper

0-471-95493-4 332pp 1995 Paperback

Visit the Wiley Home Page at http://www.wiley.co.uk

Contents

Preface

I first met Linus Pauling in 1984, during a meeting of the American Chemical Society in Seattle. I was attending as a correspondent for the *Journal of the American Medical Association* and arrived early at a session in which he was to present his latest work on megadoses of vitamin C. Every journalist there knew that Pauling was good copy, but almost everyone also shared the opinion that the vitamin C story had received more than adequate coverage during the thirteen years Pauling had been advocating its use. I was the only one in the pressroom who planned to attend.

More than hearing what he had to say, however, I was interested in seeing the person, the man who had variously been described as the century's greatest chemist, the greatest living American scientist, and a crackpot.

I was early and the only one in the seminar room when Pauling strode in, tall, erect, his long white hair forming a wispy corona around a black beret. He walked over to me, introduced himself, and to my amazement gave me a five-minute personal minilecture on the chemical binding properties of tin. Quantum chemistry was not my specialty—I was there because of what I knew about medical science and molecular biology—but the degree to which I understood what he was saying mattered less than the impression he made. He seemed to be thinking aloud as he talked, coming up with variations on his ideas, working through some theoretical problems as he spoke. I was overwhelmed that the two-time Nobel Prize–winner would choose to spend his time discussing science with me. I was flattered by his attention and charmed by his friendly, enthusiastic manner. I learned later that this reaction was common among Pauling's many admirers.

I saved the piece of yellow notepaper he used to illustrate his ideas and I determined to find out more about him. I knew that he had been born and raised in Oregon, my home state, and I talked the editor of the Sunday magazine at the *Oregonian* newspaper in Portland into sending me to Pauling's ranch at Big Sur for two days to prepare a profile of his early years. After that piece was published, I tracked his career and kept in touch. Eventually our discussions led to his cooperation in the preparation of this book.

Pauling's life was extraordinarily long, varied, tumultuous, and important for the history of twentieth-century science. During his career, Pauling, among many other achievements, described the nature of the chemical bond; discovered the structure of proteins; intuited the cause of sickle-cell anemia; engaged in this century's most famous scientific race, for the structure of DNA; won a Presidential Medal of Merit for his World War II research; advanced the fields of x-ray crystallography, electron diffraction, quantum mechanics, biochemistry, molecular psychiatry, nuclear physics, anesthesia, immunology, and nutrition; and wrote more than 500 articles and eleven books. Not to mention those two Nobel Prizes, for chemistry and for peace (Pauling remains the only person to have won two unshared Nobel Prizes).

He was recognized as a phenomenon of science at a young age—at thirty-one he became the youngest person elected to the National Academy of Sciences and at thirty-six was given control of the nation's leading department of chemistry—and continued to make seminal contributions for sixty years.

His ideas about the forces that bind atoms to other atoms and the structure of the molecules they form, expressed in groundbreaking textbooks and legendary lectures, reshaped twentieth-century chemistry. Molecular structure became a leitmotif for Pauling, a unifying concept that he used successfully to investigate and tie together physics, chemistry, biology, and medicine. He was fearless in leaping over disciplinary boundaries, and by doing so helped create new fields of research: chemical physics, orthomolecular medicine, and most important, molecular biology.

But his scientific work is only half the story. Pauling, influenced greatly by his wife, Ava Helen, used his scientific renown as a springboard to jump into political activism. Along with Albert Einstein and Leo Szilard, Pauling was a member of the Emergency Committee of Atomic Scientists, a small but important group that after World War II worked to limit the spread of atomic weapons. Pauling's increasingly outspoken views on nuclear policy led to political persecution that included a 24-year investigation by the FBI, an inquiry into revoking his government security clearance, the revocation of his passport, the loss of government grants, vilification in the press, and intimidation and threats of a contempt citation by the U.S. Senate. He fought back with articles, speeches, and legal actions, including well-publicized suits against the Hearst organization, William F. Buckley's *National Review,* and the Department of Defense.

By the early 1960s, Pauling had earned a reputation for being audacious, intuitive, stubborn, charming, irreverent, self-promoting, self-reliant, self-involved to the point of arrogance—and correct about almost everything. But within a few years, he fell from grace. Weeks after winning the Peace Prize, under pressure from an administration he had alienated with his political activities, he acrimoniously broke his association with the California Institute of Technology, his intellectual home for four decades. At an age when most people think of retiring, Pauling began the life of an academic nomad, wandering from school to school before finally starting his own institute to study nutrition and medicine. He became famous again in the early 1970s for advocating large doses of vitamin C as a palliative for everything from the common cold to cancer—claims that incurred the wrath of the medical establishment—and his former colleagues watched uncomfortably as Pauling spent his energy and money fighting what seemed to many a ridiculous battle for a cheap nutritional supplement. Over the next twenty years, Pauling's scientific image changed from brilliant individualist to monomaniacal crank.

But in the late 1980s and early 1990s new evidence emerged to form a more complete picture of the effects of vitamin C. That picture, although still fuzzy, increasingly supports what Pauling had been saying for decades.

—ⅿⅿ—

Biography is, in the end, interpretation. I started writing this book as a journalist, gathering information from as wide a range of sources as possible, attempting to present the facts in a neutral and "objective" manner. I soon found that this was impossible. On one level, there was simply too much material. Pauling's life was too long and too full to pack into a single volume without extensive condensation and selection, and every selection required a personal decision about value.

There were also too many strongly felt opinions about Pauling, and too many paradoxes and conundrums in his life—a genius whose mother was committed to a mental ward; a pacifist who patented an armor-piercing shell; a lover of humanity who practically ignored his own children—to approach neutrally. Finally, I believe that science has often been misrepresented in the past, especially by scientists, as a quest for knowledge uncolored by personality or the surrounding social milieu. But Pauling's life illustrates the importance of funding concerns, public relations, politics, and personality in the way scientific ideas are discovered and advanced. Placing his work in this context again requires careful interpretation.

I began this project as a Pauling enthusiast, and remain one, although my enthusiasm is now qualified. Pauling was a charming extrovert and an extraordinary intellect, a good storyteller and a man with a disarming way of treating all people as his equal (until proved otherwise). Below the surface charm, however, was a fiercely competitive and emotionally constricted man, a more complex character than his public persona. I have tried to present him in his complexity in this biography.

—*ᴍᴍ*—

To create this portrait of Pauling, I have relied, wherever possible, on primary sources, especially scores of interviews with Pauling, his family members, colleagues, rivals, students, and critics; Pauling's personal correspondence, manuscripts, lab books, and scientific publications; archival materials, including letters, scientific works, manuscripts, and oral histories concerning Pauling kept by his contemporaries; public government documents, including congressional and military files recently made available through the National Archives; court and county records; and more than 3,000 pages of formerly classified material newly released from the FBI, the U. S. Department of State, and the U.S. armed forces. These have been supplemented by hundreds of newspaper, magazine, and journal articles written about Pauling, his wife, his scientific work, and his political activities, as well as scores of scientific and political histories of the period. Significant sources are listed in the bibliography.

This is not an authorized biography; Pauling did not insist on editorial control in exchange for access. Although he opened his memory and his files to me, he asked only for the right to correct provable errors of fact (I am happy to say that in reviewing the first third of the manuscript before his death, he found few). Once we began working together, his cooperation was complete. I interviewed him at length a dozen times and often exchanged phone calls. He gave me permission to review and quote from the huge store of personal and professional documents in the archives at Oregon State University; encouraged colleagues, friends, and family members to talk with me; opened his files at the Linus Pauling Institute; cooperated in Freedom of Information Act requests; and shared with me private papers kept at his ranch at Big Sur.

I owe many debts to those who assisted me in the preparation of this book. The cooperation and candor of Linus Pauling; his sisters, Pauline and Lucile; daughter, Linda Pauling Kamb; and sons Crellin Pauling and Linus Pauling, Jr., were vital in the preparation of this book. Among the many people I interviewed or with whom I corresponded, I give special thanks to John Edsall, William Lipscomb, Art Robinson, Alex Rich, Matthew Mceselson, Francis Crick, Martin Karplus, Dick Marsh, Herman Mark, Richard Morgan, Elvin Kabat, Lee DuBridge, Arletta Townsend Sturdivant, John Roberts, Norman Davidson, Joseph Koepfli, Marjorie Senechal, Verner Schomaker, Dick Shoemaker, Ray Owen, Matthias Rath, Arnold Beckman, Zelek Herman, Joshua Lederberg, Richard Noyes, and Gerard and Eleanor Piel, who provided me a wonderful afternoon in New York City. Paul Engelking, Helmut Plant, and Wolfgang Leppmann at the University of Oregon assisted me in translating letters written in German. Harriet Zuckerman kindly allowed me to use the interview with Pauling she conducted as part of her preparation for *Scientific Elite*. I thank also the scores of people who responded to my requests for information in the *New York Times Book Review* and *Engineering and Science*, the magazine of Caltech.

Biographers depend on the goodwill and assistance of the keepers of records, and I owe a debt to many. Clifford Mead, head of special collections at Oregon State University's Kerr Library, and his entire staff went far beyond the expected with their unfailing courtesy and invaluable assistance with the extensive Ava Helen and Linus Pauling collection. This remarkable trove of scientific and personal papers will become even more accessible thanks to the pioneering work of Ramesh Krishnamurthy in bringing the papers on-line.

I owe a special debt, too, to Dorothy Munro, Pauling's indispensable right hand at the Linus Pauling Institute, who both guided me through the institute's sometimes confusing filing system and ensured that my days in Palo Alto were pleasant and productive. Emily Oakhill, archivist at the Rockefeller Archive Center, was particularly good at finding relevant files within that astounding collection. Rod Ross at the National Archives succeeded in locating a store of files that cast light on the internal workings of the Senate Internal Security Subcommittee. Jane Dietrich at Caltech offered friendly and useful help. My thanks also go to archivists and librarians at the University of Oregon, Harvard, MIT, Columbia, Smith College, the University of Chicago, the American Philosophical Society, the National Academy of Sciences, the American Institute of Physics, the Library of Congress, the Beckman Center for the History of Science, the Oregon Historical Society, the City of Pasadena, and Caltech.

This project was guided and informed by the viewpoints of several historians of science, among whom I particularly want to thank Daniel Kevles, whose book *The Physicists* showed me that the history of American science was also the history of politics and economics; Horace Judson, who proved in *The Eighth Day of Creation* that something as potentially dry as molecular biology can make fascinating reading; Robert Paradowski, whose doctoral dissertation, *The Structural Chemistry of Linus Pauling*, was essential in my understanding of Pauling's early chemical successes; and Robert Kargon and Lily Kay for their excellent work on the early and middle sections, respectively, of the history of Caltech.

I thank Bob Bender, my editor at Simon & Schuster, for his support of and patience with an author whose two-year project turned into a five-year marathon, and my agent Nat Sobel for placing the book with an editor as good as Bob.

Finally and mostly, I thank my wife, Lauren Kessler, who not only encouraged me to keep after Pauling until he agreed to cooperate in this project, but also acted as a sounding board for ideas, provided a sympathetic ear for complaints, and superbly edited most of the text, all while writing an award-winning book of her own.

THOMAS HAGER
Eugene, Oregon
June 4, 1995

The West

He could see everything from here.

The green Willamette River, dotted with fishing and pleasure boats, slid in a long curve right to left. The far bank was fringed with cottonwoods and oaks, and he could see beyond that to the patchwork of farms and woodlots that filled the valley and, farther still, to the foothills of the Cascades, blanketed in black-green firs. Over it all rose Mount Hood, a jagged, solitary, snow-covered peak that guarded the valley. It made sense from here, the geography of his home. He liked the sense of seeing how things fit and of being where no one else came, and he loved the height and the wind—and the sense of danger.

It was 1916, and Linus Pauling, fifteen years old, was clinging to the top of a crumbling smokestack in an abandoned smelter near the small town of Oswego, Oregon. He was a solitary boy with a quick and restless intelligence and was not afraid of much—not of exploring Sucker Creek, where his mother had warned him not to go because his father had broken his arm there when he was a boy; not of high-wiring out on the skeletal wooden railroad trestle over the Willamette while his sisters squealed in fright; not of climbing hand over hand up the rusted rungs of the smelter smokestack to its top, eight stories up in the air. He had no one to tell him no.

The smelter was his playground, a place he came often on weekends when he visited his grandparents, riding the trolley and the interurban train from his home in East Portland to theirs, a few miles south in Oswego, where his grandmother fussed over him in German and fed him cake and his grandfather let him sleep on a pallet in the shack at the smelter, where he was the night watchman. They spoiled him because he was their only son's only son and because their son was dead.

On Sunday he would ride home, sometimes with plunder. Exploring the smelter, he had found an old testing laboratory, a place where iron ore had once been assayed. Someone had left a good deal behind when the smelter closed: shelves crowded with small specimen bottles for holding ore samples; large, dark carboys of concentrated acids; various bottles and boxes of chemicals; odds and ends of laboratory glassware and equipment.

Linus brought an old, battered suitcase with him from home and began loading up everything he could carry. This was not stealing, he told himself; it was more like salvage, because the laboratory had been abandoned. Nobody wanted these things but him. He packed the suitcase with pounds of potassium permanganate and other chemicals and carried it home with him on the train, innocently looking at the other passengers while gripping between his legs five gallons of concentrated nitric acid. Another time he took apart a still for making pure water and brought it home in pieces, thinking of making a fortune supplying pure water to garages for car batteries. Then he found out how little people would pay for pure water. His greatest feat was the transport of a small, brick-lined electric furnace. Since it could not be disassembled, he talked a friend into helping him haul it down to the river, where they loaded it into a borrowed canoe, paddled miles downriver, then pushed it two miles home up Hawthorne Boulevard in a wheelbarrow.

When he was done, he had a surprisingly sophisticated laboratory in the basement of his mother's boardinghouse, in a roughly made room he had hammered together from odds and ends of salvaged lumber.

Besides his grandparents' house, this was the one place he could go to get away from his mother, whom he hated, and his sisters, who often annoyed him. This was the one place where he could make sense of things.

It was the only place that felt like home to him.

Because his real home, his true home, the place where his family had been complete and he had been truly happy, was several years in the past and several hundred miles to the east.

"Doctor" Pauling

Condon, Oregon, sits on the side of a high plateau overlooking a thousand square miles of gully-scarred brown-and-gold hills. It is a dry country. The town sits in the middle of a vast volcanic plateau that spreads east from the Cascades. The mountains lift and shred the rain-clouds as they sail inland from the Pacific, wringing out the moisture and giving it to the Willamette Valley. By the time the air gets to Condon, it is sere and crystalline, too dry to grow anything but bunchgrass and sagebrush.

To the first white pioneers, this arid land was the far end of the Great American Desert, a final barrier to be overcome on their way to the Willamette Valley a few score miles farther west. It was not until later, when some of them found the Eden at the end of the trail too crowded or too rainy, that a few trickled back east over the mountains, pushing out the local Indians and following the gullies up into the rolling hills to fatten their sheep and cattle on the bunchgrass. The creek beds held the only easy water, and the first pioneers made good ranches and farms down there, long, narrow strips of surprising green snaking through the plateau.

Outside of the creeks, one of the few substantial sources of water was Summit Springs, a large, cold font that sprang out of the rocks high on a hillside. It was here, in 1879, that Harry C. Condon, a lawyer in the nearby town of Alkali, platted a town and named it after himself.

To everyone's surprise, it boomed. An enterprising farmer discovered he could sink a well in the plateau and find ample water, then harvest two good crops of grain a year from the area's deep, wind-blown volcanic soil. Within a decade hundreds of settlers had moved in, and one observer was calling the Condon area "Kansas with hills." By the turn of the century the town had become the county seat and regional shipping center for some of the richest wheat-growing land in the world. Per capita income in the area was among the highest in Oregon. Promoters began calling the dry plateau "the Inland Empire" and Condon "Wheat City."

On a blisteringly hot summer day in 1899, Herman Henry William Pauling stepped off the stagecoach in Condon. Twenty-two years old, tall, clean-shaven, with wavy blond hair, full lips, and a penchant for dressing well—high collars, dark suits, and a pair of pince-nez—he cut a figure in the rough-and-tumble town. He had been asked to come to Condon by a group of Portland investors who wanted him to start a pharmacy. And he did not like what he saw.

Instead of the booming regional mercantile center that had been described to him, he was looking at a raw, dirty little farming town—six blocks of rough wooden buildings facing a wide dirt street, several under construction, a scattering of small houses, and a public watering trough. Chickens scratched in the road, flies were thick, and dogs roamed everywhere. Beyond the end of Main Street was nothing but wheat farms and desert. No trees, no rivers or lakes, no other towns. Just a huge sky, a thin pall of dust, and the sound of the wind.

It was disillusioning, but he wasn't there to enjoy the scenery. He set off to inspect the site that had been arranged for his new enterprise. Condon's only "drugstores" until Pauling arrived were storefronts where untrained storekeepers sold an appalling collection of sometimes useless, sometimes dangerous, patent medicines, many of which were used on both man and beast. The only other option for remedies was through the medicine shows still making the rural circuit, with quacks hawking their cure-alls from the backs of wagons.

Complaints from physicians unable to get reliable drugs and a public tired of useless, expensive medicines finally spurred regulation in Oregon in the 1890s. Reputable druggists formed associations and policed their members. A state board of pharmacy was formed early in the 1900s. In this atmosphere of change and reform, a group of Portland investors saw a chance to make money: Full-scale drugstores staffed by registered pharmacists in fast-growing towns would outsell the patent-medicine shops and make a fortune. Condon looked like a good test market. And Pauling was just the sort of young man to make their new enterprise fly.

Despite his youth, he had already earned a reputation around Portland as a well-trained, hardworking, bright, and likable pharmacist. His parents were German immigrants who had come west from New York and settled in Oswego, a little town south of Portland, drawn by the lure of employment in what was then the biggest iron foundry west of the Rockies. Herman (born "Hermann," he later dropped the second "n") was born during a stop in Missouri. An ambitious boy, he dropped out of school in the tenth grade and talked himself into an apprenticeship with an Oswego druggist who taught him the craft of compounding medicines.

Pharmacy was as much a craft in those days as a science. At the turn of the century there was no synthetic pharmaceutical industry, no Food and Drug Administration, little regulation of the purity or quality of drugs. There was, however, a self-governing pride in the quality of their work that guided the best pharmacists. Herman learned from one, a teacher who emphasized the absolute importance of careful measurement and conscientious formulation, who stressed the power that drugs had and the responsibility druggists shouldered in their preparation. Herman's Bible became the *Pharmacopoeia of the United States of America,* a recipe book for the preparation of drugs, compiled by a national convention of pharmacists, from which he learned how to assay morphine and ferment bitter wine of iron; how to compound mustard liniment and extract syrup of rose; how to pull the active essences from wild cherries, coca, dandelions, and poppies and use them to make pills, ointments, tinctures, and oils.

He was good at it, and his skill and sympathetic manner soon made Herman a town favorite: When the Oswego doctor left town, people would stop the teenager on the street and ask him to diagnose and prescribe for their medical problems. By the time he was nineteen Herman had moved to Portland and started working his way up the ladder in some of the city's biggest pharmacies. Within a few years he had earned an invitation to manage the Condon store.

⟶⟿⟵

Condon was delighted with its new pharmacist. The weekly newspaper rejoiced that "Doctor" Pauling was "a registered, reliable and experienced druggist"—in contrast to the patent-medicine peddlers. It was an image that Herman did his best to live up to. His father may have been an uneducated farmer and foundry worker, but Herman had found a way to become a professional man running his own business. He opened his doors, worked hard, and soon earned a reputation for honesty and skill in his craft. Among those who took special notice of the young druggist were Condon's young unmarried women. To them, the arrival of an eligible bachelor of Herman's caliber was cause for celebration.

This was especially true in the household of Condon businessman, attorney, and town founder Linus Wilson Darling. Darling had four daughters, his "Four Queens," he called them: Goldie Victoria, Lucy Isabelle, Estella Martha, and Elizabeth Abigail. Goldie, the eldest, had married a leading merchant in town. The next in line for matrimony was eighteen-year-old Lucy Isabelle, a handsome, dark-haired, occasionally melancholy girl whom everyone called Belle.

All through the fall and winter of 1899 the town's dashing new pharmacist was a featured guest at dinners, dances, and sleigh rides. And almost everywhere Herman Pauling went, he found himself talking to Belle Darling. By Halloween they were ardent sweethearts—Herman wrote poems to "A maiden fair with jet black hair / Her heart beats kind and true / She confides in me her every care / This maid with eyes light blue"—and by Christmas they were planning their wedding. An ornate valentine in 1900 came to Belle inscribed with a note to "my sweetest fairy" in which Herman outlined his role as a husband: ". . . You shall share my every joy equally while our sorrows I will bear alone. . . . Dear love, when life's storms are raging fiercely I offer you my arms as your protection, and you can trust in their fond yet firm embrace. When in after years the cares of home and motherhood bear upon your mind you shall find me ever an able assistant and benefactor." In May 1900 they were married. The ceremony drew a good-sized crowd of the town's leading citizens to Condon's largest church, which was beflowered, the local newspaper noted, "like a veritable Garden of Eden." One witness recalled that Herman and Belle were the handsomest couple she had ever seen.

───※───

Life's storms, however, quickly followed. Within weeks of the wedding, the Portland investors behind Pauling's drugstore received an attractive offer for the business and decided to sell out. Herman was not asked to stay on. He searched through other small towns in the area to find one where he might start his own business but couldn't come up with the right combination of affordability and opportunity. He was forced to return with his bride to Portland and take a lesser job as a clerk for a drug-supply company. It was a disappointing step down, in both position and income. Herman and Belle could afford nothing better than rooms in a cheap apartment house on the edge of Portland's Chinatown.

It was here, on February 28, 1901, that their first child, Linus Carl

Pauling, was born. His name was traditional: The Linus was taken from Belle's father; Carl, from Herman's father. The birth of a son was a joyful event for Herman, who was by nature a warm and loving family man, close to his own parents throughout his life and affectionate to children. But Belle's reaction was more mixed. She was only nineteen years old when Linus was born, and like any small-town girl brought to the big city, she wanted to immerse herself in shopping, the theater, amusement parks—all the pleasures she could never have in Condon. Now, before she had had a chance to fully enjoy any of these delights, she had to face the responsibilities and constraints of motherhood. Linus was followed within three years by two sisters, Pauline in 1902 and Frances Lucile (who later dropped her first name and was known just as Lucile) on New Year's Day, 1904. Despite—and in part because of—her deep love for Herman, Belle began to resent the children. She started hectoring her husband to bring in more money and became a complaining, sometimes indifferent mother.

Belle's difficulty adapting to parenthood was rooted in her childhood, one scarred by neglect, uncertainty, and the whims of a vain and unloving father. Her father, Linus Darling, was a self-made, self-concerned man with little time for his daughters. A Canadian by birth, at age seven he had been deserted by his own father, who ran off to fight for the Union in the U.S. Civil War. Destitute, Darling's mother moved her six children to New York State, where she died in 1867. The children were scattered, Linus Darling ending up a "bound boy" working for his room and board in New Jersey. He ran away as a teenager to work his way to Oregon, where he became a true western character: quick-witted, fun-loving, hard-drinking, peripatetic—a charming, selfish, irresponsible dreamer.

While teaching school in the lush farm country of Marion County, Oregon, Darling met his future wife, Belle's mother, Alcy Delilah Neal, among his students. The Neal side of the family was pioneer stock, sober, hardworking, and long-lived. If there was a gene for long life in Linus Pauling, it can be traced back to Cornelius O'Neal, his great-great-grandfather, an Irish immigrant who served with "Swamp Fox" Francis Marion during the Revolutionary War. According to family lore, Cornelius came west in 1844 at age eighty-three with some of his thirteen children and then trekked back to Missouri in his nineties to bring back some more family. His son, Linus's great-grandfather Calvin Neal, homesteaded a rich square mile of bottomland in the Willamette Valley and went on to sire nineteen children by three wives. (The last was thirty-one years younger than he.) Calvin, too, had the

Neal love for life: After his death at age sixty-seven the local paper reported that "fourteen hours after his supposed death, [he] revived and lived several hours longer," before the final dissolution of body and soul took place.

Calvin's daughter Alcy Delilah and her new husband, Linus Darling, moved east of the mountains in the late 1870s to try farming. They failed. When Belle was three years old, the family faced starvation and was saved only by sheer luck when her father gambled his saddle against fifty dollars in a political bet and won. A year later, Linus Darling had talked himself into the position of postmaster in the new town of Condon, where he built and ran the town's first drugstore (the patent-medicine type; he never received training as a pharmacist) and post office. Just when it looked as though their family life had stabilized, when Belle was seven years old, her youngest sister died of fever. A few months later, her mother gave birth to a stillborn son and never recovered from the trauma; tended by her four remaining young daughters, she died a month later.

Belle and her sisters were left in the care of a father whose interests centered almost entirely on himself. The girls looked after themselves, with occasional help from a hired woman, while Darling concentrated on running his businesses and teaching himself law. When Belle was twelve, the family's luck turned again: Darling married a wealthy young widow who had inherited one of Condon's finest wheat farms and brought with her a dowry of ten thousand dollars. Linus Darling suddenly found himself a gentleman farmer (although under his guidance the farm rapidly decayed), with a growing law practice. Belle spent her teenage years as one of the gentry of Condon, living in a big house, able to afford boarding school, with fine dresses and trips to Portland. But she suffered from bouts of melancholy, and she was never close to her father. After she married, Linus Darling and Belle seldom saw each other. Linus Pauling was nine years old when the man he was named for died; he would remember visiting his grandfather only once in his life.

Her own disjointed childhood left Belle ill equipped to take care of her young son and daughters. She wanted to be loved and cared for; she gave what love she had to her husband and seemed to have little for her children. Herman, desperate to make her happy, to buy her the ease and entertainment she craved, worked harder than ever. He

was extremely ambitious, and he was willing to jump from job to job
and put in punishingly long hours to make more money. The family
moved often: to Oswego for a time, to be near Herman's parents and
in a healthier atmosphere than that of the big city, then to the state
capital of Salem, fifty miles away, where Herman took a job as a traveling jewelry salesman. He was gone for days at a time, driving his horse
and buggy through hub-deep mud to the small towns scattered
through the valley.

In letters to Herman while he was on the road, Belle let him know
that she wasn't happy with the burdens of caring for the children alone
in a strange town. His letters back to her were full of reassurance and
love. "And the kidlets: bless their angel hearts. I miss them so much—
tell them their papa loves them dearly and longs for you all—tell them
to be good—and they will be always happy," he wrote, signing his letters, "Your own true love, Herman." He tried to cheer her by calling up
visions of the future they were building, inevitably one in which she
and the children would have plenty of money and few cares. In one of
his letters, written when Linus was four, his reassurances turned un-
cannily prescient: They had met for some higher purpose, he wrote
Belle. "We cannot imagine what it is but I feel that either ourselves or
our children will someday stand before the world as a specimen of a
high standard of intelligence."

And he reminded her that he was traveling for one reason—to save
enough money to open his own drugstore, this time without fickle
backers. He knew the business well enough to realize that he would
need considerable funding to compete with the well-established drug
houses in Portland. So he thought again of Condon, where there was
little competition, the bankers were friendly, and his wife's family
could provide support. In March 1905 he went there alone to see if he
could get something started and within days was writing excitedly to
Belle. Herbert Stephenson, the husband of Belle's sister Goldie and a
leading dry goods merchant in town, "gave me one side of the front of
his store and also gave me money with which to buy goods. I will have
no rent to pay—no water—no wood—no light—no phones—in fact
every cent I make will be clear profit as I will have not a cent of expense. . . . I just know that I will make boodles of money. . . . Be sure to
send all those advertising books. . . . You will be glad to get back to
Condon. I know because it is so different now, and when you see me
making money, you will be so pleased. I will have a good location and
will spend some money on advertising and it won't be long before I will
have the business. So come up old girl—pack up and come up."

Cowboys and Indians

Linus Pauling's earliest and fondest memories would center around Condon. He arrived there with his mother and sisters on a stagecoach in 1905, when he was four years old. His parents may have disliked the town, but it was a dream for a boy. Through Linus's eyes, Condon was still a piece of the Wild West. The population numbered only a few hundred. Cowboys, mule skinners, and hired hands from nearby ranches rode their horses in and drank up their pay at one of several saloons, along with a number of Scottish sheepherders, renowned for their toughness, stubbornness, hard work, and frugality, who had settled in the area. Cougars, wildcats, bears, and coyotes still outnumbered the farmers outside of town. The last remnants of the area's ancient migratory Indian tribes appeared every year out of the hills and camped at the end of Main Street, hunting, collecting native plants for food and medicine, and gathering the wool that snagged on barbed-wire fences. Grain wagons, pulled by teams of sixteen mules in belled harnesses, jangled through town all summer and fall, kicking up a perpetual haze of dust.

Within a few years the cowboys and Indians would be gone, but these links to another time were part of Linus's life. As he grew older, he sometimes played with Indian children, who taught him how to find and dig for the root of the camas plant, a staple of their diet. He remembered cowboys lounging outside his father's drugstore and teasing him as a little boy. Once, one impressed him by taking time to show the young town boy how to properly sharpen a pencil with a pocket knife. Many of the area's first settlers were still alive, and the pioneer ethos of independence, self-reliance, fortitude, and sheer stubbornness was preached at every civic gathering. New settlers were arriving every week to try their hand at homesteading the 320 acres the federal government said they could have gratis.

In order to bring out the wheat, a spur of the Northern Pacific Railroad was built to the town just months after the Paulings arrived, opening the area to a flood of farmworkers, businesspeople, and their families. Within a few years the town's population burgeoned to more than a thousand. There was a frenzy of construction, bringing Condon dozens of new houses, a confectionery and a bowling alley, a theater and a skating rink.

Young Linus spent a lot of time with an older cousin, Mervyn Stephenson. The two boys haunted the town's streets, went rabbit hunting up the deep, silent gullies near town, explored the windswept hills, and swam in the streams near his home. Linus remembered sleigh rides and the shimmering northern lights in the winter, fields of wildflowers and the hatching of hosts of insects in the spring. He and Mervyn watched the wheat being harvested in summer and sometimes brought water to the farmhands. They found arrowheads in the dust and shining rocks sparkling in the creeks.

Even though he would spend more years of his childhood in Portland than in Condon, Linus would always consider the smaller town on the hillside his spiritual birthplace.

His parents, however, hated Condon. Herman never became acclimated to the summer heat and dust storms, the tedium of the freezing winters, the primitive sanitary conditions, the recurring epidemics of diphtheria and whooping cough that killed small children. Then there was the gossipy closed-mindedness of small-town life. He tried at first to fit in—"Instead of the theater we'll attend church, thereby setting a good example for the children. Besides, I think it's good business policy here," he wrote Belle as he was setting up his shop—but from the beginning, his plan was to quickly make enough money to finance his own store back in Portland. He worked himself hard to do it, putting in twelve- and fifteen-hour days, enlarging his store, joining businessmen's associations. To please Belle and provide a good life for his children, he continued driving himself too hard.

Belle's life was hard, too. She was back in the small town from which she had only recently escaped and was left alone much of the time to care for three small children—Linus was four; Pauline, two; and Lucile, just a baby, when they returned to Condon—while Herman worked. It was no wonder she complained about the lack of money, the drudgery of motherhood, the women she imagined Herman was seeing when they were apart.

Each year during August and September, Herman would send Belle and the children to live with his parents in Oswego to spare them the ovenlike heat of late summer in Condon. During one of these separations Belle wrote him another litany of laments, and Herman, in a rare display of temper, let his feelings rush out in a reply: "I have quite enough to worry me without asking you to peck, peck, peck at me. But I guess you cannot help it, as that blessing is a characteristic of the Darling family," he wrote. "Were it not for trying to get a start financially so you and the little ones may live in an abbreviated form of luxury in

later years, I would not stay in this God for saken [*sic*] hole a moment.
You have discouraged me so often in my efforts that I would think you
would eventually come to a conclusion to encourage me a little by dis-
continuing your nonsensical jealousy."

A good father, Herman shielded his children from the strain on
the family. But the combination of business and domestic pressures
began to affect his health. Soon after returning to Condon, he started
having trouble sleeping and suffered from a string of illnesses that
kept him in bed for days at a time. On one occasion, a doctor's orders
sent him for weeks to the seashore to recover. Herman began to complain about what he called "the tummick ake"—likely an ulcer—an ailment that was to plague him for years, and he began to think about his
mortality. He wrote Belle, "We know not what day that grim monster
death may pay us a visit and do what naught else could do, break that
bond that binds us so closely made doubly strong by an undying love,
which I know exists between us, tho' not always apparent, therefore we
should strive each day to live for each other as if that day was to be the
last." Herman was thirty-one years old.

But all his work and dedication were beginning to pay off. The
Pauling drug business, founded on the motto No Cure, No Pay, grew
as fast as the town. In 1907, Herman went into partnership with a
young jeweler and opened an expanded store in one of the town's best
locations, a former bank building across from the livery stable on
Main Street. The new emporium was lavishly outfitted with mahogany
and marble and sported the largest plate-glass display window in the
county. Stock was expanded to include everything from cut crystal and
corsets to flypaper and phonographs.

The core of the business was drugs, and while Herman prided himself on the accuracy and efficacy of his medicines, he didn't shy away
from the advertising and marketing techniques that he had seen work
for patent-medicine hawkers. Reputable pharmacists of the day still
made many of their own "cures," and Condon was soon deluged with
flyers, billboards, and painted benches touting the benefits of Pauling's
Pink Pills for Pain, Pauling's Improved Blood Purifier, and Pauling's
Barb Wire Cure. The company's unceasing newspaper advertisements
were mixtures of testimonials, announcements of new stock, even occasional poetry: "When sweet Marie was sweet sixteen / She used Pauling's Almond and Cucumber Cream. / Tho' many winters since she's
seen, / She still remains just sweet sixteen."

When his partner suddenly died from pneumonia in 1908, Herman, on top of everything else, took on the management of the prof-

itable jewelry business. He imported an optician from Portland and started another moneymaking side venture in eyeglasses. A new partner was brought in to fund expansion, and the business incorporated under the name Red Cross Drug Company. Herman became active in the Foresters of America, the Woodmen of the World, and the Odd Fellows, using the fraternal organizations to make business contacts and raise his profile in the community. Belle, pleased with the respect she was given as the wife of one of the town's leading businessmen, was installed as a noble grand of the Minnehaha Lodge of the Rebekahs.

That year, Herman was put in charge of Condon's Fourth of July festivities, which he managed to make into the biggest celebration in the town's history. In the center of the day's long, noisy parade, Herman and Belle Pauling rode in the grand marshal's coach of honor.

—◆—

These were among the happiest days of Linus's life. He began to emulate his busy father. Herman wanted each of his children to become, as he termed it, "an asset to the human race," and he believed that the process required proper role models. He did his best to be that model for Linus: sober, hardworking, civic-minded, concerned about others, loving. Despite his unremitting work schedule, Herman took pains to try to make the family happy, hiring a buggy to go on picnics in the country, slipping Linus sips of beer at the dinner table, keeping Belle's fretfulness under control.

And he showed his son the business, bringing him into the sanctum of the drugstore's back room, where Linus played with the Indian skulls stored there as he watched his father making extracts of roots and leaves, making salves by working chemicals into lard, or carefully measuring, mixing, and packaging powdered herbs on a marble slab. Much of what Linus watched his father do was straightforward, if somewhat primitive, chemistry, including the careful preparation of reagents, gauging reactions with acids and alkalis, making litmus paper and test solutions. There was mystery in that room—poisons and cures in old glass bottles carefully organized and labeled with Latin names, the huge, leather-bound *Pharmacopoeia* and *Dispensatory*, with their lists of strange chemicals—and there was the imposing figure of his father making medicine.

An anecdote Linus told much later cast some light on his feelings for his father—and the nature of life in a western town. When he was about seven years old, Linus remembered, he and his cousin were caught while exploring a half-finished building by a burly workman. Linus tried to wriggle out a window, but the workman caught him by his pants, dragged him back inside, and beat him with a piece of lath. Linus ran home sobbing. He tearfully told his story to Herman, who listened carefully, then led his son by the hand through Condon's streets in search of the workman. They found the fellow eating lunch in the crowded dining room of the town's largest hotel. Herman asked him if he had beaten his son. When the man answered yes, Linus recalled, Herman knocked the fellow to the floor—and was subsequently arrested and tried for assault.

Linus's recollection of the event is both affectionate and mistaken. His father was arrested and put on trial around this time, but the charge was not assault; he was accused of bootlegging whiskey through his drugstore during a time of local prohibition. Herman Pauling was quickly found innocent of the charge. But his son's fond mixing of memories reveals his image of his father: a sympathetic protector who suffered because of loyalty to his son.

Herman's interest in Linus grew as the boy began to show signs of unusual intelligence. When Linus was five, Herman commented on the boy's talkativeness and "earnest manner" when he prattled to his elders. By age six he had already been advanced to the second grade of the little school in Condon and had learned how to express himself clearly through the written word, as his mother found out when she was emptying his overall pockets one day. She found a letter Linus had written to a girl in his class: "Dear Dorthy: I love you much better than I did saterday, why dont you right too me. I would like for you to kiss me and hug me would you. I will send you a pretty card if you will right to me. will you. I like you. do you like me. How do you like me. I love you Dorthy Dear. good by kisses love Linus Pauling"

His earnestness extended to his studies. He remembered always wanting to learn, and to learn thoroughly. In the third grade, after working furiously on one of the few mathematics problems he couldn't solve, he remembered bursting into tears from frustration. By age eight he had developed an interest in ancient civilizations, and Herman began teaching him a few words of Latin. And he showed some early interest in science. When the projector lens from Condon's one nickelodeon broke, Linus salvaged a piece and played for days focusing sunlight into a burning point. At age nine he was already reading Darwin and delighting his little sisters with miniature volcanoes he made by pushing together some sweepings in the backyard, adding some calcium carbide from a bicycle lamp, pouring water, and lighting the acetylene gas that was given off. The reaction was a common one used to provide light for bicyclists; Linus's variation on the theme was original.

From early on, Linus developed a voracious appetite for reading, racing through everything in print in the Pauling household and demanding more. Herman, whose own formal education had been cut short, was both proud and perplexed. In 1910 he wrote to the editor of the state's largest newspaper for advice:

> I am a father and have an only son who is aged 9 years, in the fifth grade, a great reader and is deeply interested in ancient history.
>
> In my desire to encourage and assist him in his prematurely developed inclinations, I ask some of the Oregonian's interested readers to advise me regarding the proper or at least the most comprehensive works to procure for him.
>
> I have obtained both public and high school books used in our schools, besides numerous other publications relating to this subject, but they all seem more or less incomplete. In order to avoid the possibility, or probability rather, of having some one advise me to have him read the Bible, I will state that it was through reading this and Darwin's theory of evolution that my son became so interested in both history and natural sciences.

The editor of the renownedly stuffy Republican paper replied: "There is nothing premature, or precocious, in a boy of nine years liking to read ancient history. The subject is fascinating, and any bright boy would naturally be fond of it had he not been spoiled by bad teaching." He then recommended Plutarch's *Lives,* Arnold's *History of Rome,* and a sampling of Herodotus. "Very likely after the boy has read these books he will not need any more advice," the editor wrote. "He can then go alone on his delightful way through the paradise of literature."

―――

As Herman was attempting to strengthen his son's intellect and moral character, his own came under attack.

Plainspokenness was common in Condon: It was hard country, and there was no profit in talking around a problem. Soon after Herman's triumphant management of the Fourth of July celebration, a competing jeweler in town attacked him in a letter to the editor of one of the newspapers. The charges were minor—something to do with the handling of advertising in a baseball-game program—but Herman, stung by the letter and feeling defensive, did what his son would often do in later years: He took an immediate, strong, public stand in order to set the record straight. The next edition of the paper contained a rambling defense of Pauling's honor titled "The Truth Will Out."

"I came to Condon just a little over three years ago, practically without funds, and embarked upon my business, and have made it a success far beyond my expectations, and I attribute my success to the fact that I have never tried to fool any of the people any of the time," Herman wrote in editorial space he paid for. "In spite of this I have made some enemies. Well, all of us have. We need them in our business. In fact I like them, providing they fight me fair and square." However, he pointed out, his competitor, "Sorehead Charlie," was not fighting fair. "Perhaps you wonder why he should try to injure my reputation for honesty and square dealing: let me tell you why; its [*sic*] because I am his competitor, and he knows that my reputation for honesty in the drug business is building up my jewelry business, and he realizes that something must be done to check this inroad on his business, so he attacks my veracity on a point absolutely insignificant. . . ."

Charlie bought his own space for a reply in the next edition, and the public debate ground on for three weeks without any resolution. In his final broadside, Herman offered this insight into the Pauling character: ". . . some people are afraid of the truth, and if telling the truth is knocking, then I must plead guilty, and what's more I shall continue doing this unfalteringly as long as I live. . . . I am going to have the last say if it takes forty years."

Herman's reputation had been blackened. Soon after came his arrest for bootlegging and then, adding injury to insult, a fire destroyed some of the stock of the Red Cross store. Linus remembered passing by on his way home from school and seeing his father sitting on the curb outside the blackened store, shards of the shattered plate-glass window scattered around him, his head in his hands.

Herman had had enough of Condon. Between insurance proceeds and the sale of his share of the company, he made enough money to move his family back to Portland and start again. He found a good building on a busy street in a fast-growing suburb of the city and began remodeling it into a dream drugstore. He had learned some lessons in Condon: Stock was cut back to items more traditionally associated with a drugstore—no more jewelry or phonographs—and a first-rate soda fountain was added. Herman rented a fine house nearby for the family.

Typically, he threw himself into his new business, working long hours to get it started right. Herman had once written Belle, "My one desire is to acquire enough wealth so that you and our darlings can live in luxury and enjoy life to its fullest extent." Now he was in a position to do it.

Then, on an unseasonably hot June day in 1910, just a few months after returning to Portland, Herman fell suddenly ill. The next day, he was dead.

Although the official cause of death was gastritis, Linus would later conclude that a perforating ulcer—the "tummick ake" Herman had complained of for so long—probably killed his father. It is likely that stress was a contributing factor. To some degree at least, Herman Pauling had, at age thirty-three, worked himself to death.

The Boardinghouse

". . . a wonder we survived"

Linus was nine years old the morning his Aunt Beth drew him aside
and told him that he must be strong, that his father had passed away.
The boy's reaction was strangely muted. He didn't fall apart or protect
himself with disbelief. He didn't even cry. When asked decades later
about the day of his father's death, he would remember that he experienced no sadness or anger, that he felt no special emotion of any sort
then or later. When asked why his reaction was so unemotional, he
said, "I suppose that I just accepted life."

In fact, he was shattered. No nine-year-old boy—even an exceptionally intelligent, well-read boy—is capable of rationalizing death
away, especially the death of his father. While Herman had not been a
perfect father—he put too much of himself into his business; he didn't
have time to know his children well—he had loved his son, had taken
pride in him, had tried to guide his development. Linus was closer to
his father than to any other member of the family. Herman was his
role model, his ideal of manhood.

And perhaps that ideal is what Linus was trying to achieve when he
learned that his father had died. It would have been typical for a boy
that age to go numb as he felt this sudden, sickening shift in his world,

as he tried to comprehend what had happened. At the same time, he saw his mother falling apart. Belle had loved Herman deeply—he was the center of her life and her sole support—and when he died, she became first distraught, then hysterical. Linus would remember her breaking down completely, screaming and crying on the way to Herman's funeral. He did as he thought he must. He choked down his feelings of sorrow and abandonment in an attempt to mimic an "adult" way of dealing with an unendurable situation. He denied himself grief.

And so, at an early age, Linus found a source of strength. He could control his emotions, he could hold steady, and in holding steady he found that he was capable of coping with his father's death. He was the man of the family now, he would have to help hold things together, and self-control was necessary. He learned this lesson well: For the rest of his life, with very few exceptions, Linus would continue to hold his emotions in check. The alternative—letting love or sorrow or any emotion engulf him—was too painful.

Herman's death was a severe shock to a family already under strain. Linus and his sisters were still adjusting to the move to a new town, the new school, the loss of friends. Linus didn't like Portland as well; the gloomy, six-month-long rainy season was especially hard to adjust to after Condon's clear skies and wonderfully snowy winters. In Condon he had been the son of a prominent businessman and a prodigy in a small school; in Portland he was one of a crowd.

Belle had an added burden: Just three months before Herman's death she had lost her father, Linus Wilson Darling. Although she and her father had never been close, the quick succession of deaths and the prospect of raising three children without financial or emotional support broke her, mentally and physically. Soon after Herman's death she fell into deep depression and chronic illness from which she never recovered.

Financially, Belle and the children were in serious trouble. After the estate was settled, Belle found herself having to fashion a new life with no house, no business skills, and no income. At first, she tried to keep Herman's drugstore going, hiring a man to manage it for her, but it didn't work. She sold the business, netting what was for that time a fair nest egg. But the money was not enough to support the family indefinitely. It had to be invested in a way that could generate enough money to keep them housed and fed. Belle finally settled on perhaps the only course of action she could take, spending almost everything she had on a house large enough to shelter her family and take in others. She would scrape by using the traditional skills of a wife and mother: cooking, cleaning, and caring for others. She would run a boardinghouse.

It was a wrenching change for the family, a fall within a period of weeks from near affluence to near poverty. The situation was worsened by Belle's poor business sense. She paid $5,250 for a three-story, six-bedroom frame house next to a meat market on the outskirts of town and assumed a $2,300 mortgage—a total more than three times the assessed value of the property. She used more of her savings to furnish it with costly appliances, including one of the first electric ranges in the city, and hired a woman to help with cleaning and cooking. A small inheritance from her father's estate helped at first; she was able to pay off the mortgage, easing some of the month-to-month financial pressure. But the income from boarders still didn't cover her costs.

Setting up the house took the last of Belle's strength. She began suffering from a general weakness that was later diagnosed as pernicious anemia, a ruinous, energy-sapping blood disorder in which the body is unable to properly absorb vitamin B_{12}. The result is exhaustion, muscle weakness in the arms and legs, and in severe cases, mood swings, memory loss, even psychosis. At the time, there was no cure. Her doctor did all he could, prescribing long periods of rest and a diet rich in red meats designed to build the blood. The children would later remember the copious amounts of liver she ate, and "cannibal sandwiches" made of raw beef scrapings and blood on bread.

Belle became increasingly a sort of living shadow, an exhausted background figure in her children's lives. At first, she tried to keep a few memories of happier times alive: She worked to provide a happy Christmas for the children, and there were weekends at Herman's parents' house in Oswego, a few singing parties (Lucile became an accomplished pianist, Pauline played the ukulele, and Linus loved to sing), and occasional short trips to the mountains with their aunts and uncles and cousins. Linus had especially happy memories of a summer month spent in the Oregon coast town of Gearhart, in a house the family got free from friends, where he fished from the dock, explored tidepools and jetties, and spent hours reading and dreaming on the beach. It was the only vacation the family had after Herman died.

But worn out, broke, worried, and sick, Belle had little happiness to impart to her children. A cousin, Richard Morgan, lived in the Pauling house around 1915, when he was a child. Not once during the year he was there, he remembered, did he see Belle smile.

~~~

At first, after their father died, the children were allowed to "run wild," as Linus's sister Pauline remembered, playing on the streets until all hours. Belle didn't know how to be a mother and, with all the pressure on her, didn't have the time or energy—and perhaps lacked the inclination—to learn. She certainly didn't know how to raise a boy or what to tell him about life or maturing into a man. And she wasn't much better with her daughters. Belle's furtive, hurried explanation of menstruation so frightened and confused Pauline and Lucile that they felt it was a scourge that afflicted only women in their family. "I thought there was something wrong with us," Pauline said.

After Belle had to let the hired woman go, she began depending on her children to help with cleaning, cooking, and other chores. She didn't have the energy to help them understand why they were asked to work so hard, and Linus and Pauline especially resented what they saw as constant nagging by their mother.

The jobs were expanded to include outside work to help with the bills. At Belle's insistence, Linus began working for wages when he was about thirteen: setting pins in a bowling alley, delivering newspapers and special delivery letters and milk, selling meat at a butcher's shop, or projecting movies at a local theater on weekends. Apart from the projectionist work—Linus loved the movies, especially comedies and adventure stories—he found each job more unbearable than the last. He seemed to take pleasure in finding a reason to quit every one within a short time.

Pauline—energetic, outgoing, pretty, flirtatious, and self-confident—took jobs every summer and dropped out of high school for a year to learn shorthand and typing at a local business college. But every penny she earned, she remembered with irritation for the rest of her life, was taken from her by Belle. Pauline's relationship with her mother became openly hostile when she was seventeen and Belle insisted that she date a well-to-do man in his mid-thirties. "My mother would have given anything if that had developed into something," she recalled. But Pauline was repelled by the thought of dating a man almost old enough to be her father. When her mother persisted, Pauline wrote a letter to the local police saying that Belle was forcing her to "go with" an older gentleman. Police detectives ("men in derbies," as Pauline remembered them) came to the house to talk with Belle, who had to do some fast talking of her own to straighten things out.

Lucile, the quietest and shyest of the three children, took on the role of peacekeeper. Linus and Pauline both left home when they were teenagers; Lucile stayed home, studied and taught piano, and cared for her increasingly dependent mother until Belle's death. Lucile would always remember a happier, more "normal" upbringing than either her older brother or sister. But whenever she talked about her mother, she would cry.

Pauline saw things more simply. "It was a wonder we survived," she said. "It was a very stark childhood."

〰〰

The children were left to find their own ways to cope. The sisters, very close in age, formed a tight community of two, talking and playing, quarreling and reuniting, throughout their childhood. When she was older, Pauline became something of a party girl, arranging and attending swimming and singing get-togethers, dating a series of boys, creating a social life that filled her need for support. Lucile devoted herself to her music and to helping Belle.

Linus withdrew into himself. He had nothing in common with his little sisters and paid as little attention to them as he could. Soon after his father's death he began distancing himself from his mother as well. Through his entire childhood, Linus could not remember having a single conversation with Belle about anything important. She had no interest in school or books, much of which she viewed as a waste of time that kept people from earning money. What communication existed was one-way, with Belle issuing requests and orders and browbeating the children, often from her bed. When Linus listened, he did so grudgingly; later, as he entered adolescence, he began openly ignoring her. "When she'd ask him to do some work around the place, like bring some wood up to the fireplace or take the garbage out or anything like that," Pauline remembered, "it would go right over his head. A week later, he still hadn't done it, you know, because he lived in a different world."

It was a world richer, more reasonable, and more controllable than the emotional chaos of the boardinghouse. It was the world inside his mind. Linus always loved learning and found that by doing well in school his teachers would provide him some of the warmth and respect that he was missing at home. His interest in reading became a passion. About fifty books of Herman's and Linus Darling's were stored on a high shelf in the living room to keep them out of reach of the children. Linus found a way to get them down and inhaled them, everything from inspirational texts and a history of the San Francisco earthquake to *Pinocchio* and Dante's *Inferno*. He memorized *Through the Looking Glass*. Linus's attitude toward reading was illustrated on the bookplate he used as a boy: a pirate and a chest of loot, with the caption "Within good books lie buried treasures."

After reading everything there was at home, he found another escape in Portland's large, marble-halled, high-ceilinged county library, a sanctuary of order and knowledge. He spent hours there every week, racing through history books, short stories, popular fiction, and volumes on natural history. He developed a special taste for science fiction, especially Jules Verne's blend of technical wizardry and high adventure. When he was asked to visit a lonely younger cousin on weekends, he entertained her for hours by reading from the *Encyclopaedia Britannica*, something he remembered as a great opportunity. "I have trouble with encyclopedias," he would say later, "because I just keep reading until I stop and haul myself back to reality."

———

By the time he was ready to enter high school—he became a freshman at age twelve after going through an accelerated program in grade school—Linus was an extremely bright, self-motivated, energetic boy on the verge of puberty. He was, in other words, ripe for some type of passion.

It would not come from social interaction. Younger and smaller than his classmates, unable to compete well in sports, bookish and painfully shy, Linus made few friends. He never dated in high school, partly because he never had money to spend on dates and partly because he didn't think of himself as very attractive. He was tongue-tied around girls and reserved around boys. "I was never much for playing or fooling around," he would say later. "I was usually by myself."

Nor would religion inspire him. Herman and Belle had been irregular churchgoers, but Linus retained vivid memories of worship from visits with his German-born grandparents, Carl and Adelheit Pauling. After Herman's death, Belle frequently took the children to Oswego on weekends to visit their grandparents, a trip the children loved. The elder Paulings had a real home in which the woodstove was always warm and the smell of rich German cakes filled the air. A sod cellar was packed with home-canned fruits and crocks of sauerkraut and pickles; their grandmother had a cow and churned her own butter. There was a large, old-fashioned flower garden in the front yard that Adelheit harvested to create the arrangements she carried two miles to Herman's grave in Oswego Cemetery. Linus was a particular favorite of his grandmother, who gave him some of the maternal attention Belle couldn't. Carl and Adelheit were devout Lutherans. Because there was no church in Oswego, every month they would invite a minister from across the river to hold services in their house. Linus sometimes sat among the small group of worshipers in the front parlor, listening to the service and hymns sung in German. As with almost everything else that came within his range of perception, he spent time thinking about God and his works.

That thinking culminated in a revelation. At his grandparents' one night, as he was drifting toward sleep, he began staring at a picture of Christ that hung on the wall in front of him. Suddenly, he jerked fully awake. Linus thought he had seen the halo around the Savior's head start to glow. Had he been more prone to belief, he might have accepted this as a minor miracle. Linus, however, checked his initial response by looking at other objects in the room and found that the glow wasn't limited to Jesus's halo. Although he didn't know the terminology, he demonstrated to himself that he had seen an optical illusion, the effect of retinal tiring from staring at the halo in the picture. Although he would think about religion off and on through his youth and would even attend a Christian Science Sunday school for a few months with a friend whose family belonged to the church, seeking a rational explanation for all phenomena came naturally to him.

His rejection of religion led to a minor philosophical crisis. "I remember when I was eleven years old that I asked myself what evidence I had that the rest of world existed anywhere except in my consciousness," he recalled from a vantage point some seventy years later. "I could not think of any convincing evidence to the contrary." After wrestling with it for a while, though, he came to the conclusion that the people around him, the other grammar school students, appeared to have roughly the same relationship with the universe as he did. "This symmetry involves so many facets as to cause me to conclude that . . . it was highly probable that I myself did not occupy a unique position in the universe," he concluded.

Having established his own philosophical position, Pauling turned his attention to everything else. He began collecting and classifying things, starting at about age eleven with a good-sized collection of insects. In this he was helped by Billy Ziegler, a drug-supply salesman and former business acquaintance of his father's who began spending considerable time at Linus's house after Herman's death. Ziegler's primary intention was to woo Belle. Although he appears never to have gotten far, perhaps because he was already married, he did make a positive impression on the children by regularly giving them little gifts (and occasionally bribing them with money to leave the house). Pauling used Ziegler as a source of supplies and convinced him to get a potentially deadly chemical, potassium cyanide, which Linus carefully mixed with plaster of paris to spread on the bottom of an insect-killing bottle.

During his first year at Portland's large and well-staffed Washington High School, Linus took his first real science course, a general introduction called "physiography," from a Smith College chemistry graduate, Pauline Geballe. Because of his eagerness to learn, Linus had a keen appreciation of teachers who were able to make their subjects coherent, logical, and interesting. He was impressed by Miss Geballe's teaching abilities, especially her use of visual aids: to demonstrate atmospheric pressure, for example, she boiled water in an old Log Cabin syrup tin, then tightened the cap and let her class watch as the steam condensed inside and air pressure crushed the can.

The class also examined the properties of minerals, which diverted Linus's attention from insects to rocks. He did a great deal of reading on the subject, carefully copying tables of properties out of books he got from the library and testing his findings in order to fit them into the logical schemes of mineralogy. "I was beginning to be a scientist, in a way, without any training," he said. His early rock collection never became substantial—the area where he lived didn't offer a great range of specimens—but it was the start of a lifelong interest in crystals and minerals.

Linus had an unusual interest in order. The hours he spent alone, studying, testing, learning about and carefully classifying minerals, were hours in which the unknown became known. There were rational relationships between things, there were logical connections, and there was a kind of ordered perfection. It was a welcome change from his home life. Rational order became his passion, and soon he was taking a scientific interest in everything. "Linus was always thinking," remembered his sister Lucile. "His mind was just active all the time wondering about this and that and the reasons for them." One cold morning, waiting for the train in Portland, she recalled, her twelve-year-old brother impressed his mother and sisters by commenting, "Mama, I know why you don't get so cold if you are moving around. Your feet aren't on the ground but half the time."

His attitude even extended to family matters. His sister Lucile remembered borrowing a neighbor's bike and running, crying, to her big brother when the boy knocked her off and took it back. Instead of avenging his sister, Linus thought awhile, then told her to stop crying. "After all," he said, "it wasn't your bike."

And it worked well in high school, where Pauling's favorite classes soon became math and science. "I got along well. I studied, did my work, and was happy. The only times that I was unhappy came when I didn't know what I was supposed to know perfectly," remembered Pauling. "It's like the story of the little boy who, when his teacher asked him, 'Willie, what is two and two?' answered, 'Four.' And she said, 'That's very good, Willie.' And he said, 'Very good? It's perfect!' I liked mathematics because you could be perfect, whereas with Latin, or in studying any language, it's essentially impossible to be perfect."

Things Happen

At around age twelve Pauling gave physical form to his emotional estrangement from the family. In the basement of his mother's boardinghouse he hammered some cheap lumber into a ten-by-ten-foot room, a rude laboratory where he could organize and protect his collections and, more importantly, create a haven from Belle where he could be free.

But he wouldn't be totally alone. Walking home from high school one day, Linus met, for the first time since Herman's death, a kindred spirit, a boy a year older than Linus but in other ways similar—bright, inward-turning, and fascinated by natural phenomena—named Lloyd Jeffress. He and Jeffress would become best friends. They overcame their shyness enough to talk about the things that interested them. They taught themselves to play chess by reading about it in an encyclopedia and making a crude game out of paper. One afternoon after school Jeffress invited Linus to his home to see his simple, homemade chemistry set. Linus watched enraptured as Jeffress performed what looked like magic tricks, mixing colored powders, making solutions bubble and change hue. Then came the grand finale. Jeffress carefully mixed common table sugar and potassium chlorate together, added a drop of sulfuric acid—and the sugar burst into flame.

At the same moment, so did Linus Pauling's mind. "As I think back, what struck me was the realization that substances are not immutable," he remembered about that afternoon. "Here he had sugar and a few chemicals and ended up with a little pile of black carbon. That phenomenon—changing substances into other substances—is what impressed me. In chemistry, things happen. Very striking things happen." He would always pinpoint that moment as the start of his chemistry career.

He had found his passion. Linus ran the mile back to his home, eager to do anything that faintly resembled chemistry. The only equipment he could find was his mother's small spirit lamp. He built a stand with his Erector set, lit the lamp, and performed his first work in chemistry: He boiled water. Unfortunately, he boiled it in the glass cap of the alcohol burner; the glass cracked, and his first foray into experimental work ended with an uncomfortable explanation to his mother.

—*mm*—

The mounted butterflies and labeled minerals were pushed aside; Linus transformed his basement sanctuary into a chemistry laboratory. "He would take Lloyd Jeffress down there and the awfulest odors would creep up occasionally from their mixtures," his sister Pauline recalled. But odors were about all his sisters or mother knew of his basement experiments. It was a strict—and strictly observed—rule that no one but Linus and a few select friends could enter his lab.

That small group included Jeffress and two other science-minded boys from the neighborhood: Lynn Anderson, the son of a local barber, and Lloyd Simon, a peppy, entrepreneurial teenager who would devote much of his time with Linus to dreaming up moneymaking schemes.

Too poor to buy his own equipment or chemicals, Linus scavenged, stole, or cajoled others to give him what he needed. Belle's married friend Billy Ziegler, eager to help, provided some chemicals from his drug-supply business. Around the corner from Linus's house lived a Mr. Yokum, a former mountain-climbing guide and semiprofessional photographer, who managed the stockroom at a local dental college. Yokum took a friendly interest in the fatherless boy; in addition to pieces of chipped laboratory glassware from the stockroom, he gave Linus his first bicycle and some early lessons in Greek, which Linus would study on his own while riding the steam train to his grandparents' house.

Most importantly, there was the abandoned laboratory at the smelter, a treasure trove of chemicals and equipment.

Chemistry had an effect on Linus that nothing had had before.

Part of it was intellectual stimulation. Linus loved puzzles and brainteasers, and chemistry was a great puzzle. There was a rough sense to the way chemicals combined and transformed into other chemicals, but a great deal was still a mystery. You could play all day at new combinations, trying to predict what would happen if instead of chemical A you used chemical B in an experiment.

Part of it was a sense of romance and adventure. He had been deeply impressed by the central roles and heroic images of scientists in the works of fiction he had read by Verne and Wells. He had been impressed by the image of scientists in these books. From Verne he learned that scientists were fearless, innovative men able to handle any danger with a combination of pluck and wit; their work was a great adventure that took them to the center of the earth, the bottom of the sea, the moon. From Wells he learned that scientists could be the key to a happier future, when rationality would supersede the petty passions of humanity, ushering in an age of reason and plenty. By playing at being a chemist, he was vicariously joining the ranks of these literary supermen.

Part of it was sheer, daring fun. "I was simply entranced by chemical phenomena," he remembered. He mixed potassium chlorate and sulfur together, wadded it in paper, set it on the trolley tracks, and ran whooping through the streets when cars set it off with a bang. (The streetcar company sent a representative to his house to put a stop it.) He prepared an unstable iodide of nitrogen that popped loudly when disturbed—a sort of junior-grade nitroglycerine—and used it to surprise his sisters at home; it worked so well that he took some to school. He accidentally sloshed concentrated sulfuric acid on himself one day, eating away his clothes and the broom he used to sweep it into a drain (although he avoided serious burns). He once set fire to wooden walls with molten phosphorous.

For Linus, chemistry was filling a need. Chemistry, he was learning, was organized in a rational way. The periodic table of the elements illustrated an underlying order to nature; the work of chemists had shown that this order extended to their science in certain ways. If you mixed the right amounts of reactants and exposed them to the right amount of energy, the same reaction would take place each time, predictably, reliably. Chemistry provided Linus with explanations and a sense of order in a life that was otherwise, in important ways, disordered and inexplicable.

Once focused on chemistry, Linus's attention never wavered. In addition to the normal load of classes and close to four years of Latin, he began to take every science and math class he could at Washington High School, including courses in advanced mathematics through the college-freshman level. In his junior year he took his first formal chemistry course under William V. Green, a small, dapper man who was impressed by Linus's eagerness for all things chemical. Green let Linus stay after school to help him determine the heat value of the school system's oil and coal. There was no second-year chemistry offered at Washington High, but in his senior year Green arranged for Linus to work independently in the lab on problems in organic chemistry.

In his last semester at Washington High School, Linus took his first physics course. The teacher, Virgil Earle, a remarkable, energetic lecturer, introduced Linus to a new level of understanding the physical world, opening his eyes to the basic laws of energy and matter that underlay chemistry. Linus was particularly impressed by Earle's precise use of language. The teacher once brought to his class's attention the wording of a story-question asked in their textbook, Millikan and Gale's *First Course in Physics*. The book read: If you were in the mountains and came across a cube of gold, one foot on each side, would you try to carry it home? Earle looked at his students. "Well?" he said. "Of course you would. Anybody would *try* to carry it home. The question ought to be, *could* you carry it home?"

This scholarly concern for accuracy was complemented by a general thoroughness in his high school classes that impressed Linus. "I think the Oregon schools had a significant effect in developing in me this feeling that if there were some pieces of information that I was missing, then I should have them," he later remembered. "That if there was something I should know, then I'd better *know* it."

One thing he would carry with him from high school was the importance of the careful use of English, and not just in science courses. Linus always had a keen ear for good language, an appreciation grounded in years of avid reading and expressed in the form of good writing. A creative-writing assignment in a high school English class even led to an attempt at fiction. A short story Linus wrote about oil exploration—complete with youthful hero, world travel, and explosive fires—was read aloud in class and proved so popular that his teacher asked for further weekly installments. "I was the only one whom she encouraged to write a novel," Linus said.

If he had lived sixty years later, Linus's shy bookishness and fixation on science might have earned him the title of "nerd." But a different set of values operated before World War I. His classmates remember him as a quiet boy but one who was well liked and respected for his exceptional abilities in class—someone who would go far. They didn't think of him as a nerd at Washington High School. They thought of him as a genius.

And Linus may have felt the same way. He coasted through Washington High without ever having to study hard, mastered every course, and impressed all his teachers. In a high school volume of Virgil's *Aeneid* that he kept his whole life, there is an illustration of a statue of Minerva. Above it, in what appears to be Linus's hand, is the note "Linus Pauling. some day." An arrow points from the note to a statuette of the Winged Victory in Minerva's hand. Above the statuette someone has drawn a halo.

When he was sixteen, a high school senior, Linus started a diary:

> August 29, 1917. Today I am beginning to write the history of my life. The idea which has resulted in this originated a year or more ago, when I thought of the enjoyment that I would have could I read of the events of my former and younger life. My children and grandchildren will without doubt hear of the events in my life with the same relish with which I read the scattered fragments written by my granddad, Linus Wilson Darling. . . . Often, I hope, I shall glance over what I have written before, and ponder and meditate on the mistakes that I have made—on the good luck that I have had—on the carefree gaiety of my younger days; and, pondering, I shall resolve to remedy these mistakes, to bring back my good luck, and to regain my happiness.

His last year of high school was a busy one. Bored by regular jobs, Linus, along with his entrepreneurial friend Lloyd Simon and another boy skilled in photography, tried to start a photo-developing service. It was not their first business venture. In addition to the distilled-water scheme, Linus and Lloyd had also tried their hand at independent chemical research, printing business cards for the "Palmon Laboratory, Research Chemists" when they were fifteen years old. Nothing panned out, but the photography idea looked like a sure thing, the right mix of commercial need (home photography was all the rage, and they would develop film for local drugstores) and an opportunity for chemical research on the side. They set up a lab in Simon's basement, supplied it with help from Belle's friend Billy Ziegler, identified the stores they would contract with for work, and planned to buy a motorcycle for deliveries. "If I get $5 to $10 a week throughout the year my college course will present few pecuniary difficulties. I might even take a year of graduate work and get the degree of Ch.E. [chemical engineer]. I will specialize in the chemistry of photography as far as possible," Linus wrote in the fall of 1917. "I enjoy day-dreaming, and building castles in Spain. But I hope these are not dreams or castles."

The following January, he annotated that entry: "They are." The high school boys found they weren't skilled enough to make salable photographic prints.

Despite some concerns about how he would finance it, Linus never doubted he would go to college. His reasons were both intellectual and practical. In the simplest sense, he needed to satisfy an almost visceral appetite for chemistry; he wanted to know much more about the field, and college was the logical place to learn it. There was also money to be made. Early in the twentieth century American business firms began to realize that basic scientific research yielded profits in the form of improved efficiency, new products, and new techniques. Chemistry was important in everything from metallurgy to pharmaceuticals, textiles to agriculture. From his wide reading Linus knew that industrial chemistry, practiced after attaining a degree in chemical engineering, could provide a good living. When he was only fifteen years old, he had already decided on his career. During a visit to his grandparents in Oswego with his friend Lloyd Jeffress, his grandmother asked him what his job plans were. Linus answered that he was going to be a chemical engineer. Jeffress then piped up prophetically, "No, he's going to be a professor."

Linus's choice of schools for advanced training was limited because he had little money, but luckily the state offered an adequate and relatively inexpensive program in chemical engineering at the Oregon Agricultural College (OAC; now Oregon State University), a land-grant institution in Corvallis, about ninety miles from his home. He applied, and OAC accepted him early in his senior year of high school. Linus had by that time already exhausted all of the science and most of the math offerings at Washington High and wanted to leave a term early to get a head start at college. State law, however, decreed that each high school student must take a full year of American history at the senior level. Linus figured that he would circumvent this by taking two terms of the class simultaneously, but the principal of Washington High School saw things differently. He refused Linus's request. Years later, Linus would remember his astonishment at this summary exercise of institutional power. "He didn't ask me, 'What are you going to do? Are you a good student?' He *just said no*," Linus said.

Instead of doing as he was told, Linus did what he thought was right. He dropped both history classes, indulged himself instead in some extra math and, as he wanted, left for college early—without a high school diploma. Using the terminology of a later time, Linus dropped out.

There would be one more defiance of authority before Linus left home. The summer before college, he took a job running a drill press and doing odd jobs at a machinery-manufacturing company, where his careful work habits soon earned him several raises. The owner offered him the then-princely wage of $125 a month if he'd come to work full-time after graduating high school. Belle was frantic for him to take the job. She had never understood her son's interest in science, she desperately needed the money, and she had no appreciation of college. At age fifteen, Belle had been sent, with her older sister Goldie, to boarding school at Pacific University in Forest Grove, Oregon, hundreds of miles from her home in Condon. She quit within a year, homesick and disenchanted with the lessons higher education offered. She could never sympathize with or understand Linus's desire to go to college.

Luckily, there were parental figures who could. Lloyd Jeffress lived with his aunt and uncle, and Linus was often invited to dinner or overnight stays at their house. They were more educated and appreciative of education than Belle; they had encouraged Jeffress to go to college and did the same for Linus. Linus told them about Belle's insistence that he work instead. "They said it was my duty to say no," Linus remembered. "They said that I must go to college." Linus told Belle he was turning down the machine-shop job and continuing his education. "I suppose it disappointed her," he remembered later. "She perhaps had started giving up on me, on understanding me."

But Belle would not let go entirely. When Linus left for OAC on October 6, 1917, he was accompanied on the train by his mother.

The Boy Professor

Rook

"I try not to think of college, because of the way it affects me," Pauling wrote in his diary the month before he left for OAC. "Why should I rush through my education in the way I am? Paul Harvey is going to OAC to study chemistry—big, manly Paul Harvey, beside whom I pale into insignificance. Why should I enjoy the same benefits he has, when I am so unprepared, so unused to the ways of man? I will not be able, on account of my youth and inexperience, to do justice to the courses and the teaching placed before me."

He was sixteen years old and understandably worried about how he would measure up to the "big, manly" types in college. "But," he added resignedly, "it is too late to change now, even if I wanted to." However, longing to get away from Belle's control, eager for the chance to learn more chemistry, and hungry for new experiences, he didn't want to.

Mervyn Stephenson, Pauling's older cousin and Condon playmate, now a junior studying engineering at OAC, met Belle and Linus at the Corvallis train station. Having Stephenson there to look after her son was a factor in Belle's decision to let him go to college; Pauling was to room with his cousin at a boardinghouse a few blocks from campus.

Belle stayed overnight to make sure her son's accommodations were satisfactory before she returned to Portland. As soon as she was gone, Stephenson gave the incoming freshman a few words of advice and left him to fend for himself. Within a few weeks Pauling had moved out of the boardinghouse to save money and after that saw little of his cousin in college.

Although Pauling had come to OAC out of necessity—it was the only college he could afford—it turned out to be a good choice. In 1917 it was the nation's second-largest land-grant institution, spread over a sprawling 349-acre campus, with more than four thousand students, two hundred instructors, and solid programs in agriculture, commerce, engineering, mining, home economics, forestry, music, pharmacy, and vocational education. Chemistry, along with most of the other arts and sciences, was a "service department," originally designed to provide future farmers, pharmacists, and housewives with the rudiments of chemical knowledge. But by the time Pauling arrived, the OAC chemistry department was rapidly growing both in size and importance as the changing American economy created a new demand for trained researchers and engineers.

During the sixteen years between Pauling's birth and his arrival at OAC, American industry had gone through an era of unprecedented expansion. Domestic petroleum production grew sixfold; steel, fivefold. The automobile and aviation industries had been born; electrification and assembly-line production had become everyday realities. Larger, more technical, more competitive industries relied increasingly on scientific research to create new products, improve old ones, and develop innovative processes for production. The early part of the twentieth century saw many of America's most forward looking industrialists become science boosters, in large part because they recognized the value of basic research in maintaining an edge in the marketplace. Led by firms such as General Electric and Bell Telephone, companies began establishing their own research facilities. In 1890, by one estimate, there were only four industrial research labs in the United States; one generation later there were more than five hundred, and new ones were being started at the rate of about fifty per year.

Universities soon made the important discovery that private industry was willing to fund professorships, programs, and campus construction as a means of ensuring a supply of skilled technical workers. Once considered havens for an aristocratic elite, universities began opening their curricula to more utilitarian subjects and their doors to the children of the growing middle class. In the three decades prior to Pauling's arrival at OAC, enrollment in American universities and colleges nearly tripled, and land-grant colleges, with their mission to "promote the liberal and practical education of the industrial classes," led the way.

Chemistry was a major beneficiary of the new order. In America, industrial chemistry had started slowly, primarily in the mining and metals industries, which relied on chemists to test and refine ores. (OAC's chemical engineering program, for instance, was part of the School of Mines.) It took the success of industrial chemistry in Germany and a world war to awaken America to the need for more—and more modern—science. The German chemical industry started in the mid-nineteenth century when organic chemists unlocked the secret of creating dyes synthetically, destroying the natural dye market and making fortunes for manufacturers quick enough to take advantage of the new techniques. By the turn of the century Germany had become the undisputed world center for chemistry, both academic and industrial. The great German universities at Berlin, Göttingen, Munich, Heidelberg, Bonn, and Leipzig were magnets for the best young minds from around the globe who came to study at the feet of the masters: Fischer, von Baeyer, Buchner, and Willstätter in organic chemistry; or, increasingly, Ostwald, Nernst, the Dutchman van't Hoff, and the Swede Arrhenius, leaders of a revolution called physical chemistry that was attempting to bridge the gap between chemistry and physics. By 1910, five of the first ten Nobel Prizes awarded in chemistry had been won by Germans—seven if you count van't Hoff and Arrhenius, who did much of their most important work in Germany.

By 1914, Germany was producing more than 80 percent of the world's dyes, and the preeminence of its chemical industry extended to such important areas as pharmaceuticals, explosives, and agricultural chemicals. America was dependent on many of these German products when the Allied blockade during World War I shut off the supply, opening the eyes of American industrialists to the need for domestic chemical research and chemical-based industries—especially with the threat of a modern war that would be fought with chemically based high explosives and poison gases. By the time Pauling was an undergraduate just after the war, chemists held about one of every three industrial research jobs in the United States, and one undergraduate student in twelve at American colleges was a chemistry major. Suddenly, research chemistry changed from a gentleman's game to a broad-shouldered, progressive, all-American career, practical, patriotic—and profitable. As one historian put it, "Becoming a scientist . . . was a means of going from the lower middle to the upper middle class." It was a climb Pauling was eager to make.

—*un*—

The first two years at OAC, Pauling took the same classes as students of mining engineering, including an overview of the mining industry and classes in explosives, forging, and metallurgy. He enjoyed the mining courses; the emphasis on metals and industrial processes built on his early interest in rock collecting and his childhood forays to the abandoned smelter and foundry in Oswego. He learned how to use a forge, hammering horseshoes and hammers and a knife out of red-hot iron; he learned the mining chemists's craft, blowpipe analysis and fire assay. There were field trips to nearby industries and talks by mining engineers and the chemists who worked with them. Like all students in the School of Mines, Pauling was a member of the Miners Club, and he went to the organization's get-togethers every two weeks to drink coffee, eat doughnuts, and hear talks by professional men.

And there were the standard introductory chemistry courses, taught in OAC's most impressive building, a three-story, towered granite-and-sandstone edifice built originally to house agricultural departments. By the time Pauling arrived, the fast-growing chemistry program had taken over most of the building. The dairy-and-stock judging area on the first floor had been converted into a huge chemistry teaching laboratory outfitted with the finest equipment and capable of accommodating 550 students in four sections. New labs were also set up for quantitative and organic chemistry. Officially the building was called Science Hall; by the time Pauling was studying there it was known as the "Chem Shack."

Presiding over the Chem Shack was Prof. John Fulton, a tubby man with an impressive shock of silver hair. Like the rest of the OAC chemistry faculty members at the time, he was not a researcher—he had never received a doctorate, and even the Harvard master's degree he claimed, Pauling found out later, was fictional—but Johnny Fulton did have sympathy for students. Although Pauling would never remember anything he learned from Fulton, he would always recall the three hundred dollars the department head later loaned him to ease his way to graduate school.

There were some good instructors. Unhappy with the chemistry class he was originally assigned to as a freshman, Pauling shopped around until he found Renton Kirkwood Brodie, "a remarkable, enthusiastic lecturer," according to Pauling. He attended Brodie's classes through his first year, solidifying his hold on the basics of chemical knowledge. And he continued to have good luck with his mathematics teachers. On his first train trip to Corvallis, Pauling met Charles Johnson, head of the OAC math department, and decided on the spot to try to take every class Johnson taught. His instincts were right: Johnson's lectures made calculus a delight.

While Fulton oversaw the chemistry department, Floyd Rowland headed the more specialized chemical engineering program after Pauling's freshman year. Pauling said that he was "not very smart, but he recognized that he wasn't." Rowland was, however, one of the few professors at OAC who had managed to get a Ph.D. (and from a good chemistry program at the University of Illinois) and was a great promoter of graduate education. With Rowland's encouragement, an unheard-of nine of the twelve OAC students who went through the undergraduate chemical engineering program with Pauling went on to graduate school.

Despite his early apprehension, Pauling soon found he could master college courses almost as easily as he had his high school work, at least when he wanted to. He earned A's in all his chemistry and math courses. "It just seemed like all he had to do was sit down at a table, look at a book, and he'd absorb the knowledge without reading it, without looking at it," remembered classmate Edward Larson.

He also began forming a feeling for what he liked and didn't like about chemistry. Qualitative analysis, for instance, which he took as a freshman, was not to his taste. "Inorganic qualitative analysis repelled me, because of its completely or nearly completely empirical character," he remembered. "Most of the methods of separation and detection of the different metals depended on the solubility of certain compounds, and there was essentially no theoretical basis for the difference. . . . I disliked qualitative analysis, whereas the precision of quantitative analysis appealed to me."

Pauling paid less attention to subjects outside the physical sciences, receiving a D in mechanical drawing (he wasn't patient enough to let the ink dry on his work, Pauling remembered, and kept smudging it) and an F in his second semester of freshman gymnasium. He failed the gym class when, in true Pauling fashion, he tried to get around the rules. He knew that members of the school athletic teams weren't required to take the standard gym classes, so he planned to join the track team instead of taking the required course. (He had thought about being a high-hurdles and high-jump competitor since high school.) Trying out for the team, however, was a disaster: He knocked over a hurdle and couldn't clear a high enough bar to interest the coach. Although he ran in one meet, he failed to make the team, got an F in the course he tried to bypass, and gave up on competitive athletics.

In most ways, he was a typical and enthusiastic underclassman. As a freshman, Pauling wore the green beanie required of all "rooks" at OAC. The school's athletic team was the Beavers, and as Pauling noted in his diary, he soon developed "lots of Beaver pep." He saluted upperclassmen, rooted at football games, sang fight songs, played billiards, and partied at freshman class "smokers." He joined the student military cadet corps, purchasing a uniform and taking classes in drill and camp cookery (eventually rising to the rank of major his senior year).

And, like most college boys, he looked for romance. Pauling was still shy around girls, a situation worsened at college by the poor opinion he had of his appearance. "The more I look at myself in the mirror, the more peculiar my physiognomy appears to me," he wrote as a freshman. "I do not look at all attractive. . . . I already have faint horizontal wrinkles in my forehead, and my upper lip projects to an unnecessarily great extent. I must remember to restrain it." He was overly critical: photos of the time show a skinny kid with a full head of wavy auburn hair, broad, expressive features, an open and engaging grin; his eyes were a bright and penetrating blue. In any case, he was young, on his own, and fully capable of overcoming fears. Pauling had his first, confused, impetuous kiss, with a girl named Gwendolyn, just before he left for college. Soon after arriving in Corvallis, while chopping wood to earn extra money, Pauling met Irene Sparks, a curly-haired seventeen-year-old who was taking business classes at OAC. Pauling was smitten and immediately asked her out to a movie. "She is the girl for me," he wrote breathlessly after the show. That diary entry was the last he ever made about her. Five years would pass before he had another significant romance.

As a sophomore Pauling was given a job working in the chemistry department's "solution room," where, bright and able, he soon made an impression on many of the professors. He was also invited to join a fraternity, Gamma Tau Beta (mainly, he thought, in order to raise the house grade-point average). Pauling was generally well accepted by his fraternity brothers, who gave him the awful nickname "Peanie" and included him in all house activities. At one party, a house member remembered, some of the boys dressed in drag, Peanie especially making "a pretty good-looking little gal."

The younger members of Gamma Tau Beta were required to have
a date every week, which Pauling remembered as "quite a problem for
me. I had a lot of trouble asking a young woman to go to a movie with
me because I was shy and didn't have a lot of money to entertain lavishly." But there was an inducement to find female companionship:
Brothers who failed their romantic duties were carried upstairs, forced
into a bathtub filled with freezing water, and held under until nearly
drowned, a quaint Greek custom called "dunking." The weekend soon
came when Pauling didn't have a date, but he had already figured out
what he called "a little subterfuge" to get around the punishment. As
the older fraternity brothers were carrying him up the stairs, he
started breathing deeply, saturating his blood with oxygen. "Then I
didn't struggle at all," he remembered. "They put me in the tub, holding me under the water, and I just lay there . . . lay there . . . lay
there . . . and the seconds went by . . . a minute went by . . . and they
pulled me out, very frightened, saying, 'He's had a heart attack or
something!' Of course, I 'recovered,' and from then on didn't have to
worry about it."

The Arrangement of Electrons

Poverty had an effect on more than Pauling's social life. He had to
work his way through college; during his freshman year he chopped
wood, mopped kitchens, and cut up quarters of beef for a girls' dormitory, putting in one hundred hours a month at twenty-five cents per
hour. "In order to do this . . . and to keep up with my studies, it was
necessary that I not waste any hours during the day," he remembered.
"So I think I developed the habit of working." Long hours of hard work
would become the norm for the rest of his life.

Following his freshman year, in the early summer of 1918, Pauling
and Mervyn Stephenson, along with a number of other OAC cadets,
were sent to the Presidio in San Francisco for six weeks of intensive officers' training. Pauling and Stephenson spent the rest of the summer
helping build wooden-hulled freighters in a shipyard on the coast of
Oregon. Whatever Pauling's opinions about war later, during World
War I he was in full support of the government's actions. Stephenson
would later remember that Pauling was a strong supporter of the war
effort, "100 percent for it."

Pauling's sophomore-year job in the chemistry department stockroom, preparing standard solutions and handing them out to students, helped him make a living and almost killed him. One day, while transferring ammonia into smaller bottles, Pauling thought he would make the job easier by creating a siphon. "I blew into the rubber tube to get up enough pressure to start the siphon and then opened my mouth, forgetting that the pressure would blow the ammonia into my mouth," he remembered. "After I had removed the mucous membrane that fell off inside my mouth, I went over to the student health service and was left to think that sometimes one mustn't be satisfied with having solved one problem but must go on and continue to think about the matter and solve the next problem that might arise." The next summer, after his sophomore year, Pauling started a job delivering milk from eight in the evening until four in the morning, physically punishing work that he could bear for only a month. He then secured a job with a contractor who had been hired by the state to test paving materials on the new network of hardtopped highways being laid across Oregon. The job of paving inspector paid well, and he enjoyed the work, traveling to out-of-the-way places with names like Wolf Creek and Grave Creek and camping out for weeks at a time in tents with the road crews. He liked the company of the workmen, who seemed to take a brotherly interest in the young whiz kid. He tested the blacktop, helped lay chain for surveying, even ran a steamroller off the road and flipped it. (Pauling didn't learn how to drive a car until he was in graduate school.) The job gave him time to think about chemistry as well. In his off hours that summer he lay on his cot in the tent and perused a chemical handbook, getting pleasure out of noting the properties of compounds, just as he had enjoyed listing the properties of minerals when he was rock collecting. He even tried some early theorizing, exercising his mind for a few weeks vainly trying to relate the magnetic properties of substances in some logical way to the periodic table. All the money he earned he sent back to Belle to bank for his coming year's tuition, and there was some left over to help his family as well.

But when he was to start his junior year, Belle gave him a shock: She told him he couldn't have the money he had earned. She needed it, she told him, to make ends meet at home. He would have to quit college for a year and work a regular job in order to make enough to finish the program.

Despite his independence in other ways, Pauling was still a dutiful son. He didn't want to live with Belle, but he did almost everything she asked. The summer before, he had even joined the Masons at her request, a prerequisite for Belle to be able to join some of her friends as a member of the allied Eastern Star women's group. (As soon as she did, he quit going to meetings of the Masons.) Now he swallowed his disappointment, telling himself that it was his obligation to help his mother, not hers to send him through college, and made plans to keep working with the highway commission through the academic year. Then he received an unusual offer from OAC. Pauling had shown himself a prodigy in the chemistry program, never receiving less than an A in any chemistry course and in the winter term of his sophomore year managing a perfect 4.0 grade-point average. The chemistry department didn't want to lose its promising student; at the same time, there was a need for teaching help to handle the mushrooming number of students taking introductory chemistry courses. The solution was simple: Pauling, at age eighteen, was offered a job as an instructor teaching quantitative chemistry, a course he had finished just the year before.

Although the teaching job paid only a hundred dollars a month — twenty-five dollars a month less than testing pavement—Pauling didn't hesitate. He had already recognized that his interests were more academic than industrial, and he realized the importance of gaining some teaching experience. As a student, he had paid enough attention to the art of teaching to know what worked and what didn't in a classroom, and his grasp of chemistry through the sophomore level was at least as good as that of most of his professors. After an initial period of nervousness, he found that he enjoyed lecturing and that the students appreciated his enthusiasm. Following his first term the mining students petitioned the department to let Pauling teach them quantitative chemistry, and the department administrators began gratefully assigning a number of courses to him, including chemistry for home-economics majors. "Lots of times the students would say, 'Well, hell, he knows more than the profs, anyway. He could conduct the class better than they did,'" remembered one of Pauling's OAC classmates. "He was regarded as quite a brain in those days."

Pauling's yearlong teaching stint gave him money, confidence as a lecturer, and time to catch up with the latest research in the field. He was given a desk next to a secretary in the small chemistry library, where he learned touch typing and pored over chemical journals between classes.

The journal reading was important. At OAC the chemistry professors not only didn't do much research themselves; they didn't teach their students much about any of the current investigations in their field. There was little attempt to place chemistry in a historical context, to outline recent trends in the field, or to transmit the excitement that comes from the pursuit of knowledge. Pauling had to find that excitement on his own, and he did—in the journals.

᠊ᢈᡰᡰ᠇᠊

One of the papers that caught his attention was written by Irving Langmuir, a General Electric Research Laboratory chemist who had made a substantial reputation for himself—and a fortune for GE—by discovering a way to greatly increase the life span of electric lights. Gifted with a roving curiosity and supported by all the power of one of the nation's leading industrial concerns, Langmuir would later become the first industrial chemist to win the Nobel Prize.

His work with electricity and its effects on metals led him to speculate on the way in which the basic unit of electricity, the electron, was involved in the structure of atoms and molecules. The paper Pauling read was a sixty-six-page *tour de force* called "The Arrangement of Electrons in Atoms and Molecules." It was an expansion, as Langmuir generously noted, of the ideas of another American chemist, the head of the University of California chemistry department, Gilbert N. Lewis, which had been published before the war. Pauling read Langmuir's work, went back and looked up Lewis's, and had his eyes opened to a new way of looking at chemistry.

The Lewis and Langmuir papers were an attempt to bring chemistry in line with some of the baffling things physicists were discovering about the structure of atoms. And atomic structure was *the* question of the day. For two thousand years atoms had been considered the ultimate units of nature, the smallest of the small. (The name atom itself means "not cut.") John Dalton in 1808 set nineteenth-century chemistry firmly on the path of atomic theory in his treatise *A New System of Chemical Philosophy,* in which he persuasively argued that unbreakable atoms formed compounds by linking with other atoms in simple whole-number proportions: one carbon with two oxygens to make carbon dioxide; one carbon with one oxygen to form carbon monoxide; one oxygen with one hydrogen to form water. (He had that one slightly wrong.) It wasn't until the 1880s and 1890s that cracks began to appear in Dalton's solid little spheres, caused by the discovery of strange new phenomena that his atomic theory couldn't explain, among them x-rays and radioactivity. In 1897 the theory of the indivisible atom was finally exploded by J. J. Thomson, the British physicist and head of the venerable Cavendish Laboratory at Cambridge, who stunned the scientific world by reporting the existence of particles one thousand times smaller than the smallest atom. Thomson called them "corpuscles." When it was quickly found that they appeared to be the elemental unit of electricity, the name that stuck was "electron."

It was the first sighting of the subatomic world. And it turned science on its head. Thomson's discovery of the electron would force a crisis of understanding in science, compel the development of a new kind of physics and a vastly revised chemistry—would in fact, perhaps more than any other single event, usher in the twentieth century.

Electrons, it seemed, were normal parts of atoms. And the new problem became figuring out what atoms were, now that they appeared to be composed of smaller pieces. Electrons, Thomson found, carried a negative charge. But under normal circumstances the atoms of which they were a part had no overall charge; therefore, there had to be a positive electrical component somewhere to neutralize the electrons. Thomson thought that perhaps the electrons were stabilized in a field of positive electricity, like raisins in a pudding. He was proved wrong by one of his former students, a brash New Zealander with a genius for laboratory work named Ernest Rutherford, who announced in 1911 that he had found evidence of a surprisingly different structure: At the center of the atom, according to his elegant experiments, was a very small, very dense nucleus that carried a positive charge. The rest of the atom, with the exception of the electrons, was empty space. Expanded to the size of a football stadium, Rutherford's atom would have a nucleus the size of a grain of rice on the fifty-yard line, with barely visible electrons orbiting the outer bleachers.

This was as astounding as Thomson's discovery of the electron. Rather than solid balls, atoms had become webs of fairy gossamer. Solid matter was mostly empty space. Rutherford's findings set off another round of theorizing. If the nucleus was that small and positively charged and the electrons were that distant and negatively charged, what held the whole thing together? Opposites attract, so why didn't electrons simply dive into the nucleus?

Physicists understood a great deal about moving objects and forces; Newton's theories and the work of his successors had given them the power to predict the movement of the planets based on a few earthly experiments. Certainly the same well-understood and proven laws of nature—the body of knowledge that would be known as classical physics—could be adapted to explain the workings of the atom. Rutherford himself proposed that atoms might be something akin to little solar systems, with electrons whizzing around the nucleus like planets around the sun. The speed of their flight could, he theorized, counterbalance the electrical attraction of the nucleus. Like most physicists, he thought in terms of fast-moving electrons; Rutherford's was a dynamic model of the atom. But his atom didn't work. One deadly shortcoming was the classical requirement that any moving charged particle lose energy. Applied to electrons, this meant that Rutherford's atom would run down like an unwound watch until the electrons spiraled into the nucleus.

If not a solar system, what was the atom like? In the early decades of the twentieth century, answering that question would become the Holy Grail for a new generation of physicists.

⁓

They were not alone in the quest. "The problem of the structure of atoms has been attacked mainly by physicists," Langmuir wrote in the paper that first caught Pauling's attention, "who have given little consideration to the chemical properties which must ultimately be explained by a theory of atomic structure. The vast store of knowledge of chemical properties and relationships, such as is summarized by the Periodic Table, should serve as a better foundation for a theory of atomic structure than the relatively meager experimental data along purely physical lines."

There was bit of jostling for position here between chemistry, the king of sciences in the nineteenth century, and physics, which would prove the dominant field of the twentieth. Both Lewis and Langmuir knew and appreciated physics—both had studied in Germany with the pioneers of physical chemistry, and Lewis was one of the first Americans to champion Einstein's theory of relativity—but they were chemists at heart.

And at the heart of chemistry, as Langmuir pointed out, was the periodic table, a Rosetta stone for chemists eager to translate nature's elemental language. The table began to take shape in the 1860s, when several chemists noticed that when they arranged the elements according to increasing atomic weight, certain properties—melting points, boiling points, chemical reactivity—seemed to rise and fall and rise again in a roughly periodic way. At least early in the table, that period seemed to be eight elements long. Start with an inert gas like helium, one of nature's most unreactive substances. Move eight steps up the table and there was another inert gas, neon. Move eight steps more and there was another, argon. It was the same with the highly reactive alkali metals: Lithium was eight steps away from sodium, which behaved much like potassium, another eight steps away.

Why eight was the magic number was unclear. Then, around 1913, it became accepted that each new element in the table represented not only an increase in weight but the addition of one electron to the preceding element. Somehow this regular increase in electrons was intimately tied to the periodic nature of the elements.

Lewis explained it in a paper he published in 1916. The inert gases were inert, he wrote, because they possessed an unusually stable grouping of electrons. Eight steps between each inert gas meant the addition of eight electrons; whatever this stable organization of electrons was, it happened eight at a time. This electronic "rule of eight" had been proposed before, but Lewis employed it to explain more about chemistry than anyone had. And he used it to create a new model of the atom. Rather than the physicists' solar system, he placed eight electrons at equal distances from one another and from the nucleus in three-dimensional space, then connected the dots. The result was a cube enclosing the nucleus, with an electron at each of the eight corners. Going up the periodic table and adding electrons, new cubes would be formed one electron at a time around the inner cubes, like boxes around boxes.

Lewis's atomic cubes did more than explain the rule of eight. They also offered explanations for phenomena that the physicists' solar-system model could not, such as how one atom could link with others to form a stable molecule. In this matter of the chemical bond, Lewis and Langmuir theorized, the explanation again came from the natural tendency of an element to want to form a perfect cube filled with eight electrons. An atom with four extra electrons beyond a perfect cube—carbon, for instance—would become most stable when it connected with some combination of other atoms that offered it four more electrons, filling its outer cube with a perfect eight. This filling of cubes could be achieved, Lewis wrote, by sharing electrons with other atoms. And his theory stated that this sharing should happen one pair at a time, using the two electrons along an edge of the cube. Four hydrogens, for instance, could each pair their single electrons with one of the four bachelors in the carbon shell, giving it the equivalent of eight in its outer cube and creating the stable molecule CH_4, methane. Sharing pairs of electrons, Lewis and Langmuir said, was the glue that held molecules together.

Their cubical picture of the atom was simple but powerful, offering at least a preliminary explanation of the character of the inert gases, the periodic table, and chemical valency, the long-known but unexplained capacity of elements to combine most stably with certain numbers of other elements.

And the Lewis and Langmuir model did something else that the physicists' atom could not: It fit with what chemists knew about the shapes of molecules. Chemists knew that molecules were not random assortments of atoms joined willy-nilly; their shapes were specific. In methane, for instance, the four hydrogens were linked to the carbon to form a tetrahedron, a three-sided pyramid. There was no plausible explanation of how a solar-system atom could lead to that sort of three-dimensional specificity, but it was easy to see how, with a cubical atom, the sharing of electrons along various edges could lead to the patterns known to exist in nature.

It was a breakthrough paper, Lewis's 1916 effort, one that Pauling always thought should have won him the Nobel Prize. Like many milestone papers in science, it planted the seeds of several important ideas. It focused chemists' attention on electrons, reinforcing the growing belief that chemistry was rooted, in general, in the structure of groupings of electrons. This emphasis on structure—"We must first of all, from a study of chemical phenomena, learn the structure and the arrangement of the atoms," as Lewis put it—would also have a great effect on chemistry. It established the chemists' place in studying atomic structure, directly challenging the physicists' solar-system atom, which could not explain valency or molecular structure. And, most importantly, it proposed that the chemical bond was made of pairs of electrons.

Lewis's cubical atom had its own problems, however. It quickly became known as the "static" model of the atom, as opposed to the physicists' "dynamic" model, because Lewis demanded that electrons stay relatively still at the cube's corners. Static electrons were impossible, the physicists argued; a negatively charged particle could not sit still at a small distance from a positively charged particle—electrostatic forces would pull them together. Lewis's characteristically audacious response was to propose that his model might be right and the accepted Newtonian laws of nature wrong. "Indeed, if we find it necessary to alter the law of force acting between charged particles at small distances," he wrote in 1916, "it will not be the first time in the history of science that an increase in the range of observational material has required a modification of generalizations based upon a smaller field of observation."

The argument was set aside as the United States entered World War I. Lewis began researching ways to defend soldiers against gas warfare, Rutherford began focusing on radioactivity, and it would be left to a new generation of young physicists to take up the problem of atomic structure after the war. On the chemists' side, it wasn't until Langmuir popularized and expanded Lewis's ideas around 1919 that they got the attention they deserved.

—*mm*—

Until he read Lewis's and Langmuir's papers, Pauling had been teaching his students the same crude chemical-bond theory developed in ancient Greece, in which atoms had a certain number of hooks and eyes with which to latch on to other atoms. Sodium, for instance, had an eye; chlorine had a hook. Sodium chloride was easily formed, and two atoms of chlorine could latch their hooks together to make Cl_2, but two atoms of sodium couldn't combine. While the theory gave a picture that satisfied Pauling at the time he was learning it, it didn't explain anything about what the hooks and eyes were, that is, the nature of the forces that held atoms into stable aggregates.

The Lewis and Langmuir model did. The idea of shared electron pairs tied chemistry to atomic physics in a way that made it possible to discuss *why* things happened in chemistry rather than simply describing *what* happened.

Even as a student, Pauling had been thinking about molecular structure in his courses in materials and metallurgy, where questions about the hardening of iron into steel and the ductility of metals were discussed in the context of crude atomic models. One idea from his classes that he later remembered was that a slip occurs along planes of atoms as a metal is stretched, with atoms in one level sliding over others. He had found something pleasing in visualizing atoms bumping along each other as the basis for an observable property.

This was a rare pleasure in chemistry, where students could read hundreds of pages of text describing the properties of substances—chemical formulas, molecular weights, densities, colors, crystalline forms, melting points, boiling points, solubilities, reactivities, refractabilities—without finding a single paragraph explaining why these properties existed: why water froze at one temperature and methane at another, why graphite was soft and diamonds hard, why neon didn't react with anything, while fluorine, one place away from it on the periodic table, reacted with almost everything. Now, through

Lewis and Langmuir, Pauling was introduced to a more sophisticated way of looking at molecules, a way that explained more. "It was then," he wrote, "that I developed a strong desire to understand the physical and chemical properties of substances in relation to the structure of atoms and molecules of which they are composed."

And Pauling was impressed by more than G. N. Lewis's ideas. He was attracted by his style. Lewis's approach to science—bold, theoretical, structural—would provide a model for Pauling. This was chemistry on a level different from what he had known. This was theoretical chemistry, the invention of a few simple, broad ideas that explained and ordered an otherwise confusing welter of phenomena. Lewis's attempts to explain all of chemistry with his electron cubes excited Pauling to think in broader terms, on a higher level than he had before.

And he wanted to share his excitement. Unlike more sophisticated universities, OAC did not offer regular chemistry-department seminars in which the faculty would spend an hour or two explaining current research to other faculty members and students. Only one, on the frozen-fish industry, had been given during the entire year Pauling taught there. But, enthusiastic about what he had read, Pauling, still a teenager, determined to raise the level of scientific discourse by giving another. He prepared carefully. Then Pauling, technically between his sophomore and junior years in college, introduced his professors to one of the most important recent advances in chemistry: the "electronic" theory of chemical bonding.

Miss Miller

His teaching year also gave Pauling time for intellectual snacking outside the sciences. Every few days he would go to the college library and check out one or two books, whatever interested him at the moment. He discovered George Bernard Shaw and read all his plays, including the prefaces and introductions. He devoured the short stories of Maupassant and read a smattering of philosophy. And he indulged his lifelong interest in popular literature as well. He bought the *Saturday Evening Post* every week, if he had an extra nickel, and read the short stories, especially enjoying anything involving mystery and adventure. He had already developed a taste for science fiction and continued to seek out anything he could find with a science-fiction flavor.

He also thought about his future. He was becoming unsatisfied with the OAC emphasis on practical training. His interest in chemistry was growing increasingly academic; Lewis and Langmuir had helped turn him toward physical chemistry in general and theoretical approaches in particular. Pauling talked with John Fulton about his concerns, and the department head showed him a flyer from a new school in Pasadena, California, the Throop Polytechnic Institute, that he thought might interest him. Pauling had already heard of it from a pair of students who had flunked out and transferred to OAC: The chemistry program in Pasadena was headed by one of the biggest names in chemistry, A. A. Noyes, founder of the phenomenally successful program in physical chemistry at Massachusetts Institute of Technology (MIT). Throop was quite small, but the program was rigorous, with a lot of tough math and physics. It sounded good, and Pauling wrote Noyes himself asking for advice on entering as an undergraduate. A Throop administrator wrote back with discouraging news about financial support, however, and Pauling decided to stick it out at OAC.

After working another summer on the highway, he reentered the chemistry program in 1920 as a junior. His teaching success had built his self-confidence; he was now closer in age to his classmates, acclimated to fraternity life, and ready to enjoy college as an upperclassman. He easily earned top marks in virtually all his courses, including, finally, a much-desired A in track. He made some money as an assistant to the school's professor of mechanics, performing calculations on the strength of materials and doing some teaching. He was invited to apply for a Rhodes scholarship, was inducted into honorary societies in engineering and the military arts, and was elected president of the chemistry honorary society, Chi Epsilon.

He also continued to build his reputation for being the smartest man on campus and something of a smart aleck. His metallography professor remembered Pauling peppering him in class with "embarrassing questions about the ultimate structure of matter." Bored with an assignment in which he was asked to describe methods of photographing metals, Pauling wrote his professor, "It is hardly necessary to describe them except briefly, as the technique of photographing metals is very similar to that required for other purposes. However, in order not to be accused of lying down on the job, I shall devote a few minutes of my valuable time to a short exposition. . . ." If he liked a professor, he would tease: "I have attempted to use words of one syllable to as great an extent as is practicable in order to prevent any mental strain," he wrote on a paper for another teacher.

"He was a bit on the cocky side," remembered Paul Emmett, a fellow chemistry major, a good friend, and an eventual brother-in-law. (Emmett would marry Pauling's sister Pauline.) "I remember one time in class our new physical chemistry teacher, in correcting problems, said, 'Well, now, since Linus Pauling and I get the same answer, when two great authorities agree, it must be right.' Linus calmly looked him in the eye and said, 'Who's the other one?'"

Pauling was disappointed in his physical chemistry class; the professor teaching it was new and unsure of himself, the textbook was poor, and there was little theory in the approach. Pauling was bored with plugging numbers into someone else's equations, especially when there wasn't a good explanation of the ideas behind the equations. He had had the same problem with organic chemistry his sophomore year, and he left OAC with a distaste for both subjects.

Public speaking was, however, becoming more of an interest. In his junior year, Pauling competed in a schoolwide oratorical contest as his class's representative. Although he was fairly comfortable speaking in front of others, Pauling also wanted to win, and he sought out additional coaching in diction and delivery from a former minister who had gone on to become an OAC professor of English. The piece Pauling wrote for the competition was a paean to scientific rationalism entitled "Children of the Dawn":

> My body slept. My mind soared. From infinite distance, attainable only by the flight of thought, I saw in the midst of the limitless universe the solar system—its sun, a pigmy amidst other pigmy suns, dimly visible as a minute radiating point—our earth, revolving about the sun, hardly to be differentiated from the myriads of other planets. That hour a thought was born in me: "The earth is not the center of the universe, but merely a tiny part of the great design."
>
> As I gazed, entranced, the vapors about the earth condensed, and oceans were born. Aeons passed. Plant and animal life appeared, simple at first, then more complex. . . . The genius of Darwin enlightened the world, so that now it is generally believed that man is an evolutionary product, with lineage extending back to the lowest forms of life. But though we know that man is immeasurably superior now to what he once was,

we do not realize the marvelous changes to come, the splendid improvements to be made.

Physical changes in man are the result of changes in his physical environment. Efficiency is Nature's goal. As conditions changed on this earth, so did the forms of life change, until man, the highest of the animals, has approached physical perfection.

Similarly, psychical changes in man are the result of changes in his mental environment. . . . A young man may now know more of geometry than Euclid, and more of calculus than Newton. . . . Is it not evident that the great mental development which has characterized the last few thousand years is still taking place? . . .

We are not the flower of civilization. We are but the immature bud of a civilization yet to come. We are the children of the dawn, witnessing the approach of day. We bask in the dim prophecies of the rising sun, knowing, even in our inexperience, that something glorious is to come; for it is from us that greater beings will grow, to develop in the light of the sun that shall know no setting.

The optimism of the piece is typical of Pauling. But his Darwinian progressivism may have been too cheery for the judges. Pauling tied for second place in the contest with the sophomore speaker, who spoke of the dangers of "Closing Our National Door" to immigrants. They both lost to the senior orator's "House Divided Against Itself." (The fellow went on to take second place in the state competition with "Our Tottering Civilization.")

The summer between his junior and senior years, while again testing paving materials, Pauling decided to apply for the Rhodes scholarship. He went all out, as always, noting in his application that since he had learned about the Rhodes the year before, "my actions and activities have to a large extent been influenced by the desire to prepare myself for Oxford." Interestingly, Pauling inquired about the possibilities of using the scholarship to study with a metallography professor at the British school. And he solicited seven letters of recommendation from his teachers at OAC, which together indicate something of the impression he had made on his mentors. Floyd Rowland, the head of the chemical engineering program, took special note of Pauling's oratorical prowess and added that the twenty-year-old "possesses one of the best minds I have ever observed in a person of his age, and in many ways is superior to his instructors." Pauling's public-speaking professor was impressed by the fact that "he seems always unwilling to accept conclusions merely because they are lying close at hand, ready-made. He has the scientific attitude. He does not expect results without hard work, but seems to delight in digging hard."

But it was his German professor Louis Bach who provided the most careful overview of Pauling's character. "To me, he is an interested and an interesting student, wide-awake, keen, critical, considerate. . . . He would make a good teacher, and nobody would be tempted to sleep under his guidance. He is endowed with a remarkable memory in combination with good judgement, sound analytical and synthetical discrimination: a brilliant mind. He likes to discuss and while discussing, shows rare originality," Bach wrote. Then he offered a mild but telling criticism: "His present tendency is to rush too quickly to conclusions. That, however, is due to lack of experience, an unavoidable condition of youth." Rushing to conclusions was one youthful tendency that some would say stayed with Pauling his whole life.

All the praise was for naught. Although Pauling became one of OAC's candidates for the Rhodes (Paul Emmett was the other), he went no further in the selection process. It was a disappointment when he received the bad tidings during the second semester of his senior year. But by then the blow to his ego didn't seem to matter so much. He was in love.

nnn

In the Corvallis railroad station on his way to spend Christmas in Portland, Pauling ran into Fred Allen, an overworked OAC professor who was teaching Pauling physical chemistry that year. Allen desperately needed someone to take over a course he was slated to teach the coming term, a section of freshman chemistry for home economics majors. He had been impressed by Pauling's work in his physical chemistry course—a chemist through and through, Allen later recalled that "the gap from Pauling to the others in the class was akin to the hardness gap from diamond to corundum"—and he knew of Pauling's teaching experience. He asked Pauling to teach the home-economics chemistry course. It was a class Pauling had taught before, and he could use the extra money, so he agreed to do the favor.

On the first day of winter term, January 6, 1922, he walked into an OAC lecture hall and faced a roomful of twenty-five young women.

They, in turn, studied their surprisingly young professor, gauging his looks (now grown to a full six feet, thin, nicely dressed) and manner (very professional and a bit stiff, perhaps trying a bit hard to come off as older than he was). Pauling, always shy around women, was extremely self-conscious. But he had taught chemistry to home-economics classes before; he knew the best way to avoid any "boy professor" sniggering was to get right to the subject. This was the second term of a three-term course, and he decided to start by measuring the class's basic knowledge. "Will you tell me all you know about ammonium hydroxide, Miss . . ." He ran his finger down the registration sheet, looking for a name he couldn't possibly mispronounce. "Miss Miller?" He looked up and into the eyes of Ava Helen Miller. She was a small, delicate, strikingly pretty girl with long, dark hair. She was barely eighteen years old. She was a flirt. And, as it turned out, she knew quite a bit about ammonium hydroxide.

Ava Helen, the tenth of twelve children, was raised on a 160-acre farm near the tiny town of Beavercreek, Oregon. Her father was a German immigrant, a rail-thin, autocratic schoolteacher who first met her mother when she was his student. Politics was a part of life in the household. Ava Helen's mother had been a suffragist, and her father was a liberal Democrat with leanings toward socialism. Her parents divorced when Ava Helen was eleven, and she and her younger brothers and sisters were raised by their mother; the combination of socialist discussions around the dinner table and the example of her self-sufficient mother engendered in Ava Helen a lifelong concern for social justice and a strong feeling that women were capable of anything they set their minds to. At age thirteen she went to live with an older sister who worked for the Oregon Supreme Court in the capital of Salem, where she breezed through high school in three years. Her mother, a believer in higher education, invested almost everything she had in putting as many of her children as possible through college.

Ava Helen entered OAC as a fun-loving, energetic, independent spirit. She also liked men. Since her family had "a great deal of respect for the teaching profession," she said later, she was especially interested in people who "looked, talked, and acted as though they knew a good bit." She and the other girls in the class were impressed by their young professor. "We thought it was very interesting that he had his curly black hair parted in the middle," she remembered. "He was very good-looking. We thought that our class would be much more interesting with this new teacher. . . . We didn't know whether he was married. We were interested in that."

She quickly found out all about Pauling from a fraternity brother, and her interest grew. She began putting in long hours in the chemistry lab, taking careful note of the products of reactions and the reactions of her professor. Pauling, on his part, thought Ava Helen was extremely bright—"smarter than any girl I'd ever met," he would later say. She enjoyed teasing him. The home-economics laboratory was on the ground floor, with windows that offered easy access. At the end of one lab session in which Pauling watched her receiving a fair number of jump-through male visitors, he asked Ava Helen, "Did you get anything done today?" She answered, "Yes, didn't you see all the help I had?"

Despite—and perhaps because of—her flirtatiousness, Pauling worked hard to appear uninterested. She thought he was avoiding looking at her; she thought he was purposefully staying clear of her desk when he walked around the classroom. Then, when Ava Helen looked inside a homework notebook Pauling had corrected, she found a short note. It was from her young professor, telling her that an OAC teacher had been severely criticized for the attentions he paid one of his students a few years before. That, Pauling wrote, was not going to happen to him. Ava Helen stormed up to him after class. "I said that he was my chemistry instructor, and so of course I expected him to teach me some chemistry, but didn't expect him to teach me anything else." And she stormed away.

Undermined, Pauling's defenses crumbled. A few weeks later, Ava Helen found another note, this time asking her out for a stroll across campus.

During their first, tremulous walk together, as he was helping Ava Helen cross a stream, Pauling's elbow cracked her across the nose. He was distraught, she thought it was funny, and the ice was broken. Soon she was bringing him treats (she later said, "My husband says I seduced him with sea foam candy") and listening intently on their long walks as he talked about chemistry—and himself. "He was the first man that I had been with who could talk about himself in my presence," she remembered. "Boys had always told me about what beautiful eyes I had or how good a dancer I was, but Linus was not overly concerned with that. He was full of ideas and dreams. He knew what he wanted to do and it all sounded so exciting."

After thinking it over for some weeks, Pauling decided that the proper way to think of the two of them was as senior and freshman rather than professor and student. In the late spring, just before giving her a final grade, he asked her to marry him. She said yes. He then lowered her grade one point below what he thought it should be in order to avoid any impression of favoritism.

—*mm*—

Most of the exciting things Pauling told Ava Helen he wanted to do depended on getting more education than was available at OAC. Spurred partly by his own instincts and ambitions and partly by Rowland's proselytizing in favor of graduate work, Pauling decided he had to go to graduate school. He applied to a number of the nation's top schools offering advanced chemistry programs, including Harvard, Illinois, and Berkeley, and wrote again to Throop Polytechnic, recently renamed the California Institute of Technology.

Berkeley was particularly attractive. The chemistry program there was headed by G. N. Lewis, the discoverer of the shared electron bond, and Berkeley was generally considered the best place in the nation to study physical chemistry. The program at Harvard, directed by America's first (and at that time only) chemistry Nobelist, Theodore Richards, was solid and well respected; Rowland's *alma mater*, Illinois, focused on organic chemistry but had a good program in physical chemistry as well. Pauling still had a strong interest in the California Institute of Technology, but it was more of a gamble: the youngest and smallest of the schools, it was just beginning to build the national reputation that would make it in a short time the best-known research center in the United States.

Timing helped Pauling decide. Harvard quickly made him an offer, but Caltech made him a better one, including a fellowship that would pay his tuition and a $350 monthly stipend for working as a teaching assistant. Caltech also accepted Pauling's friend Paul Emmett. Berkeley was too slow in making an offer. Impatient, Pauling said yes to Caltech, no to Harvard, and withdrew his other applications.

There was a great deal to do to ready himself. He borrowed one thousand dollars from an uncle, Jim Campbell, to give to his mother so he wouldn't have to worry about sending her money while engaged in his graduate studies. And he came to a decision about Ava Helen. His first impulse was to get married quickly and take his bride with him to California, but both Belle and Ava Helen's mother worked hard to discourage the idea. They wanted their children to finish their educations first, without the distractions of married life. Ava Helen's mother, determined that her daughter would have a college education, was especially persuasive. Eventually, Pauling and Ava Helen let their heads

prevail over their hearts and agreed to separate, she to finish her studies at OAC, he to return for his fiancée after receiving his doctorate.

The separation wouldn't be easy. While they were courting, Pauling had been honest enough to tell Ava Helen, "If I had to choose between you and science, I'm not sure that I would choose you." She was
becoming accustomed to straight talk from her beau, but this particular remark cut her—she would remember it for the rest of her life. She
replied with something about it being all right as long as she was part
of the package. And she went to work to make sure he wouldn't forget
her in California.

She didn't have to worry. A poem doodled on the inside of an OAC
textbook at the end of his senior year gives an insight into Pauling's
feelings:

> *April 11, 1922*
> *Fully 21 years old, and*
> *with very few regrets.*
> *Let us sincerely hope that*
> *they shall remain just as few.*
> *By the way, life is odd,*
> *My vision has increased, and*
> *I really am happy; but I wish that*
> *My little troubles didn't worry me.*
> *I wonder why* amo *is the Latin word I remember? Thus*
> Te amo
> Je t'aime
> Ich liebe dich.

A few weeks later, Pauling delivered the senior class oration at graduation. By now he had tempered his optimistic belief in progress with a
recognition of social turmoil and a sense of obligation to others. The
technological horrors unleashed during World War I had spurred a
strong reaction against, and a critique of, science. Science, the argument went, made war more deadly and the workplace less human.
Technological advances were widening the income gap between rich
and poor. Science was becoming the new god of society, but it was a
god without morals.

Pauling's response, like that of many of the day's leading scientists,
was to stress the technological nature of the problems facing society
and to ask scientists to step to the forefront in facing them. The answer, he told his fellow graduates, was a credo of service to others:

The problems looming up in the development of the state and country are enormous in volume and overwhelming in complexity. Advancement and growth depend upon the discovery and development of the resources of nature, and the investigation and interpretation of the laws of nature. In the course of progress social relations are strained, and industrial, political and educational problems arise. The country is crying for a solution of all these difficulties, and is hopefully looking to the educated man for it. This, then, is the way we can repay OAC— by service. . . . We are going into the world inspired with the resolution of service, eager to show our love for our college and our appreciation of her work by being of service to our fellow men.

Thus inspired, at the end of the summer of 1922, Pauling boarded a train and headed for Caltech.

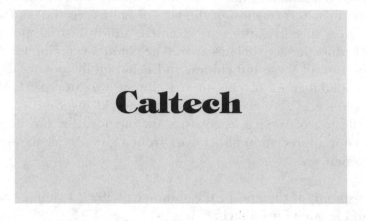

Caltech

An Idea Under Construction

Even the air was different in Pasadena, soft and warm, flower scented. The color palette was pastel: cantaloupe, orchid, ivory, and sand beneath a robin's-egg-blue sky. The town was rich, small, and quiet, nestled at the foot of the pink-and-purple San Gabriel Mountains, a well-tended bedroom community for the well-heeled of Los Angeles. A village of millionaires, it had been called, and there were sections that looked it: curved streets lined with palm trees, sprawling bungalows, and Spanish-style mansions set well back, the only sounds the snip of gardeners' shears and the hiss of sprinklers. Compared to rough-and-tumble Portland, with its dark fir forests and chilling rains, Pasadena seemed like paradise.

Pauling had arranged to room with his Oregon Agricultural College (OAC) classmate Paul Emmett, who was living with his mother in a house in town. After dropping off his suitcases, he set out immediately for Caltech, on the edge of town, across the street from the old Rose Bowl. The small campus—thirty acres of weedy fields, scrub oak, and an old orange grove—consisted of just three finished buildings: the Gates Laboratory of Chemistry and the Norman Bridge Laboratory of Physics, both relatively new, and old Throop Hall, the campus's original building, with its squat dome and Mission-style façade. An auditorium was under construction. The faculty club was a nearby farmhouse.

What mattered at Caltech, though, was not the campus but the minds gathering there. Just two decades earlier it had been an undistinguished manual training school without a major endowment or any well-known researchers. In 1907 the Chicago astronomer George Ellery Hale had adopted it as a base camp for his Mount Wilson Observatory up in the San Gabriels and, over the next decade, gradually built a network of financial support. The school became a serious center for research science only three years before Pauling arrived, when Hale lured A. A. Noyes to Pasadena by building him a fine new research building and giving him the chance to run a chemistry program as he saw fit. Noyes and Hale then rounded up enough private backing to put together another new laboratory building, a one-of-a-kind high-voltage facility, money for staff and equipment, and the offer of the presidency of the institute—a package grand enough to entice the nation's best-known physicist, Robert A. Millikan, from the University of Chicago. Millikan arrived just a year before Pauling.

When Pauling first saw it, Caltech was still an idea under construction. The faculty consisted of eighteen Ph.D.s; there were only twenty-nine graduate students, ten of them in chemistry. But the institute was poised for greatness. A number of factors were working in its favor: the economic boom in Southern California, the efficient fund-raising of Hale and Millikan, a "corporate" administrative style that gave maximum independence to researchers, and its small size, which allowed for maximum contact between students and faculty. But perhaps most important of all was the commitment of Caltech's three founders, Hale, Noyes, and Millikan, to the relatively new concept that scientific research could best be done by working across and above old disciplinary boundaries. In Pasadena chemists would regularly attend physics seminars; physicists would test theories of chemical evolution by looking out into space; astronomers would work with physicists and chemists to unlock the secrets of the stars. Interdisciplinary research would be reflected in a new approach to education, devised mainly by Noyes, that would make Caltech, in a very short time, one of the nation's best places—if not *the* best in some areas—to receive training in the physical sciences.

For four years as an undergraduate Pauling had been frustrated, asking questions about chemistry that his professors at Oregon Agricultural College couldn't answer. Now he would find himself inundated with answers—and new questions—presented by the best scientific minds in the world. At Caltech the most stimulating ideas, the latest findings, the most important issues, were discussed openly and critically on a daily basis. At Caltech, Pauling's intellect would flower. And it was due, in great part, to the sun.

———~~~———

George Ellery Hale loved the sun. That's what had brought the Chicago astronomer to Pasadena in 1903: sun to clear his daughter's bronchitis-clogged lungs and cloudless skies for the new solar observatory he wanted to build. Hale was an ambitious man, and he wanted to build the largest, best-equipped astronomical facility in the world. On a visit to California he found the clear weather, clean air, and accessible building site he was looking for—a place for what astronomers call "good seeing"—at the top of Mount Wilson in the San Gabriels. He had no money to build his new observatory and no researchers to run it. But he had an attitude, typified by his motto Make No Small Plans. And he had an uncommon ability to make big plans come true.

Hale was, like most American scientists, impressed by the success of Johns Hopkins University, which, since its founding in 1876, had changed the face of higher education in the United States. Johns Hopkins was modeled on German universities, emphasizing scholarly research among the faculty, the close association of graduate students with researchers, and the introduction of seminar-type teaching, with small groups of students attacking problems with the aid of their professor. It was a school devoted to teaching graduate students how to do independent scientific research, and the German system worked beautifully in the sciences. The rational cultivation of scientific research was of interest to industrialists as well, and oil baron John D. Rockefeller, impressed by Johns Hopkins, funded the new University of Chicago with some of the same ideas in mind. All it took to start a school was money, and the nation's growing respect for science was making money easier to get. Perhaps, Hale thought, he could create a new kind of scientific institution on the West Coast. He had made his scientific reputation by using the tools of other scientific disciplines to aid his study of astronomical phenomena and had written of creating what he called the New Astronomy, "a new science," he wrote in 1899, "which offers problems not to be solved by the astronomer alone but only by the combined skill of the astronomer, the physicist, and the chemist." In Pasadena, he thought, he could create a place devoted to this ideal of cooperative research. He went to work, persuading the board of trustees of a local vocational school called Throop Polytechnic Institute to jettison the school's elementary manual training courses and art program and concentrate instead on a bachelor's program in engineering. He arranged to have a sympathetic acquaintance selected as president. He started raising money to build new laboratories. And he began looking for scientific talent.

Hale knew how the game worked. The big-money foundations—Andrew Carnegie's and John D. Rockefeller's paramount among them—were beginning to funnel money into scientific research. But the dollars were not spread evenly; they went disproportionately to what Carnegie called "the exceptional man," a few elite scientists, proven producers who could guarantee a return on investment. If elite scientists would come to Pasadena, money would follow. But Hale didn't have a chance to attract them without decent facilities, and Throop consisted of one building unequipped for scientific research. He began building enthusiasm for expansion among the Throop board and redoubled his efforts to convince the Carnegie people to expand their funding beyond the observatory they were helping him build at Mount Wilson.

And he put out feelers in the scientific community, starting at the top. One of the first men he approached was a former Massachusetts Institute of Technology professor, now friend, the best-known teacher of chemistry in America, Arthur Amos Noyes.

───

Noyes, a Yankee born and bred, descended from Puritans who settled in Massachusetts in the 1630s. His father, a lawyer, was a gentleman more interested in history and writing than in making money. Noyes was raised in the small town of Newburyport, where, despite his family's modest circumstances, he was considered one of the gentry by right of birth. As he grew older, Noyes's Puritan inheritance became evident in his modest—some would say shy—manner, his reverence for learning, his disapproval of overt displays of wealth, and his lifelong habit of working up to sixteen hours a day. Noyes could often be found eating breakfast in his laboratory after sleeping there all night.

He also had a passion for the delights of literature, propelled in that direction by his mother, who would be his close companion until her death. Noyes would later impress students and colleagues by reciting long stretches of verse from memory—not the modern stuff, Pauling remembered, but "good old-fashioned poetry." Noyes believed in the unity of all things beautiful, both scientific and artistic; he could write a long letter about thermodynamics to a friend and sign it "Arturo."

Noyes became interested in chemistry early, but poverty delayed his entrance into MIT until he could receive a scholarship. After earning his master's degree, Noyes made what was becoming a common pilgrimage for American chemistry students in the 1880s, sailing for Germany to study with the masters. He thought he wanted to be an organic chemist. But then, in Leipzig, he came under the influence of the charismatic young firebrand Wilhelm Ostwald.

Only thirty-five, Ostwald had already earned a worldwide reputation for his research and visionary outlook. Although his gentle manner belied it, he was incredibly energetic, gifted with wide interests and talents (which included painting, making music, and philosophizing as well as working in the laboratory), and he was propelled by a vision. All of science is one, he preached, and each field should learn from others. He especially wanted to "illuminate the dark recesses of chemistry with the torch of physics." Physics, to Ostwald, was a more advanced field than chemistry, more precise, more mathematical, more theoretical. Chemists amassed facts; physicists explained them. Borrowing the techniques and approaches of physics, he and a handful of other like-minded researchers created the hybrid field eventually called physical chemistry, refocusing chemistry away from the study of chemical substances themselves to the reactions in which they participated, from the mere description and classification of compounds to the discovery of the general laws that guided their behavior. Great thoughts were born in his physical chemistry institute in Leipzig—new ideas about how chemicals behaved in solution, the effects of electricity, how catalysts worked. When Noyes was studying with him, Ostwald had not yet been rewarded for his insights; his laboratory was badly lit, poorly ventilated, and crowded with students speaking a babble of tongues. It would be twenty years before he won his Nobel Prize. But in the 1880s and 1890s it was a thrilling place to study, and the students who flocked there scattered to spread Ostwald's gospel around the world.

Noyes returned to a faculty position at MIT with a German doctorate, a respect for German preeminence in science (he would publish many of his own scientific papers first in German journals, believing that only then could they come properly to the attention of the international community), and a desire to re-create the excitement of Ost-

wald's institute in America. He asked MIT to fund a research laboratory devoted to physical chemistry, but the school was not in a financial position to do so. Fortunately for the history of chemistry in
America, in 1898, Noyes codiscovered a valuable waste-recovery
process for the photographic industry. When it was commercialized, it
brought him a thousand dollars a month for years—about five times
what he was earning as a full professor at MIT. He had no wife, no family, and apart from sailing, no expensive tastes, so he invested the
money in his dream laboratory. He struck a deal with MIT in which he
agreed to pay for half the cost of the new facility. In return, he was
granted an unusual degree of control, including a final say in decisions on faculty hiring, the use of graduate students, and the setting of
research priorities.

The MIT Research Laboratory of Physical Chemistry, christened
in 1903, was a bit of Germany in Back Bay. The German scientific institutes, such as Ostwald's, were successful because they recognized the
value of basic research both for its own sake and as part of the educational process. They were generally built around the reputation of a
central researcher, whose renown would draw students and funding.
They were often physically separate from their mother universities,
with their own libraries and teaching rooms as well as laboratories.
Freed from academic pressures and interdepartmental squabbles, institute members could devote more of their time to independent research and the introduction of advanced students to the latest
findings. Teaching was intensive, with heavy use of small seminars in
which students and teachers critically examined the latest advances.
But of course the most important education happened in the lab:
Graduate students were expected to spend long hours doing their own
original research. Today it is a cliché to say that higher education must
be tied to research, that students must be exposed to the latest advances and techniques in order to prepare them to take the next steps
in their fields. But Noyes, working in the German style, was among the
first American scientific educators to make it happen.

While the form of his laboratory was borrowed, Noyes quickly put
his own stamp on it. Many of his ideas have become common practice,
but nearly a century ago they were revolutionary: his emphasis on *how*
rather than *what* to think; his stress on basing chemistry firmly on
mathematics and physics; his real affection for students (they formed,
in a way, his surrogate family); and his creation of an atmosphere in
which students and faculty interacted constantly and informally. Many
of the foremost physical chemists of the next generation would re-

member sailing off Boston Harbor in Noyes's yacht *Research,* conversing about the latest chemical theories, smiling at spontaneous bursts of poetry. Although he had a solid research reputation, Noyes would have a much greater impact on chemistry through his dedication to altering the way chemistry students were taught. And Noyes was, Pauling remembered, "a *great* teacher of chemistry."

"It is hard to overestimate the importance of the Research Laboratory of Physical Chemistry in the development of science in America," Pauling later wrote. Noyes's lab led the way as physical chemistry's influence grew, buttressed by important findings about the mechanisms and processes involved in chemical reactions, about thermodynamics and free energies. Physical chemistry was succeeding in building a theoretical base for the field, in finding the laws that underlay chemistry. Nobel Prizes began going to physical chemists; to van't Hoff in 1901 for discovering the laws of chemical dynamics and osmotic pressure, to Arrhenius in 1903 for his electrolytic theory of dissociation, and to Ostwald himself in 1909 for his work on catalysis, chemical equilibria, and the rates of chemical reactions. Money followed success. In America, 85 percent of the Carnegie Institution chemistry funding before World War I went to physical chemists, Noyes prominent among them. MIT began drawing the best faculty and the brightest physical chemistry postdoctoral fellows from around the world—even a few, in a historic reversal, from Germany. Noyes's lab became a sort of chemical Camelot. And Noyes was given an appropriate nickname by his students: King Arthur.

Because of his self-funding and personal control over the laboratory's administration, Noyes's Research Laboratory of Physical Chemistry was allowed to develop differently from MIT, which maintained a distinctly practical approach to the education of engineers. Noyes was, of course, convinced that his new ideas about training were best for the entire institute. During a two-year stint as acting president of MIT, he tried to convince the engineers, as he said in a later speech, that "industrial research is not the main research opportunity of educational institutions. . . . The main field for educational institutions is research in pure science itself—a study of fundamental principles and phenomena, without immediate reference to practical application." The MIT engineers were not impressed. Instead, they saw his little kingdom siphoning funds from the school's main purpose—the teaching of engineering—and distracting their students.

At the same time, the research laboratory's very success was undermining it. Other institutions, eager to emulate the Noyes model, began raiding his faculty and snapping up his best graduates. The worst blow came in 1912 when Berkeley—after first approaching and being turned down by Noyes—lured away one of his star faculty members, G. N. Lewis, by promising him his own program. Lewis jump-started his California chemistry division by taking with him another of Noyes's top professors and some of the best graduate students. Other professors and fellows from the MIT program were given offers they couldn't refuse from private industry and better-funded colleges. Chronically underfunded, MIT couldn't compete,

Compared to the quality of the Berkeley offer, it was almost laughable when his former MIT student, George Ellery Hale, asked Noyes in 1909 to give up MIT to come to an unknown, underfunded school called Throop, even with Hale's extravagant promises of future support from all the rich fellows he knew. But by 1915, concerned about the increasingly industrial attitude at MIT and tempted by Hale's ever-more concrete assurances of new facilities, Noyes was ready to rethink the offer and agreed to visit Throop. In 1917, Hale's promises became reality with the dedication of a new building he had convinced a wealthy family to fund, the Gates Laboratory of Chemistry, and Noyes began spending three months during the winter in Pasadena. But he couldn't bring himself to cut his East Coast bonds entirely, to leave his home, his sailing, the lab he had built.

He would have to be kicked out. Back at MIT, Noyes's annual absences further annoyed an administration already irked by his laboratory's independence. A showdown developed between Noyes and the engineers, and the engineers won. In 1919 the president of MIT asked Noyes to withdraw from an active role in the chemistry department. Within months, at age fifty-three, Noyes resigned his post, gave up the research laboratory—"the embodiment of my love and devotion," he called it—ended the period of thirty years he had dedicated to MIT, and headed west.

In Pasadena, King Arthur was once again treated like royalty. The Gates Laboratory of Chemistry was a much larger facility than his MIT lab, and he was presented with a $200,000 fund for research, arranged by lumber magnate and Throop board chairman Arthur Fleming. The ecstatic Hale even gave Noyes his used Cadillac, a soon-to-become-legendary touring car the students called Old Mossie (short for Demosthenes, in honor of its pronounced stutter). Old Mossie, said to hold the world's record for the standing broad jump because Noyes so often tried to start off in high gear, replaced the *Research* as a vehicle for weekend trips with favorite students and colleagues, the destination now camping spots in the desert or his beach house at Corona del Mar instead of the bays and islands around Boston.

Noyes immediately started putting into effect the vision of higher education in the sciences that he had been denied at MIT. "Noyes not only originated most of the educational policies that made Caltech what it is, but he formulated them so carefully that they have served almost without change," wrote Noyes's colleague and early Caltech physics professor Earnest Watson. These policies included an insistence on small size, with a select and limited undergraduate student body; a concentration on doing a few things very well rather than becoming a broad-based university; a commitment to creative research at all levels, even undergraduate; an insistence on giving undergraduates a strong education in the humanities as well as the sciences; and an emphasis on basic rather than applied science. Noyes didn't stop there. His interest in students led him to foster a system for their self-government and to help plan their living arrangements, to provide for close contact between students and professors both academically and socially. He also supported the decision to make Caltech the first all-male institution of higher education—apart from military academies—west of the Hudson; he would have no coeds on campus to distract his budding scientists. For the chemistry division itself, Noyes adopted some elements of the German model for scientific institutes—such as an emphasis on discussing cutting-edge research in small seminars rather than large lecture classes—but purposefully rejected others, especially the German penchant for building institutes around a central charismatic researcher. Noyes believed in the primacy of the group over the individual; he was a consummate team player.

Caltech was to be a new kind of school, a monastery dedicated to research, an experimental laboratory for Noyes's theories on the creation of scientists—an institution, it was later said, for geniuses.

X-rays

And Linus Pauling was a test case.

Noyes called Pauling into his office in Gates at the beginning of the new term to have an introductory chat. They had corresponded throughout the previous spring and summer. Noyes had written first, asking about Pauling's background, especially in physical chemistry; Pauling wrote back about his disappointment in the one class he had taken at OAC. Noyes knew the author of the text Pauling had used and didn't think the book was worth much. He sent both Pauling and Paul Emmett proof sheets of the first nine chapters of a new physical chemistry text he was cowriting and asked them, in addition to reading the chapters, to solve the problems posed at the end. Instead of the standard approach, asking students to apply previously memorized equations to specific cases, Noyes's problems guided students toward deriving the equations themselves. His stress on making students think rather than memorize, giving them approaches to answers rather than the answers themselves, was a key element in his educational strategy. Once students had been forced to puzzle through a reasoning process, Noyes believed, the concepts they learned would stay with them. In the summer weekends and evenings after inspecting pavement all day on the Oregon coast, Pauling worked through all five hundred problems. "I learned a great deal about physical chemistry during the three months of the summer," Pauling remembered. Noyes's emphasis on logical and precise thinking and his technique of guiding students to discover laws and principles by themselves, Pauling wrote, "had an important effect on my own thinking about science." Noyes, for his part, was impressed by the Oregon boy's ability for independent work.

Through their correspondence Noyes also learned of Pauling's early collection of minerals and later fascination with Lewis's and Langmuir's work on chemical bonds. Extrapolating from those interests, Noyes decided that Pauling should do his doctoral research at Caltech in the laboratory of Roscoe Dickinson, a young professor who was using a new x-ray device to study the structure of crystals. At his suggestion Pauling read a book about this new technique during the summer. The process was called x-ray crystallography and involved shooting a beam of x-rays at a crystal, then figuring out from the way the rays were scattered how the crystal was structured. The concept seemed simple to Pauling, the math wasn't too difficult, and the technique could pin down bond lengths and angles—the distance between the atoms in crystals and their orientation to one another. "I'm reading *X-rays and Crystal Analysis*," Pauling wrote Paul Emmett that summer, "but not learning much. Interesting, tho. . . ."

Pauling didn't realize then that Noyes was preparing him for something special.

What distinguishes graduate from undergraduate training in the physical sciences was—and is—the expectation that graduate students will discover something new in the laboratory. At OAC, Pauling had done well in his course-related laboratory work. But like most undergraduates, he spent almost all his time in the lab learning basics: how to measure, weigh, purify, and test chemicals, repeating others' experiments rather than designing his own. He wasn't expected to find anything original, although at OAC he made one unsuccessful stab at it: During his senior year, he tried crystallizing iron in a magnetic field, hoping to learn something about the magnetic properties of atomic iron by examining the orientation of the crystals—an interesting idea, using visible crystals as a way to "see" into the invisible world of atoms. Working under the supervision of his metallography professor, he successfully deposited iron crystals on a bar of copper. But when he tried to polish them for examination under a microscope, the crystals rubbed off.

Original laboratory work required a different set of skills from those that had made Pauling a classroom prodigy. Instead of memorization and intellectual flash, it called for patience, precision, and manual dexterity, along with a knack of recognizing practical approaches to solving problems. In order to develop these skills graduate students are placed with a mentor, a major professor, under whose tutelage and in whose laboratory they are introduced to the mysteries surrounding a particular problem and are given tools with which to solve those mysteries. It is a master-apprentice relationship in which the goal is to become another master, one capable of finding out new things about nature and teaching new apprentices.

The decision about which major professor to work with is critical, and Roscoe Gilkey Dickinson was a good choice for Pauling. Dickinson was a favorite former MIT student of Noyes's who had followed his mentor to California in 1917 and earned his Ph.D. in chemistry—the first ever granted by Caltech—just two years before Pauling arrived. He was only ten years older than Pauling, close enough in age to take on the role of an older brother, and the two of them quickly became friends. The small size of Caltech at the time helped—during his first year, Pauling was Dickinson's only graduate student. Within a few weeks of the start of the first term, Dickinson and his wife were having Pauling over for dinner and taking him (and, later, Ava Helen as well) on overnight camping trips into the desert.

In the laboratory they were complementary types: Pauling effervescent with ideas, interested in almost everything, ready to go in ten directions at once; Dickinson focused, methodical, careful, "an especially clear-headed and thoughtful scientist," Pauling later wrote, "strongly critical of carelessness and superficiality." Dickinson did not have a penetrating theoretical intellect, but he would be, for Pauling, a needed counterweight, a logical, down-to-earth guide to the rigors of original laboratory research using the finicky, demanding, revolutionary technique of x-ray crystallography.

—*mm*—

Most physicists had agreed for more than a century before Pauling entered graduate school that light existed as waves of energy. A simple way to demonstrate this is to shine a beam of light through a grating made of closely ruled slits, which breaks the light waves into smaller wavelets—the way an ocean wave behaves when hitting a seawall with holes in it. If the slits in the grating are the right distance apart (they have to be spaced correctly for the wavelength of light being used), the light will form a pattern on a screen on the other side, bright spots where the wavelets of light coming out of one slit combine in rhythm with those coming out of others, reinforcing the wave pattern, dark spots where the wavelets collide out of rhythm, canceling each other. This is a diffraction pattern. When the light is a combination of many wavelengths, like sunlight, diffraction can lead to strikingly beautiful effects: the iridescent blue of butterfly wings and the glow of mother-of-pearl. Pauling, although he didn't know the nomenclature, had wondered about this optical effect as early as age thirteen when, walking down a Portland street in the rain, he looked up and saw a rainbow pattern made by the arc of a streetlight shining through the cross-hatched fabric of his umbrella. It would be several years before he learned in his first physics course that he had seen a diffraction pattern.

After x-rays were discovered in 1895, most physicists supposed they were a special kind of light—you could, after all, take amazing photographs with them of nails inside wood or bones inside a hand—and thus would also behave like waves. But no one could be certain until it could be shown that x-rays exhibited some of the definitive properties of waves, such as diffraction. The problem was that the space between the slits of a grating in a diffraction experiment had to be about the same order of magnitude as the wavelength being studied. Fine gratings, about twenty thousand lines per inch, worked for visible light. But x-rays were much more energetic than light, which meant, according to classical physics, that their wavelength would be much shorter—perhaps one one-thousandth the size of visible light. It was impossible to make a grating that fine.

The German physicist Max von Laue thought that if humans

couldn't make a proper grating, nature might. Naturally occurring crystals were thought to be made of atoms arranged in regular patterns, in sheets a few atoms thick. It was Laue's belief that these atomic sheets were about the right size to act like the slits in a diffraction grating for x-rays. The pattern coming out the other side would be complicated, of course, because crystals were made up of atomic sheets in three dimensions; it would be like what one would get by stacking a number of gratings on top of each other. But there should still be a pattern. Laue's boss at the University of Munich, Arnold Sommerfeld, thought the idea was preposterous and tried to convince him not to waste time on it. But in 1912 two students confirmed Laue's prediction by firing a beam of x-rays at a crystal of zinc sulfide and capturing the scatter on a photographic plate, creating what would later be called a Laue photograph. When the plate was developed, there was a circular pattern of light and dark spots—a diffraction pattern. Laue had proved that x-rays behaved like waves. *Nature* magazine termed his finding "one of the greatest and most far-reaching discoveries of our own age." Two years later, it won him the Nobel Prize.

The discovery was important for two reasons. First, by showing that x-rays behaved like waves, it allowed scientists to determine their size and build instruments to distinguish among various wavelengths. (X-rays come in a range of wavelengths, just like visible light.) But the second field of research pioneered by Laue turned out to be even more fruitful. Once they had a beam of a specific wavelength, researchers could use x-rays to study the spacing of the crystal gratings: X-ray crystallography became the first probe for "seeing" the three-dimensional structure of matter at the atomic level.

***

One of the fathers of chemistry, Sir Humphrey Davy, noted a century before Pauling came to Caltech that "nothing tends so much to the advancement of knowledge as the application of a new instrument. The native intellectual powers of men in different times are not so much the causes of the different success of their labours, as the peculiar nature of the means and artificial resources in their possession." X-ray crystallography proved to be an artificial resource of immense potential.

The theory behind it was simple. The researcher worked with three factors, x-rays of a certain wavelength, a crystal grating of a certain structure, and the diffraction pattern—which were linked in a straightforward mathematical relationship. Knowing the pattern and one of the two other factors, the third could be solved. Much of the early mathematics and practical technique were worked out by a British father-son team of physicists, Sir Henry and Lawrence Bragg, who made their laboratories in Cambridge and Manchester the world's foremost centers of x-ray crystallographic research.

In theory it was simple, but in practice the piecing together of crystal structures was slow, tedious, and hobbled by the complexity of the diffraction patterns. The equipment in the early days was homemade and suffered from variable quality. Crystals generally had to be unusually large, carefully prepared, cut at specific angles, and precisely positioned to get a good pattern. If you got successful Laue photographs, you had to painstakingly measure the position and intensity of scores of spots. Then came the mathematical transformations. Even with simple crystals, each structure required months of work in precomputer days. And if the crystal was too complex, if it contained more than a dozen or so atoms in the basic, repeating unit of structure called the unit cell, it would scatter the x-rays in a pattern too complex to decipher. The whole process was something like trying to puzzle out the shape of a piece of ornate wrought iron by shooting it with a homemade shotgun and analyzing the ricochet patterns.

For all these reasons it was limited to very simple crystals. But when it worked it was amazing. For the first time researchers had a tool that allowed them to understand the arrangements of individual atoms in crystals, to measure precisely the distances and angles between them. The first crystal structure the Braggs solved was rock salt, and it was a surprise. The crystal was one gigantic latticework, each sodium ion surrounded by six equidistant chlorides, each chloride by six equidistant sodiums. There were no discernible individual "molecules" of sodium chloride. The finding shook the field of theoretical chemistry, leading immediately to new ideas about how salts behaved in solution. Another early success in the Bragg lab was the discovery of the structure of diamond, pure carbon with its atoms linked, as earlier chemists had theorized, to form three-sided pyramids called tetrahedra. The Braggs went on to solve a number of other crystals (and would themselves share a Nobel the year after Laue).

A. A. Noyes was sure that more insights would come. X-ray crystallography was invented by European physicists, but Noyes would bring it to America and make it a chemists' tool. Within three years of the

Braggs' first published findings, Noyes was calling the field of x-ray crystallography "the most important one in physical chemistry today," and in 1916 he advised one of his MIT graduate students studying in Germany, C. Lalor Burdick, to stop by the Braggs' laboratory in England on his way back home to learn about their x-ray techniques. Burdick returned with enough knowledge to build America's first x-ray spectrometer at MIT, and Noyes had him build a second, improved version—"the best of its day," Burdick remembered—in Pasadena in 1917. Results began flowing quickly, and by the time Pauling arrived, x-ray crystallography was the single most important chemical research tool at Caltech, the source of fifteen of the chemistry division's first twenty published papers.

Noyes had a lot riding on the technique. Chemistry was the study of the behavior of molecules. Noyes was becoming increasingly convinced that behavior depended on structure. And now it was possible to "see" the structure of molecules. By assigning Pauling to Dickinson's laboratory, Noyes was pointing the promising student toward what he believed would be the future of chemistry.

Pauling threw himself into his laboratory work but soon found himself stymied. Noyes had suggested that Pauling try to solve the structure of lithium hydride, but after spending three weeks in October working on the problem, Pauling discovered that a team in Holland had beaten him to the structure. During the next weeks he tried a number of other compounds, making crystals by melting chemicals in an electric furnace and cooling them slowly, then cutting and mounting the good ones and taking them through an initial analysis to see if they were simple enough to solve. None of them were. (One he tried, sodium dicadmide, turned out to be one of the most complex inorganic molecules known, involving more than one thousand atoms. It would be thirty-five years before one of Pauling's colleagues solved its structure.) Pauling's frustration grew with each failure.

After two months of unsuccessful efforts with fifteen different substances, he was rescued by Dickinson. His mentor led him to the chemistry stockroom, grabbed a nodule of molybdenite—a shiny black mineral composed of molybdenum and sulfur—from the shelf, showed Pauling an innovative way of preparing thin slices mounted on glass slides, and walked him through the preparation of the Laue photographs. Why Dickinson picked molybdenite is a mystery. Perhaps he thought its relatively simple chemical formula, MoS_2, would translate into a simple crystal structure. Perhaps he was just lucky. In any case, the mounted slices were in good shape, the unit cell was small, and within a month Dickinson and Pauling had determined the structure—an interesting one, the first to be described that had six atoms of a nonmetal, sulfur, forming an equal-sided prism around a single atom of a metal, molybdenum.

Pauling was elated. "The achievement made a great impression on me. The process of structure determination involved a series of logical arguments, which were presented to me by Dickinson in a meticulous way, with emphasis on rigor," he later wrote. "I was pleased to learn that questions about the nature of the world could be answered by carefully planned and executed experiments." His pleasure was coupled with a deep sense of satisfaction—the feeling that comes from using skill and brains to bring to light one of nature's hidden things as fully and surely as the human mind is capable. He had made a discovery.

He was now a scientist.

Dickinson, of course, had analyzed crystals before, and satisfied that his student now knew the ropes, he went back to other work. Pauling assumed that the next step would be publishing his first scientific paper. But "I waited for a month and nothing happened," he remembered. So, on his own, he wrote up the results of the molybdenite work for publication and presented the paper to Dickinson.

Shortly afterward, Noyes called Pauling to his office. He sat the young man down and delicately turned the conversation to the subject of scientific attribution. Noyes noted that the molybdenite paper carried only Pauling's name; he was afraid, he said, that Pauling may have forgotten that Professor Dickinson had also been involved in the work. "This was, of course, a shock to me," Pauling said. "I realized that I had just ignored completely the efforts that he [Dickinson] had made and his activities in instructing me." The paper, "The Crystal Structure of Molybdenite," was revised and received for publication by the *Journal of the American Chemical Society* in April 1923. The authors were, in order, Roscoe G. Dickinson and Linus Pauling. "I think it was a good experience," said Pauling, "in that it pointed out to me how easy it is to underestimate the contributions that someone else has made."

After his shaky start, Pauling became a proficient crystallographer. Dickinson soon had so much faith in his student that when he went to

Europe for a year in 1924 on a fellowship, he put Pauling in charge of the x-ray lab, an experience that strengthened Pauling's independence as a researcher. Pauling also assumed the role of teacher, introducing other students to the technique and overseeing their work. After his return, Dickinson gradually became interested in other fields of research, and Pauling inherited the mantle of Caltech's resident x-ray expert. Before receiving his doctorate, Pauling would publish, on his own and with others, an impressive total of six more crystal structures.

In addition to establishing his reputation as one of the nation's more promising young crystallographers, Pauling's early work provided him with a new way of looking at the world. He spent so much time analyzing the depth, height, and width of crystal units, learning everything he could about the sizes of atoms and the lengths of the bonds between them, that from then on he would see everything chemical in terms of structure. Molecules, he began to understand viscerally, were built out of atoms, just as buildings were built out of bricks and beams. There was nothing random about their structure. They were connected at certain angles to make certain shapes; this was architecture at the scale of hundred-millionths of a centimeter.

There was a purely aesthetic pleasure in discovering and describing these forms, and there was more. The ways in which molecules were built said a great deal about how they behaved. In molybdenite, for instance, Dickinson and Pauling found that the sulfur atoms were farther apart than the Braggs had measured in other minerals. In his first paper Pauling related those stretched sulfur-sulfur bonds to molybdenite's tendency to cleave easily. He also began reviewing all known crystal structures to try to find out why the Braggs' sulfur bonds were shorter than he and Dickinson had found and developed a sense that the length of chemical bonds varied, depending on type: Bonds in which the two atoms shared electrons equally—for which Langmuir in 1919 coined the term "covalent"—were generally shorter (and stronger) than ionic bonds, in which one atom held the electrons more closely than the other. Lewis, in his papers on the cubical atom, had theorized that a range of bond types were possible, depending on how equally the electrons were shared between two atoms. And now, as he reviewed the literature and solved more structures himself, Pauling found that, as Lewis had hypothesized, it wasn't an either-or case. Some bonds appeared to be intermediate between the two general types.

Physical chemists had, for the past forty years, tended to ignore chemical structure in their concentration on reactions; after all, before crystallography there had been no way to describe structure precisely. But that was changing. Now there was a growing realization that *the properties of a substance were based on its structure.*

━━ꝏ━━

Noyes was phasing out his teaching, concentrating on administration instead. During his first term at Caltech, Pauling took the last class Noyes ever taught: chemical thermodynamics, a swan song for the nineteenth-century approach to physical chemistry based on classical Newtonian physics.

It was also the only chemistry course Pauling would take as a graduate student. He had had plenty of chemistry at OAC but was starved for physics and math. The rest of his graduate career was filled with course after course in the two fields.

Math took its place as a useful tool, a technique whose mastery was required for learning physics. And here his guide was yet another—and perhaps the most brilliant—of Noyes's MIT students, Richard Chace Tolman. After earning his doctorate in 1910, he had bounced around, from the University of Michigan to the University of Cincinnati, then four years with G. N. Lewis at Berkeley, two at the University of Illinois, and three in government service, searching for a position compatible with his wide interests. Tolman's interests were boundless: thermodynamics, statistical mechanics, kinetics, theoretical physical chemistry, even cosmology. His major interest outside of chemistry, however, was theoretical physics. He wrote the first book in English discussing Einstein's theory of special relativity and was one of a handful of American chemists—or physicists, for that matter—who understood the importance of the exciting new European advances in quantum physics. Noyes lured Tolman to Caltech the year before Pauling arrived and gave him an unusual dual title that reflected his interests: professor of physical chemistry and mathematical physics. Noyes called him "a great prize . . . a very unusual combination of experimental and theoretical knowledge. . . . Indeed, with the possible exception of G. N. Lewis of Berkeley, there is no physical chemist in the country who ranks with him." Tolman was the cornerstone in Noyes's plan to create a chemistry program fully integrated with modern physics, and during Pauling's student years he carried the brunt of graduate teaching. While Noyes became increasingly concerned with the undergraduate curriculum at Caltech in the 1920s, Tolman epitomized the spirit of the graduate program: clear, critical, and focused on the cutting edge of research.

Students saw him as an impressive intellectual, erudite in any number of fields, and he looked the part, with his high forehead and neatly trimmed mustache. He was, like Noyes, a New Englander, born into a well-to-do Massachusetts family and educated at MIT. And if it wasn't for Noyes and a few other men he felt comfortable with, members of Pasadena's private clubs, he would never have stayed at Caltech. His leftist political sympathies—Pauling remembered students reciting a ditty about "Richard the Red and his brother Ed" (Edward Tolman was a professor at Berkeley)—were at odds with Southern California's conservatism, and his sense of culture was affronted by what he saw as the region's crass commercialism. He was a Brahmin who would always feel apart from Caltech. "I feel that there is not much pressure in New England to advertise and grab, and that decisions are not made on the basis of publicity," he wrote in the late 1920s while considering an offer from Harvard. "In coming to Harvard I should feel that I was coming back to my own people, whose ways and traditions I understand." Only Caltech's unmatchable salaries kept him in place.

Whatever they paid was worth it: Tolman was the most brilliant professor at Caltech. His lectures were masterpieces of organization; he would fill blackboards with figures before class and logically, compellingly, steer his students through the complexities of the new physics. He would engage his students directly, pausing in his lecture to pick out a fellow and quiz him about a point being discussed. It kept his students awake and forced them to think quickly. Pauling followed his first Tolman class with everything else the man taught, including relativity theory and an excellent course in statistical mechanics. He impressed Tolman, as he had nearly all of his teachers, and he was soon helping Tolman prepare manuscripts for publication.

But Tolman had his greatest effect on Pauling by introducing the young chemist to quantum theory.

Bohr's Atom

Before he came to Caltech, Pauling's only college work in physics had been a three-term introductory course at OAC specially oriented to the needs of chemical engineers. It barely touched on the newest ideas from Europe, where a small group of physicists led by a young Dane named Niels Bohr were questioning how the world is made.

Bohr wanted to understand the atom, and he came to England before the war to study with Ernest Rutherford, who had just put forward his dynamic solar-system atomic model in which electrons orbited the nucleus. Bohr's first great achievement was to link Rutherford's atom to other new findings in physics, most importantly the puzzling ability of elements to give off or take in energy in specific, discrete amounts—the small packets of energy that the German physicist Max Planck in 1901 had named quanta.

Planck's heresy was to propose that energy, like light and heat, was not continuous and smooth, as Newton had thought, but instead existed in discrete bits. Planck's ideas worked to explain some paradoxical phenomena like black-body radiation but flew in the face of other cherished physical ideas. Despite mounting evidence in favor of quanta—some of the most important marshaled by a young theorist named Albert Einstein—there was still no agreement among physicists that quanta were anything more than a convenient fiction.

Bohr, however, was ready to assert that quanta were not only real but essential to understanding the atom. In 1913 he published a paper proposing a model of the atom in which electrons circled the nucleus in flat, circular orbits, as Rutherford had visualized. But Bohr said that only certain-size orbits were possible and that these were restricted by quantum rules. Add a quantum of energy and the Bohr electron "jumped" from one orbit to a more energetic one; falling back to a more stable orbit, it released energy, sometimes as visible light.

Using an instrument called the spectroscope to closely study the light given off by luminous bodies, physicists had for decades been working on a mystery. When burned, different elements emitted light not evenly across the spectrum but only at specific wavelengths. The pattern of wavelengths given off by each element was unique, a sort of glowing fingerprint. And the patterns themselves were fascinating, tantalizing, regular enough to promise some underlying order, yet complex enough to defy explanation. When seen through a spectroscope, it seemed as though each element were displaying, in notes of light, the fingering positions for a unique chord. No one, however, had figured out why the atoms were playing those particular tunes.

Until Bohr. This was the most impressive achievement of the Bohr model of the atom: He correlated the fall of an electron between quantum orbits to the frequency of the bright lines seen with a spectroscope when looking at incandescent gases.

At least for hydrogen. Hydrogen is the simplest element, with only one electron, and Bohr's atomic model could be used to calculate the most obvious of hydrogen's spectral lines. But despite years of work he couldn't get his theory to do a good job of accounting for a number of the very fine lines in the spectrum of hydrogen, nor could he get it to work for any element more complex than hydrogen—and, of course, *every* other element was more complex than hydrogen.

But his success with the hydrogen spectrum led a number of other physicists—chief among them Laue's old boss, the German theorist Arnold Sommerfeld, head of the Institute of Theoretical Physics in Munich—to work on refining his model. During World War I, Sommerfeld, with the help of two assistants detained as enemy aliens (one of them the Russian-born future Caltech professor Paul Epstein), extended Bohr's atom to include, in addition to simple circular orbits, a complex of elliptical crossing and penetrating orbits in which the movement of electrons were corrected by applying Einstein's theory of relativity. The result was a more complex model of the atom, one that could be made to fit with most of the fine structure of the hydrogen spectrum and could plausibly be extended to many-electron atoms.

What became known as the Bohr-Sommerfeld model of the atom took center stage after the war, and this was what Pauling learned from Tolman. It was a dynamic model with fast-moving electrons, as opposed to the static, cubical atom of Lewis and Langmuir that Pauling had found so appealing at OAC. By the time he was at Caltech, the chemists' static atom was becoming an object of ridicule to physicists, its "loafer" electrons, as Caltech's head Robert Millikan jeered in a 1924 speech, "sitting around on dry goods boxes at every corner, ready to shake hands with, or hold on to, similar loafer electrons in other atoms." Physicists knew that electrons had to move somehow to keep from crashing into the nucleus.

At the same time, the physicists' dynamic atom was becoming more palatable to chemists. Sommerfeld's elongated, elliptical orbits gave the Bohr atom some of the three-dimensional specificity demanded by chemists: If one end of an ellipse was closer to the nucleus, the electron's orbit would extend from the nucleus like a fat arm, offering a visualizable way of embracing other atoms in definite orientations. In the early 1920s Bohr himself remade his flat orbits into three-dimensional shells, much more like Lewis's cubes. And there was movement toward compromise from the chemist's side as well. Lewis ventured the idea that his stationary electrons might instead represent the average positions of more mobile particles. By 1923, only seven years after proposing his cubical atom, Lewis was ready to accept the Bohr-Sommerfeld model—at least in the case of the hydrogen atom—even though there was still no explanation of how atoms could form bonds with one another.

At its most refined stage in the early 1920s, the Bohr-Sommerfeld model of the atom was an appealing, captivating work of the imagination. Drawings done to Bohr's specifications showed atoms like gorgeous geometric flowers petaled with intricate layers of interpenetrating electron orbits. For the few years Pauling was a graduate student at Caltech, those complex atomic constructions, with their pulsing, wheeling, harmonious electron orbits and the chordlike sets of spectral lines, appeared to represent, as Sommerfeld said, "the true music of the spheres."

But the melody was all wrong. How could electrons disappear from one orbit and reappear in another without existing anywhere in between—a "quantum leap" deemed impossible by classical physics? No one knew. How could negatively charged electrons circle the positively charged nucleus without losing energy, as Newton demands of moving charged bodies? As great a physicist as Millikan was reduced to answering, "God did not make electrons that way." Even with Sommerfeld's corrections, there were still spectral phenomena, especially in more complex atoms, that the model couldn't explain. There was a breakdown of theory. Classical physics simply didn't seem to work at the level of the atom, but Bohr's quantum theory didn't seem to work, either. As the physicist George Gamow wrote, "It looked for a while as though either the physicists or physics itself had become completely insane."

In Tolman's classes Pauling heard some of the criticisms of the Bohr-Sommerfeld model, others from listening to talks given by visiting European physicists, especially a course on quantum physics he took from Paul Ehrenfest. As a graduate student, however, Pauling wasn't ready either to pass judgment on Bohr's model or create a new one. There was too much data on every side, too many changes happening, too many new ideas to digest. For the most part, he simply accepted what he was taught, including the general correctness of the Bohr-Sommerfeld atom. In the Caltech Seminar in Physical Chemistry, which Pauling considered the most important course Tolman taught, teacher and students worked their way chapter by chapter through the new fourth edition of Sommerfeld's influential text *Atom-bau und Spektrallinien* ("Atomic Structure and Spectral Lines"), in German, in which the German physicist detailed his ideas on the structure of the atom. Sommerfeld himself presented his model of the atom on a tour of the United States in 1922–23. Pauling heard him lecture at Caltech and became a believer: He buttonholed Sommerfeld as the professor left class one day and told him about his own ideas of atomic structure as they walked down a Caltech arcade; he even managed to show Sommerfeld some wire-and-wood models he had made demonstrating (incorrectly, as it turned out) how Bohr-Sommerfeld orbitals could explain the tetrahedral binding of carbon. At this point, Pauling was unable to differentiate between the many deficiencies in quantum theory and shortcomings in his own knowledge.

Those shortcomings were sometimes painfully evident. In one seminar Tolman asked Pauling why it was that most substances, when placed in a magnetic field, briefly develop a magnetism that is opposed to the field—a phenomenon called diamagnetism. The correct answer is that the magnetic field alters the orbital motion of the electrons in the substance. Pauling, however, unaware of the latest findings, answered that diamagnetism was simply "a general property of matter." That amused Tolman, and the teacher made a point of targeting Pauling for more questions. Once, when Tolman asked him another he couldn't answer, Pauling gave a less amusing answer. "I don't know," he said. "I haven't taken a course in that subject." After class an older, wiser postdoctoral fellow took Pauling aside and gave him some friendly advice. "Linus," he said, "you shouldn't have answered Professor Tolman the way you did. You are a graduate student now, and you're supposed to know everything."

The kinds of things Pauling wanted to know were increasingly theoretical.

Roughly speaking, scientists can be divided into two broad groups: theorists and experimentalists. Experimentalists work in the laboratory, teasing empirically provable facts from nature one small bit at a time, eventually building large collections of data showing exactly how substances behave. Theorists work in their heads, trying to make larger sense of the facts gathered by experimentalists, searching for the underlying natural laws that guide individual events. Experimentalists determine *what* happens; theorists explain *why*. Under Tolman's influence, Pauling was becoming further seduced by the excitement of theoretical thinking. It suited his temperament and talents. His interests were wide-ranging, and theoretical scientists were rewarded for thinking in broad terms. His memory was phenomenal, allowing him to draw upon a huge store of facts in a number of fields. He enjoyed solving puzzles, and making theoretical sense of seemingly unrelated bits of experimental data was the greatest puzzle in the world. And he was ambitious. Successful theorists were the stars of science, the Einsteins and Lewises and Bohrs. It was the route to the top.

This outlook, combined with his growing sense that the structure of molecules was critical to understanding their chemical behavior, led Pauling toward a goal: He wanted to discover the laws that guided the bonding of atoms in molecules. Atoms connected with specific numbers of other atoms at specific distances to form molecules with specific shapes. Why these numbers, distances, and shapes and not others? The chemical bond, whatever it was, was the key. And it was logical that quantum physics, with its growing string of successes in laying bare the inner workings of the atom, would also eventually explain the chemical bond. Whoever linked quantum theory to the chemical bond would also reconcile the physicists' dynamic atom and the chemists' static model. And whoever stole for chemistry (still primarily a descriptive science) the fire of the new methods of mathematical physics would have the chance to reshape discipline, forging a truly "physical chemistry" in which chemical phenomena could be predicted quantitatively, directly from the laws of physics. It was an enormous and important prize, and Pauling decided early in his graduate career to pursue it.

To do it, he needed to know everything about the new physics. Pauling started reading other books and papers on quantum theory and never missed one of the lively research conferences held twice each week by the physics department or jointly by physics and astronomy. Some of the talks were given by graduate students, who were asked to read about and report on their latest findings. Others were given by faculty members on their own research or by visiting scholars. There was always discussion and debate. Pauling would remember the "feeling of excitement" at these conferences. It was here that he learned of de Broglie's idea that electrons could behave like waves as well as particles. On another occasion, a graduate student, Charlie Richter (who later developed the Richter scale) rushed in to announce that two young Dutchmen, Goudsmit and Uhlenbeck, had discovered that electrons had spin. "He was more excited than I've ever see him—not even an earthquake could make him that excited," remembered Pauling. "And everybody else was excited. Things were *happening* in the fields of physics and chemistry."

Thanks to Robert Millikan, the Caltech physics division was keeping up with—and increasingly contributing to—those changes. Part of the package promised to get Millikan to Caltech was money to import to Pasadena one of the young European physicists taking part in the quantum revolution. Millikan filled the position in 1921 with one of Sommerfeld's former assistants, the mathematical physicist Paul Sophius Epstein, who brought with him the outlook, the prestige, and some of the excitement of the great European scientific centers. Epstein knew practically everybody who was anybody in European physics. At the same time, Millikan's own reputation was approaching its peak, reached in 1923 when he learned (during a class Pauling was taking from him) that he had won the Nobel Prize in physics—only the second American to be so honored.

By the early 1920s, Caltech already had an international reputation that made it a regular stop for foreign physicists touring America. Pauling heard a veritable who's who during his student years. Besides Sommerfeld and Ehrenfest there was the grand old man of physics, Hendrick Lorentz, who had investigated the effects of magnetism on light; the brilliant German mathematical physicist Max Born, who was making his institute at Göttingen one of the world centers for quantum physics; Born's friend, the experimentalist James Franck, whose work bombarding gases with electrons would help confirm the quantum nature of the atom; C. G. Darwin (grandson of Charles Darwin and an accomplished mathematical physicist) from Great Britain; and C. V. Raman from India. Lorentz had already won a Nobel Prize in physics; Born, Franck, and Raman would eventually win theirs. During the time Pauling was a graduate student, Caltech was the best place in America to learn about the new physics.

～～～

To understand quantum theory, Pauling also had to understand the advanced mathematics upon which it was based. He dived into every math course and seminar he could find at Caltech: advanced calculus, vector analysis, integral equations, complex numbers, and potential theory. Mathematics was fine as a tool, "But I never could get very interested in it," Pauling remembered. "Mathematicians try to develop completely logical arguments, formulating a few postulates and then deriving the whole of mathematics from these postulates. Mathematicians try to prove something rigorously. And I never have been very interested in rigor."

His interest was in using mathematics as a weapon to attack what he saw as more interesting problems: Pauling used his extraordinary memory to build three huge mental libraries: one of traditional chemistry, mostly gathered during his time at OAC; another of atomic sizes, bond distances, and crystal structures from his x-ray work; and a third of the mathematical equations and themes of quantum physics. As he neared the end of his graduate years, under Tolman's influence all three areas of interest began to meld into new ideas: Pauling's first theories.

It started on several fronts simultaneously. By late 1924, Noyes was letting Pauling review prepublication drafts of some papers he was writing, an unusual honor to bestow on a graduate student, especially one ostensibly working under another professor. Noyes was interested in the behavior of electrically charged atoms, or ions, in solution, and was responding to a new theory of dilute ionic solutions put forward by the team of Peter Debye and Ernst Hückel. Pauling did not let his respect for King Arthur inhibit his editorial comments. "I found a lot of things to criticize [in Noyes's drafts], and I did point out some statements Noyes had made in them that I thought did not apply really to the theory, and he changed that," remembered Pauling. Then he used Noyes's work as the basis for his own theorizing. "I thought why not do a better job, make the theory applicable to concentrated solutions?"

Pauling worked on his theory of concentrated ionic solutions for several months before showing it to Noyes. Noyes in turn arranged for Pauling to present his ideas in person to Debye, whom he had invited to visit Pasadena in the spring of 1925. Debye was then at the apex of an astonishing career in science. Born in Holland, he had given up his first love, electrical engineering, for physics, earned a Ph.D. at Munich under Sommerfeld, then succeeded Einstein as professor of theoretical physics at Zurich. But Debye's research interests were chemical. He made his reputation by discovering a way to measure the polarity of molecules (molecules which carry a positive charge on one end and a negative charge on another are polar, or said to have a dipole moment; for decades the unit used in the measurement of dipole moments was called the debye). He also recognized quickly after its discovery the immense potential of x-ray crystallography and was the first to use it on powdered solids as well as whole crystals. Even before his theory of dilute ionic solutions was published in 1923, Millikan had been impressed enough to offer Debye a Caltech professorship. Debye had turned it down. Now, visiting Pasadena four years later, he was firmly established as one of the world's greatest physical chemists.

Nervous, Pauling stood in front of a small group, including Noyes and Tolman as well as Debye, and took two hours to carefully describe his new theory. When he finished, the room was uncomfortably quiet. Tolman broke the silence to note a few reservations that he had, and the group broke up. Debye never said a word to Pauling about the presentation. Pauling eventually gathered that the problem was with his mathematics. He had developed a strong physical sense of the answer to the problem, but the mathematics he had devised to support his points had been unsatisfactory; he had made too many unsupported assumptions. He continued working on his theory for two more years before finally giving it up in the face of continuing questions about his numbers from Tolman and mathematics professor Harry Bateman. He wrote Noyes, "My treatment is rather physical and intuitive than mathematical and rigorous; . . . I have come to believe that even though I believe it to be correct, it should not be published so long as I am unable to defend it against significant adverse criticism." The experience left a bitter taste. Pauling knew he was on the right track; he could feel it.

Debye saw enough promise in Pauling to ask his help with other problems during his Pasadena visit. Pauling worked very hard for several weeks on a problem Debye had suggested concerning the behavior of a drop of liquid within another drop; it went nowhere. Then they worked together on the influence of an electric field on dilute ionic solutions; this resulted in a paper published in August 1925.

Cowriting a paper with one of the leading scientists in his field was a coup for Pauling, but it wasn't his only activity. His mind was ranging everywhere. At one point he even jotted down some thoughts about a possible connection between the Debye-Hückel theory and the structure of dwarf stars. He also began working with Tolman on another, quite different theoretical question, this time concerning an original idea of Pauling's on the residual entropy of supercooled liquids at absolute zero. The initial idea was Pauling's; he presented it "not . . . in a very sophisticated form" to Tolman, who then directed him to papers to read for more background. After Pauling wrote the first draft, Tolman asked him what he thought the order of names should be on their joint paper. The young student apparently still had something to learn about the fine points of deferring to faculty. He said that since the original idea had been his, well, his name should be first. The point was well taken—priority should be given to the person with the original insight—and Tolman, perhaps amused again by his impetuous student, agreed. Remembering the incident many years later, Pauling said that "at that time I was not very accustomed to thinking about other people, but more to thinking about myself."

Tolman would see more of that tendency in Pauling later, and his attitude would eventually turn from amusement to coolness. They would never again collaborate on a paper. Even when he became Tolman's director at Caltech, Pauling never called him "Richard"; it was always "Professor Tolman." Still, Tolman was a major figure in Pauling's development. While Pauling would later credit Dickinson with teaching him the deliberate methods of experimental work, Tolman played a more important role, that of Pauling's guide to the wide scientific landscape being opened for chemists by the latest findings of the quantum physicists. "It may be that Tolman was the one of my various teachers, many of whom were really excellent people, who influenced me more than anyone in my career," Pauling said.

–⚡–

Noyes was a different case. Pauling never considered that Noyes, the man most responsible for guiding his graduate career, had as much to do with his scientific development as had Tolman and Dickinson. His attitude was rooted in part in differences in their scientific interests. Pauling referred disparagingly to Noyes's specialty of thermodynamics as a "black box" into which chemists fed data and received answers without knowing why things happened, and Noyes never did become proficient in the new approaches to chemistry based on quantum theory that so interested Pauling. Pauling also thought Noyes was not tough enough in negotiating for the chemistry division. Moreover, Pauling liked "men's men," and Noyes was in some ways too poetic, too careful, too feminine for his tastes. (Pauling was not alone in that assessment; he would later recall Tolman calling Noyes "that old maid.") The result was a feeling, at least on Pauling's part, of distance and reserve.

But Noyes continued to grow more enthusiastic about Pauling. He had seen this young *wunderkind* quickly master the complexities of x-ray crystallography; he had seen him run the lab in Dickinson's absence. He had watched Pauling aggressively question Debye's theories, then switch gears to collaborate successfully with him. He had seen Pauling triumph in both experimental and theoretical work—an unusual accomplishment for a graduate student. In 1925, Noyes gave Pauling a final test, asking him to direct a dozen chemistry undergraduates in some original research—another part of Noyes's plan to expose budding chemists early to the realities of the laboratory. And Pauling succeeded here, too. The undergraduates did well, and one of them, a freshman named Edwin McMillan, got a publication out of his work, cowritten with Pauling. (McMillan would later win the Nobel Prize for chemistry—before Pauling won his.)

By the time he was in his third year of graduate school, Pauling's original thinking and abilities in the classroom and the laboratory had impressed not only Noyes but everyone at Caltech. He was good enough to be able to stitch together a doctoral dissertation, "The Determination with X-rays of the Structure of Crystals," from five previously published papers, and received his doctorate summa cum laude in chemistry, with minors in physics and mathematics, in June 1925.

―――

Pauling's brilliance was rooted in hard work. He remembered his schedule during the first year at Caltech: "I had, I think, forty-five hours (which at some universities would be called fifteen hours) of classwork, the advanced courses I was taking, mostly in physics and mathematics. Later on, the department made a rule that a teaching fellow could only sign up for thirty hours. In addition, I spent a lot of time on research. After dinner I would go back to the lab and work until perhaps 11 o'clock at night. On Saturday and Sunday I'd just work all day."

His roommate that first year, Paul Emmett, remembered Pauling working even more. They shared one bed, using it sequentially. Pauling, according to Emmett, routinely returned from the lab around three in the morning, when Emmett would get up to start studying.

And every evening in the laboratory Pauling would write a letter to Ava Helen. Their steady correspondence brought them closer to each other, and he found himself missing her terribly. Within months they had agreed to cut short their engagement and, despite their parents' opposition, to marry at the end of his first year.

In the spring of 1923, Pauling bought a seven-year-old Model T

Ford from Roscoe Dickinson for fifty dollars and learned to drive by taking it around the block a few times. In June he headed north to Oregon to get married. "I was planning to stop when it got dark," he remembered, "but I was eager to get to Oregon, so I thought, Why don't I just keep on driving?" Rattling over a gravel road in the Siskiyou Mountains late at night, trying to keep his speed up so the headlights would work, he drove the car off the road into a pit. When it came to rest, he was upside down, a splintered wooden roof support jammed into his leg. He extricated himself, bound the gash, and waited all night for help. When it finally arrived the next morning, he got the car repaired well enough to drive and made it in time for the wedding.

He and Ava Helen were married at her sister's home in Salem. It was a small family wedding, with both mothers putting aside their disapproval long enough to attend. Lloyd Jeffress, Pauling's high school friend, was best man. After a one-day honeymoon in the small Oregon town of Corvallis, Pauling started his summer job, again testing pavement. The newlyweds lived first with Pauling's mother in Portland, where Ava Helen worked hard to get Belle to like her—an effort that never fully succeeded. She then followed her husband through Washington State and Oregon, living in a series of rented rooms as the crew laid roads.

Ava Helen had already impressed Pauling with her intelligence. During their correspondence while he was at Caltech, for instance, Pauling had mentioned that acetic acid was present in sauerkraut; she wrote back, "Everybody knows there's no acetic acid in sauerkraut; it's lactic acid." Correcting her former professor in his field of specialty was nervy, and there was more to come. To help pass time in the evenings after his work with the road crew, he checked out a book on intelligence tests from the local library and, together with his spouse, worked the problems in it. "Much to my astonishment," he said years later in a joint interview with Ava Helen, "I found that my newly acquired wife could work these mathematical problems faster than I could, and get the right answer more often than I could. I thought afterward that it's a good thing that we didn't run across that book before we were married. . . . It might have upset my *amour-propre.*"

"You mean upset your ego," Ava Helen replied.

He brought his bride to Caltech in the fall of 1923, and they moved into a small apartment near campus. Pauling threw himself back into his old work habits, taking on a heavy class load and putting in most evenings and weekends in the lab. Ava Helen spent part of her time figuring ways to stretch their meager graduate student's stipend and the rest of it figuring ways to stay close to her hardworking husband. She had too much spirit to stay at home waiting for Pauling to finish his long hours at school. She went to school with him, accompanying him to the Friday night physics lectures, assisting him in the lab, lending a hand with crystal models, drawing out gnomonic projections, helping make calculations, and noting diffraction measurements in a lab book as Pauling called out the numbers. Data written in Ava Helen's hand are scattered through Pauling's lab research book from 1923, including the notation "I LOVE YOU" at the top of one page. Working in the laboratory was a way to be with her husband—perhaps the only way—and it also gave Ava Helen a familiarity with his work and its special vocabulary, an understanding she needed in order to talk with her husband about his deepest interests. She would not stand in the way of Pauling's pleasure in his work and his ambition to succeed, nor would she allow that ambition to come between them.

In any case, it wasn't all work. The Paulings went to concerts and movies, camping with the Dickinsons, and to the seashore. They had their first baby—a boy, Linus junior, born on March 10, 1925. They even got involved in intrigue together, helping to arrange the secret marriage of Pauling's old friend Lloyd Jeffress to a woman whose parents disapproved. Jeffress was then a graduate student in psychology at Berkeley, and the Paulings would occasionally visit him there.

On one of those visits, in 1924, Pauling walked over to the College of Chemistry and introduced himself to the man whose paper about the shared electron bond had so impressed him, Gilbert Newton Lewis. Lewis, then nearing fifty, was a scientific dynamo at the peak of his powers. Since deserting Noyes in 1912 to take over the Berkeley chemistry program, Lewis had proved himself equally adept at both research and academic management. In 1923, just before Pauling first met him, he had published both a classic text on thermodynamics (Lewis was responsible for popularizing the now-common concept of free energies) and an influential monograph summarizing his thoughts on the shared electron chemical bond. With the blessings of the school's administration, he had, during the past decade, reorganized and greatly enlarged the Berkeley chemistry program, building it into one of the most influential basic science programs in the nation.

Although they were both leading figures in physical chemistry in America, and had similar pedigrees—both descendants of English stock that came to America in the seventeenth century, both sons of scholarly-minded lawyers—Lewis and Noyes were otherwise a study in contrasts. Noyes was a New Englander steeped in Puritan tradition; Lewis was raised in the Midwest, schooled at home, and taught to think independently. Noyes, quiet and watchful, liked to operate in the background; Lewis, blunt and argumentative, pushed to the forefront. Noyes recited poetry; Lewis told jokes. He ran his department like a debating society, reveling in challenge and confrontation, "taking a boyish delight in shocking conservative prejudice," a colleague remembered. An ever-present cigar clenched beneath his walrus mustache, the Berkeley chemist was, "with or without the stimulus of ethyl alcohol, in any company . . . the focus of the liveliest discussion, and the center of the merriest group." Lewis and Pauling hit it off immediately. At their first meeting, Pauling told him of his work with crystals and then asked him if it might be possible to come to Berkeley after graduation to do postdoctoral work under his supervision. Lewis, with an eye for talent equal to Noyes's, was happy to consider it.

As soon as word reached Noyes, he began worrying. He had his own plans for Pauling. As early as Pauling's first year at Caltech, Noyes had written Hale, "One of our Fellows, who came from Oregon, is already proving quite exceptional." By the time Pauling was completing his graduate career, Noyes was touting him as "the ablest candidate for the doctor's degree in chemistry who has yet attended this Institute." Offering jobs to his own best students directly after graduation was not uncommon with Noyes—he had done it with Dickinson and other early Caltech graduates—and Noyes had decided well before Pauling received his degree that he wanted to keep him on. But it was becoming de rigueur for the best of the newly minted Ph.D.s to spend a year or two on postdoctoral fellowships at other places, learning new techniques from other masters. The most prestigious and well paid fellowships were those awarded by the National Research Council (NRC); it would be a natural next step for someone of Pauling's ability to win an NRC fellowship after graduation, go away for a time, and return to Caltech ready to take a faculty position.

The only problem was G. N. Lewis. Noyes, unwilling to take a chance on Pauling's spending months in close collaboration with as strong a program as Berkeley's and as attractive a personality as Lewis's, advised Pauling to apply to the NRC, with the unusual request that he be allowed to spend his fellowship year at his home institution. Pauling's proposed research was in x-ray crystallography, and in his letter of support Noyes stressed the fact that there were no decent facilities for that kind of research other than Caltech, threw in the offer of several graduate students to help Pauling during his fellowship, and hinted at a probable staff appointment following. "I fear that if Pauling now goes to another institution it will result in separating a rather exceptional young investigator . . . from what would be for himself an unusual research opportunity," Noyes wrote the NRC.

In the meantime, he began making backup plans. It was unlikely that the NRC would change its long-standing policy for Pauling; if they didn't, he would go to Berkeley and might possibly be lost. In the spring of 1925, Noyes heard about a new program of international fellowships just being started by the Guggenheim family foundation. Although the first official Guggenheim fellows would not be selected until April 1926, there was talk of a special-needs early group being funded for the summer of 1925. Noyes made sure his favorite student was notified, and he and Millikan advised Pauling strongly to apply so that he could go to Europe to study with the masters of quantum physics.

But Pauling was in no hurry to go to Europe. He had plenty of work to finish at Caltech and was looking forward to some time with Lewis at Berkeley. As soon as he found out he had won an NRC fellowship—which stipulated that he had to go to another institution within six months of finishing his doctorate—Pauling informed the Guggenheim Foundation that he would wait for a year before considering an international trip.

Europe was a logical destination for Pauling. In the quarter century before he received his doctorate, America had made great strides in the basic sciences, to the point where American chemistry, thanks to the work of Noyes and men like him, was as good as—and in some ways better than—that found in Europe. The same was true in experimental physics, the hands-on part of the discipline, where the expanded funding of private enterprise coupled with the skill of technologically savvy home-grown products like Millikan had made America the equal of the world. But theoretical physics, the area of thought experiments, paper-and-pencil calculations, and the discovery of new laws, remained a European hegemony. Nothing underlined that more than work in quantum theory. By 1925 it was evident that the "old" quantum theory of Bohr and Sommerfeld was breaking down as a new generation of young theorists began to make a complete break with classical physics. And virtually all of the new generation were European—primarily from Germany, France, and England. Recognizing the importance of this new wave, an increasing number of U.S. universities were sending their newly minted Ph.D.s to study at the European quantum centers: Bohr's institute in Copenhagen, Born's in Göttingen, Sommerfeld's in Munich, Schrödinger's in Zurich.

Noyes had only six months before Pauling would go to Berkeley, perhaps never to return.

Luckily for Noyes, during the summer of 1925, Pauling narrowed his attention to the great prize: the nature of the chemical bond. He began writing an ambitious theoretical paper directly linking quantum theory to the bond question, starting by marshaling crystallographic and other chemical data to reject Lewis's old model of the static atom in favor of the dynamic Bohr atom. Then, to account for the structure of benzene, he expanded the idea that pairs of rotating electrons could circle around not just one but two nuclei, thus creating a shared electron bond. Advances in quantum physics would quickly prove this a dead-end approach, but at the time, the paper was important in showing not only that Pauling could combine structural chemistry and modern physics fruitfully, but also that the newly minted Ph.D. thought about science in terms of the big picture.

~~~

Noyes, meanwhile, was busy arranging Pauling's future. He knew the man at the top of the Guggenheim hierarchy, Frank Aydelotte, and he arranged to bring Pauling and Aydelotte together at a dinner at the Caltech faculty club in the fall of 1925. By then Pauling was growing increasingly interested in the new developments in quantum physics in Europe. There was talk of an entirely new theoretical approach, an odd sort of mathematics, "matrix mechanics," that appeared to clear up some of the old problems with the Bohr-Sommerfeld atom. Even G. N. Lewis advised Pauling to go to Europe at some point to study with the founders of the quantum revolution. So Pauling sent in his application for a Guggenheim in December, proposing to study "the topology of the interior of the atom and the structure of molecules, with especial reference to the nature of the chemical bond." He wrote to both Bohr's institute in Copenhagen and Sommerfeld's in Munich asking about opportunities for study.

Although after the Aydelotte dinner Noyes had been privately assured that his boy would be among the fellows named that coming April, that still left several months during which Pauling could study with Lewis. As Pauling and Ava Helen packed their bags for Berkeley, Noyes stepped in again. He invited the Paulings to his house for Christmas dinner, a social honor that Pauling remembered came as "quite a surprise." An additional surprise came when Noyes said they should bring their nine-month-old son. The old bachelor was charming and considerate at dinner, showing a paternal side of himself that Pauling had never seen. Linus junior was asleep when they arrived, and Noyes had him put in a room near the dining room. "Every few minutes Noyes would get up from the dining table to see if the baby was asleep," Pauling remembered. "He showed great interest in him." He also showed great interest in the Paulings' leaving for Europe as quickly as possible. "You are sure to get a Guggenheim fellowship," he told Pauling, but why wait until the official notice? If the Paulings left early, he proposed, then they would have time for stopovers in Madeira, Algiers, and Gibraltar before docking in Naples, then a few weeks for touring Italy. Italy! Noyes spoke glowingly of the glories of Rome, the fabulous ruins at Paestum. "I'll give you enough money to pay the fare to Europe," he said, "and support you from the end of March until the beginning of the Guggenheim fellowship." It was a fantastic Christmas present, and the Paulings couldn't say no. Then Noyes dropped the other shoe. Of course, he told Pauling, "It really isn't worthwhile for you to move to Berkeley and then to make another move to Europe." It was a choice between G. N. Lewis or the excitement of the Continent. Lewis lost.

Later, Pauling would say, "After many years I have decided that Noyes was quite clever in getting any result that he had decided upon."

Pauling did as Noyes suggested and resigned the remainder of his NRC fellowship. His decision to toss aside one fellowship in favor of a better one led to what Pauling remembered as "a very critical letter" from the NRC in reply.

Europe it would be, but at which scientific center? The answer came by default: Bohr never answered Pauling's letter of inquiry, and Sommerfeld did. Pauling would go to Munich. There was one final question before leaving: What would they do with the baby? Pauling had assumed that Linus junior would come along on the European trip and was "shocked," he remembered, when Ava Helen proposed that they leave the boy at home. At first he argued against it. But after thinking it over he saw it made sense. He and Ava Helen would be traveling extensively and living on the cheap; they would have little room for privacy, little money for baby-sitters, little time for dealing with an infant's demands. Bringing the baby would be a strain on Ava Helen and might possibly interfere with his work. They arranged to leave him with Ava Helen's mother—a logical decision, given the deteriorating state of Linus's mother's health—providing twenty-five dollars per month for his support. They said good-bye to Linus junior at the station in Portland as they boarded an eastbound train on March 4, 1926—six days before the boy's first birthday. It would be more than a year and a half before they saw him again.

Munich

An Old Hussar Officer

Noyes, a romantic at heart, may have hoped that Pauling's Italian tour would bring to flower a latent aesthetic sensibility. But Pauling wasn't Noyes. He and Ava Helen enjoyed traveling, but he wrote that he found Naples "not spotless," Rome "a terribly crowded place," and as for the rich religious heritage of Italy, "We liked seeing St. Peter's and some other wonderful churches; but we haven't sufficient liking for the structures in general to visit the myriads mentioned by Baedeker." Pauling cut the holiday short and hurried to Munich. "We have come to the end of a very pleasant trip, and I am glad," he wrote Noyes, "for even though Italy is wonderful, and everything was new to us, traveling becomes tiresome. Moreover, I am very anxious to get back to work after nearly two months of idleness." Pauling's heart belonged to science.

Munich itself was a tourist attraction, a green and famously friendly trading center on the Isar River, rich with museums and palaces built during the days of the old kingdom of Bavaria. Before World War I it was known for its great lagers, large parks, avant-garde artists' community, and general atmosphere of tolerance—a sort of San Francisco of southern Germany. Munich was home to Thomas Mann and Bertolt

Brecht, Wassily Kandinsky, Paul Klee, and the huge Löwenbräu brewery. Germans called it the City of Beer and Art.

But World War I changed it. In 1918, as Germany was preparing to surrender, a violent revolution, led by radical socialists, swept through Munich. It became, briefly, the capital of the Bavarian People's Republic; then, for a few weeks, the first city of the Bavarian Soviet Republic. Finally, remnants of the German national army, guided by locals weary of the tyranny of artists and bolshevists, fought its way in and returned Munich to the fatherland, replacing Red terror with White. Then came the monstrous inflation of the early 1920s, with prices rising 400 percent in a few months.

Inflation-fed pessimism and uncertainty replaced Munich's traditional *Gemütlichkeit*. The most popular acts at the local beer gardens were folksingers offering up nostalgic odes to the glorious old empire. The city's shop owners and tradesmen, fearful of inflation sucking them into the ranks of the working class, began talking of how they had been betrayed in the war, sold out by Communists and Jews. A paramilitary right wing movement crystallized around the discontent in Munich. Two and a half years before Pauling arrived, an old army general named Ludendorff and a frustrated artist and former army corporal named Adolf Hitler tried to lead the group in a swift overthrow of the local government from headquarters in a Munich beer hall.

The takeover failed, and when the Paulings arrived in late April 1926—just in time to receive the official news that Linus had gotten his Guggenheim fellowship—the city had regained a surface sheen of normalcy. Inflation had been stabilized, and a short period of relative prosperity helped ease the political tension. But beneath the exterior calm there was still class and race friction, still enough Brownshirts to drive artists like Brecht out of the city. After years of war, inflation, revolution, counterrevolution, and attempted revolution, Munich was still uneasy. It was a city where life had changed and was going to change again, where anything was possible.

~un~

The Paulings settled into a tiny one-room apartment on Adelbert et Bahrerstrasse, a few blocks from the University of Munich, and Pauling immediately arranged to see Sommerfeld. He was ushered into the director's light-filled study overlooking a pleasant courtyard in the Institute of Theoretical Physics. Sommerfeld was a short man, slightly built and balding. But he commanded respect. Partly as a reflection of his upper-class family background and partly to compensate for his size, he carried himself like a Prussian aristocrat, dressing meticulously, standing ramrod straight, sporting a large, waxed mustache and a dueling scar. "Doesn't he look the old Hussar officer," one of his students remembered thinking when Sommerfeld walked into class.

When Pauling came to Munich, Sommerfeld, at fifty-eight years old, was at the height of his power and prestige, director of the Institute of Theoretical Physics in Munich, sage to generations of young students of the atom. But while his work on the Bohr atom and his influential texts on spectroscopy had given him a solid reputation as a quantum thinker, Sommerfeld would never be known as a theorist of the first rank. He was a brilliant mathematician—"If you want to be a physicist, you must do three things," he would say. "First, study mathematics; second, study more mathematics; and third, do the same"— but he used his talents to clean up and clarify the groundbreaking theories of others rather than develop his own novel approaches. This is what he had done with Bohr's atom, picking up another's broad idea and refining it mathematically to make it work better, and he had done the same earlier in his career with everything from the physics of radio waves to a theory of spinning tops. Sommerfeld would never be listed in the histories of quantum physics as more than an important supporting player; he would never win a Nobel Prize. At least one historian would dismiss him as a "mathematical mercenary."

But he was more than that. Like Noyes, he had an uncanny ability to turn raw students into talented scientists. He was an unusually open-minded man who delighted in scouting out new ideas, assessing them with his peers, and quickly presenting the most important of them to his students. He knew everyone in theoretical physics, had collaborated with many of them and corresponded regularly with the rest; the ceaseless flow of information through Munich made it a nerve center for the developing field. He used the letters and prepublication galleys of articles that came in from Einstein, Bohr, Schrödinger, Pauli, and Heisenberg as fodder for his seminars and lectures, letting his students in on new developments well before they appeared in journals.

And Sommerfeld's lectures were legendary. He was not a showman in the classroom, as Pauling would become, but was instead a paragon of organization and clarity. His speaking style was intense enough to hold students' interest, slow enough for them to take careful notes, and reasoned enough to guide them through the major themes of quantum physics without becoming lost in a thicket of paradox that edged the emerging field. At each step he would carefully correlate physical findings with their mathematical interpretations, showing on the blackboard how phenomena in the real world could be explained and illuminated through the use of numbers. During the mid-1920s, Sommerfeld's six-semester lecture cycle on quantum physics was a primer for anyone serious about the field, and Munich was considered one of the three world centers for the study of quantum physics, along with Bohr's institute in Copenhagen and Born's in Göttingen.

As important as his lecture style, however, was Sommerfeld's commitment to working with individual students. Beneath the Prussian façade was a warm, concerned, encouraging teacher, a father figure who invited students to his house for amateur musical recitals (Sommerfeld was a fair pianist), who loved to talk physics at a favorite local café, scribbling equations in pencil on the tabletop, and who made time to confer with each student individually, at length, several times each week. During these research discussions he would ask them about their progress, provide direction, and offer encouragement. Sommerfeld was an optimist of a peculiarly German type: He believed in his blood that German science, like German music and philosophy, represented a pinnacle of human achievement and that the rational application of German thinking would eventually solve the mysteries of the atom. It was just a matter of time and approach. He built his students' confidence by focusing their attention on small, solvable problems instead of allowing them to become lost in the complexities of big theories. "When kings go a-building, wagoners have more work," he would say, and he made sure his students were good carpenters before they tried on crowns. If Niels Bohr, increasingly pessimistic about the confusion surrounding his version of the atom in the mid-1920s, was becoming the gloomy philosopher of quantum physics, Sommerfeld was its cheerful engineer.

And his school was unparalleled in turning out successful physicists. "What I especially admire about you is that you have, as it were, pounded out of the soil such a large number of young talents," Einstein wrote in 1922. By one estimate, one-third of all the physicists teaching in Germany in the years before World War II had been through Sommerfeld's institute as either students or assistants. The stars included Laue, Debye, Wolfgang Pauli, Werner Heisenberg, Paul Ewald, Hans Bethe, Paul Epstein, Gregor Wentzel, Walter Heitler, Fritz London, Karl Bechert, and the foreign visitors Edward Condon, Isidor Rabi, Edward Teller, Lawrence Bragg, and Pauling. Many of his students would outdo him in research. All of them would owe him something of their sense of the possible. "I learned mathematics from Born and physics from Bohr," said Heisenberg. "And from Sommerfeld I learned optimism."

—*mm*—

Optimism was a practical necessity when dealing with the atom. It was becoming increasingly clear that the Bohr-Sommerfeld model, with its orbiting electrons, simply didn't work. The old paradoxes were still unanswered: Why didn't the moving electrons lose energy and fall into the nucleus? Why were some orbits allowed and not others? How did electrons "jump"? And now there were new mysteries. In the early 1920s a French doctoral student, Prince Louis de Broglie, theorized that electrons could behave like waves as well as particles; in other words, that matter, at least at the atomic level, could behave like light. American researchers at the Bell Laboratories proved the point in 1927 when they found that electrons could be diffracted by a crystal, just like light waves or x-rays. In 1923, another American, Arthur Holly Compton, published strong new evidence that light could also behave like a particle. Then the young Dutch researchers Goudsmit and Uhlenbeck offered evidence that electrons had "spin." How could particles also be waves and waves be particles? How could a wave "spin"?

Pauling had heard a great deal about the shortcomings of the Bohr-Sommerfeld atom at Caltech. But until it was all sorted out, he adhered to that model and everything that went with it. In the few months between December 1925, when he still believed that calculations based on the Bohr-Sommerfeld version of quantum theory were "straight-forward and well-grounded," and the summer of 1926, however, he converted to a new way of thinking about the atom.

It started with his first interview with Sommerfeld. Pauling had taken two years of German at Oregon Agricultural College in addition to what he had learned from his grandparents; between that and Sommerfeld's minimal English they were able to carry on an adequate conversation. Perhaps, Pauling asked, you remember me from your visit to the California Institute of Technology? Unfortunately, the director did not. Sommerfeld asked Pauling to outline his research interests, the things he hoped to accomplish in Munich. Pauling eagerly began talking about a problem he hoped he would be allowed to pursue, following up on work he had done at Caltech on the dielectric constant of hydrogen chloride gas. But, Pauling was surprised to find, Sommerfeld "didn't give my suggestion much heed." The director, like most German scientists, had a somewhat condescending attitude toward American physics in general. ("Don't take all this so seriously," he told one young German physics student who was worrying about going to Berkeley on a fellowship. "Life in America is not so difficult. There any young man can become an assistant professor.") In any case, it was customary in Germany for the professor to assign research projects, not the student. Sommerfeld asked Pauling to give him a few days to think it over and then assigned him a problem Pauling was less interested in, a series of austere calculations related to the spin of the electron.

Pauling pursued the project with the same enthusiasm he brought to the after-school jobs his mother had arranged for him as a teenager: He didn't accomplish much and quit as soon as he could. He was interested in other things. "I was thinking about nearly every theoretical problem that there was," he remembered.

Especially, at that time, a hydrogen chloride problem. Pauling had attempted to come up with a version of quantum theory that accurately predicted the effects of an electric field on the motion of polar molecules. His theorizing came close enough to what was found by experiment to convince Pauling that the problem was either with sloppy experimental measurements or his own theoretical tinkering, not with the Bohr-Sommerfeld model of the atom. Just before leaving for Europe he'd thought of adding a magnetic field at right angles to the electric field. If the Bohr-Sommerfeld quantum theory was right, the magnetic field would have a measurable effect on the motion of the molecules—an effect that classical theory said would not be there. This would be important new support for quantum theory. Pauling eventually convinced Sommerfeld to let him work on this problem. "He said that he would present the results next month in Zurich at a congress on magnetism called by Debye," Pauling wrote Noyes on May 22, 1926. "I shall accordingly have to work to have results by then."

Work for a budding theorist like Pauling consisted of hours of sitting at a desk, filling page after page of notebook paper with formulae and drawings, notes and scribbles. "Linus is very busy with his hydrogen chloride problem," Ava Helen wrote on June 2, "and he is at one moment very gleeful and the next very despondent." By June 10, Pauling had verified theoretically that if the Bohr-Sommerfeld model of the atom was correct, the magnetic field should have a large effect. While he waited for news of the confirming experiment from Pasadena, he drafted a paper in German, which Sommerfeld took with him to the Zurich congress on June 21. A few days later, Pauling received a telegram. Sommerfeld was calling Pauling to Switzerland to talk over his ideas.

Ava Helen remembered the late-June train ride through the Alps—the vivid green hills, the fields of red poppies, the peasant women in bright blue kerchiefs—and the excitement her husband felt. He was making an impression on Sommerfeld. His ideas were being taken seriously. When they arrived in Zurich, they were asked to dine with the director and a few others at Debye's house. During the next few days, Pauling talked about his work, listened to presentations, and chatted informally with some of the most renowned physicists of Europe. "He listens so intently and gets as excited as can be," Ava Helen wrote. "I like to watch him."

One thing he was excited about was the chance to compare notes with one of the most talked about young physicists in Europe, Wolfgang Pauli. Pauli, the son of a Viennese chemistry professor, began building a reputation at age seventeen, when he stood up after a talk by Einstein on the theory of relativity and said that he thought there was an error in the great man's conclusions. At eighteen he was writing articles on relativity for encyclopedias, and by 1925, at just twenty-five years of age, he assured his place in the history of physics by publishing his "exclusion principle," a far-reaching idea that added a fourth quantum number for describing the state of electrons to the three already postulated in the Bohr-Sommerfeld model and stated that no two electrons could have exactly the same set of quantum numbers. Goudsmit and Uhlenbeck tied Pauli's fourth quantum number to a new property of electrons they called "spin," which they described as the rotation of the electron on its axis. Spin was two-faced, either parallel to the electron's orbit or opposite it. According to the exclusion principle, then, a pair of electrons could share the same orbit as long as they had opposite spin. The idea of paired electrons immediately struck a chord with chemists, or at least those like Pauling, who were familiar with G. N. Lewis's theory of shared electron-pair chemical bonds.

Pauli was also becoming infamous for what one colleague called his "excessive honesty," a tendency to directly, sometimes brutally, attack any idea he considered sloppy. Even as mild a personality as Paul Ehrenfest was put off by Pauli's cutting criticism, telling him, "I like your papers better than you." Since Pauling's paper pointed out shortcomings in Pauli's own ideas about polar molecules, perhaps he should have expected a cool reception.

Pauling bustled up to Pauli during a break in the presentations and began outlining the results of his weeks of feverish work showing that the Bohr-Sommerfeld version of quantum physics was an improvement over the classical scheme. Pauli listened politely and then offered a two-word response: "Not interesting." Perhaps sensing the deflating effect of his comment, he added, "If you'd have thought of this two years ago, you'd be famous." Two years earlier it was still worthwhile to provide support for the Bohr-Sommerfeld atom. But now, at least to bright young European physicists such as Pauli, that version of quantum physics was dead. It had been killed during the course of the previous year by a formidable new way of thinking called quantum mechanics.

The New Mechanics

Pauli's friend Werner Heisenberg was the prime assassin. Heisenberg and Pauli were scientific siblings of complementary types, Wolfgang the restrained, analytic older brother (older, in fact, by a year and a half), Werner the impulsive revolutionary firebrand. They had parallel student careers, Heisenberg following a year or two behind Pauli: They both earned their doctorates with Sommerfeld in Munich, where first-year graduate student Heisenberg first met and befriended Pauli; both went on to Göttingen to work with Max Born; both then served as Bohr's assistant in Copenhagen. Born was one of the spiritual godfathers of the new physics; both were influenced by his consummate skepticism and utter belief in numbers. Born passed on to his postdoctoral fellows the belief that they shouldn't feel constrained when describing the atom to use concepts of space and time that worked to describe larger-scale events. He also taught them a mathematician's disdain for the messy, illogical paradoxes of the Bohr-Sommerfeld atom. By 1924, Pauli and Heisenberg were calling attempts to keep the Bohr-Sommerfeld atom patched together the "swindle."

Heisenberg would end the swindle. He thought the paradoxes arose from trying to relate the increasingly strange experimental results researchers were finding to what was, after all, a made-up model of orbiting electrons. Heisenberg decided to forget about orbits, to forget about models entirely. He wiped the Bohr-Sommerfeld atom from his mind, and on a clean mental field he began working with purely mathematical formulae based only on data that could be observed. No one could see orbiting electrons, but you could see the light they gave off. Heisenberg concentrated on spectral data. In a few legendary days, while isolated on a rocky North Sea island recuperating from hay fever, using only observable data, Heisenberg created a new mathematical approach to describing quantum physics. Cleaned up and expanded by Born and one of his students, Pascual Jordan, Heisenberg's insights became what is called matrix mechanics. The new system was a distinct improvement over the old quantum physics: It not only appeared to explain more spectral data with fewer paradoxes; it also appeared to include within itself the principles of classical physics, Newton's old mechanics, as a limiting case. Heisenberg was twenty-four when he created it.

It was also a bulky, demanding mathematical system to use. And the mathematics wasn't the only problem. Heisenberg had done too good a job of divorcing himself from models of the atom. There was a reaction against matrix mechanics because it was too abstract; it didn't relate to any visualizable thing at all. The mathematics seemed to work, but what sort of atom did the formulae describe? There was a good deal of initial skepticism based on the idea that Heisenberg's brainchild might be mathematical doodling ungrounded in physical reality, a spin of fantasy, or as Einstein succinctly termed matrix mechanics, "magic." It didn't appeal to researchers like Pauling, who worked better if they could "see" their atoms. Born had toured the United States in late 1925 explaining matrix mechanics; Pauling had heard him lecture at Caltech before he left. And Pauling, like many physicists (most *chemists* didn't understand Heisenberg's brainchild at all), wasn't ready to sign on. "It was just too difficult," he remembered. "I couldn't see any way of using matrix mechanics to attack the problems that I was interested in."

As Pauling was sailing to Europe in March 1926, the physics world was jolted again by the publication of what appeared to be an entirely independent system of quantum physics. The author was unlikely. Erwin Schrödinger was a middle-aged, rather old-fashioned Austrian theoretical physicist who had been watching the heretical progress of quantum physics with dismay. At age thirty-nine he was already past the prime age for making revolutionary theories, which generally seemed to be made by youngsters like Heisenberg. He did have his oddities: a passion for philosophy (especially Spinoza, Schopenhauer, and the ideas of the Vedanta), a Viennese sense of superiority to almost all other peoples (especially Americans), and a freethinking approach to sex (especially involving women substantially younger than himself). His colleague (and his wife's lover) Hermann Weyl once linked Schrödinger's great quantum mechanical idea to "a late erotic outburst in his life." But he was by temperament more of a reactionary

than a revolutionary, a classical physicist at heart who had an instinc-
tive dislike for the paradoxes of quantum thinking. "You surely must
understand," he once told Bohr, "that the whole idea of quantum
jumps necessarily leads to nonsense."

Schrödinger wanted to abolish Bohr's ideas and explain the atom
in classical terms. He thought he had found a way in de Broglie's idea
that electrons could behave like waves instead of orbiting like little
planets and making those nonsensical jumps. Schrödinger theorized
that the nucleus was surrounded by an electron/wave vibrating at a
certain frequency, something like the standing wave of a vibrating
drum head. Only certain stable frequencies were possible, those that
included an integer number of waves; if not, the waves would interfere
with each other. Add energy and you boost the electron/wave to the
next whole-number frequency; when it falls back, it emits a wavelength
of light. In a rush of extraordinary work, Schrödinger developed a
mathematical equation in which, by treating the electron as a wave, he
was able to derive Bohr's energy levels for the stable state of the hydrogen electron. It was incredible, but the electron, he thought, must be
in fact not a point in space but a sort of standing wave smeared around
the nucleus. He could measure the shape and density of the wave and
found that according to his calculations the hydrogen electron formed
a spherical smear of negative energy around the nucleus. His system,
which appeared to give just as complete an accounting of atomic reality as Born and Heisenberg's, became known as wave mechanics.

Sommerfeld, like many physicists of the day, quickly appreciated
the more classically recognizable ideas of wave mechanics and the relative simplicity and elegance of Schrödinger's mathematical approach
compared to matrix mechanics—Schrödinger's system was more ap-
proachable, more "user friendly" than the austere matrices of Born
and Heisenberg—although he doubted that wave mechanics actually
described a physical reality. Every young natural scientist had studied
the physics of waves in school and had a comfortable sense of what
waves were all about; even if electron waves didn't exist as such,
Schrödinger's equations still translated into a visualizable image of an
atomic nucleus surrounded by an electron "cloud" with a discernible
shape. In hydrogen the cloud formed a ball of electricity whose density
decreased exponentially with distance from the nucleus. Wave mechanics also indicated that in more complex atoms additional electrons could be idealized as forming spherical shells in layers around
the inner ball, as Bohr had predicted.

Many traditional physicists who had never liked quantum theory's

revolutionary overtones greeted the wave picture eagerly as a sub-
stantiation of traditional physics. Pauling was not old enough to be
a traditionalist, but he followed Sommerfeld's lead and employed
wave mechanics as a more easily used, visualizable tool. As Pauling
wrote to a colleague in 1926, "I find his [Schrödinger's] methods
much simpler than matrix calculation; and the fundamental ideas
more satisfactory, for there is at least a trace of physical picture behind
the mathematics." Compared to matrix mechanics, the wave picture
of the atom was, Pauling said, "*anschaulich* [clear] enough to appeal
to me."

As with any promising new idea in physics, Sommerfeld made sure
that wave mechanics was presented in Munich as quickly as possible.
Pauling attended a seminar during his first semester that analyzed prepublication proof sheets of one of Schrödinger's early wave-mechanics
papers, and Schrödinger himself arrived in Munich in the summer of
1926 to lecture on his ideas. Pauling was present when, at the end of
the Austrian's lecture, a boyish-looking young man with a shock of light
brown hair jumped to his feet in the back of the room. It was Heisenberg. Angered by the quick acceptance of Schrödinger's ideas and
worried about the possibility that his matrix system would be pushed
aside, he attacked Schrödinger directly, asking him how his electron-
wave smears could ever explain quantized processes such as the photo-
electric effect and blackbody radiation. Before Schrödinger could
answer, the head of Munich's experimental physics institute, the august Nobel Prize winner Wilhelm Wien, called back angrily, "Young
man, Professor Schrödinger will certainly take care of all these questions in due time. You must understand that we are now finished with
all that nonsense about quantum jumps." Schrödinger added calmly
that he was confident that eventually any problems would be cleared
up by his methods.

It was a clash of two worldviews. Heisenberg was increasingly convinced that the atom was, in a basic sense, unknowable, that reality at
the atomic level had little to do with anything that could be pictured
in the mind. Atomic reality was neither visualizable nor describable
in classical terms; it could only be approached through his strange
new kind of mathematics. Schrödinger was equally certain that the
atom had to make some sort of classical physical sense. While the two
were polite in their public debates, their private correspondence revealed the extent of their feelings. Schrödinger continued to term the
idea of quantum jumps "something monstrous." Heisenberg called
Schrödinger's insistence on a visualizable atom *Mist* (bullshit).

Both the matrix and wave forms of the new quantum mechanics explained far more experimental results with fewer paradoxes than the old Bohr-Sommerfeld model of the atom—the basis of what would henceforth be called the "old quantum theory." Pauli was breaking the news to Pauling that his hard work on diatomic molecules was wasted because it propped up an outmoded system. "Not interesting" indeed.

Pauli also recognized that Pauling's crossed-field system offered a good test of the new quantum mechanics. Pauling had theorized that the old quantum theory predicted a measurable magnetic-field effect on the dielectric constant of hydrogen gas. That was probably wrong, Pauli told him; the new mechanics would most likely predict no effect. If Pauling could work out the new quantum-mechanical calculations for his system, he should be able to publish the same work he had thought would support the old quantum theory. Only this time he would help demolish it.

The final piece of the puzzle fell into place when Pauling heard from Pasadena that they couldn't find the magnetic effect he had predicted. For the next several weeks Pauling reworked his calculations using the new mechanics (he referred to both Heisenberg's and Schrödinger's forms). The results demonstrated, he said, "a remarkable failure of the old quantum theory and the success of the new." For Pauling, too, the old quantum theory was dead.

"I am now working on the new quantum mechanics," he wrote Noyes two weeks after the Zurich congress, "for I think that atomic and molecular chemistry will require it." It soon became evident to Pauling, as to everyone else in physics, that the new system was a fundamental improvement. "Where the old quantum theory was in disagreement with the experiment, the new mechanics ran hand-in-hand with nature," Pauling was soon saying, "and where the old quantum theory was silent, the new mechanics spoke the truth."

Ava Helen loved their time in Europe. She and Linus were having the honeymoon they had never had, and despite his arduous work schedule—he spent most evenings doing calculations in their room while Ava Helen read or practiced German—they still had time for fun. They went to the opera and visited the galleries in Munich; they often walked to the grand new Deutsches Museum, with its extensive scientific exhibits, took weekend mountain-climbing trips to the Alps, and sometimes went dancing at Odeon's Casino. "I love to dance with Linus for he is such a good dancer," Ava Helen wrote that summer. "We get along wonderfully well and do lots of little steps that other people can't do." And she was more than a social companion. The Paulings were invited several times to Sommerfeld's house, where Ava Helen made a favorable impression. When Sommerfeld learned that she played the piano, he had one of his own moved to the Paulings' apartment. As at Caltech, Ava Helen also accompanied Linus to lectures and seminars, even to the weekly café get-togethers where the physicists talked shop. Often she was the only woman there. "One of the German boys said that including myself there are five Americans in the Institute for Theoretical Physics," she wrote proudly to Noyes that summer.

After a few months in Munich, the Paulings became fixtures in the small American student community. Together with the Guillemin brothers, a pair of U.S. postdoctoral fellows who lived in the same building as they, Linus and Ava Helen took on the role of unofficial welcoming committee for a number of visiting American students, introducing them to the city and the university, then heading to a favorite café to talk over the latest scientific findings—or more important matters, such as whether a fellowship stipend had come through.

They kept track of Linus junior's health, happiness, and progress with walking through the exchange of letters with Ava Helen's mother. And although they missed him, both Ava Helen and Pauling were glad he wasn't along because of the extra work and inconvenience he would have caused. "My respect for my wife's good sense has been steadily rising," Pauling wrote Noyes after they had been in Munich some months, "for I argued strongly against leaving the baby."

The only dark period came at the beginning of July, when they received a letter from Pauling's sister Lucile with bad news about their mother. Belle's health had worsened dramatically, and she had been sent to a state hospital in Salem used primarily for treating the insane. "The news regarding Mamma has been a great shock to me," Pauling immediately wrote back. "I shall do everything I can, so just tell me what you want me to do. . . . I have never known what to do, for I haven't ever learned the condition of affairs. . . . I am sending all the money I can put together to Uncle Jim. If more is needed I shall see about borrowing it. . . . See that Mamma has everything she needs."

But by the time the letter reached Portland, Belle was dead.

～

It was the end of an increasingly unhappy life. After Pauling had been at college for a year, Belle had married again. The groom was a tobacco-chewing soldier named Bryden whom she met on a blind date arranged by her sister Goldie. The courtship was short, and the match was doomed to failure. Pauling's sisters Pauline and Lucile both took an instant dislike to their new stepfather, who seemed to enjoy lying around the house more than working. Soon after their honeymoon Belle was hit by influenza and then developed pneumonia, both worsened by her chronic anemia. The newlyweds began quarreling. A few months after the marriage Bryden grabbed his hat and coat and said he was going to the barbershop. He never came back.

Pauline couldn't wait to leave, either. After graduating from high school, she followed in her brother's footsteps to OAC, with Linus's financial help, but she didn't like college life. She was pretty and young and eager to go someplace new. In 1925 she took a job as an assistant to the secretary in Portland's Elks Club and within a short time had attracted the admiration of the club's athletic director. Pauline encouraged him to look for opportunities in other towns, they married quickly, and a few months later they moved to Los Angeles. Belle collapsed when she learned that the couple had eloped.

Lucile, the most loving, least hardheaded of the three children, was left alone to look after her increasingly dependent mother. Belle's pernicious anemia was now entering a new phase, robbing her of movement and feeling in her legs, leading to bouts of irrationality and delusions. The pressure of making ends meet racked her nerves. Decisions had to be made about the boardinghouse, but Lucile, although she was in her early twenties, knew little about business and didn't like to make hard choices. "I left decisions, [Belle's] care, everything, up to others, being absolutely immature and irresponsible, and easily led," she later wrote Pauling.

The last time Pauling saw Belle, in March 1926 as he and Ava Helen came through Portland on their way to Europe, he recognized that his mother was increasingly incapable of caring for herself. Her hair had turned gray. She had trouble walking without help. But he would not interrupt his plans. He told her that he had deposited one thousand dollars in a Pasadena bank and that she was to tell him if she needed any of it; he also asked his uncle, Judge James Campbell, and a faithful longtime boarder, Mr. Ecklemann, to keep an eye on Belle.

Two weeks later, Belle sold her boardinghouse—at least on paper. The "buyer" was Lucile, the selling price ten dollars. Perhaps Belle wanted to avoid taxes or problems with an inheritance after her death; perhaps she wanted to reward the one child who had stayed with her. She then arranged to rent the house, and she and Lucile moved to a nearby apartment. It sapped the last of her energy. The delusions increased in frequency. She couldn't sleep. She was restless and fretful, one minute euphoric, the next suspicious and cynical. It was too much for Lucile, and Belle's older sister Goldie was called in to handle the situation.

There wasn't anything Goldie could do, either. The decision was made to commit Belle to the state hospital for the insane. After taking care of the legalities, Goldie rode with her sister sixty miles to the state hospital and filled out the admittance questionnaire when they arrived. Alcoholic drinks or drugs? "None." Natural disposition? "Moral character good. Disposition happy. Lost husband 16 years ago—raised family through great struggles." First symptoms of mental derangement? "Worried from illness and too much responsibility."

Lucile visited a few days later and was overpowered by the sight of her mother in a mental ward. In tears, she asked her Aunt Goldie to undo what had been done but was told it was too late.

Belle died a few weeks after she was admitted. She was forty-five years old.

Pauling read the news in a letter from his sister a few days later, while entertaining friends in his Munich apartment. He had heard a little about her deterioration in what he remembered as a "silly, abusive and unintelligible letter" from Goldie calling him to task for his failure to adequately support Belle, but her death still came as a shock. He broke down, crying in front of the group as Ava Helen tried to comfort him.

All of the guilt and worry Belle's children had stored up for years erupted after her death. His sister Pauline sent Pauling a scathing letter a few days later detailing the ways he had been too much of a skinflint to help Belle, noting that he was too cheap to even buy his wife decent clothes. Pauling responded carefully and coolly, noting how little he had heard about Belle's final deterioration, listing the money he had sent and outlining the arrangements he had made for Belle's care. Then, in a letter to Lucile, he let a bit of emotion show. "Perhaps you do not realize that you haven't let me know about things. I can, of course, never feel the same towards Pauline after the terrible things she said in her letter. Every one of her statements but one is a slander-ous lie. The one true statement, that Ava Helen hasn't had the beauti-ful clothes Pauline has had, arises from the fact that Ava Helen was spending about as much per year for clothes as Pauline spent per month, in order that we might pay the interest and start paying off the money that sent Pauline to an unproductive year in Corvallis and the other money I gave Mamma. . . . I have become rather accustomed to slander, and I know that people will always take Aunt Goldie's ravings with many grains of salt; but I hate to have you laboring under an illu-sion regarding me. . . . "

It was impossible to return for the funeral, and there was little more that could be done from the other side of the world. "I can think of so many things that I intended doing some day," Pauling wrote Lu-cile just after Belle's death, "but now it is too late."

A Fine Figure

Pauling's remorse was leavened with relief. He and his mother had never understood each other well or loved each other enough; his relationship with Belle had been based largely on feelings of filial duty and guilt. The weight was now lifted. At the beginning of August, Pauling and Ava Helen left for a long-planned vacation in Switzerland and France, where he did some work and had a great deal of fun. When they returned to Munich in the fall, Pauling sported a new tailor-made suit and a Scottish woolen scarf. "He looks quite dashing, especially when he carries his Italian cane," Ava Helen wrote.

He cut a fine figure professionally as well. While some Europeans expected that visiting Americans would be relatively unprepared and uncultured, experiences during the 1920s with some of the more out-standing scientific specimens, including John Slater, Edward Condon, Harold Urey, Karl Compton (later president of the Massachusetts Institute of Technology), and Pauling, helped change the image. Paul-ing's command of the local language was adequate and getting bet-ter—within a few months of arriving he could give lectures in passable German—and he was working very hard to understand the new physics. The German-born physicist Hans Bethe, finishing his doctoral work under Sommerfeld in 1927, remembered that compared to the average American, Pauling "certainly was very different. He was gener-ally recognized as really knowledgeable." Tall, friendly, and enthusias-tic, Pauling also fit the European stereotype of a Westerner, a sort of cowboy of science. "A young, lanky man who knew enormously much and was an excellent lecturer" was how Hermann Mark, a German researcher who met Pauling in Munich, remembered him at the time.

During Pauling's first semester in Munich he took a lecture class from Sommerfeld devoted to differential equations, a form of calculus essential to solving atomic problems. And as he listened, Pauling began absorbing Sommerfeld's swashbuckling mathematical approach to attacking the mysteries of the atom. The director practiced a practical, flexible style of mathematics in which finding equations that reflected and explained real-world experimental results—mathematics that worked—was more important than pure, formal rigor. He didn't worry too much about internal consistency; he used mathematical tricks. Rather than simply passing on old information or prescribing specific approaches to problems, he pointed out the holes in current theories and presented his students with a toolbox of mathematical devices that could be used to create new theoretical structures. This was an ideal approach for a rapidly changing field like quantum physics. It appealed especially to Pauling, whose own use of mathematics would always be less rigorous than practical.

Even so, Pauling's mathematical skills were sharp enough to assure his reputation as an American whiz kid. He walked into Sommerfeld's office one day in the late summer of 1926 with a problem. It concerned one of Sommerfeld's assistants, *Privatdocent* Gregor Wentzel, who had earned his Ph.D. with Sommerfeld a few years before and whose theoretical work since then had established him as a rising star of physics. Wentzel wrote a paper that Pauling found while searching for anything available on the quantum mechanics of many-electron atoms. In going through the paper, titled "A Difficulty with the Theory of the Spinning Electron," Pauling found that the problem was not with spin but with Wentzel's mathematics. The *privatdocent* had made an error in calculation: "The difficulty vanished," Pauling said, "if you did the work correctly." Pauling reworked Wentzel's calculations and came out with values closer to those found experimentally. Sommerfeld took Pauling's work to Wentzel, and it was agreed that the American was right. Pauling wrote a short paper on his correction in somewhat clumsy German; Sommerfeld threw it out, had Pauling rewrite it in English, and then had an assistant translate that into German for publication in the *Zeitschrift für Physik*. It marked a turning point in Pauling's use of quantum mechanics: He now had fashioned from the new physics a tool that could help him explain the properties of atoms. It also marked a turning point in his relationship with Sommerfeld, who now understood that the young American was someone to take seriously.

―――

When the new semester started in the fall of 1926, Pauling took Sommerfeld's first official lecture section on wave mechanics—history's first full-semester lecture course on the subject—in which Sommerfeld systematically explained the powerful mathematics of Schrödinger's wave picture of the atom. As was often the case when he presented new material for the first time, Sommerfeld taught himself about the advances along with his students. He would later remember, "My first lectures on this theory were heard by Linus Pauling, who learned as much from them as I did myself."

A new wave-mechanical universe began opening up for Pauling. One of the great failures of the Bohr-Sommerfeld atom was its inability to predict anything more than the spectra of the simplest of atoms; it did not lend itself to useful explanations of other properties, such as paramagnetism, polarity, three-dimensional structure, and chemical bonding. The first applications of the new quantum mechanics also focused on predicting the spectra of very simple atoms. The new system's quick success at this level left a number of young researchers, Pauling among them, eager to apply the techniques to more complex atoms and more varied chemical properties.

The problem was that although Schrödinger's wave equation was relatively straightforward in calculating the energy levels of a single electron around a single nucleus, each additional element had to be calculated individually, along with the effects of each on the others. Precise mathematical solutions quickly became impossible. By working with the techniques he developed in correcting Wentzel's paper and calculating screening constants, however, Pauling simplified the picture. He could concentrate on the outermost electrons only. This made it possible for Pauling to use wave mechanics to calculate light refraction, diamagnetic susceptibility, and the sizes of larger, more complex atoms—the first time wave mechanics had been applied to many of these problems and a pioneering advance in the field.

By late December he was in his room banging out a draft of a long paper on an old German typewriter, thus avoiding the double fees Munich typing agencies charged for papers in English. Ava Helen listened and waited and peered over his shoulder. "Are you sure this line on this curve should go the way it's drawn?" she asked him at one point, pointing at a figure he had created to illustrate the paper. "Of course I'm sure. I drew it," he replied. Then he looked at it again, thought a moment, and changed it.

Finally, it was ready to give to Sommerfeld. The director was impressed. He used his position as a foreign member of the Royal Society of London to offer Pauling's paper, "The Theoretical Prediction of the Physical Properties of Many-Electron Atoms and Ions," for publication in the society's *Proceedings*. In a cover note Sommerfeld wrote, "I am persuaded that these questions, which are fundamental for the structure of the atom, have never before been treated with such thoroughness and completeness."

Pauling knew he had written a good paper as well and was ready to take his screening-constants idea even further. "I believe that this work is of considerable value," he wrote Noyes. "The possible extensions and applications of the method are numerous; for example, I am now working on the sizes of ions in crystals, and the question of the occurrence of different types of crystals."

By bringing his new quantum-mechanical tools back to the study of crystals, Pauling was closing an important loop in his interests. At Caltech he had been frustrated by the inability of x-ray diffraction to solve the structures of any but the simplest crystals. To get beyond this limitation, the Braggs and other crystallographers had been building tables of the sizes of ions—electrically charged atoms such as the sodium and chlorine atoms in table salt—based on their work with simple crystals. The hope was that such tables could be used to discover some general rules or patterns that could be extended to solve the structure of crystals too complex to attack directly. Whoever came up with the most useful set of rules would make it possible to solve hundreds of these more difficult crystal structures.

Pauling was now able to attack the problem from a different angle, using quantum mechanics and the technique he had developed to correct Wentzel's paper. Within a few weeks of his Royal Society contribution, Pauling finished another major paper. The sizes of ions, he wrote, are determined by their outermost electrons; these outer electrons behave in ways determined in great part by how well more inner lying electrons shield them from the nucleus. The distances between ions in a crystal are also affected by the repulsion between the two positively charged nuclei, another factor affected by electronic shielding. Using his new screening constants, Pauling was now able to build a table of ionic sizes firmly based in quantum mechanics, and he used the values he determined to start building a set of general rules underlying crystal structures.

These two papers, both published in early 1927, helped establish Pauling's international reputation and pointed the way toward future work. In both of them he used a semiempirical method: calculating theoretical values for properties, comparing them to what was known from experiment, then correcting the theory to more closely match reality. True to Sommerfeld's teachings and his own temperament, he used whatever worked—the Royal Society paper included elements from classical, old quantum theoretical and new quantum-mechanical physics. More importantly, he consummated the marriage of two powerful scientific tools, x-ray crystallography and wave mechanics, by using each to check the accuracy of the other. "I think that it is very interesting that one can see the [psi] functions of Schrödinger's wave mechanics by means of the X-ray study of crystals," Pauling wrote Noyes. "This work should be continued experimentally. I believe that much information regarding the nature of the chemical bond will result from it."

Heitler and London

The chemical bond was one problem with which Pauling was not making much headway. He wanted more time in Europe, and that winter he applied for a six-month extension of his Guggenheim fellowship in order to further investigate "the atomic model obtained from Schrödinger's interpretation of his wave mechanics, especially with reference to the use of this model in the explanation of the chemical bond in molecules and in crystals." He planned to leave Munich in mid-February for two weeks in Göttingen with Born, then to Berlin to study crystal-structure techniques, then to Copenhagen to see Bohr for six weeks, Zurich for the three-month summer semester with Schrödinger, and finally a quick visit with the Braggs in England on the way home in September. Sommerfeld added a cover letter to Pauling's request, writing, "My colleagues and I have the impression that he is an extraordinary, productive scientist with many interests, in whom it is justified to place the greatest expectations." Pauling was granted the extension.

There remained the question of what he would do when he came back to the United States. Just after Christmas of 1926 he wrote Noyes, "I have just realized that the time will soon be here when [Caltech], as well as other universities, makes its decisions regarding the staff for the next year; so that definite arrangements regarding my position and salary will also soon be made. I have had no offers from any one, for I have thought, and accordingly expressed myself as believing, that I would return to the Institute." A week later he wrote to G. N. Lewis, hinting that he might be available for the right price: "So far I have no definite position for next year; but I promised Dr. Noyes that I would return to the Institute next year unless I received from some one else an offer better than theirs (how good it will be I do not know)." It was some months before Lewis wrote back; "I had some hopes that you might be offered a position in our Physics department, but different plans have been made, for this year at least," he wrote. "In any case I am afraid that Dr. Noyes would be quite disappointed if you did not return to him."

Lewis's looking to the physics department was logical. Pauling had thrown himself into the study of theoretical physics with such enthusiasm that there was some question as to whether he was still a chemist. During nearly a year in Munich he had never visited the university's Institute of Physical Chemistry, and with the exception of a few chats with its director, Kasimir Fajans, he ignored the chemistry faculty altogether. All his contacts and all his research were in theoretical physics.

But his own temperament and skills led him back to chemistry. At OAC and Caltech, Pauling had become accustomed to being one of the quickest and brightest students. But in Europe he found himself a lesser-known among a muster of brilliant young men about his age (Pauli, Heisenberg, Dirac, and Jordan). "I had something of a shock when I went to Europe in 1926 and discovered that there were a good number of people around that I thought to be smarter than me," he remembered, mentioning Heisenberg, Pauli, and Bethe in particular. He was beginning to feel the limits of his mathematical abilities as well, which he felt were good enough for the semiempirical approach he took to chemical questions but were not of the caliber required for rigorous mathematical physics.

On the other hand, "I got to thinking that I know some things—a lot about chemistry—that other people don't know," he said. After a year in Munich, Pauling wrote Noyes: "Most people seem to think that work such as mine, dealing with the properties of atoms and molecules, should be classed with physics, but I . . . feel that the study of chemical substances remains chemistry even though it reach the state in which it requires the use of considerable mathematics. The question is more than an academic one, for the answer really determines my classification as a physicist or chemist." Regarding his own work, he wrote, "One can hardly class this with Physical Chemistry, as ordinarily understood; possibly Molecular Chemistry would be a suitable designation."

There had never been such a thing as a "molecular chemist" before. Perhaps, Pauling seemed to suggest, he was in a field of his own. But designations didn't matter to Noyes; he wanted Pauling. Physicists wanted to discover the laws underlying atomic reality; Pauling wanted to use those laws to make chemistry more rational, more mathematical. It was the same dream that had driven Ostwald and then Noyes: chemistry illuminated by the light of physics. Only now the physics had fundamentally changed. And Pauling would bring back the new torch.

In the late spring of 1927, Noyes wrote Pauling, offering him a position at Caltech with an unusual title that reflected his hybrid interests: assistant professor of theoretical chemistry and mathematical physics.

—✐✐✐—

A few weeks after Pauling learned he had gotten the extension of his Guggenheim, he and Ava Helen were in Copenhagen at Niels Bohr's institute, the epicenter of the quantum revolution. It was already a place of legend. People talked about *Der Kopenhagener Geist* (the spirit of Copenhagen) that permeated Bohr's institute: a spirit of cooperation, collaboration, and friendship, of endless talks in which ideas from the new physics were teased out as far as they could go. Pauling had come without a formal invitation after hearing from a colleague that one didn't arrange to attend Bohr's institute; one simply appeared and was enlightened. It turned out to be bad advice. Pauling found that it was almost impossible to see the great man; Bohr's mind was on larger questions.

During the spring and summer of 1927 quantum mechanics was entering a new phase. Late in the previous year Schrödinger and the English prodigy Paul Dirac had begun healing the rift between wave and matrix mechanics by showing that the two systems were mathematically equivalent, that they gave the same answers to the same questions. But what physical reality lay behind the numbers? After a marathon meeting with Bohr, Schrödinger gave up the idea that his wave equation described an actual electron "smear," as he had originally proposed. The work of Born and others indicated that instead of an actual wave, his equation described not a physically apprehensible "thing" but a statistical probability, the mathematical likelihood of finding an electron within a certain area.

Schrödinger and Heisenberg had succeeded not in describing the atom but in trapping it with numbers, taming it so that its behavior could be predicted. This predictive ability was powerful and vitally important. With stunning swiftness, it became clear to open-minded physicists that the new quantum mechanics worked, that it pointed the way to new findings in cases where the old system had simply failed. But Heisenberg and Schrödinger would continue to argue over the reality behind the numbers.

For instance, there was the problem of how an electron could simultaneously be both a wave and a particle. After months of hammering away at the question, after countless mind-numbing discussions with Schrödinger and especially Heisenberg, Bohr decided that both descriptions had to be right. Atomic reality was (at least) two-faced: The electron you found depended on how you chose to observe it. Both wave and particle descriptions were correct, and both were needed. They were complementary. The refinement of this "Copenhagen interpretation" of quantum physics took up much of Bohr's time during the period Pauling was in Denmark.

That description also seemed to beg the question. What was an electron? It was becoming clear that no one could describe it in a way that could be visualized. The wave/particle duality and quantum jumps were unlike anything anyone had ever experienced; at the atomic level, things behaved in ways deemed impossible at the level of the senses. After endless discussions with Bohr, Heisenberg would go for long walks alone and wonder: Can nature possibly be as absurd as it seems to us in these atomic experiments?

Physics was now merging into philosophy, a process given popular impetus when Heisenberg posited his "uncertainty principle" in March 1927. In a fairly straightforward extension of his matrix ideas, Heisenberg showed that it was impossible for an observer to know both the precise position and velocity of an electron. All you could know for certain was the statistical likelihood of an electron being in a certain area, with no guarantee it would actually be there. His thoughts were practical at their core: Anyone trying to observe an electron would require some sort of light energy to do it, and even the smallest packet of light would knock the electron around, affecting the observation. We could never be certain in looking at electrons. We had reached, at the level of the atom, the limits of observability.

This raised larger questions about the understanding of nature. If what Heisenberg was saying was true, then not only had we reached the limits of precise observation, but cause and effect, as it was then conceived, didn't hold within the atom: You couldn't say an electron definitely caused something if you could only say it was "probably" somewhere in the vicinity. Physics up to this time had been built upon determinism. If the sizes, velocities, and angle of collision of two billiard balls were known, a prediction could be made about what would happen after they hit. In the same way, according to Newton's classical physics, the current positions and velocities of the particles in the universe would determine, through cause and effect, the future positions and velocities of every particle. The future was held in the present. But Heisenberg's uncertainty principle said you couldn't predict the future of a single electron, much less the universe.

Heisenberg had given Pauling proof sheets of his paper on the uncertainty principle, and Pauling was aware that the idea was spurring a lot of speculation about philosophical questions such as predestination. But to Pauling the pragmatist, these discussions were pointless. "Even if this were a classical world, it would be impossible for us to determine the positions and momenta of all the particles of the universe by experiment," Pauling pointed out in a later interview. "Even if we did know all of them, how would we carry out the computations? We can't even discuss in detail a system involving, say, 10^{20} particles or 10^{10}. I think it is meaningless to argue about determination versus free will, quite independent of the uncertainty principle." Any question that did not lead to a real world experiment or observation was not important to Pauling. If it had no operational significance, "it becomes just a matter of semantics," he said. As a result, "I have never been bothered by the detailed or penetrating discussions about interpretation of quantum mechanics."

He wasn't interested in the greater questions that concerned Bohr, and he wasn't having much success in Copenhagen with his own calculations on the chemical bond. Early in 1927 a young Danish physicist, Øyvind Burrau, had published what appeared to be a successful application of Schrödinger's wave equation to the simplest possible molecule: the hydrogen molecule-ion, two hydrogen nuclei bound by a single electron. Burrau's results showed that the electron distribution tended to concentrate between the two nuclei, the electron's attraction for the nuclei balancing their repulsion. It was the first crack in the door, an indication that the wave equation could help solve the chemical bond, and Pauling worked to extend Burrau's ideas to the next step, the hydrogen molecule with two electrons and two nuclei. But he got nowhere. The wave equation was hard enough to use in describing electrons in individual atoms, as Pauling had done in his paper on the sizes of ions. Going to the next step of complexity was much more of a challenge. You had to consider and calculate the repulsion of the two nuclei, the attraction of each electron for each of the nuclei, the repulsion of the electrons by each other; it quickly became a mathematical impossibility. Simplifications and assumptions about the form of the molecules had to be made. Heisenberg and Dirac had tackled the problem without success. And during the time he was in Copenhagen, Pauling was frustrated as well.

He did, however, make a valuable contact among the crowd of researchers flocking around Bohr: Samuel Goudsmit, one of the young codiscoverers of electron spin, who was just finishing his doctoral thesis. Pauling hit it off with "Sem," as everyone called him. Goudsmit was interested in explaining the fine structure of spectra in quantum-mechanical terms, and Pauling helped him with some theoretical calculations. Before long Pauling was suggesting that he help translate Goudsmit's doctoral thesis into English.

Finally, after several weeks in Copenhagen, Pauling was summoned to Bohr's office, along with Goudsmit. Bohr had heard they were doing calculations together, and he asked them to describe their work. As the two young men talked, he sat, impassive, his heavy eyelids drooping, occasionally saying, "Yes. Yes." When they were finished, he said, "Very well." They were dismissed. It was the only time Pauling saw Bohr during his month's stay.

On their way to see Schrödinger in Zurich, the Paulings spent a few days at Max Born's institute in Göttingen, the dominion of rigorous mathematics, the birthplace of matrix mechanics, the spiritual home of so many young theorists—Heisenberg, Pauli, Dirac, and Jordan were all in their twenties—that it became the storied land of *Knabenphysik* (boy physics). It was also a magnet for young Americans; more Guggenheim fellows in the sciences during this period ended up in Göttingen than anywhere else. Pauling was able to meet many of the major players in the quantum revolution: Dirac, Heisenberg, Jordan, and briefly, Born himself. He also ran across and spent quite a bit of time talking to a nervous, thin young research fellow from Harvard who was in Göttingen working on his doctorate, J. Robert Oppenheimer.

Pauling hoped that Schrödinger would be more accessible than Bohr, but he was disappointed. Over the course of the preceding year, wave mechanics had proved so powerful in approaching all sorts of problems that everyone was trying to learn about it. Schrödinger was asked to give lectures all over Europe, and in the spring of 1927 he toured America, including a pleasurable stop at Caltech, with side trips arranged by Paul Epstein to Hollywood and the beach at Santa Monica. While he enjoyed much of the United States, he generally disliked Americans, whom he viewed as unsophisticated, acquisitive, and pushy. All the Statue of Liberty needed, he said, was a wristwatch below the torch to make the picture complete, and Southern California would have been much improved it if had been left to the Indians and Spaniards. Worst of all was the Prohibition-caused difficulty in getting a glass of beer or wine. Soon after Pauling arrived in Zurich for the summer semester, Schrödinger was offered the most prestigious position in German science, the Berlin chair in theoretical physics being vacated by Max Planck. He had become, at age thirty-nine, an overnight scientific superstar, and he was enjoying playing the part. It included little time for visiting Americans.

By August, Pauling was feeling frustrated. "I have rather regretted the nearly two months spent here," he wrote a colleague, "for I have been unable to get in touch with Schrödinger. I saw him about once a week, at a seminar. I tried very hard to find out what he is doing, and I offered to make any calculation interesting him since he was not interested in my work; but without success. . . . As a result of two months here, I have no news regarding new developments in physics to give you."

───

But there was exciting news in chemistry. Immediately upon arriving in Zurich, Pauling found out that two young Germans, Walter Heitler and Fritz London, had found a way to apply wave mechanics to the electron-pair bond in the hydrogen molecule.

Pauling and Ava Helen had been friendly with Heitler and London while in Munich, where the four of them had celebrated one night at the Neue Börse restaurant, toasting Heitler's new doctoral degree with champagne. They had all talked about the chemical bond then, but none of them had an answer. The breakthrough happened for Heitler and London a few months later, when they went to Switzerland to work as postdoctoral fellows with Schrödinger.

When Pauling got to Zurich, he looked them up, and they began talking. The key to Heitler and London's success, he learned, was an idea developed by Heisenberg the year before, which he called electron exchange, or "resonance." The basic idea was that under the right circumstances electrons could switch places with one another very rapidly; Heisenberg had used it to explain some odd spectral lines in helium. Heitler and London adapted the concept to the chemical bond this way: They imagined two identical hydrogen atoms, each with its own electron, approaching each other. As they neared, the chances would increase that an electron from one could find itself attracted to the nucleus of the other. At a certain point, an electron would jump to the new atom, and an electron exchange would begin taking place billions of times every second. In a sense, the electrons would be unable to tell which nucleus was their own. It was this interchange, Heitler and London found, that provided the energy to draw the two atoms together. Their calculations indicated that the electron density tended to concentrate in the area between the nuclei, thus lessening the electrostatic repulsion between the two positively charged cores. At a certain point, that positive-positive repulsion would balance the energy of the electron exchange, setting up a chemical bond with a definite length.

This idea of an electron exchange was a new concept in chemistry—before Heisenberg there had been nothing like it in physics, either—but it seemed to work. The calculations based on the system very roughly corresponded to the experimental values of several technical constants for the hydrogen molecule, and the Heitler-London model made sense in other ways as well. Pauli's exclusion principle stated that two electrons could share the same orbit only if they had opposite spin, a state that Heitler and London found was necessary for their bond to occur in the hydrogen molecule. Paired electrons forming the cement between atoms: This was Lewis's shared electron bond, now given a strong quantum-mechanical foundation, a mathematical explanation. Again the new physics had pointed the way to a strange new reality.

Pauling was excited when he saw Heitler and London's results, and he spent most of his time in Zurich trying to extend their concepts.

While he talked a great deal with Heitler and London, typically he worked on his calculations alone. He didn't produce a paper during that period. But by the time he set sail on the first of September to return to America, he was committed to applying Heitler and London's resonance interpretation of chemical bonding to all types of questions about chemical structure. It would form the basis of much of his work for the next decade.

The Bond

Tetrahedra

Caltech was booming when Pauling returned. Under Robert Millikan's aggressive leadership, the number of students had grown to six hundred by the fall of 1927, including one hundred graduate students. The Caltech physics department now published more papers per year than any group in the nation. George Ellery Hale was negotiating a stupendous grant to build the world's biggest telescope atop Mount Wilson. A department of geology had been started, and an aeronautics laboratory was on the drawing board. Most importantly, word had just been released that the nation's most renowned geneticist, Thomas Hunt Morgan, was coming to start a biology division. Biology, along with physics and chemistry, would complete the triumvirate of sciences at Caltech, and Morgan, the man who had narrowed the site of the gene down to individual chromosomes—and in doing so made his experimental model, the fruit fly, famous—was the perfect leader. He was a top player, well connected and well funded, and had been lured from Columbia University in typical Caltech style, with promises of his own laboratory building and a substantial research endowment. His arrival in 1928 immediately made Caltech a national force in biology.

Pauling, Ava Helen, and Linus junior moved into a small rental house at 320 South Wilson Street, two blocks from the campus, and Pauling readied himself for his first official year as a professor. But he would not carry the grand title of assistant professor of theoretical chemistry and mathematical physics that Noyes had written him about in Munich. The "mathematical physics" part had been dropped. "I don't know what happened with the physics," Pauling remembered. "Whether Millikan objected to my having a joint appointment or whether Noyes . . . may have decided that he didn't want me to be associated with the physics department in any way, that perhaps I would shift. I didn't care." The title he ended up with, assistant professor of theoretical chemistry, was, perhaps not coincidentally, the same Noyes had had for years at MIT.

Pauling was put in charge of the Caltech x-ray laboratory, which Roscoe Dickinson had abandoned to move on to other studies. His first office was a desk in the corner of the x-ray lab, from which he could directly oversee the activities of his first official graduate student, a diligent young chemist fresh from Texas named J. Holmes Sturdivant. Pauling began preparing for his first course as an assistant professor—"An Introduction to Wave Mechanics with Chemical Applications"—by writing out 250 pages of notes in longhand. He would later turn them into a book on the subject.

The rest of his energy went to his own scientific work. As always, his mind ranged over several problems at once. Before leaving Europe, Pauling had made arrangements with Samuel Goudsmit to translate and help expand his Dutch doctoral thesis into a book on spectroscopy. The two young theorists completed the book by correspondence, with Goudsmit writing some chapters; Pauling wrote others and handled the final editing. It was published in 1930 as *The Structure of Line Spectra,* Pauling's first book but one that already carried the stamp of his unquenchable self-confidence: At least one reviewer complained that the authors' assured tone gave the impression that there was little more to be learned about line spectroscopy. Other reviews were positive, and the book became a moderate success.

But the book with Goudsmit was also a work of pure physics, which raised questions about Pauling's position at Caltech. After it was published, Pauling taught a course based on the book in the chemistry department, but it was offered only once before Noyes shut it down. He told Pauling that Millikan had complained about physics courses being taught in the wrong division, but Pauling later guessed that Noyes made the decision on his own in order to keep him focused on chemistry.

The incident underlined a problem for Noyes. Pauling was interested in many things, perhaps too many things, including theoretical physics. That was fine as far as it went—Noyes had, after all, sent him to Europe specifically to learn the new physics—but the plan now was that Pauling apply his lessons to chemistry rather than leap into physics.

For a few months after returning from Europe, Pauling was tempted to focus on pure theoretical physics. Quantum mechanics was fascinating, and Sommerfeld had given him the tools he needed to do well in the field, especially in America, where quantum physicists were hard to find. On the other hand, he had seen that the Heisenbergs and Paulis and Diracs, with their dazzling mathematics and philosophical insights, were well ahead of him in making major discoveries. Pauling was, in fact, for perhaps the only time in his life, intimidated by the competition.

He wanted to accomplish something significant, and the place to do that, he realized, was in the zone between the new physics and chemistry. If there were few quantum physicists around, the number of American researchers who could apply quantum mechanics to chemistry in the late 1920s could be counted on one hand, and most of them were not chemists but physicists with an interest in chemistry. Pauling was unique in combining both deep mathematical and physical knowledge with the training and worldview of a chemist. Quantum mechanics had opened up a new vista here, promising a vast new field of chemical applications, especially in relation to the question of the chemical bond. It was wide open and unexplored, a place to discover something big, to make a name. "I thought there was a possibility of doing something better, but I didn't know what it was that was needed to be done," Pauling remembered. "I had the feeling that if I worked in this field I probably would find something, make some discovery, and the probability was high enough to justify my working in the field." Within a few months of returning to Caltech, Pauling wrote a colleague, "I am sure that I shan't be led astray by the will-o'-the-wisp of theoretical physics." Chemistry would be his field, but a new type of chemistry, one transformed by the new physics.

~~~

Once focused, Pauling's work proceeded rapidly. On the chemical-bond question, for instance, he thought there was still much left to do. Heitler and London's resonance breakthrough with the hydrogen molecule was just a first step, to Pauling's mind, and their attempts with more complex molecules left much to be desired. These were physicists, after all, not chemists, so they could not be expected to understand how their exchange-energy concept related to the huge cornucopia of chemical phenomena, most of which they knew nothing about. Even though they had beaten Pauling to the first successful quantum-mechanical attack on the chemical bond, there was still much he could do to expand and rework their original insight.

One of the first things he did was to prepare a long article for *Chemical Reviews* in which he introduced the Heitler-London chemical-bond work and added some new insights of his own into its application to the one-electron hydrogen molecule-ion. This was the first that most chemists had ever seen of the quantum mechanical approach to their field, and it marked Pauling's entrance onto the American scientific stage in his new role of quantum-chemist.

Then he made a daring leap. In the spring of 1928 he wrote a brief note to the *Proceedings of the National Academy of Sciences* in which he outlined what he called Heitler and London's "simple theory" of the chemical bond and noted that it was "in simple cases entirely equivalent to G. N. Lewis's successful theory of the shared electron pair." Nothing new there. But at the end, in a single paragraph, he announced a significant advance. His calculations, he said, showed that quantum mechanics could explain the tetrahedral binding of carbon.

This woke readers up. Carbon was a much-studied element, the linchpin of all of organic chemistry. Strings of carbon atoms formed the backbone of proteins, fats, and starches—the major constituents of living systems. Carbo chemistry was the chemistry of life.

But physicists and chemists could not agree on carbon's electronic structure. It was known that each carbon atom carried a total of six electrons, the first two of which had nothing to do with forming bonds, since they paired to re-create the two-electron inner-electron structure of helium. The remaining four electrons should be, in theory, at the next energy level, in the so-called second shell of the atom. Chemists knew that carbon offered four bonds to other atoms and that in nature these were almost always the same size and strength and oriented to the corners of a three-sided pyramid, or tetrahedron.

But physicists said this should not happen. The most recent spectroscopic studies showed that carbon's four binding electrons existed in two different energy levels, or subshells. The two lower-level electrons should pair with each other, leaving only two to make bonds with other atoms. Carbon, the physicists said, should have a valence of two.

And there were rare cases where it did: carbon monoxide, for instance, where the carbon is double-bonded to a single oxygen atom.

Reconciling the physicists' carbon and the chemists' was a major challenge, and Pauling was determined to meet it. The physicists' spectroscopic evidence was undeniable, as was the chemists' tetrahedron. Both groups somehow had to be right.

In his 1928 note, Pauling proposed an explanation based on Heitler and London's exchange energy. Each time a new bond was created, new exchange energy was involved. The exchange energy resulting from forming four tetrahedral bonds, he wrote, was sufficient to break carbon's four binding electrons out of the physicists' subshells and allow them to assume new forms.

This was an exciting idea, but one that would have to be backed up with considerable mathematics. Pauling didn't present any in his note, however, writing that "the detailed account of the material mentioned in this note will be submitted for publication in the *Journal of the American Chemical Society*." He then sent a proof copy of his note to Lewis with a letter saying: "It pleases me very much that in the new atomic model the salient features of the Lewis atom have been reproduced as much as those of the Bohr atom."

Nearly three years would pass before Pauling's "detailed account" appeared. In 1928 he had worked out enough convoluted calculations to convince himself, at least preliminarily, that his idea was right, but "it was so complicated that I thought people won't believe it," he said. "And perhaps I don't believe it, either. . . . Anybody could see that quantum mechanics must lead to the tetrahedral carbon atom, because we have it. But the equations were so complicated that I never could be sure that I could present the arguments in such a way that they would be convincing to anybody."

Today, with computers to run the equations, precise answers are possible. But in 1930, completely solving the equations for virtually any molecular system was impossible. Pauling, like every theoretician working to apply wave mechanics to complex systems, was forced to find shortcuts, various assumptions and approximations, schemes for further simplifying the mathematics.

The same mathematical hurdle was stalling London and others interested in the field. The difference with Pauling was that he was confident enough that the mathematics would fall into place to publish his preliminary thought, thus ensuring scientific priority. He then set his graduate student, Sturdivant, an able mathematician in his own right, to work on the tetrahedral-wave-function problem. When Sturdivant got nowhere after weeks of work, Pauling, now on to other problems, set the carbon problem aside.

Pauling's Rules

Caltech continued to lure the world's foremost theoretical physicists to California for visits, and in the late 1920s, Pauling helped to welcome Heisenberg, Sommerfeld, and Dirac. He maintained a strong interest in their work and turned out a few papers of his own on physics-oriented topics, such as the momentum distribution of electrons and the influence on them of light and x-rays.

He spent most of his time, however, solving molecular structures using x-ray crystallography, and here he found himself stymied. If a structure in which he was interested involved more than a few atoms, it was almost impossible to solve. The problem was again in part mathematics, this time the terrific calculations needed to translate into a three-dimensional structure the patterns that diffracted x-rays sprayed on a photographic plate. The more atoms involved in the molecule, the more complex the pattern and the more structures were theoretically possible. Each added atom greatly increased the difficulty.

But there was also a more fundamental problem: the way x-ray crystallographers approached their work. In order to be certain of their results, researchers—nearly always physicists in the 1920s—usually started from the supposition that any arrangement of atoms that matched the compound's chemical formula should be considered as a structural possibility. Finding the correct one was a process of eliminating those that did not strictly fit the x-ray and density data. This rigorous method gave a firm answer—you could be certain you had the right structure because you had eliminated, one by one, all other alternatives—but it was also something like trying to find a needle in a haystack by picking up each stalk of hay, holding it next to a picture of a needle, and tossing it aside if it did not match. The more complex the crystal, the bigger the haystack.

As the targets of x-ray crystallographers became larger, this work became harder, more time-consuming and repetitious, requiring the employment of teams of "human computers" just to do the needed mathematical work. It was not to Pauling's taste, and he began looking for shortcuts. He had always read widely and critically; now he began to synthesize what he knew about chemistry and x-ray crystallography into a structural worldview, a sense of how atoms preferred to fit together. If he was reading an article on a crystal structure and the conclusion seemed reasonable, he added it to his mental library. But if something sounded wrong—bond angles awry or atoms misplaced—Pauling would fine-comb the work, sometimes refiguring structures from published x-ray photos, sometimes shooting and analyzing new ones. He often found that whatever seemed wrong to him was, in fact, a mistake. But occasionally, and more excitingly, the thing that struck him as wrong might actually prove to be correct. Then it was his worldview that would have to change to incorporate the new information. This was how he learned. Over the years his structural sense would become uncanny; he would be able to come up with reasonable structures and discard unreasonable ones almost instantly. Observers would later call this Pauling's "chemical intuition." The phrase is not quite right, though; it smacks too much of the emotional, the irrational. Pauling's ability was entirely rational, based on thousands of hours of careful reading, mentally sorting and filing tens of thousands of chemical facts.

This deep understanding of chemical structures allowed Pauling to break away from the old ways of doing x-ray crystallography. "My attitude was, why shouldn't I use the understanding that I have developed of the nature of crystals in inorganic substances to proceed to *predict* their structures?" he asked. The physicists doing x-ray crystallography might have to consider each structure with the right number of atoms as a possibility because they did not know any better. Pauling, however, knew that most hypothetical structures would be unlikely for one reason or another on chemical grounds. The atoms would prefer to fit in a more limited number of ways. Before starting, he could eliminate most of the chaff and get down to a small number of most likely candidates.

Prediction was the way to break out of the crystallographer's conundrum. But if accurate prediction was to be useful to other researchers, it required rules, sets of principles that could be applied to a number of cases to demonstrate why certain structures were likely or unlikely. By the late 1920s, Pauling knew that the same basic structural patterns were often repeated in different crystals. The repeated patterns happened for a reason; they had to be governed by rules. If he could find the rules, he could predict the structures of unknown crystals.

In his laboratory in Manchester, England, the British physicist William Lawrence "Willie" Bragg was thinking along the same lines.

Bragg was a complex fellow. Shy and old-fashioned, gentlemanly in the Victorian manner, fond of birds and gardening, Bragg seemed in many ways more like a country squire than a prominent scientist. Even "his outward appearance and behavior were rather like those of a prosperous farmer, dressed not quite in the latest fashion," a colleague noted.

He was also one of the brightest physicists in England and, beneath the outward reserve, gifted with a tough competitive streak. And he was under a great deal of pressure. He had achieved international fame early, perhaps too early, when he and his father, also known as William, codeveloped the science of x-ray crystallography after Laue's initial discovery. The Bragg equation for the diffraction of x-rays by a crystal was the foundation upon which the science was built; the Braggs' textbook was the bible of the field. The work with his father had earned Willie Bragg a Nobel Prize at age twenty-five, making him the youngest man ever to win one. A rush of international fame and directorship of the prestigious Manchester laboratories followed.

He did not much like administration, but he did enjoy research. Bragg was gifted with an ability to cut away extraneous details and get to the heart of a scientific problem, and he was working on a big one. In the late 1920s, Bragg's interest centered around a large and important family of minerals called the silicates, complex ionic crystals formed of silicon, oxygen, and various metal atoms. Silicates were among the most common minerals on earth—the family included everything from talc to topaz—and also the most complex. Solving their various structures would be a coup for any crystallographer. Bragg, like Pauling, was working on shortcuts and was very proud of an approach he developed in which he viewed silicate structures in terms of packing together spheres of different-sized ions, rather like packing together marbles in a jar. Bragg's work showed that ionic crystals in general kept their atoms as close together as possible, "close packing," he called it. In his scheme, the way in which larger ions like oxygen packed next to each other would determine the crystal's basic structure, and the smaller ones would tuck into the spaces in between. Using this approach, he was, he believed, on the way to making sense of all silicate structures.

As Pauling put it, "Bragg thought that that was his field." But he was in for a rude awakening. Pauling, too, was interested in silicates and intended to give Bragg some competition. Although the English researcher was only eleven years older, Pauling considered Bragg "a member of the older generation of scientists, who had blazed a trail that I was attempting to follow." And while Bragg's close-packing scheme was a good start, there were other approaches Pauling thought could bring one closer to a solution.

Like Bragg, Pauling thought of the ions in these types of crystals as spheres of distinct sizes, and he knew the sizes inside and out—after all, it had been Pauling who first developed a quantum-mechanics approach to determining ionic radii. But they differed in how they thought these spheres behaved. Whereas Bragg worked from the idea that ionic crystals had no molecular-type structure within them—he saw them instead as extended patterns of separate ions, of the sort he and his father had found in table salt—Pauling viewed silicates in terms of basic units. Silicon, for instance, behaved much like carbon; it, too, formed a tetrahedron when binding to four oxygens. Bragg had shown that oxygens for their part often packed together in ionic crystals six at a time to form an octahedron. Tetrahedra and octahedra: Pauling started with these basic building-block shapes.

In puzzling this over, Pauling made a breakthrough. He ingeniously distilled what he knew about quantum mechanics, ionic sizes, published crystal structures, and the dictates of chemistry into a set of simple rules indicating which joining patterns were most likely. The most important of these, called the electrostatic valence rule, used what was known about one element's binding capacity for others, its valency, as the basis for a formula for determining how many blocks would likely meet at a given corner. A key was the realization that in these minerals a central element's valency could be distributed in fractions to ions of opposite sign. Other rules dealt with the sharing of faces and edges. Taking all of these rules together, and considering as well Bragg's ideas about close-packing, Pauling was able to outline a relatively simple step-by-step procedure for eliminating scores of unlikely crystal structures and predicting the most likely ones.

He first published his rules in late 1928 as a contribution to a set of papers written in honor of Sommerfeld's sixtieth birthday, a fitting tribute to the man who had taught him to use whatever was needed to get to a good solution. The next year, he put them forward in more detail in the *JACS*. They were soon known widely among crystallographers as "Pauling's rules." And they worked. In his first papers, Pauling used his rules to solve the structure of two complex silicate crystals, brookite and topaz. His rules helped extend the reach of x-ray crystal-lography to tougher structures than had previously been solvable.

But more than his rules were involved. In his silicate work, Pauling developed an entire approach to solving difficult x-ray crystallography patterns, a general method that he would use time and again over the next decades. It started by using known chemical principles to set up a set of structural rules. If the rules were stringent enough, many theo-retical structures could be eliminated on the basis of chemical consid-erations alone, leaving only a few of the most plausible remaining. Pauling would then make models of those few to decide which was best. The models allowed him to view the structures in three dimen-sions, to see what worked and what did not, to fiddle and twist until things lined up right. If the models showed that certain structures packed their atoms too tightly or too loosely to seem reasonable, they, too, could be eliminated. Finally, just one would emerge as most likely. The properties of this hypothetical structure, including the x-ray dif-fraction pattern it would likely produce, could then be compared to those of the actual substance. If they matched, the structure was as-sumed to be correct.

Mustering everything he knew about chemistry and physics, and adding to it his new interest in model building, Pauling was able to leap to a solution where others were left mired in a swamp of confusing x-ray data. A few years later, Pauling was describing his approach to an acquaintance, Karl Darrow, who told him that it already had a name: the stochastic method. Darrow referred Pauling to a 1909 chem-istry text in which the author talked about the long-disused Greek term that could be translated as "to divine the truth by conjecture." In a simple way, the stochastic approach could be seen as nothing more than an educated guess, a hypothesis like any other scientific hypo-thesis. Anybody could guess at a molecular structure, and while a comparison of the molecule's properties to those calculated for the hypothetical structure might eliminate the guessed-at structure as wrong, it was difficult to say that the hypothetical structure was rigor-ously correct because the comparison between the guess and reality would be based almost invariably on limited experimental data. But the way Pauling used it, the stochastic method was not a simple guessing game. You had to know enough about chemistry and crystallography to pare away all but a single structure. As he put it, "Agreement on a limited number of points cannot be accepted as verification of the hypothesis. In order for the stochastic method to be significant the principles used in formulating the hypothesis must be restrictive enough to make the hypothesis itself essentially unique; in other words, an investigator who makes use of this method should be allowed one guess."

Pauling had broken through a very complex problem using his stochastic method, and he would continue to employ it against even tougher puzzles during the next three decades. Sometimes his one guess would be wrong; far more often he would be right. This ability to "divine the truth by conjecture" would allow him to vault over his competition in solving the thorniest chemical problems. Eventually, it would bring him his greatest triumphs and earn him the reputation of a person who could almost magically dream up solutions where others had failed. But it was all the result of very hard work, deep chemical knowledge, and a willingness, a daring, to make that one guess.

———— *m* ————

Before the publication of his rules for solving complex ionic crystals, Pauling had been known as a promising young crystallographer. Afterward, he was propelled into the first rank. Lawrence Bragg, for one, was stunned when he read Pauling's work. This young American had appeared out of nowhere and beaten him at his own game. Some of the ideas Pauling put forward were those Bragg had been using in his own attack on silicates, but much was new. The electrostatic valence rule especially was clear and very useful; years later Bragg would generously call it "the cardinal principle of mineral chemistry."

Pauling employed his rules with great success. In 1929 and 1930 he worked out the structure of mica, a silicate whose tendency to split into thin, flexible, transparent sheets Pauling discovered was due to a layered crystal structure with strong bonds in two directions and weak bonds in the third. He then compared mica to silicates that, while similar in chemical makeup, differed greatly in form. Talc, he found, also had a layered structure, but one that was held together so weakly in two directions that it crumbled instead of split. Another group of silicates called zeolites interested researchers because of their ability to absorb some gases, including water vapor, but not others. Pauling discovered that zeolites were honeycombed with passages so tiny that they formed molecular sieves, letting in only molecules small enough to squeeze through and keeping out others.

A Much-Wanted Man

Pauling's rules were important, but the young man was hungry for more. He read everything in physics and chemistry, attended every seminar given in those fields and biology as well, was interested in everything and alive to any problems he might solve. In 1930 he turned back toward physics, clearing up a puzzle that had been posed by researchers at Berkeley. In theory, heat capacity—the amount of energy needed to raise the temperature of an object—should decline to nothing for substances at absolute zero. But the Berkeley group was surprised to find that their experimental work with molecular hydrogen pointed to a significantly higher value. Pauling explained it: All you have to do, he said in a paper in the *Physical Review,* was assume that hydrogen molecules could rotate while bound into crystals. His quantum-mechanical demonstration of the point was an advance not only in the study of the heat capacity of solids but also helped to explain things like the transition from one crystalline form to another. *Scientific American* spotlighted the work as one of two "standout" discoveries in fundamental chemistry for 1930. The other for that year was Pauling's and Bragg's general solution of the structure of silicates.

Pauling's mastery of quantum mechanics and his application of it to chemistry were now becoming well known in research circles, and job offers began coming in. During the late 1920s the best American universities were snapping up young researchers who knew the new physics, preferably one of the few U.S. students who had learned it on foreign fellowships, like Pauling, John Slater, Ed Condon, John Van Vleck, or Robert Mulliken, or, failing that, immigrant Europeans such as Samuel Goudsmit. Pauling, along with a dozen or so of his quantum-literate peers, suddenly found himself much wanted.

G. N. Lewis told Pauling that he had visited Caltech in 1928—a special occasion, for he rarely traveled—intending to offer Pauling a job at Berkeley. He was waylaid by Noyes, however, who "forbade him to do so." Noyes did grant Pauling one term's leave in the spring of 1929 to serve as a visiting professor at Berkeley, and while there, Pauling received an even greater honor, a call to Harvard. The great school's chemistry department was in the midst of being restructured after the death of its longtime leader, the first American to win the Nobel Prize in chemistry, Theodore Richards. The Richards chair had been offered to both Lewis and Richard Tolman, but both had decided against going east. By the time the offer reached Pauling, the job had been downsized to an associate professorship without mention of the chair. Still, it was enticing. Harvard was the oldest, most prestigious, best-endowed university in America; its physics and chemistry departments were renowned. "The prospect of becoming associated with the Chemistry Division of Harvard University appeals to me very much," Pauling quickly wrote back. However, his teaching duties prevented his coming east for a visit until at least May, he wrote, asking for a delay.

Pauling had seen enough of academia to know how the promotion game worked. Tolman, for instance, had leveraged his Harvard offer into thousands of dollars in research moneys, support for a faculty member he wanted to hire, and a promise that he would not have to take part in publicity activities. Pauling wrote Noyes and asked him frankly what he could expect in the way of a Caltech counteroffer. Noyes did not want to lose Pauling, either. At Noyes's and Millikan's urging, the Caltech executive council in March awarded Pauling a promotion the next fall to associate professor (after only two years as an assistant professor), substantial pay raises over the coming two years, support for a laboratory assistant, two more graduate students, and travel money for a European trip.

But Harvard was serious. There was talk of building new courses in crystal structure and chemical physics around Pauling, even creating a new department devoted to the young researcher's brand of what was now being called "quantum chemistry." Pauling remembered (although no corroborating documents seem to exist) that the Harvard offer was eventually raised to full professorship, successor to the Richards chair.

So Pauling visited, arriving in Cambridge for a week in early May. He was treated royally, staying in the home of organic chemist James Bryant Conant (who was soon to become president of Harvard), touring the new chemical laboratories, presenting seminars, and attending receptions. He was twenty-eight years old and flattered by the attention, but he also found things—some big, some little—he did not like. Whereas Caltech was becoming famous for allowing researchers a free hand to develop their own unique approaches to science, at Harvard, Pauling found, subdisciplines such as organic chemistry and physical chemistry had ossified into separate fiefdoms. There was a sense of backbiting and politicking and a hoarding of talent he did not like. A product of the egalitarian American West, Pauling also received his first taste of eastern class snobbery. "Here was a society where there were a lot of important people who were important just because of birth. They had money and stature not based on their own abilities," he remembered. "I thought I would be a sort of second-class citizen at Harvard."

Pauling quickly decided against relocating. But before turning the offer down, he used it to get one more thing: the chance to work closely with G. N. Lewis. A few days after he returned from his eastern trip, the Caltech executive council granted Pauling, upon his request, an annual leave of absence of at least one month during the academic year "for the purpose of giving advanced courses of lectures or seminars at the University of California or elsewhere," expandable to a full academic term in alternate years—along with five hundred dollars per year to cover travel costs. The next day, Pauling declined Harvard's offer, then wrote G. N. Lewis, "In deciding to stay at the Institute the prospect of coming occasionally to Berkeley probably had some effect, as had perhaps also your own opinion regarding the matter. At any rate, I have regained my peace of mind."

―――

Pauling was not the only sought-after young professor. Another was J. Robert Oppenheimer, the young American physicist Pauling had met in Munich. In 1928, Millikan talked Oppenheimer into teaching physics for part of the year at Caltech, the remaining time to be spent at Berkeley, much like Pauling's new deal.

Oppenheimer made an immediate impression in Pasadena. Thin, almost frail in appearance, with strikingly large, wide-set eyes and a head of thick, dark hair, he was attractive as well as brilliant. Although raised in New York, he seemed exotically European, Bohemian, poetic, chain-smoking, prone to obscure references to literature and philosophy. His only shortcoming seemed to be that he was a dismal lecturer, mumbling, scattering cigarette ashes, talking over the heads of his listeners, and packing the blackboard with barely readable, cramped equations. Despite that, he soon attracted a devoted band of acolytes, some of the West Coast's finest students, who were able to cut through the obscurity to the essentials of the new physics and who began following him on his annual trek between Pasadena and Berkeley. He was pursued, too, by scandalous rumors that he seemed disinclined to squelch, hints of free love—perhaps homosexuality—and radical politics.

Pauling and Ava Helen found him witty, interesting, and a welcome antidote to the deadly dullness of most of the Caltech faculty.

The same age, young and brilliant, and on the way up, the Paulings and the young physicist quickly became close friends. They shared dinners and jokes, talked about European physics, and gossiped about Caltech and Berkeley professors. Oppenheimer came to Pauling for advice on how to become a better lecturer, and Pauling sought him out to talk about quantum mechanics. The two of them began to consider mounting a joint attack on the chemical bond, with Oppenheimer working on the mathematics and Pauling providing the chemistry background.

Perhaps they became too close too fast. Something began to seem odd to Pauling. Oppenheimer not only adopted some of Pauling's lecturing style; he began wearing an old fedora around campus, much like one that Pauling wore. He started to give Pauling gifts, sometimes little ones, a favorite ring on one occasion, and on another, a magnificently extravagant one, Oppenheimer's large boyhood mineral collection, the crystal treasury that had first spurred Oppenheimer's interest in science, a thousand fine specimens, including some fine calcites in which Pauling took special interest. Then there were the poems Oppenheimer gave Pauling, verse that Pauling found both obscure and troubling, mixing classical allusions with lines about mineralogy, Dante, and pederasty. Pauling had never had a friendship like this.

Neither had Ava Helen. She enjoyed Oppenheimer enormously, took pleasure in talking with him and flirting a little with him, as she did with almost everybody on social occasions. Perhaps she flirted a little more than usual, for Oppenheimer was unusually intriguing. Perhaps he felt her interest went beyond a casual friendship. It all went a little too far, in any case, when Oppenheimer came to her one day in 1929 when Pauling was at work and blurted out a clumsy invitation to join him on a tryst in Mexico. Surprised and flattered, Ava Helen told him no, of course not, she was married and took it seriously. That night, she reported the whole thing to Pauling. "I think she was somewhat pleased with herself as a femme fatale," Pauling said. Seeing how pleased she was, Pauling immediately cut off his relationship with Oppenheimer, ending any chance of collaboration on the chemical bond and leading to a coolness between the two men that would last for the rest of their lives.

Years later, Ava Helen told her husband, "You know, I don't think Oppenheimer was in love with me. I think he was in love with you." After mulling it over, Pauling concluded that she might be right.

The loss of Oppenheimer left Pauling without help in his quest to make mathematical sense of the tetrahedral bonds of carbon. The way to solve the problem—the way all problems involving the application of quantum mechanics to multiatomic systems had to be solved—was to find a set of shortcuts, approximations of terms in the wave equation, that would simplify the mathematics enough to allow progress without distorting the results too much. Pauling tried again and again to batter through the mathematics, but nothing worked.

In late 1929, stymied with the chemical bond problem, he decided to return to Europe, visit old friends in Munich, tour crystallography laboratories and get some advice on the carbon problem. After his application for a Guggenheim Foundation fellowship was turned down, he negotiated the needed travel funds from Caltech.

He and Ava Helen landed in England in May 1930, this time with five-year-old Linus junior in tow, and set off for their first scientific stop, the world's foremost center of x-ray crystallography, the Manchester laboratory of Lawrence Bragg.

Pauling had great hopes for his first meeting with Bragg. Their correspondence had been cordial, even warm, following the publication of Pauling's rules, with Bragg writing, "Your method certainly led you to the ideal structure! . . . I like your way of looking at these coordination compounds very much indeed," and Pauling becoming uncharacteristically buttery: "My wife and I think of you often. Our favorite daydream has for its theme a visit to Manchester."

The dream soured when they arrived. While Bragg was personally accommodating—setting up a flat for them, finding a maid, and arranging care for Linus junior—he was professionally distant. To Pauling's surprise, during the weeks they were there he was never asked to speak with Bragg about scientific matters, nor was he invited to give a seminar on his work, as would have been standard for a visiting professor at Caltech. "I had essentially no contact with Bragg," Pauling said, summing up his Manchester visit as "a disappointment." Although he felt confused and slighted, he tried to shrug it off, blaming it initially on Bragg's busy schedule.

Later, though, he heard from other researchers that Bragg, despite his flattering letters, thought of the young American as an unwelcome poacher in his scientific domain. Bragg had been beaten at what he thought was his own game, and he was chagrined by the experience. "I did not know then, and in fact not for many more years, that Bragg thought of me as a competitor," Pauling later wrote. There was more than that, too. Bragg's personal worries and the weight of his responsibilities were bringing him to a crisis point. A few months after Pauling left, he would suffer a nervous breakdown. If he was distant from Pauling, it was in part because he was involved in a battle with himself.

Whatever the reasons, this first visit would cast a pall over their future relationship. After Pauling returned to America, correspondence between the two fell off rapidly. He and Bragg would spend the rest of their lives as more cordial competitors than close colleagues.

Not every English researcher, however, treated Pauling as Bragg had. His hurt feelings were somewhat assuaged when the mercurial English crystallographer John Desmond Bernal asked him to give a seminar at Cambridge on the rotational motion of molecules in crystals. Then it was on to Germany, where Pauling had a pleasant time visiting friends and catching up on the latest developments. He settled down for almost three months of work in Munich, hacking away at his attempt to ease the use of quantum mechanics to explain the chemical bond, getting some help from Sommerfeld but not succeeding in making any major advances.

He did, however, make an important discovery of a different sort. During a trip to Ludwigshafen, a town a few hours' train ride away from Munich, he visited Hermann Mark, a Viennese chemist Pauling had met on his first trip to Munich. Mark had earned a considerable reputation as a crystallographer—his work included a number of preliminary studies of organic molecules—and he had been snapped up at a young age by the giant Farben chemical firm to head their research into the field of polymers and films, work that included early studies of such commercially promising products as plastics and synthetic rubber. The Farben firm provided Mark with everything he needed, and by the time Pauling visited, his spotless and efficient Ludwigshafen laboratory boasted the most sophisticated x-ray diffraction equipment on the continent. But the high point of the tour had nothing to do with x-rays. While they were looking over the facilities, Mark told Pauling that one of his assistants, a young fellow named Wierl, had developed a way to shoot a beam of electrons through a jet of gas in a vacuum tube. The molecules of gas, Wierl found, appeared to diffract the electrons, scattering them into patterns of concentric rings, the intensities and relative positions of which could be related to the distances between atoms in the molecules. This "electron diffraction" apparatus was an interesting diversion for Mark, but it could only be used on relatively small molecules that could exist as gases at room temperature, while his laboratory's focus was now on giant polymers. Farben had no interest in electron diffraction, either, because, as Mark said, "it wasn't anything that could make money."

Pauling, however, was overwhelmed by what he had heard. For some time he had been looking for a way to examine the structure of individual molecules without having to worry about the sometimes very complicated way in which they arranged themselves into crystals. Mark and Wierl's apparatus, focusing on separate molecules in a gas rather than ones welded together in a larger structure, offered a way to eliminate one level of complexity in calculating structures. Because the exposure time for electron-diffraction photographs was a few tenths of a second—rather than the hours sometimes required for x-ray crystallography—the range of substances available for structural study could be expanded to include volatile substances, especially small organic compounds difficult to hold in crystalline form. "As the impact of the significance of this discovery burst upon me I could not contain my enthusiasm, which I expressed to Mark—my feeling that it should be possible in a rather short time, perhaps ten years, to obtain a great deal of information about bond lengths and bond angles in many different molecules," Pauling said. Mark, a bit surprised by the impression his device seemed to have made, gave Pauling a set of plans for its construction and his blessings for its use.

When he returned to Pasadena in the fall of 1930, Pauling immediately put a new graduate student, Lawrence Brockaway, to work building an electron-diffraction machine. It took two years to get it running properly, but it eventually became a workhorse of Pauling's laboratory and one of the most important scientific tools at Caltech. Over the next twenty-five years, Pauling, and his students and coworkers, would use it to work out the structures of some 225 molecules.

"Euphorious"

Back home in the fall of 1930, Pauling returned to the problem of the tetrahedral carbon atom. His European trip had not helped him make any important steps forward, but he found something when he returned that did.

That year, a young American physicist named John C. Slater had found an important simplification of the Schrödinger wave equation that made it possible to better picture carbon's four binding electrons. Spurred by Slater's work, Pauling picked up his pen and started making calculations again in earnest. In order to match the chemists' reality of a carbon tetrahedron, the physicists' two sets of electron subshells had to be broken and mixed together somehow in a new, equivalent form. The central problem was finding appropriate mathematical approximations of the wave function, shortcuts that would make manageable the equations for combining the subshells' wave functions.

For weeks through the fall, though, none of Pauling's shortcuts worked. Then, on a night in December 1930, sitting at his desk in the study of his home, he tried one more approximation. This time in trying to combine the two subshells' wave functions, he chose to ignore a part of the mathematics called the radial function, a simplification that Slater's papers indicated might work. By stripping away that layer of complexity, Pauling was surprised to find that "the problem became quite a simple one from the mathematical point of view"—at least, for a Sommerfeld-trained quantum physicist.

He could now, with the right coefficients, combine the wave functions of the physicists' two carbon subshells into a mathematical description of a new hybrid form: four equal orbitals oriented precisely at the angles of a tetrahedron. Not only that, but his new hybrid orbitals were more highly directed away from the nucleus, capable therefore of overlapping more with the orbitals of other electrons from other atoms. And here was a basic insight: The greater the overlap of orbitals from two atoms, the more exchange energy was created and the stronger the bond.

He had a sudden rush of energy. From the principles and equations of quantum mechanics he had formed a tetrahedral carbon atom. The calculated angles between bonds were right; the bond lengths looked right; the energy needed to change the electron subshell orbitals into their new shapes was more than accounted for by the energy of the electron exchange.

He kept working for hours. Using the same basic approach, he found he could add more electrons to his calculations and derive the features of more complex molecules. The ability to hybridize the physicists' subshells into new orbitals opened the door to explaining the structure of a number of molecules, such as the bonding pattern found in certain cobalt and platinum compounds. One by one, under Pauling's pen, the physicists' new mechanics was proving out the chemists' ideas. "I was so excited and happy, I think I stayed up all night, making, writing out, solving the equations, which were so simple that I could solve them in a few minutes," he remembered. "Solve one equation, get the answer, then solve another equation about the structure of octahedral complexes such as the ferrocyanide ion in potassium ferrocyanide, or square planar complexes such as in tetrachloroplatinate ion, and various other problems. I just kept getting more and more euphorious as time went by."

Over the next two months he worked hard polishing and expanding his findings into what would become one of the most important papers in the history of chemistry. In it he presented six rules for the shared electron bond. The first three, restatements of Lewis's, Heitler's, London's, and his own earlier work, noted that the electron-pair bond was formed through the interaction of an unpaired electron on each of two atoms; that the spins of the electrons had to be opposed; and that once paired, the two electrons could not take part in additional bonds. His last three rules were new. One stated that the electron-exchange terms for the bond involved only one wave function from each atom; another, that available electrons in the lowest energy levels would form the strongest bonds. Pauling's final rule asserted that of two orbitals in an atom, the one that could overlap the most with an orbital from another atom would form the strongest bond and that the bond would tend to lie in the direction of that concentrated orbital. This allowed the prediction and calculation of bond angles and molecular structures.

Appropriately for his audience of mathematics-shy chemists, Pauling did not present lengthy mathematical proofs of his rules, for, as he wrote in the paper, "even the formal justification of the electron-pair bond in the simplest cases . . . requires a formidable array of symbols and equations." But he outlined the way others could work through the proofs and presented a number of examples of his reasoning at work. From the principles of quantum mechanics he was now able to derive everything from the strengths and arrangements of bonds to a complete theory of magnetism in molecules and complex ions. Using his new system, Pauling was also able to predict new electronic structures and properties for atoms. Quantum mechanics, in other words, did not just confirm what was already known; it pointed the way to new insights. In mid-February 1931, Pauling mailed his work to the *JACS*. He titled the paper, somewhat grandly, "The Nature of the Chemical Bond."

His happiness was compounded by the nearly simultaneous birth of his second son, Peter Jeffress (his middle name honoring Pauling's boyhood friend), on February 10.

———

Then came a shock. On March 1—two weeks after Pauling had submitted his new work but a month before it was published—a paper appeared in the *Physical Review* that covered much of the same ground, including the idea of maximum overlapping of wave functions to create the most stable bonds; a discussion of the relationship between ionic and covalent bonds; a description of how, in compounds where there are several ways of drawing valence bonds, it was likely that "the real situation is . . . a combination of the various possibilities, and on account of resonance the energy is lower than it would otherwise be"; and, most importantly, an explanation of the tetrahedral bond in carbon. The author was the physicist whose work had helped inspire Pauling's breakthrough, John Slater.

It looked at first as though Slater had beaten Pauling. But after reading it several times, Pauling found some important differences in their work. Slater's paper, for one thing, was more descriptive than quantitative; it did not provide a way to get hard numbers for bond strengths and lengths. Pauling dashed off a note to the *Physical Review* calling readers' attention to his *JACS* paper's "very simple but powerful approximate *quantitative* treatment of bond strengths" (Pauling's italics), briefly sketching his six rules, and stressing that it was he who had first put forward the quantum-mechanical approach to tetrahedral binding in 1928. (Slater had not referred to Pauling's earlier paper in his own work.) Pauling then quickly reviewed Slater's work and pointed out ways in which his own ideas went further.

The jockeying for position was delicately done: Pauling and Slater liked each other and respected each other's work. A few weeks before either paper came out, Slater offered Pauling a full professorship at MIT in physics, chemistry, or any combination of the two; in Pauling's "thanks but no thanks" reply (he had, by that time, been promised his own full professorship at Caltech), he wrote Slater, "There is no theoretical physicist whose work interests me more than yours." After reading Pauling's *JACS* paper, Slater wrote, "I am glad things worked out as they did, we both deciding simultaneously to write up our ideas. I haven't had a chance to read yours in detail yet, but it looked at first sight as if we were in good agreement in general." Their agreement was so good, in fact, that before Slater came to speak at a chemical-bond symposium Pauling arranged in Pasadena for the summer of 1931, he cautioned Pauling, " . . . our general points of view seem so similar that we shall want to compare notes before the meeting, to avoid saying the same things."

The two young men had hit upon the same approach to the same problems and would end up sharing credit for what would for a time be awkwardly called the Heitler-London-Slater-Pauling theory of chemical bonding—later, more gracefully, the valence-bond theory—with the consensus that Slater and Pauling had independently reached nearly the same conclusions at almost exactly the same time.

Quantum mechanics, as the physicist Victor Weisskopf later noted, had finally united the two great fields of physics and chemistry. By using the rules of the new physics to explain the bonding of atoms into molecules, Slater and Pauling consummated the marriage. The physicists had been right: Electrons moved in their orbits, they did not sit still on dry goods boxes. But in very important ways, the chemists, especially G. N. Lewis, had also been right. Electron orbitals were concentrated in certain directions, and bonds resulted from sharing electrons. Slater and Pauling showed how the physicists' new quantum principles resulted, logically and with at least approximate mathematical validity, in the molecules seen by chemists.

The importance and novelty of Pauling's work was underscored when his first paper was published just six weeks after being received by the *JACS*, a surprisingly short time compared to the normal waiting period of several months. Pauling was later told that the journal's editor, Arthur Lamb, could not think of anyone qualified to referee it and ran it without review.

To provide support and encouragement for chemists early in their careers, Dr. A. C. Langmuir (the brother of the physical chemist Irving Langmuir) in 1931 began funding an annual prize of one thousand dollars, to be awarded to the best young chemist in the nation. He left the selection to the American Chemical Society (ACS), the field's leading professional association. The first year the Langmuir Prize was offered, former ACS president A. A. Noyes made sure that his favorite young chemist was nominated, and in August 1931, Pauling was thrilled to learn that he had won. The prize recognized Pauling's unusual productivity and promise—at age thirty he had already published more than fifty papers covering a wide range of theoretical and experimental topics—and was a particularly rich award for those days, equivalent to roughly one-quarter of Pauling's annual salary. It also provided the

ACS and Caltech with the opportunity for some publicity. Pauling soon found himself a minor celebrity, interviewed by newspaper writers from Portland to New York, asked for photographs, and featured in magazines. *Scientific American* ran a large picture of him looking serious and scholarly and described him as a "prodigy of American science." Noyes told reporters that Pauling was "the most promising young man with whom I have ever come in contact in my many years of teaching." A. C. Langmuir gushed that he was "a rising star, who may yet win the Nobel Prize." At an evening plenary session of the national ACS meeting in Buffalo, New York, that September, Pauling loped across the stage to receive the award from the society's president to the sound of enthusiastic applause from two thousand of the nation's leading chemists. A cartoon of the occasion, drawn for a meeting newsletter, showed a tousle-haired young Pauling eagerly stretching his hands out toward a bag marked "$1,000." His only regret, he said later, was that Belle had not been there to see him win the award.

Four years after taking his first faculty position, Pauling had risen from promising youngster to national prominence. By the end of 1931, he was a full professor, associate editor of the *JACS,* master of crystallography, cosolver of the great problem of the chemical bond, and winner of the Langmuir Prize. He had always had a core of self-confidence; now it blossomed and filled him. He would rarely doubt himself after 1931. "I might well have become egotistical as a result" of it all, he remembered. "And I think that earlier I had developed a feeling of self-confidence in regard to science. But . . . I think that I just said I shouldn't let this go to my head. I shouldn't think I'm really better than other people even though I do this one thing better than other people."

Resonance

The Avant-Garde

In 1931, Albert Einstein, in Pasadena for several months being wooed for a faculty position at Caltech, sat in on a Linus Pauling seminar. Knowing that he had the world's greatest living scientist in his audience, Pauling worked especially hard to explain at length his new ideas about the application of wave mechanics to the chemical bond. Afterward, Einstein was asked by a reporter what he thought of the young chemist's talk. He shrugged his shoulders and smiled. "It was too complicated for me," he said.

Einstein may simply have been brushing off another newshound, but Pauling's interpretation of the chemical bond was complicated when carried out with any mathematical rigor—certainly too complicated for most chemists. Chemists were not prepared, historically, mathematically, or philosophically, for what Pauling offered them. Chemistry at that time was still a polyglot of separate disciplines and specialties rooted in the last century—organic chemistry, inorganic chemistry, physical chemistry, colloid chemistry, agricultural chemistry—each with its own champions and sets of puzzles to solve. There were ionists and thermodynamicists and now quantum chemists, separate tribes, each with its own traditions, methods, and journals, gathering together only at a few general meetings each year. In the United States only the Noyes-influenced departments at Caltech and Berkeley were able to effectively blur the old disciplinary lines with an emphasis on open communication among professors and a devotion to the general ideas underlying all of chemistry.

Pauling, with his avant-garde ideas about the quantum-based chemical bond, was in 1931 a decade ahead of his time. The vast majority of chemists neither knew what quantum mechanics was nor cared what it meant to their field. Real chemistry, to most of its practitioners, was something done in the laboratory, not on a piece of paper; discoveries were made through the hands-on experience of manipulating compounds and observing their reactions, not by dreaming up mathematical equations. X-ray crystallography was a physicists' tool they might have heard about but never used—Caltech was still one of the few places where the technique was applied in any significant way to chemistry. As for Pauling's emphasis on the importance of molecular structure, well, that was something that organic chemists thought was important, but not many other chemists believed that it played a significant role in chemistry.

What was important was getting into the lab and getting your hands dirty. The laboratory chemists' disdain of theoreticians like Pauling, who looked too much to physics for their inspiration, was expressed by the leading British chemical educator Henry Armstrong in the mid-1930s: "The fact is, the physical chemists never use their eyes and are most lamentably lacking in chemical culture. It is essential to cast out from our midst, root and branch, this physical element and return to our laboratories."

Their distrust of abstract thinking exceeded only by their ignorance of the new physics, most early-1930s chemists responded to the Heitler-London-Slater-Pauling chemical-bond ideas with a yawn. As chemical Nobelist Harold Urey recalled, they were "completely bland about the matter, didn't understand it, and largely, except for Pauling, nobody paid any attention to it."

But A. A. Noyes and G. N. Lewis made sure that Pauling's ideas were given a wide hearing at Caltech and Berkeley, where most chemistry students developed an understanding that this approach was important and a handful of the brightest began to follow Pauling into the field. From the physics side, researchers like Slater and London continued to refine the mathematics of blended wave functions, working out the structure of simple molecules from physical first principles. Their impact on chemistry was muted, however, because they had not mastered the huge masses of empirical facts important to chemists, did not share the same worldview, and did not know which questions were important. They were not, in short, chemists.

One of the few who knew both physics and chemistry was Robert Mulliken. Mulliken, the son of an MIT chemist who learned physics with Millikan at the University of Chicago, roomed next to Slater while on a fellowship at Harvard and, like Pauling, made a pilgrimage to Europe in the late 1920s to learn quantum mechanics. At Göttingen, Mulliken had come under the influence of one of Born's assistants, Friedrich Hund, who was thinking through an approach to the chemical bond different from Pauling's. Hund was interested in molecular spectroscopy, the study of the characteristic light absorbed and emitted by molecules, and he found that viewed this way, molecules behaved in important ways like individual atoms. Hund and Mulliken came up with a concept of the chemical bond that seemed radically different from Pauling's. Instead of electrons concentrating between two nuclei to bind atoms together, Hund and Mulliken theorized that binding electrons were spread around the molecule's surface, forming what Mulliken would call molecular orbitals. They conceived of the hydrogen molecule, H_2, for instance, not as two hydrogen atoms approaching each other and forming a bond by pairing their electrons, as Heitler and London had proposed, but as a two-electron helium atom splitting into two nuclei, with its surrounding electron cloud reshaping into a new molecular orbital. "In general no attempt is made to treat the molecule as consisting of atoms or ions," Mulliken wrote in 1932. "Attempts to regard a molecule as consisting of specific atoms or ionic units held together by discrete numbers of bonding electrons or electron pairs are considered as more or less meaningless." This was radical thinking; the molecular-orbital concept seemed diametrically opposed to everything chemists had thought about the nature of the chemical bond for decades. It did, however, fit the spectroscopic data, and Mulliken stuck with his ideas after returning to the United States to teach at the University of Chicago.

For a few years it looked as if chemists would be forced to choose either Pauling's view or Mulliken's. But at root the two approaches were not as different as they seemed. Both were based on Schrödinger's wave equation, and Slater and others found in the mid-1930s that if the mathematics was carried through far enough, the two approaches ended up providing the same results. It was rather like the choice physicists had to make between Heisenberg's matrix approach to quantum mechanics and Schrödinger's wave equation: Although seemingly very different, both were paths to the same destination. The choice of paths depended on which was easier to use and which worked better in a given situation.

Pauling, of course, thought his was the better approach to understanding the chemical bond. He understood that the molecular-orbital approach was useful—he had employed it in some cases while searching for a breakthrough on the chemical bond—but he largely dropped it when he found how to make his own variations on the Heitler-London theme work in 1931. Once Slater showed the essential equivalence of his and Mulliken's methods, Pauling saw no need to refer to the molecular-orbital approach. His ideas worked out of what chemists already believed about the chemical bond; Mulliken's were by comparison anti-intuitive and, Pauling thought, confusing to students.

And Pauling's notion of the chemical bond took off, while Mulliken's languished in relative obscurity. There were several reasons, prominent among them the fact that Pauling was an eloquent teacher and a persuasive writer who knew how to communicate in language chemists could understand. When Pauling spoke, the valence-bond approach seemed like revealed wisdom. When Mulliken talked, people went to sleep. He was a terrible teacher, ill at ease in front of crowds, his voice almost inaudible. He refused to pander to his chemistry students, and his lectures were notoriously digressive, heavy with mathematics, and hard to follow. He was not much better in print. As the years went by, Mulliken and a small band of followers would continue to improve their molecular-orbital approach, refining the equations and using it to successfully attack a number of problems. Twenty years later, a new generation of chemists would come to prefer it over Pauling's approach. But in the 1930s, Mulliken's ideas would be lost in a blizzard of razzle-dazzle coming from Pasadena.

———*mm*———

Pauling's taming of the wave equation in his first "Nature of the Chemical Bond" paper released a flood of new ideas. In June 1931 he submitted a follow-up paper, the second in what was to become a series, this one examining how quantum mechanics could explain the existence of relatively rare one-electron and three-electron bonds. His calculations helped distinguish among alternative explanations for the unusual bonding properties of oxygen, boron, and nitroso compounds, the rare "odd-electron" molecules that had so interested G. N. Lewis. Lewis himself helped talk Pauling through some of the ideas in this paper, the two of them scribbling sketches and formulae on a black-board in Lewis's office during Pauling's teaching stints at Berkeley, the older man puffing out clouds of cigar smoke and advice.

Then it was on to bigger mysteries. One long-standing puzzle in chemistry concerned the relationship between two seemingly different types of bonds between atoms, ionic and covalent. In Lewis's scheme, the bond was covalent when two atoms shared a pair of electrons equally and ionic when one electron-hungry atom pulled the entire electron pair to itself, resulting in a net negative charge on one atom and a positive charge on the other; the resulting bond was then due to the electrostatic attraction between the two. The question was whether ionic and covalent bonds were separate species with a sharp dividing point or merely, as Lewis thought, points along a continuum.

In Pauling's third "Nature of the Chemical Bond" paper, he showed that quantum mechanics again supported Lewis. At least in some cases, his equations showed that the existence of "partial ionic" bonds, links that had both ionic and covalent characteristics, was compatible with both quantum mechanics and observed properties. In other cases he found that the jump between bond types could be discontinuous; it depended on how strongly the elements involved attracted the electrons. He backed up his arguments with a number of real-world examples and a set of conditions necessary for such intermediate bonds to form.

Pauling was now using the term "resonance" in place of "electron exchange" when writing about the chemical bond, and he was expanding the concept into new areas. Heisenberg had used the electron-exchange idea to account for the interchangeability of electrons; Heitler and London had used it to explain the covalent chemical bond; Pauling and Slater employed it to account for the energy needed to form hybrid bonds like those in the tetrahedral carbon atom. Now Pauling proposed that when certain criteria were met, resonance could exist between the ionic and covalent forms of a molecule. Hydrogen chloride, for example, could be viewed either as a hydrogen atom linked to a chlorine atom through a purely covalent bond or as a positively charged hydrogen ion and a negatively charged chloride ion linked with a purely ionic bond. The actual molecule, Pauling proposed, is a sort of hybrid, a structure that resonates between the two alternative extremes. And whenever that happened, "whenever there is resonance between two forms," Pauling said, "the structure is stabilized."

For Pauling, the entire chemical landscape now began to shift. Resonance, he realized excitedly, could be applied as well to the relationship between single and double bonds—they did not have to be one or the other but could resonate between the two forms, leading to a stabilized partial double bond with its own peculiar properties. Resonance explained all kinds of structures that didn't fit into the old classical cubbyholes.

Virtually all of chemistry could be reevaluated in the light of this new idea, and Pauling set about doing it through the early 1930s. By applying his resonance ideas to various types of chemical bonds, then cross-checking and amending his theoretical results to fit what was known empirically about bond lengths and strengths, Pauling was able to produce a string of papers that set chemistry on a new course.

—◠◠◠—

Pauling's reputation grew with each paper. In the spring of 1932 he took up Slater's invitation to become a visiting professor for a term at MIT, leaving Ava Helen in Pasadena in the last trimester of her third pregnancy. His eastern visit introduced a number of figures in the Harvard-MIT chemical establishment to his new ideas, and he continued working on them nonstop between lectures and dinner parties. He had been thinking of ways to estimate the relative contributions of ionic and covalent bonds to any molecule, developing with a fellow Caltech faculty member, Don Yost, a system for estimating the theoretical strength of pure covalent bonds. With his new numbers in hand, Pauling could now compare his theoretical numbers to the real behavior of different pairs of elements as they formed compounds. The real-world bonds were always stronger than predicted—an added strength, Pauling assumed, from the stabilizing effect of resonance with an ionic form of the bonds. The greater the deviation, the more ionic character the bond had and the more the two elements differed in their ability to attract electrons. Using this system, it was now possible to answer old questions such as whether hydrochloric acid, HCl, was ionic or covalent—it was both, Pauling discovered, in the ratio 20:80.

One insight he worked on while in Cambridge owed something to biology. Pauling had been attending biology seminars at Caltech, and had been interested to see how the geneticists mapped the location of genes on chromosomes by measuring how frequently two independent traits were inherited together: The closer the two genes were, the greater the chance they would stay linked together during genetic crossover. Pauling now borrowed the mapping idea to create his own scale of the relationship between pairs of elements. The more ionic character he calculated in the bond between two atoms, the greater the difference in their ability to attract electrons, and the farther apart they were on his scale. Fluorine, for example—the most electron-hungry of all elements—was at the far end of the scale. Lithium was toward the other. The bond in the compound they formed, lithium fluoride, was almost 100 percent ionic. Iodine was somewhere toward the middle of Pauling's scale, and the lithium iodide bond therefore had more covalent character. By comparing a number of such pairs, he was able to map a relative property he called electronegativity and assign values to various elements. These values in turn could be used to predict bond type and strength in many molecules, including those for which no experimental data were available. Between lectures at MIT, he wrote up his ideas in a paper that would become another in the "Nature of the Chemical Bond" series, finishing it just a few days before boarding the train back to Pasadena. He arrived home on May 30, one day before the birth of his new daughter, Linda Helen.

Pauling's electronegativity scale was one of his least theoretically well founded ideas and one of his most influential. It was a number of steps removed from any rigorous grounding in quantum mechanics but was easily grasped by chemists, who recognized its practicality in addressing real-world problems. By comparing the electronegativity of two elements from his tables, researchers could for the first time roughly predict the properties of a bond formed between them without having to know the first thing about the wave equation. The scale quickly earned wide adoption.

Pauling's mixing and matching of empirical observations with ideas from quantum physics was imaginative and dangerous. At each step he added a few more assumptions and moved a little further away from a hard grounding in accepted theory. Years later this would trip him up when critics would question the justification for his schemes, but for now it appeared that everything he did worked, and worked brilliantly.

Or almost everything. One daring prediction Pauling made was that fluorine was so electronegative it would form compounds even with an inert gas like xenon. Inert gases of any sort were thought incapable of chemical combination, and the creation of a xenon compound would have made history. Experiments were needed to test his prediction. Pure xenon gas was extremely rare, but Pauling managed to obtain a little of it from a colleague and gave it to Yost, who worked through the summer of 1933 searching for the predicted compounds.

He failed to find any—a failure that Pauling found both confusing and galling. The reasons for Yost's inability to find what he was looking for are uncertain. However, thirty years later, another team would make international news by producing the xenon compounds Pauling had said were possible.

—————

The most public demonstration of the power of Pauling's resonance ideas came when he used them to solve one of the oldest problems in organic chemistry.

Benzene was a conundrum. It is composed of six carbon atoms and six hydrogen atoms, but the structure of the benzene molecule had eluded definitive analysis. In the winter of 1932–33, Pauling and his student George Wheland set out to solve the structure according to the concept of resonance. By spring they finished a paper, the fifth in Pauling's chemical-bond series, in which benzene was described as resonating between five extreme, or "canonical," structures. "The properties of the molecule," Pauling wrote, "would then be expected to be a sort of average of the properties of the individual molecules." Pauling and Wheland's approach seemed to work: The values calculated from their resonating structure fit what was known about the molecule's structure, reactivity, and stability. They expanded their approach to other aromatic molecules like naphthaline (using no fewer than forty-two canonical structures) and to hydrocarbon free radicals.

Pauling's benzene paper marked an important expansion into the realm of organic chemistry. A good deal of his subsequent work would focus on organic molecules, and George Wheland would go on to build his scientific life around it, in 1944 publishing an influential textbook, *The Theory of Resonance and Its Application to Organic Chemistry*, that he dedicated to "my first and greatest inspiration," Linus Pauling.

The powerful concept of resonance was now entering its full flower. The last two entries in Pauling's nature of the chemical-bond series, written in 1933 with postdoctoral fellow Jack Sherman, extended it to more chemical puzzles involving variations from classical single, double, and triple bonds. This work, too, was groundbreaking. Pauling showed that molecules were not restricted to whole-integer bonds but that the links between them could take on intermediate forms. Here again he melded the bond lengths and strengths from his ever-growing library of molecular structures with his ideas about the stabilizing influence of resonance, and again he came up with novel explanations for a whole slew of problems. Atoms connected by single bonds were known to be able to rotate like wheels on an axle, for instance, while those linked by double and triple bonds were held rigidly in place; Pauling postulated that those intermediate between single and double bonds—with what he called "partial double-bond character"—were also restricted from rotating, an important factor in predicting structures. Pauling explained the restriction on rotation in quantum-mechanical terms, then applied his idea of resonance between single and double bonds to explain the bond lengths and rotational properties of a number of intermediate cases.

All of chemistry began to re-form itself in Pauling's mind. Like a jazz musician, he was taking themes suggested by quantum mechanics and improvising on them with his semiempirical variations. His was a new kind of chemistry that played in the spaces between old categories. Pauling's quantum chemistry was not either/or: either this or that orbital, either ionic or covalent bonds, either single or double links. Pauling's chemical bond was a fluid, multiform thing that often resonated in between. This was exciting, beautiful music, and he was the first to play it.

The Optimist

In the early 1930s, Pauling was publishing an average of one significant piece of work every five weeks, most of it on the chemical bond or new molecular structures, moving almost entirely away from wrestling with the wave equation: "About 1933 or 1934 I gave up on the idea of myself making very complicated quantum-mechanical calculations about molecular structure," he said. "I made a lot of simple quantum-mechanical calculations and drew conclusions, and realized that if you could ever make really accurate quantum-mechanical calculations you wouldn't learn anything from them because they would just agree with the experiment."

Using his semiempirical approach, he racked up success after success, until, by 1935, he wrote, "I felt that I had an essentially complete understanding of the nature of the chemical bond."

Slowly, his new vision of chemistry began to be accepted by other chemists. The reasons were manifold: the open and accepting atmosphere for new ideas at Caltech, his ability to speak the language of chemists, his eagerness to travel widely to spread his ideas, his unique ability to blend structural studies and quantum theory, and his courage in publishing theoretical insights without a rigorous grounding in hard mathematics. But one reason stood out above all: his optimism. In 1935, two observers describing the recent advances in quantum chemistry for the *Review of Modern Physics* could have had Pauling in mind when they wrote, "To be satisfied, one must adopt the mental attitude and procedure of an optimist rather than a pessimist. The latter demands a rigorous postulational theory, and calculations devoid of any questionable approximation or of empirical appeals to known facts. The optimist, on the other hand, is satisfied with approximate solutions of the wave equation. . . . He appeals freely to experiment to determine constants, the direct calculation of which would be too difficult. The pessimist, on the other hand, is eternally worried because the omitted terms in the approximation are usually rather large, so that any pretense of rigor should be lacking. The optimist replies that the approximate calculations do, nevertheless, give one an excellent 'steer' and a very good idea of 'how things go,' permitting the systematization and understanding of what could otherwise be a maze of experimental data codified by purely empirical valence rules."

As his reputation grew, Pauling's life changed. In 1931, less than four years after taking his first appointment as assistant professor, Pauling was promoted to full professor at Caltech. By 1933 he oversaw twice the number of graduate students and postdoctoral fellows of any other chemistry professor in the division. He was awarded an honorary doctorate from his undergraduate institution, Oregon Agricultural College. As job offers kept coming in—Stanford, the University of London, Ohio State—his Caltech salary went up rapidly, and he had to teach only one seminar per term, leaving plenty of time for research. Noyes was making it clear to everyone that the young dynamo was his "white-haired boy," as one colleague remembered it, and perhaps his successor as director of the Gates Laboratory. His annual teaching stints at Berkeley cemented his friendship with G. N. Lewis—they had "wonderful arguments," Pauling remembered, sitting in Lewis's smoky office—leading to talk for a while of writing a book on valence together. (The project never came to fruition.)

But to Pauling the most significant honor of those years was his election to the National Academy of Sciences. Noyes helped engineer it, and it was an important step up. The academy was the nation's most prestigious, exclusive, and hoary scientific club; in the early 1930s, out of all the thousands of scientists in America, there were only 250 members, most of them twice Pauling's age. When he was inducted in May 1933, Pauling became the youngest person ever elected in the seventy years since the academy's founding.

He was now, at age thirty-two, ensconced in the top echelon of the nation's scientists. He was young and famous and he was doing research he loved for a good deal of money. He had healthy children and was married to a devoted wife. He was being given almost everything he wanted at Caltech, was able to travel and talk almost anywhere he wished, and was producing first-rate work.

The warm sun of success and approbation evaporated any public traces of his adolescent shyness, and he began to earn a reputation as one of the most cheerful and extroverted of scientists. At departmental parties he became, like G. N. Lewis, the center of the liveliest group. He enjoyed a stiff drink, loved a good joke, even if it was a bit off-color, and he could be heard across the room, roaring with laughter, often at his own punch lines. Pauling's wit could have a sarcastic edge to it as well, and he became known for his ability to lacerate the work of others, especially stuffed shirts, slow thinkers, and researchers whose work he did not value.

He was having a very good time, and it showed. His lecturing style had moved from confidence to bravado. He would stride into a classroom, his long, wavy hair flying, eyes sparkling, and launch into a seemingly disconnected series of observations punctuated by lightning mental calculations, jokes about colleagues, and things he had read in the paper that morning. He would wave his arms in an imitation of a hydrogen atom, perform stunts with chemicals, draw cartoons of cannons firing photons at electrons. Sometimes he would lie down on the lecture table, "Roman style," his students called it, talking with his head supported on one hand. And somehow, through it all, he would weave a coherent, eye-opening lecture.

The physicist Martin Kamen remembered seeing Pauling in classic form during a visit to the University of Chicago in the mid-1930s, on a "wonderful Monday" when it was announced that the regularly scheduled noon-seminar speaker in physical chemistry would have to yield his place because Linus Pauling was in town:

> Pauling arrived just before noon. We students were charmed, if slightly surprised, to see a bouncy young extrovert, wholly informal in dress and appearance. He bounded into the room, already crowded with students eager to see and hear the Great

Man, spread himself over the seminar table next to the black-board and, running his hand through an unruly shock of hair, gestured to the students to come closer. He noted that there were still some seats vacant at the table and cheerfully invited students pressing in at the door to come forward and occupy them. As these were seats reserved for faculty, the students hung back, but Pauling would have none of that. He insisted, and they nervously edged in, taking the seats. The talk started with Pauling leaping off the table and rapidly writing a list of five topics on which he could speak singly or all together. He described each in a few pithy sentences, including racy impressions of the workers involved. . . . The seminar he gave was a brilliant tour-de-force and made a never-to-be forgotten impression on all us students.

Pauling cared deeply about teaching, partly in reaction to what he liked and disliked about his own education, partly in response to his new understanding of his own science. He thought a chemical education should start with a sense of wonder. As early as 1930 he was advising Noyes to change the way freshman chemistry was taught at Caltech, to hold back on theories and mathematics until the students had a firm grasp on descriptive chemistry. "To awaken an interest in chemistry in students we mustn't make the courses consist entirely of explanations, forgetting to mention what there is to be explained," he said. "I know of no chemist who was attracted to this field because of theoretical chemistry. Instead, it is an interest in chemicals and their reactions which first attracted the chemist." He also proposed giving students drawings of molecules "as we now picture them," to give them a concrete feel for what they were studying. Such molecular drawings, now common in most chemistry textbooks, had not been used before.

More importantly, he thought chemistry should be taught not as a loose aggregate of facts but as a unified science with a firm and consistent underlying theory. His own ideas about the chemical bond could be used to explain a wide variety of phenomena, from thermodynamics to crystal structures, from organic to inorganic chemistry, providing a new level of order and sense, and he began organizing his classes around these basic themes.

The best of Pauling's students came away enthusiasts, provided they had a solid background in chemistry and mathematics. Those undergraduates, especially nonchemistry majors, who lacked such preparation often found Pauling obscure.

He could be rough on students who he thought did not accord him proper respect. On the first day of one freshman chemistry course, Pauling's "Roman style" position earned him a loud laugh from the students. He was not amused. Pauling "lit on the biggest guy in the class—later tackle on the football team—and sent him out," remembered one 1933 student. "From then on, it was a very sober group of freshmen." Perhaps in some ways he still looked a little too young to be taken seriously. In the summer of 1934, Pauling grew a thick auburn beard, designed in part to give him a more mature, professional air, and maintained it, off and on, for a few years.

—*um*—

As Pauling's career rocketed, his relationship with Ava Helen changed. She had once been able to help him with his work, making notes and drawing diagrams, helping to make crystal models. But as his work grew increasingly theoretical and sophisticated, she was left behind. "I helped in making the indexes of the books, and even in the beginning doing some proofreading," she remembered, "but he found people who could do this much better than I and without the effort that it took me. Moreover, I was developing my own interests more too, and my time was taken up in other ways."

The "other ways" mostly concerned children and home. By the end of 1932 the Paulings had moved to a larger house close to Caltech, which required more tending, and there were now three children to care for: the new baby Linda, one-year-old Peter, and the rambunctious seven-year-old Linus junior. As with most things, Ava Helen took to her new responsibilities wholeheartedly. "If a woman thinks honestly and clearly," she wrote to herself in 1927, "she must soon reach the conclusion that no matter what life work she chooses it could be done better by a man; and the only work in which this is not the case is the work involved in a home with children." She had been trained at college in a scientifically based form of home economics, and she determined early in her married life to create an ideal home and raise ideal children.

The pattern of the Paulings' home life became set. Ava Helen spent her days in childcare and housekeeping, cooking and cleaning; Pauling spent his doing science. He had a small study at home where he worked in the early mornings. After breakfast he walked two blocks to Caltech and worked all day at the office and lab. He walked home for dinner, then either returned to Caltech for evening seminars or retired to his home study to do more calculations late into the night. He worked weekends. He worked most holidays. When he traveled, as he did often for meetings and visiting lectureships, he did so almost always alone, mostly by train, which he enjoyed because it offered him uninterrupted time for more work.

Ava Helen felt it her duty to free as much of her husband's time as possible for work. She relieved him of home pressures, did all the cooking, kept the children away from him, handled all the details of family life to give him the time he needed. It was a domestic arrangement in keeping with the times, but it was also a conscious decision made by an intelligent woman. "A scientist, in order to be doing his work, must really be thinking about it all the time," Ava Helen said later. "Very often he doesn't want to be interrupted in that thinking. The wives of scientists are really . . . fuddy-duddy. They have to be women who are not expecting anything. You see, they don't need to be taken to the theater; they don't need to be taken out to dinner. . . . They have to have their own ability to entertain themselves and to perhaps see more deeply or understand what is really worthwhile in life."

There was a slight edge of resentment there, against the daily, almost complete separation from her husband, the creation of parallel lives that rarely touched, the sense of living in Linus's shadow. Ava Helen felt that she was Pauling's equal in most things; she, too, had a strong ego and a desire to be recognized. She loved her children; she was, her husband remembered, an "outstandingly able, excellent cook" and enjoyed the limited amount of entertaining they did at home

But home life alone, she found, was not enough for her. She would not become "fuddy-duddy." Ava Helen was restless and interested in broader issues; she read widely and thought about national and international issues. Through the 1930s the liberal-leftist thinking that had been part of her upbringing as a child flowered into a renewed interest in politics and social action.

When they were first married, Ava Helen did not talk politics with her husband, who had unreflectingly carried on the Republican party affiliation of his father. In his first two presidential elections Pauling voted for Herbert Hoover. But as the Depression went on, Ava Helen became an increasingly committed New Dealer, vocally supportive of Roosevelt and his government plans for helping the poor.

She could no longer talk science very effectively with Pauling, but she could talk politics. And she soon began making an impression. "I began listening to what she was saying about the difference between the rich and the poor, the capitalists and the workers," Pauling said.

"The Democratic Party seemed pretty clearly to correspond somewhat more closely to what I thought was right than the Republican Party." With Ava Helen's urging, Pauling switched parties, and more. Once he began to think about it, be began to see things as she saw them. The deepening economic crisis and the social unrest it engendered seemed to offer proof of the bankruptcy of capitalism. California was awash in jobless migrants and protest politics, and Pauling began listening to the complaints. By 1934, Ava Helen's influence had become so decisive that he voted for a socialist democrat, Upton Sinclair, for governor of California. From then on, he was a committed Roosevelt Democrat.

A Laboratory for Paradise

Pauling's new politics was at variance with the atmosphere at Caltech. Most scientists considered politics a messy, judgmental, value-laden minefield that anyone aspiring to objectivity should avoid, but there was a political element built into the structure of Caltech. It was exemplified by the school's leader, Robert Millikan, who thought the New Deal was left-wing paternalism that would rot the nation's self-reliance and that the Depression was a temporary jam in the social machinery, with the major effect of making it harder for scientists to create more wealth. He wasted little sympathy on those who could not find work. "Call unemployment leisure," he said, "and one can at once see the possibilities."

Millikan would have a major effect on Caltech, the institution that shaped Pauling's professional life. The son of an Iowa Congregational minister, a brilliant experimentalist and able administrator, he directed Caltech for more than a quarter of a century, building it from a promising school to one of the nation's major academic centers. To the outside world, Millikan *was* Caltech—"Millikan's School," some called it. And he was much more. For a period following his 1923 Nobel Prize for Physics, he was also the American public's image of a scientist. He had the strong-jawed, silver-haired good looks of "a witty and respected banker," as *Time* magazine described him in a 1927 cover story, the smooth delivery of a born hawker, and the soul of a middle-class technocrat. Millikan didn't talk science, he preached it, on radio, at Rotary Club lunches, in popular magazine articles, and at flower society meetings. He was one of the few scientists who publicly proclaimed his belief in God, proudly pointed out the links between science and capitalist economic development, and enjoyed talking people out of money. He exemplified the new breed of scientist/bureaucrat who would become increasingly important in academia and government through the middle of the twentieth century. And his message was simple: "The supreme question for all mankind," he said, "is how it can best stimulate and accelerate the application of the scientific method to all departments of human life."

This was a message eagerly absorbed by his favorite congregation, Southern California's banking, mercantile, industrial, and professional elite. Hale started Caltech with the support of these wealthy donors, and Millikan made sure that support not only continued but increased manyfold. He was a master money raiser, and he did it by playing off his target audiences' pride, greed, vanity, and even racism. Southern California, he said, was the meeting place of God, physics, and manifest destiny, a promised land, geographically, climatically, and demographically suited to become the great crucible in which scientific progress, business acumen, and Christian values would combine to solve current ills and meet future challenges. "California marks now, as England did three centuries ago, the furthest western outpost of Aryan civilization," Millikan told potential donors. It was here that Western white culture would interface profitably with the growing economies of the Orient. It was here that great industries would rise and the desert would be made to bloom. All of this, of course, required scientific and engineering expertise. Caltech, he believed, was the laboratory for paradise.

Millikan was a master at conjuring up compelling, albeit vague, visions of the connection between pure research and industrial profit. Without promising a single specific result in return, he could make wealthy donors feel as if a gift to Caltech were a prudent investment in the economic future of the region. They heeded his sermon. A position on the Caltech board of trustees became a badge of honor for some of the region's wealthiest men, and through the 1920s money poured in.

Caltech's corporate-style administrative structure codified this marriage of science and business. Millikan refused the standard academic title of president when he arrived, insisting instead that the school be run by an executive group, comprised equally of businessmen and faculty members. His would be a school led not by a president but by the more businesslike title he gave himself, executive director. Younger faculty more often called him by his nickname, the Chief. The school's academic divisions were each guided by councils in which full professors had votes equal to the division heads. Duties within the divisions were overseen by faculty committees. The consciously corporate structuring played down strong central leadership and emphasized group achievement. The business community loved it.

They also liked the positive press the Chief was adept at securing. In 1932 publisher Henry Luce thought the wider business community would be interested in learning about Caltech and asked Millikan to send him some information for a *Fortune* article. Press releases were not good enough for Millikan. "My reply to him was that . . . the thing to do was to send somebody out here to live for a time," he remembered. Luce sent out one of his best reporters—soon to become an editor of *Fortune*—and the Chief put him up at the faculty club for a month and a half. Millikan's weeks of working directly with the writer paid off. When an article on the wonders of Caltech appeared in July 1932, it was more than a puff piece; it was a multipart, four-color paean to scientific progress. Caltech was a "temple to . . . science reared by the rich men of business. . . . The history of Athens and Carthage, of Alexandria and Angkor, of Rome and Paris, of Chartres and London is simply repeating itself on the flatland under Mt. Wilson. . . . The institute is daring. It greets the stranger with an air of success and affluence. It is bold, in the manner of the West. It knocks brazenly on the door of the universe, like the theme in Beethoven's famous quartet." Pauling was mentioned in passing as the man "whose work on the structures of crystals and molecules earned him the Langmuir Prize last year as the nation's most brilliant young chemist."

During the Depression, on the side of a steam shovel at Caltech, a religious graffiti artist scrawled: "Jesus Saves." Beneath it, someone else chalked: "But Millikan Gets Credit."

Yet even Millikan could not spare Caltech from the Depression. As interest rates plummeted, the money generated by the institute's investments shrank; its stocks and securities melted to half their value. The evaporation of the single largest component of Caltech's private income, a huge trust fund from lumber tycoon Arthur Fleming, sent shock waves through the administration. By 1932 the school was running a deficit of $80,000. Almost all construction was halted, including a planned addition to Noyes's chemistry building. Research and travel moneys vanished, and Millikan asked all faculty to accept a 10 percent pay cut. Pauling took the pay cut, lost much of the $4,500 he had been receiving from the institute each year to support his research, and gave up five hundred dollars he had been promised each year for travel.

Pauling, deeply involved in his work and desperately in need of space for his fast-growing research group, had neither the time nor the inclination to sympathize with the budget problems faced by his higher-ups. He argued against the pay cut, refused to volunteer to give up his travel money when asked, and made it clear that he was displeased with his shrinking research support. Noyes, Millikan, and Hale struggled to keep him happy. For a time, Hale and some other trustees donated money out of their own pockets to support Pauling's research, and when construction of the new chemistry wing was delayed, rooms were found in Hale's new astrophysics building to allow for the expansion of his laboratories.

Millikan redoubled his fund-raising efforts with his large group of corporate friends, but the Depression was drying up his usual watering holes. There was little money available from the government and Millikan did not believe that scientists in any case should feed at the public trough.

But one other major source of funds was available—money that would help keep Caltech going through the Depression and would change the course of Pauling's career.

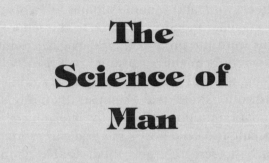

The Science of Man

Big Money

John D. Rockefeller, Sr., had a problem. The crude oil that came out of his huge Lima, Ohio, fields was laced with so much sulfur it smelled like rotten eggs. People called it skunk juice and refused to buy it. His refineries could not purify the stink away. Rockefeller was left with thousands of barrels of worthless oil.

When a group of eager chemical engineers at one of his Indiana plants asked for money to figure out a way to remove the smell, Rockefeller, disinclined to throw good money after bad, turned them down. But a few of them kept working on the problem on their own time and in 1913 succeeded in finding a way of chemically "cracking" the crude, a new refining process that got out the skunk and doubled the yield of gasoline. When he saw the results, Rockefeller had an epiphany. Almost overnight, he became a firm supporter of science.

In later years, as the aging industrialist pondered how to dispense the great wealth he had gathered, he would see to it that the aims and methods of science suffused the huge philanthropic foundations he set up. A pragmatist as well as a Christian, Rockefeller did not want to use his money to create charities to coddle those with problems; he wanted to find the causes of problems and eliminate them. He wanted results from his investment in the betterment of mankind, and science was the era's surest path to results.

During the 1920s, under the management of philosophy-professor-turned-science-enthusiast Wickliffe Rose, the Rockefeller philanthropies began the large-scale support of pure science. Rose's single biggest grant was to Caltech, for Hale's Mount Palomar telescope, one of many large sums of Rockefeller money that came to the school in the 1920s. Large lump sums were the preferred type of grant under Rose, and Caltech was a favored recipient because it was Rose's belief—as it was that of most scientists—that the best research was done by a few top men at elite institutions and that scientists themselves were better suited than foundation-funding officers to determine the disposition of money for specific projects. Rose's method was to identify the worthiest centers of basic research, give them sizable chunks of money with few strings attached, and allow the scientists themselves to figure out how to spend it. There was a great deal of money to give away. By 1932, Rockefeller philanthropies alone were providing six times as much money for academic science in the United States as the total endowment for science had been at the turn of the century. Rose had become "central banker to the world of science," as the science historian Daniel Kevles put it, and his pet phrase "Make the peaks higher" became the foundation's unofficial motto.

Fueled by Rockefeller and Carnegie grants and the money that flowed from private donors, the 1920s became a period of enormous expansion for private scientific centers like Caltech, MIT, Columbia, Harvard, and Johns Hopkins—not to mention the academic and research institutions Rockefeller's money started from scratch, the University of Chicago and the Rockefeller Institute for Medical Research in New York City. And it was not only the infrastructure, the buildings and laboratories, that grew. A network of power and influence was also expanding. Alliances formed between government, industry, and academic science during World War I—exemplified by Hale and Millikan's National Research Council (NRC)—were continued through the 1920s in the form of a growing scientific "establishment," a professional and social interweaving of men of power: university leaders, businessmen, government officials, heads of philanthropic foundations and their wealthy boards, and the presidents of such scientific organizations as the National Academy of Sciences (NAS) and the American Association for the Advancement of Science. They talked to each other at professional meetings, had dinner at each other's clubs, gave each other advice, funneled each other funds, nominated each other for high positions, and together determined the scientific agenda of the period between the world wars.

The system worked to Caltech's advantage. For example, Hale, Noyes, and Millikan, all NRC organizers, were also perennial forces in the NAS. When the Carnegie Institution—the foundation that had funded Hale's Mount Wilson Observatory—began looking for a new president in 1919, Hale and Noyes made sure their mutual friend and former NRC director John C. Merriam was nominated for the post. As Noyes pointed out to Hale, "The result of this arrangement would be that you, he, and I would together largely determine the policies of the Carnegie Institution." After Merriam was named to the position, Noyes had no trouble securing Carnegie money: $200,000 for various chemical research projects through the 1920s—one-third of the chemistry division's total annual expenditures. Some of the money supported Pauling's early work.

It was no wonder that the acerbic editor of *Science* magazine during the period, James Cattell, compared the difficulty in untangling these relationships to the famous astronomical conundrum of determining planetary involvement when several celestial bodies are involved. "Whether the Research Council belongs to the National Academy, or the National Academy belongs to the Research Council, or both are satellites of Pasadena is a problem of three bodies that is difficult of solution. . . . The Carnegie Corporation, the Rockefeller Foundation, and the National Research Council are another problem of three bodies."

⸺

By the end of the 1920s, funding from private philanthropies had become vital to Caltech—accounting for twenty cents of every dollar of total assets—and much of it was coming from the Rockefeller Foundation.

Noyes, adept at getting Carnegie money for his physical chemistry projects, targeted the Rockefeller Foundation for a major expansion of organic chemistry. This was a weak point at Caltech. The only organic chemist in Noyes's division was a holdover from the Throop days named Howard Lucas, a man Noyes considered less than stellar. But to Noyes, organic chemistry—the study of the carbon-based compounds, the molecules of life—was the cornerstone that needed to be laid before he could build other areas in which he had long been interested: biochemistry and medical research. Noyes had come to believe that this was the next great step for his branch of science, a move into crossover areas where chemistry could help revolutionize biology, just as Noyes had helped physics revolutionize chemistry. As early as 1922 he had okayed a pilot project to produce insulin at Caltech and then expanded it with Carnegie money during the next few years; he even gave thought to building a research-oriented medical school at Caltech.

But the first step was organic chemistry. Here he wanted to find a new man, a scientific star with international fame around whom an entire research group could revolve, and he went searching for money to make it happen. Noyes talked the Rockefeller Foundation out of a large grant in the mid-1920s that included money to hire a new organic chemist but then could not find anyone to fill the position. Organic chemistry was a European, especially German, specialty, and it was difficult to find any top-flight American researchers. James Bryant Conant was the number-one man in the United States, but after visiting Caltech for two months in 1927, he accepted a Harvard counteroffer. Then Noyes's health began to decline, and he put his energy elsewhere. The job was still vacant in 1930 when the Rockefeller Foundation gave Caltech another huge grant: half a million dollars, with a pledge of that much more for the development of the natural sciences, including funds to begin plans for a new organic chemistry wing on the Gates Laboratory.

Noyes now turned to Pauling. Around the time Pauling was applying his resonance ideas to benzene, Noyes asked him if he wouldn't think about changing his title to professor of organic chemistry. The benefit to Noyes was clear: He would have a proven talent to put in his new building, someone with enough spark to form the nucleus of a new department. But Pauling quickly said no. He enjoyed thinking about biology—Noyes had encouraged his faculty to attend the seminars given in the biology department, and Pauling, becoming friendly with the younger men in geneticist Thomas Hunt Morgan's group, had even given a talk of his own there based on a German genetics paper that he had been asked to translate—but his major interests still revolved around crystal structure and the chemical bond. He believed that his quantum-chemical, structural approach was the basis of *all* of chemistry, both organic and inorganic. When he was promoted to full professor, Pauling had made sure that his official title was changed from professor of physical chemistry to the more general professor of chemistry. Changing it now to organic chemistry would be a step back. He had no desire to be pigeonholed.

What Pauling called himself was less important than what he did, and Noyes was convinced that Pauling's work on the chemical bond was the most important advance being made in all of chemistry, including organic. Only Pauling had promise enough to energize an entire research program. One way or another, Pauling's group would be the centerpiece of the new building. It would help, though, if his research were oriented a little more toward biological problems.

Pauling was bright enough to see which way the wind was blowing. In February 1932 Pauling approached the foundations, making duplicate applications to the Rockefeller Foundation and the Carnegie Institute, asking for fifteen thousand dollars per year over five years to support "a unified series of investigations on the structure of inorganic and organic substances, involving both theoretical and experimental work." Much of what he requested involved x-ray crystallography and electron-diffraction studies, but he also outlined his growing interest—based on his success with benzene—in organic molecules. "I desire to solve the wave equation for simple organic crystals and molecules," he wrote, as part of a semiempirical effort to "develop a set of atomic radii and of structural principles enabling one to predict with confidence the atomic arrangement, including interatomic distances, of the normal electronic state of any molecule, and its stability relative to other molecules. This knowledge may be of great importance to biochemistry, resulting in the determination of the structure of proteins, haemoglobin, and other complicated organic substances."

Weaver

Pauling's proposal—especially the remark about proteins—caught the attention of Warren Weaver, the man hired just two months earlier by the Rockefeller Foundation to dispense its grants in the natural sciences.

Weaver was a second-rate scientist with a first-rate knack for knowing the right people. One of them was Max Mason, his electrodynamics professor while an undergraduate at the University of Wisconsin, who later became president of the Rockefeller Foundation. Another was Robert Millikan, who was sufficiently impressed by Weaver when he taught him physics at the University of Chicago to offer him a teaching job when Millikan first went to Caltech. Weaver enjoyed teaching. He spent three happy years as a junior professor in Pasadena before Mason enticed him back to teach at Wisconsin in 1920; when

Weaver left, Millikan refused to accept his resignation, saying that he should always consider himself a Caltech faculty member.

But Weaver was not good at laboratory work. "I lacked that strange and wonderful creative spark that makes a good researcher," Weaver said. "I never seemed to get a first-class original idea." So, like many scientists who failed at the bench, he shifted to teaching and administration. He got along well with a variety of people and soon worked his way up through the ranks to become head of the Wisconsin mathematics division.

He was settling down to what looked like a long career at Wisconsin when, in early 1932, Mason called him again, this time to the New York offices of the Rockefeller Foundation. Wickliffe Rose was gone now, and so was his program of lump-sum grants, Mason explained; the Depression had changed things, and the Rockefeller trustees were now less willing to dole out huge sums without a clear idea of how they would be used. The trend was going to be toward granting smaller sums for specific research programs guided by individual researchers. The trustees wanted results. That meant, of course, tighter oversight on the part of foundation officers and a keen ability to pick winners from among the many scientists who would be jockeying for grants. Mason trusted Weaver's judgment. That's why, he explained to Weaver, he wanted him to take over the natural sciences division.

Weaver was speechless. It was a dizzying prospect. At age thirty-eight, this genial, owlish-looking laboratory failure and academic middle manager was being asked to take the reins of the single most important scientific funding agency in the world. He would have the power to open new areas of research, make or break careers, dispense millions of dollars, change the course of scientific history.

He eagerly accepted.

─── ∿ ───

Weaver's personal stock of original ideas may have been low, but he had a good eye for the ideas of others. He was especially enthusiastic about a new form of biology. Although he had no background in the field himself, he was convinced that there was a scientific revolution brewing there, the birth of a new approach to the field that would contribute mightily to the betterment of man. Like Noyes, Weaver believed that the revolution would be catalyzed when the methods of the more "successful" natural sciences—mathematics, physics, and chemistry—were applied to biology. He called this "the friendly invasion of the biological sciences by the physical sciences."

When talking about his ideas in the early 1930s, he did not even use the word "biology," calling it first "vital processes," then, in 1936, inventing a label that stuck: molecular biology. This was going to change the way we think about the living world, he told the Rockefeller trustees. Whereas the old biology focused on whole organisms, molecular biology would concentrate on the unknown world inside isolated cells, the charting of metabolic pathways and the structure of individual proteins. Qualitative observations would be supported by quantitative measurements. A focus on common natural laws arising from chemistry and physics would allow biology to progress from the field into the laboratory, where a new breed of scientist, armed with fantastically powerful equipment like x-ray crystallography devices, ultracentrifuges, and ever-more powerful microscopes, would discover the ultimate stuff of life.

Weaver was not alone in his enthusiasm. H. G. Wells and Julian Huxley's best-seller *The Science of Life*, a popular overview of the field in the late 1920s, was typical of the exuberance current among a small group of British and American researchers who believed in the same vision. Soon, they wrote, "biological science . . . equipped with a mass of proved and applicable knowledge beyond anything we can now imagine," would make possible "the ultimate collective control of human destinies." Scientists would "operate directly on the germ-plasm," making possible "the practical eugenic work of the future," when man would improve every species, including his own, in the same way he had improved stocks of wheat and corn.

Weaver took the idea further, telling the Rockefeller trustees that a new, laboratory-based approach to biology and psychology could help "rationalize human behavior" by laying bare the molecular mechanisms leading to violence, unhappiness, irrationality, and sexual problems. From here on, he said, Rockefeller funds should be concentrated on solving the mysteries of the human body and mind, using the most powerful new scientific techniques possible. The trustees, conservative men for the most part, were enticed by the idea of discovering the ultimate sources of social unrest. They gave Weaver carte blanche to pursue his plan, which he packaged under the heading "The Science of Man." From that point on, the Rockefeller Foundation stopped awarding grants for mathematics, physics, and chemistry that did not relate directly to the life sciences.

Success for his new program, Weaver knew, would depend on find-

ing chemists and physicists able to translate their skills to a new setting. Pauling, with his proven abilities in chemistry and newly stated
interest in biochemical questions, was a natural. One of the first things
Weaver did as director of the Rockefeller Foundation's natural sciences
division was to give him twenty thousand dollars for two years—
enough money for Pauling to pay the salaries of five postdoctoral fellows and one full-time assistant, with some left over to buy the meters,
tubes, crystals, film, transformers, and other specialized equipment he
needed for his work. It far more than made up for Pauling's Depres-
sion-trimmed research moneys. And it marked the beginning of a long
and mutually beneficial association between the two men.

—ᷤᷤᷤ—

For Caltech, the Rockefeller Foundation's more focused funding
scheme was both good and bad. The new agenda meant the end of any
chance for funds for astronomy and geology and most of the research
in mathematics, physics, and chemistry—anything unrelated to biology and psychology, Weaver told them, would not get a penny. Not
even Millikan could convince the foundation to fund his cosmic ray research. But Thomas Hunt Morgan's genetic research would be richly
funded by the Rockefeller Foundation, and so, increasingly, would
Pauling's work.

Weaver visited Caltech soon after joining the Rockefeller Foundation and came away impressed. Noyes gave him a grand tour of the
Gates Laboratory and told Weaver of his long-term plans for the development of organic chemistry—which he was now wisely calling bio-
organic chemistry—and about his bank of talent, especially Pauling.
That night in his diary Weaver wrote, "Noyes hopes that W[arren]
W[eaver] will not think it is the normal California enthusiasm when he
says that, were all the rest of the Chemistry Department wiped away except for Pauling, it would still be one of the most important departments of chemistry in the world."

Once he met Pauling, Weaver believed Noyes might be right. Compared to the other Caltech chemistry laboratories, with one or two
graduate students quietly carrying out the professor's assignments,
Pauling's rooms in the astrophysics building crackled with energy. The
labs were crowded with nine postdoctoral fellows and five graduate
students jostling for space and engaging in animated discussion
among themselves. There was a little of G. N. Lewis's Berkeley here in
the free and open exchange of thoughts, the raw ideas quickly sketched

on blackboards, the arguments and laughter. It reminded Weaver of a European-style center of theoretical chemistry—an institute within an institute, with Pauling in charge. After visiting Caltech, Weaver wrote that Pauling "has a speculative mind of the first order, great analytical ability, and the genius to keep in close and inspiring touch with experimental work. . . . [He] has been offered lucrative professorships at Harvard, MIT, Michigan, etc. and is nearly universally rated as the leading theoretical chemist of the world."

The only drawback was that Pauling was not thinking about The Science of Man—at least not yet. Weaver proselytized for his molecular biology approach during his visit, stressing that the Rockefeller Foundation was far more interested in the structure of biological molecules than in sulfide materials. During a long talk in Pauling's office, he tried to encourage Pauling to apply his structural chemistry ideas to unraveling the mysteries of the body.

But the message did not seem to sink in. When Weaver made his second visit to Caltech some months later, in October 1933, the first two years of Pauling's original grant were almost up. Of the two dozen papers Pauling put his name on in 1932 and 1933, only the benzene article and two or three others on the structures of small carbon-based molecules were even about organic chemistry, much less molecular biology. Everything else came from Pauling's inorganic crystal work and general quantum theoretical interests. Pauling knew that Weaver was looking for something else, and he greeted his patron with a six-page report explaining how he had spent his Rockefeller money and what he planned for the future. His top priority, he said, was an attack on the structure of organic molecules, and he tantalized Weaver with a mention of future investigations of chlorophyll and hemoglobin. These hints and promises were not good enough for Weaver. He liked Pauling and thought he had great promise, but he also had to sell the value of his research to the trustees. He told Pauling bluntly that structural work in general organic chemistry would not be funded; money would flow only for work with a direct bearing on biology.

Pauling listened. When he made a formal application at the end of 1933 for a three-year grant extension, his proposal prominently mentioned biological molecules. Weaver thought he should get the money, but there was so little completed biologically related work to point to that he found it hard to convince his board. He ended up comparing Pauling to Louis Pasteur, whose abstract interests in chemical structure in the 1850s eventually led to great discoveries in biology and medicine. Even so, the board approved funds for only one additional year. Weaver broke the news to Pauling gently, telling him that economic conditions had made it "unwise" to offer longer-term support and again underlining the Rockefeller Foundation's expectations: "The possibility for favorable consideration of your request has depended largely upon the fact that your work has now developed to the point where it promises application to the study of chlorophyll, hemoglobin, and other substances of biological importance."

—*mm*—

Although biology was interesting, Pauling was not ready to orchestrate his scientific life around it. His background in organic chemistry was minimal, and he had never taken a biology course in his life. He was self-confident enough to tackle almost anything, but a move toward biology would take him out of an area of proven success and into a research field with a different set of expectations and a new group of scientists judging his success. It was risky. Besides, he felt he was close to developing a set of general rules underlying the structure of sulfide minerals, a task he felt he could complete given just a little more time and money. Early in 1934 he asked the Geological Society of America's Penrose Fund to support his research on sulfides.

The group turned him down, a surprising rejection he felt as a slap both to his research agenda and his ego. He suddenly realized just what the Rockefeller money meant. Pauling had expanded his laboratory with Rockefeller money, and the assistants and postdoctoral fellows and graduate students that he brought in and equipped with the help of that money had made him dependent on a new way of working, one in which he came up with ideas or problems to solve, handed them out for lab work, then helped to analyze the results and cowrite the paper. The system kept him out of the laboratory and in his study, where he did his best brainstorming; it expanded his reach and allowed him to indulge his wide-ranging curiosity by tackling a variety of subjects at once. Every paper he published in 1934 was cowritten, usually with someone paid with or equipped by Rockefeller money. The Depression was a long way from being over, and there was little chance of significant funds coming from other sources.

He followed the money. "It seemed pretty clear to me that I would have difficulty in getting further support from the Rockefeller Foundation unless I became interested in chemistry in relation to biology," he wrote. He dropped some of his mineralogical investigations and shifted his attention to biological molecules. "The foregoing episode," he later noted dryly, "suggests that granting agencies can influence the progress of science."

Blood

He may have been slow in starting, but once Pauling began attacking problems in organic chemistry and the structure of biological molecules, he devoted to the matter all of his usual energy and imagination. On the theoretical side, he and his student George Wheland extended their resonance ideas to important organic structures, such as the carboxyl group of organic acids and the aromatic free radicals. Lawrence Brockaway now had the electron-diffraction apparatus up and running, and a stream of papers on the structures of small organic molecules began to appear. Among them was a description of one of the subunits of hemoglobin.

Hemoglobin was an attractive target for laboratory study for a number of reasons. It was, first and above all, a protein, the most important class of molecules in the body. Hair and horn and feather, skin and muscle and tendon, were proteins, as were the most important parts of nerves and blood. Enzymes, with their unexplained ability to catalyze specific reactions, were proteins; so were antibodies and the better part of chromosomes, the tangled complexes of protein and nucleic acid that carried the secret of heredity. Proteins were involved in every reaction and formed an important part of every major structural component of the body. If there was a secret of life, it was thought, that secret would be found among the proteins.

In the early 1930s no one knew how proteins worked or even what they looked like. Yet proteins were the engines driving vital processes; it was here, at the level of these molecules, that cold chemicals became moving, breathing organisms. Discovering the secrets of the "giant protein problem," as Weaver called it, was the most important item on the Science of Man agenda.

From a practical standpoint, however, proteins were a nightmare to work with. The early data indicated that they were huge molecules, sometimes including tens of thousands of atoms—orders of magnitude larger than any molecular structure Pauling had ever solved. They were hard to purify and easily destroyed. Modest heating or treatment with acids or alkalis was enough to change a protein's native shape and kill its activity—"denaturation," it was called. Simply whipping a protein with a fork was sometimes enough to denature it, as a beaten egg white demonstrates.

Hemoglobin at least offered some advantages. It was easy to gather in bulk and in almost pure form from the red blood cells of cattle or sheep. Better yet, it could be crystallized, which meant that it had a regular, repeating structure of some sort. Anything that could be crystallized at least offered the possibility of being solved with x-ray diffraction.

Hemoglobin could also be taken apart and examined in pieces. It was a conjugated protein, a protein linked to other structures, in this case a ringlike molecule called porphyrin, which in turn was attached to an iron atom, which in turn bonded somehow to the oxygen that hemoglobin carried throughout the body. Pauling had been interested in porphyrin since 1929 when he visited Harvard and James Bryant Conant had shown him some work he was doing with it. This molecular subunit was interesting not only because of its unusual shape—it appeared to be a ring made out of smaller rings—but also because it was found across nature, binding oxygen in the chlorophyll of plants as well as the hemoglobin of a variety of animals. Porphyrin seemed to epitomize the molecular biology idea of the commonality of life at the molecular level: It showed up almost everywhere there was life, playing a similar role in very different organisms.

Prophyrin was made of four subunits, called pyrroles, linked together to make the ring. Each pyrrole itself was a ring of atoms in which single and double bonds alternated, a "conjugated" structure, it was called, a type whose chemistry Pauling had described in one of his papers on the nature of the chemical bond. Pyrrole was a natural starting place for attacking hemoglobin. From there, Pauling could look up a ladder of increasing complexity: Four pyrroles linked together to make one porphyrin ring; one porphyrin ring plus one atom of iron to form a heme; each heme attached to a globular protein to make a heme-globin unit; four heme-globins joined together to make a molecule of hemoglobin. The final structure was almost too gigantic to think about: a roughly spherical mass containing thousands upon thousands of atoms. Pauling quickly concluded that it was far too complex to attack directly with x-ray crystallography, although some optimistic British researchers, funded with Rockefeller money, were trying to do just that. But perhaps he could break the hemoglobin molecule into its component pieces, solve the subunits, and then put it back together again.

Pauling started reading everything he could find on hemoglobin, including an in-depth review of how the molecule bound oxygen. Here was a mystery. Researchers had found that oxygen did not bind to the four hemes in hemoglobin as if they were independent of one another. Instead, the binding of the first oxygen atom made it easier for the remaining three to bind, and losing one oxygen atom made it easier to lose the rest. Somehow the hemes were communicating with each other. This explained in part how hemoglobin could pick up oxygen in the lungs and drop it off elsewhere in the body, but communication within a molecule was a difficult phenomenon to explain in chemical terms.

After a few weeks mulling it over, though, Pauling came up with an ingenious idea. He devised an equation that described the data others had gathered on oxygen binding, then made a mathematical analysis of various relationships among the four heme groups in space until he came up with an orientation that seemed to fit the binding curves. The most likely orientation for the four hemes, he said, was at the corners of a flat square. His idea was later proved wrong, but when it appeared in 1935, it excited discussion among the medical researchers and biochemists who formed the majority of hemoglobin researchers. They had not seen this kind of approach in their field. It was clear that a new talent had appeared with a new way of looking at things.

When Pauling published his idea, it showed Weaver that his commitment to a new research program was real. But Pauling's other work on the hemoglobin molecule was not going as well. The new x-ray technique he was trying on porphyrins quickly proved too cumbersome to provide quick results. Pauling dropped it, telling Weaver that he was not the kind of chemist who spent two years on the detailed crystal analysis of a single compound. Solving the structure of hemoglobin would take twenty years of grinding, repetitive x-ray work and would win someone else the Nobel Prize.

Pauling's one-year Rockefeller grant was due to expire, so he applied for a new grant for more basic research. Weaver could not promise any Rockefeller money for nonbiological work, but he had another idea. He suggested that Pauling use the potential of Rockefeller support as a lever to get Millikan to pitch in five thousand dollars or so of Caltech money for fundamental studies. A display of support like that from his institution plus the progress of Pauling's recent hemoglobin work might convince the Rockefeller board of trustees to extend its grant to three years. Pauling took Weaver's advice and added a threat of his own: He would accept an offer from another university if

Millikan did not come through. He got his five thousand per year. Pauling telegraphed Weaver the good news; Weaver quickly wrote him back that the board voted to extend his grant of ten thousand dollars per year for another three years.

In three years, Weaver and Pauling had moved from patron and grantee to coconspirators and friends.

With his funding stabilized, Pauling was free to try other approaches to hemoglobin and indulge new interests. In 1935 he and a former student turned postdoctoral fellow, E. Bright Wilson, finished the three-year task of transforming the lecture notes from Pauling's wave-mechanics course into a book, *Introduction to Quantum Mechanics, with Applications to Chemistry*. Although sales were less than spectacular for the first few years after publication—quantum mechanics wasn't yet accepted as standard fare for chemists—the book would prove both durable and influential, staying in print for three decades and acquainting generations of students with the importance of the new physics.

Also in 1935, Pauling had a flash of insight that led to a paper on "orientational disorder"—a theory concerning water molecules that explained the residual entropy of ice at absolute zero. It was purely theoretical work, harkening back to his days with Tolman. Thirty years later, when sophisticated computers were finally able to run the numbers thoroughly, Pauling's theory was proven right. Now called "proton disorder," the idea became, as one student of the field said, "the most important American contribution to the modern crystallography of water."

But those were side trips: Hemoglobin was the destination.

Pauling was now finding that biology could be almost as interesting as chemistry. He spent much of the summer of 1935 at the Caltech marine research facility at Corona del Mar, extracting hemocyanin, a hemoglobin relative, from the blue blood of the keyhole limpet and becoming friends with a tall, young Caltech biology professor named Albert Tyler, who was trying to figure out the mechanism of self-sterility in sea urchins. This work of Tyler's increased Pauling's interest in another unexplained property of living systems, the ability to distinguish between self and nonself, to have molecules capable of reacting differently with one's own body than with others'. Perhaps there was a chemical connection there as well. Pauling, always looking for new ideas, filed that one away.

By the time he returned to Pasadena, Pauling had come up with a novel way to investigate hemoglobin by looking at its magnetic behavior. Pauling reasoned that when oxygen bound to the iron in hemoglobin, it probably did so covalently—the reaction was highly specific and fairly strong—which would mean that at least one of its unpaired electrons would be paired and its paramagnetism—a quality of molecules with one or more unpaired electrons—would decrease. If he could measure the change in paramagnetism, he might be able to answer the question of how oxygen bound to hemoglobin.

He already had a large, water-cooled magnet that he had borrowed for other work from Hale's private lab, and in the fall of 1935 he put Charles Coryell, an energetic, enthusiastic, newly minted Caltech Ph.D., to work with it. The experiment they set up was fairly simple: A small glass tube containing cow's blood was suspended between the poles of the magnet on a thread attached to the arm of a sensitive balance. When the magnet was switched on, a paramagnetic substance would be drawn in one direction; the balance would measure the degree of magnetic change.

They tried oxygenated blood and deoxygenated blood and appropriate controls and found that Pauling's prediction was right: The bound oxygen lost its unpaired electrons, which became involved in forming a covalent bond to the iron atom. This was an important step forward, proving that oxygen did not just adsorb nonspecifically, as some researchers had argued. But there were other surprises in the behavior of the hemoglobin molecule. Pauling and Coryell's experiments showed that the iron atom in hemoglobin underwent dramatic changes when it bound to oxygen as well, switching the bonds that held it in its porphyrin cage from ionic to covalent. "It is interesting and surprising that the hemoglobin molecule undergoes such an extreme structural change on the addition of oxygen," Pauling wrote. "Such a difference in bond type in very closely related substances has been observed so far only in hemoglobin derivatives."

The appearance of Pauling and Coryell's hemoglobin papers in 1936 continued to expand Pauling's renown. They had devised a very clever approach to solving an old problem and provided a clear indication that a physical chemist could do useful work in the field of biochemistry. He was now becoming known by researchers far removed from his original area of expertise. He had entered a new field and quickly begun to conquer it.

Hair and Horn

So far Pauling's work concerned the heme portion of the molecule, but at the same time, Pauling was thinking hard about the rest of it— the globin part, the protein. Protein chemistry was a large and some-what disjointed field, and Pauling started teaching himself about it through his usual process, conducting a vast review of the scientific literature while keeping an eye out for entry points, places where his knowledge of chemistry could offer an insight. He found that proteins were constructed out of a relatively small number of basic building blocks called amino acids, some twenty different ones, but all of them alike in one crucial respect: Each had an identical three-atom backbone, carbon-carbon-nitrogen. The end carbon was part of a carboxyl group, the end nitrogen part of an amino group. The only thing that differed among the various amino acids were side chains that were attached to the middle carbon. The great German organic chemist Emil Fischer had shown just after the turn of the century how amino acids could link up into longer chains by joining the two ends, carboxyl group to amino group, through a covalent link that Fischer called a peptide bond. The resulting long molecules he called polypeptide chains. By the 1930s, while not everyone agreed that all proteins contained polypeptide chains, it was increasingly thought that at least some proteins did.

Fischer's work looked reasonable to Pauling, and he began thinking of proteins in Fischer's terms, as long chains of peptide-bonded amino acids. But how could this long-chain structure account for the incredible variety of proteins and the dizzying assortment of roles they played in the body? Were all proteins made of various arrangements of polypeptide chains, or were there other basic structures?

Structure, as always, was Pauling's focus. The way a protein was built, he believed, had to determine its activity. But discovering how they were built seemed an impossible task. Protein structures were far too complex to solve directly with electron diffraction or x-ray crystallography. Recent work by Theodor Svedberg in Sweden, for instance, proved that hemoglobin was a molecular leviathan, a conglomeration of tens of thousands of atoms. Other proteins were almost as big.

Belle Pauling, Linus's mother, around 1900. Chronically ill, constantly worried about money, Belle was never able to give Linus the love or understanding he needed.

3

Linus's father, Herman Pauling, in his drugstore around 1899. Herman was Linus's role model; his death when Linus was nine years old was devastating.

Linus at age one, 1902.

2

4

Linus Pauling (far left) with his fraternity brothers at Oregon Agricultural College (now Oregon State University), where he started teaching chemistry while still an undergraduate. He was called "the boy professor."

High-spirited, flirtatious Ava Helen Miller (right), in costume for a play, around the time she first met Pauling at Oregon Agricultural College.

5

Ava Helen Pauling in
1925.

6

Young lovers Ava He-
len and Linus Pauling
about the time they
moved to California in
the early 1920s.

7

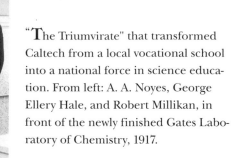

"The Triumvirate" that transformed Caltech from a local vocational school into a national force in science education. From left: A. A. Noyes, George Ellery Hale, and Robert Millikan, in front of the newly finished Gates Laboratory of Chemistry, 1917.

A. A. Noyes at the wheel of "Old Mossie," the Cadillac touring car that became legendary among Caltech students. G. N. Lewis is on the running board.

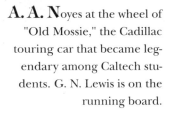

The Pauling family on the steps of their Sierra Madre house, just before World War II. Linus junior is standing next to his sister, Linda; Peter is in the foreground; and Crellin is on his mother's lap.

A monastery devoted to science: the Caltech campus in the 1950s, during the time Pauling was fighting for a nuclear test ban. The Gates Laboratory is in the background.

11

12

Pauling with George Beadle at Caltech in the 1950s. Together, the chemist and the biologist made Caltech into a world-renowned center for the study of molecular biology.

Pauling surrounded by admirers after winning the 1954 Nobel Prize in chemistry. On the right is Ava Helen; behind is daughter Linda; and to the left is his daughter-in-law Anita.

13

14

Pauling in his Caltech office around 1957, surrounded by molecular models.

15

The Pauling and Edward Teller debate about fallout from atomic tests, on San Francisco television, 1958. When it was over, Pauling refused to debate Teller again.

(Opposite page, bottom)

Pauling's blackboard at Caltech, 1963. Soon after, he left Caltech because of what he felt was a lack of appreciation for his work.

Pauling picketing the White House, 1961. The next evening, Pauling dined inside with the President and Mrs. Kennedy and a group of distinguished intellectuals. Jackie Kennedy told Pauling at the dinner that her daughter, Caroline, had looked out the window at this protest and asked, "Mummy, what has Daddy done now?"

Pauling makes his point with the Senate Internal Security Committee. He was subpoenaed to appear before them in the summer of 1960 to explain the genesis of his peace petitions; his refusal to answer questions led to a threat of a contempt citation.

19

Nobel Peace Prize winner Linus Pauling and Ava Helen Pauling join a torchlight parade given in their honor by Norwegian students during the Nobel ceremonies. The award of the prize caused a firestorm of controversy in the United States.

Linus Pauling at age eighty-six, during his long battle for acceptance of megadoses of vitamin C.

20

Still, some laboratories were trying to use x-rays to get at least a preliminary idea of the structure of proteins. The two most important sites were in Britain. At Leeds, William Astbury was investigating the molecular structure of wool and other so-called fibrous proteins, hair, horn, feathers, and muscle fibers among them. His results—a surprise to many scientists—clearly showed a regular repeating structure, a crystalline structure, in these proteins.

One mystery Astbury thought he had figured out was wool's ability to stretch without breaking and then snap back to its original length. Wool, like horn, fingernail, and human hair, fell into a general class of proteins called keratin, and by the early 1930s, Astbury, too, was convinced that keratin was made of long, stringlike polypeptide chains. "Molecular yarn," he called it. His x-ray photos showed that when wool stretched, something changed at the molecular level. Although the photos were too fuzzy to allow him to place individual atoms, he saw enough to theorize that the stretched form of keratin—he named it the beta form—was like a polypeptide string pulled fairly straight, while the unstretched or alpha form was puckered or folded. His measurements indicated that the folding occurred in two dimensions rather than three—as though in the alpha form the string were bent into a sawtooth pattern on a tabletop. Further studies showed this same basic pattern in muscle fibers.

This was an important step forward, a molecular explanation for the properties of a protein. Perhaps, Astbury thought, this molecular folding might also explain the contraction of muscle and chromosomes. He began to think of keratin as "the grandfather of all proteins," a basic structure that might explain the workings of all the others.

But he was getting carried away. X-ray diffraction was still inadequate to solve something as big as the polypeptide chain in wool keratin, with its thousands of atoms per strand. It was impossible to say precisely how keratin was built, and the nature of the forces that held it in place were still mysteries. It had not even been proved yet that keratin was made of long polypeptide chains—Astbury's work only indicated that it was probable.

Pauling made careful note of Astbury's work.

mm

While Astbury concentrated on fibrous proteins like keratin, a second British group was focusing on the molecular structure of globular proteins, those that dissolve in the body's fluids, such as hemoglobin, antibodies, and enzymes. The problem here was getting good crystals. It was not that globular proteins did not crystallize—it had been known for years that hemoglobin, for instance, when dried, would form crystals—but when x-rayed, they gave nothing but vague blurs. This led some protein chemists to postulate that globular proteins had no internal structure but were more or less random aggregates of amino acids upon which the real players in the body—nonprotein molecules like vitamins and hormones—oriented themselves.

It was not until 1934 that the Cambridge crystallographer John D. Bernal proved differently. Bernal discovered that globular proteins were like jellyfish: They needed a liquid environment to retain their structure. When dried, they collapsed. By x-raying them suspended in liquids, Bernal was able to get usable patterns, and by the late 1930s, he was the center of a small group dedicated to cracking the structure of globular proteins. He and his coworkers—among them Dorothy Crowfoot and the young Vienna-trained chemist Max Perutz—purified, crystallized, and photographed a number of globular proteins: insulin, hemoglobin, chymotrypsin, excelsin. It was a heroic effort made in miserable surroundings. Perutz remembered that their Cambridge laboratory, "a few ill-lit and dirty rooms on the ground floor of a stark, dilapidated grey building," turned into a "fairy castle" by Bernal's brilliance. They found that all the globular proteins they looked at had an ordered structure and that all of them were terrifically complex—so complex that Pauling, when he saw the photos coming from Cambridge, quickly decided that it would take decades to solve them through direct x-ray analysis, if it was possible at all. The work of Astbury and Bernal began to attract increasing attention, including the notice of Warren Weaver, who began giving them research grants in the mid-1930s. Fueled by Rockefeller money, three centers now began to coalesce around the question of precise protein structure. The first two, led by Astbury and Bernal, both of them physicists, worked from the premise that the secret could be unlocked only by painstaking, direct x-ray analysis of whole proteins. The third, in Pasadena, led by Pauling, began looking for theoretical approaches, shortcuts based on an understanding of structural chemistry. The difference in 1935 was that the British had generated a good deal of hard data from their x-ray work, while Pauling had yet to publish a single paper on the general topic of protein structure.

Hydrogen Bigamy

Pauling quickly recognized that if he wanted to perform experiments with these strange, giant protein molecules, he would need help.

A group at the Rockefeller Institute for Medical Research had the expertise he lacked. Recent experiments by two Rockefeller scientists, Alfred Mirsky and Mortimer Anson, indicated that in some cases denaturation could be reversed; hemoglobin, for instance, could be heated enough to change its shape and lose its ability to carry oxygen, but if cooled carefully, at least some of the molecules could regain their original form and properties. This link between structure and function caught Pauling's eye, but more important was the Rockefeller team's laboratory expertise. On a trip to New York in the spring of 1935, Pauling visited Mirsky, and they hit it off. Mirsky was both intrigued and taken aback when Pauling asked him to come to Caltech for a couple of years. He stammered about how that might be a very nice idea but that the institute's president, Simon Flexner, would never allow it on such short notice. Pauling said he thought Flexner might. He found the president's office, talked his way in for a meeting, and asked Flexner not only for permission for Mirsky's leave but also that the Rockefeller Institute pay for it. Flexner, a Rockefeller Foundation board member, had heard about Pauling from Weaver. Amused by the young scientist's brashness and intrigued by his application of chemical techniques to biology, he agreed.

Mirsky arrived in Pasadena at the beginning of the summer and began a further series of experiments on the denaturation of egg white, muscle, and other proteins. Pauling let Mirsky handle the laboratory work while they fed each other ideas about the chemical basis of denaturation—what the process actually did to the structure of proteins. Pauling was interested in the evidence Mirsky and Anson had gathered indicating that denaturation could be seen as a two-level process. The first, which could be caused by relatively mild heating or acid, was often reversible. The second level, caused by higher heat, harsher chemical conditions, or reaction with protein-destroying enzymes, was irreversible. Pauling quickly translated the data into chemical-bond terms. Two levels of denaturation could mean two kinds of chemical bonds, the first involving relatively weak bonds, easily broken and re-formed; the second, perhaps strong bonds that would be harder to break and more difficult to remake. The experimental evidence on the energy it took to break the strong, second-level bonds indicated they were covalent; this in turn could fit with the view of proteins as long chains of amino acids linked with covalent peptide bonds. The second level of denaturation basically tore the protein into pieces.

It was Pauling's approach to the weaker bonds that proved most fruitful. He realized quickly that the energy involved in breaking first-level bonds fit what he knew about a strange kind of link called the hydrogen bond. In 1935 he was one of the few researchers in America who understood and appreciated hydrogen bonds. The idea was that hydrogen, instead of being held by a single covalent or ionic link, as it normally was, could in certain cases be held jointly by two atoms, forming a bridge between them. Pauling saw how it worked in his scheme of chemical bonding: On one side, the hydrogen atom had to be near a strongly electronegative atom—an oxygen, for instance, or a fluorine—which would pull the hydrogen's sole electron toward it, concentrating the charge in the area in between the two nuclei, creating a small net negative charge on that side. As a result, the other side of the hydrogen would be electron-poor, creating a small positive charge, which could then form an electrostatic bond—a hydrogen bond—with nearby negatively charged atoms or parts of molecules. Pauling had written about the hydrogen-bond concept as early as 1928, tied it to his resonance theory in 1934, and used it in a major way in his 1935 paper on the entropy of ice.

Now he became convinced by Mirsky's denaturation work that hydrogen bonds were a vital component in protein structure. By the fall of 1935, the two of them had roughed out a new theory based on his reasoning. "Our conception of a native protein molecule (showing specific properties) is the following," the authors wrote. "The molecule consists of one polypeptide chain which continues without interruption throughout the molecule (or, in certain cases, of two or more such chains); this chain is folded into a uniquely defined configuration, in which it is held by hydrogen bonds. . . ." All proteins, in other words, were made of strings of amino acids, polypeptide chains, possibly in the form of the Ur-protein keratin, as Astbury thought. Strong peptide links kept the chain in one piece, but weaker hydrogen bonds between sections twisted and folded it into its final, determinative shape. This final shape was vital to the protein's function; the molecule would not perform its function unless its form was maintained. Slight heating broke the hydrogen bonds, allowing the chains to straighten out and tangle like loose yarn in a sewing box. As long as the chain remained in one piece, however, under the right conditions the hydrogen bonds could re-form and the protein could regain its original shape and activity. Stronger treatment would break the chain itself, severing peptide bonds and irreversibly denaturing the protein.

When it appeared in the *Proceedings of the National Academy of Sciences (PNAS)* in July 1936, the paper, "On the Structure of Native, Denatured, and Coagulated Proteins," was quickly recognized as an important advance in the field. At a stroke, Pauling's understanding of the chemical bond had provided a single unifying explanation for many diverse observations about protein denaturation and protein activity. Weaver was pleased: Although final acceptance of Pauling's ideas would prove slow, he had taken a major step toward solving Weaver's "giant protein problem."

But two days after the paper arrived in the offices of the *PNAS* on June 1, 1936, Pauling's life underwent a major change for reasons entirely unrelated to proteins.

King, Pope, Wizard

The Young Dictator

A. A. Noyes's health had long been fragile. During the 1920s he was diagnosed, incorrectly, with cancer, was checked for tuberculosis, tried glandular injections to pep himself up, and underwent a painful throat operation to relieve an abscess caused by choking on a crouton. As early as 1928 he believed that he was "likely to have at most five or six years of active life—perhaps less." He began then to focus his shrinking energies on fewer projects, foremost among them the perfection of Caltech's undergraduate education program. The combination of Noyes's failing health and concentration on curriculum through the early 1930s made it seem to Pauling as if the needs of the chemistry division were being slighted.

But it was typical of Noyes to place the institute first. In order to help lure Millikan to Pasadena in the early 1920s, he had agreed with Hale to devote the lion's share of Caltech's resources to physics. As a result, Millikan's empire grew rapidly; by 1927 there were sixty graduate students in physics compared with twenty in chemistry.

It was the reverse of the situation in older universities like Harvard and Cornell, where chemistry was still the king of the natural sciences, with more faculty, money, and respect than physics. Noyes, however, had come west to do something new. He believed that a small division was better for morale, more likely to crossbreed ideas and less likely to break into fractious subdisciplines, and that a small faculty could better interact with a carefully chosen student body. He was in any case a quintessential team player, temperamentally unsuited for turf battles and satisfied with chemistry's slower growth. Despite its second-place status, the overall budget for the Division of Chemistry and Chemical Engineering nearly tripled during the decade of the 1920s, helped by the Carnegie Institution's support of twenty different research projects. Even when the Depression hit, forcing cuts in research funds and the temporary abandonment of plans for a new chemistry building, Noyes did not appear to worry. Slow and steady was the plan.

It suited most of the faculty, who wanted nothing more than to teach, oversee a small laboratory, and occasionally produce an interesting paper. Only Pauling chafed at the bit. He needed things to happen; his own research group was growing as fast as the number of ideas he had; graduate students and postdoctoral fellows were flocking to work with him; he needed more space and more money to keep expanding. At Harvard he had seen how chemistry was treated compared to physics. Why was Noyes not doing a better job lobbying for his division?

For years Noyes kept his young genius satisfied by negotiating new space, backing Pauling's salary demands, and arranging promotions. He also ran interference with Millikan, who was becoming irritated by the assertive young professor. Pauling's repeated threats to leave unless he was given what he wanted gave Millikan the impression of a fellow a little too pushy, too full of himself. Perhaps he was as good as Noyes said. But in the physics department he would not have been so coddled.

Noyes, however, would pay almost any price to keep Pauling. He understood chemistry and Pauling's growing importance to the field in ways Millikan could not. Pauling's quantum-physics-based bond work, supplemented and expanded by his x-ray and electron-diffraction studies, his unique ability to correlate structure and theory, to take an idea that explained the structure of ice and apply it to the structure of proteins, represented a major leap toward the all-embracing physical chemistry that Ostwald had preached to Noyes forty years before. And the young man's energy! He dove into his work, lived and breathed chemistry like no one Noyes had seen since G. N. Lewis. There seemed no end to Pauling's ability to generate original ideas.

And he was Noyes's creation. Noyes had found him and guided

him and transformed the raw young Oregonian into an international phenomenon. Pauling was living proof of his mentor's skill in picking talent and of the power of the educational theories Noyes had put into operation at Caltech.

And there, Noyes decided, he would stay.

In order to ensure Pauling's loyalty, Noyes knew that he would have to offer more than kind words and money. He would need to offer power. So as soon as Pauling achieved the rank of full professor in the mid-1930s, Noyes made it clear to him and to important figures like Weaver that Pauling was being groomed to be the next director of the Caltech Division of Chemistry and Chemical Engineering.

On the face of it, this looked outrageous in a division gifted with so many scientists senior to Pauling in both age and academic experience—including the renowned and nationally respected Richard Tolman—but experience was less important to Noyes than promise. "Whether he is old or young is, to be sure, not the primary consideration," Noyes wrote. Instead, the director of a chemical school must be above all "a man thoroughly conversant and sympathetic with research . . . responsive to and creative of new ideas." Administrative know-how was secondary to "the ability to put through new plans of furthering science and research."

Here Pauling had no competition. Tolman's research was increasingly solitary and idiosyncratic—ruminations on cosmology had now replaced important work related to chemistry—and in any case, he had protested from the time he was hired that he had little interest in administration. William Lacey, Stuart Bates, and Dickinson, all senior to Pauling, were happy to teach and crank out relatively routine research from small laboratories. Only Pauling, with his effusion of new ideas, mastery of new techniques, ability to attract top students and run a large, productive laboratory, as well as his strong relationship with the Rockefeller Foundation, had what Noyes thought it took to lead. While any of the senior men could competently lead the division, only Pauling could make it great. As early as 1932, Noyes was telling Weaver that Pauling was his likely successor.

Then he wavered. As time went on, he saw things in Pauling that made him uncomfortable, personal traits so different from his own that he thought twice about his plan for succession. Although his nickname was King Arthur, Noyes was anything but an autocrat. He believed in cooperative, corporate-style management, with a CEO-type leader acting on the advice of strong faculty committees; the faculty, acting through their committees, actually determined much of the division's business. This was a considered response to what Noyes had found distasteful in the German chemical institutes, where the *Geheimrat*'s research was central and his decisions absolute; the German model, he thought, created followers instead of independent thinkers, "the frequent outcome of the system being one good man at the head overburdened with administrative details and a group of merely good men in subordinate positions," he said.

As Pauling's research expanded, he began in many ways to take on the attitudes that Noyes disliked. In Pauling's laboratory, Pauling determined the questions asked and the means used to answer them; he assigned others to solve problems for him rather than teaching them to think for themselves. It was good, meaningful research carried out in an exciting intellectual atmosphere, and his students and postdoctoral fellows never complained; they were learning a new approach to chemistry that would later open doors for faculty positions at the nation's best research centers.

The complaints came from other faculty members. Pauling not only ran his laboratory in the German style; he also was perceived as fighting for himself and his own research first and the needs of the division second. This "aggressive managerial style," as one professor called it, did not sit well with his fellow professors, men who were now colleagues but might soon be working under him. By the mid-1930s a reaction against Pauling was growing among members of his division. Senior faculty members viewed him as something of a prima donna; younger ones were jealous of his quick success. Suffusing it all was a sort of fraternal jealousy: everyone knew that Pauling was the King's favorite son, not just a fair-haired boy but "Noyes's white-haired boy," as one man had put it. Pauling, intensely focused on his own work, had neither the time nor the inclination to mollify his colleagues.

Noyes was concerned about that and worried, too, about Pauling's apparent lack of interest in the larger issues of the institute. The young man's devotion to his career seemed absolute. He came across as a loner, out for himself first, the division of chemistry second, and Caltech last. He had no skill or apparent interest in academic politics; he made demands of the administration instead of requests. Millikan did not like him. Noyes saw in his protégé a disturbing element of impatience and an inability to place his own needs into context. All of this seemed only to get worse as Pauling grew more successful.

On the other hand, Pauling performed his divisional committee work efficiently and was an extraordinary teacher with at least a passing interest in the curriculum of the division, especially the way in which undergraduates were taught chemistry. Perhaps he could be taught to take more of a hand in institutional affairs. In the early 1930s, Noyes drafted a plan to bring younger faculty members "into contact with the problems and ideals of the institution" by making them part of a committee on policies that would consult with Caltech's ruling executive group; Pauling and Tolman were his nominees from chemistry. On another occasion, Pauling remembered Noyes appointing him "executive officer" of the division, a position Noyes may have created as a stepping-stone to eventual directorship. "But I never did anything as executive officer," Pauling said. "He didn't turn over any duties to me."

Noyes was still hesitating when in early 1935 he received shattering news: He had cancer of the colon. His only chance, his physician explained to him, was immediate surgery. Noyes, terrified by the thought of an operation, said no. He kept his condition a secret from everyone except Hale, Millikan, and a few close friends and began to stay away from the institute, spending more time in his little house on San Pasqual Street near Caltech or his seaside place at Corona del Mar. There he could watch the gulls soar and the waves roll in, hear the wind-carried chattering of people on the beach, and remember the sea spray off Cape Cod and his sunny days in Italy. There he could put aside the worries of administration.

~~~

Despite his attempts at secrecy, soon it was whispered through the institute that Noyes was fatally ill.

Pauling's response confirmed everyone's worst fears. For several years he had expected to succeed Noyes, and now it seemed his time had come. Decisions had to be made about the development of organic chemistry, about the long-term relationship with the Rockefeller Foundation, about Depression-caused delays in the construction of the new chemistry building. Noyes seemed to have backed off from any decision making, and Pauling needed to know what was going to happen, especially regarding the time line for his assumption of the directorship. But no one seemed to be approaching him to talk about it. Noyes had gone into semiseclusion, and Millikan kept his distance. Finally, Pauling decided to act on his own. He used a job offer from Ohio State in July 1935 as a pretense to meet with Millikan to talk over his situation.

It was a disaster. Millikan was as close to Noyes as he was to any man and very concerned about his friend's illness; the last thing he wanted was to handle yet another apparent salary demand from Pauling. The meeting soured quickly when Pauling started complaining about funding, telling Millikan that more money should be allocated to chemistry and reminding him of the relative positions of chemistry and physics at other universities. Millikan did not dignify that with an answer; as far as he could see, while Noyes was still alive and chairman, divisional funding was none of Pauling's business. Then the real purpose of the meeting became clear to him: Pauling was looking for assurances about assuming the directorship when Noyes died. Millikan was infuriated. Struggling to control his temper, he told Pauling that there were no plans for expanding the chemistry division's share of institute money. Then, when Pauling kept returning to the subject of the directorship, he let himself explode. Millikan told the upstart that he was far too young to even consider the chairmanship and that as far as he was concerned, Pauling should not even bother to think about the possibility of that sort of administrative position for at least another ten or fifteen years. Then he showed him the door.

Pauling exited in a state of shock. Millikan's remarks contradicted everything he thought had been set in place for his future. And Millikan was mistaken about his youth being determinative. Pauling was now thirty-four years old, three years older than Slater had been when he took over physics at MIT and only a few years younger than Conant was when he was named president of Harvard. Something else was wrong.

After two weeks of coming to terms with his new situation, Pauling decided to find out what it was. He sent Noyes a carefully worded letter with a familiar refrain: "I feel I am forced to leave the Institute. . . . The only reason that I hesitate for a time is that there is the possibility that I have misunderstood the statements which have been made to me regarding the plans for developing the Division of Chemistry and the role that is planned for me."

Noyes read the letter in Corona del Mar. He had avoided making any decisions for a few months, but now it appeared he would have to thrash out the question of Pauling's future, a process that he feared might tear apart the chemistry division he had spent the last years of his life building. He had his secretary make a copy of Pauling's note and hand-deliver it to Hale, with a cover note of his own. "Pauling is restless, ambitious and self-seeking," Noyes wrote, "but I really believe that his desire to develop a large research center in fields of chemistry outside his own is his main thought." Then he requested an immediate emergency meeting with Tolman, Hale, and Millikan.

At the meeting, it quickly became clear that there was no simple solution. Millikan was for Tolman taking over; not only was he the senior man, but he was the right sort; he belonged to the same private clubs and moved in the same social circles as Millikan and many of Caltech's biggest donors. Everyone remembered Pauling as a penniless graduate student from the sticks living in a shabby rented house with his young wife and baby. How could he deal with the multimillionaires that Caltech needed to cultivate? Millikan was especially nervous about how the brash Pauling would mix with his board of trustees. Noyes, however, still did not believe Tolman's heart was in either chemistry or administration and argued that losing Pauling would mean a major setback for the institute. Tolman himself expressed reservations about trying to replace Noyes alone.

A compromise was finally reached: The leadership of the chemistry division would be split. Pauling would be chair in name, but his power would be shared with a new chemistry division council, a group of five faculty members who would become the final authority on appointments, promotions, salary, and budget. Tolman would deal with the trustees by serving as the chemistry division's representative to the Caltech Executive Council.

That was the plan in July, but by the time it was formally approved in November, Pauling's role was further diminished. Perhaps Noyes could not bring himself to retire; perhaps there was too much resistance to the plan from the chemistry faculty. In any case, the final version listed Noyes as chairman of the chemistry division council and Pauling as a member. The chairman's role was downgraded as well, limited to those of an *ex officio* member of the council, able to bring matters before the group but not to vote. This mechanism would ensure that Noyes's cooperative, faculty-driven model would survive his death, that no one person could run the division. Thus stripped of all meaning, the position of chairman of the chemistry division council was ready to hand to Pauling when the time came.

Pauling got the message. Just after Christmas, he wrote Conant saying that he was interested in coming to Harvard. But things had changed since the courting of Pauling seven years earlier. There were now many more young chemists trained in quantum mechanics to choose from—just the year before Harvard had hired one of Pauling's most gifted students, E. Bright Wilson—and transferring Pauling's large research group east would require a good deal of money. After two weeks of reviewing his Depression-strapped budget, Conant wrote back, "I regret to say there does not seem to be any possibility now of providing you with the opportunities here at Harvard which you would need."

Crestfallen after this double blow to his ego, Pauling threw himself back into research. Noyes helped salve his wounds by involving him in plans for a last great project he wanted to bring to fruition, a school of bio-organic chemistry, a new interdisciplinary research group that would reshape biology by using the tools of modern chemistry. Pauling, he said, would be the school's intellectual leader and would get an entire floor of a new building for his group. Other faculty, the best in the world, would be hired later. The promise of more space and a higher-profile research role helped Pauling deal with his discouragement and focus on his work.

When Warren Weaver visited Caltech in March 1936, he was delighted to learn about Pauling's progress with hemoglobin and even more happy when Pauling told him over dinner at his home about his new zeal for research on other proteins, work that might lead even to an attack on cancer.

Weaver also met with Noyes, now visibly weakened, who marshaled his failing energy to lobby for money to expand, equip, and staff his school of bio-organic chemistry. Weaver was excited about the idea—it represented, after all, a physical realization of the approach to biology that Weaver had long endorsed—and he told Noyes that he was interested in following up the idea with his board.

Feeling confident about the project and eager to put things in order before he died, Noyes asked Pauling to make a thorough study of personnel possibilities for the new school. But now it was Pauling who counseled restraint, writing Noyes that it might be better to wait to prepare a detailed plan for the Rockefeller Foundation, one that could be organized around the progress of Pauling's own research. Noyes was in no mood to wait. He had already decided that he would go to the Mayo Clinic for a colon operation, his last chance for a cure, and he quickly sent Weaver a six-page outline of proposed developments in organic chemistry, with details about the planned building, for which a private donor had already pledged funds. Then Pauling was sent on a talent-scouting trip to the East Coast, where he continued to drag his feet. He cautioned Weaver in New York that he thought Noyes "a little bit apt, in his present condition, to hurry . . . in order to assure the development during his own remaining term." Pauling still assumed that he would become chairman, in whatever emasculated form it was offered to him, and could see no sense in being bound by the last acts of a mortally ill man. He intended to make his own decisions when his time came.

He did not have long to wait. The Mayo operation was unsuccessful, and in May, Noyes returned to Pasadena. He set himself up in the bed of his house on San Pasqual Street, attended by his maid and a longtime assistant. Pauling, busy putting the finishing touches on his denaturation paper with Mirsky, visited him twice during these last weeks; on neither occasion was any mention made of his assuming the chairmanship.

On June 3, 1936, the news spread across campus: The King is dead.

m

It was the passing of an era.

Noyes's reserve, gentility, and generosity were rooted in the nineteenth century; his was a slower, more cultured, less grasping approach to life that was fast disappearing. There would be no more student-chauffeured expeditions in Old Mossie, no more cocoa at seminars, no more of what Millikan in his eulogy called Noyes's "sweetness of character." There would be no more poetry. The future now belonged to less romantic, more pragmatic, faster-moving men like Pauling—men of the twentieth century.

The moderating influence that Noyes had exerted over his division became apparent by its absence after his death. The rancor that had been festering among the faculty for the past year was now made public. Some faculty members believed Pauling had pushed Noyes too hard while he was ill, one telling Weaver that Pauling had "worried and pestered [Noyes] in an unwarranted and even unforgivable way, trying to force him into an intolerable activity of leadership for chemistry," even, perhaps, hastening Noyes's death. The senior faculty, Tolman, Dickinson, and Lacey, echoed the feeling in a frank letter to Millikan in which they "suggested" Pauling's temporary elevation to chairman—as recently redefined and rendered powerless—only because of his research importance to Caltech and "in spite of misgivings as to the complete suitability of Professor Pauling for this position. . . . We mistrust to some extent his judgment as to matters of policy and his generosity and sincerity in personal dealings."

The breadth of the anti-Pauling feeling became public at Noyes's funeral, where the honorary pallbearers included every member of the Caltech Executive Council and every member of the Division of Chemistry and Chemical Engineering—except Pauling. Embarrassed by being singled out in this way, Pauling went to Millikan demanding to know why he had been omitted. Millikan pleaded ignorance, saying that the list had been prepared by the chemistry division.

There were more insults to come. After the funeral the offer of the chairmanship was made—but to Tolman, not Pauling. This may have been a simple formality recognizing seniority, since Tolman had already made it clear that he did not want the position and quickly declined, but it had the effect of another slap in Pauling's face.

Humiliated and angry by the time the chairmanship was finally offered to him, Pauling turned it down. Without carefully considering the consequences, he dashed off a brief and blunt letter of refusal to Millikan. The new division council structure, he wrote, meant that he would carry responsibility without any authority. The proposed salary of $7,500 was too small. He would need assurances regarding the future institutional support of chemistry. And he expected to be offered not only the title of chairman but Noyes's second title of director of the Gates Laboratory. After handing in the letter on August 10, he packed up his family and left on a vacation trip to Oregon.

When he returned in two weeks, he wrote a friend: "Our Chemistry Department is still in an unorganized state, and I am afraid that we are in for a good bit of troble before things are straightened out." Millikan had expected that Pauling, perhaps chastened by Noyes's death, would give him a gracious reply to the offer of the chairmanship; he had been so taken aback by the tone of Pauling's letter that he refused to show it to the Executive Council. Here was proof of what he had thought all along: Pauling was too young and inexperienced to be a chairman, too apt to be "dictatorial" in his dealings. Millikan refused to respond in any way.

Pauling and the Chief continued trying to silently stare each other down for more than two months before Pauling blinked. In November he again requested that Millikan tell him what was going to happen.

Millikan replied frostily that he was waiting for Pauling to suggest organizational changes that would make his continued association "satisfactory."

If there were negotiations, they went nowhere. New Year's Day 1937 came and went, and the division still had no chairman.

Impatiently monitoring the situation from his office in New York City, Warren Weaver decided it was time to do something. Noyes's large bio-organic grant was in process; Weaver thought that Pauling could do great things in tandem with a top organic chemist, and he wanted that grant to go through. The bad blood at Caltech was making everything more difficult. Despite his appreciation of Pauling's shortcomings as a team player—Weaver thought Millikan should have given Pauling a "spanking" when his letter of refusal was first delivered back in August—he still considered Pauling the linchpin in his plans for Caltech.

Weaver took the train to Pasadena in January 1937 to smooth things over. He found the situation worse than he had feared. Pauling and Millikan had cut off all communication. Millikan himself had taken on management of the bio-organic grant even though he had little grasp of what it was all about. Pauling was staying proudly aloof, waiting for a favorable decision on his demands.

Weaver sat down with Pauling first, and happy to have a sympathetic ear, Pauling opened up. I am worried about balancing my time between research and administration, Pauling said. Look at what happened to Noyes—he ended up doing everything for the institute and little of value in the laboratory. This new division council setup, with the chairman's role reduced to that of a figurehead likely to be blamed for decisions he had no power to control, would require wasting hours of time on minor decisions that the chairman should be able to make on his own. Pauling also said that he resented the refusal to give him Noyes's title of director of laboratories, which, while it might seem trivial to the uninitiated, actually held significance for other scientists in his field. The salary issue was important, too, because his current pay was far below that of other division chairmen.

Pauling's concerns were justified and presented reasonably, Weaver thought, and he began to develop a new respect for the young researcher. Then Pauling showed him his August 10 letter of refusal and asked for Weaver's frank opinion. Weaver read it over and found the note "amazingly curt and even impudent." He told Pauling to remember that compared to the men on the Executive Council, he was very young; that the trustees had shown great confidence in him and done him a great honor by offering him the title of chairman. His reply not only did not acknowledge the honor but gave none of the reasons behind his decision to refuse. It looked as if Pauling were simply throwing the chairmanship back in their teeth. It was insulting. It was no wonder they were making him wait. Pauling for the first time began to see things from the other side. That night, Weaver noted in his diary, "P. seems genuinely to appreciate WW's criticisms and very soberly remarks that he has made a bad mistake."

Having chastened one side, Weaver reasoned with the other, telling Millikan of Pauling's concerns about and plans for the chemistry division, of the impressive way the young man had kept a cool head during his long wait, and especially about Pauling's importance to the Rockefeller Foundation. He asked for understanding.

After Weaver returned to New York, Millikan and Pauling began talking, working out a system that would satisfy them both. In April, almost a year after Noyes's death, Pauling wrote Weaver with good news. "After talking with you I went to Professor Millikan determined to straighten out our misunderstandings. We reached an agreement with very little difficulty and I am sure that everyone is pleased." Pauling certainly was. He would retain the title of director as well as chairman, and his salary would be raised to $9,000.

mm

Despite everyone else's fears, Pauling moved smoothly into the role of chairman, due in great part to his decision to adopt Noyes's administrative structure and concentrate his energy on his own research. As chairman he would be the big-picture man, the fellow who traveled and spoke, increasing the fame of the school, and attracting big grants. Everything else was delegated. "As an administrator," he said, "I, for some reason, developed the habit of trying to get other people to do almost everything." He made his former graduate student Holmes Sturdivant his administrative right hand, a good pick because Sturdivant—practical, efficient, mechanically inclined (he ran the chemistry division instrument shop, designing and building precise and efficient instruments in addition to his administrative duties)— was simply "one of the most competent persons I have ever known," as one professor remembered.

Most other routine decisions were handled by the division's standing committees. Even the new division council structure, such a sticking point in negotiations, was easy to solve: Pauling ignored it, calling a meeting instead of all faculty to vote on any new hires or major decisions. And here he proved adept as well: Before any vote, Pauling would test the waters and reach consensus through informal discussions, thus avoiding most public arguments. Faculty meetings were short and efficient, the way most professors liked them.

"Many thanks for your letter about my new position," Pauling wrote a friend a few weeks after being named chairman. "I do not know how it is going to work out, but so far the change has not been for the worse since I have successfully avoided taking on any duties except a few of the simplest."

The worries about Pauling's "dictatorial" tendencies proved exaggerated. There might have been a shift in overall emphasis—instead of focusing on the sort of inorganic physical chemistry that Noyes had favored, Pauling concentrated his efforts on the new bio-organic chemistry program—but the faculty soon realized that nothing much would change. Life in the division went on smoothly and, at least on the surface, congenially.

With a few exceptions. Tolman, a good friend of Noyes's, remained formal and distant with Pauling; their relationship would never warm beyond the formal. Don Yost, a highly opinionated, individualistic inorganic chemist, became "somewhat antagonistic to me," Pauling remembered, in part because of his unhappiness at the shift in emphasis away from his field and perhaps in part because of lingering bad feelings over a fiasco in which Yost failed to find the xenon compounds that Pauling had predicted should exist. Yost stayed at Caltech until he retired, often at loggerheads with Pauling, the sole dissenting vote in many divisional decisions, his rancor barely concealed and growing to the point where he and Pauling sometimes stopped speaking to each other entirely.

Those incidents aside, the Caltech chemistry department not only survived but thrived under Pauling's leadership. Within two years of assuming the chairmanship, he proudly reported to Weaver that the number of chemistry graduate students had increased from twenty-five to forty-five and that the number of postdoctoral fellows had doubled. Students were flocking to Caltech not only because Noyes had built a strong program but because Pauling was now in charge, pushing chemistry forward, leading the way with his ideas about the chemical bond and molecular structure. "They would come, many of them, because they had heard of him. And he lived up to every expectation," said Verner Schomaker, a graduate student in the mid-1930s. "He was always producing miracles and minor miracles of understanding." Richard Noyes, the son of the chemistry department chair at Illinois, could have gone anywhere for graduate school in the late 1930s, but he came to Caltech because it was "just booming on up. . . . The best structural chemistry place anywhere in the world." Pauling's students, all of the students in the chemistry division, felt during that time that they were part of a highly select, privileged group.

The feeling of being somewhere special came from both the force of Pauling's intelligence and his personal style. He did not sequester himself in his office, appearing only to address seminars or run meetings. Secure now in his new position, he roamed the halls, poked his head into labs, chatted and joked with anybody and everybody. New students who arrived expecting a distant and awe-inspiring Great Man found a friendly, relaxed, and surprisingly young fellow—barely ten years older than most of his graduate students—who asked about their interests, listened to their ideas, talked up his own, and, most surprisingly, treated them like equals. He invited students and postdoctoral fellows to his home to listen to records, eat waffle breakfasts, and join in Thanksgiving dinners. Occasionally, they served as baby-sitters. He took them on camping trips to the desert. Pauling's style was loose, jazzy, informal—Western—compared to other chemistry departments, where it was always Mister this and Professor that. At Caltech, in Pauling's orbit, real, inventive, cutting-edge chemistry could be exciting and fun.

Becoming chairman did have a slight moderating effect on him. Conscious of his new position and equipped with his new salary, Ava Helen began dressing Pauling in ever-more expensive suits, making him a fashion plate of Caltech. He stopped reclining on tables when he lectured. He was more of an equal now when he visited G. N. Lewis, who was delighted with Pauling's elevation.

Pauling still sparkled with enthusiasm. He had, at age thirty-six, achieved renown in his chosen field, ensured himself one of the highest salaries at Caltech, and assumed leadership of one of the most powerful and influential chemistry laboratories in the world. He had done it on his own terms. He was very happy.

It showed in Pauling's face, in the way he walked. Home movies taken in the late 1930s by one of his assistants, Eddie Hughes, show Pauling at Mount Wilson with friends, walking with his head down and hands clasped behind him, deep in thought, probably working on a chemical problem. But there is no tension; he ambles, tall and loose-limbed, in control and at ease. Scientists were generally expected to look serious or, at their most relaxed, faintly amused. But whenever a camera was pointed in Pauling's direction, he switched on an enormous, delighted, ear-to-ear grin of the sort found on schoolboys holding up big strings of fish. It would become a trademark.

Corey

Through his year of waiting for the chairmanship, Pauling continued traveling, speaking, teaching, and publishing a staggering amount of work, a paper every three or four weeks: more magnetic studies of hemoglobin, more organic and inorganic molecular structures, a new theory of the color of dyes, insights into the structure of metals. His quantum-mechanics textbook with Bright Wilson reached print. He also made plans to write a book on the application of his resonance ideas to organic chemistry, and together with his former student, George Wheland, wrote several chapters, but it was put aside in the press of other activities and never completed.

His number-one goal, however, was to crack the problem of the structure of proteins. He started attacking it on several levels at once. In May 1937, Astbury visited Pasadena, talked to Pauling, and showed him some of his new x-ray photographs of keratin. Both men agreed that the molecule was a long chain but disagreed on the finer points of structure. "I knew of course what Bill Astbury at Leeds had written about the structure of keratin—hair, horn, fingernail and so on. But I knew that what Astbury had said wasn't right . . . because our studies of simple molecules had given us enough knowledge about bond lengths and bond angles and hydrogen-bond formation to show that what he said wasn't right," Pauling said. "But I didn't know what *was* right."

Astbury, like Bernal and the rest of the English protein x-ray crystallographers, was trying to solve the structure directly from the complicated x-ray scatterings. Pauling preferred his own stochastic approach, the method that had worked with the silicate minerals: Learn everything possible about the sizes and shapes of the component parts, make assumptions about the bonds that hold them together, use that information to build precisely crafted models, then see if the models fit the x-ray data.

He decided to try to solve keratin that way. The building blocks were amino acids, but unfortunately there were no decent x-ray analyses of the structure of these rather complex molecules. Even without good structural data, Pauling thought he knew enough about related molecules to make a stab at how amino acids could string together to create Astbury's alpha-keratin pattern. Important among Pauling's assumptions was his earlier idea that the peptide bond had to have considerable double-bond character, thus restricting rotation and holding the atoms on either side of it in the same plane. This, together with a general idea of the basic sizes of amino acids and a belief in the importance of hydrogen bonds, gave him his starting point.

He puzzled for weeks through the summer of 1937, trying to arrange amino acid chains to match Astbury's x-ray results and provide a maximal amount of hydrogen bonding. He tried to make a flat, kinked ribbon structure like Astbury's; he could not make anything of that sort fit the x-ray data. He tried some ideas that wound the chain around in three dimensions; those did not work, either. One major problem was data of Astbury's indicating that there was some sort of major structural repeat along the chain about every 5.1 angstroms. (An angstrom is one ten-millionth of a millimeter.) Nothing Pauling built fit that.

By the time September arrived, Pauling had given up. Maybe his ideas about amino-acid structure were wrong. Maybe the bond lengths and angles he was carrying over from other structural studies did not work the same way in proteins. Maybe the peptide bond was not held flat but could twist. Maybe there was something wrong with his ideas about hydrogen bonding.

The maybes could be made certain only through the painstaking work of nailing down the precise structure of individual amino acids and confirming the way they linked together. Pauling had already started a graduate student, Gus Albrecht, growing amino-acid crystals for analysis. But he needed more talent than a graduate student alone could offer: Amino acids were bigger and more difficult than any organic molecule that had yet been subjected to x-ray analysis—even glycine, the simplest amino acid, contained ten atoms in a complicated arrangement—and success would require insight, skill, and possibly several years of grinding labor. Where would he find someone with that combination of skill and stamina?

—ⅿⅿⅿ—

Fate brought Pauling the person he needed in the thin, crooked form of Robert Corey. Corey was one of the few men in the nation highly skilled in the crystallography of proteins. After getting his Ph.D. from Cornell in 1924, he had worked for years assisting Ralph Wyckoff in the x-ray analysis of everything from porcupine quills to crystalline hemoglobin at the Rockefeller Institute for Medical Research. When Wyckoff's lab was eliminated in an administrative shake-up, Corey had been sent off with a year's pay, whatever equipment he could talk Wyckoff out of, and a good recommendation. In April 1937, Pauling got a letter from Corey asking it if might be possible for him to come to Pasadena for a year if he brought his own equipment and paid his own salary. Pauling, of course, said yes but warned Corey that there was a good possibility there would not be money enough to add him permanently to the staff.

Pauling may have had second thoughts when he met Corey, who looked older than his forty years, with his lank frame, thinning hair, and small black mustache. He had been severely crippled as a child by infantile paralysis and had never fully recovered; he limped badly and used a cane. He was also shyer, a bit more retiring than Pauling liked—"a gentle and tender man," Pauling would later say—but after talking awhile, it became clear that Corey knew all about x-ray crystallography. There was something else there, too: a furtive intelligence that shone out briefly, a sense that Corey knew a good deal more about things than he might say aloud. He told Pauling that he had already started on the first stages of an attack on glycine. Pauling recalled later: "He and I together decided that he should work on the determination of the structure of some crystals of amino acids and simple peptides." Then he corrected himself. "When I say that he and I together made this decision, I may not be quite right. It is not unlikely that he had already made the decision, and that he arranged to have me agree with him, in such a way that I would think that we had made the decision together. I learned later that he was very good at this."

It was the beginning of a long and fruitful relationship.

The Infallibility of Pasadenan Research

Soon after Corey arrived, Pauling left Caltech to spend four months at Cornell University, where he had accepted an invitation to become the George Fisher Baker Lecturer. This prestigious appointment involved giving a series of talks on a single subject, which were traditionally edited into a slim book published as one of the Baker series by Cornell University Press. Pauling's chosen topic was the nature of the chemical bond. He arrived in Ithaca at the end of September with Ava Helen, leaving the children—twelve-year-old Linus junior, six-year-old Peter, five-year-old Linda, and a new baby born just three months earlier, Edward Crellin—in the care of friends, and settled into the university's

Telluride House. Ava Helen welcomed the chance to take a break from a houseful of youngsters and looked forward to the longest time she and her husband would have alone since their first trip to Europe a decade earlier. The Paulings made the most of it, attending receptions and dinner parties and making occasional forays into New York to see the latest musicals and to go dancing.

Freed from the daily chores of chairmanship at Caltech, Pauling also had plenty of time to work on a major project he had been planning for some time, a coalescence of all of his ideas on the chemical bond into one book. He would use his Baker lectures as a starting point, but the resulting book would be much more comprehensive. He worked on the manuscript through the months of their stay in Ithaca and expanded it through 1938 after returning to Caltech.

When it appeared in 1939, *The Nature of the Chemical Bond and the Structure of Molecules and Crystals: An Introduction to Modern Structural Chemistry* became an instant classic. It was targeted to graduate-level chemistry students for use as a text in upper-division courses, but its impact went far beyond the classroom. The book would change the way scientists around the world thought about chemistry. For the first time, the science was presented not as a collection of empirical facts tied together by practical formulae but as a field unified by an underlying physical theory: Pauling's quantum-mechanical ideas about the chemical bond. By detailing how the nature of the chemical bond determined the structure of molecules and how the structure of molecules determined their qualities, Pauling showed for the first time, as Max Perutz said, that "chemistry could be understood rather than being memorized." The book also introduced chemists to the importance of x-ray and electron diffraction as important tools for determining atomic bond lengths and angles, which in turn could disclose something about the nature of the bonds between them. Before its publication, few chemists had taken notice of the arcane art of crystallography; after its publication no chemist could ignore its value.

Notably, the book was written clearly and in a language chemists could understand. Pauling purposefully left out almost all mathematics and detailed derivations of bonding from quantum mechanics, concentrating instead on description and real-world examples. The book was filled with drawings and diagrams of molecules; it was, considering the breadth of its content, amazingly readable.

The response to its publication was immediate and enthusiastic. A University of Illinois professor's letter was typical: "I cannot refrain from taking the opportunity to express to you congratulations and my personal appreciation for one of the finest contributions to chemical literature that I have ever read." G. N. Lewis, to whom Pauling had dedicated the book, wrote, "I have just returned from a short vacation for which the only books I took were half a dozen detective stories and your 'Chemical Bond.' I found yours the most exciting of the lot." Moreover, sales went well.

The Nature of the Chemical Bond would soon become a standard text at most of the nation's leading universities. It would go through three editions, be translated into French, Japanese, German, Russian, and Spanish, and stay in print for almost three decades. It would become a Bible for a new generation of chemists and one of the most cited references in the history of science.

There was, in 1939, only one criticism. The book was written with such utter self-confidence that the Harvard chemist G. B. Kistiakowsky, in an otherwise positive review in the *Journal of the American Chemical Society*, could not refrain from noting, "Dr. Pauling has been so successful in his attack upon many of the problems in the field that his advocacy of the infallibility of Pasadenan research and the somewhat pontifical style in which this book is written are understandable and should not be taken amiss."

The reference to a pontiff caught the eye of Pauling's irrepressible hemoglobin coworker Charles Coryell, who, the next time he saw Pauling on campus, loudly called a hello to "Pope Linus the First." Pauling thought that was funny, but reminded Coryell that there had already been a pope named Linus during the first years of Christian Rome. More properly, he pointed out, he would be Pope Linus the Second.

———

When he returned from Cornell in early 1938, Pauling found that Corey had, in the intervening months, made astonishing progress on the structure of amino acids. Spurred by the specter of unemployment, Corey had worked day and night on solving glycine and was already nearing his final analysis. Pleasantly surprised, Pauling agreed that he should continue his work and expand it to diketopiperazine, a compound of two glycines linked in a ring, in order to get information on the peptide bond.

Corey was vigorous, meticulous, and innovative in his use of some of the newer techniques of x-ray analysis. He quickly solved the diketopiperazine structure and followed that up in 1939 with his and Gus Albrecht's detailed description of glycine, both papers solid work and both landmarks in the development of a theory of the structure of proteins.

Corey would stay at Caltech for more than two decades, the remainder of his professional life, becoming Pauling's right hand in the x-ray laboratory. Theirs was a scientific collaboration that worked because the two partners were so different. Even-tempered thoroughness, precision, and logical analysis were Corey's strong points, and they formed a perfect complement to Pauling's flashes of theoretical insight and impulsive leaps of understanding. Corey was cautious where Pauling was bold, introspective where Pauling was outgoing, reticent where Pauling was sometimes rash. Pauling would rush ahead with the big ideas about proteins; Corey would patiently grind out the required x-ray data and rein him in until they were sure.

It was a perfect match.

—⁓⁓⁓—

On May 16, 1938, Pauling gave his first major public address as chairman of the Caltech Division of Chemistry and Chemical Engineering. The occasion was the dedication of the new Crellin Laboratory for research in organic chemistry, three floors underground and three above, a physical link between the Caltech divisions of chemistry and biology. With Pauling as shepherd, the bio-organic grant request to the Rockefeller Foundation had gone smoothly—Caltech received a quarter of a million dollars over five years, including funds for new professors, specialized equipment for the Crellin Laboratory, and ten thousand per year for Pauling's own projects in structural chemistry—and he felt a sense of pride in making Noyes's last great project a reality. The crowd included all of Caltech's top officials as well as many of the richest and most powerful men and women in Southern California.

Pauling kept his part of the program short. A spring breeze ruffling his hair, Pauling stood on the outdoor dais and spoke of the research that would take place in the new laboratory, a place where a small group of men would explore a "field of knowledge of transcendent significance to mankind which has barely begun its development. . . . the correlation between chemical structure and physiological activity . . ." The building's donor, Edward Crellin, a retired steel magnate, then spoke in plainer terms of his expectations: ". . . the search for, if not the elixir of life, a better understanding of vital processes, leading to better health and longer and happier lives." They both received polite applause. Then Pauling endured a round of hand-shaking with current and potential donors before getting back to the task of moving into his new laboratories.

The Crellin Laboratory marked a new phase of life for Pauling. Its completion not only expanded his laboratory space; it confirmed his success as a leader. He would equip it with the best men and the most sophisticated equipment available—x-ray spectrophotometers, ultra-centrifuges, electron-diffraction machines—and use it to push chemistry into new directions. He was so pleased with it and its benefactor that he and Ava Helen surprised everyone by naming their most recent child Edward Crellin Pauling. ("Not accepting the nurse's suggestion that he be named Caboose," Pauling noted.)

Their family life entered a new phase as well. With four children and a larger salary, the Paulings both needed and could afford a larger house. Just after the Crellin opening, they bought a large lot about five miles from campus in the hills below Mount Wilson, a beautiful, isolated two acres perched on the edge of an arroyo with a spectacular view, and began planning their dream home—a rambling California ranch-style house, two long wings joined at an angle, fronted with adobe-style brick. It would be a home designed to live in, not to impress people, with pleasant views and a big fireplace in the living room, bookcases everywhere, and plenty of room for the children to play. There would be six bedrooms (one apiece for the four children and the parents and one for the maid), a study for Pauling off the living room, and a large kitchen and garden space for Ava Helen. Pauling was active in every phase of the planning and presented his architect with some unusual requests. One was that Pauling's study should be crystalline in outline: octagonal, encased in bookshelves, with a view over the arroyo. Another was that the two wings of the house should join at an angle of precisely 104.67 degrees—the tetrahedral angle of carbon. The architect accommodated the first request but talked Pauling out of the second, which would have required some unusually difficult planning. They compromised and joined the wings at 120 degrees, the bond angle in benzene.

All of this was expensive, but Pauling could afford it. Nine thousand dollars a year was a fortune during the Depression, and after years of poverty growing up and more than a decade of grad-school and junior-faculty penury, Pauling intended to spend his salary, and to do so with some style. As a final reward to himself for achieving the chairmanship, he bought himself a Lincoln Zephyr, a sleek, elegant car in which he could indulge a growing passion for driving fast.

Now that the Crellin Laboratory was built, it became important to find scientists to fill it. The original intent had been to hire one world-class senior organic chemist to complement Pauling, a man around whom grants and students would coalesce, thus quickly assuring the success of the program. In addition, the Rockefeller funds provided enough money for one or two promising younger men.

The senior post was a problem. With Conant out of the picture and Pauling unimpressed with any other U.S. talent, Weaver tried to help by sending his agents to scour Europe. For a year he and Pauling courted the great Scottish organic chemist Alexander Todd, an outstanding scientist with a strong history of success and a structural viewpoint that complemented Pauling's. They paid his way to Caltech for six months in hopes that the warmth and hospitality of Southern California would work its usual magic. After visiting, however, Todd decided to stay in England.

Pauling then became enthusiastic about a Hungarian, Laszlo Zechmeister. His specialty was the purification and study of organic molecules using a recently rediscovered technique called chromatography in which individual classes of molecules could be purified out of an organic stew by dissolving them in a solvent and letting them migrate across a solid such as a piece of paper or purified silica. Depending on the solvent and the solid used, some molecules moved faster, some slower; eventually, purified forms could be separated completely. "Zecky," as he was called, was especially interested in carotenes, large molecules that give the yellow and red colors to such vegetables as carrots and tomatoes. The carotenes were conjugated molecules—they had alternating single and double bonds, like the pyrroles in hemoglobin—and Pauling was interested in their structure and chromatography as a useful tool. Despite a lukewarm response from Weaver, who thought the Hungarian was too little known to attract the support others could, Pauling hired Zechmeister for the senior post. It would turn out to be a mixed decision. Zecky would help introduce chromatography to the United States and make it an important and much-used laboratory technique. But he had little scientific ambition and would never ascend the scientific heights later scaled by Todd.

For the junior posts, Weaver suggested Carl Niemann, a young protein chemist who had quickly made a name for himself at the Rockefeller Institute for Medical Research; Pauling liked him very much and was happy to hire him. Then Pauling strongly suggested hiring a pair of brothers, R. R. and R. J. Williams, whose research interests included the B vitamins. When Weaver communicated his reaction as "not entirely enthusiastic," however, Pauling backed off. Instead, he hired one of the Williamses' young coworkers, Edwin Buchman, as the second junior man.

—◆◆◆—

A year into his chairmanship, Pauling was proving to be both a surprisingly adept leader and a person very different from A. A. Noyes. Noyes had worked quietly, cooperatively, behind the scenes, setting larger schemes into motion, changing the method of scientific education, and helping to build the institutions that would bring the United States to scientific prominence. He was the one and only King. Pauling, more adventurous, insightful, and inventive, more aggressive and involved with his own image and the success of his own research, would put a different stamp on the way chemistry was done at Caltech.

He would never be called the King. Closer to the mark was a comment Alfred Mirsky passed on from the Rockefeller Institute for Medical Research in 1938. "Oh, by the way, I was talking with Gasser [the institute's new president] about you the other day. He referred to you as a 'wizard,'" Mirsky wrote. "I hope you don't find being one a burden."

CHAPTER 10

The Fabric and the Chain

The Woman Einstein

Pauling was not the only scientist taking a theoretical approach to the molecular structure of proteins. Dorothy Wrinch was hard at work on the problem. In fact, she thought she had solved it.

Born in 1894 to a British engineer in Argentina, Wrinch started studying mathematics in Britain, then turned to philosophy, becoming a disciple of Bertrand Russell's and a minor figure in his socialist-Bohemian circle. After marrying a physicist, she became the first woman to receive a D.Sc. degree from Oxford, where she taught mathematics and published widely. She was unconventional and ahead of her time: forceful, cigarette-smoking, acid-tongued, committed to an independent career (she published under her maiden name), and interested in everything. (Among many accomplishments, she wrote a sociological tract about the problems of parenthood in two-career families.) From her time with Russell, she came to believe that all scientific progress grew directly from mathematics and logic, a belief she applied first to physics and then to biology.

But significant discoveries eluded her. By the early 1930s—nearly forty years old, separated from her husband and caring for a small daughter—Wrinch had become an intellectual Gypsy, talking herself into apprentice positions in biological laboratories throughout Europe in order to learn about genetics, embryology, and the new field of protein chemistry. She fell in with the Biotheoretical Gathering, a small, informal group of British avant-garde scientists, including the protein crystallographers John Bernal and Dorothy Crowfoot, who believed that mixing old disciplines in new ways might result in the next great leap in understanding biology. Warren Weaver, always on the lookout for new talent to fund, had his eye on that group as well, learned of Wrinch and read her papers applying mathematics to the study of the contraction of chromosomes. He gave her a generous five-year grant in 1935.

She quickly came up with results. In 1936, Wrinch proposed an entirely new and intriguing structure for proteins. She theorized that amino acids, instead of linking only end to end, might be able to connect with each other in more complex ways, forming, instead of chains, protein fabrics. She recognized that the types of bonds she was proposing had not been proved to exist but argued that so little was known about proteins at the time that the possibility of undiscovered bonding patterns was not out of the question.

She was a mathematician, not a chemist, and her fabric patterns fit some of the experimental data beautifully. Her favorite fabric was a honeycomb of hexagonal rings of amino acids that could be folded around and stitched to form closed cage structures—one of which, according to her topological calculations, would contain a total of 288 amino acids—a number that some researchers thought represented a basic unit in many proteins. This "cyclol" structure, as she called it, was one of the first detailed schemes put forward for explaining the formation of globular, as opposed to fibrous, proteins, and it generated a good deal of talk.

At first the reaction was positive. A steady stream of papers began to appear in which Wrinch detailed how her cyclol cage could explain everything from proteins' ability to create films on liquid surfaces (the cage, she argued, would open up into a flat, floating sheet) to the stimulation of antibodies in animals (amino-acid side chains, she said, would stick out from the cyclol cages, providing reactive spots). Protein experts gave her papers a serious reading. Bill Astbury was sympathetic to her model at first because one of the folded chains he had proposed for keratin came close to doubling back on itself to make hexagonal patterns like those Wrinch proposed.

Wrinch threw herself into the study of protein structure, teaching herself the basics of x-ray crystallography, knocking on doors at the

protein labs in Cambridge, suggesting experiments, engaging everyone she met in enthusiastic discussions of her work. She soon knew
enough to devise useful ideas about the mathematical interpretation
of x-ray diagrams. Her enthusiasm, love of argument, and growing obsession with her own theory kept her hammering away at anyone and
everyone she thought should be convinced about cyclols. She started
presenting her ideas at scientific conferences, and the newspapers
picked up the story of this remarkable female who, it appeared, was on
her way to solving the structure of proteins. One called her a "Woman
Einstein."

The attention paid to Wrinch and her cyclols in the period 1936–38 set
off a reaction among those most involved in the field of molecular
structure. Globular protein workers like Bernal began noting weaknesses in Wrinch's arguments due to her lack of background in chemistry and biology. Wrinch's was certainly an interesting hypothesis, but
it was only one among many, with good arguments to be made against
it. The four-way amino-acid linkage required by her model had never
been seen by organic chemists; while it was impossible to rule it out,
no new evidence appeared to support its existence. Wrinch's retort,
"Proteins are so different from other substances that it is surprising
that there is a reluctance to accept for them a structure for which no
analogue in organic chemistry can be found," didn't sit well with researchers who had a proven method of linkage with the peptide bond.
Wrinch's personal style did not help, either; she was, some thought,
rather too pushy for a scientist and certainly too pushy for a woman.
She got people thinking, but she also got on their nerves. The small
world of protein researchers began to fracture into pro-Wrinch and
anti-Wrinch groups.

High on the list of people Wrinch wanted to convince of her theories was Linus Pauling. As early as the summer of 1936 she wrote him,
"I would awfully like the chance of a conversation with you about proteins." His response was cordial; they traded research papers, and
Wrinch wrote again, "I am . . . still extremely anxious to sit at your
feet." In the spring of 1937, Pauling wrote, "She is a very clever person,
and I am sympathetic to the type of speculative consideration which
she is carrying on now. Without doubt there is a great deal of truth in
her general picture." He doubted, however, that the hexagonal rings of
amino acids she proposed were stable enough to replace the polypep-

tide chain as a preferred model, and he was growing increasingly disenchanted with the whole mathematical approach used to come up with cyclols; fifteen years before, he had seen a number of speculations about crystal structure put forward on the basis of pleasing symmetry and mathematical self-consistency rather than experimental results, and he had helped prove some of them wrong. Nature, he thought, did not work according to strict mathematical theories, or if it did, they were theories complex enough to allow a great deal of leeway and a degree of strangeness. Pauling began to believe that Wrinch was relying too heavily on the creation of "nicely symmetrical structures" rather than ones that arose naturally from the dictates of chemistry. There was no chemical reason he could see to force proteins into a cyclol cage.

—◊◊◊—

By 1938, Warren Weaver, too, was having doubts about Wrinch. He had surveyed a number of scientists about her and found no consensus—some believed her a genius; others found her ideas preposterous. Weaver himself began to think that she was "a queer fish," valuable in spurring discussion but inclined to spend too much time trying to win converts to her theory and too little time proving it. He wanted the cyclol issue resolved and asked Pauling to help him do it as "one of the few persons who will not be in the slightest awed by [Wrinch's] facility in mathematics." Weaver arranged a meeting between Pauling and Wrinch in January 1938, while Pauling was at Cornell.

By the time they sat down with each other, however, Pauling had already made up his mind about Wrinch. Soon after arriving on the Cornell campus in Ithaca, New York, Pauling saw in the *New York Times* a photo of Wrinch "fondly holding her elaborate model of a globular protein" under the headline "Architecture of the Protein Molecule." He could tell from the grainy photo that the cyclol cage was too delicate, its interior too empty to match the known high density of globular proteins. Two months before the planned meeting, Pauling, Mirsky, Max Bergmann, and Weaver talked about Wrinch at the Rockefeller Institute for Medical Research. According to Weaver's diary, Pauling not only confirmed that he thought her work was too speculative, too strongly based on a desire for symmetry; he also felt that considering the early stage of her work, she had been getting too much publicity. Bergmann added that she did not give enough emphasis to the peptide bond; the point was made that the cage structure she proposed, linked with strong covalent bonds all around, could not be broken open easily enough to explain the first stage of denaturation—the reversible step that Pauling thought involved hydrogen bonding. It was decided at the end of the discussion that Pauling would "make a serious effort to learn more accurately just what definite results [Wrinch] has," during their January meeting.

Wrinch arrived in frozen Ithaca eager to talk. But their discussions, two hours a day for two days, simply confirmed what Pauling already believed. He grilled her about the details of her structures and found out that she knew a great deal about mathematics and very little about the empirical facts of chemistry.

The private report he made to Weaver afterward was devastating. Pauling said that Wrinch was approaching the problem as a mathematician, "interested in the rigorous deduction of consequences from postulates rather than in the actual structure of proteins"; that "she did not seem to consider experimental evidence against her ideas very interesting"; and that "Dr. Wrinch is facile in the use of the terminology of chemists and biologists, but her arguments are sometimes unreliable and her information superficial."

More importantly, he attacked the whole idea of a structure devised to include 288 amino acids. There were no known chemical forces that would act to limit a protein molecule to that number, he wrote; the observation of many proteins and protein subunits roughly that size might be due to some sort of evolutionary pressure but was not the result of chemical necessity. With that prop kicked away and her knowledge of protein chemistry proved weak, Pauling concluded that Wrinch's papers were "dishonest." It was unfortunate, he wrote, that protein researchers "do not know that her feelings about science are completely different from theirs, and so they are deluded into taking her work seriously."

The only positive thing he found to say was that his talks with Wrinch had given him new energy to revisit the protein problem: "Since talking with Dr. Wrinch it has seemed to me that I should prepare a paper on my ideas. I have been averse to doing this because of their speculative nature; they are, however, superior to Dr. Wrinch's in my opinion." Weaver encouraged him to give his imagination free rein.

As far as the Rockefeller Foundation was concerned, Pauling's report finished Dorothy Wrinch. She was taken aback during their conversations by the severity of Pauling's criticisms and the closeness of his questioning and returned to England disheartened. There she encountered more attacks from Bernal and his friends. As Weaver's representative in England, W. E. Tisdale wrote soon after reading Pauling's comments, "She certainly has been a catalyst, although I'm not sure how long a catalyst should continue to exist after the reactions have been catalyzed."

—*mm*—

After his return to Caltech from Cornell, Pauling made a concerted, four-pronged attack on protein structures. Now in command of a richly equipped suite of laboratories in the Crellin building staffed by an ever-growing team of students and postdoctoral fellows, he started a program to take more x-ray photos of native proteins in hopes that something worthwhile might be discovered beyond what Astbury and Bernal had already found. He also began using Zechmeister's chromatographic techniques to separate and purify the bits and pieces that resulted from breaking proteins apart, hoping to solve the structure of a fragment as a step toward the whole protein, perhaps making it possible to reconstruct the order in which amino acids were strung in the chain.

But most of his effort still focused on the structure of the protein building blocks, amino acids. And here Corey's success with glycine and diketopiperazine was surprising because of its very lack of surprise. Amino acids, it appeared, were built very much as Pauling had thought. Most importantly, the diketopiperazine structure gave strong evidence that the peptide bond had the double-bond character Pauling theorized it should have, enough to keep the atoms from rotating around each other, holding the atoms on either side of the peptide bond rigid and flat. It proved what Pauling had assumed in his 1937 attack on the structure of keratin. So why had that attempt failed? He put Corey and Hughes and their students to work on more amino acids and small peptides, making ever-more accurate maps. Perhaps the answer was somewhere in the fine details.

Pauling's 1936 paper on protein denaturation, cowritten with Mirsky, had not after two years made much of an impression. Despite the paper's persuasive chemical arguments and firm foundation in experimental observations, it did not persuade most protein researchers that a force as little known, nonspecific, and weak as hydrogen bonds could account for the ways in which proteins were held in precise shapes. Acceptance of the hydrogen-bonding idea proved disappointingly slow. But Pauling was still convinced it was correct, and he began talking with the new colleague he had hired, the protein researcher Carl Neimann, about ways to prove it.

In the middle of this new attack on proteins a bombshell fell: Dorothy Wrinch had found proof of her cyclol structure. Instead of slinking out of the field after her talk with Pauling, Wrinch had redoubled her efforts. And she found a powerful new ally: the Nobel Prize–winning physical chemist (and codeveloper of the shared-electron-bond idea) Irving Langmuir, whose interest in molecular films led him to an interest in the cyclol hypothesis.

"Extraordinary to relate the miracle that has happened," she wrote the Rockefeller Foundation in the fall of 1938. Dorothy Crowfoot had taken new x-ray photos of the small globular protein insulin. Although Crowfoot concluded that "the patterns as calculated do not appear to have any direct relation either to the cyclol or to the various chain structures," Wrinch and Langmuir, analyzing the data with the aid of a new mathematical approach, found evidence of cyclols. Their announcement, given the weight of Langmuir's imprimatur, created shock waves among protein researchers. Langmuir confidently told Weaver that everyone should now be convinced of the cyclol hypothesis. Niels Bohr's group in Copenhagen began building cyclol cages. Wrinch began publishing a spate of new papers.

Pauling did not believe it. He thought that the new vector method of analysis Wrinch and Langmuir had used—codeveloped by one of Pauling's former students, David Harker—was too limited to provide real proof. Even when Harker wrote him that he believed Wrinch and Langmuir's analysis was correct, Pauling was unmoved.

He was not alone. In Britain, Bernal and others, including Willie Bragg, stepped up their attacks on Wrinch. In January 1939 a series of short notes appeared in *Nature*, with Bragg writing that the vector-analysis method was inadequate to give more than "vague and provisional" results with molecules as complex as proteins and Bernal calling Wrinch's ideas about insulin "demonstrably incorrect." When Wrinch responded, Bernal let loose again, writing that "no case whatever has been made out for the acceptance of the cyclol model on X-ray grounds; indeed so far as it goes, the X-ray evidence is definitely against the model." Wrinch felt betrayed; privately, she called Bernal, her old compatriot from the Biotheoretical Gathering, "jealous, brutal and treacherous."

Langmuir championed Wrinch's ideas in print and in private, cowriting papers with her, bringing her together with Harker—a special privilege to get support from one of Pauling's own students—and convincing Mirsky that denaturation might proceed in steps more closely matching those predicted by the cyclol theory. With Langmuir's help, the cyclol theory was rising from the dead.

Pauling was both confused and aggravated by the attention lavished on what he believed was a mistaken theory. This was not only a distraction from the real problems of protein research; it was an attack on Pauling's hydrogen-bonding ideas, a diminution of his reputation as a leading protein researcher, a challenge to his view of nature. He decided it was time to end it.

In the early spring of 1939 he enlisted Niemann's help in preparing a paper that would examine and demolish, one by one, every major argument in favor of the cyclol structure. They worked on it for weeks; their final product, "The Structure of Proteins," was published in the *Journal of the American Chemical Society* (*JACS*) that July. It was a tour de force, the most strongly worded attack on an opposing theory that Pauling had ever written. Chemistry was the main weapon they used, especially data on bond energies that Pauling thought clearly showed that the proposed cyclol structure was much less stable, therefore much less probable, than polypeptide chains. From energy considerations alone, Pauling and Niemann wrote, "we draw the rigorous conclusion that *the cyclol structure cannot be of primary importance for proteins; if it occurs at all* (*which is unlikely because of its great energetic disadvantage relative to polypeptide chains*) *not more than about three percent of the amino acid residues could possess this configuration*" (emphasis theirs). After highlighting what they considered Wrinch and Langmuir's other major inconsistencies and mistaken interpretations, Pauling and Niemann briefly put forward their own idea of protein structure. It had not changed much in the three years since Mirsky and Pauling's denaturation paper: Proteins were long, peptide-bonded chains held in specific shapes by proven links, a mixture of hydrogen and sulfur-sulfur bonds, and "similar interatomic interactions." What those specific shapes were, no one could yet tell. The only thing that seemed certain was that they were not cyclol cages.

"The Structure of Proteins" was devastating and immediate in its effect. "I must say that I derived enormous enjoyment from reading 'The De-Bunking of Wrinch' by Pauling and Niemann!" Alex Todd wrote after he got his copy. "It really was high time that somebody put the case against the cyclol theory in definite terms, and I think that all chemists here at least will welcome it. As far as I can see, the case is unanswerable and I shall be intrigued to see what response, if any, it will evoke from Wrinch."

—*mm*—

Ironically, a few weeks before Pauling and Niemann sent in their paper, Wrinch had decided to give up protein work. In the spring of 1939, hurt by the hostility of Bernal and the Cambridge group, she fled England for America, telling Weaver when she arrived that the conclusions she had drawn from the insulin data were premature and she was dropping any further studies. Pauling and Niemann's paper could not have appeared at a worse time. She was looking for a faculty position for herself and a home for her daughter; in order to raise her stock as a job prospect, she had to answer the attack. She stormed into the Harvard offices of Arthur Lamb, the editor of *JACS*, and demanded space for a rebuttal. Lamb explained that he would publish any correction of fact or relevant new research findings but that the journal was not a place to rehash old arguments. Her twenty-one-page riposte arrived a few weeks later, refuting Pauling and Niemann point by point, ending with the conclusion that "opponents of the cyclol hypothesis have felt compelled to fall back upon arguments which are specious (due to errors in logic), and upon experiments which are irrelevant . . . or incompetent to decide the issue." Lamb, following standard procedure, sent her manuscript to Pauling and Niemann with a cover note requesting their comments to attach to Wrinch's paper when it went out for peer review.

They in turn answered Wrinch's rebuttal paragraph by paragraph in what was becoming an escalating war of words: ". . . there is no reason why this ghost should be permitted to continue to parade across the literature of protein chemistry"; "no reason for republishing this disputed fancy"; "all we have here are further hopes and no facts." Lamb then sent the entire smoking package to two referees, whose responses so differed that everything had to be sent to two more referees. Everyone who read the papers was struck by the acidity of the debate; each suggested a different solution. Lamb and one referee thought there should be simultaneous publication of both Wrinch's work and Pauling and Niemann's response to it after both parties had reviewed the final drafts; another referee advised quickly publishing Wrinch's paper alone and then closing the issue; another compared the battle to the opening salvos of a world war and advised slowing down the process "to give each a chance for cooling down and taking second thoughts."

Then Wrinch found that Pauling and Niemann had erred in calculating the energies of formation of proteins; correcting the figures reduced the energy discrepancy between the chain and cyclol structures by about one-third. When she pointed it out in a letter to Pauling, he replied that it was too small a change to alter their conclusions and therefore that "it has not seemed to us worthwhile to correct this error in print."

Wrinch then stung Pauling from another angle. She had gotten a temporary appointment at Johns Hopkins, where David Harker worked, and the two of them began talking. Harker had had his own run-ins with Pauling as his student and listened sympathetically as Wrinch told him how Pauling had attacked her and was, to her mind, preventing her rebuttal from being published. Harker in turn told her about what he considered to be Pauling's fast-and-loose use of resonance to explain anything and everything about the chemical bond. They ended up publishing a short letter together in the *Journal of Chemical Physics* in the spring of 1940 in which they proposed an approach to chemical bonding that eliminated the need to invoke resonance. Although the letter mentioned Pauling only in footnotes, it was clearly a challenge to his basic approach.

"I have just noticed again the letter by you and Dorothy Wrinch . . . and have decided that its publication shows that you are in need of some advice," Pauling wrote Harker in the tone of a father betrayed. "The general tone of the letter indicates that it represents a criticism of the work done here. Even if there were grounds for this criticism, your personal indebtedness to this Institute should have kept you from being a party to it." After some specific criticisms, Pauling ended, "Although the casual reader might be misled by your letter into thinking it represented some small contribution to knowledge, I shall not trouble to set him straight by publishing a reply. . . . I think that you could be about better business and in better company." He then wrote the editor of the journal suggesting that it might have been wise to submit the Harker-Wrinch letter to him before publication.

Pauling was throwing his weight around, and Harker resented it. "I have heard rumors from time to time concerning your allegedly unfair attitude toward Dr. Wrinch and her right to discuss her theories in print," he wrote back. "I have invariably thought—and said—that such an attitude on your part was impossible. . . . I should be most unhappy to be forced to believe otherwise."

—*mm*—

An abbreviated form of Wrinch's rebuttal finally appeared in the *JACS* nineteen months after Pauling and Niemann's original paper. But by then both the cyclol theory and Wrinch's career were dead. Warren Weaver informed her that there would be no more Rockefeller money, telling her that five years was more than enough time to convince her colleagues about cyclols. She had trouble getting money anywhere and had trouble getting further criticisms of Pauling into print. By the end of 1940 she wrote a friend, "I get absolutely in despair, for I see the whole set-up as a power syndicate just like Hitler's and only the strong and powerful can survive. . . . This new Pauling business gets me down. He is a most dangerous fellow. . . . Even decent people hesitate to stand up to LP. He is bright and quick and merciless in repartee when he likes and I think people are just afraid of him. It takes poor [Dorothy] to point out where he is wrong: truly none of them would."

Wrinch would spend the rest of her life in scientific obscurity, still tough and outspoken, committed to the cyclol theory, and telling anyone who would listen about her beautiful protein fabrics and how Pauling and his cronies had silenced her. The Wrinch affair made anyone look bad. It ruined Wrinch's career and chained her wide-ranging intellect to a single lost cause. It deepened a rift between Pauling and Harker that was years healing. It fed rumors that Pauling was a bully who would run over those who disagreed with him. The semipublic scientific fistfight was also disturbing to the one man no one wanted to alienate: Warren Weaver. The Rockefeller director expressed his annoyance quietly but pointedly to Pauling in a letter at the end of 1939: "It is my own feeling that the very lively and somewhat contentious interest in theoretical approaches to protein problems has, perhaps up to about the present time, served a purpose which is on the whole useful; and that the time has now definitely arrived when it is of far greater importance to get a wider and more dependable body of facts. There is nothing which ever speaks so convincingly as the quiet presentation of facts."

Wrinch would later blame her problems on sexism, telling friends, "Ah, it's the Y chromosome. If I had the Y chromosome, people wouldn't talk to me like this in public journals." Gender discrimination undoubtedly played a role in the way she was treated—sexism was endemic in the sciences at the time and was institutionalized at Caltech.

But it was not an important influence on Pauling. Ava Helen made sure that Pauling was about as "liberated" as a man of the era could be; he respected the work of the few other women in his field, such as Dorothy Crowfoot Hodgkin. He was as enthusiastic in attacking Langmuir as he was in going after Wrinch. Langmuir, however, with his renown secure, did not suffer. Wrinch did.

Pauling merely put into print, more completely and strongly than anyone else, what almost every knowledgeable protein researcher who came in contact with Wrinch already thought. Not even a Y chromosome would have made the cyclol theory right.

But the Wrinch incident did illuminate less appealing sides of Pauling's character. The evidence was scanty on both sides of the debate—as Wrinch often pointed out, it was impossible to say conclusively that cyclols did not exist. During the 1950s, in fact, another researcher found that a cyclol-like structure existed in some ergot alkaloids—a discovery that Wrinch tried unsuccessfully to leverage into grants for a review of all other protein structures. Pauling, taking the role of a scientific papa silencing a noisy child, spoke with an authority that ended the argument.

It was a demonstration of his new power. Within a few years of assuming the chairmanship of the Caltech Division of Chemistry and Chemical Engineering, Pauling had become an established player in chemistry's power structure. He, like Noyes before him, sat on editorial boards, nominated people for office, selected award winners, provided advice, and spoke widely. He was invited, consulted, honored, and deferred to. He drank it in. But the prestige and acclaim brought out negative factors in his personality that became more evident as his power grew: a tendency toward self-righteousness, a desire to control situations and frame debates, and a willingness to silence those with aberrant ideas.

The Serologist

The debate with Wrinch confirmed Pauling's belief in the hydrogen-bonded chain model for proteins that he and Mirsky put forward—a belief now strong enough to lead him into an entirely new and unexpected field of research.

In the spring of 1936, after delivering a talk on hemoglobin at the Rockefeller Institute for Medical Research, Pauling was given a note:

Could he find time before he left New York to spend an hour or two discussing some research of mutual interest? It was signed by Karl Landsteiner.

Pauling knew the name. Landsteiner was an internationally respected, almost revered Austrian medical researcher who had won the Nobel Prize five years earlier for discovering the ABO blood groups, leading for the first time to safe blood transfusions and saving thousands of lives. Landsteiner had come late in life to America to continue his studies of blood, particularly the agents in the plasma serum that made up the immune system. Pauling was intrigued by his invitation and by the man himself. When he arrived at Landsteiner's laboratory the next day, he was greeted by a scientist who looked like an aristocrat: tall, mustachioed, erect, and distinguished looking, Landsteiner had short-cropped gray hair and an air of gentility and confidence retained from his early years in Vienna. In his softly accented English, he invited his visitor to sit down. Then he began telling Pauling about a mystery he was trying to solve.

It had to do with antibodies, Landsteiner explained, an unusual class of protein molecules that helped the body fight infection. Pauling's talk on hemoglobin had given Landsteiner the idea that perhaps Pauling might be able to help explain some of the observations Landsteiner had been making. For instance, antibodies were made by the body with thousands, perhaps hundreds of thousands, of different specificities, each one capable of recognizing and locking on to a different target molecule, or antigen. An antibody to *Pneumococcus* bacteria, for instance, would recognize and attach only to antigens specific to that organism and ignore antigens specific to *Streptococcus*, and vice versa. Landsteiner's own experiments using a range of man-made chemicals as antigens had shown that this specificity could be impressively precise: In some cases, antigens that differed by only a few atoms would react differently with a given antibody.

This sort of specificity was not unknown, of course; enzymes, for instance, were highly specific for their target molecules, called substrates. But each enzyme had only one substrate. Specific antibodies could be made to thousands upon thousands of targets, including artificial chemicals. There were a number of puzzling things, Landsteiner said. One was how antibodies achieved that specificity in chemical terms. How could protein molecules like antibodies tell the difference between one antigen and another? What were the forces that held an antibody molecule to an antigen? How was the body capable of making such a range of antibodies with such high precision? How could the body know how to fashion proteins directed against synthetic targets that it had never been exposed to before?

Pauling hadn't the slightest idea how to respond to these questions—beyond his immediate assumption that the answers must have to do with how the molecules were built. But he liked Landsteiner, whom he found an engaging, far-ranging thinker ("a great man," he would soon be telling others), and he was fascinated by his work. This new field Landsteiner was working in, immunochemistry, might be an effective tool with which to study protein structure and specificity. At the end of their visit, Pauling told Landsteiner he would think about his questions and they would talk again.

But he needed a quick education first. He immediately bought a copy of Landsteiner's most recent book on immunology and read it on the train back to Pasadena. He was intrigued from the opening page, where Landsteiner had written, "The morphological characteristics of plant and animal species form the chief subject of the descriptive natural sciences and are the criteria for their classification. But not until recently has it been recognized that in living organisms, as in the realm of crystals, chemical differences parallel the variation in structure." Pauling had found a kindred spirit, a man who could in two sentences tie together biology, chemistry, and crystallography. He became fascinated in what Landsteiner had been learning about the body, about how the immune system allowed each individual animal to recognize the chemical differences between self and nonself.

As the countryside blurred outside the train window, Pauling immersed himself in the book. Landsteiner, who had studied chemistry with the great Emil Fischer, had helped make the study of the immune system into a chemical science, perfecting systems for producing and measuring the activity of antibodies to known organic compounds. This was a tool that could work two ways: First, antibodies could function as fine probes for chemical structure capable of telling the difference between closely related organic molecules, including proteins; and, second, selected antigens could function as probes for investigating the structure of antibodies. Because no one knew how antibodies were made or how they attached to their targets, the field was full of gray areas, contradictory findings, and confusing experimental results. Most immunologists came to the field from biology or medicine and appeared to ignore or misunderstand chemistry. Immunology, in other words, was a field ripe for colonization.

~~~

By the time he got back to Pasadena, Pauling was ready to devote part of his time to immunology. He and Mirsky were just putting the finishing touches on their theory of protein denaturation, and Pauling began relating what he was learning about antibodies to his idea of proteins as long-chain molecules held in place by hydrogen bonds. He took it almost for granted that antibodies, like all molecules, worked the way they did because of their structure. Suppose they were built to complement the shape of a specific antigen, to form around it like a glove around a hand? This idea of complementary shapes was an old one, first put forward by Paul Ehrlich at the end of the nineteenth century—he talked about it in terms of locks and keys—and updated by others since then, but Pauling began to think of it in a new way, in terms of denaturation. What if a newly made antibody molecule was like a denatured protein, its hydrogen bonds broken, the chain opened out in a line. If it then made contact with an antigen, the two molecules would be attracted by weak, nonspecific forces—the van der Waals attraction and electrostatic attraction between oppositely charged areas on the antigen and antibody chain. Energy considerations would then tend to maximize contact between antibody and antigen; free energy would be minimized when the antibody's electrically charged atoms came close to oppositely charged areas on the antigen's surface and the greatest number of van der Waals interactions were made. The closer the fit between antigen and antibody, the more of these nonspecific weak links that snapped into place, the more stable the paired system. The antibody would naturally form itself to the antigen's shape, like soft clay pressed around a coin. Soon after returning to Caltech, Pauling roughed out a manuscript about antibody formation.

Then he put it aside. There was the paper with Mirsky to finish first. Then Noyes died, and Pauling's troubles with Millikan began. Pauling did not forget about immunology entirely—he began reading journals in the field, becoming increasingly irritated by the welter of conflicting research results—but he did not spend much time on it.

~~~

Landsteiner got him back into the game. When Pauling was at Cornell on his Baker lectureship in November 1937, he was pleasantly surprised to see Landsteiner again. The old man had made a special point of coming to Ithaca to see Pauling. Immunology was not the only thing on his agenda—Landsteiner was also sounding Pauling on the possibility of an appointment at Caltech—but once they began talking about antibodies, they could not stop. Landsteiner's brief visit turned into "the best course of instruction in a complicated field that anyone ever received," Pauling remembered, an intensive four-day miniseminar in immunology devoted primarily to answering Pauling's questions. Pauling came out of it with a head cleared of many of the contradictory research results that he had been reading for the past year. He also enthusiastically recommended to Millikan that Landsteiner, whom he called "the father of immunology," be invited to Caltech to work.

But that did not happen—Millikan grumbled something about the cost of supporting every old Nobelist who wanted to retire to sunny Southern California—and Pauling's attention was diverted again. He still thought and talked about antibodies through 1938 and 1939—in fact, his enthusiasm led members of the biology department to start experimenting with creating antibodies to fruit-fly genes and gene products—but there was the Crellin Laboratory to get started, his new house to build, the Baker lectures to give, the Dorothy Wrinch controversy to settle, and *The Nature of the Chemical Bond* to write. He was also hesitant about starting serious work in this completely new field because he had no one on staff who knew how to run immunological experiments.

In July 1939, Landsteiner nudged him again, this time with a note in *Science* that related Pauling and Mirsky's theory of protein structure to the formation of antibodies. To explain the specificity of antibodies, he wrote, "One idea to be considered among others is the possibility of different ways of folding the same polypeptide chain."

This was exactly what Pauling had been thinking, and he now set about polishing his ideas for publication before someone else beat him to it. There were already a number of papers out in which immunologists had theorized that antigens acted as templates against which antibodies were formed, but they generally proposed that the system worked by somehow ordering the sequence of amino acids in a growing protein chain, an approach Pauling thought unnecessarily complex. His idea of taking a one-sequence-fits-all protein and twisting it into a specific shape was simpler.

It also explained the controversial idea some researchers had that antibodies were two-armed or "bivalent," able to attach to two antigens at the same time, clumping them together. A common test for antibodies was to mix them with an antigen and see if they formed a fuzzy precipitate, an indication that antigen and antibody were combining. Pauling knew that chemical precipitates formed in some cases when molecules linked end to end, and he visualized the same thing happening with antibodies. Antibodies with two combining sites for antigens were the simplest way to form antigen-antibody-antigen-antibody precipitates.

The picture that began forming in Pauling's mind was this: A "denatured," fresh antibody chain would start to emerge from an antibody-producing cell. The free end would come into contact with an antigen and would attach to it. The middle part of the chain would fold into layers like a stack of pancakes, back and forth, building a roughly spherical shape needed to fit the data that showed antibodies were globular proteins. Hydrogen bonds would hold the stack together. The newly secreted back end of the chain would then be able to attach itself to another antigen, creating a "bivalent" antibody structure. This was an elegantly simple way of explaining how a myriad of antibodies could be formed from a single protein pattern, how precipitates formed, how antibodies could be raised against synthetic chemicals, and, of course, how a system of nonspecific weak forces could combine through complementary shaping to explain how antibodies attached to antigens.

In January 1940, a young assistant professor of immunology from the University of Chicago, Dan Campbell, arrived at Caltech on a fellowship, and Pauling set him to work on some confirming experiments while he drafted a final version of his antibody theory for publication. There were problems to work out. His theory was powerful not only because it was simple but because it led to specific, testable predictions. In Pauling's scheme, for instance, the two ends of an antibody molecule could form around identical reactive sites on an antigen, at two different reactive sites on the same antigen, or into two completely different antigens. But this sort of dual-action antibody, a single molecule specific for two different antigens, had never been detected. Landsteiner's own evidence weighed strongly against such configurations, and after Campbell arrived, Pauling and Landsteiner mailed sera and antigens back and forth through the spring in an unsuccessful attempt to resolve the question.

The correspondence showed Pauling that he and his immunological mentor did not think about problems in the same way. "I found that Landsteiner and I had a much different approach to science,"

Pauling remembered. "Landsteiner would ask, 'What do these experimental observations force us to believe about the nature of the world?' and I would ask, 'What is the most simple, general, and intellectually satisfying picture of the world that encompasses these observations and is not incompatible with them?'" Pauling held off publication until this point could be settled. When it proved intractable, he decided to move on, banking on the possibility that new experiments would show he was right.

A second prediction had far greater implications. If Pauling's theory was right, it should be possible to create artificial antibodies in the laboratory by carefully denaturing ordinary globulins and then renaturing them in the presence of antigens. Using easily available animal or human serum globulin as the starting material, it would then be possible to cheaply, purely, and safely produce antibodies in bulk against almost any dangerous pathogen. A physician with a patient dying of pneumonia could reach into the refrigerator, pull out a vial of antibodies directed against the specific bacterium involved, and effect a cure. Pauling imagined magic bullets made to order on an industrial scale. Artificial antibodies could revolutionize medicine. Someone would make a fortune. He started Campbell to work on this question as well.

While he waited for results in the spring of 1940, Pauling, still too unsure of his theory to publish, began distributing draft manuscripts and offering his ideas at scientific meetings. Everyone seemed to think his work was very interesting, although without confirming experiments no one was convinced. Even Landsteiner was only cautiously enthusiastic about Pauling's model of antibody formation.

Campbell's work was not helping. While his experiments buttressed Pauling's belief that antibodies were bivalent, the critical experiments—testing for dual-action antibodies and creating artificial ones—were inconclusive. But Pauling decided he had waited long enough. The inconclusive experimental work did not prove his theory, but neither did it disprove it. His was a theoretical paper, after all, meant to be a guide to productive experiments, not the final word. In June 1940, Pauling sent his paper on antibody formation to the *JACS*.

The paper appeared to be a rousing success. Written with Pauling's characteristic clarity and confidence, the paper answered the questions Pauling posed at the beginning: "What is the simplest structure which can be suggested . . . for a molecule with the properties observed for antibodies, and what is the simplest reasonable process of formation for such a molecule?" Pauling convincingly argued that a bivalent antibody molecule, with each end complementary to an area on the surface of an antigen, was both sufficient and necessary to explain the precipitation reaction. He outlined his idea of how the folding of a protein chain could result in a shape that gave an antibody its specificity. He explained how the "glue" that held antibody to antigen could be formed from a number of relatively small forces acting together: electrostatic attraction between negatively and positively charged areas, hydrogen bonds, van der Waals forces. And this was an amazing thing about his theory, that antibodies, these most precisely built proteins, achieved their specificity through an accumulation of nature's weakest and least specific bonds.

Pauling was pleasantly surprised to see his idea quickly supplant the older template schemes and become the leading theory of antibody formation. He was delighted to find himself deluged with hundreds of requests for reprints, more than he had received for any other paper.

Again he had entered a new field, bringing the power of structural chemistry to the study of immunology. And again, his coming was seen as a triumph.

~~~

Just before Pauling sent in the antibody paper for publication, he ran into physicist-turned-biologist Max Delbrück while walking across campus. Pauling liked the young German immigrant, another of the Rockefeller-funded boundary-crossers interested in the mysteries of the New Biology; he found Delbrück's approach to biological problems through the study of the simplest possible life form, viruses, "sensible." Knowing of Pauling's recent interest in antibodies, Delbrück told him that he might like to look at some papers Pascual Jordan had written during the past few years in which the German researcher promoted the idea that molecules identical with one another might, because of quantum-mechanical resonance, tend to stick together. This, he said, might help explain the ability of molecules such as genes, viruses—even antibodies, according to Jordan—to replicate exact copies of themselves. Pauling was interested, and he and Delbrück strolled to the library to review Jordan's papers. After five minutes' study, Delbrück remembered, Pauling announced that Jordan's ideas were "baloney." A few days later, Pauling told Delbrück, "I have written a little note to *Science* about this; would you like to join me in publishing this?" Delbrück had not done any real work on the paper, but he agreed with it and did not want to appear impolite. He signed on.

Pauling's "little note" was to prove prophetic. "The Nature of the Intermolecular Forces Operative in Biological Processes" by Pauling and Delbrück appeared in the discussion section of *Science* in the summer of 1940. After demolishing, in typically straightforward language, the notion of resonance as a basis for Jordan's ideas about attraction between identical molecules—"We have reached the conclusion that the theory cannot be applied in the ways indicated by him, and that his explanations of biological phenomena on this basis can not be accepted"—Pauling stated his own case: "We . . . feel that complementariness should be given primary consideration in the discussion of the specific attraction between molecules and the enzymatic synthesis of molecules." Complementary shapes, die-and-coin relationships, were how specificity was achieved in biology. Pauling made a special point of stressing the importance of the concept for cases where molecules make copies of themselves, where "complementariness and identity might coincide."

Apart from discouraging Jordan, the note sank into the literature with hardly a ripple. It was only years later that it was resurrected and hailed by historians of science as one of the founding documents of a new science, "a manifesto of molecular biology." DNA would turn out to be a molecule in which complementariness and identity coincided.

—*mm*—

After a few months of relaying to Weaver his growing excitement over immunology—especially the chance of making artificial antibodies—Pauling made an informal funding request at the beginning of 1941: twenty thousand dollars per year to start a full-blown research program in immunochemistry, enough to bring to Caltech three research assistants, three graduate assistants, a visiting professor, a roomful of research animals, and a laboratory outfitted with the best equipment available. This was as much money as Pauling's entire structural chemistry budget, and during a visit to Caltech in February, Weaver let him know that he was being "distinctly over-adventurous." Pauling cut his request nearly in half. Weaver, after checking with leaders in the field—Landsteiner and others told him that the creation of artificial antibodies would be of "revolutionary" importance—convinced the Rockefeller Foundation to award Pauling eleven thousand dollars per year for three years for his immunological work. The money enabled Pauling to hire Dan Campbell permanently, provided support for a promising young postdoctoral student, David Pressman, and bought enough equipment, rabbits, and syringes to perform the experiments he wanted.

The only minor note of warning among Weaver's contacts came from the acerbic British biochemist Norman Pirie, who hoped, Weaver noted, "that Pauling will not pile hypothesis upon hypothesis, and will not insist on speaking of this hypothesis on every conceivable occasion, but will now quietly await experimental evidence." In other words, Pirie said, he hoped that Pauling would not "Wrinch it."

The Hawk

The Orderly Organism of the World

The first of Albert Schoenflies's letters reached Pauling in December 1938. Written in German, it had a tone of controlled panic. Schoenflies was a Jew. His father had been a well-known German scientist, a pioneer of x-ray crystallography, and a friend of Laue's. Schoenflies himself had practiced law, serving ten years as a German judge before Hitler's Nuremberg Laws stripped him of his position. This was madness, he thought, but like many in Germany, he also thought it would pass. He treated his time off as an enforced holiday, spending more time with his three young children, taking a few courses in chemistry. Then he was told Jews could no longer attend classes. On a freezing November night in 1938 came the murders and beatings, the broken glass and bloodied heads of *Kristallnacht*. Schoenflies woke up. Along with thousands of others, he made a desperate attempt to leave the country. Laue told him to write to scientists in America, including Pauling, in the hope that one could get him a student visa.

Schoenflies's was one of a growing number of increasingly desperate inquiries from German academics that Pauling received in the late 1930s; his replies were unfailingly sympathetic and courteous, although there was not much that he could do to cut through the red tape of immigration restrictions. He took a special interest in the Schoenflies situation because Laue wrote him personally and asked for his help. Pauling contacted some committees that had been set up to handle German refugees but found that they acted very slowly. When Pauling tried to contact Schoenflies, he got no reply. It was four months before Pauling heard from him again, this time from a refugee camp in Holland. He was penniless, Schoenflies wrote; he was unable to withdraw any of his savings from his German bank account and had drawn an impossibly high quota number for getting into the United States. "At present I am living here without any means whatever and I am very sorrowful. . . . As my children aged 6, 8, and 10 years cannot go to any school here and as I have no opportunity to work or to find any occupation whatsoever. . . . I beg you with the request whether you can see your way clear to be of any help to me in my difficult and not enviable position." Pauling wrote back immediately with assurances that he would do everything he could to help; he wrote letters to international education boards and to committees to aid refugees. It was relatively easy to get seasoned German scientists into the United States, but ex-judges were another thing. Pauling offered to find money to support the family in Pasadena and tried to devise a way to get at least the Schoenflies children out. But he could not make the immigration bureaucracy move fast enough. When he wrote Schoenflies in the spring of 1939 to tell him that he would keep trying, his letter was returned stamped "Address Unknown."

Horror stories like this were told by the scores of Jewish scientists who began reaching the United States in the mid-1930s. Hitler was tearing apart the great German universities, using the excuse of racial purity to expel and imprison Jewish professors and those sympathetic to the Jews. In the process, he destroyed much of German science. Following Einstein's example, scores of Jewish researchers fled, many taking up residence in America. Many of the non-Jews in German science, including Sommerfeld, tried their best to help and, in the early days, spoke out against the Nazis. Others, like Heisenberg, were silent. Still others led the purges. It was nightmarish; it undermined everything Pauling believed about the rationality of science.

By 1939, Pauling believed Hitler had to be stopped. "The feeling in America is uniformly that of sympathy for England in her inability to stand for Hitlerism any longer," Pauling wrote a British friend in September. "And I hope that the democracies will line up together strong enough to put an end to the situation soon." After France fell in the spring of 1940, Pauling's concern increased. He became convinced that without direct U.S. involvement Britain, too, would fall, giving Hitler the world's largest war fleet and ultimate dominion over the seas.

～～～

The question became what to do. Scientists were traditionally apolitical, sticking to provable facts and letting the statesmen handle world affairs. Steering clear of politics was an unspoken rule of science, accepted implicitly because it was a proper and natural division of expertise: Most scientists felt that they should remain as impartial and objective in any public role as they were in their research, that they should stick to what they knew, the noble pursuit of knowledge, and leave the confusing and unverifiable concerns of politics to politicians. This was not to say that scientists did not hold political views; they simply kept them private. This had been true of Pauling, too, who, despite his move toward the left wing of the American political spectrum under Ava Helen's influence in the early 1930s, had not publicly spoken or published a word about politics.

But his feelings about a scientist's role in public debate were changing. In 1939 he read *The Social Function of Science*, a long, detailed, and devastating critique of the failure of science to grapple with world affairs written by John Desmond Bernal, the English crystallographer. The book effectively destroyed the notion of science as an island of rationality immune from less lofty human concerns. "It used to be believed that the results of scientific investigation would lead to continuous progressive improvements in conditions of life," Bernal wrote, "but first [World War I] and then the economic crisis have shown that science can be used as easily for destructive and wasteful purposes, and voices have been raised demanding the cessation of scientific research as the only means of preserving a tolerable civilization. Scientists themselves, faced with these criticisms, have been forced to consider, effectively for the first time, how the work they are doing is connected with the social and economic developments which are occurring around them." Bernal, a committed Marxist and an advocate of world government, proposed that scientists should move toward a socialist model in which their talents were used for the good of the people rather than to prop up a capitalist economy. He also understood that scientists themselves were a major impediment to the creation of a socialist utopia. In Bernal's view the typical scientist was at best a middle-class conformist, at worst a capitalist lackey, "a salaried employee of the State, of an industrial firm, or of some semi-independent institution such as a university which itself depends directly or indirectly on the State or industry. Consequently the real liberty of the scientist is effectively limited, by the needs of his livelihood, to actions which are tolerated by his paymasters." Scientific workers must organize, Bernal wrote, take control of their own work, recognize their social responsibilities and act upon them. "Set science free, and it will work for the good of humanity far more effectively than it does now for the gain of a few."

Pauling devoured the book, made it a topic of discussion in his seminar classes at Caltech, and sympathized with most of its message. His curiosity about the world had been extended by Ava Helen to questions of privilege and politics in America; now he began to believe that scientists might have something useful to say about those issues. Like Bernal, he believed that because much of the progress of the modern world was rooted in scientific advances and scientists were better informed about these advances than anyone, they could have an important rule to play in public debates. Scientists also had a technique—the scientific method—by which to analyze data coolly and rationally. He saw no reason why a scientist, given enough information, could not apply that method to think through a political or social issue, such as how to handle Hitler, in a useful way.

Ava Helen then encouraged Pauling to read *Union Now*, a book in which the American political journalist Clarence Streit outlined the dangers of totalitarianism and offered a new idea to fight it: consolidation of the world's democracies into a federation modeled on the union of American states. Streit's book, with its appealing idea of extending the basics of the U.S. Constitution to the entire world, became a miniphenomenon, spawning a Union Now movement that by 1940 claimed three thousand members in sixty chapters across the United States. Ava Helen became an enthusiastic promoter of Streit's philosophy. Both Paulings became charter members of the Pasadena chapter, and Ava Helen spent many afternoons sitting behind the counter at the group's downtown storefront office.

With his wife's urging, Pauling made the first political speeches of his life in 1940. His topic was Union Now, the containment of fascism and the need to prepare to fight the next war. At first, he was a bit uncomfortable speaking about topics that had little to do with science, but he soon found that he enjoyed it. Standing in front of small audiences in junior high school auditoriums or the living rooms of private homes, he could speak with a passion unsuited to his scientific talks. It brought back the excitement and satisfaction he had felt exercising his skills as senior orator at Oregon Agricultural College (OAC). "Should not our country help Britain now to fight the thing which is attacking her and will probably attack us when she is polished off?" he asked his audiences. "This means going to war, and we, as idealists, are by nature pacifists and opposed to war. But we are being forced into war anyway—we are vigorously preparing for war, and who among us believes that we are not going to have war sooner or later? . . . It is the cancerous growth of Nazism—of dictatorship in general—that must be eradiacted from the otherwise orderly organism of the world." He ended his speeches with a stirring vision of a planet at peace, organized and run by a stable, democratic world government.

The idea of the "orderly organism of the world" in which Hitler played the role of a disrupting cancer put Pauling's emerging political sense in line with his view of science: He believed that there existed a world of human affairs, like the world of molecules, that could be understood and made rational. Once again, structure was the key. If mankind lived in a correctly structured world—one in which nationalism was replaced with world government, capitalism with scientifically engineered socialism, and totalitarianism with democracy— suffering would decrease, and war would become obsolete. The world would be made healthy. Some of those goals were in the future, but Hitler was an imminent danger to the vision and must be dealt with immediately.

Pauling's increasingly activist left-wing beliefs placed him in the minority both at Caltech and in staunchly Republican Pasadena. In the fall of 1940, when Caltech students tried to set up an election-year debate with professors arguing for the presidential contenders, they had trouble finding anyone willing to take Roosevelt's side. Finally, they turned to Pauling, who said he would give it a try. The Caltech economics professor who championed Wendell Willkie did not have a chance. "Pauling ran rings intellectually around the other man," remembered John Edsall, a Harvard professor then visiting Caltech. "It was rather a dazzling display, a bravado performance." Willkie won Pasadena in the election, as Republican candidates did every year Roosevelt ran, but Pauling had discovered that taking on the role of gadfly could be fun.

The coming war, however, remained Pauling's main political concern. For a while he flirted with the idea of joining the American Association of Scientific Workers (AASW), the left-wing offshoot of a British association that Bernal had helped start in the late 1930s to encourage scientists to think about the social effects of their work and to mobilize them toward using science for the welfare of society and away from war projects. The AASW picked up a number of prominent supporters, but they lost Pauling when the group published a resolution in *Science* in 1940 urging the United States to remain neutral in the European war. Pauling thought that only war would defeat Hitler. He publicly protested the AASW's "peace at any price" program and joined the Committee to Defend America by Aiding the Allies and the American Friends of the Chinese People.

His feelings about fascism were shared by a majority of American scientists. As the blitzkrieg swept across Europe in the spring of 1940, the president of the National Academy of Sciences, Caltech graduate Frank Jewett, began lobbying Washington, D.C., to mobilize scientists for the coming war. The government responded by creating the National Defense Research Committee (NDRC), a group designed to organize and fund the nation's scientific war effort, the functional equivalent of the National Research Council that Hale had started during World War I. The president of the Carnegie Institution, MIT-educated electrical engineer Vannevar Bush, was picked to head it and in 1941 oversaw its amalgamation with the Committee on Medical Research to form the Office of Scientific Research and Development (OSRD).

It was the beginning of a new era of collaboration between science and government in the United States. As the rumors of war increased, Bush began gathering a core group of advisers who would determine where billions of dollars in national defense money would go. Caltech's Richard Chace Tolman was tapped to head the NDRC division on armor and ordnance, and he arrived in the nation's capital in the summer of 1940, bringing the Caltech nuclear physicist Charles Lauritsen with him as his vice chair.

Pauling was brought east, too, but for his ideas, not his administrative ability. In October 1940 he joined thirty other chemists at a discussion of wartime needs called by Division B of the NDRC in Washington. Pauling finally felt he was going to be able to do something positive to fight the Nazis, and he listened eagerly as a group of military officers presented the researchers with a wish list of needed breakthroughs, including new medicines, better explosives, and more accurate monitoring and detection devices. Pauling paid special attention when a navy officer outlined a potentially deadly problem in submarines. There was no easy way to accurately monitor the level of oxygen in those tin cans, the officer said, making it difficult to adjust levels for safety and efficiency on long underwater runs. With too little oxygen, the men would get weak and drowsy; too much increased the danger of an explosion.

On the way home on the train Pauling thought about ways to make an oxygen meter. Taking advantage of oxygen's unusual magnetic properties—its attraction to a magnet while most other common gases were slightly repelled—had worked to his advantage in his hemoglobin studies. The same properties might afford a way to make a meter. The more oxygen there was in a sample of air, the more attracted it would be to a magnet. But how could you measure it? The magnetic changes caused by slight differences in oxygen content would be very small, especially compared to the mechanical forces required to move a needle on a dial.

Then he thought about Archimedes. Two thousand years before, the Greek philosopher had discovered a way to determine how dense a liquid was by suspending a solid body in it: the denser the surrounding liquid, the more it would buoy up whatever was put in it. By measuring the difference in weight, buoyed and unbuoyed, the liquid's density could be calculated. Replace the liquid with an air sample and carefully suspend a test body in it that would react to changes in a magnetic field, Pauling reasoned, and changes in the oxygen content of the sample would cause the test body to behave differently. He began to make a sketch. The test body would have to be small and delicately balanced to measure slight changes. Pauling thought of a tiny glass dumbbell, the ends filled with air, balanced and glued onto a fine quartz fiber. The magnetic field could come from an ordinary horseshoe magnet. String the silica strand across the ends of the magnet. Then any changes in the magnetic properties of the air surrounding the test body would cause it to reorient itself in the magnetic field, to swing until it reached a new equilibrium with the torsion of the strand. The degree of swing would be very small, but perhaps it could be amplified for the viewer by reflecting a light off the test body onto a scale.

This was not a bad idea, he thought, especially for a theorist who was not known for constructing experimental apparatus. When he got back to Pasadena, Pauling gave his sketches to Reuben Wood, a more mechanically minded colleague, and Wood set to work. The hard part was making the tiny dumbbell and balancing it on the thread; once that was done, Wood glued a tiny mirror onto the dumbbell to reflect the beam of light, attached it across the magnet, and set up the whole thing inside a bell jar, with a flashlight for a light source and a piece of tissue paper pasted to the jar wall for a scale. The prototype was up and working in a matter of days.

A few weeks later, Pauling was on his way back to Washington, D.C., with the first Pauling Oxygen Analyzer carefully nested next to him in the berth of the train. He was very proud and a little nervous. In the middle of his first night out from Pasadena he awoke suddenly with a premonition that his meter was not going to work. He switched on the overhead light, carefully unboxed the device, and switched on the flashlight. The device was not behaving correctly. The reflected light on the tissue paper showed an oxygen level that was definitely too low; in the jostling to get on the train the meter must have gotten out of calibration. It was all too delicate; his design was not sturdy enough for real-world use. "I'd better get off the train and go back to Pasadena," Pauling thought. He looked out the window in despair. Then he felt a rush of relief. Everywhere he looked were mountains. The train was climbing over the Continental Divide. The meter was accurate—it was correctly reading the lower oxygen concentration at a higher elevation. He repacked his meter and happily went back to sleep.

After the top brass saw it in action, Pauling was given a contract to make several hundred Pauling Oxygen Analyzers at Caltech. He patented the design, then had Holmes Sturdivant organize a small factory in the laboratory, with workers trying to blow molten glass into tiny spheres for the dumbbells and balance them on almost invisible threads. It was very hard work. It took all the air human lungs could muster to start the tiny dab of hot glass stretching; once it started, the pressure had to drop immediately or the bulb would blow too big. They found only one virtuoso graduate student who could clamp down on the blowing tube, coordinate his diaphragm, lungs, and mouth muscles, and create a decent sphere—perhaps once every two hundred tries.

Realizing that this was not going to work, Pauling convinced the innovative Caltech chemistry professor-turned-manufacturer Arnold Beckman—inventor of the Beckman pH meter and founder of Beckman Instruments—to take over production. Beckman hired Pauling's workers, personally designed the world's smallest glassblowing machine, and found a way to draw out silica fibers so fine they could not be seen—the workers had to find them by dropping a piece of folded paper over the spot where they thought they were. The meters he made were very accurate. Although the U.S. Navy argued over technical specifications until the war was over and never became a major buyer, several hundred units were sold to the British navy. The machine was also used in aviation-medicine studies, industrial plants, and in the incubators of premature babies. Royalties from sales were shared between Caltech—for years forming a major part of its royalty income—Pauling, Sturdivant, and Wood. But the only one who made much money from it was Beckman, who, in the mid-1950s, sold the company he started to make the analyzers for a million dollars.

Dr. Addis's Diet

In March 1941, one month after his fortieth birthday, Pauling received the most significant award given him in the decade since the Langmuir Prize: the William H. Nichols Gold Medal of the New York chapter of the American Chemical Society. Pauling—"the outstanding theoretical chemist of the United States and probably of the world," the press release said—was again one of the youngest men to have ever received the medal, at the time considered American chemistry's most prestigious honor.

The awarding of the medal was cause for a chemical celebration in New York City, capped by a black-tie dinner at the Hotel Pennsylvania. As the assembled chemists sipped their coffee, Pauling's old friend and Caltech roommate Paul Emmett regaled the audience with tales of their early days together. Emmett surrendered the podium to the great Columbia chemist Joseph Mayer, who outlined Pauling's scientific work.

When Pauling's turn came to speak, everyone expected to see another knockout performance by the renowned speaker. But it quickly became apparent to those who knew him that something was wrong. Pauling's face looked bloated and puffy. His voice was flat. He mentioned at the beginning of his speech that he had been surprised to find his eyes swollen shut when he tried to open them that morning, then turned it into a joke about politicians not being able to see. But there was nothing funny about the way he seemed drained of energy. He kept his speech uncharacteristically short and went back to his hotel room early.

At a small dinner party at Alfred Mirsky's apartment the next evening, he admitted that he felt worn out and had gained about twenty pounds in the past few weeks, enough to have trouble buttoning his shirtcollar and fitting into his shoes. One of the guests, a heart specialist from the Rockefeller Medical Institute, took Pauling aside, told him that edema like his was sometimes indicative of heart trouble, and asked him if he could quickly check him over. They went into one of the Mirskys' bedrooms, where the physician laid Pauling on the floor, palpated his extremities, and listened to his heart. It was puzzling. There did not seem to be anything wrong with his cardiovascular system, but the extreme swelling was certainly enough to warrant concern. The doctor told Pauling to come to his office at the institute the next day for a complete work-up.

Now worried, Ava Helen made sure that he went and took every test the Rockefeller doctors could give him. After hours of enduring various proddings and pokings and drawings of blood, Pauling waited nervously with Ava Helen for the results. Finally, they were ushered into a room filled with somber physicians. They were asked to take a seat. It appeared, one man said, that Pauling might have a serious problem. It seemed to them that his kidneys might be affected by a condition known as Bright's disease, which caused a progressive decrease in the body's ability to filter waste products out of the blood. As a result, fluids could build up and cause bloating. But the problem was potentially more serious than that. The tests also showed that he was passing an abnormal amount of protein in his urine, a signal that the kidneys themselves were being destroyed. This was indicative of a most serious form of Bright's disease. Pauling was silent, trying to work his way through what he had just heard. Ava Helen asked if people recovered from the condition. "Some do," answered one of the physicians. But the important thing now was to pinpoint the nature of his disease and discover what was causing it.

Everything was a blur after that. They stayed another day, going through more batteries of tests. After they were done, the doctors told Pauling to cancel his remaining speaking engagements and return home immediately. They would help him find a suitable specialist in California.

On the train back, Pauling was externally calm, but inside he was shaken. Both his mother and father had died young. Grandfather Linus Darling had died of kidney disease. It looked as though he were fated to follow them. Back in Pasadena, waiting for the recommendation of a specialist, he dealt with his depressing diagnosis the only way he knew how: He threw himself into work, finishing a major grant request for the Rockefeller Foundation and reading everything he could about kidney disease. One fact stood out among the many he learned: most experts agreed that there was no effective treatment for Bright's disease.

Pauling's mood darkened, but he kept it inside and kept working. Aside from being more easily tired and twenty pounds heavier than normal, he did not feel ill. But he worked in bed, as the doctors had advised, for two weeks, until arrangements were completed for him to see the West Coast's leading kidney specialist. The name they gave him was Thomas Addis, head of the Clinic for Renal Diseases at Stanford University.

Pauling needed hope, and Addis provided it. He was a tall, handsome, charismatic Scot who looked younger than his sixty years, with a gentle, somewhat absentminded but reassuring manner and a vast background in the classification and treatment of Bright's disease. Addis's twenty years of study had convinced him that Bright's was not one disease but several, with different pathologies. His approach to diagnosis was suitably scientific in Pauling's eyes: He made a quantitative measurement of urinary sediment over time (the Addis count), which told him something about the nature of the kidney problem, and also the urinary urea clearance (the Addis urea ratio), which indicated the extent of the damage. Addis was one of the few physicians in the world who believed that Bright's could be treated. He had a theory about it, based on the idea that the disease depended on a balance of tissue destruction and restoration. The trick was letting the kidneys rest. The kidneys' major work, Addis told Pauling, consisted of concentrating urea for elimination from the body. Urea was produced from protein metabolism. In order to heal, Pauling's kidneys needed to process less urea, which meant cutting down on protein intake.

Pauling had read enough by now to know that Addis's ideas were considered controversial by other kidney experts, who pointed out that protein was required in a diet to achieve maximal kidney tissue restoration. On the other hand, the other experts also routinely gave up on Bright's patients. Addis at least attempted a cure.

For days, Addis tracked Pauling's urine output, sediment amounts, and urea clearance, sometimes bringing Pauling into his laboratory to watch the tests being analyzed firsthand. Every day, he came to talk with his star patient—they occasionally shared teatime together, a routine Addis observed religiously—and the two men found that they had much in common. Pauling was impressed with Addis's approach to the disease and his belief in scientific measurement as a basis for diagnosis. They talked about kidney function and hemoglobin metabolism and about politics: Addis, one of the Bay Area's most outspoken anti-Fascists, a supporter of civil rights and a believer in Soviet Russia, ran his clinic along socialist lines.

After two weeks together at Addis's clinic, they became good friends. Then, one day, Addis walked in and told Pauling that he should go home. His tests had shown that Pauling's condition could be treated with an extremely low protein, salt-free diet, which would lower the production of urea and reduce the swelling in his tissues. Ava Helen would make sure he stayed on it; Addis had already given her some ideas for menus. He could keep track of Pauling's progress from Stanford by looking at his urine analyses every week. Just stay in bed and eat properly, he told Pauling; don't work too much and give your kidneys a chance to repair themselves.

This sounded reasonable. Back in Pasadena, Pauling was installed in a bed in the study of his house and put on Addis's diet, with its emphasis on fruits, grains, and vegetables, along with supplemental vitamins and minerals and lots of water. He cut his correspondence to a minimum, delegated most administrative duties to Sturdivant, and tried to stop thinking about science by immersing himself in mystery novels. Ava Helen became his nurse and dietitian, carefully preparing his food, weighing each portion to the fraction of an ounce on a newly purchased postage scale, figuring total protein and salt, and noting everything in a spiral notebook. Making saltless, meatless meals interesting became her personal challenge. She found ways around the usual bananas and gelatin, supplementing the bland fare with occasional treats like escargot captured from her garden, fed for days on cornmeal and steamed in the shell. Snails, she explained to Pauling, were very low protein.

The Addis regimen seemed to work. Pauling forced himself to stay in bed, first all day, then later for half days. After four months the edema was gone; after six Pauling found his mental energy and good humor returning to normal. He corresponded often with Addis, visited him occasionally, and became an enthusiast for his methods. He later nominated Addis for the National Academy of Sciences, ensured his election, and helped him get government funding for kidney studies during the war. He stayed on his low-protein diet for almost fifteen years and attributed his survival and good health to Addis's ideas. Addis, for his part, told Pauling that Ava Helen had saved his life: Very few other patients were able to stay on his diet so religiously for so long.

~~~

To those who worked with Pauling, the cure seemed a miracle. There had been some serious talk about what the division would do without him. Now, within a year, he was back and seemingly better than ever. "We thought we might lose him," Eddie Hughes remembered. "And for many years after that, it seemed to me that he was getting younger every year instead of older as he recovered."

By September 1941 he felt well enough to go to the University of Chicago's fiftieth anniversary celebration, a great affair highlighted by the awarding of fifty honorary doctorates in fifty fields of learning. Pauling was pleased to receive the honor in chemistry. He began to throw himself into projects again, including his antibody work and the transformation of his lecture notes from freshman chemistry into a textbook.

But the book project was put aside, along with many others, when the news came that the Japanese had attacked Pearl Harbor.

Bombs and Rockets

America's formal entry into the war on December 7, 1941, merely confirmed what the Caltech community already knew was going to happen. Within days of the attack, Robert Millikan, now seventy-three years old, appointed a committee to ensure the institute's security. Japanese sabotage and bombing attacks were the major worry, and the committee went a bit overboard in the frenzy following Pearl Harbor. During a comic-opera period of a few weeks early in the war, squads of Caltech students, armed with ax handles, were put on patrol around important buildings. The suggestion was made to Pauling that an armed guard be placed outside every laboratory in Gates and Crellin, but he assured the administration that a single watchman making tours of inspection through the night would be enough. Caltech's researchers turned their thoughts from the structure of the universe to the design of homemade gas masks and methods of keeping glass from shattering during bombing raids, and Pauling, along with every other scientist working on military contracts, was fingerprinted and given a security check.

Far more important than the surface changes on campus was the flood of money the war would bring to Caltech. In Washington, D.C.,

Caltech's Charlie Lauritsen became an enthusiast for the military use of rockets and convinced the military that Caltech could become a national center in that area despite its limited prewar experience with rocket research. Three months before the Japanese attacked Pearl Harbor, the first $200,000 in federal money for rocket research was sent to Pasadena—an amount equal to about one-sixth of the institute's total prewar annual budget. Lauritsen set up a rocket-propellant plant in the foothills near Pasadena and ran it around the clock under the direction of one of Pauling's faculty members, the chemical engineer Bruce Sage. "Very few people realized we had enough high explosives up there to have blown Pasadena off the map," one participant remembered. By 1944 funding for the rocket program alone would grow to $2 million *per month*, employing thousands of workers, contracting with hundreds of businesses, and creating an entire new industry in Southern California. As Lauritsen's right-hand man on the project put it, "A large part of Caltech literally had become a branch of the Bureau of Ordnance."

The major problem with rockets was that they were undependable. Lauritsen stood at navy firing ranges and watched rocket after rocket blow up prematurely or veer off course. This, he believed, was because of the propellant being used, an American-made powder that burned erratically, far inferior to those he saw being used in England. With better propellants and more scientific design, Lauritsen believed, rockets could be made more accurate, more trustworthy, an important part of the war effort.

Pauling, too, became interested in propellants and explosives. After war was declared, he offered his expertise to the government in the area of powder research. He was made a member of the explosives division of the NDRC—now a subsidiary, along with the new Committee on Medical Research, of the OSRD—and chair of a special committee on internal ballistics for the rocket program. He traveled almost every month to Washington, D.C., to plan research and discuss objectives with the men running the war machine. Government funding began flowing to his lab as well, mostly for research into the analysis of powders and the development of more stable propellants. Pauling quickly became an expert, reading widely and spending some weeks in the spring and summer of 1942 visiting gunpowder and explosives factories in the East. The navy began sending a steady stream of captured German and Japanese fuels to Pasadena so that the Caltech scientists could analyze them. Under Pauling's supervision, new chromatographic techniques were developed that allowed the quick and accurate determination of the compounds in Axis rockets—even if it was just a few pinches scraped from a fragment. The expansion of Zechmeister's separation techniques to compounds such as those in explosives helped establish chromatography as an important tool for chemists. "We sort of revolutionized modern chemistry by introducing chromatographic analysis," Pauling said.

By the spring of 1942, Pauling, now healthy and eager to contribute to the war effort, threw himself into defense research. He invented an improved stabilizer for rocket powders, a composite grain that allowed the powder to burn more consistently and give a better trajectory. Some wag nicknamed it "Linusite," and it became widely used during the war. Pauling began working on a synthetic substitute for much-needed quartz crystals used in military sighting devices and codeveloped an armor-piercing shell that was later patented.

Whenever she could, Ava Helen still kept Pauling in bed for half a day, but it was impossible to slow him down much. His naturally restless imagination now had a thousand problems to work on, and each one he chose was funded by seemingly endless federal dollars. He was like a little boy with a blank check in a toy store. "The laboratory here has lost its leisurely air now," Pauling wrote in June 1942. "We have got so many contracts for war work that everybody is kept on the go." He toured arsenals and gave advice on the production of explosives. He analyzed chemical systems for making oxygen. He oversaw a project on aerosols. He worked on a machine for determining the molecular weights of molecules in solution and in his spare time devised what he felt was an unbreakable code (which he sent to the War Department and never heard about again). Once a month he would commute to Washington, hopping on the *Super Chief* for the three-day train trip east, spending a day or two in meetings, then returning. He enjoyed the trip, with its days of quiet thinking time as he stared out the window at the mountains and plains, and the feeling of contributing to the war effort.

As money flowed from Washington, the size of his laboratory grew. The powder project alone soon numbered about fifty young chemists packed into every available laboratory space and office, working as a team under the direction of Robert Corey. Corey was proving indispensable. The shy man who once preferred working with only one or two helpers bloomed during the war years into an efficient manager,

devising a reporting and scheduling system that made the Caltech operation a model for other war labs.

Early in 1943, Pauling's old friend J. Robert Oppenheimer stopped
by Caltech to offer Pauling a more significant chance to contribute to
the war effort. They had not spoken more than a few words in the fifteen years since Oppy had tried to talk Ava Helen into a Mexican "vacation"; but Pauling had followed the physicist's career at Berkeley and
knew through the grapevine that he was involved in a top-secret
weapons project. Oppenheimer, still gaunt and angular, still chain-
smoking and still full of himself, explained that he was in charge of a
team that was trying to build a bomb based on the nuclear fission of an
isotope of uranium. They were in a race with the Germans, he said,
who had Heisenberg working on it, so there was probably not much
standing in the Nazis' way, at least theoretically. But it had gone beyond theory here. In Chicago, a month or so earlier, Fermi and Szilard
had created a controlled fission chain reaction. It seemed certain now
that a fission bomb could be made that would loose the tremendous
energies holding together the nuclei of atoms.

The government was putting millions and millions of dollars into
the development of such a bomb, Oppenheimer explained. This was
going to be a very big project, involving hundreds of scientists, all
working together at a converted boys' school on a mesa top in New
Mexico, a place called Los Alamos, under strict security. While most of
the work would be done by physicists, there would be a fair amount of
chemistry involved. He asked if Pauling might be interested in directing the chemistry division of the project. A side benefit, he said, would
be the availability of hard-to-get radioactive tracers like tritium that
Pauling could use in his chemical biology work.

Pauling did not need long to think about it. The idea of playing
underling to a bunch of physicists—especially working directly under
Oppenheimer—was distasteful. The thought of bringing his wife and
family to a top-secret scientific boot camp in the New Mexico desert
was unappealing. He turned down the offer. "Not because I felt that it
was wrong to work on the development of nuclear weapons," Pauling
said, "rather that I had other jobs that I was doing."

⹈⹈⹈

Pauling had many other things to think about. Early in the war he became a member of the Western Committee of the OSRD's Committee
on Medical Research, where he became privy to the military's most

pressing medical needs. He learned that hundreds of wounded soldiers were dying needlessly from shock, deaths that could be prevented if only they had been given plasma. But there was not enough plasma to go around. The CMR started a crash program to develop a cheap, reliable synthetic plasma substitute, and based on his experience with hemoglobin and antibodies, Pauling won a contract for its development. He gathered a team, including Thomas Addis, who would test the artificial plasmas for clearance by the kidneys, and his immunology expert Dan Campbell. Together they explored a number of chemical approaches to making something that would fool the body. Nothing worked until Pauling came up with a way to chemically alter gelatin so that it not only mimicked the gross attributes of plasma—its density and viscosity—but could be inexpensively made and easily stored. He called his preparation oxypolygelatin. Early tests on volunteers were successful, and Pauling patented the formula, giving the government a royalty-free license to use it. He also made sure the discovery was well covered by the media, announcing his success publicly and keeping clips of the wire story that went out across the nation. It came as a great disappointment when the government refused to approve oxypolygelatin because of the wide range of sizes found in the molecules in the preparation. Then, in 1943, the entire plasma-substitute program was shut down because so many volunteers had come forward to donate the real thing.

"For the first time in medical history . . ."

By 1943, Pauling's Division of Chemistry and Chemical Engineering had been transformed: Tolman off to Washington, Niemann working on chemical warfare, faculty members Buchman and Koepfli trying to synthesize antimalarial drugs, Lucas working on plastics, Lacey on the rocket project. The students were almost all gone to war, replaced by military men taking specialized courses in explosives or rocketry. "Things are indeed much changed here," Pauling wrote a friend in the summer of 1943. "We have been trying to keep seminars going, but it has been hard to find material that can be talked about." Too much of the research was classified.

At the Rockefeller Foundation, Warren Weaver and his officers watched with some unease as the grant money they had awarded Pauling began to flow to war research. The great protein question that had spurred the most recent large foundation grants had been put aside as Corey and Hughes turned their attention to explosives and propellants. The development of the organic chemistry section was for the most part put on hold, too.

Only Pauling's work in immunology continued unchanged. Because it had arguably a more direct bearing on the war effort, he was able to carry through his basic research with the blessing of the powers in Washington. And Pauling's personal interest in the field was becoming intense. He even started dabbling in experimental work again for the first time in years, with Campbell teaching him how to inoculate rabbits and set up antibody-precipitation reactions. There were as yet no animal research facilities at Caltech, so Pauling built hutches for fifty rabbits near his garage at his home, assigning Linus junior and Peter to feed the animals and clean the cages. In the mornings before going off to work he would inject the animals with antigens and occasionally bleed them himself to collect the antibodies.

"I am happy to report that our immunochemical work is going extremely well," Pauling wrote Weaver in late 1941. One of his immediate goals was to prove that each antibody molecule had two binding sites, as he had proposed in his 1940 paper on antibody formation, and he devised an ingenious way of doing it. Landsteiner had perfected the technique of making synthetic antigens by attaching a chosen organic molecule to a protein; by doing this, antibodies could be raised to known structures and studied. Pauling had his workers make a series of these synthetic antigens with one, two, or three of the same organic molecules on each protein. By reacting the antibodies raised against the organic molecules with his various preparations and then analyzing the ratios of antigen to antibody in the resulting complexes, he was able to estimate how many antigens were attached to each antibody molecule. His results provided strong evidence that antibodies are bivalent, attaching to two antigens at a time, as he had predicted. He also found what appeared to be evidence that each of the two ends of the antibody molecule could bind to different antigens, again supporting the template theory of antibody formation.

But the most exciting news was Campbell's success by late 1941 in making artificial antibodies. The concept, based again on Pauling's 1940 paper, was that any globulin in the blood could be turned into a specific antibody by denaturing it, then allowing it to re-form around the desired antigen. This was exactly what Campbell had accomplished with beef globulin, Pauling wrote Weaver excitedly in November. This marked, he said, the preparation of what appeared to be the world's first artificial antibodies. Pauling concluded his letter by saying with some understatement, "I think that this synthesis of antibodies in vitro can be considered to be pretty important." He did not tell Weaver that he considered it important enough to apply for a patent on the process.

Campbell's experiments, however, were not as definitive as Pauling made them sound. Campbell was creating something that acted like an antibody—a protein that did, at least in Campbell's hands, bind specifically to a target antigen—but the yields of this specific product from beef globulin were low and variable. In the best cases only about one-eighth of the "manufactured antibodies," as Pauling called them, stuck to the antigen. The strength of the attachment between antibody and antigen was also less than that of natural antibodies, and the ratio of antibody to antigen in precipitates was much lower.

But that might all be explained by imperfections in the synthesis technique. The evidence might be weak, but it was there, and it fit Pauling's theories of antibody formation and of protein structure in general, with his idea of long, hydrogen-bonded chains forming into a variety of shapes. It corroborated his vision of the world. *It should work.*

He decided that it did work. The successful preparation of artificial antibodies raised all sorts of interesting possibilities. In wartime there was a crying need for all kinds of medicines, and artificial antibodies held the promise of being the most potent medicines in the world. By patenting the process, Pauling showed that he understood the commercial value of his discovery, and he underlined his sense of the money involved by taking an unusual step. In March 1942 he wrote and had released from Caltech a press release announcing that his laboratory had successfully prepared artificial antibodies. In it he noted that while it was not yet known if his discovery would be useful in medicine, the studies did "open up the possibility of a new method for use in the fight against disease."

Announcing a discovery of this importance in the popular press before anything had been published in a scientific journal was almost unheard of. But it worked to Pauling's advantage. The response was immediate. Wire services picked up the story and distributed it widely. *Science* ran the story in its news section, telling the research community: "For the first time in medical history, disease-fighting substances known as antibodies have been formed artificially in laboratory flasks." The editors of the *Journal of the American Medical Association* noted the work approvingly and looked forward to the day when networks of artificial immune human plasma banks would dispense Pauling's products. Representatives from pharmaceutical companies contacted Pauling, offering financial and technical help.

But Pauling wanted more strings-free grant money to perfect his preparatory techniques before commercializing them, and he used the burst of publicity following his press release to make certain he got it. There were two interested agencies, the OSRD's Committee on Medical Research and the Rockefeller Foundation. Pauling played them off against one another, telling the committee of his findings while simultaneously tempting Weaver with the "reasonable possibility" of developing a treatment of value against disease. Weaver got caught up in the excitement. On very short notice the Rockefeller Foundation granted Pauling thirty-one thousand dollars for his work in immunology, including twenty thousand dollars to perfect the manufacturing of artificial antibodies.

Not everyone, however, was enthusiastic. In April, Pauling wrote: "Not many people have written in for information about our experiments on the in vitro production of antibodies. Perhaps they have been too skeptical." He was right. The immunological community withheld its opinion until August, when Pauling's first complete papers on artificial antibodies appeared in *Science* and the *Journal of Experimental Medicine*. The published work showed that Pauling still had a long way to go to prove that he had done what he claimed. The experiments were described so sketchily that it was impossible to accurately replicate the work, and his control experiments looked weak. When Landsteiner and others tried to duplicate the work, they failed.

Despite the growing skepticism, Pauling still believed he was right. There were some new positive results: He and Campbell made artificial antibodies to *Pneumococcus* antigens and found that they had at least some measurable protective effect against disease when used in infected mice. But there were other signs that pointed to trouble. Campbell seemed to be the only man who could make artificial antibodies. Students and postdoctoral fellows working under his direction had no luck at all. After three months of trying, one research fellow wrote Pauling, "You have my good wishes in your endeavor to prepare artificial antibodies, but I must confess to a feeling of pessimism. . . .

Frankly, I am not impressed by experimental procedures which work sometimes but which do not at other times, and no cause can be assigned for the failure."

By early 1943 the Rockefeller Foundation was getting nervous. Frank Blair Hanson had taken over some of Weaver's duties in the natural sciences division, and he was less enthusiastic about Pauling than Weaver was. As time neared to renew the immunology grant, Hanson surveyed the nation's leading antibody experts to find out what they thought of Pauling's ideas. The responses were not encouraging. One respondent declared flatly that artificial antibodies had not been produced in Pasadena; another worried that Pauling "is not always critical of his own work." Landsteiner, while still supporting Pauling's general theory of antibody formation, told Hanson that if he were a betting man, "he would think the chances less than 50-50 that Pauling has manufactured antibodies." Famed microbiologist René Dubos summed it up: "Professor Pauling's views have received wide notoriety because of his great prestige in the field of chemistry. There are many of us, however, who feel that his claims . . . are based on very insufficient experimental evidence."

Hanson became openly skeptical himself, asking Pauling why, given the inconclusive results after a year's effort, his funding should not be decreased. Pauling did not know what to answer. There was just enough success to be tantalizing but too many failures to make things clear. After proclaiming to the world his success with artificial antibodies, he now had to admit that he was "disappointed" in their inability to fully protect animals. In further correspondence, he began downplaying the importance of artificial antibodies in his overall research scheme. The Rockefeller Foundation responded by cutting his special funding for the project by more than half. At the same time, Pauling quietly abandoned his patent application for manufactured antibodies. He would never publish another paper on the subject.

But neither would he retract his work. He had no idea why Campbell's tantalizing experiments promised success and delivered only confusion. His theory, he felt, was correct. And the small production of artificial antibodies that he had seen in Campbell's results must also be right. If it was not, someone would publicly prove it wrong.

No one did, during the war or for years afterward. In private, the top immunological researchers of the day decried Pauling's work and faulted him for not disavowing it. But they would not make their criticisms public. Only Elvin Kabat, a young immunologist just starting his career, was brash enough to attack Pauling's results in print, writing in a review article that what Pauling and Campbell were seeing was non-specific binding of antigen and globulin; Campbell, he said, had used so much globulin in his tests that the proteins stuck together randomly, dragging down some antigen with them. Privately, a number of more senior immunologists thought Kabat was probably right. So why was he the only one to publicly critique the work? As Kabat later said, "Pauling was such a powerful figure that most people did not want to get into criticizing him."

The silence ensured that Pauling's reputation would not suffer too much from his unsuccessful flirtation with artificial antibodies. Only those immunologists most familiar with the field and the officials at the Rockefeller Foundation understood the degree of his overstatement of the case.

Pauling for his part would always believe that the work he and Campbell had done was valid. Fifty years later, Pauling still insisted: "We did succeed in creating artificial antibodies—very weak ones, but still with specificity."

Why had the miraculous substances appeared only in Dan Campbell's flasks? Years later, long after giving up on the quest for artificial antibodies, Campbell offered an explanation to his close friend Ray Owen, then a member of the Caltech biology division. An overeager laboratory assistant, he said, had shaded the results to fit what he thought his bosses wanted to see. The whole incident occurred, Campbell said, "because of some technician who wanted the results to please the professor."

─────

Giving up on artificial antibodies refocused Pauling's attention on more productive immunological research. After the beginning of 1943, he returned to more fundamental questions and, working with Pressman and Campbell, began putting together a string of solid achievements. The group published more than twenty articles over the next few years, providing strong evidence for the bivalence of antibodies and the importance of specific molecular shapes in explaining the binding of antibody to antigen. By using better-defined synthetic antigens than Landsteiner's and new quantitative techniques for measuring the reaction with antibodies, the Pauling lab proved by war's end that the binding of antibody to antigen took place because the fit between them was complementary. Their work supported and extended Ehrlich's idea of lock-and-key binding, showing definitively that antibody and antigen bound to each other by fitting together like two pieces of a molecular jigsaw puzzle.

But what held them together? Studying the moderate amount of energy required to break the bond between antibody and antigen had already convinced Pauling that strong chemical bonds—covalent or ionic—were not involved. A new picture emerged in his mind. By comparing the reaction between an antibody and various antigens that differed in defined ways from the original target, Pauling's team found that changing as little as a single atom in an antigen could have a significant effect on the strength of binding. The fit, in other words, had to be astonishingly precise.

This close nuzzling together of molecules, atom to atom, brought into play another kind of glue, the van der Waals attraction between atoms. The van der Waals force, named for the Dutch scientist who outlined its effect in gases, was weak—one-tenth to one one-hundredth the strength of a covalent bond—and nonspecific, operating between almost any pair of atoms brought into close contact. Fritz London in 1930 had explained it in quantum-mechanical terms as a weak electrical attraction produced when two atoms brought close together perturbed each other's electron cloud. Pauling was familiar with it through his crystallographic work: A covalent bond held two iodine atoms tightly together as a molecule, but the molecules were bound together into a crystal by the van der Waals force. The important thing for antibodies was that the van der Waals force decreases geometrically with distance, making it operative only at very close proximity. With only a few atoms involved, it does not add up to much, but if giant molecules like proteins brought a good deal of their surfaces together, Pauling realized, the total van der Waals force could add up to something significant, enough to bind the two molecules together. Postulating this as a major factor in antigen-antibody interaction also meant that pushing the molecules apart even a little—Pauling's lab found that creating a bump on an antigen's surface that pushed the antibody away the equivalent of a fraction of the diameter of a single atom was enough —would measurably weaken the binding force. If the misfit was more pronounced, the antigen and antibody let go of each other.

Pauling found that this weak, nonspecific force, combined with some hydrogen bonding and the attraction of oppositely charged polar groups, added up to the highly specific binding of antibody and antigen. And it all worked because of structure. Precise, complementary shapes were all-important. In immunology, at least, Pauling became convinced that molecular structure determined biological specificity.

This work was valuable and important enough to keep Pauling in the forefront of immunological research despite his failure with artificial antibodies. His direct template theory of antibody formation also continued to be well accepted. It was so straightforward and sensible that despite its drawbacks it would reign as the most plausible theory of antibody formation for the next fifteen years. Even in private the same immunologists who criticized Pauling's work admitted that he brought new energy to the field, made some significant findings, and stimulated useful discussion. It would not be until the mid-1950s that his direct-template idea would be supplanted by the advent of a new theory of antibody formation based on some surprising genetics. Only then would he finally be proven wrong about the way antibodies were made.

But he was right about how they worked.

༚

Ava Helen, too, did war work. For a few months she served as a research assistant in the laboratory of a Caltech biologist searching for a way to make artificial rubber. She underwent training as an auxiliary firefighter and air-raid warden for Los Angeles County, and she dug a victory garden in front of her home. There was political work to be done, too: The proposed internment of Japanese-Americans in 1942 struck her as a blatant violation of civil rights, and she volunteered her time to the local American Civil Liberties Union (ACLU) to fight it.

At the same time, she maintained her role as mother and wife. She tried to keep the house in the hills a refuge from the war and its worries, although it was not easy. Every day, her children could hear booming explosions from one of Caltech's powder-research sites down below. In the middle of one night in 1942 the entire family was awakened by an air-raid scare. While Pauling counted the rounds of antiaircraft fire and estimated the heights of the searchlights, Ava Helen comforted the children.

They needed comforting, Linus junior, sixteen years old when the war broke out, was, he said later, "a screwed-up adolescent in many ways." He was coming to grips with his relationship to a father he felt was both distant and demanding, a man he could never please, an emotional cipher with whom he could never feel comfortable. Pauling's idea of a father-son interaction was to bring home sample problems from his freshman chemistry text and try them out on high school–aged Linus junior—who felt humiliated when he couldn't do the work. Although he got reasonably good grades, Linus junior had trouble settling down in school, going through three high schools before ending up at Flintridge, an elite boarding institution a few miles from Pasadena. When he returned home in the summers, he felt himself a stranger, six years older than his nearest brother, closer in age to the graduate students and research fellows his father commandeered as baby-sitters than to his siblings. He was unsure of his future: Although Pauling did not push him, young Linus felt that he was expected to go into science, yet he did not want to compete with his father. By the time the war started, he had made up his mind to go into medicine, a field he felt was "allied closely enough with science to satisfy what I perceived as parental requirements." Then, at age eighteen, fresh out of Flintridge, he joined the air corps and left home.

The other children were also having a tough time. Peter, also sent to boarding school at an early age, began to show signs of erratic behavior during the war years. One term he would bring home the best grades in his class at Flintridge, then fall into the B and C range the next. Despite a quick wit and verbal agility, his school reports became a litany of the same complaint: "He should and could do straight A's. . . . But his work is not nearly up to his capacity." Concerned about his progress, Pauling and Ava Helen finally took him out of Flintridge in 1945 and sent him to a public junior high school—where he easily got all A's in his core classes.

Linda was growing into a beautiful child, the apple of her father's eye—when she could catch it. And the baby, Crellie, was precocious and made much of. But the Sierra Madre house was isolated, and Linda and Crellin felt the absence of other children to play with. There was loneliness of another type as well: Their parents were often gone. Pauling was either on the road, at Caltech, or holed up in his octagonal study, where the children had strict orders never to disturb him. And while Ava Helen strove to be a perfect mother, she also enjoyed traveling and accompanied her husband as often as she could. They were gone for days or sometimes weeks at a time. The Baker Lectureship had taken the two of them to Cornell for four months, during which time they left Crellin, then a baby, and the other children at home in the care of Pauling's secretary, Arletta Townsend. Townsend became like a second mother, close to all three of the younger children, especially Linda.

Pauling was behaving as he thought a father should: working hard to provide a decent home and a few luxuries for his family and disciplining the children when necessary. Although all of his children labored to earn his love, they were children, after all. He had little patience and could be short-tempered with them if they were too rambunctious or disrespectful.

His first love was science, and his children were no match.

The Grand Plan

The Molecular Safari

Pauling was early into the war and would be early out. After reading about the surrender of the German Sixth Army at Stalingrad in mid-1943, he became convinced that the Allies were going to win. At the time, he was considering the renewal of yet another wartime federal contract, this one for the chemical analysis of systems designed to produce oxygen on demand. "And then a funny thing happened in July of '43," Eddie Hughes, who was assisting him on the project, remembered. "Pauling and I knew very well that the basic work that we were doing would never get to the battlefront for two years. And for some reason or other, we decided the war was going to be over in two years, and we refused to renew the contract. We thought it would just be a waste of taxpayers' money."

By that time, a year before D day, Pauling was already thinking about postwar projects, including one on a grander scale than anything he had done before.

───※※───

The war made even the most enormous scientific plans seem feasible. The government was spending astounding sums of money on weapons research at university centers. More than $40 million was funneled into Caltech during the four years of the war, a sum that placed the school second only to MIT in wartime federal grants to institutions. By the end of the war, there were ten times as many people on the Caltech payroll as at the start. At MIT, the legendary Radiation Laboratory, or "Rad Lab" as it became known, grew from fifteen researchers at the beginning of the war to more than four thousand by the end, turning out a much-needed new device called radar under the direction of the young physicist-administrator Lee DuBridge. The largest single wartime project, however, was Oppenheimer's secret effort to create a new kind of bomb. By the end of the war, more than $2 billion would be invested in the undertaking, making it the single most expensive scientific project in human history.

Importantly for the development of postwar science, both the Rad Lab and the Manhattan Project were capped with dramatic success. They and a host of other scientific projects proved to political leaders that big-money, large-staff research projects—an approach that would come to be called "big science"—not only worked but worked brilliantly.

Pauling was by nature disinclined toward big science—he preferred thinking alone and handing out experiments to a few hand-picked assistants—but he had been pleasantly surprised by the success of Corey's crackerjack Caltech team of fifty young powder chemists, and he thought it would be a shame to break them up when his wartime funding ended. Powder analysis would certainly not be a priority during peacetime, but there was another problem that could use a large analytic team.

In late 1943, Pauling began dropping hints with Rockefeller Foundation officials about a new, large-scale attack on the structure of proteins. The problem was as important now as it was when Weaver had pushed Pauling toward it ten years earlier; it had merely been put on hiatus because of the war. Now, with a well-organized analytic team in place, Pauling had the perfect opportunity to revisit it with some real chance of success.

When the foundation's Frank Blair Hanson visited Caltech in January 1944, Pauling pressed the plan. Hanson, the man who had cut Pauling's artificial antibody funding, put him off, telling him that the foundation would be very interested in examining it at the appropriate time—after the war had been won. Undeterred, Pauling kept lobbying, writing Hanson that summer, "Although proteins are so complex that we can not hope that a final and complete solution of the problem of their structure will ever be obtained, we can, I think, look forward to getting in our lifetime, a reasonably good insight into the general principles of protein structure." In August, as part of a general institutional effort to organize Caltech's future research priorities, he wrote a ten-page plan for Caltech's chemistry division. Only one new research area was slated for major expansion: "the analysis and explanation of physiological processes in terms of the nature and structure of the chemical substances which are involved in them." He proposed a new program, under his direction, that would not only coordinate the work of current chemists and biologists but also bring experts in physiology, bacteriology, pharmacology, enzyme chemistry, and virology to Caltech, all working on a coordinated project that would interpret life in terms of the interplay of large molecules. This was big science indeed.

In September, Weaver was back in charge of the natural sciences division, and Pauling wrote him about his ideas. Because of the excruciating slowness of x-ray crystallography calculations, he wrote, it had taken Corey and an assistant more than a year to work out the structure of a single amino acid. But with a bigger team working with the latest equipment—including the new punch-card IBM computing machines that Pauling's team was among the first to use to crunch the considerable numbers generated during the crystal analysis of large molecules—he estimated that what Corey had done in six years could now be done in one. Pauling proposed switching twenty of his powder men to a "vigorous attack" on the problem of protein structure at the end of the war. The cost, he said, with equipment and supplies, would be about $150,000 for three years' work. Would Weaver suggest making a grant request now so that the money would be available immediately at the war's end?

Despite the price tag, the head of the Rockefeller Natural Sciences Division was intrigued. This was a grand plan, a big-science approach to cracking protein structures. As Pauling well knew, Weaver was still chasing the secret of life, and he had vision enough to appreciate the idea of a full-scale assault on a problem that seemed to require nothing less. There was a problem, however. Despite Pauling's theoretical successes and Corey's work with amino acids, Caltech was still not known as a laboratory-based protein research center. In America, the Rockefeller Institute, the home of Bergmann and Mirsky and a dozen others, was still the number-one site for basic research in that field. There was also the memory of artificial antibodies, which left Weaver slightly more hesitant about Pauling's plans.

He responded in standard Rockefeller Foundation style, writing

Pauling a lukewarm letter emphasizing the foundation's continued belief in modest scientific projects done by small groups and asking Pauling to consider less costly, more flexible approaches to the problem. Then he had an officer make a few confidential phone calls to the nation's leading protein experts, asking for their frank opinion about Pauling's full-scale plan. The responses were encouragingly enthusiastic. MIT's resident protein expert, Francis O. Schmitt, even had some fun with the idea. He discussed Pauling's plan with a group of colleagues over lunch, and they started informally ranking the world's top protein research centers to help them make a decision. Over the next few days it grew into a full-scale analysis, with rankings for a dozen schools determined by their competence with nineteen different protein-related laboratory methods ranging from chromatography to ultracentrifugation. After running a statistical analysis of the results, they sent Weaver the rankings: The Rockefeller Institute was first; the Swedish group at Stockholm, second; Harvard, third; then the British group at Cambridge. Caltech was dead last. Not only did it have relatively few scientists involved in protein research, but its research seemed skewed toward diffraction work and immunochemistry at the expense of other likely techniques.

Despite Caltech's rankings, however, Schmitt endorsed Pauling's plan. "[F]ar more important than the methods used and facilities available are the men doing the work," he wrote the foundation. "I would trade all the staff at the laboratories immediately above C.I.T. . . . for one Pauling."

Weaver began to warm to Pauling's plan. But there was still the war to be won. He and Pauling informally agreed to hold off on more detailed discussions until after the defeat of Germany and Japan.

On the morning of Tuesday, August 7, 1945, Pauling walked into a drugstore a few blocks from Caltech and stopped in front of the newsrack. The headline on the Pasadena paper blared: "Tokyo Admits Atomic Havoc." He bought a paper, walked outside, shook it open, and began to read, oblivious to the foot traffic and noise around him. The front page was dominated by a story about a bombing in Japan, the destruction of the entire city of Hiroshima in a single explosion, the enormous fireball, the death and injury of tens of thousands of civilians. Pauling was stunned. He would remember that morning clearly for the rest of his life.

The project that Oppenheimer had tried to talk to him into joining had been a success.

Three days after the Hiroshima bomb was dropped, another atomic bomb destroyed Nagasaki. A few days after that came news of the Japanese surrender. The war was over. In the euphoria that followed, Pauling did not think much about the atomic bomb other than to wonder about how it worked. His focus was on a more immediate concern.

A week after V-J Day, Pauling appeared in Weaver's New York office to pitch an even bigger version of his grand plan for protein research. He was talking now about the construction of two new buildings equipped with the newest and most expensive instruments—pH meters, ultracentrifuges, electron microscopes, and electrophoresis machines—and staffed with people to do virology, pharmacology, and enzymology as well as basic structural research. Only an all-out, simultaneous effort on a number of fronts would solve the protein problem, Pauling said, and Caltech was the place to do it. Weaver was caught up in Pauling's sales pitch. He recognized that Pauling's cross-disciplinary plan, drawing in people from biology and medical research as well as chemistry, would result in something that had never existed before: "In effect," Weaver noted, "an institute of molecular biology." Despite the enormous numbers now being tossed around—$2 million for buildings; perhaps $6 million to support the whole project for fifteen years—Weaver began taking a "deepening and broadening interest" in Pauling's plan.

Money was going to be one problem, but there was another. Pauling was basing his plan on a close relationship between the Caltech divisions of chemistry and biology, and the biology division was not in good shape. After the retirement of Thomas Hunt Morgan, leadership had gone to his longtime second in command, Alfred Sturtevant, a fine scientist but someone with little capacity for administration and a limited ability to deal with people. As Pauling put it, "I think he was more interested in fruit flies than in the other members of the division." As a result, in the years following Morgan's departure, the biology division had lost both its *esprit de corps* and a number of its best young researchers.

After his meeting with Weaver, it became clear to Pauling that the success of his grand plan depended on shoring up the biology division. He knew how to do it, and he had the power.

~~~

For two years, between mid-1944 and mid-1946, Pauling held a position of unusual influence at Caltech. Millikan, now in his late seventies, had become something of a scientific relic, a living reminder of an age when scientific institutes were intimate places populated by a certain class of person. The war had changed all that, and Millikan had failed to adapt. As the war wound down, he was still calling efforts to increase government support of science "movements toward collectivism" and wondering aloud whether hiring Robert Oppenheimer might not add one Jew too many to the faculty. He was becoming an embarrassment. In response, Jim Page, Caltech's efficient and savvy chairman of the board of trustees, led a palace coup in 1944 that eased the Chief out of most decision making. Millikan was finally convinced to step down in the summer of 1945. In Pauling's opinion, it was good riddance.

Another year would pass before a new leader of the institute was found and approved. In the meantime, Caltech would be run by Page and a newly expanded executive committee of faculty and trustees. Tolman would probably have been the chemistry division's representative, but he enjoyed being a Washington, D.C., insider and one of Vannevar Bush's top advisers and stayed in the East until 1947. That meant that Pauling was named one of five faculty members on the expanded committee, and he quickly became one of the most influential. His wartime service had been impeccable, and without Millikan to remind people, much of the resentment caused by his actions around the time of Noyes's death was forgotten. His scientific reputation had never been better. Few people knew of the artificial-antibody mess, while many around Caltech were aware of his advances with rocket propellants and powders and his close relationship with the Rockefeller Foundation. Under his leadership the chemistry division had come through the war with plentiful funds, a fast-growing staff, and high morale. Biology, by comparison, did not even merit a representative on the executive committee. Taking advantage of the discrepancy in power, Pauling set out to pick his own man to head biology, someone who could understand his grand plan and help make it a reality.

―――

There was no one in the nation better suited for the job than George Beadle. Pauling had gotten to know him in the 1930s, when Beadle was one of a talented group of young geneticists clustered around Morgan.

In some important ways, Beadle and Pauling were alike: friendly, hard-working small-town boys from the West—Beadle from Wahoo, Nebraska, where he had picked up the nickname "Beets"—both favored grantees of the Rockefeller Foundation, and both believers in the same reductionist approach to biology, the way of seeing living processes in terms of biochemical reactions that science historian Lily Kay would later call the "molecular vision of life."

After five years with Morgan, Beadle had left Caltech to take genetics to the next stage of development. While Morgan had successfully used his fruit flies to pinpoint the chromosomal location of genes, Beadle wanted to know how genes worked, the biochemical pathways that connected a site on a chromosome with the color of an eye or the shape of a leaf. When he started, it was not known exactly what a "gene" was or what it did. Did a single gene, for instance, control an entire sequence of biochemical steps leading to an expressed characteristic or only a single step in that sequence? During the war Beadle, now at Stanford, and his colleague Edward Tatum used mutants of a common bread mold called *Neurospora* to find the answer. Their classic experiments showed that each gene appeared to control a single biochemical reaction, which was in turn regulated by a single enzyme. The powerfully simple concept of "one gene, one enzyme" put Beadle at the forefront of American genetics. And he was more than a good lab man. Like Pauling, he knew how to make his work appealing to funding agencies. During the war he promoted his mutant molds as biological probes for use in nutrition and agricultural studies, a politically savvy move that kept him supplied with enough Rockefeller and government money to increase the size of his operation, including luring to Stanford two of Caltech's best remaining geneticists. In 1944 he was elected to the National Academy of Sciences (NAS).

Beadle knew how to run a department, how to do top-level research, and how to get money. But more important to Pauling was his approach to biology. Beadle believed that genetics was inseparable from chemistry—more precisely, biochemistry. They were, he said, "two doors leading to the same room."

Waiting in that room was Linus Pauling. At Pauling's urging, Sturtevant offered his old friend Beadle a Caltech faculty job in the spring of 1945; when Beadle turned it down, Pauling explained to Sturtevant that one option might be stepping down so that Beadle could be offered the biology chairmanship. Sturtevant, perhaps realizing that his heart was not in administration—or that he was not up to the sorts of plans Pauling had in mind—agreed. When Beets still

balked, Pauling took the train to Stanford to have a friendly talk with him. "Don't let Pauling talk you into anything you don't want to do!" Sturtevant wrote Beadle. "What this means is that I'm a little afraid he may use *unfair* pressure on you."

Pauling would, of course, use whatever it took. He and Beadle spoke the same straightforward language, and neither one believed in wasting time. They sat in Beadle's Stanford office, and Pauling told him, in detail, about the grand plan. Pauling was now using the term "chemical biology" to describe the proposal, and he marshaled all his persuasive abilities to convince Beadle that the two of them, working together at Caltech as leaders of a successful chemistry group and a reenergized biology division, could accomplish what no other research group in the world could: mount a successful coordinated attack on the secret of life itself. Pauling created a vision of the whole sweep of biological research in the postwar era, a time when biology would be refashioned from the bottom up, revolutionized by a firm grounding in chemistry and an understanding of the molecular structure of the giant molecules, the enzymes and genes, that together constituted life. This was the chance to find out how things really worked at the molecular level. And, he added, the Rockefeller people are very interested in this kind of project now. With someone of Beadle's stature leading biology, there would be a reasonable chance at obtaining support on a scale unlike anything seen before. Pauling mentioned some numbers.

Two weeks later, Beadle accepted the chairmanship of the Caltech biology division.

‍

A month after that, in December 1945, a twenty-five-page grant request was placed on Warren Weaver's desk. Signed by both Beadle and Pauling (but written almost entirely by Pauling), it was a clarion call for a new era in science, an outline of a coordinated molecular attack "on the great problems of biology during the coming two decades." In drafting the plan, Pauling used the sort of picturesque imagery that Weaver often employed to sell ideas to his board. He wrote of "the dark forest of the unknown" that lay below the resolving powers of the electron microscope and above the limits faced by crystallographers. It was here that proteins lay, in a molecular terra incognita to be explored by Pauling and Beadle at the head of "a great expedition armed with x-rays and similar tools. . . . The answers to many of the basic problems of biology—the nature of the process of growth, the mechanism of duplication of giant molecules, genes and cells, the basis for the highly specific interactions of these structural constituents, the mode of action of enzymes, the mechanism of physiological activity of drugs, hormones, vitamins, and other chemical substances, the structure and action of nerve and brain tissue—the answers to all of these problems are hiding in the remaining region of the dimensional forest . . . and it is only by penetrating into this region that we can hope to track them down." The molecular safari would consist of chemists, a few interested physicists, and a new breed of molecular biologist to be trained at Caltech, scientists who would think naturally of the life sciences as an extension of chemistry and physics. The expedition would be equipped with all the latest instruments and techniques that were helping to turn biology into a quantitative science: ultracentrifuges, chromatographs, spectrographs, electron microscopes, radioactive tracers, "complex and very expensive apparatus," Pauling wrote, "the best . . . that can be made. . . . No one method is good enough to solve the problem, and every method must be applied as effectively as possible."

The payoff was to be substantial: not just the structure of proteins and the molecular mechanism of biochemical reactions but the birth of a new era in biology. "We believe that the science of biology is just entering into a period of great and fundamental progress, similar to that through which physics and chemistry have passed during the last thirty-five years," Pauling wrote.

Pauling then turned to costs. He figured they would need two new buildings, construction funds for which could probably be raised among Caltech trustees, but equipment, staffing, and long-term support would have to come from the Rockefeller Foundation. He estimated that the total cost of staff, equipment, and maintenance would come to $400,000 per year for fifteen years, for a total of $6 million.

It was the single largest grant request Caltech had ever made. It was the largest request Weaver had ever seen.

When an apprehensive Beadle visited Weaver a week after the grant proposal arrived, he was relieved. "I didn't have to give him a sales talk. I've never seen a fellow so enthusiastic about a place as he is about Caltech." The $6 million price tag, Beadle wrote Pauling, looked "pretty big to him." But overall, Weaver considered it "a magnificent plan." Weaver pledged that he would try it out on his board but warned the Caltech duo that it would certainly take quite a while to sell an idea this expansive. While they waited, Beadle and Pauling knocked on the doors of other granting agencies. Soon money began flowing in for the grand plan: $300,000 over five years from the National Foundation for Infantile Paralysis, smaller sums from the Public Health Service and a number of other groups.

Despite Weaver's backing, the Rockefeller Foundation could not come to a decision. While they debated the merits of the proposal, Weaver pried loose a significant amount of interim funding, fifty thousand dollars per year, for 1946 and 1947. Between that and the other grants—which now included a wide-ranging miscellany of money from government, industry, and foundations, including some grants devoted to finding cures for cancer—Beadle and Pauling had enough to get started in style. By 1947, the chemistry division's budget was double that of just six years earlier, and the biology division's was nearly triple.

For two long years, the Rockefeller Foundation's board wrangled over funding the larger proposal. The hesitation was rooted in a larger internal debate over the foundation's role in postwar science. The climate for the funding of science had changed rapidly thanks to the government's infusion of vast sums of money for wartime projects. It seemed certain that large-scale government support for basic science would continue in some form, taking away much of the perceived need for the foundation to fund projects as big as Pauling's. The social aims of the board had changed, too, since the Science of Man days during the Depression. The board was shifting its emphasis in response to a new set of perceived needs, away from basic science and toward agricultural and social-science research—especially projects related to developing nations, which were seen as seedbeds for democracy and battlefronts between capitalism and communism during the coming decades.

In that context, regardless of its merits, a basic science program on the scale of Pauling's had little chance of getting funded. As the foundation's board continued to deliberate, the numbers got smaller and smaller, until finally, in 1948, the group made its final decision: $100,000 per year for seven years.

It was a fraction of Pauling's $6 million dream, but it was still one of the largest single grants ever made to Caltech—and the biggest the foundation gave any postwar basic science program. It was enough to pay for substantial expansion of Pauling's programs for an extended period of time, and it would make his chemistry group one of the best funded in the nation. Fueled by that money and the other private funds Pauling and Beadle were obtaining, guided by their closely cooperative leadership and staffed by a group of outstanding younger scientists they were able to attract, Caltech would become during the next decade America's nursery—and arguably the most important site in the world—for the development of the infant field of molecular biology.

What made it possible? "The answer can be found in just two words," said Warren Weaver: "Beadle and Pauling. These were two nucleating centers around which ideas developed and between which ideas resonated. It is just exactly as though there were all sorts of shared electrons in the system revolving around these two great centers, with a frequency of interchange for which I hardly know a parallel anywhere else."

Grape Jelly and Hogwash

The analogy of a chemical bond between the two men was not quite right, however. Beadle and Pauling got along well and instituted a close advisory relationship between chemistry and biology at Caltech; the two divisions would attend each other's seminars and scientists would occasionally cross the disciplinary fence to help with each other's research or provide advice. But the appearance of a united front was more for funding purposes than a reflection of joint research. After the Rockefeller money was in hand, Pauling and Beadle followed generally independent lines of research. Rather then resonance, their relationship was better described by a word that became Pauling's leitmotiv during the years immediately following the war: complementarity.

Complementarity was a concept that grew directly out of his immunological work. Pauling's explanation of the binding between antibody and antigen as a matter of precise molecular fit, a complementary, hand-in-glove fit that brought the atoms on both surfaces into contact close enough to allow the formation of a number of weak van der Waals bonds, offered a way to explain other biological phenomena. Life at the molecular level, Pauling began to realize, was largely a matter of specificity, of molecules in the body being able to recognize and bind only to certain target molecules and ignore all the rest. Antibodies had to recognize and bind to specific antigens, enzymes to specific substrates, genes, in some mysterious manner, both to each other and their specific protein products. The mechanism of this exquisite biological specificity was unknown. But Pauling thought that his approach, based on precisely complementary shapes, was the key.

The major lesson from his antibody research, he was beginning to understand, was the way it illuminated the relationship between molecular structure and biological specificity. Before his death in 1943, Landsteiner had asked Pauling to write a chapter on the chemical basis of specificity for a new edition of his immunology book. Pauling's chapter, which he called "Molecular Structure and Intermolecular Forces," was a concise primer summarizing his understanding of the ways that protein molecules could recognize and attach to specific targets. In these systems, he emphasized, shape was everything, precisely complementary coin-and-die shapes that fit together and were bound through the aggregate action of weak bonds. Chemistry, as most chemists understood it—the specific reaction of molecules to form strong covalent or ionic bonds—had nothing to do with it.

When published in 1945, Pauling's chapter became not only the first review to explain clearly the relationship between modern structural chemistry and immunology, but also the first to show compellingly that most, perhaps all, biological phenomena at the molecular level could be adequately explained through the imaginative application of accepted chemical principles. Because it was published in an immunology text, it had relatively little impact on chemists. But it had a seminal influence on some of the young postwar biologists and immunologists who read it. Future Nobel Prize–winning immunologist Joshua Lederberg, for instance, thought it was one of the most important things Pauling ever wrote, a guidebook for fledgling molecular biologists hoping to understand a plethora of confusing questions.

The idea that immunological specificity was due to the ability to assume precise complementary molecular shapes fit both with what Pauling and Delbrück had proposed on a theoretical basis in their 1940 paper and with Pauling and Mirsky's concept of proteins as chain molecules held in precise shapes by hydrogen bonds. But the idea went far beyond immunology.

mm

In 1944, Erwin Schrödinger, now living in Dublin, published a small book called *What Is Life?* Because it was written by the father of the wave equation, it immediately received wide attention. It was an odd book, a somewhat poetic attempt to apply Schrödinger's creative imagination to the big questions of biology, and it was filled with what Pauling saw as woolly theorizing. In it, Schrödinger addressed an old paradox: How, in a universe that tends toward maximum entropy, could fantastically organized living systems both exist and re-create themselves? The old laws of physics, he argued, could not account for life. He proposed instead a new concept called "negative entropy." By somehow feeding upon this undiscovered substance, living organisms could counter the pull of dissolution. Within this theoretical framework, he proposed that the gene took the form of a self-replicating "aperiodic crystal." Vague as it was, Schrödinger's book exerted a powerful influence upon young postwar physicists, many of whom became attracted to biology because of it and devoted themselves to the search for the new laws of physics waiting to be discovered in the cytoplasm of living cells.

Pauling thought the book was hogwash. No one had ever demonstrated the existence of anything like "negative entropy," and the gene was most likely a protein chain, a structure that appeared to be stable enough to exist in the body in a number of forms, not whatever an "aperiodic crystal" was supposed to be. "Schrödinger's discussion of thermodynamics is vague and superficial to an extent that should not be tolerated even in a popular lecture," he said of *What Is Life?* "It was, and still is, my opinion that Schrödinger made no contribution to our understanding of life."

Pauling had his own, less exotic ideas about the nature of life. "Schrödinger says that living matter may be expected to work in a manner that cannot be reduced to the ordinary laws of physics, and that the interplay of atoms in an organism differs from the interplay in non-living matter," Pauling wrote a friend. "I do not think that such a difference will in fact be found." Life, in Pauling's view, could be reduced to "the possession of specific characteristics and the ability to produce progeny to which these specific characteristics are passed on." It was a matter of molecular specificity, and it could be adequately explained by the principles of chemistry.

While Schrödinger dreamed of streams of negative entropy, Pauling found inspiration in grape jelly. He saw his theme of molecular complementarity played out in his kitchen, on the sides of a jar left out by his children. There appeared after a few days, at the edges of the sugary goo, a sprinkling of small crystals of potassium hydrogen tartrate (cream of tartar), a common constituent of grape juice. And here was the crux of the mystery: How did the molecules of cream of tartar know how to separate themselves from the thousands of molecules present in the jelly, aggregate only with each other, and arrange themselves into highly organized, impossibly pure crystalline lattices? Of course, Pauling saw, it worked because of complementary structure. Any small aggregate of the chemical would act as a seed. On the surface of the seed crystal would be holes to fill, spaces for new molecules. But only its own kind would fit properly. Because the holes were made by potassium hydrogen tartrate molecules aligning themselves, they would fit only more of the same. Anything else would be too big or shaped wrong or so small it would float in and out; anything else would be less stable and therefore less likely to last for any period of time. Thermodynamics favored the most compact structure, the pure crystal, over a more random arrangement. Perfect crystals could arise out of grape jelly without the aid of new laws of nature. This was the way that crystals formed in the ground, in caves, in the sea, under conditions far less unusual than a living body. In the high temperatures and odd chemical environment of a living body, why shouldn't even more unusual reactions take place?

"We are so far from equilibrium that even highly improbable reactions can occur, without violation of the laws of thermodynamics. Many of these highly improbable reactions depend upon having a seed, a template, that directs the reaction. Examples are known in inanimate nature. The responsible mechanism is the same as in living organisms," Pauling believed, "detailed molecular complementariness."

No new laws were needed. Pauling was seeing now a great new piece falling into place, an extension of his worldview from inorganic crystallography to all of biology. The same concepts, the same unifying ideas from chemistry informed by modern physics, bound the universe. "We may say that life has borrowed from inanimate processes the same basic mechanism used in producing these striking structures that are crystals," Pauling said. This chemical continuum that ranged from minerals to man was beautiful and soul satisfying. He was sure he was on the right track. He could feel that he was right.

After 1945, molecular biology became as important and involving to Pauling as crystal structure or the chemical bond had been, and he brought to his new passion the same brilliance and dash that served him so well in other fields. He threw himself into it, expanding his journal reading to include biochemistry, physiology, genetics, enzymology, and a bit of bacteriology and virology, looking for soft spots, areas of least resistance where he might be able to employ his ideas about structural chemistry to answer biological questions.

Enzymes were an early target. Many important biochemical reactions seemed to proceed in unlikely environments or at rates faster than simple chemistry could explain. The agents responsible were thought to be enzymes, a family of protein molecules that acted as biological catalysts, speeding reactions without themselves being changed.

Most chemical reactions proceeded something like a train going over a hill, with a specific amount of energy—activation energy—required to boost the starting reactants to the top, where they were energized enough to combine or split apart or whatever they were going to do; the products would then fall down the other side of the energy curve to a new stable state. Catalysts appeared to work by somehow lowering the hill, reducing the activation energy needed to get a reaction going. The lower the hill, the faster the reaction could take place. It worked both ways, of course; a lower hill also made it easier for products of the reaction to re-form the original reactants. The overall effect depended on relative concentrations: If there were more reactants around than products, the catalyst would tend to push the reaction in one direction, pumping out more product until the concentrations were equalized. In the body, enzymatic reactions were kept moving in the right direction by burning up or otherwise using the product.

Enzymes were also highly specific, each one working its magic only on one set of reactants and products. The digestive enzyme trypsin, for example, catalyzed the chopping of protein chains into smaller pieces. But its point of action along the chain was precise; it worked only at the spot where two particular amino acids were linked together and at no other location. To Pauling, this specificity was easy to understand: Enzymes, like antibodies, would be shaped to fit their targets; they would have a complementary structure. But complementary to what? The necessary clue was that an enzyme worked both ways, reactant to product and product back to reactant. "The fact that it had to speed up both the forward and back reaction indicated to me that the structure that the enzyme is complementary to had to be midway between the reactants and the products," Pauling said. This correlated to a hypothetical structure enzymologists called the "activated complex," a form midway between reactant and product that would exist for only a fraction of a second during an enzymatic reaction. Then, Pauling said, "it was obvious—to me at any rate—what the answer was to why an enzyme is able to speed up a chemical reaction by as much as 10 million times. It had to do this by lowering the energy of activation—the energy of forming the activated complex. It could do this by forming strong bonds with the activated complex, but only weak bonds with the reactants or products." In Pauling's view the enzyme's binding site was a close enough fit to a target molecule to loosely grab hold of it but fit it tightly only when the target was eased into a bent or strained position. The enzyme acted somewhat like a set of molecular pliers, bending the target molecule and making it easier to break it into pieces. Once broken, the resulting products, too, would have a shape only partially complementary to the enzyme binding site, loosening the fit and making it easier to float away from the enzyme. There was no reason that the same process, Pauling saw, could not work in reverse, with the enzyme binding the products loosely, bringing them close together and easing the back-reaction to the original target. It all worked through complementary shapes.

The enzyme scheme, so much in line with Pauling's idea about antibodies, was just the beginning. Soon he was theorizing that the senses of taste and smell might work because of a complementary fit between the sensed molecule and specific sites in the body (a theory still in favor among odor researchers). The behavior viruses, too, an odd form of matter that seemed halfway between a crystallizable protein molecule and a living organism (Pauling called them "a gene that has escaped from the control of the parent organism"), he also thought could be explained on the basis of complementarity.

Pauling speculated that genes were probably large, complex protein molecules capable of making precise copies of themselves, a process called autocatalysis. His 1940 paper with Delbrück had already touched upon a possible general mechanism for genetic replication; now, between 1945 and 1947, Pauling thought more about the idea in the context of complementarity. By 1948 he had devised a general model of the simplest way a gene could replicate. "The detailed mechanism by means of which a gene or virus molecule produces replicas of itself is not yet known," he told an audience during one of the many talks he gave on complementarity during the period. "In general the use of a gene or virus as a template would lead to the formation of a molecule not with an identical structure but with a complementary structure. It might happen, of course, that a molecule could be at the same time identical with and complementary to the template upon which it is molded. . . . If the structure that serves as a template (the gene or virus molecule) consists of, say, two parts, which are themselves complementary in structure, then each of these parts can serve as the mold for the production of a replica of the other part, and the complex of two complementary parts thus can serve as the mold for the production of duplicates of itself." This prescient vision of a possible duplex nature of the gene was articulated four years before the discovery of the double helix structure of DNA.

Having done nothing less than propose a structural basis for most of molecular biology, Pauling turned to medicine. During the war, his medical interests expanded from kidney diseases, antibodies, and plasma substitutes to preliminary thoughts on the structure of drugs, the effects of nutrition, even an idea that several degenerative diseases might be caused by the clumping of red blood cells. At one point he gave thought to developing an institute for fundamental medical research in conjunction with Caltech, a place that could function as a test site for his ideas about the structure and function of biomolecules. And here, too, he thought molecular complementarity could play an important role.

Toward the end of the war, he had been asked to serve on the Palmer Committee, a group of medical experts—Pauling was the only nonphysician—convened at the behest of Office of Scientific Research and Development (OSRD) head Vannevar Bush to come up with ideas for the postwar funding of medical research. During a dinner meeting of the group in the spring of 1945 at New York's Century Club, the talk among the doctors turned to a little-known blood disease called sickle-cell anemia. A Harvard medical professor, William B. Castle, explained that the disease got its name by de-forming the red blood cells from flattened discs to misshapen crescents. These sickle-shaped cells would then clog small blood vessels, leading to the clinical effects of the disease: pain in the bones and abdomen caused by a lack of red-blood-cell-carried oxygen, blood clots in the lungs, kidney, and brain. One odd thing, Castle said, was that the sickled red blood cells appeared more in the venous blood returning to the lungs than in the more highly oxygenated arterial blood.

When Pauling heard that, something clicked. He knew from his hemoglobin work that red blood cells contain almost nothing except hemoglobin and water. If the presence or absence of oxygen played a role in the flattening of the blood cells, then hemoglobin, the molecule that binds oxygen, was probably involved. As the other committee members talked and smoked around the table, Pauling sat back quietly for a moment, imagining hemoglobin molecules, globular proteins, he knew, slightly elongated in one direction, like short, thick cylinders. Say something changed them so that a new shape was formed on the surface of the molecule, a shape complementary to an area on another hemoglobin molecule. The hemoglobins would then stick to each other. If the spots were on the ends of the molecules, they might stick together end to end, creating long chains inside the red blood cells. If enough of these chains aggregated with each other, they might form something like a hemoglobin crystal, twisting the blood cells out of shape, making them sickle. But how was oxygen involved? he wondered. Binding oxygen to the hemoglobin, Pauling thought, must change the shape of the molecule enough to distort or hide the sticky spots. Add oxygen and inhibit sickling. Take oxygen away and sickling is enhanced. Thinking out loud now, Pauling explained his ideas to the group, asked Castle a few more questions about the disease, then asked if the physician had any objections to his running a few experiments comparing normal and sickle-cell hemoglobin when he got back to Pasadena. Castle did not mind. It is unlikely that many of the other physicians, whose training in structural chemistry would have been minimal, understood much of what Pauling was talking about.

Perhaps because of his own bout with Bright's disease, medicine stayed near the forefront of Pauling's mind during this period, the themes of blood and healing becoming intertwined with his new organizing principle of complementarity. Complementarity might even explain the action of drugs. In 1940, a British researcher had proposed that sulfa drugs stopped bacterial infections by masquerading as a needed food source, taking the place of the needed metabolite and essentially starving the bacteria to death, a process that worked in theory because the drug was closely related in structure to the metabolite. Pauling, like many researchers, thought that this competition of two substances for a specific binding site on a living cell could be a central concept in designing new drugs. In October 1947 he told an audience at Yale University: "When it has become possible to determine in detail the molecular structure of the vectors of disease and of the constituents of the cells of the human body, it will be possible to draw up the specifications of a specific chemotherapeutic agent to protect the body against a specific danger, and then to proceed to synthesize the agent according to the specifications."

By then Pauling was convinced that complementarity was a sufficient explanation for all of biological specificity. He had found a way to explain the essence of life in the standard lexicon of chemistry. At a stroke, he provided a reasonable explanation for everything from enzyme action to genetic replication and eliminated the need to seek new physical laws to explain life. Life was, at its root, a matter of precise molecular structure. Pauling's down-to-earth vision, his chemical explanation of the phenomenon of life, marked one of the most profound insights in twentieth-century science. It was an affirmation of the centrality of molecular structure and an essential signpost on the path to molecular biology—a field of study that would be predicated, as Pauling foresaw, on the interaction of complementary molecules.

—⁓⁓—

At the time, however, no one seemed to be listening; rather, most listeners did not grasp the importance of what he was saying. They were not trained to understand. Biologists in the late 1940s had only a passing acquaintance with physical chemistry. Chemists, for the most part, did not think of proteins in terms of chemical substances. "The average biochemist of the day," said molecular biologist Alexander Rich, "didn't know what a van der Waals interaction was, didn't know about hydrogen bonds or electrostatic potentials." Pauling was leaping over so many disciplinary boundaries, mixing so many different scientific languages, that only a handful of other researchers could follow him.

Then, too, what he was saying was still untested. No researcher had as yet defined the sequence of amino acids in any protein, nor had any structural chemist or crystallographer even roughly outlined the sorts of complementary shapes Pauling was talking about. The detailed shapes of proteins were still a mystery. The only vaguely related structures known in three-dimensional detail were the few amino acids and peptides Pauling's group had worked out. No one knew how a gene was built, much less how it worked. Hard data on the specifics of enzyme action were just beginning to be published. In the absence of specific facts about protein structure, there was too much room for conjecture and plenty of reasons to withhold judgment. Pauling realized this, too, and generally ended his talks by noting the vital importance of learning more about the specifics of how proteins were built. Until that was done, he limited the expression of his ideas to speeches rather than major papers in refereed journals, works that might have had the influence, say, of his papers on denaturation or antibody formation. Those would come only after his general ideas had been substantiated by further experiments. Pauling set Niemann to work on proving his enzyme hypothesis in the immediate postwar period, but the younger researcher soon lost interest and moved on to other things. Pauling also kept his eye out for someone to put on the sickle-cell hemoglobin project.

In the meantime, however, he remained convinced that he was on the right track. "The evidence for the theory that specific biological forces result from complementariness in structure is very strong," he said in 1947, "and I think it highly likely that this is the only mechanism of biological specificity which has been developed in living organisms." By 1948 he was telling audiences, "I believe that we can understand these properties of living matter and that we do know what the nature of life is (apart from consciousness), in terms of molecular architecture."

Life at the Top

Pauling and Beadle exemplified the optimism and success of science in postwar America. World War II left the United States the world's undisputed leader in basic research. The German scientific community had been decimated by Hitler, and the war had damaged or demolished many of Europe's great scientific centers. Those that remained intact, like the great Cavendish Laboratory at Cambridge, were aging and impoverished. Basic science was a relatively low priority in nations dealing with bread lines and bombed-out cities.

But in America postwar scientists were showered with money and acclaim. They were the national heroes who had invented the rockets and radar and bombs that had helped the Allies win, and they were lionized during the euphoria that followed. Scientists—especially the atomic scientists—were profiled in magazines and newspapers, asked to give speeches to clubs, and made the center of attention at Capitol Hill cocktail parties. It was a heady time.

The grateful U.S. government, bewitched by dreams of a new age of plenty fueled by unlimited atomic power, was ready to keep the money flowing. Formerly unaffordable multimillion-dollar big-ticket items—atom smashers and nuclear reactors topped the list—were suddenly available to researchers. Who knew what other wonders the scientists could conjure up on short order if provided enough funds?

One of the first things Harry Truman did after assuming the presidency upon Franklin Roosevelt's death in 1945 was to ask Vannevar Bush, the man who had organized the scientists' wartime efforts as head of the OSRD, to prepare a report on the needs of postwar science. Bush saw an opportunity. He made what could have been a simple bureaucratic response into a tool to change the face of postwar science. He convened panels of experts—including the Palmer Committee on medical research, in which Pauling participated—to make recommendations for different areas of research, and melded their ideas into a long, comprehensive, and persuasive document that he called "Science—The Endless Frontier." Anchoring the plan was a proposal to create a National Research Foundation through which tax moneys would be distributed by panels of scientists, a device that would make possible the funding of science without any attendant political pressure. Only in this way, Bush argued, with scientists doling out the money to scientists, could basic research be freely pursued with government funds. Congressional critics called it a lack of accountability and gasped at the sums Bush proposed: $33 million for science the first year alone, rising to more than $120 million annually by year five. One congressman quickly dubbed it "Science—the Endless Expenditure."

Pauling enthusiastically supported the Bush plan. He was concerned especially about the interruption the war had created in the production of young scientists—by 1945 the combined junior and senior classes at Caltech included only six chemistry majors—and believed that government involvement was warranted to fix it. If something was not done, and done quickly, there was a chance that there might not be enough scientific talent to accomplish the huge tasks of the postwar years. Pauling even talked about drafting the youth of America into science training programs instead of the army. More realistic was the likelihood of using the proposed research foundation to shift money into science education while avoiding the back-room influence and mediocrity he believed characteristic of many governmental programs. Pauling joined a national "Committee to Support the Bush Report" and, after Bush turned his plan into a congressional bill, helped organize support meetings and letter-writing campaigns.

———

Pauling was rapidly becoming one of the most visible and influential scientists in the postwar world. Before the war, Pauling's ideas on the nature of the chemical bond had been beyond the reach of most chemists. But now, thanks to the growing influence of *The Nature of the Chemical Bond,* they were catching up with him. His book had become required reading for postwar graduate students and young researchers, especially those interested in molecular structure.

Pauling complemented it in 1947 with what would become an even more influential undergraduate text, *General Chemistry,* a one-volume survey of the field that would mark a milestone in chemical education. *General Chemistry* was the first introductory college text based firmly on a foundation of quantum physics, the first to take its readers logically from general theoretical principles—beginning with his valence-bond approach—to an abundance of real-world examples, and the first to use the concepts of chemical bonding and molecular structure as organizing principles. Written with his usual clarity and zest, the book also made the molecular visible through its pioneering use of illustration, including dozens of precise drawings of chemical structures made by the illustrator Roger Hayward under Pauling's supervision. In his book, molecules were not abstract notions. They were individual characters, with sizes and shapes and peculiarities. They came alive.

The book helped revolutionize the teaching of college chemistry. Pauling's reputation ensured wide early adoption, and when teachers saw how effectively it worked, the book became wildly successful—but not for its intended audience. Pauling based *General Chemistry* on his lecture notes for Caltech freshmen chemistry, which meant that much of the material was too advanced for first-year courses at other universities. After a few years, it found its niche as a best-selling text for more advanced undergraduate students, selling so well in its various editions that it propelled its relatively unknown San Francisco publisher, W. H. Freeman and Co., into the leading ranks of textbook publishers and made Pauling's name synonymous with modern chemistry for the tens of thousands of new college students who flooded campuses after the war.

Royalties from the book also gave Pauling his first taste of wealth. He was now able to make some outside investments and indulge in some luxuries, including a large in-ground swimming pool for the yard of his mountainside home—the pool that *General Chemistry* built, his children said. And he traveled. As his illness waned and his fame increased, as he responded to speaking invitations and attended more meetings than ever, his children saw less and less of him. His work schedule was back at a formidable peak level, and he made it clear that even at home he was not to be disturbed for anything other than meals. The degree of domestic organization required to accommodate his work bordered on the bizarre. A typical day started with his immediately going into his study after waking while Ava Helen fixed breakfast for the children. When they were done, she rang the doorbell to call Pauling to breakfast. He would eat and leave for Caltech, sometimes driving the children to school on the way. He returned home in the midafternoon, sometimes picking up a child from school on the way, and again isolated himself in his study, where he would work, read the newspaper, or listen to the radio news until Ava Helen rang the doorbell to call him to dinner. After helping with the dishes, he went back to his study until after the children were in bed.

This went on during the week and on weekends. Practically the only time the children talked to him was on their drives to and from school, when he would quiz them about their studies. He was impressed with young Crellin, who seemed quite bright and who surprised his father one day by telling him that he figured out that September had fifteen days in it. "How do you know that, Crellie?" Pauling asked. "We learned it in a poem," the little boy answered. "'Thirty days half September.'" Crellin would have loved to have a father like other boys, someone who would play games with him and take him places on weekends. But is was not to be. Instead, he spent his afternoons creeping up to Pauling's study door and listening to him dictating into a machine on the other side. That, Crellin remembered, was his foremost memory of his father from early childhood: "He came home and talked to 'Comma' on the dictaphone."

—⁓—

At the same time Pauling's fame was increasing, the old generation of leaders in chemistry was passing away. Roscoe Dickinson—the man who had patiently taught Pauling X-ray crystallography—died at an early age in 1945. The following year, Pauling's mentor, role model, and friend G. N. Lewis was found crumpled at the foot of his lab bench, dead of a heart attack suffered in the middle of an experiment—"a great blow to me," Pauling said. Only one year after returning to Caltech following his wartime service, Richard Tolman died of a cerebral hemorrhage in 1948.

Power was shifting to Pauling's generation. As Caltech searched for someone to succeed Millikan in early 1946, his name was put forward by at least one supporter, Ava Helen, who talked to anyone who would listen about what a great institute president Pauling would make. Pauling, however, had no desire to administrate his life away and did not lobby for the position. The trustees eventually hired the physicist Lee DuBridge, a contemporary of Pauling's and a skilled administrator who had overseen the development of radar at MIT's Rad Lab.

Well established, well respected, and well off, Pauling began to enjoy the life of a leading scientist, spending more time traveling, giving lectures, receiving awards, and directing the research of others in those areas that interested him. Immunochemistry was still one of his favorite programs, and he lavished money and attention on the work that Dan Campbell, now assisted by a brilliant postdoctoral fellow named David Pressman, was doing pinning down the final details on the interactions of antibodies and antigens. He also started Harvey Itano, a newly minted M.D. who wanted to add a Ph.D. under Pauling's direction, to work on the sickle-cell hemoglobin project. Pauling made it known that he was looking for other young physicians who were interested in trying their hand at basic research. He put Corey back to work on the structure of amino acids and small peptides.

Pauling loved to be on the road, and he had plenty of opportunity. Chemists were beginning to understand how Pauling had changed their lives for the better, and the accolades were starting. In the years just following the war he was given the profession's most prestigious honors: the Richards Medal from the northeastern section of the American Chemical Society (ACS), the Gibbs Medal from the Chicago Section, and the Davy Medal from the Royal Society in London.

The Davy was especially important to Pauling as a recognition that he had arrived not only nationally but internationally. His reputation in England after the war was "very high," he remembered, in part because of his well-known besting of Bragg—now directing the prestigious Cavendish Laboratory at Cambridge—on the question of the structure of silicates and in part because of the support of Nevil Sidgwick, a respected Oxford chemist who had been mightily impressed by Pauling on a visit to the United States in 1931 and whose influential British texts had popularized Pauling's valence-bond approach.

In 1947, Sidgwick was instrumental in awarding Pauling another great recognition from Britain: appointment to the Eastman Professorship, a yearlong teaching stint at Oxford, all expenses paid. His family was invited to accompany him. Pauling was pleased but did not see how it would be possible to relocate for an entire year. He told Sidgwick and the Oxford administration that he would be happy to come for the second and third terms of the academic year, between January and June 1948. There was only one hitch: Eastman professors had to hold a master's from Oxford. The technicality was quickly taken care of by awarding Pauling an honorary degree—the only master's degree he would ever hold.

More honors came. In April 1947 he was nominated for president of the National Academy of Sciences—an office he would have loved to hold—but Pauling was forced to withdraw his name because of the interference of his upcoming stay in England. Soon after, the same nomination was made by members of the American Chemical Society; this time he let it go forward because there would be few duties during a year as president-elect before his actual presidency started in 1949, well after his return.

The presidency of the ACS was not something that Pauling had aspired to, but being put forward for the position was welcome affirmation of his high standing in the field. Over the course of twenty years his brand of chemistry had moved from the fringes of the discipline to the mainstream, pushed there in large part by Pauling's abilities as a theorist, writer, and lecturer. He was now one of America's and the world's best-known and best-respected chemists, a man at the peak of his professional powers. When the votes were tallied in the ACS presidential election at the end of December 1947, he was put into office by a handy margin.

The only dissent came from a small group of anti-Pauling members who protested his election for what was, in this strictly professional science society, an unusual reason: They did not like his politics.

Political Science

The Jap Lover

Through the war years, except for the modicum of time spent with his family, science had been the sole focus of Pauling's life. In the postwar years, however, as his financial situation improved and his professional reputation reached its zenith, he found he had time for other things—and Ava Helen would help determine what they were.

Her own activities had grown increasingly political during the war. After Pearl Harbor she had watched, appalled, as anti-Japanese hysteria took a virulent form in California. She read of Japanese-American families threatened, children spat upon, windows broken, and graffiti scrawled on homes. When the government made plans to send all coastal Japanese citizens and Japanese Americans to inland concentration camps without any evidence of espionage or wrongdoing, Ava Helen saw the policy as sheer racism. The proposed internment of Japanese Americans became a topic around the dinner table, with Ava Helen explaining to the children how repressive governments could become in wartime. At first, Pauling took little interest—"He had been so busy that he just wasn't aware of what was going on," Ava Helen said—but her passion for the cause was infectious. Soon he, too, saw through the government argument that internment would protect both sensitive areas from Japanese sabotage and loyal Japanese Americans from angry white neighbors. Instead, Pauling saw internment as Ava Helen did: the imprisonment of a group of Americans simply because their skin was a different color. "We couldn't believe that all these things were happening in the United States," Ava Helen said. "They were very unconstitutional."

Ava Helen threw herself into the fight to prevent the internment, volunteering at the local American Civil Liberties Union (ACLU) to type letters and stuff envelopes, speaking to friends, doing anything she could to raise the public's awareness. The efforts were fruitless. In 1942, the internment order was issued, and West Coast Japanese Americans were herded together and shipped to the camps.

The seriousness of the issue was driven home for Pauling by one of his graduate students, a Japanese American named Ikeda, an expert at preparing artificial antigens for his immunological studies and one of the most talented men in his laboratory. Ikeda did not want to waste years in a barracks behind barbed wire, and he asked Pauling's help in getting out of the coastal restricted zone so that he could continue to work and study. Through 1942 Pauling helped him search for a position in the East. "Ikeda is a pleasant fellow, just like an American," he pleaded in a reference letter to a colleague at Columbia. "I have as little doubt of his loyalty as that of any other American born Japanese." With the nation at war against the Japanese, finding a school that would take Ikeda was harder than it should have been, but Pauling finally arranged a job on the East Coast that kept him out of the camps, although Pauling had to pay the young man's salary out of Caltech funds to do it.

Pauling judged people by their intelligence and ability, not their skin color, and it was disturbing to him to see evidence of racism, especially at the government level. But while Ava Helen continued to do volunteer work for the ACLU during the war, Pauling turned his mind to research. It was not until March 1945 that the Japanese-American issue came up again, this time with a vengeance. Ava Helen was asked by a Los Angeles organization if she could provide a job for a few days for a Japanese-American man newly released from camp and on his way to Camp Shelby for induction into the army. Ava Helen was happy to help and offered to take him on as a gardener. Young, shy, and very thankful, the fellow worked on a Friday and Saturday pruning and cleaning the yard around their Sierra Madre home. Then he left for the army.

On Monday morning, Pauling's fourteen-year-old son Peter ran into the house yelling for his parents. "You've got to come out here and look," he said breathlessly. "Somebody's painted stuff on the garage." Pauling could hardly believe what he saw. On the door was smeared: "AMERICANS DIE BUT WE LOVE JAPS. JAPS WORK HERE. PAULING," with a crude Japanese flag drawn above it. "JAP" was scrawled on their mailbox.

He made a quick check for other damage, called the police, then called the newspapers. "I do not know who is responsible for this un-American act," Pauling told a reporter. "I suspect, however, that this trespass on our home was carried out by one or more of those misguided people who believe that American citizens should be persecuted in the same way that the Nazis have persecuted the Jewish citizens of Germany."

After the paper printed his comparison of Pasadenans to Nazis, the Paulings began to receive hate mail and short, whispered phone calls advising them to "get rid of that Jap." Pauling tried to ignore it. Then a crudely typewritten note appeared in his Caltech office mail: "We happen to be one of a groups who fully intend to burn your home, tire [*sic*] and feather your body unless you get rid of that jap . . . Japs killed my own Father. It's too bad that some jap does not rape someone near and dear to you. well we will see that you get plenty and the more publicity you give this matter the sooner we'll take care of you just like Al Capone did some years ago." It was signed "A neighbor."

Pauling was just getting ready to take one of his many trips to Washington, D.C. When Ava Helen heard about the letter, she decided she did not want the family left unprotected while he was gone and called the local sheriff's office to find out what could be done. "Well," said the man at the other end of the line, "that's what you get for hiring a Japanese worker."

Furious, she immediately called her friends at the ACLU. The lawyers put pressure on the sheriff, got an armed guard assigned to the Pauling house, and made sure that the threatening letter was forwarded to the FBI. Federal agents arrived at the house as Pauling was preparing to leave and found Ava Helen in high dudgeon. When they asked who she thought might have written the threat, Ava Helen gave them a long harangue about the entire internment program and the threat to liberty that it represented. The agents, listening patiently, noted her conclusion that "the fabric of law and order was quite flimsy." When Pauling's turn came, he calmly listed everyone who had any way of knowing they had hired the gardener.

There were no more incidents. After two weeks, the armed guard was removed. The FBI never succeeded in finding the author of the note, and the police did not track down whoever had defaced Pauling's property.

But the experience had a profound effect. During the time Pauling was in the East he worried constantly about the safety of his wife and children. An armed guard in the driveway was not the way America was supposed to operate. The response of the local sheriff had also been unnerving: Pauling had been taught to believe that figures of authority would do the right thing, but here was a lawman who had to be forced to uphold the law. And it was an important lesson, too, that an activist organization like the ACLU, applying pressure from the outside, could make things happen.

Most importantly, if it had ever seemed to him that Ava Helen's political enthusiasms tended to be a bit extreme, he now had proof that they were not. The real extremists were those whose intolerance and prejudice had threatened his family.

It was, to use a phrase from later years, a radicalizing experience. And it was just the beginning.

The Children's Crusade

Five months later, after Hiroshima and Nagasaki were vaporized, Pauling's understanding of social justice took another step forward. The advent of the atomic bomb interested him in two ways. He immediately wanted to know the physics and mechanics of how the bomb worked, and he used some general reading, his own intuition, and an unusually informative government report, *Atomic Energy for Military Purposes,* to put together an accurate picture. He was surprised to find out how relatively simple the bomb was, at least in theory.

His technical interest was shared by many Americans. The new weapon, millions of times more powerful than anything ever seen before, set off a fireball of public interest. Everyone wanted to know how the scientists had done it. A few weeks after Hiroshima, someone who knew of Pauling's interest suggested that he might be a good speaker for a Rotary Club after-dinner talk on the bomb, a place to explain in layman's terms how the device worked. Pauling—somewhat surprised at being asked, because he was neither an atomic physicist nor one of the hundreds who had actually worked on the Manhattan Project— thought he knew enough to be helpful and agreed to speak. Other than his Union Now talks, he had rarely spoken before nonscientists. He thought he had better take along a prop.

In his garage he sawed a wooden sphere in two and hollowed the halves, then smacked them together with a satisfying loud crack. That should work. During his lecture he used a blackboard to show how atomic fission worked: large, unstable atoms like uranium and plutonium, he explained, had a great many protons and neutrons in their nucleus. When hit by neutrons, these unstable atoms could be split, releasing the enormous energy involved in holding the nucleus together and at the same time loosing more neutrons. These new neutrons in turn would split more atoms, setting off a chain reaction. If the chain reaction was controlled and slowed, atomic power could be used to make heat to drive turbines, he told his audience; this was the basis of all the talk about cheap, unlimited power from the atom.

When the reaction was much faster and less controlled, the result was a bomb, the core of which consisted of a few pounds of a special isotope of uranium or plutonium formed into the shape of a hollow sphere, like the wooden model he had made. The trick was to create a fission chain reaction that would split almost all of the atoms simultaneously. And this, the Manhattan Project engineers had figured out, was possible by surrounding the core with standard explosives and setting them off, which rapidly compressed the core from all sides. He smacked his wooden hemispheres into each other. This started the chain reaction. There was a huge, sudden energy release. Boom!

The Rotarians were impressed. Word got around that there was an egghead who could speak English, and Pauling quickly found himself one of Southern California's most requested speakers on atomic energy.

But his initial technical interest was soon outweighed by larger concerns. Even before Hiroshima, researchers working on bomb projects at laboratories in Chicago, Los Alamos, and Oak Ridge, Tennessee, began forming discussion groups to try to sort out the social and political implications of what they were doing. These atomic scientists understood better than anyone else the actual power of the bomb, and it was clear to them that U.S. control of this overwhelming weapon would alter the balance of world geopolitics. After Hiroshima, the discussion groups spread to other universities and government laboratories, where the images of mass destruction and incinerated women and children led to twin feelings of revulsion and moral outrage. Scientists felt a special sense of responsibility for creating "the Bomb."

They gathered to talk about that and about how this new source of power should be handled in the coming years.

The more Pauling read about their concerns, the more convinced he became that the new atomic age presented scientists with unprecedented social and political responsibilities. "The problem presented to the world by the destructive power of atomic energy overshadows, of course, any other problem," he wrote a friend less than two months after Hiroshima. "I feel that, in addition to our professional activities in the nuclear field, we should make our voices known with respect to the political significance of science."

In Pasadena a small group of faculty members from Caltech, the Huntington Library, and the Mount Wilson Observatory began meeting to discuss the implications of the bomb. Pauling was among them; so was Oppenheimer, newly returned to Caltech after Millikan's retirement and increasingly concerned about control of the weapon he had brought to life. Everyone in the discussion group agreed that the atomic bomb had changed the nature of warfare and made it unthinkable; most of them also agreed that the only realistic way to control it was through the institution of some form of global government. The protection of the world against "the unimaginable devastation of an atomic war," Pauling wrote University of Chicago head Robert Hutchins soon after Hiroshima, "depends upon the institution of a democratic worldwide government—a government of the people themselves, like the government of the United States of America."

These sentiments were shared to a remarkable degree by dozens of other scientists' discussion groups that sprang up spontaneously across the nation to talk over the same issues. There had never been anything like it in this traditionally apolitical profession. Suddenly, small knots of scientists and apprentice scientists were coming together in living rooms and faculty clubs, around conference tables and in taverns, sorting out the meaning of what their colleagues had done in making the bomb, working through their feelings of guilt, trying to figure out ways to ensure that what they had created was now used for the good of humankind rather than its destruction. Almost overnight, these mostly young, mostly idealistic scientists discovered a shared sense of social purpose that they had never possessed before. They also discovered a common set of solutions to the problems posed by the bomb. Scientists were children of the Enlightenment. Almost to a person, they believed, as Pauling did, in rationality, progress, the innate goodness of man, the value of the scientific method, and democracy. Their own lives were proof of those values. The unanimity of their views on dealing with the atomic bomb in the early postwar years suggested that given proper education, all rational people would come to the same conclusions they had.

The important task, then, was to educate nonscientists about the new atomic realities, to show the public how the proper application of rational thought was the best way to deal with atomic problems. The Pasadena discussion group planned to write a book "to instruct the intelligent layman on the present situation, to explain how it came about and to suggest a way out." The importance of the scientific approach would be emphasized, with its ability to "fortify the mind against the assaults of dishonest propaganda" and free people from the "intolerances and prejudices, sham ideals and false hopes" that lead to war. The desirability of international control of atomic energy was to be stressed. Pauling was put in charge of a section of the book in which writers would outline the benefits of a world at peace, a place where researchers would be free to create a cornucopia of new medicines and labor-saving devices. After the book was released, the faculty planned a series of symposia and speeches to "spread the gospel of peace."

Once awakened from their political slumber, once aware that they shared a common set of beliefs, the scientists began to think they might be able to spread the ideas that would transform the world. It was as though the bomb, the ultimate symbol of technological evil, had given them an opportunity to show the other side, the ultimate good of technological thinking.

They were, of course, hopelessly out of touch with the political realities of the day. While scientists talked of openly sharing atomic technology, politicians and the military worried about Communist expansionism, a subject most scientists seemed strangely unconcerned about. Pauling again was typical. He was not a Popular Front type; he had not come through the Depression with the idea that Russia was a necessary first step in the salvation of the world's working class. Nor did he think that Communism was evil incarnate. He saw Russia as an important ally in defeating Hitler but also as a troubled and overly authoritarian nation. He thought that the best way to change Russia for the better was to shower it with new ideas. In the middle of the war he had joined—along with such luminaries as Albert Einstein, MIT President Karl Compton, and the Guggenheim Foundation's Frank Aydelotte—the National Council of American-Soviet Friendship, a group that promoted scientific exchanges between the nations. "Let us look forward to a future when American scientists in large numbers are lecturing and working in Soviet laboratories, American students are studying in Soviet universities, and Soviet scientists and students are in America in equal numbers, carrying the most inspired teachings of each country to the other," Pauling wrote in a 1943 letter to the group's science congress. His vision could be accomplished only in an atmosphere of peace—a rational peace based on worldwide co-operation and open communication—a scientists' peace.

—*mm*—

But Pauling could be naive in his desire for peace. In early 1945 he had been named to the Research Board for National Security, a select group of twenty civilians and twenty high-ranking military men that was convened in Washington, D.C., to discuss the shape of the postwar world. Pauling considered this to be a great honor, and he eagerly attended his first meeting expecting that something truly important might happen, that the two groups might actually learn something from one another.

The meeting got off to a rocky start, however, when the architect of the Caltech rocket program, Charles Lauritsen, suggested to the generals and admirals that perhaps the board should support investigations into the causes of war and ways to avoid it. There was an uncomfortable silence until a military representative pointed out that peace studies were not on the group's agenda. Pauling jumped in to second Lauritsen, saying, "Mr. Chairman, this is a matter of the greatest importance. It would be unwise for us to decide now that it is not in the province of this board's responsibilities." Pauling felt his words important enough to write down in his pocket notebook when the meeting ended.

It was clear, however, that soldiers and scientists did not think alike, and nothing much resulted from the research board. Their approaches to the bomb exemplified the philosophical differences between the two groups. The military saw it as a weapon pure and simple, developed under military command, kept under military secrecy, and to be used for military purposes. The idea of sharing it with the world was impossible in the face of aggressive Russian actions in Eastern Europe, where the Red Army, the world's largest, seemed unlikely to give up the nations it had freed from the Germans. The world was probably headed for another war, this time between capitalism and communism, and anyone who did not see what the bomb meant in that scenario was a fool.

The scientists saw atomic power as an application of a new technology developed by scientists, one that promised wonderful benefits if shared openly. One of the first concerns raised in the discussion groups was that the military would continue to exercise sole control over the bomb and all the science that went with it, clamping down a lid of secrecy on further research and killing any chance of sharing the technology for the good of all people.

The stage was set for conflict. The prize would be the control of atomic energy.

While the nation was still celebrating its victory over Japan, the cantankerous general Leslie R. Groves—army chief of construction, builder of the Pentagon, and the man who oversaw the Manhattan Project scientists—began pushing for legislation to keep the bomb under military control. To do that, he helped the War Department draft a bill that was designed to satisfy both scientists and the military, putting the development of atomic energy under the jurisdiction of a nine-member panel, including military men, who in turn would report to a permanent, full-time administrator. On the surface, it appeared to provide a shared civilian-military framework for controlling atomic energy, and it looked innocuous enough to earn the support of many influential scientists, including Oppenheimer, Vannevar Bush, and a number of other Office of Scientific Research and Development (OSRD) and Manhattan Project bigwigs. It was introduced in Congress on October 4, 1945, under the name of its cosponsors as the May-Johnson bill. Five days later, without advance notice, it was given a short, perfunctory, and uniformly positive hearing before the House Military Affairs Committee.

The obvious haste of certain parties to pass May-Johnson set off a quick reaction in the scientific community. The discussion groups took up the issue, pointing out that the legislation was drafted in the War Department and was supported by the military. Despite its supporters' lip service to civilian control, under the bill it would be possible, even easy, for the army and navy to effectively control the proposed nine-member panel. It looked as though Groves himself were being groomed for the administrator's post. Within weeks, the discussion groups began rallying together against the May-Johnson bill.

Typical was a group of Caltech students and postdoctoral fellows that had begun meeting in the basement of the Caltech faculty club, the Athenaeum, to discuss the impact and control of atomic energy.

They soon organized themselves as the Association of Pasadena Scientists (APS), their purpose "to meet the increasingly apparent responsibility of scientists in promoting the welfare of mankind and the achievement of a stable world peace." The APS chairman, vice chairman, and a number of other founding members were all from Pauling's laboratory, and they were all opposed to May-Johnson.

Fuel for their cause came in late November 1945, when American military forces descended on laboratories in occupied Japan, tore apart five research cyclotrons, and threw the pieces into the sea. Upon learning that the atom smashers were being used strictly for nonmilitary purposes, Groves quickly issued an apology, but the anguished cries from Japanese scientists echoed through the U.S. scientific community. The military clearly did not understand the first thing about pure research. They obviously should not be allowed to control atomic research in the United States.

So the scientists came to Washington in the fall of 1945, dozens of young, energetic men like Pauling's former student Charles Coryell, who left his job at the Oak Ridge atomic laboratory to fight May-Johnson. The discussion groups formed themselves into a national organization, the Federation of Atomic Scientists (FAS), rented a one-room walk-up near the Capitol and equipped it with a single typewriter. The researchers buttonholed congressmen, sent mimeographed fact sheets to committees, and got into the newspapers by heating up the rhetoric. One of the most vocal leaders of the anti-May-Johnson forces, the Nobel Prize–winning chemist Harold Urey, called May-Johnson "the first totalitarian bill ever written by Congress. You can call it a Communist bill or a Nazi bill, whichever you think is worse." Then they put forward an alternative. In December 1945, Democratic senator Brien McMahon sponsored a bill with FAS input that called for the creation of an Atomic Energy Commission (AEC) headed by a full-time panel of civilian scientists appointed by the president, with safeguards for independent research and a civilian administrator. There were to be no military men.

mm

The debate over the May-Johnson and McMahon bills brought to light deep divisions within the scientific community. On one side were higher-level administrators who had been involved in coordinating military and scientific projects during the war and who felt that sharing responsibility for atomic decisions with the military was simply realistic, men like Vannevar Bush and Harvard president James B. Conant, who predicted that the majority of scientists would fall in line behind the bill. They were joined by hundreds of supporters around the nation who felt that May-Johnson would give adequate representation to civilians while still ensuring atomic primacy for the United States. Robert Millikan, for instance, joined some two hundred other "private citizens" in and around Caltech in signing an open letter to Congress urging the passage of May-Johnson.

The anti-May-Johnson ranks included, in addition to the young FAS firebrands, respected figures like Bell Telephone Laboratories head and National Academy of Sciences (NAS) president Frank Jewett, bomb developers Enrico Fermi and Leo Szilard, and Pauling, who joined both the APS and the FAS and wrote his own letter in support of the McMahon bill.

And the debate began to swing their way. In the spring of 1946 the FAS's membership, in part because of its opposition to May-Johnson, swelled to thousands, enhancing its standing as a lobbying force in Congress. By then the McMahon supporters had influenced a number of politicians, including President Harry Truman, who, after listening to their concerns—and sensing the postwar mood of the electorate— came down squarely in favor of civilian control of atomic energy. He was quickly followed by his secretary of war. In July, after softening its language to give the military some input into the proposed AEC, Congress passed the McMahon bill.

It was a great and surprising victory. To Pauling and the other FAS scientists, it was a triumph of reason, a sign that the military would not run the show in peacetime. Truman and his administrators were now talking of sharing atomic secrets with Russia and the rest of the world. There was a warming of international relations. There was a hope that the world might emerge from the war with a fighting chance at long-term peace.

But it would not last.

Hollywood

After the McMahon bill passed and the shock of Hiroshima began to wear off, many scientists turned their energies back to career and family. But Pauling stayed politically active. The public was still hungry for information about the bomb, and he received a steady stream of invitations to explain it. He now peppered his speeches on the technology

of the bomb with quotes from Einstein and others about the importance of civilian control, open scientific communication, and world
government. The only problem was that the more he talked about social and political issues, the less effective his speeches became.

Ava Helen saw it happening. She accompanied Pauling to almost
all of his talks, sat in the front row of the audience, and listened carefully to his delivery. She also kept an eye on the room, saw what
worked and what did not, and afterward critiqued his performance.
His problem, she thought, was one of conviction. Pauling did not feel
confident enough about his own knowledge of politics to make pronouncements on his own authority; instead, when he talked about the
control of atomic energy, he would defer to higher authorities, quot-
ing things written by or about other scientists and politicians. His talks
had none of the humor and firsthand immediacy of his scientific talks;
they sounded dry and professional. "You're not convincing," Ava Helen
told him after one particularly dismal performance. "You give the audience the impression that you are not sure about what you are saying."

As with most of her comments, Pauling took it seriously. He decided that he needed to make himself into an authority on atomic and
peace issues, the same way he had when he entered the new fields of
immunology and biochemistry. He began to study politics, history,
economics, and international relations. He read books; government
reports; newspapers, from the *L.A. Times* to the *New York Times;* magazines, including the *Nation,* the *New Yorker, Time,* and a valuable new
publication that the FAS was putting out called the *Bulletin of the Atomic
Scientists.*

He found that compared to quantum mechanics, the politics of
atomic energy was simple. A relatively small group of players determined policy: government, industry, the military, scientists, the public.
Each had its own agenda to push; each had its own concerns. It all was
fairly easy to put into order. He found that once he felt he understood
the players' motivations and modes of action, he was rarely surprised
by the statements of those who were deciding what to do with the
bomb. After a few months, he said, "I felt I could speak on my own authority." His talks caught fire.

One of the first groups that invited Pauling to speak was a political action organization, the Independent Citizen's Committee for the Arts,
Sciences, and Professions (ICCASP), which had started after the war to

serve as an artists' and intellectuals' lobby, agitating for legislation in the same way that labor unions or manufacturers' associations did for their members. Its politics were left-wing; the Hollywood chapter was composed mainly of liberal Democrats with a sprinkling of socialists and Communists, many from the film community. Lionel Trilling could have been speaking of ICCASP members when he described postwar New Dealers, with their "ready if mild suspiciousness of the profit motive, and a belief in progress, science, social legislation, planning and international cooperation, perhaps especially where Russia is in question."

Pauling's first ICCASP talk was well received. During the question period afterward, someone asked how many atomic bombs were in the U.S. stockpile, and Pauling hazarded a guess: perhaps one or two hundred, he said, with the potential to make five hundred within the next year. His estimate was far off the mark—there were fewer than ten usable bombs in the U.S. arsenal at the time—but a reporter picked up the figures, and they were reprinted widely. General Groves, then still embroiled in the fight to pass May-Johnson, was not amused and let Pauling know it. "I was, as you might suspect, misquoted on the atomic bomb matter," Pauling wrote a friend in February 1946. "Some rough estimates that I was making got misinterpreted by the press representative and spread all over the country. The General didn't think it was very funny." But Pauling didn't let the military's attempt at censure bother him. "You probably know that I have never had any connection with the atomic bomb project," he wrote. "I am just an outsider, relatively free to make guesses."

The ICCASP connection introduced the Paulings to a group of exciting, glamorous, socially concerned activists who appeared to believe in what Pauling called "just the rather liberal sort of politics that appeals to me." They both joined the organization. Rubbing shoulders with Hollywood celebrities was a thrill for a small-town couple who had always loved the movies. The local chapter was headed by John Cromwell, director of *Abe Lincoln in Illinois* and *The Prisoner of Zenda,* and members included James Cagney, Edward G. Robinson, Olivia de Havilland, Orson Welles, and Fredric March. The Paulings, through their ICCASP connections, soon found themselves visiting studios, watching films being shot, drinking cocktails in producers' mansions, and watching sneak previews in private screening rooms. They chatted with Charlie Chaplin, traded jokes over dinner at Charles Laughton and Elsa Lanchester's Hollywood cottage, and hammered out ICCASP policy at the Brown Derby with the then liberal actor Ronald Reagan.

Pauling took his ICCASP duties seriously—as opposed to the FAS, to which he devoted little time—regularly attending meetings and helping draft goals and policies. He was quickly named vice president for science of the Hollywood chapter, then was put on the group's national board of directors—along with Frank Sinatra, Thomas Mann, Duke Ellington, and Eleanor Roosevelt.

Ava Helen loved hobnobbing with this glittering crowd, so much more interesting than Caltech professors and their dowdy wives. Pauling, on the other hand, after a short period of being dazzled, considered most Hollywood people shallow and found them interested in almost anything other than science. Despite the "Sciences" in its title, ICCASP never succeeded in attracting many researchers, perhaps because it was soon labeled as a Communist front, perhaps because the FAS was available for political action. Pauling was the only Caltech member. The result was remembered by an ICCASP member who went to a patio party at a director's house attended by the Paulings. Ava Helen, he remembered, gaily chatted with people by the buffet, while Pauling sat alone at the other end of the swimming pool. The partygoers seemed intimidated by the thought of trying to talk with the great scientist. The only animated discussion the observer remembered Pauling having was with the teenage son of another guest—their topic, high school chemistry.

To the Village Square

At the beginning of October 1946, Pauling's political activities took another step forward when he received a phone call from Harold Urey asking him if he would consider joining the Emergency Committee of Atomic Scientists. This, Pauling knew, was a select group, the crème de la crème of those associated with the FAS, including Szilard and Urey and headed by Einstein himself, whose eloquent public pronouncements in favor of the open sharing of bomb technology had helped convince the public to support the McMahon bill. The committee's purpose was not to make public policy but to inform people of the new realities brought about by the bomb. As the first statement of the emergency committee put it, "Our world faces a crisis as yet unperceived by those possessing the power to make great decisions for good or evil. The unleashed power of the atom has changed everything save our modes of thinking, and thus we drift toward unparalleled catastro-

phe. . . . A new type of thinking is essential if mankind is to survive and move toward higher levels."

Apart from occasional statements on the dangers of the arms race and the need for international agreements on atomic control—which, thanks to Einstein's name, received considerable media coverage—the committee's main work was fund-raising, with the money to be given to vehicles for public education, such as the *Bulletin of the Atomic Scientists*.

Pauling thought the invitation was a great honor, and he was delighted to join. He greatly admired Einstein, and the idea of working with a small group rather than a large organization appealed to him. Nor would the emergency committee distract him too much from his research. Urey had assured him that there would not be much to do; only a few meetings each year in Princeton, near Einstein's home, to agree on public statements and strategies for raising and distributing money.

Pauling would attend almost none of them. The distance from California, his increasingly busy schedule, and perhaps his natural tendency to work by himself kept him away from the gatherings. He occasionally traveled as a committee spokesman on the West Coast—once he and Szilard braved a bumpy ride in a small plane up the Columbia River Gorge to address a Spokane electrical worker's convention—but time and again, even at major press conferences, he was the only committee board member absent from their meetings. Years later, other members would have trouble recalling ever seeing him.

Far more important to Pauling than meetings was the chance to talk privately with Einstein, a man he ranked with Newton and Darwin as one of history's greatest scientists. Einstein was a one-of-a-kind thinker, a man light-years beyond his contemporaries in devising original physical theories. His work for peace, too, Pauling found more eloquent and stirring than any other scientist's.

"Today the atomic bomb has altered profoundly the nature of the world as we know it, and the human race consequently finds itself in a new habitat to which it must adapt its thinking," Einstein told the *New York Times* a few weeks before Pauling was asked to join the emergency committee. "There is no foreseeable defense against atomic bombs. . . . America has a temporary superiority in armaments, but it is certain that we have no lasting secret. What nature tells one group of men, she will tell in time to any group interested and patient enough in asking the questions." Einstein, like Pauling, believed in the creation of a world government capable of punishing anyone who made ready for war. And he agreed that scientists had a special responsibility in educating the public to the danger. "America's decisions will not be made over a table in the United Nations. Our representatives in New York, Paris, and Moscow depend ultimately on decisions made in the village square," he said. "To the village squares we must carry the facts of atomic energy. From there must come America's voice."

Before joining the committee, Pauling had passed no more than a few words with Einstein at social occasions; afterward, he took advantage of an invitation to call on him whenever he was in Princeton. Ava Helen usually accompanied him. Einstein would meet them at the door of his old frame house on Mercer Street and escort them upstairs to his second-floor study. The three of them would spend an hour or so talking, rarely about science, mostly about world affairs, public opinion, the insanity of the bomb, and the politics of war and peace. Einstein and Ava Helen got along especially well; her energy and wit sparkled when they were together. Einstein had a wonderful sense of humor, Pauling remembered, and the three of them often traded jokes and stories.

These private talks with the great man had a profound effect on Pauling, helping him deepen and clarify his own thinking about political issues. Einstein had encouraged Roosevelt to develop the bomb—anything to defeat Hitler—and now that the genie was out of the bottle he felt a keen responsibility to encourage its rational use. He saw the atomic policy of the United States in a broader context than most scientists, blaming the current misuse of this fantastic power on surrounding economic and political conditions. The real evil was nationalism, with its irrational pride, competitiveness, and war lust. The only way to get beyond it was through the activism of an informed populace that believed in the need for world government. This was now possible, Einstein told Pauling, because creation of the bomb had opened a new age, a unique moment in world history when an awful technology might compel some form of global cooperation. It was imperative that scientists help that transition take place. The alternative was disaster.

Most scientists felt they should limit their analyses of atomic policy to what they knew specifically, to effects that could be known and measured. It would be folly for a physicist to tell an anthropologist how to do his job, much less a politician. There was a different expertise required there. But Einstein felt no such constraint. He had seen the devil firsthand in Germany in the 1930s, and he wasn't afraid to call it by name. When Einstein spoke, he spoke not of kilotonnage and inspection verification systems but of the "poison of militarism and imperialism," of officials who would "compel us to live in a universal atmosphere of fear," of a United States "drunk on victory." He said, "It is easier to denature plutonium than it is to denature the evil spirit of man." He spoke freely, from the heart.

And Pauling began speaking from the heart as well. Einstein became his model for the way a scientist could act morally in the postwar world. "It was Einstein's example," he later said, "that caused my wife and me to decide to devote much energy and effort to this activity."

The Smell of Smoke

The efforts of the emergency committee and the FAS to rationalize atomic policy were doomed, however, by a combination of Soviet aggression and American politics.

Soon after the war, Stalin sealed off the nations Russia had "liberated" in Eastern Europe, leading Winston Churchill to make his famous "Iron Curtain" speech in the fall of 1946 and providing anti-Communists with a catchphrase that would become part of the national lexicon for the next four decades. In the world's most populous nation, Chinese Communist rebels were threatening the government. The issue of Communist world domination, a potent red flag used by some U.S. politicians to attract votes ever since the Russian Revolution, was again being waved in front of the public.

Republicans used the issue to hammer the Democrats. The only thing standing between the Russians and the world was the atomic bomb. The Democratic party was full of Communist sympathizers and appeasers, one-worlders and bomb sharers, claimed Republicans. The Democratic regime in Washington was lax on security. The nation's choice, said the 1946 Republican National Committee chairman, was between communism and Republicanism.

Many voters believed it. In that year's midterm elections the Republicans grabbed scores of new congressional seats, underlining an anti-Communist shift in public opinion and giving Harry Truman and his Democrats a wake-up call.

Truman, a consummate politician, saw which way things were going. All talk of sharing atomic technology with Russia ceased. His rhetoric swerved to the right, and he began taking steps to make sure the Democratic party was seen as just as anti-Communist as the Republicans. Part of the result was Executive Order 9835, establishing in March 1947 a loyalty and security program that prohibited federal workers from belonging to or having a "sympathetic association" with any one of a number of groups deemed by the attorney general to be Fascist, totalitarian, Communist, or subversive. The real intent was to weed out government employees who were Communists or Communist sympathizers. Truman's "loyalty program," as it became known, was a model for the states, which began initiating their own loyalty checks and oath systems for teachers, policemen, and other local government employees. Appearance on the attorney general's blacklist—or others like it soon prepared by eager state commissions and committees—became a virtual death sentence for any political group that was deemed too far left.

The loyalty program system would mushroom over the next five years, providing an extralegal mechanism for investigating any federal and state employees whose political activities were deemed questionable. The House Un-American Activities Committee (HUAC), the FBI, and various state committees began keeping files on millions of Americans whose only crime may have been to join a particular political group. It was the beginning of a domestic security state.

—*mm*—

Pauling watched with growing alarm as the national political debate after the 1946 election moved away from the control of atomic energy and toward the hunting of Communists. Nowhere did the anti-Communist fever rise faster or higher than in California, where as early as 1947 Los Angeles officials ordered all Communist books removed from the county library. The leading figure in hunting Reds in the Golden State was state senator Jack Tenney, a former songwriter who stayed in the headlines by keeping his California Fact-Finding Committee on Un-American Activities—or as it soon became known, the Tenney Committee—one step ahead of HUAC in the race to see who could be most fervently anti-Communist. Tenney's group went the federal government one better by publishing its own list of California "Communist fronts"—groups defined as doing the work of Moscow without any official connection—which included the Hollywood chapter of ICCASP and a number of other organizations too mild to make it onto the U.S. attorney general's blacklist.

One of Tenney's early targets was the Hollywood Community Radio Group, an offshoot of ICCASP designed to provide left-oriented "grass-roots community programming" on the local airwaves. Pauling was on the group's board of directors. When the group's license request came up before the Federal Communications Commission (FCC) in late 1946, Tenney turned the hearing into a political circus. He called the proposed station "Joe Stalin's Charlie McCarthy" and testified that many of the station's organizers were affiliated with Communist-front groups, especially the ICCASP. Pauling testified on behalf of the radio station and later, when the Hearst papers "mistakenly" called it the Hollywood Communist Radio Group, succeeded in getting a correction published.

Tenney's committee, in turn, began gathering a file on Linus Pauling.

Even among scientists the focus of public debate had now been effectively shifted from atomic policy to anticommunism. The ICCASP, with Pauling's help, was trying to recruit more scientist members, prompting the *Chemical Bulletin* to run an anti-ICCASP article referring to the group's "Communist-like leadership." Pauling responded with an outline of his personal view of the ICCASP's motivations: "The one general characteristic which I have observed in the officers of the [Hollywood chapter of the] ICCASP," he wrote, "is a deep personal concern about the future of the United States and of the world, a sincere interest in the welfare of the human being, 'irrespective of race, color or creed,'—the possession of a social conscience." He was, of course, describing himself. Although Pauling thought some ICCASP members were not critical enough of the "ruthless policy of the Russian leaders, with its suppression of personal liberty," he reassured his fellow researchers, "I know that the organization is not dominated by Communists."

Other chemists were not so sure. *Chemical and Engineering News,* the official organ of the American Chemical Society, also editorialized against the ICCASP, prompting a flood of letters pro and con. While some readers railed against "the encroachment of Communism on our Society," Pauling harkened back to his collegiate belief in the noblesse oblige of the educated in a letter to the editor. "The problems that the world faces are great, serious and difficult. Chemists and other scientists have a social obligation which is greater than that of the ordinary citizen," he wrote. "I hope that more and more chemists, in addition to carrying on their professional activities as members of the American Chemical Society, will also devote time and effort toward the solution of social and political problems."

Despite Pauling's attempts at persuasion, few scientists would join the group. The ICCASP did not have long to live in any case. In the spring of 1947 the staff of HUAC rented a hotel suite in Los Angeles to conduct "a secret investigation of Communism in motion pictures." Fascinated by the spectacle of Hollywood on trial, Americans paid close attention in October 1947 as a string of stars, producers, writers, and directors were grilled by the HUAC committee. Dalton Trumbo, a committed pacifist and ICCASP friend of Pauling's—Pauling thought he was "one of the most gifted writers in Hollywood"—decided not to cooperate with the witch-hunters. In preparation for his appearance before the committee, Trumbo wrote an eloquent opening statement describing the atmosphere the politicians had created with their anti-Communist inquisition. Washington, D.C., he wrote, was "acrid with fear and suppression . . . a city in which old friends hesitate to recognize each other in public places; a city in which men and women who dissent even slightly from the orthodoxy you seek to impose, speak with confidence only in moving cars and the open air. You have produced a capital city on the eve of its Reichstag fire. For those who remember German history in the autumn of 1932 there is the smell of smoke in this very room."

When Trumbo tried to read his statement, he was gaveled down. He, along with nine other noncooperators, were set aside for further legal action. They would become known as the Hollywood Ten.

The film-industry hearings had been great theater and a publicity boon for HUAC. Anticommunism, as HUAC chairman J. Parnell Thomas and a number of other ambitious politicians were discovering, was a terrific way to get your name in the paper in the role of patriotic defender of America. And movie stars and federal employees were not the only targets. "Our scientists, it seems, are well-schooled in their specialties, but not in the history of Communist tactics and designs," Thomas wrote. "They have a weakness for attending meetings, signing petitions, sponsoring committees and joining organizations labeled 'liberal' and 'progressive,' but which are actually Communist fronts."

HUAC investigators began looking closely at America's researchers. Scientists, after all, were privy to atomic secrets that, if passed to the Russians, would change the balance of world power. It did not matter that most scientists agreed that it was only a matter of time until the Russians figured out how to make their own atomic bomb, spies or not—the secrets nature tells one group of men, she will not long keep from others, as Einstein said. In Thomas's view it was vital for security to ensure the loyalty of scientists, and Executive Order 9835 offered a mechanism. The ongoing shift to federal funding for science—with growing numbers of scientists receiving paychecks either as employees of government labs and agencies or through grants from the Atomic Energy Commission and the military—made tens of thousands of scientists into temporary government employees, subject to Truman's loyalty program. Hundreds of them ended up undergoing security checks and FBI field investigations.

Edward U. Condon was the first public casualty. The respected physicist, former president of the American Physical Society and current head of the National Bureau of Standards (NBS), seemed an unlikely target. He was cheerful, witty, and well liked, and his record at the NBS was good. But he had publicly helped to lead the opposition to the May-Johnson bill, which to some right-wing politicians identified him as a troublemaker. In 1947, HUAC leaked information to the press that amounted to a smear attack on Condon. It was all circumstantial facts and associations—Condon had quit the Manhattan Project because of what he called "morbidly depressing" security restrictions at Los Alamos, had proposed the international sharing of atomic technology, had been recommended for his federal job by the left-wing former vice president Henry Wallace—but it was enough to brand him "one of the weakest links in our security system." Condon's private life was dragged through the press, his associations publicized, his reputation sullied. But he refused to step down. And the scientific community, including the American Association for the Advancement of Science, the FAS, and a number of influential individuals, Pauling among them, rallied to Condon's defense. The following year, a hastily organized federal inquiry cleared him of any wrongdoing.

Still, a tremor ran through scientific circles. If Condon, a man whose only crime had been to speak out, was a target, who was next?

CHAPTER 14

England

A Hole in the Seeing

Pauling and Ava Helen embarked on a two-month trip to England and Scandinavia in the summer of 1947, happy to escape the darkening political climate. The trip was a mixture of vacation and business. Again they left the children at home with Arletta Townsend. The couple stopped first in New York, where Pauling participated in a conference on the foundation of quantum mechanics, then caught one of the new transatlantic air clippers to England. Despite the still-evident ravages of wartime bombing and continued shortages of goods, they had a wonderful time in London, where Pauling was inducted as an honorary fellow of the Royal Society. The high point of the trip came on June 12, when Pauling was granted an honorary doctorate from Cambridge in an all-afternoon ceremony in the university's ornate Senate House. Pauling, in full academic regalia, joined a former viceroy of India, the Portuguese ambassador, and eight other dignitaries in a long procession through the packed hall. Once seated, they listened as the university orator praised the honorees in Latin, noting Pauling's success in "scratching . . . the perplexities of atomic structure." It was grand.

Later, he and Ava Helen traveled to Scandinavia for a scientific congress and a long vacation along the fjords. They flew back to California in August refreshed, pleased by their reception in Europe and eager to get their affairs in order to return to England that winter for Pauling's six-month stay as Oxford's Eastman Professor.

The children were happy to have them back, and especially happy that on this next trip they were to accompany their parents. The family needed time together. Peter was continuing to have trouble at school. Linda, bright, lovely, poised, and at age fifteen desperate to please her father, never felt as if she had the chance. Crellie, still the baby of the family at age ten, was growing resentful of his parents' frequent absences.

Linus junior, however, seemed to be doing fine. He surprised his parents that fall by announcing his engagement to Anita Oser, the great-granddaughter of both Cyrus McCormick and John D. Rockefeller and heiress to one of the nation's largest private fortunes. Theirs had the trappings of a fairy-tale relationship—the quiet son of a respected scientist and the beautiful, charming daughter of America's financial elite—and their engagement was well covered in the newspapers. They were married in a simple ceremony on the lawn of the Pauling's Sierra Madre house that September. This, too, was pleasing to Pauling; it fit his vision of how the world should work. He had labored hard his entire life to achieve the American Dream, and here, spread out on the velvet lawn of his mountain home with a crowd of the wealthy and renowned drinking toasts under the brilliant Southern California sun, it seemed that he had succeeded.

In late December, Linus, Ava Helen, and their three other children took the train to New York City, where they were due to embark on the *Queen Mary* the day after Christmas. They celebrated the holiday by exchanging gifts in a midtown Manhattan hotel room and were delighted to look outside and see snow falling, giving the Paulings their first white Christmas. They all bundled up and ran outside, Pauling and Ava Helen, too, scraping up snowballs and throwing them at street signs.

But by the next morning it had turned into too much of a good thing. A blizzard had buried the city in snow. With nothing moving on the streets, their ship set to sail in a few hours and Pauling in a state of mild panic, they finally found a cabbie willing to try to get them to the dock—for an elevated fee. They made it.

The children were having the time of their lives. While the captain delayed departure to pick up late-arriving passengers, they explored the ship from end to end. Even their modest accommodations—Pauling had saved money by sailing third-class—seemed exotic and exciting. Finally, with a great blast on the steam whistle, the *Queen Mary* pulled away from the dock through the densely falling snow.

After the ship cleared the storm, the crossing was fairly calm, with the family afflicted only slightly by seasickness. Pauling spent his time on the top decks of the ship, where he ran across a fellow scientist, Erwin Chargaff, an expert on nucleic acids, who tried to interest him in a recent observation he had made about the ratios of the molecule's chemical subunits, something about the rough equivalence of purines and pyrimidines. Pauling might have been slightly interested if he had not been on vacation and had Chargaff not struck him as rather too loud, pushy, and full of himself. He cut the conversation short and fled back to his cabin. "I didn't pay enough attention to what he was saying," Pauling later remembered. It was a rare moment when Pauling's restless mind did not light upon and store new information. It was a moment he would later regret.

—*◠◠◠*—

After taking a week to settle in a London flat and enroll the children in local private schools, Pauling began what he would later remember as "one of the happiest years of my life." He was the archetypal Yank at Oxford, tall, thin, energetic, clever, and funny, his black robes and thinning hair, streaked now with gray and worn quite long for an American, flying behind him as he strode through the ancient arched and crenellated campus. Students and professors flocked to hear him. "He was a sensation. The lecture hall was too small to hold all the students who wished to attend his lectures; there was standing room only," remembered one lucky enough to get in. "I have never heard anyone quite like him, with his jokes, his relaxed manner, his seraphic smile, his slide-rule calculations, and his spontaneous flow of ideas."

In the evenings the Paulings picked through a pile of dinner and party invitations or went to plays or lectures or musical events. Pauling met an array of researchers, dignitaries, industrialists, and politicians and found that as long as the topics discussed turned on either politics or science, he could charm them all. He was showered with more honors, elected foreign member of the Royal Society, and awarded doctorates from Oxford and the University of London as well as Cambridge—the only person at that time, he was told, to have been so honored by all three.

The British Chemical Society sent him on a lecture tour of the

United Kingdom, including appearances at the University of London and a special series of three talks at Cambridge. His theme was most often molecular complementarity, which he made more dramatic by showing his audiences a standard molecular ball-and-stick model. "Here, if atoms were really this big, two or three inches across, then at the same scale, a man looking at them would be 250,000 miles high," the distance from the earth to the moon, he would tell his listeners.

This became a favorite image in his talks, the man as tall as the moon, and he used it in a number of different ways to illustrate the challenges facing scientists interested in working out the structure of giant molecules. He had his audiences imagining themselves 250,000 miles tall. Now the earth is the size of a billiard ball to you; you can pick it up in your hand and turn it around. Say you were a scientist and you wanted to study this odd little ball, especially the tiny dot, barely visible to the naked eye, that is New York City. Aided by a conventional microscope, you could see things about a thousand feet wide: Central Park, say, or Rockefeller Center. With one of the new electron microscopes you could make out the shape of the Empire State Building—although nothing of its interior structure—and cars would show up as little dots. You could measure the sizes of the cars with semipermeable membranes or ultracentrifuges. But then would come a gap. The next step would be to use x-ray crystallography or electron diffraction, techniques so incredibly precise that you could determine the shapes of bolts, rivets, and gears, but nothing bigger.

There was a hole in the seeing, a blind spot between what could be discerned with the electron microscope and what could be worked out with x-ray diffraction. To the 250,000-mile man, this would eliminate the chance of determining the shapes of things between about one foot and ten in size, including the makers of Central Park and the Empire State Building and the cars and rivets—the humans. Take the same problem back to normal scale and you find that this "dark area of the unknown," as Pauling put it, extends across the size range of proteins and other giant molecules. It was this unexplored region that now required concentrated examination.

In February 1948 he was asked to give one of the Royal Institution's Friday night lectures, a formal monthly affair attended by the cream of British science and society. Founded by Michael Faraday in 1825, the lectures were an artifact from the days when the sciences were patronized like the arts; they originally offered the wealthy of London a chance to be amused by the latest in scientific research. But now they had become much more. Only the most significant work was afforded a hearing on Friday nights—it was here, for instance, that J. J. Thomson had announced the discovery of the electron. It had become for researchers the scientific equivalent of playing Carnegie Hall. "The members are connoisseurs who have an artistic appreciation of a good discourse," remembered a regular audience member. "The traditional way in which it is conducted, with lecturer and audience in evening dress, all helps create the right atmosphere."

For his Friday night Pauling carefully prepared a talk of the requisite and precise one-hour length. The evening began with a formal dinner, after which Pauling was ushered into the carefully maintained antique office of the great Faraday himself, the father of electrochemistry, and left alone to gather his thoughts before taking the stage.

He emerged an hour later, suitably inspired, entered the small, ornate auditorium, and faced a select audience of men in black tie and women in furs and jewels. Reminding himself of the lessons he had learned in oratory at Oregon Agricultural College, Pauling took a deep breath and began:

> As I look at a living organism—at one of you or myself—I see reminders of many questions that need to answered. . . . What is skin, fingernail? How do fingernails grow? How do I feel things—how are nerves built and how do they function? How do I see things? How can I smell things, and why does benzene have one smell and iso-octane another? Why is sugar sweet and vinegar sour? How does the hemoglobin in my blood do its job of carrying oxygen from the lungs to the tissues? How do the enzymes in my body break up the food that I eat, burn it to keep me warm and to permit me to do work, and build new tissues for me from the food fragments? Why do I catch cold when exposed through contact with an ailing person, get pneumonia, and then recover after treatment with a specific antiserum or a sulfa drug? How does penicillin carry out its wonderful function of fighting disease? Why am I immune to measles, whooping cough, poliomyelitis, small-pox, whereas some other people are not? And finally, why is it that my children, as they grow and develop, become human beings, and show characteristics similar to mine, and their mother's—how have these characteristics been transmitted to them?
>
> The basic answers to all of these questions are not to be found in books. Even though Chaucer said, "For out of olde feldes, as men seith,/ Cometh al this newe corn fro yere to

yere;/ And out of olde bokes, in good feith,/ Cometh al this newe science that men lere," he was before long corrected by Francis Bacon: "Books must follow sciences, and not sciences books."

To understand all of these great biological phenomena we need to understand atoms, and the molecules that they form by bonding together.

Having gathered in his audience by mixing scientific questions, images of everyday experience, and quotes from British literary and scientific heroes, Pauling went on to outline his idea of complementarity as the central paradigm for understanding the action of biological molecules. While other Friday night speakers generally stood stock-still and read their notes, Pauling lectured from memory, pacing the theater stage, chalk in hand, scribbling out illustrations of antibody formation and enzyme action on a blackboard. He had his listeners imagine themselves as tall as the moon. He made them understand that the question of the structure of proteins was the central problem in biology. It was a flawless, seemingly spontaneous performance. And it had the desired effect. At a party given after Pauling's speech, Sir Ian Heilbrun, head of the Imperial College, remarked, "When we hear Linus giving one of his lectures, we think of a genius thinking out loud."

The Cavendish

Protein structure was also on the mind of one of the most illustrious members of the audience that night, William Lawrence Bragg. In the twenty years since Pauling had outraced Bragg to the invention of a set of rules for determining complex silicate structures, the two men's professional lives had followed parallel upward trajectories. Bragg had emerged from a mental breakdown in the early 1930s seemingly stronger and more confident than ever, and he made his Manchester x-ray crystallography laboratory the most theoretically innovative in the world. His efforts were rewarded in 1938 by the call to succeed Rutherford as head of England's greatest center for physics, the Cavendish Laboratory at Cambridge. Three years later, he was knighted.

By 1948, he had made the Cavendish into the world's foremost center for x-ray crystallography. But here the two men's interests diverged. While Pauling was interested in the results of x-ray crystallography,

Bragg was interested in the process: the perfection of equipment and mathematical techniques needed to interpret the x-ray patterns. It was the variety and power of his machines, the cleverness of the young men he attracted, and his ongoing interest in the theory of the technique that made the Cavendish Laboratory great. The molecular structures themselves Bragg left mostly to his workers. Much of their effort was spent on minerals, alloys, and small organic molecules, but there was also, when Bragg arrived, a little group led by the Austrian émigré Max Perutz that was engaged in what Bragg called "a valiant attempt" to figure out the structure of hemoglobin. Bragg was not much interested in proteins when he first arrived—he never understood biology very well and thought that proteins were in any case much too large and complex to attack with x-rays—but Perutz was a tireless and optimistic worker with enough promising results to interest Bragg in proteins as an x-ray-analysis challenge, a sort of supermineral puzzle. By the time Pauling arrived in England, Bragg had secured enough funding to sustain Perutz, a young coworker, John Kendrew, and two research assistants, and their results were beginning to show the broad structural outline of the hemoglobin molecule. This was not the only British group making headway with proteins. At other universities, Dorothy Crowfoot Hodgkin was starting her second decade of studies on insulin, and J. D. Bernal and his coworkers were beginning to pick apart the enzyme ribonuclease.

The more Pauling heard about the British work, the more concerned he became about losing the race to become the first in the world to determine the structure of a complete protein. While he had been attacking proteins from the bottom up, carefully pinning down the structures of single amino acids and small peptides as a way of building larger structures from their subunits, the British had been working from the top down, analyzing the x-ray diffraction patterns of whole proteins. Pauling had thought proteins too large, their x-ray patterns too complex, for the top-down approach to work in any reasonable length of time. But after talking with Bernal and Hodgkin, he realized that the British were getting uncomfortably close to cracking some structures.

So he began thinking again about the theoretical attack on the parent of all proteins, the keratin chain, that he had last tried in 1937. He had failed in trying to build a protein chain that matched Astbury's x-ray data and had assumed at the time that his ideas about amino-acid structure or bonding were wrong. But everything that had been done in the years since, including Corey's careful amino-acid studies, had shown him that he had not been wrong. The dimensions were all roughly as he had assumed, and the double-bond character he had predicted for the peptide bond—the factor that prevented rotation and held the atoms on either side in a plane—had been confirmed by Corey's work with diketopiperazine. He had not been off by more than a few degrees or a few hundredths of an angstrom anywhere. Why had he failed ten years earlier?

In the spring of 1948 he returned to the problem, this time with a new guiding principle. In the 1930s a structure like a spiral staircase had been proposed for long-chain starches, and in 1943 Pauling's old collaborator Maurice Huggins (the scientist with whom he had done some of the early work leading to the idea of the planarity of the peptide bond) had theorized that the same shape might be important in proteins. In Huggins's model the amino-acid chain, rather than looking like Astbury's flat, kinked ribbon, spiraled up and around like a bedspring; Huggins hypothesized that it was held in shape between turns of the chain by hydrogen bonds.

This was an exciting idea and had already become a topic of discussion among British crystallographers. It helped to explain some things. While you would expect Astbury's flat ribbon to chemically reflect a ribbon's two-sided nature, protein chains actually behaved as if they were the same all around, consistent with a spiral's overall cylindrical shape. There were theoretical arguments in favor of spirals, too: As Francis Crick, then a graduate student in Perutz and Kendrew's laboratory, put it, "It was well known that any chain with identical repeating links that fold so that every link is folded in exactly the same way, and with the same relationship to its close neighbors, will form a helix." Whether called a helix or a spiral, Huggins's idea had an important influence on the Cavendish group. Soon it seemed that every protein researcher in Britain was looking for spirals. Dorothy Hodgkin, for instance, with whom Pauling had several long conversations during his Oxford visit, had been on the lookout for evidence of the shape in her insulin molecule.

Then a week or two after his Royal Institution lecture, Pauling fell ill. The damp British spring contributed to a severe sinus infection that put him in bed in his flat. "The first day I read detective stories and just tried to keep from feeling miserable, and the second day, too," he remembered. "But I got bored with that, so I thought, 'Why don't I think about the structure of proteins?'" More specifically, he decided to make another stab at keratin, this time using the idea of a spiral. He gathered some paper, a ruler, and a pencil and began sketching out a chain of amino acids, drawing the atomic bond lengths and angles from memory. He followed a three-step plan: Draw out a chain using the known dimensions of amino acids; line the elements up in space so that hydrogen bonds could form easily and the peptide bond was kept planar; then see if the resulting model explained the x-ray data. He drew the basic carbon-carbon-nitrogen backbone of each amino acid, then a heavy line where they linked to show the peptide bond; this he would keep flat on the page. The side chains that distinguished each type of amino acid from the others he pointed outward, away from the center of the spiral, figuring that in that way they would not interfere with construction of the repeating structure that had to exist at the center.

Then he started folding, keeping the peptide-bond area flat on the page, making turns only around the single carbon in the amino-acid backbone that was not involved in the peptide bond, the one spot he thought rotation could take place. When he folded here, he tried making the angle roughly that of a tetrahedron, the most logical choice for a carbon bond. He worked his paper around, trying to line elements up so that as many hydrogen bonds as possible could form. In a few moments, much to his surprise, he came up with a spiral that looked surprisingly good. It had planar peptide bonds, roughly correct bond angles and lengths, and allowed reasonable hydrogen bonds to form between each turn. "Well, I forgot all about having a cold then, I was so pleased," he said.

It was a classic example of his stochastic method, using a few decisively limiting chemical rules to create a reasonable model. But Pauling's happiness faded when he realized that the likely x-ray pattern produced from his model would not match the patterns Astbury and others had been getting. The actual keratin pattern showed a strong reflection at 5.1 angstroms, a distance thought to be the basic repeat unit along the length of the chain—in the case of a spiral, this would mean the distance between one turn of the chain and the next above it. It would take months of careful model building to confirm this, but it appeared from his crude sketch that Pauling's spiral measured out to a different repeat distance. Playing by his own set of rules about the peptide bond and hydrogen bonding, Pauling found: "There was no way I could stretch my structure or compress it."

He went back to bed. Pauling kept quiet about his doodles, not even writing Corey about them, filing the idea of spirals away for more exploration when he got back to Caltech. For the moment, he felt, all he had was "just a piece of paper."

The Tortoise and the Hare

The sinus infection hung on for weeks, still bothering Pauling when he arrived in France with his family to give a series of scientific talks. They took an apartment in Paris, where he managed to convince a physician at the American embassy to prescribe some penicillin. He quickly recovered, and as Ava Helen and the children sallied forth to explore parks, museums, bakeries, and cathedrals, Pauling began dazzling the French scientific world.

At one of his meetings, the highlight was to be a full day devoted to comparing the advantages of Pauling's valence-bond approach to molecular chemistry to the molecular-orbital approach championed by the University of Chicago's Robert Mulliken.

For the growing community of quantum chemists, this was something akin to seeing Martin Luther take on the pope. Starting with the same gospel, the received wisdom of quantum mechanics, the two men had for nearly twenty years championed different interpretations of its chemical meaning.

In Pauling's approach, derived from the electron-interchange idea of Heitler and London, molecules were aggregates of individual atoms, each linked to its neighbors by bonds formed by electrons localized between the two nuclei. The number of bonds equaled the element's valence, or bonding capacity, and the Pauling school had come to be known as the valence-bond, or VB, approach. In theory, the total quantum-mechanical state of a molecule could be calculated by adding together the wave functions that were involved in each bond, with appropriate adjustments for the effect of each bond upon its neighbors.

During the nearly two decades that Pauling spent promoting the VB approach, Mulliken had patiently worked on his own molecular orbital (MO) theory, an approach predicated on a belief that molecules were not what VB advocates thought they were. Molecules to Mulliken were not aggregates of distinct atoms connected by distinct bonds but things unto themselves, with their own odd behavior explicable only in molecular terms. His experience studying the spectra of light absorbed and emitted by molecules had convinced him that molecules could be more profitably viewed as if their binding electrons were somewhat delocalized and spread across the surface. It was a view antiintuitive to most chemists, but one that twenty years of work had convinced Mulliken was right. Molecules to Mulliken were what they showed themselves to be, not what nineteenth-century chemists thought they ought to be. "A molecule," he said, borrowing from Gertrude Stein to encapsulate his philosophy, "is a molecule is a molecule."

The battle between the VB and MO approaches for the hearts and minds of chemists had been lopsided, in great part because of the force of Pauling's intellect and personality. Pauling knew how to present his VB ideas in ways that appealed to chemists, that correlated with the way they thought of chemical bonds, as atoms joined to each other one at a time through individual links that could be represented on paper by dashed lines between elemental symbols. Just as important was his ability to figure out shortcuts that simplified the mathematical picture. While the idea of summing a number of separate wave functions to create a quantum-mechanical picture of a molecule was sound in theory, in practice the difficult mathematics made it impossible to demonstrate in precomputer days for any but the simplest molecules. Pauling had gotten around that by improvising semiempirical variations on the VB theme, such as the calculation of resonance energy and the electronegativity scale, devices that worked in the spirit of quantum mechanics but were based as much on Pauling's imaginative way of explaining and organizing laboratory findings as they were on Schrödinger's wave equation. Chemists did not have to know how to add wave functions to make use of Pauling's ideas, and that increased the popularity of his approach through the 1930s and early 1940s, especially after publication of *The Nature of the Chemical Bond*. Chemists could use his ideas with the assurance that they were grounded in the new physics, but they did not have to learn the physics. They could get the sheen of quantum mechanics without the sweat.

Pauling himself, his brilliance and his personality, were the final and in some ways most important factors in popularizing the VB approach. He was a great teacher, a charismatic proselytizer for this interpretation of the gospel. Wherever he went, wherever his books were read and taught, chemists were converted to his approach. As a result, by the 1940s it seemed that his VB ideas had conquered the chemical world.

Mulliken was poorly equipped to compete. Not only was his basic concept alien to most chemists, not only did he offer it draped in a new and unfamiliar garb, a notation he had helped develop that used Greek symbols, superscripts, and subscripts to describe his molecular orbitals, but he was a terrible communicator—too precise, too mathematical, too qualifying to make his ideas come alive. He bored a generation of chemistry students with the worst-delivered lectures on the University of Chicago campus, shrouding his insights in a fog of timidly delivered, densely packed gobbledygook. His published papers, which appeared in the field's most physics oriented journals, were not much better.

And he watched for years as all the attention and awards went to Pauling. Mulliken saw Pauling's 1930s series of articles on the "Nature of the Chemical Bond" hailed as revolutionary, while his own fourteen-paper "Electronic Structures of Polyatomic Molecules and Valence" series, published during the same period, received relatively little attention. He saw Pauling's lectures crammed, while students avoided his. He saw Pauling receive invitation after invitation, honor after honor, while he stayed in Chicago and toiled.

It was especially galling that Pauling ignored his ideas. It was not that Pauling thought the MO approach was wrong—Slater and Pauling had decided as early as 1931 that the VB and MO approaches both represented acceptable approximations of the wave equation and that both, if taken far enough, led to the same conclusions, and Pauling had used some MO ideas himself in several early papers—but he was certain that his version of the VB approach was more usable by chemists and less confusing to teach. "One picture is enough," Pauling wrote. "Molecular orbitals just confuse the student." He devoted a substantial amount of space to discussing the VB approach in his 1935 book *An Introduction to Quantum Mechanics*, for instance, while brushing the MO approach off in a single paragraph. In *The Nature of the Chemical Bond* he noted Mulliken's ideas only in passing.

Mulliken for his part saw Pauling's popularized version of the VB approach doing real damage. Pauling was a "showman," he said, who "made a special point in making everything sound as simple as possible and in that way making it very popular with the chemists but delaying their understanding. . . . He left them with a pretty crude idea and made them feel that was satisfactory, whereas something better could have been done."

Pauling's dramatic flair had carried the VB approach to prominence through the 1930s, but by the late 1940s an increasing number of chemists were beginning to listen to Mulliken. Quantum chemistry was now moving out of its introductory phase, thanks in large part to Pauling's work, with advanced chemistry students at top schools now expected to learn basic quantum mechanics and a good deal of mathematics as part of their preparatory work for a career in chemistry. The more the new generation understood, the less they needed Pauling's shortcuts. They were hungry for a more quantitative, less intuitive approach to the field, and they found it in Mulliken's MO approach.

Some things seemed a toss-up—in the 1930s, for instance, the MO analysis of the hydrogen molecule gave a better bond length but a poorer dissociation constant than the VB method—but it was becoming clear that improved MO methods were making it the better tool for studying more complex molecules. Complaints were also surfacing about some of Pauling's VB-based ideas, such as the electronegativity scale, a useful practical device in most situations, critics said, but one with a shaky theoretical basis and a suspicious weakness in addressing metallic elements. Then there was the way Pauling used resonance between contributing structures to explain the properties of molecules. In practice, this depended on coming up with the right set of starting structures—canonical structures, they were called—between which resonance occurred, then properly weighting the contribution of each to get the final product. In general, the larger the molecule and the more atoms involved, the greater the crowd of canonical structures required to explain its character. While Pauling, blessed with peerless chemical intuition, seemed able to come up with the right mix and balance, other chemists had trouble. George Wheland, a Pauling student who had gone on to become successful in applying the VB approach to organic chemistry, further complicated matters by invoking "excited" structures—purely imaginary constructs that could not reasonably be expected to exist in nature—as resonance contributors, opening the door, some chemists thought, to any manner of wild speculation about what sorts of odd ingredients might be thrown into the canonical mix. Used this way, the VB approach seemed unnecessarily arbitrary. There was a growing sense that Pauling and his followers could pull out of their hats whatever resonance combinations they needed to explain the properties of a given molecule.

By 1947, even Wheland agreed that while the overall idea of resonance was vital in understanding chemistry, the assignment of quantitative values to canonical structures was "quite arbitrary and not at all reliable. . . . Nevertheless, I do not feel that they are therefore completely worthless; if one admits, as he must, that a rigorous treatment is impossible, and if one therefore adopts an approximate procedure, then some arbitrariness must be introduced if any progress at all is to be made. As long as one knows what he is doing, and does not take the results too seriously, he is not likely to get into serious trouble, and he may gain some insights into the problem."

That was not good enough for postwar researchers eager to make quantum chemistry a more strictly quantitative science. As Mulliken said, "The valence-bond method required great flocks of resonance

structures when the molecule got complicated, and to make any calculations with those is still just about hopeless." During the 1930s he
found a small but influential group of British quantum chemists who
thought the same way. Led by John Lennard-Jones, the first man in
Britain to hold a chair of theoretical chemistry, and Christopher
Longuet-Higgins, the Anglo-MO group actively promoted Mulliken's
ideas and extended the reach of his methods. Just before Pauling's and
Mulliken's scheduled meeting in France, for instance, Lennard-Jones
devised a simple way of using the MO approach to explain the direc-
tional nature of bonds, a gap in the method that had been one of its
major drawbacks.

By the late 1940s, as a result of the effort put into quantum chemistry by Pauling, Mulliken, and their followers, two things became increasing clear: The MO and VB approaches were at their core essentially
the same; and the MO camp had developed simpler and more useful
tools for the quantitative study of molecules. The tide was turning
from VB to MO.

That Mulliken was given equal time with Pauling in their French debate confirmed the growing influence of his MO ideas. The full-day
event also confirmed that Pauling was the more engaging and convincing speaker. But it was clear at the end that, other than the new insights he had gained into metals, Pauling had not done a great deal of
important work with his VB approach in the past ten years. He had
charged off to other things, while Mulliken had labored patiently, perfecting his MO approach, making it work in ways that the new chemists
needed. There was no immediate result, no massive change in allegiance, as a result of the day's speeches. But the debate was a confirmation of a trend that would make the MO approach the preferred one
for quantum chemists over the decade to come. The tortoise was over-
taking the hare.

After the discussion, Mulliken and his wife went to the Paulings'
Paris apartment for a party. They sat quietly as Pauling held court
among a throng of chemists and physicists. It was a gay affair, with
laughter, jokes, good-natured ribbing about chemical bonding ideas,
and, Mulliken remembered, "endless bottles of champagne." Pauling's
daughter, Linda, did an impromptu dance solo. It went on late into
the night. Mulliken, however, slipped away early. There was still time
to do a little work before bed.

A Sickled Cell

When he returned to Britain in May, Pauling delivered three lectures at Cambridge, which gave him an opportunity to assess firsthand Bragg's labs at the Cavendish. Max Perutz, who thought Pauling was one of the outstanding figures of world science, was happy to be his guide. When Perutz had been a poor student, he remembered borrowing enough money from his girlfriend to buy a used copy of *The Nature of the Chemical Bond,* a book that, he said, "transformed the chemical flatland of my earlier textbooks into a world of three-dimensional structures." Pauling was impressed by Perutz's work on hemoglobin, which indicated that the molecule had an overall oval shape but, more importantly, was made of what looked like stacks of protein cylinders, each about ten or eleven angstroms across, running parallel to the molecule's long axis. Pauling noted that this might fit the dimensions of the spiral he had folded out of paper in his sickbed a few weeks before.

But he kept that observation to himself. "I didn't say anything to [Perutz] about it," Pauling said. "I thought there is still a possibility that there is a real joker, you know, eluding me—that there is something wrong." Perutz's x-ray patterns from hemoglobin showed the 5.1-angstrom reflection that could not exist with Pauling's spiral. There was no sense muddying the water with unproved guesses—or even a new idea that could lead the Cavendish group more quickly to the final details of protein structure.

Pauling was, in fact, worried by what he saw at the Cavendish. Bragg—who received Pauling graciously but still refused to talk science—had turned it into a crystallographic showplace, with all the latest equipment and most talented researchers using it. Pauling's x-ray outfit at Caltech, by comparison, seemed shabby. "They have about five times as great an outfit as ours, that is, with facilities for taking nearly 30 x-ray pictures at the same time," he wrote his assistant Eddie Hughes. "I think that we should expand our x-ray laboratory without delay."

His competitive streak was showing. Pauling felt that he was in a race with Bragg again, this time for a greater prize, and he was concerned to see that Bragg's group had a good chance of winning. "I am beginning to feel a bit uncomfortable about the English competition," Pauling wrote Corey, describing the work Perutz and others had been doing with protein structures. "They have been driving straight at the heart of a problem, and getting its solution by hook or crook. . . . The progress that has been made seems to me to be truly astounding." In response, Pauling asked Corey to try a new tack. He had seen the British using protein-digesting enzymes to split large proteins into middle-sized pieces—strings of about twenty-six amino acids—which were thought to provide more reasonable targets for x-ray analysis; now he told Corey to do the same thing. Dutiful as always, Corey wrote back, "I am terribly impatient about getting into the protein work with a force that will really give the British some competition."

—~~~—

Their remaining time in England was very happy. Linda and Peter enjoyed their schools and their new friends, and Crellin surprised everyone by topping his schoolmates in Latin tests at London's Dragon School. Pauling continued his lectures at Oxford through the rest of the spring. In May, he heard the good news of the Rockefeller Foundation's $700,000 grant for his grand plan to launch with Beadle a combined chemical-biological attack on protein structure and other problems. In June, he and Ava Helen celebrated their twenty-fifth wedding anniversary with their children and friends at Oxford.

In July he presented his new ideas on the structure of metals at a huge symposium in Amsterdam, amusing the crowd by filling blackboards with data and then lecturing, hidden, behind them. While walking in Amsterdam, Pauling also impressed his friends when he ran after a woman he saw being dragged down the street, her coat caught in a streetcar door. Pauling held her up while pounding on the car door until the conductor stopped and freed her. He was still something of a daredevil. The family then traveled to Switzerland before returning to France for two weeks, where Pauling received yet another honorary degree, this one from the University of Paris.

By the time he was ready to return to Caltech, Pauling was buzzing with new ideas. His time away had given him both the stimulus of conversations with the most outstanding scientists in Europe and the time to mull things over. The VB approach to metallic bonds and his ideas of protein spirals had been satisfying, the debate with Mulliken, he thought, had gone well, and he had a raft of other ideas jostling for attention in his mind. "I think that it has really been very much worthwhile for me to get away for this period of time, under circumstances favorable to my thinking over questions and trying to find their solution," he wrote Corey.

The results of his European journey showed when he got back to

Pasadena. During the next months he wrote reviews of his ideas on complementarity; an important set of publications describing the new theory of the structure of metals that he had presented in Paris; and more on antibody action, the structure of uranium hydride, the stability of fibrous sulfur, the valence-state energy of bivalent oxygen, the structure of hemoglobin, and the action of x-rays on fruit flies. Subjects ranged from the very general "Chemistry and the World of Today" to the highly specific "The *Cis-Trans* Isomerization of the Carotenoids." He published in French, German, British, and American journals. The number of papers, between 1948 and 1949, topped thirty.

Within this astonishing output, one set of papers stood out. The group Pauling had set to work on discovering the cause of sickle-cell anemia had found an answer.

It had not been easy. Pauling's idea that a change in the sickle-cell hemoglobin caused it to crystallize when oxygen was removed implied a structural alteration. But for months Harvey Itano, the young physician-turned-chemist Pauling had put to work on the problem in the fall of 1946, could not find any basic difference between the blood protein from normal and sickle-cell patients. According to his tests, the hemoglobin molecules from normal and sickle-cell blood were the same size, the same molecular weight, and gave the same acid-base titration curves. His work was slowed by the fact that sickle-cell blood was hard to come by. All sickle-cell sufferers were African American, and most were from the American South; there seemed to be relatively few cases in California. Pauling and Itano first tried striking bargains with physicians in the Los Angeles black community for a small supply; for a while they lured patients to Caltech to give blood for a small sum. Eventually, Pauling found a doctor at Tulane University in Louisiana who had access to a larger supply of blood and could send what was needed.

Once they had an adequate supply, Pauling had Itano look at the effects of various chemicals on the sickle-cell hemoglobin. Itano's research confirmed that oxygen was involved in the sickling process and showed that a range of reducing agents could speed the sickling—a finding that led to a rapid diagnostic test for sickle-cell disease and the first paper that Pauling and Itano published on the subject. He also confirmed that the addition of carbon monoxide, which binds irreversibly to hemoglobin (thus blocking the attachment of oxygen), prevented sickling. As Pauling thought, the effect seemed to be localized on the hemoglobin molecule.

So why did normal and sickle-cell hemoglobin look so similar? The only detectable difference between the two was a very slight difference in the electrical charges on the molecules. Itano broke apart the hemoglobins and showed that this difference was localized in the protein part of the molecule, the globin, rather than in the iron-containing heme. But it was a very slight effect in a very large molecule. It would need an extremely sensitive probe to study any further.

To help speed the work, in the fall of 1947, Pauling started another postdoctoral fellow, John Singer, on the project. Singer was more experienced than Itano in the physical chemistry of large molecules, and he knew something about a new machine called the Tiselius Apparatus that might help them. The Swedish chemist Arne Tiselius had invented it just before the war to separate proteins out of mixtures based on the electrical properties of the molecules. Knowing that each protein carries a characteristic set of electrical charges on its surface, Tiselius devised a tool in which a protein solution in the middle of a glass tube was subjected to an electrical gradient, positive charge at one end, negative at the other. The proteins, he discovered, would move one way or another, drawn toward the positive or negative poles, at different speeds, depending on a variety of factors, but especially the mix of charges on their surfaces. It was a delicate, gentle, precise way to separate protein mixtures without harming them. During the war the Tiselius machines were rare and not commercially available, but Pauling put Sturdivant to work building one for Caltech.

By the time Pauling was in England, it was up and running, and Singer and Itano were able to try it on sickle-cell and normal hemoglobins. The Tiselius Apparatus finally uncovered a difference. The sickle-cell hemoglobin moved toward the negative end of the electric field more rapidly than its normal counterpart; it looked as though at normal pH the sickle-cell molecule carried about three extra positive charges. The results showed unequivocally that the hemoglobin molecules from sickle-cell patients differed significantly from those in normal people. Pauling's idea was right.

But this was astounding. A slight change in the electrical charge of a single type of molecule meant the difference between a healthy human and one with a deadly disease. Pauling made sure that the singularity was emphasized in the title of the first major paper to emerge from the work: "Sickle Cell Anemia, a Molecular Disease," which came out in the fall of 1949. People had theorized in broad terms about the molecular basis of disease before, but no one had ever demonstrated it the way Pauling's group did. Singer and Itano then went further. There were patients with an intermediate stage of the disease called "sicklemia," not as severe as full-blown sickle-cell anemia; Itano and Singer showed that the blood of these patients contained a mixture of normal and sickle-cell hemoglobins. An analysis of the familial relationship between normal, sicklemic, and sickle-cell patients indicated that the trait was inherited in Mendelian fashion, with the sickle-cell gene composed of two alleles, that is, two variants, one from each parent. Sicklemic patients carried one allele, or variant, for the disease and one normal allele, with full-blown cases of sickle-cell anemia carrying both alleles for the disease.

By pinpointing the source of a disease in the alteration of a specific molecule and firmly linking it to genetics, Pauling's group created a landmark in the history of both medicine and molecular biology. It validated Pauling's belief in the importance of that dark area of the dimensional unknown where proteins lay; it turned the interest of a generation of physician-researchers toward disease at the molecular level; it substantiated his idea that medical research needed to be grounded in the methods of modern chemistry; it opened up new vistas in the study of inherited medical disorders; it kicked off years of productive research into abnormal hemoglobins; and—once again—it raised Pauling's stature, especially in the medical community.

CHAPTER 15

Attack
of the
Primitives

The Dream Boys

After returning to the United States from England, Pauling resumed paying attention to politics as well as science. In the summer of 1948 the nation was gearing up for one of the most raucous and surprising presidential elections in its history, and Pauling, like many New Deal Democrats, was ready to bolt the party. He felt that Truman, by moving to the right, had sold out the ideals of Franklin Roosevelt.

Pauling's candidate was Henry Wallace, Roosevelt's former secretary of agriculture and vice president from 1940 until 1944. An aloof, intelligent, well-to-do publisher of farm journals and breeder of hybrid corn from the Midwest, Wallace was one of the most liberal of New Dealers and a strong believer in accommodation with Russia. As the anti-Communist rhetoric heated up after the war, he became pigeonholed by many politicians and most of the press as a wild idealist—one of the "post-war dream boys," as one government official labeled the liberals in government.

Truman, who made Wallace his commerce secretary, thought he was an indecisive intellectual more interested in studying foreign languages than in governing. Once he became a born-again anti-Communist, Truman fumed in his diary about Wallace, this "100 percent pacifist" who

took up cabinet-meeting time telling everyone that he "wants to disband our armed forces, give Russia our atomic bomb secrets and trust
a bunch of adventurers in the Kremlin Politburo." Truman wanted to
get rid of him, and he got his chance in late 1946 when Wallace gave a
speech in Madison Square Garden skewering Truman's "get tough"
policy against Soviet expansionism. A week after the speech, Truman
demanded Wallace's resignation.

He got it and in the process split the Democratic party. Wallace declared himself a third-party candidate for the upcoming presidential
election. He and his backers created a new Progressive party and
styled themselves the true followers of FDR. Pauling's favorite political
action group, the ICCASP, badly wounded after being attacked as a
Communist front, reformed itself as the Progressive Citizens of America and took up the Wallace cause. At first, the Wallace campaign
looked strong. He could be a forceful, intelligent speaker, and in 1947
his message of internationalism and revised New Deal policies played
well to enthusiastic and well-attended rallies. The stadiums and halls
where he spoke were filled with a polyglot of liberals and anti-Truman
Democrats, with a sprinkling of Communists. Pauling liked Wallace's
internationalism, his New Deal social conscience, and his intellectual
approach to politics, and he joined the parade, becoming a member
of a "Democrats for Wallace" group, assuming a national vice chairmanship of the Progressive Citizens of America, giving money to Wallace's campaign and introducing the candidate at a big Los Angeles
rally. There Pauling and his daughter, Linda, shared the dais with
Katharine Hepburn, who took an appreciative look at the gamine
Linda and asked why she wasn't in the movies.

Pauling and Wallace were alike in some ways, both given to solitary
thinking, both passionate about ideals, both unwilling to compromise.
Even better from Pauling's standpoint, Wallace, with his background
in hybridizing agricultural stock, understood something about science. "I think he was a good, rational person who may have had some
difficulty, the way scientists have, in being a politician," Pauling said.

That was the problem. Wallace, who always had trouble working up
the energy to glad-hand and backslap, was too remote and cool to make
a good politician. He was also unwaveringly accommodating toward
the USSR. In early 1946 it had seemed reasonable to talk about turning over atomic bombs to the United Nations and funding the massive
reconstruction of the USSR. By mid-1948, it was political suicide.

Wallace's candidacy had already begun sputtering when, while

Pauling was in England in February and March 1948, a Communist coup in Czechoslovakia brought that country firmly into the Soviet orbit. Wallace, instead of taking advantage of the anti-Communist reaction in the United States, charged that the Czech putsch was a response to a planned right-wing coup that may have involved the U.S. ambassador. Too quick to excuse Russia, too eager to criticize America, Wallace was lampooned by the Republicans, nailed by Truman, and crucified in the press. Membership in the Progressive party dwindled as it became synonymous with being soft on Communism.

Pauling was in Washington State on election day, speaking about peace and chemistry near the government's huge Hanford facility for making the raw material of the atomic bomb. Despite the fact that Ava Helen, fearing a Republican victory, had defected to Truman at the last minute and encouraged Pauling to do the same, he stuck with his man, casting an absentee ballot for Wallace. It looked as if Ava Helen had been right again. When Pauling went to bed that night, the radio commentators were sure of a Republican victory. At two in the morning, Pauling awoke, went out to his car in the motel parking lot, turned on the radio for more news, and was relieved to hear that Truman had been declared the victor. Wallace's showing, however, was dismal: He received less than 3 percent of the popular vote, and the Progressive party failed to carry a single state. Later, Pauling lamented, as would tens of thousands of Progressives, "Wallace may have been too honest to be a successful politician."

The 1948 election marked the end of the New Deal and the beginning of a new phase of intolerance in America. The Wallace candidacy had released Truman from any need to cater to the liberal wing of his own party and allowed him to move even further to the right. He had proven to himself that Democrats could win elections by getting tough on Reds, and he would continue to do it as long as it yielded victory.

The political landscape had clearly shifted, but Pauling did not move with it. Four years earlier, he would have been considered a typical New Dealer, a liberal Democrat hovering somewhere between center and left. His ideas had not changed—throughout 1947 and 1948 he continued to speak out for international control of atomic energy and against loyalty oaths, for civil liberties and against anti-Communist hysteria—but the nation had changed. Fear was driving politics now. Rooting out Communists became the national pastime. And fewer and fewer people would speak against it.

Not Any Bargain

It was a good time for FBI director J. Edgar Hoover. As the mania for security grew, so grew his power, influence, and ability to move America toward the kind of country he thought it should be. In the name of national security, Hoover collected information on citizens private and public, dangerous and innocuous, filling cabinet after cabinet with thousands of fat files, indexed and cross-indexed, the dirt and the daily routine of everyone from legislators and lawyers to longshoremen and librarians.

One FBI file carried the name of Linus Pauling. In the winter of 1947, a few weeks before Pauling left for Oxford, Hoover's intimate associate Clyde Tolson showed his boss a letter received from a member of the American Chemical Society who was worried that the group's president-elect, soon to be leaving for England, might be subversively inclined. "A quick check of the files," Tolson told Hoover, "indicates that we have never investigated Pauling but that he is closely associated with the Progressive Citizens of America and signed a resolution for the abolition of the House Un-American Activities Committee [HUAC] and is a member of infiltrated groups . . . there are sufficient references to him to indicate that he 'is not any bargain.' "

Hoover may have wanted to investigate Pauling, but he could not. While the FBI's ability to gather information on Americans had been extended through the loyalty oath program to hundreds of thousands of federal employees, including professors who received federal grants and contracts, it was not unlimited. Pauling had not been involved in any classified research since the end of the war, had not applied for federal grants, and as a researcher in a private university was currently immune from scrutiny under Executive Order 9835.

But that changed as soon as Pauling settled in London, where he was quickly approached by a representative of the Office of the Assistant Naval Attaché for Research. It was in America's interests to keep abreast of the state of British science, the young officer said, and it would be useful if Pauling could let the navy know his impressions of the labs he visited—nothing proprietary, the officer told him, nothing that would involve breaking confidences, just his general observations of the state of British science. For his role as a consultant to the government, they would pay him fifty dollars a day. All that was required was that he sign a contract. The moment Pauling signed, he became subject to the loyalty program, and the FBI began reviewing his political history.

Much of the bureau's work was easy, as Pauling never made a secret of any of his affiliations. The agents cross-checked his name in their files and came across a 1947 interview they had done with Pauling regarding the loyalty of J. Robert Oppenheimer, another scientist with a suspiciously liberal background. Pauling, who called himself a "close friend" of Oppenheimer's, told the FBI that Oppy was "volatile, complex and brilliant" and that he was certain of his loyalty to the United States. The discussion then turned to Oppenheimer's political activity, and Pauling began talking at length about his own work with the Association of Pasadena Scientists (APS), the ICCASP, the Progressive Citizens of America (PCA), and his support of Wallace. The interviewing agent noted in his report that a confidential source had called the Hollywood chapter of the ICCASP the "main political and propaganda pressure group of the Communist Party in California" and that the PCA was rife with Communists and Communist-fronters.

The FBI then borrowed the Pauling file HUAC had collected, rich with clippings from the *Daily Worker* and other Communist newspapers. There were "innumerable references," the FBI found, to Pauling's speeches on atomic policy and human rights. It was all suspicious, they thought, but the only proscribed activity under the rules of the loyalty program was Pauling's wartime flirtation with the National Council of American-Soviet Friendship, a group that had since been put on the attorney general's blacklist.

Still, it was enough for Hoover to order a full-scale field investigation. He asked the Office of Naval Intelligence to track Pauling's activities in England. He ordered FBI agents to check police and credit files and interview associates in Berkeley and Cornell. He had the Los Angeles FBI field office coordinate an investigation in Pasadena. Agents quizzed Pauling's coworkers, neighbors, and Caltech administrators. They were given permission to look through his private Caltech personnel file.

They found nothing. Everyone they spoke to defended Pauling's loyalty without reservation. His colleagues agreed that while Pauling was "very frank in his observations," "a joiner," and "an idealist who believed in the free expression of ideas," he was no Communist. The worst anyone would tell the FBI was that Pauling was "an exhibitionist" and "an intellectual parlor pink." The Los Angeles FBI office let the investigation drag on through the summer of 1948, until Hoover himself telegrammed that Pauling's was "among the most delinquent loyalty investigations in the Bureau." On September 10, a twenty-seven-page report was finally finished, and on October 14, Hoover forwarded it to the Civil Service Commission for further action.

He was too late. Pauling's contract with the navy had expired on September 1, and he was no longer subject to Executive Order 9835. Its interest renewed by the FBI investigation, HUAC—still looking for a prime scientific target—might have mounted a public investigation if J. Parnell Thomas had still been in charge. But Thomas was gone, convicted of payroll padding and sent to prison just after the 1948 elections. Hoover tried another tack, sending Pauling's report to the attorney general's office for possible criminal action. The attorney general could find no violation of the law.

The FBI investigation was over by the time Pauling returned to the United States from Oxford. When he reached Pasadena, he heard from his colleagues the unnerving news that agents had been asking questions about him, but then agents were asking questions about a number of scientists at the time, especially those involved in atomic weapons research. Pauling shrugged it off.

Ironically, as Hoover was trying to impugn Pauling's loyalty, others were honoring it. As the FBI worked to find some reason to bring him up on criminal charges, Pauling stood with four other faculty members at a special Caltech ceremony in October 1948 to receive a Presidential Medal for Merit, the highest civilian award given by the government. The citation, signed by Harry Truman, noted Pauling's "imaginative mind," his "brilliant success" with rocket powders and explosives, the oxygen meter and serum substitutes, and his "exceptionally meritorious conduct in the performance of outstanding service to the United States." Pauling was extremely proud to receive the honor.

—✒—

It was the last he would receive from the federal government for a quarter century. The nation was turning to the right. Truman's federal loyalty program was being supplemented by sometimes more repressive state-enacted loyalty oaths that extended the reach from federal employees to hundreds of thousands of state and municipal workers. The hunt was on not for spies and Communists alone but for citizens who criticized America's foreign or domestic policies and so, it seemed to witch-hunters, did the work of the Kremlin. Any statement against U.S. policy, especially from the left, was cause for suspicion. Evidence of criminal subversion was pushed aside in favor of attacking those who merely associated with the wrong groups. Dean Acheson, who endured a maelstrom of anti-Communist rhetoric during his confirmation hearings for secretary of state in early 1949, called it "the attack of the primitives." The pressure had its effect. It was becoming too dangerous to be a critic or a spokesperson for liberal causes. People stopped making their opinions known publicly. But not Pauling.

Even as it became dangerous to associate with any vaguely left wing group in 1949, he was writing, "[I]ndividuals, such as myself, must learn to get along with Communists. . . . I know extremely few people who are recognized as Communists; but I do belong to a number of organizations that have been described as Communist-front organizations, and I have been interested to see how well the members of these organizations find it possible to get along with one another. . . . I have been encouraged by my own experiences, to the extent that they do represent collaboration between Communists and non-Communists, to believe that the peoples of the world will ultimately find it possible to get along together, through the formation of an effective world government."

As the ranks of America's liberal-left political action groups continued to thin, Pauling's national stature and visibility grew. He became a champion for what remained of the Left, a respected scientist who was unafraid to speak out, sign petitions, and sponsor meetings. Increasingly, any group looking for a public name to support a liberal cause came to Pauling. Despite his atheistic tendencies, he was asked and agreed to help welcome the "Red Dean of Canterbury"—as the press had dubbed Britain's Communist party member the Right Reverend Hewlett Johnson—to the United States in the face of a right-wing protest aimed at barring his entry. Pauling received extensive newspaper coverage for his daring act of shaking Johnson's hand (but he was disappointed to find the Red Dean little more than a "stuffy old ecclesiastic"). Pauling sponsored a national conference to discuss the erosion of civil liberties and another against deportation hysteria. He donated money to the Alger Hiss defense fund. He spoke out against the persecution of eleven leaders of the U.S. Communist party on trial in New York, exhorting a crowd in Los Angeles to "fight the witch hunt and the Communist scare."

The loyalty program and its effects were especially galling. In the spring of 1949, Pauling took on the president of his alma mater, now called Oregon State College (OSC), over a loyalty case involving one of Pauling's former students, Ralph Spitzer. Spitzer had been teaching chemistry at OSC on a year-to-year contract when the college's president, A. L. Strand, fired him, using as an excuse a letter Spitzer had written to a science journal in which he argued that researchers should read and analyze the original work of the Russian geneticist T. D. Lysenko before attacking his work. But Spitzer, believing the real reason for his firing was that the president did not like Spitzer's support of Wallace and promotion of the Progressive cause among students, fought the dismissal, causing a small storm of controversy. Strand refused to reconsider, noting Spitzer's "devotion to the party line" and the "Soviet propaganda which he and his wife have promoted on the campus." Local papers supported the president, noting that "infiltration by Reds and fellow travelers in college faculties to influence the youth merits a purge of the termites." The case earned national headlines when Henry Wallace protested the firings. Strand shot back that Wallace was "intellectually dishonest." When Pauling wrote strong letters of protest, both as an alumnus and the president of the American Chemical Society (ACS), Strand took him on as well. "I would have been surprised if you had taken any other view than that which you have expressed," he wrote Pauling. "If by this action OSC has lost your respect and support, all I can say is that your price is too high. We'll have to get along without your aid." Spitzer took his case to the American Association of University Professors, but the group, concerned with being seen as too "pink," refused to back him up. Unable to get another job in chemistry, Spitzer eventually quit the field, left the country, and started a new life in Canada.

At the same time, and closer to home, the regents of the University of California announced a new loyalty oath system for employees in the spring of 1949, both to counter the public impression—fostered by much-ballyhooed HUAC and local legislative investigations—that they harbored Reds in their Berkeley atomic research establishment and to forestall what they saw as a more repressive loyalty oath program being proposed in the state legislature. The regents' plan was to have faculty members swear in writing that they were not members of the Communist party.

While most faculty members were compliant, a number refused to sign the oath. Various negotiations between the faculty and the regents shrank the number of nonsigners until only a handful were left; these were dismissed for the infraction of wanting to keep their political views private. One of them was John O'Gorman, another of Pauling's former students, who was relieved of his teaching position at UC Santa Barbara. A highly skilled chemist, O'Gorman spent a year as a hired hand on a ranch while looking for other work. Pauling helped him as much as he could, writing strong letters of recommendation and giving O'Gorman encouragement, but his academic career was irrevocably delayed.

Spitzer, O'Gorman, and a dozen other researchers who contacted Pauling after being thrown out of work because of their political beliefs made clear the human toll of the anti-Communist campaign. Seeing a series of scientific careers ruined because of the loyalty program toughened Pauling's commitment to fighting it. Without exception, he tried to help any scientist who came to him with a complaint of being unfairly treated because of the witch-hunts. He did not hire any of the men himself—he was extremely selective in choosing his research group and sensitive to the likelihood that the Caltech board of trustees would veto a politically controversial hire—but he did write dozens of letters of recommendation, using his pull as American Chemical Society president and as a well-known researcher to find work for them. It was almost impossible. Once a researcher, especially a young scientist just beginning a career, was labeled a security risk, a loyalty oath refusenik, or a pinko, most institutions refused to hire him. The risks were too great, especially for any laboratory receiving federal funds and therefore subject to the loyalty program—which, after the war, meant the majority of university labs. It was a situation analogous to that faced by blacklisted writers and directors in the movie industry, but it involved many more people and much less publicity. A few of the blacklisted scientists found work in private industrial laboratories. Others—dozens, scores, perhaps hundreds, no one knows how many—gave up.

Pauling began speaking out against the loyalty oath system whenever he could. In May 1949 he sat on an American Civil Liberties Union (ACLU) panel on academic freedom in Los Angeles, where he stated in front of reporters that he did not think teachers should be dismissed for any reason other than not doing their job—simply being a Communist, in other words, was not reason enough. The *L.A. Times* attacked Pauling's stand in an editorial, reasoning that "nobody can be a Communist and exercise academic freedom." The headline in the Pasadena paper read: "Pauling OKs Red Teachers."

In the fall of 1949, Pauling announced that he would sponsor and lead the U.S. delegation to the controversial American Continental Conference for World Peace to be held in Mexico City, a gathering of delegates from all over the Western Hemisphere designed to address the growing tension between the United States and the USSR. The conference was promptly—and, it was later shown, correctly—criticized as Communist-inspired and -organized, but that, of course, did not bother the Paulings. They loved Mexico City—Ava Helen was becoming an admirer of folk art from around the world and spent time combing the *mercados* for pieces to add to her collection—but were less enthusiastic about the meeting, which seemed to consist of speech after long-winded speech defending the Soviet Union and attacking the United States. When it came Pauling's turn, he typically went his own way. His keynote address ranged from standard socialist anti-imperialism—"We see the smaller nations of the world forced effectively to abandon their national sovereignty through the exercise of economic pressure by a rich and powerful neighbor engaged in a program of monopolistic industrial expansion and economic empire-building"—to a purposeful and carefully evenhanded denouncement of both the United States' and the USSR's policies of curtailing freedom and preparing for war. The audience, expecting another one-sided attack on the Yankees, responded with lukewarm applause.

Witch-hunts aside, there were plenty of reasons to be fearful. Three weeks after the Mexico City conference, it was announced that the Russians had successfully tested their own atomic bomb. One week after that, on October 1, 1949, the People's Republic of China was officially established, bringing the world's most populous nation under Communist control.

The Cold War began in earnest that fall, and American politicians raced to see who could make the most out of it. The Republicans blamed the "loss of China" on shortcomings in the Democrat-run State Department, possibly due to subversive influences, kicking off an internal purge that would rid State of its last New Dealers and bring a new right-wing slant to American foreign policy.

The Soviet bomb was even more frightening. In a flash it seemed that America's atomic security blanket, its only counterbalance to the huge Soviet army, had been ripped away. It was forgotten that America's atomic scientists had been telling everyone for years that it was only a matter of time until the USSR had the bomb. The cold warriors insisted that there had to be espionage involved, and the hunt was on for atomic spies. The media played up every new rumor. More than ever, it was open season on Reds and Red sympathizers.

By 1950 the combination of world events and domestic anticommunism had shifted the majority of liberals to a new, more "tough-minded" set of beliefs. But Pauling changed neither his message nor the manner in which it was delivered. The Chinese people had a right to determine their own method of government, through revolution if necessary, he insisted. The Soviet atomic bomb was not a threat, he said, but "a warning to the people of the world and a potent incentive to the nations of the world to resume negotiations, through the United Nations organization, for the establishment of an effective system of international control of atomic energy."

As others melted away from the old causes, Pauling became a target. In California, the Tenney Committee's file on him grew fat with newspaper reports of his speeches on atomic energy and civil rights. Many of the clippings were from the Communist press, papers like the *Daily Worker*—a major source of information for committee researchers—that carried glowing reports each time Pauling gave a speech or participated in a protest. By late 1949, the Tenney Committee had decided Pauling was a leader of "the California agitation."

Pauling's file was shared enthusiastically with the FBI and the anti-Communist press, and Pauling's name began to appear regularly in right-wing lists of suspected Reds. Stubbornly independent, secure in his work, and confident that he was right, Pauling ignored it all.

Proper Restraint

But Caltech's president, Lee DuBridge, could not. The son of a YMCA athletics instructor from the Midwest, DuBridge, according to one science historian, was a man with "simple tastes, boundless energy, and an uncomplicated eagerness to do something important." DuBridge was relatively young—just Pauling's age—slight, a bit boyish-looking, a good fund-raiser, an outstanding administrator with strong Washington connections, and a man whose enormous self-confidence matched even Pauling's. Of his wartime success guiding the Rad Lab, for example, he was fond of saying, "The atom bomb only ended the war. Radar won it."

After arriving to great fanfare, DuBridge threw himself into modernizing Caltech. He started by rethinking the institute's creaky administrative system, quickly disbanding the joint faculty-trustee Executive Council in which Pauling had been prominent and replacing it with a separate board of trustees and a committee of division chairmen with reduced power. This was a mixed blessing for Pauling, effectively stripping him of much of the institutional influence he had enjoyed since the end of the war but also freeing him from unwanted administrative duties. DuBridge then won the hearts of the faculty by streamlining and updating Millikan's idiosyncratic salary system, giving almost everyone a 30 percent raise. It was the start, remembered one Caltech chemistry professor, of "a golden era."

Pauling withheld judgment. He had known DuBridge since the 1920s, when the young physicist had come to Caltech for two years as a National Research Council (NRC) fellow. Although not close friends, they were on a first-name basis, saw each other socially, and admired each other professionally.

Whatever warmth there had been, however, began to cool soon after DuBridge arrived. Pauling and the new president simply did not get along well. Part of the reason was scientific. DuBridge was a physicist, and he put a great deal of effort and money into revitalizing the Caltech physics division, which had lost its preeminent position under the aging Millikan. He was less comfortable with chemistry, and especially with Pauling's approach to it. Millikan and many of the older trustees would have given DuBridge an unflattering version of Pauling's actions around the time of Noyes's death, and the new president was also able to talk with Tolman, Yost, and other Noyes-era faculty members unhappy with Pauling's commitment to chemical biology, a fascination, they thought, that was taking the division too far from its roots in physical chemistry. There was a feeling that Pauling worked hard to get funding for only his own pet projects, making poor relations of chemical engineering and inorganic chemistry. DuBridge would also have heard about Pauling's troubled foray into immunology and ongoing difficulty in producing artificial antibodies.

So, while DuBridge publicly called Pauling's and Beadle's grand plan to mount a joint chemical-biological attack on the molecular basis of life "one of the most important enterprises in the country," privately he was cool toward Pauling's scheme. When Pauling wrote him enthusiastically about angling for a huge bequest to fund a basic research attack on cancer, for instance, DuBridge's initial thought was to make sure that physical chemistry and chemical engineering were funded first. Pauling understood quickly that he did not have DuBridge's full confidence, and the relationship between the two men became reserved and somewhat distant.

Politics also came between the president and his chemistry chairman. Although raised in a Republican household, DuBridge considered himself a liberal and proved it by fighting hard against early drafts of the May-Johnson bill, supporting the dissemination of information by the Federation of Atomic Scientists (FAS) about the atomic bomb and speaking out strongly against the witch-hunts. He was for peace as much as the next man and thought there was a role for scientists in bringing it about. "It is not the job of the scientist to be primarily a politician, a sociologist, a military leader or a preacher," he told the audience in a Caltech commencement speech in 1947. But "the scientist or engineer—like every other human being—bears also the responsibility of being a useful member of his community... and should speak on issues which can be addressed with competence—including joining hands with other citizens when called to tasks of peace."

That sounded good to Pauling, but DuBridge's politics was tempered by his skill as a consummate team player. A president had to be, and DuBridge shuttled easily between conservative Caltech trustees, liberal faculty, and numerous governmental and scientific advisory groups. He became an archetypal postwar insider-scientist, a man at home in classroom, boardroom, laboratory, and government office. From that standpoint, he realized that there had to be some rules, even if unspoken, guiding the political activities of scientists. In the years following the war, the American public—dazzled by the magic of atomic power, worried about enormous questions of national security, and concerned about the technical details of arms development—asked scientists for answers. For a time, scientists were thought of as mental supermen, and their opinions were given special attention.

In DuBridge's mind, that also conferred on researchers what he called "special obligations." He wrote his faculty soon after arriving as president that Caltech was not in the business of censoring the right of its scientists to speak as private citizens, but warned that they should strive to be accurate and balanced, and exercise "proper restraint." Special care should be taken to ensure that private opinions were not confused with institutional positions. If these guidelines were followed by a faculty member, he wrote, "the Institute is prepared to defend his freedom of speech, of teaching, and of research."

The key phrase was "proper restraint." When the Cold War swung into full gear, the vast majority of scientists translated the phrase as "silence." By 1949, scientists, like everyone else, were having second thoughts about any political action that could be perceived as left-wing. No one talked about them, but most researchers began observing a set of unwritten rules: If possible, confine your political activities to the Washington advisory system; limit political activities to a small proportion of your time; restrict your comments to your areas of expertise; keep your political opinions moderate. As long as everyone played by the rules, the relationship between science, government, and the public would be smooth, and money would continue to flow.

—*wm*—

By DuBridge's definition, Pauling seemed incapable of proper restraint. And DuBridge began to hear about it. As early as 1946, Reese Taylor, the conservatively inclined executive vice president of Consolidated Steel and an important Caltech trustee, began complaining about Pauling. One month after DuBridge started his presidency, Taylor sent him a clip of a newspaper ad signed by supporters of Henry Wallace. He highlighted Pauling's name and noted, "I do question the propriety of prominent members of the faculty of a privately endowed institution participating publicly in politics on any side." DuBridge replied that while it would be wrong for him as Caltech's president to participate in any way directly in political activities, "I cannot in conscience deny this privilege to members of the faculty serving in their private capacity as citizens." He then assured Taylor, "I do not, myself, at all agree with the statement which Dr. Pauling signed."

As Pauling became increasingly visible off campus, a group of trustees, most prominently Taylor, Herbert Hoover, Jr., and John McCone, became increasingly angered by his political statements and concerned about what they thought these statements meant for Caltech. There was talk of disciplining Pauling, perhaps firing him. But DuBridge, supported by the head of the board, Jim Page, cautioned patience. Right now he might seem a bit off-track, they said, but give him time to come around. DuBridge called Pauling to his office and spoke to him privately, asking him to be more moderate in his public pronouncements and cautioning him to leave the institute's name out of it when he spoke politically. It was a chilly meeting. Pauling thought DuBridge was using euphemisms to mask the real issue, which was Pauling's right to speak as he saw fit. DuBridge saw Pauling as an inflexible character with a rigid political agenda and a love of seeing his own name in print.

Within Caltech, Pauling scrupulously divided his roles as teacher and activist, making certain that he never mentioned politics in class and asking that his Caltech affiliation not be used in publicity for his political talks. But inevitably there were problems. When invited by a Caltech student group to give a talk on world government, Pauling accepted, reasoning that it was on his own time and constituted an extracurricular activity, although it obviously mixed politics and academia. Occasionally, an endorsement of, or advertisement for, one of his political speeches would slip by with his Caltech title on it.

Increasingly, it was becoming impossible for Pauling to keep his political and professional lives completely separate. In the late 1940s the press learned that he was a good story and began covering him in earnest. Whenever the reporters mentioned one of Pauling's talks, he was always identified as a Caltech professor and head of the chemistry division.

That was true of the coverage of his 1949 speech in Mexico City. When Reese Taylor heard a conservative radio commentator ranting about Pauling's attendance, he wrote Page and DuBridge demanding to know why, if Pauling was not a Communist, he was speaking at such a gathering. Page and DuBridge tried to calm Taylor again, but they, too, were growing uncomfortable with Pauling's outspokenness. DuBridge was now being peppered with letters complaining about Pauling. When the president of a local sash-and-balance company asked why Caltech had this Communist on the faculty, DuBridge tried a new tack, sending Pauling out to dine with him and demonstrate firsthand that he was not a dangerous radical. Pauling tried to keep the luncheon conversation apolitical, turning it to his ideas about medical research and lobbying for a donation. Pauling thought it had gone well. Then the businessman wrote him a note: "Remember my friendly warning: Don't get too far out on a limb with some of these 'questionable' groups. Some of us have saws and can use them."

―――

In 1950 things only got worse. A string of revelations shocked the public and intensified the Cold War: the perjury conviction of Alger Hiss on January 21; the public disclosure of British physicist Klaus Fuchs's atomic spying on February 3; and Joe McCarthy's waving of a list of 205 alleged Communists in the State Department a few days later, a publicity stunt that gave the junior senator from Minnesota his first national headlines. In April, the National Security Council (NSC) recommended a massive military buildup to contain communism and counter the growing threat of atomic espionage.

But far the worst of all, to Pauling and the remaining FAS scientists—the group's membership had shrunk to half its level of four years before—was Truman's announcement in January that the United States was going to develop a "super bomb" to maintain the American weapons advantage. It was top secret, but Pauling quickly put together enough information to learn that its energy would come not from tear-ing atoms apart, as in an old-style atomic bomb, but from fusing light atoms together. Hydrogen was the likeliest energy source, and the new weapon was quickly dubbed the hydrogen bomb. "An H-bomb consists of an old-fashioned atomic bomb surrounded by a ton, or perhaps ten tons or more, of hydrogen or other light elements, the nuclei of which can fuse together to form heavier nuclei, with the liberation of around five times as much energy, on a weight basis, as in a fission bomb," Pauling told a radio audience in May. There was, he told his listeners, no theoretical limit to its power.

To Pauling, Einstein, and most of the members of the Emergency Committee of Atomic Scientists, the development of the H-bomb did not change the basic rules of the atomic war game —it was still irra-tional and unthinkable—but it needlessly upped the stakes. There was to be more money thrown away on killing more people. By now, how-ever, even the emergency committee was splitting apart. The Nobel Prize–winning chemist and staunch liberal Harold Urey broke ranks, unhappily concluding that the Russians would build the H-bomb if the United States did not. "We should not intentionally lose the arma-ments race," he concluded. Pauling's reply was simple—"Harold—you're wrong," he was quoted as saying in the *Daily Worker*—but the damage had been done. Pauling and Leo Szilard considered forming a new committee without Urey, but it looked like too much work, too much time for members already tired after years of fighting. Einstein wanted to keep the committee going, but the other members were ready to drop it. What good was it doing? The information and warn-ings they had been issuing were doing little good. Donations were dry-ing up. In the end, the emergency committee voted to disband.

The threat of the new bomb seemed only to reenergize Pauling. Public discussion of the enormous destructive capabilities of the H-bomb had led to a new concern about a senseless arms race with Russia, and new audiences began listening to Pauling's message of peace and international cooperation. On February 13, 1950, he gave one of his finest political speeches to a packed Carnegie Hall peace rally, calling for negotiations with the USSR and advising Congress to appropriate millions of dollars to the National Science Foundation for studies into the causes and prevention of war. "The problem of an atomic war must not be confused by minor problems such as Commu-nism versus capitalism," he said. "An atomic war would kill everyone, left, right, or center." His voice gaining strength, he exhorted the thou-sands of activists: "The world has finally come to the critical point in time at which the ultimate, irrevocable decision has to be made. This is the decision between, on the one hand, a glorious future for all humanity, and, on the other, death, devastation, and the complete destruction of civilization." At the end, he looked over the hall, drinking in the thunderous applause that rolled over him. He was not alone, after all.

Through the spring of 1950 he spoke to group after group about the arms race, the need for peace, and the new bomb and what it meant to the world. He always ended with a call for negotiations with the USSR and the need for world government.

Every talk was monitored by reporters for the anti-Communist press, by local informants for the California Committee on Un-American Activities (still called the Tenney Committee, although Tenney had given up its chairmanship to an equally fervent anti-Communist legislator) or by the FBI. The FBI's interest in Pauling had been piqued again in February, when naval intelligence sent them an anonymous note from an informant—perhaps one of Pauling's neighbors—who claimed to have seen "high-powered radio equipment" filling one wall of the Paulings' garage. "Maybe some of these proffessors [*sic*] could stand a little secret investigation," the informant suggested. Although the spy equipment turned out to be a ham-radio outfit operated by one of Pauling's sons, the FBI was back on his case. Hoover was especially interested in a talk Pauling gave to a small audience organized by the Pasadena Non-Partisan Committee for Peace on May 18. A reporter for the right-wing publication *Alert* sent the FBI's Los Angeles office a memo noting that Pauling "went into extensive details as to how the atomic bomb was made and later described how the H-bomb was made." An FBI agent was dispatched to his Caltech office to quiz him about the sources of his information. Pauling told the truth: He had read enough in public documents and published scientific reports to figure it out on his own. Hoover then suggested to the Atomic Energy Commission (AEC) that Pauling may have violated national security. AEC representatives looked over the notes of the speech and were not worried. The estimates had been so vague, they told Hoover, that it did not appear that any security restrictions had been violated.

Rabid

The FBI could not nail Pauling, but they were about to make a case against someone close to him. Sidney Weinbaum, a Pauling research assistant for fifteen years, was a Communist. Pauling had hired him in the late 1920s to make the complex mathematical calculations needed to solve crystal structures, and Weinbaum was good at it, a meticulous "human computer," as they were later called. He was interesting, besides, an accomplished pianist and two-time chess champion of Los Angeles, yet happy to work in Pauling's shadow, carefully filling research books with his neat, spidery computations. Pauling was always friendly, in a boss-worker sort of way, inviting Weinbaum and his wife over to the house for parties. But according to Weinbaum, they never talked politics.

That, it turned out, was a good thing. The son of Russian Jews who had fled the Revolution, Weinbaum became a leftist radical in the 1930s, joining a "Communist club" at Caltech, where he had plenty of opportunity to talk politics with other students and young faculty. He quit the group in 1941, then two years later quit Pauling's lab to work in the aviation industry. After the war he found a job at Caltech's Jet Propulsion Laboratory (JPL).

In 1949, Weinbaum's past caught up with him. He had held a security clearance for classified work ever since the war, but now his clearance was denied when it was discovered that he had had questionable contacts in his youth. The JPL immediately dropped him. Pauling took him back into his lab to work on unclassified material while Caltech appealed the case to a military review board, where Weinbaum testified that he had never been a Communist. The FBI knew better and pressured him to name names, hoping to uncover a Caltech spy ring. When he refused, he was arrested on perjury charges in the spring of 1950.

The case created a small sensation in Southern California. Although no espionage was ever proved, Weinbaum, because of his work at the top-secret JPL, was the closest thing Southern California had to a Communist spy, and his case made local headlines almost daily.

Out on bail awaiting trial, Weinbaum came to Pauling for help, "distraught," Pauling remembered, with very little money to support his wife and young daughter. Weinbaum told Pauling that his wife, Lena, whom Pauling and Ava Helen knew was high-strung, was not taking the strain well. Pauling promised that he would help raise money to cover legal costs and began working with other faculty members to build a legal defense fund.

The Weinbaum-Pauling link was all that some of the more conservative members of the Caltech Board needed to convince them that Pauling himself was a Communist. They went to DuBridge and insisted that something be done about him before more bad publicity hit the school. "What the Institute had at that time were some people who were just so opposed to Communism that they were almost rabid on it," remembered Arnold Beckman, a trustee then. "And Linus's behavior bothered them a great deal, particularly when Sidney Weinbaum was accused and then convicted of being a Communist, and he was one of Linus's close friends. So many people thought Linus was a Communist. And Linus, being the independent character he is, didn't do anything to mollify them." Jim Page and DuBridge continued to advise moderation and patience, asking that the board wait for proof. DuBridge told the board that if it was ever proven that any Caltech faculty member was a Communist Party member, he would fire him on the spot—party members, after all, were under discipline and could not be expected to tell the truth to their students—but that the case had not been proven against Pauling. The issue split the board between those who wanted Pauling fired and those who wanted to wait. "I don't know of any issue that divided them quite as strongly as that," Beckman recalled.

It was a disaster for DuBridge no matter how it turned out. On the one hand, Pauling's recent work, especially the sickle-cell hemoglobin results and the whole idea of molecular disease, was bringing his scientific reputation—and, by association, that of Caltech—to new heights. Getting rid of junior faculty was one thing, but no American scientist of Pauling's stature had ever been fired because of politics; any public move against him would certainly raise a storm of criticism within the international scientific community. On the other hand, doing nothing would enrage some important trustees and make it appear that DuBridge was soft on Communists. He placated the trustees and bought some time by monitoring the Weinbaum trial through the spring for any hints that Pauling might have been involved with the Communist Party. There were none.

Then, on June 25, 1950, Weinbaum was pushed off the front pages when Communist North Korea invaded the south. Two days later, Harry Truman announced that the United States would send in troops to repel the Reds, setting off a new round of anti-Communist fervor. The Cold War had turned hot. This was no time to coddle possible traitors.

Two days after Truman committed U.S. troops to Korea, the Caltech board of trustees moved in private to appoint a committee "to investigate and report to the board whether Dr. Pauling's services are detrimental to the Institute, and whether his appointment should be terminated." Concerned that a committee comprised solely of businessmen might be seen as one-sided, DuBridge set up a parallel committee of faculty members to provide an independent check. It was all to be done secretly and quickly. It was a way, DuBridge hoped, to close the issue without any publicity. It was the first time Caltech had ever run an internal political investigation.

—⁓⁓—

The same day, a secret panel met in a nondescript room in Washington, D.C. Before them sat a pale, nervous white-haired man in a dark suit. He was a paid FBI informer named Louis Budenz. He was naming names.

Budenz, a former Communist Party member and managing editor of the *Daily Worker,* had already earned national fame and a fair amount of money testifying against his old comrades. After opening his heart to HUAC in 1946, Budenz spent three thousand hours "consulting" with the FBI, then went on the "I was a former Communist" lecture circuit and began writing books about the internal Red threat. It was a decent living, but one that required coming up with new revelations every once in a while. And Budenz, like many caught up in the anti-Communist craze, had a habit of taking things a little too far. In one of his books, *Men Without Faces,* he had claimed to know the identities of four hundred "concealed Communists" in high places in American society. The panel he faced in Washington, D.C., on that June day in 1950 wanted all four hundred names. After running through all of the real Communists he knew, Budenz began listing anyone he could think of who might possibly be a Communist. One of the names was Linus Pauling.

His testimony was kept out of the papers while J. Edgar Hoover ran checks on the named individuals. The FBI found Budenz's testimony about Pauling particularly satisfying; with a sworn statement like this, the FBI was now free to work outside of the loyalty program restrictions. Hoover ordered another full-scale investigation of Pauling. For three months, through the summer and early fall of 1950, his agents attended Pauling's speeches; grilled his associates; combed through his Caltech personnel file; photocopied his Tenney Committee file; checked with HUAC, where the researchers had thickened their own Pauling dossier with thirty-five recent clips from the *Daily People's World;* took another look at their files on the Red Dean of Canterbury visit; reviewed his support of Weinbaum; and cross-checked every group he had joined against "known Communist fronts."

They could find no evidence of membership in the Communist Party. Hoover again could not take any legal action, but when the twenty-seven-page FBI report was completed on October 17, he recommended that Pauling's name be placed on the agency's Security Index, the newly created list of America's highest-profile "fellow travelers," people whom Hoover deemed dangerous to national security. The index had been created in response to the recently passed Internal Security Act, legislation that gave the government unprecedented peacetime powers to control internal political activities. Those on the FBI's index would be monitored constantly, and their files would be updated every six months.

‑‑‑‑

A week after the FBI report was completed, Pauling got a call from a wire-service reporter. "Are the charges true that Senator McCarthy leveled at you?" the reporter asked. Pauling had heard nothing of any charges. "He called you a security risk, along with six other Communist-linked atomic scientists," the reporter said. "He said you had a 'well nigh incredible record' of membership in Communist-front organizations. Is that true?" Pauling had been watching the meteoric rise of McCarthy, an ascent fueled by flimsy and outrageous accusations eagerly spread by the press. He had not heard of any charges, he repeated. "I have been working in support of the international policy that would lead to peace and avert an atomic war, and I assume that that is what Senator McCarthy is referring to."

His name was in every major paper in the nation the next day. "McCarthy Says Reds Infiltrate Atom Projects," blared the *New York Herald Tribune*. This was a random shot by McCarthy, with Pauling's name pulled from the Budenz testimony and inserted among the names of researchers who were actually working on bomb projects. The charges were vague, no evidence was presented, and nothing more would come of it; after the headlines were made, the senator would swivel his sights to other targets.

But the damage had been done. Pauling was now nationally infamous as a security threat and a defender of communism while American boys were dying in Korea. He could handle the resulting hate mail—there had been crank letters every so often since the Japanese-American incident at the war's end—but then something more disturbing happened. A letter arrived from the Eli Lilly pharmaceutical company, a group that Pauling had served as a consultant since 1946.

In 1949 the company had renewed Pauling's contract for three years and raised his payment to $4,800 annually, a significant sum for the limited consulting he did, but a salary warranted by his "exceptional service." Now, barely a year later, they told him that his contract was being canceled. "No reason was given in the letter," Pauling said. "But I was later told by the assistant director of research and the former director of research that the contract had been cancelled because of my political activities, and that if I were to state that I would in the future refrain from all political activities, it was probable that the contract could be reinstated."

It was not the only indication that his politics would affect his scientific work. That same year, the head of the chemistry branch of the Office of Naval Research (ONR) had invited Pauling to chair a committee that would review the progress of chemical investigations funded by the ONR and help formulate new directions for research. It was a prestigious post. But the ONR commander in Pasadena protested when he found out about the invitation, sending his superiors a ten-point list of Pauling's Communist-front associations culled from ONR and FBI files. "Having a person of questionable loyalty as the chairman of this ONR committee is most undesirable," the commander wrote, not only because of possible espionage but also because the ONR would be placed "in a most embarrassing position" if a congressional investigation revealed that the navy had named a "fellow traveler" to a sensitive position. The head of the chemistry branch, greatly embarrassed, was forced to withdraw the invitation.

─ⅿⅿ─

The Caltech internal investigation dragged on through the fall. The Paulings tried to carry on life as usual, but it was increasingly difficult. Pauling took refuge in his molecular structures and newly refined protein models. He and Ava Helen continued to go to faculty functions and parties. Most of their friends saw the political pressure for what it was and tried to help the Paulings laugh it off, but there was a coolness among others, and it was getting worse. After Weinbaum was convicted of perjury and sent to prison, Pauling noticed people looking away when he passed them on campus, becoming distant, especially during the time of the internal investigation. Pauling was a man of many acquaintances but few close friends; still, he depended on being liked and respected by his colleagues. When he saw them avoiding him, it hurt.

The pressure of being investigated by his own school, the hate mail, the loss of the Lilly contract, the hostility on campus, all began to add up. Pauling never showed his concern in public, but Ava Helen could tell that her husband was suffering. And she was, too. Soon after the McCarthy allegations a friendly former student asked her at a faculty tea how she was doing. For a moment her composure broke, and Ava Helen's eyes filled with tears. "I don't know how my husband can hold up much longer," she said.

The internal investigation finally closed that fall. The two committees found no evidence of Communist Party membership or malfeasance of any sort. Although some trustees still felt strongly that Pauling should be fired, the faculty committee made a solid case for keeping him on, arguing that discharging him without evidence of wrongdoing would not only lose the school one of the world's leading chemists but would be seen as disgraceful behavior by scientists around the world. From DuBridge's standpoint, the investigation was a success: It both channeled the anger of conservative trustees and gave him what he needed to defend Pauling. When he received yet another letter asking why he did not cleanse his institute of Pauling and other Reds, DuBridge could explain that Pauling had been cleared of wrongdoing and could add, "I hope in this country we have not come to the place where a man is persecuted for holding unpopular political beliefs."

To Convince Him of His Errors

But the country had come to such a place—even if Pauling behaved as if it had not. Through 1950 he continued his political activities as if nothing had happened: Raising money for Sidney Weinbaum's defense (although he was out of town for most of the trial, thus avoiding testifying); agreeing to serve as a parole adviser for the Hollywood Ten writer Dalton Trumbo; joining the American Association of Scientific Workers, an offshoot of a leftist international organization headed by the French atomic scientist Frédéric Joliot-Curie, who was a Communist; maintaining his leading role in the Progressive Citizens of America and the Arts, Sciences, and Professions board; and continuing to speak widely on the same topics that had gotten him in trouble.

During this period, he was one of a very small group of American public figures who remained outspoken in their dedication to peace and civil rights causes, taking a personal and professional risk that millions of others easily avoided. And he did this despite a natural tendency to the contrary. He would have loved to have spent his time exclusively on science, avoiding any political controversy in favor of solving nature's puzzles and enjoying the personal satisfaction, stature, money, and accolades it brought him. Scientifically, at least, Pauling was no rebel. He was daring in the way he crossed disciplinary boundaries, but his daring was rooted in the fundamental norms and expectations of his profession. He succeeded not because he battled the scientific establishment but because he worked well within it, laboring harder and pushing his ideas further than others. He wanted very much, in fact, to be a part of the establishment. He wanted—and in some ways needed—the accolades, the awards and prizes, bestowed by the academy and professional societies. In this way, he would later say, he was a conformist.

His political work, by contrast, appeared distinctly nonconformist. Here he battled the establishment, openly and defiantly. As he put it, during the McCarthy period "there were two qualities of my personality pushing in opposite directions: the one to conform, and the other to rely on my own assessment of the situation."

In the political arena, his desire to fit in was overcome by something more powerful: his belief in himself. On one level, he could say simply, as he often did during this period, "I felt that it was my duty as a citizen of the United States of America and as a scientist to take part in politics." But deep within he had to justify the risks he was taking, the stress to which he was subjecting himself and his family. He thought hard about his political convictions, and he thought about them like a scientist.

Pauling was a product of the Enlightenment, as were all scientists. Like many Enlightenment philosophers, he had replaced God with Reason, and he believed in the steady upward progress of society based on the application of rational thought and the scientific method. Knowledge was the key. Pauling's morality grew out of what he knew to be true; he knew that he was a rational person, and he believed that other rational persons would, with sufficient knowledge, come to similar conclusions.

His beliefs mirrored those of many other leftists and liberals during the period from the Depression to the early 1960s. A number of scientists flirted with communism and stayed with left-wing politics because these were systems based on reason and rationality. Researchers like Bernal and the Joliot-Curies in France turned to the Left because they found there a scientific approach to human affairs. The socialist idea of greatest good for the greatest number made statistical sense. The Soviet Union might not be perfect in this analysis, but at least it had taken a brave and necessary step on the path of human advancement by applying reason to human affairs, by elevating scientists to the top of the social hierarchy and making rational five-year plans. Capitalism, by comparison, elevated industrialists and rewarded greed.

Pauling complemented his beliefs in scientific humanism and socialism with a peculiarly American devotion to free speech. Here he operated on a simple theory of politics that he derived in the same way he did his scientific ideas: basing it on a proven body of information, breaking down the problem into constituent parts, focusing on those that were most important, and reassembling them with a new understanding. In politics the underlying information, the received wisdom, he believed, was the U.S. Constitution and the Bill of Rights, documents which he revered as monuments to the philosophy of the Enlightenment. During the McCarthy period, he saw representative democracy and free speech take on special importance, and Pauling analyzed those concepts from a scientific standpoint. The way he saw it, American politics could be thought of, like quantum mechanics, as a matter of statistics. "The principle upon which a true democratic system operates is that no single man is wise enough to made the correct decisions about the very complex problems that arise, and that the correct decisions are to be made by the process of averaging the opinions of all the citizens in the democracy," he wrote. "These opinions will correspond to a probability distribution curve extending from far on the left to far on the right. If, now, we say that all of the opinions that extend too far to the right . . . are abnormal, and are to be excluded in taking the average, then the average that we obtain will be the wrong one. An understanding of the laws of probability would accordingly make it evident to the citizen that the operation of the democratic system requires that everyone have the right to express his opinion about political questions, no matter what that opinion might be."

That he was now at the far left end of the probability curve therefore did not matter. He was still a valid data point. He had the right to express any opinions he liked. This was, as far as Pauling was concerned, a scientific fact.

That kept him going. And there was another reason he continued to speak out. "Most other scientists had stopped. I could understand that. I could understand why some thought it was just too much of a sacrifice. They knew they could lose their jobs. They might not be able to continue their scientific work. I felt the same way," he said of the McCarthy period, "but I kept on in order to retain the respect of my wife."

―ᴍᴍ―

In August, Pauling received a letter from representatives of the Berkeley Academic Assembly asking his support in fighting the UC regents' loyalty oaths. "A contagion of fear, hatred and suspicion infects the entire University," they wrote him. "Scholars have been forced by economic necessity to give mute acceptance to something they know destroys the very meaning of their profession and their lives."

Pauling responded strongly. "The University has already suffered great harm through the introduction by the Regents of a political test, which restricts freedom of thought and the search for truth," he proclaimed in a public statement. "Unless the Regents rescind their earlier actions, the University will never regain its former preeminent position." He sent a copy of his words to the Academic Assembly, with a cover note suggesting that the regents—an appointed board with heavy representation from industrial, financial, and agricultural interests—should be replaced with a group of "intelligent men and women who understand education and scholarship." The Berkeley group made sure his ideas received wide play in the newspapers.

Eleven weeks later, at nine-thirty on the morning of November 13, 1950, a man walked into Pauling's Caltech office and handed him a subpoena to appear before the California State Investigating Committee on Education in Los Angeles. Pauling read it twice before he realized that his appearance was set for ten-thirty the same day. Still, a subpoena was a subpoena. He canceled his appointments for the day, grabbed his jacket, and headed for the car.

Pauling thought he had a rough idea of what was going on. The committee was holding hearings on the possible effects of loyalty oaths on public school teachers, and as a well-known opponent of the oaths, he figured he was being called to give expert testimony. The suddenness of the subpoena seemed unusual, but he was eager to let the committee know what he thought. As he drove toward downtown in his Lincoln, he thought about how he might phrase his criticisms.

What he did not realize was that this committee had been formed out of the Tenney Committee, was chaired by a member of the Tenney

Committee, and was counseled by a lawyer for the Tenney Committee. The purpose was not as much to gather expert testimony as it was to hunt Reds.

At 10:30 A.M., Pauling entered the large hearing room of the State Building in Los Angeles, took an oath to tell the truth, and sat down to give the committee an opening statement. Speaking from the heart, Pauling began, "I think there is nothing more important than preserving our national security by the proper security measures. . . . However, this must be done in such a way as to preserve our individual liberties." He explained the danger of cutting off the far ends of the bell curve of opinion and how, in his opinion, loyalty oaths enforced a dangerous conformity. The loyalty oaths would not help curb subversion, he said, because real subversives would merely sign the oath and go on with their activities. Pauling had by now changed his opinion of the Communist Party, agreeing with the Berkeley faculty that party members were too narrowly doctrinaire to be allowed to teach. "I think that in the case of Communist activities any of them should be brought to the attention of the authorities and a hearing and trial should be held, and if there is evidence that the man or woman involved is a Communist he can be fired," Pauling testified. "I don't think this oath has anything to do really with Communist activities. . . . It is only the people who have strong fundamental American convictions, who believe we must preserve democracy and keep to the spirit of our ancestors who fought at the time of the Revolution, who objected to signing it." With an ending flourish, he compared the enforcement of oaths to the forced adoption of Lysenkoism in Russia and the Nazi persecution of scientists in the 1930s.

The committee then got down to its real business. The committee's counsel asked if Pauling had seen any evidence of subversive activities at Caltech. Pauling answered no. The counsel reminded Pauling about Sidney Weinbaum, a convicted Communist that he had employed. Startled at this shift in the tone of the hearing, Pauling said that Weinbaum had not been convicted of subversion but of perjury. "There was no suggestion that he was disloyal to this country in any way," he said.

For the next two hours the committee grilled Pauling on his views of communism, how he could stomach the thought of Reds pressing the party line on helpless youngsters, and why he could not agree that saving children was more important than due process. Finally, Pauling had enough:

SENATOR DONNELLY: I think a good many taxpayers of the state of California feel perhaps we can get along without some of the higher education better than we can by having our children indoctrinated with communism and the professors in a subtle way instilling it into the minds of the children when they are in a formative stage.

PAULING: Yes. You believe it is not right to adhere to the principles of democracy.

SENATOR DONNELLY: No, I did not say anything such as that. I don't believe any such thing.

PAULING: The right decision to be made is from the average decisions of all people without precluding those whom you would suppress because of their opinion and political beliefs.

SENATOR DONNELLY: That is entirely a different matter, for a person to have an opinion and then to take a position of trust such as teachers have. As one of the professors stated who appeared here today, they are entrusted with the most precious things that parents have in this world, their children, and then to have them teach those children in their underhanded manner the principles of communism when they are not supposed to teach the subject at all, I don't think it is necessary to have that kind of teacher.

PAULING: Good. Then if you have any case of a teacher of that sort, why not bring them before the board and present evidence?

The committee, worried that the Caltech professor might be getting the better of them, broke for lunch. Pauling was asked to return at two o'clock.

The afternoon session was a nightmare. The committee returned to Weinbaum: When did he work for you? Who recommended him? Did you investigate his background? Why not? They then turned to Pauling's own political work. Armed with the Tenney Committee's file, the chairman began ticking off Pauling's suspect associations. Was he aware that the Progressive Citizens of America, for which he had served as a vice chairman, was found by the California Senate Committee on Un-American Activities to be Communist controlled? What about your support of the Red Dean of Canterbury? Henry Wallace? The Arts, Sciences, and Professions Council? What are your opinions of the tactics of the Communist Party? What about your criticisms of the recent trial of Communist Party leaders? Pauling patiently answered each question.

And then, late in the afternoon, came the central question.

COUNSEL: Dr. Pauling, I have just one more question. Are you now a member of the Communist Party?

PAULING: Well, now, this sounds like an inquiry into my political beliefs. Of course, it is a foolish question, but I suppose it is part of the routine.

COUNSEL: Yes, I would like to have you answer. . . .

PAULING: It seems to me that as I was thinking about my colleagues at the University of California who were cut off one by one—after thousands of them had voted in opposition to the loyalty oath, they were cut off one by one by the successive advocation of threats that they would lose their jobs and were required to give up their principles as good American citizens, their beliefs—that this was political pressure being imposed, as I have thought about them. Finally, there were left just this little residue of the original number that were finally fired, a hundred or thereabouts. And as I have thought about them, I have tried to decide how long I would stick to my principles about the loyalty oath. I wasn't able to decide how much strength of character I would have. You never know what you will do until the time arrives for you to do it. I saw man after man, who had spoken strongly against this loyalty oath, sign it when it became evident that he would lose his job if he did not sign it. Now, I feel that the same principle applies here, and I find it hard to decide myself whether to subject myself, perhaps legalistically, just because of a principle, to the difficulties that might arise. Nevertheless, it seems to me that the beliefs that I have about the proper working of Democracy, the way that we can save this nation by preserving Democracy against attacks that are being made against it, require that I refuse to answer any question as to my political beliefs and affiliations. And so I say that I shall not answer.

The committee broke for a short recess to ponder strategy. Pauling had made a choice faced by many witnesses in front of congressional panels of the day: whether to answer the question; to invoke the Fifth

Amendment, the constitutional protection against self-incrimination; or to maintain that the question was outside the committee's charge and refuse to answer. Pauling had no intention of answering a question that had sent his friends to jail or internal exile. At the time he faced the committee there was a risk in taking the Fifth, too, which was widely seen as an admission of guilt and often resulted in the witness's being fired. So he took the last course, the course that Dalton Trumbo and the Hollywood Ten had taken. This, however, carried a risk as well: Refusal to answer a legislative committee's question could lead to a contempt citation.

When the committee reconvened, the counsel tried bullying Pauling, reminding him of legal decisions that appeared to show it was in his best interest to answer the question. Pauling had read too widely to be taken in. He stuck with his refusal. If the committee wanted anything more, it would have to cite him. The counsel backed off, and the grilling continued. Pauling answered every question coolly, logically, and clearly.

They were getting nowhere. Finally, one frustrated committee member brought the discussion back around:

> SENATOR DONNELLY: Well, Doctor, at the present time we are engaged in a war, whether it is a declared war on Russia or not, our country is fighting the Communists, we will have to recognize that, and that American boys are giving up their lives on a foreign soil. What is all this to avail us if we permit Communists to infiltrate into our universities and colleges and teach our youths the Communist doctrine? . . . You continually refer to political pressure and to politics when any one mentions communism or asks whether you are a member of the Communist Party . . . I don't believe you are fair in calling the Communist Party a political organization, or if you have any allegiance to the Communist Party, I don't believe that it is fair to call that political views. I think that is subversive and it is traitorous, especially at a time when we are engaged in war.

> PAULING: Well, I am interested to know what you think, but I don't believe that it is determinative. Here again, I would say that if I am guilty of some illegal act, I should be called to justice for it.

> SENATOR DONNELLY: Well, don't you think it is an illegal act to refuse to state whether or not you are a Communist and be

considered in contempt of the senate of the state of California? . . .

PAULING: It seems to me, and I must say that I am speaking without knowledge of the law or benefit of legal advice, that it is not justifiable for an inquiry to be made into my political beliefs and affiliations and that this principle is important enough . . . even though I put myself in jeopardy, I should adhere to it. . . .

SENATOR DONNELLY: If you are a member of the Communist Party and if you are paying dues, if you are a part and parcel of an organization that advocates the overthrow of the United States government by force and violence, now, all the pretty words you say do not change the complexion of that at all.

The inquiry ended in *Catch-22* fashion:

SENATOR WEYBRET: Where would we land if every one of us went over and supported these Communists, knowing that they were here under the supervision, or whatever you might call it, of a foreign country? Where would we land if we all took the same attitude?

PAULING: You mean all of the people in the nation?

SENATOR WEYBRET: Yes, where would we be?

PAULING: Well, then, we would presumably have a different form of government as a result of the choice of the people.

Outmaneuvered, disgusted, and tired, the panel finally dismissed him.

An FBI agent in the audience closed his notebook. Later that week, he would send a complete report to J. Edgar Hoover.

―᭶᭶᭶―

Despite his composure before the committee, Pauling was deeply shaken by the inquisition and especially by the threat of a contempt citation. He had seen firsthand the effect that tangling with a congressional committee had had on Dalton Trumbo's life—a wife and three children left in limbo while the screenwriter served his year in the penitentiary as a result of a conviction for contempt of Congress. At the state level, he was not sure what the penalties would be except for one: A conviction for contempt of an official state committee would certainly get him fired from Caltech.

The next day, Pauling's refusal to answer the question was all over the papers and all over campus. Unsure of what to do, Pauling turned for advice to the liberal and well-connected Caltech physics professor Charlie Lauritsen, who came up with a simple idea: It was against Pauling's principles to tell the committee about his politics under duress, but nothing prevented him from voluntarily telling his friends and colleagues. The Caltech internal investigation had already shown that Pauling was not a member of the Communist Party, and everyone knew it. Write DuBridge a note, Lauritsen suggested, make the statement that you are not a party member. Then let DuBridge figure a way around the committee.

Pauling thought about it, then drafted a long statement and sent it to DuBridge that same day with a cover note, "Dear Lee: I enclose this statement about my political beliefs. You are free to use it in any way." In the three-page document he restated his reasons for not testifying about his political beliefs before the committee, offered a critique of the loyalty-oath program, and concluded, "I believe that a citizen has the right to announce his political beliefs if he desires, and that he also has a right to keep them to himself if he desires. I may say that I am not personally sympathetic to the extremes of belief and policy that I understand some Communists to hold; but I feel that we must staunchly support the basic principles of our Democracy, including the right of people to hold even extreme political beliefs."

Buried in the middle Pauling had written, "I am not a Communist. I have never been a Communist. I have never been involved with the Communist Party." This was what DuBridge needed to hear. He was already getting another round of complaints from his trustees about the latest Pauling flap, and he was happy to see his chemistry head make this statement. He suggested a few edits to Pauling—a section was added saying, "I am not opposed to loyalty oaths in general. I have voluntarily taken many loyalty oaths in connection with my services to the Nation"—and then told Pauling he would take care of things. DuBridge contacted the education committee and arranged for Pauling to appear when it convened for more hearings in Pasadena in two days. When the panel was gaveled to order, Pauling walked in, read his statement under oath, turned, and began walking out as the legislators buzzed. On his way out the door Pauling thought he heard somebody say, "All I know is that he's made a monkey out of this committee." It might have been Senator Donnelly, whose staff had been busy preparing Pauling's contempt citation.

Press coverage of the hearings kicked off the usual flurry of anti-Pauling mail to DuBridge's office, but he was now able to counter with an incontrovertible fact: Pauling had testified under oath that he was not a Communist. In Pauling's case, he could write disgruntled alumni that even though there may be violent disagreement on Pauling's opinions, as long as he acted within the law and kept politics out of the classroom, "our best course is to try to convince him of his errors rather than to take more radical steps."

The Secret of Life

Off the Deep End

Pauling's attention switched rapidly between politics and science now, with research becoming a refuge from the attacks and pressure brought about by his political activities. At the urging of his publisher, in 1949 he finished a simpler version of *General Chemistry,* more suited for the wider audience of college freshmen who were not of Caltech caliber, extemporizing entire chapters into his dictaphone and letting his secretary rough out the drafts for minor corrections. *College Chemistry,* as it was called when it appeared in 1950, became another big seller. For her birthday in 1950, Pauling bought Ava Helen a brand-new, British-racing-green, two-seat MG roadster.

Protein structures continued to occupy Pauling's thoughts. At the time the Weinbaum case was breaking in the spring of 1950, a long paper by Sir Lawrence Bragg, John Kendrew, and Max Perutz appeared in the *Proceedings of the Royal Academy.* Pauling had a vertiginous moment when he saw the title: "Polypeptide Chain Configurations in Crystalline Proteins." It looked as though Bragg's team might have made a breakthrough, beating him to the great prize of being the first to describe a protein atom by atom.

He felt better as he read it. It was a strangely unfocused paper for

Bragg's group, a laundry list of possible structures for the basic protein pattern found in Astbury's alpha-keratin chain with no overwhelming evidence in favor of any one. Some were spirals; others, kinked chains. Almost all of them, Pauling realized, could be easily dismissed on chemical grounds. Bragg and his team dismissed them, too. They could come to no firm conclusion about an ultimate structure and ended up weakly endorsing Astbury's old idea of a folded ribbon.

Reading between the lines, Pauling found the paper more interesting. The entire menagerie of models had been built as Pauling would have built them, using an understanding of the structural elements involved—especially, Pauling noted with satisfaction, detailed information from Caltech on the shapes and sizes of amino acids—and a consideration of the forces that would hold them in a final shape, placing special emphasis on the notion of hydrogen bonding.

It was obvious that Bragg had learned something in the fifteen years since he had been beaten by Pauling's rules. The time Pauling had spent at the Cavendish Laboratory in 1948 had also had an effect; soon after Pauling returned home, Bragg complemented the top-down approach of Perutz and Kendrew, which emphasized the structure of whole proteins, with a Pauling-like attack on the structures of individual amino acids.

But Pauling was relieved to see that Bragg still did not know how to play the stochastic game correctly. In his 1950 paper Bragg did not place enough chemical restrictions on his structural guesses to narrow them down sufficiently. The British apparently did not believe, for instance, that the peptide bond had to be held rigid and flat, and almost all of their models twisted or bent that bond in a way Pauling believed impossible—one reason they came up with twenty possibilities instead of just a few. And one restriction they did impose Pauling thought unnecessary. The Cavendish team assumed that there had to be a whole number of amino acids—three or four seemed most likely—in every full turn of their spiral models. Huggins had made this integral-number mistake, too, in his 1943 paper. The thinking was that if protein spirals crystallized as they did, then the basic repeating unit—the space group, it was called—had to exhibit a sort of symmetry describable by whole numbers. Because the space group in an alpha-keratin spiral was thought to consist of one whole turn, repeated ad infinitum up the chain, space-group symmetry thinking made it seem logical that there was an integer number of amino acids in each turn; that way, each whole turn would start and end at the same point on the amino-acid backbone.

It was not obvious to Pauling, however. When folding his paper spirals in Oxford, he had concentrated on chemical rules, not crystallographic dogma. The model he had roughed out had not involved a whole number of amino acids in each turn, and once he thought about it, he could see no reason why it should have to. After reading Bragg's 1950 paper, he began to think that this integral-number fixation was akin to the "magic number" mania of protein researchers in the 1930s, the mistaken belief in nice, whole numbers that had led Dorothy Wrinch to her cyclols. Nature did not work that way, Pauling thought, spinning out living things according to mathematical equations. Nature was sloppier than that, more opportunistic—nature took the easiest way out, the way that required the least energy—the way that built the most stable chemical structures.

Bragg's team had missed the prize, and their paper succeeded only in refocusing Pauling on the race. Proteins had been his top priority when he returned from England two years before, and he had assigned a number of researchers to it: Corey and coworkers continuing to lead the world in the structural study of amino acids and small peptides, with results continuing to support Pauling's idea of the planar peptide bond; Corey and a small team working on a whole globular protein, lysozyme, breaking it down into smaller pieces, separating them on chromatographic columns and analyzing the fragments; Pauling directing an effort to ease x-ray analysis by placing easily located atoms of heavy elements like mercury into the protein chain; a new faculty member, Jack Kirkwood, gathering information on the charge distribution and general properties of globular proteins, using the Tiselius apparatus. When a visiting professor of physics, Herman Branson, arrived in the winter of 1948–49, Pauling put him to work on an exhaustive review of all possible spiral protein models that accommodated his restrictions—a planar peptide bond and maximum hydrogen bonding—"to see if there were any that I had missed." Importantly, he eliminated one restriction that Bragg's group had imposed. There was no good reason, he told Branson, to assume that there had to be an integral number of amino acids in each turn of the spiral. Branson, with the help of Sidney Weinbaum (this was prior to his perjury conviction), started to work, using his grasp of mathematics and extremely accurate model-building equipment to construct dozens of variations on the spiral theme.

Then Pauling turned his attention to other things. His year as president of the American Chemical Society (ACS) began in January 1949. His political work was claiming more of his workday. The sickle-cell-anemia work had blossomed, and for a few months in late 1949 and early 1950, Pauling put a great deal of effort into using it as the jumping-off point for a concerted, molecular-level attack on such medical problems as cancer and heart disease. "I feel sure that significant progress in attacking disease can be made by bringing medical research into more intimate contact with the most advanced outposts in basic science," he wrote, "and that the only way in which this can be done is to have medical research become an intrinsic part of the activities in laboratories in which basic science is being advanced." He wanted to create a place where young M.D.s like Harvey Itano could come to develop a new approach to medicine based on an understanding of molecular action, and he started dreaming of a new building to house it, a laboratory of medical chemistry that would extend between his Crellin Laboratory of Chemistry and Beadle's Kerckhoff Laboratory of Biology, using staff from both divisions to reshape medical research.

In January 1950, with Beadle's help, Pauling put together a proposal for the Rockefeller Foundation to build such a place. Weaver shot down their idea, however, explaining that biology and chemistry needed to consolidate their research, not expand it, and that in any case the foundation was not in the business of financing buildings. Pauling and Beadle spent weeks that spring writing letters and pounding the streets of New York seeking support from other foundations and drug companies—including asking the Kresge Foundation for $1.5 million—to no avail. Physicians and philanthropists, who barely had time to come to grips with the notion of a molecular disease, found the term "medical chemistry" a "disturbing description," the Caltech pair discovered—too vague on the one hand, too newfangled on the other. They would offer the Caltech team nothing but short-term, limited support.

Giving that up, Pauling turned back to protein spirals. The previous fall, after a year's study, Branson and Weinbaum had concluded that only two spirals—including the one Pauling had come up with in Oxford—provided maximal hydrogen bonding and accommodated the planar peptide bond while still keeping atoms close but not overlapping. The tighter of the two numbered roughly 3.7 amino acids in each turn of the spiral; the looser, 5.1 amino acids. Only two possible, but still Pauling would not publish. The problem was the same he had seen in England: Neither of the two spirals matched the 5.1-angstrom x-ray reflection present in alpha keratin, which most researchers assumed represented the distance along the axis between each full turn, a very important marker for the structure. Branson and Weinbaum's work confirmed that the tighter spiral, the one Pauling now thought might represent the structure of alpha keratin, had about 5.4 angstroms between each turn. "I felt so strongly that the structure must explain the x-ray data," Pauling remembered, "that I took a chance by waiting."

But one of the spirals that Bragg's team postulated, the one with four amino acids per turn, came perilously close to Pauling's 3.7-residue spiral, and Pauling felt that it was only a matter of time until they corrected their approach. In the spring of 1950, he threw himself back into his protein work, overseeing Corey's final systematic analysis of possible structures, building models out of wire, balls, and sticks, and a showy new modeling system carved out of wood in the Caltech shop in which atoms appeared as spheres at their full van der Waals radius, with hollows whittled into the sides to allow them to fit together like masses of soap bubbles—space-filling models, they were called, another Pauling innovation that would become standard equipment in hundreds of chemistry labs and classrooms. Playing strictly by the rules he had imposed on protein structures, making sure that every possible hydrogen bond was formed, that every peptide bond was flat, that there was no undue strain and no atoms jostling too close to others, Pauling and Corey confirmed the chemical plausibility of the two spirals. And they discovered new insights this time—including a way to stretch one structure to account for the properties of silk. But a basic puzzle remained after all the fine tuning: The tighter of Pauling's two basic spirals, the form he believed was most likely that of alpha keratin, still did not explain the observed 5.1-angstrom x-ray reflection. The difference between this and the 5.4-angstrom reflection predicted by Pauling's theoretical spiral—one-sixth the width of a single hydrogen atom—was the only thing standing between him and the honor of being the first man to describe the structure of a protein. It might as well have been the Grand Canyon.

Through the summer and fall of 1950, through Budenz's accusations and the Caltech internal investigation, Pauling worked on solving that problem and outlining structures for other proteins. His sense of urgency was heightened in September 1950 when he learned that his former student (and Dorothy Wrinch confidant) David Harker was setting up an East Coast laboratory for protein structure research, with the backing of Irving Langmuir and the promise of major financial support. The competition was becoming more fierce. Pauling needed to work even harder, and to do so began using a technique he had developed for harnessing his dreams. Between the time he turned out his reading light at night and the time he fell asleep, he would focus his mind on whatever scientific problem most puzzled him. He found that by doing this his subconscious would work on the problem all night, in dreams now haunted by whirling protein spirals and ghostly x-ray diagrams. It also kept him from having nightmares about political persecution.

Despite everything, no answer to the 5.1-angstrom dilemma appeared. So Pauling made a fateful decision. Feeling "forced into it by the Bragg, Kendrew and Perutz paper," he resolved to ignore this essential piece of contradictory experimental evidence and publish at least a preliminary note about his models. There was no sense waiting any longer. If he was right—if there was some as-yet-to-be-discovered explanation for the discrepancy between his models and the x-ray data—he had to get into print first or risk losing his place in history. If he was wrong, it would not make any difference when he published.

On October 16, 1950, Pauling and Corey sent the *Journal of the American Chemical Society* (*JACS*) a short note to establish priority, mentioning that they had come up with two spiral models, one with 3.7 amino-acid residues per turn, the other with 5.1, with a mention of the hydrogen-bonding scheme and the assertion that strong evidence existed that the proposed structures were present in a variety of proteins. They hinted as well at their model for silk. That was all; at the end, the authors promised that "a detailed account of this work will be published soon."

Then came good news. Pauling got wind of new data from a British firm called Courtaulds, a manufacturer of artificial fibers. The company's researchers had succeeded in making wholly synthetic polypeptide chains made of only one type of amino acid. These man-made chains behaved in some ways like natural keratin but in other ways were tantalizingly different. The Courtaulds scientists found that their synthetic chains packed together like pencils in a box—to Pauling, this looked like evidence in favor of a spiral configuration, which would give an overall shape like a long, thin cylinder—and they also found that there appeared to be hydrogen bonding along the length of the chains. The best news of all, however, came from the group's most detailed x-ray pictures: The new fibers gave no 5.1-angstrom reflection.

Pauling was elated. Here was a structure that appeared to be a spiral—or more precisely a "helix," a word that Pauling began using around this time after he was introduced to it by one of his postdoctoral fellows, Jack Dunitz—yet did not show evidence of that con-

founding repeat distance. Perhaps the 5.1-angstrom reflection in natural keratin was not as important as everyone thought. Perhaps it was
an artifact or due to some higher level of structure in natural keratin
and he was justified in ignoring it. With renewed vigor, Pauling and
Corey continued their model building, constructing final versions of
their two helixes, the tighter of which Pauling termed alpha, the looser
gamma, and two versions of the extended silklike patterns, which he
and Corey now called pleated sheets.

The news circulated at Caltech that Pauling's team was constructing protein models precise to the finest detail. This especially interested the institute's biologists. When Pauling gave a seminar to them
that winter on his ideas, the large lecture room in the Kerckhoff Laboratory building was packed, the audience buzzing. "Everybody knew
this was going to be pretty hot stuff," biology professor Ray Owen remembered.

Pauling delivered the talk with his usual dramatic flair. He entered
flanked by assistants carrying a variety of props, one of which was
something tall wrapped in cloth and bound with string like a piece of
statuary about to be unveiled. Everyone knew that it was "the Model."
Pauling began his talk, going over the basics of protein structure,
drawing diagrams to illustrate the importance of hydrogen bonding
and the flat peptide bond. He held up a child's set of soft plastic pop-
beads and snapped them together to show how amino acids connected. After a suitable introduction, he started moving toward the
Model, taking a jackknife from his pocket and opening it, reaching for
the string. The audience members leaned forward in their seats. Then
Pauling, the master showman, thought of something else and backed
off. Everyone sat back. Noting the effect this had, he repeated the trick
several times. "He really built up a great deal of suspense," Owen said.

Then, when he had had enough fun, Pauling unveiled it with a
grand flourish: a beautiful, multicolored model of his tight spiral, the
alpha helix. It was the first time many in the audience had seen a
space-filling molecular model, and it had an effect. It looked "real," a
knobby skein of close-packed atoms painted bright red, white, and
black, twisting up and around to form a thick, knurled column. The
helix's gentle curve could be traced with the eye, atom by atom; it had
depth and weight and density, a kind of visual impact that no other
models had ever approached. It was Pauling's intuitive structural-
chemical vision made manifest. It was a sensation. Pauling ended his
talk with evidence of its existence in a variety of natural substances,
and afterward the Caltech professors and students crowded around,

shaking his hand, asking questions, looking close, reaching out to touch the helix model.

Shows like the Kerckhoff seminar were something like out-of-town previews, giving Pauling a chance to respond to any criticisms before writing more detailed papers. But there were no significant criticisms. Everyone seemed very impressed. Pauling was now feeling better about his structures, especially the alpha helix.

With growing confidence, Pauling and Corey expanded their repertoire through the winter of 1950–51, coming up with models for proteins like collagen, feather rachis, gelatin, and muscle, many of them involving the alpha helix as a component in more complex structures. Their collaboration had settled into a routine: Pauling coming up with the basic ideas for structures, Corey patiently and exactingly turning these insights into precise, finished models. They would talk over the rough spots, the places where Corey's work showed weaknesses in Pauling's vision, and together they would smooth them out. Structure after structure fell into place in this way, and rumors of success sped around the world. At the Cavendish, Bragg's people, who had paid little attention to Pauling and Corey's early, rather cryptic note in *JACS*, waited nervously for Pauling's more detailed papers to appear. And in New York, Warren Weaver, eager for news of this string of breakthroughs, dispatched a Rockefeller Foundation officer familiar with protein work to Pauling's laboratory in February 1951. W. F. Loomis found it a place full of wild ideas. "He certainly is imaginative, daring, and brilliant," Loomis noted in his diary after spending a day with Pauling. "But he has gone off the deep end in some cases (such as the 'artificial antibody' story) and his many stimulating pictures, models, etc. may be largely figments of his own imagination rather than lasting and sound science."

A Broadside

The deep end! Pauling might well have agreed. He was taking a chance at a number of levels. The Courtaulds data might simply be a peculiarity of artificial polypeptides; the absence of a 5.1-angstrom repeat might have nothing to do with real proteins, which always seemed to offer the x-ray reflection that Pauling's models could not. He still had no good explanation for that. By deciding to move forward despite that discrepancy, he was taking a chance that Bragg's group, for example, would never take. At the Cavendish, they followed their x-ray data slavishly, letting the spots on the photographic plates determine their models. In Pasadena, however, with its inferior x-ray equipment and smaller staff of crystallographers, it was necessary to take a chance to win. It was daring to play the game at the level Pauling had chosen, to demand precision in protein models down to the tenth or hundredth of an angstrom for molecular structures hundreds of times more complex than anyone had ever analyzed. Anyone else would have equivocated like Bragg or waited until the data were more settled.

But there was no one like Pauling. Now middle-aged, at a time in life when many scientists were content to rest on their youthful accomplishments or try their hand at administration, Pauling found himself more energetic, more focused, and more self-confident than ever.

And self-confidence would prove the deciding factor. He had an unbounded belief in his grasp of chemistry; he understood the discipline in its entirety as well as or better than anyone else on earth. And of all the subfields of chemistry, he understood best how atoms formed themselves into molecules. All of his chemical understanding told him that the alpha helix and his other protein structures had to be right. They had been built upon solid rules; months and months of careful model building had confirmed their strength. He had a choice between believing in himself—in his approach to solving large molecules, in his stochastic method of setting up rules and building models—or in believing a spot on the x-ray photos. He chose to believe in himself.

Belief was becoming a necessity for Pauling. His growing political troubles had forced him to examine the depth of his beliefs in that sphere; he had already faced the choice of following them or knuckling under to an investigatory committee. And he held firm—while still finding a way to avoid a contempt citation. When pushed, he pushed back harder. He was stubborn, sure of himself, and not shy. He was at the top of his game and had no intention of letting up. Not when the secret of life was within his reach.

On his fiftieth birthday, February 28, 1951, Pauling blew out the candles on the cake his staff had baked for him, accepted the good wishes of his coworkers, and mailed a manuscript to the *Proceeding of the National Academy of Sciences* (*PNAS*). "The Structure of Proteins: Two Hydrogen-Bonded Helical Configurations of the Polypeptide Chain," by Pauling, Corey, and Branson, was a complete, extremely detailed description of the structure of the alpha and gamma helixes.

Excited and unable to hold back the good news until the paper was published, he immediately started telling others about the singularity and significance of his work. "The difference between our two predicted configurations and the others that have been described in the literature is that ours are precise, whereas the others are more or less vague," Pauling wrote Warren Weaver a few days after sending in his paper. "I feel in a sense that this represents the solution of the problem of the structure of proteins." Weaver, elated with this justification of his twenty years of support for Pauling, immediately sent the Rockefeller Foundation's resident science writer and publicist, George Gray, to Caltech to prepare a full report for the trustees. Gray found Pauling a publicist's dream, a scientist who knew how to communicate his research in simple, colorful language. ("I try to identify myself with the atoms," Pauling told him. "I ask what I would do if I were a carbon atom or a sodium atom.") Weaver began reconsidering the desirability of a multi-million-dollar grant for chemistry and biology at Caltech. Before his paper appeared in print, Pauling also wrote Dennis Flanagan, the editor of *Scientific American*, that he and Corey had cracked the protein structure problem, adding, "It seems to me to be just about the most important step forward that has been made during the last 25 years or perhaps 50 years in this field." Flanagan quickly wrote back asking more about this "bombshell" and begging Pauling to write an article on protein structure for the magazine.

The first paper was just a prelude. It was as though the alpha and gamma helixes, once published and out of the way, cleared his mind for all the other protein structures he had been thinking about. Everything began falling into place, and he spent March finishing more protein papers with Corey. "I am having a hard time keeping my feet on the ground now," Pauling wrote a former student in the middle of March. "I have been working night and day, neglecting almost everything else." It was the most exhilarating scientific work he had done since the early days of the chemical bond twenty years before. And he surprised even himself with what he produced.

⁓〰〰⁓

In early April, Pauling and Corey sent the *PNAS* one of the most extraordinary sets of papers in the history of twentieth-century science. There were seven altogether, and they appeared dramatically as a unified group that dominated the journal's May issue. There was a detailed description of the pleated sheet. There was a new model for feather rachis, which they proposed was a mixture of pleated sheets and helixes. There were new ideas about the structures of synthetic polypeptides, globular proteins, and muscle. Most exciting of all for Pauling was what he called "an astounding structure" for collagen, a major protein in tendon. In collagen, he believed, three helixes were twisted around each other to form a single cable.

Every protein researcher in the world immediately recognized the magnitude of Pauling's work. The proposed structures were complete and extraordinarily detailed; in a field where nothing like this had ever appeared, suddenly everything had appeared: It was as if a lifetime's worth of respectable work for any other researcher had exploded into view at one time; it was as though a single composer had debuted seven symphonies on the same day.

In Britain, Bragg read the papers, became almost apoplectic, and rushed to the Cambridge chemistry office of Alexander Todd, the eminent organic chemist and an old friend of Pauling's. Todd had never before seen Sir Lawrence in that part of the university and immediately took note of the physicist's red face and the papers—Pauling's—that he clutched in one hand. "I said it was nice to see him in chemistry and asked what had led to this unexpected visit," Todd remembered. Bragg, "in a somewhat agitated state of mind," demanded to know how anyone could make a decision between Pauling's spirals and the ones he had proposed earlier. Todd, who had already seen Pauling's manuscript, said he would certainly pick Pauling's because of its planar peptide bond. When Bragg said the bond could not be planar, Todd explained to him about resonance structures and double-bond character. "If you had checked with me before, I'd certainly have told you so," he said. Nonplussed, Bragg returned to the physics department.

"I judge that he did not read *The Nature of the Chemical Bond* carefully enough," Pauling crowed when he heard the anecdote from Todd.

Perutz devoured all the Pauling-Corey papers in a single Saturday morning and set off for his laboratory. If the Caltech crew was correct and there were 3.7 amino acids in every turn of the alpha helix, then each individual amino acid along the chain should account for about 1.5 angstroms of the spiral's length. This amino-acid repeat distance in the protein's backbone should show up on x-ray pictures, but the 1.5-angstrom distance was so small that it would take special experiments to look for it. It was worth it, however, because of all the many structures proposed for alpha keratin only Pauling's spiral would create this particular spot; it would act as a sort of fingerprint for the alpha helix. Perutz placed a horsehair in his x-ray apparatus, curved a piece of film around it in a way that would catch the expected reflections, and shot it. He scanned the film as soon as it was developed. There it was: a fuzzy spot out on the far margins of the photo, a reflection that indicated a structural repeat every 1.5 angstroms. Perutz x-rayed a porcupine quill and found the reflection again, and again in synthetic polypeptides and hemoglobin. He even found it on the far margins of years-old x-ray pictures of proteins, where it had been ignored. Perutz, an unusually unselfish researcher, a man almost as happy to confirm the work of others as he was to make his own discoveries, wrote Pauling, "The fulfillment of this prediction and, finally, the discovery of this reflection in hemoglobin has been the most thrilling discovery of my life." He then published his confirmatory findings, concluding, "The spacing at which this reflexion appears excludes all models except the 3.7 residue helix of Pauling, Corey and Branson, with which it is in complete accord." In tandem with the Pasadena group's other data, he wrote, "it leaves little doubt about their structure being right."

With that proof from his own shop, Bragg admitted by June that the alpha helix appeared to have some validity—although it still did not explain why natural keratin gave the 5.1-angstrom reflection—and congratulated Pauling on his "broadside" of protein papers, especially the one on the alpha helix. It was gratifying to Pauling when his old competitor wrote: "I do congratulate you most warmly on what I feel is a very real and vital advance toward the understanding of proteins." The parts of the broadside beyond the alpha helix were, however, not as settled, and the English protein community started the laborious process of dissecting Pauling's other papers, one by one.

Erroneous and Vicious

Pauling's protein-structure research took so much time in the first half of 1951 that he devoted relatively little time to political work. That did not matter, however, to those ferreting out Reds in public life. Thanks to the sharing of information between the FBI, the Tenney Committee, and HUAC, Pauling was now among the select group of prominent Americans at the top of every investigating committee's list of suspected Communists. Anytime mention needed to be made of Red subversion of the sciences or the peace movement, Pauling was there to point to, and fingers were leveled regularly during 1951. The anti-Communist newsletter *Alert* spent three issues informing readers about Pauling's appearance before the California education subcommittee, with a copious listing of his front activities.

Then on April 1, the day after Pauling and Corey sent in their seven protein papers for publication, HUAC named Pauling one of the foremost Americans involved in a "Campaign to Disarm and Defeat the United States" through his participation in a phony "Communist Peace Offensive." There was nothing new in the charges— the evidence was the already-public list of the left-wing groups and causes he had joined—but the invective reached new heights. "His whole record . . . indicates that Dr. Linus Pauling is primarily engrossed in placing his scientific attainments at the service of a host of organizations which have in common their complete subservience to the Communist Party of the USA, and the Soviet Union," HUAC's press release read. "Professor Pauling has not deviated a hair's breadth from this pattern of loyalty to Communist causes since 1946." Pauling responded by telling reporters, "I have associated myself in a smaller or larger way with every peace movement that has come to my attention. I shall continue to act in the way that my conscience tells me is best."

A few days after the accusations made front-page news, Pauling opened a letter from the president of Marshall College in West Virginia noting his regret at having to withdraw an invitation to Pauling to address scientists in the area. The problem, the president wrote, was not, of course, Pauling's political beliefs but the possibility of "vigorous protests" by local citizens and the resulting potential embarrassment for Pauling and his wife. Pauling did not buy it. "I am disgusted that you should have acted in this way," he wrote back. But his suggestion that he be reinvited received no reply.

Even more unconscionable from Pauling's point of view were the actions of the regents of the University of Hawaii. He had been scheduled to dedicate a new chemistry building on campus, but the regents—alerted by state antisubversive officials who had received a copy of Pauling's Tenney Committee file from their helpful counterparts in California—forced the chemistry department to withdraw the invitation. Pauling learned about it from a reporter and again was blunt in his response: "I am very surprised that the regents of a university, who are supposed to be men of enlightenment and principle, would put a man on trial and publicly announce his conviction without having told him of the charges or given him an opportunity to refute them." When the controversy hit the papers and the media came to DuBridge for comment, the president kept his distance, saying only that he could not see that the issue had anything to do with Caltech.

Left on his own, Pauling wrote the Hawaiian regents of his "deep indignation" at their action. "Do you think that an American who insists on making up his own mind, who objects to being told what to do, to being pushed around by officious officials, is thereby made un-American?" he wrote. "I do not. I think that he is being more American than people who do not object." He enclosed a copy of his statement of political beliefs—including his denial of membership in the Communist Party—asked to be reinvited, and hinted at legal repercussions if he was not. The regents stood firm.

Pauling decided to go the islands anyway. It was a good time for a vacation. His protein papers had just appeared in print, the political heat was being turned up, and he was ready for a rest. Going to Hawaii was also a good way to demonstrate his disdain for intolerance. "I thought that it would be worthwhile to go to Honolulu and to give some scientific talks, just to make it clear to the people of the Islands just how big a mistake the Board of Regents of the University of Hawaii made in withdrawing their invitation to me," he wrote a friend. He convinced the Hawaiian chapter of the American Chemical Society to invite him for a series of talks and flew to Honolulu with Ava Helen at the end of May. It turned out to be a delightful break. Wherever he spoke, he was greeted by enthusiastic groups of scientists eager to hear about his newest discoveries. Many shook his hand afterward and thanked him for his courage in speaking out against intolerance. The Honolulu newspaper took Pauling's side and began to question the regents' actions.

It gave Pauling hope. For a brief moment it seemed that by standing up for his beliefs, he was not only preserving his reputation but giving heart to others.

―⁓―

A few weeks after his return, however, the atmosphere darkened again. Pauling had managed since 1948 to avoid any projects that would bring him back under the scrutiny of the loyalty program, but it was becoming more difficult. In 1951, with the Korean War in full flame and the Rosenberg trial refocusing attention on the question of atomic spies, Truman signed another executive order expanding his loyalty standards so that mere doubt of loyalty, rather than hard evidence, became the standard for dismissal of government employees. Hundreds of cases were reopened, including Edward Condon's. This time the long-suffering physicist had had enough and quit his post as head of the National Bureau of Standards.

With the expansion of government funding for science, especially classified defense research, enormous numbers of scientists, technicians, and engineers found themselves required to go through the mechanism of the loyalty program in order to find work. Originally, the military had overseen loyalty reviews and hearings, but now, faced with a new influx of civilian cases, the system had been revamped to provide more nonmilitary input. Behind the window dressing, however, the loyalty program still amounted to a shadow legal system. Nonmilitary scientists applying for work on classified government contracts would have their security files reviewed by the area commanding general. Questionable activities or associations would send the subjects' files to a regional personnel security board. The board had the power to revoke clearance—discharging the subject from any classified project—without ever seeing the person or presenting evidence. The only recourse for blacklisted scientists was to appeal to the Industrial Employment Review Board (IERB), where for the first time they were offered the chance to present their cases in person, with counsel. IERB hearings were not exactly trials—they were held outside the legal system after a verdict had already been passed and involved military men judging the political activities of civilians—yet they were very like trials, with questioning and cross-examination and lawyers. It was a system out of *Alice in Wonderland*. After the IERB passed judgment, there was nowhere else to go. The decision of the panel was final.

Tens of thousands of researchers were caught in this topsy-turvy mechanism. Once denied clearance for any reason—and the reason could be as simple as joining a suspect group—they found it difficult to get employment anywhere, whether on a government project or not. The loyalty program did not turn up any atomic spies, but it had the practical effect of silencing dissent. The basic blacklisting techniques that had worked efficiently in whipping the film industry into line five years earlier now worked to prevent researchers from making their politics known.

Then Pauling himself was sucked into the loyalty program.

Although he steered clear of classified defense work, Pauling served on the Caltech faculty committee on contracts, a position that required him to review the classified grant requests of others. The air force requested that everyone who looked at its contracts, even in a review capacity, be cleared to look at classified materials at a low level, one sufficient to see "confidential" or "restricted" materials as opposed to the higher-level "secret" or "top secret" documents. This type of lower-level clearance was routinely rubber-stamped; it rarely involved the type of full review that brought people before the IERB. In early 1951, Caltech sent Pauling's name, along with a number of trustees and faculty, for low-level clearance. All of them were granted without a problem—except Pauling's.

In late July he received a letter from the local military security board notifying him that a request for access to classified material at Caltech was being denied. According to "information" in the board's possession, "you have been a member of the Communist Party and a close associate of Communist Party members . . . you have also been affiliated with or a member of numerous organizations which espouse Communist Party ideologies and on many occasions you have openly defended known Communists and Communist ideologies."

This was not true. Pauling immediately appealed the decision to the IERB, and a hearing was set for November.

Ironically, at the same time he was being denounced in America as a Communist, news reached Caltech that Pauling was being denounced by Soviet chemists for his "erroneous and vicious" resonance-based theory of chemical structure. The Lysenko-era Russian researchers, intent on boosting the reputation of Russian achievements in structural chemistry, had for two years been tearing away at Pauling's "reactionary, bourgeois" chemical ideas, especially his use of idealized resonance structures with no real independent existence. Resonance theory, it was decided, was antimaterialistic and hence anti-Soviet. The chemists' division of the Soviet Academy of Sciences in the summer of 1951 formally resolved that Pauling's approach was "pseudo-scientific" and "idealistic" and should be rejected. *Pravda* trumpeted the decision, which was echoed in Soviet scientific publications with appropriate denunciations of Pauling's approach to chemistry as "contrived, a made-up convenience, an economy of thought that bore no relation to reality." A contemporary observer wrote in *The American Journal of Chemical Education,* "The intensity and crudeness of this invective appear to be without parallel in the annals of chemistry." Soviet chemistry would henceforth be anti-Pauling.

It was a bizarre position to be in, reviled simultaneously by Americans for being a Communist and by Soviets for being a reactionary. Privately, Pauling was "deeply concerned" about the Russian invective, writing a friend, "I have not been able to gain any understanding whatever of the meaning or cause for such an attack." Publicly, it provided a damage-control opportunity eagerly pounced upon by Lee DuBridge. When a *New York Times* reporter telexed the Russian chemists' anti-Pauling resolution to Caltech for a response, Caltech replied with a three-page news release decrying the effects of Lysenkoism and emphasizing Pauling's criticism of Communist science: "If Russian chemists are not allowed to use the resonance theory, or are deprived of scientific freedom in any other direction, Russian scientists will fall behind Western science and Russian technology will also suffer," Pauling was quoted as saying. Subsequent coverage in the *Times* and *Time* magazine helped portray Pauling as a defender of Western science against Russian attempts to stifle the truth.

The Rules of the Game

While Russians and Americans combed through Pauling's activities for evidence of political incorrectness, Bragg, Astbury, and other English researchers were sifting his protein papers for scientific blunders. By the fall of 1951 they felt that they had found an abundance. While Perutz had confirmed the existence of the alpha helix and its presence in many proteins with his 1.5-angstrom alpha-helix fingerprint, he could not find it in feather-rachis protein, as Pauling had predicted he should; Perutz concluded that Pauling and Corey's proposed feather structure must be wrong. Perutz also thought the proposed model for muscle contraction, which Pauling had hypothesized involved the contraction of pleated sheets into alpha helixes, could not be right because evidence of the alpha pattern was found in both the extended and contracted forms. Bernal was ready to accept the alpha helix for fibrous proteins but was fairly certain that it was not a contributor to the structure of two globular proteins he was working with, ribonuclease and chymotrypsin. The Courtaulds team did not agree with what Pauling had said about the dimensions of their synthetic polypeptides. Pauling's looser gamma helix was being criticized because it had a hole down the center large enough to let in small molecules that could destabilize it. Most disappointingly for Pauling, his proposed structure for collagen—the three-helix cable that he thought did a good job of explaining the substance's resistance to stretching—did not gain support from the English x-ray results.

　　Pauling spent much of his time in the latter part of 1951 conceiving answers to these criticisms and revising his structures. He felt the work so important that he turned down the offer of a visiting professorship at Harvard to concentrate on the task; he also put off a planned trip to Europe until he felt more secure about his ideas. The alpha-helix fingerprint in feathers might be hidden because the helixes are out of phase, he noted; muscle might also contain "non-contractile alpha-keratin" which remained in the alpha form all the time. He cleared up a misunderstanding with the Courtauld's group and soon got them to agree that the alpha helix seemed reasonable for their synthetic polypeptides. The gamma helix, however, he was ready to abandon. Pauling had always been uneasy about its stability; by the fall Pauling was backing off from it entirely. As the evidence against his collagen structure mounted, he fell back to a new position, concluding by the end of 1951 that "the structure that we have suggested . . . is not quite right. I think that its general aspects are correct, but some small changes will be necessary." Meanwhile, he and Corey came up with two new pleated sheet structures and were also thinking about what they called a "rippled sheet" for some proteins.

All of these criticisms, however, were overshadowed by the towering achievement of Pauling's alpha helix. Despite Astbury's continuing concern that Pauling had yet to explain the absence of the 5.1-angstrom repeat, the evidence for his proposed helix was overwhelming. The confounding x-ray reflection, it appeared, must be due to something unrelated to the basic structure itself. Pauling's extended versions of the alpha helix, the various pleated sheets, looked good as well. In England it began to be accepted that while Pauling may have moved a bit too fast on his other structures, he had solved the big one, the contracted and extended forms of keratin, the substance that Astbury believed was the progenitor of all proteins. As Pauling wrote at the time, "I am sure that these discoveries will introduce a new era in the protein field."

They did. Pauling's protein work had changed the rules of the game. It was Pauling who had insisted on the importance of hydrogen bonding. It was Pauling who showed the power of model building based on precise chemical rules—the stochastic approach that allowed complex x-ray patterns to be solved by making a highly educated guess at the answer. It was Pauling who insisted on structural precision down to the hundredth of an angstrom, raising the level of play to a point where loose, general ideas about protein structures could no longer compete. From now on, any proposed structure would have to match Pauling's precision. And, importantly, it was Pauling who shattered the English preoccupation with integral patterns of symmetry, the formal crystallographic paradigm that insisted on symmetrical space groups, the sort of thinking that had led Bragg and Perutz astray. After the alpha helix, crystallographers studying biological molecules would be free to think in new ways about them, free to look for nonintegral patterns—free to see their targets for what they were.

∿∿

It was an immense achievement, and Pauling made sure he was properly credited. In September 1951, eighteen thousand chemists from forty-two nations—the largest gathering of chemists in history—met in New York City for the World Chemical Conclave, the International Congress of Pure and Applied Chemistry, and the celebration of the American Chemical Society's Diamond Jubilee. The size of the meetings and their location in the heart of Manhattan ensured plenty of news coverage. Pauling was scheduled to give several talks, including a major speech on protein structures, and he prepared by helping the Caltech news department write a six-page release outlining the importance of his discoveries. This document was, for its day, a masterwork of scientific public relations, outlining Pauling's discoveries at some length, emphasizing the effort behind them and their impact on science and medicine. It was all presented in language reporters could understand, including eye-catching phrases like "the secret of life." The ACS public relations staff, eager to bring maximum coverage to their event and aware of Pauling's charisma and accessibility, helped promote his work.

As a result, Pauling stole the show. The most heavily attended presentation of the entire affair was his talk on protein structures, delivered in a large assembly room at the Roosevelt Hotel. Pauling spoke with his usual gusto to an overflow crowd, including reporters from several major papers and a *Life* magazine photographer. It was a flawless performance—until the end, during the question-and-answer session, when a balding, nondescript man in a gray suit stood up in the back of the room and said that he had discovered the alpha helix first. The man was Maurice Huggins, the scientist who sent everyone off after helixes by proposing a spiral structure for proteins in 1943. There was an awkward moment as Pauling's mind raced, trying to come up with the details of Huggins's work. Then he recovered, pointing out that while Huggins's basic idea of a spiral shape was correct, he had, like Bragg, missed both the necessity of the planar peptide bond and the importance of a nonintegral repeat pattern. Huggins was not mollified. He and Pauling went back a long way—in the 1920s he had helped Pauling with some early ideas about the chemical bond and also promoted the idea of hydrogen bonding—but in every case Pauling had gone on to fame and fortune, while Huggins's career, by comparison, languished. He did not want to see Pauling again steal his thunder with proteins. It took Pauling weeks to convince him that his model had been relatively vague and incorrect in some important respects.

Instead of casting doubt on Pauling's work, the brief verbal fireworks underlined the dramatic nature of his discoveries for the attending reporters. The next day, the *New York Times* headline read: "Chemists Unravel Protein's Secrets—Aid to Fight on Diseases—Discovery Marks First Inroads on Mysterious Protoplasm—May Solve Basic Riddles." The accompanying story, with its D day–flavored language describing this "first major beachhead on nature's major stronghold—the structure of protoplasm, physical basis of life—which until now had remained impregnable," was spread across the nation. Two weeks later, 5 million readers opened *Life* magazine to find an enormous photo of a grinning Pauling pointing to his space-filling model of the alpha helix, with the headline "Chemists Solve a Great Mystery." His success with proteins made him one of the world's most famous scientists.

The IERB

Two months later, he was hauled in front of the IERB to fight for his reputation.

Pauling's political stands had continued to come under attack from the right wing, both publicly and in a series of letters delivered to Lee DuBridge. DuBridge knew that distaste for Pauling among the most conservative—and in some cases wealthiest—backers of the school was costing him large amounts of money in lost gifts. His attitude toward Pauling—and that of many others at Caltech—was summarized in an FBI report that October: "None of the faculty at Cal Tech feel that Pauling is actually a Communist, but have characterized him as a diluted [*sic*] exhibitionist and pointed out that his constant desire to see his name in print has caused Cal Tech a great deal of grief," the agent wrote. "Cal Tech is very unhappy with Pauling's recent bad publicity, which has reflected on the Institute in general. [Blacked out] feel that he is an irreplaceable scientist, but are more convinced than ever that sooner or later something will have to be done in that it

is costing the Institute millions of dollars in potential endowments." So
while he continued to defend Pauling publicly, privately DuBridge redoubled his efforts to convince Pauling to tone down his activities.

His ambivalence toward Pauling was demonstrated during preparations for the IERB hearing. Pauling had requested that DuBridge assign him a lawyer, but the Caltech president delayed so long in
responding that Pauling felt it necessary to hire his own man, local
ACLU firebrand Abraham Lincoln Wirin. The Paulings knew Wirin
from his work fighting anti-Japanese hysteria during the war, and he
had since earned a name for himself as an unusually combative radical
lawyer, always ready to take the gloves off with investigating committees. Wirin's reputation was assured in civil libertarian circles when, at
a HUAC hearing, he was grabbed by security guards and thrown out
for refusing to stay quiet. On the Thursday before the hearing,
DuBridge called Pauling, told him that Wirin would not be acceptable,
and offered a substitute lawyer. Pauling replied that it was too late. "I
shall try to represent the Institute as well as myself in a satisfactory
manner, and I have confidence that Mr. Wirin will also do so," he
said. He advised DuBridge to hire a lawyer to represent Caltech at the
hearing.

On Monday, Pauling entered room 810 of the Federal Building in
Los Angeles followed by Wirin and a group of character witnesses they
had assembled. He sat down before the panel and, after the hearing
was called to order, read a thirteen-page statement summarizing his
life and political beliefs. He told the board how the incident with his
Japanese-American gardener had made him more aware of social
questions and how he had independently formed his political views by
reading newspapers and historical studies. "I am free from commitment of any sort to any political party or other group," he told them. "I
have never been a Communist. I am not a Communist. I have never
been involved with the Communist Party."

He was, he said, an American. He believed in representative democracy, the preservation of peace between nations, the rights of man as
expressed in the Constitution, and the acceptance of the highest ethical principles. He then outlined the price he had paid for his political
activities. He told the board how he had lost the Eli Lilly consultantship
and how "very strong pressure to cause me to cease my political activities has been applied by my present employer, the California Institute
of Technology." He finished with a long recital of his many services
to the nation, his receipt of a medal from Truman, a typically self-
confident assessment of his skills as a scientist—"I have, I think, a

broader grasp of science as a whole—mathematics, physics, chemistry, biology, and geology (mineralogy)—than any other man in the United States," he said—and a plea for clearance. "I recognize that my political activities and associations are such as to indicate unreliability as a repository of classified information," he told the board. "I myself feel that my personal character and integrity and the value of my possible services to the country are such as to permit clearance to be given to me."

The IERB spent two days questioning Pauling in Los Angeles in a routine that was now becoming depressingly familiar, trotting out the usual list of "suspect" groups, speeches, and endorsements. The only amusement came when the board's counsel asked, "Are you or are you not a member of the Save the Redwoods League?" Pauling could not help laughing aloud. Finally, after hearing the unqualified support of his character witnesses, the board decided to continue the hearings in Washington, D.C., early in December. This was a big case—Pauling was one of the most prominent scientists ever to come before the IERB—and they did not want to hurry it.

But the Washington hearings never happened. The day after the Los Angeles hearing ended, DuBridge sent Pauling a surprising letter. He had discovered, he said, "a slip" in the way Pauling's request for clearance had been handled by the Caltech personnel office. It seemed that Pauling was appearing before the IERB because his name had, "through a misunderstanding," been included with a batch of top-secret clearance requests for scientists working on an H-bomb research program called Project Vista. It was all a mistake. The IERB was investigating him for the wrong thing. DuBridge had his personnel administrator write a *mea culpa,* and when Pauling presented it to the IERB in Washington, D.C., the entire case was dismissed.

———

Pauling was deeply shaken. Being taken to task by a gaggle of local anti-Communist politicians, as he had been by the California education committee, was one thing. Having his ability to conduct his scientific work threatened at the national level was another. Losing his security clearance would have crippled Pauling's ability to operate efficiently as a high-ranking Caltech administrator; he would not, for instance, have been able to review any classified grant requests made by his own faculty members. Added to his already shaky position at the institute, it might have been enough to persuade DuBridge and the anti-Pauling trustees that he should be stripped of some degree of

power, perhaps demoted. His political work, it was now clear, was interfering in important ways with his ability to be a productive scientist.

Pauling had always maintained a careful balance between conformity and independence, between wanting to be liked and wanting to
be right. The IERB hearing, with its bizarre climax, was enough to shift
that balance. Now, he decided, it was clear that the importance of belonging to politically suspect groups was outweighed by the trouble
they caused.

After a long talk with Ava Helen, he decided to pull back.

Within a few days of DuBridge's discovery of the clerical error,
Pauling sent letters of resignation to the National Council of the Arts,
Sciences and Professions and the American Association of Scientific
Workers, two groups under attack for being Communist-dominated.
He told the American Peace Crusade—a group he had helped start
but which was also accused of being dominated by Communists—that
he could not serve as an officer. A few months later he resigned from
the World Federation of Scientific Workers, the international group
headed by the French physicist and Communist Frédéric Joliot-Curie,
after having accepted a position as vice president the year before. He
was "too busy," he said, "to devote proper attention" to their concerns.
During the remainder of 1951 and most of 1952, Pauling would not
give a strictly political talk, would not make political pronouncements
to the press, would not participate in any group that was identified as
pro-Communist. He would, like most liberals, lower his head and wait
for better times.

Pauling's IERB hearing might have been aborted, but it had the
desired effect. When it was over, Pauling had been made keenly aware
of the saws and had sought out a safer place on the limb.

The Triple Helix

The Pauling Point

Amazingly, Pauling seemed able to handle his political travails with no apparent effect on his scientific work. In 1951 and 1952 alone, forty-three of his scientific papers—journal articles, popular pieces, notes, and reviews—reached print: his epochal series on protein structures, fundamental papers on the bonding of elementary phosphorus and the structure of oxygen acids, the borides of transition elements and the alloys of lead, the resonance of the hydrogen molecule and the nature of intermetallic compounds. He made a major advance in the field of hydrate chemistry by showing how water molecules could link themselves into elegant crystalline cages around a central kernel of a gas atom. He reviewed the structural chemistry of molybdenum. He began work on a new theory of ferromagnetism. He published an idea he had implemented at Caltech for modifying examinations for doctoral students. He began writing a new, heavily revised second edition of *General Chemistry* and explained to readers of the popular magazine *Science Digest* why "It Pays to Understand Science."

Awards and honors continued to shower in: election as vice president of the illustrious American Philosophical Society, the intellectuals' club that Benjamin Franklin had started; first recipient of the G. N.

Lewis Medal, awarded by the Berkeley chapter of the American Chemical Society (ACS); named to the Panel on Research of the President's Commission on the Health Needs of the Nation; featured in the "Half-Century Hall of Fame" of *Popular Mechanics;* a continuing string of honorary degrees. He even became a movie star in a small way, enduring the application of pancake makeup and the rigor of being directed by Frank Capra for a Caltech recruiting film.

Things were happy at home as well, at least as far as Pauling could see. The Sierra Madre house was often the site of the annual start-of-the-school-year divisional party, which Pauling would hold on his lawn, with simple food and plenty to drink, the punch served once, someone recalled, from the nose cone of a rocket. He and Ava Helen entertained a cavalcade of dinner guests, mostly faculty or visiting scholars, and Ava Helen held occasional teas at the house for faculty wives despite the fact that she did not get along well with most of them—too dowdy and domestic for her tastes—and they found her too sharp-tongued and politically opinionated for theirs. More to her liking was a monthly folk-dance group that met at the house in the years following their return from England. Ava Helen had always loved music, and with the furniture pushed back and the record player turned up, she and a group of friends and children would dance for hours—with such enthusiasm that on one occasion Ava Helen tripped and broke her wrist.

Folk art became a minor interest of hers, and because she chose her husband's wardrobe, it soon showed up in Pauling's style as well. In the early 1950s his tailored suits and ties often gave way to slacks and sport shirts, even at the office, some of the shirts outlandishly colorful, with boldly stated ethnic patterns. He wore his thinning gray hair longer now, more like Einstein, so that it formed a wispy corona around his head. Age led to another addition to his personal style as well: Ben Franklin–style half-frame spectacles that he would push up over his forehead when talking or down on his nose so that he could peer over them to make a point. Occasionally, he wore a beret. In the gray-suit 1950s, it all added to the image of a liberal rebel, a man so at ease with himself that he did not care what others thought about him. And that was fine with Pauling.

His children seemed to be thriving. After taking his residency in psychiatry at a hospital in Honolulu, firstborn Linus junior had decided to settle in Hawaii with his wife, partly because of the paradisiacal climate, partly to keep enough distance between him and his parents. There were grandchildren now, the first, Linus III, born in

1948. Because of the distance, Pauling and Ava Helen saw him and the siblings that followed only rarely.

Peter made up for his older brother's remoteness by modeling himself after his father, entering Caltech as an undergraduate and taking up the study of physics and chemistry, a development that made Pauling proud, although Peter's siblings worried about his attempts to fill his father's shoes. Peter seemed to do all right, however, making passing grades and developing a typical college-level interest in beer and parties. He became friends with a number of Pauling's graduate students and postdocs, and around 1950 a small social scene began developing at the Paulings' house, with a half-dozen young would-be scientists making their way up into the hills on warm afternoons for a beer, a dip in the pool, some jokes with Peter, and a chance to flirt with tall, slim, blond teenaged Linda Pauling.

She enjoyed the attention not only for all the usual reasons but also because it helped to balance a growing feeling of neglect. Linda had always doted on Pauling and wanted to impress him. She tried to be the perfect daughter, respectful, polite, quiet. But nothing seemed to bring her more than a perfunctory pat on the head. Pauling's attention was focused on research, Ava Helen, and politics, in that order, and Linda would always be at best a distant fourth. She tried to impress her father by taking an interest in science at her private prep school, working a summer job at age eighteen x-raying alloys in a Caltech lab and telling her family that she wanted to major in chemistry in college. That was fine, Pauling said. She became jealous of the time Ava Helen spent traveling with Pauling and the way he looked to her for approval and opinions. Linda would always remember the afternoon she waltzed into Pauling's study to show him a new dress she thought was particularly attractive. Pauling took a quick look, said, "You know, that dress would look wonderful on your mother," and went back to his calculations.

But now Linda was starting to get plenty of attention from her father's students, and she encouraged it. When Pauling and Ava Helen were away, Peter's and Linda's poolside gatherings sometimes turned into small and sometimes raucous parties.

But the young visitors, a mix of students and postdocs, liked it almost as much when Pauling was there. They were the select, the privileged, the few disciples of science allowed into one of its private sanctums. There was the fun around the pool, of course, but there was also the opportunity to talk about research with Pauling in his octagonal study or to discuss science, politics, or their futures when Pauling, taking a break from his theoretical work, would stride across the lawn, sit down with that trademark grin on his face, and start up a conversation. Entire lives could be changed in the course of a brief poolside chat. It happened to Matt Meselson, a friend of Peter's up for a swim in the summer of 1952. Meselson, a talented young former Caltech student who had just spent a year in graduate school at Berkeley, was planning to switch to the University of Chicago until Pauling, fully dressed in a suit and tie, walked out into the hot yard, kneeled by the edge of the pool, looked straight at the young man as he treaded water, and asked, "Well, Matt, what are you going to do next year?" Meselson told him his plans for Chicago. "But, Matt," Pauling said, "that's a lot of baloney. Why don't you come to Caltech and be my graduate student?" The vision of the world-renowned scientist looming over him at poolside was awe-inspiring. Meselson looked up at him and said, "Okay, I will." After studying with Pauling, Meselson went on to a distinguished career in molecular biology at Harvard. It was like that, the great man appearing, dropping some bit of wisdom, then heading back to the house to leave them to their fun. It was unbelievably exhilarating, the cutting edge, a heady mixture of unconventional politics, unorthodox science, and sparkling people, all packaged as a Southern California pool party. Pauling's house was, one remembered, "the hot spot."

Pauling was an extremely popular professor among his students. Most of them thought of him as a guru who did his thinking up in the hills, received enlightenment, then descended to share the revealed truth with the multitudes. His now-legendary freshman lectures were still studded with parlor tricks—Pauling would calculate a needed number to six figures on a five-inch pocket slide rule, inevitably sending a group of disbelieving freshmen to a mechanical calculator to check his work (he was always right)—but they now also seemed like the free flow of pure wisdom from the greatest teacher in chemistry. A Pauling lecture was "like going to a great concert," one listener remembered.

His students began modeling themselves after him. The great trick in becoming another Pauling had something to do with recognizing what they called "the Pauling Point." "This is when you do things only up to a certain level to get the right answer—or another way, if you go further and deeper it looks much more complicated and the answer becomes more diffuse," said Martin Karplus, another Harvard professor who was once one of the young fellows sitting around Pauling's pool. "The Pauling Point is just to take the right level of approach to get the correct answer." This was the master's essential art, the ability to see the big picture, to stop worrying at just the right moment about niggling details, to achieve victory over a problem without beating it to death. It was science done with grace and timing. And, most of them found out, it was almost impossible to emulate.

Pauling had never been one to hover over his students and post-doctoral fellows, marking each movement and providing careful directions—"It was a sink or swim environment," one remembered—but with his increased fame the few interactions he did have with them took on the overtones of a conversation with a Zen master. Alex Rich, a recently graduated M.D. who joined Pauling's lab to try his hand at research, was having trouble settling into a project, jumping from sickle-cell work to theoretical studies of the binding of carbon. Nothing captured his imagination. Restless and unsure of what to do, he found himself one evening in 1950 in Pauling's study, having a talk about science in general and nothing in particular. Then Pauling picked up a book that had just been mailed to him, the proceedings of the transaction of a meeting of the Royal Society on quantum chemistry, a volume of nothing but the sort of theoretical calculations Rich had been sweating over. Pauling looked at it and threw the book down. "Worthless," he said. "Rubbish." When Rich asked why, Pauling said, "Well, in the thirties I worked hard to see if I could find a closed solution, to solve these equations in a way that gave you these answers. I couldn't find them, and since then people have used different kinds of approximations to try and do this or do that. There are many methods of making approximations. It's like whipping a dead horse." It was not until he was driving down the hill that Rich realized that Pauling was telling him something about his future. "Linus can't solve these problems," he said to himself. "Why do I think I can do a better job?" Based on the oblique conversation, Rich decided to learn x-ray crystallography, a career change that led to an outstanding career at MIT.

Meselson compares Pauling's style to Socrates' admonition that virtue cannot be taught; it can only be set by example. "That's the way Linus, I think, affected people."

The young men around him in the early 1950s, in the privileged group, including a number who would go on to significant careers in science, would be deeply affected and bound together by his example. They would become closer to Pauling than any students since his first batch back in the early 1930s.

The Secret of Life, Part 2

Being a father figure to budding scientists was satisfying to Pauling, but his greatest satisfaction, as always, came from his research. After 1951, Pauling began applying the lessons he had learned with proteins to the structures of other long-chain biomolecules, including starches and nucleic acids. These were certainly less important than proteins in terms of the body's functions, but they also appeared to be much simpler structurally, which might make them relatively easy to solve with his model-building approach.

In the summer of 1951, Pauling started reading in some depth and talking to others about deoxyribonucleic acid—everyone called it DNA—the most common form of nucleic acid in chromosomes. Astbury had done some smeary x-ray work in the late 1930s that indicated that DNA was a long-chain molecule with a repeating pattern. It might well be a helix. But it was composed of just four subunits, called nucleotides, all of which appeared to be present in all DNA from all animals in approximately equal amounts, compared to protein's twenty-some amino acids, which varied widely in occurrence in various molecules. Each nucleotide consisted of a sugar, a phosphate group, and one of four carbon-and-nitrogen ring structures called bases: adenine, guanine, thymine, and cytosine. Pauling had theorized a structure for guanine in the early 1930s as part of his work on resonance; it was a flat plate, and the other three bases appeared to be too. The key to DNA would be figuring how each base joined with a sugar and a phosphate to make a nucleotide; then how the nucleotides joined to form chains. Compared to protein structures, Pauling thought, that should not be too hard to work out.

It was not a top-priority problem in any case. DNA was by weight an important component of chromosomes, but so was protein, and it seemed likely to most researchers that the protein portion carried the genetic instructions. Protein had the variety of forms and functions, the subunit variability, the sheer sophistication to account for heredity. DNA by comparison seemed dumb, more likely a structural component that helped fold or unfold the chromosomes. Beadle believed it. Pauling believed it. At the beginning of 1952, almost every important worker in genetics believed it.

The only evidence to the contrary was a little-appreciated paper published in 1944 by Rockefeller Institute researcher Oswald Avery, who had found that DNA, apparently by itself, could transfer new genetic traits between *Pneumococcus* bacteria. But for years no one paid much attention to Avery's work. Pauling knew about it—he had been in contact with Avery during the war through his work with *Pneumococcus* antigens and artificial antibodies—but thought it unimportant. "I knew the contention that DNA was the hereditary material," Pauling said. "But I didn't accept it. I was so pleased with proteins, you know, that I thought that proteins probably are the hereditary material rather than nucleic acids—but that of course nucleic acids played a part. In whatever I wrote about nucleic acids, I mentioned nucleoproteins, and I was thinking more of the protein than of the nucleic acids."

So the structure of DNA was simply an interesting question in modeling techniques when Pauling talked with Gerald Oster, a professor visiting Caltech from Brooklyn Poly in the summer of 1951, about his research. Oster had been doing some studies on the effect of water content on DNA, and after returning east, he sent Pauling some of his data. At the end of one letter, Oster added a quick idea. "I hope you'll write to Prof. J. T. Randall, King's College, Strand, London," he wrote. "His coworker, Dr. M. Wilkins, told me he had some good fibre pictures of nucleic acid."

Good pictures of DNA were hard to come by. While any strand of hair could provide a decent x-ray photo of keratin, DNA had to be extracted from cell nuclei and separated from its attendant protein, a difficult process. The techniques of the day for isolating DNA in general degraded the molecule somewhat, and the final product was the sodium salt of DNA, called sodium thymonucleate. But there was some doubt as to how the isolation process altered the molecule's structure, and even purified sodium thymonucleate was difficult to use for x-ray diffraction. At the time, Astbury's first x-ray patterns from the 1930s— and one new photograph he had published in 1947 with his own ideas about DNA structure—were the only usable ones in print. And they were not worth much. While x-ray patterns from globular proteins provided too much data to analyze successfully, Astbury's DNA photos provided too little. Pauling could get some rough ideas of dimensions and the size of repeating units from these pictures, but they were too muddy to get much more.

He needed better x-ray photos and decided to write Wilkins. It would be somewhat uncommon for a researcher involved in an active program to give up raw data before publishing it in some form, but Oster had led Pauling to believe that Wilkins was not interested in doing much with the photos he had, which Oster thought had been taken some time ago. So Pauling took a chance and wrote to Randall's laboratory sometime in the late summer of 1951 asking if he could see what Wilkins had.

—⁓⁓⁓—

Maurice Wilkins was not sure what to do when he read Pauling's letter.

A thin, bespectacled physicist whose career had so far failed to produce much of significance, Wilkins had succeeded a year earlier in one endeavor: finding a way to get the world's best x-ray photos of DNA. It had happened while he was working with a solution of sodium thymonucleate. When dissolved in water, the substance formed a kind of viscous solution that Wilkins found could be drawn out into spider-web-thin fibers by carefully dipping the end of a glass rod in the solution and pulling it slowly. The very long DNA strands apparently aligned themselves along the fibers. By keeping in mind Bernal's discovery that globular proteins photographed better when wet, Wilkins kept his x-ray camera set up at a high humidity and was able to string his fibers up and take x-ray photos. The results were dramatically better than Astbury's, with a wealth of sharp spots. Wilkins's work immediately confirmed that DNA had a repeating crystalline structure and was therefore solvable.

But he could not solve it alone. Wilkins was a man of many talents—he got his start separating uranium isotopes for the Manhattan Project—but was not well trained in the interpretation of x-ray photos and was hampered by inadequate equipment for fiber x-ray work at King's College. He decided in 1950 not to publish his pictures until he had a chance to analyze his data more thoroughly and replicate them with better equipment. The delay that Oster read as lack of interest was really time spent arranging for a better laboratory setup and some help.

By January 1951, Wilkins had his new equipment and someone to run it, Rosalind Franklin, a talented young crystallographer who had earned a reputation for her meticulous x-ray work with hard-to-study coal derivatives. Unfortunately, the relationship between Wilkins and Franklin got off to a rocky start. Wilkins thought Franklin had been hired to assist him and turned over to her his photos, his fiber x-ray setup, and one of his graduate students. Franklin, however, was under the impression that she had been hired to work independently. By the time Pauling's letter arrived, the two had had a falling-out, leaving the question of how to proceed with DNA somewhat up in the air and making it more difficult to answer Pauling's request. Franklin had taken a proprietary interest in solving DNA's structure from the steadily better photos she was taking, and Wilkins was also interested in solving the structure—with, he hoped, Franklin's help. Wilkins was well aware that given his photos, Pauling would probably beat them both to it. His fears were increased by his suspicion that DNA might be a helix, the form that Pauling had already used to embarrass the English. He held on to Pauling's letter for a week while he mulled over alternatives. Then he wrote back that he was sorry but he wanted to look more closely at his data before releasing the pictures.

Undeterred, Pauling wrote Wilkins's superior, J. T. Randall, with the same request. Randall was sorry, too, replying, "Wilkins and others are busily engaged in working out the interpretation of the desoxyribosenucleic acid x-ray photographs, and it would not be fair to them, or to the efforts of our laboratory as a whole, to hand these over to you."

That was in August. Pauling put DNA aside until November, when an article on its structure by a fellow named Edward Ronwin was published in the *Journal of the American Chemical Society (JACS)*. Pauling could see at a single glance that Ronwin's work was wrong. The molecule's phosphate groups, which should have consisted of a phosphorus atom surrounded by a tetrahedron of four oxygens in Pauling's opinion, showed each phosphorus connected to five oxygen atoms. Pauling had just finished reviewing phosphorus chemistry for a paper of his own, and it seemed to him that Ronwin's model was nonsense. He wrote a letter to the *JACS* about it. Pauling, as it turned out, was right.

More importantly, it started him thinking about how DNA might be built. Ronwin had put his phosphates down the middle of the molecule, with the flat bases sticking out to the sides. This was certainly possible—Astbury's x-ray photos did not rule out such an arrangement—and it would solve a major problem. The four bases of DNA came in two different sizes: two double-ring purines and two smaller pyrimidines with single rings. Say that it was a helix, as Astbury's photos indicated it might be. Trying to arrange the different-sized bases on the inside of a long helical molecule would create all sorts of fitting and stacking problems. Facing the bases out would make the molecule easier to solve, just as facing the amino-acid side chains away from the center of the protein spiral had made the alpha helix much easier to work with.

If the bases faced out, Pauling hypothesized, then the core of the helix would be packed with phosphates. Phosphates up the middle, bases facing out. It fit the available x-ray data. After Ronwin's paper, the problem of the structure of DNA began reducing itself in Pauling's mind to a question of packing phosphates together.

—*mm*—

He had gotten that far when Pauling put DNA aside again and returned to proteins. In the fall of 1951 he received an invitation to a special meeting of the Royal Society designed specifically to address the many questions British researchers had raised about his structures. The date was set for May 1, 1952.

Pauling was eager to go. In preparation, through the end of 1951 and on into the first months of 1952, he and Corey tested, refined, and rethought their structures, especially muscle and collagen. Part of the problem with muscle was that it rarely gave clear x-ray patterns, so Pauling collected and dried two hundred samples himself, mostly from mussels gathered at the Caltech marine station at Corona del Mar. He concluded from his new pictures that muscle was mostly composed of alpha helixes, with about 10 percent of something else that gave an odd look to the x-ray patterns; he and Corey would later try to figure out what that was. As for collagen, Corey prepared a twenty-page in-house review of data supporting their three-helix cable structure. Corey also redoubled his efforts on a multistage attack on lysozyme, working to become the first person to determine the complete structure of a globular protein. Here again, Pauling's lab was racing with Bragg's, with Corey pitted against Perutz and Kendrew, who were doing the same thing with hemoglobin and myoglobin.

In January 1952, Pauling began making arrangements for a spring European trip that would include the May Royal Society meeting, an honorary doctorate from the University at Toulouse, and a tour of Spanish universities. He sent in an application to renew his passport.

Then came another distraction.

Mrs. Shipley

On Valentine's Day, 1952, Mrs. Ruth B. Shipley, head of the State Department's passport division, wrote a note. "My dear Dr. Pauling: You are informed that your request for a passport has been carefully considered by the Department. However, a passport of this Government is not being issued to you since the Department is of the opinion that your proposed travel would not be in the best interests of the United States."

When he read it, Pauling was irritated but not surprised. Passports had become another political weapon since the passage of the Internal Security Act of 1950 broadened the government's power to refuse political dissidents the right to travel. Shipley, a fervent anti-Communist and security-minded sister of a pre-Hoover FBI director, took advantage of her position as head of the State Department's Passport Division to refuse passports to anyone she and the State Department's security personnel—or the FBI, with which she kept in close contact—suspected of being too far left and too loud about it.

After 1950, her power to refuse passports was almost unlimited, and Shipley wielded her new weapon like a committed Cold Warrior. In a one-year period following May 1951, her office barred three-hundred Americans from going abroad, sometimes on the flimsiest of excuses. Targets ranged from African-American singer and admitted pro-Communist Paul Robeson to Indiana University virus researcher and moderate leftist Salvador Luria. Suspicious foreigners were also refused visas to enter the United States, resulting in embarrassing situations for the organizers of international meetings, including the huge World Chemical Conclave. Pauling publicly protested the visa denials and joined a group formed specifically to protest the Internal Security Act. But passport interference was especially hard to deal with because there was no clear route for appeals.

Shipley had been keeping an eye on Pauling, and her interest deepened when she saw his name among those speaking out against her policies. In late October 1951, in response to an earlier request Pauling made for a passport for a possible trip to Europe and India, she initiated a State Department Security Office investigation. The process was short and to the point. State Department officials read his FBI files and interviewed a single anonymous source, who told them that Pauling was "a professional do-gooder" driven into politics by his wife, "a complete fool with regard to politics," who "assures her husband daily on the hour that he has one of the three greatest minds in the world today, and that he should not deny the uninformed and ignorant his leadership and ability."

On the basis of that information, Shipley concluded that "there is good reason to believe that Dr. Pauling is a Communist" and refused him a passport. Pauling responded to his Valentine's Day denial by firing off a letter to Harry Truman, asking him to "rectify this action, and to arrange the issuance of a passport to me. I am a loyal and conscien-

tious citizen of the United States. I have never been guilty of any unpa-
triotic or criminal act." He attached a copy of the Medal of Merit citation Truman had signed. The president's secretary wrote back that it
was strictly a Passport Division decision but that the White House was
requesting a reexamination. When Shipley stood firm, Truman's office
did nothing more.

In April, Pauling decided to simplify matters by restricting his trip
to England only and wrote an exceedingly polite letter to Shipley offering to meet with her at her convenience later in the month when he
would be in the East. The purpose of his trip to Washington, D.C., he
mentioned pointedly, was to chair a meeting of an Office of Naval Research committee. Then he put lawyer Abraham Lincoln Wirin on the
case. Wirin and Pauling peppered the passport office with transcripts
of his IERB hearing, information about the Russian attack on Pauling,
and copies of his many awards.

But Shipley's mind was made up. On April 18, she again wrote him
that his passport was being refused.

Time was now getting short. The Royal Society meeting was set for
May 1. On April 21, Pauling and Ava Helen paid a personal visit to the
Passport Office. After a short wait in the lobby, they were ushered into
the presence of a tightly controlled, tight-lipped Ruth Shipley. The
Paulings assumed that she was a public servant and adopted an appropriately polite but forceful tone. They asked her for the specific reasons
Pauling's passport was being denied. Her response, Pauling remembered, was "a rather vague general statement" about his Communist-
front activities. She brushed aside their further questions and made it
clear that the decision to deny his passport had been hers to make and
she had made it. There would be no further debate. She then showed
them into the office of the director of security and consular affairs,
who asked Pauling to provide written evidence that supported his
claim that he was not a Communist. Pauling had some relevant documents airmailed overnight from Pasadena and took them in the next
day, including his statement under oath that he was not a member of
the Communist Party. He was told brusquely that a decision would be
reached as soon as it was reached but that there was no telling when.

By now Pauling felt that this was more than frustrating; it was insulting. He had arrived as a distinguished citizen ready to solve a problem and was being treated like a truant schoolboy.

He rearranged his travel plans to take a later flight and continued
his protest, going so far as to get the president of the National Academy of Sciences (NAS) to write a letter on his behalf. Nothing did any

good. On April 28, two hours before the last plane that would get him to London on time was to leave, he received final word that his passport would not be granted. The next day, Pauling wired the Royal Society that he would not be able to attend the meeting being held in his honor.

The English sponsors of the meeting were incredulous. Many of the attendees learned about it at a formal tea that Pauling had been slated to attend the day before the meeting's start. One of them later recalled "the shock that it produced, the outrage at the stupidity of the State Department at detaining the great man as if he were a dangerous character."

—*m*—

Corey, who was slated to give a talk of his own, and Caltech crystallographer Eddie Hughes were already in London when the news broke. Pauling had told Hughes to be prepared to stand in for him, but it was laughable to think that it would really happen. This, after all, was going to be one of the most important presentations in the history of the study of protein structure, and of course Pauling would be there to deliver it. Not hearing any news, Hughes went to Heathrow Airport to meet the last plane Pauling could have taken, and it was only when his boss did not come down the ramp that it began to sink in that he was going to have to make the speech himself. In his hotel room that night Hughes nervously read and reread the manuscript Pauling had prepared, with notations to indicate where to show the twenty slides that went with it. It was a long talk, but Hughes practiced until it just fit within the standard hour-long slot.

The next morning, adrenaline flowing, he walked into the ornate meeting room of the Royal Society, mounted the dais, and was informed that he would have twenty minutes to speak. "There I was, standing before the Royal Society, with Charles the Second's oil painting looking over my shoulder, wondering what I should leave out," he said. Hughes slashed furiously at his copy of the speech while Corey went first with a talk about amino-acid structures. He was not done editing when his time came to speak, and he managed only to stumble through a review of Pauling's chemical approach to structure—the importance of the planarity of the peptide bond, correct interatomic distances and bond angles, maximum formation of hydrogen bonds—when he ran out of time. Seeing a disaster in the making, a member moved that Hughes should have an extra ten minutes. That gave him time to read Pauling's conclusion: "In view of the success that has thus far been obtained by this method of attack, it seems justified to assume that proposed configurations of polypeptide chains that deviate largely from the structural principles that have now been formulated . . . may be ruled out of consideration." Pauling would have delivered the lines with ringing confidence. Hughes sat down with a sigh of relief. There was scattered applause.

For the rest of the day, Hughes remembered, "the Englishmen sat there, telling us what was wrong." Astbury led the attack, reminding everyone that the alpha helix did not explain the 5.1-angstrom reflection, while his own kinked-ribbon model did; that Pauling's density calculations left "discrepancies . . . much too great to be reasonable," that Pauling ignored side-chain interactions; that too much reliance was being placed on data from artificial polypeptides. Dorothy Hodgkin remained neutral, reporting that her insulin-diffraction patterns could support either Astbury's model or Pauling's. Bernal reiterated the lack of proof for the presence of the alpha helix in any globular protein. Ian MacArther pointed out that Pauling had been rather free with his numerical corrections in response to criticisms, noting that "on occasion, the alpha helix has been as deft in explaining error as well as fact." Bragg did not need to say anything.

Only John Edsall, an American hemoglobin researcher given the honor of speaking last, came to Pauling's defense. He lauded Pauling's chemical approach as "one of the major landmarks in our thinking about acceptable configurations for polypeptide chains in proteins" and called the alpha helix "one of the great creative triumphs of thinking in the field of protein chemistry."

But the damage was done. Hughes felt that the Caltech team had been bushwhacked, especially when at the end of the day he and Corey, eager to rebut the English critics, were allowed just five minutes to do it. "I was very angry," Hughes remembered. "I wrote Pauling and told him I thought we'd gotten a dirty deal."

Bragg, too, had regrets. Everyone at the meeting was very sorry indeed that Pauling had not been there, he wrote Pauling immediately afterward. "There was much discussion about your model of the alpha helix; a number of people are still doubtful about it and you ought to have been there to answer their questions personally." As for himself, Bragg added, he was convinced of the alpha helix's "essential correctness"—at least in artificial polypeptides.

Despite the tough reception for his protein ideas, Pauling's passport plight was widely deplored in England. It started at the May 1 meeting, where U.S. State Department science adviser Joe Koepfli found himself cornered by irate English scientists who told him that his government's travel policies were suspiciously and unacceptably like Russia's. The left-wing press in England made the case a cause célèbre, with the *Daily Worker* (London) headline blaring: "Iron Curtain Round Scientist."

On May 5, Secretary of State Dean Acheson read a telexed copy of a letter published that morning in the *Times* (London) by Sir Robert Robinson, Britain's leading organic chemist, winner of the Nobel Prize and a man known generally for his reserve. Sir Robert took the State Department to task for its "deplorable" actions in the Pauling case. "It would be insincere to pretend that we have no inkling of the reason for the drastic action taken by the American authorities," he wrote, "but that does not lessen our surprise and consternation." In a cover note, a U.S. embassy attaché in London stressed that "this one case is resulting in a definite and important prejudice to the American national interest."

The news from France was no better. Two days after the Royal Society meeting, in a slap directed at the U.S. government, the French elected Pauling "Honorary President" of a biochemistry symposium scheduled for Paris that summer. French scientists were united in their criticism of the Pauling case; the U.S. science attaché in Paris was informed by one physiologist that the Americans must be "losing their minds." The Pauling case was splashed across the front page of the left-wing *L'Humanité*, along with the story of French scientists denied visas to visit the United States. "The accumulating number of such cases is causing strong feelings and is resulting in considerable mistrust as to our motives," the attaché wrote his superiors in Washington, D.C.

The European outcry was heard in the offices of the *New York Times,* which ran a pair of news stories in early May along with an editorial, "Dr. Pauling's Predicament," calling for an investigation of passport policy. The State Department was quickly peppered with pro-Pauling protest letters. Bernal and thirty other British scientists signed one; Harold Urey, Enrico Fermi, Edward Teller, Bill Libby, and other leading atomic scientists from the University of Chicago wrote another, asking Dean Acheson, "What harm, what information, what tales could Professor Pauling take with him to England, even if he were so inclined, that can compare in damage to the incredible advertisement that this country forbids one of its most illustrious citizens to travel?" Einstein wrote Acheson to protest and then sent Pauling a note of personal support. "It is very meritorious of you to fight for the right to travel," he wrote. "The fact that independent minds like you are being rebuked equally by official America and official Russia is significant and to a certain degree also amusing." Even DuBridge could not ignore the issue and noted publicly that the Pauling case was "not in keeping with our democratic traditions."

The State Department was not alone in hearing from aggrieved citizens. Spurred by angry letters and telegrams from their constituents, a half-dozen U.S. senators and representatives, from Henry Cabot Lodge to Richard Nixon, asked for more details on the case.

And Pauling, too, buoyed by his supporters, renewed his fight. He sent in another passport application for travel to England and France that summer, talked to the press—telling one reporter, "This whole incident, to be blunt, stinks"—wrote Acheson and Truman letters of protest, and brought his case to the attention of Oregon's maverick senator Wayne Morse, who became "incensed," Pauling remembered. Morse thundered on the Senate floor that the State Department's passport policies were "tyrannical" and Acheson was "an undesirable employee of the government." He then began drawing up new legislation to create a process for appeals of passport decisions. The nation's news and thought magazines picked up the issue.

Through it all, Ruth Shipley was not moved. She referred inquiring congressmen to the House Un-American Activities Committee pamphlet "A Campaign to Disarm and Defeat the United States," which detailed Pauling's Communist-front activities, and brushed off everyone else. When one scientist got through to her on the telephone to ask why Pauling's passport had been denied, she cut him short, saying, "As I had to defer to the scientists on scientific matters on which they were expert, they would have to defer to the Department in so technical a matter as the refusal of a passport."

Secretary of State Acheson, however, could not ignore the issue. He wanted to defend his passport policy, but when he studied it, he realized that there existed neither clear guidelines for the decision to revoke a passport nor any proper appeals process. By late May, the Pauling case had spurred the State Department to outline publicly for the first time its policy on refusing passports, but the language used was so broad and vague that the press would not buy it. A few weeks later, Acheson released a longer explanation, including details of how appeals should be handled step by step, with those refused retaining the right to bring in counsel. The wording made it appear that the process had been in place for months, but it was news to Pauling, especially the part about his right to a lawyer. He immediately wrote Acheson that his explanation "does not correspond to my own experience."

The furor resulted in special attention to his new passport application. Shipley routinely refused it in June, but when she sent it up for the usual rubber-stamp approval from Acheson's office, there was a review. During the next week, the Pauling case was discussed intensively at the highest levels of the State Department. The decision was made to end what had become a public relations fiasco with minimal fanfare. Shipley was overruled. Pauling was to be granted a limited passport—good for a short period of time for travel only in England and France—provided that he sign a new affidavit denying membership in the Communist Party. No public announcement was to be made. If reporters asked, the official line was to be that "new evidence" had altered the case. Although Acheson had been involved in making the decision, his name was not to be attached to it in any way. No other details were to be provided.

Pauling was surprised and jubilant when he heard the news. On July 11 he showed up at the Los Angeles field office to sign the affidavit. On July 14, his passport was granted.

Not everyone was pleased. Ruth Shipley fumed at being overruled. J. Edgar Hoover, his long-standing interest in Pauling reawakened, dispatched an agent to her office to ask what the "new evidence" was. Shipley told him that the FBI knew as much about it as she did and then let Hoover's agents comb through Pauling's State Department records. After a thorough search, the agents concluded: "A review of the file fails to disclose exactly what this new evidence is, unless it refers to the volume of letters and comments in the file protesting the previous refusal of a passport to the subject."

Pauling was once again heartened. His was the first case in which public protest had made a difference in passport policy. Ruth Shipley was now under scrutiny, and a new passport appeals process was being developed to ensure a more reasonable and fair hearing for anyone else denied the right to travel.

Variety Act

Pauling's unexpected arrival at the Paris International Biochemical Congress caused a sensation. News of his political troubles and defiance of the government had made him a hero in France, and his hastily arranged talk on protein structures drew an overflow crowd. Afterward, he was swarmed by researchers eager to shake the honorary president's hand and express their admiration for his principles. He and Ava Helen received a stream of friends and well-wishers in their rooms at the Trianon.

A week or so after the Congress, Pauling attended the International Phage Colloquium at the centuries-old Abbey of Royaumont outside Paris, where he heard the American microbiologist Alfred Hershey describe an ingenious experiment that had everyone talking. In an attempt to settle the question of whether DNA or protein was the genetic material, Hershey and a coworker, Martha Chase, had found a way to tag the DNA and protein of a bacterial virus with separate radioactive labels. By tracking the labels, they were able to show persuasively that the protein did nothing. DNA alone directed the replication of new viruses.

While Oswald Avery's work had been presented tentatively and made little impact, the "Waring blender experiment," as it became known, after a piece of decidedly nontechnical machinery that was used in the experiment, clearly showed that DNA was the genetic material. What worked with viruses might well work with higher organisms as well, and as word of the Hershey-Chase experiment spread, phage researchers, geneticists, and biochemists interested in replication began to switch their focus from protein to DNA. Pauling, too, quickly realized that he had been on the wrong track. It was not that proteins were unimportant; they were still critical in the functioning of the body. But it was clear now that the genetic master molecule, the one that directed the making of proteins, was DNA.

It was an unnerving realization, but Pauling took it in stride. He was confident that he could solve DNA. He had already started thinking about it, and it looked fairly simple. The only problem would be if someone beat him to it, but he could not take the possibility very seriously. Wilkins and Franklin were at work on it—Corey, in fact, had visited Franklin's laboratory while over for the Royal Society meeting in May and had seen some excellent x-ray photos she was getting of DNA—but there was no indication that either of them knew enough chemistry to be a serious threat. If Bragg were involved, that would be a different matter, but the only indication from the Cavendish that anyone was looking at DNA came from one of Delbrück's protégés, there on a postdoctoral fellowship, twenty-two-year-old James Watson, who had written Delbrück something about looking for a DNA model a few months earlier. Delbrück had read Watson's letter to Pauling. It did not sound very serious. Although Delbrück thought Watson was promising, he had not been good enough to get admitted to Caltech when he applied for graduate work. The gentlemen at the Cavendish had, in any case, not yet beaten Pauling in any race.

At the Royaumont meeting, Pauling talked with a group about solving DNA the way he had solved the alpha helix: using precise x-ray work to confirm the structure of its building blocks, as Corey and his coworkers had done with amino acids. Nail down the precise form of the bases and their relationship to the sugars and phosphates, he said; then make a model of the most chemically probable long-chain structure that they would form.

James Watson was among the group gathered around Pauling at Royaumont, and he listened closely. He already knew that Pauling's approach was the way to solve DNA, and he had already tried to do it.

Watson was at Royaumont ostensibly because he was part of "the phage group," an informal array of researchers gathered around Delbrück at Caltech and Salvador Luria at Indiana University, researchers who believed that bacterial viruses were as close as you could get to "naked genes," stripped-down versions of living organisms capable of nothing but replication. The simpler the system, the easier it was to study, and the phage group was convinced that viruses represented the next great genetics tool, following Morgan's fruit flies and Beadle's molds.

And Watson realized earlier than most that DNA was the key to learning about genes. After getting his Ph.D. under Luria, Watson had left on a European fellowship to study microbial metabolism and nucleic acid biochemistry, but he had quickly tired of it and began bouncing around looking for inspiration. He found it in Naples, at a meeting in the spring of 1951 where Wilkins displayed some of his x-ray photos of DNA. Although he did not know much about x-ray crystallography, Watson realized that Wilkins's work showed that DNA had a regular, repeating structure. It could form fibers that gave x-ray patterns, which meant that its structure was solvable—but Watson would need to learn x-ray crystallography to solve the structure. He tried to talk his way into Wilkins's lab but knew nothing about what they were doing and was turned down; with Delbrück's help he ended up instead, in the fall of 1951, learning how to diffract x-rays from proteins with Kendrew at the Cavendish.

It was thought wise to give someone with such changeable interests as Watson as much guidance as possible, so he was assigned to share an office with a graduate student of Perutz's who knew crystallography inside and out. His name was Francis Crick.

The two men hit it off immediately. They made quite a pair: Crick, in his mid-thirties, old for a graduate student—his scientific progress delayed by wartime work—but self-confident and outgoing, talkative to a fault, with fashionably long sideburns and a love of three-piece suits; Watson, young, thin, and shy, with his American tennis shoes and crew cut. Erwin Chargaff painted an unkind contemporary picture of them: "One 35 years old, with the looks of a fading racing tout . . . an incessant falsetto, with occasional nuggets gleaming in the turbid stream of prattle. The other, quite undeveloped . . . a grin, more sly than sheepish . . . a gawky young figure." Crick and Watson, he said, looked like "a variety act."

But they impressed each other. Crick soon understood why Watson "was regarded, in most circles, as too bright to be really sound." Watson wrote Delbrück a few weeks after meeting Crick that he was "no doubt the brightest person I have ever worked with and the nearest approach to Pauling I've ever seen." This was high praise, given both men's high regard for the wizard of Pasadena. Watson had first been exposed to Pauling's charisma in the summer of 1949, when he worked with Delbrück at Caltech for a few months and got to know some of the young men in Pauling's lab. Watson saw Pauling only from afar, but it was enough to make an impression. "There was no one like Linus in all the world," Watson later wrote. "Even if he were to say nonsense, his mesmerized students would never know because of his unquenchable self-confidence." Pauling had presence and style, he did great science, had an intriguing family, and loved to drive foreign sports cars very fast. To the nineteen-year-old Watson, Pauling was someone to emulate.

Crick started out not as a Pauling fan but as a competitor. He had been present during the discussions between Bragg, Perutz, and Kendrew that led to the misbegotten 1950 paper on protein structures, had failed, as they all did, to note the importance of the planar peptide bond, and had shared in the humiliation that resulted when Pauling beat them to the alpha helix. He learned three indelible lessons from that experience: The first was that Pauling's approach, with its guess at a reasonable solution based on firm chemical principles and its reliance on model building, was the fastest way to solve giant biomolecules. The second was that no single piece of experimental evidence should serve to dissuade one from a theory—witness Pauling's decision to ignore the anomalous 5.1-angstrom reflection. The third was that helixes were the form to look for.

By the time Watson arrived, Crick was ripe for a project that would free him from endless attempts at the mathematical interpretation of hemoglobin diffraction patterns. Within a few days, Watson provided him with what he was looking for, a relatively simple and potentially more important target: DNA. They quickly agreed on a method of attack: Rather than devising complex mathematical schemes to directly and unambiguously interpret x-ray results, they would use chemical common sense to build a model structure. As Watson put it, they would "imitate Linus Pauling and beat him at his own game."

The story of Crick and Watson's first attempt to solve the structure of DNA in the fall of 1951 has been told many times, most entertainingly in Watson's book *The Double Helix*. Suffice it to say that it was brief and unsuccessful. Using Pauling's approach, within a few weeks they came up with a model of three helixes wound around each other, phosphates at the core. It seemed to fit the density data, the x-ray data was compatible with anything from two to four strands per molecule, and it solved a theoretical problem. If DNA was the genetic material then it had to say something specific to the body; it had to have a language that could be translated somehow into the making of proteins. It was already known that the sugars and phosphates were simple repeating units, unvarying along the DNA strands. The bases were the variables. The bases varied, but the x-ray pattern indicated a repeating crystalline structure; ergo, the core—the part of the structure giving rise to the repeating patterns—must contain the repeating subunits, the sugars or phosphates, with the bases sticking out where they would not get in the way. DNA was, in other words, like the alpha helix. Watson and Crick were thinking very much like Pauling.

The problem was explaining how one could pack phosphates into the middle when at normal pH they would be generally expected to carry a negative charge. All those negative charges at the core would repel each other, blowing the structure apart. The triple helix they had devised was so pretty, though, and fit so much of the data that Crick and Wilson figured there had to be a place for positive ions at the core to cancel out the negative charges. They grabbed a copy of *The Nature of the Chemical Bond,* searched for inorganic ions that would fit their needs, and found that magnesium or calcium might fit. There was no good evidence for the presence of these positive ions, but there was no good evidence against them, either. They were trying to think like Pauling, after all, and Pauling would certainly have assumed that the structure came first and the minor details fell into place later.

The two young men, euphoric about cracking this problem so quickly, invited Wilkins and Franklin to come to the Cavendish to see their triumph. Franklin tore it apart. The problem was not only the assumption that their molecule was helical—Franklin was not convinced that the x-ray data proved that it was—but their idea that positive ions cemented the center together. Magnesium or any other ions, she pointed out, would undoubtedly be surrounded by water molecules in a cell nucleus and rendered neutral. They could not hold the phosphates together. And water was important. Crick and Watson, she pointed out, had gotten some data wrong. According to Franklin, DNA was a thirsty molecule, drinking up ten times more water than their model allowed. The molecule's ability to soak up water indicated to Franklin that the phosphates were on the outside of the molecule, where they would be encased in a shell of water. The wrong water content also meant that Crick and Watson's density calculations were off.

She was, as it turned out, right. The two men tried to convince Wilkins and Franklin to collaborate with them on another attempt but were turned down. When news of the fiasco reached Bragg, he quickly sent Crick back to proteins and Watson to something more in keeping with his background, a crystallographic study of tobacco mosaic virus.

But the pair, Watson in particular, did not stop thinking about nucleic acids. Pauling remembered Watson as "something of a monomaniac" where DNA was concerned, and rather than give up on the problem, he and Crick took it underground, talking it over quietly in their office or over drinks at a local pub. They might have gotten one model wrong, but they were certain their approach was right. Perhaps all they needed was a little more chemistry. For Christmas 1951, Crick gave Watson a copy of *The Nature of the Chemical Bond.* "Somewhere in Pauling's masterpiece," Watson remembered, "I hoped the real secret would lie."

Coiled Coils

Pauling, after his meetings in France, arrived in England eager to make up for the time lost because of his passport problems. Through August 1952 he toured the English protein centers, talking with his critics and answering their questions. New evidence had been found that the alpha helix was an important component of a number of natural proteins, including globular proteins, and the pleated sheet structures were also being confirmed. Pauling considered the alpha-helix case proved and was on to new ideas now about how his structure could bend around corners and fold back on itself to make the densely packed spheroid shapes of globular proteins. He found the English, too, more ready to accept his alpha helix as evidence of it turned up in their own investigations. "In this way I made up, I think, for the failure to attend the Royal Society meeting in May—at any rate, so far as I myself am concerned, in that the doubts that some of these people had about the correctness of our protein structures were strongly expressed to me," he wrote Arne Tiselius. Doubts strongly expressed could be strongly answered, and Pauling set about convincing the British on some points, modifying his own thinking on others.

While visiting the Cavendish, Pauling was introduced to a number of the younger researchers and was especially interested in meeting Crick. Crick had been spending most of his time since being directed away from DNA on a problem Bragg had set his team working on after reading Pauling's protein papers, that of finding a mathematical formula for predicting how helixes would diffract x-rays. In the spring of 1952, Crick and two coworkers published a paper that provided the necessary mathematical treatment. It was Crick's first significant scientific success and proved immensely useful. He had proudly sent Pauling an advance copy. He then started thinking about how his formula might help explain the 5.1-angstrom reflection that was missing from Pauling's alpha helix.

Crick was interested in coming to Caltech on a postdoctoral fellowship and found himself discussing the possibility with Pauling while sharing a car ride around Cambridge. For once the voluble Crick found himself tongue-tied. He was filled with an admixture of awe—here he was, a mere graduate student, in the presence of the man he felt was the world's leading scientist—and wariness. DNA was not a subject of conversation; after all, Crick was not supposed to be working on it. But he had devised a new theory to explain why Pauling's alpha helix did not provide the 5.1-angstrom reflection observed in most natural substances. He knew that Pauling was thinking about that, too, and he did not want to give too much away, but at the same time he wanted very much to impress his visitor. He did not have to worry; Pauling already had his eye on Crick, and invited him to spend a year at Caltech working with him. Thus warmed, Crick felt confident enough to ask, "Have you thought about the possibility that alpha helixes are coiled around one another?" Pauling, who had been considering a number of schemes for the higher-level protein organization, including some in which individual helixes wound around each other, remembers answering, "Yes, I have," before letting the matter drop. He felt that he was almost ready to publish his ideas and had no intention of sharing them with a Cavendish student, no matter how promising.

According to Crick, however, Pauling gave no indication that he had been working on the problem at all.

〜〜〜

Proteins were still in the forefront of Pauling's mind. During his month in England, Pauling thought so little about DNA that he did not even make an effort to visit King's College to see Wilkins and Franklin's increasingly valuable x-ray photographs. The reason was twofold, he later remembered: He was preoccupied with proteins, and he still assumed that Wilkins did not want to share his data.

It was a historic mistake. Franklin had new pictures now, crisp, focused patterns from DNA in its pure, extended, wet form, clearly showing both twofold symmetry—thus ruling out three-stranded structures—and the crosslike reflections of a helix. If Pauling had seen these—and there was no reason to think she would not have shown him; she had, after all, shown Corey her work during his May visit—if he had talked to Franklin, who was not shy about presenting her strong ideas about water content and its effect on the form of the molecule, if he had heard the ideas that had capsized the Crick-Watson model, he would undoubtedly have changed the nature of his later approach. At the very least, a visit with Franklin would have impressed upon him that Astbury's earlier photos, the ones he was using, showed a mixture of two forms of the molecule.

Historians have speculated that the denial of Pauling's passport for the May Royal Society meeting was critical in preventing him from discovering the structure of DNA, that if he had attended that meeting he would have seen Franklin's work and had a better shot at following the right path. The idea nicely illustrates the scientific view that bureaucrats should not interfere in open communication between researchers. But the real problem was not the passport policy. Instead, three unrelated factors combined to set Pauling wrong. The first was his focus on proteins to the exclusion of almost everything else. The second was inadequate data. The x-ray photos he was using were taken of a mixture of two forms of DNA and were almost worthless. The third was pride. He simply did not feel that he needed to pursue DNA full tilt. After talking to Perutz and Bragg, he was likely aware that Crick and Watson had made a stab at the structure and failed; he knew for certain that Wilkins was after it. But he did not consider them to be real competition. How could they be? Events had proven that he was the only person in the world capable of solving large biological molecules.

"I always thought that sooner or later I would find the structure of DNA," Pauling said. "It was just a matter of time."

After missing his chance to see Franklin's data, Pauling returned to Caltech in September and threw himself into finishing his work on higher-level helical structure. "The field of protein structure is in a very exciting stage now," he wrote. "I have a hard time to keep from spending all of my time on this problem, with the neglect of other things." He worked out a way that his alpha helix could itself be twisted, like a piece of yarn wound around a finger, into the sort of coiled coil Crick had mentioned, and how this form could provide the missing x-ray reflection that the alpha helix alone did not. Then he went further, proposing ways in which these coiled coils could wind about each other to form cables of various numbers of strands. He published his new ideas in October.

Crick, however, knew Pauling's ideas already via Pauling's son Peter, who arrived at Cambridge in the fall of 1952 to work as a graduate student in Kendrew's laboratory. Peter, twenty-one, breezy, fun loving, more interested in the structure of Nina, Perutz's Danish au pair girl, than in the structure of myoglobin—"slightly wild," according to Crick—immediately fell in with Crick and Watson and their new office mate, Jerry Donohue, another Caltech expatriate who arrived that fall on a Guggenheim after working for years with Pauling.

Their office became an unofficial communication center between Cambridge and Pasadena. Peter and Donohue were both in correspondence with Pauling, and their office talk provided Crick and Watson with at least a small idea of what Pauling was up to. He wrote his son, for instance, that he was working hard on a structure for natural keratin made of helix ropes. When Peter told Crick, Crick's first thought was that Pauling had stolen his idea after he had let it slip during their car ride. He immediately refocused his own efforts. Within a month he had solved the last mathematical problems and on October 22 sent a short note to *Nature* describing the general outlines of his idea. It arrived just a few days after Pauling's longer manuscript on the same subject reached the same journal.

Crick's piece, however, arrived with a cover note requesting expeditious publication and, since notes are generally published more quickly than full papers in any case, reached print well before Pauling's. There was grumbling on both sides of the Atlantic for a few weeks about who had priority until the Cavendish crew conceded that Pauling's set of ideas went significantly beyond Crick's. Pauling, unsurprised by Crick's work when it appeared, was only irritated that *Nature* did not publish the two papers together. Finally, a gentleman's agreement was reached that the two men had come to the same point independently.

That was minor. The important fact was that the final major hurdle to acceptance of the alpha helix had been cleared away. By late fall Pauling was certain that his structure, with its various coiled-coil permutations, was the basic substance in hair, horn, and fingernail. It gave him a new idea about the structure of feathers as well. Evidence that the alpha helix existed in a number of globular proteins continued to mount. By late November, Pauling felt that his belief in the alpha helix had been fully confirmed. The alpha helix had been shown to be a principal structural feature in hemoglobin, serum albumin, insulin, pepsin, lysozyme, and a dozen other globular proteins, he happily wrote a colleague. "In fact, all of the globular proteins that have been investigated have been found to contain the alpha helix as their principal structural feature."

A Beautiful Structure

But the alpha helix was no longer the prize it once seemed. It was a breakthrough in methodology, a vindication of Pauling's stochastic approach, an important part of bigger things, but in the end it was only, as Pauling said, "a structural feature." The alpha helix appeared to be a stable arrangement that polypeptide chains assumed to get from point

A to point B. As the molecular biologist Gunther Stent later put it, "No matter how great Pauling's triumph was, the discovery of the alpha helix did not immediately suggest to anyone very many new ideas about proteins, about how they work or are made. It did not seem to lead to very many new experiments, or to open new vistas to the imagination."

The real prize, the true secret of life, Pauling now knew, was DNA, and it was here that he next turned his attention.

On November 25, 1952, three months after returning from England, Pauling attended a Caltech biology seminar given by Robley Williams, a Berkeley professor who had done some amazing work with an electron microscope. Through a complicated technique he was able to get images of incredibly small biological structures. Pauling was spellbound. One of Williams's photos showed long, tangled strands of sodium ribonucleate, the salt of a form of nucleic acid, shaded so that three-dimensional details could be seen. What caught Pauling's attention was the obvious cylindricality of the strands: They were not flat ribbons; they were long, skinny tubes. He guessed then, looking at these black-and-white slides in the darkened seminar room, that DNA was likely to be a helix. No other conformation would fit both Astbury's x-ray patterns of the molecule and the photos he was seeing. Even better, Williams was able to estimate the sizes of structures on his photos, and his work showed that each strand was about 15 angstroms across. Pauling was interested enough to ask him to repeat the figure, which Williams qualified by noting the difficulty he had in making precise measurements. The molecule Williams was showing was not DNA, but it was a molecular cousin—and it started Pauling thinking.

The next day, Pauling sat at his desk with a pencil, a sheaf of paper, and a slide rule. New data that summer from Alexander Todd's laboratory had confirmed the linkage points between the sugars and phosphates in DNA; other work showed where they connected to the bases. Pauling was already convinced from his earlier work that the various-sized bases had to be on the outside of the molecule; the phosphates, on the inside. Now he knew that the molecule was probably helical. These were his starting points for a preliminary look at DNA. He did not know how far he would get with this first attempt at a structure, especially because he still had no firm structural data on the precise sizes and bonding angles of the base-sugar-phosphate building blocks of DNA, but it was worth a look.

Pauling quickly made some calculations to determine DNA's molecular volume and the expected length of each repeating unit along its axis. Astbury's photos showed a strong reflection at 3.4 angstroms—according to Pauling's calculations, about three times his estimated length of a single nucleotide unit along the fiber. Repeating groups of three different nucleotides seemed unlikely; a threefold chain structure would explain the repeat more easily. His density calculations indicated that three chains would need to pack together tightly to fit the observed volume, but that was all right. In crystallography, the tighter the packing, the better. After five lines of simple calculations on the first page of his attack on DNA, Pauling wrote, "Perhaps we have a triple-chain structure!"

He was immediately captivated by the idea: three chains wound around one another with the phosphates in the middle. Sketching and calculating, he quickly saw that there was no way for hydrogen bonds to form along the long fiber axis, holding the windings of the chain in place, as in the alpha helix. Without them, what held the molecule in shape? One place that hydrogen bonds could form, he saw, was across the middle of the molecule, from phosphate to phosphate. That was a surprise, but everything else seemed to be working out. After six pages of calculations, he wrote, "Note that each chain has . . . roughly three residues per turn. There are three chains closely intertwined, and held together by hydrogen bonds between PO_4's." The only problem was that there did not seem to be quite enough space in the center of the molecule, where the phosphates came into closest contact. He put down his pencil for the night.

Three days later, he came back to the problem. According to Astbury's figures, DNA was a relatively dense molecule, which implied tight packing at the core. But trying to jam three chains' worth of phosphates into Astbury's space restrictions was like trying to fit the stepsisters' feet into Cinderella's glass slipper. No matter how he twisted and turned the phosphates, they wouldn't fit. *"Why are the PO_4 in a column so close together?"* he wrote in frustration. If Astbury's estimates on distances could be relaxed a bit, everything would fit, but Pauling could not do that without deviating too far from Astbury's x-ray data. Pauling next tried deforming the phosphate tetrahedra to make them fit, shortening some sides and lengthening others. It looked better, but still not right. He stopped again.

Next, he had an assistant go back through the literature in the chemistry library and pick up everything he could find on the x-ray crystallography of nucleic acids. There was not much to go on besides Astbury's work and that of Sven Furberg, a Norwegian crystallographer who had studied under Bernal and had found that the bases in

DNA were oriented at right angles to the sugars. There was not one detailed structure of any purine or pyrimidine, much less a nucleotide.

On December 2 he made another assault, filling nine pages with drawings and calculations. And, he thought, he came up with something that looked plausible. "I have put the phosphates as close together as possible, and have distorted them as much as possible," he noted. Even though some phosphate oxygens were jammed uncomfortably close in the molecule's center, not only did it all just fit, but Pauling saw that the innermost oxygens packed together in the form of an almost perfect octahedron, one of the most basic shapes in crystallography. It was very tight, but things were lining up nicely. It had to be right. It had been less than a week since he first sat down with the problem.

The next day, Pauling excitedly wrote a colleague, "I think now we have found the complete molecular structure of the nucleic acids." During the next several weeks he ran downstairs every morning from his second-story office in Crellin to Verner Schomaker's office, "*very* enthusiastic," Schomaker remembered, bouncing ideas off the younger man, thinking aloud as he checked and refined his model. He began working with Corey to pinpoint the fine structure.

Then came trouble. Corey's detailed calculation of atomic positions showed that the core oxygens were, in fact, too close to fit. In early December, Pauling went back to twisting and squeezing the phosphate tetrahedra. Someone brought up the question of how his model allowed for the creation of a sodium salt of DNA, in which the positive sodium ions supposedly adhered to the negative phosphates. There was no room for sodium ions in his tightly packed core, was there? Pauling had to admit he could find no good way to fit the ions. But that would sort itself out later. The other results were positive. Running the proposed structure through Crick's mathematical formula indicated that his model helix would fit most of the x-ray data, although not all of it. Schomaker played with some models on his own and found a way to twist the phosphate tetrahedra so that they were not quite so jammed, but for the moment Pauling saw no reason to change his ideas. The core phosphates were too neatly close-packed not to be true.

And this was what the central problem had reduced itself to in his mind: a question of phosphate structural chemistry. The biological significance of DNA would be worked out later, he thought; if the structure was right, the biological importance would fall out of it naturally in some way. At this point it was his business to get the structure, not the function. So he ignored the larger context surrounding the molecule and focused single-mindedly on one thing: finding a way to fit those phosphates into the core so that the resulting helixes fit the available data.

His faith in that approach had been justified by his success with the alpha helix. He had built his protein spiral from strict chemical principles, published it in the face of contradictory data, and later found the facts he needed to answer his critics. He was confident now about his ability to jump ahead of the pack, to use his intuitive grasp of chemistry to tease out a structure that felt right. If you waited for every doubt to be answered first, you would never get credit for any discovery. And his DNA triple helix felt right.

A week before Christmas, he wrote Alex Todd at Cambridge, "We have, we believe, discovered the structure of nucleic acids. I have practically no doubt. . . . The structure really is a beautiful one." Pauling knew that Todd had been working with purified nucleotides and asked him to send samples for x-ray analysis. "Dr. Corey and I are much disturbed that there has been no precise structure determination reported as yet for any nucleotide. We have decided that it is necessary that some of the structure determinations be made in our laboratory. I know that the Cavendish people are working in this field, but it is such a big field that it cannot be expected that they will do the whole job." He then wrote his son Peter and Jerry Donohue that he was hoping soon to complete a short paper on nucleic acids.

But the structure still was not quite right. Everything would seem to fall into place when Corey came up with another set of calculations showing that the phosphates were packed just a little too tightly, their atoms jostling each other a little too closely to be reasonable. Pauling would readjust and tinker, bend and squash, so close to the answer yet unable to make it all fit perfectly.

mm

He was becoming frustrated with it when another distraction cropped up: On December 23, professional FBI informer and darling of the congressional investigating committees Louis Budenz testified publicly, before a House special committee investigating charitable foundations, that Pauling, a member of the advisory board of the Guggenheim Foundation, was a concealed Communist. Budenz outdid himself, pouring out the names of twenty-three grantees of various organizations and three other officials, most of whom had no more to do with communism than did Pauling. His testimony would enrage a number of influential people associated with powerful foundations and eventually help spur a backlash against McCarthyism, but in the short term the timing of the announcement—two days before Christmas, at a time when the news media would be hungry for headlines but without the staff to do follow-up—did maximum damage to those named with little chance for response.

Pauling, who had for the most part abided by his decision a year before to pull out of active politics, felt as if he had been sucker punched. His response was characteristically straightforward. "That statement is a lie," he told the press. "If Budenz is not prosecuted for perjury, we must conclude that our courts and Congressional committees are not interested in learning and disclosing the truth." When he discovered that Budenz was not liable for perjury because his testimony was protected by congressional privilege, Pauling tried another tack to get his accuser into court, calling Budenz a "professional liar" in the press in hopes that Budenz would sue him. Budenz did not take the bait.

—✺—

Depressed about this unexpected political attack, Pauling took the unusual step of inviting some colleagues into his laboratory on Christmas Day to have a look at his work on DNA. He was tired of the niggling problems with his model and ready for some good news. He got it from his small audience, who expressed enthusiasm for his ideas. Much cheered, Pauling spent the last week of the year working with Corey on the finalization of a manuscript.

On the last day of December 1952, Pauling and Corey sent in their paper, "A Proposed Structure for the Nucleic Acids," to the *Proceedings of the National Academy of Sciences*. This was, they stressed, "the first precisely described structure for the nucleic acids that has been suggested by any investigator"—thus positioning the work as the nucleic acid equivalent to the alpha helix. He went through his reasoning for the core structure. Most of the paper concentrated on precisely stacking phosphate tetrahedra, but there was a little biology, too. In Pauling's model, the bases, the message-carrying portion of nucleic acids, were directed outward, like leaves along a stalk, with room enough to be put into any order, providing maximum variability in the molecule and thus maximum specificity in the message. Astbury had already noted that the 3.4-angstrom repeat in nucleic acid was about the same as the distance per amino acid along an extended polypeptide chain, raising the idea that new proteins might be struck directly off a nucleic acid mold. Pauling noted that his model allowed the same thing to happen, with the sides of four adjacent bases along his chains forming a space just right for fitting an amino acid.

There was, however, an uncharacteristic tentativeness in the piece. This was "a promising structure," Pauling wrote, but "an extraordinarily tight one"; it accounted only "moderately well" for the x-ray data and gave only "reasonably satisfactory agreement" with the theoretical values obtained by the Crick formula; the atomic positions, he wrote, were "probably capable of further refinement."

—*mm*—

It was, in fact, a rush job. Pauling knew that DNA was important; he knew that Wilkins and Franklin were after it and that Bragg's group had already made at least one stab at it. He knew that it was a relatively simple structure compared to proteins. And he knew that whoever got out a roughly correct structure first—even if it was not quite right in all its details—would establish priority. That is what he was aiming for, not the last word on DNA but the first, the initial publication that would be cited by all following. It did not have to be precise. He wanted credit for the discovery.

The hurried haphazardness of the nucleic-acid paper can best be understood by comparison to Pauling's protein work. Pauling's alpha helix was the result of more than a decade of off-and-on analysis and thousands of man-hours of meticulous crystallographic work. Before he published his model, his lab pinned down the structure of the amino-acid subunits to a fraction of a degree and a hundredth of an angstrom. There was an abundance of clean x-ray work available on the subject proteins, allowing Pauling to scrutinize and eliminate dozens of alternative structures. Two years passed between the time he came up with the rough idea for his helix and the time he published it. Much of that interval was spent with Corey, overseeing and refining the precise construction of a series of elaborate three-dimensional models.

None of that went into DNA.

"The only doubt I have . . ."

Crick and Watson were downcast by the news from Peter in late December that Pauling had solved DNA. Alternating between bouts of despair and denial—trying to figure out how he could have beaten them and then deciding that he certainly could not have without seeing Wilkins and Franklin's x-ray work and then thinking, well, of course, he is Pauling, so anything is possible—they continued working on the problem themselves. If they could come up with something independently before Pauling's paper appeared, at least they might share credit.

The previous spring, a few months after they had been warned off DNA and a few months before Pauling's visit to the Cavendish, Crick and Watson had been introduced to Erwin Chargaff, the acerbic and opinionated Austrian-born biochemist who had been using chromatography to analyze the chemical composition of nucleic acids. Chargaff was not impressed. "I never met two men who knew so little and aspired to so much," he said. "They told me they wanted to construct a helix, a polynucleotide to rival Pauling's alpha helix. They talked so much about 'pitch' that I remember I wrote it down afterwards, 'Two pitchmen in search of a helix.'" But this conversation was critical to Crick and Watson. Chargaff told them that there was a simple relationship between the occurrence of different bases in DNA, that adenine and thymine were present in roughly the same amounts and so were guanine and cytosine. One of each pair was a larger purine; the other, a smaller pyrimidine. It was the same relationship that he had told Pauling about during their Atlantic crossing in 1947 and that Pauling had ignored.

But it made all the difference to Crick and Watson. Franklin's criticisms had already pointed them toward putting the phosphates on the outside of the molecule; now they had the clue of a one-to-one relationship between the bases on the inside. They began thinking about helixes in which the purines and pyrimidines lined up somehow down the core of the molecule.

When Pauling's much anticipated DNA manuscript arrived via Peter in early February 1953, both researchers were surprised to see something that looked like their own abortive three-chain effort, only more tightly put together. A few minutes' reading showed that there was no room at the core for the positive ions needed to hold together the negatively charged phosphates. Crick and Watson were dumbfounded. Pauling's structure depended on hydrogen bonds between the phosphate groups, but how could there be a hydrogen there when the phosphates in DNA lost their hydrogens at normal pH? "Without the hydrogen atoms, the chains would immediately fly apart," Watson said. They had already been through this with their own model, but they checked it again, and there it was in black and white in a respected text: The phosphates had to be ionized. The book they were looking at was Pauling's *General Chemistry*.

There was an immense feeling of relief. "If a student had made a similar mistake, he would be thought unfit to benefit from Caltech's chemistry faculty," Watson later said. He and Crick immediately went off to confirm their criticism with Cambridge's chemists. Before the day was out, Pauling's mistake was the talk of the college: Linus's chemistry was wrong.

Just as importantly for Watson, when he told Wilkins of Pauling's mistake and his idea that DNA was helical, he was given a reward: his first look at the more recent x-ray patterns Franklin had gotten from the molecule. She had found that DNA existed in two forms, a condensed dry form and an extended wet form the structure assumed when it drank up all that water. Astbury's photos, the ones Pauling had used, had been of a mixture of the two forms. Franklin's recent shots, much clearer and of only the extended form, immediately confirmed to Watson that the molecule was a helix and gave him several vital parameters for its solution.

With obvious satisfaction, Crick, still smarting a bit from the coiled-coil affair, wrote Pauling, to thank him for providing an advance copy of his nucleic acid paper. "We were very struck by the ingenuity of the structure," he wrote. "The only doubt I have is that I do not see what holds it together."

Pauling's apparent misstep pleased Bragg so much that he agreed to let Crick and Watson go back full-time to DNA. There was a window of opportunity here, and he wanted the Cavendish to take advantage before Pauling had time to regroup.

Pauling, however, had already moved on to a new project, a theory of ferromagnetism that he worked on through the spring. He also began making plans for a major international protein conference in Caltech the next fall and was drawn back to DNA only when Peter wrote him in mid-February about the English hooting at his structure. Corey had by now finally finished checking Pauling's atomic coordinates, some of which appeared again to be unacceptably tight. "I am checking over the nucleic acid structure again, trying to refine the parameters a bit," Pauling wrote Peter back. "I heard a rumor that Jim Watson and Crick had formulated this structure already sometime back, but had not done anything about it. Probably the rumor is exaggerated." In late February he finally tried Schomaker's suggestion of twisting the phosphate groups forty-five degrees and found that it eased some of the strain.

Something was still wrong. When Pauling gave a seminar on his DNA structure at Caltech, the reception was cool; afterward, Delbrück told Schomaker that he thought Pauling's model was not convincing. He mentioned a letter he had gotten from Watson saying that Pauling's structure contained "some very bad mistakes" and in which Watson had added, "I have a very pretty model, which is so pretty that I am surprised that no-one ever thought of it before." Pauling wanted to know more. He quickly wrote Watson, inviting him to his fall protein conference, mentioning that he had heard from Delbrück about his DNA work, and encouraging him to keep working on the problem. "Professor Corey and I do not feel that our structure has been proven to be right," he wrote, "although we incline to think that it is." In early March he drove with Ava Helen to the University of California at Riverside to examine a collection of organic phosphates there, finding candidates for structural analysis that would be similar to the phosphate groups in DNA, looking for models to tell him how much he could deform his tetrahedra. Crick's barb about what held the molecule together led him to gather chemical precedents for the existence of adjoining negative charges in the same molecule, and he began to reason to himself that perhaps the DNA core environment was a special one that allowed the phosphates to exist as he had proposed. It was still, to Pauling, a matter of phosphate chemistry. Meanwhile, Todd had sent him the requested samples of nucleotides, and Pauling started their x-ray analysis.

He was finally laying the groundwork for a reasonable structure. But it was too late.

—⁓—

Given the go-ahead to return to DNA, thanks to Pauling's paper, Crick and Watson each began feverishly devising models, focusing more on two-stranded models now that Chargaff had gotten them thinking of bases somehow pairing with each other. The "very pretty model" of which Watson had written Delbrück was one attempt, but it was wrong, as Jerry Donohue pointed out.

Donohue's input turned out to be critical. A magna cum laude graduate of Dartmouth who had worked and studied with Pauling at Caltech since the early 1940s, Donohue knew structural chemistry inside and out. Hydrogen bonding had been a specialty of his, and he saw that Crick and Watson, chemical novices that they were, had been playing with the wrong structures for guanine and thymine. He set them right, switching the hydrogen atoms essential for cross-bonding into their correct positions, destroying their earlier model and pushing them toward the correct solution.

With Donohue's corrections, Crick and Watson could now see hydrogen bonds forming naturally between specific pairs of purines and pyrimidines: adenine to thymine and guanine to cytosine. That was the last piece of the puzzle, and the result was dazzling. Matching a large with a small base not only smoothed the structure's outline but provided a simple explanation for Chargaff's findings. The resulting structure, a sort of ladder with base pairs as the steps and the sugar-phosphate backbone as the runners, formed easily into a helix that matched the x-ray data.

More than beautiful, the structure had meaning. Each strand was a complementary mirror image of the other; if separated, each could act as a mold for forming a new double helix identical with the original. This immediately provided ideas about replication that Pauling's model, with its bases facing out and unrelated to each other, could not.

On March 12, Watson sent Delbrück a letter, illustrated with rough sketches, discussing their new model. He warned his mentor not to tell Pauling about it until they were more certain of their results, but Delbrück, never one to keep secrets, immediately showed the letter around. Pauling's mind raced as he read it. He saw immediately that the Cavendish structure was not only chemically reasonable but biologically intriguing. "The simplicity of the structural complementariness of the two pyrimidines and their corresponding purines was a surprise to me—a pleasant one, of course, because of the great illumination it threw on the problem of the mechanism of heredity," he said. In it he could see echoes of many of the things he had been thinking and writing about complementarity since his 1940 paper with Delbrück.

The same day that Alex Rich first heard about the Watson-Crick structure, he awoke in the middle of the night, got out of bed, went into his office, and began building a rough version of the Watson-Crick double helix out of the pieces of molecular models he had there. All he knew was that they had paired the DNA bases across the center of the molecule, but knowing that was enough. He quickly paired the correct bases, saw that it worked beautifully, and went back to bed shaking his head.

Pauling, while not yet ready to concede the race, was impressed. A few days after seeing Watson's letter, he wrote a colleague, "You must, of course, recognize that our proposed structure is nothing more than a proposed structure. There is a chance that it is right, but it will probably be two or three years before we can be reasonably sure. . . ." A few days later, he received an advance copy of the Watson and Crick manuscript, which started by attacking his DNA model and ended by thanking Jerry Donohue for his help. Pauling looked it over and wrote his son, "I think that it is fine that there are now two proposed structures for nucleic acid, and I am looking forward to finding out what the decision will be as to which is incorrect. Without doubt the King's-College data will eliminate one or the other."

He still had not seen any of Franklin's or Wilkins's recent x-ray photos and withheld final judgment until he did. His chance would come soon: He was planning to go to Brussels in April for a Solvay Conference on proteins and intended to stop off in England on the way to see the Watson-Crick model and the photos from Wilkins's and Franklin's laboratories. When he applied for a passport, his old nemesis Ruth Shipley again recommended denial, this time based on her belief that Pauling's Industrial Employment Review Board (IERB) testimony proved that he was refusing to be considered for top-secret clearance. After Pauling explained that he had been cleared for top-secret material in the past and would be willing to be again, but only if it was required for his work—and after he once more swore in her presence that he was not a Communist—his passport was approved.

In early April, a few days after Crick and Watson submitted their paper for publication, Pauling arrived in Cambridge. After spending the night with Peter, he walked into Crick's office and for the first time saw the three-dimensional model they had wired together out of die-cut metal plates. Crick chattered nervously about the features of the double helix while Pauling scrutinized it. He then examined Franklin's photo of the extended form of the molecule. Watson and Crick waited. Then, "gracefully," Watson remembered, "he gave the opinion that we had the answer."

It was a joyful moment for the two young men and a deflating one for Pauling. He was amazed that this unlikely team, an adolescent postdoc and an elderly graduate student, had come up with so elegant a solution to so important a structure. If they were right, his own model was a monstrous mistake, built inside out with the wrong number of chains. But he recognized now that the Cavendish team was almost certainly right.

There was only one thing left for him to do: Show the world how to handle defeat with style.

Pauling left Crick's office and met Bragg for lunch, during which Sir Lawrence vainly tried to restrain his ebullience. After so many years of coming in second, his team had finally beaten Pauling! Later, Pauling joined the Cricks at a pleasant dinner at their house at Portugal Place. Through it all he remained charming and funny and remarkably accepting of the new DNA structure, a true gentleman, both wise enough to recognize defeat and great enough to accept it with good humor. A day or two later both Bragg and Pauling went to the Solvay meeting—an occasional select gathering of the world's top researchers funded by a Belgian industrialist—where Bragg provided the first public announcement of the double helix. Pauling was generous in his support. "Although it is only two months since Professor Corey and I published our proposed structure for nucleic acid, I think that we must admit that it is probably wrong," he told the group. "Although some refinement might be made, I feel that it is very likely that the Watson-Crick structure is essentially correct."

—————

Inside, however, Pauling was burning. Despite his generous crediting of Watson and Crick's work in England, he still thought there was an outside chance that some variation of his own idea would still prove correct. Soon after returning home in mid-April he put Alex Rich to work taking new x-ray photos of DNA and returned to fine-tuning the atomic positions in his model.

It was hopeless. It quickly became clear that he had taken a pratfall on the world scientific stage. After the Watson-Crick paper was published, they were showered immediately with worldwide acclaim, while Pauling's model was shoved aside and forgotten. He had been wrong before—about artificial antibodies especially and a few relatively unimportant, small molecular structures—but never wrong as publicly and on such an important topic as this. It was all the more humiliating for the world's leading structural chemist to be beaten by a pair of beginners.

What had gone wrong?

Everyone seemed to have an opinion. Peter thought the problem was Pauling's strictly chemical approach to DNA, with his fascination with phosphate packing taking precedence over thoughts about biological function. "To my father, nucleic acids were just interesting chemicals, just as sodium chloride is an interesting chemical," he wrote. This was not strictly true, however. Thanks to Morgan's influence at Caltech, Pauling had been interested in genes ever since the early 1930s. He talked of "a chemical attack on the structure of chromosomes" in 1937 and had made the replication of the gene a central image in his late-1940s talks on complementarity. He had a strong idea about how genes duplicated themselves: They started as a complex of two complementary structures, each of which served as the mold for creating the other, together re-creating the complex. He simply got carried away by his pretty structure and figured that the biological facts would fall into place later.

Chargaff concluded that the problem was obvious: Pauling "failed to take account of my results." Wilkins thought Pauling "just didn't try. He can't really have spent five minutes on the problem himself." Verner Schomaker theorized that Pauling did not put enough people onto the problem to gather sufficient hard data, and Alex Rich added that the Caltech coworkers who reviewed Pauling's model were partly to blame for being insufficiently critical. "In a way," he said, "the people around him let him down."

Pauling had his own thoughts about how he had been led astray. At first, he blamed the x-ray photos he had used. Pauling wrote Delbrück a week or so after he visited the Cavendish, saying that poor crystallographic data had put him off track. "The x-ray photographs that we had, which had been made by Dr. Rich, and which are essentially identical with those obtained some years ago by Astbury and Bell, are really the superposition of two patterns. . . . Corey and I had tried to find the structure that accounted for one of the principal features of one pattern, and simultaneously for one of the principal features of the second pattern."

Later, he put more emphasis on misreading DNA's density, the error that led to the idea of a three-chain structure. "The reason that I got off on this three-strand binge is that I did not know how much water of hydration there was in those preparations," he said. "More than a third of the material in the preparation was water and only two-thirds was nucleic acid. So the calculation that I made ignoring the water gave three strands. And if you correct for the water—I just hadn't realized there was so much hydration—then it turns out to be two strands."

He also blamed his lack of knowledge of the DNA subunits. "If we had also done some work on some purines or pyrimidines, I might well have had the background information that would have pushed me in the right direction. But we didn't do any purine or pyrimidine work."

Each excuse contained a measure of truth. But each was a symptom of a problem, not the problem itself.

There were two reasons Pauling failed with DNA: hurry and hubris. He rushed because DNA was the biggest prize around and if he did not crack it, someone else—probably someone in England—soon would. Although he later denied he was competing with the British researchers for the DNA structure—"I did not feel that I was in a race with Watson and Crick," he said. "They felt that they were in a race with me"—the fact was that he *was* in a race, perhaps not with the unknown Watson and Crick but certainly with Wilkins and Franklin and, above all, with his oldest rival, Sir William Lawrence Bragg. Pauling wanted to publish his DNA structure quickly in order to beat Bragg's group, and Wilkins, too, and he took a chance doing it without having done his homework.

Pauling had no precise structures for the nucleotide subunits. The x-ray photos he used, those that Astbury had done years before, were muddy and vague, and Pauling never attempted to make x-ray photos of his own prior to publication. He started with one idea, the phosphate-core model, and never deviated from it. No three-dimensional models were ever built. Pauling did not even have Corey check his figures a final time before sending in the paper. He wanted the credit for solving DNA, and to get it he had to publish first.

More importantly, he rushed because he thought he could get away with it. His success with the alpha helix had given him faith that he could jump ahead successfully. All of the basic assumptions that he had made in the late 1930s had been right; fifteen years of further research had only proved it. He was right about hydrogen bonding and the planar peptide bond and the nonintegral repeat. As long as he stuck with what he knew about chemistry, he was always right.

The alpha helix had graced him with success and cursed him with overweening pride. After its solution, he believed he no longer needed to do the homework required by others. It was clear that he was the best person in the world at solving the structure of giant molecules— any molecules, for that matter. He knew that he had put together the correct basic structure of the alpha helix two years before he published it, two long years during which Bragg might have come up with the answer and beaten him to it. Pauling had hesitated then because of his doubts about the 5.1-angstrom x-ray reflection, an experimental observation that turned out to be irrelevant. The lesson was clear: In certain cases he had to trust himself, not the experimental results. He had to trust his intuition, his nose for a good structure. He knew that his triple-stranded DNA structure was very tight and that it begged the question of how the negatively charged phosphates could keep from repelling each other, but he believed that those matters would work themselves out, as the missing reflection in his alpha helix had worked itself out as a matter of coiled coils. The phosphate packing in the center of his model was too pretty, too clever not to be right.

He wanted the prize, he gambled, and he lost.

He regretted it, of course, the remainder of his life, although he was soon back to his usual cheerful self around the lab. Within a few months he could joke with Alex Rich about it, asking him how his new project on a special form of DNA was going, then adding, "You work hard on that problem, Alex, because I like *most* of the important discoveries to be made in Pasadena."

The encounter with DNA would become the stuff of legend in the literature that would spring up around its discovery. Watson and Crick would take center stage, with Pauling assuming the smaller part of an offstage voice, a legendary Goliath in a far land felled by two unlikely Davids. A year would rarely go by after 1953 without someone, a scientist or writer, asking him where he had gone wrong.

Ava Helen finally tired of it. After hearing the questions and explanations over and again, she cut through the excuses with a simple question. "If that was such an important problem," she asked her husband, "why didn't you work harder on it?"

The Prize

Silence

The story going around Caltech in the summer of 1953 was that Pauling's new building was the payoff from an old racing debt.

This was the Norman Church Laboratory of Chemical Biology, a sizable research facility that would physically link Pauling's chemistry buildings to Beadle's biology labs—a bricks-and-mortar manifestation of his and Beadle's grand plan. The money for the building had come from the will of a wealthy longtime Caltech trustee whose passions had included breeding racehorses. DuBridge often told the story of how Church, accused in the 1930s of doping winners, had asked his friend Milliken if there was anyone at Caltech who could run scientific tests on his horses and clear his name. Milliken sent him to Pauling, who, according to DuBridge's story, figured out how to screen Church's Thoroughbreds for the suspected drugs and showed that the horses were clean. "Norman Church never forgot that," DuBridge said. "He owed a debt to Milliken and Pauling for getting him out of trouble." The debt was paid twenty years later, according to the story, with a $1.5 million bequest for Pauling's new building.

That was a large chunk of money, but not enough to finish the building Pauling wanted. The Church Laboratory was to be a symbol of everything Pauling now recognized as the future of chemistry, a future in which the old science inspired a new biology. He envisioned a grand five-story temple to basic research, the biggest building on campus, two floors of laboratories underground and three above, with spacious laboratory suites arranged and equipped in the most modern manner, to be shared equally between biology and chemistry.

It had to be big. Pauling desperately needed space, and so did Beadle. Fed by the postwar boom in science funding, the staffs of their two Caltech divisions had grown by 50 percent in less than five years. Pauling's innovative research program was drawing scores of postdoctoral fellows, each in need of lab and study space; the lion's share of the old Gates and Crellin laboratories was devoted to their work. The other faculty were starting to grumble about being squeezed out by things as nonchemical as Campbell's immunology program.

So Pauling designed a laboratory twice as big as the Church bequest could pay for—going against the wishes of President DuBridge, who argued that he and Beadle should build only what they could afford. The first $1.5 million paid for the shell of the building, and in the early 1950s, Pauling began looking for an equal sum to finish it, furnish it, and pay its operating expenses. It was not easy to find. All of the large foundations had already said no two years earlier when he and Beadle had hit the streets looking for funds for their laboratory of medical chemistry, and the federal government at that time was not funding large capital projects.

There was only one rather unlikely place left to turn. Through the early summer of 1953, Pauling worked with Beadle to finish a massive 100-page grant request to the Rockefeller Foundation in which they asked for the extraordinary sum of $1.5 million to finish Church and keep it running for more than a decade. It was in many ways a reiteration of their 1945 grand plan, now expanded to include joint research into fifteen areas of inquiry for molecular biology—everything from protein structure to the properties of viruses, enzyme chemistry to experimental plant ecology, general physiology to a concentrated attack on the chemistry of nucleic acids. It was a long shot—Pauling knew from his conversations with Weaver that the foundation was moving away from such large-scale grants for the sciences—but Pauling bet that his recent success with protein structures, a triumph as important to Weaver as it had been to Pauling, would pave the way for his request. In July 1953, Pauling's request was forwarded to Weaver, and everyone held their breath.

Putting his energy into finishing the Church Laboratory helped Pauling move beyond the sting of his loss to Watson and Crick.

Still, the DNA episode altered the trajectory of his scientific interests. The most important effect was the loss of his enthusiasm for solving the structure of giant biomolecules. Although he kept part of his team at work on solving the complete structure of a globular protein, gave more thought to how proteins might aggregate into larger structures, and continued toying with a new model for collagen—joking to colleagues that although his stochastic approach dictated only one guess per structure, he and Corey deserved in this case one each— these were the tail ends of projects; they ran on inertia. Pauling had lost much of his enthusiasm.

Without a great research project on which to focus, Pauling busied himself with odds and ends. He organized an international meeting of protein chemists to be held in Pasadena in the fall of 1953. He wrote a few review articles and finished updating what would prove to be an even more successful second edition of *General Chemistry*. He wrote some entries on chemical subjects for a new edition of the *Encyclopaedia Britannica*—a welcome honor for someone who had been entranced by the volumes as a boy.

His only significant new scientific work was the publication of his new theory of ferromagnetism, which appeared in the *Proceedings of the National Academy of Sciences (PNAS)* near the middle of the year. Magnetism had been one of Pauling's interests since his college days in Oregon, when he had tried one summer to explain the magnetic properties of elements from the facts he found in an old chemical handbook. He thought his new theory, which correlated a number of observations with a clever underlying theory, was an important piece of work.

After it was published, however, no one seemed to pay much attention. A few weeks later, perplexed by the lack of reaction, Pauling wrote Slater to find out what he thought. The reply he received was uncharacteristically blunt. The new work was "extremely sketchy," Slater wrote. "This is the same objection which I have to many of your papers. I feel that such oversimplified theories do a great deal of harm, in that they tend to make the uncritical reader feel that problems have been worked out completely, when as a matter of fact I think we have hardly made a beginning toward their solution." Well, Pauling thought,

Slater has always been a number cruncher, a man so enamored of working out problems to ten decimal places that he had trouble seeing the big picture.

But Slater had a point. The same criticism could have been advanced a decade earlier with Pauling's immunological theory, but at that time other scientists had been afraid to do so.

Now, with his DNA error a matter of public record, he no longer appeared invincible.

―――

Through all the excitement over proteins and DNA, J. Edgar Hoover was watching for Pauling to make the mistake that would unveil him as a Communist. When Pauling—using a passport granted after the usual delays and eventual State Department overruling of Ruth Shipley's recommendations—traveled to Europe again in the summer of 1953, Hoover alerted the CIA, army and navy intelligence, the Atomic Energy Commission (AEC), and the security office of the Department of State that the outspoken chemist would be loosed on the world stage. He was watched in Paris in June when he visited Irène Joliot-Curie, the daughter of Marie Curie and a Nobel Prize–winning physicist in her own right. Pauling was distressed to learn that she had just been denied foreign membership in the American Chemical Society (ACS) because of her Communist leanings. This, he felt, was an insult to a great French scientist and a chilling indication that politics was now to play a part in supposedly apolitical scientific societies. Pauling became disgusted with the ACS and considered quitting.

In Stockholm in July, where Pauling attended the International Congress of Pure and Applied Chemistry, his every move was tracked. And here Hoover thought he had something: A report came in that Lars Sillen, a Swedish chemistry teacher and strong believer in world government, had entertained both Pauling and some of the Russian delegates at a dinner at his house. Who knew what secrets might have been passed? Hoover quickly notified the criminal division of the U.S. attorney general's office, attaching Budenz's statement about Pauling's Communist Party membership and suggesting, "The above is furnished for your information and in order that you may consider the possible prosecution of the subject for denial of his Communist Party membership."

After due consideration, the Justice Department decided that trading toasts with Russian scientists did not constitute proof of party membership. In the absence of further evidence, the attorney general again dropped the case.

—mm—

Returning to Pasadena in September, Pauling put the finishing touches on arrangements for his international protein conference. Everyone who was anyone in the field had agreed to attend, and the combination of Pauling's personality, California sunshine, and the magnitude of the achievements of the past three years made it an ebullient event.

Pauling made certain that the meeting was the antithesis of the Royal Society affair, with its drastically limited presentation and rebuttal times. In Pasadena only two or three papers were presented each day, each followed by unlimited discussion. Pauling talked about the biological meaning of his alpha helix and ways it might affect research in globular proteins; Watson reviewed the latest findings with DNA; Perutz gave an overview of a promising new approach to the x-ray study of large proteins involving heavy atom diffusion. Pauling and Ava Helen took Bragg and his wife on a thousand-mile, four-day motor tour of the Golden State, showing off everything from Yosemite to Big Sur. Everyone had enough time to enjoy the beach and the mountains, and Pauling threw a terrific party at his house that spilled onto the lawn and down to the pool.

The scientific discussions were far ranging. Much attention was given to the DNA discovery and the huge new areas of research it opened up. A few months earlier, the English biochemist Frederick Sanger had announced his success in separating the globular protein insulin into four separate chains and determining the order of amino acids in each one—final proof that globular proteins were composed of polypeptide chains, as Pauling had argued for nearly twenty years. Most of the objections to Pauling's protein ideas that the British had raised at the Royal Society meeting a year earlier had been answered to everyone's satisfaction; general agreement had been reached about the correctness and importance of the alpha helix and pleated sheets, and the Caltech team had given up on their earlier proposals for structures that the British had attacked, such as collagen and muscle. Instead of a rancorous debate, the Pasadena conclave became, as Hughes put it, "one big love-fest."

A photo of the fifty or so attendees standing in rows on the steps of the Caltech Athenaeum is a snapshot of the founding fathers of molecular biology. At the time, Bragg was the only Nobel laureate in the group. But ranged around him were more than a half-dozen researchers who would win their own during the next decade: Delbrück, Beadle, Watson and Crick, Perutz and Kendrew. And, of course, Pauling.

The only dark cloud was the absence of the x-ray crystallographer Dorothy Crowfoot Hodgkin, another future Nobelist, who was denied entry to the United States by the State Department. She assumed, she wrote Pauling, that the reason was because she and her husband were active in too many left-wing British political groups.

mm

Pauling was beginning to chafe at his self-imposed political silence. After his Industrial Employment Review Board (IERB) hearing in late 1951, he had quit several blacklisted organizations and given up all public appearances except those dealing with science. For two years he had forgone all opportunities to speak out against the madness of the Cold War—and there had been a number. In December 1951, a few weeks after his decision to go on political hiatus, Richard Lippman— the young physician who had taken over as Pauling's kidney specialist after Addis's death—phoned Pauling "in great agitation," saying that he, along with two other physicians, had been dropped from the staff of Cedars of Lebanon Hospital in Los Angeles. The reason, Lippman said, was "dislike of my political beliefs." More than doctor and patient, Pauling and Lippman were good friends, with Pauling impressed both by Lippman's kidney research—Pauling thought him "one of the most able young scientific men in the country"—and by their shared interest, in the days before Pauling quit the group, in the goals of the National Council of the Arts, Sciences and Professions (NCASP).

Pauling looked into the matter and quickly concluded that Lippman was being blacklisted. Within weeks of being named a suspected Communist in a HUAC hearing, Lippman's U.S. Public Health Service (USPHS) grant for kidney research had been suspended. Then the hospital let him go. Pauling quickly wrote a letter to the chairman of the hospital's board of trustees expressing his "great indignation" at the board's action and attended a meeting held by some of Lippman's patients and other supporters to organize a protest.

A few years earlier, Pauling would have carried the torch for the Lippman support group, speaking louder and longer than anyone about the mistreatment of an idealistic young man whose career was being ruined by right-wing politics. But now he held his tongue. He pulled out of the group entirely when he saw that it was becoming dominated by Communist members of the NCASP, a group he had just quit. When the Lippman defense group invited him to a public protest meeting, Pauling declined, saying that he was too ill to attend.

It was a failure of nerve, and it was hard on Pauling. He had now joined the mass of liberals who silently waited for the anti-Communist mania to pass, biding their time, biting their tongues, sympathetic to those who became casualties of the times but unwilling to do more than offer condolences. He vented some of his frustration indirectly, spending some time planning a nonprofit foundation "devoted to the discovery and development of outstanding young men, a haven of open-mindedness" that would encourage "independence of spirit, self-confidence, and freedom from restriction by convention." It was his way of honoring men like Lippman, but it never came to fruition.

Then he found another, more direct way to provide support. Lippman found that the blacklist extended to New York, where he was dropped from a new job just as he was to start. He returned to California and came to Pauling in despair, asking for advice about positions. Pauling decided on direct action and found Lippman a staff position at Caltech as an assistant on one of his research projects. This was done quietly, with no public fanfare, and served to both assuage Pauling's conscience and keep Lippman working. Soon Pauling did the same for another talented political refugee with a medical degree, Thomas Perry. There was more low-key grumbling in the chemistry division about Pauling's taking on men whose qualifications for chemical research were at best questionable, but Pauling was not doing this strictly for science. It was his way of proving to himself that despite his silence on political issues, he was still honorable.

His political restraint through 1952, however, did not seem to make his life any easier. He was called on the carpet by DuBridge, who had been contacted by the Cedars of Lebanon board chairman after Pauling attacked the board for firing Lippman. Pauling had to assuage him by reminding DuBridge that this was a private action, not a public political statement. Pauling remained on the FBI's Security Index, and Los Angeles agents tracked every appearance of his name in the *Daily Worker*, used its informers in the NCASP to monitor his activity in the Lippman case, and sent a full report every six months to J. Edgar Hoover. When his passport case blew open in the spring of 1952, an FBI informant reported that the Caltech board of trustees again discussed getting rid of Pauling, this time considering the possibility of buying out his contract by offering him four or five times his annual salary. The scheme was shelved when his passport was restored. Then, toward the end of the year, Budenz named him as a concealed Communist before the House committee investigating charitable foundations, and again—after a year of silence—his name was in the headlines.

The pressure was never-ending. Pauling had stopped almost all of his political work, yet his reputation remained constantly under attack. What was the point in remaining mute?

—*mm*—

Pauling broke his silence in a small way after Eisenhower's election. He wrote a private letter to outgoing president Harry Truman asking him to extend executive clemency to the Rosenbergs, whom Pauling believed had been singled out and tried unfairly in a hysterical search for atomic spies. He signed public letters advocating the repeal of the Internal Security Act of 1950 and the Smith Act. And in late November 1952 he gave a speech to a small gathering of the New Deal faithful at the local FDR Club, a restatement of his old left-wing idealism, a call for tolerance, a rekindling of some of his old fire. It felt wonderful to speak his heart again. And it was especially encouraging to receive a letter afterward from a housewife who was there. "May I express my deep admiration and gratitude for the way you can stand up and speak like a man," she wrote. "The courage of your actions and the honesty of your thinking—in public—is such a heartening thing. I believe the candle you keep burning casts its beams into far corners."

Then he fell silent again. It quickly became clear that the early days of the Eisenhower administration were not the time to raise his profile as a leftist. Eisenhower seemed intent on outdoing Truman as an anti-Communist. He appointed right-wingers to a number of government posts, including replacing Dean Acheson at State—the department was still under constant attack as a stronghold of left-wing sympathizers—with the fervently anti-Communist John Foster Dulles. Another of his appointments was Oveta Culp Hobby, a woman who, as secretary of the new Department of Health, Education, and Welfare (HEW), quickly began withholding federal moneys from suspected Communists.

Hobby's ascension had a direct effect on Pauling. Sometime in the late fall of 1953, he was notified, without further explanation, that his research grants from the USPHS—about sixty thousand dollars to support his work with oxypolygelatin and the structure of proteins—were being suspended. The USPHS was a subunit of Hobby's new HEW.

Confused by the canceling of his grant, Pauling called the USPHS to ask for more information.

Eventually he was put in contact with a sympathetic manager who advised Pauling to reapply, but in a new way. Instead of one large grant request with multiple authors (including Pauling), he told Pauling to send in separate smaller requests under the names of individual researchers. When Pauling tried it, preparing one under Dan Campbell's name and another under Corey's, both were immediately funded—for longer periods of time and for more money than requested. When he tried one under his name, however, his application was ignored.

Pauling was not the only scientist apparently blacklisted by the USPHS. The funds of other left-wing researchers at Caltech were also cut off, prompting the school's administration to warn Washington that they would sue for breach of contract if something was not done. At least forty scientists nationwide were punished for their political beliefs through the cancellation of USPHS grants; there is no record of how many more were denied approval of their initial applications.

It is an indication of both a surprising naïveté in Pauling's political vision and the degree of his separation from the Caltech administration that he did not immediately realize the reasons behind the USPHS's actions. It was not until he told Beadle about the agency's odd behavior that things became clear. After giving Pauling a long look, Beadle told him that of course it was all political. "Don't you know what has happened?" he asked. "They just don't want your name on the list of grant recipients." Pauling was dumbfounded. Despite his substantial experience with the domestic side of the Cold War, it was still unimaginable that a government office dedicated to scientific funding could be tainted by anti-Communist mania. As he later said, "You see how unsophisticated I was even at that time."

Pauling's USPHS grant request was delayed for more than two years, until he received notice of its approval—the day that Oveta Culp Hobby resigned.

~mn~

Still he maintained his political silence. The granting of his passport had now become a long-running farce. Every time he applied, Ruth Shipley would recommend denial. Pauling would send a series of polite reminders about his departure date, followed by more urgent reminders. Shipley, after many delays, would be overruled. Pauling would pack his bags and wait, and his passport would be validated a day or two before he was to leave.

This was the routine that preceded his trip to Israel a few weeks after the big Pasadena protein conference in the fall of 1953. Pauling had been invited to participate in the dedication of the new Weizmann Institute for scientific research, and his short trip allowed him to see a new nation in which he was quite interested and to meet Prime Minister David Ben Gurion and his wife at a reception at the King David Hotel.

But his Mideast trip rang alarm bells at Dulles's Department of State. A new head of passport security had just been appointed, an ex-FBI agent and hard-line anti-Communist named R. W. Scott McLeod, who quickly found that he and Shipley thought alike. Together they started tightening restrictions on the right to travel. McLeod opened lines of communication with HUAC and Senator McCarthy as well as the FBI, and from every source he began hearing about Linus Pauling. McLeod made sure that Pauling's trip to Israel was monitored closely by army intelligence; his suspicions were lessened only slightly by the report that Pauling had said nothing remotely controversial.

A few days after returning in early November, Pauling reapplied for an around-the-world trip he wanted to take with Ava Helen, including spending some time in India, where he had been invited by the government to attend the Indian Science Congress, give several weeks of scientific talks, and dedicate a new laboratory in Bombay. The plan was to leave in mid-December. The Paulings were eager to see India, which under Nehru was becoming a leader of the so-called Third World, the emerging nations aligned with neither the United States nor the USSR. Pauling saw hope in Nehru of a way to a middle road between communism and capitalism.

The State Department was interested in India, too, for much the same reasons, but with a less sanguine attitude. Its analysis was that India was moving leftward, out of the Western orbit. Given that situation, it would do no good to have dissident Americans like Pauling traveling there to paint a dismal picture of the United States, especially considering that the science congress he would be attending would also feature a dozen Russian scientists. Shipley's recommendation to deny Pauling's passport was given a fresh look.

When he heard nothing back about his passport by early December, Pauling enlisted the help of Detlev Bronk, the president of the National Academy of Sciences. Concerned about the impression a new passport refusal to Pauling would have on world scientific opinion, Bronk met with Shipley. It was a chilly conversation. Shipley told him that India was "a sensitive spot" and that any decision about Pauling's trip would include the opinions of others, such as security chief McLeod. She could not say when the decision would be final. When Bronk called Pauling with the news, he warned him that McLeod was one of McCarthy's men. A few hours after Bronk's call, a State Department official called Pauling to say that no decision would be made in time for his planned departure date.

Incensed, Pauling called Shipley directly. Trying to control his temper, he explained that the trip was purely for science and pleasure, that he would not be giving any political talks. She responded by asking him how he could explain recommending clemency for convicted atomic spies. He told her about the bad publicity that would result if his passport was denied. She told him that it was in the hands of higher-ups.

This had now gone beyond the usual delays. Still, Pauling could not imagine that Shipley's office would make the same mistake they had made in 1952, risking the wrath of the world scientific establishment by refusing him the right to travel. In addition, he had controlled himself, cutting his ties with Communist-front groups and abandoning his political talks. Surely he would not be denied a passport now.

He and Ava Helen canceled some early dates and rearranged their departure for a week later, on the twenty-second. Pauling wrote Dulles and offered to come to Washington to talk anytime during the week before Christmas. There was no reply. He wrote again, relaying his flight schedule and noting that he would inquire at the New York passport office at 9:00 A.M. on the day of departure. There was no reply.

On December 21, the Paulings flew into New York, their bags packed for a three-month trip. The next morning, Pauling appeared at the passport office. There was no passport, and there was no explanation. Seething, he returned to his hotel and put in a call to John Foster Dulles. The secretary of state, he was told, could not speak to him. Pauling talked instead with the department's science adviser, who told him that a final decision about his passport had been made but that he could not tell him what it was.

Later that afternoon, two hours after the Paulings' flight had taken off without them, a representative of the State Department called to say that his passport was being refused. Pauling could, he was told, appeal the decision in writing to the chairman of the board of passport appeals.

Pauling had no intention of doing that. He talked with his lawyer—who told him that an informal hearing with State officials would be set up on the twenty-ninth—and he and Ava Helen flew to Washington, D.C. He tried unsuccessfully to set up a meeting with Shipley. Then he spent a joyless Christmas with Ava Helen at the Hay-Adams House waiting for his hearing.

In the meantime, he asked Vannevar Bush and Karl Compton to vouch for him; both men wrote the secretary of state, assuring Dulles of Pauling's integrity and loyalty despite the fact that "some years ago he went off the deep end in political activities." When the day finally came for his hearing, Pauling and Ava Helen arrived expecting to finally talk with Shipley, but they were ushered instead into a room where one of her underlings, sitting at a table behind a large pile of papers, "would leaf through them once in a while and ask a question," Pauling remembered. Pauling was asked about his membership in Communist-front groups; he explained that he had quit them. He was asked about the Rosenbergs; he explained that he was concerned about the manner in which their trial had taken place, not with supporting the Communist cause. He was asked about sending ten dollars to a defense fund for an academic who had been fired for being a Communist; he explained that he had sent a similar amount to help intellectual refugees behind the Iron Curtain. He was asked again if he had joined the Save the Redwoods League. Pauling could not believe the question.

The next day, he and his lawyer prepared an affidavit countering each of the State Department's concerns. He was then told, on December 31, that there were many other concerns going back many years. He was asked to answer for everything in his political past, in detail and in writing.

There was no way he could do that on short notice, Pauling said; he had no idea that he would be asked to make so comprehensive a review. All of his records and papers were in Pasadena. There was no way he could respond in time to make his appointments in India.

He and Ava Helen withdrew their passport application and flew home.

〜

"A miserable time," Pauling remembered. The whole affair cost them two weeks and two thousand dollars spent on fruitless travel.

But this time there was no international outcry. This time Pauling kept quiet about his troubles, stayed away from the press, and limited his protest to a few letters to influential people, such as former Supreme Court justice Owen Roberts, now president of the American Philosophical Society. "I think that it is possible that the action of the State Department is the result of fear of McCarthy," Pauling wrote Roberts in January, "but perhaps more likely that it is just the result of a feeling of irritation on the part of Mrs. Shipley because of the action of the Secretary of State in over-ruling her about my passport in the spring of 1952."

He planned to play by the rules, lining up invitations to speak professionally in Japan, Greece, and Thailand around the end of 1954 as part of a strategy of making another run at a passport, only this time applying well ahead of time and with all his supporting documentation in hand. He would play this hand quietly, with as little controversy as possible. He would keep DuBridge and the trustees happy.

There was good reason not to rock the boat. The Rockefeller Foundation, to almost everyone's surprise, approved Pauling and Beadle's $1.5 million grant request, clearing the way for completion of the Church Laboratory. This was the largest grant that Pauling had ever obtained, an affirmation of his continuing clout at Caltech and a great piece of news, but somehow it seemed an anticlimax. He still had no focus on exactly what he wanted to do in his new building. He spent much of January and February, the months he had expected to be traveling around the world, looking for new molecular approaches to disease; poking away at the frustrating collagen problem; arranging a few details on the outfitting of his new building. He read a bit about the chemical functioning of the brain, a wide-open research area that might be fruitful. He chaired a symposium on hemoglobin at the 125th national meeting of the ACS, leading the meeting's keynote speaker, former president Harry Truman, to quip the next day that Pauling might be better off if he stuck to the study of white blood cells rather than red. The joke got a round of applause from the audience and a small laugh from Pauling. But here was another example of how little good it did to stay away from politics. After more than two years denying himself the right to speak as a citizen, his grants were still canceled, his right to travel still denied; he was still the butt of jokes.

He was tired of being silent. And in the spring of 1954 he felt compelled to speak again.

~~~

The trigger was another bomb. On March 1, the United States obliterated an entire Pacific island, Bikini Atoll, by exploding a device that surprised almost everyone with its power.

Ninety miles from the bomb site, on the day of the test, undetected by American observers, fishermen on a Japanese tuna boat called the *Lucky Dragon* saw the sky light up. Hours later the skies misted over, and a fine white ash began to fall, covering the boat and its crew with a hard-to-remove residue. By the time they reached their home port two weeks later, the crewmen were nauseous and fevered, their gums bleeding, their skin darkened and burned, their hair coming out in clumps—the classic symptoms of radiation poisoning. Japanese authorities quickly hospitalized the sickest crew members and impounded their catch, but a radiation scare swept over the islands. The people of Japan, remembering what had happened in Hiroshima and Nagasaki, demanded that their fish be tested with Geiger counters. Student demonstrations against America flared up.

Then came even worse news. Japanese physicians and scientists told the world that radioactive dust from the American bomb test, particles that had apparently been sucked up into the high levels of the atmosphere by the explosion, was being carried around the earth by high-altitude winds. It could fall anywhere. Its effects were unknown. A new word entered the lexicon of the press: fallout.

As the Japanese reports filtered into the American press, it quickly became clear that the Bikini explosion involved a bomb much bigger than anything previously tested. The public began demanding more details, and at a press conference on March 24, President Eisenhower did nothing to allay fears when he said: "It is quite clear that this time something must have happened that we have never experienced before, and must have surprised and astonished the scientists."

It certainly surprised Pauling. And it roused him from his self-imposed silence. The exorbitant amounts and exotic varieties of radioactive by-products being measured by the Japanese indicated that this was no simple H-bomb. It was something new, something much more dangerous. On April 15 he delivered his first talk on bomb policy in two and a half years. Before a crowd of a thousand listeners at the Los Angeles Unitarian Church, he went over the new bomb scare, talked about the reckless increase in the power of weaponry represented by this new Bikini-style "super bomb," and stressed that this unbridled rush toward unlimited killing capacity made it necessary to once again take up the causes of peace and disarmament. Much of his talk centered on the themes that had been sounded by the Emergency Committee of Atomic Scientists after Hiroshima—the need for world government, the importance of opening a dialogue with the Communist nations—but there was a new sense of urgency spurred by the high levels of radiation released at Bikini.

Warming to the audience, Pauling expanded his speech to a related topic, the threat to American freedom represented by the recent attacks on J. Robert Oppenheimer, who was being blacklisted, denied access to classified materials, and brought up before a security board. The reasons, it appeared, were a rehash of old charges—the same Communist associations that had spurred the 1947 FBI investigation in which Pauling had vouched for Oppenheimer's loyalty—and one new charge: that Oppenheimer had hindered the development of the H-bomb by counseling a go-slow policy. Oppenheimer had been lionized for his work on the Manhattan Project, and the prospect of having the security clearance stripped from a scientist of his stature made national headlines throughout the early months of 1954.

Pauling felt strongly about the Oppenheimer case. Although eight years before, he had recommended against Oppenheimer being nominated for the AEC board—because, he said, of an impression of unreliability associated with what he called Oppenheimer's "personal characteristics"—he now sympathized with his former friend's situation. Everyone who knew Oppenheimer was certain he was a leftist. By the early 1950s, the FBI had compiled a file, which took up ten feet of shelf space, detailing Oppenheimer's sympathies toward, and associations and friendships with, Communists. While there was no indication of espionage, there was evidence that at various times Oppenheimer had hidden facts or lied to make himself seem more conformist than he was—a "lack of candor," as those investigating him put it. Had Oppenheimer been a nonentity, a scientific underling, he would have been denied a security clearance years ago. But he was too important a scientist, too vital to the national effort, to be treated like a nonentity. Despite his record, he was given a complete security clearance for years—until Eisenhower came into office.

It seemed ridiculous to pillory Oppenheimer now, and it seemed to Pauling that the causes were strictly political: Oppenheimer was seen as an impediment to the production of more and bigger bombs. As Oppenheimer defended himself and the affair blossomed into a national debate, Pauling joined scores of scientists flocking to his defense. Having found his political voice again, Pauling wrote a short, impassioned piece that ran in the *Nation* on May Day, 1954. "The suspension as a security risk of Dr. J. Robert Oppenheimer . . . constitutes a disgraceful act on the part of the government of the United States," he wrote. "The conclusion that Dr. Oppenheimer is a loyal and patriotic American must be reached by any sensible person who considers the facts. It must have been reached by the officials of the AEC, and by President Eisenhower himself. We are accordingly forced to believe that the recent action is the result of political considerations—that Dr. Oppenheimer has been sacrificed by the government." Pauling then urged the United States to lead a concerted scientific and political search for "a practical alternative to the madness of atomic barbarism."

Later that month, Oppenheimer was stripped of his clearance.

The case served as another example to scientists that they had better stay in line. But Pauling paid no attention. "For a couple of years I have greatly restrained myself with respect to political action," he wrote a friend who complimented him on his piece in the *Nation*. "I have decided that not only is it wrong to permit oneself to be stifled, but it isn't worthwhile."

—*um*—

Pauling launched himself back into the political fray. The new "super-bomb" and its attendant fallout became the primary theme of a series of talks he gave, with the Oppenheimer case and its meaning for scientific freedom a close second. In a commencement speech at Reed College in Oregon in June—his daughter, Linda, was graduating—Pauling lambasted Washington for its "inability to think clearly" in the Oppenheimer case. Science cannot flourish when scientists are punished for saying what they believe, Pauling told the students and their parents. "You must always search for truth. Truth does not depend upon the point of view. If your neighbor does not see things as you do, then you must search for the truth. If a statement is made in one country but not another, then you must search for the truth."

The truth seemed increasingly hard to find in the growing national debate over radioactive fallout. The AEC, under its new head,

Lewis Strauss, exacerbated the problem by deciding to hold back most of the relevant data on the extent and effects of fallout, choosing instead to issue vague, reassuring, and occasionally misleading statements about the importance and safety of the bomb-test program. Through the spring and summer of 1954, it was almost impossible to find out anything definitive about fallout, and in the absence of hard data, supposition became popular. Pauling started his usual process of reading widely and putting together what facts he could find. The picture he started forming of the effects of fallout was frightening. The additional load of radiation released by bomb tests in the form of fallout added only a fraction to the "background" radiation from natural and medical sources—radioactive elements in the earth, x-rays, and cosmic radiation. But radiation damages DNA, and even a slight increase in total radiation exposure could be enough, Pauling figured, to increase the mutation rate in humans a small but significant amount. He began to speak and write about the link between fallout and mutations and continued to read more about low-level radiation and its effects, especially on genes.

In June, Pauling made another passport request for his around-the-world trip scheduled for that winter, this time asking for a precise, written list of the reasons his passport had been denied. He wanted to leave plenty of time for an appeal. When he received from Shipley a list of twenty-four allegations pulled from his FBI file, Pauling and his lawyers prepared a new affidavit answering each one. His response was sent to the passport office with a letter noting, "Most of the allegations . . . are trivial." The only one Pauling considered serious was the first on the list, that he was a concealed member of the Communist Party. "I find it hard to believe that the Department of State of the United States of America should make such an allegation," he wrote. "The slightest serious investigation of such a charge . . . would surely have shown that there is no truth behind it." Shipley knew that already. In the most recent FBI reports on Pauling that she had reviewed, the agency had noted that it had found no evidence after two years of searching to corroborate Budenz's charge that Pauling was a party member.

On October 1, after reviewing Pauling's affidavit, Shipley wrote back: "The Department . . . has concluded on the basis of evidence at hand that your activities during the years following World War II have demonstrated a consistent and prolonged adherence to the Communist Party line." Pauling might not be a Communist, but he was close enough. His passport was refused. She included a form for an appeal.

Pauling had no intention of mounting an appeal. He did not feel that he should have to plead his case before a panel of strangers, to endure again the humiliating trial by character assassination that had happened with the IERB. He wrote the secretary of state a few days later, "I have decided, after consideration of my experience with the Department of State last year, not to attempt to make the trip." Citing the expense and personal embarrassment of his last try for a passport, Pauling wrote: "I feel that I cannot take the chance of a repetition of this experience." He withdrew his application.

By then he had another plan.

The Road to Stockholm

It had been twenty-three years since A. C. Langmuir said that Pauling "may yet win the Nobel Prize," and during that time his colleagues and students had increasingly wondered when he would receive the highest honor bestowed in science. As time went by and other, less prolific researchers won the Nobel Prize for chemistry—including Edwin McMillan, who did research as a student under Pauling at Caltech—Pauling began to think he might never get one. This was a disappointment, a sore point. Many people considered Pauling one of the century's most important chemists; he was fifty-three years old, and recognition of his scientific achievements seemed long overdue. He reasoned that he had been ignored by the committee in Stockholm because Nobel's will said specifically that the science prizes were to be given not for a body of work but for a single discovery made during the preceding year. Pauling's achievement was a body of work, an edifice of structural chemistry made of many parts. "That was the trouble," Pauling said. "What was the single great discovery that I had made?"

At the end of 1952, Albert Szent-Györgyi, a biologist who had won his own Nobel Prize for his work with vitamin C, wrote Pauling that he was planning to nominate him for the 1953 Nobel Prize in chemistry. "In my opinion you should have had it long ago, but better late than never," he said. The only problem was, what single discovery should he list on the nomination? Pauling replied, "I think that my own most important work was done during the period 1928 to 1932. It involved the discovery of fundamental principles about the nature of the chemical bond and the configuration of molecules." To be helpful, he also sent a short biography and a newly written eight-page summary of his scientific work that emphasized his discovery of the hybridization of bond orbitals, the theory of directed valence, and the relation between structure and magnetic properties—all of this leading to his work with hemoglobin, antibodies, and the structure of proteins.

When, in November 1953, the Nobelists for that year were announced, however, the chemistry winner was Hermann Staudinger, an elderly German chemist whose research on polymers had influenced Pauling's own ideas about long-chain structures. Pauling shrugged off his disappointment. But now there were rumors in the air. In the summer of the next year a visiting chemist, a member of the Swedish Academy of Science, told Pauling that Staudinger had gotten the nod only because he was twenty years older than Pauling and the committee felt he might not last another year. He then indicated that Pauling might expect good news in a few months. The buzz increased when a Swedish television team visiting Caltech—to take footage, they said, of notable scientists—spent most of their time with Pauling. In October, around the time Pauling withdrew his passport application, the Caltech News Bureau sent out a packet on Pauling with the news that he was expected to win the prize.

Pauling tried to put it all out of his mind when he left on a lecture tour to Cornell and Princeton in early November 1954. But he was hoping. The prizes were always announced at the beginning of November. He would know soon.

A few minutes before Pauling was to deliver a lecture at Cornell on the afternoon of November 3, a reporter tracked him down by phone. "What is your reaction to winning the Nobel Prize in chemistry?" he asked. Pauling took a deep breath. Then he asked the reporter what he had won it for. "Chemistry," the reporter replied. "No, what does the citation say?" Pauling wanted to know which of his discoveries was being honored. The reporter read his wire copy: ". . . for research into the nature of the chemical bond . . . and its application to the elucidation of complex substances." Pauling gave a wide grin, told the reporter something about how proud he was to have won, and rang off.

He was elated. The prize was being given in recognition of everything he had done with the chemical bond from 1928 to the alpha helix. The Nobel officials had broken precedent and given him a lifetime award. Cornell professors were slapping him on the back and offering congratulations, but Pauling was so excited he hardly noticed it. He walked in a happy daze to the classroom to give his scheduled lecture—"I had a little difficulty calming down enough to enter," he remembered—where the students and professors greeted him with a standing ovation.

Calls started coming in immediately from reporters and well-wishers who heard the news on the radio. Pauling told the *New York Times* how appreciative he was of the honor and "appreciative also of the contributions made by my outstandingly able collaborators. I have been fortunate in having been for thirty-two years a member of the staff of the Institute, where there are unusually favorable conditions for carrying on scientific research." He used his new bully pulpit as a Nobelist to assail the government's policy in the Oppenheimer case. And he sent Ruth Shipley a thinly disguised message. When asked if he thought he would have any trouble getting a passport to attend the ceremonies in Stockholm, he told reporters, "I don't think there will be any trouble. Nazi Germany once caused trouble for its Nobel Prize winners, but I would not expect the United States to do so."

He was back in full voice. He was having fun again.

Keeping to his schedule despite being dogged by reporters, Pauling traveled to Princeton to deliver the Vanuxem Lectures on the structure and biological properties of molecules. While there he paid what would be his last visit to Einstein. The old physicist was frail now and easily tired, but he was happy to see Pauling and was especially pleased to see that his younger friend was using his newfound fame to speak out about the Oppenheimer case. They discussed the new super-bombs, their mutual regret that the Emergency Committee of Atomic Scientists had fallen apart, their perplexity at the spectacle of current American foreign policy. Einstein told Pauling, "I made one great mistake in my life, when I signed the letter to President Roosevelt recommending that atom bombs be made." The only excuse, he said, was that he thought the Germans were doing the same thing. There was a silence. Then Einstein told Pauling an anecdote about Count Oxenstierna, a seventeenth-century chancellor of Sweden. "As Oxenstierna said to his son," Einstein said, " 'You would be astonished to know with how little wisdom the world is governed.' " Pauling was happy to see that the two of them still thought the same way about the world.

Einstein died five months later.

_⁓⁓⁓_

The day Pauling's Nobel Prize was announced, his irrepressible former student Charles Coryell circulated a congratulatory letter around the MIT chemistry department for signatures. He was happy to see that the entire department signed with enthusiasm. "I doubt that many Nobel Prizes have been so popular with the masses in science," Coryell wrote. "Out of 86 approached, 86 signed without hesitation, and almost all are delighted that the Nobel Prize embarrasses the State Department." The MIT letter was one of more than one hundred telegrams and letters from around the world. Pauling answered each one when he returned to Caltech.

And there, too, he found almost universal jubilation. Everyone, from DuBridge to the division janitor, offered their congratulations. Ava Helen invited his staff and close friends to their hillside house for a celebration. Many toasts were drunk, and Carl Niemann's wife read a poem in Pauling's honor. "Everybody was just elated," one attendee remembered. There was a bigger party on December 3, when the entire Caltech community arrived on campus to honor Pauling. More than 350 faculty, trustees, and friends of the institute ate a catered dinner, heard DuBridge outline Pauling's accomplishments, and laughed uproariously at a skit lampooning Pauling and Caltech presented by the "Chemistry and Biology Stock Company."

"The Road to Stockholm," as they titled it, managed to capture the lighter side of the school's attitude toward Pauling: a mixture of admiration, love, and complete irreverence. There were radio announcers making fun of Pauling's loose lecturing style and bebopping students comparing Pauling's idea of resonating molecules to jazz. ("Boy, you ought to hear how a hydrocarbon molecule operates. Man, it's solid murder. It's the end.") But the high points were a series of song satires sung to popular tunes of the day, such as "Tavern in the Town."

> Pauling's courses can't be beat, can't be beat.
> Pauling's courses are a treat, are a treat.
> They will teach you all the facts you need to know,
> And maybe some that are not so.

Ava Helen was portrayed as a lovesick student singing to her teacher (to the tune of "Put Your Arms Around Me, Honey"):

> Dr. Linus Pauling is the man for me.
> He makes violent changes in my chemistry.
> Oh fie, when he rolls his eyes
> All my atoms ionize.
> When he's near, blood molecules rush to my face,
> And I couldn't tell an acid from first base.
> Oh joy, you'll never see
> Such affinity.

Dr. Pauling lectures with such piquancy
He disturbs my resonating frequency.
All my valences are changed,
All my orbits rearranged.
When he smiles I only want to clutch and cling,
Sharing two electrons in his outer ring.
Oh joy, you'll never see
Such affinity.

Finally, there was a reading of imaginary telegrams from well-wishers: "REACTIONARY CAPITALISTIC DOG: I HAVE TOLD YOU FIFTY TIMES ALREADY THAT RESONANCE DOES NOT FIT WITH QUANTUM MECHANICS. FUI. Signed Vladimir Ivanovich Lubeschevsky." Pauling laughed especially hard at "DEAR DOCTOR PAULING: YOU HAVE BEEN CLEARED TO ACCEPT THE NOBEL PRIZE. WE'RE NOT MAD IF YOU'RE NOT. Signed Oveta Culp Hobby and Ruth Shipley."

It was a joyous evening, full of warmth and laughter and generous high spirits. There had been few nights like it in the school's history. For Pauling, there would never be another.

───ⁿⁿⁿ───

The Ruth Shipley joke was especially funny given the circumstances. The day after his prize was announced, while traveling from Cornell to Princeton, Pauling wrote a number of influential people, including Senators Wayne Morse and Paul Douglas and former Supreme Court justice Owen Roberts, asking for their help in restoring his right to travel. He wrote a similar letter to Herbert Hoover, Jr., a longtime Caltech trustee who had just been named undersecretary of state. Hoover, however, had been highly critical of Pauling at Caltech and would do nothing to help him.

Once again, publicity worked in Pauling's favor. The U.S. ambassador to Sweden warned Secretary of State Dulles soon after the awards had been announced that Pauling's passport difficulties were already a topic of discussion in Stockholm. "While we have no information here regarding Pauling's political sympathies or past activities, I must emphasize that if passport is refused effect on Swedish public opinion of all shades will be catastrophic," he wrote. "Hope I may receive assurances promptly that passport will be issued."

Assurances would be a while coming. The FBI ordered another investigation, uncovering the unsavory fact that Pauling was back in the business of giving speeches, in one of which he had advocated creating a "Department of Peace" in the cabinet. The results were shipped to Shipley. For a week, as Pauling's passport difficulties became a popular topic of discussion in the Scandinavian press, the State Department did nothing, hoping that Pauling would make the first move by initiating a formal appeal. Once he appealed, the process could be delayed for months, using the excuse that Pauling was being given the same attention as any other American and that everything was going through proper channels.

Pauling knew better. Letters from his supporters began arriving, along with a wire from a U.S. Information Agency official in Europe "urgently recommending" that Pauling be allowed to travel in order to counter negative publicity. Pauling-related memos ricocheted around the State Department, with some staff advocating the minimization of damage by giving Pauling his passport—"Being a sarcastic and peculiar kind of person, Pauling has once refused to go before an Appeals Board and may prefer an attempt to embarrass the Department," one staffer noted—while others, especially Shipley and security head McLeod, advocated holding out. The department's legal adviser concluded that a strong case could not be made for withholding Pauling's passport under current regulations, which indicated that he would have to be shown to be under the direction of the Communist Party— something the FBI had been unable to do in six years. In an attempt to close the issue, an emergency meeting was held on November 15 attended by McLeod, Shipley, and three more moderate State Department officials. When the suggestion was made to bypass the appeals process, Shipley came out of her seat. "The passport division has had long experience in dealing with Communist cases," she said, "and we know the pitfalls inherent in any departure from established policy and procedure." A departure from procedure two years earlier had given Pauling his passport over her objections. She would not have it happen again. What about writing something into the passport so that Pauling could travel to Stockholm but was limited to doing nothing more than accepting the prize? That can't be done, Shipley said flatly. The meeting ended without consensus, McLeod and Shipley strongly recommending denying the passport, the three other officials—categorizing Pauling as more of an "imprudent and foggy-minded left-winger" than a threat to national security—recommending issuance to avoid adverse publicity.

Dulles decided to give Pauling his passport.

Herbert Hoover, Jr., was not happy about it. This meant bypassing the appeals process that had been set up in great part specifically because of Pauling, a move that could expose the department to criticism. He called a friend in the FBI later that day, asking the agency to review the letter of issuance he planned to send. Venting his anger, Hoover told his FBI friend that he had been trying to have Pauling ousted from Caltech for the past ten years and that it grated on him to give him a passport without an appeal being mounted. Soon after, Hoover resigned from the Caltech board of trustees, citing Pauling as his major complaint.

J. Edgar Hoover took one look at Dulles's public relations problem and told his staff, "We should most certainly not get into it."

A short letter notifying Pauling that he would be allowed to go to Stockholm was sent later that day by the undersecretary for administration.

The same day, the State Department's legal adviser found Ruth Shipley sitting alone in the cafeteria. He sat down with her. They had a long talk about Pauling, Communists, and the importance of proper procedure. Shipley, the counsel noted, was downcast at being overruled again, very disappointed in the way things had gone, and repeated that Pauling's passport should be refused.

Within a few weeks, Ruth Shipley announced that she was retiring as head of the passport division.

Scott McLeod developed something of a sense of humor about the Pauling affair. Asked shortly afterward by a congressional committee how Pauling had managed to get a passport without going through the appeals process, he answered that the issuance was the result of a "self-generating appeal." Asked to interpret that phrase, he smiled and said that it meant that "the State Department reads the papers, too."

―――

Pauling was given a passport valid not only for Sweden, but for the world.

As happy as he had ever been in his life, he, Ava Helen, Crellin, and Linus junior and his wife, Anita, flew out of Los Angeles on December 5. They met Peter and Linda in Copenhagen. Then the entire family, "a joyous crowd," Ava Helen remembered, traveled together to Stockholm.

Pauling had never seen anything like the Nobel ceremonies. It started on December 9 with a reception for the winners held by the royal high chamberlain of Sweden. Here Pauling chatted briefly with the winners in physics—Max Born, the mathematical sage of Göttingen he had met on his first trip to Europe, being honored belatedly for his contributions to quantum mechanics, sharing the prize with Walther Bothe, a German experimental physicist whose best work was also done in the late 1920s—and members of the three-man American team who shared the prize in medicine for their research on polio. Ernest Hemingway, winner in literature, was eagerly awaited by the European press but was unable to make it to Stockholm because of injuries sustained during an African safari.

The next day, the awards were presented before two thousand people in the Stockholm Concert Hall in a ceremony that Pauling called "one of the most impressive . . . held in the modern world." Each new Nobelist was lauded in a speech outlining his work. Pauling's was delivered by a long-winded Swedish crystallographer who took the opportunity to present an overview of chemical history from Berzelius onward, ending with Pauling's view of the chemical bond and his application of it to all of chemistry and much of biology and medicine. When he was done and the applause had died down, King Gustavus VI of Sweden handed Pauling his gold Nobel medal and accompanying scroll. Instead of accepting it with the stiff formality common to the occasion, Pauling, dressed in tails and white tie and obviously enjoying the moment, gave the king one of his ear-to-ear grins, evidencing "such beaming pleasure," the European papers reported, "that everyone in the hall rejoiced with him."

The ceremony was followed by the Nobel dinner in the Gold Room of Stockholm's city hall, a spacious turn-of-the-century room named because of the twenty-four-carat gold mosaics lining its walls. Here the ritual continued as the king proposed a toast to each new laureate and each responded with a short speech of appreciation. Pauling's—in which he expressed his long-standing admiration for Sweden and his desire to be thought of as an "honorary Swede"—earned the most enthusiastic applause. After dinner, the king led the Nobelists to the top of a marble staircase overlooking a crowd of hundreds of cheering Swedish university students waving flags and torches. After the students serenaded the winners with a song, it was customary for one Nobelist to address them with a few words of inspiration, and Pauling had been elected to speak by his fellow laureates. His address was reprinted in all the papers in Sweden:

"Perhaps as one of the older generation, I should preach a little sermon to you, but I do not propose to do so," he called out to the crowd. "I shall, instead, give you a word of advice about how to behave toward your elders. When an old and distinguished person speaks to you, listen to him carefully and with respect—*but do not believe him. Never put your trust in anything but your own intellect.* Your elder, no matter whether he has gray hair or has lost his hair, no matter whether he is a Nobel Laureate, *may be wrong.* . . . So you must always be skeptical—*always think for yourself.*"

Pleasantly surprised, the students cheered wildly.

The next day, Saturday the eleventh, Pauling delivered his Nobel lecture, a review in which he focused especially on the concept of resonance. In it, he talked confidently about valence-bond concepts that were under increasing critical attack, using the Nobel Prize as a validation of his approach to chemistry.

That evening came the grand finale of the Nobel celebration, a formal dinner at the royal palace as guests of the king and queen. Pauling entered the dining room looking tall and elegant in his black evening clothes; on his arm was Princess Margaretha of Sweden. Ava Helen, escorted by the prime minister of Sweden, was happy to find herself seated at the left hand of the king. She was happy, but in her down-to-earth socialist fashion, not overly impressed. "I discussed politics with the Prime Minister—and gardening with the King," she wrote in her diary that night. "Very interesting."

As a final honor, Pauling and the three American winners in medicine were feted at a party thrown by the American embassy—an encouraging sign, Pauling thought, that perhaps the U.S. government was ready to accept him as a worthwhile citizen.

After it was over, the embassy counsel wired Washington, D.C., that Pauling's visit had passed without incident. "The Stockholm press has given him much publicity, both because of his own cheerful and attractive personality and the photogenic qualities of his family," the counsel wrote with an almost audible sigh of relief. "Neither in his press conference following his arrival nor in his remarks at the banquet . . . did Professor Pauling make any remarks which could be objected to."

Far from being objectionable, Pauling earned America a new level of respect. Part of it accrued from the fact that he had been allowed to travel to Stockholm at all, demonstrating that individual achievement could overcome the tensions of the Cold War. But more important was his personal charm and warmth. "There has rarely been a Nobel Prize winner who knew so well how to captivate the whole world as this modest, cordial and cosmopolitan savant," one European paper reported, calling the Nobel ceremonies "a 'festive performance' whose 'principal actor,' Hemingway, did not attend. But nevertheless it had a 'star' in the modest professor from Pasadena."

The same feeling of goodwill followed Pauling around the globe. After two weeks of sightseeing with the family in Sweden and Norway, Pauling and Ava Helen flew to Israel for a week, where they visited universities and talked to researchers in Haifa and Jerusalem. They spent Christmas in Bethlehem, an experience that did nothing to alter Pauling's atheism, then flew to India for several weeks. This long-delayed visit became a high point of their trip. As guests of the Indian government they toured the nation's leading universities and laboratories, traveling from New Delhi to Calcutta to Allahabad, visiting the Taj Mahal, the caves at Ajanta, and the temples at Benares.

In Baroda, Pauling attended the Indian Science Congress, where he found scientific diplomacy in full flower, with large delegations of Russian and Chinese scientists bearing gifts of minerals and equipment. The American presence was limited to him and a few nonsponsored Yankees. As the only American invited to address the full congress, Pauling gave a talk on hemoglobin and sickle-cell anemia, then ended it with some broader concerns. He made reference to the need for world peace and then reminded the international audience that the majority of American researchers were working not on atomic and hydrogen bombs and the means of delivering them, as many in the Russian orbit were saying, but on problems like sickle-cell anemia, investigations related to the peaceful development and welfare of all people on earth. He added, as a pointed barb aimed at the Communist-bloc delegates, that American scientists were also lucky enough to work freely.

Pauling's talk was greeted with wild applause. Afterward, an Indian scientist told a friend from the United States, "Your Dr. Pauling has done more tonight to dispel the notion that Americans are international war-mongers than have all the official releases through your State Department."

The Paulings also shared a dinner and conversation about politics, bombs, and peace with Nehru, a man whom Pauling thought extraordinary, graced with "great mental powers, excellent judgement and complete sincerity. . . . In my opinion, Nehru is one of the greatest men in the world."

After a few days in Bangkok, the Paulings flew to Japan in February. Pauling was known there not only for his scientific work but for his work against the bomb. He was mobbed. In Tokyo and Kyoto his lectures were so popular that hundreds of people had to be turned away—in two cases leading to damage as people tried to force their way in. Away from the cities, however, the Paulings were able to visit Buddhist temples, take long walks in the snow, tour a number of universities and industrial plants, try out a Japanese bath, and enjoy a few days in a private home by the sea. Pauling became interested in the country's economics and politics. Japan was still impoverished, its universities quite poor compared with those in the United States, and Pauling was impressed by the popular support he saw for opening trade with the USSR and the People's Republic of China.

He also heard a great deal about radioactive fallout. The crew of the *Lucky Dragon* was still under observation, and Japanese scientists analyzing the radioactive elements that fell to earth after the Bikini bomb test were finding some unexpected isotopes. There was talk that the unusually high levels of radioactivity released by the test were due not only to the power of the bomb, its ability to push fallout up into the stratosphere for wider distribution, but also to its very nature. It appeared that it might involve a new combination of fission and fusion. Pauling listened closely.

Only one incident marred their visit. Professor Mizushima, a Japanese chemist who had helped arrange some of Pauling's lectures, was also in charge of educating the emperor's second son, Yoshi. Through his contacts with the imperial household, Mizushima had received permission to arrange an audience between Pauling and the emperor, provided that it was approved through official channels on the U.S. side. This was a very great distinction, and Mizushima immediately wrote the U.S. embassy for guidance. The request was forwarded up the ladder to Washington, D.C., where it ended up on the desk of security head Scott McLeod. "This Bureau is of the opinion that it is ridiculous for the Department to entertain ideas of official sanction or to pave the way for an individual of Pauling's background to be accorded such privileges by various chiefs of state in different parts of the world," McLeod responded. The U.S. embassy in Japan refused to cooperate, and Pauling's imperial audience never materialized.

That was, however, a relatively minor matter. By the time Pauling flew back to Pasadena after nearly five months of world travel, he was a slightly different man. From the time he learned of the Nobel Prize until he returned home in April, Pauling had been honored and feted, applauded and attended. He had dined with kings and prime ministers. He had delivered more than fifty speeches to enthusiastic audiences.

And he had learned that his concerns were the world's concerns. Once outside the United States, he could see the dismay with which the rest of the world viewed nuclear weapons testing, the degree of anxiety about fallout, the depth of worry over the Cold War between the United States and the USSR, the extent to which his ideas were mirrored throughout the globe. He returned home secure in his beliefs. He returned home ready to fight.

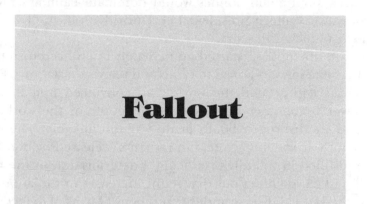

Fallout

The U-bomb

The Nobel Prize changes scientists. For some it marks a sudden leap from nonentity to international fame. For others it represents a ticket to explore new areas. For almost all, it means a period of disruption, a lessening of output, a loss of focus.

Pauling was accustomed to fame and was unfazed by the piles of mail, stacks of invitations, and calls from the media that greeted him when he returned home. But the prize did change his life. Winning it brought Pauling to the acknowledged pinnacle of scientific achievement; he no longer needed to worry about proving himself professionally. The thirty-five thousand dollars that came with the prize also helped make him more financially independent.

As a result, he was free to throw himself again into political activism. He had muzzled himself politically in part because he did not want to lose his job and in part because DuBridge had convinced him that his activism was bad for Caltech. The great prestige of the prize now made these, in Pauling's mind, moot points. Caltech did not fire Nobel Prize winners. The generous praise during the previous few months made it seem that the old wounds might be healed, that his school could once again be proud of him despite his political views.

The Bikini bomb test and the Oppenheimer case had already started Pauling back on the road to social activism. Now the prize made it possible for him to follow that path wholeheartedly. For the next six years antibomb politics would dominate Pauling's thoughts and actions. As Caltech president Lee DuBridge put it, "For a while there he lost touch with science."

The shift in emphasis started immediately upon his return to California. In a statement released to radio and television stations, Pauling said that his trip around the world had convinced him that there would never be another world war. The people of the world loved peace, and the hydrogen bomb made war unthinkable. The danger now was not war, Pauling wrote, but radiation released by bomb tests. "Are we justified in willfully producing a deterioration in the human race?" he asked, pointing out that slight increases in radiation might increase the rates of disease and the number of births of defective children. "The time has come when it is essential that international negotiations be carried out with the aim of limiting or stopping all atomic bomb tests."

He believed his statement reasonable, given what he had learned about the dangers of radiation from his reading, conversations with geneticists, and his talks with Japanese scientists. Experiments on various plants and animals had proved that genes were damaged by radiation, and there was some preliminary evidence that the greater the exposure, the greater the damage. As exposure decreased, damage decreased along a straight line. The best evidence showed that the damage did not reach zero until the radiation did. Very small increases in radiation exposure, therefore, were probably associated with very small but real increases in the risk of health problems.

That was what the data seemed to indicate, but much more needed to be done to prove this point, especially for humans. Still, there was enough troubling evidence to convince Pauling and a great many other scientists that bomb tests and the increased radiation from fallout were a danger to human health. It was evident from animal studies that radiation could damage the DNA in egg and sperm cells, causing birth defects. There was also some evidence that radiation could affect the body's other cells, increasing the rate of diseases like cancer. But almost no studies had been done directly examining the effects of very slight increases in radiation exposure, such as those caused by fallout.

Pauling, however, presented little uncertainty in his remarks. He received national attention by asserting in an NBC interview that "leukemia is one of the great dangers," claiming that fallout might be sufficient to trigger this form of blood cancer in susceptible victims.

During the spring of 1955, what Pauling had heard in Japan became more widely known. Japanese researchers made it clear that the Bikini test involved no ordinary hydrogen bomb. Not only was it several times more powerful than a standard hydrogen bomb—strong enough to break through the lower reaches of the atmosphere and pump fallout into the stratosphere, where it remained suspended, able to spread around the world—but it produced a great deal more fallout than any previously tested bomb.

The Bikini bomb, it appeared, represented something new. More evidence came from an analysis of the fallout done by the Japanese. Among the strange mix of radioactive isotopes in the dust were some that could be made only as a by-product of splitting apart common uranium. This was confusing because common uranium was not volatile enough to use in a standard atomic bomb, which was why scientists during the war had spent so much time and money purifying a rare and more explosive isotope. According to physicists, common uranium could only enter into an explosive reaction if it was set off by an enormous input of energy.

And that, it now appeared, was what had occurred at Bikini. The bomb tested there, it became clear, was a new type of three-stage device: A Hiroshima-style fission bomb was used to set off a fusion-type H-bomb, which provided the energy needed to fission a coating of common uranium. This fission-fusion-fission design was ingenious, a way of enormously increasing the power of an H-bomb for very little money. In theory—and this was part of what frightened observers like Pauling—such a bomb could be made as powerful as desired by simply packing on cheaper, easily available uranium.

The resulting "U-bomb," as it became known, was both incredibly powerful and incredibly dirty. Its development spurred a new period of worldwide activism against the development of nuclear weapons.

In July 1955, the British philosopher, mathematician, and pacifist Bertrand Russell, spurred to action by the release of radioactivity in the Bikini test, released a resolution against nuclear war signed by himself, Albert Einstein—it was the last public document Einstein signed before dying—and eight other prominent scientists. Pauling, who had been away when Russell's letter arrived seeking his help, cabled his endorsement a few days later, becoming the eleventh signatory of what was to become known as the Russell-Einstein Manifesto.

"It is feared that if many H-bombs are used there will be universal death—sudden only for a minority, but for the majority a slow torture of disease and disintegration," the manifesto read. "There lies before us, if we choose, continual progress in happiness, knowledge and wisdom. Shall we, instead, choose death, because we cannot forget our quarrels? We appeal, as human beings, to human beings: Remember your humanity and forget the rest. If you can do so, the way lies open to a new paradise; if you cannot, there lies before you the risk of universal death."

The rhetoric was reminiscent of the early days of the Emergency Committee of Atomic Scientists, with the same impetus of a vastly powerful new weapon, the same sense of urgency, the renewed feeling that if scientists could only get the word out to the public, the resulting distaste for nuclear war would bring about a new world order. Einstein's death created a vacuum in moral leadership among scientists dedicated to peace. Russell would take his place in Britain. In the United States, Pauling would pick up the banner.

—*wm*—

By 1956, Pauling was spending, he estimated, half of his time reading and giving talks about bombs and fallout, poring over government reports, books on nuclear war, scientific studies on genetic effects, and popular accounts of bomb tests, spending hour after hour trying to find the truth.

Atomic Energy Commission (AEC) spokespersons were trying to calm public fears by pointing out that natural radiation surrounded everyone, every day, in the form of natural radioactive isotopes in the ground from solar radiation and cosmic rays. An increase of 1 percent in this "background radiation"—the increase due to bomb tests—was negligible for any one person, they said. In any case, hard data on any direct link between low-level radiation and human disease did not exist. In June, AEC commissioner Lewis Strauss assured a convention of physicians that the total fallout released by all nuclear tests to date had not increased any individual's exposure by as much as a single chest x-ray. Those who were claiming that the tests poisoned the atmosphere and produced future generations of monsters were committing, he said, "an act of irresponsibility."

Pauling realized that the AEC's interpretation of the data was skewed because it focused on individuals rather than groups. The individual effects of low-level radiation exposure were small—so small that they were invisible unless measured over an entire population. If, Pauling said, you assume that all of the 1.5 million birth defects around the world each year are caused by natural background radiation—a major assumption but one arguable given the genetic evidence—then an increase in background radiation of only 1 percent from bomb tests would cause another fifteen thousand defective children to be born every year. The individual risk was small, but the cumulative picture of fifteen thousand defective babies was compelling. These were the kind of numbers Pauling and others began using.

The more that became known about fallout—despite the AEC's reluctance to release definitive data, researchers around the world were now busy analyzing the radioactive dust—the more unsettled the public became. The outer coating of the U-bomb created a riot of weird radioactive products when it exploded, including one that quickly caught the attention of the American public: strontium 90, a long-lived isotope that had never been seen on earth before the atomic tests. Strontium 90 was especially dangerous because of its unfortunate resemblance to calcium. Researchers quickly showed that when rain fell through a fallout cloud, strontium 90 was deposited on grass, where it could be eaten by cattle and passed through their milk to humans, where it was deposited in bones, especially in the growing bones of children. Once in the bone, it decayed, exposing the tissue around it to radiation. Through 1956, Pauling and a number of other activists sharply etched the image of children's milk poisoned with radioactivity in the minds of millions of families. Testing a bomb was no longer a local matter; its effects now were spread worldwide on the wind.

—*mm*—

Pauling's renewed political activism went beyond antibomb statements. He joined the Society of Social Responsibility in Science, a pacifist, leftist organization of scientists, and renewed his activism in the area of civil rights, signing a petition urging Congress to declare the Internal Security Act of 1950 unconstitutional and pitching in as a sponsor of the Citizens Committee to Preserve American Freedoms. In November 1955 he was called to Washington, D.C., this time as a friendly witness, to testify about his passport difficulties before a congressional subcommittee on First Amendment rights headed by longtime McCarthy opponent Thomas Hennings.

The Hennings committee hearings brought his name back into the press ("Pauling Says 'Something Rotten' in State Dept.," blared the Pasadena paper) and engendered the usual reaction. Fulton Lewis, Jr., a conservative newspaper columnist who worked closely with the FBI, attacked Pauling's testimony as biased because of his Communist-front activities, which were enumerated in numbing detail. The next month, the Senate Internal Security Subcommittee (SISS), HUAC's counterpart on the other side of the Capitol, issued "The Communist Party of the United States of America: What It Is, How It Works, A Handbook for Americans," listing eighty-two "most active and typical sponsors of Communist Fronts." One of them was Pauling. The Nobel Prize, it seemed, was no defense against witch hunters.

Pauling also found that the Caltech board of trustees' murmur of complaint once more rose to a howl. Two important members, Reese Taylor and Herbert Hoover, Jr., had already resigned because of Pauling; now John McCone, an important figure in Southern California's burgeoning defense industry, led a new charge to oust the controversial scientist. DuBridge held firm to his usual policy: publicly supporting Pauling's right to speak out—especially about bomb tests, which DuBridge agreed were of doubtful military value—while privately pressuring his recalcitrant division head to tone it down.

And once more Pauling's friends rallied to his defense. On NBC television, Harold Urey revealed that Pauling, whom he called "exceedingly brilliant and upright," had been stripped of his U.S. Public Health Service grant for political reasons. George Beadle published an unusual defense of Pauling in the Caltech alumni magazine, praising Pauling's independence, excoriating the security and loyalty system, then noting pointedly, "I am proud that Caltech has a President who knows the true meaning of academic freedom. . . . I am grateful for a board of trustees that has not succumbed to the disease of mistrust and suspicion."

Even Pauling's secretaries came to his defense. When making a purchase at a local department store, one of them chatted with a clerk. After learning that she worked for Linus Pauling, the clerk said, "You work for that *Commie?*"

"Well, he isn't a Communist," his secretary answered. "If anyone should know, I should know, because I've had access to his private files for a number of years, and I have never seen anything in his correspondence that would indicate that he was a Communist." She threw her purchase down and left.

Pauling was used to all this by now, accustomed, too, to the stern talks by DuBridge about academic responsibility. He made it very clear, both privately and in a public speech, that he was not advocating political activism or spreading leftist ideas among Caltech students. Instead, he advised them to listen to the words of Aristotle: "Young men should be mathematicians, old men should be politicians."

Then he continued his work for peace and an end to bomb tests.

Mongols and Idiots

Despite his increasingly heavy load of political work, Pauling still found some time for science. He oversaw his research group's work on protein structures, tinkered a bit with nucleic acids—eventually making, with Corey, his own contribution to Watson's and Crick's double helix: the addition of a hydrogen bond between one base pair—and finally finished furnishing the Church laboratory.

For years he had talked about the discoveries that could be made by applying chemistry to medicine, using the model of molecular disease that he had devised to explain sickle-cell anemia. He had even heard talk in Stockholm about how he had been considered for a Nobel Prize in physiology and medicine for that work. The sickle-cell work was enormously important, he knew, and certainly there were many more diseases that would benefit from a similar analysis. Although Harvey Itano had recently left Pasadena to work for the National Institutes of Health, taking the abnormal hemoglobin project with him, there were other areas where the molecular model could be applied. Pauling briefly considered an attack on cancer, but then figured that that territory had been too well settled by researchers already. He thought about muscular dystrophy but decided against it.

In the summer of 1955 he found what he had been looking for. He had been reading a little about the physiology of the brain, focusing especially on the way in which specific molecules might be involved in mental functions. He had come across a discussion of a rare biochemical defect in which an inability to metabolize the amino-acid phenylalanine led to a buildup of that substance and its by-products in the blood and urine. Somehow this biochemical imbalance caused mental deficiency. The condition eventually became known as phenylketonuria (PKU).

What he read immediately suggested to Pauling that the condition was caused by a defect in an enzyme specific for metabolizing phenylalanine. PKU was, in other words, a molecular disease. It was the opening he was looking for. Perhaps he could verify that the cause was an enzyme deficiency, then isolate the defective enzyme and study it. "It is, of course, not to be expected that a study of this sort would lead immediately to a therapy for the disease—we would be interested primarily in obtaining basic information about the nature of mental disease, which would later be useful in the effort to develop new therapeutic methods," he wrote his cousin Richard Morgan, a statistician with the state mental health division.

PKU, with its suggestion of a link between a specific enzyme and severe cognitive problems, opened the door to a vast, new area of inquiry: the molecular basis of mental disease. Pauling asked Morgan's help in laying the groundwork, and his cousin responded by getting him into contact with mental health experts who might be able to provide other possibilities of similar biochemical abnormalities in mental patients. Mental diseases, Pauling found, constituted perhaps 10 percent of all hospitalizations in the United States, yet virtually nothing had been done along the lines he proposed. Using his model of molecular disease, there was the chance for sudden, important discoveries about the workings of the brain.

Morgan set up a meeting between Pauling and some local psychiatrists at the Pacific State Hospital, a Los Angeles–area facility for mental defectives. The visit was a sobering one for Pauling. He toured ward after ward of retarded and mentally defective children, kids suffering from PKU, gargoylism, and retardations of unknown origin. The ability to think had been something Pauling always had taken for granted; seeing the effects of a loss of that ability struck a chord inside him. He saw the deformities in speech and reasoning, the distorted motion, the characteristic physical traits that mirrored the interior dysfunction in mental processes. This tragic loss of human intelligence was the result of a damaged double helix or malfunctioning enzyme, he believed; this was the mental result of misbuilt molecules. He could help find out what was happening here. He might be able to cure or prevent at least some of this suffering.

The majority of the patients at the facility were Mongoloid idiots, as they were called at the time, a condition that the facility's medical director believed was due to a genetic defect inherited from their parents. Although such parents might seem normal, he told Pauling, they could be identified by certain signs—the shape of their ears, their hands, and so forth. This, too, he told Pauling, might be a fertile area for research, and there were hundreds of Mongoloid idiots at the facility, compared to only fourteen PKU cases.

Pauling had seen all he needed to see. Less than a month after his visit to the mental hospital, he finished drafting a massive grant proposal requesting from the Ford Foundation more than $800,000 for a seven-year investigation into the molecular basis of mental disease. A portion of the money would go toward looking for the abnormal enzyme in PKU, with the ultimate aim of devising a simple diagnostic test for the condition. Part of the research would involve ongoing urinalysis to check the progress of the disease; part would be devoted to finding biochemical abnormalities underlying Mongoloidism and other mental deficiencies.

While he did not get everything he asked for, Pauling's grant request was rewarded handsomely: The following spring, he was informed that the Ford Foundation would award him $450,000 over five years. It was another massive grant, another pioneering extension of Pauling's chemical viewpoint into a new field, another indication that the Caltech Division of Chemistry and Chemical Engineering was the most forward looking in the world.

But the reaction around campus was strangely muted. Pauling's own group, the newer faculty and students who had helped him with his protein research, understood what he was doing, but the older members of the faculty, those hired by Noyes, were derisive. What did collecting urine specimens from retarded children have to do with chemistry? This was medical research, and what business did the Caltech chemistry division have to do with medical research? Noyes had created a temple to physical chemistry, and Pauling was letting it crumble while he devoted all of his time and effort as director to these increasingly tangential pursuits. Look at the way space was allocated in the Church laboratory, with large new suites given to immunochemistry and now this medical project, while the physical and analytic chemists, true to the heart of the science, stayed cooped up in the aging Gates and Crellin labs. In the minds of the old faculty, Pauling had upset the balance of the division. There was a question of quality as well. Many of Pauling's hires had been made to support his research goals, and, the thinking went, jobs had gone to men who might be good experimentalists but were certainly not professorial material. Then there were the left-wing doctors he hired for his medical projects. The only really good recent hire, in the minds of the older faculty, had been Jack Roberts, a young rising star of organic chemistry, an expert in the uses of nuclear magnetic resonance. Roberts was one new man the older professors could get along with.

The internal grumbling reached the office of Lee DuBridge, who listened sympathetically. He was not opposed to the mental research project, although he agreed it represented another move away from the basic core of chemistry. He was, however, very concerned about the overall performance of his chemistry chair. Pauling seemed not to care any more about his division. After winning the Nobel Prize, he seemed to be away from Caltech almost as much as he was there, traveling the country, adding to his already crowded political and chemical lecturing schedule talks to various psychological and mental health associations. And here, too, he seemed a bit out of control. This was the heyday of Freudianism and its offshoots, and many psychiatrists and psychologists were convinced that mental diseases were rooted in experience, not molecules. In May 1956, Pauling outraged much of the audience at a national conference of the American Psychiatric Association by stating, "I am sure that most mental disease is chemical in origin." He went on to assert that schizophrenia in particular was the result of a molecular imbalance. On questioning afterward, he admitted that he had no proof, but that he was working on a "hunch."

DuBridge didn't know whether Pauling's speculations were off the mark or not. Far more important—and annoying—to him and his board were Pauling's political activities. Some instances were minor, for example when, in 1956, Pauling, appearing on the television program *Youth Wants to Know,* told the children of America that his scientific work had caused him to doubt the existence of God. More important was his continuing and growing agitation against the testing of nuclear weapons. By mid-1956 there was general scientific agreement with Pauling's view that adding radiation to the atmosphere was undesirable—in June the National Academy of Sciences (NAS) released a report saying that "the concept of a safe rate of radiation simply does not make sense" and warning especially against the long-term genetic effects that might result from the buildup of strontium 90 in the bones—but there was also general disagreement with his view that this represented an important risk to health. The NAS panels found no proof of increased rates of leukemia or other illnesses from fallout, and although they concluded that a minor effect on average life spans could not be ruled out, the consensus was that there was more danger to human health from medical x-rays than fallout.

Pauling restudied, refined, and stuck with his statistical extrapolations of the limited radiation-exposure data from animal studies. He concluded that each added radiation load to which a population was exposed shortened someone's life by triggering cancer or leading to "premature aging." Averaged over the population, he came up with a figure that each roentgen of added exposure would shorten the average life by two or three weeks, a figure that he began using in dozens of speeches and articles.

And he knew how to get headlines. Spurred by a telephone call he received from a woman in Tonopah, Nevada, who told him that she thought that heavy fallout there had led to the death from leukemia of her seven-year-old son and sore eyes among many people—observations that the local paper had refused to print—Pauling wrote the editor of the Tonopah *Times-Bonanza* with his estimate of the damage that local residents might have suffered. The added 5 roentgens of radiation deposited in that high-fallout area would shorten the average life by about three months, Pauling said. Multiply that by the population, he told the editor, and you can estimate that the tests have robbed Nevadans of one thousand years of life. That got headlines. Pauling then tipped an investigative journalist to the incidence of cancer in the Nevada fallout area, which led eventually to stories in the national press.

The majority of scientists followed the NAS line—fallout radiation was bad, but not too bad—and Pauling once again found himself marginalized as the leader of an unnecessarily noisy and somewhat hysterical minority that was using the fallout issue as a lever for obviously political and pacifist ends. Only among the minority of antibomb activists was he viewed as a hero.

On the other side, proponents of a strong defense accelerated their campaign to reassure the public that fallout was safe. AEC head Lewis Strauss and his chief scientific adviser, the respected radiation physicist William Libby, spoke widely about the infinitesimal addition to background radiation caused by bomb tests and downplayed the effects of strontium 90. They framed the issue as a choice between unproven and probably negligible health effects on a tiny minority of the human race and the Communist domination that would result if bomb testing were stopped and the United States lost the arms race. Adding weight to their arguments was the Cold War emphasis on national security: The Russian ground forces were so much stronger than the Western powers that only American and British atomic weapons held them in check. If tests were stopped, the West would lose this critical military advantage, and the Red tide would rise.

It was an effective public relations campaign that succeeded in linking those like Pauling, who proposed an end to bomb tests, with anti-Americanism and pro-communism. It worked to derail the presidential candidacy of Adlai Stevenson, who advocated a test ban as part of his campaign strategy in the fall of 1956, and it caused most antibomb scientists to remain mute. "There is a surprising popular lack of interest in some of the suppressive actions of the government," Pauling told a television interviewer in 1956. "I have estimated that of ten scientists who, ten years ago, were talking over problems, about the problems of the atomic bomb and war and peace, only one remains nowadays. The others have become silent."

In their absence, Pauling became the nation's leading antitest advocate, speaking widely, publishing his ideas about the effects of low-level radiation in as many outlets as possible, and countering the AEC's assurances with shocking estimates of damage to human health, which he now dramatized by extrapolating over several generations. Despite the renewed attacks on his credibility by politicians and journalists, he felt terrific about fighting the good fight once again. No one had yet shown that his statistical analysis of the danger to human health was wrong, and until they did, he would stick with it.

Ava Helen, Linda, and Deer Flat Ranch

With the children grown and out of the house—the youngest, Crellin, now in college—Ava Helen's influence on Pauling increased. She was now at his side constantly, traveling with him everywhere, assessing every speech, building his confidence, emphasizing his growing importance as a national figure. Ava Helen was Pauling's closest friend and political mentor as well as his cheerleader, and her opinion was more important to him than those of a thousand politicians, administrators, and commentators. Their relationship had weathered some extremely difficult times, and the problems and successes they had faced together seemed only to bring them closer.

Ava Helen, too, now had time for political activity, and she became more active in helping Pauling refine his thoughts on issues, pushing him toward greater activism, and broadening the scope of his concerns. Pauling was for the moment still the spokesman for the pair, the one who put forward publicly the feelings that they both shared. But Ava Helen was important in guiding what he said. She was quiet about it, however, taking credit only in later years when she said simply, "I think I've introduced him to a number of things that he may not have been aware of."

After the Nobel Prize, the two of them began searching for a country place, perhaps near the sea, where they could be alone and escape the smog and pressures of Pasadena. While driving the coast highway between Los Angeles and San Francisco, through a gorgeous and isolated stretch of rugged seashore called Big Sur, they found what they wanted. Stopping to rest at a place where the highway clung high on the mountainside above the ocean, they looked down and saw a large, beautiful emerald-green triangle of level land jutting out into the water. There was a creek down there and a small cabin sitting near the shore. "Something like this would be perfect," Pauling said to his wife.

They found that former cattle ranch, all 122 acres of it, was for sale. They drove down the rutted, bone-jarring access road with a real estate agent, looked it over, and found it to their liking. The turn-of-the-century cabin was still furnished with a big wood cookstove and some well-used furniture; there was a weatherbeaten barn, cattle still roaming, and a couple of horses. They both fell in love with it.

They used Pauling's Nobel Prize money to buy it, lock, stock, and cookstove. They called it Deer Flat Ranch, and soon were spending as much time as they could there. It was a refuge for the two of them, a place without a phone where they could avoid seeing another human for a week at a time. Here, perched on a ledge over the sea, with nothing but the muffled sound of the surf, the wind, and birdcalls to distract him, Pauling concentrated on problems without interruption, Ava Helen baked bread, and together they took long walks, holding hands and talking endlessly.

―�‐

The children may have been grown, but they could still be cause for concern. In the summer of 1956, after the usual delays, Pauling was granted a passport to go to Europe, ostensibly to give the keynote speech at ceremonies in Rome surrounding the hundredth anniversary of the death of the great Italian chemist Amadeo Avogadro. But Pauling also needed to check on his children.

Peter, newly married to a woman his parents had never seen, was having difficulty finishing his doctorate at the Cavendish Laboratory. Pauling's first stop was England, where he talked the situation over with Kendrew. It appeared clear after their discussion that his second son was not succeeding in the field of protein studies, and Peter ended up switching to inorganic chemistry at the University of London.

Linda was an even bigger puzzle. She had changed from doting daughter to free spirit soon after she started attending Reed College, a small liberal arts university in Portland, in 1951, taking on new friends and new attitudes about social relationships. "I find that I have some difficulty understanding the younger generation," Pauling confessed to a friend. After graduation, Linda left on what her parents thought was going to be a short trip to visit Peter in England. But after becoming a welcome addition to Peter's group of friends—young and party-loving American students and postdocs, with a sprinkling of interesting young men from England—she ended up staying. At first, Pauling sent her one hundred dollars per month, but then, when he saw that she had no intention of coming home, he sent her a plane ticket and orders to return. She cashed in the ticket and stayed, taking a job as an au pair with Francis Crick and his wife, Odile, ironing Crick's shirts and taking care of children at their house, now known as the Golden Helix. At night, Linda, willowy, blond, and exotically American, became a hit of the Cambridge social scene. She was young and beautiful and on her own in Europe. She had many boyfriends and at least one fiancé. She ran off to Scotland for a few weeks with a professor of zoology, living with him and a friend in an attic flat in Edinburgh, then ended up in Florence in the spring of 1956, taking an occasional art class and enjoying the cafés and museums.

It had been two years since Linda had seen her parents when they finally caught up with her in Rome in June 1956. "Confusion confounded," Ava Helen noted in her diary the day Linda arrived, but the two parents resolved not to let their disapproval of her recent actions ruin their relationship. Linda watched as Pauling received the Order of the Italian Republic in an elaborate ceremony during the Avogadro celebration, then accompanied her parents for a month as they toured Italy, staying in first-class hotels and dining at the finest restaurants. When they asked her to come back with them to Pasadena, however, Linda refused. She stayed in Italy for another month, until a combination of chronic poverty and a severe respiratory infection sent her home.

After nursing her to health, the Paulings tried a different tack with their daughter. From the moment she arrived, they threw her together as often and as long as possible with a favorite graduate student of Pauling's, a handsome and brilliant young geologist named Barclay Kamb. By the summer of 1957, Linda had settled down: She was living at home, making money by assisting Corey at Caltech, and occasionally cooking dinner for Kamb, who was, Pauling was happy to note, "hanging around our house quite a bit." The matchmaking worked. On a beautiful day in September 1957, Pauling walked across the front lawn of his Sierra Madre home with Linda on his arm, in front of two hundred guests, and delivered her to Barclay Kamb—now a Caltech assistant professor of geology—for the purpose of marriage.

The Right to Petition

Pauling's political work and well-publicized foray into mental disease left him busier than ever through 1957. His desk was covered with invitations from high school groups, women's associations, hospitals, universities, professional societies, and activist organizations to speak on chemical, medical, and nuclear issues. The teachers union of the city of New York gave him an award for outstanding service to the cause of freedom in education; the Roswell Park Memorial Institute invited him to be on their advisory board; the American Association of Clinical Chemists made him an honorary member; the National Science Foundation made him the star of a series of color films on the chemical bond for science teachers. At the same time, he was working on yet another edition of *The Nature of the Chemical Bond* and arranging another summer trip to Europe.

Pauling's continued advocacy of a ban on bomb tests and his incessant reiteration of the health risks of fallout—coupled with similar efforts by Russell and others—appeared to be having an effect. In March the Japanese government sent an expert on radiation on a worldwide trip to urge a halt in tests. In April, alarmed by evidence of rising levels of strontium 90, the British Labor party moved in favor of a test ban. Nehru appealed to the world to support a ban, and the reclusive Albert Schweitzer, the saintly physician who devoted his life to treating people in the heart of Africa, made a worldwide radio appeal—"a great document," Pauling called it—asking the public to demand an end to tests. The World Council of Churches, the West German Bundestag, and the pope all joined in to demand the end of testing.

Their sentiments were supported by a report from the British Atomic Scientists Association in which it was estimated that one thousand people would die of various diseases for every megaton tested. Pauling took that evidence even further, telling a crowd in Chicago that his estimates of fallout damage led him to conclude that ten thousand people were dead or dying of leukemia because of bomb tests and that the current rate of testing would lead to a 1 percent increase in human genetic mutations. AEC scientific spokesman Bill Libby immediately wrote Pauling demanding to know where he got his estimates, adding, "I am most seriously charged with responsibility in connection with weapons tests, and I am most anxious to learn whether we have made any mistakes." Pauling replied that his comments had been made off the cuff in response to a question after his speech and referred Libby to public reports and a calculation he made based on new estimates of levels of strontium 90 in the food chain.

All estimates of radiation damage were uncertain; they were all based on preliminary scientific evidence, and the data could be twisted different ways to suit specific political ends. "There is considerably uncertainty about estimated values in this field," Pauling wrote in 1957, "but I think that we should consider the worst possible case, rather than the best possible case." His worst-case pronouncements were made as dramatic as possible by extrapolating them to entire populations, often over many generations, and by repeating them as often as possible through whatever means would get them to the most people.

The AEC used the same data, but emphasized on the other end of the margin of error and focused on the increased risk to individuals with the purpose of reassuring the public that bomb tests were less dangerous than wearing a radium-dial watch.

Both sides, as it turned out, were right. But Pauling's population-based statistical estimates—the idea that each bomb tested led to thousands of defective babies in the future—proved more compelling to the public. In the fall of 1956 the majority of Americans were against a test ban. By the spring of 1957 almost two-thirds approved of a ban, if other nations joined in.

Feeling the tide turning, on May 15, Pauling gave a fiery antibomb speech to an honors day assembly at Washington University in St. Louis. He talked about the link between mutated genes and sickle-cell anemia and phenylketonuria, tied the increased risk of such mutations to fallout, cited the Schweitzer appeal, and got loud applause when he told his audience, "I believe that no human beings should be sacrificed to the project of perfecting nuclear weapons." He ended with one of his favorite quotations from Benjamin Franklin: "'The rapid progress true Science now makes occasions my regretting sometimes that I was born so soon. It is impossible to imagine the height to which may be carried, in a thousand years, the power of man over matter. O that *Moral* science were in as fair a way of improvement, that men would cease to be wolves to one another, and that human beings would at length learn what they now improperly call *humanity.*'" The students and faculty rose to their feet in a prolonged, cheering ovation. He was swamped afterward with listeners eager to find out what they could do to help.

Pauling got together later that day with two like-minded faculty members, the physicist Edward Condon and biologist Barry Commoner, and put together a plan. From his many talks around the nation, Pauling believed that there was a consensus on the dangers of testing among scientists but that it was muted by the government's stifling of dissent and distorted in the public mind by the AEC's tactic of downplaying risks.

Pauling, with Condon's and Commoner's help, decided to give scientists a voice through a petition appeal to stop nuclear testing. Each of the three wrote a draft petition, then together decided that Pauling's brief and moderate "Appeal by American Scientists to the Governments and Peoples of the World" was the one to send.

"We, the American scientists whose names are signed below, urge that an international agreement to stop the testing of nuclear bombs be made now," it began. In its five short paragraphs, the appeal noted the long-term danger of an increase in the number of genetic mutations (avoiding any mention of more controversial effects, such as cancer); warned of the danger of nuclear proliferation; urged a test ban as a first step toward disarmament; and ended with: "We have in common with our fellow men a deep concern for the welfare of all human beings. As scientists we have knowledge of the dangers involved and therefore have a special responsibility to make those dangers known. We deem it imperative that an immediate action be taken to effect an international agreement to stop the testing of all nuclear weapons."

That evening, they mimeographed and retyped some copies of the original and started mailing them to scientists they thought would sign. Within a week they had received more than two dozen signatures, including that of Hermann J. Muller, one of the nation's most respected geneticists and the discoverer of the mutagenic effects of radiation. That was just the start. Pauling took the project back to Pasadena, where, with the help of Ava Helen and some volunteers, he mailed hundreds of copies of the petition to universities and scientific laboratories around the nation. Within a few weeks, he had received back two thousand more signatures.

Pauling was ecstatic. The signatories included more than fifty NAS members, a few Nobelists, and a heavy representation of leading geneticists. There were abstentions for various reasons, researchers who did not like one or another of the specific points in the appeal or who believed that scientists should stay out of politics in general, but over-all the response was heartening proof that American scientists op-posed nuclear testing. On June 3, Pauling released his petition to the press, sending copies as well to the United Nations and President Eisenhower.

There had not been a mass outcry from scientists like this since the fight for civilian control of atomic energy ten years before, and the ef-fect was electric. The sudden appearance of the Pauling petition made national headlines as government officials and media commentators struggled to make sense of this dramatic new turn in the test-ban de-bate. Pauling seized the moment to inject a bit more drama, telling an interviewer on an ABC television medical program that fallout would cause mental or physical defects in 200,000 children over the next twenty generations and that a million people would lose five to ten years of life apiece.

There was an immediate attempt to downplay Pauling's petition and cast suspicion on its author. In a press conference a few days after its release, Eisenhower told reporters, "I noticed that in many in-stances scientists that seem to be out of their own field of competence are getting into this argument about bomb testing, and it looks almost like an organized affair." Conservative columnists and editorial-page editors in the U.S. press quickly decided that "organized affair" meant "Communist inspired." Gen. Leslie Groves addressed the question of Pauling's expertise, saying, "I don't know what his goals are, other than that he has won a Nobel Prize. I would never ask a football coach how to run a major league baseball team."

The next step was predictable. The head of HUAC blasted Pauling on the floor of the House of Representatives for spreading Soviet propaganda; a few days later, Pauling was subpoenaed by the Senate Internal Security Subcommittee, which wanted to know whether Com-munist organizations were behind his petition. "I would be pleased to have the opportunity to help educate some of our representatives in Washington on this matter," Pauling told reporters. Washington poli-tics denied him the opportunity. Senators Clinton Anderson and Lyn-don Johnson were setting up joint hearings on atomic energy at the same time and did not want SISS chair James Eastland horning in on their issue. Pauling's appearance in Congress was delayed indefinitely after Anderson "blew his top" with Eastland.

There was also a negative response from a few scientists. Two re-spected Berkeley chemists, Ken Pitzer and Joel Hildebrand, publicly pointed out that not 1 percent of Pauling's signers had a specialist's knowledge of radiation effects, prompting Pauling to respond that practically all of his petitioners had specialized knowledge related in some way to the issue of bomb testing and all relied on the published studies of others who were radiation experts—as I myself, he reminded reporters, all rely on the judgment and experiments of professors Hildebrand and Pitzer. AEC spokesmen continued to downplay the hazards of testing. Bill Libby reminded a congressional panel a few days after the petition appeared that the risk from fallout was "very small" compared to everyday risks tolerated by humans—or the risk of annihilation if the United States surrendered its atomic superiority.

Pauling fired back as he was leaving for Europe on June 11. "My conscience will not permit me to remain silent when Dr. Libby and other representatives of the Atomic Energy Commission make misleading statements about these superlatively important questions." He informed reporters that he would be seeking contacts to help him with a new petition—this one to be signed by scientists from around the world.

His petition, it appeared, had put the entire U.S. government on the defensive. Talks were under way in London at which for the first time the USSR and the United States were seriously discussing a test ban, a development unthinkable a year or two earlier. Public opinion had shifted squarely to his side. Perhaps, Pauling began to hope, the summer of 1957 might see a test ban agreement.

—*mm*—

The Paulings' European trip was highlighted by their first visit to the Soviet Union. Pauling had for years wanted to observe the Soviet experiment firsthand, and when he was invited to attend an international conference on biochemistry in Moscow, along with nine other American scientists, he eagerly said yes. During his visit, Pauling was as outspoken as ever. He planned in his biochemical presentations to review the Mendel-Morgan theory of genetics—still in disfavor in Russia, where Lysenko's ideas were official dogma—and indignantly refused to back down when a translator tried to convince him that promoting Western genetics would be a mistake. On the contrary, he found that his Russian audience did not seem to mind even when he attacked Lysenko's ideas directly. In addition to his professional lectures, he gave a popular talk in a Moscow auditorium on molecular disease, taped a radio address on peace, and spoke against nuclear testing. He and Ava Helen were able to travel a bit and found that the vast reaches of farmland outside the major cities seemed strangely familiar. "I was astonished by the memories it brought back of my life in Eastern Oregon when I was seven or eight years old," Pauling said. "The Russian people seemed to be much like Americans—not those Easterners, you know, from New York and those places, but like real Americans from the West . . . just like us, only more eager for peace."

There also appeared to be no crime. A German virologist Pauling met at the Moscow conference, for instance, was distraught at losing his bag and all his money in a cab until the cabbie showed up the next day and returned it with apologies for not having done so earlier. The Paulings were impressed by that display of honesty and impressed as well with the way scientists were treated in the USSR. They were "top dogs," Pauling found, the most highly respected and handsomely paid professionals in the nation. This was the mark of a good, rational society.

His tour was official, of course. He did not see the "psychiatric hospitals" for political dissidents, nor was he invited to review conditions in the Gulag.

<hr />

When he returned to the United States in the fall, things had changed. The antitest momentum that seemed so strong a few months earlier had suddenly dissipated.

Pauling knew at least one reason why. While he had been touring the Soviet Union, the Hungarian-born physicist and media-proclaimed "Father of the H-bomb," Edward Teller, speaking for the AEC, had convinced a great many people that more tests were needed in order to perfect a "clean bomb." Teller was a committed anti-Communist whose family had suffered in Hungary because of communism. He was certain that without the development of atomic weapons, the Russians would not hesitate to take over the world, and he saw it as a personal duty to prevent it. A clean bomb, Teller said, would be almost entirely fusion in its action, eliminating almost all radioactive fallout. Such a bomb, he told Eisenhower, was a perfect battlefield tool, allowing the destruction of enemy soldiers without the danger of drifting radioactivity, without even damaging equipment or buildings. Such a bomb, he said, could be perfected within four or five years if testing was allowed to continue.

Teller's "clean bomb" idea in the summer of 1957 "seemed to serve effectively as propaganda to stop, for a while, the growing concern about the horrors of nuclear weapons and nuclear war," Pauling said. The combined vision of this low-fallout nuclear weapon and the intransigence of the Soviet negotiators derailed the London weapons talks, which fell apart entirely in September. The public's attention turned to new issues—the race riots in Little Rock, the launching of Sputnik—and away from concerns about nuclear testing.

The major powers took advantage of the situation to start an orgy of bomb testing in the fall, blasting more than twice as many bombs in a few months as they had the entire previous year. Sputnik jarred the American government into a new level of respect for its competitors on the world stage and also demonstrated that the Soviets knew enough about rockets to send nuclear warheads to America on the backs of ballistic missiles. The arms race heated up, with America announcing another major series of bomb tests for 1958.

Pauling, deeply disappointed by the shift in attitude toward testing, responded by trying to write popular articles on the dangers of fallout—he was turned down, however, by both the *Ladies' Home Journal* and the *Saturday Evening Post* "because there are so many grey areas involved in such a discussion"—and continued working on his worldwide antitesting petition.

In the fall of 1957 the names began coming in. When he saw how large the response was among European scientists, Pauling began combing through scientific directories for more likely signatories. He hired a part-time secretary, paid from his own pocket, to oversee the job of typing, making copies, getting translations done, and mailing the petitions. Together with Ava Helen and the help of a few friends, he made certain that the petition was circulated properly both in the United States and internationally—Pauling wanted to make sure that at least one scientist from each of the forty-eight states was included, for instance—and that the names were tallied correctly.

The results were encouraging. By early January 1958 more than nine thousand signatures had been collected from scientists in forty-three nations, including many in the Eastern bloc. Not everyone signed—typical of many of the nonrespondents was Sir Lawrence Bragg, who wrote Pauling that he did not sign simply because "I had not got enough knowledge," and the university president who wrote, "Dear Linus: In reference to your letter of November 6, and to the enclosed petition, as you probably imagine, I couldn't disagree with you more heartily. I, therefore, have high hopes that you will fail completely in your undertaking!!!"—but enough did, including thirty-five Nobelists and hundreds of members of the planet's most august scientific societies, to give the petition the weight Pauling thought it needed to shift the world toward a test ban.

On January 13, 1958, in New York to attend a Nobelists' banquet, he handed a copy of his petition with all the signatures attached to Dag Hammarskjöld, the secretary-general of the United Nations. He then held a press conference telling the world about the scientists' desire for peace and an end to fallout.

It proved to be another great publicity coup. Pauling appeared to have single-handedly mobilized the bulk of world scientific opinion behind the need for a test ban. His effort underlined the essential harmony of the global research community, made headlines around the world, and gave renewed heart to antibomb activists.

Then, once again, the reaction started.

Teller

To J. Edgar Hoover, Pauling had long been prominent among those "creating fear, misunderstanding, and confusion in the minds of the public" on the fallout issue. As the controversy continued, he made certain that Pauling's Communist-front associations were made available to conservative columnists, who in turn began asking how Pauling had raised all the money needed to circulate such a huge petition. As one newspaper editor wrote, "Anybody who has tried to get a dozen or two names for a local school board petition knows that an operation of the Pauling scale takes thousands of man hours and tens of thousands of dollars." Pauling answered the first round of attacks by explaining that he had organized his petition drive over the kitchen table in his home and that total costs came to about $250, mostly for postage. "When people understand an important question and are eager to do something about it, as the scientists of the world are about this most important question, it is easy to obtain thousands of signatures," he said.

The most serious attack, however, came from Edward Teller, who responded to Pauling's petitions by writing a piece for *Life* magazine entitled "The Compelling Need for Nuclear Tests." The editors added their own cover line in the February issue: "Dr. Teller Refutes 9,000 Scientists." Pauling was incensed when he read it. There was nothing in the article showing that any statement in his petition was wrong; instead, it was a rambling rehash of the AEC's dismissals of fallout fears coupled with a strong argument for continued testing in order to perfect "clean bombs" to hold the Communists at bay.

Pauling had known Teller slightly since his first days in Munich, where the young Hungarian was learning his ABCs of quantum physics, and he admired him as a scientist. But as Teller became the world's most visible scientific proponent of bomb development, he lost his respect for him as a person. It was Teller who pushed for the development of the hydrogen bomb when others advised caution; whose testimony helped strip Oppenheimer of his security clearance; whose close advisory relationship with Lewis Strauss and Eisenhower made him the nation's most powerful scientist in deciding the direction of the U.S. bomb program; passionate, obsessive, tenacious Teller, with his hints of omnipotent knowledge gleaned from highly classified files, who came up with the "clean bomb" idea just in time to derail history's first test-ban negotiations. If Einstein had been ashamed of the bombs his colleagues created, Teller was proud of them. "To my mind, the distinction between a nuclear weapon and a conventional weapon," he said, "is the distinction between an effective weapon and an outmoded weapon." And Teller distrusted those who talked peace. He had seen Hitler do that before conquering Hungary, and he believed the Russians were doing it now as well as they prepared to swallow up even more of the world. Only the U.S. nuclear arsenal prevented them. "If we renounce nuclear weapons," Teller said simply, "we open the door to aggression."

Teller and Pauling were at once diametrically opposed and much alike. Both held tight to a simplified political vision, both were dogged in their quests, both marshaled impressive scientific facts to support their political positions. They went to war with each other in the spring of 1958.

The arena was the studio of an educational TV station in San Francisco, where the management had arranged a one-hour debate between Teller and Pauling. On camera Pauling looked tall and thin, tailored and immaculate, in an expensive suit. Teller, compact and dark, with prominent, bushy eyebrows, looked by comparison like someone's rumpled old uncle.

Both men were allowed an opening statement, and Pauling started. He immediately went on the offensive, tearing at Teller's *Life* article for its "many statements that are not true and many statements that are seriously misleading." For instance, Teller had accused Pauling of saying that the development of a clean bomb was impossible when he would certainly never have said that because he did not know enough about the topic.

Teller, his voice a soothing, gravelly rumble, still heavily flavored with a Hungarian accent, used his opening time to calmly answer Pauling's points. He had seen Pauling's comments about the clean bomb in the *New York Times,* he said. Perhaps the reporters had misunderstood Pauling. (The *Times* did report that Pauling had termed the production of a clean bomb "impossible.") But these points are minor, Teller said. Everyone agrees on the need for peace but not on how to achieve it. World War II, after all, was caused when the decent nations disarmed, allowing Hitler to flourish. The Russians have said they want to bury us, Teller said, and we can't stop them without developing bombs. With more testing we can develop clean bombs for digging canals and excavating mines; we can put the atom to work for mankind. "This alleged damage which the small radioactivity is causing—supposedly cancer and leukemia—has not been proved, to the best of my knowledge, by any decent and clear statistics," Teller concluded. "It is possible that there is damage. It is even possible, to my mind, that there is no damage; and there is the possibility, further, that very small amounts of radioactivity are helpful." How, after all, would evolution occur without mutation?

"If we proceeded with everything with as great a caution as we are proceeding in the case of nuclear testing, there would be very little progress in the world," he concluded, a smile playing across his face. "Dr. Pauling, as a great progressive, surely does not want that."

Thrown off guard by Teller's calm and wit, Pauling's responses began sounding shrill, his voice high-pitched and piping compared to Teller's. He made the tactical error of trying to defend Khrushchev's use of the phrase "We will bury you," explaining that the Russian premier was talking about political evolution, not warfare. He then pointed out that Teller and his associates themselves had estimated that fallout might cause fifteen hundred defective mutations a year— one-tenth of Pauling's own current estimate but a recognition of danger nonetheless.

Teller shot back that this divergence in estimates highlighted the extent of their current ignorance, that with such wide swings in numbers it was not unreasonable to think that there may not even be a single case. Even if there is a risk from testing, Teller said reassuringly, we take risks all the time. Spewing more smog into the air or adding a new food additive to our diet exposes us to a much greater risk. He had even seen a story about how tight pants might cause a significant number of mutations by increasing the temperature in the sperm plasm. According to this, the pants we wear might be far more dangerous than fallout.

The debate went on in this pattern: Pauling raising specific criticisms based on statistical analysis, Teller countering with witticisms, irrelevant comparisons, and visions of bomb-dredged harbors. Pauling ended up sounding humorless and critical; Teller, relaxed and funny.

When it was over, Pauling felt as though he had debated the devil. Teller had deflected real issues and used public relations tricks to make everything sound fine and trick the American people into a false sense of complacency. Teller exemplified everything that was wrong about the AEC and the military-industrial complex, made up of men to whom atomic war was somehow thinkable, who were making plans for tactical nuclear attacks and calculating how many millions would die, who would willingly sacrifice thousands of children in future generations to push their political and economic agendas instead of putting a fraction of that time or money into the study of peace.

But Teller was worse than most of them, Pauling thought, because he was a scientist. Scientists in general, his petitions showed, favored curtailing the arms race. Scientists were supposed to lead the way to a rational, peaceful future. After the debate, however, Pauling realized that Teller was a different type of scientist. "Dr. Teller argues in support of continuing nuclear tests because he believes in war, nuclear war," Pauling wrote, almost with a sense of disbelief, after the debate. This ran contrary to everything Pauling believed about the positive role scientists could play in the world, in his schemes for scientific parliaments and a world run happily along scientific lines. In Pauling's mind, Teller was a brilliant physicist who was also a warmonger; he was a dark angel fallen from the firmament of science.

It was the only time the two most public opponents in the nuclear-test-ban controversy would debate face-to-face. "Since that time I have refused to meet or debate [Teller] further because I consider his debating methods improper," Pauling said.

Instead, he tried to battle him in the press. And here Pauling quickly found that he was outmaneuvered as well. While Teller could get an article published in mainstream magazines like *Life* almost at will, Pauling was denied entry on the grounds that the entire field was too controversial and hazy. When Pauling wrote a piece for *Life* to rebut Teller's, it was rejected, as his pieces had been by a number of other mass-market magazines. The only place he could get it published was in *I. F. Stone's Weekly*.

He tried another route. The media might be able to keep him out, but what if he published a book? Teller was just about to release a book, *Our Nuclear Future;* Pauling thought he could write one that would help counter whatever influence that had as well as serving as a full public answer to Teller's *Life* article. Dictating, madly, from dawn to dusk, over two long weekends in March 1958, he completed the bulk of the manuscript, a distillation of everything he had learned over the past years about nuclear bombs and fallout.

The book, published as *No More War!*, was an unusual mixture of science primer, political tract, and jeremiad. The opening chapters were flat and straightforward, a lecture by Professor Pauling on atomic fission and fusion, the creation of fallout, and the link between genetic mutations and radiation. There were occasional eye-openers, such as the fact that all 100,000 genes from all 3 billion people on earth—the entire gene pool of the human race—would form a ball 1/25 inch in diameter, but generally Pauling was careful to avoid controversy, couching all of his estimates of genetic damage moderately and meticulously outlining his reasoning in each case. Only occasional barbs were thrown at Teller and the AEC crowd. Pauling answered Teller's comment that a little radiation might be good for the genes, for instance, by paraphrasing, J. B. S. Haldane: My clock is not keeping perfect time. It is conceivable that it will run better if I shoot a bullet through it, but it is much more probable that it will stop altogether.

Then, halfway through, the book changed gears to become a direct attack on Teller, Strauss, the AEC, and the arms race. "The public has been given the impression that there is a great disagreement among scientists about the facts," Pauling wrote. "I think that the explanation of this situation is that the spokesmen for the Atomic Energy Commission have often made statements that seem to be misleading. Though many of the statements are true, they may convey the wrong impression. Sometimes the statements have turned out to be wrong." He then stated each misleading statement, one by one, and demolished them.

Teller had said that the danger from fallout was no more dangerous to human health than being one ounce overweight. But who could say, Pauling asked, what the health effects of being one ounce overweight were? Teller's point, Pauling said, was "ludicrous." AEC spokesman Bill Libby had said that there was no evidence that people in Denver had higher cancer rates than anyone else despite the increased cosmic radiation due to the altitude. But that was ridiculous, Pauling countered, because medical science is not precise enough to detect the small predicted increase in cancer rates. Libby had said,

"There is no single provable case of any person being injured or seriously affected by any of the slightly extra radiation created in the United States by these tests." That might be accurate in a sense, Pauling wrote, because you can't make a firm cause-and-effect connection between fallout and any individual case of cancer or birth defect. But it is misleading because it implies no danger, when in fact every scientist, Libby included, agreed that fallout would lead to at least a slight increase in genetic defects and other health dangers to the entire population.

The final pages of the book, harkening back to the rhetoric of the Emergency Committee of Atomic Scientists, presented Pauling's call for a new world order. "Does the Commandment 'Thou Shalt Not Kill' mean nothing to us? Are we to interpret it as meaning 'Thou shalt not kill except on a grand scale,' or 'Thou shalt not kill except when the national leaders say to do so'?" Immorality was loose in the world, Pauling said, a lust for power and profit and war, and only a return to morality would save humankind. "May our great Nation, the United States of America, be the leader in bringing *morality* into its proper place of prime importance in the conduct of world affairs," Pauling wrote. This, however, was not enough by itself. Even if the United States were to become righteous overnight, the rest of the world might not. How then do we achieve peace? "I propose that the great world problems be solved in the way that other problems are solved," Pauling wrote, "by working hard to find their solution—by carrying on *research for peace*." He advised setting up a secretary for peace in the U.S. cabinet, with a budget equal to 10 percent of the military's, the funds used for "a great international research program involving thousands of scientists, economists, geographers, and other experts working steadily year after year in the search for possible solutions to world problems, ways to prevent war and to preserve peace." Every nation should have its own peace office, which could work together through a World Peace Research Organization overseen by the United Nations to clear the way for international agreements like the test ban and then conduct research to end all wars between nations. Newer, bigger weapons could never bring us peace, Pauling wrote. Only international law could do that.

~ww~

As Pauling was writing his book, fallout from the previous six months of heavy bomb tests began to descend around the world, increasing public fears as well as levels of radioactivity. The news reports of rising strontium 90 levels helped bring public opinion again to Pauling's side. Dozens of local protest groups had now merged into a new national organization, the National Committee for a Sane Nuclear Policy, better known as SANE. Antibomb protests were flowering across Europe and in Japan as well, exerting new pressure on national governments to do something about fallout.

His manuscript completed, Pauling began thinking of new ways to halt the tests. His petitions and speeches had now made him an internationally recognized leader in the antitesting movement, and as his web of correspondents grew, so did the number of schemes he juggled. Albert Szent-Györgyi, the Hungarian-American discoverer of vitamin C and a scientist with interests almost as far ranging as Pauling's, had written Pauling with the idea of convening representatives from the premier science academies in the United States, the Ukraine, and the USSR in a sort of scientific summit meeting to discuss ways to modernize their nations' "antiquated" economic and political systems as a first step toward peace. Pauling was enthusiastic about the idea and quickly expanded it into a proposed "World Scientific Parliament" in which representatives from many nations would gather to "study the question of how the political structure of the world should be adjusted to the progress of science."

In March, as he read of plans to arm U.S. submarines with nuclear weapons, Szent-Györgyi became more impassioned about the need for the parliament, writing Pauling, "There will be no guarantee that the commanders of these subs belong to some very high ethical group. What we can be sure of is that they will be laying on the bottom of the sea, bored to death and drunk all the time. The fate of the world will thus be in the hands of a few score of drunken people, any of whom may want to cheer himself with fireworks." Pauling and Szent-Györgyi forwarded their idea for a world conclave to the NAS.

Pauling had been in contact as well with Bertrand Russell and the loose international network of concerned scientists who had coalesced around him to fight the bomb. As a follow-up to the Russell-Einstein Manifesto, these activists had arranged in the summer of 1957 the world's first independent conference of scientists from East and West designed to discuss concerns about nuclear weapons without the hindrance of nationalist concerns. The first meeting—called "Pugwash," after the Canadian estate of wealthy industrialist Cyrus Eaton, where it was held—turned out to be so valuable that Russell thought it should be expanded into a series. Pauling, as one of the original signers of the manifesto, had been expected to be among the twenty or so delegates to the first Pugwash meeting but had been unable to attend because of a European trip. In 1958, however, he met with Russell and a number of others to make arrangements for the next Pugwash meeting in Vienna.

And he continued his public appearances. He debated Bill Libby on Edward R. Murrow's *See It Now* program and made himself available to a number of radio interviewers.

In March 1958 the Soviets dropped a political bombshell by calling for an immediate halt to all nuclear testing. It was a masterstroke of timing, coming just as the Soviets had finished their own long and very dirty test series and before the Americans were to start one, and just as world concern about fallout (much of it from Soviet tests) was reaching another peak. The timing, however, was less important to Pauling than the fact that a serious test-ban proposal had been forwarded.

He and the Pugwash group gave the antitesting process a push. On April 4, three days after the Soviet initiative, Pauling, Russell, Clarence Pickett, Norman Thomas, and a miscellany of others—including sixteen Marshall Islanders—filed suit in federal district court to enjoin the AEC from conducting the planned series of bomb tests. In a unique legal move, Pauling and the others argued that Congress had never given the government authority to threaten "the right to life and the right to raise normal children" by releasing fallout radiation into the atmosphere. Similar legal efforts, Pauling announced at a press conference, were being mounted in the Soviet Union and Great Britain.

Taking on an agency of the federal government in court was a quixotic maneuver, designed primarily for publicity, but it pleased Pauling. If the government was behaving crazily, why not use the courts to provide therapy? He had his favorite lawyer, Abraham Lincoln Wirin, on the case, but Wirin told him to expect it to drag through the courts for years.

Antitest work was now taking up almost all of Pauling's time, but it was time spent in a good cause, one to which he could give every fiber of his being. Even the negative press he got seemed somehow unimportant. When *Time* magazine ran photos of Pauling and other antibomb activists with the caption "Defenders of the unborn . . . or dupes of the enemies of liberty?" he could even manage a wry smile. There was new momentum building against the tests; perhaps the time had come when the old attacks, the Red-baiting and innuendo, would no longer work.

In early April 1958, while combing through the most recent fallout literature, Pauling came across some amazing information. In a speech to the Swiss Academy of Medical Sciences, Bill Libby himself had identified a previously unreported source of radioactive contamination in fallout: a long-lived isotope called carbon 14. This was a substance Libby knew well; his professional career had taken off years earlier when he discovered that the decay of naturally occurring carbon 14 could be used to accurately date artifacts.

But Pauling was more interested in the new information that a great deal of this substance was being spewed into the air—about 160 pounds of it with each good-sized nuclear blast. Carbon was the backbone of almost all biomolecules. Pauling knew that the body would treat carbon 14 like regular carbon, incorporating it into tissues in whatever proportion it existed in nature. Carbon 14 also had a very long half-life, in excess of eight thousand years, making it a threat far into the future. Pauling quickly calculated that bomb tests to date had increased the total carbon 14 on earth by somewhere around 10 percent. If it were incorporated into human bodies at the same rate, its radioactive decay would dramatically increase the mutation rate. No "clean bomb" would eliminate it as a problem, because carbon 14 was produced not by fission but by the reaction of neutrons with nitrogen in the air. And no one had yet pointed out the danger. Pauling hastily calculated the long-term results.

On April 28, Pauling called a press conference at a meeting of the NAS in Washington, D.C., to announce his discovery of "a new threat in atomic fallout." Pauling told reporters that the carbon 14 produced by bomb tests to date would create 5 million defective children over the next three hundred years, with millions of additional cases of cancer. The next day, Pauling's "new threat" was on the front pages of papers across the nation.

Libby was outraged. He immediately responded that Pauling's estaimates were far off the mark, that most carbon 14 ended up in the oceans, and that total carbon 14 exposure for humans had been raised less than 1 percent by testing so far—which would lead only to "a very minute effect," he told reporters. Two days later, a group of Columbia geologists wrote the *New York Times* that Pauling had confused his estimates by using figures based on total carbon 14 in the earth instead of in the atmosphere alone; their calculations showed that Pauling had overestimated the amount of carbon 14 by a factor of fifty. The actual threat from carbon 14, they wrote, was equivalent to the increased radiation risk represented by going up a few feet in height. They ended with: "Exaggerated statements by respected scientists only add to the public's confusion and do not contribute to the solution of the problem."

Pauling realized that he had made a mistake in his calculations and adjusted his estimate of damage downward by a factor of five—while still insisting that carbon 14 was a long-term threat to unborn children.

His original estimate had been off, but his revised number was right. Six months later, the AEC quietly released a report in which the commission's own estimates of the long-term genetic damage caused by fallout of carbon 14 closely matched Pauling's revised figures.

But damage had been done to Pauling's reputation. He had been caught making exaggerated claims, a mistake that would be remembered by his critics far longer than the fact that he was essentially right about carbon 14.

On May 11, 1958, Pauling appeared on *Meet the Press,* the nationally televised public affairs show, in order, he thought, to explain his views on fallout. He seemed unaware of the fact that the show's host, Lawrence Spivak, had built his show's ratings by routinely giving his guests a tough grilling.

When the show started, the four-reporter panel immediately asked Pauling about his motivations in opposing the bomb tests. When Pauling tried to explain the difference between his approach to data and Libby's, he was interrupted by a reporter from the Hearst newspapers. Why shouldn't Americans believe Libby and Teller, he asked, scientists "who have not been tainted . . . with a rather prolonged association with Communist fronts and causes, as you appear to have been?" When Pauling tried to answer that the majority of scientists agreed with his views on fallout, the reporter cut him off with more Communist-front questions. The others joined in: Wasn't it odd how he came up with the carbon-14 data just in time to impugn the clean-bomb tests? Hadn't he supported the Rosenbergs? Pauling got into a minidebate with Spivak over the fine points of the Rosenberg case. Then the questions turned to how he raised money for his petitions. When Pauling answered that he raised it himself, he was asked, "Then how does it happen that the same day the Communist press all over the world blazoned this thing?" "The newspaper services—" Pauling answered. "I am afraid you know more about that than I do."

His half hour was over, and he had been unable to say anything substantive about fallout. Pauling stalked out of the studio with Ava Helen. It was not a public affairs show. This was an inquisition. They were both outraged.

Resignation

So was Lee DuBridge. The spectacle of his chemistry head noisily defending convicted spies on national television made it more difficult than ever for DuBridge to continue defending Pauling.

DuBridge had watched Pauling change after the Nobel Prize, becoming, to his mind, less responsible and more outspoken, lavishing time and energy on fighting bomb tests instead of performing his Caltech duties. He had seen Pauling make outrageous statements, push politically unpopular positions, fight government agencies on which Caltech depended for research support, and alienate his board of trustees.

The relationship between the two men had grown increasingly chilly as Pauling's political commitments deepened, but not because DuBridge disagreed with Pauling's stands. Both he and Caltech physics head Robert Bacher had been vocal opponents of nuclear testing, as had a number of other Caltech professors. "I think that there was some—the word would be somewhere between resentment and discomfort—that Linus didn't make an effort to generate a consensus of the other faculty members who had, in their own quiet way, been involved in advising the government about peace issues," said Pauling's colleague Norman Davidson. Pauling had ebulliently gone off on his own and forgotten to acknowledge the good work of the rest of the Caltech family.

DuBridge disagreed with his tactics. Pauling hardly ever seemed to be around to perform the routine duties expected of a chairman: the presentations, the socializing, the cultivation of prospective donors. Nor was his research going well. His old triumphs with the chemical bond were fraying around the edges as more chemists tilted toward the molecular-orbital theory—which Pauling continued to ignore completely—and much of his current scientific work, such as the attempt to find the molecular roots of mental disease, seemed to be going nowhere. There was grumbling among his faculty about space allocation and research priorities. Pauling never seemed to be around to hear it.

Instead, he was globe-trotting, getting himself in the headlines.

The count of Caltech trustees who resigned because of their frustration over Pauling was now up to three, including John McCone. The Republican party bigwig had left the board after an early-morning blowup occasioned by his opening his newspaper and reading yet another column about Pauling's Communist-front peace activities. He called DuBridge to complain. It was 6:30 A.M., and the phone woke DuBridge out of a deep sleep. McCone harangued him about his errant chemist, then hung up and called other board members. Some of the more moderate trustees were so angry at this latest in a string of McCone complaints that they stopped speaking to him. He finally quit the board.

Now, in 1958, however, DuBridge heard that McCone was slated to succeed Lewis Strauss as the head of the AEC. DuBridge and his physics head, Bob Bacher, were both heavily involved in the commission's business.

In early June, Pauling was asked into DuBridge's office. There was no point in any small talk. DuBridge went back over sore points, telling Pauling, "Just because you know science doesn't mean that you should pose as an authority on international affairs." Pauling reiterated his right to speak on issues he believed were important. They agreed that Pauling was causing the institute a good deal of trouble. DuBridge asked Pauling again if he would moderate his activities. Pauling refused. But DuBridge needed to give his trustees a sign that Pauling was still somewhat under control. Noting that Pauling had offered to resign as department head a year before, DuBridge said, "Now I think I'll take you up on it." Pauling got up and walked out.

He had chaired the chemistry division for more than two decades, and there was no doubt that it would be something of a relief to be freed from administrative headaches. It was true that he had brought up the option himself a year earlier. Quitting would mean that he could devote more time pursuing world peace.

On June 10, he wrote DuBridge, "I feel that, after having served as Chairman . . . for 21 years, I should like to turn this job over to someone else. . . . Let me take this opportunity to express again to you and the Board of Trustees my deep feeling of appreciation of the privilege that I have had in the past and continue to have to carry on scientific work in the California Institute of Technology. . . . I am happy to have been a member of the staff for 36 years, and I expect to be happy in continuing for another decade."

Later, he put it differently. "I was asked to resign as Chairman of the Division of Chemistry and Chemical Engineering and Director of the Gates and Crellin Laboratories of Chemistry," Pauling said, "and I did resign."

The Subcommittee

No More War!

Pauling was very quiet about his resignation. He told none of his colleagues about DuBridge's pressure. To everyone at Caltech he said the same thing: He had simply decided to cut back on his administrative duties in order to devote more time to research and politics. He did not want it made public that, at the end, he had been forced out.

DuBridge replaced Pauling with Ernest Swift, a stern and courtly Virginian, a low-profile veteran chemist who had idolized Noyes and suffered quietly under Pauling. Swift viewed Pauling's brand of biological and medical chemistry as something that "just insidiously grew," shadowing the older emphases in the division. He saw his job as restoring balance. He quickly reinstated the Chemistry Division Council that Noyes had first proposed back in the 1930s, giving representation to all the chemical subdisciplines, including those like physical and inorganic chemistry, which Pauling had long ignored. A review of laboratory space was started with an eye toward reducing the substantial square footage controlled by Pauling's people. Pauling himself was moved out of his large office to smaller faculty quarters, and his salary was cut from a chairman's eighteen thousand dollars to a standard professor's fifteen thousand dollars.

That was a slap in the face. The money was not so important—Pauling's rising book royalties exceeded his salary—but the way in which it was done was, Pauling thought, purposefully humiliating. It seemed to him that DuBridge, instead of holding to the free-speech ideals he mouthed on public occasions, was buckling under pressure. He was punishing Pauling for his political views. As a result, after this time, Pauling and DuBridge would have little to do with one another, limiting their interaction to the minimum required on social occasions. Typically, however, Pauling did not make his feelings of resentment and abandonment public. He presented an outer façade of control, making it appear that the things that were happening were the result of his choices. He did this because he was still a good Caltech soldier and because he still believed something he had learned as a child in Oregon: Real men did not complain.

—⁓⁓—

The resignation did not cause Pauling to miss a beat in his peace work. He still spoke everywhere, giving two or three peace talks each week at high schools and on local talk shows, at Jewish community centers, and to local antibomb organizations. He also continued speaking to a wide variety of medical and psychological groups about his idea of molecular psychiatry, although his own research had so far provided little of value. He was now so well known that he got mail from individuals wanting to help him stop the bomb tests, high school students looking for words of wisdom on how to conduct their lives, and people asking for medical advice on rickets, epilepsy, smoking, and fluoridation. Autograph hounds began asking for his signature. Television's *Ellery Queen* show wrote asking if they could use some of his molecular models in a scene. A worried mother wrote that she was afraid to bear more children because of fallout and the threat of a nuclear holocaust. Pauling replied that he was optimistic there would not be another war. Publishers wrote asking him to write an autobiography. Pauling said that he might if he ever found the time. The only letters he left unanswered were the cramped, multipage missives with key phrases underlined in red, the nut mail: the wild rantings about cancer cures and special clays that promote long life; a fellow with a scheme for breeding cows to give milk with more unsaturated fat; and another who had invented something called "the science of connexionology" that united religion, atomic physics, and the study of human behavior.

Pauling also received a steady stream of offers to speak in Lompoc,

San Jose, Portland, and local grade schools, and official invitations to Brazil, Cuba, Africa, and Bulgaria. It seemed that every variety of peace and scientific and medical group wanted him as an honorary member.

Pauling was so busy, he generally said no to everything, pleading a lack of time. He was no longer a joiner, especially of political groups. Even SANE, a group designed to be a mainstream voice for antinuclear concerns that achieved wild success in the late 1950s, could not get him to join. Pauling spoke at the group's meetings but told a recruiter that he preferred to carry out his actions as an "independent human being without the aid of any organization."

Sometimes honors were thrust upon him. In late June, Pauling received word that he was one of the first two Americans, along with National Academy of Sciences (NAS) head Detlev Bronk, ever elected to full membership in the Soviet Academy of Sciences. Pauling was well aware that there were few higher honors in the USSR than the title of "Academician," and he told the press that he was "pleased and honored." In turn, the press noted that "it is impossible in today's world position simply and naively to ignore the political implications" of such an honor.

—*mm*—

The world position, however, was changing in a fundamental way. Despite Teller's influence and the hard-line stance of the Atomic Energy Commission (AEC) against all talk of a test ban, Eisenhower was changing course. Part of the reason was the influence of moderate advisers; part was his sensitivity to the ongoing public outcry against fallout, which, thanks in part to Pauling's publicity campaign, remained strong. The president was also looking at the last eighteen months of his administration and wanted to do something substantive to promote world peace before he left office.

So, for a variety of reasons, the U.S. government in the summer of 1958 officially became suddenly receptive to talk of a nuclear test ban. In July 1958 a conference of scientific experts was convened in Geneva to study the technical feasibility of detecting violations—a first step toward assuring both sides that if an agreement was put in place, a nation cheating on it would be caught. The bomb tests continued as the experts talked that summer.

By late August, however, Pauling heard good news: The Geneva conference of experts had decided that it was technically possible to detect an illicit nuclear explosion, even underground. The door was now open to serious negotiations for a test ban, and with their own most recent test series complete, the United States and Great Britain immediately announced that pending such negotiations, they were prepared to stop tests for one year if the Soviets would do the same.

Six months earlier, promoting the idea of a test ban was considered evidence of Communist subversion. Now it was official government policy.

This stunning shift elated Pauling, and it happened just when Pauling's new book *No More War!* hit the bookshelves. Hoping for a strong public response, Pauling began a whirlwind promotion tour. But the change in U.S. policy may have robbed the book of some of its punch. While it was widely and generally respectfully reviewed, with most critics commending Pauling for his courage in taking a stand against testing and his "simply stated, forceful presentation," sales were disappointingly slow. Pauling ended up buying several hundred copies himself and distributing them to anyone he thought might have some influence on the test-ban issue, sending copies to national leaders around the world, presenting one to each member of the U.S. Senate, even leaving copies on colleagues' desks at Caltech.

His new status as a proponent of Ike's policies did not, however, mean that Pauling was no longer controversial. At the end of August, when he arrived in England to attend scientific meetings, make appearances to support the British publication of *No More War!,* and address the Campaign for Nuclear Disarmament, the activist peace group headed by Bertrand Russell, immigration officials forced him to cut his visit short enough to prevent his appearance at the antibomb rally. Pauling and Russell made certain the incident received wide coverage as an example of Cold War hysteria. The publicity had its desired effect: The British government backed down and allowed Pauling to return and address the rally. As a result of all the noise, Pauling's appearance became a sensation, helping him make, as one newspaper put it, "the most profound impression of all the notables who have spoken to British anti-H-bomb campaigners."

By now Pauling had perfected a standard and very effective hourlong antibomb stump speech. The beginning was always the same: "We live in a wonderful world," he would tell his audience, "a beautiful world! I like this world. I like everything in it: the stars, the mountains, the seas, lakes and rivers, the forests, the minerals, the molecules—and especially the human beings. Scientists have discovered many wonderful things about the world during recent centuries. . . ." After a brief mention of some recent discovery that had caught his interest, the molecular structure of myoglobin or how neutrinos had been found to behave like little propellers, he would relate how science had helped make society better, with advances in medicine, transportation, and communications.

But there had been other scientific advances, he would say, that had completely thrown the world into unprecedented danger. Pauling would then launch into the meat of his talk, a discussion of how "the two great discontinuities" of the atom bomb in 1945 and the U-bomb in 1954 had made war unthinkable. He would horrify his audiences with descriptions of the damage caused by fallout and the catastrophe of an all-out nuclear war, then enrage them with figures on how much the United States was spending to achieve this holocaust, with the latest news on weapons development and proliferation. "Why are more weapons of destruction being made?" he would ask. "Are these weapons going to be used? Are the leaders of the great nations of the world going to sacrifice all of the people in the world because they are not willing to negotiate in a rational way with one another to solve world problems by the application of man's power of reason? I think that the politicians and diplomats are still living in the world of the nineteenth century. They do not know how greatly the world has changed. They are still living in the old world of power politics rather than in the real world of today."

The new scientific advances in warfare, he insisted, demanded a new approach to politics. "We need to have the spirit of science in international affairs," he would say, "to make the conduct of international affairs the effort to find the right solution, the just solution, of international problems, not the effort by each nation to get the better of other nations, to do harm to them when it is possible. I believe in morality, in justice, in humanitarianism. . . . The time has now come for morality to take its proper place in the conduct of world affairs; the time has now come for the nations of the world to submit to the just regulation of their conduct by international law." Finally, if his audience was American, he would wave the flag. "I am an American," he would conclude, "born in Oregon, resident in California for many years. I am proud of our great country. I hope that the United States of America will take the lead in bringing morality into its proper place of prime importance in the conduct of world affairs."

This basic stump speech worked wonderfully around the world. Everywhere he went, in England, Germany, Scandinavia, Austria, France, he was greeted enthusiastically by growing groups of antibomb

protesters. He became a counterweight to the standard caricatures of
Yankees: the imperialistic Washington bureaucrat or a fat, loud, ugly
American tourist. He was the tall, intelligent, plain-spoken westerner
who would not be silenced, the man who was not afraid to speak the
truth despite what his government did to him.

—

The incident with British immigration marked the last public harassment Pauling would suffer for a while. With the new tilt in official U.S.
policy in favor of a test ban, only the press of the far right continued to
attack antibomb activists. Privately, Pauling was still tracked by the FBI,
and the Senate Internal Security Subommittee continued building a
file on his activities. But the worst that the FBI could conclude after its
twelve years of investigation was that "for years Pauling has been an intense publicty seeker. . . . He is a highly individualistic, egotistical personality." Egotism was not evidence of treason, and Pauling was quietly
removed from the agency's Security Index.

The Geneva test-ban talks were slated to start on the last day of October 1958—a date when it was expected that an informal halt in testing would begin as well. In preparation, all parties concerned rushed
ahead with what might be the last bomb tests possible for some time.
The United States called its series "Operation Deadline." In the first
three weeks of October alone, the Soviets set off fourteen bombs,
spewing clouds of fallout that sent radiation readings in Los Angeles
soaring to 120 times normal rates, the highest ever recorded outside of
nuclear test ranges. By the time Halloween arrived, the three nuclear
powers had tested sixty-three bombs in 1958—one-third of the total
number tested since World War II, all in the space of ten months.

At the same time, a UN expert committee, after reviewing all the
evidence, supported Pauling's findings by concluding that bomb tests
probably caused between four hundred and two thousand cases of
leukemia per year and that "even the smallest amounts of radiation are
likely to cause deleterious genetic . . . effects."

News reports of the movements of clouds of fallout from the 1958
tests kept public anxiety high as the Geneva talks started, and Pauling
kept up his pressure. He knew that talks had broken down before and
that Teller and the new AEC chairman, John McCone, were still pushing hard to resume testing, and he realized more than anyone that
only continued public pressure would keep the negotiators on track.
His speaking schedule remained full, and he continued skirmishing

with AEC-funded researchers who questioned his numbers on the health effects of fallout. Dozens of letters went back and forth that fall between Pauling and those who thought his estimates were farfetched or politically motivated; in each case Pauling backed up his thinking with published figures from carefully run studies, reports like the United Nation's or the AEC's own published figures. The outcome of these debates was always the same: In the absence of better data, Pauling's figures were as solid as anyone else's. The arguments and facts that he put forward in *No More War!* were still valid. "I am pleased to say that none of my statements has been disproved by any new information that has been published since the publication of the book," he wrote in January 1959.

As the Geneva talks continued through the spring, Pauling stumped the country, speaking to peace groups, church groups, student groups, labor groups, any group he could find. His words were given added power by the fallout that continued to drift down from the previous fall's frenzied bomb testing. The headlines brought the issue into people's homes almost daily: "Jetliner Found Coated with Radioactivity After U.S. Flight"; "Strontium 90 in Minnesota Wheat Beyond Permissible Levels"; "Strontium 90 Levels Rise Sharply in Milk and Children's Bones"; "Strontium 90 Levels in New York Double in Four Years." The AEC, now launching a new effort to encourage people to build bomb shelters, could not send out reassuring press releases fast enough and was itself under attack for conflict of interest. How could the same agency both develop nuclear weapons and be responsible for monitoring their health effects, critics asked. Political pressure grew to strip the AEC of its health-related responsibilities, which Pauling recommended be given to the U.S. Public Health Service.

Antibomb audiences were growing in size and enthusiasm. In the spring, a Brooklyn SANE rally drew an audience of twenty-four hundred at a local auditorium to hear Pauling's dire message: The United States had stockpiled enough nuclear weapons to kill everybody in the world twenty times over; all the talk of bomb shelters and civil defense was "just silly"; the AEC was a "schizophrenic" agency; "the only safe amount of strontium 90 in the bones of our children is zero."

Perhaps, Pauling thought, resigning as chairman of the division had not been such a bad thing. He was free to speak his mind, to work as hard as he liked against the bomb tests and for peace. Real progress was being made. "I have felt pretty pleased with my changed situation," he wrote in April. By June, he sounded positively optimistic. "There has been a great change from a year ago," he said. "A year ago I was making recommendations that were running counter to government policy. My feelings haven't changed at all, but they have now become a part of government policy."

Lambaréné

Pauling had met presidents and prime ministers, philosophers and kings. But he had yet to meet the man he considered the world's most potent force for peace and morality: Albert Schweitzer. He intended to correct that in the summer of 1959.

Schweitzer was a strange and driven man. A French-born paradigm of Western culture—scholar of Bach and the historical Jesus, author of books on Kant and the Apostle Paul, holder of four earned doctorates in theology, music, philosophy, and medicine—Schweitzer gave up Europe and all its glories to work in obscurity treating natives at a primitive hospital in the jungles of French Equatorial Africa. For thirty-five years he disappeared from sight, until the story of his self-sacrifice hit the press after World War II and made him a sudden hero. Schweitzer became a symbol, the "Great White Wizard" who helped those most in need, a secular saint who gave up the trappings of academic success for a life of Christian service. After winning the Nobel Peace Prize in 1952, Schweitzer was universally admired as the greatest living European. Schweitzer's endorsement of an idea gave it unmatched moral power. Schweitzer's name on a document—such as his signature on Pauling's petition to end nuclear testing—was worth a thousand others.

Schweitzer and Pauling had been exchanging letters about nuclear testing and appeals for a ban since Pauling approached him to sign his petition in 1957. Schweitzer had invited Pauling to visit Africa. The death of Einstein had left Pauling without an older mentor to provide advice and guidance on moral issues; who better than a secular saint to take that role?

In July 1959, the Paulings flew from Germany to the small central African village of Lambaréné, then traveled by jeep to the banks of a nearby river, where they boarded a dugout canoe and, paddled by chanting boatmen, floated the last few miles to Schweitzer's hospital.

The Paulings were immediately struck by the primitiveness of the place: a series of huts along dirt paths in the forest, the smell of cooking, the sound of pigs grunting, parrots screaming, and the constant wailing of children. It was exotic. There were tame toucans and monkeys, a large vegetable garden, and everywhere, just at the edge, the enveloping, smothering presence of the jungle, raucous with birdcalls. "It is beautiful here, and chaotic," Ava Helen noted in her diary.

After a brief hello from Schweitzer and his staff, they settled into their accommodations in one of the huts that had been given over to house the stream of visitors who seemed to come and go daily. The Paulings stayed longer than most. Over the next week, guided often by Schweitzer's charming, handsome young chief medical officer, Frank Catchpool, they toured the hospital and the huts where the native patients stayed, talked with the staff, chatted with the newsmen, writers and photographers, heads of state, movie stars, and the wealthy who made the canoe trip in search of stories or inspiration. Schweitzer considered most of his visitors an exhausting imposition on his time; he would often pretend not to understand English to avoid conversations.

But the Paulings were different. "Of all the visitors who came to Lambaréné, Linus Pauling was the most at home," Catchpool said. "He seemed unaffected by the noise, the filth, and the confusion of an African bush hospital." As a result, he soon found himself favored by Schweitzer. They started by eating dinner with him and his staff every afternoon—Ava Helen tartly noting that blacks and whites dined separately—and stayed afterward to hear Schweitzer deliver lectures in French on religious topics. After a week, Pauling was asked to deliver an after-dinner talk on sickle-cell anemia, a disease endemic to the area but about which the staff knew surprisingly little. His forty-five-minute speech in excellent German impressed the medical staff. Schweitzer, however, slept through most of it, awakening at the end in time to deliver a little sermon on the letters of the Apostle Paul.

Then Schweitzer began inviting Pauling to his house for an hour or so of private conversation every evening. They would talk in German about nuclear testing and the need to stop fallout, about the health effects of radiation or world politics. As had Einstein, Schweitzer "impressed me very greatly," Pauling said, "and as I recall, we concurred on everything."

In other ways, however, the Paulings were less impressed. Ava Helen was never asked to Schweitzer's house; he spoke to her only at the dinner table. "In this respect he was more old-fashioned than Einstein," Pauling noted. And Schweitzer's attitude toward his patients was also a disappointment. "It was also clear that he did not think that they were his equals," Pauling said. "He made little effort to improve their education or to change their style of life." Later, they came to understand better how Schweitzer's medical approach grew out of and fit with the culture of Africa, but at the time they were disillusioned. Rather than a saint, the Great White Wizard appeared to be a segregationist who pontificated on obscure religious topics to his small European staff. If Pauling was looking for a replacement for the sort of father figure that Einstein had been, Schweitzer was not it.

He and Ava Helen traveled from Africa to the Fifth World Conference Against Atomic and Hydrogen Bombs in Hiroshima, where Pauling delivered a keynote speech, "Our Choice: Atomic Death or World Law." Underlining his growing worldwide stature, Pauling led an effort to come up with a simple statement to encapsulate the conference's concerns and make them easier to publicize.

But his brand of scientific pacifism did not appeal to everyone. When the original draft of the Hiroshima Appeal, written largely by Pauling, was read aloud to the gathering, it was heckled by leftists in the audience as too mild. A prolonged and noisy debate ensued, with some activists calling for a document with more teeth, others supporting Pauling's reasonable approach. At one point, the radically activist representatives of Britain's Campaign for Nuclear Disarmament walked out of the proceedings. Pauling was taken aback by the rancor of the arguments, but he helped forge a compromise that finally resulted in an appeal—including specific condemnation of the U.S.-Japan security treaty and opposition to placing any nuclear warheads in Japan—that was adopted unanimously. "We were very well pleased with this conference," Pauling wrote Bertrand Russell afterward.

As DuBridge noted, Pauling seemed to have forgotten almost entirely about science. The only significant new research he had done in the past two years was to answer questions about the fallout controversy: two journal articles on the health effects of carbon 14 and strontium 90 and an unusual piece on the relationship between longevity and obesity—written to answer Teller's comment that fallout was about as dangerous as being one ounce overweight. Everything else was summaries of old work, book reviews, and an increasing number of "popular" pieces for leftist magazines about the menace of atomic tests.

With the change in attitude in Washington, the mainstream press was finally printing some pro-ban articles. In late August, the *Saturday*

Evening Post published a two-part feature, "Fallout: The Silent Killer," that for the first time in a mass-circulation magazine gave credence to the claims of Pauling and other antitesting scientists, although it also called Pauling's figures pessimistic and quoted critics as saying that his estimates of damage were higher than the evidence allowed. The consensus of the series, however, was that fallout was dangerous and that testing should be stopped. Pauling himself was able to at least get into print a steady stream of letters to the editors of popular magazines, as well as longer articles in liberal-thought magazines.

He worked tirelessly to keep the pro-ban momentum going. He and Ava Helen traveled to Canada, Australia, and New Zealand in the fall of 1959, giving scores of speeches to peace groups from Sydney to Saskatchewan. His voice was now often joined by Ava Helen's. She had started to make her own speeches, at first handling some of Pauling's overflow, then in answer to an increasing number of requests by such women's groups as the Women's International League for Peace and Freedom (WILPF), a pacifist organization that was started in 1915 by Jane Addams. By 1959 she was making almost as many speeches as her husband, delivering more than thirty during the Australia and New Zealand trip alone. She was pleased to find that as one of the few women speaking publicly on political issues, she was warmly received.

Their schedules were sometimes arranged now by sponsoring groups like the American Friends Service Committee, which took full advantage of having two speakers in one package. But it could get frantic. At many stops the Paulings now found themselves working around each other's schedules, with Ava Helen lecturing at one site while Pauling made his way to another, the two of them seeing each other only in motel rooms, train compartments, or the backseats of cars between engagements. They flew to New York, where Pauling gave the keynote address at a huge SANE rally in Carnegie Hall. They drove to Hollywood for the all-star premiere of the movie *On the Beach*, followed by a klieg-lighted midnight press conference at Grauman's Chinese Theatre, where Pauling, English novelist Aldous Huxley, and ten other of what the press called "assorted thinkers" discussed the issue of disarmament.

The Cliff

In the fall of 1959, the Geneva test-ban talks started breaking down. The culprit was Edward Teller—at least in the minds of Pauling and a number of other observers. Just as everything seemed to be moving smoothly toward a comprehensive ban on all bomb tests, in the air, on the sea, and under the ground, the father of the H-bomb publicized a critical flaw: Bomb tests underground could be hidden by conducting them in huge underground caverns. According to a theory by a researcher named Albert Latter, the blast energy would be masked by caves of the appropriate size, making tests up to three hundred times more difficult to detect with seismographs. This "Big Hole" theory, as the press called it, was given serious consideration thanks to Teller's support. When the theory turned out to be correct—theoretically feasible although unlikely due to the enormous expense of excavating a cave large enough to mask a test—Teller magnified it into a serious impediment to further negotiations. The issue of inspection for violations of a test ban was always a sensitive one, and Teller emphasized that the Big Hole theory offered a new way for the Soviets to get around any sort of inspection or detection. It made the cost of putting in a foolproof system of seismographs astronomical. The Soviets, already balking over the number of Western observers and seismograph stations that would be allowed in their territory, were now being asked to allow in many more.

Once off track, the test-ban negotiations stalled. While the Russians and Americans argued, the one-year moratorium that had gone into effect when the talks had started expired. Although all sides agreed to extend it for another two months while the talks limped on, the extra time did no good. At the end of 1959, the Eisenhower administration announced that the voluntary test moratorium was over.

~mm~

It was an unhappy New Year for Pauling. Although the Geneva talks were slated to resume in mid-January, they would be crippled; Teller's Big Hole theory had effectively stopped talk of a comprehensive ban on all nuclear weapons testing. Because of the difficulty in detecting underground shots, the discussion in 1960 would turn to a partial ban, one that would stop tests in the atmosphere or under the sea but allow underground tests to continue. This was still a step in the right direction—underground tests would release little or no fallout—but it would allow the continued development of nuclear weaponry. This was, to Pauling and many other antibomb activists, the second time they had seen the goal of a full test ban within their reach, only to have it pulled away.

Pauling suffered a personal blow as well at the end of the year when Richard Lippman died. In the last few years—after Pauling had rescued the young M.D. from the blacklist by hiring him as a research assistant and giving him oversight of the mental-deficiency project—the two men had grown close, sharing political passions and scientific interests. By 1959, Lippman was the best friend Pauling had had since the death of Lloyd Jeffress a decade before. He was only forty-three years old when he died suddenly at Christmastime, a loss that devastated Pauling, although, as usual, he hid his feelings.

But the twin disappointments of the reversal in the test-ban negotiations and the death of his friend left Pauling in an uncharacteristically dark frame of mind when he and Ava Helen retreated to their Big Sur ranch in January 1960. He spent a lot of time alone on that trip, thinking by the kitchen table next to the big wood stove or walking by himself down to the sea.

On Saturday morning, the thirtieth, Pauling told Ava Helen that he was going to go for a walk to check their fence lines; she watched him hiking with his long stride toward the hills that rose sheer from the ocean's edge south of the cabin. When he did not return for lunch, Ava Helen began to worry, but figured he might have lost track of time. By six o'clock she was frantic. It was dark, Pauling was not answering her calls; she thought he must have slipped somewhere, was injured, perhaps had fallen into the ocean. She had no telephone at the house and drove to the local forest ranger's office—the nearest link to the outside world—and reported her husband missing.

Within an hour, a handful of searchers were scattered through the hills, picking their way across the steep terrain with flashlights. At midnight they called off the impromptu search. There was no sign of Pauling. The next morning, a larger search started at first light. A helicopter was called in. A few reporters, hearing that a search had been mounted for the controversial Nobelist, arrived from San Francisco. After more hours passed without a sign of Pauling, the rangers began to talk of searching the rocks at the foot of the cliffs. Overhearing their talk, an overeager reporter called in a story saying that Pauling's body had been sighted at the foot of a precipice and he was presumed dead. The news was broadcast on at least one San Francisco radio station; both Linda and Crellin were told by someone who heard it that their father was dead.

Pauling could hear the searchers above him in the darkness and tried to call out to them, but the wind carried his voice out to sea. He tried to move toward them, but when he did, some more of the loose rock around him skittered down the slope and disappeared over a cliff. He stopped moving. He was "ledged," as climbers call it, stuck on a steep hillside that fell three hundred feet to the surf line, caught in a position where he did not feel that it was safe to move in any direction.

He had gotten there by following a deer trail across a seaside hill. The trail petered out, then dead-ended below an overhanging outcropping of rock, and he was turning around when the rock and gravel under his feet started to give away. He was in a section of loose blue shale, a slick, slippery rock—climbers call rock like that "greasy"—that suddenly, sickeningly, started sliding toward the edge. Remembering a climbing trick he had learned in Germany in the twenties, he sat down and jammed his walking stick into the scree. The rocks stopped moving.

After he caught his breath, he tried to crawl off the shale, but any movement sent a new batch of gravel skittering downward. All he could do was maneuver himself slowly to a small level area where he felt a little more secure. Every movement threatened to start another slide. His heart was drumming—he "got the jitters," as he put it afterward—and it took time for him to regain his calm. Then he assessed his situation. He was on a very steep slope, an angle, he figured, of around eighty degrees. There was no place he could reach without starting another slide. There was nothing below him for thirty stories but loose rock and the ocean.

He decided not to move.

How long, he wondered, would it take Ava Helen to call in the searchers? As evening approached, he used his walking stick to dig a small depression in the gravel, eight inches or so deep and large enough to lie down in. He pushed his stick into the scree on the ocean side to keep from rolling over and out if he fell asleep. He had had nothing to eat since breakfast. It was getting cold, and Pauling had only a light jacket; he opened a map he had in his pocket and tucked it around himself to conserve warmth. And he waited. When the searchers passed by above him a few hours after dark, he was elated; he thought he would soon have some hot dinner and be in a warm bed. But the rangers could neither see him nor hear his calls under the overhanging rock, and they went away.

Pauling's jitters came back. He decided that he had better not fall asleep, after all—too much danger of moving in his sleep—and he started performing mental exercises to stay awake. He counted as high as he could go in as many languages as he could remember. He "gave a little lecture to the surf on chemical bonds." He moved his limbs to keep warm, first one arm, then the other, then one leg and the other. He reviewed the periodic table of the elements. He listened to the waves pounding below him. He was more frightened than he had ever been in his life.

When they found him at noon the next day, Pauling was emotionally shaken and physically exhausted. But he swallowed all that—almost as a matter of habit, without thinking about it, internalizing and hiding away this and any other disturbing experience, any sign of weakness—and put up a good front for his rescuers when they pulled him off the shale. He walked out of the hills under his own power, joking with the rangers. "Unharmed and in high spirits," the reporters said. After drinking some coffee, eating lunch, and explaining what had happened, he seemed himself again, even deciding that he felt well enough to drive back to Pasadena to teach the class he was scheduled to give the next day. Ava Helen, who had been put through her own kind of hell by the ordeal—"but no one thought of me," she said—thanked the searchers, shooed the reporters away, radioed her children to tell them Linus was safe, and helped him pack up the car. Her husband was, she thought, remarkably strong.

On Monday morning, less than twenty-four hours after his rescue, Pauling walked into his office area at Caltech. The news of his disappearance had been carried nationwide on the news wires, and everyone in his research group had been worried. Now they festooned his office door with a large "Welcome Back, Dr. Pauling" banner, and one of the secretaries baked a cake decorated with a little toy man on a cliff and a mermaid in the water below. There was a small cheer when he arrived. Pauling looked at the cake, then, without a word to anyone, walked into his private office and shut the door. The little crowd that had gathered to greet him was stunned. A moment later, a sheet of notepaper was pushed under the door; it was a request from Pauling to cancel his class and all other appointments.

No one knew quite what to do. Pauling's son-in-law, Barclay Kamb, was as close to him as anyone; he was called in, and the situation was explained to him. Kamb knocked softly on Pauling's door, then went inside to talk with him. Something was seriously wrong. Pauling seemed aware of his surroundings but unable to say a word. Kamb decided to take him home.

Pauling did not say a word all the way back to his house and remained mute as Ava Helen put him to bed. The trauma of the cliff episode had put him in a state of shock, his physician said after examining him; it was nothing too serious, and a few days of bed rest should bring him around.

Those few days were the strangest in Pauling's life. He was silent most of the time, lying in bed, letting Ava Helen tend him. When Linda visited with his new grandchildren, he began to cry. It was the first time anyone had seen him emotionally vulnerable, in anything less than full control.

The night on the cliff seemed to have cracked open a tightly sealed place inside, a place where he hid everything painful, his feelings of hurt and humiliation, everything from his father's death to the ignominy of being forced out of his chairmanship at Caltech, every insult, every political attack on his character, every barb that had been absorbed and ignored. He had forced all these things inside. He had refused to be hurt by them. But in fact, he had been hurt by his critics at Caltech and in Washington and in the press, his pride had been stung, his ego battered. He had never expressed this to anyone except perhaps Ava Helen. He had swallowed it all, but it had not disappeared. It was only hidden, this tight, concentrated unhappiness, and now for a short time the shock of the incident on the cliff brought it to light.

Pauling was, for those few days, for the first time in his life, at the mercy of his emotions.

✺

It restored a kind of balance. He did not—seemingly could not—deal with his emotions once they were released. He was, above all, through four decades of training and practice, a rationalist, and he would not allow himself to get trapped in the quicksand of his irrational feelings. He pulled back from strong emotions almost instinctively, as a measure of self-preservation, as a way to avoid pain.

But the episode functioned as a kind of therapy, giving him a rest he badly needed, releasing enough psychological pressure to allow him to regain control. Over the next two weeks, he began to talk, got out of bed, read a newspaper, did a little work on the new edition of *The Nature of the Chemical Bond,* and wrote a few letters. He was soon seemingly back to normal and began thinking about honoring some of his many outstanding speaking engagements.

On February 13 he made his first public appearance since the night on the cliff, speaking about fallout and international agreements to a small Hollywood gathering. Earlier that day, France tested its first atomic bomb in the Sahara, becoming the fourth nation to join the atomic club and sending the first fallout into the atmosphere since the test moratorium started in late 1958. At this provocation from the West, the Soviets immediately announced that it was now free from its pledge not to test.

Pauling threw himself back into a full speaking schedule to fight this reversal, making more than forty major speeches during the spring to any sizable group that would listen: liberal forums and peace groups, Kiwanis and Rotary clubs, high school assemblies and church congregations. Despite the French test and Soviet blustering, the Geneva talks seemed to progress encouragingly for a few months; Eisenhower seemed determined to get something signed before he left office, and hopes were high that the final barriers might be overcome at a May summit meeting between the leaders of the East and West in Paris.

It all fell apart, however, in early May when a top-secret U.S. spy plane called U-2 was shot down over Russia. It was humiliating for Eisenhower, who had sworn that such flights were not taking place, and it killed any chance of a test ban being finalized at the Paris summit. The AEC's McCone and Teller used the resulting breakdown in international negotiations to launch another round of pressure for renewed testing. The pendulum of public opinion began swinging again, this time toward taking a harder line with the Soviets and putting off even a limited test ban.

To Pauling, the U-2 incident was more proof that the United States was the recalcitrant partner in the test-ban talks, the nation that seemed always to find a way to throw things off track. It was almost as though there were a conspiracy to continue the Cold War. Pauling's talks now began to center not only on the horrors of nuclear war but on the military-industrial cabal he saw running U.S. policy. Leading it were Teller and what Pauling called "the small but highly influential group of people" centered around him, "the militarists, industrialists, H-bomb scientists, and politicians in all countries who are striving to find a way to continue to wage war, to impose their national will upon the rest of the world." This military-industrial clique, he said, "are our enemies."

In mid-May, Pauling and Ava Helen were driving up to Berkeley for more speeches when they heard over the radio that the scheduled San Francisco appearance of a HUAC panel had triggered a noisy protest outside city hall, mostly made up of students. They listened as the reporters described how the protest had turned into a small-scale riot when police used fire hoses and clubs to clear the area; the entire melee, replete with screaming students being dragged by the hair to paddy wagons, was broadcast that night on television to a shocked America.

The Paulings were excited. Any anti-HUAC action was fine, in Pauling's view, but especially one that involved American college students, a group that had been politically passive through the 1950s. The San Francisco riot was, in fact, the beginning of a new kind of student antigovernment activism and a seminal event in the development of the New Left. The next day, after delivering a scheduled speech to a Union Square peace rally, Pauling and Ava Helen gave their blessing to the event by joining thousands of anti-HUAC protesters who were picketing city hall to protest the treatment of the students. Telling reporters that HUAC was immoral and should be abolished, Pauling added, "American students during recent years have been pretty backward about protesting or demonstrating or taking part in political action. I think that it is really encouraging that students in the United States are beginning to wake up."

SISS

In Washington, D.C., during an East Coast peace lecture swing in June, Pauling delivered a speech to one of Ava Helen's favored groups, the Women's International League for Peace and Freedom (WILPF). Afterward, he was mobbed by admiring attendees thanking him for his inspirational talk, asking his advice, and pushing papers into his hand: newspaper clippings, announcements of upcoming events, a poem someone had written to him. He thanked them all and shoved most of the papers into his pocket. It wasn't until he got back to his hotel room and was undressing that he emptied his pockets and started looking through the detritus. Then everything stopped. Among the papers pressed upon him after the meeting was a subpoena commanding him to appear before an executive session of the Senate Internal Security Subcommittee (SISS). He had to look at the date twice. He was to appear on the morning of Monday, June 20—the day after tomorrow.

Being served papers in this way was a surprise, but harassment from the SISS was not. Pauling knew a little about the subcommittee. It had been started by the Senate in 1951 to complement HUAC. which was getting all the anti-Communist headlines. Under a string of conservative chairmen, the SISS had staged through the 1950s a series of spectacular hearings on Communist influence in the Foreign Service, in youth organizations, and in the television industry. The subcommittee had listed Pauling as one of the nation's leading fellow travelers in 1956 and threatened to bring him before them in 1957 to answer questions about whether Communists were behind his petitions against testing. More recently, SISS acting chairman Thomas Dodd had threatened to hold hearings on Communist influences in SANE unless the group purged itself of suspected Reds; the group's leader, Norman Cousins, had, in Pauling's words, "knuckled under" to Dodd and instituted something akin to a loyalty check on its members. The decision fractured SANE's leadership and crippled the nation's largest and most effective peace group. The SISS ranked with HUAC, in Pauling's estimation, as an example of government gone bad.

But why a subpoena now? The most obvious answer appeared to be Thomas Dodd. Dodd was an unusual senator, a first-term Democrat from Connecticut who appeared to be trying to carve out a unique place for himself in the national scene as a conservative member of a traditionally liberal party, an unusual combination, especially from a northern state. He came into the Senate swinging, speaking out strongly against the Soviets and backing the development of Teller's "clean bomb." He quickly became the Democratic party's most outspoken proponent of continued bomb testing to keep America strong. When he was offered the acting leadership of the SISS, he used it to investigate and attack SANE and other antibomb groups. Pauling was a natural next target.

Dodd was encouraged in his pursuit by the SISS director of research, Benjamin Mandel, a former HUAC star investigator who had tracked Pauling since 1951. Pauling was one of Mandel's pet projects. He had been encouraged by the SISS to subpoena the dissident scientist in 1957; when that fell through because of political considerations, he continued to thicken his files with everything he could find on Pauling's anti-bomb activism. "You have probably noted the item in the paper to the effect that Linus Pauling has gone over the head of the American Government in the usual Communist style," Mandel memoed SISS chief counsel Jules Sourwine after Pauling announced his international scientists' petition in 1958. "It would be interesting to inquire of Pauling regarding the details of this apparatus."

When Mandel showed Dodd the Pauling file, the new senator quickly decided that Pauling was a probable "fellow traveler" who had larded his 1958 petition with signatures from behind the Iron Curtain.

Even though the petition was two years old, Pauling was more active than ever in criticizing America's militarism. If testing was ever going to resume, efforts like Pauling's would have to be shown for what they were, Dodd reasoned, part of the Communist "peace offensive." Dodd's attack on SANE had worked. Putting Pauling under scrutiny would serve as another blow to the peace crowd and might also help shore up the Democratic party's reputation for anti-Communist toughness during an election year. Dodd okayed the subpoena.

He did not know what he was getting into.

The first thing Pauling did after finding the subpoena was to call Abraham Lincoln Wirin, who flew to Washington the next day. After hours of conferring in Pauling's hotel room, they decided that the language in the subpoena—calling Pauling to testify "with respect to Communist participation in, or support of, a propaganda campaign against nuclear testing, and other Communist or Communist-front activities with respect to which you may have knowledge"—indicated that the subcommittee was going to dredge up his entire record, all the old McCarthy charges. But it was difficult to plan a strategy on short notice without knowing exactly what Dodd was going to ask. Both Pauling and Wirin had been through this type of thing before; they both knew how an open-ended witch-hunt could harm a person's reputation without ever proving anything. Dodd was going on a fishing expedition. The only way to be anything other than prey would be to put him on the defensive. For the moment, they decided to use the technique that had worked so well in Pauling's passport cases: to mount a strong public relations offensive waged through the press.

The day before he was scheduled to appear, Pauling called a press conference, where he told the hastily gathered reporters that the SISS inquiry was clearly an attempt to interrupt the flow of information to the public on nuclear tests and represented an attack on the Bill of Rights. It was the first salvo in what would become a bitter public battle.

When Pauling and Wirin arrived for the hearing, they were angered to learn that the proceedings had been delayed for a day because the Senate was in session. They were also informed that the first hearing would be held in executive session, closed to the press and public, a common first step that allowed the subcommittee to gather and sift through information before going to public hearings.

They immediately decided that this was unacceptable. Both Pauling and Wirin recognized that a private session gave the SISS control over the release of information, and therefore control over the press, robbing Pauling of his strongest weapon. They immediately and noisily demanded open hearings.

The subcommittee members, after reading the next morning's *Washington Post* editorial castigating Dodd for this "foolish piece of political harassment," agreed after a quick huddle to make the hearing public. The doors to the hearing room in the new Senate Office Building were opened, and in flooded a wave of WILPF activists led by Ava Helen. Whatever else happened, Pauling would have a sympathetic audience.

After gaveling the session to order, the silver-haired Dodd opened the hearing by assuring Pauling that there was "nothing hostile about our presence here, nothing hostile to you at all," that "I have personally no ill will toward you," and that the hearing was not in any sense an "attempt to torment you or harass you or trouble you." So far, Pauling and Wirin's tactics were working.

Then Pauling was sworn in, and SISS counsel Jules Sourwine got down to business. It quickly became clear why Pauling was there. Sourwine's interrogation centered on a single question: How had Pauling managed to get all those names on his UN petition without a large, possibly Communist, organization behind him? Pauling, nattily dressed in a tailored business suit, answered every question politely and completely.

Would he provide to the subcommittee copies of the names on his petition to the United Nations? He would, although he should not have to; the names, as the subcommittee should know, were available at the United Nations.

Would he provide to the subcommittee the names of those to whom he sent letters asking for signatures? Yes, he would be happy to, once he returned home to Pasadena and found the lists.

Would he provide to the subcommittee the names of those who had helped fill the petitions, those who had sent back more than one name? Here Pauling hesitated. "I feel some concern about my duty to the people who worked for this petition," he said. "I feel concern that they may be subpoenaed before this subcommittee, subjected to the treatment that I have been subjected to." He asked why the request was being made. Dodd answered that there had been some discrepancies discovered in the way the petition had been delivered to the United Nations. For instance, he had a letter before him saying that the num-

ber of signatures Pauling claimed to have delivered to the United Nations had not actually been received there, and he wanted to provide
Pauling the chance to clear that up. That did not sound right to Pauling. He was certain that the number he said were delivered were delivered. (Pauling was right; Dodd was acting on misinformation from his
own research staff.)

Sourwine repeated the request for the names of those who helped
circulate the petitions. After a short, whispered conversation with
Pauling, Wirin asked for a short recess. Outside the hearing room, the
two men talked. Pauling felt that he had to hold firm to his refusal to
provide the names of his petition circulators. The subcommittee was
sure to subpoena a number of them and inquire into their backgrounds and beliefs. These people had helped Pauling in an idealistic
cause; asking him to provide their names now was akin in his mind to
the old McCarthy demands to name names. Pauling would not be an
informer. But, Wirin cautioned, recognize what you're getting into: If
you refuse to give the subcommittee requested information, they can
cite you for contempt, which means a jail sentence if it sticks. The only
tested legal way to get out of answering a direct question was to cite the
Fifth Amendment. But, Pauling said, anyone who says they refuse to
answer on the grounds that it may incriminate them is immediately
presumed to be guilty of something. I won't take the Fifth. What's another strategy?

Together they decided on a riskier course of action. Instead of the
Fifth, Pauling would base his refusal on his First Amendment right to
freedom of speech and petition. A First Amendment defense had
never beaten a congressional contempt citation yet, Wirin told Pauling, but we can try it. There was not much else to do. At least the First
Amendment always received a welcome response in the press. Pauling
and Wirin hastily put together a written statement.

When the hearing resumed, Pauling put on his half-glasses and
read to the subcommittee: "The circulation of petitions is an important part of our democratic process. If it is abolished or inhibited, it
would be a step toward a police state. No matter what assurances the
subcommittee might give me concerning the use of names, I am convinced the names would be used for reprisals against these enthusiastic, idealistic, high-minded workers for peace." There was an eruption
of applause from Ava Helen's contingent.

Pauling was reminded by Sourwine that a refusal to answer could
result in a citation for contempt of Congress. One senator asked pointedly if he was aware of the case of Willard Uphaus, a professor who was

then serving a one-year jail sentence for refusing to answer a similar request. Pauling knew about Uphaus. He knew what the senator was trying to tell him. He set his heels, continuing to answer questions and continuing to refuse the subcommittee's request for the names of those who circulated his petition.

The hearings ended after Dodd told Pauling he would have until August 9 to come up with the requested names.

Pauling, civil and polite in the hearing room, vented his anger to the press in the hallway afterward. His petitions "were not Communist inspired," he told reporters: "I inspired them." He attacked Dodd and the SISS for attempting to stifle free speech and the freedom to petition the government. "Do you think anybody tells me what to do—with threats? I make up my mind. If I want to take a chance, I take a chance."

His words appeared in papers across the nation, along with a surprising outpouring of support for Pauling among the nation's editorial writers. By 1960 there was growing recognition of the fact that congressional investigating committees had been trampling over the rights of witnesses for years in the name of national security, turning their investigations into a form of public theater in which committee counsels were free to stain reputations by subpoenaing whomever they wanted on short notice, dragging them into a public forum, and making whatever statements they liked. Witnesses were forced to appear and forced to answer.

McCarthy's misuse of this power had started a reaction, and Pauling's defiance of Dodd coincided with a growing feeling that investigatory committees should be reined in. Almost every major daily newspaper in the nation voiced anger at the SISS on its editorial pages: The *Honolulu Advertiser:* "Since it's official U.S. policy to seek an end to nuclear testing . . . the inquiry seems superfluous." The *Hartford Times,* in Dodd's home state of Connecticut: "Dr. Pauling is obeying his conscience. The Senate should not interfere." The *Austin American,* in Texas: "My blood tingles with pride now as I read Dr. Pauling's refusal to bow to this bullying committee." The *Washington Post:* "Justice is best served at times by those who defy authority. Professor Pauling offered a splendid illustration of the point." Even the reliably anti-Communist *Time* magazine softened its attitude toward Pauling, calling into question Dodd's decision to put on public display this "kind of kook" whose "naive flirtation with the left has made him a highly controversial figure." The SISS was supported by only a few newspapers, mostly in the Deep South.

Seeing a political debacle in the making, Dodd started writing lengthy rebuttals to the papers that attacked him, noting Pauling's Communist-front history and making his request for names sound innocent and innocuous. But he could not outwrite, outfight, or outwork Pauling. On the night of June 21, just hours after his SISS hearing, Pauling got wild applause from an overflow crowd of peace activists at Johns Hopkins when he called to them to write Dodd "and say you don't want me to go to jail for contempt." The next morning, he told the story of his harassment to the viewers of NBC's *Today* show and started working on a series of articles and letters about his case. Support flooded in from everywhere, with people he had never met sending small donations to help defray his legal costs.

Wirin got the August SISS hearing postponed until October, giving Pauling and Ava Helen time to continue their speechmaking and traveling. The threat of the subcommittee seemed only to energize the Paulings. Together they led a mass "Walk for Disarmament" in Los Angeles that drew four thousand people on July 9—the first protest march most Angelenos had ever seen. They then left for a short European tour. Both Paulings spoke to large and enthusiastic audiences across the Continent, then spent time in Geneva, where Pauling held private conversations with the American, British, and Soviet ambassadors about the progress of the test-ban talks. Instead of diminishing his effectiveness, Dodd's actions seemed only to have enhanced Pauling's importance. The Geneva visit was especially encouraging, with all of the ambassadors assuring Pauling that they were close to a final agreement and, according to Pauling's notes, encouraging him to continue the process of influencing public opinion.

When he returned in August, Pauling opened another front in his battle with Dodd. He mounted a legal attack on the SISS, asking a judge to make a declaratory judgment affirming his right to refuse to answer the subcommittee's request on the basis that it was not pertinent to their inquiry and would constitute unreasonable search and seizure. This was a clever constitutional move, adding a Fourth Amendment argument to the First and using the judicial branch of government to fight the perceived abuses of Congress. But it was not successful. In district court, government lawyers argued that a ruling in Pauling's favor "would be the death of any legislative process," allowing every hearing witness to run to the courts before answering a question. In late August the judge agreed, dismissing the case because it was a legislative matter not appropriate for judicial review. Pauling and Wirin appealed the decision.

In the meantime, Pauling continued his public relations pressure. He attacked the SISS in every speech he made, and hundreds of protest letters began coming to Dodd and his Senate colleagues. Many carried dozens of signatures; some, scores. At Washington University in St. Louis, the birthplace of Pauling's petitions, more than a hundred faculty members signed a letter of protest; 178 professors at the University of Pennsylvania sent another. Pasadena residents and Caltech faculty members sent in scores of letters. And there were cries of protest from around the world, from Germany and Japan, Norway and Mexico, England and India, and from Nobelists, nationally known peace activists, and ordinary citizens, the writers lauding Pauling's "rugged individualism" and decrying the harassment of this "great American . . . caught in the ebb tide of McCarthyism."

Dodd was kept busy through the summer and early fall sending out responses and overseeing the preparation of a report on Pauling's June appearance. When Pauling saw the galley proofs, he was incensed. For one thing, Dodd was planning to title the report "Communist Infiltration and Use of Pressure Groups." Then, by carefully comparing the galleys to a stenographic transcript of the hearing, Pauling discovered not only that some of his testimony was missing—edited out, he felt, because it was favorable to him—but that the senators had been allowed to edit their remarks for clarity, while he had not. Reading it over, Pauling saw indications as well that Dodd had purposely asked misleading questions. Dodd had made much of the discrepancy between the number of signatures that Pauling claimed to have sent the United Nations versus the number that actually showed up, for instance, but now Pauling saw that a full and correct copy of the petition from the United Nations—proving that he had reported the number correctly—had been placed into the record on the day of the hearing. Similarly, Sourwine had implied that Pauling had for some reason hidden the fact that Russians had signed his petitions, but it was clear from documents in the subcommittee's hands that he had not.

All of this and other matters—"known by you to be false," Pauling told Dodd in a long letter of correction that he asked be attached to his testimony—made Pauling believe that Dodd and his subcommittee were less than honest. He held yet another press conference where he accused the SISS of harassment and called it "a discredit to the United States and to the people of America."

"One way or another, we shall be busy with this thing for some time yet, but we haven't much anxiety about the final outcome," Ava

Helen told a friend. "It is just a shame for Linus to be wasting his talents in this way."

—///—

By the end of summer, Dodd had had his fill of Pauling's insults and decided to fight back in his own way, in his own forum. A contempt citation was looking less likely—it would have to be approved by the full Senate, and many senators had received pro-Pauling letters from constituents—but there were other ways to make Pauling uncomfortable and display to the nation what his true motivations were. His staff began putting together a master list of Pauling's Communist-front activities.

The public relations battle reached a climax in the days leading up to Pauling's second appearance before the subcommittee, scheduled for October 11. Pauling prepared a half-page newspaper advertisement detailing Dodd's harassment and asking the help of all Americans to rid the nation of congressional committees "that exceed their authority and subvert the Constitution and the Bill of Rights." The *New York Times* rejected the ad as libelous, but the *Washington Post* ran it. Dodd countered with another long release defending his "simple request for cooperation on the basis of honor and reasonableness." Pauling asked for a delay in the hearing; Dodd refused. The Emergency Committee for Civil Liberties ran an advertisement supporting Pauling signed by scores of liberals; Dodd had his research staff comb through the names to uncover those linked to Communists. *New York Times* editors called the SISS's pursuit of Pauling "part of its usual policy of harassment"; Dodd sent out unsolicited copies of the June hearing transcript to people he thought might have influence over public opinion.

Outside his Washington hotel on the night of October 10, Pauling was served a subpoena commanding him to appear the next morning and to bring the requested signatures and letters of transmittal.

—///—

The hearing room was packed with reporters and onlookers, including Ava Helen in a prim dress and hat, but the subcommittee's chairs were empty. Dodd was the only member who showed up for the October 11 hearing. Everyone else, it seemed, had pressing business that urgently required their presence elsewhere. The lack of support did not seem to trouble the senator from Connecticut, who opened the proceedings by reading a twelve-page statement defending the integrity of his inquiry. Six pages into it, he asked Pauling and Wirin if they minded if he cut it short and simply put the rest into the record. Wirin agreed, with the stipulation that Pauling have a chance to read and respond to it before it was published. Then Dodd moved briskly to the main questions. Have you brought the requested original signatures? Pauling had, in volumes bound in red covers.

Then came the main event: Have you brought the requested letters of transmittal with the names of the petition circulators?

Before Pauling could answer, a nondescript man in the back of the chamber stood and announced in a loud voice that he himself was proud to be one of the people who had circulated a petition. Pauling turned around. As applause rippled through the chamber, Herbert Jehle, a local university professor, gave a deep bow to Dodd, another to the audience, and sat down. Pauling smiled.

Pauling then turned to Dodd and gave him his answer. "I am unwilling to subject these people to reprisals by this subcommittee," he said. "I could protect myself by agreeing, but I am fighting for other persons who could not make a fight themselves." He refused to provide the names of the circulators.

This was the point at which Dodd was expected to rise up and cite Pauling for contempt. There was an expectant hush in the hearing room. And there was an anticlimax. Dodd simply said, "Very well," and motioned to his chief counsel, Sourwine.

The real purpose of the second hearing then became apparent. There was to be no citation for contempt, no further chance for Pauling to appear in the role of a martyr. Instead, there was going to be an old-fashioned loyalty inquiry. Sourwine asked nothing about the circulation of the petition and everything about Pauling's background as a supporter of Communist causes. Have you ever been to East Berlin? Have you ever met Ethel Rosenberg? Did you not participate in the San Francisco HUAC protests?

At the noon break Pauling was confronted in the hall by an angry young man who told him he should be deported. Pauling replied that that would be problematical, since he was native born and would have nowhere to go.

In the afternoon Sourwine's questions droned on—some ridiculous—Are you aware that there were known Communists among the members of the Soviet Academy of Sciences who signed your petition?—some pointed, all dedicated to proving that Pauling was guided by and aligned with Communist goals and aims. Did you know that one of the signers of your petition, Dr. Hideki Yukawa of Japan, had won the Lenin Prize? No, Pauling replied, he knew Dr. Yukawa only as a winner of the Nobel Prize for physics. Didn't you support the passport fight of Martin Kamen, whose right to travel was denied after he had been investigated for passing secrets on to the Russians? Pauling replied that he had, then reminded Sourwine that Kamen had been cleared of all charges, had won a lawsuit on the issue, and had had his passport reinstated. It appeared, as *New York Post* columnist Murray Kempton put it, that Pauling was "on trial in this place where, of course, everyone knew he was not on trial."

During the afternoon session, Wirin got a copy of Dodd's complete opening statement and saw that the last six pages constituted a direct attack on Pauling, including a list, "Affiliations with Communist-Controlled Organizations or Activities Supporting the Communist Party," of more than twenty suspect organizations with which Pauling had been associated. The SISS staff had already distributed it to the press at the noon break. Senator Dodd, it appeared, was making certain that it was Pauling who would be put on the defensive this time.

The hearing dragged on, with Sourwine questioning Pauling about more than thirty organizations and twenty-five individuals. It took on the stylized format and rhythm established back in the days of the Hollywood Ten: Do you know Mr. X, who signed your petition? Do you know that Mr. X has been accused of membership in a known Communist-front organization? Have you ever been a member of organization Z? Are you aware that organization Z has been listed by HUAC as a Communist-front organization? It was an exercise in character assassination through association. It was a smear.

After five hours, when it was finally over, Dodd strode up to Pauling and said, "That wasn't such a strain, was it?" Without an answer, Pauling turned and walked out.

Peace

Egghead Millionaires

Publicly, it appeared that Pauling had won. He had forced the Senate Internal Security Committee to back down from its threat of a contempt citation. Dodd's last-day attempt at a smear did not even seem to have much effect; the media for the most part ignored his litany of old charges. Less than a month after it was over, John F. Kennedy would win the White House, and American politics would take a new direction. The Pauling hearing would prove to be the last of the Communist witch-hunts.

Pauling's resolute stand made him an even greater hero in the peace movement. Two weeks after his SISS ordeal, a SANE rally in New York turned spontaneously into a Pauling testimonial. More than two thousand people jammed the Hotel Commodore ballroom after it was announced that Pauling would speak, hundreds more overflowed to nearby rooms fitted with loudspeakers, and several hundred had to be turned away. Everyone wanted to see the man who had defeated the SISS. They clapped as Pauling accepted a petition signed by one thousand local university students supporting his defiance of Congress, listened avidly as he talked about his experiences with the subcommittee, and cheered when he called for an end to war and a rebirth of civil rights. His experience had taught him something. "The fight for peace," he told the crowd, "cannot be carried on independently of the fight for freedom."

—∿∿∿—

He should have walked away from the SISS hearings in triumph and put the experience behind him. But Pauling could not. The hours of grilling and the concerted attempt to smear his reputation constituted a deep personal insult, and one that Pauling, in his anger, elevated to a symbol of the rebirth of McCarthyism rather than its last gasp. Instead of walking away, he overreacted, continuing to attack Dodd in speeches and television appearances, calling the SISS and the House Un-American Activities Committee "immoral" and the senator "an evil person."

"We have, I understand, only a few thousand Communists in the United States, as compared to many millions in France and Italy," Pauling wrote soon after the Dodd hearings. "I don't see how the sensible American people could be endangered by a few thousand Communists. Communists may represent a threat to our civil rights and liberties that we should be aware of and prepared to guard ourselves against if it ever becomes serious . . . [but] the anti-Communist forces of repression that are now in positions of great authority are more than a threat—they are taking our rights away from us right now." He devoted part of his time now working for the abolition of the investigatory committees, throwing himself against old enemies who were already close to dying a natural death.

And Dodd fought back. When Pauling succeeded in delaying publication of the report on his last SISS appearance—arguing through early 1961 over the inclusion of the unread portion of Dodd's opening statement and other matters—Dodd's committee released a separate report on the Pugwash movement outlining the suspect backgrounds of the participants, including more than nine pages devoted to Pauling's "marked bias for Communist causes and . . . willingness to aline [sic] himself with Communist-held views having no scientific bearing or interest." When the SISS report was finally published in March 1961, it included all of Dodd's opening statement and was accompanied by an SISS press release noting that there was "reason for suspecting that the Communist apparatus played an important role in circulating the [Pauling] petition in the United States and other free countries." The evidence offered was primarily Pauling's history of left-wing associations. "Dr. Pauling has figured as the number one scientific name in virtually every major activity of the Communist Peace offensive in this country," the report concluded, a series of links that "have not been entirely accidental or unconscious on his side." To make certain that Pauling's peers got the message, Dodd sent unsolicited copies of his report to National Academy of Sciences (NAS) members and other prominent scientists.

"Scandalous . . . offensive . . . the worst smear job I've ever seen," Wirin told Pauling after he saw the report. Pauling agreed. In a speech to the American Humanist Association the next day, he lashed out at Dodd, daring him or any other member of the subcommittee to come out from behind congressional immunity so he could sue them. In an earlier time, he said, he would have challenged Dodd to a duel.

His reaction extended to anyone and anything that echoed Dodd's attack, including publications that hewed too closely to the SISS line and made what Pauling considered defamatory statements about his character. "The newspapers have been partners in the resurgence of McCarthyism," he said. "They need to be stopped." He launched a one-man war to do it. He and his lawyers mounted five libel suits during the next year, seeking $60,000 from the Bellingham, Washington, *Herald* for printing letters to the editor that questioned Pauling's patriotism; $100,000 from the Anti-Communist League of York County, Pennsylvania, for publishing a pamphlet based on the SISS report; $300,000 from the St. Louis *Globe-Democrat* for an anti-Pauling editorial; $500,000 from the New York *Daily News* for calling Pauling a pro-Communist "semi-prominent American loudmouth"; and $1 million from the Hearst organization and King Features Syndicate for a piece by right-wing columnist and chronic Pauling critic Fulton Lewis, Jr.

The SISS episode, coupled in some way, perhaps, to the emotional trauma of the cliff experience, seemed to have thinned Pauling's skin. He moved from routinely ignoring criticism to being highly sensitive to it, whether it came from the Right or Left. In the two years following the SISS appearance Pauling also took on many of his former allies in the fight for peace. He quit his position as a sponsor of SANE and stopped speaking with founder Norman Cousins, who Pauling felt had given in to Dodd. He seriously considered bringing a $1 million lawsuit against the *Bulletin of the Atomic Scientists,* a magazine he had helped support through Einstein's Emergency Committee of Atomic Scientists, after it printed an article in which prominent bomb-control activist Bentley Glass lumped him with Teller as two scientists whose political aims colored their interpretation of bomb-test data. It took weeks of effort by members of the magazine's editorial board to talk Pauling out of bringing suit, and for years after that he had little use for either the *Bulletin* or its editor, Eugene Rabinowitch. He had a falling out with the organizers of the Pugwash conferences for continuing to invite Glass, Rabinowitch, and others he disapproved of to their meetings; the Pugwash discussions, he felt, had degenerated from a free and open airing of new ideas from outside the political process into a parroting of official government lines.

Another factor in his shift in sensitivity may have been Ava Helen, who had always been a more doctrinaire left-winger than her husband. She personally considered most of the old religious-based peace groups "reactionary" and the newer ones like SANE not much better. None of them seemed willing to place their antibomb activism in the context of a critique of capitalist society. How could you end war, she thought, unless you transformed the economic systems that spawned war? Now Pauling, too, was more pointed in his critique of American society. Capitalism was a factor, coupled with the obscene deals made between the defense industry and Washington. Why was there a continued opposition to a test ban? "No doubt cold-war profits are an important motive," he noted.

There was no one more despicable in his mind than an educated person, especially a scientist, who made money from war and suffering. From a news magazine Pauling picked up a new term that he began to use in his speeches, "egghead millionaires," a hundred or so scientists who had parlayed their research talents into fortunes in the defense industry. To Pauling, the egghead millionaires, along with Teller, were the ultimate symbols of the betrayal and corruption of a once-noble calling.

But from the lofty vantage point now occupied solely by himself, Ava Helen, Bertrand Russell, and a handful of their activist friends, it looked as if almost no one measured up to their standards of antibomb purity.

Pauling was still popular—in 1960 the Rationalist Society named him Rationalist of the Year, for instance, and he made the cover of *Time* as one of the scientists named "Men of the Year' in January 1961—but to the leaders of the peace movement he was beginning to appear less a hero than a loose cannon, a popular speaker and a necessary counterweight to Teller, but also unreliably independent, increasingly litigious, and ever more comfortable in the farther fringes of the left wing.

Kennedy, Oslo, and Brain Ice

The nation's new president did not escape Pauling's critical eye. Pauling had been a longtime Stevenson supporter, and his enthusiasm for the dashing young senator from Massachusetts had never risen above lukewarm. There had even been some talk in 1960 about running Pauling as a peace candidate (in a straw vote of Stanford University students, he had received 152 write-in votes out of 3,000 votes cast), but he recognized the idea as laughable, telling his supporters—some of whom later proposed that he run for senator or mayor of Los Angeles—that he was no politician.

Kennedy at least offered the right sentiments about trying to push forward the long-stalled Geneva test-ban negotiations and early in his term created the U.S. Arms Control and Disarmament Agency. "I myself have a high opinion of our new President's wish to achieve disarmament," Pauling wrote soon after the election. And Kennedy had style, inviting Pauling and 166 other "creative Americans" to the inaugural festivities in Washington, D.C., in early 1961. Previous engagements made it impossible for Pauling to attend, but he was impressed by the gesture after twelve years of being cold-shouldered by the White House. He sent his RSVP with a personal note: "I am happy to join in welcoming you and congratulating you. You are our great hope for peace in the world."

His hope seemed borne out by Kennedy's September 1961 address to the United Nations in which the president challenged the Soviet Union "not to an arms race but to a peace race," starting with a ban on atmospheric bomb tests. At the same time, JFK reenergized the U.S. peace team in Geneva, providing what his chief negotiator, Arthur Dean, called "a new drive and sense of determination."

Despite the positive signs, Pauling believed that he would have to keep applying pressure. Kennedy was talking about a test ban, but his people were also talking about supplying nuclear weapons to NATO as a further reminder to the Soviets that they could not win a land war in Europe. Reports were surfacing that the Chinese were developing atomic bombs. These potential expansions of nuclear technology represented a new and, Pauling thought, distinctly dangerous trend. The greater the number of nations that had nuclear arms or the means to produce them, the greater the chance of an accident, thievery, or a madman setting off a holocaust.

So, assured that Kennedy was effectively pushing on the test-ban front, in early 1961 Pauling turned his efforts toward a new goal: stopping the proliferation of nuclear weapons.

The best method, the Paulings decided, would be a new petition. With the help of a small group of activist friends, the Paulings drafted a call for a halt in the nuclear arming of NATO, a move toward universal disarmament, and the strengthening of the United Nations as a force for world peace. The "Appeal to Stop the Spread of Nuclear Weapons," as they called it, was sent out immediately to two thousand scientists who had signed their earlier petition, with the Paulings stuffing envelopes at their kitchen table.

Within a month Pauling had collected more than seven hundred signatures from around the world, including those of thirty-eight Nobelists and 110 members of the NAS. That was good for a start. On February 16, Pauling presented the petition to Dag Hammarskjöld at the United Nations, careful to hand out on the same day a press release detailing how the petition had been initiated and paid for.

In a clever move, Pauling then used the publicity of the UN presentation to solicit support from people throughout the world, asking them via the press to send in several hundred thousand more signatures by mid-April, just before NATO representatives were scheduled to meet in Oslo to discuss the nuclear-arms issue. A petition effort on this scale had never before been mounted.

But even history's largest petition was not enough for Pauling. In order to focus world attention on the issue, he decided to hold his own international peace meeting in Oslo on the eve of the NATO meeting. It would be a return to the spirit of the first Pugwash meetings, with respected scientists from both sides of the Iron Curtain demonstrating that militarism was not the only answer to international tensions. The conference could be set up from Pasadena, using his group of activist friends as organizers. They hoped, they wrote in the minutes of an organizational meeting held at Pauling's house, to raise "a great roar of protest" from the people of the world.

Planning the meeting, finding attendees, arranging their travel, and finding ways to pay for it all took a great deal of Pauling's time through the remainder of the spring. He first wrote Gunnar Jahn, head of the Norwegian Nobel Committee, and persuaded him to open the Norwegian Nobel Institute for his meeting. He convinced Albert Schweitzer, Bertrand Russell, and twenty other notables to act as sponsors of what he called the "Conference to Study the Problem of the Possible Spread of Nuclear Weapons to More Nations or Groups of Nations"—but which everybody else called the Oslo Conference—and began searching for $30,000 to pay for it. The Paulings would end up paying for a great deal of the conference themselves.

In the middle of it all, Pauling celebrated his sixtieth birthday at a party Ava Helen arranged. He had a wonderful evening, surrounded by old friends, colleagues, and former students from all over, many of whom he had not seen in years. One especially welcome partygoer was David Harker, Pauling's student in the 1930s and later a competitor in protein studies. Harker and Pauling had had their ups and downs, but now the crowd laughed as Harker told anecdotes about his student days. One that stuck in everyone's mind later became a signature quote of Pauling's. "Dr. Pauling, how do you have so many good ideas?" Harker remembered asking his mentor. Pauling thought a moment and said, "Well, David, I have a lot of ideas and throw away the bad ones."

It was still true. Although his peace efforts alone constituted enough work for most committees, Pauling still found some time to devote to science.

He revised a new edition of his *College Chemistry* text and told friends he was planning a new book on the molecular basis of civilization. His mental health project was nearing the end of its five-year Ford Foundation funding, and Pauling had little to show for it. The endless rounds of urinalysis and blood testing of mental defectives had turned up a few tantalizing leads, but nothing that represented as simple an answer as the PKU model had led him to believe might be operative. There were simply too many chemicals in urine and blood to analyze efficiently with available technology. What analyses were possible indicated that the chemical makeup of these complex biological solutions varied so widely from person to person that it was difficult to pinpoint any one factor related to a condition as ill defined as mental retardation.

The only significant new idea Pauling developed about brain function was tangential to the mental health project. For years he had wondered about something he had heard in a 1952 talk by a physician, who had said that xenon gas was a wonderful anesthetic agent. Pauling had pricked his ears because xenon, he knew from personal experience, was one of the most unreactive elements in nature. How could something that reacts with nothing have this profound biological effect?

Seven years passed before an answer came to him. He was scanning a paper on the crystal structure of a long-chain, alkyl-substituted ammonium-salt hydrate when he realized that the answer to his anesthesia question might be water. He had already shown that water molecules could organize themselves around other molecules of the right sizes and types to form hydrates, sort of polygonal cages around the central molecule, that had properties quite distinct from ordinary water. Hydrates behaved in some ways like crystals of ice. Hydrates, he suddenly realized, could form around and be stabilized by xenon. What if xenon acted as an anesthetic by stabilizing the formation of hydrates around the side chains of proteins in the brain? The formation of these water cages, these crystals in the brain, might impair the movement of nearby side chains and ions, lower the amplitude of electrical oscillations, and lead to unconsciousness. Xenon would, in a manner of speaking, freeze the mind.

By reading the literature during the following year, he saw not only that his theory was something completely new in the field of anesthesia but that it fit roughly with what was known about the structures of many other hydrate-forming anesthetics like chloroform and nitrous oxide. It also was supported by the observation that lowering the temperature of the brain produced effects similar to anesthesia. In both cases, Pauling thought, the result might be linked to the formation of microcrystals. By the spring of 1960 he was drafting a paper—working on it at the Big Sur ranch during the visit when he was stranded on the cliff—and had started a new student, Frank Catchpool, Schweitzer's former medical chief, who had followed Pauling to Caltech, to work looking for evidence. Pauling was so encouraged by the reception his ideas received at a couple of meetings where he presented it in preliminary form—"intriguing and attractive," one leading anesthesiologist said—that despite Catchpool's failure to come up with any strongly corroborating evidence, Pauling decided to publish, anyway. His paper, "A Molecular Theory of General Anesthesia," appeared in *Science* in July 1961. He considered it one of his most important efforts since the protein-structure work a decade earlier, and he began putting more people in his laboratory to work proving that it was correct.

To test the idea that lower temperatures would ease the formation of crystals, thus lessening the need for anesthetic, a group of Pauling's researchers used goldfish as test animals in a series of experiments. Scores of goldfish were put in separate bowls equipped with sensitive temperature controls and anesthetic drips. The investigators would peer into bowl after bowl, checking the temperatures and debating whether a given goldfish was truly unconscious. The sight left the older chemists in the division shaking their heads.

Pauling's other scientific work was not going well. The third edition of *The Nature of the Chemical Bond,* rushed through to meet a deadline in the middle of his peace work and his SISS appearances, was published to less than enthusiastic reviews. Information about Mulliken's molecular-orbital theory was once again conspicuous by its absence despite growing acceptance among chemists. This time reviewers took Pauling to task for ignoring the obvious. He offered the defense that the MO approach was too math-heavy for his general treatment—"I am determined to keep my book unsophisticated," he wrote one critic—but after several correspondents provided him with examples of simple MO applications that did not need strenuous calculations, Pauling recanted and began talking of preparing a fourth edition that would pay more attention to molecular orbitals.

But by then the damage had been done. Pauling, the pioneer of chemical-bond theory, now appeared to be out of date. "In the third edition he basically didn't—or didn't want to—cover the subject at the stage that it was at the time. It's very much his views instead of an overview," said one of his former students. "My feeling, and I think the feeling of other people who are admirers of Pauling, is that it was a little bit sad."

But the Oslo Conference that spring renewed Pauling's spirits. About thirty-five physical and biological scientists and twenty-five social scientists and others from fifteen nations participated in the meetings, including four representatives from the USSR. Gunnar Jahn and representatives of the Nobel Institute watched appreciatively as Pauling ran a smooth meeting, culminating in agreement on a public synopsis of goals. The "Oslo Statement" called for a ban on the transfer of nuclear weapons from existing nuclear powers to other groups or nations, a complete test ban, general and complete disarmament, and study of the transition from a militarized to a demilitarized economy. It was read aloud when the conference ended to a public meeting that drew five hundred people to the great Aula meeting hall of the University of Oslo. Thanks to Pauling's flair for public relations, the conference also received wide coverage in the U.S. press. "Everything has gone along almost perfectly," Pauling enthused when it was over. "The Aula meeting was grand." The capping event was a torthlight parade of

Norwegian students and believers in peace that wound through Oslo in honor of Pauling and his meeting.

No Shelter

In September 1961, the Soviets started testing again. As soon as he heard the announcement on the news, Pauling telegrammed Khrushchev, asking "in the name of science" that the Soviets reconsider their decision.

Khrushchev did not, and Kennedy followed with his own announcement that the United States might be forced to resume tests as well—underground, he said, with no release of radiation. Pauling wrote anguished telegrams and letters to both leaders, pointing out the dangers of fallout, urging them in the name of humanity to stop. Khrushchev answered him with a rambling eight-page letter blaming everything on the West's apparent determination to rearm Germany. Kennedy did not respond.

Between September and the end of November, the Soviets indulged in the greatest orgy of nuclear testing the world has ever seen. One test alone measured an enormous fifty-eight megatons, the largest man-made explosion ever created, three thousand times more powerful than the Hiroshima blast.

By the time the testing frenzy ended in late November, the Soviet Union had tested fifty bombs—roughly one nuclear blast every two days. Pauling estimated that the resulting radiation would create 160,000 birth defects and that the increase in carbon 14 alone would cause 4 million aborted pregnancies, stillbirths, and birth defects over the next several score generations. "This is premeditated murder of millions of people," he told the press. "It compares with the consignment of Jews to the gas chambers."

—*mm*—

Then he made plans to visit the Soviet Union.

He had been invited before the new round of tests to come to Moscow to celebrate the 250th anniversary of the founding of Russian science by the chemist Lomonosov. Instead of protesting the Soviet tests by declining, Pauling decided that it would be better to use the opportunity to keep lines of communication open, to lecture the Soviets about peace, and to remind Soviet chemists that his view of the chemical bond was correct. The timing might have been bad, but Pauling always felt that the way to handle international problems was through increased, rational discussion; 1961 may have been the year of the Bay of Pigs and the building of the Berlin Wall, but Pauling would demonstrate through his visit that there was an alternative to bluster and threats when it came to international relations. He would carry on his own kind of diplomacy.

When he arrived at the Russian embassy in Paris to secure his visa, however, the staff, without explanation, turned him down. His trip in jeopardy, he traveled on as planned to a scientific meeting in Yugoslavia, where a Russian scientist told him why: "In Paris, when you went to the Embassy, you said that you were Leenus Pauling [a pronunciation Pauling was in the habit of using in Europe]. Leenus Pauling is the idealistic representative of the capitalistic West who has developed theories in chemistry that are incompatible with dialectical materialism such that no patriotic Soviet scientist will use them. You should have said that you were Linus Pauling. Linus Pauling is a great friend of the Soviet Union and a worker for World Peace." He corrected his pronunciation and got his visa.

The Paulings arrived in Moscow in late November in time to attend the grand Lomonosov celebration, then stayed in the country nearly a month to sightsee and give lectures. Pauling gave about a dozen scientific talks—two specifically on the advantages of his "corrupt" theory of resonance—and addressed about a thousand Muscovites who gathered to hear him give a public lecture about peace. He and Ava Helen both spoke against the resumption of tests. The Russian press made much of them—especially Ava Helen, portrayed in magazines as an exemplar of peace-loving American womanhood—and they had a wonderful time, seeing the Bolshoi Ballet, visiting churches and schools, talking with peace activists, and sharing feasts. The only disappointment was that despite repeated requests, they did not see Khrushchev, although they had tea with Madame Khrushchev and shared the stage with her at one event.

In the United States, Pauling was often accused of being "soft" on the USSR, an impression buttressed by the American press, which ignored the protests Pauling made to Khrushchev but trumpeted his similar protests to Kennedy. And in a way, especially compared to mainstream American opinion, Pauling *was* soft. He certainly did not feel that communism was any worse than capitalism; he saw the two systems as the political-economic equivalents of matrix and wave mechanics or of the valence-bond and molecular-orbital approaches to chemistry: concepts that seemed radically different on the surface but when fully developed would become much the same. Eventually, he believed, both would end up looking very much like Swedish-style socialism.

Although he could be harshly critical of the Soviet government—pointing publicly to the mistreatment of Jews, the suppression of the Hungarian revolt, Stalin's purges, the restriction of science by political dogma, the use of the death penalty to punish "economic crimes," examples, he said, "of the immorality of action of a great power"—he found that he liked the Russian people, their friendliness and down-to-earth manner, their apparently sincere desire for peace. And he and Ava Helen were impressed by the reasons they heard from the Soviets about their need to engage in an arms race: the United States, they were told, was constantly leaping ahead with new weapons—first with the A-bomb, first with the H-bomb, first with the U-bomb—forcing the USSR to play catch-up as a matter of national survival. This analysis of the United States as the primary reason for the arms race became part of Pauling's thinking in the early 1960s.

And there was a commonsense reason for Pauling to concentrate his attention on U.S. policies. "While I am critical of the Soviet government," he said, "I feel that I should be especially critical of the American government because I am an American. . . . Just as I think it is proper for me to be more critical of myself and of my wife and my children than I am of some other person and his wife and children, so I think it is proper for me to be more critical of the American government than the Soviet government." Besides, he added, "I have little expectation of having influence on the Soviet government through criticism."

~uun~

The sputtering Geneva test-ban talks resumed again in late November, but without much optimism on either side.

Pauling continued to apply pressure for a test ban through an increasing series of public talks, undeterred even when he was denied a forum. Protests by the local American Legion led to the cancellation of one of his talks on science education in Cincinnati. When the Associated Students at the University of California's Riverside campus invited him to speak on nuclear issues in early 1962, the campus administration refused to allow the talk, arguing that it was "basically political in nature" and "outside the competence of a chemist." Pauling appealed to UC system president Clark Kerr, letting him know that unless the decision was reversed he would take legal action. The pressure worked: Kerr spoke to the Riverside chancellor and got Pauling reinvited.

But he was speaking to hundreds at a time in auditoriums while Teller and the Atomic Energy Commission (AEC) spoke to millions through the mass media. By early 1962 public opinion again began to shift toward the resumption of tests, which Kennedy, after his announcement a few months earlier, had so far delayed. Everything the Paulings had spent seven years fighting for appeared to be in jeopardy. "We feel rather depressed," Ava Helen wrote a friend in the peace movement in February. "Each day brings more backward steps. I try to think of a new approach or new words and it seems we have used them all and still events bring us closer and closer to the final agony."

On March 2, President Kennedy announced that he was approving the resumption of U.S. atmospheric bomb tests in late April—the first such American tests since 1958 and a great blow to Pauling, who had hoped Kennedy would hold firm.

This was a betrayal of Kennedy's promises during the election, Pauling thought, and proof that the president was ruled by his military advisers and political expediency rather than morality. It was a triumph of the military-industrial complex, of the egghead millionaires, of the members of the Democratic party who thought Kennedy had to get tough. So much for the nation's great hope for peace. Pauling fired off a strident telegram to the White House—"Are you going to give an order that will cause you to go down in history as one of the most immoral men of all time and one of the greatest enemies of the human race? . . . Are you going to be guilty of this monstrous immorality, matching that of the Soviet leaders, for the political purpose of increasing the still-imposing lead of the U.S. over the Soviet Union in weapons technology?"—and followed it with a series of white-hot public speeches. "Anger and shame—anger with my government and shame for my country," Pauling cried to the crowds. "It is with shame that I now, for the first time, make the statement that it is not our government, but the Soviet that has led in striving for peace. . . . Not Khrushchev, but President Kennedy who is the most evil." The United States, he said, had been first to develop and explode the atomic bomb, first to test the hydrogen bomb, first with the superbomb. The United States had the greatest stockpile of nuclear weapons on earth and the most sophisticated systems for delivering them. Why in the name of humanity was it necessary to test again?

But he was now conspicuously out of step with public opinion. Most Americans thought that Kennedy had been admirably patient on the nuclear-testing issue, holding U.S. tests underground while the Russians exploded massive bombs in the atmosphere, refusing to go to above-ground tests even while the AEC cried loudly through the winter that the United States was falling behind. When he did announce the April resumption, the president pointed out that the American tests would be conducted high in the atmosphere, where less dust would be sucked up, lessening the resulting fallout. Despite all this, the Soviets were still delaying progress in the Geneva negotiations. Perhaps the resumption of atmospheric testing by the United States would get their attention.

Kennedy's decision was widely supported across the political spectrum. Even the Federation of Atomic Scientists, the old anti-A-bomb activists, came out publicly in favor, as did Hans Bethe, the respected physicist and government adviser who had previously been a staunch opponent of atmospheric tests. SANE was muted in its response, expressing more regret than protest, mirroring the general feeling among peace workers that the tests were an unfortunate necessity required to force the Soviets to engage more seriously in negotiations in Geneva.

Pauling stood alone, the only figure of national importance to vehemently and vocally oppose the president's decision. His month in the USSR and his immoderate telegram to Kennedy brought him a great deal of criticism from a wide spectrum of columnists and readers—"I suggest you inform yourself on more than chemistry before you attempt to dictate Presidential decisions" and "You should get down on your knees and crawl to Moscow" were typical of the letters sent to his office—and some scattered letters of support.

But he persevered. Through March and April he escalated his solo attack on the administration. Pauling and Ava Helen went on a whirlwind speaking tour arranged by the American Friends Service Committee, racing across the country by car, train, and plane on an intense schedule that left them both exhausted. They sent out scores of letters in an attempt to start a grassroots campaign to get Kennedy to rethink his decision but got little response. Pauling and Albert Szent-Györgyi lobbied the NAS unsuccessfully to take a stand in opposition to the new tests.

Kennedy responded by inviting the Paulings to dinner as guests at an evening honoring the best and most creative minds in the nation. Scheduled for April 29—a few days after the planned resumption of American atmospheric tests—the dinner was to be the largest the Kennedys ever held, 175 guests, including forty-nine Nobel Prize winners, seven Pulitzer Prize winners, and a leavening of assorted writers, actors, university presidents, celebrities, and media bosses. The young president and his wife raised eyebrows in Washington not only by inviting notorious leftists like Oppenheimer and the Paulings but also by deciding to bar politicians from the event—with the exception of Robert Kennedy, Vice President Lyndon Johnson, and a few White House staffers. The Paulings, eager to take advantage of their first invitation to the White House, happily accepted.

And they took advantage of the situation. The day before the dinner, Pauling joined three thousand picketers organized by Women Strike for Peace and circled the White House several times. A reporter snapped a photo that was sent over the wire and appeared in papers from New York to Los Angeles: Pauling in shirtsleeves, grinning that trademark grin, holding aloft a placard he had been handed by one of the marching women: "Mr. Kennedy, Mr. Macmillan, We Have No *Right* To Test." It would turn out later to be an unfortunate choice of sentiment.

The next morning, he picketed the White House again, then went to his hotel, rested, changed into evening clothes, and returned for dinner.

⁓⁓⁓

If there was ever an event in the Kennedy White House that approximated the myth of Camelot, it was this sparkling evening.

The Paulings first met the Kennedys in the reception line. "I'm pleased to see you," Kennedy said to Pauling, smiling, then quipped, "I understand you've been around the White House a couple of days already." Pauling grinned and answered yes. Then Kennedy added gracefully, "I hope you will continue to express your feelings." The two men shook hands. Pauling took the hand of Jackie Kennedy, who impressed all the guests with her off-the-shoulder Oleg Cassini gown and long white gloves. She gave him one of her dazzling smiles and asked, "Dr. Pauling, do you think it's right to march back and forth out there in front of the White House carrying a sign?" Silence fell over that part of the line; for a moment Pauling did not know what to answer. Then she added, "Caroline could see you, and she asked, 'Mummy, what has Daddy done now?'" Everyone laughed.

The Paulings knew almost everyone there and were friends with many. Everyone was ushered into the State Dining Room for a sumptuous feast with plenty of wine. Couples were seated separately to ensure maximum conversation. Whether by accident or design, Ava Helen was seated near the AEC's Bill Libby—both of them managing to avoid talk of fallout during the course of the dinner—and Pauling sat near Mitzi Newhouse, wife of the publisher of the St. Louis *Globe-Democrat*, which Pauling was suing for libel. According to one gossip columnist the next day, "Pauling admired Mrs. Newhouse's chic attire, particularly her jewels. He studied her necklace, then turned to Mrs. Pauling and said, 'I'll get one of these for you, dear—as soon as I win my million-dollar libel suit.'" Pauling insisted the story was apocryphal.

Kennedy rose at the end of dinner to make a few remarks. One reporter, he said, had termed this dinner "the President's Easter egghead roll." When the laughter subsided, Kennedy said, "I deny that. I regard this as the most distinguished and significant dinner we have had in the White House since I have been here, and I think in many, many years . . . the most extraordinary collection of talent, of human knowledge, that has ever been gathered at the White House— with the possible exception of when Thomas Jefferson dined alone."

After dinner, the guests were on their way to the East Room for a reading of Hemingway's work when they passed through the entrance hallway where the air force's strolling strings orchestra was playing dinner music. Ava Helen asked Jackie if it was proper to dance and was told no, but Eleanor Piel, an attorney and wife of *Scientific American* publisher Gerard Piel, took Pauling by the arm and began waltzing him around the marble-floored hall. Several other couples joined in the impromptu dance, a scene immortalized by a photographer from *Life* magazine. Talent, beauty, grace, and a breaking of old barriers— the Kennedy White House shone that night.

~~~

And Pauling got much of the attention. "This action of demonstrating outside the White House and then on the same day attending a dinner inside the White House attracted much attention," Pauling wrote Schweitzer. "I think that probably every newspaper in the United States made some mention of it, almost always favorable."

He was right about the attention he received but off-base about its nature. A number of commentators found it unseemly to break bread with the president after protesting his policies as harshly as Pauling had. One columnist called Pauling's actions "loony."

Even the sign Pauling carried when he picketed the White House led to a misunderstanding. The geneticist Hermann J. Muller, who had won the Nobel Prize for showing that x-rays increased the rate of genetic mutations—research essential to Pauling's arguments about the deleterious effects of bomb-test radiation—had been an important early backer of a test ban but more recently had joined Bethe and many others in moving to a regretful acceptance of the need to test. Muller made his pro-test views public in several magazine articles in May and June, telling readers that while radiation was dangerous, the threat of war with the USSR if the United States did not prove its toughness was far more so. Muller positioned himself as a moderate, criticizing Teller for underestimating the dangers of fallout and Pauling for advocating that the United States stop testing unilaterally. "Fortunately for America," he wrote, "President Kennedy doesn't lean toward either the Teller or Pauling sides."

Pauling was outraged. He wrote Muller, pointing out that he had never advocated unilateral U.S. action and had always promoted international treaties. He demanded an apology. Muller replied that he inferred Pauling's position based on the wire photo he'd seen in which Pauling's sign said that only Western leaders had no right to test. Correspondence between the two scientists continued in private and through the letters to the editors of the magazines where Muller's articles had appeared, until Muller, concluding, "Certainly, I think it would be foolish to continue this argument in public," publicly apologized.

Pauling had straightened the record, but again at a price. Muller was America's most respected geneticist; his careful work had demonstrated to a generation of followers that radiation causes mutations. Geneticists, in turn, had been among Pauling's strongest and most effective supporters in the fight against testing. Pauling's public argument with the even-tempered and thoughtful Muller—even though it was over politics, not science—eroded some of that support and added to the growing impression that Pauling was a crusader who had lost the ability to compromise.

This lessened appreciation among his peers was not pleasant, but to Pauling it was irrelevant. Instead of moderating his position, he helped organize another lawsuit against both the Soviet and U.S. governments to halt testing and began trying to build a coordinated world peace organization that would include both Communist and non-Communist activists. His one bow to public opinion was to make certain that he criticized the Soviet Union at least as much as he did the United States.

━━ーイイイー━━

But none of his efforts seemed to work. At the end of 1962 America was testing in the atmosphere again; the amount of radioactive pollution on earth according to Pauling's calculations had doubled in just over a year; Kennedy had risked nuclear war with his brinksmanship in the Cuban Missile Crisis; Pauling's most recent suit against the Department of Defense had been thrown out of court; he was squabbling with other peace workers; his libel cases were getting nowhere; his work for peace and an end to testing was marginalized, ignored, derided.

How had it all gone wrong?

The Molecular Clock

Pauling's work with the genetic effects of radiation had increased his interest in the whole process of mutation, especially given Teller's assertion that a little extra mutation might be good for evolution. The majority of mutations were, of course, deleterious—this was the basis of his argument against nuclear testing and fallout—but they also formed the steps through which organisms changed over time to adapt to their environment. How could negative mutations add up to positive evolution? Pauling thought about that. Many lower organisms, like bacteria, for instance, could live on the simplest of foodstuffs, synthesizing everything they needed from a single food source as simple as gelatin. Humans, however, had lost the ability to make everything they needed; they required a diet that provided a variety of vitamins and amino acids they could no longer synthesize. Somehow along the evolutionary track mutations had occurred that altered the enzymes needed to synthesize these substances. That would be deadly if there was no other option for getting the needed nutrients but was all right as long as the nutrients could be found in other foods.

And there was a positive side to the equation. The energy freed by no longer having to synthesize certain substances could be used for other metabolic reactions, thus making possible more complex organisms. What seemed at first like a "metabolic disease"—losing the ability to make a vitamin—could turn out to be a positive evolutionary move.

Evolution, then, could be seen as a molecular process, and Pauling put Emile Zuckerkandl, a French postdoctoral fellow, to work investigating it. The test molecule was to be Pauling's old favorite, hemoglobin. Zuckerkandl went to the San Diego Zoo and got blood from gorillas, chimpanzees, and rhesus monkeys. Then he collected more from horses, cows, cats, dogs, and fish. The idea was to track the evolution not of a species but of a molecule by comparing its size and structure in various animals.

The most striking discovery that resulted from this work, published in 1962, was that hemoglobin could be used as an evolutionary clock. A detailed study of horse hemoglobin, for instance, showed that it differed from the human form by about eighteen amino-acid substitutions in each of its four chains. When this was correlated with what paleontologists knew about the time when the human and horse lines diverged, it offered an average baseline value of about one evolutionarily effective mutation every 14.5 million years. Using that as a yardstick and comparing the hemoglobins of other animals, Pauling and Zuckerkandl estimated that man and gorillas—whose hemoglobins were much more similar—diverged over 11 million years ago, an estimate of divergence millions of years more recent than most researchers thought. Although Pauling recognized that important mutations might occur not at a steady state but in clusters, he concluded that "it will be possible, through the detailed determination of amino-acid sequences of hemoglobin molecules and of other molecules, to obtain much information about the course of the evolutionary process, and to illuminate the question of the origin of species."

Pauling and Zuckerkandl's basic idea of molecular evolution and the use of a biomolecule to track events in the past—a concept that now forms its own research subspecialty, with DNA replacing hemoglobin as the molecule of choice—was groundbreaking. As Alex Rich, Pauling's former student and nucleic-acid expert, put it, "At one stroke he united the fields of paleontology, evolutionary biology and molecular biology."

It also put him briefly at the forefront of the debate over eugenics. Pauling and Zuckerkandl's notions of molecular evolution, combined with Pauling's long history of research into such heritable diseases as sickle-cell anemia, led Pauling naturally to the question of eliminating harmful genes from the world population. In a number of speeches and several papers between 1959 and 1962, he strongly advocated preventing the passage of congenital abnormalities from one generation to the next. While he and Zuckerkandl opposed directed eugenics, in which people would use sperm banks to create children of whatever personality types were in vogue at the moment, they were in favor of another approach.

"The human race is deteriorating," he told one crowd. "We need to do something about it." That "something" involved the identification and control of carriers of defective genes. "No objection can be legitimately raised, it seems to us, against the ambition to eliminate from human heredity those genes that lead to clearly pathological manifestations and great human suffering," he and Zuckerkandl wrote. Carriers of the sickle-cell gene, for example, should be discouraged from marrying each other, and if only one partner carried it, they should have fewer children than average. The same went for PKU carriers and those of other molecular diseases. "Enterprise in love combined with blind ignorance," they wrote, should not be allowed to lead to a polluted gene pool. If voluntary action did not work, Pauling said, legal rules might have to be put in place.

This flirtation with eugenics was a reminder of what might happen if scientists really did run society. But it was a small side issue to Pauling, a subcategory of his greater interest in using molecules to track evolution.

To Pauling, the idea of the "molecular clock" was simply more proof of what he had been saying for forty years: Everything grew out of molecular structure. Chemistry, medicine, evolution, and brain function were matters of molecular structure. "The appearance of the concept of good and evil that was interpreted by Man as his painful expulsion from Paradise probably was a molecular disease that turned out to be evolution," he said. There was no reason to invoke superstition or "élan vital" or religious dogma to explain life. "Life," he wrote in 1962, "is a relationship between molecules."

Space Wars

Pauling was operating on a level that Ernest Swift cared little about. What Swift cared about as director of the Caltech Division of Chemistry and Chemical Engineering was that Pauling was rarely there to teach his classes, take part in administrative duties, or oversee his laboratories. He was always off in another part of the world making trouble about nuclear testing and writing inflammatory telegrams to the president. Swift would walk the halls and peer into Pauling's research suites and raise an eyebrow at what he saw there: medical doctors running around with tubes of urine and gorilla blood, biochemists giving knockout drops to goldfish.

Under Swift's guidance, the chemistry division was changing, and Pauling's people did not fit in. "Some of them," he suggested, "were not of the caliber and their projects were not of the nature that we would normally welcome." Corey was a good researcher, as were Schomaker and a few others from Pauling's earlier days. "But there were others," Swift said, "particularly those doing more medical or biochemical things, that were problems."

Swift was hiring more orthodox chemists, and he was short on space. Pauling's labs in Church were the most likely target for expansion—some of them seemed half empty, after all—and there was agreement among most of the division members that some should be offered to more productive researchers. But Swift would not confront Pauling. Despite his feelings about what was right for the division, he had served under him for too many years and seen him achieve too much to reward him at the end of his career by stripping him of his laboratory facilities. "[Swift] was terribly distressed about it and hated to push Pauling around," DuBridge remembered. He retired in early 1963 and left the problem to his successor.

Jack Roberts, a talented organic chemist, took the reins of the division. He was relatively young, did not much care about Pauling's political work one way or another, had a history of independent thinking, and, in his new role, was eager to prove himself to the Caltech president and board of trustees. If more space was needed, as Swift and DuBridge claimed, he would provide it. One of the first things Roberts did as chair was to meet with Pauling and explain to him the needs of the division. He remembered that Pauling, while not happy with the conversation, civilly agreed to reduce his space.

Pauling's memories were more detailed. Roberts, he said, told him, "This medical stuff is out of place," demanded that he stop the mental disease project within two months, and insisted that he give up half his lab space. Pauling, unwilling to fire research people on such short notice, countered with a proposal to give up his own office and gradually phase out the anesthesia work. The dispute went to an appropriate chemistry division committee, which brokered a compromise in which Pauling gave up a smaller amount of space.

It was a nasty incident and an indication of just how badly Pauling's relationship with his own division had deteriorated. "Pauling just choked at this," DuBridge remembered. "This, he thought was the ultimate insult—to ask him to give up his research space."

It was a new era at Caltech, a time when the stars again were physicists, for example, Richard Feynman and Murray Gell-Mann, a period marked by a relative decline in chemistry. The men of Pauling's era were disappearing; an especially deep loss was that of his old friend and grand plan coconspirator George Beadle, who left in 1961 to become chancellor of the University of Chicago—a decision made easier, Beadle would later say, because of how badly Caltech treated Pauling. Although the division of biology, with Delbrück still around, remained close to and impressed by Pauling's research, it now seemed that the rest of Caltech had forgotten what he had done for it. But Pauling continued to hold his tongue about internal policy decisions at his school. He gave up the space he controlled in the lab he had built and did not say a negative word in public about any of it.

Privately, he decided it was time to leave Caltech. This was not an entirely new notion; he had been thinking about it ever since DuBridge had bounced him out of the chairmanship five years earlier. In 1960 he had considered starting a private West Coast institute similar to Princeton's Institute for Advanced Studies, even looked at sites for it near Monterey, but he had given up on the idea when it became clear how much money it would take. Early the next year he explored the idea of joining the staff of Stanford's Hopkins Marine Station at Pacific Grove, then in the fall of 1961 seriously considered joining the University of California Medical School in San Francisco as a lecturer in the Department of Pharmacology. That, too, fell by the wayside as Pauling threw himself into peace work.

But after the raid on his lab space, Pauling began looking in earnest. He wrote Warren Weaver, now head of the Sloan Foundation, asking if there was any chance of grant money to pay his salary for five years so he could relocate. (There was not.) He talked with Chester Carlson, the Xerox inventor who had given money for the Oslo Conference, and asked for private support. He hoped to arrange things so that he could leave Caltech by the summer of 1964 and pursue his research independently.

It was not easy to think of leaving the place in which he had spent his entire professional life, to consider ending a relationship that had spanned more than forty years. But it was something he now felt he had to do.

⁓

Then came great and unexpected news on the test-ban front. The United States and the USSR, both sobered by the events of the Cuban Missile Crisis, began talking seriously. On June 10, 1963, Kennedy announced that the United States would stop conducting atmospheric tests as a sign of support for the ongoing Geneva talks. A few weeks later, Khrushchev sent a countersignal, announcing Soviet approval of the idea of a partial test ban, one that would get around the thorny issue of detecting underground blasts by exempting them from the ban.

Suddenly, in the summer of 1963, everything began moving quickly. By allowing underground tests, a number of Soviet objections were removed at a stroke. Both sides would have the option of continuing to develop nuclear weapons while at the same time preventing fallout.

On August 5, after five years of negotiation, the United States and the USSR signed a treaty to ban all tests of nuclear weapons in the atmosphere, in outer space, and under the sea. This first significant weapons-limitation treaty of the Cold War period was "a shaft of light," as Kennedy put it, an end to the era of bomb-test fallout and a good omen for future negotiations. It was ratified by the U.S. Senate on September 24 and signed by the president on October 7.

Everyone was in favor—even, with some reservations, Pauling. "We are very happy about the ratification of the bomb-test treaty by the United States Senate," Pauling wrote Schweitzer. It was not perfect—underground testing allowed the arms race to continue—but it did stop the dangers of fallout. It would not end war, but it was a step, an important first step, in the right direction.

⁓

In early October the Paulings returned home from a long South American trip: they had been greeted like foreign diplomats by the presidents of several nations. Clifford and Virginia Durr, peace and civil rights activists from Virginia, were visiting and giving lectures and talks in California, and the Paulings invited them to their Deer Flat Ranch in Big Sur for a short visit. In the small cabin, sitting around a rough table in front of the stove, the four raised their glasses in a dinner toast: The bomb-test treaty had gone into effect that day, October 10.

The next morning, as they were eating breakfast, they were surprised by a knock at the door. It wasn't often that anyone made it to the ranch, especially that early in the morning. It was a forest ranger from the nearby Salmon Creek station, who said that the Paulings' daughter had called—the ranch still had no telephone—and asked that he fetch Pauling to call her back. Pauling, thinking there was some sort of emergency, was ready to leave without finishing his meal, but the ranger assured him that it wasn't that serious. After the Paulings and Durrs finished their breakfast, Linus and Ava Helen walked the mile up the hill and down the road to the ranger station.

When they finally got Linda on the line, she said, "Daddy, have you heard the news?"

"No," Pauling said. "What news?"

Linda's voice rose on the other end of the line. "You've been awarded the Nobel Peace Prize!"

Pauling held the receiver in his hand without saying anything. Then he handed it to his wife.

For perhaps the first time in his life, he was speechless.

Nomads

The Peacenik Prize

Pauling found his voice. As media calls inundated the tiny ranger station, he was told what had happened: The Norwegian Parliament's Nobel Prize Committee had made an unprecedented announcement the day the limited-test-ban treaty went into effect. Two Nobel Peace Prizes were being awarded: one to Linus Pauling, for the previous year, 1962—a year in which, without explanation, the committee awarded no Peace Prize—and the 1963 prize to the International Red Cross.

The news caught Pauling completely off guard. He spent four hours expressing amazement to the reporters from around the world who managed to get through to the station. He was pleased, he said again and again, that his work for peace had been so honored. During one interview, a strange voice broke in and exclaimed, "God bless you, Dr. Pauling!" The abashed ranger explained that they were on a party line and that people up and down that stretch of coast were probably sharing vicariously in the excitement.

An American winning the Nobel Peace Prize was not unheard of— George C. Marshall and Ralph Bunche had won during the fifties— but it was rare enough to make big news, and by the time Pauling had hung up the phone and returned to his cabin, the media circus had started in earnest. Reporters and photographers, flying into small airstrips in Monterey and at the Hearst Castle in San Simeon, descended on the remote ranch in rented cars. The Paulings decided that they had better drive back to Pasadena.

They arrived to find reporters setting up camp in Ava Helen's garden, television cameras whirring and flashbulbs popping, telegrams arriving by the score, the phone ringing nonstop. Pauling held a short news conference in which he thanked the Nobel Committee and offered his opinion that the award might now make it respectable to work for peace in the United States. Then they pushed out the reporters and tried to come back to earth.

Pauling was jubilant. For years he had been snubbed, maligned, and pressured because of his peace work. Now he was vindicated. How could anyone say he had been misguided when the world recognized the value of his efforts in this way? As he and Ava Helen talked about it, he realized something else: No one in history had ever won two unshared Nobel Prizes. Ava Helen was quick to point out that Marie Curie had also won two, but Pauling noted that she had shared one of hers. His were solo.

At least they were solo technically. Pauling certainly agreed with a number of congratulatory notes that mentioned that Ava Helen should have been a cowinner, and she herself was not shy about sharing in the glory. "We think of this honor as an indication of the rightness of our position during these many years," Ava Helen wrote a friend, gently alluding to her own role in Pauling's political activism. "You know, of course, my husband would have preferred to have remained quietly in his laboratory thinking about his scientific problems. However, people are more important than scientific truths. . . ." In every public statement Pauling made about the prize, he was also careful to say that it should be seen as a recognition of the work of Bertrand Russell and the efforts of antibomb peace workers throughout the world.

But when all was said and done, the prize was his, and it meant more to Pauling than any of the many other awards he had ever won. "I got the Nobel Prize in chemistry just because I had been doing something that I liked to do and could do pretty effectively . . . and having a good time. I was doing what I would have preferred to do if I could have done anything at all in the whole world, and to get the Nobel Prize for doing something you like to do, well, it's nice, but as I say, I would have done it anyway," he told an interviewer. On the other hand, "I gave over 500 public lectures about radioactive fallout and nuclear war and the need for stopping the bomb tests in the atmosphere and the need for eliminating war ultimately. You know, I didn't enjoy giving these lectures. . . . I was doing something that I didn't care to do very much, except for reasons of morality and conviction. I sort of got pushed into this. . . . So when I received word in 1963 that I had been given the Nobel Prize, I felt that that showed that the sacrifice that I had made was worthwhile."

_ᵐᵐ_

The Nobel Peace Prize expanded Pauling's options. The monetary award was fifty thousand dollars—three years' worth of Caltech salary—and he and Ava Helen immediately started planning how it could be used to build a new, modern home to replace the old cabin at Deer Flat Ranch.

It also solidified his decision to leave Caltech.

The morning Pauling returned to Pasadena, the local paper carried DuBridge's reaction to the latest honor for his brilliant and troublesome professor: "The Nobel Peace Prize is a spectacular recognition of Dr. Pauling's long and strenuous efforts to bring before the people of the world the dangers of nuclear war and the importance of a test ban agreement," the Caltech president said. But then he made the mistake of adding, "Though many people have disapproved of some of his methods and activities, he has, nevertheless, made a substantial impact on world opinion, as this award clearly proves."

Pauling was looking for reasons to leave Caltech, and DuBridge's statement provided him with a decisive one. In Pauling's mind, he had just lifted Caltech to a new height of international fame by making it home to the only living double Nobelist. DuBridge's response was to emphasize that many people thought his "methods and activities" were wrong. There was no word of personal congratulations, no indication of institutional pride. When Ava Helen read the statement, she was furious, and Linda phoned the president's office "in high dudgeon," to excoriate DuBridge for his treatment of her father.

Elsewhere at Caltech the response was mixed. Pauling's research group was overjoyed, decorating his office with placards—"Pauling Puts Pace in the Peace Race"—and crowding around with champagne, cake, and congratulations. An especially poignant moment came when Corey, who knew better than anyone what Pauling's commitment to peace had cost him in scientific terms, walked into Pauling's office and gave him a silent embrace.

But the rest of the chemistry division and the Caltech administration were strangely quiet. Congratulations were few and perfunctory, and there was no indication of any plan for a celebration of any sort.

The public reaction to Pauling's prize was also deeply split. The small papers of the left-wing press and a few big papers, most notably the *Washington Post*, were congratulatory, but most of the mainstream media—generally slavish in its adulation of new Nobelists—was unusually critical. If anyone deserved the prize, the editorial argument went, it was Kennedy, whose tough stand during the Cuban Missile Crisis had put the Soviets on notice that they'd better negotiate. Kennedy had achieved peace the way Americans liked: by staring down an adversary. Pauling, by contrast, was an appeaser, a "placarding peacenik," as the *New York Herald-Tribune* put it. The *Chicago Tribune* and the *Wall Street Journal* said that Pauling's prize was really a reward for the U.S. pro-Communist movement. The Luce magazines were especially harsh, with *Time* using the occasion of the award as an excuse to once again list Pauling's record of Communist-front associations and *Life* titling its editorial about the award "A Weird Insult from Norway." The *Life* piece was unprecedented in its viciousness: "However distinguished as a chemist, the eccentric Dr. Pauling and his weird politics have never been taken seriously by American opinion." It concluded that the award was "an extraordinary insult to America." Instead of basking in adulation, Pauling found himself a few days after the prize announcement writing Henry Luce "to express my indignation, and my contempt for your magazine."

As a former president of the American Chemical Society (ACS), he expected that the organization would congratulate him, but he was disappointed here as well. The ACS magazine snubbed him, virtually ignoring his prize, running only a single paragraph about it buried in the back pages of one issue.

This chorus of disapproval was surprising to Pauling, and hurtful. As usual, however, he swallowed his emotional response and moved briskly ahead as though it did not matter.

But it did matter, deeply. The unexpectedness of the prize, followed quickly by his disappointment at how it was received both nationally and at Caltech, upset Pauling. He reacted quickly, rashly, and in ways that would change the course of his life.

On October 18, exactly one week after learning he had won the Nobel Peace Prize, Pauling held a press conference in the living room of his Sierra Madre house. As cameras whirred and clicked, he read a prepared statement. He was taking a leave of absence from Caltech, he said, to take a position at the Center for the Study of Democratic Institutions (CSDI), a Santa Barbara–based think tank devoted to studying political and social issues. In answer to questions, Pauling insisted that there was "no rift" between him and Caltech; the decision to move on, he said, reflected a change in his personal priorities and had been planned before the prize. He cut the questions short and ushered out the press.

The brief public statement covered a great deal of pain.

A few days earlier, just after the DuBridge statement hit the press, Pauling notified chemistry division head Jack Roberts that he was planning to leave Caltech permanently—"Not without regret," he wrote Roberts, "after more than 41 years that I have spent as a staff member"—and Roberts had taken the news to DuBridge. Over the next few days there were some muddled attempts at negotiating the terms of Pauling's departure—at one point it looked as if Pauling were hoping DuBridge would try to talk him out of leaving—but DuBridge was not in a negotiating mood. He was about to have a thorn removed, and it is likely he did not want to delay the process.

Outside of his family and a few administrators, Pauling's press conference surprised everyone at Caltech. Most of the chemistry division, including people who had worked with Pauling for forty years, learned he was leaving from the newspapers. A series of quick meetings ensued as Pauling assured the staff working on his projects that they would be taken care of, that he had arranged for them to carry on at Caltech until his grants ran out.

And then, suddenly, he was gone.

Most of the faculty were stunned. DeBridge forged ahead as though Pauling had never been there, giving nothing more than a perfunctory institutional response of regret to Pauling's announcement. After a few weeks, Max Delbrück and his colleagues in the biology division—scientists who understood the value of Pauling's recent research and had supported his antitesting work—lured him back to attend a small party in honor of the Nobel Peace Prize in the patio between the Kerckhoff and Church laboratories. It was not much compared to the grand jubilee that had accompanied Pauling's first Nobel. Many biologists showed up; a number of chemists did not. Everyone put on a happy face. But the afternoon was tinged with a feeling of sadness and loss, for Pauling and for Caltech.

—*m*—

A few weeks after he quit Caltech, as Pauling was making arrangements to move to Santa Barbara, he told the ACS that he was quitting that organization as well.

In spite of the media disapproval—perhaps because of it—he was famous now, able to make a life outside of chemistry. The Associated Press voted him 1963's top newsmaker in science, and peace activists were encouraging him to run for president or at least senator from California.

He made sure that he stayed in the headlines, stealing the show at the Washington, D.C., centenary celebration of the National Academy of Sciences in late October by attacking President Kennedy's recently announced plan to send a man to the moon. Pauling called the moon project "pitiful" and said that the same amount of money needed to answer one question about the moon could answer a thousand important questions about the human body. His remarks, quoted on the front page of the *Washington Post*, threatened to overshadow the NAS's centennial, and the group's president, Frederick Seitz, felt compelled to snatch Pauling away from a group of reporters the next day, haul him into an empty room, and explain to him the importance of avoiding attacks on the administration during an event that was designed to highlight scientific achievements. Pauling agreed to quiet down for the good of the NAS. When they emerged, a reporter asked, "Did Dr. Seitz spank you?" Pauling looked at him for a moment, smiled, and asked, "Who can spank me?"

People could encourage him to do things, but no one could tell him what to do. At age sixty-two, Pauling was quitting the job he had held for four decades, giving up the laboratories he had designed and built, resigning from the professional society he had once headed, and starting over.

That was the way he looked at it. But to many it would seem

that Pauling had cut his moorings and would spend the next decade adrift.

Oslo Again

The rest of 1963 was busy. Ava Helen went house hunting in Santa Barbara, eventually finding a small place with a beautiful garden that suited her on Hot Springs Road in the exclusive area of Montecito, and began to make moving plans. It was decided that the Pasadena house, rather than being sold on the market, would go to Linda and Barclay Kamb. Ava Helen and Pauling were also talking with an architect about a new house at Deer Flat Ranch and making arrangements for a December trip to Norway for the Nobel ceremonies.

Everything came to a halt for several days in late November when the Paulings, along with the rest of the nation, learned that President Kennedy had been assassinated. Despite Pauling's public differences of opinion with Kennedy regarding international policy, he had been impressed by the young president's sense of style, his panache in inviting Pauling to the White House, his ability to treat Pauling graciously despite their differences. "I liked Kennedy," Pauling would later say, "even though I quarreled with him." During the next several months, in every speech he gave about peace throughout the world, Pauling went out of his way to praise Kennedy's role in the adoption of the test-ban treaty.

〜〜〜

Kennedy's assassination had a direct effect on Pauling when he arrived in Oslo. A crowd of reporters and Nobel Committee officials met the Paulings as they debarked from the plane, but there was no official American delegation. The excuse was that the embassy was in mourning for the president, but it was the first time anyone could remember that the representatives of a Nobel Peace Prize winner's nation had not greeted their honored citizen upon their arrival in Norway. The head of the Nobel Committee, Gunnar Jahn, was outraged. Pauling shrugged it off as more Cold War posturing by the State Department; he was used to that.

All four of Pauling's children and his grandson Linus III joined him to enjoy three days of parties, torchlight parades, and speeches as Pauling beamed in the middle of all the attention.

The prize was awarded before a large crowd in the Festival Hall of the University of Oslo. In a brief acceptance address, Pauling credited the work of Einstein, Russell, and "thousands of others" who had labored for peace. He ended by sharing his prize with one special worker for justice: Ava Helen. "In the fight for peace and against oppression, she has been my constant and courageous companion and coworker," he told the crowd. "On her behalf, as well as my own, I express my thanks."

Instead of returning home after the festivities, the Paulings toured Scandinavia again, spending Christmas with friends in Oslo, enjoying the snowy countryside of Sweden and Norway, then celebrating New Year's in Copenhagen. In early January they flew back to New York. By then the world community of peace activists had had time to organize a tribute for Pauling, sponsored by Bertrand Russell, Norman Cousins, Albert Schweitzer, and a dozen other luminaries, held at the Grand Ballroom of the Commodore Hotel. Three thousand people, including the ambassadors from Hungary, Ceylon, Czechoslovakia, Poland, and Indonesia and official representatives from Canada, Algeria, Brazil, the USSR, Israel, India, and Norway, jammed into the room to hear the historian Henry Steele Commager compare Pauling to the ancient citizens of Athens. The Athenians, he said, like Pauling, "knew the secret of happiness to be freedom and the secret of freedom to be a brave heart." Pauling capped the evening with a version of his Nobel address. At the end he was given a prolonged standing ovation.

It was a wonderful occasion, but a tiring one after their travels. Pauling was behaving as though he had the energy of a young man—he had committed himself to a strenuous series of lectures in the East after the tribute—but all of the activity and the stresses of the changes in his life started to take their toll. A blizzard hit New York, forcing the Paulings to walk on one occasion more than a mile through the snow to get back to their hotel, and both of them fell ill with colds. By the time they finished their lecture tour—met everywhere, they were happy to see, by large and enthusiastic crowds—the colds had turned into severe sinus infections.

They were ill and exhausted by the time they returned to California in February. Then they began the process of uprooting themselves, moving their household, and starting a new life.

Santa Barbara

"Terribly busy," Ava Helen wrote a friend in the summer of 1964. "We have attempted too much in too short a time. Moreover, our move to Santa Barbara was much more of a task than we anticipated." Linda and Barclay had moved into the Sierra Madre house before Ava Helen had finished moving out, resulting in a bedlam of grandchildren, packing boxes, telephone calls, and moving men. It was a task to shoehorn all of Pauling's books and their personal effects into the smaller Santa Barbara house. At the same time, they were finishing plans for the new house at the ranch, lecturing widely, and trying to get settled in a new town.

When all the Nobel hubbub settled down, the Paulings found that Santa Barbara was a disappointment. It was hard to find the sort of liberal support group they had developed in Los Angeles, and as cosmopolitan as they now were, they began to feel a bit stifled by the small-town feeling. "It seems rather an out-of-the-way place," Ava Helen wrote a friend, "and we miss all of our friends."

The Center for the Study of Democratic Institutions was also not what Pauling had imagined. An outgrowth of the Ford Foundation's Fund for the Republic, it had been established "to promote the principles of individual liberty expressed in the Declaration of Independence and the Constitution of the United States." This vague charter was carried out through a series of symposia, publications, and conferences.

In other words, there was a great deal of talk. Pauling had been attracted to the Center for the Study of Democratic Institutions because it was led by Robert Hutchins, the former head of the University of Chicago, a leading liberal and a man Pauling respected, and he had hoped to use the center and its brainpower to put together, finally, what he had been pursuing for years: a scientifically based ethical system that could be used to answer political and social questions the way scientists answered questions about the natural world. He noted to himself: "I suggest a program of (1) Analyzing the world problem; (2) Deciding on some basic questions or possible axioms; (3) Discussing them, and approving or rejecting them (those approved would constitute a system of ethics); (4) Then using them to reach, one by one, a series of theorems, conclusions about the world that would have to be accepted."

This was grand, optimistic, naive thinking. And it would never come to fruition at the CSDI. Soon after arriving in Santa Barbara, Ava Helen became concerned that her husband would find the Center "altogether too superficial. Hutchins is a brilliant and witty person," she wrote, "but I think he is rather superficial himself. He gives the impression of thinking that almost anything can be solved if one is just witty enough."

After a few months, Pauling was agreeing with his wife. Talking things over was fine as long as it was a means toward an end. But at the CSDI there were endless rounds of discussion and nothing but discussion. "My complaint about the Center," he noted, "is that the great amount of talk leads to little in the way of accepted conclusions."

In addition to political work, Pauling had planned to continue some scientific studies as well. But the CSDI had neither laboratory facilities nor a history of supporting science, points that became important when Pauling applied for grant funding. The National Science Foundation (NSF), for instance, delayed one of Pauling's grant requests in 1964 because he had no laboratory; his affiliation with the center made no sense in scientific terms. When the NSF asked Oppenheimer's opinion, he replied that while Pauling was brilliant, "the institutional arrangements proposed seem idiotic."

So Pauling began looking elsewhere. For a time it looked as if the University of California at Santa Barbara (UCSB) might work out; one of Pauling's former students, Fred Wall, had just been named head of the department of chemistry there and was thrilled with the idea of snagging a Nobelist, even part-time. Wall quickly offered Pauling an adjunct appointment and sent what he thought would be a routine recommendation up the administrative ladder for approval.

He was shocked when the UCSB chancellor rejected it. It appeared, he told Pauling with embarrassment, that Pauling's political activities had made him too controversial to work at Santa Barbara. Pauling immediately went at it with the chancellor via telephone and letter, and the issue eventually went to UC system head Clark Kerr for resolution. As Wall remembers it, a few of Kerr's trustees—perhaps remembering how Pauling had taken on the system during the loyalty-oath controversy—said they would allow Pauling to become a teacher in the UC system only over their dead bodies. The chancellor's decision held.

Pauling told Fred Wall that he would never set foot on the UCSB campus again.

Santa Barbara was not turning out well.

ᴀᴀᴀ

But Pauling was less a citizen of Santa Barbara than he was a citizen of the world. In 1964 he and Ava Helen traveled on peace tours to Mexico, England, France, Germany, and Australia. Ava Helen, now a well-known peace activist in her own right, went on a solo trip to a Women Strike for Peace meeting in The Hague. At the airport she was delayed and eventually denied entrance to the country because "they did not want demonstrators," as one official told her. It took calls to Pauling in the United States, then his calls to the Dutch embassy in Washington, D.C., before the situation was corrected and she was admitted.

At home, they both threw themselves into a variety of projects. Pauling spent time working on an ambitious CSDI-supported project called "The Triple Revolution," a liberal proposal to change American society in response to recent advances in weaponry, automation, and human rights. When published, the ideas—including a guaranteed wage for all Americans and massive public investments in rapid transit, education, and low-cost housing—were either attacked as the work of "leftwingers, socialists, pacifists, and far-out economic theorists," or, more commonly, ignored. It was another example of the failure of the CSDI method.

In their spare time, the Paulings tried unsuccessfully to arrange a tour of Cuba, pored over everything they could find about the Kennedy assassination—the evidence convinced Pauling that the killing was organized by a cabal of Texas industrialists, right-wingers, and pro-Johnson supporters—and spent increasing amounts of time studying and speaking about a new issue: Vietnam.

"I am not quite sure why we decided to do all of this at once, but I suppose we thought we could do five times more than people usually attempt to do," Ava Helen wrote. "I am not sure this is correct, however." Her letters from this period refer constantly to her worries about the amount of stress in their lives, the way that Pauling was working himself to death, and their pessimism over Republican Barry Goldwater's presidential candidacy. "Everything is fine here," Ava Helen wrote, "except that the fascists get braver all the time. . . . Perhaps the name of the Center should be 'The Center for the Study of the Malfunctioning of the Democratic Institutions of the United States.'"

The only bright spot came during the 1964 election. Not because Johnson won—"Those people who say LBJ is President but Goldwater won the election have some truth," Ava Helen wrote—but because Pauling received more than twenty-five hundred write-in votes for governor of California.

~

The next two years were not happy ones. Pauling spent a decreasing fraction of his time at the CSDI and an increasing portion traveling and working on his own. The Vietnam War had now replaced the test-ban issue as their primary focus. Pauling deplored the war as both un-constitutional—Johnson was waging war, he argued, without a declara-tion from Congress—and unnecessary. He made a strong public attack on U.S. policy in February 1965 at a CSDI-sponsored event in New York called Pacem in Terris and followed it with an appeal to world leaders, signed by eight of the ten living Peace Nobelists, to sup-port a political settlement starting with an immediate cease-fire. Paul-ing sent his Vietnam Appeal to a slate of world leaders, then tried to play peacemaker by forwarding Ho Chi Minh's response to LBJ. His ef-forts were ignored by the White House.

His only scientific tools now a pencil, paper, and slide rule, Pauling turned in the summer of 1965 to pure physics, working on a new the-ory of the structure of atomic nuclei. Here again, he took on the task from the viewpoint of an atomic architect. The result, which he called the "close-packed spheron theory," described the nucleus in the same way he described the structure of crystals, as an aggregate of particles that logically assumed a certain form because of size and charge con-siderations. It was his attempt to do for nuclear physics what Pauling's rules had done for crystallography in the 1920s. It was an interesting simplification of existing theories, but it did not really break much new theoretical ground and received only modest interest from physi-cists when it was unveiled at the NAS meeting in the fall of 1965.

By the time he celebrated his sixty-fifth birthday in February 1966, Pauling was increasingly restless and unfocused. He had no research group, no definitive scientific problem to work on, no absorbing polit-ical fight to which to devote himself.

There were fights, however, that he had started in other areas, no-tably the courtrooms hearing his lawsuits. Some had died a natural death during the preceding years. The second suit he had helped initi-ate against the Department of Defense, for instance, had gone all the way to the Supreme Court, which finally made it clear in mid-1964 that the plaintiffs had no standing to sue.

Libel suits, however, were still absorbing Pauling's time and money. Two of the suits he had initiated against the Bellingham paper and the Hearst syndicate had been settled out of court for a fraction of what Pauling had sought—he received around thirty-five thousand dollars instead of more than $1 million. Two other papers, the St. Louis *Globe-Democrat* and the New York *Daily News,* decided to battle him in court. The cases, which took years to prepare, finally were argued in lengthy jury trials. Both were decided in the newspapers' favor.

Pauling appealed both decisions, setting off more months of talking to lawyers, providing depositions, and rounding up character witnesses. The strain on Pauling, Ava Helen, and their friends—some of whom began to balk at the time and trouble it took to fly across the country to repeatedly testify that Pauling was a great scientist and no Communist as far as they could see—was considerable. The *Daily News* case did not end until 1965, when the U.S. Supreme Court refused to review the decision against Pauling; the *Globe-Democrat* suit wound its agonizing way through the courts until 1966, when it was definitively settled in the newspaper's favor.

But Pauling's suits—and threats of suits—had some effect. He often got corrections or retractions printed by simply holding the threat of a suit over the heads of publishers. Despite his failures in court, Pauling was now known to publishers and editors as someone who would spend a great deal of time and money pursuing them legally if they used the wrong words to describe him. As a result of his litigiousness the major media became slightly more careful in their descriptions of his political work.

And Pauling kept on suing. In 1963 he engaged a Reno lawyer to sue *Nevadans on Guard,* a tiny anti-Communist newsletter, for raising the old Budenz accusations of being a concealed Communist in an article following his Nobel Peace Prize. And in 1966, after years of pretrial preparation, Pauling went to court with his smartest, toughest adversary yet: William F. Buckley.

Buckley, Sullivan, and "The Collaborators"

Buckley had made a career out of needling liberals and their policies. His upstart conservative journal of opinion, the *National Review,* showed that conservatism could be fun: It was witty, biting, and full of ideas. Although the magazine reached only a small readership (even in the mid-1960s it had a paid circulation base of about 100,000), Buckley's influence was far greater: His ability to handle himself in public, his Yale-influenced patrician acerbity, and his ability to demolish opponents in debates had by the early 1960s made him into a leading spokesman for the right.

Pauling had been a favorite target of the *National Review* since 1957, when the editors termed him an "old-hand fellow traveler" for his activity in pulling together the first antitesting petition. At various times during the next five years, the journal lampooned Pauling's use of "genetic hocus-pocus" in arguing for a test ban, saying that his estimation of risk was "grotesquely exaggerated" and that he was a man "in the clutch of an irrational obsession" who was "the spokesman for a fraud and a lie."

Pauling ignored it all, until he read a July 1962 *National Review* editorial entitled "The Collaborators." It lumped Pauling with other activists the editors considered to be espousing a pro-Communist line, calling him "a megaphone for Soviet policy" and someone who had for years "given his name, energy, voice and pen to one after another Soviet-serving enterprise."

It was no worse than what the *National Review* had been saying for years. But Pauling's reaction changed. During the summer of 1962, in the months following his picketing the White House, Pauling was being increasingly marginalized within the peace movement as an intemperate crusader whose zeal for a test ban had gone too far. His reaction to Buckley's needling may have arisen from a sense of frustration coupled with opportunity: In 1962, his other libel suits seemed to be going well, and going to the courts appeared to be an effective way of shutting up inaccurate reports about his activities.

In August 1962, William F. Buckley received a letter from Michael Levi Matar, Pauling's lawyer in New York, informing him that if a correction and apology were not forthcoming for the statements in "The Collaborators," Pauling would bring suit for this "vicious libel." Buckley referred the letter to the magazine's publisher, William Rusher, who replied that "Dr. Pauling is in error if he believes that the *National Review* bears him malice. No one at the *National Review* knows Dr. Pauling or has even met him." The magazine would be happy, Rusher said, to correct any factual inaccuracy. A few weeks later the *National Review* published a short editorial, "Are You Being Sued by Linus Pauling?" noting that Pauling, "brandishing his lawyers . . . seems to be spending his time equally between pressing for a collaborationist foreign policy, and assailing those who oppose his views. . . ." Lest there be any doubt about the magazine's stand, the editorial ended by chastising those papers that had settled with Pauling out of court, saying they "may simply have been too pusillanimous to fight back against what some will view as brazen attempts at intimidation of the free press by one of the nation's leading fellow-travelers."

The gauntlet thrown, lawyers on both sides began preparing, and on January 17, 1963, Pauling's suit was filed: He was asking $1 million for the reckless and malicious damage done to his good reputation by Buckley, Rusher, and the editorial's author, *National Review* senior editor James Burnham.

In public, Buckley responded with bravado. "The *National Review* is prepared to defend its opinions, and its right to give them, against the harassments of any man," a *National Review* editorial read when the case became public. "It certainly will not be intimidated by a litigious publicist who, in the sober words of a Senate subcommittee, 'had over a period of many years, evinced a general readiness to collaborate with Communists.'"

Internally, however, there was concern. At that point, Pauling's batting average on suits was good: He had settled out of court in two cases and had forced retractions and corrections in several others. He had not yet lost a case. And the *National Review* was operating on a shoestring. Anything approaching a million-dollar judgment would put the magazine out of business. The legal costs alone were problematic.

But after careful reviewing what had been written about Pauling, the decision was made to tough it out. After meetings with Rusher and Burnham, Buckley felt reassured that calling Pauling a fellow traveler, based on his record, was "akin to identifying Harry Truman as a Democrat." If Pauling wanted to argue the point, he was in for a fight with a group of men adept at argument.

The lawyers jockeyed over technicalities for months. By the time Pauling was finally to be deposed in the case, the Nobel Peace Prize had been announced—bad news for Buckley's side—and he delayed his appearance before the lawyers in New York until his return from Oslo in early 1964. Legal preparations continued for months more, with both sides becoming so frustrated in their attempts to obtain background documentation from the other that a referee was finally appointed in 1965 to sort it all out.

The delay worked to the *National Review*'s advantage. In 1964, a landmark libel case called *New York Times v. Sullivan* was decided by the

U.S. Supreme Court, setting into effect a fundamental shift in U.S. libel law. In order to protect robust public debate, the judges in the *Sullivan* case reasoned, politicians and other public figures should be subject to a different standard of libel than their private counterparts. It should no longer be considered libelous for a newspaper to call one candidate in an electoral race a "nincompoop," for instance—a statement that might be considered libelous if leveled at a private citizen— unless it could be shown that the paper did so with "actual malice," defined as knowledge of the falsity of the statement or reckless disregard of the truth.

The *Sullivan* decision made it much more difficult for politicians to win libel cases. But it left open the question of how far it could be extended beyond the electoral realm, to public figures such as entertainers and lobbyists or activists like Pauling.

Because of their timing and Pauling's stature, his libel suits—especially the *National Reivew* case—would help define the limits of the *Sullivan* ruling. After *Sullivan* was decided, the *National Review* lawyers immediately began arguing that it dictated a dismissal of the Pauling suit. The judge was not sure that Pauling qualified as a public figure and denied their request. Then, in the fall of 1965, Buckley ran for mayor of New York City, and the case was delayed again as he argued for a change of venue, saying that he could not get a fair trial in Manhattan because of the "invidious" press coverage of his campaign. More delay followed as the magazine tried to consolidate the Pauling case with another libel suit it was fighting. That, too, ended in failure.

By the time the case came before a jury in March 1966, everyone involved was tired of it—a feeling that would intensify as the arguments dragged out over the next six weeks. Pauling's lawyers, led by Matar, were meticulous to a point that threatened to alienate the judge in the case, Samuel J. Silverman. They took days to establish that Pauling had a good reputation to start with, even calling Ava Helen to the stand with a suitcase full of scrolls and medals—including Pauling's Nobel medals—that Matar passed to the judge and jurors. Each and every one of his many accomplishments, including his twenty-five or so honorary degrees, was read into the record. Pauling himself took the stand for ten hours, always looking straight at the jury when testifying about his background, his achievements, and his politics. "I never associated with organizations that had members I knew or even suspected of being dedicated to Communism," he said. "I have no knowledge of or interest in Marxism myself." He testified that the *National Review* editorials might well have affected his income, as he received no raise at Caltech in 1962 and his book income had been down slightly. He testified that he had been given a cold shoulder by the president of Caltech and others on campus, that the editorials had resulted in a loss of self-confidence.

The *National Review* lawyers were equally painstaking in their presentation, taking days to review in numbing detail Pauling's history of left-wing associations and the results of various congressional inquiries. They showed that Pauling's overall income had not decreased in the past few years; including his prize money, it had increased. Pauling's attorneys bogged down the testimony with so many objections that Silverman lost patience. "If the jury should happen to hear both sides say they rest," the weary judge said after four weeks of testimony, "remember it's April first."

Two more weeks went by before Judge Silverman had had enough. When the *National Review* team made a new motion for dismissal based on the *Sullivan* ruling, Silverman shocked the Pauling side by ruling in their favor. He had now heard enough, he said, to decide both that Pauling was a public figure who fell within the *Sullivan* ruling and that the *National Review* had not acted in reckless disregard of the truth. Under *Sullivan*, without actual malice there could be no libel ruling in Pauling's favor. "Dr. Pauling has added the prestige of his reputation to aid the causes in which he believes," Silverman told the jury. "I merely hold that by so doing he also limited his legal remedies for any claimed libel of his reputation. Perhaps this can be deemed another sacrifice that he is making for the things he believes in."

Pauling was ordered to pay just over one thousand dollars to the *National Review* for legal costs (the journal's attorneys' fees totaled more than fifty thousand dollars). The jury was dismissed.

Pauling, commenting only that he was "disappointed," let his lawyer go and found a better one to mount his appeal: superattorney Louis Nizer. Nizer's group was pessimistic from the start, but with Pauling's strong encouragement and the chance that the extension of the *Sullivan* decision to those who were not public officials might be overturned, they agreed to take the case.

Silverman's ruling in the Pauling case, however, was soon confirmed by rulings from other courts in other cases where the public figures involved were not politicians. In 1967, the broader interpretation of *Sullivan* was upheld by the U.S. Supreme Court, and by the time Nizer finally brought Pauling's appeal to court in the spring of 1968, it was a lost cause. *Sullivan* was also a determining factor in Pauling's libel losses against the *Globe-Democrat* and the New York *Daily News*.

The *National Review* celebrated Silverman's decision by running a savagely mocking seven-page rehash of the trial for their readers. William F. Buckley's magazine not only survived the Pauling scare; it thrived.

And Pauling, disarmed by *Sullivan,* never mounted another libel case.

The Orthomolecular Shift

The failure of his libel suits, with the attendant drain on his time, energy, and money, left Pauling depressed. So he worked harder.

By the end of 1966, Pauling and Ava Helen were now spending half their time in their house on Hot Springs Road, the other half at their beautiful, newly finished house at Big Sur. Isolated, with plenty of time to work on whatever new ideas caught his attention, Pauling was ready to give up on the CSDI and spend his time working on theoretical science. He published papers on the structure of graphite and boron nitride, examined baryon resonances as rotational states and electron transfer in intermetallic compounds, and surveyed yet again the necessity of a scientific approach to world problems. For a few days he toyed with the idea of making a thorough study of the phenomenon of unidentified flying objects, with a critical analysis of everything from the credibilty of observers to the possibility of the extraterrestrial origin of humankind.

And out of this intellectual roaming came a new unifying idea.

It started in late 1965, during a visit with some friends, one of them a psychiatrist, in Carmel. During some spare time before dinner, Pauling, searching for something interesting to read in the guest room, settled on a book that had been written about treating schizophrenia. The title, *Niacin Therapy in Psychiatry,* interested him because he had not heard much about using vitamins (niacin is one of the B vitamins) to treat mental disease. The author was a Canadian researcher, Abram Hoffer, director of psychiatric research for the province of Saskatchewan, and the book summarized years of experiments done by Hoffer and a colleague, Humphry Osmond, that appeared to show clearly that very high doses of niacin and related compounds could have a significant positive effect on the mental functioning of schizophrenics. The doses the Canadians gave were astonishing—in some cases more than a thousandfold higher than the recommended daily allowance. But there seemed to be no significant negative side effects, and there was marked improvement in symptoms and readmittance rates. Abram and Hoffer called their treatment "megavitamin therapy."

Pauling's decade-long concern with the biochemistry of mental disease gave him an appreciation for the arguments in the book, but there was something about it that bothered him as well.

After a week of thinking it over, the answer hit him. Most drugs, he knew, are safe and effective in only a very limited range of concentrations; even with aspirin, too much is fatal. In Hoffer and Osmond's work, niacin was being used like a drug, but it appeared to be both safe and increasingly effective over an enormous range of doses, orders of magnitude greater than anything recommended by physicians. It was surprising to Pauling, and he began to wonder if other vitamins might act the same way.

A few months later, his interest was reinforced by a personal experience with megavitamin therapy. In a speech he gave after receiving the Carl Neuberg Medal—awarded for his work in integrating new medical and biological knowledge—in March 1966, Pauling mentioned that he wanted to live another fifteen or twenty years in order to see the wonderful new medical advances that would surely come. A few days later, he received a letter from Irwin Stone, a gregarious Staten Island biochemist he had met briefly at the Neuberg dinner.

Stone told him how much he appreciated his talk and then wrote that asking for twenty more years of life was asking for too little. Why not live another fifty years? It was possible, if Pauling listened to his advice.

He then told him the story of vitamin C.

—*mm*—

Irwin Stone had been interested in vitamin C since 1935, when he began publishing papers and taking out patents on the use of ascorbic acid, or ascorbate (both synonyms for vitamin C), as a food preservative. Over the years his interest grew as he read a series of scattered reports from around the world indicating that ascorbate in large doses might have some effect on treating a variety of viral diseases as well as heart disease and cancer. Convinced of its health-giving power, Stone and his wife started taking up to 3 grams of the vitamin per day— many times the daily dose recommended by the government.

Stone felt better as a result, but it took a car crash to make him a true believer. In 1960 Stone and his wife, driving in South Dakota, both nearly died when they were hit head-on by a drunk driver. They not only survived the crash, however, Stone told Pauling, but healed with miraculous rapidity. This he attributed to the massive doses of vitamin C they took while in recovery.

He emerged from the hospital ready to convince others about the value of ascorbate. He began to read widely, noting that among mammals, only man, closely related primates, and guinea pigs were unable to synthesize their own vitamin C internally because they lacked an enzyme critical in producing the vitamin. As a result, humans had to obtain it through their diet. If there was none available, the result was scurvy, the dreaded ailment that had killed thousands of sailors before a British physician discovered it could be prevented by providing lime juice or fresh oranges. The U.S. government had duly set the minimum daily requirement for vitamin C at a level just sufficient to prevent scurvy.

But Stone believed that it was not enough. Scurvy was not a simple nutritional deficiency, it was a genetic disease, the lethal end point of an inborn error of metabolism, the loss of an enzyme that robbed humans of the ability to produce a needed substance. And it appeared from animal studies that simply preventing scurvy might not be enough to ensure optimal health. Only one good biochemical assessment of ascorbic acid production in another mammal had been done, on rats, and it indicated that on a weight-adjusted basis, a 150-pound adult human would need between 1.4 and 4 grams of vitamin C per day to match what rats produced to keep themselves healthy. Stone was convinced that taking less than this amount could cause what he called "chronic subclinical scurvy," a weakened state in which people were more susceptible to a variety of diseases. In a paper he had written—and which had already been rejected by six medical journals— he concluded, "This genetic-disease concept provides the necessary rationale for the use of large doses of ascorbic acid in diseases other than scurvy and opens wide areas of clinical research, previously inadequately explored, for the therapeutic use of high levels of ascorbic acid in infectious diseases, collagen diseases, cardiovascular conditions, cancer and the aging process."

In other words, to Stone, giving someone enough vitamin C to prevent scurvy was like feeding them just enough to keep them from starving. Full, robust health demanded more. He advised that Pauling start with about one and a half grams per day. It was especially good, Stone said, for preventing viral diseases like colds.

"I didn't believe it," Pauling later said jokingly of Stone's letter.

After all, Stone was no physician, nor was he a nutritionist exactly or a professional medical researcher. His background had been in the brewing industry as a biochemist. But Stone's theoretical framework—the idea of a genetic mutation causing the need for vitamin C—was directly in line with Pauling's own thinking. Beadle had shown with his *Neurospora* mutants how genetic mutations led to variants with new nutritional requirements for vitamins and amino acids, and Pauling had taken Beadle's ideas to heart. "Every vitamin we need today bears witness to a molecular disease our ancestors contracted some hundreds of millions of years ago," Pauling had written in 1962. A year or two earlier, he might have ignored Stone's advice as just another crank fan letter, but now, especially given his recent awakening of interest in megavitamin therapy for schizophrenia, vitamin C seemed at least worth a try.

He began taking 3 grams per day.

The results were miraculous. Colds had for decades been the bane of Pauling's existence, and the colds he caught never seemed to be mild. They were debilitating, hacking, phlegm-drenched affairs that put him in bed for a week. Then many of them would progress to full-blown sinus infections. Colds intefered with his work, forced him to put off travel plans, made his life miserable. In the past, he had found only one way to prevent them—a daily dose of penicillin, a practice he followed off and on for years, from 1948 until the early 1960s.

Then came vitamin C. After starting to take it at Stone's recommended levels, he and Ava Helen both found that they had greater energy, an increased sense of well-being, and no more colds. This cure for a condition that had plagued Pauling for four decades, as much as anything written in the scientific literature, made Pauling a believer in vitamin C.

But he was a quiet believer. For three years he took his vitamin C every day and enjoyed the benefits without writing a word about it. Not that he was not interested in it from a biochemical standpoint; he even started measuring the vitamin C in his urine while at Santa Barbara—but he was less interested in ascorbate as a cure-all than he was in expanding Hoffer and Osmond's ideas about mental health and vitamins.

Pauling was now synthesizing another great theory, a grand plan of the mind that occupied his imagination for the next year. Hoffer and Osmond's use of megavitamins in treating schizophrenia was the catalyst, but there was more to it. The mind, Pauling had concluded after years of research, was a firestorm of molecular-electrical energy firing a complex biochemical system fed by metabolites, governed by enzymatic reactions, and orchestrated in some as yet unknown way—most likely, Pauling thought, following the most advanced current thinking, by the creation of favored patterns of neuronal connections.

His interest centered on the underlying biochemical system. His first forays into the mysteries of the mind, his studies a decade earlier on mental deficiency and PKU patients, had focused on discovering and defining enzyme deficiencies that would explain the molecular causes of mental deficiency. The tools he had used, urinalysis and blood analysis, had been too crude to find what he was looking for; the search had ended in failure. But now, in late 1966 and early 1967, he broadened his approach. Another overarching theory was emerging from his renewed interest in mental health, one that he believed would explain—like all of his great theories—a variety of confusing, sometimes contradictory, observations.

If mental functioning depended on the presence of the correct amounts of certain molecules—enzymes, coenzymes, substrates, and products—then optimal mental functioning was likely to depend on maintaining some type of molecular balance in the brain, "the right molecules in the right amounts," as he would later say. If one important enzyme was inactive or malfunctioning—as in PKU patients—it could throw off the entire mechanism. The effects of a poorly functioning enzyme could, however, be counterbalanced by a great increase in its substrate. This might be what Hoffer and Osmond had done with niacin—greatly increased the substrate or cofactor needed in a malfunctioning enzymatic reaction to push it in the right direction.

He came up with a catchy new name for his theory, "orthomolecular" psychiatry, and began preparing his ideas for publication.

"Orthomolecular psychiatric therapy is the treatment of mental disease by the provision of the optimum molecular environment for the mind, especially the optimum concentrations of substances normally present in the human body," he explained in his first paper on his theory, written in the spring of 1967. The treatment of PKU with a protein-free diet was one example of orthomolecular therapy: The result was a lowering of the concentration of the amino acid that caused mental problems. Hoffer and Osmond's megavitamin therapy was another. There were others. It was known that a variety of nutritional deficiencies, including vitamin deficiencies like pellagra and scurvy, could lead to mental derangement of various sorts. "The functioning of the brain and nervous tissue is more sensitively dependent on the rate of chemical reactions than the functioning of other organs and tissues," Pauling wrote. "I believe that mental disease is for the most part caused by abnormal reaction rates, as determined by genetic constitution and diet, and by abnormal molecular concentrations of essential substances."

There was something tremendously exciting to Pauling about this new theory. It was an important theory, yes, one that postulated an entirely new way of looking at the optimal functioning of the mind, but there was more to it than that. It offered a way of going back and helping understand, in some way correct, something irrational and incomprehensible in his life. He remembered his mother, Belle, pernicious anemia eating away at her mind, pushing her into a mental ward. She had suffered a molecular imbalance in her brain. Orthomolecular psychiatry could help make sure that did not happen to anyone else.

And there was more. The orthomolecular concept could be applied to the entire body. Diabetes, for instance, could be seen as an orthomolecular disease, treatable by providing the right amount of a naturally occurring molecule, insulin, to the patient. Goiter was treated by providing needed iodine. Fluoridated water could prevent cavities. Life was a complex series of chemical reactions; the body was the vessel in which they took place. Like any chemical reaction, everything depended on having the right amounts of starting material, catalyst and product. Pauling quickly expanded his theory from the brain to an all-encompassing orthomolecular vision of health.

San Diego and Stanford

Pauling now needed a laboratory to test his theory, a facility that would help him get grant funding. Santa Barbara could not provide him one, so he looked elsewhere. In the summer of 1967, an opportunity arose at the new and growing UC campus at San Diego, to which Pauling had been invited as a one-year visiting professor of chemistry and physics. The San Diego chemistry department seemed interested in allowing this visit to evolve into a permanent appointment. Pauling took a leave of absence from the CSDI, Ava Helen found a house in La Jolla, and in September 1967, Pauling started to work at San Diego.

For a while it seemed like a return to happier days, with a laboratory—a tiny fraction of the space he had at Caltech but still a laboratory—scientific colleagues to work with, and the reassuring rhythm of the academic calendar.

San Diego, however, would prove no more secure a resting place than Santa Barbara. Pauling had barely cobbled together some research funds and hired a research assistant to work on some problems when it became apparent that his chances of a permanent appointment were in trouble. The reason again was politics.

Disgusted by the Vietnam policies of both major political parties, Pauling had become vehemently more radical. In 1967 he joined the Peace and Freedom Party—its presidential nominee was Black Panther Eldridge Cleaver—and adopted the rhetoric of the left-wing Students for a Democratic Society (SDS), whose aims and tactics he applauded. He supported Black Power. He called for continued and vigorous mass demonstrations. And he now talked of revolution. "I believe in nonviolence," he told an antiwar rally in May 1968. "But The Establishment believes in violence, in force—in Mace, napalm, police power, aerial bombing, nuclear weapons, war. As long as the selfishness of the Establishment remains determinative, our hope that the coming revolution will be nonviolent has little basis in reality."

His escalating rhetoric brought him again to the attention of the UC regents. There had been rumors from the time he arrived in San Diego that a few regents, the usual longtime Pauling critics, would never agree to a long-term appointment for him at any UC school. Then an added difficulty arose when he celebrated his birthday in February 1968. The age he had now reached, sixty-seven, was the standard retirement age for UC professors. Pauling was in perfect health, bursting with ideas, and had not given much thought to retirement. But age was now used as a factor to hold up his reappointment. At the same time, a rule change went into effect giving the UC board of regents direct power to veto any exception to the retirement-age rule, and it was clear to Pauling that the regents would never support him. His future at San Diego was now in limbo, which made it difficult for Pauling to secure grants. Without grants, he had little chance of being seen as a productive faculty member, one worth keeping on after retirement age.

After months of hesitation and internal squabbling, UCSD finally reappointed Pauling for a second one-year stint a few weeks before the start of fall term, in 1968. But it was clear now that anything beyond one year was unlikely. Pauling began looking for other places to go. He considered, then rejected, an offer from his old friend Beadle to come to the University of Chicago. His home was in California

Then he made a decision. In February 1969, Pauling announced that he was leaving San Diego at the end of the academic year. His destination, he said, was Stanford University, where he had been offered an appointment as a consulting professor in chemistry, starting in July.

_~~~_

In May 1969, hundreds of San Diego students gathered in a school gymnasium to mourn the death of a Berkeley student who had been killed by police gunfire during the confrontation over the People's Park. The question at hand was whether to go on strike and shut the campus down.

Some faculty members pleaded moderation. Then Pauling came to the front of the gathering. His voice as strong as it had been in his anti-testing speeches, his sentiments clear, he told the students that the Berkeley killing was part of the pattern of U.S. militarism, economic exploitation, and disregard for human rights that was being played out in Vietnam. "The strike is a way for exploited and suppressed people to express their objection to the exploitation and suppression," he cried, his voice growing stronger as he went along. "Everyone in the whole University of California, all the students, the faculties, the employees, should strike against the immorality and injustice of the act at Berkeley."

It was his way of saying good-bye to the regents of the University of California.

_~~~_

Stanford was a great improvement in several ways. Palo Alto was much closer to the ranch at Big Sur, for one thing, making his and Ava Helen's frequent trips there less onerous. The chemistry faculty members were happy to have him, there were no problems at the private school with his retirement age or with regents, and the San Francisco–area political climate was amenable.

But financial considerations had forced Pauling to strike a deal in which he paid half of his own salary and all of his expenses out of his own research grants. There was no guarantee of any salary at all after the first year. And the only laboratory space available was small and separate from the main chemistry building.

But once grant money started coming in for his orthomolecular work, he thought, all that could be improved. Pauling and Ava Helen found an unassuming and comfortable house, with a big rock fireplace and natural-wood highlights—in a way much like their old house in Pasadena—in Portola Valley, in the hills five miles west of the university.

Perhaps now, he thought, he could quit wandering, settle down, and make some significant advances in his work.

Vitamin C

The End of the Common Cold

Pauling did not dislike physicians. For the most part, however, he did not respect them.

Part of the reason became clear to him in the late 1950s, when he gave a dinner talk about molecular disease to the San Diego Medical Association. He was mildly irritated during his lecture by the way the doctors continued conversing and clinking their glasses while he spoke. Then afterward, when he and Ava Helen attended a reception at the home of one of the association's officers, they overheard someone commenting that since Pauling had agreed to speak without a fee, the group could now afford to pool their money and bring in a really outstanding physician as a speaker next month. The Paulings were both insulted and enlightened about the priorities of the medical profession. "The result of our having overheard this discussion was that I decided that I would not accept invitations from organizations of physicians unless they were accompanied by an offer to pay a stipend or honorarium comparable, in my judgment, to what they would have paid a physician," he said.

The medical profession's attitude toward money was only part of the problem. It seemed to Pauling that physicians were also in some cases unable to fully appreciate the value of their own research findings, an inability that became critical in Pauling's decision to involve himself in a public debate over vitamin C.

He had been generally silent about ascorbic acid and its benefits through the late 1960s, limiting his few comments to ideas about how it might be used, along with other nutrients, in the treatment of schizophrenics. In late 1969, however, convinced by the theoretical arguments of Irwin Stone and impressed by his own success in preventing colds, Pauling began expanding his comments to include the subject of ascorbate and general health, noting in a speech he gave to physicians at the Mt. Sinai Medical School his success with the use of vitamin C as a cold preventive. His comments were reported in the newspapers, and afterward he received a "very strongly worded" letter from Dr. Victor Herbert, a leading clinical nutritionist and a man who helped set the U.S. recommended daily allowances (RDAs) for vitamins, who assailed Pauling for giving aid and comfort to the quacks who were bleeding the American public with unsupported claims about the benefits of vitamins. Where, Herbert asked, were the carefully controlled clinical studies to prove that ascorbic acid had a real effect on colds?

Pauling was taken aback. He had not, in fact, carefully reviewed the literature on vitamin C, limiting his reading to a few of the citations in Irwin Stone's original papers. But now, "sufficiently irritated by this fellow Herbert," he began a typically comprehensive tour of the scientific journals.

At the same time, a writer for *Mademoiselle* magazine contacted Pauling to get his comments on vitamin C for an article on its health benefits. Pauling offered the general observation that "optimal amounts of vitamin C will increase health and intelligence" and referred readers to his paper on orthomolecular psychiatry. When the article appeared in November 1969, he found his statement rebutted by Frederick Stare, a professor of nutrition at Harvard, who said Pauling "is not an authority on nutrition" and that there was no evidence that increased C helped prevent the common cold; in fact, just the opposite was true. A large-scale study done with five thousand students in Minnesota twenty years earlier, Stare said, had proven definitively that vitamin C had no effect on colds.

Stung, Pauling quickly tracked down the study and found that Stare had gotten his facts wrong. The 1942 University of Minnesota study Stare referred to involved 363 student subjects who had been given either a placebo or some extra ascorbic acid over a period of twenty-eight weeks. It was true that the authors had concluded in their summary that there was no "important effect" of vitamin C on infections of the upper respiratory tract. But when Pauling took a closer look at their data, he decided they were wrong. Despite what Pauling considered the very low dose of vitamin C given the students—an average of 180 mg per day compared to the 3,000 mg Pauling was now taking—the researchers had in fact seen an effect: Subjects receiving the extra vitamin had 15 percent fewer colds, and the colds they got were 30 percent less severe than those receiving the placebo. Vitamin C was not a preventive or cure, but the results were, Pauling estimated, statistically significant.

It was confusing, especially when Pauling saw the same thing happening in other reports he found on vitamin C and colds: Partial effects were discounted. The physicians who ran the studies seemed to be looking for total cures, not an indication of an effect. The doses they used were low (150–250 mg was common in these early studies—several times the current RDA but many times lower than what Pauling and Stone considered a protective dose), and the effects they looked for were too strong.

The problem, Pauling decided, was that the researchers were looking for vitamin C to act like a drug. In traditional drug testing, small differences in dosage could have tremendous effects, and overdoses were deadly. The tendency was to use relatively small amounts and look for big effects.

But to Pauling, vitamin C was a nutrient, not a drug. When the medical researchers saw a small effect, he thought the logical next step should have been to follow up with larger doses. His literature search uncovered at least one study that showed what might happen if they did. In 1961 a Swiss researcher named Ritzel had given half of a group of 279 skiers 1,000 mg per day of vitamin C—more than five times the Minnesota dose—and the other half a placebo. Ritzel found that those skiers receiving ascorbic acid had 61 percent fewer days of illness from upper respiratory tract infections and a 65 percent decrease in the severity of their symptoms compared to the placebo group.

This, Pauling thought, was very strong evidence in favor of his ideas. Plot the dose of vitamin C along the bottom of a graph and the effects on colds up the side and you could draw a straight line from the Minnesota results (a small effect with small dose) to the Swiss findings (a larger effect with larger dose). He found a few other papers in which the results fit the pattern. True, some of the research he looked at showed no effect at all—most of these studies, Pauling estimated, were flawed because they used too low doses, too short duration, shoddy oversight, or improper blinding—but the important thing was that a small group of careful clinical studies existed that supported Pauling and Stone's general theory of vitamin C and health: The more C you took, approaching megadose levels, the lower your chances of getting sick, and the less sick you got. Although Pauling's literature review also turned up hints of ascorbic acid's beneficial effects on a number of other diseases, everything from heart disease to polio to cancer, the common cold was the best-documented example of its effects.

—✍—

In the spring of 1970, Pauling decided to go public with his findings.

He did not feel he could wait. He had, he thought, good evidence that a cheap, apparently safe, easily available nutrient could prevent at least an appreciable fraction of a population from suffering through an affliction that made millions of people miserable. And there might be even greater results. Pauling had read of small villages, snowbound in the winter, where no one got colds because there was no reservoir of respiratory viruses to pass around. When visitors arrived in the spring, they would bring colds with them, and everyone would suffer. What if, through the use of vitamin C, a great many more people strengthened their resistance to colds? The two hundred or so cold viruses rampant in the world would have many fewer places to replicate themselves. The spread of colds would lessen; the population of cold viruses would decrease. "If the incidence of colds could be reduced enough throughout the world," Pauling thought, "the common cold would disappear, as smallpox has in the British Isles. I foresee the achievement of this goal, perhaps within a decade or two, for some parts of the world." Vitamin C, properly and widely used, might mean the end of the common cold.

This, of course, would not only greatly lessen the amount of suffering in the world; it would increase the fame of Linus Pauling. He was nearing seventy years of age. It had been nearly twenty years since he had captured international attention with the alpha helix and won the Nobel Prize for chemistry. There had been talk at that time of a third Nobel Prize in physiology and medicine for his sickle-cell work, but it had not materialized. His efforts had gone to politics in the years since, and none of his recent scientific work had had much impact. Science was moving on without him. He was becoming a historical figure.

Pauling did not feel like one. He was not ready for emeritus status, trotted out at honorary occasions, shunted aside while the young men made the discoveries. He was still strong, still smart, still a fighter. Orthomolecular medicine was the newest of his grand plans, and no one had shown that his ideas about creating an optimal molecular environment for the body and mind were wrong. The evidence he had uncovered about ascorbic acid and colds, evidence that showed human health could be improved by increasing the amount of vitamin C in the body, was the strongest indication yet that he was right. Bringing it to the public's attention would not only be good for the public; it would be a striking example of the correctness of his general theory.

On March 31, 1970, he signed a contract with his longtime textbook publisher, W. H. Freeman & Co., to produce a short book on the common cold. This was to be the popular explication of his ideas, a direct—and possibly profitable—communication to the public along the lines of *No More War!* While working on it at the ranch in Big Sur over the next two months, he also drafted a more technical version of his findings to be submitted to *Science.*

―――

Pauling's book *Vitamin C and the Common Cold,* written in his usual clear, well-organized, straightforward style, presented the results of his literature search. He discussed the findings of five controlled trials that supported his idea, several anecdotal instances of physicians who had treated colds with vitamin C, and evidence that ascorbic acid was safe in large doses. Pauling felt confident that a several-gram daily dose would do no more harm than to cause loose stools, that vitamin C was safe, especially compared with potentially toxic, commonly available over-the-counter medications such as aspirin. The rest of the book was a summary of his orthomolecular thinking and Stone's ideas about evolution. A good deal of space was devoted to the topic of biochemical individuality, which resulted in a wide personal variation in the need for vitamin C and other nutrients.

On November 18, 1970, prepublication galleys were released to the press, and an unprecedented public roller-coaster ride began. The next day, the *New York Times* quoted Pauling as saying that humans needed between 1 and 4 grams of vitamin C per day to achieve optimal health and prevent colds. Pauling also took the occasion to slam the medical establishment—from drug companies to medical journals and physicians—for attempting to quash the evidence in favor of ascorbic acid. Why would they do that? the reporter asked. Look at the cold-remedy industry, Pauling said: It was worth $50 million per year, and that bought a lot of advertising space in medical magazines.

This quickly alienated both physicians and the editors of medical journals, neither of whom liked the implication that profits were more important than health. The medical establishment felt it necessary to respond, and respond quickly, once they saw how Pauling's idea took off.

The book sold wildly, and so did vitamin C. Pauling's timing, at least on the public side, was superb. The 1960s had seen a resurgence of interest in "natural" health based on a holistic attitude that said body, mind, and soul were one. Many streams fed into this alternative health movement: a back-to-the-land, organic-foods orientation; a fascination with yoga, acupuncture, meditation, and other Eastern health practices; the rediscovery of the lost Western arts of naturopathy and homeopathy. Pauling's message about vitamin C resonated with millions of people who were reacting against corporate, reductionistic, paternalistic medicine, with its reliance on drug therapy, with people taking a renewed responsibility for their own health and trying to do it naturally. It was delivered just as natural food stores were popping up on corners in every town in America, each one stocked with a section for herbal remedies, a rack for magazines on alternative health regimens, and plenty of shelf space for vitamins.

The publication of Pauling's book triggered a nationwide run on vitamin C. Sales skyrocketed, doubling, tripling, quadrupling, within a week of its appearance. Druggists interviewed in newspapers across the nation told of people coming in to buy all the vitamin C they had. Wholesale stocks were depleted. "The demand for ascorbic acid has now reached the point where it is taxing production capacity," said a drug company spokesman less than a month after Pauling's book appeared, adding, "It wouldn't pay to increase production capacity since we're sure it's just a passing fad."

The reaction was swift. The physician-head of the Food and Drug Administration (FDA), Charles C. Edwards, announced to the press that the national run on vitamin C was "ridiculous" and that "there is no scientific evidence and never have been any meaningful studies indicating that vitamin C is capable of preventing or curing colds." The FDA, Pauling found, had proposed in 1966 that no vitamin C tablets over 100 mg be available without a prescription, and he responded to Edwards with sarcasm. If the FDA had its way and he wanted to take 10 grams of vitamin C to fight off a cold without going to a physician for a prescription, Pauling said, he would have to take 100 tablets. "I think I would have as much trouble swallowing all these tablets as I would swallowing some of the statements made by the Food and Drug Administration in proposing these regulations," he said.

The medical press was equally critical of Pauling. The *American Journal of Public Health* said that Pauling's book was "little more than theoretical speculation." The *Journal of the American Medical Association,* said of Pauling's book, "Here are found, not the guarded statements of a philosopher or scientist seeking truths, but the clear, incisive sentences of an advertiser with something to sell. . . . The many admirers of Linus Pauling will wish he had not written this book." *The Medical Letter* launched the harshest attack yet, saying Pauling's conclusions "are derived from uncontrolled or inadequately controlled clinical studies, and from personal experience" and pointing out that there was no good evidence that vitamin C was safe when taken over a long period of time in large doses.

Pauling could do nothing about the aesthetic judgments of book reviewers, but he could fight errors of fact. "I ask that you publish a correction, retraction, and apology of the false, misleading, damaging and defamatory statements made about my book," Pauling began a twelve-page missive to the head of the *Medical Letter's* editorial board. He rebutted their article point by point, stressing that he had cited perfectly adequate controlled trials, from the Swiss and Minnesota studies to a 1970 Irish report of a double-blind trial of more than 100 schoolgirls that showed that 200 mg per day of ascorbic acid during the winter significantly reduced the incidence, duration, and severity of colds. As for the safety of megadoses of vitamin C, all of the evidence to date showed that the worst a high dose could cause was mild stomach irritation or diarrhea, which could be controlled by monitoring the dose and building up tolerance gradually. He challenged the journal to bring forward any case in which someone taking large doses of vitamin C had been harmed by it.

None were forthcoming, but neither was an apology. Instead, the *Medical Letter* piece was picked up by the popular press, including *Consumer Reports,* which reiterated the *Medical Letter's* points, roundly condemned Pauling's book, and added that in the absence of more safety data, Pauling's actions were not "socially responsible." The Paulings, who had subscribed to *Consumer Reports* for decades, were shocked by the harsh tone of the piece, which Pauling called "intemperate and completely unreliable." They argued their point in a meeting with the president and members of the board of directors of the magazine's sponsoring body, but a correction was never published.

Bad news came from the journal *Science* as well, which rejected Pauling's paper on the evolutionary need for vitamin C. Pauling immediately sent it to the *Proceedings of the National Academy of Sciences,* where he knew that as a member of the NAS there was no doubt of his getting it published.

━━ⅈⅈⅈ━━

The controversy over Pauling's book arose from a simple fact: He had not made his case. The book was a combination of his interesting but unproven speculations about orthomolecular medicine and the human evolutionary need for ascorbic acid, coupled with a select handful of studies that indicated that vitamin C could prevent or ameliorate colds in a fraction of a population. That might make an interesting conference paper, but it was little reason to advocate a wholesale change in the dietary habits of a nation. His critics pointed out that he had no clear theory of how vitamin C exerted it powers and that there was no good study—no study at all—establishing that the long-term ingestion of megadoses of vitamin C was safe. The current dogma in the medical profession was that vitamins were needed only in the small amounts provided by a well-balanced diet. Taking grams of vitamin C every day might cause everything from gastric upset to kidney stones, and who knew what else?

The way he had gone about publicizing his ideas, sidestepping the normal channels of scientific peer review to publish a popular book, also fueled criticism. He was behaving like a health faddist, not a scientist. In the eyes of most physicians—generally conservative about new therapies, disdainful of the holistic health movement, trained to believe that vitamin C was needed only to prevent scurvy—Pauling looked like a nutritional quack, a vitamin pusher who was essentially prescribing without a license.

Sure, he was a Nobelist, but most physicians did not know much about his illustrious scientific career. He was old, he was out of his field, he was obsessed with vitamin C and convinced he could not be wrong. Victor Herbert even diagnosed the case on television: Pauling, he said, suffered from something like senile megalomania.

It was the medical profession's duty to shut him down.

—*mm*—

The debate over *Vitamin C and the Common Cold* raged through 1971. To every charge leveled by the medical profession, Pauling found an answer. No, he did not know exactly how vitamin C prevented colds, but there was evidence that it had antiviral and immune-building powers, and in any case, as he wrote in the book, "we may make use of ascorbic acid for improving health in the ways indicated by experience, even though a detailed understanding of the mechanisms of its action has not yet been obtained." All of the published literature showed that high doses of vitamin C over an extended period of time were benign. The worst that happened was transitory diarrhea or stomach upset that could be controlled by increasing intake slowly. There was not one proven case of kidney stones resulting from vitamin C. The FDA made a great deal of the danger of taking one form of it, the sodium ascorbate salt, because it could put too much sodium into the diet, but that was easily countered by taking the more common nonsalt form of pure ascorbate. The specter of long-term health problems was, Pauling felt, a red herring. Besides, he pointed out, physicians had no trouble telling patients to take aspirin, another substance without a defined mechanism of action and one that had been proven much more toxic than vitamin C. As for his method of publication, he had tried to get his ideas published simultaneously in a juried journal, *Science,* and had been turned down. But the promise offered by vitamin C to aid human health was too great—and Pauling's age was too advanced—to wait for the normal channels of scientific communication. He went public to help the public. Physicians might think of doing the same thing.

In his counterattack, Pauling stressed two things. The most important was that rather than touting a miracle cure for the common cold, he was simply promoting a strategy to control it. From the beginning he stressed that individuals varied widely both in their natural resistance to colds and their need for vitamin C. Some lucky people never developed colds whether they had vitamin C or not. Others apparently remained susceptible to colds regardless of how much they took. These two groups, the immune and the highly susceptible, were at the ends of a bell curve. In the middle were the great majority of people, and Pauling believed that the evidence showed firmly that it was here that vitamin C could help increase resistance. He wanted to shift the bell curve, make millions of people less miserable, and help decrease the total sum of human suffering.

In this he was being hampered, he believed, by the medical profession's drive to make money and their tendency toward conformity. Physicians were too busy earning their fees, he said, to read carefully the literature on vitamin C, so they relied on the pronouncements of experts in their own field like Stare and Herbert. "They are willing to make their statements without ever going back to see just what the facts are," Pauling told a journalist. "They just pick up bits of information or misinformation from one another, the authorities, instead of checking the facts and drawing their own conclusion."

This was an argument, in other words, not only over scientific facts but over worldviews. Meanwhile, the book sold so well that a paperback edition was quickly arranged, for which Pauling added two new chapters specifically responding to his medical critics. His belief in ascorbate was even stronger now because he had taken a closer look at the data to answer some points. He found that even if he accepted only those trials that best conformed to the physicians' own definition of proof—double-blind trials (ones in which neither the patient nor the physician knew during the test who was getting the placebo and who the test substance)—and adding his own stricture that they involved doses of more than 100 mg of vitamin C per day and tracked naturally occurring colds over a long period of time, the evidence was "overwhelming": The four published trials that met the qualifications all showed that vitamin C had a significant effect in preventing and ameliorating the common cold. The right thing for the medical profession to do now was not to argue the point but to investigate it fully with well-controlled trials of high-dose vitamin C.

By the time the paperback edition appeared in December 1971, sales of vitamin C began soaring again as the winter cold season hit. Not all the evidence was in Pauling's favor. At the University of Maryland, researchers announced the results of a study in which eleven prisoners were given a Pauling-sized dose of ascorbic acid, 3 grams per day for two weeks, before inoculating them with cold viruses. All eleven developed colds, as did the ten controls who received a placebo. The Maryland study was widely reported as proof that Pauling was wrong—despite the fact that there was no indication that the small-scale study was double-blind and the report had surfaced at a scientific meeting, not in a juried journal. Pauling dismissed it for other reasons, because the prisoners had been hit with an artificial inoculation of viruses that could well have been great enough to overwhelm any protective system in the body, whether reinforced by vitamin C or not.

The general public believed Pauling. Overall demand for vitamin C shot up 15 percent in 1971, a rate three times faster than expected. By the mid-1970s vitamin C was by far the biggest seller in the burgeoning vitamin market, with an estimated 50 million Americans taking at least some extra daily supplementation. The very happy manufacturers of vitamin C labeled this "the Linus Pauling Effect."

The Vale of Leven

While the medical profession in general dismissed Pauling's work, his arguments struck a chord with at least some individual physicians. Pauling received a steady stream of letters from practitioners who had seen positive effects in their patients who took extra vitamin C or who found that a gram or two helped them fight their own colds.

And it went beyond colds. In November 1971, Pauling received a letter from Ewan Cameron, a surgeon who practiced in a little hospital called the Vale of Leven outside Glasgow, Scotland, describing some amazing results he had seen when using high-dose ascorbic acid in the treatment of cancer. Very high doses, 10 grams per day or more, he wrote, seemed to slow the progress of cancer, in some cases even shrinking tumors. He had only tried it on a small number of terminal patients, but he thought Pauling might be interested in his preliminary work because he also had an idea about ascorbate's mechanism of action. Cameron had proposed in a book five years earlier that vitamin C might play a role in strengthening the interstitial ground substance, the thick, gel-like, collagen-reinforced mucopolysaccharide that acted as the glue holding cells together in the body. A strong ground substance was important in keeping cancer in check, Cameron hypothesized, because tumors tended to invade the body by breaking down the glue between normal cells. The stronger the glue, the less invasive the cancer and the more easily controlled and treated.

Cancers defeated this natural protective mechanism, Cameron wrote Pauling, by producing an enzyme, hyaluronidase, that dissolved the ground substance and opened the way to invasion of the body. Vitamin C helped defeat cancer by helping form an antihyaluronidase molecule. Details of this theoretical scheme had to be worked out, but Cameron was excited about his findings and the clinical results he had seen in his small group of terminal patients. He was as much an enthusiast about vitamin C as Pauling was. "I am unashamedly optimistic that with your help we could soon conquer cancer," he wrote Pauling.

Pauling was impressed by Cameron's findings and eager to explore this new clue about vitamin C's mode of action. Strengthening the substance that held cells together could account not only for a few studies that indicated vitamin C had an anticancer effect but also fit with what was known about scurvy (where one symptom was the breakdown of tissues, bleeding of gums, and so forth) and observations as wideranging as the fact that vitamin C seemed to help people with slipped discs. Vitamin C might be an overall tissue strengthener, a substance that helped bind the body together.

He began corresponding with the Scottish surgeon and quickly established that Cameron was no kook. Mild-mannered and capable, Cameron was a graduate of the University of Glasgow medical school and a fellow of the Royal Colleges of Surgeons of Edinburgh and Glasgow. He had treated cancer efficiently as a surgeon for many years and had published a number of papers on cancer treatment. The 1966 book he had written, *Hyaluronidase and Cancer*, had been well reviewed. After reading it, Pauling wrote Cameron, "I am tremendously interested to learn about the observations that you have made. . . . I feel that your ideas are really important and supported by much evidence."

A month later, a less promising note from Scotland arrived. "We seem to have had several days of unmitigated clinical disaster over here," Cameron wrote. Three of his small group of vitamin C patients had died within seventy-two hours for various reasons—one from massive hemorrhaging, caused perhaps by the vitamin C working so well that the tumors self-destructed, kicking off the bleeding, Cameron wrote. His initial enthusiasm suddenly turned to doubt. Cameron wrote, "It is becoming obvious that even if ascorbic acid 'works' the associated clinical problems are going to be considerable but hopefully not insurmountable."

Pauling responded by urging his new colleague to continue his efforts. "The attack you are making on the cancer problem is the most important and promising of all those that I have heard about," he wrote Cameron. "It is essential that a thorough test be made of the value of ascorbic acid." Something should be published about this exciting new theory as well. The best way, he wrote Cameron, would be to conduct a double-blind test in his terminal patients, giving some vitamin C and others a placebo. But Cameron refused. After the small cluster of deaths, the remaining vitamin C patients in his original cohort and new ones that he added to the list continued to do better than expected. He felt now that it would be ethically wrong to do anything but provide all his terminal patients with vitamin C.

Even without a double-blind trial there was enough to publish, Pauling thought. As with the work on vitamin C and colds, he felt that Cameron's work with vitamin C and cancer needed to be made public as quickly as possible in order to spur further studies.

Pauling helped Cameron refine and write up his hyaluronidase theory and a review of his success with cancer patients for publication in the United States, and they decided as joint authors to submit it to the *Proceedings of the National Academy of Sciences,* a perfect vehicle for the paper not only because it would be published more quickly than in most journals but also because there was no chance of rejection. The journal's policy had long been that if someone was good enough to get into the NAS, he or she was good enough to publish ideas without peer review. The only member-submitted articles that had not been published in the past half century had been two or three that directly attacked the work of another NAS member—this was considered less than gentlemanly—and one less than adequate paper submitted by a member who had recently suffered a stroke. Everything else saw print.

So it was a complete shock a few weeks later when Pauling received a letter from John Edsall, the head of the *PNAS* editorial board, informing him that the journal was rejecting the cancer paper. The decision had been reached, Edsall wrote, at a stormy meeting of the editorial board in which it had been decided that papers advocating therapeutic procedures in areas as controversial as cancer treatment belonged in medical journals, where they could be better evaluated. Edsall himself had been the deciding factor. He had known Pauling for forty years and respected him greatly—it had been Edsall who defended Pauling's alpha helix at the Royal Society meeting in 1952—but he was also the son of a physician who had impressed upon him the importance of not implying great value in a treatment without a thorough and exhaustive examination of the evidence. He did not see that sort of care in Pauling and Cameron's paper. "It was a very troubling and quite painful decision," Edsall later recalled.

It was also unprecedented. "I do not know what to do next," Pauling wrote Cameron after hearing the news. "I do not have any idea about its publication in the United States. I have published nothing in the medical journals, and I have little confidence of being successful."

Pauling and Cameron finally tried resubmitting the piece to the *PNAS,* slightly altered to play down the therapeutic recommendations.

It was rejected again, this time with the backing of the council of the academy. Meanwhile, rumors of the extraordinary *PNAS* rejection filtered out into the scientific community and came to national attention when a news review of the controversy ran in *Science* in early August. The story reinforced the impression that Pauling had lost sight of science in his enthusiasm for vitamin C. Why else would the *Proceedings*, which never rejected any paper, reject his?

The only good thing to come of this latest controversy was an offer from a sympathetic editor of *Oncology*, a journal for cancer physicians, to publish the piece. Pauling and Cameron accepted eagerly.

—*mm*—

The incident seemingly did nothing to dampen Pauling's enthusiasm. Cameron continued to find that vitamin C helped his terminal cancer patients live longer, with less pain and more energy. It improved their quality of life. And there were rare cases where it seemed to do more, where the cancer disappeared almost entirely after high-dose vitamin C therapy. Buoyed by anecdotal reports like this and continuing to find old reports of ascorbic-acid therapy as useful in other conditions, Pauling now asserted his belief that vitamin C in high doses was of likely value in "almost every disease state," as he wrote Cameron. "I do not think of it as being a wonder drug," he added, not an immediate cure for diseases, but at optimal doses it was a strengthener of the body's tissue structure and immune system, making it more likely that diseases could be fought off or their symptoms eased. It was valuable orthomolecular therapy to counter a genetic lack of ascorbate in the body. It was a tonic for a vitamin C–starved animal.

Pauling was convinced that vitamin C was effective. Now all he had to do was the research to prove it.

The Institute

Art Robinson was a bright young freshman at Caltech around 1960 when he took freshman chemistry. The class was then being taught by Jurg Waser, but Robinson sometimes saw Pauling deliver a guest lecture. Everybody knew vaguely about Pauling and his reputation and his fight against the U.S. government, and here he came striding into the lecture room, tall, ramrod-straight, a sort of chemist's Don Quixote trailed by his Sancho Panza, Waser, struggling under a load of props and models. To the students, Pauling was a legend. One day when they knew he was coming in, someone scrawled on the blackboard behind his podium, "Pauling is God and Waser is his Prophet."

Pauling saw it, paused for a moment, Robinson remembered, erased the words "and Waser is his Prophet," and continued his lecture.

That made an impression on everyone and a strong impression on Robinson. Two years later, when he was offered the chance to work on Pauling's anesthesia project, he jumped at it. Even as an undergraduate, the young man displayed a marked talent in the laboratory, where he helped devise an innovative way of using brine shrimp instead of goldfish to measure the effects of anesthetics. He got a paper published in *Science* as a result. And he caught Pauling's eye.

Robinson went on to do his Ph.D. work at the University of California at San Diego (UCSD) under the direction of physicist Martin Kamen, who remembered Robinson as the brightest graduate student he had ever had—so bright that UCSD hired him as an assistant professor right out of graduate school. It was here that he and Pauling crossed paths again, when Pauling arrived for his short stay in San Diego in the late 1960s. They began talking at UCSD about orthomolecular medicine and schizophrenia and about the reasons Pauling's earlier attempts to find a biochemical key to mental diseases by screening blood and urine had failed. They made an odd pair, the two of them, the old theorist and the young experimentalist. Politically they were polar opposites, Robinson from conservative Houston, Texas, a self-defined "libertarian/conservative." But science overwhelmed any differences. Robinson thought he knew how to fix the problems with Pauling's schizophrenia project, using newer methods that coupled gas chromatography, an exquisitely sensitive way of separating and measuring the chemical components in a complex biological mix like urine, to computers that could store and compare massive amounts of data from hundreds of individuals. Pleased with the chance to work with Pauling and interested in the experimental challenge, Robinson shifted his research to match Pauling's. The two of them became close at San Diego, and Robinson soon was spending most of his time perfecting ways to pinpoint the biochemical changes associated with various diseases. Pauling and Robinson got funds for a urinalysis project on schizophrenia from the National Institute of Mental Health. Robinson, whose own parents died at about this time, took on the Paulings as surrogate parents and was a frequent guest at the Big Sur ranch, even spending Christmas with them.

When Pauling moved to Stanford, Robinson—much to the dismay

of his mentors at UCSD—followed him, taking a leave of absence and trekking north with Pauling to set up his increasingly complex urinalysis equipment. By early 1972, just as Pauling's interests were turning to vitamin C and cancer, Robinson had outgrown the small temporary laboratory Pauling had been given in Palo Alto—he was by then running sixteen gas chromatographs and various pieces of computer paraphernalia—and he and Pauling asked Stanford for more space.

The school was not inclined to provide it. For one thing, Pauling was not being a quiet, well-mannered faculty member. Although the FBI had decided finally in 1972 that Pauling was no longer a threat to national security—closing its quarter-century-long investigation of the scientist, archiving the twenty-five-hundred page file it had gathered, and concluding that there was no good evidence, after all, that he had ever been a Communist—Pauling had continued his political activism. He attacked President Nixon for everything from the bombing of Cambodia to his policy in Pakistan—then told reporters that Nixon should take more vitamin C; strongly criticized the Stanford administration for firing a faculty member who had made speeches calling for an end to the university's involvement with military research; and exhorted Stanford students repeatedly to take a stand against the war in Vietnam.

That was bad enough, but by 1972, Pauling had added this apparently nonsensical obsession with vitamin C. He and Robinson were doing vitamin-loading tests on schizophrenics, giving them large doses of vitamin C, then tracking its presence in their urine (the idea was that a deficiency of ascorbic acid in the body would lead to higher uptake, thus reduced excretion), and Pauling had been pestering people at the medical school for months with requests to help him test the effects of vitamin C on patients. The continued anti-Pauling broadsides from the medical community were beginning to become embarrassing for Stanford.

When Pauling, stymied in his request for a move to larger quarters, suggesting building a modest structure for his and Robinson's work, to be funded in part by the university, in part with money he would raise himself, the administration hesitated, then reminded Pauling that he was already past the usual retirement age for Stanford professors. Finally, at the end of 1972, they said a new building was out of the question.

Art Robinson came up with the idea for a solution. He and Pauling had already arranged to get their part of the money for the proposed Stanford building, fifty thousand dollars, from Keene Dimick, the re-

tired head of a gas chromatography company and an enthusiastic believer in Pauling's vitamin ideas. Why not tell Stanford to go to hell
and use Dimick's money to rent laboratory space off campus? This was
a chance, Robinson and Pauling decided, to get out of academia entirely and set up their own research institute.

The two of them talked it over with Dimick and on May 15, 1973,
announced that their work would henceforth be carried out at a new
research facility in Menlo Park, a few miles from Stanford. They called
it the Institute of Orthomolecular Medicine.

—_www_—

Pauling was now seventy-two years old, but he threw himself into the
new venture with the energy of a young man. Within a few months, he
had resigned his position at Stanford, Robinson severed his last ties
with UCSD, and both men began looking for money. Pauling first lobbied his friends and colleagues to join the institute's board of associates—a position that meant little more than that their names appeared
on the letterhead but which would lend an air of prestige to fund-
raising efforts—and thirty of them obliged, including Francis Crick,
Maurice Wilkins, and a number of other Nobelists.

Dimick's initial stake had secured the new institute a building, but
Pauling and Robinson, with only their old National Institutes of
Health (NIH) urinalysis grants to fall back on, had to use their own
money in part to staff and equip it. The two main areas of research
were to be Robinson's urinalysis project and new proposals from Pauling for research into vitamin C. Robinson did not have much trouble
getting more grant support for his side, but Pauling's attempts were
less successful.

Typical was his trip to the National Cancer Institute (NCI) in
March 1973. Pauling and Ava Helen arrived in Bethesda carrying
Cameron's case histories of the first forty cancer patients he had
treated in Scotland, which they presented to a dozen NCI officials.
Pauling suggested that perhaps it was time for controlled trials to be
carried out in the United States, but the officials, after a two-hour discussion, said they could do nothing until animal tests had indicated
that the treatment was both safe and effective. Once again, Pauling
thought, the physicians were treating vitamin C like a drug rather than
a food, but he was willing to go through the steps. He quickly applied
for a $100,000 grant to carry out animal studies at the new institute.
The proposal was scored too low by NCI reviewers to receive funding.

Pauling tried to correct the shortcomings noted by the reviewers and applied again in 1974. He was turned down. He applied again in 1975 and then in 1976. He was turned down each time.

Cameron himself visited NCI later in 1973, during a trip on which he met Pauling for the first time. But the two of them together could accomplish little more than Pauling had alone. The attitude of the NCI researchers seemed to be similar to that of other physicians: A few anecdotal observations at a little Scottish hospital were not enough to warrant large-scale research support. Cameron's own feelings about the National Cancer Institute were expressed in a letter to Pauling. After viewing the "really distressing" way that chemotherapy, radiation, and surgery were used in Bethesda, he wrote, "I do not know what kinds of results they are achieving, but they are certainly causing much mutilation and human suffering along the way."

In the summer of 1973, Pauling suffered another setback when a task force of the American Psychiatric Association (APA) released a long report that tore into the concept of orthomolecular psychiatry, especially Hoffer and Osmond's ideas, saying their theoretical basis was "found wanting," their experimental results were too individualized and short-term to provide good data, and their use of publicity was "deplorable." In a spirited defense Pauling wrote for the APA journal, he charged that the membership of the task force was skewed and that the report had ignored some important studies: "Neither the general theory of orthomolecular psychiatry, as presented in my 1968 paper, nor any of the special arguments about the value of ascorbic acid is presented or discussed in any significant way," he wrote; the report's conclusions, he said, were "unjustified." But by the time his article saw print the next year, the damage had been done. Again the medical establishment had spoken; again it had ruled that Pauling's orthomolecular ideas were ill-founded.

"It is hard to understand physicians, I must say," Pauling told a reporter. "They accept what they are told. . . . They believe in authoritarianism, and they apparently find it hard to understand that the world changes."

_〰〰_

In the summer of 1973, Pauling and Cameron tried a different approach to spurring interest in vitamin C and cancer. Moving away from Cameron's hard-to-prove antihyaluronidase theory, they now emphazised vitamin C as an immune-response booster that could help ease the side effects of chemotherapy and radiation therapy—an adjunct to accepted cancer treatments rather than a radical alternative. It was a clever move, both less threatening to the cancer establishment and better grounded in experimental fact, including the observation that vitamin C helped improve the functional ability of phagocytes, the white blood cells involved in the immune reaction to cancer.

But it was too late. By now, Pauling was almost completely ostracized from the medical profession. It did not help that he continued to argue his case in the popular press instead of scientific journals, even giving interviews to sensationalist tabloids like the *National Enquirer* and *Midnight*. Now he was saying that proper use of optimal doses of vitamins, coupled with a decrease in sugar consumption and quitting cigarette smoking, could lengthen the average American life span by somewhere around twenty years. He had upped his own daily dose of vitamin C to 6 grams. To physicians, he appeared increasingly strident and a little sad. What a shame it was, they agreed, to see such a great man turning into a crackpot.

By mid-1974, both Pauling's reputation and the financial condition of his fledgling institute had reached a nadir. In a medical echo of the McCarthy days, a talk Pauling had been scheduled to give on vitamin C to students at UC Santa Cruz was canceled when the sponsoring body, a local cancer society, told the students who had invited Pauling that they would not pay to bring him in. The campus chancellor, deciding that no outside body was going to determine what his students heard, paid for Pauling's visit out of university funds. As if in answer to Pauling, the U.S. RDA for vitamin C was lowered from 60 mg per day to 45 in 1974.

In the spring, two more of Cameron's papers on vitamin C's effects on cancer patients were rejected by one of America's leading cancer journals. The major criticism was that he had not carried out a contemporaneous double-blind trial, but had gauged the effect instead by comparing his vitamin C patients to similar cases pulled out of the hospital's files—"historical controls," as they were called in the profession. His results were also less than definitive because he used his high-dose regimen only in terminal patients, who would die of heart failure or kidney problems, conditions probably unrelated to vitamin C but which threw off the statistical analysis of his results. Pauling and Ava Helen flew to the Vale of Leven in June to see Cameron's work firsthand and to help him revise his manuscript. Later, by beefing up the theoretical side and adding his own name to the manuscript, Pauling was able to shepherd Cameron's findings through publication in the journal *Chemical and Biological Interactions*.

That was good news at least, and Pauling's institute needed it. He and Robinson had had little success in raising any significant amount of money from scientific agencies for work on vitamin C and cancer, and their failure resulted in a fiscal crunch so severe that they had to support the operation out of their own pockets. It was obvious that something would have to be done.

In July 1974, the institute's small board of directors decided to make some major changes. The medical-scientific establishment might not fund their work, but there was another source of money: the public. The public had consistently responded more favorably to Pauling's ideas on vitamin C than physicians had. They could be appealed to directly for money, as various cancer fund-raising charities had done for decades. If fund-raising went well, far from closing down the institute, they could expand it and open a small medical clinic to conduct their own studies. To capitalize on the institute's most important asset, they would rename it, dropping the "orthomolecular" part, which was tainted by the APA's attack and in any case required too much explanation to prospective donors. From now on, it would be the Linus Pauling Institute of Science and Medicine—a change to which Pauling acceded because, as he put it, "there seemed to be advantages to having my name attached to the institute in connection with raising funds."

Pauling's feelings about the institute were mixed. While it was a necessary structure for pursuing the right course with vitamin C, in other ways it was a headache. He was by title the institute's president, but he did not like administration and tended to ignore day-to-day problems. "I don't waste time on needless details," he told an interviewer proudly around this time. "I think that, too, is a secret for success in life." He preferred to spend his time traveling and speaking on scientific issues and vitamin C, keeping up his theoretical work on the chemical bond and other problems by publishing a few papers every year, and spending time with Ava Helen.

And Ava Helen was taking more of his attention. Her health had been a matter of concern off and on for years; she had suffered a small stroke in late 1967—a frightening episode with a midnight ambulance ride to the hospital in San Diego, but followed by a quick and complete recovery—then in 1972 had had a cataract removed. She and Pauling spent quite a bit of time together at the ranch during the period of her eye problems and the next year took together a long-awaited trip to the People's Republic of China, where they toured communes and returned home with hand-forged tools given to them by appreciative farmworkers.

His continued traveling and desire to be with his wife, combined with the ongoing fiscal crisis at the institute, made it clear to Art Robinson that someone with a more direct interest in the day-to-day running of the facility would have to be put in charge. To Pauling, the institute might have been a grace note on a long career, but to Robinson, it was his entire future. It had to be run efficiently. "Pauling wasn't doing anything as president," said Robinson. "I got frustrated, and I don't know how I got my nerve up for this because I usually treated him with great deference, but one day I said, 'Look, why don't you do the job? This makes it very hard for us.' And he looks at me and says, 'Well, why don't you do the job? You be president.' So I became president."

That was the way things were done at the institute. In the summer of 1975, Robinson became president and director of the Linus Pauling Institute of Science and Medicine, with Pauling himself taking the role of fellow.

—*mm*—

As it turned out, Robinson was not the right man for the job, either. While Pauling continued traveling to speak about vitamins and accept more honors—capped with the first official honor bestowed on him by a president since Harry Truman's postwar award almost thirty years before, the National Medal of Science, awarded at the White House by President Ford in the fall of 1975—Robinson labored to put the institute on a stable funding course. There simply weren't enough dollars. Salary cuts were distributed among what few institute employees there were, with Robinson and Pauling leading the way by donating portions of their salaries. By the end of the year, Pauling had given up his salary entirely.

That did not make for a happy workforce, a situation worsened by Robinson's poor administrative skills. He was a laboratory man, good at writing grants and performing experiments but unskilled in management. Neither was he a fund-raiser at heart, for he had little patience dealing with prospective donors and lacked Pauling's persuasiveness in one-on-one conversations. He quickly found himself unhappy as president, spending half his time in airplanes with a briefcase looking for money instead of being where he wanted to be. "I was the best guy in the lab," he remembered, "and I wasn't in the lab."

It was an opportune moment for Richard Hicks to appear. The polished, well-dressed executive assistant to the chairman of the board of the Dean Witter brokerage firm in San Francisco was interested in a career change, possibly to the health field. He had first met Pauling when the scientist spoke to the Dean Witter board on vitamins and health. Hicks himself was a vitamin enthusiast, and in late 1975 he approached Pauling and Robinson with a scheme to help them raise money. They should do a direct-mail campaign, he said, which he would capitalize himself in exchange for 15 percent of whatever he raised and the title of executive vice president of the institute—that was how sure he was of their potential success. "He presented himself very well, he knew his way around the corporate world in terms of how to look and how to act, he was going to pay for everything, 15 percent looks good," Robinson said, "and I'd go back to the lab." Hicks was hired on March 1, 1976.

—∿∿∿—

While the institute struggled, Pauling continued the public fight for vitamin C. When *JAMA* published an analysis of existing studies concluding that vitamin C had little effect against colds, Pauling pointed out the shortcomings and underlined the importance of a new, double-blind Canadian study—set up in part, he noted with satisfaction, to disprove his ideas—showing that people receiving 1 gram per day had fewer and less severe colds. When *Modern Medicine* published an editorial railing against "self-deception" among scientists like Pauling—whom it accused of putting forward an unproven thesis, then demanding that others prove him wrong—Pauling threatened a libel suit and drafted for the editors a retraction he wanted to see printed. The editorial had indeed gone too far; the editor apologized for not having read Pauling's book more carefully, then published almost verbatim the retraction Pauling had provided.

Those were rearguard actions, however. Pauling wanted to move forward with new evidence, especially about vitamin C and cancer. Pauling and Robinson undertook animal studies of vitamin C in 1975, buying hundreds of hairless mice, putting them on different diets featuring various combinations of vitamins C and E and other antioxidants, and irradiating them to produce skin cancer. One group also received a formulation of high-dose vitamins and minerals called "the Linus Pauling Super Pill," an item there was some talk of marketing as a way to raise money for the institute. A final group of mice were fed seawater as well. The seawater idea came from a letter to Pauling by a Caltech alumnus who noted that marine invertebrates rarely suffered from cancer, so perhaps there was some trace element in seawater that protected them. Pauling decided to follow up the lead.

The test was ongoing when in the spring of 1976, an NCI site-visit team arrived to review the institute. They duly noted the small staff, Pauling's frequent absences, and staff complaints about Robinson's poor managerial abilities. Their report would help sink the institute's future grant requests.

At the same time, however, Pauling received some good news from the Vale of Leven. By the early summer, a new analysis by Cameron showed that his vitamin C–treated cancer patients lived more than four times longer—210 days versus 50 days—than the historical controls to whom he compared them. Pauling helped write up the results in a paper that he submitted to both the *PNAS* and the *Journal of the National Cancer Institute*. "It will be interesting to see what happens," Pauling wrote Cameron.

The editors of both journals quickly voiced concerns about the study's design, especially the way the control group was chosen. How could the paper's reviewers be sure that similar criteria were used in all cases to determine who was included in the control group, and how far their cancers had progressed? All cases were supposed to be "terminal," but how could anyone be sure in the historical controls that the same definition had been consistently applied? The referees for the paper at the *PNAS* took "severe exception" to the fact that randomized concurrent controls had not been used.

As Pauling argued his case with the journals through the summer, saying that the large size of the control group—Cameron had used ten controls for every vitamin C subject—and Cameron's care in picking them had resulted in effective randomization, the story of Cameron's success hit the press. Britain's *New Scientist* magazine interviewed Cameron (who refused to be identified by name "to avoid causing mental distress to our many local patients") and reported that 15 of his 100 vitamin C–treated patients had lived more than one year after being deemed terminal, versus only four of one thousand control patients. In nearly 10 percent of the patients receiving vitamin C, Cameron said, there had been clear evidence of tumor regression. The article also quoted other cancer experts as saying that the study would have trouble getting published in any juried journal because of the inadequate information available for the control group. As the respected Oxford epidemiologist Richard Peto put it, "Historical controls are the source of more horseshit than anything else in the world."

Pauling's response to the criticisms was simple and aggressive. "I am beginning to think that the attitude of oncologists toward new ideas is largely responsible for the fact that, despite the expenditure of billions of dollars during the last 20 years, there has been essentially no change in the survival time of cancer patients," he said.

—᷈᷈᷈—

To Pauling's consternation, Ava Helen's health had continued to decline, with unspecified ailments keeping her at home in bed at times when Pauling was traveling, and forcing her to miss the big celebration Caltech threw for his seventy-fifth birthday in 1976.

The root of her problem was finally diagnosed a few months later: She had stomach cancer. In mid-July, she underwent surgery to remove the tumor as well as most of her stomach. Ignoring the advice of oncology experts, she and Pauling decided that instead of additional chemotherapy or radiation, she would take vitamin C in the dose recommended by Cameron, 10 grams per day. And it seemed to work. Soon her strength returned, and she felt well enough to once again accompany Pauling on his many speaking trips.

Pauling would not have known what to do without her. They were closer now than ever, so much a part of each other's lives that being apart was difficult. Yes, they had arguments at times, "the hottest of arguments," Ava Helen had once told a reporter. But "to live with someone with whom one always agreed would be unbearable. Surely one would have to be a nincompoop and the other a tyrant. Or possibly both could be liars."

Pauling and Ava Helen were none of these. They were instead an evenly matched pair of bright, loving, humorous, intelligent, witty people. Their relationship at its best was caught on tape by a film crew in the mid-1970s as they shot a segment on Pauling for the science show *Nova*.

INTERVIEWER: Does he have an ego?

AVA HELEN: Oh yes he does, a very well-developed one. [Turning to Pauling] Don't you agree?

PAULING: Yes, I'm sure that's right.

INTERVIEWER: Is he hard to live with?

AVA HELEN: Yes, he is [laughter]. . . .

PAULING: Hard to live with? I thought I was just about the easiest-going person that there was in the world.

AVA HELEN: Well, that may be—that could be true, too, but still be hard to live with.

PAULING: Well, in a sense, I think you are hard to live with. Your principles are so high, your standards are so high, that I have to behave myself all the time.

AVA HELEN: [Laughing] And that's a great burden on you.

PAULING: Yes.

AVA HELEN: Well now, you tell me the next time you want to misbehave. [Laughter]

PAULING: Okay.

AVA HELEN: And we'll see. We'll just see what—

PAULING: It'll be with you, though.

Pauling was shaken by her cancer and by the way the operation had affected her. Her energy was returning but the loss of much of her stomach necessitated changes in diet, and she suddenly seemed smaller, frailer, her face more deeply lined than before. She did travel with Pauling, but she also seemed to treasure even more her time at the ranch at Big Sur, where she took up music again, learning to play folk songs on the guitar and buying a grand piano. She had her children and grandchildren over as often as she could, their visits made easier and more enjoyable when family members, led by Linus junior, helped build a guest cottage just out of sight of the main house. Those days in the late 1970s were good ones at Big Sur, full of love and music, and best of all, the weeks when Linus and Ava Helen were alone, just the two of them, old lovers listening to the sea.

Resurrection

A Very Persuasive Man

Ava Helen's illness made the question of the use of vitamin C in the treatment of cancer more than scientific; it was a personal cause, and Cameron's most recent work buttressed Pauling's opinion that it was more important than anyone realized. The same week in 1976 that his and Cameron's *Proceedings of the National Academy of Sciences* paper saw print, Pauling gave a presentation to the Royal Society in London. Instead of a moderate call for further research, Pauling now stated, "It is my opinion that ascorbic acid may turn out to be the most effective and most important substance in the control of cancer." Proper use of the vitamin could, he estimated, lead to a 75 percent reduction in incidence and mortality from the disease.

Blue-sky estimates like that, with as little data as Pauling had to base them on, only hardened the medical profession's disdain for his ideas.

But Pauling was nothing if not an optimist. He next prepared with Robinson two of the largest grant requests he had ever made. Robinson was to be the primary investigator on the first: a $5.8 million plan to work with the Kaiser-Permanente health-care system to set up a national bank of tens of thousands of urine and blood samples linked to clinical data. Pauling was leading the charge on the second, a request to the National Cancer Institute (NCI) for $2.5 million "to support basic studies on vitamin C, animal work, and controlled trials with patients" in Scotland.

The basic strategy was simple: If funding agencies thought that his institute was too small to support major studies, he would ask for enough grant money to make it bigger. Being turned down four times in a row hadn't seemed to deter him. As one incredulous National Institute of Health (NIH) researcher said, "The guy doesn't give up. He just keeps coming at you."

With an air now of inevitability, both grants were turned down in early 1977. Pauling's was rejected in part because of what the reviewers saw as inadequate controls and a description of treatment methods too vague to reproduce. Both were faulted for being overambitious: Asking more than $8 million for an institute that had administrative and funding problems and numbered only four full-time researchers—counting Pauling—was simply asking too much.

The grant rejections made news. "Like other aging scientists, Pauling doesn't want to wait," explained John Kalberer, NCI's program planner. "He doesn't want to go by the protocols—the building block approach to scientific investigation—that he would have abided by earlier in his career." Albert Szent-Györgyi had attempted to get NCI funding for research on the health benefits of vitamin C as well, and Kalberer was no kinder to him. "I would love to give Linus Pauling or Albert Szent-Györgyi money, but we just do not have money for grand old men," he said, "and they refuse to submit an application that is reviewable."

Pauling responded by sending copies of his proposal and a letter about its rejection to two dozen members of Congress, including Senators Ted Kennedy and George McGovern, respective heads of subcommittees on health and nutrition. He and Robinson contacted a lawyer about the possibility of suing the NCI for bias but were counseled that Americans had not been awarded the legal right to get a grant request funded. The lawyer advised them that their chances of success in suing a federal agency were "less than slim."

But Pauling's activities were beginning to make an impression on at least one person who mattered: the head of the NCI, Vincent DeVita. "It is my opinion, which has grown stronger and stronger during the past four years, that the use of ascorbic acid in controlling cancer may well turn out to be the most important discovery about cancer that has been made in the last quarter century," Pauling wrote DeVita in early 1977. At first as disdainful as most of his peers about the value of vitamin C—DeVita's own background had focused on the development of chemotherapeutic treatments for cancer—the NCI head began to think it might be good to put the issue to rest once and for all with a carefully controlled clinical trial. "Dr. Pauling began contacting me personally," he remembered. "He wrote me a couple of times and came to visit me. He convinced me that his data are suggestive. . . . Dr. Pauling can be a very persuasive man."

Public opinion also may have played a role in persuading the NCI to give vitamin C a trial. DeVita commanded the much ballyhooed "War on Cancer," a campaign that had brought hundreds of millions of federal dollars to the NCI. But he was, according to a number of critics, short on victories. As Pauling delighted in pointing out, mortality rates for the most common and deadly forms of cancer had not budged appreciably in years. DeVita knew that if he continued to ignore Pauling entirely, the venerable scientist's public pressure, congressional lobbying, and attacks on the NCI would continue.

In March 1977, DeVita wrote Pauling that he was arranging to give vitamin C the test Pauling wanted. The investigator would be an authority beyond reproach: Charles Moertel, professor of oncology at the Mayo Medical School and director of the Mayo Comprehensive Cancer Center. In April, Pauling visited the NCI to discuss the way in which the tests would be carried out. The trial would be double-blind, include a significant number of late-stage cancer patients, and involve high doses of vitamin C. In correspondence with Moertel, Pauling stressed the importance of using patients with intact immune systems (patients who had not received heavy doses of chemotherapy or radiation beforehand) in order to maximize vitamin C's immune-enhancing abilities, and of continuing the vitamin C therapy until the patients died. This last point would avoid a rebound effect that Cameron and others had observed when high-dose vitamin C was suddenly cut off and the blood level of C, instead of merely returning to normal, dropped much lower. The rebound effect, Pauling worried, might kill patients taken off vitamin C. Moertel seemed open to his suggestions. The Mayo study was scheduled to start later in the year.

mm

The Paulings were now spending roughly equal amounts of time in Palo Alto, at the Big Sur ranch, and traveling. In the summer of 1977, Pauling and Ava Helen went to Iceland, where he had been made hon-

orary president of a conference on the environment (he had continued to make a number of strong statements about the dangers of over-
population, nuclear power, and environmental degradation); to a
meeting of Nobelists in Switzerland; to Munich for lectures and a fiftieth anniversary of their first trip there; to London to visit Peter and
talk with British scientists about vitamin C and cancer; and finally to
the Vale of Leven for another visit with Cameron. Pauling was trying
hard to talk his Scottish colleague into joining him in California, but
Cameron continued to turn him down.

Back at the institute, things were in their standard state of unrest.
An investigative report published in the summer of 1977 in *New Scientist* magazine painted a picture of a research facility in disarray, with
the NCI grants rejected, a staff dissatisfied with the autocratic Robinson—the fledgling medical clinic had shut down after only eight
months, for instance, reportedly after its director squabbled with
Robinson over who was in charge—and Pauling shying away from decision making.

On the other hand, fund-raising was beginning to take off. A series
of clever institute advertisements in financial periodicals like *Barron's*
and the *Wall Street Journal* proved successful: "For Sale—One Thousand Mice with Malignant Cancer—$138 Apiece," one headline read;
"Linus Pauling—Nobel Prize Chemistry 1954, Nobel Prize Peace 1963,
Nobel Prize Vitamin C 19??," another. A professional direct-mail company was hired to supervise a series of appeals to target audiences like
the readers of *Prevention* magazine, and these, too, were terrifically successful.

The influx of donations made a sudden and profound change in
the institute's financial picture. In 1977, just over half the institute's
income came from nongovernment funds; the next year, when the
direct-mail campaign hit high gear, that figure rose to 85 percent. In
1978 alone almost $1.5 million flooded in from private donors.

The sudden riches, instead of stabilizing the institute, tore it apart.
Much of the fund-raising success was due to Hicks, but he and Robinson had never gotten along well, and their rift widened as Robinson
began making plans about how to spend the money. With such a flow
of income, Robinson thought, why not get out of their rented building
and construct a place of their own, away from the increasing conges-
tion of the South Bay area of California? He began talking with Pauling and the trustees of the institute about buying land in Oregon—a
state that had recently declared a "Linus Pauling Day"—and building a
great new research institution devoted to Linus Pauling's brand of

medicine, a facility in Robinson's vision that would rival the Salk Institute or the Scripps Institute. He found a beautiful, rural two-thousand-acre site on a hill a few miles south of Oregon State University. He met with local hospital officials, who seemed agreeable to the idea of cooperating in clinical work. Meetings were held with the governor of the state. An earnest money agreement was drafted. Robinson saw his future suddenly become clear and grand. He would be the head of a large and respected research nexus. "We'd have a campus like Stanford," Robinson said.

But his dream was not shared by everyone. Robinson had recently married, and his visits with the Paulings had declined as a result; his relationship with them, which at one point had almost seemed to be that of another son, had cooled. He and Pauling were not communicating well. Robinson assumed, for instance, that Pauling was thinking about pulling back even more from the institute's day-to-day operations, retiring to the Big Sur ranch with Ava Helen, working on theoretical papers, and checking in only occasionally. It was not an unreasonable supposition. Pauling was, after all, seventy-six years old and had named Robinson the institute's president precisely because he wanted fewer administrative responsibilities. So Robinson felt free to take charge. The institute was his life. And now was his chance to take it to another level.'

Before charging off after his dream of a Stanford in the firs, however, Robinson failed to build a consensus about the wisdom of the move. Richard Hicks was not eager to uproot himself and move to Oregon. He liked the Bay Area, its big money and its social scene, and he wanted to stay. So did a good number of the staff and some key board members.

Hicks and some board members began talking with Pauling about Robinson's shortcomings as president, his poor communication skills, and the wisdom of moving to Oregon.

Pauling was irritated but did not want to be bothered. He wanted the people at the institute to work it out among themselves. By early 1978, when dissension at the institute was reaching its height, he was more interested in traveling with Ava Helen—to Scotland again early in the year, where he continued his efforts to lure Cameron to the United States, then to Cuba for a few days—than he was in getting into the middle of an administrative fight.

Then Robinson went too far, in Pauling's opinion. Robinson had been overseeing the mouse study on diet, vitamin C, and cancer that he and Pauling had designed. The idea had been to vary only the amounts of vitamin C among the various test groups (and, in one group, seawater). By 1978, however, Robinson had, on his own, expanded the scope of the experiment. The impetus came from talks he had with Arnold and Eydie Mae Hunsberger, a wealthy couple interested in alternative medicine. Eydie Mae had survived cancer, she was convinced, by putting herself on a diet of raw fruits, juices, and vegetables, an experience she related in a book, *How I Conquered Cancer Naturally*. The couple then started The Orthomolecular Institute in Santa Cruz to promote their ideas.

Robinson decided to test the diet of raw fruits and vegetables with vitamin C in some of his mouse groups. When Pauling was told about it, he was not pleased, either with the association with the Hunsbergers, for whom he had little respect, or with the data Robinson was getting. Preliminary data from the mouse study indicated that very high doses of vitamin C, equivalent to a human dose of about 50 grams per day, were very effective in lowering the number and size of cancerous lesions in mice. But lower amounts, closer to a human dose of between 3 and 10 grams per day—levels that Pauling was recommending to prevent colds and treat cancer—appeared to do just the opposite, increasing the susceptibility to cancer, almost doubling its rate in one group. Robinson came up with an explanation, reassuring Pauling that this was probably due to the fact that mice synthesized their own ascorbic acid. When getting moderate amounts in their diet, they might shut down their internal production, leaving a net deficit unless the vitamin C added to their diet reached a very high level.

More interesting to Robinson was the observation that the Hunsbergers' diet of raw fruits and vegetables seemed to work as an adjunct, increasing the protective effects of vitamin C alone. Robinson's relationship with the Hunsbergers grew closer. There was talk of promoting treatments for cancer based on these findings, dietary protocols that would carry the stamp of approval of the Linus Pauling Institute of Science and Medicine.

When Pauling heard that, he hit the roof. "I called [Robinson] in and said, 'You can't do this—connecting the institute to people who are going to practice medicine in some unconventional way. You just can't do that, so you must withdraw your connection," he remembered saying. On top of everything else Hicks and others had been telling him, it now appeared to Pauling that his former protégé, the man he had made president of his institute, had taken a research project and turned it into something other than what Pauling had planned.

On June 12, 1978, Pauling sent Robinson a memo asking that he consult with him and Hicks before making any substantive decisions. Within a few hours of reading it, Robinson fired Hicks.

On June 19, in his role as chairman of the board of trustees, Pauling asked Robinson to resign his post as president and to leave the institute for a period of time in order to avoid interfering with the creation of a new administrative structure. Robinson asked for thirty days to consider his alternatives, which Pauling granted.

In early July, Pauling issued a memo to the institute staff asking them to ignore any orders Robinson might issue and informing them that Richard Hicks was now the institute's chief executive officer. The next day, Robinson issued a memo of his own: "I am the chief executive officer under the Articles of Incorporation and the By-Laws of the Institute," he wrote. "Neither Dr. Pauling nor Mr. Hicks have any authority to remove me from my position."

As rumors flew back and forth and lawyers were called in, on August 15 the institute board elected Linus Pauling president and director. The next day, Pauling informed Robinson that he was taking over control of the mouse study.

Nine days later, Art Robinson sued the Linus Pauling Institute and five trustees, including Linus Pauling, for $25.5 million.

‒‒‒‒

Why did the breach occur? Both sides later offered different reasons. Robinson pointed to the mouse study, saying that Pauling did not want any results published indicating that vitamin C had anything other than cancer-fighting effects. But Robinson himself had offered a possible reason for his results, and Pauling later published the mouse study with that explanation in place.

Personality conflicts played a part, especially between Hicks and Robinson, and the fact that everyone viewed Robinson as a relatively poor administrator also entered in. "I think that the nature, the origin of the conflict, probably was in Art Robinson's authoritarian nature," said Emile Zuckerkandl, Pauling's collaborator on the molecular-evolution papers and Robinson's eventual successor as president of the institute. "He wanted to make the main decisions concerning the institute himself . . . without involving Pauling enough."

There may have been deeper reasons as well. The institute was

Robinson's life and his future. As he was seizing the reins of the institute, he was taking control of his life, breaking free of Pauling's influence and defining himself in terms other than simply Pauling's second
in command. If he had been a son to Pauling, he had now also become
a rival. It was almost Oedipal, with Robinson pushing his father figure
aside in order to take command of what they both loved: the institute.

But no protégé was as important to Pauling as his reputation and
his work. When it looked as if he were being pushed, Pauling pushed
back. "Someone here pointed out that Art had gotten into the habit of
thinking of the institute as his institute," Pauling told a reporter. "Perhaps he thought I had gotten to an age where I should be sitting under
a tree smoking a pipe."

Once forced out of the institute, Robinson proved a formidable legal
opponent. His lawsuits, often revised—eight in all, totaling at one
point $67.4 million—dragged on for years. He devoted himself to
them, making it his task to tear down the edifice he had helped create,
to make Pauling and the board pay for ruining his academic and professional career.

The institute might have thought that it would be possible to wear
Robinson down, force him to give up his suits through sheer exhaustion of energy and money. But, like Pauling, Robinson just kept coming back. He turned the computers he had bought to use for his
research toward making money, transforming them from instruments
to track urinalysis patterns into tools for playing the commodities market. He made, he estimated, a half million dollars this way over the
next several years, enough to support him and his wife and keep their
legal battle going.

It was a disaster for the institute. Hundreds of thousands of dollars—much of it from the fund-raising success—went for legal fees.
Coverage of the case in financial papers like *Barron's* and in the scientific press did incalculable damage to the reputation of the institute.
And Robinson wouldn't give up.

It wasn't all bad news. Toward the end of 1978, Ewan Cameron, after
years of invitations, finally arrived in California to take up a one-year
visiting professorship at the institute. For many workers it was like a

breath of spring. Robinson was gone, and with him much of the tension that had electrified the air. Cameron was by comparison gentle, gracious, and warm. He and Pauling had been busily revising their paper on Cameron's treatment of cancer patients with high-dose vitamin C; in response to criticisms, they excluded cases with poor matching controls and redefined the point at which they started measuring survival. Now the results looked even better than before. Patients taking high-dose vitamin C lived almost a year longer, on average, than similar patients who did not. Eight of Cameron's vitamin C patients were alive more than three years after being deemed "untreatable"; none of the controls were. After the usual delay, the newly reevaluated results were published in the *PNAS* in September 1978, along with a critical comment by an editorial board member emphasizing that historical controls were not as valid as those from randomized double-blind trials.

Then Pauling and Cameron began working to expand their ideas into a book, a project that helped take Pauling's mind off his ongoing legal troubles. Things outside the institute were looking up as well, with Pauling's status as a founding father of modern chemistry recognized by a new series of awards. *Time* magazine even credited Pauling in a special article in which notable Americans listed those leaders they thought most effective in changing life for the better. The historian Henry Steele Commager nominated Pauling, telling readers that he provided leadership "in an almost eighteenth-century fashion by combining great distinction in scientific inquiry and in the moral arena." Caltech president Lee DuBridge nominated the astronomer Carl Sagan.

—◆—

Just as he once had a standard stump speech promoting a test ban, Pauling now had a stump speech promoting vitamin C. He would go through Irwin Stone's evolutionary argument for high doses of ascorbic acid, then criticize the U.S. government for its irrational nutritional policy in regard to vitamins. Laboratory monkeys, he would point out, eat a standardized diet that the federal authorities dictated should have ninety times as much vitamin C per day as the equivalent recommended daily allowance for humans. Perhaps the authorities wanted to keep their research monkeys in better health, he would tell the crowd, because, unlike humans, they were expensive to replace.

He would then display a set of large test tubes containing various amounts of powdered vitamin C, illustrating how much the various animal species would produce in a day if they were the size of an average human. A 70-kg goat, he told the crowds, would produce in its body 13 grams of vitamin C per day, about half a test tube full. A similar-size human being produces this much, he said, holding up an empty tube. And the FDA recommends we take this much to make up for it. He would hold up a tiny pinch of powder. "The goat manufactures 330 times as much as the Food and Drug Nutrition Board recommends," he said. "I think that the goat knows more about this matter than the board does."

Then he would tell the crowds that he himself was now taking 10 grams per day, an amount that had risen steadily the more he learned about vitamin C. Why was he taking this much when his books recommended only 2 grams or so? "You can neglect what you read in my books," he said, "because I had to be sort of cautious when I was writing the books—approach the problem gradually and not frighten all the physicians."

Despite all the scientific controversy, the public listened to Pauling. Tens of thousands had discovered, as Pauling had, that taking a gram or more of vitamin C per day made them feel better and helped them fight off infections. Consumption continued to climb, with demand rising so high during the 1970s that the bulk price of ascorbic acid tripled despite an increase in supply. The world's largest producer of vitamin C, Hoffmann-LaRoche, doubled its production capacity over the decade by building new plants—and every year, as a way of saying thank you, donated $100,000 to the Linus Pauling Institute.

Crocodile Dung and Mummy Dust

In March 1979, Pauling and Cameron published an extensive review article on vitamin C and cancer in the journal _Cancer Research,_ summarizing what they had found in a literature search of more than 350 scientific articles and books and concluding with a statement of their current understanding of the role of vitamin C in controlling cancer. "There is evidence from both human and experimental animal studies that the development and progress of cancer evokes an increased requirement for ascorbic acid," they wrote. "Ascorbic acid is essential for the integrity of the intercellular matrix. . . . There is good evidence that high intakes of ascorbate potentiate the immune system in various ways. Ascorbate may also offer some protection against a variety of chemical and physical carcinogens and against oncogenic viruses and is also involved in a number of other biological processes believed to be involved in resistance to cancer."

They concluded that it is "essential that extensive studies of ascorbic acid in cancer be made without delay."

―――ᴍᴍ―――

Six months later, the first such study was published, and the news was not good. Pauling received an advance copy on September 12, 1979, and could tell almost everything he needed to know from the title: "Failure of High-Dose Vitamin C (Ascorbic Acid) Therapy to Benefit Patients with Advanced Cancer."

This was the Charles Moertel/Mayo Clinic study that the NCI had set up, and the results appeared to refute Cameron's work in Scotland. But in reading the paper, Pauling and Cameron could see, if not holes in Moertel's study, certainly ways in which it failed to replicate Cameron's work. The most important difference was that Moertel had included a number of patients who had significant prior chemotherapy, a factor Pauling had warned Moertel would weaken their immune systems. Moertel had given sixty terminal patients 10 grams per day of vitamin C for some time, but only five of the group had received no previous chemotherapy or radiation. Their failure to respond to vitamin C did not indicate that it was ineffective, Pauling wrote Cameron. "I think the conclusion to be drawn from this result, together with your observations, is that cytotoxic chemotherapy destroys the immune system to such an extent as to prevent ascorbate from being effective."

Cameron's patient population was quite different—in Scotland it was not common practice to give terminal patients the kind of aggressive therapy given in the United States—but that difference was not mentioned in Moertel's paper. Moertel stated that half of Cameron's patients had previously received radiation and/or chemotherapy, but that was wrong, Cameron said. The number of patients receiving those treatments at the Vale of Leven came nowhere near 50 percent.

This was a significant point, and Pauling pointed out the error to Moertel, asking that it be corrected before the paper reached print in the *New England Journal of Medicine (NEJM)*. He was told that it was already in production and too late to change.

When published, the Moertel study was taken as proof that Pauling's ideas about vitamin C and cancer were quackery. "No Vitamin C Benefits Found in Cancer Trial," headlined the *Medical World News*. "Dr. Linus Pauling's much-publicized claim that vitamin C can prolong and improve the lives of terminal cancer patients has collided head-on with the scientific method." The same tone was picked up by newspapers nationwide.

Pauling answered with rebuttals, noting differences in the Moertel and Cameron studies in letters and interviews with the *New York Times,* the *Wall Street Journal,* and the *Washington Post.* Moertel expressed his feelings about the issue in a note to the *NEJM* correcting his statement about Cameron's use of other therapies. "Any contention that previous chemotherapy prevented our patients from achieving the extraordinary survival increases claimed by Drs. Cameron and Pauling must be considered highly speculative at best. . . . On the basis of available evidence, we do not consider it conscionable to withhold oncologic therapy of known value to give the patients large amounts of vitamin C."

The battle lines were now drawn between Moertel and Pauling, who after this point gave up personal communication in favor of public attacks on each other's work. Pauling referred to Moertel's work as part of the establishment conspiracy against vitamin C and claimed that most physicians were unwilling to try something new for fear of a malpractice suit. Moertel in his public statements would lump vitamin C with quack cancer remedies like laetrile, holy water, crocodile dung, and mummy dust.

It was strangely like Pauling's battle with Dorothy Wrinch over the cyclol theory of proteins forty years before, with Pauling taking Wrinch's role. Pauling was now the outsider in an established field, the intruder whose ideas were dismissed by those in power. He saw his opponents' papers quickly published in respected journals, while his and Cameron's work was often rejected. Pauling now experienced what it felt like to have his ideas and his grant requests rejected outright not because they were fully disproven but because the case was considered closed.

Perhaps he could better understand Wrinch's feelings when she wrote to a friend in 1940 comparing Pauling and his supporters to a "power syndicate just like Hitler's" that only those who were strong and powerful could survive.

—⁓⁓—

Everyone else might take Moertel's work as the last word, but Pauling did not. His and Cameron's book *Cancer and Vitamin C* was published a few weeks after Moertel's study appeared. Despite negative reviews like that in the *Times Literary Supplement*—which noted Pauling's "almost obsessive preoccupation with vitamin C" and concluded that the book was "totally unacceptable, the more so, since it may raise hopes which are unsupported by proper scientific evidence"—sales were brisk, in part because Pauling himself bought fifteen thousand copies to send to physicians and one thousand more for members of Congress and government officials. He pressured NCI director DeVita to fund a second clinical trial that would more accurately duplicate the Vale of Leven work.

And again he got results. To put the issue to rest again, DeVita's agency would eventually okay a second trial, stipulating that the patients were not to have received prior chemotherapy or radiation. The only problem from Pauling's standpoint was that the second trial was to be conducted again by Charles Moertel.

—⁓—

The combination of bad publicity from the Moertel trial and the drain of the Robinson suit had put the institute again on shaky financial ground. In 1980 the owner of the institute's leased home notified Pauling that he would have to move by next year. The only affordable space that could be found in the area was a leaky, twenty-year-old warehouse near a busy Palo Alto intersection. A few years earlier, Pauling would never have considered it. "It is an old building, and not very attractive," Pauling wrote a friend. But it was roomy, inexpensive, and available on short notice. With some remodeling, it would do for a short time, Pauling told himself, until fund-raising picked up again.

—⁓—

It had been five years since Ava Helen's stomach cancer operation, and they had been good years. She had traveled extensively with Pauling, and she had received a few recognitions of her own: an honorary doctorate from San Gabriel College and guest-of-honor invitations to a number of fund-raisers for peace, environmental issues, and women's rights.

Then, as the controversy over ascorbate raged, her health began to flag. In the summer of 1981, during a second trip to China with Pauling, she fell so ill with abdominal pain that they had to alter their travel plans. When they returned to California, her doctors recommended that she undergo exploratory surgery.

The results were not good. She was suffering a recurrence of her stomach cancer, the physicians told them. The disease had spread far enough, surrounding some important arteries, to make surgery impossible.

Standard U.S. oncological therapy at this point dictated chemotherapy, but Ava Helen, after talking with Pauling, Cameron, her children, and her physicians, decided against it. She apparently now qualified as a terminal cancer patient, and she understood quite clearly what her choices were. She decided that her only therapy, aside from pain control, would be to increase her intake of vitamin C.

She then went to the ranch, shooed aside most sympathy, and tried to take care of Pauling. She knew better than anyone how poorly he dealt with emotional distress, and so she encouraged him to work hard and to travel, to keep up his schedule of speaking engagements. While he was on his trips, the children came and stayed with her. On one long weekend, she talked with Linda about things Pauling did not want to hear: the type of memorial service she wanted, the music to play, her wish to be cremated. As she weakened through the fall, Ava Helen was the calmest one in the household. Linda, who tended to cry now every time she saw her mother, only saw Ava Helen weep once, when she read a letter written by Linda's son Sasha, a simple, loving letter expressing how much she meant to him.

Finally, Ava Helen arranged one last public appearance. She was pleased to learn that she had been named winner of the Ralph Atkinson Award for Civil Liberties, which was to be presented by the Monterey chapter of the American Civil Liberties Union on November 1, and she decided that regardless of how weak she felt, she would attend. She made certain that her children and friends knew about it as well. "She knew she was dying, and she wanted us there," her son Crellin remembered. "She knew this was her last hurrah."

The award ceremony went well. But nine days later, while Pauling was off on his way to England, Ava Helen began vomiting blood. She was hemorrhaging internally, the doctors at the Stanford University Hospital intensive care unit told the family; the cancer was eating away at her tissues, causing the bleeding into her gastrointestinal tract. Pauling returned immediately. Ava Helen's bleeding was stopped, and she went back to the Portola Valley house and began making plans to celebrate Thanksgiving with the entire family down at Big Sur. But on November 23, there was another hemorrhage. She couldn't be moved. Thanksgiving was held at the Portola Valley house.

Pauling hung on to the hope that Ava Helen would live, that massive doses of vitamin C would perform a miracle, as it had with a few of Cameron's patients, that somehow the cancer would simply disappear.

He had added to her diet raw fruits and vegetables, carrot and celery and tomato juices freshly squeezed at home, everything he could think of to restore her to health. "Daddy was convinced that he was going to save her," said Linda. "And that was, I think, the only reason he was able to survive. . . . He said to me after she died that until five days before, he thought he was going to be able to save her."

Ava Helen knew better. The hemorrhages were getting worse and more frequent. Finally, she had enough. She had been receiving transfusions to replace the blood she had lost. Now, at the beginning of December, in bed in her house at Portola Valley, she said to stop the transfusions.

Pauling stayed with her as much as he was able, holding her hand. The children were nearby.

On December 7, Ava Helen died.

The Sea

Pauling spent a good deal of time now out on the deck at the house in Big Sur, looking down at the kelp-rich sea and then out to where it turned a pure and simple blue before meeting the sky. It was a good place to sit quietly and think.

Thought was his savior now, pure thought, pure theory, the application of his mind to problems as difficult and abstract as possible. The atomic nucleus had caught his attention again, the attempt to build a reasonable picture of the core of matter through ideas about building blocks of subunits, the spheron theory, structural thinking. He published three papers on the nucleus of the atom in 1982.

Most of her things were still inside, the pieces of folk art on the walls and bookshelves, the grand piano, now engulfed by stacks of journals and papers. He still talked to her, holding phantom conversations as he spooned his vitamin C powder into his juice in the morning. He still looked for her, expecting to see her in the doorway, asking him to stop and take a walk, to come to lunch. He would cry and look out to sea. Then he would get back to work.

He was lost for a while after her death. His children guided him through the memorial service, then watched him anxiously, wondering what to do next. They hired him a full-time housekeeper, figuring that he would want someone to cook and clean for him. Pauling fired her. They hired a gardener to take care of the plantings Ava Helen had tended. Pauling fired him.

They took the hint, let Pauling determine his own actions, and watched. He started cooking for himself, making a big pot of spaghetti and eating it for three days, then cooking something else that would last. He tried to keep his schedule as normal as possible through the spring of 1982, making appearances at the institute, traveling and giving speeches, going through the motions. He seemed to be doing all right.

But he wasn't. Ava Helen's death seemed to have split him in two, bifurcating him into the rational and the emotional, the scientist and the little boy. The first half observed the second half with some interest. Sitting in an airplane on his way to a meeting, he was surprised to note that he was moaning aloud. The same thing happened at home, he noticed, unexpected, unbidden periods of moaning. When someone asked about Ava Helen, he would begin to cry.

It was as though it were another person doing these things, but Pauling understood, also, who it was. He had never really known how to react emotionally, so he was doing the only thing possible, responding unconsciously, subconsciously, in ways that surprised him. He wrote his children a letter to let them know how he grieved.

And with enough time, he began to heal. By June, he felt well enough to attend his sixtieth class reunion at Oregon State University, and this, too, became part of the healing process. Almost without thinking, he set off alone in his car days before the reunion, driving fast, ending up in Dayton, Washington, a little town where he had worked with the paving crew and where he and Ava Helen had spent a month in a rented room just after being married. He looked for the places where they had walked. He remembered how she had surprised him that summer by outscoring him on an intelligence test. The smartest girl he had ever met.

He rewound his life, driving from there to Condon and Lonerock, where he found the grave of Linus Wilson Darling, then over to the Oregon coast, where he had spent time as a boy. There was nothing there that he remembered. He finally made it to Corvallis, where he spent a few days, seeing his old classmates at the reunion and walking the campus. He visited the lecture room in the science building where he had first seen Ava Helen; it was still very much as it had been that day. He walked to the front of the room where the lectern had been, stood and looked out over the empty seats. He saw a class of young women dressed in the styles of the 1920s. And he said aloud, "Tell me what you know about ammonium hydroxide, Miss Miller."

He went to Salem and looked for the house where he and Ava

Helen had been married, then to Portland, where he participated in the presentation of Linus Wilson Darling's diaries to the Oregon Historical Society. He visited places on the way south where he had helped pave roads to work his way through college. Then he returned home. He had driven twenty-four hundred miles. And he had laid Ava Helen to rest.

⁓ﬀﬀ⁓

He made changes after he got back. He rented an apartment close to Stanford University, just a short way from the institute, and told his son Crellin that he could live in the Portola Valley house. He decorated the apartment with pictures of Ava Helen and himself, framed awards, and pieces of furniture from their travels. It was small and comfortable. He spent half his time there and half at the ranch at Big Sur.

He became involved once again in the institute and made some changes here as well. In early 1983 the Robinson suit was entering its fifth year, the complaints ranging from tenure violation to mental distress, slander, libel—"everything but the kitchen sink," as Robinson said. Legal costs on each side had reached somewhere in the neighborhood of $1 million. It was finally nearing a court date.

But the suit never reached a trial. In February, the institute board, weary of the cost in both dollars and negative publicity, decided to settle out of court. On the advice of his lawyers, Robinson accepted something between $500,000 and $600,000—just enough to clear his remaining legal debts and buy a new car, he later said—and walked away. He ended up trying unsuccessfully to start his own health institute at a ranch outside of Cave Junction, Oregon, where he continued to carry on some scientific work, home-schooled his children, and researched and published articles about the benefits of bomb shelters.

⁓ﬀﬀ⁓

Pauling's life took on a rhythm. He rose early, often around 4:00 A.M., built a fire in the fireplace if he was at the ranch, had some breakfast, and put in a full day's reading and theoretical work. At about four in the afternoon he would knock off for cocktail hour and watch a little television, the news mostly or *The People's Court*, which he enjoyed. He would fix himself dinner, oxtail soup or some pasta dish, and go to bed at about seven, where he would read until he fell asleep. He no longer enjoyed science fiction—he felt that he knew all of the plots and permutations by now and did not enjoy the new emphasis on extraterrestrial sex—but would occasionally read a Louis L'Amour western or a mystery. He enjoyed the British humor magazines Peter would sometimes send. He drank a little more vodka than before and took less care of his appearance; his outfits, topped always now with his black beret, were often poorly matched combinations of fraying sport coats, well-worn sweaters, and stained pants. He did not exercise beyond an occasional walk or a nude dip in the pool at the ranch. But his health—in part, he was certain, because of the megadoses of vitamins he took—was excellent.

He traveled incessantly, delivering a steady stream of speeches about peace and world affairs, endorsing the nuclear-freeze campaign, decrying Reagan's "senseless militarism" and the folly of the Star Wars program, traveling to Russia—where he was unable, despite his repeated attempts, to meet with Andrei Sakharov—and to Nicaragua, where he arrived on a peace ship loaded with medicine and food from Norway and Sweden and rode in a Land Cruiser to Managua with President Daniel Ortega.

He found that if he did not enjoy living alone, at least he could become accustomed to it. Ava Helen's death had thrown his life off balance, and he missed her desperately. But he righted himself and went on.

—◦◦◦—

The institute never recovered the momentum it had achieved in 1978. Any money that might have gone into an endowment to provide stable funding had been siphoned off by the Robinson suit. Richard Hicks began focusing his energy on cultivating a few wealthy donors, such as Armand Hammer, the Japanese philanthropist Ryoichi Sasakawa, and Danny Kaye, who had helped entertain the crowd at Pauling's eightieth birthday party. The institute began giving a "Linus Pauling Medal for Humanitarianism" to one or another wealthy potential donor at a black-tie dinner every year. Some of the efforts worked. After he received a medal from Pauling's institute, Hammer donated a significant sum of money. But it was never enough to move out of the warehouse.

Pauling did not help to promulgate an air of scientific integrity when he continued to tout vitamin C in the pages of supermarket tabloids and on television talk shows. An appearance on *Donahue* became especially embarrassing when Pauling was paired with fellow guest Jack La Lanne, an aging fitness advocate with a line of nutritional products to hawk.

Pauling seemed unconcerned. He had no trouble dealing directly with the public, even if many of his scientific colleagues thought it was inappropriate. His institute depended on the public now. If his ideas were adequately funded by the science establishment, he wouldn't have to take to the airwaves to promote them.

A low point in his professional image came in the spring of 1983, when Pauling took the stand at a San Francisco hearing held by a postal judge to investigate the alleged false and misleading claims of one Oscar R. Falconi, a mail-order vitamin dealer. Falconi, operating as the "Wholesale Nutrition Club," had advertised that vitamin C could protect against bladder cancer, stop urinary tract infections, help users kick tobacco and alcohol addictions, and cleanse the system of the ill effects of caffeine. His hearing would have drawn no attention but for the appearance of Pauling, whose testimony was tracked by the San Francisco papers and was then picked up in the news section of the science journal *Nature,* which brought it to his colleagues around the world. According to the *Nature* story, Pauling "appeared willing to defend even the most extreme of Falconi's claims," especially concerning vitamin C's effects in preventing cancer. The reporter also noted the testimony of Irwin Stone, described as "a retired brewing chemist" who testified that "all clinical diseases have as their cause a lack of vitamin C."

Dubious of Pauling's fixation on vitamin C, most scientists chose to ignore it in favor of remembering his earlier achievements. His career was now being rewarded with a string of tributes and honors, capped in 1984 by the award of the most prestigious honor given by the American Chemical Society, the Priestley Medal. On the day of the award, *USA Today* noted, "For years a pariah, Linus Pauling tonight gets the scientific equivalent of the Good Housekeeping Seal of Approval." This sign of Pauling's "returning respectability," as the *Washington Post* put it, was welcome. But to Pauling respectability was less important than his effort to make the world realize that cheap, safe vitamin C could greatly reduce human suffering.

The Main Kook

Then Moertel released his second study. Pauling had heard nothing about it until he was called by reporters in January 1985. They had received a news release, they told Pauling, saying that the second study had again shown that vitamin C had no effect on cancer patients.

Pauling had not even received the courtesy of a prepublication copy. But when he got one and read it, he was outraged. Yes, Moertel had answered Pauling's earlier criticism by using only patients who had received no previous anticancer drugs or radiation—in this case a hundred advanced colorectal cancer patients for whom no other known therapy was effective. The randomized, double-blind test adhered to all the rules of standard clinical testing. But Moertel had made a major error in Pauling's estimation. When the investigators saw no indication of an effect, defined as a decrease in tumor size, they immediately took the patients off vitamin C and in some cases put them on chemotherapy. Stopping the administration of a new test drug when it was shown ineffective was standard procedure—a lack of quick effect coupled with potentially severe side effects was good reason to revert to proven techniques—but it was wrong in the case of vitamin C, Pauling argued. Vitamin C was not a drug; it was a food. Taking patients off of it in mid-test could result in a rebound effect, where blood levels of C could drop dangerously low. Cameron had kept his patients on vitamin C until they died, giving the vitamin maximum time to do its work; by taking them off early, Moertel had not only failed to replicate Cameron's work; he may have hastened his patients' deaths.

When the Moertel study appeared in the *NEJM* on January 17, the results were accompanied by an editorial written by an NCI official who called them "definitive" and offered the suggestion that Cameron's findings were the result of "case selection bias." Vitamin C produced no significant increase in survival time. Pauling and Cameron were wrong. Case closed.

"I have never seen him so upset," Cameron wrote about Pauling a few weeks after the Moertel paper appeared. "He regards this whole affair as a personal attack on his integrity." But it was more than that, more even than the fact that the Moertel study might spell the end of any significant financial support for the Pauling institute's work on cancer. There may have been an emotional dimension to Pauling's reaction as well. By saying that vitamin C was worthless, Moertel's study cast doubt on everything Pauling had done to save Ava Helen's life.

So, at age eighty-four, Pauling fought the second Moertel study as hard as he had ever fought anything in his life. He sent out a press release calling the Mayo group's claim to have replicated Cameron's work "false and misleading." He wrote letters to DeVita, Moertel and his five coauthors, the author of the accompanying editorial, and the editor of the *NEJM*, Arthur Relman, demanding a "correction, retraction and apology" for their work. He threatened to sue the *NEJM*, the NCI, and the Mayo Clinic. He put together a slide show of flaws in the Moertel study and showed it to health groups. He wrote a paper showing that taking the patients off vitamin C increased their death rate and submitted it to the *NEJM*. He tried to spur congressional hearings. He went to the media—looking, Cameron said, "tired, old and upset" in his television interviews.

None of it worked. Pauling's frenzied attack allowed Moertel to take the high ground, saying, "We should move on to more hopeful areas of treatment and not remain dead set on a worthless treatment." Moertel had followed all the proper procedures for the clinical testing of a new drug; by saying now that vitamin C shouldn't be treated like a new drug, Pauling was attempting to change the rules in mid-game. He stopped responding to Pauling's letters. At the NCI, DeVita considered the matter closed. Pauling's lawyer talked him out of any legal action, noting that a judge was unlikely to take sides in such a technical, scientific problem. At the *NEJM*, Relman refused to print the two letters of refutation Pauling wrote—one for Moertel's study, the other for the accompanying editorial—saying one was enough. Pauling argued with him about it for almost a year, so alienating Relman that the influential editor also stopped communicating. Neither Pauling's letter nor his death rate paper saw print in the *NEJM*.

By the summer, Pauling had lost the battle in the scientific and popular arenas. The mainstream medical community could now say that it had gone out of its way to test Pauling's ideas and they had been twice disproven. Pauling's angry response only underlined his lack of objectivity. The popular press, incapable in general of analyzing the counterarguments Pauling presented would from now on always qualify their reports on Pauling with a mention of the Moertel results. The only group that stuck with Pauling was the alternative health crowd, a development that further marginalized him within the medical community. As one respondent to a fund-raising appeal from the institute scrawled across the reply form, "Are you guys whacked out? I respect Dr. Pauling, but you don't settle medical controversies by suing a medical journal."

Even Cameron thought Pauling's claims of bias and conspiracy were extreme, saying privately, "I think we are dealing with a bunch of fools rather than a bunch of knaves." He was careful to disassociate himself from Pauling's threats against Relman while he tried to get some of his own research published in the *NEJM*. Cameron's opinion moved more toward Pauling's, however, a year later, after he had revised his *NEJM* paper three times in response to reviewers' comments and still saw it rejected.

―――

But Pauling still had a case. The Mayo study was not a definitive refutation of Cameron's work. As the Australian science historian Evelleen Richards pointed out in a recent book-length analysis of the vitamin C and cancer controversy, Moertel had not only treated his patients differently by taking them off vitamin C earlier than Cameron, he had used a different scale for determining results. Moertel was treating vitamin C like an anticancer drug, where proof of efficacy is determined by a measurable change in the disease's progression: in this case, shrinkage of the tumor. Cameron had worked within a different framework, looking as well for an easing of pain, heightened energy, and increased survival time—improved quality of life, in other words. Sometimes tumors had shrunk in Cameron's experience, but that was only one effect out of several. Making it the only measuring stick of success skewed Moertel's study.

Rather than the final word on vitamin C and cancer, Richards said, "the history of this dispute has become an almost paradigmatic instance of the limitations of the clinical trial in resolving issues of medical controversy."

―――

If not the final word in fact, the Moertel studies proved, for the moment, the final word in practice. Two months after the second Mayo study came out, Pauling struck up a conversation with a cattle rancher sitting next to him on an airplane. The rancher, not knowing who he was talking to, mentioned that it's dangerous to visit a doctor because "you might get in with one of those kooks who talk about massive doses of vitamin C." Pauling looked at him for a moment and said, "I am the main kook."

He was, he noted to himself later, surprised to find that people thought of vitamin C this way.

So he decided to educate the public again. Pauling made plans to write a health book for the mass market, a popular overview that would distill everything he knew about the field and bring it to the public. The book, *How to Live Longer and Feel Better,* was finished in the fall of 1985 and published in early 1986 by Pauling's longtime publisher, Freeman. The front cover was its best advertising: A full-color close-up of Linus Pauling in his eighties: vibrant, ruddy, bright-eyed, glowing with evident good health as he grinned into the camera. Inside was a typically clear and straightforward review of nutrition, vitamins, and orthomolecular medicine. An entire chapter was spent discussing the way his ideas had been treated by the medical profession, with special attention paid to the Moertel studies, which Pauling called "the Mayo Clinic fraud." But the tone was upbeat in the end, with Pauling noting that the American Orthomolecular Medical Association now had five hundred members and that his ideas were being given a serious hearing in at least some medical schools.

Pauling recommended eating what you like in moderation—including eggs and meat—enjoying a drink or two every day, cutting down on sugar, and taking large doses of most vitamins. "You should eat some vegetables and fruits," too, he wrote. A little exercise couldn't hurt, smoking was out, and stress should be avoided. The only thing "alternative" about his approach to health was the megavitamin recommendation; Pauling was now advising between 6 and 18 grams of vitamin C per day, plus 400–16,000 IU of vitamin E (40–160 times the RDA), 25,000 IU of vitamin A (five times the RDA), and one or two "super B" tablets for the B vitamins, along with a basic mineral supplement.

The book was well received critically and sold well—for a short time even making the *New York Times* best-seller list—a modest success that helped raise morale at the institute and brought in some money as well. Fund-raising at the institute had again nosedived after the second Moertel study, with direct-mail appeals bringing in only one-quarter as much as they had just a few months earlier. Part of Pauling's book income was devoted to keeping the institute running.

At the same time, Pauling's personal morale was boosted by a party Caltech threw for his eighty-fifth birthday. The relationship between the school and its distinguished alumnus had been strained ever since his decision to leave more than twenty years earlier, but now it seemed that all that was forgotten. Caltech declared an academic holiday for the occasion. A banquet was given at which the speakers praised Pauling as the greatest chemist of the twentieth century, a man who deserved a third Nobel for his sickle-cell work, and the true father of molecular biology. Francis Crick was there to help celebrate. For the first time in many years, Pauling felt welcome in his own academic home.

To the Heart

In April 1989, the new head of the NCI, Samuel Broder, agreed to have a short chat with Pauling. Two and a half hours later, Broder had altered his thinking about vitamin C.

During that talk, Pauling brought his persuasive powers to bear, convincingly marshaling all of his arguments for vitamin C, new statistical interpretations of Cameron's data, and attacks on the Moertel studies. It was a tough sell. Broder, he remembered, "was not interested whatever in what I said during the first two hours." But by the end of the meeting, Broder was asking Pauling to send him some of Cameron's case histories and inviting him to speak to bigwigs in the NCI division of cancer prevention and control.

Then better news came. A few months after Cameron's data arrived, in January 1990, the NCI announced that it would cosponsor an international symposium on vitamin C and cancer later that year. The featured speaker would be Linus Pauling.

It was the result of a great deal of work on Pauling's part. He had never given up after the second Moertel trial, although for a while his attention had focused less on vitamin C than on other topics. During 1987, at age eighty-six, Pauling accomplished as much as three average scientists half his age, publishing six letters to editors, four forewords to books, three long historical reviews, and fifteen original scientific papers—about one publication every three weeks—in journals from *Nature* to the *Physical Review*, on topics from crystal structure to nuclear physics, superconductivity to metabolism, chemical bonding to world peace.

Vitamin C had not shown up much in his publications, but it was constantly on his mind. Research at the institute continued to buttress the idea that ascorbic acid could be of benefit in a wide variety of conditions—new research was now focusing on its effect on AIDS—and Pauling personally had been working with a colleague at the institute, Zelek Herman, on a new way to statistically analyze clinical trial data. When they used their new method on Moertel's and Cameron's cancer trials, they again found a strong positive effect of vitamin C. A version of their paper about this research had been delayed, rejected after months of consideration by the *NEJM*, but now, buoyed by his talk with Broder, Pauling submitted it to the *PNAS*. It was the start of a new campaign to legitimize the use of vitamin C in cancer treatment. On the same day the paper was published, in September 1989, Pauling made a sortie into the heart of the enemy camp, giving a talk on cancer and vitamin C at the Mayo Clinic. He followed the talk with a televised news conference.

The international conference on "Ascorbic Acid: Biologic Functions in Relation to Cancer" that the NCI helped arrange in the fall of 1990 in Washington, D.C., was a tremendous success from Pauling's standpoint. It was, first of all, a legitimization of his ideas, a recognition by the establishment that it was worthwhile discussing the value of vitamin C in preventing and treating cancer. This in itself was a major step forward. But there was more. The breadth of effects presented by scores of researchers from around the world surprised even the conference organizers. There were presentations on vitamin C's importance in enzymatic and nonenzymatic reactions, its effect in delaying tumor onset and growth, prolonging survival times, reducing treatment toxicity, and increasing the efficacy of other treatments. Special attention was focused on its action as an antioxidant to quench free radicals implicated in cancer genesis. "It was great! A great affair! Very exciting!" Pauling said when it was over.

Gladys Block, a conference organizer, was pleased with the general results of the meeting—"There is no question that the status of vitamin C has changed in a lot of researchers' minds," she said—but she was less happy about the response within the NCI. She had invited all the branch chiefs at the NCI, and out of that group "essentially nobody came," she said. The proceedings were also shunned by virtually all the major medical journals, with the exception of *Journal of the American Medical Association*. Although the conference raised some excitement about vitamin C as a way of relieving the toxicity of chemotherapy, the NCI's interest continued to center around vitamins as components of foods—there was no disagreement that foods high in vitamin C lowered the risk of cancer—and in its antioxidant action, not in the value of megadoses. That was reinforced when the panel of experts Broder gathered to review Cameron's clinical data concluded that, given the use of historical controls, the results were inconclusive.

—◆◆◆—

It was a halting step, but the NCI conference was the start of a shift in the attitude toward vitamin C. It was no longer a taboo subject at the NCI, and other researchers were beginning to get interested. Part of the growing legitimacy of vitamin C was rooted in a new interest in its role as an antioxidant capable of sopping up a dangerous class of molecules called free radicals inside the body. Free radicals, bits of molecular debris formed during chemical reactions, had been implicated in cell damage at a number of levels, and there was a growing consensus that they were contributors to everything from cancer and heart disease to the aging process. Antioxidants, it appeared, could lessen the threat, and vitamins C and E were excellent antioxidants.

Symbolic of the change in attitude—and toward Pauling—was a special meeting of the New York Academy of Sciences in early 1992 devoted to discussing high-dose vitamins and other nutrients. After multiple sessions addressing the antioxidant abilities of vitamin C and its value in other ways, a nutrition professor from Alabama said to the group during the discussion period, "For three days I have been listening to talks about the value of large intakes of vitamin C and other natural substances, and I have not heard a single mention of the name Linus Pauling. Has not the time come when we should admit that Linus Pauling was right all along?" The congregation of researchers responded, the professor wrote Pauling, by bursting into loud and enthusiastic applause.

In May of that year, a longtime Pauling collaborator, James Enstrom of UCLA, published an epidemiological study showing that men taking an average of 500 mg of extra vitamin C per day could expect to live on average five years longer than those who did not. *Time* magazine ran a cover story about the amazing properties of vitamins, with an emphasis on antioxidants such as vitamin C. The *Medical World News* told its readers in a cover story, "We may be in the midst of a grand upheaval that gives a handful of vitamins a protective role if consumed in higher-than-dietary amounts," and pointed to a recent NCI review that showed that vitamin C had a protective effect in thirty-four of forty-seven studies examined, helping prevent or control various cancers, including those of the lung, stomach, colon, and rectum.

All the good news was coming too late for Pauling's institute, which in 1991 suffered a financial crisis. There was not enough money to pay the staff, who were nonetheless loyal enough to Pauling to donate their retirement benefits to the institute and in some cases work without pay to keep the place going. But by the end of 1991, even that wasn't enough. The operation was several hundred thousand dollars in debt. Hicks said that if they didn't get $3 million in short order, the institute would have to close.

When asked by reporters about the financial problems, Pauling, now ninety years old, responded by turning the conversation to something more upbeat.

Vitamin C, he said, could help prevent heart disease.

Pauling had known about a link between vitamin C and heart disease almost from the beginning, when he first read studies that increased ascorbic acid could help lower cholesterol in the body, especially the LDL cholesterol linked to atherosclerosis. Around 1981 he had talked about starting research into vitamin C and heart disease at the institute. But cancer had captured his attention.

It wasn't until 1989 that his interest was revived by a visit from a charmingly enthusiastic young German physician named Matthias Rath. Rath had met Pauling years before, when Rath was still a student, when they had shared a car ride during one of Pauling's peace tours in Germany. Inspired, Rath had followed Pauling's career. After he earned his M.D. and decided to relocate in the United States, he visited Pauling and told him about a great theory he had. Vitamin C, he was convinced, was somehow intimately related to lipoprotein (a), a carrier of cholesterol in the blood and a component of the plaque that forms on artery walls during atherosclerosis. A lot of interest was centering on Lp(a), as it was called, because of its increasingly well understood role as a risk factor in heart disease. Lp(a), according to Rath's theory, was an evolutionary tool used by the body in part to strengthen artery walls that had been weakened hundreds of thousands of years ago when man's predecessors lost the ability to produce vitamin C. With increased doses of vitamin C, Rath said, levels of Lp(a) would decrease. The risk of heart disease would be reduced.

With his usual enthusiasm for any new proposal that supported the value of vitamin C, Pauling took the idea and ran with it. He also took on Rath as a researcher in his institute, and together they published a paper in the *PNAS* outlining the Lp(a)/vitamin C link. Soon Pauling was discussing vitamin C in relation to heart disease in the same way he had talked about colds and cancer a decade earlier. At the institute, Rath began testing the idea in guinea pigs. He also worked hard to stay near Pauling, making sure that his work on heart disease remained close to the top of the great scientist's priority list.

It was exciting work. Evidence presented at a National Heart, Lung and Blood Institute (NHLBI) conference in September 1991 showed that antioxidants such as vitamin C could prevent atherosclerotic lesions in rabbits and indicated that the same might be true in humans. The theory about why that happened was different—the NHLBI researchers related it more to the oxidation of LDL—but the effect was the same.

◈

In December 1991, age finally caught up with Linus Pauling. He had been experiencing intestinal discomfort which he thought might be diverticulitis. After a series of tests, however, his physician told him the bad news: he had cancer of both the prostate and the rectum.

Pauling underwent two surgeries for the rectal cancer in the winter of 1991–92 and spent much of the time during that period recovering in bed, either at the ranch or his Stanford apartment. Rath was constantly by his side, giving him medical advice, boosting his spirits, keeping his enthusiasm up for the advances they would make in controlling heart disease. Rath now wrote papers with titles such as "Solution to the Puzzle of Human Cardiovascular Disease: Its Primary Cause Is Ascorbate Deficiency Leading to the Deposition of Lipopro tein(a) and Fibrinogen/Fibrin in the Vascular Wall" and "A Unified Theory of Human Cardiovascular Disease Leading the Way to the Abolition of This Disease as a Cause for Human Mortality." He convinced Pauling to add his name as an author. But the writing was unlike Pauling's.

Rath's growing influence over Pauling began to concern those who had worked with Pauling longer at the institute. It especially worried one of the institute's trustees, Linus Pauling junior.

◈

Linus junior had been a member of the board of trustees since the beginning of the institute and had watched with increasing concern as his father fell ill and, after the 1991 fiscal crisis, the institute began to fall apart. By 1992 the staff had been cut by a third, including some of the top researchers. In February, Pauling had announced publicly that he had cancer. Richard Hicks resigned as vice president in March, and Rath was put in charge of handling the institute's financial affairs. Zuckerkandl left in July to start his own research institute. He was succeeded as president by Linus Pauling junior.

A power struggle developed over what was left of the institute, with Pauling's eldest son on one side and Rath on the other. During the spring, Rath—now sporting a vanity license plate on his car that read "NBL4MATT"—traveled with the increasingly frail Pauling to meetings in Denver and Toronto, caring for him, constantly impressing upon him the importance of his heart-disease research. In Toronto he applauded as Pauling announced the formation of the Linus Pauling Heart Foundation.

The relationship between Rath and Pauling had grown very close, very fast. It was capped on July 22, when Pauling signed a paper saying, "It is understood that Dr. Rath will continue the life work of Dr. Linus Pauling."

But Rath's influence was about to wane. On July 23, at a meeting of the institute's newly reformulated board of trustees that had been called to respond to a financial crisis at the institute, Linus Pauling stepped down and Linus Pauling junior succeeded his father as chairman of the board. Soon after, Rath left the institute.

―〰―

Pauling no longer cared much. He was, after all this time, after all his work, ready to rest. He was treating his own cancer with vitamin C, raw fruits, vegetables, juices, and an experimental immune-system-boosting therapy. He was spending his time doing what he liked at the ranch: making calculations and looking out to sea. If he had pain, he took some Tylenol. If there was too much, he had Darvocet and Valium.

"I am most interested in the human being's right to die with dignity," he had recently written. "If illness or injury puts me in a hopeless condition, I wish to be allowed to die, without unnecessary suffering, but with dignity."

That was the way he intended it to be. He stayed at the ranch as much as he could, still writing, this time a final version of his theory of the atomic nucleus, and seeing old friends who had heard about his illness and came to see him one last time.

―〰―

His children cared for him at the end, at the ranch and at Crellin's home in Portola Valley, the place where Ava Helen had died. He was as active as possible. During the last few weeks he met with friends, worked a little on problems, and gave a deposition, from his bed, to lawyers representing Matthias Rath, who had announced a lawsuit against both Pauling and the institute.

In the summer of 1994, at a meeting of the American Association for the Advancement of Science in San Francisco, Crellin arranged a special afternoon symposium to honor his father. The large lecture room was half-filled with an audience that appeared split in thirds among older, buttoned-down scientists, long-haired students, and natural-fiber-clothed health devotees. Pauling had to be brought to the event in a wheelchair, but once there, he insisted on walking into the room. The pain was so bad that his face beneath the black beret was ashen. When he entered, the audience started to applaud. The applause grew, and the audience rose to its feet, cheering. Pauling stopped and waved. Then he gave the crowd one of his trademark ear-to-ear grins.

―ᴜᴜᴜ―

Pauling died at the ranch at Big Sur on August 19, 1994.

Notes

KEY TO SOURCES

AHQP   Archive for the History of Quantum Physics, Niels Bohr Library, American Institute of Physics, New York City

CIT   Archives of the California Institute of Technology, Pasadena, California

FBI   Pauling's FBI file, released to the author through the Freedom of Information Act

LPI   Linus Pauling Institute of Science and Medicine, Palo Alto, California (Many of these documents have since been relocated to OSU.)

Nova   Transcripts of taped interviews made during the preparation of a *Nova* television program on Pauling in 1977 (housed at OSU)

OSU   The Ava Helen and Linus Pauling Papers, Kerr Library, Oregon State University

RAC   Rockefeller Archive Center, Tarrytown, New York

State FOIA   Pauling's Department of State file, released to the author through the Freedom of Information Act

CHAPTER 1: THE WEST

19 *Condon, Oregon, sits on the side of a high plateau:* The history of Condon is outlined in *The History of Gilliam County, Oregon* (1981); *An Illustrated History of
Central Oregon* (1905); *A Pictorial History of Gilliam County* (1983); and issues
of the Condon *Times* and Condon *Globe* newspapers between 1876 and 1910.
More detailed information comes from interviews with family members and
the correspondence of Herman Pauling.

21 *By the time he was nineteen Herman:* Information on Herman Pauling's early
life was gathered from interviews with family members as well as published
accounts in *The History and Genealogy of the Allied Families of Neal, Rossell,
Bilyeau, McNeil, Nash* (1970); *In Their Own Words: A Collection of Reminiscences
of Early Oswego, Oregon* (1976); and correspondence from Herman to Belle
Pauling in the possession of Linus Pauling.

23 *But Belle's reaction was more mixed:* The relationship between Belle and Herman Pauling is spelled out in Herman's many letters to Belle, in the possession of the Pauling family; information on her relationship with her
children comes from the author's interviews with Linus, Pauline, and Lucile.

23 *Her father, Linus Darling:* The Darlings were descendants of a Loyalist family
that emigrated to Canada from the United States during the Revolution.
(Ethan Allen was a relative by marriage.) Linus Darling thought for years
that his father, William Allen Darling, had been killed in the war but later
learned that he had settled in Michigan, married again, and lived a long
life. Father and son even had a reunion in Tacoma, Washington, near the
turn of the century. Linus Darling worked at bookkeeping, store clerking,
surveying, and farming and as a justice of the peace, book salesman, hotel
clerk, postmaster, newspaperman, and schoolteacher. (He was kicked out of
a teaching job in Lone Rock for drinking and gambling with his students.)
Eventually he made some money as a druggist in one of the first businesses
started in Condon; taught himself law and practiced it successfully (for
many years without a license); married a rich grass widow; even ran as a
Democrat in a heavily Republican county for county surveyor and other offices, losing every time. (He sought political office even before he remembered that he was Canadian by birth and quietly secured U.S. citizenship in
another county.) In addition to his three-volume diary kept at the Oregon
Historical Society, Linus Wilson Darling left a paper trail through county
courthouses and small-town newspapers across Oregon. Much of the information here comes from the Condon *Globe* and Condon *Times* newspapers
of the time. It was reported in the Portland *Oregonian* on March 2, 1877, that
he shot a man named "Champagne Charlie" to death; the man allegedly
sold Darling a ranch and then came back to reclaim it by force. There is no
evidence for the shooting other than the newspaper report. Darling was
good-looking, full of dreams, egotistical, disputatious with adversaries, and
generous with friends. His drinking and gambling with students in Lone
Rock, Oregon, led to a number of complaints against him, dated 1882 and
filed in the Wasco County Courthouse. Among the documents is a note to

the school district office from local school board member Charles Wick that reads: "The Charges against Mr. Darling are corect he don't deny them but promises to do better if given a chance, he shall have it, but if he dont proof it, out he goes like lightning."

23 *Belle's mother, Alcy Delilah Neal: The History and Genealogy of the Allied Families of Neal, Rossell, Bilyeu, McNeil, Nash* (1970).

28 *Pauling's Pink Pills for Pain:* Pauling's advertisements and business growth are documented in the Condon *Globe* and Condon *Times* newspapers of the years 1905 to 1910.

31 *"I am a father and have an only son:"* The letter, published on page 10 of the May 13, 1910, issue of the Portland *Oregonian,* was signed "P.W.P" (an apparent typographical error; it should have read H.W.P.). The letter's authorship was confirmed by Linus Pauling.

32 *Herman's reputation had been blackened:* Herman's arrest and trial were documented in the legal records kept at the Gilliam County Courthouse and in the Condon newspapers of the day.

CHAPTER 2: THE BOARDINGHOUSE

35 *He denied himself grief:* Pauling interview with author. Additional comments about that response are based on the opinions of child psychologists and family grief counselors.

37 *the children were allowed to "run wild":* Details about Belle Pauling's activities following her husband's death were provided through the author's interviews with her children and through county assessment and taxation records and archival documents at the Oregon Historical Society.

40 *His rejection of religion:* Linus Pauling, "Note to self," February 16, 1981 (LPI).

46 *They thought of him as a genius:* Albert Bauer, a classmate of Pauling's at Washington High School, noted in an interview with the author that Linus was "a student, out-and-out, all the time" who "kept pretty much to himself" and socialized little. But, Bauer added, Pauling's intellectual abilities were widely appreciated, noting, "The students in the class were as impressed with him [Pauling] as I was."

CHAPTER 3: THE BOY PROFESSOR

50 *America's most forward looking industrialists become science boosters:* Servos (1990), pp. 90–96, 204–19; see also relevant sections of Kevles (1987), Ihde (1964), and the original papers gathered in Farber (1966). Statistical information is from Thackray et al. (1985).

52 *"going from the lower middle to the upper middle class":* Reingold (1979).

53 *"I disliked qualitative analysis":* Linus Pauling, "Foreword," in McLachlan and Glusker (1983), p. v.

56 *"After I had removed the mucous membrane":* Pauling (1969), pp. 2–3.

57 *"hell, he knows more than the profs":* Edward Larson, interview with author.

58 *Pauling read Langmuir's work:* Langmuir (1919) and Lewis (1916) are wonderful introductions both to the chemists' views of atomic structure at the time and to a discursive, almost flow of consciousness style of scientific writing that is now rarely seen.

59 *a crisis of understanding:* By focusing on the history of atomic structure using Thomson as a starting point, I do not mean to slight the importance of Roentgen's discovery of x-rays or Becquerel's work with radioactivity, the development of spectroscopy, the decades of work on solution chemistry, or any of the many other threads from physical science that eventually became the fabric of quantum physics—merely to tell a simple story leading directly to Pauling's introduction to structural chemistry.

61 *This electronic "rule of eight":* The "rule of eight" was first proposed in 1904 by the German chemist Richard Abegg. The German physicist Walther Kössel related Abegg's rule to a proposed atomic structure with ringlike electron shells, but it took Lewis to tie it to the shared electron bond.

62 *It was a breakthrough paper:* Stranges (1982) provides an excellent overview of the development of ideas of chemical binding in relation to subatomic structure during this period.

69 *"Miss Miller?":* The anecdote about their meeting is from personal and published interviews with Pauling and Ava Helen. Ava Helen's flirtatiousness extended throughout her life: Interviews with Pauling's colleagues and students indicate that she knew how to make a man feel noticed. "She knew how to use her eyes" is a comment that was made more than once.

70 *"Boys had always told me":* quoted in *The Cambrian,* November 8, 1979, p. 17.

CHAPTER 4: CALTECH

75 *Caltech was still an idea under construction:* A general overview of the early history of Caltech is presented in Goodstein (1991). Kargon (1977) focuses on the importance of interdisciplinary research in its early history.

75 *his professors at Oregon Agricultural College couldn't answer:* Pauling would muse later that his lack of training at OAC might have been for the best, that his intellectual fermentation as an undergraduate may have contributed to his later success by bringing his curiosity to a fever pitch just as he arrived at a place where—hungry for answers, more mature—he could benefit from a new level of instruction. There is no statistical evidence, however, that a poor undergraduate school is an advantage. Sociologist of science Harriet Zuckerman has found that American-educated Nobelists are far more likely than other scientists to have graduated from "elite," generally Ivy League undergraduate schools.

79 *Noyes, working in the German style:* The first seminar in the United States was given at the University of Michigan in 1871. The first American Ph.D., another German innovation, was granted by Harvard in 1873. Johns Hopkins, the first U.S. university devoted solely to graduate education in the German research university style, was founded in 1876.

80 *King Arthur:* I am indebted to the science historian John Servos for his extensive historical work on Noyes's role in the development of physical chemistry in America, upon which much of this section is based. The essential texts are Servos (1976) and Servos (1990). Additional early Noyes material is from Pauling (1976) and Pauling (1958), Watson (1968), Kargon (1977), and Noyes material in the Caltech Archives.

83 *"I learned a great deal":* Pauling interview with author.

88 *x-ray crystallography was the single most important chemical research tool at Caltech:* Linus Pauling, "X-Ray Crystallography in the California Institute of Technology," in McLachlan and Glusker (1983), p. 29.

89 *"This was, of course, a shock to me":* This anecdote was related to the sociologist Harriet Zuckerman in a 1964 oral-history interview with Pauling (Columbia University Archives).

90 *he would see everything chemical in terms of structure:* Pauling's structural outlook built upon decades of work by other chemists. Kekulé (a former architecture student) dreamed up the circular structure of benzene in 1865 and invented a way of presenting chemical formulae in a structural manner (at least in two dimensions); his student van't Hoff and the French chemist Le Bel then brilliantly put forth the idea of the three-dimensional tetrahedral shape of carbon bonds, which helped explain Pasteur's stereoisomers; G. N. Lewis certainly had three dimensions in mind when he proposed his cubic atom. But Pauling was one of the first nonorganic chemists who used detailed three-dimensional structural thinking as an approach to almost every chemical problem.

90 *the term "covalent":* Stranges (1982), p. 248.

92 *"Richard the Red":* See R. A. Millikan to Noyes, August 1, 1921 (CIT).

92 *"pressure in New England to advertise and grab":* Tolman to Harvard Chemistry Department, May 30, 1928 (Harvard Archives).

96 *"you're supposed to know everything":* Pauling interview with author.

98 *"not even an earthquake":* Pauling interview with author.

98 *Paul Sophius Epstein:* Millikan would have preferred hiring C. G. Darwin or Peter Debye for Epstein's position, but they turned him down.

99 *"I never have been very interested in rigor":* Pauling interview with author.

100 *"My treatment is rather physical and intuitive":* Pauling to Noyes, November 22, 1926 (OSU).

100 *the structure of dwarf stars:* "Inter-ionic attraction theory in Dwarf Stars," a note dated 1924 in the notes and memoranda collection of the AHQP Pauling collection.

101 *"I was not very accustomed to thinking about other people":* Pauling interview with author.

102 *Edwin McMillan:* It's interesting to note Pauling's attitude toward credit for scientific work in relation to his work on x-ray studies of the alloys of lead and thallium with McMillan. Pauling was on his way to Europe when the paper was ready to be sent to the *Journal of the American Chemical Society,* and he wrote Noyes from New York on March 10, 1926, "The experimental work was done by McMillan alone, who also measured the photographs and made the computation. As a matter of fact, he was helped only a little bit in the interpretation of results. Hence, it might be desirable to have McMillan

send in the paper as his own, which would satisfy me. Or if you feel it better not to do this, possibly you could write, 'By Edwin McMillan with Linus Pauling' in case you approve of this method of designation. You must not interpret this to mean I am unwilling to have my name connected with this research, for I am not" (OSU). The paper as published was credited to both, with McMillan's name first. This accommodating attitude contrasts with Pauling's handling of the theoretical paper with Tolman.

102   *stitch together a doctoral dissertation:* All the papers were published in the *Journal of the American Chemical Society.* The five chapters include two corrections of structures made by others and three original determinations: his molybdenum work with Dickinson, magnesium stannide, and the isomorphous compounds ammonium fluoferrate, fluo-aluminate, and oxyfluomolybdate. One of the structures in the last paper was a mistake: The compound he thought was ammonium fluo-aluminate was later shown to be a fluosilicate whose structure had already been determined (Marsh and Schomaker [1991] p. 44).

105   *"a boyish delight in shocking":* Hildebrand (1958), p. 212.
105   *Lewis, with an eye for talent:* Pauling (1983a), p. 334.
105   *"the ablest candidate":* Noyes to National Research Council, March 24, 1925 (Archives of the National Academy of Sciences).
106   *study with the masters of quantum physics:* See records at OSU and the Archives of the National Academy of Sciences. Pauling had thought of applying to the International Education Board for funding also.
107   *the structure of benzene:* Pauling (1926a). Pauling credited Knorr with the idea of enclosing two nuclei within the orbits of a pair of electrons.
107   *"the topology of the interior of the atom":* Pauling's description of his work is found in the (1925–26) treasurer's report to the Guggenheim Foundation, p. 37.
108   *"Noyes was quite clever":* Pauling (1976).

CHAPTER 5: MUNICH

110   *Pauling's heart belonged to science:* It seems obvious that Pauling was trying to impress Noyes with his eagerness to get to work; indeed, later he and Ava Helen enjoyed traveling above almost anything else. While his heart may have belonged to science, his head was inclined to be free roaming. He was reading widely at this time in both popular science and studies of history. A 1926 notebook of Pauling's in the OSU collection includes a list of "Books to buy" that include I. A. Richards's *Science and Poetry,* Henry Breasted's *Human Adventure* and *The Conquest of Civilization,* James Henry Robinson's *Ordeal of Civilization,* and H. N. Russell's *Astronomy: Revision of a Young Man's Manual.*
111   *his Guggenheim fellowship:* Pauling was one of thirty-eight recipients selected from more than nine hundred applicants for the first "official" Guggenheim fellowships, announced in April 1926. Fifteen more had been selected in the "early" group. The total of fifty-three fellows included, in addition to

Pauling, writer Stephen Vincent Benét, composer Aaron Copland, cybernetics pioneer Norbert Weiner, and future physics Nobelist Arthur Holley Compton.

112 *"the old Hussar officer"*: Mehra and Rechenberg (1982), p. 17.

112 *"First, study mathematics"*: Kevles (1987), p. 200.

112 *Sommerfeld would never be listed:* In an interview with the author, Pauling said, "It's a little surprising that Sommerfeld didn't receive the Nobel Prize in my opinion, even though of course his theory of elliptical orbits under the fine structure of spectral lines wasn't quite right—it didn't involve the spinning electron. So it was probably proper for the Nobel Committee to postpone decision about Sommerfeld."

113 *"pounded out of the soil"*: Thanks to the science historian Russell McCormach for both suggesting and translating this quotation.

114 *he adhered to that model:* Pauling (1926a). Here Pauling wrote, "The continued success of the Bohr atom has led all physicists except the most cautious to attribute a certain reality to the physical concept underlying the theory; namely, that the atom is composed of electrons rotating in stable orbits about the positive nucleus. . . . Hence, in attempting to explain the chemical properties of substances on the basis of the structure of the atom it would seem desirable to assume the Bohr theory to be true." It is clear that when Pauling arrived in Munich he was hoping to pursue an old quantum theory approach to the chemical bond. In a letter to Noyes, April 25, 1926 (OSU), he tried to predict which theoretical problem Sommerfeld would give him, writing: "He [Sommerfeld] and Grimm have published a paper in which they discuss very specifically and satisfactorily certain cases of crystals in which atoms are connected by two electrons in orbits around two nuclei, and Dr. Niessen, from Holland, a fellow of the Rockefeller Foundation, is just publishing the first calculations regarding such orbits. Probably my problem shall be in this field."

114 *"straight-forward and well-grounded"*: Pauling (1926b), p. 34.

115 *"Life in America is not so difficult"*: from Jeremy Bernstein's "Profiles: Physicist," *New Yorker,* October 13, 1975, p. 88.

115 *"I was thinking about nearly every theoretical problem"*: For example, Pauling's "Abstracts of papers and research problems" for 1926 (OSU) lists more than fifty questions to attack, including various projects concerning the properties and crystal structures of alkaline-earth halides and other crystal-structure problems; dielectric constant problems; "the diamagnetic susceptibility of electrons in motion about a number of nuclei arranged regularly in space must be studied"; various notes concerning chemical bonding (including the notes "Solve the wave mechanics problem of penetrating orbits" and "Burrau's result permits a first approximation to the H_2 molecule to be made. . . . This will not be good for energy, but will give moment of inertia with some certainty (done by Condon)"; relative dissociation constants of complex ions; approaches to paramagnetism; notes on making new apparatus; expanding his screening constants work; explanations of various spectral data; etc.

115 *the magnetic field should have a large effect:* In a letter to G. N. Lewis, June 10, 1926 (UC Archives, College of Chemistry Records), Pauling wrote, "At pres-

ent I am calculating the motion of a molecule of a substance such as hydrogen chloride in crossed electric and magnetic fields, and am reaching the
same conclusion as that I announced in Pasadena before I left. . . . An effort
is being made to observe the effect experimentally in Pasadena. It will be
most interesting if it is successful; for as far as I can see the phenomenon
could not by any means whatever be explained on the basis of the classical
theory."

116   *"He listens so intently"*: Ava Helen Pauling to Belle and Lucile Pauling, June
23, 1926 (LP).

116   *Pauli was also becoming infamous:* Weisskopf (1989), p. 159.

118   *Heisenberg created a new mathematical approach:* Heisenberg did not create the
idea of using only observable quantities himself; the concept in physics had
a distinguished lineage going back through Einstein to Mach. But Heisenberg applied it most effectively to the question of quantum physics.

119   *"the whole idea of quantum jumps"*: Moore (1989), p. 227.

119   *Sommerfeld, like many physicists of the day:* "Have I mentioned before that he
[Sommerfeld] accepts completely the wave mechanics, as a good mathematician would, for all quantum theory problems are thus reduced to the
boundary conditions of the old mathematical physics?" Pauling to Noyes,
December 17, 1926 (OSU).

120   *"a trace of physical picture behind the mathematics"*: Pauling to Van Vleck, July
29, 1926 (OSU).

120   *"we are now finished with all that nonsense"*: Moore (1989), p. 222.

120   *bullshit:* Moore (1989), p. 221.

121   *That was probably wrong, Pauli told him:* I am relying on Pauling's correspondence of the time rather than his later memories. In various interviews and
Pauling (1981a), Pauling insisted that he was "reasonably sure" he intended
to use quantum mechanics on the HCl problem before meeting Pauli, explaining, in an interview with the author, "I had carried out the discussion
on the basis of the old quantum theory because there had been quite a bit
of effort to find examples of problems where the old quantum theory gave
the wrong answers, and I was adding one more example." Pauling's contemporaneous letters, however, give no indication that he intended to find a
"wrong answer" or that he had much of an idea of how to use quantum mechanics. Although Sommerfeld had been presenting quantum mechanical
concepts in Munich, prior to the Zurich meeting there is no mention of
quantum mechanics in Pauling's letters or research notes. As late as June 10,
less than two weeks before the Zurich meeting, he wrote Lewis about his
reasoning for thinking the old quantum effect he was predicting would
occur, adding, "An effort is being made to observe this effect experimentally in Pasadena. It will be most interesting if successful. . . ." (Pauling to
Lewis, June 10, 1926, University of California Archives, College of Chemistry records). In a later letter to Lewis, Pauling termed the failure to discover the magnetic-field influence an "unexpected result" (Pauling to
Lewis, January 8, 1927; UC Archives, College of Chemistry Records). His letters after the congress credit Pauli specifically with suggesting a quantum-
mechanical approach. "We went to Zurich June 22–26 for a congress on
magnetism, called by Debye. Professor Sommerfeld presented my work on

the influence of a magnetic field on the dielectric constant of HCl; later W. Pauli jr. showed me that probably the effect definitely predicted by the old quantum theory would not be predicted by the new quantum mechanics. . . ." (Pauling to Noyes, July 12, 1926, OSU). "I have just finished some calculations on the dielectric constant of HCl. The old quantum theory . . . gave directly and unequivocally the prediction that with easily realizable magnetic field strengths the application of a magnetic field to HCl at right angles to the electric field should change the dielectric constant noticeably. . . . At Pauli's suggestion, I have just finished the calculations with the new quantum mechanics, which says no change should occur. The fact that Mott Smith and Daily in Pasadena have just shown no change to occur experimentally shows that we have a pronounced failure of the old quantum theory and success of the new" (Pauling to Loeb, July 27, 1926; Bancroft Library, UC Berkeley).

121   *"a remarkable failure of the old":* Pauling (1927). The paper was received for publication on September 10, 1926.

121   *"the new mechanics spoke the truth":* Linus Pauling, "Notes for lecture course, 'Introduction to Wave Mechanics with Chemical Applications'" (Fall 1927, p. 2; AHQP collection, Bohr Library).

124   *"Worried from illness and too much responsibility":* Details of Belle's hospitalization are from her admissions records from the Oregon State Hospital.

124   *"silly, abusive and unintelligible letter":* Pauling to Lucile Pauling, August 1, 1926 (Linus Pauling personal collection).

125   *"I have become rather accustomed to slander":* Pauling to Lucile Pauling, August 1, 1926 (Linus Pauling personal collection).

125   *a long-planned vacation in Switzerland and France:* In Paris, Pauling spent some time visiting and trading editing services with John Van Vleck, a young American editor of the *Physical Review.* Pauling and Van Vleck had corresponded concerning diatomic molecules in electric fields, a problem Van Vleck was also interested in at the time, after Van Vleck happened across the manuscript of Pauling's earlier paper in the *Physical Reviews* office and contacted him concerning a mathematical error.

125   *"He looks quite dashing":* Ava Helen Pauling to Lucile Pauling, October 27, 1926 (Linus Pauling personal collection).

125   *"recognized as really knowledgeable":* Hans Bethe oral history, AHQP, January 17, 1963, p. 8.

125   *"A young, lanky man":* Herman Mark, interview with the author.

126   Privatdocent *Gregor Wentzel:* Bethe remembered Wentzel as "probably the most interesting of the whole group," at Munich during the time Pauling was there. "I had the impression here was a man who really knew things," he said, "and who probably knew more than Sommerfeld." Hans Bethe oral history, AHQP, January 17, 1963, p. 8.

126   *Pauling wrote a short paper on his correction:* Received for publication October 27, 1926. See Pauling (1981a) for a discussion of his work with Wentzel's paper.

128   *"I am persuaded that these questions":* Sommerfeld to J. W. Jeans, December 24, 1926 (OSU); translation courtesy of Wolfgang Leppmann.

128   *"I believe that this work is of considerable value":* Pauling to A. A. Noyes, December 17, 1926 (OSU).

128   *the Braggs and other crystallographers:* Pauling referred to the atomic sizing work of Wasastjerna and Goldschmidt especially. See Servos (1976), pp. 992–93.

129   *the Royal Society paper included:* A more detailed discussion of these works is found in Paradowski (1972), pp. 208–11, 294–302.

129   *"I think that it is very interesting":* Pauling to Noyes, December 17, 1926 (OSU).

129   *a six-month extension of his Guggenheim:* Pauling to the John Simon Guggenheim Memorial Foundation, December 27, 1926 (OSU).

129   *"My colleagues and I have the impression":* Sommerfeld to the Guggenheim Foundation, December 23, 1926 (OSU). Thanks to Helmut Plant for the translation from German.

130   *"I would return to the Institute":* postscript dated December 28, 1926, appended to letter, Pauling to Noyes, December 17, 1926 (OSU).

130   *"So far I have no definite position":* Pauling to G. N. Lewis, January 8, 1927 (UC Archives, College of Chemistry Records).

130   *"Dr. Noyes would be quite disappointed":* G. N. Lewis to Pauling, June 14, 1927 (UC Archives, College of Chemistry Records).

130   *During nearly a year in Munich:* "I practically ignored the chemical institutes of the University of Munich. They were in a different part of town. . . . I would go to the chemical laboratory once in awhile to look things up in the literature, to see the chemical journals. I didn't introduce myself there. . . . I don't believe I ever visited the Institute of Physical Chemistry, and I wasn't invited to give a seminar there, or to speak." After Pauling's paper on the sizes of ions and the structure of ionic crystals came out, Fajans asked Pauling to his apartment (all from Pauling interview with Zuckerman, p. 19).

130   *"I had something of a shock":* Pauling interview with author.

131   *"Molecular Chemistry":* postscript dated December 28, 1926, appended to letter, Pauling to Noyes, December 17, 1926 (OSU).

131   Der Kopenhagener Geist: Weisskopf (1991), p. 65.

132   *Heisenberg . . . would wonder:* Cline, 1987, p. 200.

133   *"it is meaningless to argue about determination versus free will":* Pauling oral history, AHQP, March 27, 1964, pp. 9–10, 27. Pauling favored at this time the "operational" philosophy of Harvard physicist Percy W. Bridgman, whose well-known 1927 book *The Logic of Modern Physics* redefined physical concepts in terms of sets of operations.

134   *It was the only time Pauling saw Bohr:* Pauling also spent several days in Copenhagen at Bohr's suggestion with the Japanese theorists Nishima and Sugiura, "talking with them and trying to help in the work they were doing . . . on a problem that involved some aspects of structural chemistry" (Pauling interview with Zuckerman, p. 17).

134   Knabenphysik: Mazumdar (1989), p. 1195.

135   *All the Statue of Liberty needed, he said, was a wristwatch:* Moore (1989), pp. 231–32.

135   *"I have rather regretted":* Pauling to John Van Vleck, August 9, 1927 (OSU).

137 *While he talked a great deal with Heitler and London:* Handwritten introduction to a collection of papers on "Quantum Mechanical Work in Europe, 1926–1927" (AHQP Pauling Collection microfilm notes).

137 *he worked on his calculations alone:* There are, however, a few lines of notes in Heitler's hand among Pauling's calculations from this period (AHQP Pauling Collection microfilm notes, 1927).

CHAPTER 6: THE BOND

138 *published more papers per year than any group in the nation:* Between July 1925 and August 1926, for example, Caltech contributed more than one-fifth of the total published physics research in the United States, outstripping such old centers as Harvard, MIT, and Princeton (Goodstein 1991, p. 106).

138 *Thomas Hunt Morgan, was coming:* Goodstein (1991), p. 117.

139 *his first official graduate student:* Pauling had overseen the graduate work of one of Dickinson's students, Sterling Hendricks, when Dickinson went to Europe during the time Pauling was still a graduate student himself and would sometimes refer to Hendricks as "my first graduate student." But Sturdivant was the first whose work he directed as a professor.

139 *Goudsmit writing some chapters, Pauling wrote others:* Samuel Goudsmit oral history, AHQP, December 7, 1963, pp. 50–51.

139 *Millikan had complained:* Pauling oral history, AHQP, March 27, 1964, p. 25.

139 *Noyes made the decision on his own:* Line spectroscopy was one of Millikan's personal fields of interest, and he may have resented the intrusion of a chemist. Evidence against Millikan's meddling, however, comes from Fred Allen, a former OAC teacher of Pauling's who went on to a productive career at Purdue. Allen remembered, "Robert A. Millikan, visiting at Purdue in the early twenties, told me with a twinkle in his eye, 'Linus is too good a man to waste on chemistry. I'm going to make a physicist of him.' In 1956 I told this to Linus, who said, 'He tried. He offered me the headship at Caltech.' I said, 'Why didn't you take him up?' Linus replied, 'Chemistry made me a better offer'" (Allen's annotated 1921–22 OAC grade book, Purdue Chemistry Library). Pauling has never mentioned being offered the head of the physics division in any other place.

140 *intimidated by the competition:* "I recognize that many physicists are smarter than I am—most of them theoretical physicists. A lot of smart people have gone into theoretical physics, therefore the field is extremely competitive. I console myself with the thought that although they may be smarter and may be deeper thinkers than I am, I have broader interests than they have" (Pauling [1991], p. 69).

140 *"I am sure that I shan't be led astray":* Pauling to W. L. Bragg, May 31, 1928 (OSU).

141 *the one-electron hydrogen molecule-ion:* Pauling (1928b).

141 *Pauling's entrance onto the American scientific stage:* See Sturdivant (1968), p. 5.

142 *his 1928 note:* Pauling (1928a).

142   *"the salient features of the Lewis atom"*: Pauling to Lewis, March 7, 1928 (OSU). It is interesting to note that Lewis's reply to Pauling included a molecular-orbital-type criticism: "I am sorry that in one regard my idea of valence has never been fully accepted. It was an essential part of my original theory that the two electrons in a bond completely lose their identity and can not be traced back to the particular atom or atoms from which they have come; furthermore that this pair of electrons is the only thing which we are justified in calling a bond. Failure to recognize this principle is responsible for much of the confusion now prevailing in England on this subject, where they still talk of polar bonds and semi-polar bonds, and so on. I think that in London's paper and in yours a little too much emphasis is placed upon the origin of the paired electrons" (Lewis to Pauling, May 1, 1928 [OSU]).

142   *"it was so complicated"*: Pauling interview with author.

144   to predict *their structures?"*: Pauling interview with author.

145   *"a prosperous farmer, dressed not quite in the latest fashion"*: Thomas and Phillips (1990), p. 89.

145   *"close packing,"* he called it: Pauling recognized that he was building on the Braggs' work. He sent Lawrence Bragg, along with a copy of his brookite manuscript, a note saying, "We . . . are pleased to have begun work in the field which you recently opened—the study of complex ionic crystals." (Pauling to W. H. Bragg, May 31, 1928 [OSU]).

145   *"Bragg thought that that was his field"*: Pauling interview with author.

146   *"the older generation of scientists"*: Pauling to R. J. P. Williams, January 10, 1990 (LPI). A good deal of the perceived generation gap, Pauling thought, was due to Bragg's refusal to learn quantum mechanics, which left him, in one important way, back in the nineteenth century.

146   *the electrostatic valence rule:* This approach built upon Alfred Werner's coordination theory for inorganic compounds built around metal ions. Briefly, Pauling's electrostatic valence rule states that the state of maximum stability of an ionic crystal is that in which the valence of each anion, with changed sign, is equal to the sum of the strengths of the electrostatic bonds to it from the adjacent cations.

146   *He first published his rules:* Pauling (1928b); followed by a more detailed treatment in Pauling (1929).

147   *two complex silicate crystals:* Pauling was especially impressed with the topaz gem he used in his x-ray work at this time, a large crystal he borrowed from Tiffany's in New York and kept until they demanded it back. Pauling interview with author.

147   *the stochastic approach:* Pauling (1955a), p. 297.

148   *"the cardinal principle of mineral chemistry"*: Bragg (1937), p. 35.

149   Scientific American *spotlighted the work:* news item, *Scientific American,* March 1931, p. 13.

149   *found himself much wanted:* Goudsmit and Uhlenbeck, for instance, were imported to the University of Michigan. Notable among Pauling's American-born peers—first of the new generation of quantum physicists and chemists—were John Slater, J. H. Van Vleck, Robert Mulliken, Edward Condon, Carl Eckart, D. M. Dennison, and J. R. Oppenheimer—about a dozen

in the late 1920s. See Sopka (1980), 3.55, for a list of those teaching quantum mechanics in America at the time.

149 *"forbade him to do so":* Pauling oral history, AHQP, March 27, 1964, p. 31.

150 *"The prospect of becoming associated with the Chemistry Division of Harvard":* Pauling to Gregory Paul Baxter, February 28, 1929 (Chemistry Department files, Harvard University Archives).

150 *a promotion the next fall to associate professor:* Caltech Executive Council minutes, March 23, 1929 (Pauling personal collection).

150 *building new courses in crystal structure:* F. A. Saunders to G. P. Baxter, April 5, 1929 (Chemistry Department files, Harvard University Archives).

151 *"a sort of second-class citizen at Harvard":* Pauling interview with author.

151 *the Caltech executive council granted Pauling:* Caltech Executive Council minutes, May 17, 1929 (Pauling personal collection).

151 *"I have regained my peace of mind":* Pauling to G. N. Lewis, May 18, 1929 (College of Chemistry Records, UC Archives, Berkeley).

151 *Oppenheimer made an immediate impression:* Kevles (1987), p. 218. During this time, Oppenheimer came to Pauling, already known as a fine speaker, for advice on lecturing. "Decide what it is you want to talk about, then find some agreeable subject of contemplation not remotely related to your lecture," Pauling said, "and then interrrupt that from time to time to say a few words" (Smith and Weiner [1980], p. 131).

152 *Oppenheimer's large boyhood mineral collection:* Smith and Weiner (1980), p. 112; also Cassidy (1992), p. 119.

152 *minerology, Dante, and pederasty:* Oppenheimer's poems to Pauling are in the OSU collection.

152 *"I think he was in love with you:"* The Oppenheimer affair is a matter of Pauling family legend. Author's interviews with Linus Pauling and Linus Pauling, Jr.

153 *"Your method certainly led":* W. L. Bragg to Pauling, August 8, 1928 (OSU).

153 *"Our favorite daydream":* Pauling to W. L. Bragg, August 3, 1928 (OSU).

153 *"essentially no contact with Bragg":* Thomas and Phillips (1990), p. 87.

154 *"Bragg thought of me as a competitor":* Pauling to R. J. P. Williams, January 10, 1990 (LPI). See also Judson (1979), p. 76.

154 *Hermann Mark:* Pauling (1981c), p. 63.

155 *"it wasn't anything that could make money":* Herman Mark, interview with author.

155 *Pauling, however, was overwhelmed:* Pauling (1984), p. 337. See also Pauling (1965a), p. 11.

156 *Spurred by Slater's work:* Of this period in 1930, Pauling has said, "Slater pointed out that the $2p$ wave functions, in their real form rather than the complex form with imaginary numbers, could be described as pointing in the directions of the three Cartesian coordinates, 90 degrees from one another. . . . In my earlier work I was trying to hybridize, I guess I would say now, the complex functions in the x/y plane. It hadn't been clear to me that it was only for special applications that these complex functions were the important ones, and that the real functions are just as good, or even better, for other purposes. So I think that the fact that Slater had just published a paper, or given a lecture, in which he made use of these three equivalent real functions—not imaginary, or not complex—stimulated me to go back to the calculations I had made and referred to in my 1928 paper" (Pauling interview with author).

156 *"the problem became quite a simple one"*: Pauling interview with author.

157 *"I just kept getting more and more euphorious"*: Nova, side 9.

158 *a paper appeared in the* Physical Review: Slater (1931).

158 *Pauling dashed off a note:* "Three of these results have been independently obtained by Slater and announced in a preliminary communication. He points out the possibility of the formation of four equivalent tetrahedral bonds by a carbon atom (as I did in 1928) without giving the tetrahedral eigenfunctions and without recognizing that tetrahedral eigenfunctions are also important even when fewer than four bonds are formed. . . ." (Pauling [1931a]).

158 *"There is no theoretical physicist"*: Pauling to Slater, February 9, 1931 (American Philosophical Society Library files).

158 *"our general points of view seem so similar"*: Slater to Pauling, April 11, 1931 (American Philosophical Society Library files).

159 *could not think of anyone qualified to referee it:* Pauling interview with author.

160 *A cartoon of the occasion:* Redepicted on the cover of *Bulletin of the History of Chemistry* 7 (1990).

160 *His only regret:* Pauling and Ikeda (1992), p. 12.

160 *"I shouldn't let this go to my head"*: Pauling interview with author.

CHAPTER 7: RESONANCE

161 *Einstein was asked by a reporter:* Pauling thought that Einstein was interested in understanding molecular structure only "in a rather general way rather than in the detailed way in which I am interested" (Pauling 1981, p. 133). After a vacation at Caltech's expense—hobnobbing with movie stars, walking the Pacific beaches, and enduring meal after meal with Robert Millikan—Einstein turned down a Caltech salary offer so munificent it sent shock waves throughout the institute's board of trustees. He settled instead in Princeton.

162 *X-ray crystallography was a physicist's tool:* Max Perutz wrote, "Few chemists took much notice of x-ray crystallography's new insights until 1939, when Pauling published *The Nature of the Chemical Bond.*" Max Perutz, "How Lawrence Bragg Invented X-Ray Crystallography." In Thomas and Phillips (1990), p. 79.

162 *"the physical chemists never use their eyes"*: quoted in Brock (1993), p. 388.

162 *"except for Pauling, nobody paid any attention to it"*: Harold Urey, AHQP oral history.

163 *"In general no attempt is made"*: Ramsay and Hinze (1975), p. 451.

164 *Lewis himself helped talk Pauling through:* At the end of the paper Pauling thanked Lewis "for his valuable suggestion relative to the structure of the nitroso compounds and for his stimulating interest in the work as a whole" (Pauling [1931b], 3236).

165 *In Pauling's third "Nature of the Chemical Bond" paper:* Pauling (1932a).

165 *Pauling was now using the term "resonance":* "The principle of resonance says that if a molecule can be described in two (or more) equally acceptable ways (where 'acceptable' effectively means states with the same energy, different versions of the lowest possible energy state for that molecule) then the molecule has to be thought of as existing in both (or all) of those states simultaneously. The 'real' molecule is a hybrid of all the possible structures with the same lowest energy" (Gribbin [1987], p. 129).

167 *a relative property he called electronegativity:* Pauling was careful to point out that his concept of electronegativity "is not analogous to the electron affinity of atoms, but is closely related to the intuitive conception of electronegativity possessed by the chemist" (Pauling [1932c], 3582).

167 *another in the "Nature of the Chemical Bond" series:* Pauling (1932c).

167 *By comparing the electronegativity:* The general idea of electronegativity had been discussed before Pauling, but not in a quantitative manner.

167 *the creation of a xenon compound:* On the xenon fluoride fiasco, see Pauling to Fred Allen, September 13, October 12, and November 16, 1932; July 12, 1933; October 24, 1962; Gary Schrobilgen to Pauling, May 30, 1986, and Pauling to Schrobilgen, June 12, 1986 (all LPI).

168 *benzene was described:* Pauling (1970), p. 996.

168 *They expanded their approach to other aromatic molecules:* Pauling and Wheland (1933).

168 *The last two entries in Pauling's nature of the chemical-bond series:* Pauling and Sherman (1933a); Pauling and Sherman (1933b).

169 *"I made a lot of simple quantum-mechanical calculations":* Pauling interview with author.

170 *"an optimist rather than a pessimist":* Van Vleck and Sherman (1935), p. 167.

170 *By 1933 he oversaw:* "Chemistry Division List—1933–34" (OSU).

170 *job offers kept coming in:* Pauling interview with author.

170 *his Caltech salary went up rapidly:* Pauling interview with author: "My salary went up rapidly in the early thirties because they got worried about—well, I'd been offered a professorship at Harvard which I turned down—but they got worried about my leaving." In the mid-1930s Pauling remembered receiving a salary of $7,000 per year, which, he thought at the time, seemed like a lot compared to his Uncle James Campbell's circuit court judge salary of $4,000 per year.

170 *His annual teaching stints at Berkeley:* Pauling AHQP interview, part 2, tape 103b.

170 *writing a book on valence together:* W. A. Noyes to Lewis, April 30, 1932; Lewis to Noyes, May 20 1932; Pauling to Lewis, June 24, 1932 (all OSU).

170 *The academy was the nation's most:* The average age of NAS members at the time of Pauling's election, according to figures from the NAS Archives, was over sixty. Pauling would hold the "youngest-ever" title for membership in the NAS until 1976. His extraordinarily early election was likely linked to the active roles that Noyes, Millikan, and Hale took in NAS administration.

171 *"Pauling arrived just before noon":* Kamen (1985), p. 57.

172 *"To awaken an interest in chemistry":* Pauling to Noyes, November 18, 1930 (OSU).

173 *Pauling "lit on the biggest guy in the class":* Robert C. Davidson to author.

173   *"I helped in making the indexes":* Nova, side 18, p. 4.
173   *"If a woman thinks honestly and clearly":* "Note, 1927." Ava Helen Pauling papers, OSU.
174   *"A scientist, in order to be doing his work":* Nova, side 7, p. 2.
174   *"I began listening to what she was saying":* Nova, side 14, p. 3.
175   *"Call unemployment leisure":* Kargon (1982), 162.
176   *"California marks now, as England did three centuries ago":* "California Institute of Technology: Its Aims, Accomplishments, Needs and Financial Condition," 1923, p. 4, a promotional piece prepared by Robert A. Millikan's office (CIT archives, RAM 30). Millikan, like many other scientists and non-scientists of the time, discriminated against Jews. His attitude is exemplified by his description of Paul Ehrenfest: "His suavity and ingratiating manner are a bit Hebraic (unfortunately), and to be fair perhaps I ought to say too that his genial open-mindedness, extraordinarily quick perception and air of universal interest and inquiry are also characteristic of his race." On the subject of bringing Paul Epstein to Caltech, Millikan wrote Hale, "Do you still think we want to get Epstein, anyway? Even though a Jew?" After making absolutely sure a Gentile of the same caliber couldn't be found, Millikan hired Epstein (Goodstein [1991], p. 98). For more on Millikan, see Kargon (1977 and 1982) and the extensive Millikan collection in the Caltech Archives.
176   *A position on the Caltech board of trustees:* Among the most important backers of the school during the 1920s were Arthur Fleming (lumber), Henry Robinson (oil, telephone, railroads, lumber, eventual director of Southern California Edison Co.), Harry Chandler (head of the *Los Angeles Times,* among other things), William Kerckhoff (lumber), and Allan Balch (electricity). Those who could not get on the board were in the 1930s offered a position as a California Institute Associate in exchange for a donation of $1,000 per year for ten years, in return for which they were given the run of the Institute, access to its faculty, and memberships in the beautiful new faculty club, the Athenaeum, with its luncheons on the piazza and dinners in the baronial dining hall.
177   *The business community loved it:* For more on Caltech's corporate structure, see Servos (1976) and Kay (1987), p. 116.
177   *"My reply to him":* Millikan to Robert Marsh, Jr., undated (RAM 31, CIT).
177   *Caltech was a "temple to . . . science":* "Seat of Science," *Fortune,* July 1932.
177   *Research and travel moneys vanished:* Goodstein (1991), pp. 239–40; Anonymous (1932), p. 23.
177   *Pauling took the pay cut:* Kohler (1991), p. 343; Pauling to Millikan, June 1, 1933 (RAM 30, CIT).
178   *For a time, Hale:* Goodstein (1991), p. 240; Noyes to Hale, October 8, 1931 (RAM 30, CIT); Pauling to Millikan, June 1, 1933 (RAM 30, CIT).

CHAPTER 8: THE SCIENCE OF MAN

179   *John D. Rockefeller, Sr., had a problem:* Yergin (1991), p. 111.
180   *"Make the peaks higher":* Weaver (1967), pp. 25 and 36. For more on the devel-

opment of the Rockefeller philanthropies and their effect on science, see Fosdick (1952); Jonas (1989); Kevles (1987), 192; and the extensive records at the Rockefeller Archive Center.

180 *a growing scientific "establishment":* Kargon (1977), pp. 15–19. The National Research Council, formed largely by Hale during World War I as a scientific advisory system for government, was especially important in forging links between scientists, government officials, and public-minded businessmen, all of whom would play a role in the philanthropic funding of science during the 1920s and 1930s. Examples: Carnegie Corporation of New York president J. R. Angell was a former NRC chair; Hale, offered the top position at the Carnegie Institution, turned it down and made sure it went to his friend and NRC associate John C. Merriam; Max Mason, longtime friend of Millikan's, went directly from the presidency of the Rockefeller Foundation to an academic post at Caltech; Noyes was AAAS president in 1927; T. H. Morgan in 1930 simultaneously served as president of the NAS and of the AAAS; Millikan, Noyes, and Hale were active in NAS and NRC policy making.

181 *"The result of this arrangement would be":* Noyes to Hale, April 21, 1919 (Hale Collection, microfilm roll 28).

181 *$200,000 for various chemical research projects:* Servos (1976), pp. 181–83.

181 *"Whether the Research Council belongs to the National Academy":* quoted in Kay (1993), p. 68.

181 *By the end of the 1920s, funding:* Funding details for this period are found in the Caltech collection at RAC. For the sake of brevity the name "Rockefeller Foundation" is used here to subsume the various subunits and divisions that awarded funding.

181 *Noyes, adept at getting Carnegie money:* Noyes had some misgivings about the medical school idea, although it was an active topic until 1930, when Morgan said he would not participate. See Noyes to Hale, December 22, 1922; Noyes to Hale August 17, 1923; Noyes to Henry Pritchett, January 30, 1925; Morgan to Hale, December 4, 1930 (all CIT).

182 *Pauling, becoming friendly with the younger men in geneticist Thomas Hunt Morgan's group:* Pauling (1986), p. 2.

183 *"a unified series of investigations":* Linus Pauling, "A Program of Research in Structural Chemistry" (RAC 1.1, 205, Box 5, Folder 70).

184 *Weaver's personal stock of original ideas:* See Abir-Am (1982), p. 348, for sources on Weaver and the Rockefeller Foundation's plans in the early 1930s.

185 *"the friendly invasion of the biological sciences":* Weaver (1967b), pp. 227–40.

185 *Weaver was not alone in his enthusiasm:* Wells, Huxley, and Wells et al. (1934), pp. 1478–79.

185 *"The Science of Man":* See Kohler (1979), p. 263, and especially Kay (1993), pp. 44–47.

186 *Not even Millikan could convince the foundation:* Kevles (1987), p. 248.

186 *"were all the rest of the Chemistry Department wiped away":* Weaver diary notes, October 23–25, 1933 (RAC 1.1, 205, Box 5, Folder 71).

187 *"a speculative mind of the first order":* Weaver diary notes, October 23–25, 1933 (RAC 1.1, 205, Box 5, Folder 71).

187 *Weaver proselytized for his molecular biology approach:* Pauling (1986), p. 3.

187   *But the message did not seem to sink in:* See Linus Pauling, "Brief Account of Research in Chemistry Supported by Grant from the Rockefeller Foundation," October 24, 1933 (RAC 1.1, 205, Box 5, Folder 71); Linus Pauling, "Rockefeller Fund," October 24, 1933 (OSU).

187   *He ended up comparing Pauling to Louis Pasteur:* Abir-Am (1982), p. 358; Weaver to Pauling, December 19, 1933 (OSU).

188   *He followed the money:* See Pauling to Bragg, April 11, 1962 (OSU); and Pauling's own interpretation of the incident in Pauling (1968a), pp. 528–29.

189   *the "giant protein problem":* Weaver (1970), p. 59.

191   *he came up with an orientation that seemed to fit the binding curves:* Pauling (1935a, p. 421). Pauling's conclusions were later proven wrong by more sophisticated structural analysis.

191   *Pauling dropped it:* Warren Weaver Diary, April 5, 1935 (RAC 1.1, 205, 6.74).

192   *Weaver and Pauling had moved from patron and grantee to coconspirators:* Weaver to Pauling, November 23, 1934 (RAC 1.1, 205, 6.73), Frank Blair Hanson to Warren Weaver, November 20, 1934 (RAC 1.1, 205, 6.73).

192   Introduction to Quantum Mechanics: Wilson wrote about one third of the manuscript, especially the sections dealing with his specialty, molecular vibrations. His memories of Pauling and the book are recounted in Wilson (1980), pp. 19–21.

192   *a paper on "orientational disorder":* Pauling (1935b). See also Barclay Kamb's comments in the essay "Crystallography of Water Structures," in McLachlan and Glusker (1983), p. 336.

192   *He spent much of the summer of 1935:* Kay (1987), p. 124.

193   *They tried oxygenated blood and deoxygenated blood:* A good description of these experiments is found in Judson (1979), p. 523.

193   *"It is interesting and surprising":* Pauling and Coryell (1936), p. 213.

195   *"the grandfather of all proteins":* Astbury (1936), p. 803.

195   *X-ray diffraction was still inadequate:* Kohler (1991), pp. 334–36.

196   *"a few ill lit and dirty rooms":* quoted in Olby (1974), p. 263.

198   *a hydrogen bond:* A good review of the early history of Pauling's work with the hydrogen bond can be found in Quane (1990).

198   *the two of them had roughed out a new theory:* In the resulting 1936 paper, Mirsky and Pauling did not credit a 1931 paper by the Chinese researcher Hsien Wu, who proposed that the compact form of native proteins was maintained by what he called "secondary forces"—bonds weaker than covalent bonds—that were disrupted during denaturation.

CHAPTER 9: KING, POPE, WIZARD

200   *"likely to have at most five or six years of active life":* Noyes to Hale, October 20, 1928, and following, in Millikan Collection (CIT).

201   *the overall budget for the Division of Chemistry and Chemical Engineering:* Servos (1976), p. 179; Kay (1987), p. 118.

202   *"Whether he is old or young":* Noyes to E. W. Washburn, February 4, 1929 (CIT).

203 *"one good man at the head overburdened with administrative details"*: A. A. Noyes, "Faculty Participation in College Management," undated address (CIT).

203 *"aggressive managerial style"*: Borsook oral history, p. 43 (CIT).

203 *"Noyes's white-haired boy"*: Joseph Koepfli, interview with author.

204 *"But I never did anything"*: Pauling interview with author.

205 *Millikan told the upstart:* Noyes to Hale, July 27, 1935 (CIT); Pauling to author, May 3, 1991.

206 *"Pauling is restless"*: Noyes to Hale, July 27, 1935 (CIT).

206 *A compromise was finally reached:* "Organization of Division of Chemistry," hand dated July 31, 1935; Chemistry Division papers (CIT).

207 *When Warren Weaver visited Caltech in March 1936:* Warren Weaver diary, March 6, 1936 (RAC 1.1, 205, 6.75); Pauling notes headed "March 6, 1936" (OSU).

207 *Weaver also met with Noyes:* Kay (1987), p. 125; Noyes to Pauling March 21, 1936 (OSU).

207 *But now it was Pauling who counseled restraint:* Pauling to Noyes, April 11, 1936 (OSU); Weaver diary, May 5, 1936 (RAC 1.1, 205, 6.75).

208 *Pauling had "worried and pestered [Noyes]"*: Weaver diary, undated, headed "Pasadena" (RAC 1.1, 205, 6.76).

209 *"in spite of misgivings"*: Dickinson, Tolman, and Lacey to Millikan, June 12, 1936 (RAM Collection, microfilm roll 22, CIT).

209 *he dashed off a brief and blunt letter of refusal:* Pauling to Caltech Executive Council, August 19, 1936 (RAM Collection, microfilm roll 30, CIT Archives).

209 *"Our Chemistry Department is still in an unorganized state"*: Pauling to J. H. Van Vleck, August 26, 1936 (OSU).

209 *too apt to be "dictatorial"*: Weaver diary entry, September 21, 1936 (RAC 1.1, 205, 6.75).

210 *Millikan replied frostily:* Millikan to Pauling, November 17, 1936 (RAM Collection, microfilm roll 30, CIT).

211 *"P. seems genuinely to appreciate"*: Weaver diary, January 31, 1937 (RAC 1.1, 205, 6.75).

211 *"I am sure that everyone is pleased"*: Pauling to Weaver, April 16, 1937 (RAC 1.1, 205, 6.76).

211 *"I, for some reason, developed the habit"*: Pauling interview with author.

211 *"one of the most competent persons"*: John Roberts, interview with author.

212 *"Many thanks for your letter"*: Pauling to A. E. Mirsky, May 25, 1937 (OSU).

212 *Life in the division went on smoothly:* See Swift oral history, 54 (CIT); Beckman oral history, pp. 33–34 (CIT); Koepfli interview with author.

212 *Yost stayed at Caltech:* On Yost and Pauling see author's interviews with Pauling, John Roberts, Verner Schomaker, and Richard Noyes; Ernest Swift oral history, p. 74 (CIT), Yost to Pauling, January 5, 1953 (Yost Collection, CIT).

212 *Students were flocking to Caltech:* Pauling to Warren Weaver, October 14, 1939 (OSU); for students' feelings about Pauling, see author's interviews with Richard Noyes, Verner Schomaker, and Aaron Novick; and Wilson (1980), p. 21.

214 *He also made plans to write a book:* Pauling to R. H. Fowler, June 26, 1942 (OSU).

214 *"I knew of course what Bill Astbury"*: quoted in Judson (1979), p. 81.

216   *"he arranged to have me agree with him":* Linus Pauling, "Notes for Corey Memorial Meeting, Caltech," dated May 5, 1971 (OSU).

217   *few chemists had taken notice of the arcane art of crystallography:* Max Perutz, "How Lawrence Bragg Invented X-ray Analysis." In Thomas and Phillips (1990), p. 79.

218   *"I have just returned from a short vacation":* Lewis to Pauling, August 25, 1939 (OSU)

218   *Pope Linus the Second:* anecdote related to author by John Edsall and confirmed by Pauling in interviews.

219   *the bio-organic grant request to the Rockefeller Foundation:* Report, "A Program for the Development of Organic Chemistry at the California Institute of Technology and for an Attack on Biological Problems by the Methods of Organic Chemistry and Structural Chemistry," dated August 7, 1937 (RAC 205, 6.77).

219   *a "field of knowledge of transcendent significance":* Pauling (1938), p. 563.

219   *"if not the elixir of life, a better understanding":* E. Crellin, "Mr. Crellin's Address" (OSU).

221   *For the junior posts, Weaver suggested:* Pauling to Weaver, June 1, 1937; Weaver to Pauling, June 16, 1937; Pauling to Weaver, June 21, 1937 (all OSU).

222   *"Oh, by the way, I was talking with Gasser":* Mirsky to Pauling, January 6, 1938 (OSU).

CHAPTER 10: THE FABRIC AND THE CHAIN

223   *Dorothy Wrinch:* Wrinch background is from Abir-Am (1987); Senechal (1977 und 1980); Kohler (1991), pp. 338–41; and the Wrinch papers in the Sophia Smith collection at Smith College.

225   *"Proteins are so different":* Wrinch (1939), p. 482.

225   *"I would awfully like the chance":* Wrinch's correspondence with Pauling is found in the OSU and Smith College collections.

226   *"nicely symmetrical structures":* Pauling to Warren Weaver, March 6, 1937 (OSU).

226   *"a queer fish":* Kohler (1991), p. 340.

226   *He wanted the cyclol issue resolved:* Warren Weaver diary, November 1, 1937 (RAC).

226   *Pauling saw in the* New York Times: *New York Times,* September 5, 1937, p. 13; Pauling's comment on the photo is from an interview with the author.

227   *Pauling would "make a serious effort":* Warren Weaver diary, November 1, 1937 (RAC).

227   *The private report he made to Weaver:* Linus Pauling, "Notes on talks between Dr. D. M. Wrinch and Linus Pauling. January 26 and 27, 1938. Cornell" (OSU). Pauling's opinion of Wrinch was set before they ever met, on the basis of his reading her work and what he had heard from his contacts in Britain. He knew, for instance, that Wrinch had alienated Bernal, a man whose opinion Pauling valued.

227   *"Since talking with Dr. Wrinch":* Pauling to Weaver, February 23, 1938 (OSU); Linus Pauling, "Report on the Work of Dr. Dorothy Wrinch," March 31,

1938 (OSU). See also Pauling to Weaver, April 11, 1938 (RAC); and Weaver to Pauling, March 2, 1938 (OSU).

228 *"She certainly has been a catalyst":* W. E. Tisdale to Warren Weaver, April 25, 1939 (RAC).

228 *a concerted, four-pronged attack on protein structures:* Pauling to Weaver, June 10, 1938 (RAC); Pauling to Weaver, July 29, 1938 (OSU). In a postscript Pauling noted that there was no indication this approach had been used before. It was technically challenging, and he gave it up before Zechmeister arrived.

228 *Acceptance of the hydrogen-bonding idea:* See, for example, Bernal (1939a), an overview of the state of protein knowledge in the early part of that year that doesn't mention Pauling's and Mirsky's paper; see also Srinivasan, Fruton, and Edsall (1979), p. 108.

229 *Pauling did not believe it:* Pauling to David Harker, October 17, 1938 (OSU).

229 *In January 1939 a series of short notes:* W. L. Bragg, *Nature* 143:73 (1939); J. D. Bernal, *Nature* 143:74 (1939); J. D. Bernal, I. Fankuchen, and D. Riley, *Nature* 143:897 (1939).

229 *"jealous, brutal and treacherous":* Quoted in W. E. Tisdale to Warren Weaver, November 21, 1938 (RAC).

229 *Langmuir championed Wrinch's ideas:* See papers cowritten by Langmuir and Wrinch in the late 1930s; also Mirsky to Pauling, January 6, 1938 (OSU).

230 *"The Structure of Proteins":* Pauling and Niemann (1939).

230 *"'The De-Bunking of Wrinch'":* Alex Todd to Pauling, July 28, 1939 (OSU).

231 *Wrinch had decided to give up protein work:* Dorothy Wrinch interview with Warren Weaver, April 3, 1939 (RAC).

231 *Lamb explained:* Wrinch's correspondence with Lamb is found in the Sophia Smith Collection at Smith College; Pauling's and Niemann's with Lamb is in the OSU collection. There is no evidence that it made any difference to Lamb that Pauling was one of the *Journal's* associate editors; he appeared to use standard procedure in giving Wrinch a chance to make her case.

232 *"it has not seemed to us worthwhile":* Pauling to Wrinch, January 31, 1940 (OSU).

232 *Harker had had his own run-ins with Pauling:* Pauling described Harker in an interview with the author as "unable to accept responsibility or supervision of any sort" while a student.

232 *"you are in need of some advice":* Pauling to David Harker, July 6, 1940 (OSU); Harker to Pauling, July 16, 1940 (OSU).

233 *"I get absolutely in despair":* Senechal (1977), p. 22.

233 *the quiet presentation of facts":* Weaver to Pauling, November 1, 1939 (RAC).

233 *"Ah, it's the Y chromosome":* quoted by David Harker in Senechal (1980), p. 14.

234 *another researcher found that a cyclol-like structure:* Apart from the ergot alkaloids, cyclols have not been found elsewhere in nature.

236 *"a great man":* Pauling to Weaver, January 12, 1939 (RAC); for more on Landsteiner, see Heidelberger (1969).

236 *Landsteiner's most recent book on immunology:* Landsteiner (1936).

237 *This idea of complementary shapes:* A good discussion of the history of the template theories of immunology from Ehrlich to Pauling is found in Silverstein (1989), pp. 64–71.

238 *"the best course of instruction":* Pauling interview with author.

238 *"One idea to be considered among others":* Landsteiner and Rothen (1939), p. 66.

239 *"I found that Landsteiner and I":* Pauling (1970), p. 1005.

240 *"What is the simplest structure which can be suggested":* Pauling (1940), p. 2643.

241 *he found Delbrück's approach:* Of Delbrück. Pauling said in 1938, "His training in physics is good and he attacks biological problems in a sensible way. He understands their nature, whereas Dr. Wrinch does not" (Pauling to Weaver, February 23, 1938 [RAC]).

241 *"I have written a little note":* quoted in Fischer and Lipson (1988), p. 157.

243 *"Pauling will not pile hypothesis upon hypothesis":* Weaver interview with Pirie, April 3, 1941 (RAC).

CHAPTER 11: THE HAWK

245 *"my difficult and not enviable position":* The correspondence between Schoen-flies and Pauling is cataloged at OSU.

245 *"The feeling in America".* Pauling to Leslie Sutton, September 11, 1939 (OSU).

246 *"It used to be believed":* Bernal (1939b), p. xiii.

246 *"a salaried employee of the State":* Bernal (1939b), p. 387.

247 *"Set science free":* Bernal (1939b), p. 404.

247 *Pauling devoured the book:* Ralph Spitzer to Pauling, January 26, 1948 (OSU): "I am finally reading Bernal's book on the social function of science. I remember your bringing it up in the seminar when it first came out."

248 *"Should not our country help Britain":* Pauling, handwritten Union Now speech excerpts (OSU).

248 *"Pauling ran rings intellectually":* John Edsall, interview with author.

249 *He publicly protested:* "A Counter-Statement," *Science* 91:504–5 (1940). Pauling signed with eighteen others, including T. H. Morgan and most of his research group. See also Pauling to A. H. Compton, May 14, 1940 (OSU).

249 *a discussion of wartime needs:* Pauling to Robert L. Taylor, November 29, 1949 (OSU).

250 *Pauling gave his sketches to Reuben Wood:* Pauling, Wood, and Sturdivant (1946), pp. 795–96; also Pauling to D. A. Mills, December 27, 1955 (OSU).

251 *"I'd better get off the train":* Pauling interview with author.

251 *had Holmes Sturdivant organize a small factory:* "Interview with Arnold Beckman," Beckman Center for the History of Chemistry, pp. 21–22.

252 *he admitted that he felt worn out:* Pauling, interview with author; Pauling to C. Lockard Conley, November 17, 1969 (LPI).

254 *The name they gave him was Thomas Addis:* For background on Addis, see the manuscript "Thomas Addis" prepared for the *Biographical Memoirs of the NAS* by Pauling and Kevin Lemley (LPI files) and the Addis correspondence files at OSU.

255 *Ava Helen became his nurse:* Pauling interview with author.

256 *"We thought we might lose him":* Edward Hughes *Nova* interview, side 27, p. 3 (OSU).

256 *squads of Caltech students, armed with ax handles:* Rubel (1992) provides an amusing overview of Caltech during the war.

257 *"blown Pasadena off the map":* Earnest Watson, quoted in Goodstein (1991), p. 255; for the funding effect the war had on Caltech, see Goodstein (1991), pp. 244–45.

257 *"A large part of Caltech":* William Fowler, quoted in Goodstein (1991), p. 245.

258 *"We sort of revolutionized modern chemistry":* Pauling interview with author.

258 *"everybody is kept on the go":* Pauling to T. Eyster, June 14, 1942 (OSU).

259 *a model for other war labs:* Information on the wartime powder project came from author's interviews with Pauling, Walter Schroeder, and Garmon Harbottle.

259 *Pauling did not need long to think about it:* Pauling interview with Keith Riggs, p. 2 (OSU); interviews with author. I can find no written evidence to corroborate Oppenheimer's visit and job offer to Pauling other than Pauling's own memory. The chemistry section of the Manhattan Project involved subjects outside of Pauling's area of expertise; it was more appropriate for inorganic chemists like Don Yost, who was eventually asked to direct it. Perhaps Oppenheimer offered it to Pauling first because he felt it was his duty to an old friend. Perhaps he wanted to make up for past transgressions. Perhaps he knew that Pauling would turn it down and offered it merely as a courtesy.

260 *oxypolygelatin:* See Pauling to Addis, March 3, 1942, and May 3, 1943; Pauling to John Warren Williams, March 23, 1943 (all OSU); Pauling interviews with author. Despite losing his funding for this project in 1943, Pauling continued for twenty years to push for the adoption of oxypolygelatin. Although it was eventually used by veterinarians, was carried for a while by L.A. motorcycle police for use in accidents, and was reportedly widely used in the People's Republic of China, Pauling never made much money.

260 *"Things are indeed much changed here":* Pauling to C. D. Russell, August 31, 1943 (OSU).

261 *"I am happy to report that our immunochemical work":* Pauling to Weaver, November 18, 1941 (OSU).

262 *"the possibility of a new method":* Pauling to W. Huse, March 3, 1942 (OSU).

262 *"For the first time in medical history":* Science supplement, March 20, 1942, p. 12; see also news coverage in the *Journal of the American Medical Association* 119:1377 (1942), in which the editors noted that similar work had been done in Russia and Germany many years earlier.

263 *tempting Weaver with the "reasonable possibility":* Pauling to Weaver, March 25, 1942 (RAC); Frank Blair Hanson to Pauling, May 7, 1943 (RAC).

263 *"Not many people have written":* Pauling to Merck Research, April 18, 1942 (OSU).

263 *"a feeling of pessimism":* Henry Bull to Pauling, June 17, 1943 (OSU).

264 *"he would think the chances less than 50-50":* Frank Blair Hanson diary, May 3, 1942 (RAC); see also Hanson to Pauling, May 7, 1943, and Pauling to Hanson, May 17 and 28, 1943 (all RAC).

264 *"Professor Pauling's views have received wide notoriety":* René Dubos to F. B. Hanson, July 14, 1943 (RAC).

264 *Pauling quietly abandoned his patent application:* Pauling to California Institute Research Foundation, May 29, 1943 (OSU).

265   *"Pauling was such a powerful figure":* Elvin Kabat, interview with author. Kabat had also confronted Pauling in person during a visit Pauling made to Michael Heidelberger's laboratory at Columbia during the war. Heidelberger left the two of them alone for a few moments and was horrified upon his return to find Kabat engaged in a loud argument over the artificial antibody work. Heidelberger later dressed down Kabat for his ungentlemanly conduct.

265   *The silence ensured that Pauling's reputation would not suffer:* Only in private conversation, rippling out to researchers in other fields in the form of gossip, would the degree of Pauling's overstatement of the antibody case filter out. Possible reasons that senior immunologists kept quiet: The background of most researchers in the field prior to Pauling was biological, and there may have been a reticence to take on a major figure whose knowledge of chemistry was so much greater; Pauling's stature in general would tend to mute criticism; it was unhealthy in 1943, as it is now, to take on someone whose help you might need in the future. In the case of Landsteiner's public silence, there may have been a more specific reason: In 1943 he was trying to get Pauling to write a chapter on molecular structure for the new edition of his book on serology.

265   *"We did succeed in creating artificial antibodies":* Pauling interview with author. In the absence of strong public criticism, Pauling's idea of artificial antibodies died a slow death, still occasionally appearing in the literature years later. Ironically, although antibodies are not formed in the way Pauling suggested, his general ideas about forming specific complementary molecules have been borne out in recent experiments in a field called "molecular imprinting" in which polymers are cross-linked around substrate molecules; one such experiment was carried out successfully at Pauling's suggestion with silica-based polymers. "The irony is," Joshua Lederberg said in an interview with the author, "that Pauling's principle has been validated." It is possible to demonstrate, in other words, that Pauling's general idea was correct but not with the system he was using during the war.

265   *"because of some technician":* Ray Owen, interview with author.

267   *it would reign as the most plausible theory:* Silverstein (1989), pp. 126–27.

268   *"to satisfy what I perceived as parental requirements":* Linus Pauling, Jr., interview with author.

CHAPTER 12: THE GRAND PLAN

270   *"a funny thing happened":* Hughes oral history, p. 6 (CIT).

271   *More than $40 million was funneled into Caltech:* Goodstein (1991), pp. 245, 262.

271   *"Although proteins are so complex":* Pauling to Frank Blair Hanson, June 27, 1944 (OSU).

272   *he wrote a ten-page plan:* Linus Pauling, "The Division of Chemistry and Chemical Engineering at the California Institute of Technology: Its Present State and Future Prospects," August 15, 1944 (OSU).

273   *a lukewarm letter:* Weaver to Pauling, September 21, 1944 (RAC).

273   *"I would trade all the staff":* F. O. Schmitt to F. B. Hanson, November 1, 1944 (RAC).

273   *He would remember that morning:* See Pauling's interview with Keith Riggs (1986) and Pauling interviews with author.

274   *"an institute of molecular biology":* Weaver interview notes, September 10, 1945 (RAC).

274   *"he was more interested in fruit flies":* Pauling interview with author. "Of course," he added, "I'm sure that *I* was criticized as being more interested in crystals and molecules than in the other members of the chemistry division." Pauling's opinion on the decline of the Caltech biology division is found in Warren Weaver's interview notes, September 10, 1945 (RAC).

275   *"movements toward collectivism":* R. A. Millikan to V. Bush, April 2, 1945 (OSRD Collection, National Archives).

275   *palace coup:* See Goodstein (1991), p. 265; author's interview with Lee DuBridge; Millikan to Page, July 25, 1945 (CIT); Pauling interview with Warren Weaver, September 10, 1945 (RAC).

276   *Beadle knew how:* See Weaver (1967b), p. xii; Kay (1987), pp. 190–93.

277   *"Don't let Pauling":* Alfred Sturtevant to Beadle, October 13, 1945 (CIT). Pauling's attempts to bring Beadle to Caltech are outlined in correspondence in the Beadle files at CIT.

277   *Beadle accepted the chairmanship:* As Pauling succinctly put it in an interview with the author, "I went to Stanford and talked him into accepting."

277   *written almost entirely by Pauling:* Beadle to Pauling, March 7, 1946 (CIT).

277   *"the dark forest of the unknown":* from an undated handwritten draft of Pauling's Rockefeller Foundation proposal (CIT Chemistry Division, file 1.7). Pauling would later use the "safari" analogy widely in talks about his protein work. See also Pauling to Weaver, December 4, 1945 (OSU).

278   *"I didn't have to give him a sales talk":* Beadle to Pauling, December 12, 1945 (CIT).

278   *"a magnificent plan":* Weaver to Beadle, January 28, 1946 (CIT).

279   *National Foundation for Infantile Paralysis:* The NFIP, founded by Franklin Roosevelt in 1938, was immensely rich at the time. Beadle had gotten wind of the fact that the group was interested in funding basic research and told Pauling to visit them while in New York. Pauling and Beadle originally asked for $3 million over twenty years, but received only a fraction of it, science historian Lily Kay has written, in part because the NFIP "considered Pauling's work on artificial antibodies to be nonsense, and objected to a lack of viable research in virology at Caltech" (Kay [1987], p. 233).

279   *By 1947, the chemistry division's budget:* Kay (1987), p. 236.

280   *"The answer can be found":* Weaver (1961), p. 337.

281   *one of the most important things Pauling ever wrote:* Joshua Lederberg interview with author. Pauling was neither the originator of the idea of complementarity in immunological reactions nor the only researcher advocating it in the 1940s. But he, Pressman, and Campbell were the first to quantify and clearly outline the nature of the forces involved, and Pauling stated the case for complementarity more strongly than others. "It may be emphasized that this explanation of specificity, as due to a complementariness in structure which permits non-specific intermolecular forces to come into fuller operation than would be possible for non-complementary structures, is the only explanation which the present knowledge of molecular structure and intermolecular forces provides," he wrote (Pauling [1945a], p. 293). Most importantly, Pauling was the first to take the idea of complementarity and apply it imaginatively to other biological systems.

282 *"Schrödinger's discussion of thermodynamics is vague":* Pauling (1987a), p. 229. This was a blunt assessment, since it appeared in what was supposed to be a celebratory volume lauding the centenary of Schrödinger's birth.

282 *"Schrödinger says that living matter":* Pauling to Ralph N. Lewis, October 9, 1957 (OSU).

282 *Life, in Pauling's view:* Pauling (1948d), p. 1.

283 *"We are so far from equilibrium":* Pauling (1987a), p. 232.

283 *"We may say that life has borrowed":* Pauling (1948f), p. 708.

284 *"it was obvious—to me at any rate":* Pauling (1990), 63.

285 *a set of molecular pliers:* For an outline of Pauling's ideas about enzymes, see Pauling (1990), p. 63. Pauling's enzyme hypothesis was linked to antibodies in another way: In the late 1940s he figured that it should be possible to create artificial enzymes by making antibodies to enzyme inhibitors, which theoretically worked because their structure was similar to the strained form of the target molecule, the "activated complex." His first experiment along this line—an attempt to make antibodies to malonic acid, an inhibitor of catalase—didn't work, so Pauling gave it up. "I just got busy with other things and never repeated the experiment," he remembered. "It was a very busy time for me." Forty years later, making artificial enzymes in this way became a very active research field.

285 *senses of taste and smell:* "Even the sense of taste and odor are based upon molecular configuration rather than upon ordinary chemical properties," he wrote in 1946. "A molecule that has the same shape as a camphor molecule will smell like camphor even though it may be quite unrelated to camphor chemically" (Pauling [1946a], p. 1064).

285 *The behavior of viruses, too:* Pauling (1948d), pp. 5–6.

285 *"The detailed mechanism by means of which a gene":* Pauling (1948d), p. 10.

286 *Pauling turned to medicine:* See Pauling to R. O. Roblin, Jr., March 17, 1941; to Manuel Morales, February 26, 1945; to Seeley G. Mudd, November 6, 1945; to Willis Whitney, November 20, 1945; to Thomas Midgely, Jr., March 3, 1942 (all OSU).

286 *When Pauling heard that, something clicked:* The most complete account of Pauling's initial thoughts about sickle-cell anemia are found in Pauling (1955b); see also Pauling (1970), p. 1011; Pauling to William Castle, May 28, 1963; to Anthony Allison, November 5, 1969; and to C. Lockard Conley, November 17, 1969 (all OSU).

287 *a central concept in designing new drugs:* Pauling (1949a), p. 109. The inhibition of bacterial growth by competitive substances, or antimetabolites, proved later to be less effective than antibiotics because in part what was food for the bacterium was also food for the host. (The sulfa drug's tar-

get, para-aminobenzoate, happened not to be an essential metabolite in man.) The general concept, however, is the basis of much of cancer chemotherapy.

287   *"When it has become possible":* Pauling (1948b), p. 57.

287   *the path to molecular biology:* Much later, Pauling would aver, "Molecular biology is a branch of chemistry, just as biochemistry is a branch of chemistry" (Academy of Achievement interview, 1990).

288   *"The average biochemist":* Alex Rich, commentary accompanying Pauling (1990).

288   *"The evidence for the theory":* Pauling (1947a), p. 2970.

288   *By 1948 he was telling audiences, "I believe that we can":* Pauling (1948d), p. 1.

289   *"Science—the Endless Expenditure":* quoted in Penick, Pursell, and Sherwood (1965), p. 143. A review of the genesis of the Bush report can be found in England (1976).

290   *only six chemistry majors:* Pauling to Carl Hinshaw, May 7, 1945 (OSU).

290   *back-room influence and mediocrity:* Pauling (1945b), p. 3.

291   *The degree of domestic organization:* Author's interviews with Crellin Pauling and Linda Pauling Kamb.

292   *"a great blow to me":* Pauling to Wendell M. Latimer, April 4, 1946 (OSU).

292   *one supporter, Ava Helen:* See, for instance, Joseph Koepfli interview with author.

293   *the support of Nevil Sidgwick:* For example, see Sidgwick (1933), in which Pauling is referenced in the index more than any other source other than Debye, Goldschmidt, and the author. See also Paradowski (1972), p. 445.

CHAPTER 13: POLITICAL SCIENCE

295   *"He had been so busy":* quoted in *The Cambrian,* November 8, 1979, p. 17.

296   *"Ikeda is a pleasant fellow":* Pauling to Martin Heidelberger, March 12, 1942 (OSU).

297   *"Somebody's painted stuff":* Details of the graffiti incident are from local news reports, the Paulings' *Nova* interviews, author's interviews with Pauling, Linus Pauling, Jr., and Linda Pauling Kamb, and Pauling's FBI files; and Pauling (1951a), p. 2.

300   *" we should make our voices known":* Pauling to A. R. Todd, September 29, 1945 (OSU).

300   *"the unimaginable devastation of an atomic war":* Pauling to Robert Hutchins, September 25, 1945 (OSU).

301   *The Pasadena discussion group:* "G.D." to Pauling, January 5, 1946 (OSU).

301   *"Let us look forward":* note by Pauling titled "To The Council of the Tenth Anniversary Congress of the National Council of American Soviet Friendship," attached to letter to Walter B. Cannon, November 2, 1943 (OSU).

302   *"Mr. Chairman, this is a matter":* Pauling handwritten note, Pauling biography files (LPI).

303   *The discussion groups took up the issue:* see Greenberg (1967), pp. 117–18.

304 *the Association of Pasadena Scientists:* Information on the founding of the group is found in the APS collection (CIT).

304 *"the first totalitarian bill":* Harold Urey, quoted in Greenberg (1967), p. 118.

304 *The debate over the May-Johnson:* See, for example, Hershberg (1994), pp. 259–60.

306 *"You're not convincing":* quoted in Paradowski (1991), p. 199.

306 *"I felt I could speak":* Pauling interview with author.

307 *"I was, as you might suspect":* Pauling to Paul Emmett, February 25, 1946 (OSU).

307 *"just the rather liberal sort of politics":* Pauling interview with author.

308 *"Our world faces a crisis":* quoted in Nathan and Norden (1968), p. 376.

309 *the committee's main work:* For more on the ECAS, see Nathan and Norden (1968), pp. 376–77. Besides Pauling, the group's members in 1947 included Einstein, Urey, Szilard, Hans Bethe, Harrison Brown, Thorfin Hogness, Philip M. Morse, Frederick Seitz, and Victor Weisskopf.

309 *Years later, other members:* Author's interviews with Hans Bethe and Victor Weisskopf.

309 *"Today the atomic bomb":* Albert Einstein, "The Real Problem Is in the Hearts of Men," *New York Times Sunday Magazine,* June 23, 1946.

311 *"It was Einstein's example":* The full quote is: "It may well be that my work for world peace would not have been very effective if I had not been invited to become a member of the board of trustees of the Emergency Committee of Atomic Scientists. I had been making some public talks about nuclear weapons and nuclear war before that time, but I think that it was Einstein's example that caused my wife and me to decide to devote much energy and effort to this activity" (Ikeda [1988], p. 8).

311 *The nation's choice:* B. Carroll Reece, June 1946, quoted in Caute (1978), p. 26.

312 *Hollywood Community Radio Group:* See Alvin Wilder to Pauling, August 29, 1946, Pauling to Wilder, August 30, 1946 (both OSU).

313 *"The one general characteristic":* Linus Pauling, "ICCASP? Yes" draft manuscript attached to letter to John Cromwell, November 6, 1946 (OSU).

313 *"The problems that the world faces":* Linus Pauling, letter to the editor, *Chemical and Engineering News* 24:3108 (1946).

314 *"one of the most gifted writers":* Pauling to Louis Finkelstein, September 19, 1946 (OSU).

314 *"Our scientists, it seems":* J. Parnell Thomas, *Liberty,* June 21, 1946.

315 *Edward U. Condon:* A good review of the Condon case can be found in Wang (1992).

CHAPTER 14: ENGLAND

318 *"I didn't pay enough attention":* Pauling interview with author.

318 *"He was a sensation":* quoted in Dunitz (1991), p. 11.

319 *"dark area of the unknown":* This image is fully presented in Pauling (1990).

320 *"The members are connoisseurs":* Sir William L. Bragg, *Times Educational Supplement,* June 3, 1955.

320 *"As I look at a living organism":* Pauling (1948f), p. 707.

321   *"When we hear Linus":* anecdote related by Joseph Koepfli in interview with author.

321   *By 1948, he had made the Cavendish:* On Bragg, Perutz, and the rise of molecular biology at the Cavendish, see Judson (1979), pp.104–8; Olby (1974), p. 267; Thomas and Phillips (1990), p. 44.

323   *"It was well known that any chain":* Crick (1988), p. 54; on Huggins and the ubiquity of helical thinking, see also Olby (1974), pp. 234, 287. According to Olby, Crick called Huggins's helix "seminal," and Bragg later said that if Huggins had gotten the planarity of the peptide bond right, he would have solved the alpha helix.

323   *"The first day I read detective stories":* Nova interview, N9. Pauling often told the story of how his enforced idleness in England led to the discovery of the protein helix. Other versions are found in Pauling (1970), p. 1004; Pauling (1986), p. 6; and Pauling interviews with author. In all of these later versions, Pauling claims that he sketched two helixes, one of which would later become the immensely important alpha helix, the other the looser gamma helix, which proved of no biological importance. He tells a different story, however, in his earliest published version of the incident (Pauling 1955a, pp. 293–94): "Then one day in March 1948, while I was at home in Oxford (where I was serving as Eastman Professor) recuperating from a cold, I decided again to attack the problem of the configuration of polypeptide chains . . . . Within an hour, with the aid of a pencil and a piece of paper, I had discovered a satisfactory helical structure. It did not, however, explain the details of the x-ray diagram of hair and other alpha-keratin proteins, and nothing more was done along these lines for several months. After my return to Pasadena, Professor Corey and I suggested to Dr. H. R. Branson, who was interested in the application of mathematics to chemical problems, that he make a search for other satisfactory helical configurations. He found only one, and in 1951 a description of the two helixes, the alpha helix and the gamma helix, was published." I am using this earliest version as the basis of my text. In it, Pauling explicitly says he found only one helix in Oxford, and Branson the other in Pasadena. Pauling is careful not to distinguish which was the alpha helix.

324   *"There was no way I could stretch":* Nova interview, N36.

324   *"just a piece of paper":* Pauling, unpublished notes for lecture on the history of proteins, titled "UCLA, 28 February 1968" (LPI).

327   *And he watched for years:* Mulliken (1989), p. 88.

327   *the VB and MO approaches both represented:* See Paradowski (1972), p. 431; Mulliken (1965), p. S14.

327   *"One picture is enough":* Linus Pauling, handwritten notes for Honolulu lecture on "The Chemical Bond and the Structure of Molecules," dated April 3, 1979 (LPI).

327   *Pauling was a "showman":* Quoted in Ramsay and Hinze (1975), p. 9.

328   *it was becoming clear that improved MO:* On criticisms of the VB approach and its eclipse by MO, see Coulson (1970), p. 259; Paradowski (1972), p. 450; Bykov (1965), p. 233. Van Vleck and Sherman (1935), p. 186, called Pauling's resonance energy concept "fundamental and interesting . . . but we believe that only an empirical significance can be given to the purported comparison of theoretical and observed resonance energies, much of the trouble being with the latter. The so-called observed values are obtained by assuming bond additivity. . . . Pauling and collaborators attribute all the departures from bond additivity to resonance. There are, however, other factors which can cause deviations from additivity; i.e. the electronic environment in other parts of the molecule." There is as well the 1947 correspondence between Pauling, Kasimir Fajans, and George Wheland (in the Fajans collection at the Michigan Historical Collections, Bentley Historical Library, University of Michigan). Fajans—the former head of the physical chemistry school at Munich (and the man whom Pauling had more or less ignored while studying with Sommerfeld)—had emigrated to the University of Michigan and become a caustic detractor of Pauling's ideas of resonance. In 1947 he, Pauling, and Wheland engaged in a lively debate through the mail over Pauling's assignment of percentage contributions from various canonical structures in the resonance picture of H_2O. Fajans pushed for a more precise understanding of the underlying logic behind assigning percentages to various ionic and covalent forms but was dissatisfied with Pauling's explanations and continued to attack Pauling's resonance ideas whenever he could. It was, however, generally agreed that Fajans did not have a clear grasp of quantum mechanics. The majority of professors at Fajans's own university continued to teach Pauling's brand of chemistry.

328   *By 1947, even Wheland agreed:* G. W. Wheland to K. Fajans, July 21, 1947 (Fajans Collection, Bentley Historical Library, University of Michigan).

328   *"The valence-bond method required great flocks":* quoted in Ramsay and Hinze (1975), pp. 9–10.

329   *The tide was turning:* See, for instance, Coulson (1970), pp. 359–60, in which it is estimated that a mere handful of MO papers in the 1930s were followed by about seventy in the 1940s, six hundred in the 1950s, and perhaps five thousand in the 1960s.

329   *"endless bottles of champagne":* Mulliken (1989), p. 126.

330   *"transformed the chemical flatland":* Perutz (1991), p. 10.

330   *"I didn't say anything":* quoted in Olby (1974), p. 281. Pauling felt he was in a race with Bragg and consciously withheld information he thought might be useful to the Cavendish group. "I was very careful not to talk to the people in Britain about it [the alpha helix]," he said in an interview with the author. In 1951, just as he was convinced of the correctness of his alpha helix, Pauling wrote his former student David Harker, "I feel that it is all right for me to have kept these ideas to myself until I could check up on them. If I had told Perutz about them, or Bragg, they probably would have checked up on them, and . . . might well have published, perhaps about now, the papers that we are now publishing" (Pauling to Harker, March 8, 1951 [OSU]).

330   *"I am beginning to feel a bit uncomfortable":* Pauling to Robert Corey, February 18, 1948 (OSU).

331   *"I am terribly impatient":* Corey to Pauling, February 25, 1948 (OSU).

331   *a woman he saw being dragged down the street:* David Shoemaker, interview with author.

331   *"I think that it has really been":* Pauling to Robert Corey, March 3, 1948 (OSU).

332   *a rapid diagnostic test for sickle-cell disease:* Itano and Pauling (1949).

333   *Pauling's idea was right:* He was not exactly right, however, about the mechanism of sickling. Pauling had supposed that hemoglobin crystallization occurred because of the sticking together of complementary regions formed by the change in structure; eventually it was shown that areas on the hemoglobin molecule are created that react differently to the water in the cell's aqueous environment, leading to the formation of threadlike aggregates.

334   *An analysis of the familial relationship:* J. V. Neel published his idea of the genetic basis of sickle-cell anemia before Pauling and Itano, but as Pauling noted in Pauling, Itano, Singer and Wells (1949), p. 546: "Our results had caused us to draw this inference before Neel's paper was published."

CHAPTER 15: ATTACK OF THE PRIMITIVES

335   *"post-war dream boys":* Yergin (1977), p. 245.

335   *Truman fumed in his diary:* McCullough (1992), p. 517.

336   *"I think he was a good, rational person":* Pauling interview with author.

337   *"Wallace may have been too honest":* Pauling interview with author.

338   *"A quick check of the files":* Clyde Tolson to J. Edgar Hoover, November 26, 1947 (FBI).

339   *Still, it was enough for Hoover:* Details of the FBI's early interest in Pauling is detailed in the agency's Pauling files for 1947, 1948, and 1949.

341   *"the attack of the primitives":* quoted in Yergin (1977), p. 407.

341   *"[I]ndividuals, such as myself":* Pauling to Milton Burton, February 28, 1949 (OSU).

341   *"stuffy old ecclesiastic":* Pauling interview with author.

341   *Ralph Spitzer:* See A. L. Strand to Pauling, March 4, 1949 (OSU). The Spitzer case was also immortalized in literature: In Bernard Malamud's *A New Life,* a novel that arose from Malamud's teaching experience at OSU at that time, Spitzer and another fired OSU professor have been said to constitute together the model for the powerful character of Duffy, a symbol of dispossessed integrity. The Spitzer file in the OSU Archives contains the relevant correspondence and newspaper coverage of the affair.

342   *a new loyalty oath system:* On the California regent's loyalty oath program, see Reitman (1975), p. 158.

343   *Pauling began speaking out: Los Angeles Times,* May 10, 1949, (Sec. II, p. 4); *Pasadena Independent,* May 10, 1949; clips from the files of the FBI during 1949.

343   *American Continental Conference for World Peace:* Pauling's speech is found in typescript as "Address by United States Delegate, Linus Pauling," September 5, 1949 (OSU). The U.S. press reported that Pauling's Mexico City speech was met with "stony silence." Pauling felt that the speech, although it "did not cause great excitement," was "very well received. . . . The newspapers had to try hard to put an unfavorable aspect on the conference" (Pauling to I. M. Kolthoff, November 3, 1949 [OSU]).

344 *"tough-minded" set of beliefs:* on the liberal shift to the right, see O'Reilly (1983), p. 168.

345 *The Soviet atomic bomb:* Pauling quoted in *Bulletin of the Atomic Scientists* 5 (November 1949): 323.

345 *Lee DuBridge:* For background on DuBridge and his early impact on Caltech, see Kevles (1987), pp. 303, 308; Goodstein (1991), pp. 271–74; Caute (1978), p. 462; Smith (1965), pp. 122, 148; and the Norman Horowitz oral history, p. 14 (CIT).

346 *"one of the most important enterprises":* quoted in Kay (1993), p. 236.

346 *DuBridge's initial thought:* While considering how to handle funding difficulties in 1947, DuBridge wrote the Caltech dean of faculty that appointments in physical chemistry and chemical engineering were more urgent than hiring a protein chemist (DuBridge to dean of faculty, June 6, 1947 [OSU]). Correspondence between Pauling and DuBridge in 1946–47 regarding divisional priorities can also be found in the DuBridge collection at CIT.

347 *"It is not the job of the scientist":* DuBridge (1947), p. 1.

347 *an archetypal postwar insider-scientist:* While president of Caltech, DuBridge served at various times on the General Advisory Board of the Atomic Energy Commission, the Naval Research Advisory Board, the Air Force Science Advisory Board, the President's Communications Policy Board, the top advisory body of the National Science Foundation, the Science Advisory Committee of the Office of Defense Mobilization, and the National Manpower Council.

347 *"proper restraint":* "Appointments, Obligations and Tenure of Faculty Members," from the CIT Office of the President, February 27, 1947 (CIT). On the unspoken rules guiding scientific behavior at the time, see Goodell (1977), pp. 91–92.

348 *"I do question the propriety":* Reese Taylor to DuBridge, October 10, 1946; DuBridge to Taylor, October 11, 1946 (CIT).

349 *why, if Pauling was not a Communist:* Reese Taylor to Jim Page, September 21, 1949 (CIT).

349 *"Remember my friendly warning":* Dudley Steele to Pauling, November 8, 1949 (OSU).

350 *"An H-bomb consists":* Linus Pauling, typescript titled "Radio Talk," dated May 1949 (OSU).

350 *"We should not intentionally lose":* Harold Urey, quoted in Lapp (1965), p. 106; Pauling's reply quoted in the *Daily Worker,* February 14, 1950, p. 1.

350 *Pauling and Leo Szilard:* Szilard to Pauling, February 8, 1950 (OSU). Pauling said, "Einstein and I were among the members who felt that the Committee should continue to work to educate the people of the United States about the need for controlling nuclear weapons and for preventing war. When the Cold War started, there was enough of a difference of opinion that the Committee ceased to exist" (Pauling interview with author).

350 *"The problem of an atomic war":* quoted in the *New York Times,* February 14, 1950, p. 1; *Daily Worker,* February 14, 1950, p. 2.

351 *"Maybe some of these proffessors* [sic] *":* February 2, 1950 memo, Office of Naval Intelligence to SAC/L.A. (FBI).

351 *An FBI agent was dispatched:* From Pauling's FBI files and Pauling interview with author.
352 *Weinbaum came to Pauling:* From Pauling deposition for the *National Review* libel case, January 6, 1964 (LPI).
353 *"What the Institute had":* Beckman oral history, p. 46 (CIT).
353 *"to investigate and report":* board of trustees abstract, June 29, 1950 (DuBridge collection [CIT]).
354 *Louis Budenz:* background from O'Reilly (1983), pp. 236–37; Belfrage (1973), p. 62.
355 *"I have been working in support":* quoted in the *New York Times,* October 23, 1950.
355 *"McCarthy Says Reds":* New York Herald Tribune, October 24, 1950, p. 1.
356 *his contract was being canceled:* Pauling to E. C. Kleiderer, October 20, 1950 (OSU); Pauling interview with author. "I must say that if I had known . . . that my political activities would cause me such a great financial loss, I am not sure that I would have engaged in them," Pauling told one investigatory board. Pauling (1951a), p. 7.
356 *"Having a person of questionable loyalty":* Office of Naval Research (ONR) commander, Pasadena, to chief, ONR, January 23, 1950 (FBI).
357 *"I hope in this country":* DuBridge to Dewey, December 4, 1950 (CIT). The official results of Pauling's Caltech investigations are sealed by the school, but in the Department of State's Division of Security files is a contemporaneous memo in which an anonymous but apparently well connected Caltech informer states that the Trustees backed off from firing Pauling because (1) it would bring disgrace upon the school; (2) "as a dismissed educator, Pauling would probably develop a persecution complex and go completely to the Communist cause"; (3) Pauling must be kept in the American camp; (4) American chemistry needs Pauling; and (5) no one takes him too seriously, anyway (Department of State Division of Security Report, August 27, 1951, obtained by the author through the Freedom of Information Act [FOIA]).
357 *Through 1950 he continued his political activities:* Pauling's reaction to Weinbaum's conviction for perjury is found in a letter to David Harker, February 6, 1951 (OSU): "Sidney seems to have felt that he was innocent, but it seems to me that he may have been relying upon some technicality." On Dalton Trumbo: see Cleo Trumbo to Pauling, August 16, 1950 (OSU), and Dalton Trumbo to Cleo Trumbo, December 10, 1950, in Manfull (1970); on the AASW: Pauling to Melba Phillips, March 27, 1950 (OSU); on Joliot-Curie, the son-in-law of Madame Curie, who oversaw the first successful French atomic chain reaction and then announced his intention of publishing the method openly: Gellhorn (1950), p. 11; and Joliot-Curie's correspondence with Pauling (OSU).
358 *"there were two qualities":* Pauling recognized his conformist tendencies as a scientist and emphasized them to the author during interviews.
358 *"I felt that it was my duty":* Pauling (1951a), p. 3.
358 *a product of the Enlightenment:* For an analysis of the link between Enlightenment philosophy and fellow traveling, see Caute (1973), pp. 250–57.

359   *"The principle upon which":* Pauling (1951c), p. 12.

359   *"Most other scientists had stopped":* quoted in Dye (1985), p. 12.

360   *"A contagion of fear":* UC Academic Assembly to Pauling, August 9, 1950 (OSU).

360   *"The University has already suffered":* Pauling "Public Statement," August 28, 1950 (OSU).

361   *"I think there is nothing":* All quotes from the State of California's Ninth Report of the Senate Investigating Committee on Education (1951). See also Barrett (1952), p. 20.

365   *An FBI agent:* SAC/L.A. to J. Edgar Hoover, November 21, 1950 (FBI).

366   *"All I know":* Pauling interview with author; on the preparation of a contempt citation, see Pauling stories in the *Los Angeles Times,* November 17, and *Los Angeles Mirror,* November 16, 1950.

367   *In Pauling's case, he could write:* DuBridge to Frederick Llewellyn, December 4, 1950 (CIT).

CHAPTER 16: THE SECRET OF LIFE

368   *extemporizing entire chapters:* During the writing of *College Chemistry,* Caltech student Alex Rich recalls walking into Pauling's office. "And there he was, feet on the table, dictating. . . . When I said, well, how do you get to final copy? 'Oh,' he says, 'I read it over and just correct the mistakes that [secretary] Bea Wulf made in transcribing.' The point is, he could dictate and out would come perfectly readable, almost final text. That impressed me a lot" (Alex Rich interview with author).

368   *a strangely unfocused paper:* The Cavendish team did not think much of it, either. "It was one of those papers you publish mainly because you've done all that work," Perutz later said (Judson [1979], p. 85; Olby [1974], pp. 289–91).

369   *a Pauling-like attack:* Olby (1974), p. 292.

370   *easily located atoms of heavy elements:* Pauling to Elliot Wayer, April 15, 1950 (OSU).

370   *Herman Branson:* Branson's role in the discovery of the alpha-helix structure has become controversial since Pauling's death. Branson has recently claimed the alpha helix as his own. There is no doubt that Pauling was thinking about protein structures in England in 1947–48; both a former student, David Shoemaker, and Pauling's daughter, Linda, remember seeing folded-paper models of protein structures in Pauling's room in England at the time. Pauling would have wanted Branson to keep an open mind so as not to miss any potential structures; he would purposefully have avoided tipping him to the alpha-helix structure. Most importantly, Pauling gave Branson the essential limiting factors in his search: The requirements for a planar peptide bond and maximum hydrogen bonding and the nonnecessity of an integral repeat. Without these limits, Bragg's team failed. With them, the alpha helix was, as Branson found, a logical structure. It is important, too, that Branson reviewed and approved the manuscript of Pauling, Corey, and Branson (1951), in which he accepts the position of third author.

371 *"significant progress in attacking disease"*: Pauling to E. C. Kleiderer, March 8, 1950 (OSU).

371 *Weaver shot down their idea:* See Kay (1993), p. 259; Kay (1987), p. 264; and the Chemistry Division files for 1950–51 (RAC).

372 *"I took a chance by waiting"*: Pauling interview with author.

372 *His sense of urgency:* see Harker to Pauling, September 6, 1950 (OSU).

373 *Feeling "forced into it"*: Pauling interview with author.

373 *a British firm called Courtaulds:* Judson (1979), p. 87.

373 *more precisely a "helix"*: Pauling used the word "spiral" in his 1950 *JACS* paper with Corey. Jack Dunitz, then a researcher working in Pauling's labs, says that he told Pauling about the term "helix" in the winter of 1950, arguing that it was more correct for a three-dimensional structure than spiral, which he said was more correct for two-dimensional representations (Dunitz [1991], p. III). Pauling thought they were equivalent but switched to helix sometime that winter.

374 *"pretty hot stuff"*: Ray Owen, interview with author.

375 *"He certainly is imaginative"*: quoted in Kay (1993), p. 263.

376 *"The Structure of Proteins"*: Pauling, Corey, and Branson (1951).

377 *"The difference between our two"*: Pauling to Weaver, March 8, 1951 (OSU).

377 *"I try to identify myself with the atoms"*: George W. Gray interview with Pauling, July 12, 1951 (RAC).

377 *"the most important step forward"*: Pauling to Dennis Flanagan, March 8, 1951 (OSU).

377 *"I am having a hard time"*: Pauling to E. B. Wilson, March 15, 1951 (OSU).

378 *"an astounding structure"*: Pauling to E. Bright Wilson, March 15, 1951 (OSU).

378 *"I said it was nice to see him"*: "A Recollection of Sir Lawrence Bragg," by A. R. Todd, in Thomas and Phillips (1990), p. 95. After this incident, Bragg regularly checked organic structures with Todd, including Watson and Crick's model of the DNA helix.

378 *"I judge that he did not read"*: Pauling interview with author.

379 *"The fulfillment of this prediction"*: Perutz to Pauling, August 17, 1951 (OSU).

379 *"The spacing at which"*: Perutz (1951), p. 1054.

379 *"I do congratulate you"*: Bragg to Pauling, June 13, 1951 (OSU).

380 *"His whole record"*: quoted in the California legislature's Ninth Report of the Senate Investigating Committee on Education, 1951, p. 54.

380 *"I have associated myself"*: Los Angeles Times, April 5, 1951, p. 1.

380 *Marshall College:* See M. L. Vest to Pauling, April 6, 1951; Pauling to M. L. Vest, April 9, 1951; Leland Taylor to Pauling, April 18, 1951; Pauling to I. M. Kolthoff, May 8, 1951 (all OSU).

380 *"I am very surprised"*: Los Angeles Times, March 29, 1951, p. 15.

381 *"Do you think that an American"*: Pauling to board of regents, University of Hawaii, March 30, 1951 (OSU).

381 *"I thought that it would be worthwhile"*: Pauling to T. W. J. Taylor, June 13, 1951 (OSU).

381 *Truman signed another executive order:* Wang (1992), p. 261.

382 *a shadow legal system:* For more on the loyalty oaths and IERB procedures and the effect on scientists, see Gellhorn (1950), pp. 100–6; Wang (1992), p. 257. Pauling had a brush with the loyalty program in 1950, when he accepted an invitation to give a series of talks at the Oak Ridge National Laboratory, one of the major government sites for atomic research. The head of the chemistry program there, unaware or unconcerned about Pauling's political standing, sent Pauling's name to the AEC for security clearance and was quickly informed that clearance could not be granted without special action at the top levels of government. The abashed administrator wrote Pauling that he could still deliver the talks but without clearance he would be barred from visiting the laboratories themselves. Pauling decided not to push the issue and declined the invitation to speak, writing, "I do not think I would like an environment in which some scientific information is made available to me and some is not. The best way of handling the situation is, I think, just not to get into it." (Henri Levy to Pauling, December 30, 1949, and January 24, 1950; Pauling to Levy, June 8, 1950 [all OSU]).

383 *According to "information":* The security board's information was apparently from Pauling's FBI file, which J. Edgar Hoover had passed on to the AEC a month earlier. See Hoover to AEC, June 13, 1951 (FBI FOIA).

383 *"contrived, a made-up":* quoted in Lapp (1965), p. 239.

384 *"The intensity and crudeness":* Hunsberger (1954), p. 506.

384 *"I have not been able":* Pauling to Holland Roberts, October 25, 1951 (OSU).

384 *"If Russian chemists are not":* For more on the Russian resonance controversy, see Pauling (1950b), p. 232; 272; and Pauling (1970), pp. 998–99.

384 *Bernal was ready:* Bernal to Pauling, June 22, 1951 (OSU).

385 *"non-contractile alpha-keratin":* Pauling and Corey (1951), pp. 550–51.

385 *"the structure that we have suggested":* Pauling to George Boyd, December 18, 1951 (OSU).

385 *"rippled sheet":* Pauling to Perutz, August 29, 1951 (OSU).

385 *"I am sure that these discoveries":* Pauling to N. V. Sidgwick, May 1, 1951 (OSU).

385 *Pauling's protein work had changed the rules:* As Bernal later put it, "It can be said that, by and large, Pauling's idea played an essential role in the working out of protein structure. But it did far more. It broke away from the limitation imposed by crystallographers on the integral nature of the turns of a helix. It eventually led to a new generalization of crystallography that was to have immense repercussions. It might be said, 'Only a crystallographer could have predicted this development, but if they were good crystallographers, they would have been bound to reject it.' Indeed, Pauling's generalization opened the field to a new and much more wide-sweeping account of semiregular structures that are similar to the helical" (Bernal [1968], p. 376).

387 *The man was Maurice Huggins:* See Olby (1974), pp. 286–287; Pauling to Huggins, April 2, 1952 (OSU).

387 *"Chemists Unravel Protein's Secrets":* New York Times, September 5, 1951, p. 33.

387 *"Chemists Solve a Great Mystery":* Life, September 24, 1951, p. 77.

388 *"a diluted [sic] exhibitionist":* "Report on Linus Pauling, October 17, 1951" (FBI FOIA).

388   *"I shall try to represent the Institute":* Pauling to DuBridge, November 15, 1951 (OSU).

388   *He told the board:* Pauling (1951a).

389   *He had discovered:* Lee DuBridge to Pauling, November 21, 1951 (CIT). Pauling's strange IERB case raises some interesting questions, including how Pauling's papers were first misfiled; how the process could have gone so far under a mistaken classification; how and why DuBridge discovered the "mistake" when he did; and why this easy way out of the IERB hearing came just days before Pauling resigned from groups which might be embarrassing to Caltech. DuBridge refused in an interview with the author to comment on Pauling's IERB hearing, and Pauling recalled only that the whole affair was "nonsensical."

390   *He was "too busy":* See Pauling to National Council of the Arts, Sciences and Professions, November 24, 1951; to the American Peace Crusade, November 27, 1951; to the American Association of Scientific Workers, November 27, 1951; and to the World Federation of Scientific Workers, July 11, 1952 (all OSU). Pauling later talked little about his hiatus from political activism, relegating it to a few notes at the time he got back into the fray. See, for instance, Pauling to Bernard Schaar, May 10, 1954 (OSU): "For a couple of years I have greatly restrained myself with respect to political action."

CHAPTER 17: THE TRIPLE HELIX

393   *She became jealous:* Linda Pauling Kamb interview with author.

394   *"Well, Matt":* Matthew Meselson, interview with author. The Pauling poolside scene in the early 1950s was described in author's interviews with Alex Rich, Martin Karplus, Linda Pauling Kamb, and Crellin Pauling.

394   *"the Pauling Point":* Martin Karplus interview with author.

395   *"Worthless," he said:* Alex Rich interview with author.

396   *a structure for guanine:* Pauling and Sherman (1933b).

396   *the protein portion carried the genetic instructions:* On the protein paradigm, see Kay (1993), p. 210; Gunther Stent, "The DNA Double Helix and the Rise of Molecular Biology," in Watson (1980), p. xiv; Judson (1979), p. 63.

396   *Oswald Avery:* Avery's 1944 DNA findings were widely ignored because they were published in wartime, he couched his results tentatively, and he worked at the Rockefeller Institute, one of the strongholds of the protein paradigm. (Alfred Mirsky, who worked with Pauling on proteins in the mid-1930s, was one of the protein-gene's most unshakable supporters.) See Gribben (1987), p. 205; Judson (1979), p. 40.

397   *"I knew the contention":* quoted in Olby (1974), pp. 376–77.

397   *Oster added a quick idea:* Gerald Oster to Pauling, August 9, 1951 (OSU).

399   *given his photos, Pauling would probably beat them:* On Wilkins's early DNA work, see Olby (1974), pp. 341–51; Watson (1980), p. 36.

399 *"Wilkins and others are busily engaged":* J. T. Randall to Pauling, August 28, 1951 (OSU).

399 *He wrote a letter to the* JACS: On the phosphorus row, see Ronwin (1951); Pauling and Schomaker (1952a and 1952b).

400 *muscle was mostly composed of alpha helixes:* Pauling and Corey (1952); Pauling to Paul Emmett, January 16, 1952 (OSU).

400 *Corey also redoubled his efforts:* Corey's lysozyme project received little attention after Kendrew and Perutz beat him with their Nobel Prize–winning work on myoglobin. Corey's methods—including amino-acid sequencing and isomorphous replacement of heavy atoms in the protein to ease x-ray work—paralleled the British team's. But Corey's meticulous, precise mind, perfect for solving single amino acids and small peptides, was not up to the job of cracking a complete protein. "The problem was that Corey didn't have the same temperament as Kendrew," Pauling told the author. "He was perhaps not imaginative enough." Pauling, however, also kept an active hand in Corey's lysozyme work, including offering the suggestion of using chromatography to separate breakdown components for analysis. Lysozyme was a good target, though, and became the third globular protein solved— by a team at Britain's Royal Institution. See Pauling (1986a), p. 6.

401 *After 1950, her power to refuse passports:* Caute (1978), p. 246.

401 *"a professional do-gooder":* State Department files released through the FOIA.

401 *a letter to Harry Truman:* Pauling to Harry Truman, February 29, 1952; William McWilliams to William Hassett, March 8, 1952 (both State Department FOIA).

402 *"a rather vague general statement":* Pauling interview with author.

403 *"the shock that it produced":* John Edsall, interview with author.

403 *"There I was":* Edward Hughes oral history (CIT). The papers delivered at the Royal Society meeting were published as a special issue of *Proceedings of the Royal Society of London* [B] 141 (1953).

404 *very sorry indeed:* Bragg to Pauling, May 5, 1952 (OSU).

405 *"this one case is resulting":* Hans Clarke to State Department, May 5, 1952 (State Department FOIA).

405 *"The accumulating number of such cases":* Jeffries Wynan to State Department, May 5, 1952 (State Department FOIA).

405 *"Dr. Pauling's Predicament": New York Times* coverage of the case is found in the issues of May 12, 13, and 19, 1952.

406 *"What harm, what information":* Edward Teller et al. to Dean Acheson, May 22, 1952 (State Department FOIA).

406 *"It is very meritorious of you":* Einstein to Pauling, May 21, 1952 (OSU).

406 *"This whole incident, to be blunt":* Pauling quoted in the California Institute of Technology *Tech*, May 15, 1952, p. 1.

406 *"As I had to defer":* internal memo from Ruth Shipley, dated May 16, 1952 (State FOIA).

407 *the Pauling case was discussed intensively:* Details are from a score of June and July 1952 memos obtained from the State Department through the FOIA.

407 *"A review of the file":* Memo, SAC/WDC to J. Edgar Hoover, November 30, 1953; and internal memorandum dated July 22, 1952 (both FBI FOIA).

409 *Delbrück had read Watson's letter to Pauling:* In June, just before Pauling left for Europe, Delbrück had read him a letter of Watson's saying that he wanted to stay in Cambridge for an extra year because he was so excited about learning x-ray crystallography. In that letter Watson had also mentioned Wilkins's "extremely excellent" DNA photos (Olby [1974], p. 378).

409 *At the Royaumont meeting:* Watson remembered Pauling talking about solving DNA either at Royaumont or at the Trianon the day after his talk on protein structures. See Judson (1979), p. 145; and Watson (1980), p. 179.

410 *"the looks of a fading racing tout":* quoted in Donohue (1978), p. 134.

410 *"too bright to be really sound":* Crick (1974), p. 144.

410 *"the nearest approach to Pauling":* quoted in Olby (1974), p. 354.

410 *"There was no one like Linus":* Watson (1980), pp. 24–25.

411 *"imitate Linus Pauling":* Watson (1980), p. 32.

411 *DNA was, in other words, like the alpha helix:* Putting the bases outside let Crick and Watson ignore the problems caused by trying to figure out what would hold the bases together if they faced each other at the core. They were convinced at the time that the bases existed in tautomeric forms that would make hydrogen bonding between them difficult if not impossible. See Olby (1974), pp. 357–59; Watson (1980), p. 77.

412 *"something of a monomaniac":* Pauling interview with author.

412 *"Somewhere in Pauling's masterpiece":* Watson (1980), p. 62.

413 *"In this way I made up":* Pauling to Arne Tiselius, October 17, 1952 (OSU).

413 *sharing a car ride around Cambridge:* This anecdote is from author's interviews with Crick and Pauling, whose memories of the discussion about coiled coils differ in both substance and place. Pauling wrote Robert Olby in 1970 (LPI) that they talked during the car ride: "I remember what happened. Crick did not tell me that he was working on the problem. He simply said to me, 'Have you thought about the possibility that alpha helixes are coiled around one another?' I answered, 'Yes, I have.' He did not say anything more, nor did I. I assumed that he had been working on this idea, as I had. . . . I was in fact working on it at the time, and had nearly completed my arguments at the time. I did not tell Crick what I was doing. . . ." Crick, however, recalls that his mention of the coiled-coil idea occurred in his office at the Cavendish and that Pauling did not respond with any mention of his own thinking. See also Watson (1980), p. 85.

415 *"The field of protein structure":* Pauling to Leonora Bilcher, September 18, 1952, and to E. A. Doisy, November 19, 1952 (both OSU).

415 *"slightly wild":* Crick interview with author.

416 *Pauling, unsurprised by Crick's work:* See Donohue to Pauling, November 9, 1952 (OSU); Pauling to Robert Olby, June 23, 1970 (LPI).

416 *The alpha helix had been shown:* Pauling to Richard Block, November 26, 1952 (OSU).

417 *"No matter how great Pauling's triumph":* Gunther Stent, "The DNA Double Helix and the Rise of Molecular Biology," in Watson (1980), p. xvii.

418 *"Perhaps we have a triple-chain structure!":* From Pauling's laboratory notes on the DNA investigation (OSU).

419 *"I think now we have found":* Pauling to E. B. Wilson, December 4, 1952 (OSU).

420 *"The structure really is a beautiful one"*: Pauling to Alexander Todd, December 19, 1952 (OSU). Pauling also wrote Todd that he was writing Bragg with the news that he had discovered the structure of DNA, but if he did, the resulting letter has not been located.

421 *"That statement is a lie"*: See *New York Times,* December 29, 1952, p. 1; Pauling to R. Milton Smith, January 23, 1953 (OSU); G. B. Van Niel to DuBridge, December 27, 1952 (OSU); Caute (1978), p. 124.

421 *into his laboratory on Christmas Day:* Judson (1979), p. 154.

421 *"A Proposed Structure for the Nucleic Acids"*: Pauling and Corey (1953).

423 *"I never met two men"*: quoted in Judson (1979), p. 142.

424 *"If a student had made a similar mistake"*: Watson (1980), pp. 93–94.

424 *"The only doubt I have"*: Crick to Pauling, March 2, 1953 (CIT).

424 *"I am checking over"*: Pauling to Peter Pauling, February 18, 1953 (OSU).

425 *"I have a very pretty model"*: quoted in Olby (1974), pp. 488–89.

425 *"Professor Corey and I do not feel"*: Pauling to James Watson, March 5, 1953 (CIT).

425 *perhaps the DNA core environment:* Pauling to Peter Pauling, March 10, 1953 (OSU).

425 *Donohue's input turned out to be critical:* As Watson said, "If he had not been with us in Cambridge, I might still have been pumping for a like-with-like structure. . . . But for Jerry, only Pauling would have been likely to make the right choice and stick by its consequences" (Watson [1980], p. 122). Pauling later told the author that Donohue should perhaps have shared the resulting Nobel Prize.

426 *"The simplicity of the structural"*: Pauling (1970), p. 1010.

427 *"You must, of course, recognize"*: Pauling to Walter S. Vincent, March 19, 1953 (OSU).

427 *"there are now two proposed structures"*: Pauling to Peter Pauling, March 27, 1953 (OSU).

427 *"gracefully," Watson remembered:* Watson (1980), p. 129.

428 *"Although it is only two months"*: Judson (1979), p. 179.

428 *"To my father"*: Peter Pauling (1973), p. 560.

429 *"a chemical attack on the structure of chromosomes"*: quoted in Kay (1993), p. 155. In his fourth chemical bond paper in 1932, Pauling compared the linear separation of atoms on his electronegativity scale to "the way that genes are mapped in a chromosome from crossover data."

429 *"failed to take account of my results"*: quoted in Judson (1979), p. 144.

429 *"just didn't try"*: quoted in Judson (1979), p. 101.

429 *"the people around him let him down"*: Verner Schomaker and Alex Rich interviews with author.

429 *Pauling wrote Delbrück:* Pauling to Delbrück, April 20, 1953 (OSU). It is interesting to note how in this letter Pauling makes it sound as though Alex Rich's DNA photos had been taken at the beginning of the process of dissecting the structure of DNA—this would have been standard procedure—when in fact Rich's laboratory notebooks show that he took his first DNA x-ray photo on April 17, 1953—three days before Pauling wrote the letter (Alex Rich interview with author).

429 *"The reason that I got off"*: Pauling interview with author.

429   *"If we had also done some work":* Pauling interview with author.

431   *"If that was such an important problem":* Pauling has related Ava Helen's comment many times in interviews, including those with the author. "I should have worked harder on it" also became one of his stock answers to DNA questions.

CHAPTER 18: THE PRIZE

432   *"Norman Church never forgot":* DuBridge oral history, p. 31 (CIT). The story may be apocryphal. Pauling, when asked, remembered nothing about testing Church's horses and offered that it was more likely that Millikan had gone to Arnold Beckman with the problem.

433   *So Pauling designed a laboratory:* On planning for the Church building, see Pauling and Beadle (1953); Pauling to Ben May, June 22, 1953; Sturdivant to Beadle, July 19, 1952; Pauling to Leonora Bilger, October 11, 1953; Sturdivant to Pauling, August 19, 1953 (all OSU).

434   *"extremely sketchy":* Slater to Pauling, December 16, 1953 (American Philosophical Society Library).

435   *Irène Joliot-Curie:* See Pauling to David Todd, October 19, 1959 (OSU).

435   *"The above is furnished":* J. Edgar Hoover to Criminal Division, September 23, 1953 (FBI FOIA).

436   *his international protein conference:* On the September 1953 protein conference, see Thomas and Phillips, p. 120; Judson (1979), p. 258; Pauling to Peter Pauling, September 24, 1953 (OSU); and Dorothy Hodgkin to Pauling, July 12, 1953 (CIT Chemistry Division files).

436   *"one big love-fest":* Edward Hughes oral history (CIT).

437   *Lippman was being blacklisted:* See Pauling to Ben Meyer, January 4, 1952; Pauling to DuBridge, March 4, 1952 (OSU); the Lippman files at OSU; and Pauling's FBI files for 1951–52, which contain details on his political activities at the time.

438   *"a haven of open-mindedness":* Pauling to Myron A. Bantrell, February 8, 1952 (OSU).

438   *buying out his contract:* See FBI report dated April 21, 1952 (FBI FOIA). At least one Caltech trustee or someone privy to their deliberations was an FBI informant.

439   *"The courage of your actions":* Mary W. to Pauling, November 21, 1952 (OSU).

440   *Pauling was not the only scientist:* On the U.S. Public Health Service blacklist, see Greenberg (1967), p. 129; Caute (1978), p. 472; Pauling to John Edsall, May 11 and July 21, 1955 (OSU); Pauling interview with author. The Henry Borsook Oral History at Caltech also addresses the blacklist. Pauling has said—although I have so far found no corroborating evidence—that at least one of his grants from the National Science Foundation was also cut off during this period.

440   *"You see how unsophisticated":* Pauling interview with author.

441 *R. W. Scott McLeod:* On McLeod, see O'Reilly (1983b), p. 195; Caute (1978), p. 246; and the McLeod mentions in Pauling's State Department FOIA files for 1953 and 1954.

442 *Bronk met with Shipley:* "Notes, Telephone call Dr. Cornell," December 14, 1953, hand numbered 41 and 42 (OSU).

443 *board of passport appeals:* The long-promised passport appeals board was not instituted until December 23, 1953—the day after Pauling's passport was refused. Although a director was named, there was no actual board until sometime later. The timing indicates that the board was started partly in response to Pauling's case and partly in response to that of Martin Kamen, another left-wing scientist who threatened to bring suit when he was denied a passport.

443 *"he went off the deep end":* Karl Compton to Dulles, December 30, 1953 (State Department FOIA).

444 *"the result of fear of McCarthy":* Pauling to Owen Roberts, January 18, 1954 (OSU).

444 *white blood cells rather than red:* New York Times, March 27, 1954, p. 10.

445 *"surprised and astonished the scientists":* quoted in Divine (1978), p. 8. On the *Lucky Dragon* episode, see also Lapp (1965), pp. 122–25.

446 *On April 15 he delivered:* FBI Los Angeles office report, April 28, 1954 (FBI FOIA).

446 *Oppenheimer's "personal characteristics":* Pauling to Harlow Shapley, July 3, 1946 (OSU).

447 *"a disgraceful act":* Pauling (1954), p. 370.

447 *"I have greatly restrained myself":* Pauling to Bernard Schaar, May 10, 1954 (OSU).

448 *"I find it hard to believe":* Pauling to State Department, September 3, 1954 (State Department FOIA).

449 *"That was the trouble":* Pauling interview with author.

450 *the Nobel Prize in chemistry:* On winning the 1954 Nobel Prize, see Szent-Györgyi to Pauling, November 8, 1952, and Pauling's reply, November 21 (both OSU); Paradowski (1993); and Pauling interviews with author.

451 *Pauling told the* New York Times: New York Times, November 4, 1954, p. 1.

451 *his last visit to Einstein:* See Pauling to Ronald W. Clark, July 28, 1969 (LPI); Pauling (1981b), p. 133; and Pauling's handwritten notes for an ACLU tribute to Einstein, dated May 12, 1955 (OSU).

451 *"I doubt that many Nobel Prizes":* Charles Coryell to J. R. Oppenheimer, November 2, 1954 (APS Library Collection).

452 *"The Road to Stockholm":* The playlet was written over a two-week period by Caltech humanities professor Kent Clark with the help of some of Pauling's coworkers and students.

454 *Pauling-related memos ricocheted:* Details about the State Department's deliberations over Pauling's right to travel to the 1954 Nobel ceremonies are found in Pauling-related 1954 State Department and FBI documents released through the FOIA.

454 *"we know the pitfalls":* Mrs. Shipley to Mr. McLeod, November 16, 1954 (State FOIA).

458   *"Your Dr. Pauling has done more tonight":* Alfred Ingersoll to Thomas Hennings, November 23, 1955 (OSU).
458   *"great mental powers":* Pauling (l955c), p. 16.
459   *"it is ridiculous for the Department":* Scott McLeod to Robert J. McClurkin, January 3, 1955 (State FOIA).

CHAPTER 19: FALLOUT

461   *The Nobel Prize changes scientists:* See Zuckerman (1977).
462   *"For a while there":* quoted in Dye (1985), p. 12.
462   *"Are we justified":* Linus Pauling, "Statement for Radio and Television Transmission," dated March 1955 (OSU).
464   *"an act of irresponsibility":* quoted in Divine (1978), p. 47.
465   *fifteen thousand defective children:* Pauling's estimates of biological damage from low-level radiation were based on his interpretations of the experimental and theoretical work of biologists and geneticists Hardin Jones, Alfred Sturtevant, E. B. Lewis, and Hermann J. Muller.
465   *Pauling's renewed political activism:* On the Russell-Einstein Manifesto, see Carlson (1981), p. 377; Pauling to Heinz Norden, December 3, 1956 (OSU); and Pauling and Ikeda (1992), p. 71. The Mainau Declaration is reprinted in Pauling (1958b). On civil liberties work, see Pauling to Edward Condon, September 2, 1955 (OSU), and the *New York Times,* September 16, 1955, p. 3. On the Hennings Committee see Belfrage (1973), p. 244; Pauling's handwritten introduction to his Hennings testimony dated November 15, 1955 (OSU) and coverage in the *New York Times,* November 16, 1955, p. 22.
466   *"exceedingly brilliant and upright":* quoted in the *New York Times,* January 17, 1955, p. 25.
466   *"I am proud that Caltech":* Beadle (1955), p. 14.
466   *"Well, he isn't a Communist":* Judy Schomaker, *Nova* transcripts (OSU).
467   *"Young men should be mathematicians":* Matthew Meselson interview with author.
467   *his own contribution to Watson's:* Pauling and Corey (1956).
467   *an attack on cancer:* See Thomas (1978), p. 17; Pauling to H. R. Kent, December 10, 1958 (OSU).
468   *the Ford Foundation:* "Biochemical and Structural Chemical Factors in Relation to Mental Disease, Especially Mental Deficiency," Ford Foundation grant request, dated August 15, 1955 (OSU). See also Pauling to Richard Morgan, June 20, 1955 (OSU).
470   *"most mental disease":* New York Times, May 3, 1956, p. 25. See also Pauling to Sam T. Gibson, September 10, 1957 and to Eric Sandahl, June 5, 1957 (both OSU).
470   *doubt the existence of God: New York Times,* January 2, 1956, p. 2. Pauling's comment came in answer to a question referring to Millikan's statement that the more he learned, the more he was sure of the existence of God. Pauling said, "My experience has been different, in a sense almost the opposite, of Professor Milliken."

470 *The NAS panels:* Divine (1978), p. 78.

471 *robbed Nevadans of one thousand years:* Pauling to George Beadle, October 25, 1956; Pauling to Roy Popkin, October 26, 1956; and Richard G. Elliott to *Tonopah Times-Bonanza,* November 9, 1956 (all OSU).

471 *"There is a surprising":* Lundberg (1956), p. 3.

472 *"I think I've introduced him": The Cambrian,* November 8, 1979, p. 17. Ava Helen added in this interview, "The whole nuclear ban and disarmament treaty was initiated by me."

474 *"I find that I have some difficulty":* Pauling to Fred West, June 25, 1951 (OSU).

475 *ten thousand people were dead: New York Times,* May 1, 1957, p. 31.

475 *"I am most seriously charged":* William Libby to Pauling, May 2, 1957, and Pauling's reply, May 10, 1957 (both OSU).

476 *"There is considerable uncertainty":* Pauling to Reino Hakala, March 6, 1957 (OSU).

476 *"I believe that no human beings":* On the genesis of the Appeal by American Scientists, see Pauling's *Nova* tape transcripts, side 14, p. 2 (OSU); the *Bulletin of the Atomic Scientists* 13(1957):264–65; Pauling (1958b), pp. 170–73; Divine (1978), p. 126; Pauling and Ikeda (1992), p. 68. The petition idea may have been spurred by a letter Pauling received two years earlier from a Scripps College professor: "It seems to me there must be hundreds, even thousands of American scientists who, like me, may not be articulate spokesmen, yet who want desperately to stand up and be counted in the present crisis; who feel that perhaps, just perhaps, government officials might take heed if many individual scientists all over the country were to warn us publicly of the dangers of our present attitude" (Isabel Fothergill to Pauling, March 22, 1955 [OSU]). Pauling had also been invited to sign an American Friends Committee antitest petition in the weeks just before devising his own. His petition, however, was the first to focus exclusively on scientists.

478 *ABC television medical program: New York Times,* June 3, 1957, p. 11.

478 *"almost like an organized affair":* quoted in the *Washington Star,* June 9, 1957, p. 6.

478 *"I would be pleased": New York Times,* June 7, 1957, p. 5.

478 *Anderson "blew his top":* "A couple of days after they [SISS] had subpoenaed Pauling, Sen. Clinton Anderson literally blew his top with [SISS chair] Eastland and Morris. He accused both Eastland and Morris of engaging in a personal attack on both Senator Anderson and Lyndon Johnson since the Joint Committee on Atomic Energy was having fallout hearings. Both Eastland and Morris rejected this and finally agreed to put out a statement that since Pauling could not come on June 18, they would postopne indefinitely his hearing" (FBI internal memo, L. B. Nichols to Clyde Tolson, June 13, 1957 [FBI FOIA]).

479 *Bill Libby reminded: New York Times,* June 8, 1957, p. 5.

479 *"My conscience will not permit": New York Times,* June 12, 1957, p. 6.

480 *"I was astonished":* Pauling interview with author.

480 *They were "top dogs":* Pauling interview with John Spender, February 4, 1965 (typescript; LPI), pp. 26–27; *Nova* tape transcripts, side 14, pp. 4–5 (OSU).

480 *"seemed to serve effectively as propaganda":* Pauling (1958b), p. 153.

481 *"there are so many grey areas":* Richard Thruelson to Pauling, December 23, 1957 (OSU).

481   *"I had not got enough knowledge":* Lawrence Bragg to Pauling, October 13, 1958 (OSU).

481   *"high hopes that you will fail":* quoted in Lapp (1965), p. 134.

482   *"creating fear, misunderstanding, and confusion":* confidential FBI report, "Communist Exploitation of Radiation 'Fall-Out' Controversy," sent by J. Edgar Hoover to John Foster Dulles, June 19, 1957 (FBI FOIA).

482   *"Anybody who has tried":* Sacramento Union, February 10, 1958, p. 15.

482   *"When people understand":* Pauling to editor, *Sacramento Union*, March 12, 1958, p. 16.

483   *It was Teller:* On Teller, see Bernstein (1982), p. 233; Divine (1978), pp. 147, 192.

483   *a one-hour debate between Teller and Pauling:* transcript published as "Fallout and Disarmament," 1958.

485   *"Since that time I have refused":* Pauling and Ikeda (1992), p. 81.

485   I. F. Stone's Weekly: Pauling (1958c).

488   *"cheer himself up with fireworks":* Albert Szent-Györgyi to Pauling, March 9, 1958 (OSU).

489   *Taking on an agency of the federal government:* The idea of an injunction suit against the AEC and the U.S. government to prohibit further tests was first proposed to Pauling in May 1956 by Philip Isely, publisher of a newsletter on atomic dangers. "Regardless of the legal success of such a suit, it might be a device for organizing effective public opinion on the matter," Isely wrote (Philip Isely to Pauling, May 2, 1956, [OSU]). Pauling replied at the time that he did not know enough about the law and did not have enough time to pursue it (Pauling to Isely, June 5, 1956 [OSU]).

491   *"Exaggerated statements":* On the C-14 controversy, see *New York Times* articles on April 29 and 30 and May 2, 1958.

491   *Pauling appeared on* Meet the Press: National Broadcasting Company (1958).

492   *"somewhere between resentment and discomfort":* Norman Davidson interview with author.

493   *McCone harangued him:* Author's interview with Joseph Koepfli.

493   *"I feel that":* Pauling to DuBridge, June 10, 1958 (OSU).

494   *"I was asked to resign":* Pauling to Iris Chang, February 28, 1992. DuBridge refused to talk about Pauling's resignation. This version of Pauling's resignation is derived from Pauling's accounts given in interviews with the author and other published interviews.

CHAPTER 20: THE SUBCOMMITTEE

495   *He did not want it made public:* A good deal of correspondence around the time of his departure (OSU) and interviews with several chemistry faculty members of the day supports this interpretation of his behavior.

495   *"just insidiously grew":* Ernest Swift oral history, pp. 54–55, 96–97 (CIT).

497   *"pleased and honored":* Pauling to Elmo Roper, June 9, 1958 (OSU).

497   *"it is impossible":* New York Times, June 22, 1958, p. 1.

498 *Pauling and Russell made certain:* See the *National Catholic Weekly,* July 5, 1958, p. 1; *New York Times,* September 22, 1957, p. 1; *Peace News* (London), September 12, 1958, p. 1; and Pauling handwritten statement on immigration difficulty in Bertrand Russell collection, McMaster University Archives.

498 *"the most profound impression":* National Guardian (Britain), September 25, 1958, p. 9.

498 *"We live in a wonderful world":* This compiled "basic stump speech" uses material from Pauling (1958b) and typescripts of several speeches of the period by Pauling, especially an address he gave to the National Conference of Social Workers in Chicago, May 13, 1958, attached to a letter from Pauling to Mary Temple, June 10, 1958 (OSU).

501 *"I am pleased to say":* Pauling to Lester Pearson, January 6, 1959 (OSU).

501 *"I have felt pretty pleased":* Pauling to Robert F. Loeb, April 13, 1959.

501 *"There has been a great change":* quoted in the *Oregonian,* June 9, 1959, p. 1.

502 *In July 1959, the Paulings flew:* Accounts of the Schweitzer visit are found in the Ava Helen Pauling diary entries for the dates of the visit (LPI); Pauling's "memo book" notes for the dates (OSU); Pauling and Ikeda (1992), p. 8; Ikeda (1988), p. 12; Catchpool (1986), pp. 231–32; *Nova* tape transcript interviews with Frank Catchpool and Ava Helen Pauling (OSU); and Pauling interviews with author.

504 *"We were very well pleased":* Pauling to Russell, August 27, 1959 (OSU); on the Hiroshima Appeal see also the *New York Times,* August 8, 1959, p. 13; and *National Guardian,* September 21, 1959, pp. 6–7.

504 *the health effects of carbon 14 and strontium 90:* Pauling (1958c, 1958d); Kamb and Pauling (1959).

506 *Once off track:* On the stalling of the Geneva talks in 1959, see Divine (1978), p. 296.

507 *reported her husband missing:* Information on the cliff episode comes from author's interviews with Pauling, Linda Pauling Kamb, Barclay Kamb, and Crellin Pauling; and news reports of the day, especially *New York Times,* February 1, 1960, p. 1.

510 *a tightly sealed place inside:* This interpretation of the events following Pauling's night on the cliff is the author's, on interviews with Linda Pauling Kamb, and Barclay Kamb.

511 *"the militarists, industrialists, H bomb scientists":* from "The World Must Now Choose Peace," typescript of an address to International Peace Pageant and Musical Festival, Santa Monica, California, May 7, 1960 (OSU).

512 *a seminal event:* In order to point out how Communists influenced the protests, HUAC made a forty-minute film, "Operation Abolition," using news footage of the San Francisco riot. Later, SDS organizers were grateful to the committee for distributing the film because the scenes of police clubbing students helped radicalize viewers (O'Reilly [1983], p. 282).

512 *"American students":* typescript of San Francisco interview with Pauling, dated September 10, 1960 (OSU).

512 *SISS:* The best information on the subcommittee's Pauling investigation and hearings is found in the Pauling name files (Boxes 84 and 85) in the National Archives collection of the U.S. Senate Judiciary Committee, Internal Security Subcommittee individual name files (identified here as SISS). This includes a comprehensive collection of news clippings of the day as well as all of the correspondence between Pauling and the subcommittee and internal memos from the subcommittee's investigators, counsel, and members. Other sources are the SISS's publication of the hearing ("Testimony of Dr. Linus Pauling, Tuesday, June 21, 1960" published by the U.S. Senate Committee on the Judiciary [1961]); Kalven (1960 and 1961); "My Experiences with the Internal Security Subcomittee of the U.S. Senate," a typescript manuscript by Pauling dated September 1960 (OSU); and typescript of a Pauling interview with Virginia Mill, dated October 4, 1960 (CIT).

513 *"Linus Pauling has gone over the head":* memo, Ben Mandel to J. G. Sourwine, January 15, 1958 (SISS).

519 *"a discredit to the United States":* New York Times, September 27, 1960, p. 5.

519 *"One way or another":* Ava Helen Pauling to Mrs. P. G. Briggs, September 1, 1960 (OSU).

521 *The real purpose of the second hearing:* See Kalven (1960); *I. F. Stone's Weekly;* 8:1; "The Pauling Case: End of an Inquiry?" by Anthony Lewis, *New York Times,* October 16, 1960, p. 10; and the transcript of the hearing, published by the U.S. Senate.

522 *Pauling was "on trial":* Murray Kempton, *New York Post,* October 12, 1960, p. 39.

CHAPTER 21: PEACE

524 *"The fight for peace":* National Guardian, November 7, 1960, p. 5.

524 *"an evil person":* excerpts from *At Random,* a television program from New York City, October 16, 1960 (OSU).

524 *"We have, I understand":* Pauling to Donald Harrington, November 11, 1960 (OSU).

524 *"marked bias for Communist causes":* "The Pugwash Conferences" staff analysis for SISS, 1961, p. 55 (SISS).

524 *"reason for suspecting":* SISS press release dated March 17, 1961 (SISS).

525 *"The newspapers have been partners":* Pauling to William H. Fisher, March 23, 1961 (OSU).

525 *He quit his position:* On Pauling's decision to quit SANE, see Pauling to Nicholas Cheronis, March 8, 1961; to Clark Foreman, November 8, 1960; to Charles Coryell, December 19, 1962 (all OSU).

525 *Bentley Glass:* Glass (1962); Pauling (1962c); Pauling (1963b); author's interview with Aaron Novick; Pauling to Anita Hammar Cumming, August 7, 1962 (OSU).

526 *the Pugwash discussions, he felt, had degenerated:* Pauling to Bertrand Russell, May 19, 1962 (OSU).

526 *"Men of the Year":* Richard Feynman told the story of sharing a car ride with three Las Vegas prostitutes around the time of Pauling's being named one of the "Men of the Year." After telling them he worked at Caltech, one said,

"Oh, isn't that the place where that scientist Pauling comes from?" . . . "Yeah!" Feynman answered, astonished. . . . "I couldn't believe it. I was riding in a car full of prostitutes and they knew this stuff!" The women told him they had learned Pauling's name while looking through the "Men of the Year" issue and picking out the youngest and handsomest scientists (Feynman [1986], p. 203).

527 *"I myself have a high opinion"*: Pauling to P. P. Ewald, February 10, 1961 (OSU).

528 *international peace meeting in Oslo:* Complete notes and letters concerning the planning of the Oslo Conference are on file at OSU.

529 *"I have a lot of ideas"*: Pauling quotes this in the *Nova* transcripts, N3.

529 *xenon gas was a wonderful anesthetic:* Pauling recalls his interest in this problem in the *Nova* transcripts, side 2, pp. 4–5 and N2 (OSU), and in Pauling (1969); (1981b), pp. 143–44; and (1991c), p. 83. See also Catchpool (1968), pp. 343–47; Pauling memos to Catchpool dated January 26 and February 15, 1960 (both OSU); Pauling to Chauncey Leake, February 8, 1960, and to Graham DuShane, February 2, 1961 (both OSU); and Pauling (1961).

530 *"intriguing and attractive"*: *New York Times*, April 6, 1961, p. 37.

531 *"I am determined to keep my book unsophisticated"*: See, for example, Pauling's correspondence with D. P. Craig and H. C. Longuet-Higgins in the summer and fall of 1961 (OSU).

531 *"In the third edition"*: Martin Karplus, interview with author.

531 *"The Aula meeting was grand"*: Pauling to Joan Harris, May 10, 1961 (OSU).

532 *the Soviets started testing again:* See Divine (1978), pp. 315–16; Keating's Research Report (1972), pp. 16–18; Lapp (1965), p. 143; Dean (1966), p. 90.

532 *"This is premeditated murder"*: Portland *Oregonian*, February 26, 1962, p. 4.

533 *"Leenus Pauling"*: Pauling interview with author.

534 *Swedish-style socialism:* See Pauling's handwritten notes, "Political and Economic Systems," dated October 1, 1962 (OSU).

534 *"While I am critical of the Soviet government"*: typescript: "Transcript of Discussion Between John Spender and Linus Pauling," dated February 4, 1965, p. 64 (LPI).

534 *"basically political in nature"*: See Pauling to Polycarp Kusch, November 8, 1960; Pauling to Jerome Rozen, Jr., April 13, 1962 (both OSU).

535 *"We feel rather depressed"*: quoted in Serafini (1989), p. 208.

535 *"Are you going to give an order"*: Handwritten text of telegram from Pauling to J. F. Kennedy, 1962 (OSU).

535 *"Anger and shame"*: typescript of undated Pauling antiwar speech (OSU).

537 *Kennedy responded by inviting:* Details on the Kennedy dinner are found in Pauling's interviews with author; author's interviews with Gerard and Eleanor Piel; Pauling, *Nova* transcript, N44; Ava Helen Pauling, *Nova* transcript, side 19, p. 5; coverage in the *Washington Star*, April 30, 1962, p. B6; *Washington Daily News*, May 1, 1962, p. 20; and *New York Post*, May 9, 1962, p. 51.

539 *"Fortunately for America"*: Muller and Pollack (1962) and a three-part series Muller wrote for *Saga* magazine in 1962.

540 *criticized the Soviet Union:* *New York Times*, June 24, 1962, p. 5, and September 11, 1962, p. 32; *Look*, July 17, 1962, p. 14.

541   *the evolution not of a species but of a molecule:* The original idea of using hemoglobin as a marker for species divergence was not Pauling's. As early as 1907
researchers had compared hemoglobin crystals from different animals and
found that certain morphological characteristics were common to specific
families and genera; in the 1920s, Landsteiner and later others used immunological cross-reactions with the blood of different animals to show a
crude set of evolutionary relationships.

541   *"the question of the origin of species":* Pauling (1962d), p. 8. On the concept of
the molecular clock, see also Zuckerkandl and Pauling (1962); Pauling
(1991c), pp. 73–74; Edelstein (1986), pp. 26–27.

542   *"The human race is deteriorating":* I thank Lily Kay for bringing this issue to my
attention. On Pauling and eugenics, see Zuckerkandl and Pauling (1962), p.
221; Pauling (1962d), p. 1; Kay (1993), pp. 156, 276; *Pediatric Herald,* March
3, 1962, p. 1; Henahan 1966, p. 51; Eugene *Register-Guard,* January 21, 1959,
story on Pauling's address at the University of Oregon's Religious Evaluation
Week.

542   *"the concept of good and evil":* Zuckerkandl and Pauling (1962), p. 189.

543   *"Some of them," he suggested:* Ernest Swift oral history, p. 79 (CIT).

543   *"This medical stuff is out of place":* Pauling interview with author; information
on Roberts's thinking is from Roberts interview with author. See also Pauling to Eddie Hughes, December 12, 1966 (CIT).

544   *"Pauling just choked":* DuBridge oral history, pp. 43–45 (CIT). DuBridge in
an interview with the author denied being involved in the decision to pare
Pauling's lab space, but Roberts has said that DuBridge was consulted at
every step, often through the Caltech dean of faculty, Robert Bacher.

544   *a private West Coast institute:* See Pauling to Linus Pauling, Jr., December 7,
1960 (OSU).

544   *joining the staff at Stanford's:* Pauling to J. E. Wallace Sterling, January 25, Feb-
ruary 24, and March 31, 1961 (OSU). On the pharmacology staff idea, see
Pauling to I. S. Edelman, September 26, 1961 (OSU). On the Sloan grant,
Pauling to Weaver, June 4, 1963 (OSU).

546   *"Daddy, have you heard the news?"* Anecdote related in *Nova* transcripts, side
14 (OSU); and in author's interviews with Linda Pauling Kamb.

CHAPTER 22: NOMADS

548   *Ava Helen should have been a cowinner:* "Many people have suggested that the
Prize should have been officially awarded to both of us," Ava Helen wrote a
friend around the time of the Peace Prize, "but I am afraid I cannot concur
in that. Of course, any man who has lived or shared his life with his wife the
number of years my husband and I have been together must surely share his
honors with her. . . . We feel that this is a prize to the peace workers of the
world" (Ava Helen Pauling to Mrs. James Patrick Murphy. Transcript of undated dictabelt recording [OSU]).

548 *"We think of this honor":* Ava Helen Pauling to Victoria Orellana, transcript of undated dictabelt recording (OSU).

548 *"I got the Nobel Prize": Nova* transcripts, side 3, p. 3 (OSU).

549 *"Though many people have disapproved": Pasadena Star-News,* October 11, 1963, p. 1.

550 *"placarding peacenik": New York Herald-Tribune,* October 11, 1963, editorial page. The *New York Times* did not comment editorially until December 11, when the editors commended Pauling's "courage in running against the crowd," but then added that he "has not always been wise in his choice of tactics and . . . has sometimes been reckless."

550 *The Luce magazines:* "A Weird Insult from Norway," *Life* editorial, October 25, 1963; Pauling to Henry Luce, October 16, 1963 (OSU). In the face of this mass-media assault, it was small solace for Pauling when a midsized paper like the St. Louis *Post-Dispatch* reminded its readers, "No man worked harder, throughout the harshest years of the Cold War, to persuade people of every country that for the sake of humanity nuclear testing should be stopped. . . . May Dr. Pauling's prize inspire in others the courage to dissent."

552 *"Who can spank me?": Washington Post,* October 23, 1963, p. 1; October 24, 1963, p. 1.

552 *resigning from the professional society:* See Pauling to Alden Emery, November 19, 1963 (OSU).

554 *"In the fight for peace":* "Response by Linus Pauling." Typescript of Nobel acceptance address, dated 1:00 P.M., December 10, 1963 (OSU). See also Pauling (1964).

554 *a tribute for Pauling: The Minority of One,* February 1964, pp. 12–15.

554 *"knew the secret of happiness":* Commager (1964), p. 17.

555 *"Terribly busy":* Ava Helen Pauling undated letter, transcription of dictabelt recording (OSU).

555 *"I suggest a program":* Linus Pauling. Undated, handwritten notes titled "Center" (OSU).

555 *Ava Helen became concerned:* Ava Helen to James Higgins, undated dictabelt transcription (OSU). Ava Helen's low regard for Hutchins was a likely factor in Pauling's own dissatisfaction with the center. On one occasion, Ava Helen introduced Hutchins to some visiting Russian women, who, unimpressed by his wit, asked him how many women he had on staff at the center. Ava Helen took great delight in Hutchins's discomfiture when he replied that he had none.

556 *"My complaint about the Center":* Linus Pauling, undated, handwritten notes titled "Center" (OSU).

556 *"the institutional arrangements proposed seem idiotic":* Oppenheimer papers, Library of Congress, Box 56: Pauling correspondence.

556 *He was shocked:* On the UCSB incident, see Pauling to Chester Carlson, April 30, 1964 (OSU); Fred Wall oral history, Beckman Center for the History of Chemistry, pp. 72–73; and Pauling interviews with the author.

557 *"The Triple Revolution":* See typescript press release titled "The Ad Hoc Committee on the Triple Revolution," dated March 22, 1964 (OSU); Jack Steele column in the *Washington Daily News,* March 24, 1964, p. 4

557 *"we thought we could do five times more":* transcript of undated Ava Helen Pauling dictabelt letter (OSU).

557 *"the fascists get braver all the time":* transcript of undated AHP dictabelt letter (OSU).

557 *"Those people who say LBJ":* Ava Helen Pauling to Mary Sterns, March 27, 1965 (LPI).

558 *"close-packed spheron theory":* Pauling (1965b).

559 *settled out of court:* Pauling to Richard Kenyon, May 24, 1962 (OSU); Pauling testimony in Buckley libel suit.

559 *he engaged a Reno lawyer:* Pauling to Fred Okrand, November 19, 1963 (OSU).

560 *"The Collaborators": National Review,* July 1962, p. 8.

560 *"vicious libel":* Michael Levi Matar to William F. Buckley, August 23, 1962 (LPI).

560 *"Dr. Pauling is in error":* William Rusher to Matar, August 28, 1962 (LPI).

560 *"Are You Being Sued by Linus Pauling?": National Review,* September 25, 1962, p. 218.

561 *"The* National Review *is prepared": National Review,* June 4, 1963, p. 442.

561 *"akin to identifying Harry Truman as a Democrat": National Review* fund-raising letter, signed by William F. Buckley, February 17, 1966 (LPI).

562 *"I never associated with organizations": New York Post,* March 30, 1966, p. 28. Other details of the *National Review* libel trial come from "Linus Pauling Takes the Stand," a review of the trial in the *National Review,* May 17, 1966, pp. 459–66; the *New York Herald-Tribune,* April 20, 1966, p. 27; *Time,* April 29, 1966, p. 80; *New York Times,* April 24, 1966, p. 46; and other news coverage of the event.

563 *the* Sullivan *ruling:* On the importance of Pauling's case in extending Sullivan, see Lawhorne (1971), pp. 233–34.

564 *unidentified flying objects:* "A Study of Unidentified Flying Objects," typescript memo dated July 16, 1966 (LPI).

565 *niacin was being used like a drug:* On the birth of Pauling's interest in vitamin therapy for mental disease, see Pauling (1979); Pauling (1981b), p. 158; Pauling interviews with author.

565 *Irwin Stone:* On Stone's theories of vitamin C and the birth of Pauling's interest, see Stone (1966), pp. 133–34; Stone (1986), p. 53; Dye (1985), p. 14; Thomas (1978), p. 17; Pauling's interviews with author.

566 *"I didn't believe it":* Thomas (1978), p. 17.

569 *"The functioning of the brain":* Pauling (1968b), p. 266.

570 *"I believe in nonviolence":* "Protest Politics," handwritten speech dated May 9, 1968 (OSU). When questioned about the consistency of advocating both global law and disruptive student demonstrations, Pauling answered, "I do not think that [the students'] actions have been nearly so violent or as basically unlawful as those of their elders. . . . I estimate that the ratio of violence done by the government to that done by the revolting students is about one million to one" (Pauling to Frank Chilson, July 3, 1969 [OSU]).

571 *"The strike is a way":* Linus Pauling, "Note to myself," dated May 1969 (LPI).

571 *"But financial considerations":* William Johnson to Pauling, February 20, 1969 (OSU).

CHAPTER 23: VITAMIN C

573 *"The result of our having overheard":* Linus Pauling, "Biographical Note" dated April 11, 1970 (LPI).

574 *He had not, in fact, carefully reviewed the literature:* Thomas (1978), p. 17.

574 *"optimal amounts of vitamin C":* Mademoiselle, November 1969, p. 189.

575 *no "important effect":* Cowan, Diehal, and Baker (1942), p. 1267.

575 *vitamin C was a nutrient:* Pauling (1971), p. 69.

576 *"the common cold would disappear":* Pauling (1971), p. xiii.

578 *"it's just a passing fad":* New York Times, December 5, 1970, p. 68.

579 *"I think I would have as much trouble swallowing":* Oregon Journal, December 29, 1970, p. 5.

579 The Medical Letter: *The Medical Letter* 12(26):1–4; Pauling to Harold Aaron, February 1, 1971 (OSU).

579 *Pauling's actions were not "socially responsible":* Consumer Reports 36(2):113–114; Pauling to Colston Warne, February 10, 1971 (LPI); Pauling (1971), pp. 79–80.

580 *Bad news came:* See Pauling laboratory notebook 288, dated July 28, 1971 (OSU); *Medical Tribune* 14(1973).28.

580 *senile megalomania: Heretic: Linus Pauling.* London: BBC Television, 1994.

581 *"we may make use of ascorbic acid":* Pauling (1971), p. 20.

582 *"They are willing to make their statements":* transcript of *Nova* interview, side 9 (OSU).

582 *the evidence was "overwhelming":* Pauling (1971), p. 84.

582 *The Maryland study was widely reported:* For example, *New York Times*, November 28, 1971, p. 77; *Parade*, December 26, 1971, p. 5.

583 *Overall demand for vitamin C:* Figures from *U.S. News & World Report*, December 4, 1972.

583 *"the Linus Pauling Effect":* Richards (1991), p. 49.

584 *"I am unashamedly optimistic":* Ewan Cameron to Pauling, November 30, 1971 (LPI); on Cameron and Pauling's early contact, see also Richards (1991), pp. 73–79.

584 *"I am tremendously interested":* Pauling to Ewan Cameron, December 14, 1971 (LPI).

584 *"We seem to have had several days":* Ewan Cameron to Pauling, January 5, 1972 (LPI).

584 *"The attack you are making":* Pauling to Ewan Cameron, January 11, 1972 (LPI); Richards (1991), p. 84.

585 PNAS, *a perfect vehicle:* Pauling to Ewan Cameron, February 8 and April 5, 1972 (both LPI).

585 *"It was a very troubling":* Edsall interview with author; on the *PNAS* rejection, see also Edsall to Pauling, April 26, 1972 (LPI); Richards (1991), p. 90.

585 *"I do not know what to do":* Pauling to Ewan Cameron, May 8 and June 12, 1972 (both LPI).

587 *"Pauling is God":* Art Robinson interview with author. Additional information on Robinson's early years with Pauling is from author's interviews with Pauling and Martin Kamen.

588 *exhorted Stanford students: New York Times,* January 26, 1972, p. 36.

588 *the effects of vitamin C on patients:* See Richards (1991), p. 93; Pauling to Ewan Cameron, November 27, 1972 (LPI).

589 *rent laboratory space off campus:* transcript of *Nova* interview, side 1 (OSU); Pauling and Robinson (1978), p. 98.

589 *Institute of Orthomolecular Medicine:* Pauling to Ewan Cameron, November 27, 1972 (LPI).

590 *He was turned down each time:* Richards (1991), p. 93; Pauling and Robinson (1978), p. 100.

590 *"causing much mutilation":* quoted in Richards (1991), p. 95.

590 *a task force of the American Psychiatric Association: Psychiatric News,* July 18, 1973; *Science News,* July 28, 1973, pp. 59–60; *American Journal of Psychiatry* 131(1973):1251–57.

590 *"It is hard to understand physicians": Medical Tribune* 14(1973):1.

591 *an adjunct:* Richards (1991), p. 98.

591 *UC Santa Cruz:* Pauling personal communication to author, January 30, 1994.

592 *"there seemed to be advantages":* Pauling and Robinson (1978), p. 100; transcript of *Nova* interview no. 1 (OSU); Richards (1991), p. 40.

592 *"I don't waste time on needless details":* Clip dated "1974" from *National Enquirer,* Lucile Pauling scrapbook.

593 *"Pauling wasn't doing anything as president":* Art Robinson, interview with author.

593 *National Medal of Science: Los Angeles Times,* September 19, 1975, p. 1. The story notes that Pauling's criticism of Nixon's foreign policy prevented him from winning the honor twice before, when the Nixon administration ignored the recommendation of its own advisory group and refused to name Pauling a medal winner. "The government had to knuckle under because of the 'revolt,' essentially, by scientists at the refusal to give me the National Medal of Science," Pauling said in an interview. "I think that it was pure political pressure on the part of the scientists. It made it necessary for the President to give in."

594 *"I was the best guy in the lab":* Arthur Robinson, interview with author.

594 *"He presented himself very well":* Richard Hicks and Arthur Robinson, interviews with author.

594 *"self-deception" among scientists: Modern Medicine,* January 15, 1976, and July 1, 1976; *Medical Tribune,* September 8, 1976, p. 3; transcript of *Nova* interview, side 18, p. 2 (OSU); typescript of American Academy of Achievement interview with Pauling, November 11, 1990, p. 19 (OSU).

595 *buying hundreds of hairless mice:* Information on the mouse studies is from Pauling and Robinson (1978); Richards (1991), pp. 100–6; Hussain (1977), p. 218; and author's interviews with Robinson and Pauling.

595 *"It will be interesting to see what happens":* Pauling to Ewan Cameron, July 14, 1976 (LPI); Richards (1991), p. 103.

596 *"Historical controls are the source of more horseshit": New Scientist,* July 1, 1976, pp. 30–31.

596 *"I am beginning to think":* quoted in Richards (1991), p. 105.

596 *"the hottest of arguments"*: Santa Barbara News-Press, August 16, 1964.
597 *"Does he have an ego?"*: Transcript of *Nova* interview, side 18, p. 5 (OSU).

CHAPTER 24: RESURRECTION

598 *"It is my opinion"*: Hussain (1977), p. 217.
599 *"The guy doesn't give up"*: Collier (1978), p. 22.
599 *"Like other aging scientists"*: Collier (1978), p. 22.
599 *"I would love to give Linus"*: Hussain (1977), p. 220.
599 *"less than slim"* : Francis Heisler to Pauling Institute, March 9, 1977 (LPI).
599 *"It is my opinion"*: Richards (1991), p. 111.
600 *"Dr. Pauling began contacting me"*: Collier (1978), p. 22.
601 *An investigative report:* Hussain (1977).
601 *In 1978 alone almost $1.5 million:* Grant (1979), p. 4; Collier (1978), p. 24.
602 *"We'd have a campus like Stanford"*: Art Robinson interview with author.
604 *Art Robinson sued:* Information on the Robinson affair is from Grant (1979); Richards (1991), pp. 42–44; Paradowski (1991), pp. 208–9; and author's interviews with Linus Pauling, Art Robinson, Emile Zuckerkandl, and Richard Hicks.
606 *"in an almost eighteenth century fashion"*: Time, August 6, 1989, p. 29.
607 *"I think that the goat knows more"*; Pauling (1979).
607 *demand rising so high during the 1970s:* Richards (1991), p. 49.
607 *"There is evidence"*: Cameron, Pauling, and Leibovitz (1979), p. 664.
608 *"Failure of High-Dose Vitamin C"*: Creagan, Moertel, et al. (1979).
608 *"I think the conclusion"*: Pauling to Cameron, May 7, 1979 (LPI).
608 *"No Vitamin C Benefits Found"*: Richards (1991), p. 119.
609 *"Any contention that previous chemotherapy"*: Creagan, Moertel, et al. (1979). Note *NEJM* 301:1399.
610 *He pressured NCI:* Richards (1991), pp. 124–25.
610 *"It is an old building"*: Pauling to Lloyd Jeffress, January 25, 1981; Pauling to Armand Hammer, November 7, 1980 (both LPI).
611 *"She knew she was dying"*: Information on Ava Helen's last months is from author's interviews with Linda Pauling Kamb, Linus Pauling, Jr., Crellin Pauling, and Linus Pauling; and Paradowski (1991), pp. 209–10.
614 *settle out of court:* author's interview with Art Robinson.
616 *"appeared willing to defend"*: Nature 303:275 (1983). See also coverage in the San Francisco Chronicle, May 12, 1983.
617 *When the Moertel study appeared:* Moertel et al. (1985).
617 *"I have never seen him so upset"*: Richards (1991), p. 142.
618 *Pauling's frenzied attack:* Richards (1991), pp. 141–60.
619 *The Mayo study was not a definitive refutation:* After an interesting comparison of the response to vitamin C among cancer researchers to their investment in the much more toxic drugs interferon and 5-fluorouracil, Richards ([1991], pp. 203, 209–12) concludes that vitamin C was afforded much less research support because, as a cheap, nonpatentable, low-tech treatment,

"it fundamentally threatens the cognitive and social authority of oncologists. . . . It does not fit easily into the established cancer research tradition or paradigm; it is freely available over the counter and does not require a professional's prescription or intervention for its administration. . . . It therefore threatens to take the treatment of cancer out of the hands of the professionals, the experts, and into the hands of nonprofessionals, even into the hands of patients."

619   *"the history of this dispute":* Richards (1991), p. 7.

619   *"you might get in":* Linus Pauling, typescript "Note to Myself" titled "Episode in a plane," dated March 30, 1985 (LPI).

620   How to Live Longer: Pauling (1986c).

621   *"was not interested whatever":* Pauling interview with author.

621   *a new way to statistically analyze:* Pauling and Herman (1989); Richards (1991), p. 237.

622   *"Ascorbic Acid: Biologic Functions in Relation to Cancer":* See Barinaga (1991), p. 374; Davidson (1991), p. 61; Pauling interview with the Academy of Achievement, p. 16. The entire proceedings of the conference were published in a special supplement to the *American Journal of Clinical Nutrition* 54 (1991).

623   *"For three days":* Anecdote related by Pauling in "Our First 20 Years," Linus Pauling Institute Newsletter, spring/summer 1993, p. 1.

623   *the institute would have to close:* San Francisco Chronicle, September 23, 1991, A17; *Science* 254(1991):192–93.

624   *a link between vitamin C and heart disease:* See Rath and Pauling (1990); author's interviews with Matthias Rath and Pauling.

625   *Rath's growing influence:* author's interviews with Linus Pauling, Linus Pauling, Jr., Zelek Herman, Matthias Rath.

626   *"Dr. Rath will continue the life work":* "Pauling Gate," undated news release from Matthias Rath (LPI).

626   *"die . . . with dignity":* Pauling and Ikeda (1992), pp. 58–59.

Bibliography

Abir-Am, Pnina. 1982. "The Discourse of Physical Power and Biological Knowledge in the 1930s: A Reappraisal of the Rockefeller Foundation's 'Policy' in Molecular Biology." *Social Studies of Science* 12:341–82.

———. 1984. "Beyond Deterministic Sociology and Apologetic History: Reassessing the Impact of Research Policy upon New Scientific Disciplines. Reply to Fuerst, Bartels, Olby and Yoxen." *Social Studies of Science* 14:252–63.

———. 1987. "Synergy or Clash: Disciplinary and Marital Strategies in the Career of Mathematical Biologist Dorothy Wrinch." In *Uneasy Careers and Intimate Lives*, edited by Pnina Abir-Am and Dorinda Outram. New Brunswick, N.J.: Rutgers University Press.

Ada, G. L. 1989. "The Conception and Birth of Burnet's Clonal Selection Theory." In *Immunology 1930–1980*, edited by Pauline Mazumdar. Toronto: Wall & Thompson.

Allen, Garland. 1975. *Life Science in the Twentieth Century*. New York: Wiley.

———. 1978. *Thomas Hunt Morgan*. Princeton, N.J.: Princeton University Press.

An Illustrated History of Central Oregon. 1905. Spokane, Wash.: Western Historical Publishing Co.

Armstrong, E. F., ed. 1924. *Chemistry in the Twentieth Century*. London: Ernest Benn Ltd.

"Artificial Antibodies." 1942. *Journal of the American Medical Association* 119:1376–77.

Asimov, Isaac. 1974. *Asimov on Chemistry*. Garden City, N.Y.: Doubleday.

———. 1982. *Asimov's Biographical Encyclopedia of Science and Technology*. 2d ed. Garden City, N.Y.: Doubleday.

Astbury, W. T. 1953. "Introduction to a Discussion on the Structure of Proteins." *Proceedings of the Royal Society of London* [B] 141:1–9.

———. 1936. "X-Ray Studies of Protein Structure." *Nature* 141:803.

Barinaga, Marcia. 1991. "Vitamin C Gets a Little Respect." *Science* 254:374–76.

Barrett, Edward L., Jr. 1952. "California: Regulation and Investigation of Subversive Activities." In *The States and Subversion*, edited by Walter Gellhorn. Ithaca, N.Y.: Cornell University Press.

Bartels, Ditta. 1984. "The Rockefeller Foundation's Funding Policy for Molecular Biology: Success or Failure?" *Social Studies of Science* 14:238–43.

Beadle, George. 1955. "Portrait of a Scientist." *Engineering and Science* XVIII:11–14.

Belfrage, Cedric. 1973. *The American Inquisition 1945–1960*. Indianapolis: Bobbs-Merrill.

Bengelsdorf, Irving S. 1986. "The Lysenko-Pauling-Sakharov File." In *The Roots of Molecular Medicine*, edited by Richard Huemer. New York: Freeman.

Bernal, J. D. 1939a. "The Structure of Proteins." *Nature* 143:663.

———. 1939b. *The Social Function of Science*. New York: Macmillan.

———. 1953. "The Use of Fourier Transforms in Protein Crystal Analysis." *Proceedings of the Royal Society of London* [B] 141:71–85.

———. 1962a. "Crystallography in Britain During and After World War II." In *Fifty Years of X-Ray Diffraction*, edited by P. P. Ewald. Utrecht: N.V.A. Oosthoek's.

———. 1962b. "Biochemical Evolution." In *Horizons in Biochemistry*, edited by Michael Kasha and Bernard Pullman. New York: Academic Press.

———. 1968. "The Pattern of Linus Pauling's Work in Relation to Molecular Biology." In *Structural Chemistry and Molecular Biology*, edited by Alexander Rich and Norman Davidson. San Francisco: Freeman.

Bernstein, Barton J. 1982. "In the Matter of J. Robert Oppenheimer." *Historical Studies in the Physical Sciences* 12:195–252.

Bernstein, Jeremy. 1982. *Science Observed*. New York: Basic Books.

Berry, A. J. 1968. *From Classical to Modern Chemistry*. New York: Dover.

Bragg, W. L. 1937. *Atomic Structure of Minerals*. Ithaca, N.Y.: Cornell University Press.

———. 1962. "Personal Reminiscences." In *Fifty Years of X-Ray Diffraction*, edited by P. P. Ewald. Utrecht: N.V.A. Oosthoek's.

Brock, William H. 1993. *The Norton History of Chemistry*. New York: Norton.

Burdick, C. L. 1962. "The Genesis and Beginnings of X-ray Crystallography at Caltech." In *Fifty Years of X-Ray Diffraction*, edited by P. P. Ewald. Utrecht: N.V.A. Oosthoek's.

Burhop, E. H. S. 1964. "Scientists and Public Affairs." In *The Science of Science*, edited by Maurice Goldsmith and Alan Mackay. London: Souvenir Press.

Bykov, G. V. 1965. "Historical Sketch of the Electron Theories of Organic Chemistry." *Chymia* 10:229–47.

Cameron, Ewan, L. Pauling, and B. Leibovitz. 1979. "Ascorbic Acid and Cancer: A Review." *Cancer Research* 39:663–81.

Campbell, Dan H. 1968. "Antibody Formation: From Ehrlich to Pauling and Return." In *Structural Chemistry and Molecular Biology*, edited by Alexander Rich and Norman Davidson. San Francisco: Freeman.

Carey, Charles Henry. 1922. *History of Oregon*. Portland: Pioneer Historical Publishing Co.

Carlson, Elof Axel. 1981. *Genes, Radiation, and Society: The Life and Work of H. J. Muller.* Ithaca, N.Y.: Cornell University Press.

Caroe, G. M. 1978. *William Henry Bragg, 1862–1942.* Cambridge, Eng.: Cambridge University Press.

Carpenter, Kenneth J. 1986. *The History of Scurvy and Vitamin C.* Cambridge, Eng.: Cambridge University Press.

Cassidy, David C. 1992. *Uncertainty: The Life and Science of Werner Heisenberg.* New York: Freeman.

Castle, William B. 1974. "From Man to Molecule and Back to Man." In *Proceedings of the First National Symposium on Sickle Cell Disease.* Bethesda, Md.: National Institutes of Health.

Catchpool, J. F. 1968. "The Pauling Theory of General Anesthesia." In *Structural Chemistry and Molecular Biology,* edited by Alexander Rich and Norman Davidson. San Francisco: Freeman.

———. 1986. "The Evolution of a Scientist's Conscience." In *The Roots of Molecular Medicine,* edited by Richard Huemer. New York: Freeman.

Caute, David. 1973. *The Fellow-Travellers.* New York: Macmillan.

———. 1978. *The Great Fear.* New York: Simon & Schuster.

Cline, Barbara Lovett. 1987. *The Men Who Made a New Physics.* 2d ed. Chicago: University of Chicago Press.

Collier, Peter. 1978. "The Old Man and the C." *New West,* April 24, pp. 21–25.

Commager, Henry Steele. 1964. "Social Function of Dissent." *The Minority of One,* February, pp. 16–17.

Coulson, C. A. 1970. "Recent Developments in Valence Theory." *Pure and Applied Chemistry.* 24:257–87.

Cousins, Norman. 1971. "Linus Pauling and the Vitamin Controversy." *Saturday Review,* May 15, pp. 37–44.

Cowan, D. W., H. S. Diehl, and A. B. Baker. 1942. "Vitamins for the Prevention of Colds." *Journal of the American Medical Association* 120:1267.

Cowan, P. M., and Dorothy Crowfoot Hodgkin. 1953. "Some Observations on Peptide Chain Models in Relation to Crystallographic Data for Gramicidin B and Insulin." *Proceedings of the Royal Society of London* [B] 141:89–92.

Creagan, E. T., C. G. Moertel, et al. 1979. "Failure of High-Dose Vitamin C (Ascorbic Acid) Therapy to Benefit Patients with Advanced Cancer; a Controlled Trial." *New England Journal of Medicine,* September 27.

Crease, Robert P., and Charles C. Mann. 1986. *The Second Creation.* New York: Collier Books.

Crick, Francis. 1952. "Is Alpha-Keratin a Coiled Coil?" *Nature* 170:882–83.

———. 1974. "The Double Helix: A Personal View." *Nature* 248:766–71.

———. 1988. *What Mad Pursuit.* New York: Basic Books.

Cruikshank, D. W. J. 1992. "Time-Resolved Macromolecular Crystallography: Introductory Remarks and a Little History." In *Time-Resolved Macromolecular Crystallography.* Oxford, Eng.: Oxford University Press.

Curtin, Deane W., ed. 1980. *The Aesthetic Dimension of Science.* New York: Philosophical Library.

Danton, George H. 1928. *Germany Ten Years After.* Boston: Houghton Mifflin.

Davidson, Kay. 1991. "The Nobel Pursuits of Linus Pauling." *California* 16(2):58–63.

Dean, Arthur H. 1966. *Test Ban and Disarmament: The Path of Negotiation.* New York: Harper & Row.

Divine, Robert A. 1978. *Blowing on the Wind.* New York: Oxford University Press.

Donnan, F. G., et al., eds. 1951. *Memorial Lectures Delivered Before the Chemical Society.* Vol. 4. London: Chemical Society.

Donohue, Jerry. 1978. "Fragments of Chargaff." *Nature* 276:133–35.

———. 1983. "Hydrogen Bonding: Some Glimpses into the Distant Past." In *Crystallography in North America,* edited by Dan McLachlan and Jenny P. Glusker. New York: American Crystallographic Association.

DuBridge, Lee A. 1947. "The Responsibility of the Scientist." *California Institute Forum* 1:1–8.

Dunitz, Jack. 1991. "From Quantum Mechanics to Biochemistry: Homage to Linus Pauling." *Croatica Chemica Acta* 64:I–III.

Dye, Lee. 1985. "The Deeply Personal War of Linus Pauling." *Los Angeles Times,* June 2, Sec. VI, p. 1.

Edelstein, Stuart J. 1986. *The Sickled Cell: From Myths to Molecules.* Cambridge, Mass.: Harvard University Press.

Edsall, J. T. 1952. "Some Comments on Proteins and Protein Structure." *Proceedings of the Royal Society of London* [B] 141:97–103.

———. 1979. "The Development of the Physical Chemistry of Proteins, 1898–1940." In *The Origins of Modern Biochemistry, A Retrospect on Proteins,* edited by P. R. Srinivisan, Joseph Fruton, and John T. Edsall. New York: New York Academy of Sciences.

England, J. Merton. 1976. "Dr. Bush Writes a Report: Science—The Endless Frontier." *Science* 191:41–47.

Farber, Eduard. 1963. *Nobel Prize Winners in Chemistry 1901–1961.* 2d ed. London: Abelard-Schuman.

———, ed. 1966. *Milestones of Modern Chemistry.* New York: Basic Books.

Feld, Bernard. 1984. "Leo Szilard, Scientist for All Seasons." *Social Research* 51:675–90.

Feynman, Richard P. 1986. *Surely You're Joking, Mr. Feynman!* New York: Bantam.

Fischer, Ernst Peter, and Carol Lipson. 1988. *Thinking About Science: Max Delbrück and the Origins of Molecular Biology.* New York: Norton.

Fosdick, Raymond B. 1952. *The Story of the Rockefeller Foundation.* New York: Harper & Brothers.

Franklin, Jon. 1987. *Molecules of the Mind.* New York: Dell.

Fruton, Joseph. 1972. *Molecules and Life.* New York: Wiley.

Fuerst, John A. 1984. "The Definition of Molecular Biology and the Definition of Policy: The Role of the Rockefeller Foundation's Policy for Molecular Biology." *Social Studies of Science* 14:225–37.

Gellhorn, Walter. 1950. *Security, Loyalty, and Science.* Ithaca, N.Y.: Cornell University Press.

Gillispie, C. C., ed. 1980. *Dictionary of Scientific Biography.* New York: Charles Scribner's Sons.

Glass, Bentley. 1962. "Scientists in Politics." *Bulletin of the Atomic Scientists* 18:2–7 (May).

Goertzel, Ted. 1992. *Turncoats and True Believers.* Amherst, N.Y.: Prometheus Books.

Goertzel, Ted, and Mildred and Victor Goertzel. 1980. "Linus Pauling: The Scientist as Crusader." *Antioch Review*, Summer 1980, pp. 371–82.

Goodell, Rae. 1977. *The Visible Scientists*. Boston: Little, Brown.

Goodstein, Judith R. 1984. "Atoms, Molecules, and Linus Pauling." *Social Research* 51:691–708.

———. 1991. *Millikan's School*. New York: Norton.

Grant, James. 1979. "Of Mice and Men: The Linus Pauling Institute is Plunged into Controversy." *Barron's*, June 11, pp. 4–5.

Gray, George. 1949. "Pauling and Beadle." *Scientific American* 180(5):16–21.

Greenberg, Daniel. 1967. *The Politics of Pure Science*. New York: New American Library.

Gribbin, John. 1984. *In Search of Schrödinger's Cat*. London: Wildwood House.

———. 1987. *In Search of the Double Helix*. New York: Bantam.

Gurin, Joel. 1977. "Pauling: Just Try to Find an Answer." *Science Digest*, August, pp. 54–57.

Haurowitz, Felix, et al. 1946. "The Mutual Precipitation of Proteins and Azoproteins." *Archives of Biochemistry and Biophysics* 11:515–20.

Heater, Sheila Neal. 1970. *History and Genealogy of the Allied Families of Neal, Rossell, Bilyeu, McNeil, Nash, Walker, Wirth, McKee and Underwood*. Self-published.

Heidelberger, Michael. 1969. "Karl Landsteiner." *Biographical Memoirs of the National Academy of Sciences* XL:177–86.

Heilbron, J. L. 1986. *The Dilemmas of an Upright Man*. Berkeley and Los Angeles: University of California Press.

Henahan, John F. 1966. *Men and Molecules*. New York. Crown.

Herman, Zelek. 1986. "The 25 Most Cited Publications of Linus Pauling." In *The Roots of Molecular Medicine*, edited by Richard Huemer. New York: Freeman.

———. 1991. "Some Early (and Lasting) Contributions of Linus Pauling to Quantum Mechanics and Statistical Mechanics." In *Molecules in Natural Science and Medicine: An Encomium for Linus Pauling*, edited by Zvonimir B. Maksic and Mirjana Eckert-Maksic. New York: Ellis Horwood.

Hershberg, James. 1994. *James B. Conant*. New York: Knopf.

Hildebrand, Joel. 1952. "The Professor and His Public." *Chemical and Engineering News* 30:4934–37

———. 1958. "Gilbert Newton Lewis." *Biographical Memoirs of the National Academy of Sciences* 31:209–35.

The History of Gilliam County, Oregon. 1981. Dallas: Gilliam County Historical Society.

Hodgkin, Dorothy Crowfoot. 1979. "Crystallographic Measurements and the Structure of Protein Molecules as They Are." In *The Origins of Modern Biochemistry, A Retrospect on Proteins*, edited by P. R. Srinivisan, Joseph Fruton, and John T. Edsall. New York: New York Academy of Sciences.

Holton, Gerald. 1978. *The Scientific Imagination: Case Studies*. Cambridge, Eng.: Cambridge University Press.

Horgan, John. 1993. "Profile: Linus C. Pauling—Stubbornly Ahead of his Time." *Scientific American*, March, pp. 36–37.

Huemer, Richard P. 1986. "Preface." In *The Roots of Molecular Medicine: A Tribute to Linus Pauling*, edited by Richard P. Huemer. New York: Freeman.

Hunsberger, I. Moyer. 1954. "Theoretical Chemistry in Russia." *Journal of Chemical Education* 31:504–14.

Hussain, Farooq. 1977. "The Linus Pauling Institute: An Investigation." *New Scientist* 75:216–21.

Hutchins, Robert M. 1963. *Science, Scientists and Politics.* Occasional papers published by the Center for the Study of Democratic Institutions, San Francisco.

Ihde, Aaron J. 1964. *The Development of Modern Chemistry.* New York: Harper & Row.

Ikeda, Daisaku. 1992. *A Lifelong Quest for Peace: A Dialogue between Linus Pauling and Daisaku Ikeda.* Boston: Jones and Bartlett.

In Their Own Words. 1976. Lake Oswego: Lake Oswego Public Library.

Itano, Harvey, and Linus Pauling. 1949. "A Rapid Diagnostic Test for Sickle Cell Anemia." *Blood* 4:66–68.

Jacobson, Harold Karan, and Eric Stein. 1966. *Diplomats, Scientists, and Politicians.* Ann Arbor: University of Michigan Press.

Jaffe, Bernard. 1976. *Crucibles: The Story of Chemistry.* New York: Dover.

James, R. W. 1962. "Early Work on Crystal Structure at Manchester." In *Fifty Years of X-Ray Diffraction,* edited by P. P. Ewald. Utrecht: N.V.A. Oosthoek's.

Jonas, Gerald. 1989. *The Circuit Riders.* New York: Norton.

Judis, John B. 1988. *William F. Buckley, Jr.: Patron Saint of the Conservatives.* New York: Simon & Schuster.

Judson, Horace. 1979. *The Eighth Day of Creation.* New York: Simon & Schuster.

Kabat, Elvin. 1943. "Immunochemistry of the Proteins." *Journal of Immunology* 47:513–87.

Kalven, Harry, Jr. 1960. "Congressional Testimony of Linus Pauling, Part I: The Legal Framework." *Bulletin of the Atomic Scientists* 16:383–90.

———. 1961. "Congressional Testimony of Linus Pauling, Part II: Sourwine in an Old Bottle." *Bulletin of the Atomic Scientists* 17:12–19.

Kamb, Barclay, and Linus Pauling. 1959. "The Effects of Strontium-90 on Mice." *Proceedings of the National Academy of Sciences* 45:54–69.

Kamen, Martin D. 1985. *Radiant Science, Dark Politics.* Berkeley: University of California Press.

Kargon, Robert H. 1977. "Temple to Science: Cooperative Research and the Birth of the California Institute of Technology." *Historical Studies in the Physical Sciences* 8:3–31.

———. 1982. *The Rise of Robert Millikan.* Ithaca, N.Y.: Cornell University Press.

Kasha, Michael. 1990. "Four Great Personalities of Science: G. N. Lewis, J. Franck, R. S. Mulliken and A. Szent-Györgyi." *Pure and Applied Chemistry* 62:1615–30.

Kasha, Michael, and Bernard Pullman, eds. 1962. *Horizons in Biochemistry.* New York: Academic Press.

Kay, Lily E. 1987. "Cooperative Individualism and the Growth of Molecular Biology at the California Institute of Technology, 1928–1953." Ph.D. diss., Johns Hopkins University.

———. 1989. "Selling Pure Science in Wartime: The Biochemical Genetics of G. W. Beadle." *Journal of the History of Biology* 22:73–101.

———. 1989. "Molecular Biology and Pauling's Immunochemistry: A Neglected Dimension." *History and Philosophy of the Life Sciences* 11:211–19.

———. 1991. *Life as Technology: Representing, Intervening, and Molecularizing.* Monograph. Boston: MIT.

———. 1993. *The Molecular Vision of Life.* New York: Oxford University Press.

Keating's Research Report. 1972. *Disarmament Negotiations and Treaties, 1946–1971.* New York: Charles Scribner's Sons.

Keller, Evelyn Fox. 1990. "Physics and the Emergence of Molecular Biology: A History of Cognitive and Political Synergy." *Journal of the History of Biology* 23:389–409.

Keller, William W. 1989. *The Liberals and J. Edgar Hoover.* Princeton, N.J.: Princeton University Press.

Kendrew, John. 1966. *The Thread of Life.* Cambridge, Mass.: Harvard University Press.

———. 1969. "Physics, Molecular Structure, and Biological Function." In *Biology and the Physical Sciences,* edited by Samuel Devons. New York: Columbia University Press.

Kevles, Daniel J. 1987. *The Physicists.* Cambridge, Mass.: Harvard University Press.

Klug, Aaron. 1968. "Rosalind Franklin and the Discovery of the Structure of DNA." *Nature* 219:808–10, 843–44.

Kohler, Robert. 1979. "Warren Weaver and the Rockefeller Foundation Program in Molecular Biology: A Case Study in the Management of Science." In *The Sciences in the American Context: New Perspectives,* edited by Nathan Reingold. Washington, D.C.: Smithsonian Institution Press.

———. 1991. *Partners in Science: Foundations and Natural Scientists 1900–1945.* Chicago: University of Chicago Press.

Kohn, Alexander. 1988. *False Prophets.* Oxford, Eng.: Basil Blackwell.

Kragh, Helge. 1990. *Dirac.* Cambride, Eng.: Cambridge University Press.

Lachman, Arthur. 1955. *Borderland of the Unknown.* New York: Pageant Press.

Landsteiner, Karl. 1936. *The Specificity of Serological Reactions.* Springfield, Ill.: Thomas.

Landsteiner, Karl, and A. Rothen. 1939. "Adsorption of Antibodies by Egg Albumin Films." *Science* 90:65–66.

Langmuir, Irving. 1919. "The Arrangement of Electrons in Atoms and Molecules." *Journal of the American Chemical Society* 41:686–734.

Langone, John. 1982. "Linus Pauling: Vim, Vigor and Vitamins." *Discover,* November, pp. 45–54.

La Paglia, S. R. 1971. *Introductory Quantum Chemistry.* New York: Harper & Row.

Lapp, Ralph E. 1965. *The New Priesthood.* New York: Harper & Row.

Lawhorne, Clifton O. 1971. *Defamation and Public Officials: The Evolving Law of Libel.* Carbondale: Southern Illinois University Press.

Lehmann, H., and R. G. Huntsman. 1966. *Man's Haemoglobins.* Amsterdam: North-Holland Publishing.

Lewis, Gilbert N. 1916. "The Atom and the Molecule." *Journal of the American Chemical Society* 38:762–85.

Lilge, Frederic. 1948. *The Abuse of Learning.* New York: Macmillan.

Liveridge, Anthony. 1993. "Heresy! Three Modern Galileos." *Omni* 15:44–46.

Lundberg, Dan. 1956. "Text of Broadcast: Hometown Scene, KCOP-TV Los Angeles, January 29, 1956." New York: Radio Reports, Inc.

MacArthur, Ian. 1953. "The Pauling-Corey Models and Fibrous Proteins." *Proceedings of the Royal Society of London* [B] 141:33–39.

MacKinnon, Edward. 1977. "Heisenberg, Models and the Rise of Matrix Mechanics." *Historical Studies in the Physical Sciences* 8:137.

Macnab, Gordon. 1975. *A Century of News and People in the* East Oregonian, *1875–1975.* Pendleton: East Oregonian Publishing Co.

Manfull, Helen. 1970. *Additional Dialogue: Letters of Dalton Trumbo.* New York: M. Evans.

Marsh, Richard E., and Verner Schomaker. 1991. "The Early Crystallographic Works of Linus Pauling." In *Molecules in Natural Science and Medicine: An Encomium for Linus Pauling,* edited by Zvonimir B. Maksic and Mirjana Eckert-Maksic. New York: Ellis Horwood.

Mazumdar, Pauline. 1989. "Working Out the Theory." In *Immunology 1930–1980,* edited by Pauline Mazumdar. Toronto: Wall & Thompson.

McClelland, Charles E. 1980. *State, Society and University in Germany, 1700–1914.* Cambridge: Cambridge University Press.

McCormmach, Russell. 1982. *Night Thoughts of a Classical Physicist.* Cambridge, Mass.: Harvard University Press.

McCullough, David. 1992. *Truman.* New York: Simon & Schuster.

McLachlan, Dan, Jr., and Jenny P. Glusker, eds. 1983. *Crystallography in North America.* New York: American Crystallographic Association.

Meduski, J. W., J. D. Meduski, Khashayar Khakmahd, Akbar Azad, and Claude Cruz. 1986. "Photon Counting in Nutritional Biochemistry." In *The Roots of Molecular Medicine: A Tribute to Linus Pauling,* edited by Richard P. Huemer. New York: Freeman.

Mehra, Jagdish, and Helmut Rechenberg. 1982. *The Historical Development of Quantum Theory.* 2d ed. New York: Springer-Verlag.

Mendelssohn, K. 1973. *The World of Walther Nernst.* Pittsburgh: University of Pittsburgh Press.

Millikan, Robert A. 1938. "The Development of Chemistry at the California Institute of Technology." *Science* 87:2269.

Moertel, C. G., et al. 1985. "High-Dose Vitamin C Versus Placebo in the Treatment of Patients with Advanced Cancer Who Had No Prior Chemotherapy." *New England Journal of Medicine* 312:137–41.

Moore, Walter. 1989. *Schrödinger: Life and Thought.* Cambridge: Cambridge University Press.

Morrison, J. L. 1953. "The Nonspecific Precipitation of Proteins by Polyhaptenic Dyes." *Canadian Journal of Chemistry* 31:216–26.

Moyer, Albert E. 1991. "P. W. Bridgman's Operational Perspective on Physics: Part 1: Origins and Development." *Studies in the History and Philosophy of Science* 22:237–58.

Muller, Hermann J., with Jack Harrison Pollack. 1962. "Let's Face the Truth About Nuclear Testing." *This Week,* June 10, pp. 4–6.

Mulliken, Robert S. 1965. "Molecular Scientists and Molecular Science: Some Reminiscences." *Journal of Chemical Physics* 43:S2–11.

———. 1967. "Spectroscopy, Molecular Orbitals, and Chemical Bonding." *Science* 157:13–24.

———. 1989. *Life of a Scientist.* Berlin: Springer-Verlag.

Nachtrieb, Norman. 1975. "Interview with Robert S. Mulliken." *Journal of Chemical Education* 52:560–64.

Nathan, Otto, and Heinz Norden, eds. 1968. *Einstein on Peace.* New York: Schocken Books.

National Broadcasting Company. 1958. "Guest: Dr. Linus Pauling." *Meet the Press* 2(17):1–9.

Ninth Report of the Senate Investigating Committee on Education, California Legislature 1951 Regular Session. 1951. Sacramento: State of California.

Nossal, G. J. V. 1989. "The Coming of Age of the Clonal Selection Theory." In *Immunology 1930–1980*, edited by Pauline Mazumdar. Toronto: Wall & Thompson.

Olby, Robert. 1974. *The Path to the Double Helix*. Seattle: University of Washington Press.

———. 1984. "The Sheriff and the Cowboys: or Weaver's Support of Astbury and Pauling." *Social Studies of Science* 14:244–47.

O'Reilly, Kenneth. 1983. *Hoover and the Un-Americans*. Philadelphia: Temple University Press.

Oshinsky, David M. 1983. *A Conspiracy So Immense*. New York: Free Press.

Pais, Abraham. 1982. "Max Born's Statistical Interpretation of Quantum Mechanics." *Science* 218:1193–98.

———. 1986. *Inward Bound*. New York: Oxford University Press.

Palmer, W. G. 1965. *A History of the Concept of Valency to 1930*. Cambridge, Eng.: Cambridge University Press.

Paradowski, Robert. 1972. "The Structural Chemistry of Linus Pauling." Ph.D. diss., University of Michigan.

———. 1991. "Chronology." In *Linus Pauling: A Man of Intellect and Action*. Japan: Cosmos Japan International.

———. 1993. "Linus Carl Pauling." In *Nobel Laureates in Chemistry, 1901–1992*, edited by Laylin James. Washington, D.C.: American Chemical Society and the Chemical Heritage Foundation.

Pauling, Linus. 1926a. "The Dynamic Model of the Chemical Bond and its Application to the Study of Benzene." *Journal of the American Chemical Society* 48:1132.

———. 1926b. "The Quantum Theory of the Dielectric Constant of Hydrogen Chloride and Similar Gases." *Proceedings of the National Academy of Sciences* 12:32–35.

———. 1927. "The Influence of a Magnetic Field on the Dielectric Constant of a Diatomic Dipole Gas." *Physiological Reviews* 29:145–60.

———. 1928a. "The Shared-Electron Chemical Bond." *Proceedings of the National Academy of Sciences* 14:359.

———. 1928b. "The Coordination Theory of the Structure of Ionic Crystals." In *Festschrift zum 60. Geburtstage Arnold Sommerfelds*. Leipzig: Verlag von S. Hewrzel.

———. 1928c. "The Application of the Quantum Mechanics to the Structure of the Hydrogen Molecule and Hydrogen Molecule-Ion and to Related Problems." *Chemical Reviews* V:173–213.

———. 1929. "The Principles Determining the Structure of Complex Ionic Crystals." *Journal of the American Chemical Society* 51:1010–26.

———. 1931a. "Quantum Mechanics and the Chemical Bond." *Physiological Reviews* 37:1185.

———. 1931b. "The Nature of the Chemical Bond. II. The One-Electron Bond and the Three-Electron Bond." *Journal of the American Chemical Society* 53:3225–37.

———. 1932a. "The Nature of the Chemical Bond. III. The Transition from One Extreme Bond Type to Another." *Journal of the American Chemical Society* 54:988–1003.

———. 1932b. "Interatomic Distances in Covalent Molecules and Resonance Between Two or More Lewis Structures." *Proceedings of the National Academy of Sciences* 18:293–97.

———. 1932c. "The Nature of the Chemical Bond. IV. The Energy of Single Bonds and the Relative Electronegativity of Atoms." *Journal of the American Chemical Society* 54:3570–82.

———. 1935a. "The Oxygen Equilibrium of Hemoglobin and Its Structural Interpretation." *Science* 81:421.

———. 1935b. "The Structure and Entropy of Ice and Other Crystals with Some Randomness of Atomic Arrangement." *Journal of the American Chemical Society* 57:2680–84.

———. 1938. "The Future of the Crellin Laboratory." *Science* 87:563.

———. 1939. *The Nature of the Chemical Bond and the Structure of Molecules and Crystals.* Ithaca, N.Y.: Cornell University Press.

———. 1940. "A Theory of the Structure and Process of Formation of Antibodies." *Journal of the American Chemical Society* 62:2643–57.

———. 1945a. "Molecular Structure and Intermolecular Forces." In *The Specificity of Serological Reactions* by Karl Landsteiner, 2d ed. Cambridge, Mass.: Harvard University Press.

———. 1945b. "Proposed Federal Aid to Research in Science and Medicine." *Engineering and Science* 8:3–16.

———. 1946a. "Analogies between Antibodies and Simpler Chemical Substances." *Chemical and Engineering News* 24:1064.

———. 1946b. "Modern Structural Chemistry." *Chemical and Engineering News* 24:1788–89.

———. 1947a. "Unsolved Problems of Structural Chemistry." *Chemical and Engineering News* 25:2970.

———. 1947b. "Molecular Architecture and Medical Progress." In *The Scientists Speak,* edited by Warren Weaver. New York: Boni & Gaer.

———. 1948a. *The Chemical Bond.* 2d ed. Ithaca, N.Y.: Cornell University Press.

———. 1948b. "Chemical Achievement and Hope for the Future." *American Scientist* 36:51–58.

———. 1948c. "Antibodies and Specific Biological Forces." *Endeavour* 7:43–53.

———. 1948d. *Molecular Architecture and the Processes of Life.* Nottingham, Eng.: Sir Jesse Boot Foundation

———. 1948e. "Molecular Structure and Biological Specificity." *Chemistry and Industry* (suppl.: XI International Congress of Pure and Applied Chemistry):1–4.

———. 1948f. "The Nature of Forces between Large Molecules of Biological Interest." *Nature* 161:707–9.

———. 1949a. "Chemical Achievement and Hope for the Future." In *Science in Progress,* edited by George Baitsell. New Haven: Yale University Press.

———. 1949b. "Chemistry and the World of Today." *Engineering and Science* 13:5–8.

———. 1950a. "Structural Chemistry in Relation to Biology and Medicine." *Medical Arts and Sciences* 4:84–88.

———. 1950b. "Academic Research as a Career." *Chemical and Engineering News* 28:3970.

————. 1951a. "Statement by Professor Linus Pauling For Presentation to the Industrial Employment Review Board." Typescript, OSU.

————. 1951b. *The Future of Structural Chemistry* (Address on the Receipt of the Gilbert Newton Lewis Medal). Monograph.

————. 1951c. "The Significance of Chemistry." *Engineering and Science,* January, p. 10.

————. 1954. "Linus Pauling: A Disgraceful Act . . ." *Nation* 178:370.

————. 1955a. "The Stochastic Method and the Structure of Proteins." *American Scientist* 43:285–97.

————. 1955b. "Abnormality of Hemoglobin Molecules in Hereditary Hemolytic Anemias." Vol. 49 of *The Harvey Lectures.* New York: Academic Press.

————. 1955c. "News from Around the World." *Engineering and Science,* April, pp. 15–17.

————. 1958a. "Fact and Fable of Fallout." *Nation* 186:537–42.

————. 1958b. *No More War!* New York: Dodd, Mead.

————. 1958c. "The Relation Between Longevity and Obesity in Human Beings." *Proceedings of the National Academy of Sciences* 44:619–22.

————. 1958d. "Genetic and Somatic Effects of Carbon-14." *Science* 128:1183–86.

————. 1961. "A Molecular Theory of General Anesthesia." *Science* 134:15–21.

————. 1962a. "Problems of Inorganic Structures." In *Fifty Years of X-Ray Diffraction,* edited by P. P. Ewald. Utrecht: N.V.A. Oosthoek's.

————. 1962b. "Early Work on X-Ray Diffraction in the California Institute of Technology." In *Fifty Years of X-Ray Diffraction,* edited by P. P. Ewald. Utrecht: N.V.A. Oosthoek's.

————. 1962c. "Genetic Effects of Weapons Tests." *Bulletin of the Atomic Scientists* 18(December):15–18.

————. 1962d. "Molecular Disease and Evolution." Typescript of the Rudolph Virchow Lecture, dated November 5, 1962 (OSU).

————. 1963a. "The Genesis of Ideas." In *Specific and Nonspecific Factors in Psychopharmacology,* edited by Max Rinkel. New York: Philosophical Library.

————. 1963b. "Genetic Effects." *Bulletin of the Atomic Scientists* 19(September):30–32.

————. 1964. *Linus Pauling on Science and Peace.* New York: Fund for the Republic, Inc.

————. 1965a. "Fifty Years of Physical Chemistry in the California Institute of Technology." *Annual Review of Physics and Chemistry* 16:1–13.

————. 1965b. "The Close-Packed Spheron Model of Atomic Nuclei and Its Relation to the Shell Model." *Proceedings of the National Academy of Sciences* 54:989–94.

————. 1968a. "Acceptance of the Roebling Medal of the Mineralogical Society of America." *American Mineralogist* 53:524–28.

————. 1968b. "Orthomolecular Psychiatry: Varying the Concentrations of Substances Normally Present in the Human Body May Control Mental Disease." *Science* 160:265–71.

————. 1969. "The Advancement of Knowledge: Orthomolecular Psychiatry" (February 25, 1969). Typescript, OSU.

————. 1970. "Fifty Years of Progress in Structural Chemistry and Molecular Biology." *Daedalus,* Fall, pp. 988–1014.

———. 1971. *Vitamin C and the Common Cold.* 2d ed. New York: Bantam Books.

———. 1974. "The Molecular Basis of Biological Specificity." *Nature* 248:769–71.

———. 1975. "For the Best of Health: How Much Vitamin C Do You Need?" *Executive Health* 12:1–4.

———. 1976. "Arthur Amos Noyes." *Proceedings of the Robert A. Welch Foundation Conferences on Chemical Research,* Vol. 20. Houston: Robert A. Welch Foundation.

———. 1977. "The Theory of Resonance in Chemistry." *Proceedings of the Royal Society of London* [A] 356:433–41.

———. 1978. "Vitamin C and Heart Disease: Can Vitamin C Protect You, and How Much Should You Take?" *Executive Health* 14:1–4.

———. 1979. "A Lecture by Linus Pauling in Honor of Roger J. Williams" (November 5, 1979). Typescript, OSU.

———. 1981a. "Early Work on Chemical Bonding in Relation to Solid State Physics." *Proceedings of the Royal Society of London* [A] 378:207–18.

———. 1981b. "Chemistry." In *The Joys of Research,* edited by Walter Shropshire, Jr. Washington, D.C.: Smithsonian Institution Press.

———. 1981c. "Herman F. Mark and the Structure of Crystals." In *Polymer Science Overview: A Tribute to Herman F. Mark,* edited by G. Allan Stahl. Washington, D.C.: American Chemical Society.

———. 1983a. "Pauling on G. N. Lewis." *Chemtech* 13:334–37.

———. 1983b. "On Vitamin C and Infectious Diseases." *Executive Health* 19:1–4.

———. 1984. "Herman Mark and the Structure of Crystals." *Chemtech* 14:334–37.

———. 1985. "Why Modern Chemistry Is Quantum Chemistry." *New Scientist* 108:54–55.

———. 1986a. "Early Days of Molecular Biology in the California Institute of Technology." *Annual Review of Biophysics and Chemistry* 15:1–9.

———. 1986b. "The Future of Orthomolecular Medicine." In *The Roots of Molecular Medicine: A Tribute to Linus Pauling,* edited by Richard P. Heumer. New York: Freeman.

———. 1986c. *How to Live Longer and Feel Better.* New York: Freeman.

———. 1987a. "Schrödinger's Contribution to Chemistry and Biology." In *Schrödinger: Centenary Celebration of a Polymath,* edited by C. W. Kilmister. Cambridge, Eng.: Cambridge University Press.

———. 1987b. "My Indebtedness to Herman Mark." In *Polymer Science in the Next Decade: An International Symposium Honoring Herman F. Mark on His 90th Birthday,* edited by Otto Vogl and Edmund H. Immergut. New York: Wiley.

———. 1990. "Research Landmarks: Molecular Architecture and Biological Reactions." *Journal of NIH Research* 2:59–64.

———. 1991a. "The Meaning of Life." In *The Meaning of Life,* edited by David Friend and the editors of *Life.* New York: Little, Brown.

———. 1991b. "The Value of Rough Quantum Mechanical Calculations." *Foundations of Physics* 22:829–38.

———. 1991c. "An Extraordinary Life: An Autobiographical Ramble." In *Creativity: Paradoxes and Reflections,* edited by Harry A. Wilmer. Wilmette: Chiron Publications.

Pauling, Linus, and George Beadle. 1953. "Chemical Biology at the California Institute of Technology: A Statement Submitted to the Rockefeller Foundation in

Support of an Application for Continued Financial Support." Typescript grant request, OSU.

Pauling, Linus, and Robert B. Corey. 1950. "Two Hydrogen-Bonded Spiral Configurations of the Polypeptide Chain." *Journal of the American Chemical Society* 72:5349.

———. 1951. "Configurations of Polypeptide Chains." *Nature* 68:550–51.

———. 1952. "The Lotmar-Picken X-ray Diagram of Dried Muscle." *Nature* 169:494–95.

———. 1953. "A Proposed Structure for the Nucleic Acids." *Proceedings of the National Academy of Sciences* 39:84–97.

———. 1956. "Specific Hydrogen-Bond Formation Between Pyrimidines and Purines in Deoxyribonucleic Acids." *Archives of Biochemistry and Biophysics* 56:164–81.

Pauling, Linus, Robert B. Corey, and H. R. Branson. 1951. "The Structure of Proteins: Two Hydrogen-Bonded Helical Configurations of the Polypeptide Chain." *Proceedings of the National Academy of Sciences* 37:205–10.

Pauling, Linus, Robert B. Corey, and Roger Hayward. 1954. "The Structure of Protein Molecules." *Scientific American* 191:51.

Pauling, Linus, and Charles Coryell. 1936. "The Magnetic Properties and Structure of Hemoglobin, Oxyhemoglobin and Carbonmonoxyhemoglobin." *Proceedings of the National Academy of Sciences* 22:210–16.

Pauling, Linus, and Samuel Goudsmit. 1930. *The Structure of Line Spectra.* New York: McGraw-Hill.

Pauling, Linus, and Zelek Herman. 1986. "The Nature of the Chemical Bond Fifty Years Later: The Relative Electronegativity of Atoms Seen in Perspective." In *Molecular Structure and Energetics,* edited by Joel Liebman and Arthur Greenberg. Deerfield Beach, Fla.: VCH Publishers.

———. 1989. "Criteria for the Validity of Clinical Trials of Treatments of Cohorts of Cancer Patients Based on the Hardin Jones Principle." *Proceedings of the National Academy of Sciences* 86:3466–68.

Pauling, Linus, and Daisaku Ikeda. 1992. *A Lifelong Quest for Peace.* Boston: Jones and Bartlett.

Pauling, Linus, Harvey A. Itano, S. J. Singer, and Ibert C. Wells. 1949. "Sickle Cell Anemia, a Molecular Disease." *Science* 110:543–48.

Pauling, Linus, and Carl Niemann. 1939. "The Structure of Proteins." *Journal of the American Chemical Society* 61:1860–67.

Pauling, Linus, and Arthur Robinson. 1978. "The Linus Pauling Institute—A Reply." *New Scientist,* January 12, pp. 98–100.

Pauling, Linus, and Verner Schomaker. 1952a. "On a Phospho-Tri-Anhydride Formula for the Nucleic Acids." *Journal of the American Chemical Society* 74:1111.

———. 1952b. "On a Phospho-Tri-Anhydride Formula for the Nucleic Acids." *Journal of the American Chemical Society* 74:3712.

Pauling, Linus, and Jack Sherman. 1933a. "The Nature of the Chemical Bond. VI. The Calculation from Thermochemical Data of the Energy of Resonance of Molecules Among Several Electronic Structures." *Journal of Chemical Physics* 1:606–17.

———. 1933b. "The Nature of the Chemical Bond. VII. The Calculation of Resonance Energy in Conjugated Systems." *Journal of Chemical Physics* 1:679–86.

Pauling, Linus, and G. W. Wheland. 1933. "The Nature of the Chemical Bond. V. The Quantum-Mechanical Calculation of the Resonance Energy of Benzene and Naphthalene and the Hydrocarbon Free Radicals." *Journal of Chemical Physics* 1:362–74.

Pauling, Linus, and E. Bright Wilson. 1935. *Introduction to Quantum Mechanics with Applications to Chemistry*. New York: McGraw-Hill.

Pauling, Linus, Reuben E. Wood, and J. H. Sturdivant. 1946. "An Instrument for Determining the Partial Pressure of Oxygen in a Gas." *Journal of the American Chemical Society* 68:795–98.

Pauling, Linus, and Don Yost. 1932. "The Additivity of the Energies of Normal Covalent Bonds." *Proceedings of the National Academy of Sciences* 18:414–16.

Pauling, Peter. 1973. "DNA—The Race That Never Was?" *New Scientist,* May 31, pp. 558–60.

Penick, J. L., Jr., C. W. Pursell, Jr., M. B. Sherwood, and D. C. Swain. 1965. *The Politics of American Science 1939 to the Present*. Chicago: Rand McNally.

Perutz, Max. 1951. "New X-Ray Evidence on the Configuration of Polypeptide Chains." *Nature* 167:1053–54.

———. 1991. "Foreword." In *Molecules in Natural Science and Medicine,* edited by Zvonimir B. Maksic and Mirjana Eckert-Maksic. New York: Ellis Horwood.

A Pictorial History of Gilliam County. 1983. Portland: Gilliam County Historical Society.

Piel, Gerard. 1962. *Science in the Cause of Man*. New York: Knopf.

Pimentel, George C., and Richard D. Spratley. 1969. *Chemical Bonding Clarified Through Quantum Mechanics*. San Francisco: Holden-Day.

Platt, John R. 1966. "Nobel Laureate in Chemistry: Robert S. Mulliken." *Science* 154:745–47.

Pullman, Albert, and Bernard Pullman. 1962. "From Quantum Chemistry to Quantum Biochemistry." In *Horizons in Biochemistry,* edited by Michael Kasha and Bernard Pullman. New York: Academic Press.

Quane, Denis. 1990. "The Reception of Hydrogen Bonding." *Bulletin of the History of Chemistry* 7:3–12.

Ramsay, D. A., and J. Hinze, eds. 1975. *Selected Papers of Robert S. Mulliken.* Chicago: University of Chicago Press.

Rath, M., and Linus Pauling. 1990. "Hypothesis: Lipoprotein(a) Is a Surrogate for Ascorbate." *Proceedings of the National Academy of Sciences* 87:6204–7.

Reingold, Nathan, ed. 1979. *The Sciences in the American Context: New Perspectives.* Washington, D.C.: Smithsonian Institution Press.

Reitman, Alan, ed. 1975. *The Pulse of Freedom.* New York: Norton.

Reminiscences of Oregon Pioneers. 1937. Pendleton, Ore.: East Oregonian Publishing Co.

Rhodes, Richard. 1986. *The Making of the Atomic Bomb.* New York: Simon & Schuster.

Rich, Alexander, and Norman Davidson, eds. 1968. *Structural Chemistry and Molecular Biology*. San Francisco: Freeman.

Richards, Evelleen. 1991. *Vitamin C and Cancer: Medicine or Politics?* New York: St. Martin's Press.

Rider, Robin E. 1984. "Alarm and Opportunity: Emigration of Mathematicians and Physicists to Britain and the United States, 1933–1945." *Historical Studies in the Physical Sciences* 15:107–76.

Rigden, John S. 1987. *Rabi, Scientist and Citizen*. New York: Basic Books.

Rimland, Bernard. 1986. "Foreword." In *The Roots of Molecular Medicine: A Tribute to Linus Pauling*, edited by Richard P. Huemer. New York: Freeman.

Roberts, Jack. 1989. Remarks at the Dinner for the First Linus Pauling Lecture, November 28, 1989.

Roe, Anne. 1953. *The Making of a Scientist*. New York: Dodd, Mead.

Ronwin, Edward. 1951. "A Phospho-tri-anhydride Formula for the Nucleic Acids." *Journal of the American Chemical Society* 73:5141–44.

Rubel, John H. 1992. "The Committee." *Engineering and Science* 55:28–35.

Russell, C. A., ed. 1985. *Recent Developments in the History of Chemistry*. Great Britain: Whitstable Litho, Inc.

Sackett, Robert Eben. 1982. *Popular Entertainment, Class and Politics in Munich, 1900–1923*. Cambridge, Mass.: Harvard University Press.

Schrecker, Ellen W. 1986. *No Ivory Tower*. New York: Oxford University Press.

Scott, William T. 1967. *Erwin Schrödinger: An Introduction to his Writings*. Amherst: University of Massachusetts Press.

Senechal, Marjorie. 1977. "A Prophet Without Honor: Dorothy Wrinch, Scientist, 1894–1976." *Smith Alumnae Quarterly*, April, pp. 18–23.

———, ed. 1980. *Structures of Matter and Patterns in Science*. Cambridge, Mass.: Schenkman Publishing Co.

Serafini, Anthony. 1989. *Linus Pauling: A Man and His Science*. New York: Paragon House.

Servos, John W. 1976. "The Knowledge Corporation: A. A. Noyes and Chemistry at Cal-Tech, 1915–1930." *Ambix* 23:175–86.

———. 1986. "History of Chemistry." In *Historical Writing on American Science: Perspectives and Prospects*. Baltimore, Md.: Johns Hopkins University Press.

———. 1990. *Physical Chemistry from Ostwald to Pauling*. Princeton, N.J.: Princeton University Press.

Serwer, Daniel. 1977. "Unmechanischer Zwang: Pauli, Heisenberg, and the Rejection of the Mechanical Atom, 1923–1925." *Historical Studies in the Physical Sciences* 8.189.

Sidgwick, Nevil V. 1933. *Some Physical Properties of the Covalent Link in Chemistry*. Ithaca, N.Y.: Cornell University Press.

Silverstein, Arthur M. 1989. *A History of Immunology*. San Diego: Academic Press, Inc.

Slater, John. 1931. "Directed Valence in Polyatomic Molecules." *Physical Review* 37:481–89.

———. 1965. "Molecular Orbital and Heitler-London Methods." *Journal of Chemical Physics* 43:S11–17.

Smith, Alic Kimball. 1965. *A Peril and a Hope*. Chicago: University of Chicago Press.

Smith, Alice Kimball, and Charles Weiner, eds. 1980. *Robert J. Oppenheimer: Letters and Recollections*. Cambridge, Mass.: Harvard University Press.

Snow, C. P. 1964. "J. D. Bernal, A Personal Portrait." In *The Science of Science*, edited by Maurice Goldsmith and Alan Mackay. London: Souvenir Press.

Sopka, Katherine Russell. 1980. *Quantum Physics in America 1920–1935*. New York: Arno Press.

Srinivasan, P. R., Joseph S. Fruton, and John T. Edsall, eds. 1979. *The Origins of Modern Biochemistry, A Retrospect on Proteins*. New York: New York Academy of Sciences.

Stearn, Marshall B., ed. 1991. *Portraits of Passion*. Sausalito, Calif.: Park West Publishing.

Stone, Irwin. 1966. "Hypoascorbemia, The Genetic Disease Causing the Human Requirement for Exogenous Ascorbic Acid." *Perspectives in Biology and Medicine* 10:133–34.

———. 1972. *The Healing Factor*. New York: Grosset & Dunlap.

———. 1982. *Scurvy, The Most Misunderstood Epidemic Disease in 20th Century Medicine*. Self-published pamphlet.

———. 1986. "Scurvy, The Cosmic Connection: An Ancient Supernova and the Practice of Medicine in the Twentieth Century." In *The Roots of Molecular Medicine: A Tribute to Linus Pauling*, edited by Richard P. Huemer. New York: Freeman.

Stranges, Anthony N. 1982. *Electrons and Valence*. College Station: Texas A&M University Press.

Sturdivant, J. H. 1968. "The Scientific Work of Linus Pauling." In *Structural Chemistry and Molecular Biology*, edited by Alexander Rich and Norman Davidson. San Francisco: Freeman.

Talmadge, David W. 1989. "Is This Theory Really Necessary?" In *Immunology 1930–1980*, edited by Pauline Mazumdar. Toronto: Wall & Thompson.

Teller, Edward, and Albert L. Latter. 1958. *Our Nuclear Future*. New York: Criterion Books.

Thackray, Arnold, Jeffrey L. Sturchio, P. Thomas Carroll, and Robert Bud, eds. 1985. *Chemistry in America, 1876–1976*. Dordrecht, Holland: D. Reidel.

Thomas, John M., and Sir David Phillips, eds. 1990. *Selections and Reflections: The Legacy of Sir Lawrence Bragg*. Northwood, England: Science Reviews, Ltd.

Thomas, Kas. 1978. "The Plowboy Interview: Dr. Linus Pauling." *Mother Earth News* 49:16–22.

Van Vleck, J. H., and A. Sherman. 1935. "The Quantum Theory of Valence." *Review of Modern Physics* 7:167–86.

Wadleigh, H. R. 1910. *Munich*. London: T. Fisher Unwin.

Walz, John A. 1936. *German Influence in American Education and Culture*. Philadelphia: Carl Schurz Memorial Foundation.

Wang, Jessica. 1992. "Science, Security, and the Cold War." *Isis* 83:238–69.

Wasowicz, Lidia. 1985. "Linus Pauling at 84: Maverick in the Lab." *Los Angeles Times*, February 10, Sec. I, p. 3.

Watson, Ernest, "A. A. Noyes," *Engineering and Science*, November 1968, pp. 23–27.

Watson, James. 1980. *The Double Helix*. A Norton Critical Edition, edited by Gunther Stent. New York: Norton.

Weaver, Warren. 1961. "Reminiscences." Transcript of Interviews Conducted by Oral History Research Office, Columbia University.

———. 1967a. *U.S. Philanthrophic Foundations*. New York: Harper & Row.

———. 1967b. *Science and Imagination*. New York: Basic Books.

———. 1970. *Scene of Change*. New York: Charles Scribner's Sons.

Weinbaum, Sidney. 1991. "Sidney Weinbaum: Politics at Mid-Century." *Engineering and Science* 55:30–38.

Weisskopf, Victor. 1989. *The Privilege of Being a Physicist*. New York: Freeman.

———. 1991. *The Joy of Insight: Passions of a Physicist*. New York: Basic Books.

Wells, H. G., Julian Huxley, and George P. Wells. 1934. *The Science of Life*. New York: Literary Guild.

Wheaton, Bruce R. 1983. *The Tiger and the Shark*. Cambridge, Eng.: Cambridge University Press.

Wheland, George Willard. 1944. *The Theory of Resonance and Its Applications to Organic Chemistry*. New York: Wiley.

White, Florence Meiman. 1980. *Linus Pauling: Scientist and Crusader*. New York: Walker.

Wilmer, Harry A., ed. 1991. *Creativity: Paradoxes and Reflections*. Wilmette, Ill.: Chiron Publications.

Wilson, E. Bright. 1968. "Some Remarks on Quantum Chemistry." In *Structural Chemistry and Molecular Biology*, edited by Alexander Rich and Norman Davidson. San Francisco: Freeman.

———. 1980. "Some Personal Scientific Reminiscences." *International Journal of Quantum Chemistry: Quantum Chemistry Symposium* 14:17–29.

———. 1986. "One Hundred Years of Physical Chemistry." *Sigma Xi*, January–February, pp. 70–77.

Winchell, Mark Royden. 1984. *William F. Buckley, Jr.* Boston: Twayne.

Wolf, Fred Alan. 1981. *Taking the Quantum Leap*. San Francisco: Harper & Row.

Wrinch, Dorothy. 1939. "The Structure of Globular Proteins." *Nature* 143:482.

Wyckoff, W. G. 1962. "The Development of X-ray Diffraction in the U.S.A.," and "Problems of Biochemical Structures." In *Fifty Years of X-Ray Diffraction*, edited by P. P. Ewald. Utrecht: N.V.A. Oosthoek's.

Yergin, Daniel. 1977. *Shattered Peace*. Boston: Houghton Mifflin.

———. 1991. *The Prize*. New York: Simon & Schuster.

Yoxen, E. J. 1984. "Skepticism about the Centrality of Technology Transfer in the Rockefeller Foundation Programme in Molecular Biology." *Social Studies of Science*. 14:248–52.

Zuckerkandl, Emile, and Linus Pauling. 1962. "Molecular Disease, Evolution, and Genic Heterogeneity." In *Horizons in Biochemistry*, edited by Michael Kasha and Bernard Pullman. New York: Academic Press.

Zuckerman, Harriet. 1977. *The Scientific Elite*. New York: Free Press.

Index